AF516892

IFS : MATHEMATICS FOR INDIAN FOREST SERVICE

TEJASKAR PANDEY
Jubilee. Hall Delhi University
PANKAJ K. PANDEY 'SAREYASKAR'
Delhi University

Language Editor :
OJASKAR PANDEY

CBS Publishers & Distributors
485, Jain Bhawan, Bhola Nath Nagar, Shahdara, Delhi 110032 (India)

Book Useful for

1. State Forest Service Examination
2. State Civil Service Mains (Pure Maths)
3. Civil Service (IAS) Prilims
4. CSIR-Section Officer Examination
5. JNU and DU MCA Test
. JNU, Pune M. Tech Computor Science ntrance Test
7. BSC (Mathematics)
. BPSC Maths (Pure)
9. Rajasthan PCS Maths (Pure)
10. B Tech
11. AMIE (Section A)
12. M.P. (Prilims)

ISBN 81-239-0285-9

First Edition 1994

Published by:

Satish Kumar Jain for CBS Publishers & Distributors
485, Jain Bhawan, Bhola Nath Nagar,
Shahdara, Delhi-110 032. (India).

Printed at:

R.N. Printers, Ram Nagar,
Shahdara, Delhi-110 032

Preface

Dear Students

We are happy to inform you that this book will fulfill the demands of the Students appearing in IFS/BPSC/IAS(P)/and MCA test examinations of Indian Universities.

We think that more material will be added in the next edition.

All the formulaes which appeared in the book will be provided to you as a seperate book. We thank the publisher, printer and other friends who helped us in this connection. The error which creeps up in this book will be removed in next edition.

Yours
TEJASKAR PANDEY

Note: For the Formulae Book and extra Materials for IFS Mathematics please send Rupees 80/- to the Publisher Writing the Name of the Book, by Money Order Writing Your Adress. Book will be send by VPP, or you can collect personally.

Writer and Publisher

Our Address is :
CBS Publisher and Distributor
11 Daryaganj, New Delhi
Behind Employment Exchange,
New Delhi-110002

Syllabus

PART A

Algbra :

Algebra of sets, relations and functions, inverse of a function, composite function, equivalence relation.
Numbers: integers, rational numbers, real numbers (statement and properties) complex numbers.
Groups, sub-groups, cyclic and permutation groups: Lagrange's theorem isomorphism.
De-Moivre's theorem for rational index and its simple applications.
Theory of Equation; Polynomial equations, transformation of equations, symmetric function of roots of cubic and biquadratic equations, location of roots and Newton's method for finding roots.
Matrices: Algebra of matrices, determinants—simple properties of determinants.
Products of determinants, adjoint of a matrix, inversion of matrices, rank of matrix. Application of matrices to the solution of linear equations (in three unknowns).
Inequalities: Arithmetic and geometric means, Cauchy Schwarz inequality (only for finite sums).
Analytic Geometry of two dimensions: Straight lines, pair of straight lines, circles, systems of circles, Ellipse, parabola, hyperbola (referred to principal axis).
Reduction of a second degree equation to standard form, Tangents and normals.
Analytic Geometry of three dimensions: Planes, straight lines and spheres (Cartesian Co-ordinates only).

Calculus and Differential Equation

Differential calculus: Concept of limit; continuity and differentiability of a function of one real variable, derivative of standard functions, successive differentiation. Roll's theorem. Mean value theorem, Maclaurin and Taylor series (proof not needed) and their application; Binomial expansion for rational index expansion of exponential logarithmic trigonometrical and hyperbolic functions. Indeterminate forms. Maxima and Minima of a function of a single variable, geometrical applications such as tangent, normal, subtangent, subnormal, asymptotic curvature (Catesian co-ordinates only) Envelopes, partial differentiation. Euler's theorem for homogeneous functions

Integral calculas: Standard methods of integration. Riemann definition of definite integral of continuous functions, fundamental theorem of Integral calculus. Rectification, quadrature, volumes and surface area of solids of revolution. Simpson's rule for numerical integration.

Convergence of sequence and series, test of convergence of series with positive terms Ratio, Root and Gauss' tests.

Alternating series

Differential Equation: Solution of standard first order differential equation. Solution of second and higher order linear differential equations with constant co-efficients. Simple applcations of problems of growth and decay, simple harmonic motion. Simple pendulum and the like.

PART B

Machanics: (Vector Methods may be used)

Statics—Representation of a force, parallelolgram of forces; composition and resolution of forces and conditions of equilibrium coplanar and concurrent forces. Triangle of forces. Like and unlike parallel forces. Moments, Couples, General conditions for equilibrium of coplanar forces, centre of gravity of simple bodies. Friction—static and limiting friction, angle of friction equilibrium of a particle on a rough inclined plane simple problems, simple machines (lever, system of Pullyes, gear), Virtual work (two dimensions).

Dynamics: Kinematics—displacement, speed. velocity and acceleration of a particle, relative velocity, Motion in a straight line under constant acceleration. Newton's laws of motion. Central orbits. Simple harmonic motion, motion under gravity (in vacuum) Impulse, work and energy, conservation of energy and linear momentum. Uniform circular motion.

Astronomy: Spherical Trigonometry—Sine and cosine formulae, properties of right- angled spherical triangles.

Spherical Astronomy—Celestial sphere, Coordinate systems and their conversion. Diurnal motion. Sidereal and solar times, mean solar time, local and standard times, equation of time. Rising and setting of the sun and stars, dip of the horzon. Astronomical refraction. Twilight. Parallax, abberration, prcssion and mutation. Kepler's—laws, planetary orbits and stationary points Apparent motion of the moon phases of the moon. Astronomical Instruments—sextant tranxit instrument.

Statistics: Probability – Classical and statistical definition of probability, calculation of prabability of combinatorial methods, addition and multiplication theorcms. Conditional probability Random variables (discrete and continous density function. Mathematical expectation.

Standard distribution—Binomial—definition, mean and variance, skewness limiting form, simple applications; Poisson—definition, mean and variance, additive property. fitting of poisson distribution to given data; Normal—simple properties and simple applications fitting a normal distribution given data.

Bivariate distribution—Coorelation; linear regression involving two variables fitting of straight line, parabolic and exponential curves, curves, properties of correlation coefficient.

Simple sampling distributions and simple tests of hypothesis: Random sample, statistic, sampling distribution and standard error. Simple application of the normal *t*, *chi*^{2} and *F* distributions for test of significance.

Note. Candidates will be required to answer compulsorily from Part A of the syllabus one question on each of the three topics viz. (1) Algebra (2) Analytic Geometry of two and three dimensions and (3) Calculas and differential equation. From Part B of the syllabus it will be compulsory to answer at least one question on any one of the three topics viz. (1) Mechanics (2) Astronomy and (3) Statistics.

Contents

1

Mathematics

De-Moivre's theorem for rational index and its simple application:

(i) State and prove De-Moivre's theorem.

(ii) State and prove De-Moivre's Theorem for a positive integral index.

(iii) State and prove De-Moivre's Theorem for a negative integral index.

Solution If n be a positive integer or a negative integer then

$$(\cos\theta + i\sin\theta)^n = \cos n\theta + i\sin n\theta$$

and (ii) If n be a fraction, positive or negative then one of the values of $(\cos\theta + i\sin\theta)^n$ is $\cos n\,\theta + i\sin n\,\theta$.

Proof: let n be a positive integer

By actual multiplication we have

$$(\cos\theta_1 + i\sin\theta_1)(\cos\theta_2 + i\sin\theta_2) = (\cos\theta_1\cos\theta_2 - \sin\theta_1\sin\theta_2) + i(\sin\theta_1\cos\theta_2 + \cos\theta_1\sin\theta_2)$$

$$= \cos(\theta_1 + \theta_2) + i\sin(\theta_1 + \theta_2)$$

Also $(\cos\theta_1 + i\sin\theta_1)(\cos\theta_2 + i\sin\theta_2)(\cos\theta_3 + i\sin\theta_3)$

$$= [\cos(\theta_1 + \theta_2) + i\sin(\theta_1 + \theta_2)](\cos\theta_3 + i\sin\theta_3)$$

$$= \cos(\theta_1 + \theta_2 + \theta_3) + i\sin(\theta_1 + \theta_2 + \theta_3)$$

Proceeding in this way, the product of n similar factors is

$$(\cos\theta_1 + i\sin\theta_1)(\cos\theta_2 + i\sin\theta_2)\ldots(\cos\theta_n + i\sin\theta_n)$$

$$= \cos(\theta_1 + \theta_2 + \ldots + \theta_n) + i\sin(\theta_1 + \theta_2 + \ldots + \theta_n)$$

Putting $\theta_1 = \theta_2 = \theta_3 = \ldots = \theta_n = \theta$ we have

$$(\cos\theta + i\sin\theta)^n = \cos n\theta + i\sin n\theta$$

This proves De Moivre's Theorem, when n is a positive integer

Case 2 let n be a negative integer

let $n = -m$ where m is a positive integer

Now $(\cos\theta + i\sin\theta)^n = (\cos\theta + i\sin\theta)^{-m}$

$$= \frac{1}{(\cos\theta + i\sin\theta)^m}$$

$$= \frac{1}{\cos m\theta + i\sin m\theta}$$

$$= \frac{\cos m\theta - i\sin m\theta}{(\cos m\theta + i\sin m\theta)(\cos m\theta - i\sin m\theta)}$$

$$= \frac{\cos m\theta - i\sin m\theta}{(\cos^2 m\theta + \sin^2 m\theta)}$$

$$= (\cos m\theta - i\sin m\theta)$$

$$= \cos(-n)\theta - i\sin(-n)\theta$$

$$= \cos n\theta + i\sin n\theta$$

Case 3 Let n be a fraction, positive or negative

let q be a positive integer and let

$$n = \frac{P}{q} \quad \text{where } P \text{ is either +ve or −ve}$$

Therefore

$$\left(\cos\frac{\theta}{q} + i\sin\frac{\theta}{q}\right)^q = \cos q\frac{\theta}{q} + i\sin q\frac{\theta}{q}$$

$$\left(\cos\frac{\theta}{q} + i\sin\frac{\theta}{q}\right) = (\cos\theta + i\sin\theta)^{1/q}$$

Taking the q th roots on both sides.

Now since P is + ve or − ve so from De-Moivre's theorem case (i) and (ii) suggests that

$$\left(\cos\frac{\theta}{q} + i\sin\frac{\theta}{q}\right)^P = (\cos\theta + i\sin\theta)\frac{P}{q}$$

$$\cos\frac{P}{q}\theta + i\sin\frac{P}{q}\theta = (\cos + i\sin\theta)\frac{P}{q}$$

i.e. One of the values of $(\cos\theta + i\sin\theta)\frac{P}{q}$ is $\cos\frac{P}{q}\theta + i\sin\frac{P}{q}\theta$

(Proved)

Problem 1 If $\alpha = 15°$, find the value of

$$\frac{(\cos\alpha + i\sin\alpha)(\cos 2\alpha + i\sin 2\alpha)}{\cos 3\alpha - i\sin 3\alpha}$$

Solution We have

$$\frac{(\cos \alpha + i \sin\alpha)(\cos 2\alpha + i \sin 2\alpha)}{(\cos 3\alpha - i \sin 3\alpha)}$$

$$= (\cos \alpha + i \sin \alpha) (\cos 2\alpha + i \sin 2\alpha) (\cos 3\alpha - i \sin 3\alpha)^{-1}$$

$$= (\cos \alpha + i \sin \alpha) (\cos 2\alpha + i \sin 2\alpha) (\cos (3) \alpha + i \sin 3\alpha)$$

$$= (\cos \alpha + i \sin \alpha) (\cos 2\alpha + i \sin 2\alpha) (\cos 3\alpha + i \sin 3\alpha)$$

$$= \cos (\alpha + 2\alpha + 3\alpha) + i \sin (\alpha + 2\alpha + 3\alpha)$$

$$= \cos 6\alpha + i \sin 6\alpha$$

$$= \cos 90° + i \sin 90° = (0) + i \times 1 = i$$

Problem 2 Prove that

$$(1 + \cos \theta + i \sin \theta)^n - (1 + \cos \theta - i \sin \theta)^n$$
$$= 2^{n+1}\, i \cos^n \frac{\theta}{2} \sin \left(\frac{n\theta}{2}\right)$$

Solution LHS

$$(1 + \cos \theta + i \sin \theta)^n - (1 + \cos \theta - i \sin \theta)^n$$

$$= \left[2 \cos^2 \frac{\theta}{2} + 2i \sin \frac{\theta}{2} \cos \frac{\theta}{2}\right]^n - \left[2 \cos^2 \frac{\theta}{2} - 2i \sin \frac{\theta}{2} \cos \frac{\theta}{2}\right]^n$$

$$= \left[2 \cos \frac{\theta}{2} \left(\cos \frac{\theta}{2} + i \sin \frac{\theta}{2}\right)\right]^n - \left[2 \cos \frac{\theta}{2} \left(\cos \frac{\theta}{2} - i \sin \frac{\theta}{2}\right)\right]^n$$

$$= 2^n \cos^n \frac{\theta}{2} \left[\left(\cos \frac{\theta}{2} + i \sin \frac{\theta}{2}\right)^n - \left(\cos \frac{\theta}{2} - i \sin \frac{\theta}{2}\right)^n\right]$$

$$= 2^n \cos^n \frac{\theta}{2} \left[\cos \frac{n\theta}{2} + i \sin \frac{n\theta}{2} - \cos \frac{n\theta}{2} + i \sin \frac{n\theta}{2}\right]$$

$$= 2^n \cos^n \frac{\theta}{2} \cdot 2i \sin \frac{n\theta}{2}$$

$$= 2^{n+1}\, i \cos \frac{^n\theta}{2} \sin \left(\frac{n\theta}{2}\right)$$

Hence $(1 + \cos \theta + i \sin \theta)^n - (1 + \cos \theta - i \sin \theta)^n$ is wholly imaginary.

Problem 3 Prove that

$$(1 + \cos \theta + i \sin \theta)^n + (1 + \cos \theta - i \sin \theta)^n$$
$$= 2^{n+1} \cos^n \frac{\theta}{2} \cos \frac{n\theta}{2}$$

[*I.F.S. 82*]

Solution $\quad (1 + \cos\theta + i\sin\theta)^n + (1 + \cos\theta - i\sin\theta)^n$

$$= \left(2\cos^2\frac{\theta}{2} + 2i\sin\frac{\theta}{2}\cos\frac{\theta}{2}\right)^n + \left(2\cos^2\frac{\theta}{2} - 2i\sin\frac{\theta}{2}\cos\frac{\theta}{2}\right)^n$$

$$= \left[2\cos\frac{\theta}{2}\left(\cos\frac{\theta}{2} + i\sin\frac{\theta}{2}\right)\right]^n + \left[2\cos\frac{\theta}{2}\left(\cos\frac{\theta}{2} - i\sin\frac{\theta}{2}\right)\right]^n$$

$$= 2^n\cos^n\frac{\theta}{2}\left[\cos\frac{n\theta}{2} + i\sin\frac{n\theta}{2} + \cos\frac{n\theta}{2} - i\sin\frac{n\theta}{2}\right]$$

$$= 2^n\cos^n\frac{\theta}{2}\,2\cos\frac{n\theta}{2} = 2^{n+1}\cos^n\frac{\theta}{2}\cos\frac{n\theta}{2}$$

Problem 4. If $x_r = \cos\frac{\pi}{2^r} + i\sin\frac{\pi}{2^r}$ prove that

$$x_1 x_2 x_3 \ldots \text{ to infinity} = -1$$

or

$$\lim_{n\to\infty} (x_1 x_2 \ldots x_n) = -1$$

Solution $\quad x_r = \cos\frac{\pi}{2^r} + i\sin\frac{\pi}{2^r}$

putting $\quad r = 1, 2 \ldots$ we have

$$x_1 = \cos\frac{\pi}{2} + i\sin\frac{\pi}{2}$$

$$x_2 = \cos\frac{\pi}{2^2} + i\sin\frac{\pi}{2^2}$$

$$x_3 = \cos\frac{\pi}{2^3} + i\sin\frac{\pi}{2^3}$$

$$\ldots \quad \ldots \quad \ldots$$

$$\ldots \quad \ldots \quad \ldots$$

$$\ldots \quad \ldots \quad \ldots$$

$$x_n = \cos\frac{\pi}{2^n} + i\sin\frac{\pi}{2^n}$$

$$x_1 x_2 \ldots \text{ to infinity}$$

$$= \left(\cos\frac{\pi}{2} + \sin\frac{\pi}{2}\right)\left(\cos\frac{\pi}{2^2} + i\sin\frac{\pi}{2^2}\right)\ldots$$

$$= \cos\left[\frac{\pi}{2} + \frac{\pi}{2^2} + \ldots\right] + i\sin\left[\frac{\pi}{2} + \frac{\pi}{2^2} + \ldots\right],$$

$$= \cos\left[\frac{\pi}{2}\left(1 + \frac{1}{2} + \frac{1}{2^2} + \ldots\right)\right] + i\sin\left[\frac{\pi}{2}\left(1 + \frac{1}{2} + \frac{1}{2^2} + \ldots\right)\right]$$

$$= \cos\left[\frac{\pi}{2}\left(\frac{1}{1-\frac{1}{2}}\right)\right] + i\sin\left[\frac{\pi}{2}\left(\frac{1}{1-\frac{1}{2}}\right)\right]$$

$$= \cos\frac{\pi}{2}\cdot 2 + i\sin\frac{\pi}{2}\cdot 2$$

$$= \cos\pi + i\sin\pi \quad = -1 + i\times 0$$

$$= -1 + 0 = -1$$

i.e. $\quad x_1\, x_2\, x_3 \ldots \quad \ldots$ to infinity $= -1.$

Problem 5 Prove that one of the values of

$$(a+ib)^{m/n} + (a-ib)^{m/n}$$

$$= 2\,(a^2+b^2)^{m/2n}\cos\left(\frac{m}{n}\tan^{-1}\frac{b}{a}\right)$$

Solution We have

$$(a+ib)^{m/n} + (a-ib)^{m/n}$$

putting $\quad a = r\cos\theta$

$$b = r\sin\theta$$

$$a^2+b^2 = r^2 \qquad r = (a^2+b^2)^{1/2}$$

$$\tan\theta = \frac{b}{a} \qquad \to \theta = \tan^{-1}\left(\frac{b}{a}\right)$$

So $\quad (a+ib)^{m/n} + (a-ib)^{m/n}$

$$= (r\cos\theta + ir\sin\theta)^{m/n} + (r\cos\theta - ir\sin\theta)^{m/n}$$

$$= r^{m/n}(\cos\theta + i\sin\theta)^{m/n} + r^{m/n}(\cos\theta - i\sin\theta)^{m/n}$$

$$= r^{m/n}\left[\cos\frac{m}{n}\theta + i\sin\frac{m}{n}\theta + \cos\frac{m}{n}\theta - i\sin\frac{m}{n}\theta\right]$$

$$= 2r^{m/n}\cos^{m/n}\theta$$

$$= 2\,(a^2+b^2)^{m/2n}\cos\left(\frac{m}{n}\tan^{-1}\frac{b}{a}\right)$$

R.H.S. (*proved*)

Problem 6 If n is a positive integer, prove that

$$(1+i)^n + (1-i)^n = = 2^{(n/2)+1}\cos\frac{n\pi}{4}$$

Solution Putting $1 = r\cos\theta$ $1 = r\sin\theta$ we have

$$(1+i)^n + (1-i)^n$$

$$= (r\cos\theta + ir\sin\theta)^n + (r\cos\theta - ir\sin\theta)^n$$

$$= r^n(\cos\theta + i\sin\theta)^n + r^n(\cos\theta - i\sin\theta)^n$$

$$= r^n[\cos n\theta + i\sin n\theta + \cos n\theta - i\sin n\theta]$$

$$(1+i)^n + (1-i)^n = 2r^n\cos n\theta$$

Now $\quad 1^2 + 1^2 = r^2 \cos^2\theta + r^2 \sin^2\theta$

$$2 = r^2$$

$$r = 2^{1/2}$$

$$\tan\theta = 1 \qquad \theta = \frac{\pi}{4}$$

$$(1 + i)^n + (1 - i)^n = 2 \cdot 2^{n/2} \text{ eos } n\frac{\pi}{4}$$

$$= 2^{(n/2)+1} \cos\frac{n\pi}{4} \qquad \text{R.H.S. } (\textit{proved})$$

Problem 7 If n be a $+vc$ integer prove that

$$(1 + \sqrt{3}\,i)^n + (1 - \sqrt{3}\,i)^n = 2^{n+1} \cos\frac{n\pi}{3}$$

Solution Putting $1 = r\cos\theta$, $\quad \sqrt{3} = r\sin\theta \Rightarrow \tan\theta = \sqrt{3}$

$$\theta = \pi/3$$

$$1^2 = r^2\cos^2\theta \qquad 3 = r^2\sin^2\theta$$

$$1 + 3 = r^2(\cos^2\theta + \sin^2\theta)$$

$$4 = r^2 \qquad r = 2$$

Now $\quad (1 + \sqrt{3i})^n + (1 - \sqrt{3i})^n$

$$= (r\cos\theta + ri\sin\theta)^n + (r\cos\theta - ri\sin\theta)^n$$

$$= r^n[(\cos\theta + i\sin\theta)^n + (\cos\theta - i\sin\theta)^n]$$

$$= r^n[\cos n\theta + i\sin n\theta + \cos n\theta - i\sin n\theta]$$

$$= r^n\, 2\cos n\theta$$

$$= 2^n\, 2\cos n\theta$$

$$= 2^{(n/2)+1} \cos^{n\pi/3} \qquad \text{R.H.S. } (\textit{proved})$$

Problem 8 If $\quad x = \cos\alpha + i\sin\alpha,\ y = \cos\beta + i\sin\beta,$

$z = \cos y + i\sin y$ and if $x + y + z = 0$, then

prove that $\quad \dfrac{1}{x} + \dfrac{1}{y} + \dfrac{1}{z} = 0$

Solution $\quad x + y + z = 0$

$$\Rightarrow \cos\alpha + i\sin\alpha + \cos\beta + i\sin\beta + \cos\gamma + i\sin\gamma = 0$$

$$\Rightarrow (\cos\alpha + \cos\beta + \text{eos}\,\gamma) + i(\sin\alpha + \sin\beta + \sin\gamma) = 0 + i0$$

Equating real and imaginary parts we have

$$\cos\alpha + \sin\beta + \cos\gamma = 0$$
$$\sin\alpha + \sin\beta + \sin\gamma = 0$$

Now $\dfrac{1}{x}+\dfrac{1}{y}+\dfrac{1}{z}$

$$= \frac{1}{(\cos\alpha + i\sin\alpha)} + \frac{1}{(\cos\beta + i\sin\beta)} + \frac{1}{(\cos\gamma + i\sin\gamma)}$$
$$= (\cos\alpha + i\sin\alpha)^{-1} + (\cos\beta + i\sin\alpha)^{-1} + (\cos\gamma + i\sin\gamma)^{-1})$$
$$= \cos\alpha - i\sin\alpha + \cos\beta - i\sin\beta + \cos\gamma - i\sin\gamma$$
$$= (\cos\alpha + \cos\beta + \cos\gamma) - i(\sin\alpha + \sin\beta + \sin\gamma)$$
$$= 0 - i \times 0$$
$$= 0$$

Thus $\dfrac{1}{x} - \dfrac{1}{y} + \dfrac{1}{z} = 0$ ***(Proved)***

Problem 9 If $(a_1 + ib_1)(a_2 + ib_2).\ldots.(an + ibn) = A + iB$, prove that

(i) $\tan^{-1}\dfrac{b_1}{a_1} + \tan^{-1}\dfrac{b_2}{a_2} + \ldots + \tan^{-1}\dfrac{bn}{an} = \tan^{-1}\dfrac{B}{A}$

(ii) $(a_1^2 + b_1^2)(a_2^2 + b_2^2)\ldots(an^2 + bn^2) = A^2 + B^2$

Solution Let

$$a_1 = r_1\cos\theta_1 \qquad b_1 = r_1\sin\theta_1$$
$$o_2 = r_2\cos\theta_2 \qquad b_2 = r_2\sin\theta_2$$
$$\ldots\ldots \qquad \ldots\ldots$$
$$\ldots\ldots \qquad \ldots\ldots$$
$$a_n = r_n\cos\theta_n \qquad b_n = r_n\sin\theta_n$$

Then $a_1^2 + b_1^2 = r_1^2 \quad a_2^2 + b_2^2 = r_2^2\ldots$

$$a_n{}^2 + b_n{}^2\, r_n{}^2 \quad \text{and} \quad \tan\theta_1 = \frac{b_n}{a_n}$$

Now we have

$$(r_1\cos\theta_1 + ir_1\sin\theta_1)(r_2\cos\theta_2 + ir_2\sin\theta_2) \ldots$$
$$(r_n\cos\theta_n + ir_n\sin\theta_n) = A + iB$$
$$\Rightarrow r_1 r_2\ldots r_u[\cos(\theta_1 + \theta_2 + \ldots + \theta_n) + i\sin(\theta_1 + \theta_2 + \ldots + \theta_n)]$$
$$= A + iB$$

Equating real and imaginary parts we have

$$r_1 r_2 \ldots r_n \cos(\theta_1 + \theta_2 + \ldots + \theta_n) = A \tag{1}$$

$$r_1 r_2 \ldots r_n \sin(\theta_1 + \theta_2 + \ldots + \theta_n) \quad B \tag{2}$$

squaring and adding (i) and (ii)

$$r_1^2 + r_1^2 \ldots r_n^2 = B^2 + A^2$$

$$(a_1^2 + b_1^2)(a_2^2 + b_2^2) \ldots (a_n^2 + b_n^2) = A^2 + B^2$$

Dividing equation (2) by (1) we have

$$\tan \quad (\theta_1 + \theta_2 + \ldots + \theta_n) = \frac{B}{A}$$

$$\Rightarrow \theta_1 + \theta_2 + \ldots + \theta_n = \tan^{-1}\left(\frac{B}{A}\right)$$

$$\Rightarrow \quad \tan^{-1}\frac{b_1}{a_1} + \tan^{-1}\frac{b_2}{a_2} + \ldots + \tan^{-1}\frac{b_n}{a_n} = \tan^{-1}\frac{B}{A}$$

(Proved)

Problem 10 If α and β be Ihe roots of the equation $x^2 - 2x + 4 = 0$, prove that

$$\alpha^n + \beta^u = 2^{n+1}\cos\frac{n\pi}{3}$$

Solution Since α and β are the roots of $x^2 - 2x + 4$ then

$$\alpha = \frac{2 + \sqrt{4 - 4 \cdot 1 \times 4}}{2}$$

$$\beta = \frac{2 - \sqrt{4 - 16}}{2}$$

$$\alpha = \frac{2 + \sqrt{-12}}{2} = \frac{2 + 2i\sqrt{3}}{2}$$

$$= 1 + \sqrt{3}\, i$$

$$\beta = (1 - \sqrt{3}\, i)$$

$$\alpha = 2\left(\frac{1}{2} + \frac{\sqrt{3}}{2}\, i\right)$$

$$\beta = 2\left(\frac{1}{2} - \frac{\sqrt{3}}{2}\, i\right)$$

$$\alpha = 2\left(\cos\frac{\pi}{3} + i\sin\frac{\pi}{3}\right)$$

$$\beta = 2\left(\cos\frac{\pi}{3} - i\sin\frac{\pi}{3}\right)$$

Then $\alpha^n + \beta^n = 2^n\left[\left(\cos\frac{\pi}{3} + i\sin\frac{\pi}{3}\right)^n + \left(\cos\frac{\pi}{3} - i\sin\frac{\pi}{3}\right)^n\right]$

$$= 2^n\left[\cos\frac{n\pi}{3} + i\sin\frac{n\pi}{3} + \cos\frac{n\pi}{3} - i\sin\frac{n\pi}{3}\right]$$

$$= 2^n \cdot 2\cos\frac{n\pi}{3} = 2^{n+1}\cos\frac{n\pi}{3}$$ R.H.S. (*Proved*)

Problem 11 Find the equation whose roots are the nth powers of the roots of the equation

$$x^2 - 2x\cos\theta + 1 = 0$$

Solution The given equation is

$$x^2 - 2x\cos\theta + 1 = 0$$

$$x = \frac{2\cos\theta \pm \sqrt{4\cos^2\theta - 4}}{2}$$

$$x = \frac{2\cos\theta \pm \sqrt{-4(1-\cos^2\theta)}}{2}$$

$$x = \frac{2\cos\theta \pm i\,2\sin\theta}{2}$$

$$x = (\cos\theta \pm i\sin\theta)$$

$$\alpha = \cos\theta + i\sin\theta;\ \beta = \cos\theta - i\sin\theta$$

We have to find the equation whose roots are α^n and β^n then

$$\alpha^n + \beta^n = (\cos\theta + i\sin\theta)^n + (\cos\theta - i\sin\theta)^n$$

$$= \cos n\theta + i\sin n\theta + \cos n\theta - i\sin n\theta$$

$$\alpha^n + \beta^n = 2\cos n\theta$$

product of roots

$$= \alpha^n \cdot \beta^n = (\cos\theta + i\sin\theta)^n(\cos\theta - i\sin\theta)^n$$

$$= (\cos n\theta + i\sin n\theta)(\cos n\theta - i\sin\theta)$$

$$= \cos^2 n\theta - i^2\sin^2 n\theta$$

$$= \cos^2 n\theta + \sin^2 n\theta = 1$$

Then the equation can be of the form

$$x^2 - (\alpha^n + \beta^n)\, x + \alpha^n \beta^n = 0$$

i.e. $$x^2 - 2x \cos n\theta + 1 = 0 \text{ Ans.}$$

Problem 12 Obtain the roots ef

$$x^4 - x^3 + x^2 - x + 1 = 0$$ [I.F.S. 84]

Solution Since $x^4 - x^3 + x^2 - x + 1 = 0$

$\Rightarrow (x + 1)(x^4 - x^3 + x^2 - x + 1) = 0$

$\Rightarrow x^5 - x^4 + x^3 - x^2 + x + x^4 - x^3 + x^2 - x + 1 = 0$

$\Rightarrow x^5 + 1 = 0$

$\Rightarrow x^5 = -1 = \cos \pi + i \sin \pi$

$\Rightarrow x^5 = \cos (2n\pi + \pi) + i \sin (2n\pi + \pi)$

$\Rightarrow x^5 = \cos (2n + 1)\pi + i \sin (2n + 1)\pi$

$\Rightarrow x = [\cos (2n + 1)\pi + i \sin (2n + 1)\pi]^{1/5}$

$\Rightarrow x = \cos \dfrac{(2n + 1)\pi}{5} + i \sin \dfrac{(2n + 1)\pi}{5}$

where $n = 0, 1, 2, 3, 4$

putting the values of n we have

$$x = \cos \frac{\pi}{5} + i \sin \frac{\pi}{5},\ \cos \frac{5\pi}{5} + i \sin \frac{5\pi}{5}$$

$$= \cos \pi + i \sin \pi$$

$$= -1$$

$$\cos \frac{7\pi}{5} + i \sin \frac{7\pi}{5},\ \cos \frac{2\pi}{5} + i \sin \frac{2\pi}{5}$$

Problcm 13, Apply De Moivre's theorem to solve the equation

$$x^7 + x^4 + x^3 + 1 = 0$$

Solution. $$x^7 + x^4 + x^3 + 1 = 0$$

$\Rightarrow x^4 (x^3 + 1) + 1 (x^3 + 1) = 0$

$\Rightarrow (x^4 + 1)(x^3 + 1) = 0$

So either $x^4 + 1 = 0$ or $x^3 + 1 = 0$

$\Rightarrow x^4 = -1$ $\quad x^3 = -1$

$\Rightarrow x^4 = \cos\pi + i\sin\pi$ $\quad \Rightarrow x^3 = \cos\pi + i\sin\pi$

$\Rightarrow x^4 = \cos(2n\pi + \pi) + i\sin(2n\pi + \pi)$ $\quad \Rightarrow x^3 = \cos(2n\pi + \pi) + i\sin(2n\pi + \pi)$

$\Rightarrow x = [\cos(2n+1)\pi + i\sin(2n+1)\pi]^{1/4}$ $\quad \Rightarrow x^3 = \cos(2n+1)\pi + i\sin(2n+1)\pi$

$\Rightarrow x = [\cos(2n+1)\pi + i\sin(2a+1)\pi]^{1/3}$

$$\Rightarrow x = \cos\frac{(2n+1)\pi}{4} + i\sin\frac{(2n+1)\pi}{4} \qquad \Rightarrow x = \cos\frac{(2n+1)\pi}{3} + i\sin\frac{(2n+1)\pi}{3}$$

$n = 0, 1, 2, 3$ $\qquad n = 0, 1, 2$

Problem 14 If $\sin\alpha + \sin\beta + \sin\gamma = \cos\alpha + \cos\beta + \cos\gamma = 0$ prove that

$$\cos 3\alpha + \cos 3\beta + \cos 3\gamma = 3\cos(\alpha + \beta + \gamma)$$

and
$$\sin 3\alpha + \sin 3\beta + \sin 3\gamma = 3\sin(\alpha + \beta + \gamma)$$ [*IFS 85*]

Solution Let $x = \cos\alpha + i\sin\alpha$, $\quad y = \cos\beta + i\sin\beta$

$z = \cos\gamma + i\sin\gamma$

Then

$$x + y + z = (\cos\alpha + i\sin\alpha) + (\cos\beta + i\sin\beta) + (\cos\gamma + i\sin\gamma)$$
$$= (\cos\alpha + \cos\beta + \cos\gamma) + i(\sin\alpha + \sin\beta + \sin\gamma)$$
$$= 0 + i \times 0 = 0$$

Now
$$x^3 + y^3 + z^3 - 3xyz$$
$$= (x + y + z)(x^2 + y^2 + z^2 - xy - yz - zx)$$
$$= 0 \times (x^2 + y^2 + z^2 - xy - yz - zx)$$
$$= 0$$

$$(\cos\alpha + i\sin\alpha)^3 + (\cos\beta + i\sin\beta)^3 + (\cos\gamma + i\sin\gamma)^3 - 3(\cos\alpha + i\sin\alpha)(\cos\beta + i\sin\beta)(\cos\gamma + i\sin\gamma) = 0$$

$$\Rightarrow (\cos 3\alpha + i\sin 3\alpha) + (\cos 3\beta + i\sin 3\beta) + (\cos 3\gamma + i\sin 3\gamma) = 3[\cos(\alpha + \beta + \gamma) + i\sin(\alpha + \beta + \gamma)]$$

$$\Rightarrow (\cos 3\alpha + \cos 3\beta + \cos 3\gamma) + i(\sin 3\alpha + \sin 3\beta + \sin 3\gamma) = 3[\cos(\alpha + \beta + \gamma) + i\sin(\alpha + \beta + \gamma)]$$

Equating real and imaginary parts on both sides, we have

$$\cos 3\alpha + \cos 3\beta + \cos 3\gamma = 3 \cos (\alpha + \beta + \gamma)$$

$$\sin 3\alpha + \sin 3\beta + \sin 3\gamma = 3 \sin (\alpha + \beta + \gamma) \qquad \textit{(proved)}$$

Problem 15. If $x + iy = \dfrac{3}{2 + \cos \theta + i \sin \theta}$

then prove that

$$(x - 1)(x - 3) + y^2 = 0$$

Solution we have

$$x + iy = \frac{3}{2 + \cos \theta + i \sin \theta}$$

$$= \frac{3}{[(2 + \cos \theta) + i \sin \theta} \cdot \frac{[(2 + \cos \theta) - i \sin \theta]}{[(2 + \cos \theta) - i \sin \theta]}$$

$$= \frac{6 + 3 \cos \theta - 3 i \sin \theta}{4 + \cos^2 \theta + 4 \cos \theta - i^2 \sin^2 \theta}$$

$$= \frac{6 + 3 \cos \theta - 3 i \sin \theta}{4 + \cos^2 \theta + 4 \cos \theta + \sin^2 \theta}$$

$$= \frac{(6 + 3 \cos \theta) - 3 i \sin \theta}{4 + 1 + 4 \cos \theta}$$

$$x + iy = \frac{(6 + 3 \cos \theta) - 3 i \sin \theta}{5 + 4 \cos \theta} = \frac{6 + 3 \cos \theta}{5 + 4 \cos \theta} - \frac{i\, 3 \sin \theta}{5 + 4 \cos \theta}$$

Equating real and imaginary parts on both sides we have

$$x = \frac{6 + 3 \cos \theta}{5 + 4 \cos \theta} \qquad y = -\frac{3 \sin \theta}{5 + 4 \cos \theta}$$

Now

$$(x - 1) = \frac{6 + 3 \cos \theta}{5 + 4 \cos \theta} - 1$$

$$= \frac{6 + 3 \cos \theta - 5 - 4 \cos \theta}{5 + 4 \cos \theta}$$

$$= \frac{1 - \cos \theta}{5 + 4 \cos \theta}$$

$$(x - 3) = \frac{6 + 3 \cos \theta}{5 + 4 \cos \theta} - 3$$

$$= \frac{6 + 3 \cos \theta - 15 - 12 \cos \theta}{5 + 4 \cos \theta}$$

$$= \frac{-9 - 9 \cos \theta}{5 + 4 \cos \theta} = \frac{-9(1 + \cos \theta)}{5 + 4 \cos \theta}$$

Now $(x - 1)(x - 3) + y^2$

$$= \frac{(1 - \cos\theta)}{(5 + 4\cos\theta)} x - \frac{9(1 + \cos\theta)}{(5 + 4\cos\theta)} + y^2$$

$$= \frac{-9(1 - \cos^2\theta)}{(5 + 4\cos\theta)^2} + \frac{9\sin^2\theta)}{(5 + 4\cos\theta)^2}$$

$$= \frac{-9\sin^2\theta}{(5 + 4\cos\theta)^2} + \frac{9\sin^2\theta}{(5 + 4\cos\theta)^2} = 0$$

$$\Rightarrow (x - 1)(x - 3) + y^2 = 0 \qquad \textit{(proved)}$$

Solution 16 If α and β are the roots of the equation $t^2 - 2t + 2 = 2$, show that

$$\frac{(x + \alpha)^n - (x + \beta)^n}{\alpha - \beta} = \frac{\sin^n\phi}{\sin^n\phi}$$

where $\cot\phi = x + 1$

Solution Since α and β are the roots of the equation

$$t^2 - 2t + 2 = 0, \quad \text{then}$$

$$\alpha = \frac{2 + \sqrt{4 - 4.1.2}}{2}$$

$$\alpha = \frac{2 + \sqrt{4 - 8}}{2} = \frac{2 + \sqrt{-4}}{2} = \frac{2 + 2i}{2} = 1 + i$$

and $\beta = \frac{2 - \sqrt{4 - 4.1.2}}{2} = \frac{2 - 2i}{2} = 1 - i$

$$\alpha = 1 + i \qquad \beta = 1 - i$$

Now $\frac{(x + \alpha)^n - (x + \beta)^n}{\alpha - \beta} = \frac{(x + 1 + i)^n - (x + 1 - i)^n}{1 + i - 1 + i}$

$$= \frac{(x + 1 + i)^n - (x - 1 - i)^n}{2i}$$

$$= \frac{(\cot\phi + i)^n - (\cot\phi - i)^n}{2i}$$

$$= \frac{\left(\frac{\cos\phi}{\sin\phi} + i\right)^n - \left(\frac{\cos\phi}{\sin\phi} - i\right)^n}{2i}$$

$$= \frac{\frac{(\cos\phi + i\sin\phi)^n}{\sin^n\phi} - \frac{(\cos - i\sin\phi)^n}{\sin^n\phi}}{2i}$$

$$= \frac{\cos n\phi + i\sin n\phi - \cos n\phi + i\sin n\phi}{2i\sin^n\phi}$$

$$= \frac{2i\sin n\phi}{2i\sin^n\phi} = \frac{\sin n\phi}{\sin^n\varphi} \qquad \textit{RHS} \quad \textit{(proved)}$$

Problem 17 prove that the nth roots of unity forms a series in geometric progression.

Solution Let x be the nth roots of unity then

$$x^n = 1$$

$$\Rightarrow \quad x^n = \cos 0 + i \sin 0$$

$$\Rightarrow \quad x^n = \cos (0 + 2 r\pi) + i \sin (0 + 2r \pi)$$

$$\Rightarrow \quad x^n = \cos 2r \pi + i \sin 2r \pi$$

$$\Rightarrow \quad x = (\cos 2r \pi + i \sin 2 r\pi)^{1/n}$$

where $\quad r = 0, 1, 2 \ldots n - 1$

$$\Rightarrow \quad x = \cos \frac{2r \pi}{n} + i \sin \frac{2r \pi}{n}$$

$$\Rightarrow \quad x = e^{i(2 r\pi)/n}$$

where $\quad r = 0, 1, 2. \ldots n - 1$

The nth roots of unity

$$= e^0, \; e^{i(2\pi)/n}, \; e^{i(4\pi)/n}, \; e^{i(6\pi)/n} \ldots \; e^{i2(n-1)\pi/n}$$

$$= 1, \; e^{i(2\pi)/n}, \; e^{i(4\pi)/n}, \; e^{i(6\pi)/n} \ldots \; e^{i2(n-1)/\pi/n}$$

which are evidently in G.P. have common rotio $e^{i(2\pi)/n}$ *(proved)*

Problem 18 If $\quad x = \cos \theta_1 + i \sin \theta_1, \quad y = \cos \theta_1 + i \sin \theta_2,$

$z = \cos \theta_3 + i \sin \theta_3$ and $x + y + z = xyz$

then prove that $\cos (\theta_2 - \theta_3) + \cos (\theta_3 - \theta_1) + \cos (\theta_1 - \theta_2) = -1$

Solution we have

$$x + y + z = xyz$$

$$(\cos \theta_1 + i \sin \theta_1) + (\cos \theta_2 + i \sin \theta_2) + (\cos \theta_3 + i \sin \theta_3)$$
$$= (\cos \theta_1 + i \sin \theta_1) (\cos \theta_2 + i \sin \theta_2) (\cos \theta_3 + i \sin \theta_3)$$

$$\Rightarrow \quad (\cos \theta_1 + \cos \theta_2 + \cos \theta_3) + i (\sin \theta_1 + \sin \theta_2 + \sin \theta_3)$$
$$= \cos (\theta_1 + \theta_2 + \theta_3) + i \sin (\theta_1 + \theta_2 + \theta_3)$$

$\Rightarrow$ Equating real and imaginary parts on both sides we have

$$\cos \theta_1 + \cos \theta_2 + \cos \theta_3 = \cos (\theta_1 + \theta_2 + \theta_3) \quad (1)$$

$$\sin \theta_1 + \sin \theta_2 + \sin \theta_3 = \sin (\theta_1 + \theta_2 + \theta_3) \quad (2)$$

squaring (1) and (2) and adding we have

$$1 + 1 + 1 + 2 \cos (\theta_1 - \theta_2) + 2 \cos (\theta_2 - \theta_3) + 2 \cos (\theta_3 - \theta_1) = 1$$

$$2 \cos (\theta_1 - \theta_2) + 2 \cos (\theta_2 - \theta_3) + 2 \cos (\theta_3 - \theta_1) = -2$$

$$\Rightarrow \quad \cos (\theta_1 - \theta_2) + \cos (\theta_2 - \theta_3) + \cos (\theta_3 - \theta_1) = -1$$

(proved)

Problem 19 If $\cos\alpha + \cos\beta + \cos\gamma = \sin\alpha + \sin\beta + \sin\gamma = 0$, show that

$$\sum \cos^2\alpha = \sum \sin^2\alpha = \frac{3}{2}$$

Solution. Let $x = \cos\alpha + i\sin\alpha \qquad z = \cos\gamma + i\sin\gamma$

$y = \cos\beta + i\sin\beta$

Now
$$\begin{aligned} x + y + z &= (\cos\alpha + i\sin\alpha) + (\cos\beta + i\sin\beta) \\ &\quad + (\cos\gamma + i\sin\gamma) \\ &= (\cos\alpha + \cos\beta + \cos\gamma) \\ &\quad + i(\sin\alpha + \sin\beta + \sin\gamma) \\ &= 0 + i \times 0 = 0 \end{aligned}$$

$$\begin{aligned} \frac{1}{x} + \frac{1}{y} + \frac{1}{z} &= \frac{1}{\cos\alpha + i\sin\alpha} + \frac{1}{\cos\beta + i\sin\beta} \\ &\quad + \frac{1}{\cos\gamma + i\sin\gamma} \\ &= (\cos\alpha + i\sin\alpha)^{-1} + (\cos\beta + i\sin\beta)^{-1} \\ &\quad + (\cos\gamma + i\sin\gamma)^{-1} \\ &= \cos\alpha - i\sin\alpha + \cos\beta - i\sin\beta + \cos\gamma - i\sin\gamma \\ &= (\cos\alpha + \cos\beta + \cos\gamma) - i(\sin\phi + \sin\beta + \sin\gamma) \\ &= 0 - i \times 0 \\ &= 0 \end{aligned}$$

Now
$$\begin{aligned} (x + y + z)^2 &= x^2 + y^2 + z^2 + 2xy + 2yz + 2zx \\ &= x^2 + y^2 + z^2 + 2xyz\left(\frac{1}{x} + \frac{1}{y} + \frac{1}{z}\right) \\ &= x^2 + y^2 + z^2 + 2xyz \times 0 \end{aligned}$$

$$\Rightarrow \quad x^2 + y^2 + z^2 = 0$$

$$\Rightarrow \quad (\cos\alpha + i\sin\alpha)^2 + (\cos\beta + i\sin\beta)^2 + (\cos\gamma + i\sin\gamma)^2 = 0$$

$$\Rightarrow \quad \cos 2\alpha + i\sin 2\alpha + \cos 2\beta + i\sin 2\beta + \cos 2\gamma + i\sin 2\gamma = 0$$

$$\Rightarrow \quad (\cos 2\alpha + \cos 2\beta + \cos 2\gamma) + i(\sin 2\alpha + \sin 2\beta + \sin 2\gamma) = 0$$

Equating real and imaginary parts on both sides we have

$$\cos 2\alpha + \cos 2\beta + \cos 2\gamma = 0$$

$$\sin 2\alpha + \sin 2\beta + \sin 2\gamma = 0$$

since
$$\cos 2\alpha + \cos 2\beta + \cos 2\gamma = 0$$
$$2\cos^2\alpha - 1 + 2\cos^2\beta - 1 + 2\cos^2\gamma - 1 = 0$$
$$2(\cos^2\alpha + \cos^2\beta + \cos^2\gamma) = 3$$
$$\Rightarrow \quad \cos^2\alpha + \cos^2\beta + \cos^2\gamma = \frac{3}{2}$$

Again
$$1 - \sin^2\alpha + 1 - \sin^2\beta + 1 - \sin^2\gamma = \frac{3}{2}$$
$$3 - \frac{3}{2} = \sin^2\alpha + \sin^2\beta + \sin^2\gamma$$
$$\frac{3}{2} = \sin^2\alpha + \sin^2\beta + \sin^2\gamma$$
$$\Rightarrow \quad \sin^2\alpha + \sin^2\beta + \sin^2\gamma = \frac{3}{2} \qquad \textit{(proved)}$$

Problem 20] If $x = \cos\theta + i\sin\theta$ and $1 + \sqrt{1 - a^2} = na$, prove that
$$(1 + a\cos\theta) = \frac{a}{2n}(1 + nx)\left(1 + \frac{n}{\alpha}\right)$$

Solution
$$RHS = \frac{a}{2n}\left[(1 + nx)\left(1 + \frac{n}{x}\right)\right]$$
$$= \frac{a}{2n}\left[1 + \frac{n}{x} + nx + n^2\right]$$
$$= \frac{a}{2n}\left[1 + n^2 + n\left(x + \frac{1}{x}\right)\right] \qquad (1)$$

Now
$$x = \cos\theta + i\sin\theta$$
$$\frac{1}{x} = \cos\theta - i\sin\theta$$
$$x + \frac{1}{x} = 2\cos\theta$$

Again
$$1 + \sqrt{1 - a^2} = na$$
$$\sqrt{1 - a^2} = na - 1$$

squaring both sides we have

$$1 - a^2 = (na - 1)^2$$

$$1 - a^2 = n^2 a^2 + 1 - 2na$$

$$2na = n^2 a^2 + a^2$$

$$2na = a^2 (1 + n^2)$$

$$\frac{2n}{a} = 1 + n^2$$

putting the values of $x + \frac{1}{x}$ and $\frac{2n}{a}$ in equation (1)

$$RHS = \frac{a}{2n}\left[\frac{2n}{a} + n\, 2\cos\theta\right]$$

$$= 1 + a\cos\theta \quad LHS$$ *(proved)*

Problem 21 If $x + \frac{1}{x} = 2\cos\theta$, show that $x^n + \frac{1}{x^n} = 2\cos n\theta$

Solution $x + \frac{1}{x} = 2\cos\theta$

$$\Rightarrow x^2 + 1 = 2x\cos\theta$$

$$\Rightarrow x^2 - 2x\cos\theta + 1 = 0$$

Then

$$x = \frac{2\cos\theta \pm \sqrt{4\cos^2\theta - 4.1.1}}{2}$$

$$x = \frac{2\cos\theta \pm \sqrt{4(\cos^2\theta - 1)}}{2}$$

$$x = \frac{2\cos\theta \pm \sqrt{-4(1 - \cos^2\theta)}}{2}$$

$$x = \frac{2\cos\theta \pm \sqrt{-4\sin^2\theta}}{2}$$

$$x = \frac{2\cos\theta \pm 2i\sin\theta}{2}$$

$$x = \frac{2(\cos\theta \pm i\sin\theta)}{2}$$

$$x = \cos\theta \pm i\sin\theta$$

let $$x = \cos\theta + i\sin\theta$$

$$\frac{1}{x} = \cos\theta - i\sin\theta$$

Now $$x^n + \frac{1}{x^n} = (\cos\theta + i\sin\theta)^n + (\cos\theta - i\sin\theta)^n$$

$$= \cos n\theta + i\sin n\theta + \cos n\theta - i\sin n\theta$$

$$x^n + \frac{1}{x^n} = 2\cos n\theta \qquad \textit{(proved)}$$

Problem 22 If $(1 + x)^n = P_0 + P_1 x + P_2 x^2 + P_3 x^3 + \ldots$ show that

$$P_0 - P_2 + P_4 - P_6 + \ldots = 2^{n/2} \cos^{n\pi/4}$$

and $$P_1 - P_3 + P_5 - P_7 + \ldots = 2^{n/2} \sin^{n\pi/4}$$

Solution $(1 + x)^n = P_0 + P_1 x + P_2 x^2 + P_3 x^3 + \ldots$

putting $x = i$ we have

$$(1 + i)^n = P_0 + P_1 i + P_2 i^2 + P_3 i^3 + \ldots$$
$$= P_0 + P_1 i - P_2 - P_3 i + P_4 - P_5 i + \ldots$$
$$= (P_0 - P_2 + P_4 - P_6 + \ldots$$
$$+ i(P_1 - P_3 + P_5 - P_7 + \ldots)$$

Now

$$(1 + i)^n = \left[\sqrt{2}\left(\frac{1}{\sqrt{2}} + i\frac{1}{\sqrt{2}}\right)\right]^n$$

$$= \left[2^{1/2}\left(\frac{1}{\sqrt{2}} + i\frac{1}{\sqrt{2}}\right)\right]^n$$

$$= 2^{n/2}\left[\cos\frac{\pi}{4} + i\sin\frac{\pi}{4}\right]^n$$

$$= 2^{n/2}\left[\cos\frac{n\pi}{4} + i\sin\frac{n\pi}{4}\right]$$

$$= 2^{n/2}\cos\frac{n\pi}{4} + i2^{n/2}\sin\frac{n\pi}{4}$$

Equating real and imaginary parts on both sides we have

$$P_0 - P_2 + P_4 - P_6 + \ldots = 2^{n/2}\cos n\pi/4$$

$$P_1 - P_3 + P_5 - P_7 + \ldots = 2^{n/2}\sin n\pi/4$$

Problem 23 If $2\cos\alpha = a + \frac{1}{a}$, $2\cos\beta = b + \frac{1}{b}$,

$$2\cos\gamma = c + \frac{1}{c} \quad \text{etc.}$$

prove that

$$2\cos(\alpha + \beta + \gamma + \ldots) = abc \ldots + \frac{1}{abc \ldots}$$

Solution.

$$2\cos\alpha = a + \frac{1}{a}$$

$$2\cos\alpha = \frac{a^2 + 1}{a}$$

$$\Rightarrow a^2 - 2a\cos\alpha + 1 = 0$$

$$a = \frac{2\cos\alpha \pm \sqrt{4\cos^2\alpha - 4}}{2}$$

$$= \frac{2\cos\alpha \pm \sqrt{-4(1 - \cos^2\alpha}}{2}$$

$$= \frac{2\cos\alpha \pm 2i\sin\alpha}{2}$$

$$a = (\cos\alpha \pm i\sin\alpha)$$

Taking only positive sign we have

$$a = \cos\alpha + i\sin\alpha$$

Similarly

$$b = \cos\beta + i\sin\beta$$

$$c = \cos\gamma + i\sin\gamma$$

etc.

Now

$$\text{RHS} = abc \ldots + \frac{1}{abc} \ldots$$

$$= (\cos\alpha + i\sin\alpha)(\cos\beta + i\sin\beta)\ldots$$

$$+ \frac{1}{(\cos\alpha + i\sin\alpha)}\,\frac{1}{(\cos\beta + i\sin\beta)}$$

$$= \cos(\alpha + \beta + \gamma \ldots) + i\sin(\alpha + \beta + \gamma + \ldots)$$
$$+ \cos(\alpha + \beta + \gamma + \ldots) - i\sin(\alpha + \beta + \gamma + \ldots)$$

$$= 2\cos(\alpha + \beta + \gamma + \ldots)$$ LHS (*proved*)

Problem 24 If $\cos\theta = \frac{1}{2}\left(a - \frac{1}{a}\right)$; $\cos\phi = \frac{1}{2}\left(b + \frac{1}{b}\right)$, show that $\cos(\theta + \phi)$ is one of the values of $\frac{1}{2}\left(ab + \frac{1}{ab}\right)$

Solution we have

$$\cos\theta = \frac{1}{2}\left(a + \frac{1}{a}\right)$$

$$2\cos\theta = \frac{a^2 + 1}{a}$$

$$a^2 - 2a\cos\theta + 1 = 0$$

$$\Rightarrow \quad a = \frac{2\cos\theta \pm \sqrt{4\cos^2\theta - 4}}{2}$$

$$\Rightarrow \quad a = \frac{2\cos\theta \ \pm 2\,i\sin\theta}{2}$$

$$\Rightarrow \quad a = \cos\theta \pm i\sin\theta$$

Taking positive sign we have $a = \cos\theta + i\sin\theta$

similarly $b = \cos\phi + i\sin\phi$

Now $\frac{1}{2}\left(ab + \frac{1}{ab}\right) = \frac{1}{2}$ [($\cos\theta + i\sin\theta)(\cos\phi + i\sin\phi)$

$+ (\cos\theta + i\sin\theta)^{-1} \ (\cos\phi + i\sin\phi)^{-1}$

$= \frac{1}{2}[\cos(\theta + \phi) + i\sin(\theta + \phi) + \cos(\theta + \phi) - i\sin(\theta + \phi)]$

$= \frac{1}{2}[2\cos(\theta + \phi)] = \cos(\theta + \phi)$ *(proved)*

Problem. 25 Solve $x^6 + x^5 + x^4 + x^3 + x^2 + x + 1 = 0$

Solution. We have $x^6 + x^5 + x^4 + x^3 + x^2 + x + 1 = 9$

$\Rightarrow (x - 1)(x^6 + x^5 + x^4 + x^3 + x^2 + x + 1) = 0$

$\Rightarrow x^7 + x^6 + x^5 + x^4 + x^3 + x^2 + x$

$\quad - x^6 - x^5 - x^4 - x^3 - x^2 - 1 = 0$

$\Rightarrow x^7 - 1 = 0$

$\Rightarrow x^7 = 1$

$\Rightarrow x^7 = \cos 0 + i\sin 0$

$\Rightarrow x^7 = \cos(0 + 2n\pi) + i\sin(0 + 2n\pi)$

$\Rightarrow x^7 = \cos 2n\pi + i\sin 2n\pi$

$\Rightarrow x = [\cos 2n\pi + i\sin 2n\pi]^{1/n}$

$$\Rightarrow \quad x = \cos\frac{2n\pi}{7} + i\sin\frac{2n\pi}{7}$$

$$n = 0, 1, 2 \ldots . 6.$$

Problem 26 Apply Dc-Maivre's theorem to solve.

$$x^7 + x^5 + x^2 + 1 = 0$$

Soution.

$$x^7 + x^5 + x^2 + 1 = 0$$

$$\Rightarrow \quad x^5 (x^2 + 1) + 1 (x^2 + 1) = 0$$

$$\Rightarrow \quad (x^5 + 1)(x^2 + 1) = 0$$

Now either

$$x^5 + 1 = 0$$

$$x^5 = -1$$

$$\Rightarrow \quad x^5 = \cos \pi + i \sin \pi$$

$$\Rightarrow \quad x^5 = \cos (2n\pi + \pi) + i \sin (2n\pi + \pi)$$

$$\Rightarrow \quad x = \cos \frac{(2n+1)\pi}{5} + i \sin \frac{(2n+1)\pi}{5}$$

$$x = 0, 1, 2, \ldots 4$$

or

$$x^2 + 1 = 0$$

$$x^2 = -1$$

$$x^2 = \cos (2n+1)\pi + i \sin (2n+1)\pi$$

$$x = \cos \frac{(2n+1)\pi}{2} + i \sin \frac{(2n+1)\pi}{2}$$

$$n = 0, 1$$

Problem 26. Prove, by use of De-Moivre's theorem that the roots of the equation $(x-1)^n = x^n$, $n$being a+ve integer are

$$\frac{1}{2}\left\{1 + i \cot \frac{r\pi}{n}\right\}$$

where $\quad r = 0, 1, 2, \ldots (n-1)$

Solution We have $\quad (x-1)^n = x^n$

$$\Rightarrow \quad \left(\frac{x-1}{x}\right)^n = 1$$

$$\Rightarrow \quad \left(\frac{x-1}{x}\right)^n = \cos 0 + i \sin 0$$

$$\Rightarrow \quad \left(\frac{x-1}{x}\right)^n = \cos (0 + 2r\pi) + i \sin (0 + 2r\pi)$$

$$\Rightarrow \quad \left(\frac{x-1}{x}\right) = \cos \frac{2r\pi}{n} + i \sin \frac{2r\pi}{n}$$

$$\Rightarrow \quad 1 - \frac{1}{x} = \cos \frac{2r\pi}{n} + i \sin \frac{2r\pi}{n}$$

$$\Rightarrow \quad \frac{1}{x} = 1 - \cos \frac{2r\pi}{n} - i \sin \frac{2r\pi}{n}$$

$$\Rightarrow \quad x = \frac{1}{1 - \cos \frac{2r\pi}{n} - i \sin \frac{2r\pi}{n}}$$

$$\Rightarrow \quad x = \frac{1}{2\sin^2\frac{r\pi}{n} - i\sin^2\frac{r\pi}{n}}$$

$$\Rightarrow \quad x = \frac{1}{-2i\sin\frac{r\pi}{n} - 2i\sin\frac{r\pi}{n}\cos\frac{r\pi}{n}}$$

$$\Rightarrow \quad x = \frac{1}{-2i\sin\frac{r\pi}{n}\left(\cos\frac{r\pi}{n} + i\sin\frac{r\pi}{n}\right)}$$

$$\Rightarrow \quad x = \frac{\left(\cos\frac{r\pi}{n} - i\sin\frac{r\pi}{n}\right)}{-2i\sin\frac{r\pi}{n}}$$

$$\Rightarrow \quad x = \frac{i^2\left(\cos\frac{r\pi}{n}\ i\sin\frac{r\pi}{n}\right)}{2i\sin\frac{r\pi}{n}}$$

$$\Rightarrow \quad x = \frac{i}{2}\left(\cot\frac{r\pi}{n} - i\right)$$

$$\Rightarrow \quad x = \frac{1}{2}\left(i\cot\frac{r\pi}{n} - i^2\right)$$

$$\Rightarrow \quad x = \frac{1}{2}\left(i\cot\frac{r\pi}{n} + 1\right)$$

where $\quad r = 0, 1, 2, \ldots (n-1)$

Problem 28. Show that the roots of $8x^3 - 4x^2 - 4x + 1 = 0$ are $\cos\frac{\pi}{7}$, $\cos\frac{3\pi}{7}$, and $\cos\frac{5\pi}{7}$ and deduce from it the equation whose roots are $\sec^2\frac{\pi}{7}$, $\sec^2\frac{3\pi}{7}$, $\sec^2\frac{5\pi}{7}$.

Solution. Let

$$7\theta = (2n+1)\pi$$

$$\theta = \frac{(2n+1)\pi}{7}$$

$$\cos\theta = \cos\frac{(2n+1)\pi}{7}$$

$$n = 0, 1, 2, 3, 4, 5, 6$$

The distinct values of $\cos\theta$ can be obtained by putting $n = 0, 1, 2, 3$. The distinct vallues of cos are

$$\cos\frac{\pi}{7}, \cos\frac{3\pi}{7}, \cos\frac{5\pi}{7}, \cos\pi = -1$$

Now $\quad 7\theta = (2n + 1)\pi$

$$4\theta + 3\theta = (2n + 1)\pi$$

$$4\theta = (2n + 1)\pi - 3\theta$$

$$\cos 4\theta = \cos[(2n + 1)\pi - 3\theta]$$

$$\cos 4\theta = -\cos 3\theta$$

$$2\cos^2 2\theta - 1 = -(4\cos^3 c - 3\cos\theta)$$

$$[2(2\cos^2\theta - 1)^2 - 1] = 3\cos\theta - 3\cos^3\theta$$

$$\Rightarrow \quad [2(4\cos^4\theta - 4\cos^2\theta + 1) - 1] = 3\cos\theta - 4\cos^3\theta$$

$$\Rightarrow \quad 8\cos^4\theta - 8\cos^2\theta + 2 - 1 = 3\cos\theta - 4\cos^3\theta$$

$$\Rightarrow \quad 8\cos^4\theta + \cos^3\theta - 8\cos^2\theta - 3\cos\theta + 1 = 0$$

$$\Rightarrow \quad 8x^4 + 4x^3 - 8x^2 - 3x + 1 = 0 \qquad (i)$$

where $x = \cos\theta$

since $x = -1$

so $(x + 1)$ must be a factor of the equation (l)

$$\Rightarrow \quad 8x^4 + 8x^3 - 4x^3 - 4x^2 - 4x^2 - 4x + x + 1 = 0$$

$$\Rightarrow \quad 8x^3(x + 1) - 4x^2(x + 1) - 4x(x + 1) + 1(x + 1) = 0$$

$$\Rightarrow \quad (x + 1)(8x^3 - 4x^2 - 4x + 1) = 0$$

$$\Rightarrow \quad 8x^3 - 4x^2 - 4x + 1 = 0 \qquad - (2)$$

Thus the roots of $8x^3 - 4x^2 - 4x + 1 = 0$

are $\cos\frac{\pi}{7}$, $\cos\frac{3\pi}{7}$ and $\cos\frac{5\pi}{7}$.

Now we have to deduce the equation whose roots

are $\sec^2\frac{\pi}{7}$, $\sec^2\frac{3\pi}{7}$, $\sec^2\frac{5\pi}{7}$

Now substituting $\quad \frac{1}{x^2} = \gamma$ we have

$$\Rightarrow \quad x^2 = \frac{1}{\gamma}$$

$$8x^3 - 4x^2 - 4x + 1 = 0$$

$$\Rightarrow \quad 8x^3 - 4x = 4x^2 - 1$$

$$\Rightarrow \quad 4x(2x^2 - 1) = 4x^2 - 1$$

$$\Rightarrow \quad 4x\left(\frac{2}{\gamma} - 1\right) = \left(\frac{4}{\gamma} - 1\right)$$

$$\Rightarrow \quad 4x\frac{(2-\gamma)}{\gamma} = \frac{(4-\gamma)}{\gamma}$$

$$\Rightarrow \quad 4x(2-\gamma) = (4-\gamma)$$

squaring both sides we have

$$\Rightarrow \quad 16x^2(4 - 4\gamma + \gamma^2) = (16 - 8\gamma + \gamma^2)$$

$$\Rightarrow \quad \frac{16}{\gamma}(4 - 4\gamma + \gamma^2) = (16 - 8\gamma + \gamma^2)$$

$$\Rightarrow \quad 64 - 64\gamma + 16\gamma^2 = 16\gamma - 8\gamma^2 + \gamma^3$$

$$\Rightarrow \quad \gamma^3 - 8\gamma^2 + 16\gamma - 64\gamma - 16\gamma^2 - 64 = 0$$

$$\Rightarrow \quad \gamma^3 - 24\gamma^2 + 80\gamma - 64 = 0$$

Thus the equation whose roots are $\sec^2\frac{\pi}{7}$, $\sec^2\frac{3\pi}{7}$, $\sec^2\frac{5\pi}{7}$

is given by

$$\gamma^3 - 24\gamma^2 + 80\gamma - 64 = 0 \qquad \textit{(proved)}$$

Problem 29 (*i*) Prove that the roots of the equation

$$8x^3 + 4x^2 - 4x - 1 = 0 \text{ are}$$

$$\cos\frac{2\pi}{7}, \cos\frac{4\pi}{7}, \text{ and } \cos\frac{6\pi}{7}$$

(*ii*) prove that $\cos\frac{2\pi}{7}, \cos\frac{4\pi}{7}, \cos\frac{6\pi}{7} = \frac{1}{8}$

(*iii*) $\cos\frac{2\pi}{7} + \cos\frac{4\pi}{7} + \cos\frac{6\pi}{7} = -\frac{1}{2}$

(*iv*) Evaluate $\sec\frac{2\pi}{7} + \sec\frac{4\pi}{7} + \sec\frac{6\pi}{7}$

Solution Let

$$7\theta = 2n\pi$$

$$\theta = \frac{2n\pi}{7}$$

$$\cos\theta = \cos\frac{2n\pi}{7} \qquad n = 0, 1, 2, 3, 4, 5, 6$$

The distinct values of $\cos\theta$ is given by

$$\cos 0 = 1, \cos\frac{2\pi}{7}\ \cos\frac{4\pi}{7}\ \cos\frac{6\pi}{7}$$

Now $$7\theta = 2n\pi$$

$$4\theta + 3\theta = 2n\pi$$
$$4\theta = 2n\pi - 3\theta$$

$$\cos 4\theta = \cos(2n\pi - 3\theta$$

$$\cos 4\,\theta = \cos 3\,\theta$$

$$2\cos^2 2\theta - 1 = 4\cos^3\theta - 3\cos\theta$$

$$2(2\cos^2\theta - 1)^2 - 1 = 4\cos^3\theta - 3\cos\theta$$

$$\Rightarrow\quad 2[(4\cos^4\theta - 4\cos^2\theta + 1)] - 1 = 4\cos^3\theta\cos\theta$$

$$\Rightarrow\quad 8\cos^4\theta - 8\cos^2 + 2 - 1 = 4\cos^3\theta - 3\cos\theta$$

$$\Rightarrow\quad 8\cos^4\theta - 4\cos^3\theta - 8\cos^2\theta + 3\cos\theta + 1 = 3$$

$$\Rightarrow\quad 8x^4 - 4x^3 - 8x^2 + 3x + 1 = 0 \qquad (1)$$

since $x=1$ so $x - 1$ must be a factor of the equation (*i*)

$$\Rightarrow\quad 8x^4 - 8x^3 + 4x^3 - 4x^2 - 4x^2 + 4x - x + 1 = 0$$

$$\Rightarrow\quad 8x^3(x-1) + 4x^2(x-1) - 4x(x-1) - 1(x-1) = 0$$

$$\Rightarrow\quad (x-1)(8x^3 + 4x^2 - 4x - 1) = 0$$

$$\Rightarrow\quad 8x^3 + 4x^2 - 4x - 1 = 0$$

Thus the equation whose roots are $\cos\frac{2\pi}{7}$, $\cos\frac{4\pi}{7}$ and $\cos\frac{6\pi}{7}$

is given by

$$8x^2 + 4x^2 - 4x - 1 = 0 \qquad (2)$$

which is of the form

$$a_0 x^3 + a_1 x^2 + a_2 x + a_3 = 0$$

$$a_0 = 8, a_1 = 4\ a_2 = -4, a_, = -1$$

then sum of the roots taken once a tatime

$$= (-1)^1 \frac{a_1}{a_0}$$

$$\cos\frac{2\pi}{7} + \cos\frac{4\pi}{7} + \cos\frac{6\pi}{7} = (-1)^1\ \frac{4}{8} = -\frac{1}{2}$$

sum of the roots taken thrice at a time

$$= (-1)^3 \frac{a_3}{a_0}$$

$$\cos\frac{2\pi}{7}, \cos\frac{4\pi}{7}, \cos\frac{6\pi}{7} = -1\frac{(-1)}{8} = \frac{1}{8}$$

Now we have to find the equation whose roots are

$$\sec\frac{2\pi}{7}, \sec\frac{4\pi}{7} \text{ and } \sec\frac{6\pi}{7}$$

substituting $\frac{1}{x} = y$ in equation (2) we have

$$\frac{8}{y^3} + \frac{4}{y^2} - \frac{4}{y} - 1 = 0$$

$$8 + 4y - 4y^2 - y^3 = 0$$

$$\Rightarrow y^3 + 4y^2 - 4y - 8 = 0$$

Thus the equation whose roots are

$$\sec\frac{2\pi}{7}, \sec\frac{4\pi}{7} \text{ and } \sec\frac{6\pi}{7} \text{ is given}$$

$$y^3 + 4y^2 - 4y - 8 = 0$$

and hence sum of the roots taken once at a time

$$\sec\frac{2\pi}{7} + \text{seec}\frac{4\pi}{7} + \sec\frac{6\pi}{7} = (-1)^1\frac{a_1}{a_0}$$

$$= -1\frac{4}{1}$$

$$= -4$$

i.e. $\sec\frac{2\pi}{7} + \text{se}\frac{4\pi}{7} + \text{see}\frac{6\pi}{7} = -4$ *(Proved)*

Problem 30 Show that

$$\left\{\frac{(1 + \sin\theta) + i\cos\theta}{(1 + \sin\theta) - i\cos\theta}\right\}^n = \cos\left(\frac{n\pi}{2} - n\theta\right) + i\sin\left(\frac{n\pi}{2} - n\theta\right)$$

Solution. $= \left\{\frac{(1 + \sin\theta) + i\cos\theta}{(1 + \sin\theta) - i\cos\theta}\right\}^n$

$$= \left\{\frac{\cos^2\theta + \sin^2\theta + \sin\theta + i\cos\theta}{1 + \sin\theta - i\cos\theta}\right\}^n$$

$$= \left\{\frac{\sin^2\theta - i^2\cos^2\theta + \sin\theta + i\cos\theta}{1 + \sin\theta - i\cos\theta}\right\}^n$$

$$= \left[\frac{(\sin\theta + i\cos\theta)(\sin\theta - i\cos\theta) + (\sin\theta + i\cos\theta)}{1 + \sin\theta - i\cos\theta}\right]^n$$

$$= (\sin\theta + i\cos\theta)^n \left\{\frac{1 + \sin\theta - i\cos\theta}{1 + \sin\theta - i\cos\theta}\right\}^n$$

$$= (\sin\theta + i\cos\theta)^n$$

$$= \left[\cos\left(\frac{\pi}{2} - \theta\right) + i\sin\left(\frac{\pi}{2} - \theta\right)\right]^n$$

$$= \cos n\left(\frac{\pi}{2} - \theta\right) + i\sin n\left(\frac{\pi}{2} - \theta\right)$$

$$= \cos\left(\frac{n\pi}{2} - n\theta\right) + i\sin\left(\frac{n\pi}{2} - n\theta\right) \qquad \textit{RHS (proved)}$$

Problem 31 If $\alpha = \cos\frac{2\pi r}{n} + i\sin\frac{2\pi r}{n}$ and if r and p are prime to n, prove that $1 + \alpha^P + \alpha^{2P} + \ldots + \alpha^{(n-1)P} = 0$

Solution LHS $1 + \alpha^P + \alpha^{2P} + \ldots \alpha^{(n-1)P}$

$$= \frac{1 - (\alpha^P)^n}{1 - \alpha^P} = \frac{1 - (\alpha^n)^P}{1 - \alpha^P}$$

$$= \frac{1 - \left[\left(\cos\frac{2\pi r}{n} + i\sin\frac{2\pi r}{n}\right)^n\right]^P}{1 - \left(\cos\frac{2\pi r}{n} + i\sin\frac{2\pi r}{n}\right)^P}$$

$$= \frac{1 - \left[\cos\frac{2\pi r}{n} + i\sin\frac{2\pi r}{n}\right]^P}{1 - \left(\cos\frac{2\pi^K r}{n} + i\sin\frac{2\pi Pr}{n}\right)}$$

$$= \frac{1 - (\cos 2\pi r + i\sin 2\pi r)^P}{1 - \left(\cos\frac{2\pi^P r}{n} + i\sin\frac{2\pi Pr}{n}\right)}$$

$$= \frac{1 - 1^P}{1 - \left(\cos\frac{2\pi Pr}{n} + i\sin\frac{2\pi Pr}{n}\right)}$$

$$= \frac{1 - 1}{1 - \left(\cos\frac{2\pi Pr}{n} + i\sin\frac{2\pi Pr}{n}\right)}$$

$$= 0 \text{ since } \cos\frac{2\pi r}{n} + i\sin\frac{2\pi Pr}{n} \neq 1$$

because r and P are primeton.

Thus $1 + \alpha^P + \alpha^{2P} + \ldots + \alpha^{(n-1)P} = 0$ *(Proved)*

Problem 32 If $(1 + x)^n = a_0 + a_1 x + a_2 x^2 + \ldots$ (n = +ve enteger) prove that

$$a_0 + a_4 + a_3 + \ldots = 2^{n-2} + 2^{n/2-1} \cos \frac{n\pi}{4}$$

Solution We have

$$(1 + x)^n = a_0 + a_1 x + a_2 x^2 + \ldots \tag{1}$$

since (1) is an identity so

putting $x = i$ we have

$$(1 + i)^n = a_0 + a_1 i + a_2 i^2 + a_3 i^3 + a_4 i^4 + \ldots$$

$$(1 + i)^n = a_0 + a_1 i - a_2 - a_3 i + a_4 + a_5 i - a_6 - a_7 i + .$$

$$= (a_0 - a_2 + a_4 - \ldots -) + i (a_1 - a_3 + a_5 - \ldots)$$

Now we have

$$(1 + i)^n$$

$$= \left[\sqrt{2} \left(\frac{1}{\sqrt{2}} + i \frac{1}{\sqrt{2}}\right)\right]^n$$

$$= \left[\sqrt{2} \left(\cos \frac{\pi}{4} + i \sin \frac{\pi}{4}\right)\right]^n$$

$$= 2^{\frac{n}{2}} \left(\cos \frac{n\pi}{4} + i \sin \frac{n\pi}{4}\right)$$

so $$2^{\frac{n}{2}} \cos \frac{n\pi}{4} + i\, 2^{\frac{n}{2}} \sin \frac{n\pi}{4}$$

$$= (a_0 - a_2 + a_4 - a_6 + \ldots) + i (a_1 - a_3 + a_5 - \ldots)$$

Now equating the real and imaginary parts on both sides we have

$$a_0 - a_2 + a_4 - a_6 + \ldots$$

$$= 2^{\frac{n}{2}} \cos \frac{n}{4} \tag{2}$$

Again putting $x = +1$ we have

$$2^n = a_0 + a_1 + a_2 + \ldots \tag{3}$$

putting $x = -1$ we have

$$0 = a_0 - a_1 + a_2 - \ldots \tag{4}$$

Adding (3) and (4) (4) we have

$$2^n = 2\,a_0 + 2a_2 + \ldots$$

$$a_0 + a_2 + a_4 + \ldots = 2^{u-1} \qquad (5)$$

Adding (2) and (5)

$$2\,(a_0 + a_4 + a_8 + \ldots) = 2^{n-1} + 2\,\frac{n}{2}\cos\frac{n\pi}{4}$$

$$a_0 + a_4 + a_8 + \ldots = 2^{n-2} + 2^{n/2-1}\cos\frac{n\pi}{4} \quad \text{RHS } (\textit{Proved})$$

Problem 33 If $\cos\alpha + 2\cos\beta + 3\cos\gamma = \sin\alpha + 2\sin\beta + 3\sin\gamma = 0$ prove that

$$\cos 3\alpha + 8\cos 3\beta + 27\cos 3\gamma = 18\cos(\alpha + \beta + \gamma)$$
$$\sin 3\alpha + 8\sin 3\beta + 27\sin 3\gamma = 18\sin(\alpha + \beta + \gamma)$$

Solution Let

$$x = \cos\alpha + i\sin\alpha$$
$$y = 2\cos\beta + 2\,i\sin\beta$$
$$z = 3\cos\gamma + 3\,i\sin\gamma$$

$$x + y + z = (\cos\alpha + i\sin\alpha) + (2\cos\beta + 2i\sin\beta) + (3\cos\gamma + 3i\sin\gamma)$$

$$x + y + z = (\cos\alpha + 2\cos\beta + 3\cos\gamma) + i\,(\sin\alpha + 2\sin\alpha + 3\sin\gamma)$$
$$= 0 + i \times 0$$
$$= 0$$

Again xyz

$$= 2.3\,(\cos\alpha + i\sin\alpha)(\cos\beta + i\sin\beta)(\cos\gamma + i\sin\gamma)$$
$$= 6\cos(\alpha + \beta + \gamma) + i\sin(\alpha + \beta + \gamma)$$

Now

$$x^3 + y^3 + z^3 - 3\,xyz$$
$$= (x + y + z)(x^2 + y^2 + z^2 - xy - yz - xz)$$
$$= 0$$

$$\Rightarrow x^3 + y^3 + z^3 = 3\,xyz$$

$$\Rightarrow (\cos\alpha + i\sin)^3 + 8\,(\cos\beta + i\sin\beta)^3 + 27\,(\cos\gamma + i\sin\gamma)^3 = 3 \times 6\,[\cos(\alpha + \beta + \gamma) + i\sin(\alpha + \beta + \gamma)]$$

$$\Rightarrow (\cos 3\alpha + i\sin 3\alpha) + (\cos 3\beta + i\sin 3\beta) + 27\,(\cos 3\gamma + i\sin 3\gamma) = 18\,[\cos(\alpha + \beta + \gamma) + i\sin(\alpha + \beta + \gamma)]$$

$$\Rightarrow (\cos 3\alpha + 8 \cos 3\beta + 27 \cos 3\gamma)$$
$$+ i (\sin 3 \alpha + 8 \sin 3 \beta + 27 \sin 3\gamma)$$
$$= 18 [\cos (\alpha + \beta + \gamma) + i \sin (\alpha + \beta + \gamma)]$$

Equating real and imaginary parts we have

$$\cos 3\alpha + 8 \cos 3\beta + 27 \cos 3\gamma$$
$$= 18 \cos (\alpha + \beta + \gamma)$$
$$\sin 3\alpha + 8 \sin 3\beta + 27 \sin 3\gamma$$
$$= 18 \sin (\alpha + \beta + \gamma)$$

(Proved)

Problem 44 Solve $x^5 = 1$, by De-Moivre's theorem and prove that the sum of nth powers of the roots of the equation, n being an integernot divisible by 5 is zero.

Solution We have $x^5 = 1$

$$x^5 = \cos 0 + i \sin 0$$
$$x^5 = \cos (0 + 2r\pi) + i \sin (0 + 2r\pi)$$
$$x^5 = \cos 2r\pi + i \sin 2r\pi$$
$$x = [\cos 2r\pi + i \sin (+ 2r\pi]^{1/5}$$
$$x = \cos \frac{2r\pi}{5} + i \sin \frac{2r\pi}{5} \qquad r = 0, 1, 2, 3, 4$$

so the different values of x are

$$1, \cos \frac{2\pi}{5} + i \sin \frac{2\pi}{5}, \cos \frac{4\pi}{5} + i \sin \frac{4\pi}{5}$$
$$\cos \frac{6\pi}{5} + i \sin \frac{6\pi}{5}, \cos \frac{8\pi}{5} + i \sin \frac{8\pi}{5}$$

Now we have to show that the sum of nth powers of these are zero

Now

$$1^n + \left(\cos\frac{2\pi}{5} + i \sin\right)^n + \left(\cos \frac{4\pi}{5} + i \sin \frac{4\pi}{5}\right)^n$$
$$+\left(\cos\frac{2\pi}{5} + i \sin \frac{6\pi}{4}\right)^n + \left(\cos \frac{8\pi}{5} + i \sin \frac{8\pi 5}{5}\right)^n$$
$$=1 + \left(\cos \frac{2\pi n}{5} + i \sin \frac{2\pi n}{5}\right) + \left(\cos \frac{2\pi n}{5} + i \sin \frac{2\pi n}{5}\right)^2$$
$$+\left(\cos\frac{2\pi n}{5} + i \sin \frac{2\pi n}{5}\right)^3 + \left(\cos + i \sin\frac{2\pi n}{5}\right)^4$$

which is the sum of 5 terms in Geometric progression whose common ratio is $\cos\frac{2n\pi}{5} + i\sin\frac{2n\pi}{5}$

$$\text{sum} = \frac{1 - \left(\cos\frac{2\pi n}{5} + i\sin\frac{2\pi n}{5}\right)^5}{\cdot - \left(\cos\frac{2\pi n}{5} + i\sin\frac{2\pi n}{5}\right)}$$

$$= \frac{1 - \left(\cos\frac{2\pi 5n}{5} + i\sin\frac{2\pi 5n}{5}\right)^5}{1 - \left(\cos\frac{2\pi n}{5} + i\sin\frac{2\pi n}{5}\right)}$$

$$= \frac{1-1}{1 - \left(\cos\frac{2\pi n}{5} + i\sin\frac{2\pi n}{5}\right)} = 0$$

since n is not disible by zero

so $\qquad \cos\frac{2\pi n}{5} + i\sin\frac{2\pi n}{5} \neq 1$

Problem 45 Solve $\quad x^9 - x^5 + x^4 - 1 = 0$

$$x^9 - x^5 + x^4 - 1 = 0$$

$$\Rightarrow \quad x^5(x^4 - 1) + 1(x^4 - 1) = 0$$

$$\Rightarrow \quad (x^5 + 1)(x^4 - 1) = 0$$

so either

$$x^5 + 1 = 0, \text{ or } x^4 - 1 = 0$$

$$x^5 + 1 = 0$$

$$\Rightarrow \quad x^5 = -1$$

$$\Rightarrow \quad x^5 = \cos\pi + \sin\pi$$

$$\Rightarrow \quad x^5 = \cos(\pi + 2r\pi) + i\sin(\pi + 2r\pi)$$

$$\Rightarrow \quad x^5 = \cos(2r+1)\pi + i\sin(2r+1)\pi$$

$$\Rightarrow \quad x = [\cos(2r+1)\pi + i\sin(2r+1)\pi]^{1/5}$$

$$\Rightarrow \quad x = \cos\frac{(2r+1)\pi}{5} + i\sin\frac{(2r+1)\pi}{5} \qquad (1)$$

where $\qquad r = 0, 1, 2, 3, 4$

or $\qquad x^4 - 1 = 0$

$$\Rightarrow \quad x^4 = 1$$

$$\Rightarrow \quad x^4 = \cos + i \sin 0$$

$$\Rightarrow \quad x^4 = \cos(0 + 2r\pi) + i \sin(0 + 2r\pi)$$

$$\Rightarrow \quad x^4 = \cos 2r\pi + i \sin 2r\pi$$

$$\Rightarrow \quad x = \cos [\cos 2r\pi + i \sin 2r\pi]^{1/4}$$

$$\Rightarrow \quad x = \cos \frac{2r\pi}{4} + i \sin \frac{2r\pi}{4}$$

$$\Rightarrow \quad x = \cos \frac{r\pi}{2} + i \sin \frac{\pi r}{2} \qquad (2)$$

where $r = 0, 1, 2, 3$

Equation (1) and (2) will give the solution of the given equation.

Problem 46. Express $\left(\frac{\cos \;+ i \sin x)}{\sin x \;+ i \cos x}\right)^5$ in the form $\cos A + i \sin A$

Solution $\left(\frac{\cos x + i \sin x}{\sin x + i \cos x}\right)^5 = \left[\frac{\cos x + i \sin x}{\cos\left(\frac{\pi}{2} - x\right) + i \sin\left(\frac{\pi}{2} - x\right)}\right]^5$

$$= \left[(\cos x + i \sin x)\left\{\cos\left(\frac{\pi}{2} - x\right) - i \sin\left(\frac{\pi}{2} - x\right\}\right]^5$$

$$= \left[(\cos x + i \sin x)\left\{\cos\left(-\left(\frac{\pi}{2} - x\right)\right) + i \sin\left(-\left(\frac{\pi}{2} - x\right)\right\}\right]^5$$

$$= \left[\cos\left(x - \overline{\frac{\pi}{2} - x}\right) + i \sin\left(x - \overline{\frac{\pi}{2} - x}\right)\right]^5$$

$$= \left[\cos\left(2x - \frac{\pi}{2}\right) + i \sin\left(2x - \frac{\pi}{2}\right)\right]^5$$

$$= \cos\left(10x - \frac{5\pi}{2}\right) + i \sin\left(10x - \frac{5\pi}{2}\right) \qquad \textbf{Ans.}$$

Problem 47 Obtain the three values of

$$\sqrt[3]{1 + \sqrt{-3}} + \sqrt[3]{1 - \sqrt{-3}}$$

Solution Putting $1 = r \cos \theta$ (1)

and $\sqrt{3} = r \text{ sine } \theta$ (2)

The expression is

$$\sqrt[3]{1+\sqrt{-3}}+\sqrt[3]{1-\sqrt{-3}}$$

$$= 3\sqrt{r\cos\theta + i\,r\sin\theta} + 3\sqrt{r\cos\theta - i\,r\sin\theta}$$

$$= (r\cos\theta + i\,r\sin\theta)^{1/3} + (r\cos\theta - i\sin\theta)^{1/3}$$

$$= r^{1/3}(\cos\theta + i\sin\theta)^{1/3} + (r\cos\theta - i\sin\theta)^{1/3}$$

$$= r^{1/3}[\{\cos(\theta+2n\pi) + i\sin(\theta+2n\pi)\}^{1/3} + \{\cos(\theta+2n\pi) - i\sin(\theta+2n\pi)\}]^{1/3}$$

$$= r^{1/3}\left[\cos\frac{(2n\pi+\theta)}{3} + i\sin\frac{(2n\pi+\theta)}{3} + \cos\frac{(2n\pi+\theta)}{3} - i\sin\frac{(2n\pi+\theta)}{3}\right]$$

$$= 2r^{1/3}\cos\frac{(2n\pi+\theta)}{3}$$

where $n = 0, 1, 2$

squaring (1) and (2) and adding

$$1 + 3 = r^2 \qquad r^2 = 4 \Rightarrow r = 2$$

Then expression

$$= 2\cdot 2^{1/3}\cos\frac{(2n\pi+\theta)}{3}$$

$$= 2^{1+1/3}\cos\frac{(2n\pi+\theta)}{3} = 2^{4/3}\cos\frac{(2n\pi+\theta)}{3}$$

where $n = 0, 1, 2$

Problem 48 If
$$x_1 = \cos\alpha_1 + i\sin\alpha_1$$
$$x_2 = \cos\alpha_2 + i\sin\alpha_2$$
$$x_3 = \cos\alpha_3 + i\sin\alpha_3$$
and if $x_1 + x_2 + x_3 = 0$ prove that
$$\sum\cos(\alpha_2 - \alpha_3) = -\frac{3}{2}$$

Solution $x_1 + x_2 + x_3 = 0$

$$(\cos\alpha_1 + i\sin\alpha_1) + (\cos\alpha_2 + i\sin\alpha_2) + (\cos\alpha_3 + \sin\alpha_3) = 0$$

$$(\cos\alpha_1 + \cos\alpha_2 \cos\alpha_3) + i(\sin\alpha_1 + \sin\alpha_2 + \sin\alpha_3) = 0$$

Equating the real and imaginary partson both sides we have

$$\cos\alpha_1 + \cos\alpha_2 + \cos\alpha_3 = 0 \tag{1}$$

$$\sin\alpha_1 + \sin\alpha_2 + \sin\alpha_3 = 0 \tag{2}$$

squaring and adding (1) and (2) we have

$$1+1+1+2\cos(\alpha_2-\alpha_3)+2\cos(\alpha_3-\alpha_1)+2\cos(\alpha_1-\alpha_2)=0$$

$$\Rightarrow \quad 2[\cos(\alpha_2-\alpha_3)+\cos(\alpha_3-\alpha_1)+\cos(\alpha_1-\alpha_2)]=-3$$

$$\Rightarrow \quad \cos(\alpha_2-\alpha_3)+\cos(\alpha_3-\alpha_1)+\cos(\alpha_1-\alpha_2)=-\frac{3}{2}$$

$$\Rightarrow \quad \sum\cos(\alpha_2-\alpha_3)=-\frac{3}{2}$$

Problem 49 Determine all possible values of the real angle θ, which satisfy the equality :

$$(\cos\theta+i\sin\theta)^{1/7}=\left(\cos\frac{\pi}{3}+i\sin\frac{\pi}{3}\right)^2$$

Solution We have

$$(\cos\theta+i\sin\theta)^{\frac{1}{7}}=\left(\cos\frac{\pi}{3}+i\sin\frac{\pi}{3}\right)^2$$

$$\cos(2n\pi+\theta)+i\sin(2n\pi+\theta)^{\frac{1}{7}}=\cos\frac{2\pi}{3}+i\sin\frac{2\pi}{3}$$

where $\qquad n=0,1,2\ldots 6$

$$\cos\frac{2n\pi+\theta}{7}+i\sin\frac{2n\pi+\theta}{7}=\cos\frac{2\pi}{3}+i\sin\frac{2\pi}{3}$$

Equating real and imaginary parts on both sides we have

$$\cos\frac{2n\pi+\theta}{7}=\cos\frac{2\pi}{3}$$

$$\sin\frac{2n\pi+\theta}{7}=\sin\frac{2\pi}{3}$$

$$\frac{2n\pi+\theta}{7}=\frac{2\pi}{3}$$

$$n=0,1,2\ldots 6$$

$$2n\pi+\theta=\frac{14\pi}{3}$$

$$\theta=\frac{14\pi}{3}-2n\pi$$

$$\theta=2\pi\left(\frac{7}{3}-n\right)$$

$$\theta=2\pi\left(\frac{7-3n}{3}\right)$$

$$\theta=\frac{2\pi}{3}(7-3n)$$

$$n=0,1,2,\ldots 6$$

Problem 50 If $2\cos\alpha = a + \frac{1}{a}$, $2\cos\beta = b + \frac{1}{b}$ etc. prove that

$$2\cos(p\alpha + q\beta + r\gamma + \ldots) = a^p b^q c^r \ldots + \frac{1}{a^p b^q c^r \ldots}$$

Solution Since $2\cos\alpha = a + \frac{1}{a}$

$$\Rightarrow \quad 2\cos\alpha = \frac{a^2+1}{1}$$

$$\Rightarrow \quad a^2 - 2a\cos\alpha + 1 = 0$$

$$\Rightarrow \quad a^2 - 2a\cos\alpha + \cos^2\alpha + \sin^2\alpha = 0$$

$$\Rightarrow \quad a^2 - 2a\cos\alpha + \cos^2\alpha = -\sin^2\alpha$$

$$\Rightarrow \quad (a - \cos\alpha)^2 = i^2\sin^2\alpha$$

$$\Rightarrow \quad a - \cos\alpha = \pm i\sin\alpha$$

$$\Rightarrow \quad a = \cos\alpha \pm i\sin\alpha$$

similarly $\quad b = \cos\beta \pm i\sin\beta$

$$c = \cos\gamma \pm i\sin\gamma \text{ etc}$$

Now taking + ve sign only

$$a = \cos\alpha + i\sin\alpha$$

$$b = \cos\beta + i\sin\beta$$

$$c = \cos\gamma + i\sin\gamma \text{ etc}$$

Now $\quad a^p b^q c^r \ldots + \frac{1}{a^p b^q c^r \ldots}$

$$= (\cos\alpha + i\sin\alpha)^p(\cos\beta + i\sin\beta)^q(\cos\gamma + i\sin\gamma)^r \ldots$$

$$+ \frac{1}{(\cos\alpha\ i\sin\alpha)^p(\cos\beta + i\sin\beta)^q(\cos\gamma + i\sin\gamma)^r} \ldots$$

$$= (\cos p\alpha + i\sin p\alpha)(\cos q\beta + i\sin q\beta)(\cos r\gamma + i\sin r\gamma) \ldots$$

$$+ (\cos\alpha - i\sin\alpha)^p(\cos\beta - i\sin\beta)^q(\cos\gamma - i\sin\gamma)^r \ldots$$

$$= \cos(p\alpha + q\beta + r\gamma + \ldots) + i\sin(p\alpha + p\beta + r\gamma + \ldots)$$

$$+ (\cos p\alpha - i\sin p\alpha)(\cos q\beta - i\sin q\beta)(\cos r\gamma - i\sin r\gamma) \ldots$$

$$= \cos(p\alpha + q\beta + r\gamma + \ldots) + i\sin(p\alpha + q\beta + r\gamma + \ldots)$$

$$+ \cos(p\alpha + q\beta + r\gamma + \ldots) - i\sin(p\alpha + q\beta + r\gamma + \ldots)$$

$$= 2\cos(p\alpha + q\beta + r\gamma + \ldots) \text{ LHS}$$ (*Proved*)

Problem 51 Reduce

$$\frac{(1+\sqrt{2}+i)^{10}}{1+\sqrt{2}-i)^{10}} \text{ to a simple form}$$

Solution let $1+\sqrt{2} = r\cos\theta$ (1)

$$1 = r\sin\theta \quad (2)$$

squaring (1) and (2) we have

$$1+2\sqrt{2}+2+1 = r^2$$

$$4+2\sqrt{2} = r^2$$

and $\tan\theta = \dfrac{1}{1+\sqrt{2}}$

$$\theta = \tan^{-1}\left(\frac{1}{1+\sqrt{2}}\right)$$

Then the expression reduces to

$$\frac{r(\cos\theta + ir\sin\theta)^{10}}{r\cos\theta - ir\sin\theta)^{10}} = \frac{r\cos\theta + i\sin\theta)^{10}}{(\cos\theta - i\sin\theta)^{10}}$$

$$= (\cos\theta + i\sin\theta)^{10}(\cos\theta + i\sin\theta)^{10}$$

$$= (\cos\theta + i\sin\theta)^{20} = \cos 20\theta + i\sin 20\theta$$

where $\theta = \tan^{-1}\dfrac{1}{1+\sqrt{2}}$ **Ans.**

Problem 52 If $x_r = \cos\theta_r + i\,sin\,\theta_r, (r = 1)\,2\ldots n)$ and if $x_1 + x_2 + x_3 + \ldots + x_n = 0$, then prove that

$$x_1^{-1} + x_2^{-1} + w_3^{-1} + \ldots + x_n^{-1} = 0$$

Solution We have

$$x_1 + x_2 + x_3 + \ldots + x^n = 0$$

$$(\cos\theta_1 + i\sin\theta_1) + (\cos\theta_2 + i\sin\theta_2) + (\cos\theta_3 + i\sin\theta_3) + \ldots + (\cos\theta_n + i\sin\vartheta_n) = 0$$

$$\Rightarrow (\cos\theta_1 + \cos\theta_2 + \ldots + \cos\theta_n) + i(\sin\theta_2 + \sin\theta_2 + \ldots + \sin\theta_n) = 0$$

$$\Rightarrow \cos\theta_1 + \cos\theta_2 + \ldots + \cos\theta_n = 0 \quad (1)$$

and $\sin\theta_1 + \sin\theta_2 + \ldots + \sin\theta_n = 0$ (2)

Now $x_1^{-1} + x_2^{-1} + x_3^{-1} + \ldots x_n^{-1} = 0$

$$(\cos\theta_1 - i\sin\theta_1) + (\cos\theta_2 - i\sin\theta_2) + \ldots + (\cos\theta_n - i\sin\theta_n)$$

$$= (\cos\theta_1 + \cos\theta_2 + \ldots + \cos\theta_n) - i(\sin\theta_1 + \sin\theta_2 + \ldots + \sin\vartheta_n)$$

$$= 0 - i \times 0 = 0$$

(Proved)

2

Theory of Equations

Polynomial equations, transformation of equations, relations between roots and coefficients of a polynomial equation, symmetric function of roots of cubic and biquadratic equations, location of roots and Newton's method for finding roots.

Relations between the roots and coefficients,

Theorem *In an equation with real coefficients, imaginary roots occur in conjugate pair.*

i.e. $\alpha + i\beta$ $(\beta \neq 0)$ be a root of the equation $f(x) = 0$ in which the coefficients are real, then $\alpha - i\beta$ must also be a root of the equation

$$f(x) = 0$$

since $\alpha + i\beta$ is a root of the equation

$$f(x) = 0$$

i.e.

$$f(\alpha + i\beta) = 0 \tag{1}$$

let us divide $f(x)$ by $[(x - \alpha)^2 + \beta^2]$ i.e. by $[x - (\alpha + i\beta)]\,[x - (\alpha - i\beta)]$ let the quotient be θ and the remainder is $Rx + R^1$. Then we have

$$f(x) \equiv \{(x - \alpha)^2 + \beta^2\}\, Q + Rx + R^1 \tag{2}$$

Now since $\alpha + i\beta$ is a root of the equation $f(x) = 0$ hence it will satisfy the expression (2)

Thus
$$\begin{aligned} f(\alpha + i\beta) &= [(\alpha + i\beta - \alpha)^2 + \beta^2]\, Q + Rx + R^1 \\ &= [(i\beta)^2 + \beta^2]\, Q + R(\alpha + i\beta) + R^1 \\ &= [-\beta^2 + \beta^2]\, Q + R(\alpha + i\beta) + R^1 \end{aligned}$$

$$(f(\alpha + i\beta) = R(\alpha + i\beta) + R^1$$

From equation (1) we have

$$R(\alpha + i\beta) + R^1 = 0$$

$$\Rightarrow (R\alpha + R^1) + iR\beta = 0$$

Equating the real part and imaginary part to zero we have

$$R\alpha + R^1 = 0$$

$$R\beta = 0$$

$$\Rightarrow R = 0 \text{ since } \beta \neq 0$$

otherwise the roots will be real

and $\quad R\alpha + R^1 = 0$

$\Rightarrow \quad 0\alpha + R^1 = 0$

$\Rightarrow \quad R^1 = 0$

Thus R and R^1 equals to zero

Hence from relation (2) we have

$$f(x) \equiv \{(x-\alpha)^2 + \beta^2\}\, Q$$

$$f(x) \equiv [x - (\alpha + i\beta)]\,[x - (\alpha - i\beta)]\, Q$$

This shows that $\quad x - (\alpha - i\beta)$ is a factor of $f(x)$

and consequently $\quad x = \alpha - i\beta \quad$ is a root of the equation

$$f(x) = 0$$

Cor I. Every equation of odd degree has at leat one real root

let $f(x) = 0$ be an equation of odd degree. let n be the degree of the equation $f(x) = 0$

$\Rightarrow$ n must be an odd integer let $f(x)$ have r real and s imaginary roots. Since imaginary roots occurs in conjugate pair and hence every equation of odd degree has at least one real root.

Cor II. On the same ground we can prove that in an equation with rational coefficients irrational roots occurs in conjugate pair [i.e. if $\alpha + \sqrt{\beta}$ is one root the other root must be $\alpha - \sqrt{\beta}$.

Note 1 If we want to find the common roots of any two polynomials then we have to find the Highest Commen Factor (HCF) the HCF is factorised and the common roots are obtained.

Relation between the roots and coefficients

Note 1 let $\alpha_1, \alpha_2, \alpha_3, \ldots \alpha_n$ be the roots of the polynomial equation

$$a_0 x^n + a_1 x^{n-1} + a_2 x^{n-2} + \ldots + a_n = 0$$

then sum of the product of the roots taken at a time

i.e.

$$\alpha_1 \alpha_2 \ldots \alpha_n = (-1)^n \frac{a_n}{a_0}$$

$$\alpha_1 + \alpha_2 + \ldots + \alpha_n = -\frac{a_1}{a_0}$$

$$\Sigma \alpha_1 \alpha_2 = \frac{a_2}{a_0} = (-1)^2 \frac{a_1}{a_0}$$

$$\Sigma \alpha_1 \alpha_2 \alpha_3 = -\frac{a_2}{a_0} = (-1)^3 \frac{a_2}{a_0}$$

Example 1 let

α, β and γ be the roots of the equation

$$ax^3 + 3bx^2 + 3cx + d = 0 \quad \text{then}$$

$$\alpha + \beta + \gamma = -\frac{3b}{a}$$

$$\alpha\beta + \beta\gamma + \alpha\gamma = \frac{3c}{a}$$

$$\alpha\beta\gamma = -\frac{d}{a}$$

Problen 1 Solve the equation $x^3 - 9x^2 + 14x + 24 = 0$, two of whose roots are in the ratio $2 : 3$.

Solution Let the roots of the equation be

2α, 3α and β then we have

$$2\alpha + 3\alpha + \beta = \frac{9}{1}$$

i.e.
$$5\alpha + \beta = 9 \tag{1}$$

$$2\alpha \cdot 3\alpha + 3\alpha \cdot \beta + 2\alpha \cdot \beta = 14$$

i.e.
$$6\alpha^2 + 5\alpha\beta = 14 \tag{2}$$

$$2\alpha\ 3\alpha\ \beta = -24$$

i.e.
$$\alpha^2\ \beta = -4 \tag{3}$$

Now Multiplying (1) by 5α we have

$$25\alpha^2 + 5\alpha\beta = 45\alpha$$

$$6\alpha^2 + 5\alpha\beta = 14$$

$$- \quad - \quad -$$

$$19\alpha^2 = 45\alpha - 14$$

i.e.
$$19\alpha^2 - 45\alpha + 14 = 0$$

on solving we get

$$\alpha = \frac{45 \pm \sqrt{(45)^2 - 4 . 19 . 14}}{38}$$

$$= \frac{45 \pm \sqrt{2025 - 1064}}{38}$$

$$= \frac{45 \pm \sqrt{961}}{38} = \frac{45 \pm 31}{38} = 2 \text{ or } \frac{7}{19}$$

If $\quad \alpha = 2 \quad \beta = 9 - 5\alpha = 9 - 5 \times 2 = 9 - 10 = -1$

If $\alpha = \frac{7}{19}$ $\beta = 9 - 5\alpha = 9 - 5 \times \frac{7}{19} = 9 - \frac{35}{19}$

$$= \frac{171 - 35}{19} = \frac{136}{19}$$

But $\alpha = \frac{7}{19}$ and $\beta = \frac{136}{19}$ do not satisfy (3)

Hence we take $\alpha = 2$ and consequently $\beta = -1$ so the roots are $3\alpha, 3\alpha, \beta$ i.e. $4, 6, -1$ **Ans.**

Problem 2 Solve the equation $2x^3 + 15x^2 + 37x - 30 = 0$ whose roots are in A.P.

Solution Let $\alpha - \delta$, α and $\alpha + \delta$ be the roots of the given equation

$$2x^3 - 15x^2 + 37x - 30 = 0$$

Then $\alpha - \delta + \alpha + \alpha + \delta = \frac{15}{2}$

$$3\alpha = \frac{15}{2}$$

$$\alpha = \frac{15}{2 \times 3} = \frac{5}{2} \quad (1)$$

Again $(\alpha - \delta)\, \alpha\, (\alpha + \delta) = \frac{30}{2}$

$$\alpha(\alpha^2 - \delta^2) = 15$$

$$\frac{5}{2}\left(\frac{25}{4} - \delta^2\right) = 15$$

$$\frac{25}{4} - \delta^2 = 6$$

$$\delta^2 = \frac{25}{4} - 6 = \frac{25 - 24}{4}$$

$$\delta^2 = \frac{1}{4} \Rightarrow \delta = \pm\frac{1}{2}$$

Thus the roots are $\alpha - \delta \quad \alpha \quad \text{and } \alpha + \delta$

$$\frac{5}{2} - \frac{1}{2} \quad \frac{5}{2} \quad \frac{5}{2} + \frac{1}{2}$$

$$\frac{4}{2} \quad \frac{5}{2} \quad \frac{6}{2}$$

i.e. $2 \quad \frac{5}{2} \quad 3$

If we take $\delta = -\frac{1}{2}$ we get the same roots.

Promblem 3 Solve the equation

$$4x^4 - 28x^3 + 51x^2 - 7x - 20 = 0$$

whose roots are in A. P.

Solution Let the roots of the given equation be

$$\alpha - 3\delta,\ \alpha - \delta\ \ \alpha + \delta\ \ \alpha + \delta$$

Now $$\alpha - 3\delta + \alpha - \delta + \alpha + \delta + \alpha + 3\delta \frac{28}{4}$$

$$4\alpha = \frac{28}{4} = 7 \Rightarrow \alpha = \frac{7}{4}$$

Again $(\alpha - 3\delta)(\alpha - \delta) + (\alpha - \delta)(\alpha + \delta) + (\alpha - 3\delta)(\alpha + 3\delta)$

$$+ (\alpha + \delta)(\alpha - 3\delta) + (\alpha + \delta)(\alpha + 3\delta)(\alpha - \delta)(\alpha + 3\delta) = \frac{51}{4}$$

$$\Rightarrow \alpha^2 - 4\alpha\delta + 3\delta^2 + \alpha^2 - \delta^2 + \alpha^2 - 9\delta^2 + \alpha^2 - 2\alpha\delta - 3\delta^2$$

$$+ \alpha^2 + 4\alpha\delta + 3\delta^2 + \alpha^2 + 2\alpha\delta - 3\delta^2 = \frac{51}{4}$$

$$\Rightarrow 6\alpha^2 - 10\delta^2 = \frac{51}{4}$$

$$6 \cdot \frac{49}{16} - 10\delta^2 = \frac{51}{4}$$

$$\Rightarrow \frac{147}{8} - 10\delta^2 = \frac{51}{4}$$

$$\Rightarrow 10\delta^2 = \frac{147}{8} - \frac{51}{4} = \frac{45}{8}$$

$$\Rightarrow \delta^2 = \frac{45}{81 \times 0} = \frac{9}{16}$$

$$\Rightarrow \delta = \pm \frac{3}{4}$$

thaking the +ve sign we have the root

$$\alpha - 3\delta,\ \alpha - \delta\ \alpha + \delta,\ \alpha + 3\delta$$

$$\frac{7}{4} - 3 \cdot \frac{3}{4}\ \ \frac{7}{4} - \frac{3}{4},\ \frac{7}{4} + \frac{3}{4},\ \frac{7}{4} + 3 \cdot \frac{3}{4}$$

$$\frac{7}{4} - \frac{9}{4},\ \frac{4}{4},\ \frac{10}{4}\ \ \frac{7}{4} + \frac{9}{4}$$

$$-\frac{2}{4},\ 1,\ \frac{5}{2},\ 4 \text{ or } -\frac{1}{2},\ 1,\ \frac{5}{2},\ 4$$ **Ans.**

Problem 4 Find the condition that the roots of the cubic $ax^3 + 3bx^2 + 3cx + d = 0$ be ingeometric progression

Solution The roots of the cubic in G.P. is given by

$$\frac{\alpha}{\lambda}, \alpha, \alpha\lambda$$

Now
$$\frac{\alpha}{\lambda} \cdot \alpha \cdot \alpha\lambda = -\frac{d}{a}$$

$$\alpha^3 = -\frac{d}{a}$$

Since α is a root of the cubic

$ax^3 + 3bx^2 + 3cx + d = 0$ so it will satisfy this equation. Hence

$$a\alpha^3 + 3b\alpha^2 + 3c\alpha + d = 0$$

$$\Rightarrow \quad a\left(-\frac{d}{a}\right) + 3b\alpha^2 + 3cd + d = 0$$

$$\Rightarrow \quad -d + 3b\alpha^2 + 3c\alpha + d = 0$$

$$\Rightarrow \quad 3b\alpha^2 + 3c\alpha = 0$$

$$\Rightarrow \quad 3\alpha(b\alpha + c) = 0$$

$$\Rightarrow \quad b\alpha + c = 0$$

$$\Rightarrow \quad h\alpha = -c$$

Taking cubic on both sides we have

$$b^3\alpha^3 = -c^3$$

$$b^3\left(-\frac{d}{a}\right) = -c^3$$

$$b^3 d = a c^3$$

$$\Rightarrow \quad b^3 d - c^3 a = 0$$

which is the required condition **Ans.**

Problem 5 Find the condition that the roots of the biquadratic

$$x^4 + Px^3 + qx^2 + rx + S = 0$$

may be in geometrical progession.

Solution. Let the roots of the biquadratic equation which are in GP is given by

$$\frac{\alpha}{\delta^3}\ \frac{\alpha}{\delta}, \alpha\delta\ \ \alpha\delta^3$$

Now
$$\frac{\alpha}{\delta^3} + \frac{\alpha}{\delta} + \alpha\delta + \alpha\delta^3 = -p$$

$$\alpha\left(\frac{1}{\delta^3} + \frac{1}{\delta} + \delta + \delta^3\right) = -p \qquad (1)$$

Again $\frac{\alpha}{\delta^3} \cdot \frac{\alpha}{\delta} + \frac{\alpha}{\delta^3} \cdot \alpha\delta + \frac{\alpha}{\delta^3} \cdot \delta^3 + \frac{\alpha}{\delta} \cdot \alpha\delta + \frac{\alpha}{\delta} \cdot \delta^3 + \alpha\delta \cdot \alpha\delta^3 = q$

$$\alpha^2\left(\frac{1}{\delta^4} + \frac{1}{\delta^2} + 1 + 1 + \delta^2 + \delta^4\right) = q$$

$$\Rightarrow \alpha^2\left(\frac{1}{\delta^4} + \frac{1}{\delta^2} + 2 + \delta^2 + \delta^4\right) = q \quad (2)$$

$$\frac{\alpha}{\delta^3} \cdot \frac{\alpha}{\delta} \cdot \alpha\delta + \frac{\alpha}{\delta^3} \quad \frac{\alpha}{\delta} \cdot \alpha\delta^3 + \frac{\alpha}{\delta^3} \cdot \alpha\delta\, \alpha\delta^3 + \frac{\alpha}{\delta} \cdot \alpha\delta\, \alpha\delta^3 = -r$$

$$\Rightarrow \alpha^3\left[\frac{1}{\delta^3} + \frac{1}{\delta} + \delta + \delta^3\right] = -r \quad (3)$$

and $\frac{\alpha}{\delta^2} \cdot \frac{\alpha}{\delta} \quad \alpha\delta \,.\, \alpha\delta^3 = s$

$$\alpha^4 = s \quad (4)$$

Now dividing (3) by (1) $\alpha^2 = \frac{r}{p}$ (5)

From (4) we have $(\alpha^2)^2 = s$

$$\left(\frac{r}{p}\right)^2 = s \qquad \frac{r^2}{p^2} = s$$

$$\Rightarrow \quad r^2 - p^2 s = 0$$

Problem 6 Find the condition that the cubic $x^3 - px^2 + px - r = 0$ should have its roots in harmonic progression.

Solution. Let α, β and γ be the roots of the cubic

$x^3 - px^2 + qx - r = 0$ Then

$$\alpha + \beta + \gamma = p \quad (1)$$

$$\alpha\beta + \beta\gamma + \alpha\gamma = q \quad (2)$$

$$\alpha\beta\gamma = r \quad (3)$$

α, β and γ are in H.P.

$$\Rightarrow \frac{1}{\alpha}, \frac{1}{\beta}, \frac{1}{\gamma} \text{ are in A.P.}$$

$$\Rightarrow \frac{1}{\alpha} + \frac{1}{\gamma} = \frac{2}{\beta}$$

$$\Rightarrow \frac{\gamma + \alpha}{\alpha\gamma} = \frac{2}{\beta}$$

$$\Rightarrow \alpha\beta + \beta\gamma = 2\alpha\gamma$$

$$\Rightarrow \alpha\beta + \beta\gamma + \alpha\gamma = 3\alpha\gamma$$

$$\Rightarrow \quad 9 = 3\alpha\gamma$$

$$\Rightarrow \quad \alpha\gamma = \frac{q}{3} \quad (4)$$

Putting the values of $\alpha\gamma$ from (4) in (3) we have

$$\beta \frac{q}{3} = r$$

$$\beta = \frac{3r}{q}$$

since β is the root of the Cubic equation $x^3 - px^2 + qx - r = 0$ so it will satisfy this equation

$$\beta^3 - p\beta^2 + q\beta - r = 0$$

$$\Rightarrow \left(\frac{3r}{q}\right)^3 - p\left(\frac{3r}{q}\right)^2 + \left(\frac{3r}{q}\right) - r = 0$$

$$\Rightarrow 27\frac{r^3}{q^3} - p\frac{9r^2}{q^2} + 3r - r = 0$$

$$\Rightarrow \frac{27r^3 - 9pqr^2 + 3q^3 r - q^3 r}{q^3} = 0$$

$$\Rightarrow 27r^3 - 9pqr^2 + 2q^3 r = 0$$

$$\Rightarrow r(27r^2 - 9pqr + 2q^3) = 0$$

$$\Rightarrow 27r^2 - 9pq + 2q^3 = 0$$

which is the required condition.

Problem 7 Find the condition that $\alpha, \beta, \gamma, \delta$ of the equation that the roots $x^4 + px^3 + qx^2 + rx + s = 0$ should be connected by the relation

$$\alpha\beta = \gamma\delta$$

Solution $\alpha, \beta, \gamma, \delta$ be the roots of the biquatratic equation

$$x^4 + px^3 + qx^2 + rx + s = 0$$

Then

$$\alpha + \beta + \gamma + \delta = -p \quad (1)$$

$$\alpha\beta + \alpha\gamma + \alpha\delta + \beta\gamma + \beta\delta + \gamma\delta = q \quad (2)$$

$$\alpha\beta\gamma + \alpha\beta\delta + \beta\gamma\delta + \alpha\gamma\delta = -r \quad (3)$$

$$\alpha\beta\gamma\delta = s \quad (4)$$

since $\alpha\beta = \gamma\delta$ so from (4) we have

$$(\alpha\beta)^2 = s$$

$$\Rightarrow \alpha\beta = \sqrt{s}$$

$$\Rightarrow \alpha\beta = \gamma\delta = \sqrt{s} \quad (5)$$

From equation (3) we have

$$\alpha\beta\gamma + \alpha\beta\delta + \beta\gamma\delta + \alpha\gamma\delta = -r$$

$$\Rightarrow \alpha\beta(\gamma + \delta) + (\beta + \alpha)\gamma\delta = -r$$

$$\Rightarrow \sqrt{s}(\gamma + \delta) + \sqrt{s}(\alpha + \beta) = -r$$

$$\Rightarrow \sqrt{s} \times (\alpha + \beta + \gamma + \delta) = -r$$

$$\Rightarrow \alpha + \beta + \gamma + \delta = \frac{r}{\sqrt{s}}$$

$$\Rightarrow -p = \frac{r}{\sqrt{s}}$$

$$\Rightarrow -p\sqrt{s} = -r$$

squaring both sides we have

$$(-p\sqrt{s})^2 = (-r)^2$$

$$\Rightarrow p^2 S = r^2$$

which is the required condition.

Problem 8 Solve the equation

$$x^4 - 18x^3 + 136x^2 - 720x + 1600 = 0$$

whose roots are connected by the relation

$$\alpha\beta = \gamma\delta$$

Solution Let $\alpha_1 \beta, \gamma, \delta$ be the roots of the biquatratic equation

$$x^4 - 18x^3 + 136x^2 - 720x + 1600 = 0$$

Then $\alpha + \beta + \gamma + \delta = 18$ (1)

$$\alpha\beta + \alpha\gamma + \alpha\delta + \beta\gamma + \beta\delta + \gamma\delta = 136 \quad (2)$$

$$\alpha\beta\gamma + \alpha\beta\delta + \beta\gamma\delta + \alpha\gamma\delta = 720 \quad (3)$$

$$\alpha\beta\gamma\delta = 1600 \quad (4)$$

since $\alpha\beta = \gamma\delta$

so $(\alpha\beta)^2 = (\gamma\delta)^2 = 1600$

$$\alpha\beta = \gamma\delta = 40$$

Now from equation (2) we have

$$\alpha\beta + \alpha\gamma + \alpha\delta + \beta\gamma + \beta\delta + \gamma\delta = 136$$

$$40 + \alpha(\gamma + \delta) + \beta(\gamma + \delta) + 40 = 136$$

$$(\alpha + \beta)(\gamma + \delta) = 136 - 80$$

$$(\alpha + \beta)(\gamma + \delta) = 56$$

$$\alpha + \beta + \gamma + \delta = 18$$

then let $u = \alpha + \beta, \quad v = \gamma + \delta$

$$u + v = 18$$

$$uv = 56$$

$$(u - v)^2 = (u + v)^2 - 4uv$$
$$= (18)^2 - 4 \times 56$$
$$= 324 - 224 = 100$$
$$(u - v)^2 = 100 \quad \Rightarrow u - v = 10$$

$$u + v = 18$$
$$u - v = 10$$

Adding $\quad 2u = 28$ $\quad$ Subtracting

$u = 14$ $\quad 2v = 8$

$v = 4$

$\alpha + \beta = 14$ $\quad \gamma + \delta = 4$

$\alpha\beta = 40$ $\quad \gamma\delta = 40$

Now (α, β) is the root of the equation

$$x^2 - (\alpha + \beta)\,x + \alpha\beta = 0$$

i.e.
$$x^2 - 14x + 40 = 0$$

then
$$\alpha, \beta = \frac{14 \pm \sqrt{(14)^2 - 4.40}}{2}$$
$$\alpha, \beta = \frac{14 \pm \sqrt{196 - 160}}{2}$$
$$= \frac{14 \pm \sqrt{36}}{2} = \frac{14 \pm 6}{2}$$

i.e. $\quad \alpha = 10, \quad \beta = 4$

Again $(\gamma_1\ \delta)$ is the root of the equation

$$x^2 - (\gamma + \delta)\,x + \delta\gamma = 0$$
$$\Rightarrow x^2 - 4x + 40 = 0$$

then
$$x = \frac{4 \pm \sqrt{16 - 4.40}}{2} = \frac{4 \pm \sqrt{16 - 160}}{2}$$
$$x = \frac{4 \pm \sqrt{-144}}{2} = \frac{4 \pm \sqrt{144\, i^2}}{2}$$
$$= \frac{4 \pm 12\, i}{2} = 2 \pm 6\, i$$

i.e. $\quad \gamma = 2 + 6\,i, \quad \delta = 2 - 6\,i$

Problem 9 Find the condition that the equation $x^4 + px^3 + qx^2 + rx + s = 0$ should have two roots connected by the relation $\alpha + \beta = 0$, Determine in that case two quadratic equations which shall have for roots (,) $\alpha_1\,\beta$ and (,,) $\gamma_1\delta$.

Solution Let $\alpha, \beta, \gamma, \delta$ be the roots of the biquactratic equation

$$x^4 + Px^3 + qx^2 + rx + \delta = 0 \text{ such that}$$

$$\alpha + \beta = 0$$

we have
$$\alpha + \beta + \gamma + \delta = -p \quad (1)$$

$$\alpha\beta + \alpha\gamma + \alpha\delta + \beta\gamma + \beta\delta + \gamma\delta = q$$

$$\alpha\beta\gamma + \alpha\beta\delta + \beta\gamma\delta + \alpha\gamma\delta = -r \quad (3)$$

and
$$\alpha\beta\gamma\delta = \delta \quad (4)$$

From equation (1)
$$\gamma + \delta = -p \quad (5)$$

From (2)

$$\alpha\beta + (\alpha + \beta)\gamma + (\alpha + \beta)\delta + \gamma\delta = q$$

$$\alpha\beta + 0\,\gamma + 0\cdot\delta + \gamma\delta = q$$

$$\alpha\beta + \gamma\delta = p$$

and
$$\alpha\beta(\gamma + \delta) + \gamma\delta(\alpha + n) = -$$

$$\alpha\beta(\gamma + \delta) = -r$$

i.e.
$$\alpha\beta(-p) = -r$$

$$\alpha\beta = \frac{r}{p}$$

since
$$\alpha\beta\gamma\delta = s$$

$$\Rightarrow \gamma\delta = \frac{s}{\alpha\beta}$$

$$\Rightarrow \gamma\delta = \frac{s}{\frac{r}{p}}$$

$$\Rightarrow \gamma\delta = \frac{ps}{r}$$

Putting the values of $\alpha\beta$ and $\gamma\delta$ in equation (r) we have

$$\frac{r}{p} + \frac{ps}{r} = q$$

$$\Rightarrow \frac{r^2 + p^2 s}{pr} = q$$

$$\Rightarrow r^2 + p^2 s = pqr$$

which is the required condition. For the second part we have to find the :quation whose roots are $\alpha_1\ \beta$ since

$$\alpha + \beta = 0$$

$$\alpha\ \int = \frac{r}{p}$$

Hence α, β are the roots of the equation

$$x^2 - (\alpha + \beta) n + \alpha\beta = 0$$

i.e. of
$$x^2 + \frac{r}{p} = 0$$

$$\Rightarrow px^2 + r = 0$$

Again
$$\gamma + \delta = - p$$

$$\gamma\delta = \frac{ps}{r}$$

so γ, δ are the roots of the equation

$$x^2 - (\gamma + \delta) x + \gamma\delta = 0$$

i.e.
$$x^2 + px + \frac{ps}{r} = 0$$

i.e. of $rx^2 + prx + ps = 0$ **Ans.**

Problem 10 Find the condition that the sum of two roots of the equation
$$x^4 + px^3 + qx^2 + rx + s = 0$$
is equal to the sum of her two.

Solution Let $\alpha, \beta, \gamma, \delta$ be the roots of the biquadtratic equation

$$x^4 + px^3 + qx^2 + rx + s = 0$$

$$\alpha + \beta + \gamma + \delta = - p \tag{1}$$

$$\alpha\beta + \alpha\gamma + \alpha\delta + \beta\gamma + \beta\delta + \gamma\delta = q \tag{2}$$

$$\alpha\beta\gamma + \alpha\beta\delta + \beta\gamma\delta + \alpha\gamma\delta = - r \tag{3}$$

$$\alpha\beta\gamma\delta = s \tag{4}$$

Given that
$$\alpha + \beta = \gamma + \delta$$

so from equation (1) we have

$$\alpha + \beta = \gamma + \delta = \frac{p}{2} \tag{5}$$

$$\alpha\beta (\gamma + \delta) + (\alpha + \beta) \gamma\delta = - r \tag{6}$$

$$\alpha\beta \left(-\frac{p}{2}\right) + \gamma\delta \left(-\frac{p}{2}\right) = - r$$

$$-\frac{p}{2} (\alpha\beta + \gamma\delta) = - r$$

$$\alpha\beta + \gamma\delta = \frac{2r}{p} \tag{7}$$

From equation (2)

$$\alpha\beta + \gamma\delta + (\alpha + \beta)(\gamma + \delta) = q$$

$$\frac{2r}{p} + \left(-\frac{p}{2}\right)\left(-\frac{p}{2}\right) = q$$

$$\frac{2r}{p} + \frac{p^2}{4} = q$$

$$\frac{8r + p^3}{4P} = q$$

$$\Rightarrow p^3 + 8r - 4pq = 0$$

$$\Rightarrow p^3 - 4pq + 8r = 0$$

which is the required condition.

Problem 11 Solve $18x^4 + 9x^3 - 41x^2 + 24x - 4 = 0$ having given that the sum of two of the roots is unity.

Solution Let α_1 β_1, γ and δ be the roots of the biqudratic equation

$$18x^4 + 9x^3 - 41x^2 + 24x - 4 = 0$$

Then we have

$$\alpha + \beta + \gamma + \delta = \frac{9}{18} = -\frac{1}{2}$$

igiven that $\alpha + \beta = 1$

$$\Rightarrow 1 + \gamma + \delta = -\tfrac{1}{2}$$

$$\Rightarrow \gamma = \delta = -\frac{1}{2} - 1 = -\frac{3}{2}$$

let $\alpha\beta = K$ and $\gamma\delta = K'$

x_1 β are the roots of the equation

$$x^2 - (\alpha + \beta)x + \alpha\beta = 0$$

.e. of $x^2 - x + K = 0$ (1)

and γ_1 δ are the roots of the equation

$$x^2 - (\gamma + \delta)x + \gamma\delta = 0$$

i.e. of $x^2 + \frac{3}{2}x + k^1 = 0$ (2)

i.e. $2x^2 + 3x + k^1 = 0$ (3)

Now $9(x^2 - x + k)(2x^2 + 3x + 2k^1)$

$$= 18x^4 + 9x^3 - 41x^2 + 24x - 4$$

$$18x^4 + 9x^3\, 9x^2(2k^1 - 3 + 2k) + 9x(3k - 2k^1) + 18kk^1$$

$$= 18x^4 + 9x^3 - 41x^2 + 24x - 4$$

Therefore equating the coefficients of x^2. x and the constant term on both sides of the above identity. we get

$$9(2k^1 - 3 + 2k) = -41 \quad (2)$$

$$-9(2k^1 - 3k) = 24 \quad (3)$$

$$18kk^1 = -4 \quad (4)$$

From (2)

$$\begin{aligned} 18k^1 - 27 + 18k &= -41 \\ -18k^1 \qquad + 27k &= 24 \\ \hline -27 + 45k &= -17 \\ 45k &= -17 + 27 \\ k &= +\frac{10}{45} \\ k &= \frac{2}{9} \end{aligned}$$

Again

$$18 \times \frac{2}{9} k^1 = -4$$

$$k^1 = -\frac{4}{4} = -1$$

so (α, β) is the roots of the equation

$$x^2 - (\alpha + \beta)\, x + \alpha\beta = 0$$

i.e. of $x^2 - x + \frac{2}{9} = 0$ i.e. of $9x^2 - 9x + 2 = 0$

α, β are the roots of $9x^2 - 9x + 2 = 0$

$$\alpha, \beta = \frac{9 \pm \sqrt{81 - 4\,9.2}}{2.9}$$

$$\alpha, \beta = \frac{9 \pm \sqrt{81 - 72}}{2,9} = \frac{9 \pm 3}{2.9}$$

$$\alpha = \frac{6}{9}, \beta = \frac{3}{9}; \alpha = \frac{2}{3}, \beta = \frac{1}{3}$$

γ, δ are the root of the equation

$$x^2 - (\gamma + \delta)\, x + \gamma\delta = 0$$

i.e. of $x^2 + \frac{3}{2}x - 1 = 0$

i.e. of $2x^2 + 3x - 2 = 0$

$$\gamma, \delta = \frac{-3 \pm \sqrt{9 - 4.2.(-2)}}{4}$$

$$= \frac{-3 \pm \sqrt{9+16}}{4} = \frac{-3 \pm 5}{4}$$

$$= \gamma = \frac{1}{2}, \delta = -2$$

Thus $\frac{2}{3}, \frac{1}{3}, \frac{1}{2}, -2$ are the roots of the biquadratic

$$13x^4 + 9x^3 - 41x^2 + 24x - 4 = 0$$

Problem 12 Solve the equation

$$3x^4 - 25x^3 + 50x^2 - 50x + 12 = 0$$

having given that the product of two roots is 2.

Solution Let $\alpha, \beta, \gamma, \delta$ be the roots

$$3x^4 - 25x^3 + 50x^2 - 50x + 12 = 0$$

and given that $\alpha\beta = 2$

$$\alpha + \beta + \gamma + \delta = \frac{25}{3}$$

$$\alpha\beta\gamma\delta = \frac{12}{3}$$

$$2 \times \gamma\delta = 4$$

$$\gamma\delta = 2 \text{ since } \alpha\beta = 2$$

Let $\alpha + \beta = k, \gamma + \delta = k^1$

α, β are the roots of the equation

$$x^2 - (\alpha + \beta)x + \alpha\beta = 0$$

i.e. of $x^2 - kx + 2 = 0$

γ, δ are the roots of the equation

$$x^2 - (\gamma + \delta)x + \gamma\delta = 0$$

i.e. of $x^2 - k^1x + 2 = 0$

Now

$$3(x^2 - kx + 2)(x^2 - k^1x + 6)$$

$$\equiv 3x^4 - 25x^3 + 50x^2 - 50x + 12$$

$$\Rightarrow \quad 3[x^4 - (k + k^1)x^3 + (4 + kk^1)x^2 - (2k^1 + 2k)x + 4]$$

$$= 3x^4 - 25x^3 + 50x^2 - 50x + 12$$

Equating the coefficients of x^3. x^2 x and constant terms on both sides we have

$$3(k + k^1) = 25 \quad (1)$$

$$3(4 + kk^1) = 50 \quad (2)$$

$$3(2k^1 + 2k) = 50 \quad (3)$$

From equation (1)

$$k + k^1 = \frac{25}{3}$$

$$12 + 3kk^1 = 50$$

$$3kk^1 = 50 - 12$$

$$3kk^1 = 38$$

$$kk^1 = \frac{38}{3}$$

Now $\quad (k - k^1)^2 = (k + k^1)^2 - 4kk^1$

$$= \left(\frac{25}{3}\right)^2 - 4 \cdot \frac{38}{3} = \frac{625}{9} - \frac{152}{3}$$

$$(k - k^1)^2 = \frac{625 - 456}{9}$$

$$(k - k^1)^2 = \frac{169}{9}$$

$\Rightarrow \quad (k - k^1) = \frac{13}{3}$ more Taking + vesign

$\Rightarrow \quad k + k^1 = \frac{25}{3}$

$$k - k^1 = \frac{13}{3}$$

$$2k = \frac{38}{3}$$

$$k = \frac{38}{6} = \frac{19}{3}$$

$$k^1 = \frac{12}{6} = 2$$

α, β are the roots of

$$x^2 - (\alpha + \beta)x + \alpha\beta = 0$$

i.e. of $\quad x^2 - \frac{19}{3}x + 2 = 0$

i.e. of $$3x^2 - 19x + 6 = 0$$

$$\alpha, \beta = \frac{19 \pm \sqrt{(19)^2 - 4.3.6}}{2 \cdot 3} = \frac{19 \pm \sqrt{361 - 72}}{6}$$

$$= \frac{19 \pm \sqrt{289}}{6} = \frac{16 \pm 17}{6}$$

$$\alpha = \frac{19+17}{6} = \frac{36}{6} = 6$$

$$\beta = \frac{19-17}{6} - \frac{2}{6} = \frac{1}{3}$$

γ, δ are the roots of the equation

$$x^2 - (\gamma + \delta)\, x + \gamma\delta = 0$$

i.e. of $$x^2 - 2x + 2 = 0$$

$$\gamma, \delta = \frac{2 \pm \sqrt{4 - 4 \cdot 1 \cdot 2}}{2}$$

$$= \frac{2 \pm \sqrt{-4}}{2} = \frac{2 \pm 2i}{2}$$

$$\gamma, \delta = 1 + i$$

$$\gamma = 1 + i\,,\ \delta = 1 - i$$

Thus $6, \frac{1}{3}, 1 + i, 1 - i$ are the roots of the biquadratic equation

$$3x^4 - 25x^3 + 50x^2 - 50x + 12 = 0$$

Problem 13 Solve the equation $4x^3 - 8x^2 - 31x + 35 = 0$, **having given** that the sum of its roots is unity.

$$\left[1, \frac{7}{2} - \frac{5}{2}\right]$$

Find the condition that the roots of the equation $x^3 + px^2 + qx + r = 0$, be in Arithmetic progression.

Solution Let $\alpha - \delta$, α and $\alpha + \delta$ be the roots of the cubic equation

$$x^3 + px^2 + qx + r = 0$$

$$\alpha - \delta + \alpha + \alpha + \delta = -p$$

$$\Rightarrow 3\alpha = -p$$

$$\Rightarrow \alpha = -\frac{p}{3}$$

Since α is a root of the cubic equation so it will satisfy this

$$\Rightarrow \alpha^3 + p\alpha^2 + q\alpha + r = 0$$

$$\Rightarrow \left(-\frac{p}{3}\right)^3 + p\left(-\frac{p}{3}\right)^2 + q\left(-\frac{p}{3}\right) + r =$$

$$\Rightarrow -\frac{p^3}{27} + \frac{p^3}{9} - \frac{p^q}{3} + r = 0$$

$$\Rightarrow \frac{2p^3}{27} - \frac{p^q}{3} + r = 0$$

$$\Rightarrow 2p^3 - 9p^q + 27\,r = 0$$

which is the required equation

Problem 14 Solve the equation $27x^3 + 42x^2 - 28x - 8 = 0$ whose roots are in Geometric progression.

Solution Let the roots are $\frac{\alpha}{\lambda}$, α and $\alpha\lambda$ then

$$\frac{\alpha}{\lambda} + \alpha + \alpha\lambda = -\frac{42}{27}$$

$$\alpha\left(\frac{1}{\lambda} + 1 + \lambda\right) = -\frac{42}{27} \qquad (1)$$

$$\frac{\alpha}{\lambda}\cdot\alpha\cdot\alpha\lambda = \frac{8}{27}$$

$$\Rightarrow \alpha^3 = \frac{8}{27}$$

$$\Rightarrow \alpha = \frac{2}{3} \qquad (2)$$

Putting the value of α from equation (2) in relation (1) we have

$$\frac{2}{3}\left(\frac{1 + \lambda + \lambda^2}{\lambda}\right) = -\frac{42}{27}$$

$$9 + 9\lambda + 9\lambda^2 = -21\lambda$$

$$\Rightarrow 9\lambda^2 + 30\lambda + 9 = 0$$

$$\Rightarrow 3\lambda^2 + 10\lambda + 3 = 0$$

$$\Rightarrow 3\lambda^2 + 9\lambda + \lambda + 3 = 0$$

$$\Rightarrow 3\lambda(\lambda + 3) + 1(\lambda + 3) = 0$$

$$\Rightarrow (3\lambda + 1)(\lambda + 3) = 0$$

$\Rightarrow$ either $3\lambda + 1 = 0$ or $\lambda + 3 = 0$

$$\Rightarrow \lambda = -\frac{1}{3} \quad \text{or} \quad -3$$

let $\lambda = -3$ then the roots are

$$-\frac{2}{9}, \frac{2}{3}, -2$$

Ans.

Problem 15 Solve the equation $70x^3 - 107x^2 + 54x - 9 = 0$ whose roots are in Harmonic progression.

Solution Let α, β, γ be the roots of the cubic equation

$$70x^3 - 107x^2 + 54x - 9 = 0$$

which are in HP.

$$\alpha + \beta + \gamma = \frac{107}{70} \quad (1)$$

$$\alpha\beta + \alpha\gamma + \beta\gamma = \frac{54}{70} \quad (2)$$

$$\alpha\beta\gamma = \frac{9}{70} \quad (3)$$

since α, β, γ are in Harmonic progression

$$\Rightarrow \frac{1}{\alpha}, \frac{1}{\beta}, \frac{1}{\gamma} \text{ are in Arithmetic progression}$$

$$\Rightarrow \frac{1}{\alpha} + \frac{1}{\gamma} = \frac{2}{\beta}$$

$$\Rightarrow \frac{\alpha + \gamma}{\alpha\gamma} = \frac{2}{\beta}$$

$$\Rightarrow \alpha\beta + \beta\gamma = 2\alpha\gamma$$

$$\Rightarrow \alpha\beta + \beta\alpha + \alpha\gamma = 3\alpha\gamma \quad \text{[Adding } \alpha\gamma \text{ on bothsides]}$$

$$\Rightarrow 3\alpha\gamma = \frac{54}{70}$$

$$\Rightarrow \alpha\gamma = \frac{54}{70 \times 3}$$

since $\alpha\beta\gamma = \dfrac{9}{70}$

$$\frac{54}{70 \times 3}\beta = \frac{9}{70}$$

$$\beta = \frac{9 \times 3}{54} = \frac{1}{2}$$

From relation (2) we have

$$\beta(\alpha + \gamma) + \alpha\gamma = \frac{54}{70}$$

$$\frac{1}{2}(\alpha + \gamma) + \frac{18}{70} = \frac{54}{70}$$

$$\frac{1}{2}(\alpha + \gamma) = \frac{54}{70} - \frac{18}{70} = \frac{54 - 18}{70} = \frac{36}{70}$$

$$\alpha + \gamma = \frac{36}{35}$$

α, γ are the roots of the equation

$$x^2 - (\alpha + \gamma)\, x + \alpha\gamma = 0$$

i.e. of $$x^2 - \frac{36}{35}x + \frac{9}{35} = 0$$

i.e. $35x^2 - 36x + 9 = 0$

i.e. $$x = \frac{36 \pm \sqrt{(36)^2 - 4\cdot 35 \times 9}}{2\cdot 35}$$

$$= \frac{36 \pm \sqrt{1296 - 1260}}{2\cdot 35}$$

$$= \frac{36 \pm \sqrt{36}}{2\cdot 35}$$

$$= \frac{36 + 6}{2\cdot 35} = \frac{42}{2 \times 35} \text{ or } \frac{30}{2\cdot 35}$$

i.e. $\alpha = \frac{3}{5}, \quad \gamma = \frac{3}{7}$

Thus the roots of the equation

$$70x^3 - 107x^2 + 54x - 9 = 0 \text{ are}$$

$$\frac{3}{5}, \frac{1}{2} \text{ and } \frac{3}{7}$$ **Ans.**

Problem 16 Find the conditions that the equation

$$x^4 + px^3 + qx^2 + rx + s = 0$$

should have its roots in A.P. Hence solve the equation

$$x^4 + 2x^3 - 21x^2 - 22x + 40 = 0$$

Solution Let $\alpha, \beta, \gamma, \delta$ are the roots of the equation

$$x^4 + px^\beta + qx^2 + rx + s = 0$$

since $\alpha, \beta, \gamma, \delta$ are in A.P. so they are $x - 3\delta, \alpha - \delta, \alpha + \delta, \alpha + 3\delta$ then

$$\alpha - 3\delta + \alpha - \delta + \alpha + \delta + \alpha + 3\delta = -p \quad (1)$$

i.e. $4\alpha = -p$

$$\Rightarrow \quad \alpha = -\frac{p}{4}$$

$$(\alpha - 3\delta)(\alpha - \delta) + (\alpha - 3\delta)(\alpha + \delta) + (\alpha - 3\delta)(\alpha + 3\delta)$$
$$+ (\alpha - \delta)(\alpha + \delta) + (\alpha - \delta)(\alpha + 3\delta) + (\alpha + \delta)(\alpha + 3\delta) = q \quad (2)$$
$$(\alpha - 3\delta)(\alpha - \delta)(\alpha + \delta)(\alpha + 3\delta) = s \quad (3)$$

and $$(\alpha - 3\delta)(\alpha - \delta)(\alpha + \delta) + (\alpha - 3\delta)(\alpha - \delta)(\alpha + 3\delta)$$
$$+ (\alpha - \delta)(\alpha + \delta)(\alpha + 3\delta) + (\alpha - 3\delta)(\alpha + \delta)(\alpha + 3\delta) = -r \quad (4)$$

From relation (2) we have

$$\alpha^2 - \alpha\delta - 3\alpha\delta + 3\delta^2 + \alpha^2 + \alpha\delta - 3\alpha\delta - 3\delta^2 + \alpha^2 + 3\alpha\delta$$
$$- 3\alpha\delta - 9\delta^2 + \alpha^2 + \alpha\delta - \alpha\delta - \delta^2 + \alpha^2 + 3\alpha\delta - \alpha\delta - 3\delta^2$$
$$+ \alpha^2 + 3\alpha\delta + \alpha\delta + 3\delta^2 = q$$

$$6\alpha^2 - 10\delta^2 = q$$

$$6\,\frac{p^2}{16} - 10\delta^2 = q$$

$$\frac{3}{8}\,p^2 - 10\delta^2 = q$$

$$10\delta^2 = \frac{3p^2}{8} - q$$

$$\delta^2 = \frac{3p^2 - 8q}{80}$$

From relation (3)

$$(\alpha^2 - 9\delta^2)(\alpha^2 - \delta^2) = s$$

$$\left[\frac{p^2}{16} - 9\,\frac{(3p^2 - 8q)}{80}\right]\left[\frac{p^2}{16} - \frac{(3p^2 - 8q)}{80}\right] = s$$

$$\Rightarrow \frac{(5p^2 - 27p^2 + 72q)}{80} \cdot \frac{(5p^2 - 3p^2 + 8q)}{80} = s$$

$$\Rightarrow \frac{(-22p^2 + 72q)}{80} \cdot \frac{(2p^2 + 8q)}{80} = s$$

$$\Rightarrow 4\,(36q - 11p^2)(p^2 + 4q) = 80 \times 80s$$

$$\Rightarrow (36q - 11p^2)(p^2 + 4q) = 1600s \qquad (5)$$

From (4) we have

$$(\alpha - 3\delta)(\alpha^2 - \delta^2) + (\alpha^2 - 9\delta^2)(\alpha - \delta) + (\alpha^2 - \delta^2)(\alpha + 3\delta)$$
$$+ (\alpha^2 - 9\delta^2)(\alpha + \delta) = -r$$

$$\Rightarrow (\alpha^2 - \delta^2)(\alpha - 3\delta + \alpha + 3\delta) + (\alpha^2 - 9\delta^2)(\alpha - \delta + \alpha + \delta) = -r$$

$$\Rightarrow (\alpha^2 - \delta^2)\,2\alpha + (\alpha^2 - 9\delta^2)\,2\alpha = -r$$

$$\Rightarrow 2\alpha\,(2\alpha^2 - 10\delta^2) = -r$$

$$\Rightarrow 2\left(-\frac{p}{4}\right)\left[\frac{2p^2}{16} - \frac{3p^2}{8} + q\right] = -r$$

$$\Rightarrow -\frac{p}{2}\left[-\frac{2p^2}{8} + q\right] = -r$$

$$\Rightarrow \quad -\frac{p}{2}\left[-\frac{p^2+4q}{4}\right] = -r$$

$$\Rightarrow \quad +p^3 - 4pq = -8r$$

$$\Rightarrow \quad p^3 - 4pq + 8r = 0 \tag{6}$$

(5) and (6) will give the required condition. Now we have to solve

$$x^4 + 2x^3 - 21x^2 - 22x + 40 = 0$$

The roots of this equations are in A.P. They are

$$\alpha - 3\delta, \alpha - \delta, \alpha + \delta, \alpha + 3\delta$$

Here $p = 2$, $q = -21$ $r = -22$, $s = 40$

$$\alpha = -\frac{p}{4} = -\frac{2}{4} = -\frac{1}{2}.$$

$$\delta^2 = \frac{3p^2 - 8q}{80}$$

$$\delta^2 = \frac{3(2)^2 - 8(-21)}{80}$$

$$\delta^2 = \frac{3 \times 4 + 168}{80}$$

$$\delta^2 = \frac{12 + 168}{80}$$

$$\delta^2 = \frac{180}{80}$$

$$\delta^2 = \frac{9}{4} \qquad \delta = \frac{3}{6} \text{ (taking + ve sign)}$$

Hence the roots are

$$-\frac{1}{2}-\frac{9}{2}, -\frac{1}{2}-\frac{3}{2}, -\frac{1}{2}+\frac{3}{2}, -\frac{1}{2}+\frac{9}{2}$$

i.e. $-\frac{10}{2}, -\frac{4}{2}, \frac{2}{2}, \frac{8}{2}$

i.e. $-5, \quad -2, \quad 1, \quad 4$ **Ans.**

Problem 17 Solve the equation

$$x^4 + 15x^3 + 70x^2 + 120x + 64 = 0$$

whose roots are in Geometric progression.

Solution Let a, ar, ar^2, ar^3 be the roots of the biquadratic equation

$$x^4 + 15x^3 + 70x^2 + 120x + 64 = 0$$

let $\alpha = a, \beta = ar^3, \gamma = ar, \delta = ar^2$

Here we see that

$$\alpha\beta = aar^3 = a^2 r^3$$

$$\gamma\delta = ar\, ar^2 = a^2 r^3$$

i.e.
$$\alpha\beta = \gamma\delta$$

$$\alpha + \beta + \gamma + \delta = -15$$

$$\alpha\beta + \alpha\gamma + \alpha\delta + \beta\gamma + \beta\delta + \gamma\delta = 70$$

$$\alpha\beta\gamma + \alpha\beta\delta + \beta\gamma\delta + \alpha\gamma\delta = -120$$

$$\alpha\beta\gamma\delta = 64$$

Then $\alpha\beta = \gamma\delta = 8$ or -8

let $\alpha + \beta = l, \quad \gamma + \delta = m$

α, β are the roots of the equation

$$x^2 - (\alpha + \beta)\, x + \alpha\beta = 0$$

i.e. of
$$x^2 - lx + 8 = 0$$

γ, δ are the roots of the equation

$$x^2 - (\gamma + \delta)\, x + \gamma\delta = 0$$

i.e. of
$$x^2 - mx + 8 = 0$$

Then $(x^2 - lx + 8)(x^2 - mx + 8) = x^4 + 15x^3 + 70x^2 + 120x + 64$

$$\Rightarrow \quad x^4 - (l + m)\, x^3 + (16 + lm)\, x^2 - 8\,(l + m)\, x + 64 = x^4 + 15x^3 + 70x^2 + 120x + 64$$

Compairing the coefficients of x^3, x^2 and x on both sides we have

$$l + m = -15 \qquad lm + 16 = 70 \qquad lm = 54$$

l, m are the roots of the quadratic eqn.

$$x^2 - (l + m)\, x + lm = 0$$

i.e. of
$$x^2 + 15x + 54 = 0$$

$$l, m = \frac{-15 \pm \sqrt{225 - 4.54}}{2}$$

$$= \frac{-15 \pm \sqrt{225 - 216}}{2}$$

$$= \frac{-15 \pm \sqrt{9}}{2} = \frac{-15 \pm 3}{2}$$

$$l = -9 \qquad\qquad m = -6$$

$$\alpha + \beta = -9 \qquad\qquad \gamma + \delta = -6$$

$$\alpha\beta = 8 \qquad\qquad \gamma\delta = 8$$

α, β are the roots of the equation

$$x^2 - (\alpha + \beta)\, x + \alpha\beta = 0$$

$$x^2 + 9x + 8 = 0$$

$$\alpha, \beta = \frac{-9 \pm \sqrt{81 - 4 \times 8}}{2}$$

$$= \frac{-9 \pm \sqrt{81 - 32}}{2}$$

$$= \frac{-9 \pm \sqrt{49}}{2} = \frac{-9 \pm 7}{2} = \frac{-16}{2} \text{ or } \frac{-2}{2}$$

i.e. $\alpha = -8 \qquad \beta = -1$

γ, δ are the roots of the equation

$$x^2 - (\gamma + \delta)\, x + \gamma\delta = 0$$

$$x^2 + 6x + 8 = 0$$

$$x^2 + 4x + 2x + 8 = 0$$

$$x\,(x + 4) + 2\,(x + 4) = 0$$

$$(x + 4)\,(x + 2) = 0$$

$$\gamma = -4 \qquad \delta = -2$$

Thus the roots are

$$-8, -4, -2, -1$$

Problem 18 Solve the equation

$$6x^4 - 5x^3 - 27x^2 + 5x + 21 = 0$$

sum of two of its roots being equal to zero.

Solution Let α, β, γ. δ be the roots of the biquadratic equation

$$6x^4 - 5x^3 - 27x^2 + 5x + 21 = 0$$

such that $\qquad \alpha + \beta = 0$

then $\qquad \alpha + \beta + \gamma + \delta = \frac{5}{6} \qquad (1)$

$$\alpha\beta\gamma + \alpha\beta\delta + \beta\gamma\delta + \alpha\gamma\delta = \frac{-5}{6} \qquad (2)$$

$$\alpha\beta\gamma\delta = \frac{21}{6} \qquad (3)$$

since $\qquad \alpha + \beta = 0 \Rightarrow \gamma + \delta = \frac{5}{6}$

From equation (2) we have

$$\alpha\beta(\gamma+\delta)+(\alpha+\beta)\gamma\delta=-\frac{5}{6}$$

$$\alpha\beta\left(\frac{5}{6}\right)=-\frac{5}{6}$$

$\Rightarrow$ $$\alpha\beta=-1$$

$$\alpha\beta=-1$$

$$\alpha\beta\gamma\delta=\frac{21}{6}$$

$$(-1)\gamma\delta=\frac{21}{6} \quad \Rightarrow \quad \gamma\delta=-\frac{21}{6}$$

$$\alpha+\beta=0 \qquad \alpha\beta=1$$

α and β are the roots of the equation

$$x^2-(\alpha+\beta)x+\alpha\beta=0$$

i.e. $$x^2-(0)x+(-1)=0$$

$\Rightarrow x^2=1$ $\qquad \Rightarrow x=\pm 1$

i.e. $\alpha=1,\ \beta=-1$

Again γ, δ are the roots of the equation

$$x^2-(\gamma+\delta)x+\gamma\delta=0$$

i.e $$x^2-\frac{5}{6}x-\frac{21}{6}=0$$

$$6x^2-5x-21=0$$

$$\gamma,\delta=\frac{5\pm\sqrt{25-4.6(-21)}}{2\cdot 6}$$

$$=\frac{5\pm\sqrt{25+504}}{2\cdot 6}=\frac{5\pm\sqrt{529}}{2\cdot 6}=\frac{25\pm 23}{2\cdot 6}$$

$$\gamma=\frac{28}{2\cdot 6}=\frac{7}{3}$$

$$\delta=\frac{5-23}{2\cdot 6}=\frac{-18}{2\cdot 6}=-\frac{3}{2}$$

Thus $1,-1,\frac{7}{3},\ -\frac{3}{2}$ are the roots of the biquadratic equation

$$6x^2-5x^3-27x^2+5x+21=0$$

Problem 19 If $Z^4 + 6H^2 + 4GH + a_0^2 I - 3H^2 = 0$ has two poirs of equal roots, prove that $G = 0$ and $a_0^2 I = 12H^2$.

Solution Let $\alpha, \alpha, \beta, \beta$, be the roots of the biquardratic equation

$$Z^4 + 6HZ^2 + 4GZ + a_0^2 I - 3H$$

i.e. of

$$Z^4 + 0Z^2 + 6HZ^2 + 4GZ + a_0{}^2 I - 3H^2 = 0$$

$$\alpha + \alpha + \beta + \beta = 0$$

$$2\alpha + 2\beta = 0 \qquad \Rightarrow 2(\alpha + \beta) = 0 \Rightarrow \alpha + \beta = 0$$

and

$$\alpha \cdot \alpha \cdot \beta \cdot \beta = a_3^2 I - 3H^2$$

$$\beta \beta = k$$

α, β are the roots of the equation

$$Z^2 - (\alpha + \beta) x + \alpha\beta = 0$$

i.e. of

$$Z^2 + \cdot\cdot = 0$$

Thus $Z^4 + 6HZ^2 + 4GZ + a_0^2 I - 3H^2 = (Z^2 + K)^2$

$$= Z^4 + 2Z^2 k + k^2$$

Equating the ccefficient of equal powers of Z we have

$$36H = 2K \qquad 4G = 0 \qquad \Rightarrow G = 0$$

$$a_0{}^{:} I - 3H^2 = K^2$$

$$a_0^2 I - 3H^2 = (3H)^2$$

$$a_0^2 I - 3H^2 = 9H^2$$

$$\Rightarrow a_0^2 I = 12H^2$$

(*proved*)

Problem 20 Find the condition that the biquadratic

$$x^4 + px^3 + qx^2 + rx + s = 0$$

may have two pairs of equal roots.

Solution. Let α, β: α, β be the roots of the biquadratic equation

$$x^4 + px^3 + qx^2 + s = 0$$

Then

$$\alpha + \beta + \alpha + \beta = -p$$

$$\Rightarrow 2(\alpha + \beta) = -p$$

$$\Rightarrow \alpha + \beta = -\frac{p}{2}$$

$$\alpha^2\beta^2 = s \qquad \Rightarrow \alpha\beta = \sqrt{5}$$

α, β are the roots of the equation

i.e. α, β are the roots of the equation

$$x^2 + \frac{p}{2} x + \sqrt{s} = 0$$

Then $x^4 + px^3 + qx^2 + rx + S = \left((x^2 + \frac{p}{2}\, x + \sqrt{s}\right)^2$

$$= \left(x^2 + \frac{p}{2}\, x\right)^2 + 2\left(x^2 + \frac{p}{2}\, x\right)\sqrt{s} + s$$

$$x^4 + 2x^2 - \frac{p}{2}\, x + \frac{p^2}{4}\, x^2 + 2x^2\sqrt{5} + px\sqrt{s} + s$$

Comparing the coefficients of equal powers of x on both sides we have

$$\frac{p^2}{4} + 2\sqrt{s} = q \text{ and } p\sqrt{s} = r$$

$$p^2 + 8\sqrt{s} = 4q$$

$$p^2 - 4q = -8\sqrt{s} \qquad \text{and } p\sqrt{s} = r$$

squaring we have

$$(p^2 - 4q)^2 = 64s \qquad \text{and } p^2 s = r^2$$

which are the required condition.

Problem 21 Find the condition that the equation

$$x^4 + px^3 + qx^2 + rx + s = 0$$

may have allits root equal.

Solution Let $\alpha, \alpha, \alpha, \alpha$ be the roots of the biquadratic equation

$$x^4 + px^3 + qx^2 + rx + s = 0$$

Then $\alpha + \alpha + \alpha + \alpha = -p$

$$\Rightarrow 4x = -p$$

$$\Rightarrow \alpha = -\frac{p}{4}$$

since $x = \alpha$ is a root of the biquadratic equation so $(x - \alpha)$ must be a factor. Then

$$x^4 + px^3 + qx^2 + rx + s = (x - \alpha)^4$$

$$x^4 + px^3 + qx^2 + rx + s \equiv [x^2 - 2x\alpha + \alpha^2]^2$$

$$\equiv (x^2 - 2x\alpha)^2 + \alpha^4 + 2(x^2 - 2x\alpha)\,\alpha^2$$

$$\equiv x^4 - 2\cdot x^2\cdot 2x\alpha + 4x^2\alpha^2 + \alpha^4 + 2x^2\alpha^2 - 4x\alpha^3$$

$$\equiv x^4 - 4x^3\alpha + 6x^2\alpha^2 - 4x\alpha^3 + \alpha^4$$

Equating the similar powers of x on both sides we have

$$p = -4\alpha \qquad \Rightarrow \alpha = -\frac{p}{4}$$

$$6\alpha^2 = q, \qquad -4\,\alpha^3 = r \qquad \alpha^4 = s$$

since $\quad p = -4\alpha$

$$p^2 = 16\alpha^2 \qquad p^2 = 16\frac{q}{6}$$

$$\Rightarrow p^2 = \frac{8}{3}q$$

$$\Rightarrow 3p^2 = 8q \tag{1}$$

$$p^3 = -64\alpha^3$$

$$p^3 = -64\left(-\frac{r}{4}\right) = 16r$$

$$p^3 = 16r \tag{2}$$

Again $\quad p^4 = 256\alpha^4$

$$\Rightarrow p^4 = 256s \tag{3}$$

Equation (1) (2) and (3) are the required condition.

Problem 22 Find the condition that the cubic

$$x^3 - px^2 + qx - r = 0$$

may have (*i*) two roots equal (*ii*) three roots equal.

Solution let $\quad f(x) = x^3 - px^2 + qx - r = 0$

it have two equal roots say α so $(x - \alpha)^2$ must be a factor. Then

$$f^1(x) = 3x^2 - 2px + q \text{ must have factor } (x - \alpha)$$

Thus $(x - \alpha)$satisfies both $f(x) = 0$ and $f^1(x) = 0$

i.e. $$\alpha^3 - p\alpha^2 + q\alpha - r = 0 \tag{1}$$

and $$3\alpha^2 - 2p\alpha + q = 0 \tag{2}$$

multiplying (1) with 3 we have

$$3\alpha^3 - 3qx^2 + 3q\alpha - 3r = 0$$

multiplying (2) by α we have

$$3\alpha^3 - 2p\alpha^2 + q\alpha = 0$$

substituting (3) from (4) we have.

$$3\alpha^3 - 2p\alpha^2 + q\alpha - 3\alpha^3 + 3p\alpha^3 - 3qr + 3r = 0$$

$$p\alpha^2 - 2q\alpha + 3r = 0$$

From cross-wise multiplication of (2) and (5) we have

$$3\alpha^2 - 2p\alpha + q = 0$$

$$p\alpha^2 - 2q + 3r = 0$$

$$\frac{\alpha^2}{-6pr + 2q^2} = \frac{\alpha}{pq - 9r} = \frac{1}{-6q + 2p^2}$$

$$\frac{\alpha^2}{2q^2 - 6pr} = \frac{\alpha}{pq - 9r} = \frac{1}{2p^2 - 6q}$$

$$\alpha = \frac{pq - 9r}{2p^2 - 6q}$$

$$\alpha^2 = \frac{2q^2 - 6pr}{2p^2 - 6q}$$

$$\left(\frac{pq - 9r}{2p^2 - 6q}\right)^2 = \frac{2q^2 - 6pr}{2p^2 - 6q}$$

$$(pq - 9r)^2 = (2q^2 - 6pr)(2p^2 - 6q)$$

$$(pq - 9r)^2 = 4(q^2 - 3pr)(p^2 - 3q)$$

which is the required condition

Again let $x^3 - px^2 + qx - r = 0$ have three roots equal and let they are α, α and α

$$\alpha + \alpha + \alpha = p$$

$$3\alpha = p \qquad \alpha = \frac{p}{3}$$

since α is a root so $(x - \alpha)$ must be a factor so

$$x^3 - px^2 + qx - r \equiv (x - \alpha)^3$$

$$x^3 - px^2 + qx - r \equiv (x^2 - 2x\alpha + \alpha^2)(x - \alpha)$$

$$x^3 - px^2 + qx - r \equiv (x^3 - x^2\alpha - 2x^2\alpha + 2x\alpha^2 + \alpha^2 x + \alpha^3$$

$$x^3 - px^2 + qx + r \equiv x^3 - 3x^2\alpha + 2x\alpha^2 + \alpha^2 x - \alpha^3$$

$$x^3 - px^2 + qx - r \equiv x^3 - 3x^2\alpha + 3x\alpha^2 - \alpha^3$$

Compairing the equal powers of x an both sides we have

$$p = 3\alpha \qquad q = 3\alpha^2 \qquad r = \alpha^3$$

$$p^2 = 9\alpha^2 \qquad p^2 = 9\frac{q}{3} \qquad p^2 = 3q \tag{1}$$

$$\alpha = \frac{p}{3}$$

so $$r = \left(\frac{p}{3}\right)^3$$

$$r = \frac{p^3}{27} \qquad p^3 = 27r \tag{2}$$

and $$\alpha^3 = \alpha \cdot \alpha^2$$

$$\alpha^3 = \frac{p}{3} \cdot \frac{q}{3} \qquad r = \frac{pq}{9}$$

i.e. $$pq = 9r \tag{3}$$

(1) (2) and (3) will give the required contition.

3

Symmetric Function of Roots of Cubic and Biquadratic Equation

If an expression involving the roots of an equation remains unaltered when any two of the roots are interchanged, then such an expression is called a symmetric function of the roots of the given equation.

Problem 1 Calculate the values of the following symmetric functions for the cubic equation $x^2 + px^2 + qx + r = 0$ whose roots are α, β, γ

(i) $\sum\alpha^2$ *(ii)* $\sum\alpha^2\beta^2$
(iii) $\sum\alpha^2\beta$ *(iv)* $\sum\alpha^3$
(*v*) $\sum\alpha^3\beta^3$ (*vi*) $\sum\frac{\beta^2+\gamma^2}{\beta\gamma}$ (*vii*) $\sum\frac{\beta^2+\gamma^2}{\beta+\gamma}$

Solution (i) we know that

$$(\sum\alpha)^2 = (\alpha+\beta+\gamma)^2$$
$$= \alpha^2+\beta^2+\gamma^2+2(\alpha\beta+\beta\gamma+\alpha\gamma)$$
$$= \sum\alpha^2 + 2\sum\alpha\beta$$
$$\sum\alpha^2 = (\sum\alpha)^2 - 2\sum\alpha\beta$$

since α, β, γ are roots of the cubic $x^3 + px^2 + qx + r = 0$

$$\sum\alpha = -p \qquad \sum\alpha\beta = q \qquad \alpha\beta\gamma = -r$$
$$\sum\alpha^2 = (-p)^2 - 2q$$
$$\sum\alpha^2 = p^2 - 2q \quad \textbf{Ans.}$$

(ii) $$(\sum\alpha\beta)^2 = (\alpha\beta+\beta\gamma+\alpha\gamma)^2$$
$$= \alpha^2\beta^2+\beta^2\gamma^2+\alpha^2\gamma^2+2\alpha\beta^2\gamma+2\alpha\beta\gamma^2+2\alpha^2\beta\gamma$$
$$= \sum\alpha^2\beta^2 + 2\alpha\beta\gamma(\alpha+\beta+\gamma)$$
$$= \sum\alpha^2\beta^2 + 2\alpha\beta\gamma(\sum\alpha)$$
$$\sum\alpha^2\beta^2 = (\sum\alpha\beta)^2 - 2\alpha\beta\gamma(\sum\alpha)$$
$$\sum\alpha^2\beta^2 = q^2 - 2(-r)(-p)$$
$$= q^2 + (-2pr) = q^2 - 2pr$$

(iii) $\sum\alpha^2\beta = ?$

We have $\sum\alpha \sum\alpha\beta = (\alpha + \beta + \gamma)(\alpha\beta + \beta\gamma + \gamma\alpha)$

$$= \alpha^2\beta + \alpha\beta\gamma + \alpha^2\gamma + \alpha\beta^2 + \beta^2\gamma + \alpha\beta\gamma + \alpha\beta\gamma + \beta\gamma^2 + \alpha\gamma^2$$

$$= \alpha^2\beta + \alpha^2\gamma + \alpha\beta^2 + \beta^2\gamma + \beta\gamma^2 + \alpha\gamma^2 + 3\alpha\beta\gamma$$

$$= \sum\alpha^2\beta + 3\alpha\beta\gamma$$

$$\sum\alpha^2\beta = \sum\alpha\sum\alpha\beta + 3\alpha\beta\gamma$$

$$= (-p)q - 3(-r) = 3r - pq$$

(iv) $\sum\alpha^3 = ?$

We have $\sum\alpha\sum\alpha^2 = (\alpha + \beta + \gamma)(\alpha^2 + \beta^2 + \gamma^2)$

$$= \alpha^3 + \beta^3 + \gamma^3 + \alpha\beta^2 + \alpha\gamma^2 + \alpha^2\beta + \beta\gamma^2 + \alpha^2\gamma + \beta^2\gamma$$

$$= \sum\alpha^3 + \sum\alpha^2\beta$$

$$\sum\alpha^3 = \sum\alpha\sum\alpha^2 - \sum\alpha^2\beta$$

$$= (-p)(p^2 - 2q) - (3r - pq)$$

$$= -p^3 + 2pq - 3r + pq$$

$$= -p^3 + 3pq - 3r = 3pq - 3r - p^3$$

(v) $\sum\alpha^3\beta^3 = ?$

we have

$$\sum\alpha\beta(\sum\alpha^2\beta^2) = (\alpha\beta + \beta\gamma + \alpha\gamma)(\alpha^2\beta^2 + \beta^2\gamma^2 + \alpha^2\gamma^2)$$

$$= \alpha^3\beta^3 + \alpha\beta^3\gamma^2 + \alpha^3\beta\gamma^2 + \alpha^2\beta^3\gamma + \alpha^2\beta\gamma^3 + \alpha^3\beta^2\gamma + \alpha\beta^2\gamma^3 + \beta^3\gamma^3 + \alpha^3\gamma^3$$

$$= \sum\alpha^3\beta^3 + \alpha\beta\gamma(\alpha\gamma^2 + \alpha^2\beta + \beta\gamma^2 + \beta^2\gamma + \alpha^2\gamma + \beta^2\alpha)$$

$$\sum\alpha^3\beta^3 = \sum\alpha\beta\sum\alpha^2\beta^2 - \alpha\beta\gamma\sum\alpha^2\beta$$

$$= q(q^2 - 2pr) - (-r)(3r - pq)$$

$$= q^3 - 2pqr + 3r^2 - pqr$$

$$= q^3 - 3pqr + 3r^2$$

(vi) $$\sum\frac{\beta^2+\gamma^2}{\beta\gamma} = \frac{\beta^2+\gamma^2}{\beta\gamma} + \frac{\alpha^2+\beta^2}{\alpha\beta} + \frac{\alpha^2+\gamma^2}{\alpha\gamma}$$

$$= \frac{\alpha(\beta^2+\gamma^2) + \gamma(\alpha^2+\beta^2) + \beta(\alpha^2+\gamma^2)}{\alpha\beta\gamma}$$

$$= \frac{\sum\alpha^2\beta}{\alpha\beta\gamma} = \frac{3r - pq}{(-r)} = \frac{pq - 3r}{r}$$ **Ans.**

(vii) $\sum \dfrac{\beta^2+\gamma^2}{\beta+\gamma} = \dfrac{\beta^2+\gamma^2}{\beta+\gamma} + \dfrac{\alpha^2+\beta^2}{\alpha+\beta} + \dfrac{\alpha^2+\gamma^2}{\alpha+\gamma}$

$$= \frac{(\alpha+\beta)(\alpha+\gamma)(\beta^2+\gamma^2)+(\beta+\gamma)(\alpha+\gamma)(\alpha^2+\beta^2)+(\alpha+\beta)(\beta+\gamma)}{(\alpha+\beta)\,(\beta+\gamma)\,(\alpha+\gamma)}$$

$$= \frac{\sum(\beta^2+\gamma^2)\,(\alpha+\beta)\,(\alpha+\gamma)}{(\alpha+\beta)\,(\beta+\gamma)\,(\alpha+\gamma)}$$

Numerator

$$= \sum(\beta^2+\gamma^2)\,(\alpha+\beta)\,(\alpha+\gamma)$$
$$= \sum(\beta^2+\gamma^2)\,(\alpha^2+\alpha\beta+\alpha\gamma+\beta\gamma)$$
$$= \sum(\beta^2+\gamma^2)\,(\alpha^2+\sum\alpha\beta)$$
$$= \sum(\beta^2+\gamma^2)\,(\alpha^2+q)$$
$$= \sum\alpha^2\,(\beta^2+\gamma^2)+q\sum(\beta^2+\gamma^2)$$
$$= \alpha^2\,(\beta^2+\gamma^2)+\beta^2\,(\alpha^2+\gamma^2)+\gamma^2\,(\alpha^2+\beta^2)$$
$$+\ 2(\beta^2+\gamma^2+\alpha^2+\beta^2+\alpha^2+\gamma^2)$$
$$= 2(\alpha^2\beta^2+\beta^2\gamma^2+\alpha^2\gamma^2)+2q\,(\alpha^2+\beta^2+\gamma^2)$$
$$= 2\sum\alpha^2\beta^2+2q\sum\alpha^2$$
$$= 2(q^2-2pr)+2q\,(p^2-2q)$$
$$= 2q^2-4pr+2p^2q-4q^2$$
$$= 2p^2q-2q^2-4pr$$

and Denominator

$$= (\alpha+\beta)\,(\beta+\gamma)\,(\alpha+\gamma)$$
$$= (\alpha+\beta)\,(\alpha\beta+\beta\gamma+\alpha\gamma+\gamma^2)$$
$$= \alpha^2\beta+\alpha\beta\gamma+\alpha^2\gamma+\alpha\beta^2+\gamma\beta^2+\alpha\beta\gamma+\beta\gamma^2$$
$$= \sum\alpha^2\beta+2\alpha\beta\gamma$$
$$= (3r-pq)+2(-r)$$
$$= 3r-pq-2r$$
$$= (r-pq)$$

Thus $\sum \dfrac{\beta^2+\gamma^2}{\beta+\gamma} = \dfrac{2p^2q-2q^2-4pr}{r-pq}$

Problem 2 If $\alpha, \beta, \gamma, \delta$ be the roots of the biquadratic equation

$$x^4 + px^3 + qx^2 + rx + s = 0$$

Find in terms of the coefficients, the value of the following symmetric function.

(i) $\sum \alpha^2$ (ii) $\sum \alpha^2\beta$

(iii) $\sum \alpha^2\beta\gamma$ (iv) $\sum \alpha^3$

(v) $\sum \alpha^2\beta^2$ (vi) $\sum(\alpha - \beta)^2 (\gamma - \delta)^2$

(vii) $\sum(\gamma\alpha + \beta\delta)(\alpha\beta + \gamma\delta)$ (viii) $(\beta\gamma + \alpha\delta)(\gamma\alpha + \beta\delta)(\alpha\beta + \gamma\delta)$

Solution (1) $\sum \alpha^2 = ?$

We have $(\sum \alpha) = (\alpha + \beta + \gamma + \delta)^2$

$$= \alpha^2 + \beta^2 + \gamma^2 + \delta^2 + 2\alpha\beta + 2\alpha\gamma + 2\alpha\delta + 2\beta\gamma + 2\beta\delta + 2\gamma\delta$$

$$= \sum \alpha^2 + 2\sum \alpha\beta \qquad \sum \alpha = -p$$

$$\Rightarrow \sum \alpha^2 = (\sum \alpha)^2 - 2\sum \alpha\beta \qquad \sum \alpha\beta = q$$

$$\Rightarrow \sum \alpha^2 = (-p)^2 - 2q$$

$$\Rightarrow \sum \alpha^2 = p^2 - 2q$$

(ii) We have

$$\sum \alpha \sum \alpha\beta = (\alpha+\beta+\gamma+\delta)(\alpha\beta + \alpha\gamma + \alpha\delta + \beta\gamma + \beta\delta + \gamma\delta)$$

$$= \alpha^2\beta + \alpha^2\gamma + \alpha^2\delta + \alpha\beta\gamma + \alpha\beta\delta + \alpha\gamma\delta$$
$$+ \alpha\beta^2 + \alpha\beta\gamma + \alpha\beta\delta + \beta\gamma\delta + \beta^2\delta + \beta\gamma\delta + \alpha\beta\gamma + \alpha\gamma\delta$$
$$+ \beta\gamma^2 + \beta\gamma\delta + \gamma^2\delta + \alpha\beta\delta + \alpha\gamma\delta + \alpha\delta^2 + \beta\gamma\delta + \beta\delta^2 + \gamma\delta^2$$

$$= \sum \alpha^2\beta + 3\sum \alpha\beta\gamma$$

$$\sum \alpha = -p \quad \sum \alpha\beta = q \quad \sum \alpha\beta\gamma = -r \quad = \alpha\beta\gamma\delta = s$$

$$\Rightarrow \quad \sum \alpha^2\beta = \sum \alpha \sum \alpha\beta - 3\sum \alpha\beta\gamma$$

$$\Rightarrow \quad \sum \alpha^2\beta = (-p)(q) - 3(-r)$$

$$\sum \alpha^2\beta = -pq + 3r = 3r - pq \quad \textbf{Ans.}$$

(iii) We have

$$\sum \alpha \sum \alpha\beta\gamma = (\alpha + \beta + \gamma + \delta)(\alpha\beta\gamma + \alpha\beta\delta + \beta\gamma\delta + \alpha\gamma\delta)$$

$$= \alpha^2\beta\gamma + \alpha^2\beta\delta + \alpha\beta\gamma\delta + \alpha^2\gamma\delta + \alpha\beta^2\gamma + \alpha\beta^2\delta$$
$$+ \beta^2\gamma\delta + \alpha\beta\gamma\delta + \alpha\beta\gamma^2 + \alpha\beta\gamma\delta + \beta\gamma^2\delta + \alpha\gamma^2\delta$$
$$+ \alpha\beta\gamma\delta + \alpha\beta\delta^2 + \beta\gamma\delta^2 + \alpha\gamma\delta^2$$

$$= \sum \alpha^2\beta\gamma + 4\alpha\beta\gamma\delta$$

$$\sum \alpha^2\beta\gamma = \sum \alpha \sum \alpha\beta\gamma - 4\alpha\beta\gamma\delta$$

$$\sum \alpha^2\beta\gamma = (-p)(-r) - 4s$$

$$\sum \alpha^2\beta\gamma = pr - 4s \quad \textbf{Ans.}$$

(iv) $\sum \alpha^3 = 2$ we have

$$\sum \alpha \cdot \sum \alpha^2 = (\alpha + \beta + \gamma + \delta)(\alpha^2 + \beta^2 + \gamma^2 + \delta^2)$$

$$= \alpha^3 + \alpha\beta^2 + \alpha\gamma^2 + \alpha\delta^2 + \alpha^2\beta + \beta^3 + \beta\gamma^2 + \beta\delta^2 + \alpha^2\gamma + \beta^2\gamma + \gamma^3 + \gamma\delta^2 + \alpha^2\delta + \beta^2\delta + \gamma^2\delta + \delta^3$$

$$\sum \alpha \sum \alpha^2 = \sum \alpha^3 + \sum \alpha^2\beta$$

$$\sum \alpha^3 = \sum \alpha \sum \alpha^2 - \sum \alpha^2\beta$$

$$= (-p)(p^2 - 2q) - (3r - pq) = -p^3 + 2pq - 3r + pq$$

$$\sum \alpha^3 = 3pq - p^3 - 3r \quad \textbf{Ans.}$$

(v) $\sum \alpha^2\beta^2 = ?$

We have

$$\left(\sum \alpha\beta\right)^2 = (\alpha\beta + \alpha\gamma + \alpha\delta + \beta\gamma + \beta\delta + \gamma\delta)^2$$

$$= \sum \alpha^2\beta^2 + 2\sum \alpha^2\beta\gamma + 6\,\alpha\beta\gamma\delta$$

$$\Rightarrow \sum \alpha^2\beta^2 = \left(\sum \alpha\beta\right)^2 - 2\sum \alpha^2\beta\gamma - 6\,\alpha\beta\gamma\delta$$

$$\Rightarrow \sum \alpha^2\beta^2 = q^2 - 2(pr - 4s) - 6s$$

$$= q^2 - 2pr + 8s - 6s$$

$$= q^2 - 2pr + 2s$$

(vi) $\sum (\alpha - \beta)^2 (\gamma - \delta)^2$

$$= \sum (\alpha^2 - 2\alpha\beta + \beta^2)(\gamma^2 - 2\gamma\delta + \delta^2)$$

$$= (\alpha^2 - 2\alpha\beta + \beta^2)(\gamma^2 - 2\gamma\delta + \delta^2) + (\beta^2 - 2\beta\gamma + \gamma^2)(\alpha^2 - 2\alpha\delta + \delta^2) + (\beta^2 - 2\beta\delta + \delta^2)(\alpha^2 - 2\alpha\gamma + \gamma^2)$$

$$= \alpha^2\gamma^2 - 2\alpha^2\gamma\delta + \alpha^2\delta^2 - 2\alpha\beta\gamma^2 + 4\alpha\beta\gamma\delta - 2\alpha\beta\delta^2 + \beta^2\gamma^2 - 2\beta^2\gamma\delta + \beta^2\delta^2 + \alpha^2\beta^2 - 2\alpha\beta^2\delta + \beta^2\delta^2 - 2\alpha^2\beta\gamma + 4\alpha\beta\gamma\delta - 2\beta\gamma\delta^2 + \alpha^2\gamma^2 - 2\alpha\gamma^2\delta + \gamma^2\delta^2 + \alpha^2\beta^2 - 2\alpha\beta^2\gamma + \gamma^2\beta^2 - 2\alpha^2\beta\delta + 4\alpha\beta\gamma\delta - 2\beta\gamma^2\delta + \alpha^2\delta^2 - 2\alpha\gamma\delta^2 + \gamma^2\delta^2$$

$$= 2\sum \alpha^2\beta^2 - 2\sum \alpha^2\beta\gamma + 12\alpha\beta\gamma\delta$$

$$= 2(q^2 - 2pr + 2s) - 2(pr - 4s) + 12s$$

$$= 2q^2 - 4pr + 4s - 2pr + 8s + 12s$$

$$= 2q^2 - 6pr + 24s$$

(vii) $\sum (\gamma\alpha + \beta\delta)(\alpha\beta + \gamma\delta)$

$$= (\alpha\gamma + \beta\delta)(\alpha\beta + \gamma\delta) + (\alpha\delta + \beta\gamma)(\alpha\gamma + \beta\delta) + (\alpha\beta + \gamma\delta)(\alpha\delta + \beta\gamma)$$

$$= \alpha^2\beta\gamma + \alpha\gamma^2\delta + \alpha\beta^2\delta + \beta\gamma\delta^2 + \alpha^2\gamma\delta + \alpha\beta\delta^2 + \alpha\beta\gamma^2 + \gamma\beta^2\delta + \alpha^2\beta\delta + \alpha\beta^2\gamma + \alpha\gamma\delta^2 + \beta\gamma^2\delta$$

$$= \sum \alpha^2\beta\gamma = pr - 4s$$

(viii) $$(\beta\gamma + \alpha\delta)(\gamma\alpha + \beta\delta)(\alpha\beta + \gamma\delta)$$
$$= (\beta\gamma + \alpha\delta)(\alpha^2\beta\gamma + \alpha\gamma^2\delta + \alpha\beta^2\delta + \beta\gamma\delta^2)$$
$$= \alpha^2\beta^2\gamma^2 + \alpha\beta\gamma^3\delta + \alpha\beta^3\gamma\delta + \beta^2\gamma^2\delta^2 + \alpha^3\beta\gamma\delta + \alpha^2\gamma^2\delta^2 + \alpha^2\beta^2\delta^2 + \alpha\beta\gamma\delta^3$$
$$= \alpha\beta\gamma\delta(\alpha^2 + \beta^2 + \gamma^2 + \delta^2 + \alpha^2\beta^2\gamma^2\delta^2 \left(\frac{1}{\alpha^2} + \frac{1}{\beta^2} + \frac{1}{\gamma^2} + \frac{1}{\delta^2}\right)$$
$$= \alpha\beta\gamma\delta\left(\sum \alpha^2\right) + \alpha^2\beta^2\gamma^2\delta^2 \sum\frac{1}{\alpha^2}$$

Now we have to find the values of

$\sum \alpha^2$ and $\sum\frac{1}{\alpha^2}$ we have

$$\left(\sum \alpha\right)^2 = (\alpha + \beta + \gamma + \delta)^2$$
$$= \alpha^2 + \beta^2 + \gamma^2 + \delta^2 + 2\sum \alpha\beta = \sum \alpha^2 + 2\sum \alpha\beta$$
$$\Rightarrow \quad \sum \alpha^2 = \left(\sum \alpha\right)^2 - 2\sum \alpha\beta \tag{1}$$
$$= (p^2 - 2q)$$
$$\Rightarrow \quad \left(\sum \frac{1}{\alpha^2}\right)^2 = \left(\frac{1}{\alpha} + \frac{1}{\beta} + \frac{1}{\gamma} + \frac{1}{\delta}\right)^2$$
$$\sum \alpha = -p; \quad \sum \alpha\beta = q; \quad \sum \alpha\beta\gamma = -r; \quad \alpha\beta\gamma\delta = s$$
$$= \frac{1}{\alpha^2} + \frac{1}{\beta^2} + \frac{1}{\gamma^2} + \frac{1}{\delta^2} + 2\sum\frac{1}{\alpha\beta}$$
$$= \sum\frac{1}{\alpha^2} + 2\sum\frac{1}{\alpha\beta}$$
$$\Rightarrow \quad \sum\frac{1}{\alpha^2} = \left(\sum\frac{1}{\alpha}\right)^2 - \sum\frac{2}{\alpha\beta} \tag{2}$$
$$\Rightarrow \quad \sum\frac{1}{\alpha^2} = \left[\left(\frac{1}{\alpha} + \frac{1}{\beta} + \frac{1}{\gamma} + \frac{1}{\delta}\right)\right]^2 - 2\left(\frac{1}{\alpha\beta} + \frac{1}{\beta\gamma} + \frac{1}{\alpha\delta} + \frac{1}{\beta\delta} + \frac{1}{\alpha\gamma} + \frac{1}{\gamma\delta}\right)$$
$$\Rightarrow \quad \sum\frac{1}{\alpha^2} = \left[\frac{(\beta\gamma\delta + \alpha\gamma\delta + \alpha\beta\delta + \alpha\beta\gamma)}{\alpha\beta\gamma\delta}\right]^2 - 2\frac{(\gamma\delta + \alpha\delta + \beta\gamma + \alpha\gamma + \beta\delta + \alpha\beta)}{\alpha\beta\gamma\delta}$$
$$\Rightarrow \quad \sum\frac{1}{\alpha^2} = \left[\frac{\sum\alpha\beta\gamma}{\alpha\beta\gamma\delta}\right]^2 - 2\frac{\sum\alpha\beta}{\alpha\beta\gamma\delta}$$
$$= \left(-\frac{r}{s}\right)^2 - 2\frac{q}{s}$$
$$= \frac{r^2}{s^2} - \frac{2q}{s} = \frac{r^2 - 2qs}{s^2}$$

so $(\beta\gamma + \alpha\delta)(\gamma\alpha + \beta\delta)(\alpha\beta + \gamma\delta)$

$$= s(p^2 - 2q) + s^2\left(\frac{r^2 - 2qs}{s^2}\right)$$

$$= s(p^2 - 2q) + r^2 - 2qs$$

$$= p^2 s - 2qs + r^2 - 2qs$$

$$= r^2 - 4qs + p^2 s$$

Problem 3 If α, β, γ are the roots of $ax^3 + 3bx^2 + 3cx + d = 0$ prove that

(i) $a^2(1 + \alpha^2(1 + \beta^2)(1 + \gamma^2) = (a - 3c)^2 + (3b - d)^2$

(ii) $a^2\{(\beta-\gamma)(\gamma-\alpha) + (\gamma-\alpha)(\alpha-\beta) + (\alpha-\beta)(\beta-\gamma)\} = 9(ac - b^2)$

[*Forest Service 88*]

Solution Let α, β, γ, be the roots of cubic equation

$ax^3 + 3bx^2 + 3cx + d = 0$ then

$$\sum \alpha = \alpha + \beta + \gamma = -\frac{3b}{a} \quad (1)$$

$$\sum \alpha\beta = \alpha\beta + \beta\gamma + \alpha\gamma = \frac{3c}{a} \quad (2)$$

$$\alpha\beta\gamma = -\frac{d}{a} \quad (3)$$

Now we have to find the value of

$$a^2(1 + \alpha^2)(1 + \beta^2)(1 + \gamma^2)$$

$$= a^2[1 + \alpha^2 + \beta^2 + \gamma^2 + \alpha^2\beta^2 + \alpha^2\gamma^2 + \beta^2\gamma^2 + \alpha^2\beta^2\gamma^2]$$

$$= a^2[1 + \sum \alpha^2 + \sum \alpha^2\beta^2 + (\alpha\beta\gamma^2] \quad (4)$$

Now we have to find the value of $\sum \alpha^2$, $\sum \alpha^2 \beta^2$

$$(\sum\alpha)^2 = (\alpha + \beta + \gamma)^2$$

$$= \alpha^2 + \beta^2 + \gamma^2 + 2(\alpha\beta + \beta\gamma + \alpha\gamma)$$

$$= \sum \alpha^2 + 2\sum \alpha\beta$$

$$\sum \alpha^2 = (\sum \alpha)^2 - 2\sum \alpha\beta$$

$$= \left(-\frac{3b}{a}\right)^2 - 2\cdot\frac{3c}{a}$$

$$= \frac{9b^2}{a^2} - \frac{6c}{a} = \frac{(9b^2 - 6ac)}{a^2}$$

Again $\quad (\sum \alpha\beta)^2 = (\alpha\beta + \beta\gamma + \alpha\gamma)^2$

$$= \alpha^2\beta^2 + \beta^2\gamma^2 + \alpha^2\gamma^2 + 2(\alpha^2\beta\gamma + \alpha\beta^2\gamma + \alpha\beta\gamma^2)$$

$$= \sum \alpha^2\beta^2 + \alpha\beta\gamma(\alpha + \beta + \gamma)$$

$$\sum \alpha^2\beta^2 = (\sum \alpha\beta)^2 - 2\alpha\beta\gamma(\alpha + \beta + \gamma)$$

$$= \left(\frac{3c}{a}\right)^2 - 2\left(-\frac{d}{a}\right)\left(-\frac{3b}{a}\right)$$

$$= \frac{9c^2}{a^2} - \frac{6bd}{a^2} = \frac{(9c^2 - 6bd)}{a^2}$$

Now from (4) we have

$a^2(1 + \alpha^2)(1 + \beta^2)(1 + \gamma^2)$

$$= a^2\left[1 + \frac{(9b^2 - 6ac)}{a^2} + \frac{(9c^2 - 6bd)}{a^2} + \frac{d^2}{a^2}\right]$$

$$= a^2\left[\frac{a^2 + 9b^2 - 6ac + 9c^2 - 6bd + d^2}{a^2}\right]$$

$$= a^2 + 9b^2 - 6ac + 9c^2 - 6bd + d^2$$

$$= (a^2 - 6ac + 9c^2) + (9b^2 - 6bd + d^2)$$

$$= (a - 3c)^2 + (3b - d)^2 \qquad \textit{(Proved)}$$

(ii) $\quad (a^2\{(\beta - \gamma)(\gamma - \alpha) + (\gamma - \alpha)(\alpha - \beta) + (\alpha - \beta)(\beta - \gamma)\}$

$$= a^2[\beta\gamma - \gamma^2 - \alpha\beta + \alpha\gamma + \gamma\alpha - \alpha^2 - \beta\gamma$$
$$+ \alpha\beta + \alpha\beta - \beta^2 - \alpha\gamma + \beta\gamma]$$

$$= a^2[\sum\alpha\beta - \sum\alpha^2]$$

$$= a^2\left[\frac{3c}{a} - \frac{(9b^2 - 6ac)}{a^2}\right]$$

$$= a^2\left[\frac{3ac - 9b^2 + 6ac}{a^2}\right]$$

$$= (9ac - 9b^2) = 9(ac - b^2) \qquad \textit{(Proved)}$$

Problem 4 If α. β, γ be the roots of the equation
$\alpha x^3 + 3bx^2 + 3cx + d = 0$

Find the value in terms of the coeffiients of

$$(2\alpha - \beta - \gamma)(2\beta - \gamma - \alpha)(2\gamma - \alpha - \beta)$$

Solution $(\alpha, \beta, \gamma$ be the roots of the cubic equation

$$ax^3 + 3bx^2 + 3cx + d = 0$$

then $\quad \sum\alpha = \alpha + \beta + \gamma = -\dfrac{3b}{a} \qquad (1)$

$$\sum\alpha\beta = \sum\alpha\beta = \alpha\beta + \beta\gamma + \alpha\gamma = \frac{3c}{a} \quad (2)$$

$$\alpha\beta\gamma = -\frac{d}{a} \quad (3)$$

Now $2\alpha - \beta - \gamma = 3\alpha - (\alpha + \beta + \gamma)$

$$= 3\alpha + \frac{3b}{a} = \left(\alpha + \frac{b}{a}\right)$$

Again

$$2\beta - \gamma - \alpha = 3\beta - (\alpha + \beta + \gamma)$$

$$= 3\beta + \frac{3b}{a} = 3\left(\beta + \frac{b}{a}\right)$$

and $2\gamma - \alpha - \beta = 3\gamma - (a + \beta + \gamma)$

$$= 3\gamma + \left(\gamma + \frac{b}{a}\right)$$

Now $(2\alpha - \beta - \gamma)(2\beta - \gamma - \alpha)(2\gamma - \alpha - \beta)$

$$= 27\left(\alpha + \frac{b}{a}\right)\left(\beta + \frac{b}{a}\right)\left(\gamma + \frac{b}{a}\right)$$

$$= 27\left[\alpha\beta\gamma + \frac{b}{a}(\alpha\beta + \beta\gamma + \alpha\gamma) + \frac{b^2}{a^2}(\alpha + \beta + \gamma) + \frac{b^3}{a^3}\right]$$

$$= 27\left[-\frac{d}{a} + \frac{b}{a}\frac{3c}{a} + \frac{b^2}{a^2}\left(-\frac{3b}{a}\right) + \frac{b^3}{a^3}\right]$$

$$= 27\left[-\frac{d}{a} + \frac{3bc}{a^2} - \frac{3b^3}{a^3} + \frac{b^2}{a^3}\right]$$

$$= 27\left[\frac{-da^2 + 3abc - 3b^3 + b^3}{a^3}\right]$$

$$= \frac{27[-da^2 + 3abc - 2b^3]}{a^3}$$

$$= -\frac{27}{a^3}[a^2 d - 3abc + 2b^3] \quad \textbf{Ans.}$$

Problem 5 If $\alpha, \gamma, \gamma, \delta)$ be the roots of the biquadratic
$x^4 + px^3 + qx^2 + rx + s = 0$

prove that

$$(\alpha^2 + 1)(\beta^2 + 1)(\gamma^2 + 1)(\delta^2 + 1) = (1 - q + s)^2 + (p - r)^2$$

Solution Let α, β, γ, δ be the roots of the biquadratic equation

$$x^4 + px^3 + qx^2 + rx + s = 0$$

Then $x^4 + px^3 + qx^2 + rx + s$

$$\equiv (x - \alpha)(x - \beta)(x - \gamma)(x - \delta)$$

Putting $x = i$ we have

$$1 - pi - q + ri + s$$
$$= (i - \alpha)(i - \beta)(i - \gamma)(i - \delta)$$
$$(1 - q + s) - (p - r)i$$
$$= (i - \alpha)(i - \beta)(i - \gamma) i - \delta) \qquad (1)$$

Again putting $x = -i$ we have

$$1 + pi - q - ri + s$$
$$= (i + \alpha)(i + \beta)(i + \gamma)(i + \delta)$$
$$(1 - q + s) + (p - r)i$$
$$= (i + \alpha)(i + \beta)(i + \gamma)(i + \delta)$$

Multiplying (1) and (2) we have

$$(1 - q + s)^2 + (p - r)^2 = (1 + \alpha^2)(1 + \beta^2)(1 + \gamma^2)(1 + \delta^2)$$

(Proved)

Problem 6 Find the numerical value of

$$(\alpha^2 + 2)(\beta^2 + 2) + 2)(\gamma^2 + 2)(\delta^2 + 2)$$

where α, β, γ, δ are the roots of the equation

$$x^4 - 7x^3 + 8x^2 - 5x + 10 = 0$$

Solution Since α, β, γ, δ are the roots of the biquadratic equatiyn

$$x^4 - 7x^3 + 8x^2 - 5x + 10 = 0$$

so we have the Identity

$$x^4 - 7x^3 + 8x^2 - 5x + 10 = (x - \alpha)(x - \beta)(x - \gamma)(x - \delta)$$

Putting $x = \sqrt{2}i$ we have

$$(\sqrt{2}i)^4 - 7(\sqrt{2}i)^3 + 8(\sqrt{2}i)^2 - 5(\sqrt{2}i) + 10$$
$$= (\sqrt{2}i - \alpha)(\sqrt{2}i - \beta)(\sqrt{2}i - \gamma)(\sqrt{2}i - \delta)$$
$$\Rightarrow 4 + 14\sqrt{2}i - 16 - 5\sqrt{2}i + 10$$
$$= (\sqrt{2}i - \alpha)(\sqrt{2}i - \beta)(\sqrt{2}i - \gamma)(\sqrt{2}i - \delta)$$
$$\Rightarrow -2 + 9\sqrt{2}i = (\sqrt{2}i - \alpha)(\sqrt{2}i - \beta)(\sqrt{2}i - \gamma)(\sqrt{2}i - \delta) \qquad (2)$$

similarly putting $x = -\sqrt{2}i$ we have

$$-2 - 9\sqrt{2}i = (\sqrt{2}i + \alpha)(\sqrt{2}i + \beta)(\sqrt{2}i + \gamma)(\sqrt{2}i + \delta) \qquad (3)$$

Multiplying (2) and (3) we have

$$4 - 81 \times 2i^2 = (\alpha^2 + 2)(\beta^2 + 2)(\gamma^2 + 2)(\delta^2 + 2)$$

$$4 + 162 = (\alpha^2 + 2(\beta^2 + 2)(\gamma^2 + 2)(\delta^2 + 2)$$

Thus we have $(\alpha^2 + 2)(\beta^2 + 2)(\gamma^2 + 2)(\delta^2 + 2) = 166$ **Ans.**

Problem 6 For thc cubic $x^3 + px^2 + qx + r = 0$, calculate the value of the following symmetric functions.

(i) $\sum(\alpha - \beta)^2$ (ii) $\sum\alpha^4$ (iii) $\sum(\beta + \gamma - \alpha)^3$

(iv) $\sum \dfrac{\alpha^2 + \beta\gamma}{\beta + \gamma}$.

Solution α, β, γ be the roots of the cubic equation

$$x^3 + px^2 + qx + r = 0$$

$$\sum(\alpha - \beta)^2 = (\alpha - \beta)^2 + (\beta - \gamma)^2 + (\gamma - \alpha)^2$$

$$= \alpha^2 + \beta^2 - 2\alpha\beta + \beta^2 - 2\beta\gamma + \gamma^2 + \gamma^2 + \alpha^2 - 2\gamma\alpha$$

$$\sum(\alpha - \beta)^2 = 2\sum\alpha^2 - 2\sum\alpha\beta$$

Again $(\sum\alpha)^2 = (\alpha + \beta + \gamma)^2$

$$\sum\alpha^2 = (\sum\alpha)^2 - 2\sum\alpha\beta \quad (2)$$

so $\sum(\alpha - \beta)^2 = 2(\sum\alpha)^2 - 6\sum\alpha\beta$ $\qquad \sum\alpha = p$

$\sum(\alpha - \beta)^2 = 2(-p)^2 - 6q$ $\qquad \sum\alpha\beta = q$

$\sum(\alpha - \beta)^2 = 2p^2 - 6q$ $\qquad \alpha\beta\gamma = r$

$= (2p^2 - 3q)$ **Ans.**

(ii) $\sum\alpha^4 = \alpha^4 + \beta^4 + \gamma^4$

We have $(\sum\alpha^2)^2 = \alpha^2 + \beta^2 + \gamma^2)^2$

$$= \alpha^4 + \beta^4 + \gamma^4 + 2(\alpha^2\beta^2 + \beta^2\gamma^2 + \alpha^2\gamma^2)$$

$$= \sum\alpha^4 + 2\sum\alpha^2\beta^2$$

$$\sum\alpha^4 = (\sum\alpha^2)^2 - 2\sum\alpha^2\beta^2 \quad (1)$$

Again $(\sum\alpha)^2 = (\alpha + \beta + \gamma)^2$

$$= \alpha^2 + \beta^2 + \gamma^2 + 2\alpha\beta + 2\beta\gamma + 2\alpha\gamma$$

$$= \sum\alpha^2 + 2\sum\alpha\beta$$

$$\sum\alpha^2 = (\sum\alpha)^2 - 2\sum\alpha\beta$$

$$= (-p)^2 - 2q$$

$$\sum\alpha^2 = (p^2 - 2q) \quad (2)$$

$$(\sum\alpha\beta)^2 = (\alpha\beta + \beta\gamma + \beta\gamma)^2$$
$$= \alpha^2\beta^2 + \beta^2\gamma^2 + \alpha^2\gamma^2 + 2\alpha\beta^2\gamma + 2\alpha^2\beta\gamma + 2\alpha\beta\gamma^2$$
$$= \sum\alpha^2\beta^2 + 2\alpha\beta\gamma(\alpha + \beta + \gamma)$$
$$\sum\alpha^2\beta^2 = (\sum\alpha\beta)^2 - 2\alpha\alpha\gamma\sum\alpha$$
$$= (q)^2 - 2(-r)(-p)$$
$$= q^2 - 2pr$$

Thus $\sum\alpha^4 = (p^2 - 2q)^2 - 2(q^2 - 2pr)$
$$= (p^4 - 4p^2q + 4q^2 - 2q^2 + 4pr$$
$$= p^4 - 4p^2q + 4pr + 2q^2 \quad \textbf{Ans.}$$

(iii) $(\alpha + \beta - \gamma)^3 + (\alpha + \gamma - \beta)^3 + (\beta + \gamma - \alpha)^3 = \sum(\beta + \gamma - \alpha)^3$

let $A = \beta + \gamma - \alpha \qquad B = \alpha + \beta - \gamma$

$C = \alpha + \gamma - \beta$

$A + B = 2\beta \qquad B + C = 2\alpha$

$C + A = 2\gamma \qquad A + B + C = \alpha + \beta + \gamma$

Remember

Now $A^3 + B^3 + C^3 = (A + B + C)^3 - 3(A + B)(B + C)(C + A)$
$$= (\sum\alpha)^3 - 24\,\alpha\beta\gamma = (-p)^3 - 24(-r)$$
$$A^3 + B^3 + C^3 = 24r - p^3$$

i.e. $(\beta + \gamma - \alpha)^3 + (\alpha + \beta - \gamma)^3 + (\alpha + \gamma - \beta)^3$
$$= 24r - p^3 \quad \textbf{Ans.}$$

(iv) $\sum\dfrac{\alpha^2 + \beta\gamma}{\beta + \gamma} = \dfrac{\alpha^2 + \beta\gamma}{\beta + \gamma} + \dfrac{\beta^2 + \alpha\gamma}{\alpha + \gamma} + \dfrac{\gamma^2 + \alpha\beta}{\alpha + \beta}$

$$= \frac{\sum(\alpha^2 + \beta\gamma)(\alpha + \gamma)(\alpha + \beta)}{(\beta + \gamma)(\alpha + \gamma)(\alpha + \beta)}$$
$$= \frac{\sum(\alpha^2 + \beta\gamma)(\alpha^2 + \alpha\beta + \alpha\gamma + \beta\gamma)}{(\beta + \gamma)(\alpha + \gamma)(\alpha + \beta)}$$
$$= \frac{\sum(\alpha^2 + \beta\gamma)(\alpha^2 + q)}{(\beta + \gamma)(\alpha + \gamma)(\alpha + \beta)}$$
$$= \frac{\sum\alpha^4 + \alpha^2 q + \alpha^2\beta\gamma + q\beta\gamma}{(\beta + \gamma)(\alpha + \gamma)(\alpha + \beta)}$$
$$= \frac{\sum\alpha^4 + q\sum\alpha^2 + \sum\alpha^2\beta\gamma + q\sum\beta\gamma}{(\beta + \gamma)(\alpha + \gamma)(\alpha + \beta)}$$

$$N^r = \sum \alpha^4 + q\sum \alpha^2 + \sum \alpha^2 \beta\gamma + q\sum \beta\gamma$$
$$= p^4 - 4p^2 q + 4pr + 2q^2 + q(p^2 - 2q) + \alpha\beta\gamma \sum\alpha + q(q)$$
$$= p^4 - 4p^2 q + 4pr + 2q^2 + p^2 q - 2q^2 + pr + q^2$$
$$= p^4 - 3p^2 q + 5pr + q^2$$
$$D^r = (\beta + \gamma)(\alpha + \gamma)(\alpha + \beta)$$
$$= (\alpha + \beta + \gamma - \beta)(\alpha + \beta + \gamma - \alpha)(\alpha + \beta + \gamma - \gamma)$$
$$= (-p - \beta)(-p - \alpha)(-p - \gamma)$$
$$= -(p + \beta)(p + \alpha)(p + \gamma)$$
$$= -[p^3 + p^2(\alpha + \beta + \gamma) + p(\alpha\beta + \beta\gamma + \alpha\gamma) + \alpha\beta\gamma]$$
$$= -[p^3 + p^2(-p) + p(q) - r]$$
$$= -[p^3 - p^3 + pq - r]$$
$$= -[pq - r] = (r - pq)$$

so $\sum \dfrac{\alpha^2 + \beta\gamma}{\beta + \gamma} = \dfrac{p^4 - 3p^2 q + 5pr + q^2}{r - pq}$ **Ans.**

Problem 7 If α, β, γ are the roots of the cubic $ax^3 + 3bx^2 + 3cx + d = 0$, prove that

(i) $(\beta + \gamma)(\gamma + \alpha)(\alpha + \beta) = \dfrac{1}{a^2}(ad - 9bc)$

(ii) $(\alpha\beta + \beta\gamma)(\beta\gamma + \alpha\gamma)(\gamma\alpha + \alpha\beta) = \dfrac{d}{a^3}(9bc - ad)$

Solution α, β, γ are the roots of the cubic $ax^3 + 3bx^2 + 3cx + d = 0$ then

$$\sum \alpha = \alpha + \beta + \gamma = -\frac{3b}{a}$$
$$\sum\alpha\beta = \frac{3c}{a} \qquad \alpha\beta\gamma = -\frac{d}{a}$$

Now (i) $(\beta + \gamma)(\gamma + \alpha)(\alpha + \beta)$

$$= (\alpha + \beta + \gamma - \alpha)(\alpha + \beta + \gamma - \beta)(\alpha + \beta + \gamma - \gamma)$$
$$= \left(-\frac{3b}{a} - \alpha\right)\left(-\frac{3b}{a} - \beta\right)\left(-\frac{3b}{a} - \gamma\right)$$
$$= -\frac{1}{a^3}(3b + a\alpha)(3b + a\beta)(3b + a\gamma)$$
$$= -\frac{1}{a^3}[27b^3 + 9ab^2(\alpha + \beta + \gamma) + 3a^2 b(\alpha\beta + \beta\gamma + \alpha\gamma) + a^3 \alpha\beta\gamma]$$
$$= -\frac{1}{a^3}\left[27b^3 - 27b^3 + 3a^2 b\,\frac{3c}{a} + a^3\left(-\frac{d}{a}\right)\right]$$
$$= -\frac{1}{a^3}[9abc - a^2 d] = \frac{(ad - 9bc)}{a^2} \qquad \textit{(Proved)}$$

(ii) $(\alpha\beta + \beta\gamma)(\beta\gamma + \alpha\gamma)(\gamma\alpha + \alpha\beta)$

$$= (\alpha\beta + \beta\gamma + \alpha\gamma - \alpha\gamma)(\alpha\beta + \beta\gamma + \alpha\gamma - \alpha\beta)(\alpha\beta + \beta\gamma + \gamma\alpha - \beta\gamma)$$

$$= (\sum\alpha\beta - \alpha\gamma)(\sum\alpha\beta - \alpha\beta)(\sum\alpha\beta - \beta\gamma)$$

$$= \left(+\frac{3c}{a} - \alpha\gamma\right)\left(\frac{3c}{a} - \alpha\beta\right)\left(\frac{3c}{a} - \beta\gamma\right)$$

$$= \frac{1}{a^3}(3c - a\alpha\gamma)(3c - a\alpha\beta)(3c - a\beta\gamma)$$

$$= \frac{1}{a^3}[27c^3 - 9ac^2 \sum\alpha\beta + 3a^2 c\, \alpha\beta\gamma(\alpha + \beta + \gamma) + a^3(\alpha\beta\gamma)^2]$$

$$= \frac{1}{a^3}(27c^3 - 27c^3 + 9bcd - ad^2)$$

$$= \frac{1}{a^3}(9bcd - ad^2) = \frac{d}{a^3}(9bc - ad) \qquad \textit{(Proved)}$$

Problem 8 If α, β, γ, be the roots of the biquadratic

$$x^4 + px^3 + qx^2 + rx + s = 0$$

find the value of $(\alpha^2 + 3)(\beta^2 + 3)(\gamma^2 + 3)(\delta^2 + 3)$

Solution Since $\alpha, \beta, \gamma, \delta$ be the roots of the biquadratic

$$x^4 + px^3 + qx^2 + rx + s = 0$$

then

$$x^4 + ax^3 + qx^2 + rx + s$$

$$\equiv (x - \alpha)(x - \beta)(x - \gamma)(x - \delta) \qquad (1)$$

since (1) is an identify so putting $x = \sqrt{3}\,i$ we have

$$x = \sqrt{3}\,i)^4 + p(\sqrt{3}\,i)^3 + q(\sqrt{3}\,i)^2 + r(\sqrt{3}\,i) + s$$

$$= (\sqrt{3}\,i - \alpha)(\sqrt{3}\,i - \beta)(\sqrt{3}\,i - \gamma)(\sqrt{3}\,i - \delta)$$

or $\quad 9 - 3\sqrt{3}\,pi - 3q + r\sqrt{3}\,i + s$

$$= (\sqrt{3}\,i - \alpha)(\sqrt{3}\,i - \beta)(\sqrt{3}\,i - \gamma)(\sqrt{3}\,i - \delta)$$

$$(9 - 3q + s) - \sqrt{3}\,i(3p - r)$$

$$= (\sqrt{3}\,i - \alpha)(\sqrt{3}\,i - \beta)(\sqrt{3}\,i - \gamma)(\sqrt{3}\,i - \delta) \qquad (2)$$

Again substituting

$$x = -\sqrt{3}\,i \text{ we have}$$

$$(9 - 3q + s) + \sqrt{3}\,i(3p - r)$$

$$= (-\sqrt{3}\,i - \alpha)(-\sqrt{3}\,i - \beta)(-\sqrt{3}\,i - \gamma)(-\sqrt{3}\,i - \delta)$$

$$= (\sqrt{3}\,i + \alpha)(\sqrt{3}\,i + \beta)(\sqrt{3}\,i + \gamma)(\sqrt{3}\,i + \delta) \qquad (3)$$

Multiplying (2) and (3) we have

$$(\alpha^2 + 3)(\beta^2 + 3)(\gamma^2 + 3)(\delta^2 + 3) = (9 - 3q + s)^2 + 3(3p - r)^2$$

Problem 9 If $\alpha, \beta, \gamma, \delta$ be the roots of the equation

$$x^4 + px^3 + qx^2 + rx + s = 0$$

find the values of the following symmetric functions

(i) $\sum \frac{1}{\alpha^2}$ (ii) $\sum(\alpha - \beta)^2$

(iii) $\sum \alpha^3 \beta$ (iv) $\sum \alpha^3 \beta\gamma$

(v) $\sum \frac{\beta^2 + \gamma^2}{\beta\gamma}$ (vi) $\sum \alpha^4$

(vii) $\sum \frac{\alpha^2}{\beta^2}$

Solution (i) We have

$$\left(\sum \frac{1}{\alpha}\right)^2 = \left(\frac{1}{\alpha} + \frac{1}{\beta} + \frac{1}{\gamma} + \frac{1}{\delta}\right)^2$$

$$= \sum \frac{1}{\alpha^2} + 2\sum \frac{1}{\alpha\beta}$$

$$\Rightarrow \sum \frac{1}{\alpha^2} = \left(\sum \frac{1}{\alpha}\right)^2 - 2\sum \frac{1}{\alpha\beta}$$

Now to find $\sum \frac{1}{\alpha}$ and $\sum \frac{1}{\alpha\beta}$ we have to find the equation whose roots are

$$\frac{1}{\alpha}, \frac{1}{\beta}, \frac{1}{\gamma}, \frac{1}{\delta}$$

i.e. we have to transform the equation

$$x^5 + px^3 + qx^2 + rx + s = 0$$

For this putting $\frac{1}{x}$ for we have

$$\left(\frac{1}{x}\right)^4 + p\left(\frac{1}{x}\right)^3 + q\left(\frac{1}{x}\right)^2 + r\frac{1}{x} + s = 0$$

i.e. $$\frac{1}{x^4} + \frac{p}{x^5} + \frac{q}{x^2} + \frac{r}{x} + s = 0$$

i.e. $$sx^4 + zx^3 + qx^2 + px + 1 = 0 \qquad (1)$$

The roots of the transformed equation (1)

$$\frac{1}{\alpha}, \frac{1}{\beta}, \frac{1}{\gamma}, \frac{1}{\delta}$$

Then $\sum \frac{1}{\alpha} = -\frac{r}{s}$

$$\sum \frac{1}{\alpha\beta} = \frac{q}{s}$$

Thus $\sum \frac{1}{\alpha^2} = \left(\sum \frac{1}{\alpha}\right)^2 - 2s \times \frac{1}{\alpha\beta} = \left(-\frac{r}{s}\right)^2 - 2\left(\frac{q}{s}\right)$

$$= \frac{r^2}{s^2} - \frac{2q}{s} = \frac{r^2 - 2qs}{s^2}$$

(ii) $\sum(\alpha - \beta)^2 = (\alpha - \beta)^2 + (\beta - \gamma)^2 + (\beta - \delta)^2 + (\alpha - \delta)^2 + (\gamma - \delta)^2 + (\alpha - \gamma)^2$

$$= 3\alpha^2 + 3\beta^2 + 3\gamma^2 + 3\delta^2 - 2\left(\sum \alpha\beta\right)$$

$$= 3\sum \alpha^2 - 2\sum \alpha\beta$$

Now $\left(\sum \alpha\right)^2 = \sum \alpha^2 + 2\sum \alpha\beta$

$$\sum \alpha^2 = \left(\sum \alpha\right)^2 - 2\sum \alpha\beta$$

$$= (-p)^2 - 2q = p^2 - 2q$$

$$\sum(\alpha - \beta)^2 = 3(p^2 - 2q) - 2q$$

$$= 3p^2 - 6q - 2q$$

$\sum(\alpha - \beta)^2 = 3p^2 - 8q$ **Ans.**

(iii) $\sum \alpha^3\beta = ?$

We have

$\sum \alpha^2 \sum \alpha\beta = (\alpha^2 + 1\beta^2 + 1\gamma^2 + \delta^2)(\alpha\beta + \beta\gamma + \gamma\delta + \alpha\gamma + \alpha\delta + \beta\delta)$

$$= \sum \alpha^3\beta + \sum \alpha^2\beta\gamma$$

$\sum \alpha^3\beta = \sum \alpha^2 \sum \alpha\beta - \sum \alpha^2\beta\gamma$ (1)

Again $\sum \alpha \sum \alpha\beta\gamma$

$$= (\alpha + \beta + \gamma + \delta)(\alpha\beta\gamma + \alpha\beta\delta + \beta\gamma\delta + \alpha\gamma\delta)$$

$$= \sum \alpha^2\beta\gamma + 4\alpha\beta\gamma\delta$$

$\sum \alpha^2\beta\gamma = \sum \alpha \sum \alpha\gamma - 4\alpha\beta\gamma\delta$ (2)

or $\sum \alpha\beta^2 = \sum \alpha^2 \sum \alpha\beta - \sum \alpha \sum \alpha\beta\gamma + 4\alpha\beta\gamma\delta$ (3)

We have

$\left(\sum \alpha\right)^2 = (\alpha + \beta + \gamma + \delta^2) = \sum \alpha^2 + 2\sum \alpha\beta$

$\Rightarrow \sum \alpha^2 = \left(\sum \alpha\right)^2 - 2\sum \alpha\beta$

$\Rightarrow \sum \alpha^2 = (-p)^2 - 2q = p^2 - 2q$

$\sum \alpha\beta = q$ $\sum \alpha\beta\gamma = -r$ $\alpha\beta\gamma\delta = s$

$\alpha^3\beta = (p^2 - 2q)q - (-q)(-r) + 4s$

$= p^2q - 2q^2 - pr + 4s$ **Ans.**

(iv) $\sum\alpha^3 \beta\gamma = ?$

We have

$$\sum\alpha^2 \sum\alpha\beta\gamma = (\alpha^2 + \beta^2 + \gamma^2 + \delta^2)(\alpha\beta\gamma + \beta\gamma\delta + \alpha\gamma\delta + \alpha\beta\delta)$$
$$= \sum\alpha^3\beta\gamma + \alpha^2\beta\gamma\delta + \beta^2\alpha\gamma\delta + \gamma^2\alpha\beta\delta + \delta^2\alpha\beta\gamma$$
$$= \alpha^3 \beta\gamma + \alpha\beta\gamma\delta(\alpha + \beta + \gamma\ \delta)$$
$$\sum\alpha^3\beta\gamma = \sum\alpha^2 \sum\alpha\beta\gamma - \alpha\beta\gamma\delta(\alpha + \beta + \gamma + \delta)$$
$$= (p^2 - 2q)(- r) - s(-p)$$
$$= p^2r + 2qr + ps$$
$$= 2qr - p_2r + ps \quad \textbf{Ans.}$$

(v)
$$\sum \frac{\beta^2 + \gamma^2}{\beta\gamma} = \frac{\beta^2 + \gamma^2}{\beta\gamma} + \frac{\alpha^2 + \beta^2}{\alpha\beta} + \frac{\alpha^2 + \gamma^2}{\alpha\gamma} + \frac{\beta^2 + \delta}{\beta\delta} + \frac{\gamma^2 + \delta^3}{\gamma\delta} + \frac{\alpha^2 + \delta^2}{\alpha\delta}$$
$$= \frac{(\beta^2 + \gamma^2)\alpha\delta + (\alpha^2 + \beta^2)\gamma\delta + (\alpha^2 + \gamma^2)\beta\delta}{\alpha\beta\gamma\delta}$$
$$(\gamma^2 + \delta^2)\alpha\beta + (\beta^2 + \gamma^2)\alpha\delta + (\alpha^2 + \delta^2)\beta\gamma$$
$$\sum \frac{\beta^2 + \gamma^2}{\beta\gamma} = \frac{\sum\alpha^2 \beta\gamma}{\alpha\beta\gamma\delta}$$

Now we have to find the value of $\sum\alpha^2 \beta\gamma$.

$$\sum\alpha \sum\alpha\beta\gamma = (\alpha + \beta\ \gamma + \delta)(\alpha\beta\gamma + \beta\gamma\delta + \alpha\gamma\delta + \alpha\beta\delta)$$
$$= \sum\alpha^2 \beta\gamma + 4\alpha\beta\gamma\delta)$$
$$\Rightarrow \sum\alpha^2 \beta\gamma = \sum\alpha\sum\alpha\beta\gamma - 4\alpha\beta\gamma\delta$$
$$\sum\alpha^2 \beta\gamma = (-p)(-r) - 4s$$
$$= pr - 4s$$
$$\sum \frac{\beta^2 + \gamma^2}{\beta\gamma} = \frac{\sum\alpha^2\beta\gamma}{\alpha\beta\gamma\delta}$$
$$= \frac{pr - 4s}{s} = \frac{pr}{s} - 4$$

(vi) $\sum\alpha^4 = ?$

We have

$$(\sum\alpha^2)^2 = (\alpha^2 + \beta^2 + \gamma^2 + \delta)^2$$
$$= \sum\alpha^4 + 2\sum\alpha\beta^2$$
$$\sum\alpha^4 = (\sum\alpha^2)^2 - 2\sum\alpha^2 \beta^2 \qquad (1)$$

Again we have

$$= (\sum\alpha)^2 = (\alpha + \beta + \gamma + \delta)^2$$
$$= \sum\alpha^2 + \sum 2\alpha\beta$$
$$\sum\alpha^2 = (\sum\alpha)^2 - 2\sum\alpha\beta = (-p)^2 - 2q$$
$$\sum\alpha^2 = p^2 - 2q \quad (2)$$

Again $(\sum\alpha\beta)^2 = (\alpha\beta + \beta\gamma + \gamma\delta + \alpha\delta + \beta\delta + \alpha\gamma)^2$

$$= \sum\alpha^2\beta^2 + 2\sum\alpha^2\gamma\gamma + 6\alpha\beta\gamma\delta$$
$$\sum\alpha^2\beta^2 = (\sum\alpha\beta)^2 - 2\sum\alpha^2\beta\gamma - 6\alpha\beta\gamma\delta$$
$$= q^2 - 2(pr - 4s) - 6s$$
$$= q^2 - 2pr + 8s - 6s$$
$$= q^2 - pr + 2s$$

Hence $\sum\alpha^4 = (p^2 + 2q\}^2 - 2[q^2 - 2pr + 2s]$

$$= p^4 - 4p^2q + 4q^2 - 2q^2 + 4pr - 4s$$
$$= p^4 - 4p^2q + 4pr + 2q^2 - 4s$$

(vii) $\sum\frac{\alpha^2}{\beta^2}$

We have

$$\sum\alpha^2\sum\frac{1}{\alpha^2} = (\alpha^2 + \beta^2 + \gamma^2 + \delta^2)\left(\frac{1}{\alpha^2} + \frac{1}{\beta^2} + \frac{1}{\gamma^2} + \frac{1}{\delta^2}\right)$$
$$= \sum\frac{\alpha^2}{\beta^2} + 4$$
$$\sum\frac{\alpha^2}{\beta^1} = \alpha^2 \quad \sum\frac{1}{\alpha^2} - 4$$

since $\alpha, \beta, \gamma, \delta$ be the roots of the biquadratic

$$x^4 + px^3 + qx^2 + rx + s = 0$$

Then $\sum\alpha^2 = (\sum\alpha)^2\, 2\sum\alpha\,\beta = (-p)^2 - 2q = (p^2 - 2q)$

Again $\frac{1}{\alpha}, \frac{1}{\beta}, \frac{1}{\gamma}, \frac{1}{\delta}$ be the roots of the biquadratic

$$sx^4 + rx^3 + qx^2 + px + 1 = 0$$
$$\sum\frac{1}{\alpha^2} = \left(\sum\frac{1}{\alpha}\right)^2 - 6\sum\frac{1}{\alpha\beta} + \left(-\frac{r}{s}\right)^2 - 2\left(\frac{q}{s}\right)$$
$$= \frac{r^2}{s^2} - \frac{2q}{s} = \left(r^2 - \frac{6qs}{s^2}\right)$$

Thus $\sum\frac{\alpha^2}{\beta^2} = (p^2 - 2q)\frac{(r^2 - 2qs)}{s^2} - 4$

$$= \frac{(p^2 - 2q)(r^2 - 2qs)}{s^2} - 4$$

Problem 10 For the cubic $x^3 + px^2 + qx + r = 0$, calculate the value of $(\alpha^2 + 1)(\beta^2 + 1)(\gamma^2 + 1)$ where α, β, γ are the roots of the cubic.

Solution. Since α, β, γ be the roots of the cubic equation so we have idenitity

$$x^3 + px^2 + qx + r \equiv (x - \alpha)(x - \beta)(x - \gamma)$$

Putting $x = i$ we have

$$-i - p + qi + r = (i - \alpha)(i - \beta)(i - \gamma)$$

$$(r - p) - 1(i - q) = (i - \alpha)(i - \beta)(i - \gamma) \quad (1)$$

Again substituting $x = i$ we have

$$i - p - qi + r = (-i - \alpha)(-i - \beta)(-i - \gamma)$$

$$(r - p) + i(1 - q) = -(i + \alpha)(i + \beta)(i + \gamma) \quad 2)$$

Multiplying equation (1) and (2) we have

$$(r - p)^2 + (1 + q)^2 = -(1 + \alpha^2)(1 + \beta^2)(1 + \gamma^2)$$

$$(1 + \alpha^2)(1 + \beta^2)(1 + \gamma^2) = (1 - q)^2 + (r - p)^2$$

$$(1 + \alpha^2)(1 + \beta^2)(1 + \gamma^2) = (p - r)^2 + (1 - q)^2 \quad \textbf{Ans.}$$

Problem 11 If $\alpha + \beta + \gamma = 6$, $\alpha^2 + \beta^2 + \gamma^2 = 14$, $\alpha^3 + \beta^3 + \gamma^3 = 36$, Eind the value of $\alpha^4 + \beta^4 + \gamma^4$.

Solution Let α, β, γ be the roots of the cubic equation

$$x^3 + px^2 + qx + r = 0$$

Therefore $s_1 = \sum\alpha = \alpha + \beta + \gamma = -p = 6$

or $p = -6$

Again $s_2 \sum\alpha^2 = (\sum\alpha)^2 - 2\sum\alpha\beta$

$$= (-p)^2 - 2q = p^2 - 2q = 14$$

$$p^2 - 2q = 14$$

$$(-6)^2 - 2q = 14$$

$$36 - 2q = 14$$

$$2q = 36 - 14$$

$$2q = 22$$

$$q = 11$$

we have the cubic

$$x^3 + px^2 + qx + r = 0 \quad (1)$$

since α β, γ are the roots of the cubic so they will satisfy (1)

$$\alpha^3 + p\alpha^2 + q\alpha + r = 0$$

$$\beta^3 + p\beta^2 + q\beta + r = 0$$

$$\gamma^3 + p\gamma^2 + p\gamma + r = 0$$

Adding $(\alpha^3 + \beta^3 + \gamma^3) + p(\alpha^2 + \beta^2 + \gamma^2)$

$$+ q(\alpha + \beta + \gamma) + 3r = 0$$

$$36 + p14 + 6q + 3r = 0$$

$$36 + 14(-6) + 6 \times 11 + 3r = 0$$

$$102 - 84 + 3r = 0 \Rightarrow 3r = -18$$

$$r = -6$$

Thus the cubic equation is given by

$$x^3 - 6x^2 + 11x - 6 = 0 \quad (1)$$

Multiplying (1) with x we have

$$x^4 - 6x^3 + 11x^2 - 6x = 0$$

Putting $x = \alpha, \beta, \gamma$ and then adding we have

$$(\alpha^4 + \beta^4 + \gamma^4) - 6(\alpha^3 + \beta^3 + \gamma^3)$$

$$+ 11(\alpha^2 + \beta^2 + \gamma^2) - 6(\alpha + \beta + \gamma) = 0$$

$$\alpha^4 + \beta^4 + \gamma^4 - 6 \times 36 + 11 \times 14 - 6 \times 6 = 0$$

$$\alpha^4 + \beta^4 + \gamma^4 - 216 + 154 - 36 = 0$$

$$\alpha^4 + \beta^4 + \gamma^4 - 252 + 154 = 0$$

$$\alpha^4 + \beta^4 + \gamma^4 - 98 = 0$$

so $\alpha^4 + \beta^4 + \gamma^4 = 98$ **Ans.**

Problem 12 If α, β, γ be the roots of the equation $x^3 + 3x + 9 = 0$ Find the value of $\alpha^9 + \beta^9 + \gamma^9$.

Solution α, β, γ be the roots of the cubic equation

$$x^3 + 0x^2 + 3x + 9 = 0$$

Thus $\sum\alpha = \alpha + \beta + \gamma$

Again $(\sum\alpha)^2 = \sum\alpha^2 + 2\sum\alpha\beta$

$$\Rightarrow \sum\alpha^2 = (\sum\alpha)^2 - 2\sum\alpha\beta^3 = 0 - 2(3) \quad (3)$$

$$= -6$$

$$\alpha + \beta + \gamma = 0$$

$$\alpha^2 + \beta^2 \gamma^2 = 6$$

$$x^3 + 3x + 9 = 0$$

$$\alpha^3 + 3\alpha + 9 = 0$$

$$\beta^3 + 3\beta + 9 = 0$$

$$\gamma^3 + 3\gamma + 9 = 0$$

Adding we have, $(\alpha^3 + \beta^3 + \gamma^3) + 3(\alpha + \beta + \gamma) + 27 = 0$

$$(\alpha^3 + \beta^3 + \gamma^3) + 3 \times 0 + 27 = 0$$

$$s_3 = \alpha^3 + \beta^3 + \gamma^3 = -27$$

Again $\quad x^3 + 3x + 9 = 0$

$$\Rightarrow x^3 = -(3x + 9)$$

$$\Rightarrow x^3 = -3(x + 3)$$

Cubing both sides we have

$$x^9 = -27(x + 3)^3$$

$$x^9 = -27[x^3 + 27 + 3x \cdot 31 (x + 3)]$$

$$x^9 = -27[x^3 + 9x^2 + 27x] + 27$$

$$x^9 = -27[x^3 + 9x^2 + 27x + 27]$$

must be satisfied with α, β and γ and so

$$\alpha^9 = -27[\alpha^3 + 9\alpha^2 + 27\alpha + 27]$$

$$\beta^9 = -27[\beta^3 + 9\beta^2 + 27\beta + 27]$$

$$\gamma^9 = -27[\gamma^3 + 9\gamma^2 + 27\gamma + 27]$$

Adding the three equation we have

$$\alpha^9 + \beta^9 + \gamma^9 = -27[(\alpha^3 + \beta^3 + \gamma^3) + 9(\alpha^2 + \beta^2 + \gamma^2) + 27(\alpha + \beta + \gamma) + 81]$$

$$\alpha^9 + \beta^9 + \gamma^9 = -27[-27 + 9(-6) + 27 \times 0 + 81]$$

$$= -27[-27 - 54 + 81]$$

$$= -27[-81 + 81] = -27 \times 0 = 0$$

i.e. $\quad \alpha^9 + \beta^9 + \gamma^9 = 0$

Problem 13 If α, β, γ be the roots of the equation $x^3 + 2x + 6 = 0$ prove that

$$s_7 = 2(s_4 - s_6)$$

Solution α, β, γ be the roots of the cubic equation

$$x^3 + 0x^2 + 2x + 6 = 0$$

$$s_1 = \sum\alpha = \alpha + \beta + \gamma = 0 \quad \Big| \quad \sum\alpha\beta = 2$$

$$s_2 = \sum\alpha^2 = \alpha^2 + \beta^2 + \gamma^2$$

and we have

$$(\sum\alpha)^2 = \sum\alpha^2 - 2\sum\alpha\beta$$

$$(\sum\alpha^2 = (\sum\alpha)^2 - 2\sum\alpha\beta = (0)^2 - 2\,(2) = -4$$

$$S_2 = -4$$

Now we have $x^2 + 2x + 6 = 0$

Since α, β, γ are the roots of this cubic equation so they will satisfy the equation

$$\alpha^3 + 2\alpha + 6 = 0$$

$$\beta^3 + 2\beta + 6 = 0$$

$$\gamma^3 + 2\gamma + 6 = 0$$

Adding we have

$$(\alpha^3 + \beta^3 + \gamma^3) + 2\,(\alpha + \beta + \gamma) + 18 = 0$$

$$s_3 + 2s_1 + 18 = 0$$

$$s_3 + 2 \times 0 + 18 = 0$$

$$s_3 = -18$$

i.e. $\sum\alpha^3 = \alpha^3 + \beta^3 + \gamma^3 = -18$

Again $x^3 + 2x + 6 = 0$

Multiplying this equation by x we have

$$x^4 + 2x^2 + 6x = 0$$

Putting $x = \alpha, \beta, \gamma$ and adding we have

$$\alpha^4 + \beta^4 + \gamma^4 + 2\,(\alpha^2 + \beta^2 + \gamma^2) + 6\,(\alpha + \beta + \gamma) = 0$$

$$s_4 + 2s_2 + 6s_1 = 0$$

$$s_4 + 2\,(-4) + 6 \times 0 = 0$$

$$s_4 - 8 = 0$$

$$s_4 = 8$$

we have $x^3 + 2x + 6 = 0$

$$x^3 = -2x - 6$$

$$x^3 = -2\,(x + 3)$$

Squaring both sides we have

$$x^6 = 4\,(x^2 + 6x + 9) \qquad (1)$$

Putting $x = \alpha, \beta, \gamma$ and adding there by we have

$$\alpha^6 + \beta^6 + \gamma^6 = s_7 = 4[s_2 + 6s_1 + 27]$$

$$s_7 = 4\,[-4 + 6 \times 0 + 27]$$

$$s_7 = 4 \times (23)$$

$$s_7 = 92$$

Multiplying (1) by x we have

$$x^7 = 4\,(x^3 + 6x^2 + 9x)$$

putting $x = \alpha, \beta, \gamma$ and adding thereby we have

$$s_7 = 4\,[s_3 + 6s_2 + 9s_1]$$

$$s_7 = 4\,[-18 - 24 + 9 \times 0]$$

$$= 4\,(-42) = -168$$

$$= 2\,(s_4 - s_6)$$

$$= 2\,(8 - 92) = 2 \times (-84) = -168 = s_7$$

Thus $\quad s_7 = 2\,(s_4 - s_6)$

Problem 14 If α, β, γ, be the roots of the equation $x^3 + px + q = 0$, prove that $6s_5 = 5s_2s_3$

Solution α, β, γ be the roots of the cubic equation

$$x^3 + 0\,x^2 + px + q = 0 \qquad \sum\alpha\beta = +p$$

$$s_1 = \sum\alpha = \alpha + \beta + \gamma = 0 \qquad \alpha\beta\gamma = -q$$

$$s_2 = \sum\alpha^2 = \alpha^2 + \beta^2 + \gamma^2 = (\sum\alpha)^2 - 2\sum\alpha\beta = (0)^2 - 2p$$

$$s_2 = -2p$$

$$x^3 + px + q = 0$$

since α, β, γ are the roots of the above equation so they will satisfy the equation

$$\alpha^3 + p\alpha + q = 0$$

$$\beta^3 + p\beta + q = 0$$

$$\gamma^3 + p\gamma + q = 0$$

Adding we have $(\alpha^3 + \beta^3 + \gamma^3) + p\,(\alpha + \beta + \gamma) + 3q = 0$

$$s_3 + ps_1 + 3q = 0$$

$$s_3 + p \times 0 + 3q = 0$$

$$s_3 = -3q$$

$$x^3 + px + q = 0$$

$$x^2(x^3 + px + q) = 0$$

$$\Rightarrow x^5 + px^3 + qx^2 = 0$$

$$\alpha^5 + p\alpha^3 + q\alpha^2 = 0$$

$$\beta^5 + p\beta^3 + q\beta^2 = 0$$

$$\gamma^5 + p\gamma^3 + q\gamma^2 = 0$$

Adding we have,

$$(\alpha^5 + \beta^5 + \gamma^5) + p(\alpha^3+\beta^3+\gamma^3) + q(\alpha^2 + \beta^2 \gamma^2) = 0$$

$$s_5 + ps_3 + qs_2 = 0$$

$$s_5 + p(-3q) + q(-2p) = 0$$

$$s_5 - 3pq - 2pq = 0$$

$$s_5 - 5pq = 0$$

$$s_5 = 5pq$$

$$6s_5 = 30\,pq$$

$$6s_5 = 5 \times 6\,pq$$

$$6s_5 = 5(-2p)(-3q)$$

$$6s_5 = 5s_2\,s_3 \qquad \textit{(proved)}$$

Problem 15 Express $\sum \alpha\beta$ and $\alpha\beta\gamma$ in terms of a, b, c where

$$\alpha + \beta + \gamma = a,\ \alpha^2 + \beta^2 + \gamma^2 = b,\ \alpha^3 + \beta^3 + \gamma^3 = c$$

Solution Let as suppose that α, β, γ be the roots of the cubic

$$x^3 + px^2 + qx + r = 0$$

Then
$$s_1 = \sum \alpha = \alpha + \beta + \gamma$$
$$= -p$$
$$\sum \alpha\beta = q \qquad \alpha\beta\gamma = -r$$

Now we have to find the value of q and $-r$

we have
$$(\sum \alpha)^2 = \sum \alpha^2 + 2\sum \alpha\beta$$
$$\Rightarrow \sum \alpha^2 = \sum (\alpha)^2 - 2\sum \alpha\beta$$
$$\Rightarrow \quad s_2 = \alpha^2 + \beta^2 + \gamma^2$$
$$= (-p)^2 - 2q = p^2 - 2q$$

since α, β, γ are the roots of the cubic equation

$$x^3 + px^2 + qx + r = 0$$

Then they will satisfy this equation

$$\alpha^3 + p\alpha^2 + qr + r = 0$$

$$\beta^3 + p\beta^2 + q\beta + r = 0$$

$$\gamma^3 + p\gamma^2 + q\gamma + r = 0$$

Adding all these we have

$$(\alpha^2 + \beta^3 + \gamma^3) + p(\alpha^2 + \beta^2 + \gamma^2) + q(\alpha + \beta + \gamma) + 3r = 0$$

$$s_3 + ps_2 + qs_1 + 3r = 0 \qquad (1)$$

Again
$$a = -p$$
$$\Rightarrow p = -a \qquad (2)$$

Since
$$s_2 = p^2 - 2q$$
$$b (= p^2 - 2q$$
$$b = (-a)^2 - 2q$$
$$b = a^2 - 2q$$
$$2q = a^2 - b$$
$$q = \tfrac{1}{2}(a^2 - b) \qquad (3)$$

Equation (1) gives
$$s_3 + ps_2 + qs_1 + 3r = 0$$
$$c + p(b) + qa + 3r = 0$$
$$c + (-a)b + \tfrac{1}{2}a(a^2 - b) + 3r = 0$$
$$\Rightarrow c - ab + \left| \frac{a^3 - ab}{2} + 3r = 0 \right.$$
$$\Rightarrow 2c - 2ab + a^3 - ab + 6r = 0$$
$$\Rightarrow 2c - 3ab + a^3 + 6r = 0$$
$$\Rightarrow 6r = -(2c - 3ab + a^3)$$
$$\Rightarrow -r = \frac{(a^3 - 3ab + 2c)}{6}$$

Thus
$$\sum \alpha\beta = q = \tfrac{1}{2}(a^2 - b)$$
$$\alpha\beta\gamma = -r = \frac{1}{6}(a^3 - 3ab + 2c)$$

Problem 16 Calculate s_4 for the equation
$$x^8 - 1 = 0$$

Solution we have
$$x^8 - 1 = 0$$
$$\Rightarrow (x^4 - 1)(x^4 + 1) = 0$$
$$\Rightarrow \text{either} \quad x^4 - 1 = 0$$
or
$$x^4 + 1 = 0$$
Adding both we have
$$2x^4 = 0$$
$$x^4 = 0$$
Putting all the values of x (ve roots) and adding
$$s_4 = 0 \qquad \textbf{Ans.}$$

Remember the Newten's Theorem on the sums of the powers of the roots,

Let $\alpha_1, \alpha_2, \alpha_3, \ldots \alpha_n$ be the equation
$$f(x) \equiv a_c x^n + a_1 x^{n-1} + a^{n-1} + a_2 x^{n-2} + \ldots + a_n - 1\, x + a_n = 0$$
Then
$$a_o\, s_n - 1 + a_1\, s_{n-1} + a_2\, s_{n-3} + \ldots + n\, a_{n-1} = \{n - (n-1)\}\, a_{n-1}$$
$$a_0\, s_{n-1} + a_1\, s_{n-2} + o_2\, s_{n-3} + \ldots ; + na_{n-1} = a_{n-1}$$

Putting $n = 2_1\, 3 \ldots$ we can find s_1, s_2 s_3 etc, successively in terms of $a_o, a_1, a_2 \ldots a_{n-1}$.

Problem 17 Calculate the values of s_3 and s_4 for the equation.

$$x^4 + 4x^3 - 6x + 2 = 0$$

Solution Let $\alpha_1, \beta, \gamma, \delta$ be the roots of biquadratic equation

$$x^4 + 4x^3 + 0x^2 - 6x + 2 = 0 \qquad \sum\alpha\beta = 0$$

$$s_1 = \sum\alpha = -4 \qquad (1) \quad \sum\alpha\beta\gamma = 6$$

$$s_2 = \sum\alpha^2 = (\sum\alpha)^2 - 2\sum\alpha\beta \qquad \alpha\beta\gamma\delta = -2$$

$$= (-4)^2 - 2 \times 0$$

$$s_2 = 16$$

From Newton's theorem for the sum of roots we have

$$a_o\, s_{n-1} + a_1\, s_{n-2} + \ldots + (n)_{n-1} = (n - (n-1)\}\, 0_{n-1}$$

Here $\qquad n = 4$

$$a_0 = 1 \quad a_1 = 4 \quad a_2 = 0 \quad a_3 = -6 \quad a_4 = 2$$

$$a_0\, s_3 + a_1\, s_2 + a_2\, s_1 + 4a_3 = a_3$$

$$s_3 + 4s_2 + 4\,(-6) = (-6)$$

$$s_3 + 4s_2 - 24 = -6$$

$$s_3 + 4s_2 = 18$$

$$s_3 + 4\,(16) = 18$$

$$s_3 = 18 - 64 = -46$$

Again since $\alpha, \beta, \gamma, \delta$ be the roots of the biquadratic equation

$$x^4 + 4x^3 - 6x + 2 = 0$$

Soputting $x = \alpha, \beta, \gamma, \delta$ and adding we have

$$\sum\alpha^4 + 4\sum\alpha^3 - 6\sum\alpha + 8 = 0$$

$$s_4 + 4s_3 - 6s_1 + 8 = 0$$

$$s_4 + 4\,(-46) - 6\,(-4) + 8 = 0$$

$$s_4 - 184 + 24 + 8 = 0$$

$$s_4 = 184 - 32$$

$$s_4 = 152$$

Thus $\qquad s_3 = -46, \; s_4 = 152$

Problem 18 If $\alpha + \beta + \gamma = 0$ prove that

(i) $\qquad \alpha^5 + \beta^5 + \gamma^5 = -5\alpha\beta\gamma\,(\beta\gamma + \gamma\alpha + \alpha\beta)$

(ii) $\qquad \alpha^7 + \beta^7 + \gamma^7 = 7\alpha\beta\gamma\,(\beta\gamma + \gamma\alpha + \alpha\beta)^2$

(iii) $\qquad \dfrac{\alpha^5 + \beta^5 + \gamma^5}{5} = \dfrac{\alpha^2 + \beta^2 + \gamma^2}{2} \times \dfrac{\alpha^3 + \beta^3 + \gamma^3}{3}$

Solution α, β, γ be the roots of a cubic equation

$$x^3q + px^2 + qx + r = 0$$

such that $\sum\alpha = \alpha + \beta + \gamma = 0$

i.e. $s_1 = 0$

$$\alpha + \beta + \gamma = -p = 0 \qquad \sum\alpha\beta = q$$

i.e. $p = 0 \qquad \alpha\beta\gamma = -r$

so the cubic equation reduces to $x^3 + qx + r = 0$

$$s_2 = \sum\alpha^2 = (\sum\alpha)^2 - 2\sum\alpha\beta$$

$$s_2 = (0)^2 - 2(+q)$$

$$s_2 = -2q \tag{2}$$

$$x^3 = -(qx + r) \tag{3}$$

muliiplying both sides with x^2

We have $x^5 = -(qx^3 + rx^2)$ (4)

From equation (3) we have

$$s_3 = -(qs_1 + 3r)$$

$$s_3 = -(q \times 0 + 3r)$$

$$s_3 = -3r \tag{5}$$

From equation (4) we have

$$s_5 = -(qs_3 + rs_2)$$

$$s_5 = -[-q3r + r(-2q)]$$

$$s_5 = -[-3qr - 2qr)$$

$$s_5 = 5qr$$

$$\frac{s_5}{5} = qr$$

$$\frac{s_5}{5} = -\frac{s_2}{2} \times -\frac{s_3}{3}$$

$$\frac{s_5}{5} = \frac{s_2}{2} \times \frac{s_3}{3}$$

i.e. $\dfrac{\alpha^5 + \beta^5 + \gamma^5}{5} = \dfrac{(\alpha^2 + \beta^2 + \gamma^2)}{2} \dfrac{(\alpha^3 + \beta^3 + \gamma^2)}{3}$

Again $s_5 = 5qr$

$$s_5 = 5\sum\alpha\beta(-\alpha\beta\gamma)$$

$$\alpha^5 + \beta^5 + \gamma^5 = -5\alpha\beta\gamma(\alpha\beta + \beta\gamma + \alpha\gamma)$$

Again $\qquad x^3 = -(qx + r)$

squaring both sides we have

$$x^6 = (-)^2 (q^2 x^2 + 2qxr + r^2)$$

Multiplying both sides with x we have

$$x^7 = +(q^2 x^3 + 2qrx^2 + r^2 x)$$

putting $\qquad x = \alpha, \beta, \gamma$ and adding we have

$$s_7 = 4 (q^2 s_3 + 2qrs_2 + r^2 s_1)$$

$$s_7 = + [q^2 (-3r) + 2qr (-2q) + r^2 0]$$

$$s_7 = + [-3q^2 r - 4q^2 r]$$

$$s_7 = 7 (-r) q^2$$

$$= \alpha^7 + \beta^7 + \gamma^7 = 7 \alpha\beta\gamma (\alpha\beta + \beta\gamma + \alpha\gamma)^2 \quad \textit{(Proved)}$$

4

Transformation of Equations

Problem 1 Find the equation whose roots are the squares of the roots $\alpha, \beta, \gamma, \delta$ of the equation $x^4 + px^3 + qx^2 + rx + s = 0$. Hence find the value of

(i) $\sum \alpha^2 \beta^2$ (ii) $\sum \alpha^2 \beta^2 \gamma^2$

Solution From the given equation we have

$$x^4 + qx^2 + s = -(px^3 + rx)$$

$$x^4 + qx^2 + s = -x(px^2 + r)$$

squaring both sides we have

$$(x^4 + qx^2 + s)^2 = [-x(px^2 + r]^2$$

$$[(x^2)^2 + qx^2 + s]^2 = x^2(px^2 + r)^2$$

puttnig $x^2 = y$ we have

$$(y^2 + qy + s)^2 = y(py + r)^2$$

$$y^4 + q^2 y^2 + s^2 + 2qy^3 + 2y^2 s + 2qys = y[p^2 y^2 + 2pry + r^2]$$

$$y^4 + q^2 y^2 + s^2 + 2qy^3 + 2y^2 s + 2qys - y^3 p^2 - 2pry^2 - r^2 y = 0$$

$$y^4 + (2q - p^2) y^3 + (q^2 + 2s - (p^2) y^2 + (2qs - r^2) y + s^2 = 0$$

$$\therefore \quad y^4 - (p^2 - 2q) y^3 + (q^2 - 2pr + 2s) y^2 - (r^2 - 2qs) y + s^2 = 0$$

which is the required equation whose roots are the squares of the roots of equation

$$x^4 + px^3 + qx^2 + rx + s = 0$$

Now $\sum \alpha^2 \beta^2 = (q^2 - 2pr + 2s)$

$\sum \alpha^2 \beta^2 \gamma^2 = (r^2 - 2qs)$ **Ans.**

Problem 2 Show that the cubes of the roots of the equation

$$x^3 + ax^2 + bx + ab = 0$$

are given by the equaeion

$$x^3 + a^3 x^2 + b^3 x + a^3 b^3 = 0$$

Solution Let α, β, γ be the roots of the cubic equation

$$x^3 + ax^2 + bx + ab = 0$$

Now we have to find the equation whose roots are $\alpha^3, \beta^3, \gamma^3$

$$x^3 + ax^2 + bx + ab = 0$$

$$x^3 + ab = -(ax^2 + bx)$$

$$x^3 + ab = -x(ax + b)$$

$$\Rightarrow (y + ab = -x(ax + b)$$

cubing both sides we have

$$(x^3 + ab)^3 = -[x(ax + b)]^3$$

$$(x^3 + ab)^3 = -x^3(ax + b)^3$$

Putting $\quad x^3 = y$ we have

$$(y + ab)^3 = -y(ax + b)^3$$

$$y^3 + a^3 b^3 + 3yab(y + ab) = -y[(a^3 x^3 + b^3 + 3axb(ax + b)$$

$$y^3 + a^3 b^3 + 3y^2 ab + 3y a^2 b^2 = -[a^3 y + b^3 + (-)3ab(y + ab)]xy$$

$$y^3 + a^3 b^3 + 3y^2 ab + 3yo^2 b^2 = -y[a^3 y + b^3 - 3aby - 3a^2 b^2]$$

$$y^3 + a^3 b^3 + 3y^2 ab + 3ya^2 b^2 = -a^3 y^2 - b^3 y + 3aby^2 + 3ya^2 b^2$$

$$y^3 + a^3 y^2 + b^3 y + a^3 b^3 = 0$$

Thus the cubes of the roots of the equation $x^3 + ax^2 + bx + ab = 0$ are given by the equation $x^3 + a^3 x^2 + b^3 x + a^3 b^3 = 0$ *(Proved)*

Problem 3 If α, β, γ be the roots of the equation $x^3 + px^2 - 1 = 0$ Find $\sum \alpha^3 \beta^3$.

Solution α, β, γ are the roots of the cubic equation $x^3 + px^2 - 1 = 0$ we have to find the equation whose roots are $\alpha^3, \beta^3, \gamma^3$ since

$$x^3 + px^2 - 1 = 0$$

$$x^3 - 1 = -px^2$$

using both sides we have

$$(x^3 - 1)^3 = [-px^2]^3$$

putting $\quad x^3 = y$

$$(y - 1)^3 = -p^3 (x^3)^2$$

$$(y - 1)^3 = -p^3 y^2$$

$$y^3 - 1^3 - 3y \cdot 1(y - 1) = -p^3 y^2$$

$$y^3 - 1 - 3y^2 + 3y + p^3 y^2 = 0$$

$$\Rightarrow y^3 + (p^3 - 3)y^2 + 3y - 1 = 0 \tag{1}$$

The roots of the equation (1) are $\alpha^3, \beta^3, \gamma^3$

Then $\quad \sum \alpha^3 \beta^3 = 3$ **Ans.**

Problem 4 Find the equation whose roots are the cubes of the roots of the equation $x^3 + 3x^2 + 2 = 0$

Solution Let α, β, γ be the roots of the cubic equation

$$x^3 + 3x^2 + 2 = 0$$

we have to find the equation whose roots are α^3, β^3, γ^3

$$x^3 + 3x + 2 = 0$$

$$x^3 + 2 = -3x^2$$

$$(x^3 + 2)^3 = -27x^6$$

$$(x^3 + 2)^3 = -27(x^3)^2$$

Substituting $x^3 = y$

$$(y + 2)^3 = -27y^2$$

$$y^3 + 8 + 3 \cdot y^2 (y + 2) = -27y^2$$

$$y^3 + 8 + 6y^2 + 12y + 27y^2 = 0$$

$$y^3 + 33y^2 + 12y + 8 = 0$$

which is the required equation whose roots are the cubes of the roots of the equation $x^3 + 3x^2 + 2 = 0$. **Ans.**

Problem 5 Find the equation whose roots are the cubes of the roots of the equation $x^3 + px^2 + qx + r = 0$ and if α, β, γ be the roots of the given equation. Find the valne of $\sum\alpha^3$, and $\sum\alpha^3\beta^3$.

Solution Let α, β, γ, δ be the roots of the cubic equation $x^3 + px^2 + qx + r = 0$ we have to find the equation whose roots are α^3, β^3, γ^3,

we have $x^3 + px^2 + qx + r = 0$

$$(x^3 + r) = -(px^2 + qx)$$

$$\Rightarrow (x^3 + r) = -x(px + q$$

Cubing both sides we have

$$(x^3 + r)^3 = -x^3 (px + q)^3$$

$$(x^3 + r)^3 = -r^3 [p^3 x^3 + q^3 + 3pxq(px + q)^2]$$

$$(x^3 + r)^3 = -x^3 [p^3 x^3 + q^3 + 3p^2 x^2 q + 3pxq^2]$$

substituting $x^3 = y$ we have

$$(y + r)^3 = -y[p^3 y + q^3 + 3pxq(px + q)]$$

$$y^3 + r^3 + 3yr(y + r) = -y[p^3 y + q^3 - 3pq(x^3 + r)]$$

$$y^3 + r^3 + 3y^2 r + 3yr^2 = -p^3 y^2 - q^3 y + 3pqy(y + r)$$

$$y^3 + r^3 + 3y^2 r + 3yr^3 + p^3 y^2 + q^3 y - 3pqy^2 - 3pqry = 0$$

$$y^3 + (p^3 + 3(r - 3pq) y^2 + (3r^2 - 3pqr + q^3) + r^3 = 0$$

$$\sum\alpha^3 = 3pq - 3r - p^3$$

$$\sum\alpha^3\beta^3 = q^3 - 3pqr + 3r^2$$ **Ans.**

Problem 6 If α, β, γ be the roots of the equation $x^3 + px^2 + qx + r = 0$ Find the equation whose roots are $(\beta + \gamma), (\gamma + \alpha), (\alpha + \beta)$ and hence find the value of $(\beta + \gamma)(\gamma + \alpha)(\alpha + \beta)$.

Solution Let α, β, γ be the roots of the cubic equation

$$x^3 + px^2 + qx + r = 0$$

$$\sum\alpha = \alpha + \beta + \gamma = -p$$

let
$$y = \beta + \gamma$$
$$y = (\alpha + \beta + \gamma) - \alpha$$
$$y = -p - \alpha$$
$$\Rightarrow -\alpha = p + y$$
$$\Rightarrow \quad \alpha = -(p + y)$$

since α is the root of the equation

$$\alpha^3 + p\alpha^2 + q\alpha + r = 0$$

$$\{-(p + y)\}^3 + p\{-(p + y)\}^2 + q\{-(p + y)\} + r = 0$$
$$-(p + y)^3 + p(p + y)^2 - q(p + y) + r = 0$$
$$-[p^3 + y^3 + 3py(p + y)] + p(p^2 + y^2 + 2py) - pq - qy + r = 0$$
$$p^3 + y^3 + 3p^2y + 3py^2 - p^3 - py^2 - 2p^2y + pq + qy - r = 0$$
$$y^3 + p^2y + 2py^2 + qy + (pq - r) = 0$$
$$y^3 + 2py^2 + (p^2 + q)y + (pq - r) = 0$$

which is the required equation. Hence the product of its roots

$$(\beta + \gamma)(\gamma + \alpha)(\alpha + \beta) = -(pq - r) = r - pq \quad \textbf{Ans.}$$

Problem 7 The roots of the cubic $x^3 + qx + r = 0$ are α, β, γ. Form the equation whose roots are $\beta^2 + \beta\gamma + \gamma^2) \gamma^2 + \gamma\alpha + \alpha^2, \alpha^2 + \alpha\beta + \beta^2$.

Solution α, β, γ are the roots of the cubic equation

$$x^3 + qx + r = 0$$

let
$$y = \beta^2 + \beta\gamma + \gamma^2$$
$$y = (\beta + \gamma)^2 - \beta\gamma \tag{1}$$

Completing the cubic equation we have

$$x^3 + 0x^2 + qx + r = 0$$

i.e. $\quad \sum x = \alpha + \beta + \gamma = 0$

$$\Rightarrow \quad \beta + \gamma = -\alpha$$
$$\sum\alpha\beta = q$$
$$\alpha\beta\gamma = -r$$

From equation (1) we have

$$y = (\beta + y)^2 - \beta y$$

$$y = (-\alpha)^2 - \frac{\alpha\beta y}{\alpha}$$

$$y = \alpha^2 - \frac{(-r)}{\alpha}$$

$$\gamma = \alpha^2 + \frac{r}{\alpha}$$

$$\alpha y = \alpha^3 + r$$

i.e. $\alpha^3 - \alpha y + r = 0$ (2

since α is *a* root of the cubic

$$x^3 + qx + r = 0$$

then it will satisfy this

i.e. $\alpha^3 + q\alpha + r = 0$ (3)

Now eliminating α from (2) and (3) subtracting (3) from (2) we have

$$-\alpha y - q\alpha = 0$$

i.e. $\alpha y + q\alpha = 0$

$$\Rightarrow \alpha(y + q) = 0$$

since $\alpha \neq 0 \Rightarrow y + q = 0$

since $\beta^2 + \beta\gamma + \gamma^2, \gamma^2 + \gamma\alpha + \alpha^2, \alpha^2 + \alpha\beta + \beta^2$ are the roots of a cubic equation so the cubic equation is $(y + q)^3 = 0$

i.e. $y^3 + q^3 + 3yq^2 + 3y^2 q = 0$ **Ans.**

Problem 8 If α, β, y be the roots of the equation $x^3 - 2x - 3 = 0$ find the equation whose roots are

$$\frac{1 + \alpha}{1 - \alpha}, \frac{1 + \beta}{1 - \beta}, \frac{1 + y}{1 - y}$$

α, β, γ be the roots of the cubic $x^3 - 2x - 3 = 0$

i.e. of the equation $x^2 + 0 \cdot x^2 - 2 \cdot x - 3 = 0$

then $\sum\alpha = \alpha + \beta + y = 0$

$$\sum\alpha\beta = -2$$

$$\alpha\beta\gamma = 3$$

since α is *a* root of the equation

$$x^3 - 2x - 3 = 0$$

i.e. $x^3 - 2\alpha - 3 = 0$ (1)

let $$y = \frac{1 + \alpha}{1 - \alpha}$$

$$y - y\alpha = 1 + \alpha$$

$$y - 1 = \alpha + y\alpha$$

$$y - 1 = \alpha\,(1 + y)$$

$$\Rightarrow \quad \alpha = \frac{y - 1}{y + 1}$$

putting the value of α in equation (1), we have

$$\left(\frac{y-1}{y+1}\right)^3 - 2\left(\frac{y-1}{y+1}\right) - 3 = 0$$

$$\frac{(v - 1)^3 - 2\,(y - 1)\,(y + 1)^2 - 3}{(y - 1)^3} = 0$$

$$\frac{[y^3 - 1 - 3y1\,(y - 1)] - 2\,(y - 1)\,(y^2 + 2y + 1) - 3\,(y + 1)^3}{(y + 1)^3} = 0$$

$$\frac{y^3 - 1 - 3y^2 + 3y - 2\,(y^3 + 2v^2 + y - y^2 - 2y - 1) - 3\,(y^3 + 1 + 3y^2 + 3y}{(y + 1)^3} = 0$$

$$y^3 - 1 - 3y^2 + 3y - 2\,(y^3 + y^2 - y - 1) - 3y^3 - 3 - 9y^2 - 9y = 0$$

$$y^3 - 1 - 3y^2 + 3v - 2y^3 - 2y^2 + 2y^2 + 2y + 2 - 3y^3 - 3 - 9y^2 - 9y = 0$$

i.e. $$-4y^3 - 14y^2 - 4y - 2 = 0$$

$$\Rightarrow 4y^3 + 14y^3 + 4y + 2 = 0$$

$$\Rightarrow 2y^3 + 7y^2 + 2y + 1 = 0$$

which is the required equation.

Problem 9 If α, β, γ be the roots of the equation $x^3 + qx + r = 0$, **find** the equation whose roots are

(i) $\dfrac{\beta + \gamma}{\alpha^2}$, $\dfrac{\gamma + \alpha}{\beta^2}$, $\dfrac{\alpha + \beta}{\gamma^2}$

(ii) $\dfrac{\beta}{\gamma} + \dfrac{\gamma}{\beta}$, $\dfrac{\gamma}{\alpha} + \dfrac{\alpha}{\gamma}$, $\dfrac{\alpha}{\beta} + \dfrac{\beta}{\alpha}$

Solution α, β, γ be the roots of tqe cubic equation

$$x^3 + qx + r = 0$$

i.e. of the equation $x^3 + 0 \cdot x^2 + qx + r = 0$

then $$\sum\alpha = \alpha + \beta + \gamma = 0$$

$$\sum\alpha\beta = q$$

$$\alpha\beta\gamma = -r$$

(i) Let
$$y = \frac{\beta + \gamma}{\alpha^2}$$
$$y = \frac{\alpha + \beta + \gamma - \alpha}{\alpha^2}$$
$$y = \frac{0 - \alpha}{\alpha^2} = -\frac{\alpha}{\alpha^2} = -\frac{1}{\alpha}$$
$$\alpha = \left(-\frac{1}{y}\right)$$

since α is a root of the cubic equation
$$x + qx + r = 0$$
so
$$\alpha^3 + q\alpha + r = 0$$
i,e.
$$\left(-\frac{1}{\gamma}\right)^3 + q\left(-\frac{1}{\gamma}\right) + r = 0 - \frac{1}{y^3} - \frac{q}{y} + r = 0$$
$$\frac{-1 - qy^2 + ry^3}{y^3} = 0$$

i.e. $ry^3 - qy^2 - 1 = 0$ which is the required equation.

(ii) Let
$$y = \frac{\beta}{\gamma} + \frac{\gamma}{\beta}$$
$$y = \frac{\beta^2 + \gamma^2}{\beta\gamma}$$
$$y = \frac{(\beta + \gamma)^2 - 2\beta\gamma}{\beta\gamma}$$
$$y = \frac{(\beta + \beta)^2}{\beta\gamma} - 2$$
$$y = \alpha\,\frac{(-\alpha)^2}{\beta\gamma} - 2$$
$$y = \frac{\alpha \cdot \alpha^2}{\alpha\beta\gamma} - 2$$
$$y = \frac{\alpha^3}{\alpha\beta\gamma} - 2$$
$$y = \frac{\alpha^3}{-r} - 2$$
$$(y + 2) = -\frac{\alpha^3}{r}$$
$$ry + 2r + \alpha^3 = 0 \qquad (1)$$

we have the cubic equation

$$\alpha^3 + q\alpha + r = 0 \qquad (2)$$

substracting (2) from equation (1) we have

$$ry - q\alpha + r = 0$$

$$r(y + 1) = q\alpha$$

$$\alpha = \frac{r(y + 1)}{q} \qquad (3)$$

since α is a root of the cubic equation

$x^3 + qx + r = 0$ so it will satisfy this

i.e. $\alpha^3 + q\alpha + r = 0 \qquad (2)$

putting the value of (3) in (2) we have

$$\left\{\frac{r(y + 1)}{q}\right\} + r(y + 1) + r = 0$$

$$r^3(y + 1)^3 + r(y + 1)q^3 + rq^3 = 0$$

$$r^2(y + 1)^3 + (y + 1)q^3 + q^3 - 0$$

$$r^2(y + 1)^3 + q^3(y + 2) = 0$$

$$r^2(y^3 + 1 + 3y^2 + 3y) + yq^3 + 2q^3 = 0$$

$$r^2 y^3 + r^2 + 3y^2 r^2 + 3yr^2 + yq^3 + 2q^3 = 0$$

$$r^2 y^3 + 3r^2 y^2 + (3r^2 + q^3)y + (r^2 + 2q^3) = 0$$

which is the required equation.

Problem 10 If α, β, γ be the roots of the equation

$$x^3 + px^2 + qx + r = 0$$

find the equation whose roots are

(i) $\dfrac{\alpha}{\beta + \gamma}, \dfrac{\beta}{\gamma + \alpha}, \dfrac{\gamma}{\alpha + \beta}$

(ii) $\alpha(\beta + \gamma). \beta(\gamma + \alpha), \gamma(\alpha + \beta)$

Solution Let α, β, γ be the roots of the cubic

$$x^3 + px^2 + qx + r = 0$$

$$\alpha + \beta + \gamma = -p \qquad \sum\alpha\beta = q \qquad \alpha\beta\gamma = -r$$

Now we have to find the equation whose roots are

$$\frac{\alpha}{\beta + \gamma}, \frac{\beta}{\alpha + \beta}, \frac{\gamma}{\alpha + \gamma}$$

Let $$y = \frac{\beta}{\gamma + \alpha}$$

$$y = \frac{(\alpha + \beta + \gamma) - (\gamma + \alpha)}{(\alpha + \gamma)}$$

$$y = \frac{\alpha + \beta + \gamma}{\alpha + \gamma} - 1$$

$$y = \frac{-p}{(\alpha + \alpha + \gamma) - \beta} - 1$$

$$y + 1 = \frac{-p}{-p - \beta}$$

$$y + 1 = \frac{p}{p + \beta}$$

$$\frac{p + \beta}{p} = \frac{1}{y + 1}$$

$$1 + \frac{\beta}{p} = \frac{1}{y + 1}$$

$$\frac{\beta}{p} = \frac{1}{y + 1} - 1 = \frac{1 - y - 1}{y + 1} = -\frac{y}{y + 1}$$

$$\beta = -\frac{py}{(y + 1)} \tag{1}$$

since β is a root of the cubic equation $x^3 + px^2 + qx + r = 0$ hence it will satisfy this equation. Hence $\beta^3 + p\beta^2 + q\beta + r = 0$ (2)
putting the value of β from (1) in equation (2)

$$\left[\frac{-py}{y + 1}\right]^3 + p\left[\frac{-py}{y + 1}\right]^2 + q\left[\frac{-py}{y + 1}\right] + r = 0$$

$$-\frac{p^3y^3}{(y + 1)^3} + \frac{p^3y^2}{(y + 1)} - \frac{p \cdot q \cdot y}{y + 1} + r = 0$$

$$-p^3y^3 + p^3y^2(y + 1) - pqy(y + 1)^2 + r(y + 1)^3 = 0$$

$$-p^3y^3 + p^3y^3 + p^3y^2 - pqy[y^2 + 2y + 1] + r[y^3 + 3y^2 + 3y + 1] = 0$$

$$p^3y^2 - pqy^3 - 2pqy^2 - pqy + ry^3 + 3ry^2 + 3ry + r = 0$$

$$\Rightarrow (r - pq)y^3 + (p^3 - 2pq + 3r)y^2 + (3r - pq)y + r = 0$$

which is the required equation.

(ii) Let $y = \alpha(\beta + y)$

$$y = \alpha\beta + \alpha\gamma$$

$$y = (\alpha\beta + \beta\gamma + \alpha\gamma) - \beta\gamma$$

$$y = q - \frac{\alpha\beta\gamma}{\alpha}$$

$$y = q - \frac{(-r)}{\alpha}$$

$$\Rightarrow y = q + \frac{r}{\alpha}$$

$$\Rightarrow y - q = \frac{r}{\alpha} \Rightarrow \alpha = \frac{r}{y - q} \quad (1)$$

since α is root of the cubic equation

$$x^3 + px^2 + qx + r = 0$$

so it will satisfy this

i.e. $x^3 + p\alpha^2 + 2\alpha + r = 0$ (2)

putting the value of (α) from equation (1) in equation (2)

$$\left[\frac{r}{y - q}\right]^3 + p\left[\frac{r}{y - q}\right]^2 + q\left[\frac{r}{y - q}\right] + r = 0$$

$$\frac{r^3}{(y - q)^3} + \frac{pr^2}{(y - b)^2} + \frac{2r}{(y - q)}\Bigg] + r = 0$$

$$r^3 + pr^2(y - q) + qr(y - q)^2 + r(y - q)^3 = 0$$

$$r^3 + pr^2 y - pqr^2 + qr(y^2 - 2yq + q^2)$$
$$+ r[y^3 - q^3 - 3yq(y - q)] = 0$$

$$r^3 + pr^2 y - pqr^2 + qry^2 - 2yq^2 r + q^3 r$$
$$+ ry^3 - rq^3 - 3y^2 qr + 3yq^2 r = 0$$

$$\Rightarrow ry^3 - 2qry^2 + (pr^2 + q^2r)y + (r^3 - pqr^2) = 0$$

$$\Rightarrow y^3 - 2qy^2 + (pr + q^2)y + (r^2 - pqr) = 0$$ **Ans.**

Problem 11 If α, β, γ be the roots of $x^3 - x - 1 = 0$. Find the equation whose roots are

$\dfrac{1 + \alpha}{1 - \alpha}, \dfrac{1 + \beta}{1 - \beta}, \dfrac{1 + y}{1 - y}$ and Hence find the value of

$$\frac{1 + \alpha}{1 - \alpha} + \frac{1 + \beta}{1 - \beta} + \frac{1 + \gamma}{1 - \gamma}$$

α, β, γ by the roots of the cubic equation $x^3 - x - 1 = 0$

i.e. $\alpha^3 - \alpha - 1 - 0$

Again let $y = \dfrac{1+\alpha}{1-\alpha}$

$$\Rightarrow y - y\alpha = 1 + \alpha$$

$$\Rightarrow y - 1 = y\alpha + \alpha$$

$$\Rightarrow y - 1 = \alpha(y+1)$$

$$\Rightarrow \frac{y-1}{y+1} = \alpha \qquad (2)$$

putting the value of α from equation (2) in equation (1) we have

$$\left(\frac{y-1}{y+1}\right)^3 - \left(\frac{y-1}{y+1}\right) - 1 = 0$$

i.e. $(y-1)^3 - (y-1)(y+1)^2 - (y+1)^3 = 0$

i.e. $(y-1)^3 - (y-1)(y^2+2y+1) - (y+1)^3 = 0$

i.e. $y^3 - 1 - 3y(y-1) - (y^3 + 2y^2 + y - y^2 - 2y - 1) - (y^3 + 3y^2 + 3y + 1) = 0$

i.e. $y^3 - 1 - 3y^2 + 3y - y^3 - 2y^2 - y + y^2 + 2y + 1 - y^3 - 3y^2 - 3y - 1 = 0$

i.e. $-y^3 - 7y^2 + y - 1 = 0$

i.e: $y^3 + 7y^2 - y + 1 = 0$

which is the required equation and

$$\frac{1+\alpha}{1-\alpha} + \frac{1+\beta}{1-\beta} + \frac{1+y}{1-y} = -7 \qquad \textbf{Ans.}$$

Problem 12 If α, β, γ be the roots of a cubic $x^3 + 3x + 2 = 0$, find the equation whose roots are

$$(\alpha-\beta)(\alpha-\gamma),\ (\beta-\gamma)(\beta-\alpha),\ (\gamma-\alpha)(\gamma-\beta)$$

Solution Let $y = (\alpha-\beta)(\alpha-\gamma)$

$$= \alpha^2 - \alpha\gamma - \alpha\beta + \beta\gamma$$

$$= \alpha^2 - \alpha\gamma - \alpha\beta - \beta\gamma + 2\beta\gamma$$

$$= \alpha^2 - (\alpha\beta + \beta\gamma + \alpha\gamma) + 2\beta\gamma$$

$$y = \alpha^2 - (\alpha\beta + \beta\gamma + \alpha\gamma) + \frac{2\alpha\beta\gamma}{\alpha}$$

since α, β, γ are the roots of the cubic

$$x^3 + 3x + 2 = 0 \quad \text{of} \quad x^3 + 0x^2 + 3x = -2$$

so $\alpha + \beta + \gamma = 0, \qquad \alpha\beta + \beta\gamma + \alpha\gamma = 3\ \alpha\beta\gamma = -2$

Thus $$y = \alpha^2 - 3 + \frac{2(-2)}{\alpha}$$

$$y = \alpha^2 - 3 - \frac{4}{\alpha}$$

$$y = \frac{\alpha^3 - 3\alpha - 4}{\alpha}$$

$$\Rightarrow y\alpha = \alpha^3 - 3\alpha - 4$$

$$\Rightarrow \alpha^3 - (3 + y)\,\alpha - 4 = 0 \qquad (1)$$

Again α is a root of a cubic

$$x^3 + 3x + 2 = 0$$

so $$\alpha^3 + 3\alpha + 2 = 0 \qquad (2)$$

subtracting (1) from (2) we have

$$3\alpha + 2 + 3\alpha + y\alpha + 4 = 0$$

$$6\alpha + 6 + y\alpha = 0 \Rightarrow (6 + y)\,\alpha + 6 = 0$$

$$\Rightarrow \alpha = -\frac{6}{(6 + y)}$$

substituting the value of α in (2) we have

$$\left(-\frac{6}{6+y}\right)^3 + 3\left(-\frac{6}{6+y}\right) + 2 = 0$$

i.e. $$-\frac{216}{(6 + y)^3} - \frac{18}{6 + y} + 2 = 0$$

i.e. $$-216 - 18(6 + y)^2 + 2(6 + y)^3 = 0$$

i.e. $$-216 - 18(y^2 + 12y + 36) + 2[216 + y^3 + 18y(6 + y)] = 0$$

i.e. $$-216 - 18y^2 - 216y - 648 + 432 + 2y^3 + 36y(6 + y) = 0$$

i.e. $$-216 - 18y^2 - 216y - 648 + 432 + 2y^3 + 216y + 36y^2 = 0$$

i.e. $$2y^3 + 18y^2 - 432 = 0$$

i.e. $$2(y^3 + 9y^2 - 216) = 0$$

i.e. $$y^3 + 9y^2 - 216 = 0$$ **Ans.**

Which is the required equation.

Problem 13 If α, β, γ be the roots of the cubic

$$ax^3 + 3bx^2 + 3cx + d = 0$$

Find the equation whose roots are

$$\frac{\beta\gamma - \alpha^2}{\beta+\gamma-2\alpha}, \frac{\gamma\alpha - \beta^2}{\gamma+\alpha-2\beta}, \frac{\alpha\beta - \gamma^2}{\alpha+\beta-2\gamma}$$ [I.F.S. 83]

Solution. Let $y = \dfrac{\beta\gamma - \alpha^2}{\beta + \gamma - 2\alpha}$

$$\alpha y = \frac{\alpha\beta\gamma - \alpha^3}{\alpha + \beta + \gamma - 3\alpha}$$

since α, β, γ be the roots of the cubic

$$ax^3 + 3bx^2 + 3cx + d = 0$$

$$\Rightarrow \sum\alpha = \alpha + \beta + \gamma = -\frac{3b}{a}$$

$$\sum\alpha\beta = \frac{3c}{a}$$

$$\alpha\beta\gamma = -\frac{d}{a}$$

so $$\alpha y = \frac{-\frac{d}{a} - \alpha^3}{-\frac{3b}{a} - 3\alpha} = \frac{-(d + a\alpha^3)}{-(3b + 3a\alpha)}$$

$$\alpha y = \frac{d + a\alpha^3}{3(b + a\alpha)}$$

$$\Rightarrow 3\alpha y(b + a\alpha) = d + a\alpha^3$$

$$\Rightarrow 3\alpha yb + 3\alpha^2 ya = d + a\alpha^3$$

$$\Rightarrow a\alpha^3 - 3ya\alpha^2 - 3yb\alpha + d = 0$$

sinee α is a root of the cubic equation

$$ax^3 + 3bx^2 + 3cx + d = 0$$

$$\Rightarrow a\alpha^3 + 3b\alpha^2 + 3c\alpha + d = 0 \qquad (2)$$

subtracting (1) from equation (2) we have

$$a\alpha^3 + 3b\alpha^2 + 3c\alpha + d - a\alpha^3 + 3ay\alpha^2 + 3yb\alpha - d = 0$$

$$\alpha(3b\alpha + 3c + 3ay\alpha + 3by) = 0$$

$$\Rightarrow 3(b\alpha + c + ay\alpha + by) = 0$$

$$\Rightarrow b\alpha + c + ay\alpha + by = 0$$

$$\Rightarrow \alpha(ay + b) + (by + c) = 0$$

$$\Rightarrow \alpha(ay + b) = -(by + c)$$

$$\Rightarrow \alpha = -\frac{(by + c)}{(ay + b)}$$

substituting the value of α in equation (2) we have

$$a\left[-\left(\frac{by+c}{ay+b}\right)\right]^3 + 3b\left[-\frac{(by+c)}{(ay+b)}\right]^2 + 3c\left[\frac{-(by+c)}{(ay+b)}\right] + d = 0$$

$$-\left(\frac{by+c}{ay+b}\right)^3 + 3b\left(\frac{by+c}{ay+b}\right)^2 - 3c\left(\frac{(by+c)}{ay+b}\right) + d = 0$$

$$-a(by+c)^3 + 3b(by+c)^2(ay+b) - 3c(by+c)(ay+b)^2 + d(ay+b)^3 = 0$$

i.e. $$d(ay+b)^3 - 3c(by+c)(ay+b)^2 + 3b(by+c)^2(ay+b) - a(by+c)^3 = 0$$ **Ans.**

Reciprocal roots

Let $\alpha_1, \alpha_2, \alpha_3 \ldots \alpha_n$ be the roots of the equation

$$x^n + p_1 x^{n-1} + p_2 x^{n-2} + \ldots + p_{n-1} x + p_n = 0$$

Then $\frac{1}{\alpha_1}, \frac{1}{\alpha_2}, \frac{1}{\alpha_3} \ldots \frac{1}{\alpha_n}$ are the roots of the equation

$$p_n y^n + p_{n-1} y^{n-1} + \ldots + p_1 y + 1 = 0$$

Rule Take the last coefficient of the given equation to be the first coefficient of the transformed equation, last but one to be the second and so on after making the given equation complete if it is not so.

Problem 14 Find the condition that the roots of the equation

$$x^3 - px^2 + qx - r = 0$$ be in H.P. [I.F, S. *81*]

The equation whose roots are the recoprocals of the given equation is

$$-rx^3 + qx^2 - px + 1 = 0$$

i.e. $$rx^3 - qx^2 + px - 1 = 0$$

Its roots are therefore in A.P.

let $\alpha - \delta, \alpha, \alpha + \delta$ be its roots

$$\alpha - \delta + \alpha + \alpha + \delta = \frac{q}{r}$$

$$3\alpha = \frac{q}{r} \qquad \alpha = \frac{q}{3r} \qquad (1)$$

since α is a root of the cubic equation

$$r x^3 - qx^2 + px - 1 = 0$$

i.e. $$r\alpha^3 - q\alpha^2 + p\alpha - 1 = 0$$

i.e. $$r\left(\frac{q}{3r}\right)^3 - q\left(\frac{q}{3r}\right)^2 + p\left(\frac{q}{3r}\right) - 1 = 0$$

i.e. $$r\,\frac{q^3}{27r^3} - \frac{q^3}{9r^2} + \frac{pq}{3r} - 1 = 0$$

$$\frac{q^3}{27r^2} - \frac{q^3}{9r^2} + \frac{pq}{3r} - 1 = 0$$

$$\frac{q^3 - 3q^3 + 9pqr - 27r^2}{27r^2} = 0$$

$$-2q^3 + 9pqr - 27r^2 = 0$$

i.e. $$27r^2 - 9pqr + 2q^3 = 0$$

which is the required condition that the roots of the equation

$$x^3 - pq^2 + qx - r = 0$$

are in Harmonical progression. *(Provea)*

5

Inequalities

Arithmetic and Geometric means, Caucny'-Schwartz inequality (only for finite sums.

Lheorem 1. Show that Arithmetic mean of two five quantities is greater than their geometric mean.

let a, b be two positive quantities. Their

$$AM = \frac{a+b}{2}$$

$$GM = (ab)\frac{1}{2} = \sqrt{ab}$$

Then
$$AM - GM = \frac{a+b}{2} - \sqrt{ab}$$

$$= \frac{a+b-2\sqrt{ab}}{2}$$

$$= \frac{(\sqrt{a}-\sqrt{b})^2}{2} = +\text{ ve quantity}$$

$$\geqslant 0$$

i.e.
$$AM - GM \geqslant 0$$

$$\Rightarrow AM \geqslant GM$$ (*proved*)

Theorem 2 prove that the AM of any number of positive quantities is greater than $G.M.$ (IFS. 82)

Solution let $a_1, a_2, a_3 \ldots a_n$ be n factors and let their sum be constant and equal to s

since $\frac{a_1+a_2}{2}, \frac{a_1+a_2}{2}$ are two number whose $(a_1 + a_2)$ and their product $\frac{a_1+a_2}{2} \times \frac{a_1+a_2}{2} > a_1 a_2$, so if we replace the two equal factors

a_1 and a_2 by two equal factors $\frac{a_1 + a_2}{2}$, $\frac{a_1 + a_2}{2}$, . . . we find that

$$\frac{a_1 + a_2}{2} \times \frac{a_1 + a_2}{2} \cdot a_3\, a_4\, a_5 \ldots a_{n-1}\, a_n$$

$$> a_1\, a_2\, a_3 \ldots a_n$$

but their sum remains unchanged similarly

$$\frac{a_1 + a_2 + a_3}{3} \cdot \frac{a_1 + a_2 + a_3}{3} \cdot \frac{a_1 + a_2 + a_3}{3}\, a_4 \ldots a_n$$

$$> a_1\, a_2 \ldots a_n$$

while their sum remains constant

$$\frac{a_1 + a_2 + \ldots + a_n}{n} \ldots \frac{a_1 + a_2 + \ldots + a_n}{n} \ldots \frac{a_1 + a_2 + \ldots + a_n}{n}$$

$$> a_1\, a_2 \ldots a_n$$

while their sum is same

$$s = a_1 + a_2 \ldots + a_n$$

or
$$\left(\frac{a_1 + a_2 + \ldots + a_n}{n}\right)^n > a_1\, a_2 \ldots a_n \tag{2}$$

i.e.
$$\left(\frac{a_1 + a_2 + \ldots + a_n}{n}\right)^n \text{ or } \left(\frac{s}{n}\right)^n$$

where $a_1, a_2\, a_3 \ldots a_n$ are in equal quantities

or
$$\frac{a_1 + a_2 + a_3 + \ldots + a_n}{n} > (a_1\, a_2 \ldots a_n)^{1/n}$$

But we know the *AM* of $a_1, a_2, \ldots a_n$

$$\frac{a_1 + a_2 + \ldots + a_n}{n}$$

and *GM* is $(a_1\, a_2\, a_3 \ldots a_n)^{1/n}$

Hence $A \cdot M$ of any finite number of quantities is greater the *G.M.*

Theorem 3 let $a_1\, a_2 \ldots a_n, b_1, b_2, b_3 \ldots b_n$ be two sets of arbitary real numbers, show that

$$\left(\sum_{i-1}^{n} a_i\, b_i\right)^2 \geqslant \left(\sum_{i-1}^{n} a_i^2\right) \left(\sum_{i-1}^{n} b_i^2\right)$$

the equality sign only holding if the numbers ar, br are proportional to each other i.e. when

$$\lambda ar + \mu br = 0 \qquad [I.F.S.\ 80, 81]$$

Solution We have from schwarth inequality

$$a_1^2 + a_2^2 + \ldots + a_n^2)(b_1^2 + b_2^2 \ \ldots + b_n^2)$$
$$- (a_1b_1 + a_2b_2 + a_nb_n)^2$$
$$= \sum_{i \neq j} (ai^2bj^2 + aj^2bi^2 - 2\ aibi\ ajbj)$$
$$= \sum (aibj - ajbi)^2 \geqslant 0$$

i.e. $$\sum_{i=1}^{n} ai^2 \sum_{i=1}^{n} bi^2 \quad \geqslant \quad (\sum_{i=1}^{n} aibi)^2)$$ *(proved)*

Definition of Inequality

Let a and b be real numbers. If $a - b$ is negative we say that a is less than b and write $a < b$. If $a - b$ is positive then a is greater than b i.e. $a > b$

Elementary properties of inequalities

(i) For any two real numbers a and b, we have

$$a < b \quad \text{or} \quad a = b \quad \text{or} \quad a > b$$

(ii) If $a > b$ and $a > c$ $\Rightarrow a > c$

(iii) If $a > b$, then $a + m > b + m$, for any real number m

(iv) When we multiply both sides of the inequality by a neative quantity, the sign of inequality is reversed.

(v) If $a \neq 0, b \neq 0$ and $a > b$ then $\frac{1}{a} < \frac{1}{b}$.

(vi) If $a_1 > b_1, a_2 > b_2 \ldots a_n > b_n$

then $$a_1 + a_2 + \ldots + a_n > b_1 + b_2 + \ldots + b_n$$

and $$a_1\, a_2 \ldots a_r > b_1\, b_2 \ldots b_n$$

Some Important Properties

(i) If $x > 0$ and $a > b > 0$; then $a^x > b^x$

(ii) If $a > 1$ and $x > y > 0$ then $a^x > a^y$

(iii) If $0 < a < 1$ and $x > y$ then $a^x < a^y$

(iv) If $a > 1$ and $x > y$ then $\log_a x > \log_a y$

(v) If $0 < a < 1$ and $x > y$ then $\log_a x < \log_b y$

Theorem Remember If $a_i \geqslant 0 \qquad i = 1, 2, \ldots n$ then

(i) $$\frac{a_1^m + a_2^m + \ldots + a_n^m}{n} \geqslant \left(\frac{a_1 + a_2 + \ldots + a_n}{n}\right)^m$$

if $$m \geqslant 0$$

and $$\frac{a_1^m + a_2^m + \ldots + a_n^m}{n} \leqslant \left(\frac{a_1 + a_2 + \ldots + a_n}{n}\right)^m$$

That is, arithmetic mean of the mth powers of n positive puantities is greater than the mth power of their arithmetic mean in all cases except when $0 < m < 1$.

Inequalities Arithmetic and geometric means Cauchy schewarz inequality (only for finite sums).

Problem 1 Prove that $n^n > \{1, 3, 5, 7 \ldots (2n-1)\}$

Solution We consider n quantities $1, 3, 5, 7 \ldots (2n-1)$

Then $$AM = \frac{1+3+5+7+\ldots+(2n-1)}{n}$$

$$= \frac{\frac{n}{2}[2\cdot 1 + (n-1)\cdot 2]}{n}$$

$$= \frac{\frac{n}{2}[2+2n-2]}{n} = \frac{\frac{n}{2}\cdot 2n}{n} = \frac{n^2}{n} = n$$

AM of $(1, 3, 5 \ldots (2n-1)\} = n$ (1)

GM of $\{1, 3, 5 \ldots (2n-1)\} = \{1\cdot 3\cdot 5 \ldots (2n-1)\}^{1/n}$ (2)

since we know that $AG > GM$

so from (1) and (2) we have

$$n > \{135 \ldots (2n-1)\}^{1/n}$$

or $$n^n > \{1\cdot 35, \ldots (2n-1)\}$$ *(Proved)*

Problem 2 If $a > b > 0$ and n is a positive integer, prove that

$$a^n - b^n > n(a-b)(ab)^{(n-1)/2}$$

Solution We consider the numbers

$$1, \frac{b}{a}, \left(\frac{b}{a}\right)^2 \ldots \left(\frac{b}{a}\right)^{n-1}$$

Their Arithmetic mean

$$AM = \frac{1 + \left(\frac{b}{a}\right) + \left(\frac{b}{a}\right)^2 + \ldots + \left(\frac{b}{a}\right)^{n-1}}{n}$$

$$= \frac{1 - \left(\frac{b}{a}\right)^n}{n\left(1 - \frac{b}{a}\right)} = \frac{a^n - b^n}{a^n \cdot n\left(\frac{a-b}{a}\right)}$$

$$\boxed{a > b > 0 \Rightarrow \frac{b}{a} < 1}$$

so $1 + r \ldots + r^{n-1} = \dfrac{1 - r^n}{1 - r}$

$$AM = \frac{a^n - b^n}{n\,(a - b)\cdot a^{n-1}}$$

$$GM = \left[1 \cdot \frac{b}{a} \cdot \frac{b^2}{a^2} \cdots \frac{b^{n-1}}{a^{n-1}}\right]^{1/n}$$

$$= \left[\left(\frac{b}{o}\right)^{1+2+\cdots+n-1}\right]^{1/n}$$

$$= \left(\frac{b}{a}\right)^{(n-1)n/2 \cdot 1/n} = \left(\frac{b}{a}\right)^{n-1/2}$$

sinee $\quad AM > GM$

$$\Rightarrow \frac{a^n - b^n}{n\,(a-b)\,a^{n-1}} > \left(\frac{b}{a}\right)^{(n-1)/2}$$

$$\Rightarrow a^n - b^n > n\,(a - b)\,a^{n-1}\left(\frac{b}{a}\right)^{(n-1)/2}$$

$$\Rightarrow a^n - b^n > n\,(a - b)\,(ab)^{(n-1)/2}$$

$$\Rightarrow a^n - b^n > n\,(ab)^{(n-1)/2}\,(a - b)$$ *(Proved)*

Problem 3 If s is the sum of a set $a_1, a_2 \ldots a_n$ of positive numbers,

Prove that $\dfrac{s}{s - a_1} + \dfrac{s}{s - a_2} + \ldots + \dfrac{s}{s - a_n} \geqslant \dfrac{n^2}{n - 1}$ [*IFS* 78, 87]

Solution Given that $s = a_1 + a_2 \ldots + a_n$

where $\quad a_1 > 0, a_2 > 0 \ldots a_n > 0$

let us consider n quantities $s - a_1, s - a_2, \ldots s - a_n$

AM of these n quantities

$$= \frac{(s - a_1) + (s - a_2) + \ldots + (s - a_n)}{n}$$

$$= \frac{ns - (a_1 + a_2 + \ldots + a_n)}{n}$$

$$AM = \frac{ns - s}{n} = s\left(\frac{n - 1}{n}\right)$$

GM of these n quantities

$$= [(s - a_1)(s - a_2) \ldots (s - a_n)]^{1/n} \tag{2}$$

But we known that $\quad AM > GM$

i,e. $\quad s\left(\dfrac{n - 1}{n}\right) \geqslant \{(s - a_1)(s - a_2) \ldots (s - a_n)\}^{1/n}$

$$\Rightarrow s \geqslant \frac{n}{n - 1}\{(s - a_1)(s - a_2) \ldots (s - a_n)\}^{1/n} \tag{A}$$

Again we consider n quantities

$$\frac{1}{s-a_1}, \frac{1}{s-a_2}, \ldots \frac{1}{s-a_n}$$

Their $$AM = \frac{\frac{1}{s-a_1} + \frac{1}{s-a_2} + \ldots \frac{1}{s-a_n}}{n}$$

$$= \frac{1}{n}\left[\frac{1}{s-a_1} + \frac{1}{s-a_2} + \ldots + \frac{1}{s-a_n}\right]$$

Their $$GM = \left[\frac{1}{(s-a_1)} \cdot \frac{1}{(s-a_2)} \cdots \frac{1}{(s-a_n)}\right]^{1/n}$$

$$= \frac{1}{[(s-a_1)(s-a_2)\ldots(s-a_n)]^{1/n}}$$

Again $$AM \geqslant GM$$

$$\frac{1}{n}\left[\frac{1}{s-a_1} + \frac{1}{s-a_1} + , . . + \frac{1}{s-a_n}\right]$$

$$\geqslant \frac{1}{[(s-a_1)(s-a_2)\ldots(s-a_n)]^{1/n}} \qquad \text{(B)}$$

Multiplying corresponding sides of (A) and (B) we have

$$s\frac{1}{n}\left[\frac{1}{s-a_1} + \frac{1}{s-a_2} + \frac{1}{s-a_3} + \ldots + \frac{1}{s-a_n}\right] \geqslant \frac{n}{n-1}$$

$$\Rightarrow \quad \frac{s}{s-a_1} + \frac{s}{s-a_2} + \frac{s}{s-a_3} + \ldots \frac{s}{s-a_n} \geqslant \frac{n^2}{n-1}$$

(proved)

Problem If a and b are positive and $a + b = 1$ prove that

$$\left(a + \frac{1}{a}\right)^2 + \left(b + \frac{1}{b}\right)^2 \geqslant \frac{25}{2}$$

Solution Here $\left(a + \frac{1}{a}\right)^2 + \left(b + \frac{1}{b}\right)^2$

$$= a^2 + 2 + \frac{1}{a^2} + b^2 + 2 + \frac{1}{b^2} = (a^2 + b^2) + \left(\frac{1}{a^2} + \frac{1}{b^2}\right) + 4$$

$$= (a^2 + b^2) + \left(\frac{b^2 + a^2}{a^2 b^2}\right) + 4 = (a^2 + b^2)\left[1 + \frac{1}{a^2 b^2}\right] + 4$$

$$= [(a+b)^2 - 2ab]\left[1 + \frac{1}{(ab)^2}\right] + 4$$

$$= [1 - 2ab]\left[1 + \frac{1}{(ab)^2}\right] + 4 \qquad [a + b = 1]$$

$$\left(a + \frac{1}{a}\right)^2 + \left(b + \frac{1}{b}\right)^2 = (1 - 2ab)\left(1 + \frac{1}{a^2 b^2}\right) + 4 \qquad (1)$$

Again $a > 0,\ b > 0$

$$AM = \frac{a+b}{2} \quad GM = \sqrt{ab}$$

We know that $AM \geqslant GM$

i.e. $$\frac{a+b}{2} \geqslant \sqrt{ab}$$

$$\left(\frac{a+b}{2}\right)^2 \geqslant ab$$

i.e. $$ab \leqslant \left(\frac{a+b}{2}\right)^2$$

i.e. $$ab \leqslant \frac{1}{4}$$

Thus $$\left(a+\frac{1}{a}\right)^2 + \left(b+\frac{1}{b}\right)^2 \geqslant \left(1-2\,\frac{1}{4}\right)\left(1+\frac{1}{1/16}\right)+4$$

$$\left(a+\frac{1}{a}\right)^2 + \left(b+\frac{1}{b}\right)^2 \geqslant \left(1-\frac{1}{2}\right)(1+16)+4$$

$$\left(a+\frac{1}{a}\right)^2 + \left(b+\frac{1}{b}\right)^2 \geqslant \frac{1}{2} \times 17 + 4$$

$$\left(a+\frac{1}{a}\right)^2 + \left(b+\frac{1}{b}\right)^2 \geqslant \frac{17+8}{2}$$

i.e. $$\left(a+\frac{1}{a}\right)^2 + \left(b+\frac{1}{b}\right)^2 \geqslant \frac{25}{2}$$ *(proved)*

Problem 5 If n is a positive integer > 2 prove that

$$1^1\ 2^2\ 3^3\ 4^4 \ldots n^n < \left(\frac{2n+1}{3}\right)^{n(n+1)/2}$$

Solution Consider the quantities

$$1,\ 2,\ 2,\ 3,\ 3,\ 4,\ 4,\ 4,\ 4 \ldots n,\ n,\ n \ldots n$$

The number of terms $= 1+2+3+4\ldots+n\ \dfrac{n(n+1)}{2}$

Now $G.M. = \{1 \cdot 2^2\, 3^3\, 4^4 \ldots n^n\}^{1/(n+1)/2}$ (1)

$$A.M. = \frac{1+(2+2)+(3+3+3)+(4+4+4+4)+\ldots+(n+n+\ldots+n)}{1+2+3+4+\ldots+n}$$

$$= \frac{1+2\cdot 2+3\cdot 3+4\cdot 4+\ldots n\cdot n}{1+2+3+\ldots+n}$$

$$= \frac{1^2+2^2+3^2+4^2+\ldots+n^2}{1+2+3+\ldots+n}$$

$$= \frac{n(n+1)(2n+1)}{6} \cdot \frac{2}{n(n+1)} = \frac{(2n+1)}{3}$$

Now since $GM < AM$

i.e. $\{1^1\, 2^2\, 3^3\, 4^4 \ldots n^n\}^{2/n(n+1)} < \dfrac{2n+1}{3}$

$$\{1^1\, 2^2\, 3^3\, 4^4 \ldots n^n\} < \left(\frac{2n+1}{3}\right)^{n(n+1)/2}$$ *(proved)*

Problem 6 If $a > b > 0$ prove that $(a+b)\left(\frac{1}{a} + \frac{1}{b}\right) > 4$

Proof ;

$$a > b > 0$$

$$\Rightarrow \quad a - b > 0$$

$$\Rightarrow \quad (a-b)^2 > 0$$

$$\Rightarrow \quad (a+b)^2 - 4ab > 0$$

$$\Rightarrow \quad (a+b)(a+b) - 4ab > 0$$

$$\Rightarrow \quad (a+b)(a+b) > 4ab$$

$$\Rightarrow \quad \frac{(a+b)(a\ a+b)}{ab} > 4$$

$$\Rightarrow \quad (a+b)\left(\frac{1}{a} + \frac{1}{b}\right) > 4$$ *(proved)*

Problem 7 Prove that

$$(ab + bc + ca) < (a+b-c)^2 + (a+c-b)^2 + (b+c-a)^2$$

Solution We have to prove that

$$(a+b-c)^2 + (a+c-b)^2 + (b+c-a)^2 - (ab+bc+ca) > 0$$

LHS $(a+b-c)^2 + (a+c-b)^2 + (b+c-a)^2 - (ab+bc+ca)$

$= a^2 + b^2 + c^2 + 2ab - 2bc - 2ca + a^2 + c^2 + b^2$

$\quad + 2ac - 2bc - 2ab + b^2 + c^2 + a^2 + 2bc - 2ac - 2ab$

$\quad - (ab + bc + ca)$

$\quad 3a^2 + 3b^2 + 3c^2 - 2ab - 2bc - 2ac - (ab + bc + ca)$

$= (a^2 + b^2 - 2ab) + (b^2 + c^2 - 2bc) + (a^2 + c^2 - 2ac)$

$\quad + (a^2 + b^2 + c^2) - (ab + bc + ca)$

$= (a-b)^2 + (b-c)^2 + (c-a)^2 + (a^2 + b^2 + c^2)$

$\quad - (ab + bc + ca)$

$= +\text{ve quantity} + (a^2 + b^2 + c^2) - (ab + bc + ca)$

We know that

$$a^2 + b^2 > 2ab$$
$$b^2 + c^2 > 2bc$$
$$c^2 + a^2 > 2ac$$

Adding $\quad 2\,(a^2 + b^2 + c^2) > 2\,(ab + bc + ca)$

$$a^2 + b^2 + c^2 > ab + bc + ca$$

Hence

$$(a + b - c)^2 + (a + c - b)^2 + (b + c - a)^2 - (ab + bc + ca) > 0$$

Thus $\quad (ab + bc + ca) < (a + b - c)^2 + (a + c - b)^2 + (b + c - a)^2$

(proved)

Problem 8 Prove that $(a^2 + b^2 + c^2)(x^2 + y^2 + z^2) > (ax + by + cz)^2$

Solution We have $\quad (a^2 + b^2 + c^2)(x^2 + y^2 + z^2) - (ax + by + cz)^2$

$$= a^2x^2 + a^2y^2 + a^2z^2 + b^2x^2 + b^2y^2 + b^2z^2 + c^2x^2 + c^2y^2 + c^2z^2 - a^2x^2 - b^2y^2 - c^2z^2 - 2abxy - 2bcyz - 2acxz$$

$$= (ay - bx)^2 + (bz - cy)^2 + (az - cx)^2$$

$= +$ve quantity

i.e. $\quad > 0$

$$(a^2 + b^2 + c^2)(x^2 + y^2 + z^2) - (ax + by + cz)^2 > 0$$

$$(a^2 + b^2 + c^2) + (x^2 + y^2 + z^2) > (ax + by + cz)^2 \quad \textit{(proved)}$$

Problem 9 $2 \cdot 4 \cdot 6 \ldots 2n < (n + 1)^n$

Solution Consider numbers $2, 4, 6 \ldots 2n$

AM of these n numbers

$$= \frac{2 + 4 + 6 + \ldots + 2n}{n} = \frac{2\,(1 + 2 + 3 + \ldots + n)}{n}$$

$$= \frac{2 \cdot n\,(n + 1)}{2n} = (n + 1)$$

GM of these n numbers $= [2, 4 \cdot 6 \ldots 2n]^{1/n}$

Again as we know $\quad AM > GM$

$$(n + 1) > [2 \cdot 4 \cdot 6 \ldots 2n]^{1/n}$$

i.e. $\quad 2 \cdot 4 \cdot 6 \ldots 2n < (n + 1)^n \quad$ *(proved)*

Problem 10. Prove that $[1^r + 2^r + 3^r \ldots + n^r] > n^n\,(n!)^r$

Solution Let us consider n numbers $1^r, 2^r, 3^r \ldots n^r$

AM of the numbers $= \dfrac{1^r + 2^r + 3^r + \ldots + n^r}{n}$

GM of these n numbers

$$=[1^r, 2^r \cdot 3^r \ldots n^r]^{1/n}$$
$$= [1 \cdot 2 \cdot 3 \ldots n]^{r/n}$$
$$= [n\,!]^{r/n}$$

since $AM > GM$

so $$\frac{1^r + 2^r + 3^r + \ldots + n^r}{n} > [n\,!]^{r/n}$$

$$\Rightarrow \left[\frac{1^r + 2^r + 3^r + \ldots + n^r}{n}\right]^n > (n\,!)^r$$

$$\Rightarrow 1^r + 2^r + 3^r + \ldots + n^r > n^n (n\,!)^r$$ (*Proved*)

Problem 11 If $a > b$, prove that

$$\left(1 + \frac{x}{a}\right)^a > \left(1 + \frac{x}{b}\right)^b$$

Solution We have $\left(1 + \frac{x}{a}\right)^a - \left(1 + \frac{x}{b}\right)^b$

$$= 1 + a\frac{x}{a} + \frac{a(a-1)}{21}\left(\frac{x}{a}\right)^2 + \ldots$$

$$-1 - b\left(\frac{x}{b}\right) - \frac{b(b-1)}{2\,i}\left(\frac{x}{b}\right)^2 \ldots$$

$$= \left[\frac{(a-1)}{2\,!}\left(\frac{x^2}{a} - \frac{b-1}{2\,!}\right)\frac{x^2}{b}\right] + \ldots$$

$$= x^2\left[\frac{a-1}{2a} - \frac{b-1}{2b}\right] + \ldots = x^2\left[\frac{ab-b-ab+a}{2ab}\right] + \ldots$$

$$= x^2\frac{(a-b)}{2ab} \ldots = \frac{x^2}{2}\left(\frac{1}{b} - \frac{1}{a}\right) + \ldots$$

since $a > b \Rightarrow \frac{1}{a} < \frac{1}{b}$

.e. $\frac{1}{b} - \frac{1}{a} > 0$ (a + ve quantity)

so $\left(1 + \frac{x}{a}\right)^a - \left(1 + \frac{x}{b}\right)^b > 0$

i.e. $\left(1 + \frac{x}{a}\right)^a > \left(1 + \frac{x}{b}\right)^b$ (*Proved*

Problem 12 Show that

$$\left(\frac{x^2 + y^2 + z^2}{x + y + z}\right)^{x+y+z} > x^x\, y^y\, z^z$$

Solution Take the series $x, \ldots x, y \ldots y, z \ldots z$

i.e. x occuring x times y occuring y times z occuring z times

$$AM = \frac{(x+x+\ldots+x \text{ times})+(y+y+\ldots+y \text{ times})+(z+z+\ldots+z \text{ times})}{x + y + z}$$

$$= \frac{x\cdot x + y\cdot y + z\cdot z}{x + y + z} = \frac{x^2 + y^2 + z^2}{x + y + z}$$

$$GM = \{x\cdot x \ldots \text{ to } x \text{ times } y\cdot y \ldots y \text{ times } z\cdot z\cdot z \ldots \text{ to } z \text{ times}\}^{1/x+y+z}$$

$$= [x^x\, y^y\, z^z]^{1/x+y+z}$$

We know that $AM > GM$

$$\frac{x^2 + y^2 + z^2}{x + y + z} > [x^x\, y^y\, z^z]^{1/x+y+z}$$

$$\left[\frac{x^2 + y^2 + z^2}{x + y + z}\right]^{x+y+z} > x^x.y^y.z^z \qquad \textit{(Proved)}$$

Problem 13 Prove that $3\,(a^3 + b^3 + c^3) \geqslant (a + b + c)\,(a^2 + b^2 + c^2)$

Solution We know that for any two integers a and b

$$(a - b)^2 > 0$$

$$a^2 + b^2 - 2ab > 0$$

$$a^2 + b^2 > 2ab$$

$$a^2 + b^2 - ab > ab$$

$$\Rightarrow (a + b)\,(a^2 + b^2 - ab) > (a + b)\,ab$$

$$\Rightarrow a^3 + b^3 > ab\,(a + b) \qquad (1)$$

similarly

$$b^3 + c^3 > bc\,(b + c) \qquad (2)$$

$$c^3 + a^3 > ca\,(c + a) \qquad (3)$$

Adding equation (1), (2) and (3) we have

$$2\,(a^3 + b^3 + c^3) > ab\,(a + b) + bc\,(b + c) + ca\,(c + a)$$

$$2\,(a^3 + b^3 + c^3) > a^2 b + ab^2 + b^2 c + bc^2 + c^2 a + ca^2$$

$$2\,(a^3 + b^3 + c^3) > a\,(b^2 + c^2) + b\,(c^2 + a^2) + c\,(a^2 + b^2)$$

$$3\,(a^3 + b^3 + c^3) > a\,(a^2 + b^2 + c^2) + b\,(a^2 + b^2 + c^2) + c\,(a^2 + b^2 + c^2)$$

on adding $a^2 + b^2 + c^2$ on both sides

$$3\,(a^3 + b^3 + c^3) > (a + b + c)\,(a^2 + b^2 + c^2) \qquad \textit{(Proved)}$$

Problem 14 $a^2 + b^2 + c^2 = 1$ and $x^2 + y^2 + z^2 = 1$ show that

$$ax + by + cz < 1$$

or $$1 - (ax + by + cz) > 0$$

Solution $$\frac{a^2 + x^2}{2} > (a^2 x^2)^{1/2}$$

$$a^2 + x^2 > 2ax$$

Similarly $$b^2 + y^2 > 2by$$

$$c^2 + z^2 > 2cz$$

$$\Rightarrow (a^2 + b^2 + c^2) + (x^2 + y^2 + z^2) > 2\,(ax + by + cz)$$

$$\Rightarrow 1 + 1 > 2\,(ax + by + cz)$$

$$\Rightarrow 2 > 2\,(ax + by + cz)$$

$$\Rightarrow 1 > (ax + by + cz)$$

i.e. $ax + by + cz < 1$ *(proved)*

Problem 5.15 Prove that

$$(1 + x^3)(1 + y^3)(1 + z^3) > (1 + xyz)^3$$

Solution We have to prove that

$$(1 + x^3)(1 + y^3)(1 + z^3) > (1 + xyz)^3$$

i.e. to prove that

$$(1 + x^3)(1 + z^3 + y^3 + y^3 z^3)$$

$$> [1 + x^3 y^3 z^3 + 3xyz\,(1 + xyz)]$$

$$1 + z^3 + y^3 + y^3 z^3 + x^3 + x^3 z^3 + x^3 y^3 + x^3 y^3 z^3$$

$$> 1 + x^3 y^3 z^3 + 3xyz + 3x^2 y^2 z^2$$

i.e. to prove $(x^3 + y^3 + z^3) + (x^3 y^3 + y^3 z^3 + x^3 y^3 z^3)$

$$> \quad 3xyz + 3x^2 y^2 z^2$$

Let us consider three numbers

$$x^3,\ y^3,\ z^3$$

$$AM = \frac{x^3 + y^3 + z^3}{3}$$

$$GM = (x^3 y^3 z^3)^{1/3}$$

$$AM > GN$$

$$\Rightarrow \frac{x^3 + y^3 + z^3}{3} > xyz$$

$$\Rightarrow x^3 + y^3 + z^3 > 3xyz \tag{1}$$

Agrin let us consider the three numbers

$$x^3 y^3,\ y^3 z^3,\ x^3 z^3$$

$$AM = \frac{x^3 y^3 + y^3 z^3 + x^3 z^3}{3}$$

$$GM = (x^3 y^3 y^3 z^3 x^3 z^3)^{1/3} = x^2 y^2 z^2$$

$$\frac{x^3 y^3 + y^3 z^3 + x^3 z^3}{3} > x^2 y^2 z^2$$

$$x^3 y^3 + y^3 z^3 + x^3 z^3 > 3x^2 y^2 z^2 \qquad (2)$$

Adding eqquation (1) and (2) we have

$$(x^3 + y^3 + z^3) + (x^3 y^3 + y^3 z^3 + x^3 z^3) > 3xyz + 3x^2 y^2 z^2$$

which means that

$$(1 + x^3)(1 + y^3)(1 + z^3) > (1 + xyz)^3$$

Problem 5.16 If a, b, c are sides of the triangle, then $\frac{ab + bc + ca}{a^2 + b^2 + c^2}$ can not greater than 1 or less than $\frac{1}{2}$.

Solution a, b, c are sides of the triangle then we have to prove that

$$\frac{1}{2} \leqslant \frac{ab + bc + ca}{a^2 + b^2 + c^2} \leqslant 1$$

we know that in a triangle

$$c^2 = a^2 + b^2 - 2ab \cos c$$

$$2ab \cos c = a^2 + b^2 - c^2$$

$$a^2 + b^2 - c^2 = 2ab \cos c$$

$$\Rightarrow a^2 + b^2 - c^2 \leqslant 2ab \qquad (1)$$

$$\text{since } |\cos c| \leqslant 1$$

similarly $\quad b^2 + c^2 - a^2 \leqslant 2bc \qquad (2)$

and $\quad a^2 + c^2 - b^2 \leqslant 2ca \qquad (3)$

Adding we have

$$a^2 + b^2 + c^2 \leqslant 2(ab + bc + ca)$$

$$\Rightarrow \frac{ab + bc + ca}{a^2 + b^2 + c^2} \geqslant \frac{1}{2} \qquad (4)$$

Again $\quad \frac{a^2 + b^2}{2} > (a^2 b^2)^{1/2}$

$$\frac{a^2 + b^2}{2} > ab$$

$$\Rightarrow a^2 + b^2 > 2ab \qquad (5)$$

similarly $b^2 + c^2 \geqslant 2bc$

and $c^2 + a^2 \geqslant 2ac$

Adding we have

$$2(a^2 + b^2 + c^2) \geqslant 2(ab + bc + ca)$$

$$(a^2 + b^2 + c^2) \geqslant ab + bc + ca$$

$$\frac{ab + bc + ca}{a^2 + b^2 + c^2} \leqslant 1$$

Thus $\frac{1}{2} \leqslant \frac{ab + bc + ca}{a^2 + b^2 + c^2} \leqslant 1$ *(proved)*

Problem 17 Prove that

$$6abc < a^2(1 + b^2) + b^2(1 + c^2) + c^2(1 + a^2)$$

Solution Consider the numbers

$$a^2, b^2, c^2, \; a^2 b^2, \; b^2 c^2, \; c^2 a^2$$

Arithmetic mean

$$AM = \frac{a^2 + b^2 + c^2 + a^2 b^2 + b^2 c^2 + c^2 a^2}{6}$$

Geometric mean

$$GM = [a^2 b^2 c^2 a^2 b^2 b^2 c^2 c^2 a^2)^{1/6} = [a^6 b^6 c^6]^{1/6} = abc$$

We know that $AM > GM$

$$\frac{a^2 + b^2 + c^2 + a^2 b^2 + b^2 c^2 + c^2 a^2}{6} > abc$$

$$a^2 + b^2 + c^2 + a^2 b^2 + b^2 c^2 + c^2 a^2 > 6abc$$

$$a^2(1 + b^2) + b^2(1 + c^2) + c^2(1 + a^2) > 6abc$$

$$\Rightarrow \quad 6abc < a^2(1 + b^2) + b^2(1 + c^2) + c^2(1 + a^2)$$

(proved)

Problem 18 If $s = a + b + c + d$ prove that

$$(s - a)(s - b)(s - c)(s - d) > 8/abcd$$

Solution

$$s - a = a + b + c + d - a = b + c + d$$

$$s - b = a + b + c + d - b = a + c + d$$

$$s - c = a + b + c + d - c = a + b + d$$

$$s - d = a + b + c + d - d = a + b + c$$

we have

$$\frac{b+c+d}{3} > (bcd)^{1/3}$$

$$b + c + d > 3\,(bcd)^{1/3} \qquad (1)$$

Again $\quad a + c + d > 3\,(acd)^{1/3} \qquad (2)$

$$a + b + d > 3\,(abd)^{1/3} \qquad (3)$$

$$a + b + c > 3\,(abc)^{1/3} \qquad (4)$$

Multiplying (1), (2), (3) and (4) we have

$$(s-a)(s-b)(s-c)(s-d) > 81\,(a^3 b^3 c^3 d^3)^{1/3}$$

$$(s-a)(s-b)(s-c)(s-d) > 81\,(abcd) \qquad \textit{(proved)}$$

Problem 18 If x, y, z are +ve and $x + y + z = 1$, prove that

$$\left(\frac{1}{x}-1\right)\left(\frac{1}{y}-1\right)\left(\frac{1}{z}-1\right) \geqslant 8$$

[*IFS 83*]

Solution

$$\frac{1}{x}-1 = \frac{1-x}{x} = \frac{y+z}{x} = \frac{y}{x}+\frac{z}{x} \geqslant 2\left(\frac{y}{x}\cdot\frac{z}{x}\right)^{1/2}$$

$$\frac{1}{y}-1 = \frac{1-y}{y} = \frac{x+z}{y} = \frac{x}{y}+\frac{z}{y} \geqslant 2\left(\frac{x}{y}\cdot\frac{z}{y}\right)^{1/2}$$

$$\frac{1}{z}-1 = \frac{1-z}{z} = \frac{x+y}{z} = \frac{x}{z}+\frac{y}{z} \geqslant 2\left(\frac{x}{z}\cdot\frac{y}{z}\right)^{1/2}$$

$$\left(\frac{1}{x}-1\right)\left(\frac{1}{y}-1\right)\left(\frac{1}{z}-1\right) \geqslant 8\left[\frac{xz}{x^2}\;\frac{xz}{y^2}\;\frac{xy}{z^2}\right]^{\frac{1}{2}}$$

$$\left(\frac{1}{x}-1\right)\left(\frac{1}{y}-1\right)\left(\frac{1}{z}-1\right) \geqslant 8 \qquad \textit{(proved)}$$

Problen 5.19 If $x + y + z = 1$ show that the least value of

$$\frac{1}{x}+\frac{1}{y}+\frac{1}{z} \text{ is 9 and that}$$

$$(1-x)(1-y)(1-z) > 8\,xyz$$

[*IAS 84*]

Solution We have $\quad x + y + z = 1$

$$1 - x = y + z > 2\sqrt{yz}$$

$$1 - y = x + z > 2\sqrt{xz}$$

$$1 - z = x + y > 2\sqrt{xy}$$

$$\Rightarrow \quad (1-x)(1-y)(1-z) > 8\,xyz \qquad \textit{(proved)}$$

Problem 20 If $x\, y$, z are three (+ ve) quantities prove that

$$(x+y+z)\left(\frac{1}{x}+\frac{1}{y}+\frac{1}{z}\right)>9$$

Problem 21 Prove that

$$\frac{2}{a+b}+\frac{2}{b+c}+\frac{2}{c+a}>\frac{9}{a+b+c}$$

Solution We have to prove that

$$\frac{2}{a+b}+\frac{2}{b+c}+\frac{2}{c+a}>\frac{9}{a+b+c}$$

i.e. to prove that

$$(a+b+c)\left(\frac{1}{a+b}+\frac{1}{b+c}+\frac{1}{c+b}\right)>\frac{9}{2} \quad (1)$$

Now since $AM > GM$

$$\frac{a+b+c}{3}>(abc)^{1/3}$$

i.e. $a+b+c>3\,(abc)^{1/3}$ (2)

and $$\frac{\frac{1}{a+b}+\frac{1}{b+c}+\frac{1}{c+a}}{3}>\left(\frac{a+b+b+c+c+a}{3}\right)^{-1}$$

because we have the in equality

$$\frac{\frac{1}{x}+\frac{1}{y}+\frac{1}{z}}{3}>\left(\frac{x+y+z}{3}\right)^{-1}$$

so $$\frac{1}{a+b}+\frac{1}{b+c}+\frac{1}{c+a}>3\left[\frac{2}{3}\;(a+b+c\right]^{-1}$$

$$\frac{1}{a+b}+\frac{1}{b+c}+\frac{1}{c+a}>\frac{9}{2}\,(a+b+c)$$

i.e. $$(a+b+c)\left[\frac{1}{a+b}+\frac{1}{b+c}+\frac{1}{c+a}\right]>\frac{9}{2}$$ *(Proved)*

Problem 22 $2\,(a^3+b^3+c^3)>bc\,(b+c)+ca\,(c+a)+ab\,(a+b)$

Solution Since $AM > GM$

$$\Rightarrow \frac{a^2+b^2}{2}>(a^2\,b^2)^{1/2}$$

$$\Rightarrow \frac{a^2+b^2}{2}>ab$$

$$\Rightarrow \quad a^2 + b^2 > 2ab$$

$$\Rightarrow \quad a^2 + b^2 - ab > ab$$

$$\Rightarrow \quad (a + b)(a^2 - ab + b^2) > ab(a + b)$$

$$\Rightarrow \quad a^3 + b^3 > ab(a + b) \qquad (1)$$

similarly we have

$$b^3 + c^3 > bc(b + c) \qquad (2)$$

$$a^3 + c^3 > ac(a + c) \qquad (3)$$

Adding (1), (2) and (3) we have

$$2(a^3 + b^3 + c^3) > ab(a + b) + bc(b + c) + ca(c + a) \qquad \textit{(Proved)}$$

Problem 23 Prove that

$$\frac{b + c}{a} + \frac{c + a}{b} + \frac{a + b}{c} > 6$$

Solution i.e. we have to prove that

$$bc(b + c) + ca(c + a) + ab(a + b) > 6abc$$

i.e. to prove

$$bc(b + c) + ca(c + a) + ab(a + b) - 6abc > 0$$

We have $bc(b + c) + ca(c + a) + ab(a + b) - 6abc$

$$= b^2c + bc^2 + c^2a + ca^2 + a^2b + ab^2 - 6abc$$

$$= b^2c + bc^2 + c^2a + ca^2 + a^2b + ab^2 - 2abc - 2abc - 2abc$$

$$= c(b^2 + a^2 - 2ab) + b(c^2 + a^2 - 2ac) + a(b^2 + c^2 - 2bc)$$

$$= c(b - a)^2 + b(c - a)^2 + a(b - c)^2 = + \text{ve quantity}$$

so $$\frac{b + c}{a} + \frac{c + a}{b} + \frac{a + b}{c} > 6 \qquad \textit{(Proved)}$$

Problem 24 Prove that

$$\left\{\frac{1}{3}(n + 1)\left(n + \frac{1}{2}\right)\right\}^{n/2} > n!$$

Solution Consider the numbers $1^2, 2^2, 3^2 \ldots n^2$

$$AM = \frac{1^2 + 2^2 + 3^2 + \ldots + n^2}{n}$$

$$GM = (1^2 \cdot 2^2 \cdot 3^2 \ldots n^2)^{1/n} = (1 \cdot 2 \ldots n)^{2/n} = (n!)^{2/n}$$

As we know that $AM > GM$

$$\frac{1^2 + 2^2 + 3^2 + \ldots + n^2}{n} > (n!)^{2/n}$$

$$\frac{n(n+1)(2n+1)}{6n} \geq (n!)^{2/n}$$

$$(n+1)\left(\frac{2n+1}{6}\right) > (n!)^{2/n}$$

$$(n+1)\left(\frac{n}{3}+\frac{1}{6}\right) > (n!)^{2/n}$$

$$(n+1)\frac{1}{3}\left(n+\frac{1}{2}\right) > (n!)^{2/n}$$

$$\Rightarrow \left[\frac{(n+1)(n+\frac{1}{2})}{3}\right]^{n/2} > n! \qquad \textit{(Proved)}$$

Problem 25 Prove that $(a_1+a_2+a_3+\ldots+a_n)\left(\frac{1}{a_1}+\frac{1}{a_2}+\ldots+\frac{1}{a_n}\right)>n^2$

Solution We have $\frac{a_1+a_2+\ldots+a_n}{n} > (a_1 a_2 \ldots a_n)^{1/n}$ (1)

$$\frac{\frac{1}{a_1}+\frac{1}{a_2}+\ldots+\frac{1}{a_n}}{n} > \left(\frac{1}{a_1 a_2 \ldots a_n}\right)^{1/n} \qquad (2)$$

Multiplying (1) and (2) we have

$$(a_1+a_2+\ldots+a_n)\left(\frac{1}{a_1}+\frac{1}{a_2}+\ldots+\frac{1}{a_n}\right) > n^2 \qquad \textit{(Proved)}$$

Problem 26 Prove that $\left(\frac{a\alpha+b\beta+c\gamma}{a+b+c}\right)^{a+b+c} > \alpha^a \beta^b \gamma^c$

Solution We consider quantities such as

$\alpha\ \alpha, \ldots a$ times

$\beta\ \beta \ldots b$ times

$\gamma\ \gamma \ldots c$ times

Their

$$AM = \frac{(\alpha+\alpha+\alpha\ldots a \text{ times})+(\beta+\beta+\ldots b \text{ times})+(\gamma+\gamma+\ldots c \text{ times})}{a+b+c}$$

$$AM = \frac{a\alpha+b\beta+c\gamma}{a+b+c} \qquad (1)$$

$$GM = \{\alpha^a \beta^b \gamma^c\}^{1/a+b+c}$$

$$AM > GM$$

$$\Rightarrow \frac{a\alpha+b\beta+c\gamma}{a+b+c} > [\alpha^a \beta^b \gamma^c]^{1/a+b+c}$$

$$\left[\frac{a\alpha+b\beta+c\gamma}{a+b+c}\right]^{a+b+c} > \alpha^\alpha \beta^b \gamma^c \qquad \textit{(Proved)}$$

Problem 27 Prove that

(i) $[(n-1)!]^2 > n^{n-2}$

(ii) $(n!)^2 > n^n$ if $1 < r < n$

Solution Since $1 < r < n$

$\Rightarrow (n-r) > 0, (r-1) > 0$

$\Rightarrow (n-r)(r-1) > 0$

$\Rightarrow nr - n - r^2 + r > 0$

$\Rightarrow nr - r^2 + r > n$

$\Rightarrow r(n-r+1) > n$

putting $r = 2, 3 \ldots (n-2)(n-1)$

i.e. $2(n-1) > n$

$3(n-2) > n$

$4(n-3) > n$

$\ldots \quad \ldots \quad \ldots$

$(n-2)\, 3 > n$

$(n-1)\, 2 > n$

Multiplying we get

$[2 \cdot 3 \cdot 4\, (n-1)]\, [(n-1)(n-2) \ldots 3 \cdot 2 \cdot 1] > n^{n-2}$

$(n-1)!\, (n-1)! > n^{n-2}$

$\Rightarrow [(n-1)!]^2 > n^{n-2}$ [*First Part Proved*]

$\Rightarrow n^2\,](n-1!)]^2 > n^n$

$\Rightarrow [n\,(n-1)!]^2 > n^n$

$\Rightarrow (n!)^2 > n^n!$ [*Second part proved*]

Problem 28 If $n > 2$

Prove that $(n!)^2 > n^n$ [IFS 86]

Solution Here $1 < r < n$

$r = 2 > 1$ and $n > 2$

i.e. $1 < 2 < n$

so the above relation $(n!)^2 > n^n$ is true

Problem 29 If a, b, c, are positive and the sum of any two is greater than the third, then prove that

$$\left[1 + \frac{b-c}{a}\right]^a \left[1 + \frac{c-a}{b}\right]^b \left[1 + \frac{a-b}{c}\right]^c < 1$$

Solution Let us consider the numbers

$$(\alpha - \alpha \ldots a \text{ times})\ (\beta \cdot \beta \ldots b \text{ times})\ (\gamma \cdot \gamma \ldots \text{times})$$

$$AM = \frac{(\alpha+\alpha+\ldots a \text{ times}) + (\beta+\beta \ldots \text{to } b \text{ times})+(\gamma+\gamma+\ldots c \text{ times})}{a+b+c}$$

$$AM = \frac{a\alpha + b\beta + c\gamma}{a+b+c}$$

$$GM = \{\alpha \cdot \alpha \ldots a \text{ times } \beta \cdot \beta \ldots b \text{ times } \gamma \cdot \gamma \ldots c \text{ times}\}^{1/a+b+c}$$

$$= [\alpha^a \beta^b \gamma^c]^{1/a+b+c}$$

As we know that $AM > GM$

$$\Rightarrow \frac{a\alpha + b\beta + c\gamma}{a+b+c} > [\alpha^a \beta^b \gamma^c]^{1/a+h+c}$$

i.e.
$$\left[\frac{a\alpha + b\beta + c\gamma}{a+b+c}\right]^{a+b+c} > \alpha^a \beta^b \gamma^c$$

i.e.
$$\alpha^a \beta^b \gamma^c < \left[\frac{a\alpha + b\beta + c\gamma}{a+b+c}\right]^{a+b+c}$$

let us put
$$\alpha = 1 + \frac{b-c}{a}$$

$$\alpha = \frac{a+b-c}{a}$$

$$a\alpha = a + b - c$$

since $a + b > c$

$\Rightarrow a + b - c > 0$

$\Rightarrow a\alpha > 0 \Rightarrow \alpha > 0$

similarly $\beta > 0$

and $\gamma > 0$

$$\beta = 1 + \frac{c-a}{b}$$

$$\beta = \frac{b+c-a}{b}$$

$$b\beta = b + c - a$$

and
$$\gamma = 1 + \frac{a-b}{c}$$

$$\gamma = \frac{c+a-b}{c}$$

$$\Rightarrow c\gamma = c + a - b$$

Then
$$\alpha^a \beta^b \gamma^c < \left[\frac{a+b-c+b+c-a+c+a-b}{a+b+c}\right]^{a+h+c}$$

$$= (1)^{a+b+c} = 1$$

i.e.
$$\alpha^a \beta^b \gamma^c < 1$$

Therefore
$$\left[1 + \frac{b-c}{a}\right]^a \left[1 + \frac{c-a}{b}\right]^b \left[1 + \frac{a-b}{c}\right]^c < 1 \quad \textit{(Proved)}$$

Problem 30 Prove that

$$\frac{b^4 + c^4}{b + c} + \frac{c^4 + a^4}{c + a} + \frac{a^4 + b^4}{ab} > 3abc$$

Solution We have

$$\frac{b^4 + c^4}{2} > \left(\frac{b + c}{2}\right)^4 = \left(\frac{b + c}{2}\right)\left(\frac{b + c}{2}\right)^3$$

i.e. $$\frac{b^4 + c^4}{b + c} > \left(\frac{b + c}{2}\right)^3$$

but since $$AM > GM$$

so $$\frac{b + c}{2} > \sqrt{bc}$$

i.e. $$\frac{b^4 + c^4}{b + c} > (\sqrt{bc})^3 \qquad (1)$$

similarly $$\frac{c^4 + a^4}{c + a} > (\sqrt{ca})^3 \qquad (2)$$

and $$\frac{a^4 + b^4}{a + b} > (\sqrt{ab})^3 \qquad (3)$$

$$\Rightarrow \frac{b^4 + c^4}{b + c} + \frac{c^4 + a^4}{c + a} + \frac{a^4 + b^4}{a + b} > (\sqrt{bc^3}) + (\sqrt{ca})^3 + (\sqrt{ab})^3$$

$$\frac{b^4 + c^4}{b + c} + \frac{c^4 + a^4}{c + a} + \frac{a^4 + b^4}{a + b} > 3\{(bc)^{3/2}(ca)^{3/2}(ab)^{3/2}\}^{1/3} = 3abc$$

i.e. $$\frac{b^4 + c^4}{b + c} + \frac{c^4 + a^4}{c + a} + \frac{a^4 + b^4}{a + b} > 3abc \qquad \textit{(Proved)}$$

Problem 31 For any real $x \neq 0$, prove that

$$\left|x + \frac{1}{x}\right| \geqslant 2$$

or $$\left|\frac{1 + x^2}{2x}\right| \geqslant 1$$

Solution since both sides of the inequality are positive

so $\left|x + \frac{1}{x}\right| \geqslant 2$ is equivalent to

$$\left|x + \frac{1}{x}\right|^2 \geqslant 4$$

i.e. $$\left(x + \frac{1}{x}\right)^2 \geqslant 4$$

i.e. $$x^2 + \frac{1}{x^2} + 2 \geqslant 4$$

$$\Rightarrow x^2 + \frac{1}{x^2} - 2 \geqslant 0$$

i.e. $$\left(x - \frac{1}{x}\right)^2 \geqslant 0$$

which is true for $x \neq 0$

Problem 32 For all $x > 0$, prove that $x + \frac{1}{x} \geqslant 2$

Solution Let us consider two numbers x and $\frac{1}{x}$

$$AM \text{ of } x \text{ and } \frac{1}{x} = \frac{1}{2}\left(x + \frac{1}{x}\right)$$

$$GM \text{ of } x \text{ and } \frac{1}{x} = \left(x \cdot \frac{1}{x}\right)^{1/2} = 1$$

Therefore $$AM \geqslant GM$$

$$\Rightarrow \frac{1}{2}\left(x + \frac{1}{x}\right) \geqslant 1$$

$$\Rightarrow x + \frac{1}{x} \geqslant 2$$ *(Proved)*

Problem 32 For $a > 0$, $b > 0$, $c > 0$ prove that

(i) $(a + b)(b + c)(c + a) \geqslant 8\,abc$

(ii) $\frac{bc}{a} + \frac{ca}{b} + \frac{ab}{c} \geqslant a + b + c$

Solution We have $\frac{a + b}{2} \geqslant (ab)^{1/2}$

$$\frac{a + b}{2} \geqslant \sqrt{ba}$$

$$a + b \geqslant 2\sqrt{ab} \quad (1)$$

similarly $$b + c \geqslant 2\sqrt{bc} \quad (2)$$

$$c + a \geqslant 2\sqrt{ac} \quad (3)$$

Multiplying (1), (2) and (3) we have

$$(a + b)(b + c) + c + a) \geqslant 8\,abc$$ *(Proved)*

(Ii) Use $AM \geqslant GM$ in pairs

Problem 33 Show for any triangle with sides a, b and c

$$3(ab + bc + ca) \leqslant (a + b + c)^2 < 4(bc + ca + ab)$$

Solution Let a, b, c are three sides of a triangle let us suppose without loss of any generally $a > 0, b > 0, c > 0$

and $a \geqslant b \geqslant c$

We know that in a triangle, difference of two sides is less than the third side i.e. $a - b < c$

$$\Rightarrow (a - b)^2 < c^2$$

$$\Rightarrow a^2 - 2ab + b^2 < c^2$$

$$\Rightarrow a^2 + b^2 - c^2 < 2ab$$

similarly $b^2 + c^2 - a^2 < 2bc$

$$a^2 + c^2 - b^2 < 2ac$$

Adding all the above in equality we have

$$a^2 + b^2 + c^2 < 2(ab + bc + ca)$$

adding $2(ab + bc + ca)$ on both sides we have

$$(a + b + c)^2 < 4(ab + bc + ca) \tag{1}$$

Again $(a - b)^2 > 0$

$$a^2 - 2ab + b^2 > 0$$

$$\Rightarrow a^2 + b^2 > 2ab$$

similarly $b^2 + c^2 > 2bc$

$$c^2 + a^2 > 2ca$$

Adding we have $2(a^2 + b^2 + c^2) > 2(ab + bc + ca)$

$$a^2 + b^2 + c^2 > ab + bc + ca$$

Adding both sides $2ab$, $2bc$, $2ac$

$$(a + b + c)^2 > 3(ab + bc + ca) \tag{2}$$

From in equalities (1) and (2) wc have

$$3(ab + bc + ca) < (a + b + c)^2 < 4(ab + bc + ca) \quad \textit{(Proved)}$$

Problem 34 If $x^2 + y^2 = 1$, prove $-\sqrt{2} \leqslant x + y \leqslant \sqrt{2}$

Solution Let us suppose that $x > y$

$$\Rightarrow x - y > 0$$

$$(x - y)^2 > 0$$

$$x^2 + y^2 - 2xy > 0$$

$$x^2 + y^2 \geqslant 2xy$$

$$\Rightarrow x^2 + y^2 + x^2 + y^2 > x^2 + y^2 + 2xy$$
$$\Rightarrow 2(x^2 + y^2) > (x + y)^2$$

i.e. $(x + y)^2 < 2(x^2 + y^2)$

i.e. $(x + y)^2 < 2 \cdot 1$ i.e. $|x + y| \leqslant \sqrt{2}$

$\Rightarrow (x + y)^2 < 2$ i.e $-\sqrt{2} \leqslant (x + y(\leqslant \sqrt{2}$

Problem 35 If x, y, z are all positive and $x < y < z$, show that

$$\frac{x^2}{z} < \frac{x^2 + y^2 + z^2}{x + y + z} < \frac{z^2}{x}$$

Solution $x > 0, y > 0$ and $z \geqslant 0$

$$x < y < z$$
$$\Rightarrow x^2 < y^2 < z^2$$
$$3x^2 < x^2 + y^2 + z^2 < 3z^2 \qquad (1)$$

Again $x < y < z$

$$\Rightarrow 3x < x + y + z < 3z$$
$$\Rightarrow \frac{1}{3x} \geqslant \frac{1}{x + y + z} \geqslant \frac{1}{3z}$$
$$\Rightarrow \frac{1}{3z} < \frac{1}{x + y + z} < \frac{1}{3x} \qquad (2)$$

Multiplying the inequalities (1) and (2) we have

$$\frac{x^2}{z} < \frac{x^2 + y^2 + z^2}{x + y + z} < \frac{z^2}{x} \qquad \textit{(Proved)}$$

Problem 36 If a, b, c are real numbers such that $a^2 + b^2 + c^2 = 1$ show that $ab + bc + ca \geqslant -\frac{1}{2}$.

Solution a, b, c are real numbers then $(a + b + c)^2 \geqslant c$

$$a^2 + b^2 + c^2 + 2ab + 2bc + 2ca > 0$$
$$2(ab + bc + ca) > (a^2 + b^2 + c^2)$$
$$ab + bc + ca \geqslant -\tfrac{1}{2} \qquad \textit{(Proved)}$$

Problem 37 It $a^2 + b^2 = 1$

$m^2 + n^2 = 1$ prove that

$|am + bn| \leqslant 1$.

Solution Since $a^2 + b^2 = 1$we can find an angle α such that

$$a = \alpha, b = \sin\alpha$$

Similarly we can find an angle β such that

$$m = \cos\beta, n = \sin\beta$$

we then have

$$|am + bn| = |\cos\alpha \cdot \cos\beta + \sin\alpha \cdot \sin\beta| = |\cos(\alpha - \beta)| \leqslant 1$$

Problem 38 If $x > 0, y > 0, z > 0$ prove that

(i) $(x + y + z)^3 \geqslant 27\ (y + z - x)(z + x - y)(x + y - z)$

(ii) $xyz \geqslant (y + z - x)(z + x - y)(x + y - z)$

Solution Consider that $y + z - x = a,\ z + x - y = b,\ x + y - z = c$

Then $a + b = 2z,\ b + c = 2x,\ c + a = 2y$

$$2(a + b + c) = 2(x + y + z)$$

$$\Rightarrow a + b + c = x + y + z$$

$$AM \text{ of } a, b, c = \frac{a + b + c}{3}$$

GM of $(abc)^{1/3}$

Since $AM \geqslant GM$

$$\Rightarrow \frac{a + b + c}{3} \geqslant (abc)^{1/3}$$

$$\Rightarrow \left(\frac{a + b + c}{3}\right)^3 \geqslant abc$$

$$\Rightarrow (a + b + c)^3 \geqslant 27\ abc$$

$$\Rightarrow (x + y + z)^3 \geqslant 27\ (y + z - x)(z + x - y)(x + y - z)\ [F.P.P.]$$

Again $\dfrac{b + c}{2} \geqslant (bc)^{1/2}$

$$\frac{c + a}{2} \geqslant (ca)^{1/2}$$

$$\frac{a + b}{2} \geqslant (ab)^{1/2}$$

Multiplying we have

$$(b + c)(c + a)(a + b) \geqslant 8\ abc$$

$$2x \cdot 2y \cdot 2z \geqslant 8\ abc$$

$$8xyz \geqslant 8\ (y + z - x)(z + x - y)(x + y - z)$$

i.e. $xyz \geqslant (y + z - x)(z + x - y)(x + y - z)$ *(Proved)*

Problem 39 If $x_i > 0\ (i = 1, 2 \ldots n)$ and $x_1 x_2 x_3 \ldots x_n = 1$ *(Proved)*

$$x_1 + x_2 + x_3 + \ldots + x_n \geqslant n$$

Solution Let us consider n numbers $x_1\ x_2\ x_3 \ldots x_n$

Then $AM = \dfrac{x_1 + x_2 + x_3 + \ldots + x_n}{n}$

$$GM = [x_1\, x_2\, x_3 \ldots x_n]^{1/n}$$

since
$$AM \geqslant GM$$

$$\frac{x_1 + x_2 + x_3 + \ldots + x_n}{n} \geqslant [x_1\, x_2\, x_3 \ldots x_n]^{1/n}$$

$$\Rightarrow x_1 + x_2 + x_3 + \ldots + x_n \geqslant n \qquad \textit{(proved)}$$

Problem 40 If a, b, c are in HP and $n >_1$ show that $a^n + c^n > 2b^n$.

Solution a, b. c are in Harmonical progression then b is the Harmonic mean of a and c

$$GM \text{ of } a, c = \sqrt{a\,c}$$

$$GM > HM$$

$$\Rightarrow \sqrt{a\,c} > b \qquad (1)$$

Let us consider the numbers a^n and c^n we have

$$AM \text{ of } a^n \text{ and } c^n = \frac{a^n + c^n}{2}$$

$$GM \text{ of } a^n \text{ and } c^n = (a^n\, c^n)^{1/n}$$

Then since $AM > GM$

$$\Rightarrow \frac{a^n + c^n}{2} > (a^n\, c^n)^{1/2}$$

$$\Rightarrow \frac{a^n + c^n}{2} > (\sqrt{a\,c})^n \qquad (2)$$

From (1) and (2) we have

$$\frac{a^n + c^n}{2} > b^n$$

$$\Rightarrow a^n + c^n > 2b^n \qquad \textit{(proved)}$$

6

Complex Number, Algebra of Complex Number

Complex Numbers

Definition. A complex number may be defined as an ordered pair of real numbers and may be denoted by tne symbol (x, y). If we write $z = (x, y)$. then x is called the real part and y the imaginary part of the complex number z and may be denoted by $R(z)$ and $I(z)$ respectively.

It is clear from the definition that the two complex numbers (x, y) and (x^1, y^1) are equal if and only if $x = x^1$ and $y = y^1$ we shall denote the set of all complex numbers by the letter C.

Sum of two complex numbers

The sum of two complex numbers (x, y) and (x^1, y^1) is defined by the equality

$$(x, y) + (^1, y^1) = (x + x^1, y + y^1)$$

Product of two complex numbers

The product is defined by the equality

$$(x, x)(x^1\ y^1) = (xx^1 - yy^1\ xy^1 + yx^1)$$

The complex number $z = (x_1\ y)$ is also denoted by $x + y$ where i is the square root of real number. We denote the complex number i by the symbol (0, 1) with this notation

$$1^2 = (0, 1)(0, 1) = (00 - 1\cdot 1, 0\cdot 1 + 1\cdot 0)$$
$$= (-1, 0) = -1 + i\,0 = -1$$

Remark

$$\therefore \qquad i = \sqrt{-1} \text{ and } i^2 = -1 \text{ we have}$$

$$(\sqrt{-1})^2 = \sqrt{-1} \times \sqrt{-1} = -1$$

$$\sqrt{-a} \times \sqrt{-b} = \sqrt{a}\, i^2 \times \sqrt{b}\, i^2 = \sqrt{a}\, i \times \sqrt{b}\, i.$$
$$= \sqrt{ab}\, i^2 = -\sqrt{ab}$$

Thus $\sqrt{-a} \times \sqrt{-b} = -\sqrt{ab}$

since $\sqrt{-a} = \sqrt{ai^2}$ so apure imaginary $= \sqrt{a}i$ number can be expressed as the product of i and a real number.

Difference of two complex numbers

The difference of two complex numbers $z=(x, y)$ and $z^1=(x^1, y^1)$ is defined by the equality

$$z - z^1 = (x, y) - (x^1, y^1) = (x. y) + (-x^1, -y^1)$$
$$z - z^1 = (x - x^1, y - y^1)$$

Division It is defined by the equality $\frac{z}{z^1} = z\ (z^1)^{-1}$ provided $z^1 \neq 0$ we have $\frac{z}{z^1} = (x, y)\ (x^1, y^1)^{-1}$

$$= (x, y) \left(\frac{x^1}{x'^2 + y'^2}, -\frac{y^1}{x'^2 + y'^2}\right)$$

$$= \left(\frac{xx' + yy'}{x'^2 + y'^2}, \frac{yx' - xy'}{x'^2 + y'^2}\right)$$

provided $\quad x'^2 + y'^2 \neq 4$

Modulus and argument of a complex number

Let $z = x + iy$ be any complex number. If $x = r \cos \theta$, $y = r \sin \theta$, then $r = +\sqrt{x^2 + y^2}$ s called the modulus of the complex number z written as $|z|$ and $\theta = \tan^{-1} \frac{y}{x}$ is called the argument or amplitude of z written as arg (z).

It follows that
$$|z| = 0 \text{ iff } \sqrt{x^2 + y^2} = 0$$
$$\text{iff } \quad x^2 + y^2 = 0$$
$$\text{iff } \quad x = 0 \quad \text{and} \quad y = 0$$

Again
$$|z| = \sqrt{x^2 + y^2}$$
$$= \sqrt{(x-0)^2 + (y-0)^2}$$

Geometrically, $|z|$ is the distance of the point z from the origin i.e. from (x, y) from $(0, 0)$.

It can be easily proved that

$$|z|^2 = |z| \qquad R^e(z) \leqslant |z|$$
$$I^m(z) \leqslant |z|$$

Argument of a complex number is not unique, since if θ be a value of the argument so also is $2n\pi + \theta$, where $n = 0, \pm 1, \pm 2 \ldots$ The value of the argument which satisfies the inequality.

$-\pi < \theta \leqslant \pi$ is called the principal value of the argument. We remark that the argument of 0 is not defined.

Remark. It is evident from the definitions of difference and modulus that $|z_1 - z_2|$ is the distance between the points z_1 and z_2

Because if

$$z_1 = x_1 + iy_1$$

$$z_2 = x_2 + iy_2$$

$$z_1 - z_2 = (x_1 - x_2) + i(y_1 - y_2)$$

$$|(z_1 - z_2| = |(x_1 - x_2) + i(y_1 - y_2)|$$

$$= \sqrt{(x_1 - x_2)^2 + (y_1 - y_2)^2}$$

If follows that for fixed complex number z_0 and real number r, the equation $|z - z_0| = r$ represents aeircle with contre z_0 and radius r.

Polar from of a complex number

If r is the modulus and θ, the argument of a complex number z, then

$$z = r\cos\theta + ir\sin\theta$$

$$z - r(\cos\theta + i\sin\theta)$$

which is the polar from or trigonometrical form of z.

Since $e^{i\theta} = \cos\theta + i\sin\theta$ we can write $z = re^{i\theta}$. This is known as the exponential form of z.

The geometrical rcprcsentation of complex numbers

We represent the complex number $z = x + iy$ by apoint P whose cartesian co-ordinates are $(x_1\ y)$ referred to rectangular axes OX and OY, usually called *real* and *imaginary* axes respectively clearly the polar co-ordinates of P are $(r_1\ \theta)$ where r is the modulus and θ the argument of complex number z. The plane whose points are represented by complex numbers is called Argand plane or Argand diagram.

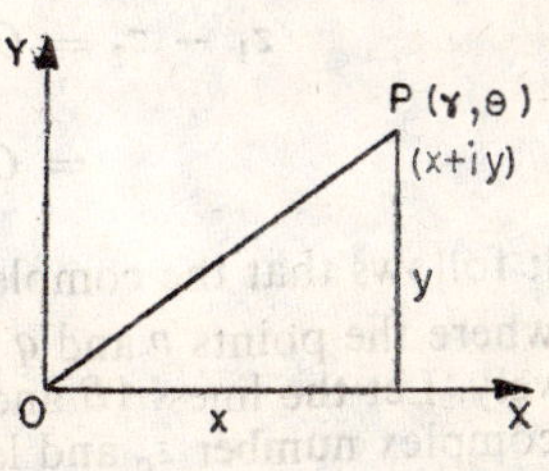

It is also called Complex plane or Gaussian plane. The Complex number z is known as the offix of the point $(x_1\ y)$ which represents if.

Vector representation of complex numbers

If P is the point $(x_1\ y)$ on the Argand plane Corresponding to the complex number $z = x + iy$ referred to Ox and OY as co-ordinate axes, the modulus and argument of z are represented by the magnitude and direction of the vector $\overrightarrow{OP}$ respectively and *vice-versa*.

The points on the Argand plane representing the sum and difference, of two complex numbers

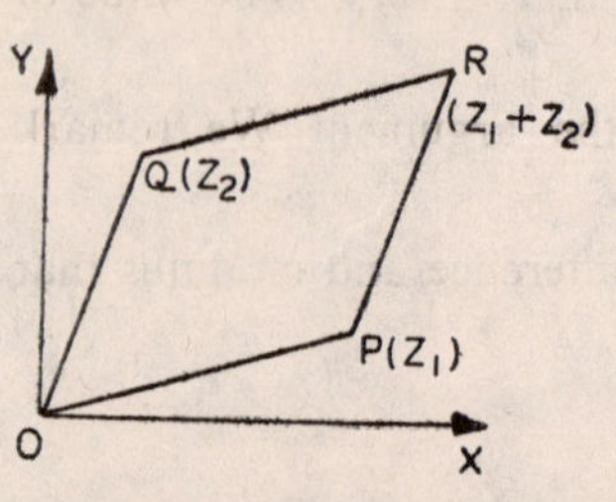

Sum. Let the complex numbers z_1 and z_2 be represented by the points P and Q on the Argand plane.

Complete the parallelogram $OPRQ$. Then the mid points of PQ and OR are the same. But mid point of PQ is

$$\left(\frac{x_1 + x_2}{2}, \frac{y_1 + y_2}{2}\right)$$

so the co-ordinates of R are $(x_1 + x_2, y_1 + y_2)$. Thus the point R corresponds to the sum of complex numbers z_1 and z_2. In vector addition we have

$$z_1 + z_2 = \overrightarrow{OP} + \overrightarrow{OQ} \quad = \overrightarrow{OP} + \overrightarrow{PR} = \overrightarrow{OR}$$

Difference

We first represent $-z_2$ by Q^1 so that QQ^1 is bisceted at O. Complete the parallclogram $OPRQ^1$. Then the point R represent the complex number $z_1 - z_2$ since the mid point of PQ^1 and OR the same.

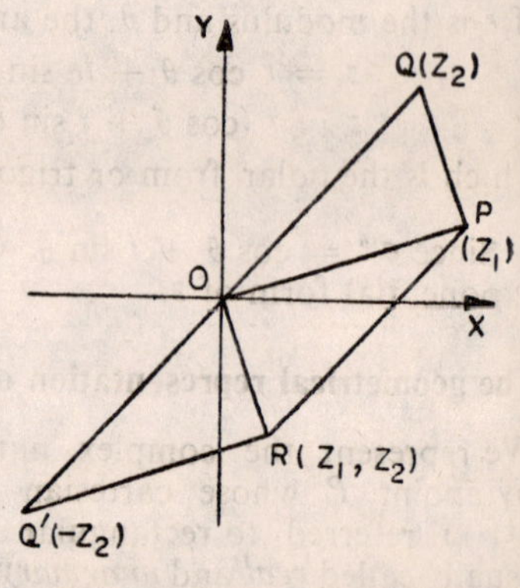

As OQ is equal and parallel to RP, we see that $ORPQ$ is a parallelogram, so that

$$\overrightarrow{OR} = \overrightarrow{QP}$$

Thus we have in vectorial notatian

$$z_1 - z_2 = \overrightarrow{OP} - \overrightarrow{OQ}$$

$$= \overrightarrow{OP} + \overrightarrow{QO}$$

It follows that the complex number $z_1 - z_2$ is represented by vector $\overrightarrow{QP}$ where the points p and q represent the complex numbers z_1 and z_2 respectively. Let the lines AB and CD interest at the point PO represented by the complex number z_0 and let p_1, p_2 be any two points on AB and CD represented by z_1 and z_2 respectively. Then the angle θ between the lines is given by

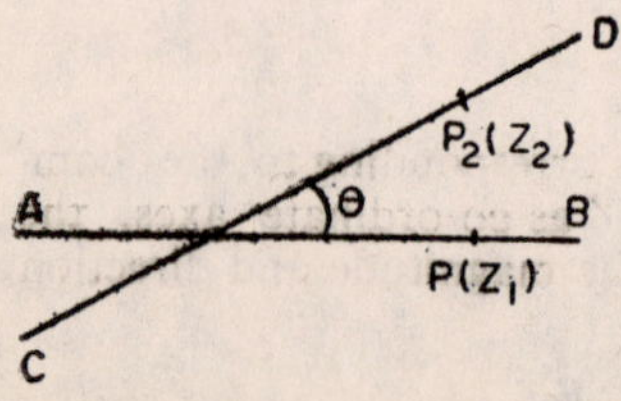

$$\theta = \arg(z_2 - z_0) - \arg(z_1 - z_0)$$

$$= \arg\left(\frac{z_2 - z_0}{z_1 - z_0}\right)$$

Here only principal values of the arguments are considered.

Conjugate Complex numbers :

If $z = x + i\,y$, then the complex number $x - i\,y$ is called the conjugate of the complex numbers z and is written as $\bar{z}$.

Conjugate of $z_1 + z_2$ and $z_1\,z_2$

Let $z_1 = x_1 + i\,y_1$

$z_2 = x_2 + i\,y_2$ be any two complex numbers. Let

$\bar{z}_1 = x_1 - i\,y_1$

and $\bar{z}_2 = x_2 - i\,y_2$ be the conjugates of z_1 and z_2 respectively.

Then $z_1 + z_2$ repsesents the sum of two complex numbers z_1 and z_2

$$\overline{(z_1 + z_2)} = \overline{[(x_1 + i\,y_1) + (x_2 + iy_2)]}$$
$$= \overline{(x_1 + x_2) + i\,(y_1 + y_2)}$$
$$= \overline{x + i\,y} = x - i\,y$$

where $x = x_1 + x_2 \quad y = y_1 + y_2$

$$\overline{(z_1 + z_2)} = x - i\,y$$
$$= (x_1 + x_2) - i\,(y_1 + y_2)$$
$$= (x_1 - i\,y_1) + (x_2 - i\,y_2)$$
$$\overline{(z_1 + z_2)} = \bar{z}_1 + \bar{z}_2$$ [*Important Note*]

Again we have

$$\overline{(z_1\,z_2)} = \overline{[x_1 + i\,y_1)\,(x_2 + i\,y_2)]}$$
$$= \overline{(x_1\,x_2 - y_1\,y_2) + i\,(x_1\,y_2 + x_2\,y_1)}$$
$$= (x_1\,x_2 - y_1\,y_2) - i\,(x_1\,y_2 + x_2\,y_1)$$
$$= (x_1 - i\,y_1)\,(x_2 - i\,y_2)$$
$$= \overline{x_1 + iy_1)}\ \overline{x_2 + i\,y_2} = \bar{z}_1\,\bar{z}_2$$
$$\overline{z_1\,z_2} = \bar{z}_1\,\bar{z}_2$$ [*Important Note*]

Q. Prove that

(i) $|z|^2 = z\bar{z}$

(ii) $2R\,(z) = z + \bar{z}$

(iii) $2\,i\,I\,(z) = z - \bar{z}$

Let (i) $z = x + i\,y \qquad \bar{z} = x - i\,y$

$$z\bar{z} = (x + i\,y)\,(x - i\,y) = x^2 - i^2\,y^2 = x^2 + y^2$$
$$= (\sqrt{x^2 + y^2})^2 = (|z|)^2 = |z|^2$$

i.e. so $|z|^2 = z\bar{z}$

(ii) $z + \bar{z} = (x + i\,y) + (x - i\,y) = 2x = 2R(z)$

i.e. $2R(z) = z + \bar{z}$

(iii) $z - \bar{z}$

$$(x + i\,y) - (x - i\,y) = x + i\,y - x + i\,y$$
$$= 2\,i\,y = 2\,i\,I(z)$$

i.e. $2\,i\,I(z) = z - \bar{z}$ (*proved*)

Q. Prove that (i) $|\bar{z}| = |z|$

(ii) $\overline{(\bar{z})} = z$

Let $z = x + i\,y$ $\quad |z| = \sqrt{x^2 + y^2}$

$\bar{z} = x - i\,y$ $\quad \bar{z} = \sqrt{x^2 + (-y)^2} = \sqrt{x^2 + y^2}$

Thus $|\bar{z}| = |z|$

(ii) $|\bar{z}| = \overline{(x - iy)} = \overline{x + i\,(-y)}$

$$= x - i\,(-y) = x + iy = z$$

Thus $\overline{(\bar{z})} = z$

Q. Prove that amp $(z) = -$amp $(\bar{z})$

Let $z = x + iy$ $\quad \bar{z} = x - iy$

$$\arg z = \tan^{-1}\frac{y}{x} \qquad \arg(\bar{z}) = \tan^{-1}\left(-\frac{y}{x}\right)$$

$RHS = -\text{amp}\,(\bar{z})$

$$= -\tan^{-1}\left(-\frac{y}{x}\right) = \tan^{-1}\left(\frac{y}{x}\right) = \text{amp}\ (z)$$

Thus amp (z) $= -$amp $(\bar{z})$

Properties of moduli

Theorem 1 The modulus of the sum of two complex numbers can never exceed the sum of their moduli. or

prove that $|z_1 + z_2| \leqslant |z_1| + |z_2|$

Proof. We have $|z_1 + z_2|^2 = (z_1 + z^2)\,\overline{(z_1 + z_2)} = (z_1 + z_2)\,(\bar{z}_1 + z_2)$

$$= z_1\,\bar{z}_1 + z_1\,\bar{z}_2 + z_2\bar{z}_1 + z_2\,\bar{z}_2$$
$$= z_1\,\bar{z}_1 + z_2\,\bar{z}_2 + (z_1\,\bar{z}_2 + z_2\,\bar{z}_1$$
$$= |z_1|^2 + |z_2|^2 + (z_1\,\bar{z}_2 + z_2\,\bar{z}_1)$$

Let $z_2 = x_1 + iy_1 \qquad \bar{z}_1 = x_1 - iy_1$

$z_2 = x_2 + iy_2 \qquad \bar{z}_2 = x_2 - iy_2$

Now $z_1\,\bar{z}_2 + z_2\bar{z}_1 = (x_1 + iy_1)\,(x_2 - iy_2) + (x_2 + iy_2)\,(x_1 - iy_1)$

$$= x_1\,x_2 - ix_1\,y_2 + ix_2\,y_1 - i^2\,y_1\,y_2$$
$$+ x_1\,x_2 - i\,x_2\,y_1 + i\,y_2\,x_1 - i^2\,y_1 y_2$$
$$= 2x_1\,x_2 + 2y_1\,y_2 = 2\,(x_1\,x_2 + y_1\,y_2)$$

$$z_1 \bar{z}_2 = (x_1 + iy_1)\overline{(x_2 + iy_2)} = (x_1 + iy_1)(x_2 - iy_2)$$
$$= (x_1 x_2 + y_1 y_2) - ix_1 y_2 + ix_2 y_1$$
$$= (x_1 x_2 + y_1 y_2) - i(x_1 y_2 - x_2 y_1)$$
$$2R(z_1 \bar{z}_2) = 2(x_1 x_2 + y_1 y_2)$$

Thus $|z_1 + z_2|^2 = |z_1|^2 + |z_2|^2 + 2R(z_1 \bar{z}_2)$

since $R(z) \leqslant |z|$

$$\Rightarrow R(z_1 \bar{z}_2) \leqslant |z_1 \bar{z}_2|$$
$$\Rightarrow 2R(z_1 \bar{z}_2) \leqslant 2|z_1 \bar{z}_2|$$

Thus $|z_1 + z_2|^2 \leqslant |z_1|^2 + |z_2|^2 + 2|z_1 \bar{z}_2|$

$$= |z_1|^2 + |z_2|^2 + 2|z_1||\bar{z}_2|$$
$$= |z_1|^2 + |z_2|^2 + 2|z_1||z_2|$$

because $|z| = |\bar{z}|$

$$= (|z_1| + |z_2|)^2$$

Thus $|z_1 + z_2|^2 \leqslant (|z_1| + |z_2|)^2$

i.e. $|z_1 + z_2| \leqslant |z_1| + |z_2|$

which shows that the modulus of the sum of two complex numbers can never exceed the sum of their moduli.

Problem 2 Prove that If z_1 and z_2 are two complex numbers then

$$|z_1 + z_2|^2 + |z_1 - z_2|^2 = 2(|z_1|^2 + |z_1|^2)$$ *[IFS 88]*

Solution At first prove $|z_1 + z_2|^2 = |z_1|^2 + |z_2|^2 + 2R(z_1 \bar{z}_2)$

$$|z_1 - z_2|^2 = |z_1|^2 + |z_2|^2 - 2R(z_1 \bar{z}_2)$$

then add them

We have $|z_1 + z_2|^2 = (z_1 + z_2)\overline{(z_1 + z_2)} = (z_1 + z_2)(\bar{z}_1 + \bar{z}_2)$

$$= z_1 \bar{z}_1 + z_1 \bar{z}_2 + z_2 \bar{z}_1 + z_2 \bar{z}_2$$
$$|z_1 + z_2|^2 = |z_1|^2 + |z_2|^2 + z_1 \bar{z}_2 + z_2 \bar{z}_1$$

let $z_1 = x_1 + iy_1,\ \bar{z}_1 = x_1 - iy_1$

$$z_2 = x_2 + iy_2\ \ \bar{z}_2 = x_2 - iy_2$$
$$z_1 \bar{z}_2 = (x_1 + iy_1)(x_2 - iy_2)$$
$$= x_1 x_2 - ix_1 y_2 + iy_1 x_2 - i^2 y_1 y_2$$
$$= (x_1 x_2 + y_1 y_2) + i(x_2 y_1 - x_1 y_2)$$
$$z_2 \bar{z}_1 = (x_2 + iy_2)(x_1 - iy_1)$$
$$= x_2 x_1 - ix_2 y_1 + iy_2 x_1 - i^2 y_1 y_2$$
$$= (x_1 x_2 + y_1 y_2) - i(x_2 y_2 - x_1 y_2)$$

Now we have $z_1 \bar{z}_2 + z_2 \bar{z}_1 = 2(x_1 x_2 + y_1 y_2)$

Again $\quad Re(z_1 \bar{z}_2) = Re\,(x_1 + iy_1)(x_2 - iy_2)]$

$$= Re\,[(x_1 x_2 + y_1 y_2) + i(x_2 y_1 - x_1 y_2)]$$

$$= x_1 x_2 + y_1 y_2$$

so $\quad 2(x_1 x_2 + y_1 y_2) = 2Re\,(z_1 \bar{z}_2)$

Thus $\quad |z_1 + z_2|^2 = |z_1|^2 + |z_2|^2 + 2Re\,(z_1 \bar{z}) \qquad (1)$

since $\quad Re\,(z) \leqslant |z|$

so $\quad Re\,(z_1 \bar{z}_2) \leqslant |z_1 \bar{z}_2| = |z_1| |\bar{z}_2| = |z_1| |z_2|$

$$|z_1 + z_2|^2 \leqslant |z_1|^2 + |z_2|^2 + 2|z_1| |z_2| = (|z_1| + |z_2|)^2$$

$$|z_1 + z_2|^2 \leqslant (|z_1| + |z_2|)^2$$

i.e. $\quad |z_1 + z_2| \leqslant |z_1| + |z_2|$

so similarly we have

$$|z_1 - z_2|^2 = (z_1 - z_2)\overline{(z_1 - z_2)} \qquad \Big| \; \overline{(z_1 - z_2)} = \bar{z}_1 - \bar{z}_2$$

$$= (z_1 - z_2)(\bar{z}_1 - \bar{z}_2)$$

$$= z_1 \bar{z}_1 + z_2 \bar{z}_2 - (z_2 \bar{z}_1 + z_1 \bar{z}_2)$$

$$= |z_1|^2 + |z_2|^2 - 2Re\,(z_1 \bar{z}_2) \qquad (2)$$

Adding equation (1) and (2) we have

$$|z_1 + z_2|^2 + |z_1 - z_2|^2 = 2|z_1|^2 + 2|z_2|^2 = 2(|z_1|^2 + |z_2|^2)$$

So for any two complex numbers z_1 and z_2

$$|z_1 + z_2|^2 + |z_1 - z_2|^2 = 2(|z_1|^2 + |z_2|^2) \qquad \textit{(Proved)}$$

Theorem 3 If z_1 and z_2 be two complex numbers, then show that

$$\arg(z_1 z_2) = \arg z_1 + \arg z_2$$

Proof $\quad$ Let $z_1 = x_1 + iy_1 \qquad z_2 = x_2 + iy_2$

$x_1 = r_1 \cos\theta_1 \qquad y_1 = r_1 \sin\theta_1$

$x_2 = r_2 \cos\theta_2 \qquad y_2 = r_2 \sin\theta_2$

$z_1 = r_1(\cos\theta_1 + i\sin\theta_1)$

$z_1 = r_1 e^{i\theta 1}$ similarly $z_2 = r_2 e^{i\theta 2}$

where r_1 and r_2 are the modulus of z_1 and z_2 respectively and θ_1 and θ_2 are the argument of z_1 and z_2 respectively

$$\theta_1 = \arg(z_1) \qquad \theta_2 = \arg(z_2)$$

$$z_1 z_2 = r_1 e^{i\theta 1} r_2 \; e^{i\theta 2} = r_1 r_2 e^{i(\theta_1 + \theta_2)}$$

Thus $\quad \arg(z_1 z_2) = \theta_1 + \theta_2$

$$\arg(z_1 z_2) = \arg z_1 + \arg z_2 \qquad \textit{(Proved)}$$

heorem 4 Prove that

$$\arg\left(\frac{z_1}{z_2}\right) = \arg z_1 - \arg z_2$$

vhere the symbols have their usual meaning

$$z_1 = r_1\, e^{i\theta_1} \qquad z_2 = r_2\, e^{i\theta_2}$$

vhere r_1 and r_2 are the modulus of z_1 and z_2 respectively θ_1 and θ_2 are the ırgument of z_1 and z_2 respectively

$$\frac{z_1}{z_2} = \frac{r_1\, e^{i\theta_1}}{r_2\, e^{i\theta_2}} \qquad \arg z_1 = \theta_1, \quad \arg z_2 = \theta_2$$

$$= \frac{r_1}{r_2}\, e^{i(\theta_1-\theta_2)}$$

$$\arg\left(\frac{z_1}{z_2}\right) = \theta_1 - \theta_2$$

$$\arg\left(\frac{z_1}{z_2}\right) = \arg(z_1) - \arg(z_2)$$

(Proved)

Theorem 5 If z_1, z_2 are any two complex numbers then prove that

(i) $R(z_1 + z_2) = R(z_1) + R(z_2)$

(ii) $I(z_1 + z_2) = I(z_1) + I(z_2)$

(iii) $R(z_1 - z_2) = R(z_1) - (z_2)$

(*iv*) $I(z_1 - z_2) = I(z_1) - I(z_2)$

Proof Let $z_1 = x_1 + iy_1$ $z_2 = x_2 + iy_2$ be any two complex numbers

$$I(z_1) = y_1 \qquad I(z_2) = y_2$$

$$R(z_1) = x_1 \qquad R(z_2) = x_2$$

$$z_1 + z_2 = (x_1 + iy_1) + (x_2 + iy_2) = (x_1 + x_2) + i(y_1 + y_2)$$

$$R(z_1 + z_2) = x_1 + x_2$$

$$R(z_1 + z_2) = R(z_1) + R(z_2) \qquad (1)$$

$$I(z_1 + z_2) = y_1 + y_2 = I(z_1) + I(z_2) \qquad (2)$$

$$z_1 - z_2 = (x_1 + iy_1) - (y_2 + iy_2) = (x_1 - x_2) + i(y_1 - y_2)$$

$$R(z_1 - z_2) = x_1 - x_2$$

$$R(z_1 - z_2) = R(z_1) - R(z_2) \qquad (3)$$

$$I(z_1 - z_2) = y_1 - y_2$$

$$I(z_1 - z_2) = I(z_1) - I(z_2) \qquad (4)$$

(Proved)

heorem 6 If a and b are complex numbers, prove that

$$|a + \sqrt{a^2 - b^2}| + |a - \sqrt{a^2 - b^2}| = |a + b| + |a - b|$$

[*IFS 83*]

7

Differential Calculas

Partial differentiation, Euler's theorem for homogeneous functions.

Definition let $u = f(x, y)$ be a function of two variables x and y.

The partial derivative of u *w.r.t* x is denoted by the symbol $\frac{\partial u}{\partial x}$ and this means that u has been differentiated $w \cdot r$ to x only and the remaining variable y has been treated as constant.

Problem If $u = \log \frac{x^2 + y^2}{xy}$, verify that $\frac{\partial^2 4}{\partial y\, \partial x} = \frac{\partial^2 u}{\partial x\, \partial y}$

We have $\quad u = \log \frac{x^2 + y^2}{xy}$

$$u = \log (x^2 + y^2) - \log (xy)$$

$$\frac{\partial u}{\partial x} = \frac{1}{(x^2 + y^2)} \frac{\partial}{\partial x} (x^2 + y^2) - \frac{1}{xy} \cdot \frac{\partial}{\partial x} (xy)$$

$$\frac{\partial u}{\partial x} = \frac{1}{(x^2 + y^2)} (2x) - \frac{1}{xy} y$$

$$\frac{\partial u}{\partial x} = \frac{2x}{x^2 + y^2} - \frac{1}{x}$$

$$\frac{\partial^2 u}{\partial y\, \partial x} = \frac{\partial}{\partial y}\left[\frac{\partial u}{\partial x}\right] = \frac{\partial}{\partial y}\left[\frac{2x}{x^2 + y^2} - \frac{1}{x}\right]$$

$$= 2 \frac{\partial}{\partial y}\left[\frac{x}{x^2 + y^2}\right] - \frac{\partial}{\partial y}\left(\frac{1}{x}\right)$$

$$= 2\left[\frac{(x^2 + y^2)\frac{\partial}{\partial y}(x) - x\frac{\partial}{\partial y}(x^2 + y^2)}{(x^2 + y^2)^2}\right] = 0$$

$$= 2\left[\frac{(x^2 + y^2) \cdot 0 - x\,(2y)}{(x^2 + y^2)^2}\right] = -\frac{4xy}{(x^2 + y^2)^2} \tag{1}$$

Again $\quad u = \log(x^2 + y^2) - \log(xy)$

$$\frac{\partial u}{\partial y} = \frac{2y}{(x^2 + y^2)} - \frac{x}{xy}$$

$$\frac{\partial u}{\partial y} = \frac{2y}{x^2 + y^2} - \frac{1}{y}$$

$$\frac{\partial^2 u}{\partial x \partial y} = \frac{\partial}{\partial x}\left[\frac{\partial u}{\partial y}\right]$$

$$= \frac{\partial}{\partial x}\left[\frac{2y}{x^2 + y^2} - \frac{1}{y}\right] = 2\frac{\partial}{\partial x}\left(\frac{y}{x^2 + y^2}\right) - \frac{\partial}{\partial x}\left(\frac{1}{y}\right)$$

$$= 2 \cdot \frac{\left[(x^2 + y^2)\frac{\partial}{\partial x}(y) - y\frac{\partial}{\partial x}(x^2 + y^2)\right]}{(x^2 + y^2)^2} - 0$$

$$= \frac{2[0 - 2xy]}{(x^2 + y^2)^2} - 0$$

$$\frac{\partial^2 u}{\partial x \partial y} = \frac{-4xy}{(x^2 + y^2)^2} \tag{2}$$

From equation (1) and (2) it is clear that

$$\frac{\partial^2 u}{\partial y \partial x} = \frac{\partial^2 u}{\partial x \partial y} \qquad \textit{(proved)}$$

Problem 2 $\quad u = \sin^{-1}\frac{x}{y} + \tan^{-1}\frac{y}{x}$ prove that $x\frac{\partial u}{\partial x} + y\frac{\partial u}{\partial y} = 0$

Solution We have

$$u = \sin^{-1}\frac{x}{y} + \tan^{-1}\frac{y}{x}$$

$$\frac{\partial u}{\partial x} = \frac{\partial}{\partial x}\left[\sin^{-1}\frac{x}{y} \quad \tan^{-1}\frac{y}{x}\right]$$

$$= \frac{\partial}{\partial x}\left[\sin^{-1}\frac{x}{y}\right] + \frac{\partial}{\partial x}\left[\tan^{-1}\frac{y}{x}\right]$$

$$= \frac{1}{\sqrt{1 - \frac{x^2}{y^2}}} \cdot \frac{\partial}{\partial x}\left(\frac{x}{y}\right) + \frac{1}{1 + \frac{y^2}{x^2}} \cdot \frac{\partial}{\partial x}\left(\frac{y}{x}\right)$$

$$= \frac{y}{\sqrt{y^2 - x^2}} \cdot \frac{1}{y} + \frac{x^2}{x^2 + y^2}\left(-\frac{y}{x^2}\right)$$

$$= \frac{1}{\sqrt{y^2 - x^2}} - \frac{y}{(x^2 + y^2)}$$

$$x\frac{\partial u}{\partial x} = \frac{x}{\sqrt{y^2 - x^2}} - \frac{xy}{(x^2 + y^2)} \tag{1}$$

Again $$\frac{\partial u}{\partial y} = \frac{\partial}{\partial y}\left[\sin^{-1}\frac{x}{y} + \tan^{-1}\frac{y}{x}\right]$$

$$= \frac{\partial}{\partial x}\left[\sin^{-1}\frac{x}{y}\right] + \frac{\partial}{\partial y}\left[\tan^{-1}\frac{y}{x}\right]$$

$$= \frac{1}{\sqrt{1-\frac{x^2}{y^2}}}\frac{\partial}{\partial y}\left(\frac{x}{y}\right) + \frac{1}{1+\frac{y^2}{x^2}}\frac{\partial}{\partial y}\left(\frac{y}{x}\right)$$

$$= \frac{y}{\sqrt{y^2-x^2}}\left(-\frac{x}{y^2}\right) + \frac{x^2}{x^2+y^2}\,\frac{1}{x}$$

$$= -\frac{x}{y\sqrt{y^2-x^2}} + \frac{x}{x^2+y^2}$$

$$y\frac{\partial u}{\partial y} = -\frac{xy}{y\sqrt{y^2-x^2}} + \frac{xy}{x^2+y^2}$$

$$y\frac{\partial u}{\partial y} = -\frac{x}{\sqrt{y^2-x^2}} + \frac{xy}{x^2+y^2} \qquad (2)$$

Adding equation (1) and (2) we have

$$x\frac{\partial u}{\partial x} + y\frac{\partial u}{\partial y} = \frac{x}{\sqrt{y^2-x^2}} - \frac{xy}{(x^2+y^2)} - \frac{x}{\sqrt{y^2-x^2}} + \frac{xy}{x^2+y^2}$$

i.e. $$x\frac{\partial u}{\partial x} + \frac{\partial u}{\partial y} = 0 \qquad \textit{(proved)}$$

Problem 3 If $z(x+y) = x^2+y^2$, show that

$$\left(\frac{\partial z}{\partial x} - \frac{\partial z}{\partial y}\right)^2 = 4\left(1 - \frac{\partial z}{\partial x} - \frac{\partial z}{\partial y}\right)$$

Solution $$z(x+y) = x^2+y^2$$

$$z = \frac{x^2+y^2}{x+y}$$

$$\frac{\partial z}{\partial x} = \frac{1}{\partial x}\left[\frac{x^2+y^2}{x+y}\right]$$

$$= \frac{(x+y)\frac{\partial}{\partial x}[x^2+y^2] - (x^2+y^2)\frac{\partial}{\partial x}(x+y)}{(x+y)^2}$$

$$\frac{\partial z}{\partial x} = \frac{(x+y)\,2x-(x^2+y^2)\cdot 1}{(x+y)^2}$$

$$\frac{\partial z}{\partial x} = \frac{2x^2+2xy-x^2-y^2}{(x+y)^2}$$

$$\frac{\partial z}{\partial x} = \frac{x^2 + 2xy - y^2}{(x + y)^2} \tag{1}$$

$$\frac{\partial z}{\partial x} = \frac{\partial}{\partial y}\left[\frac{x^2 + y^2}{x + y}\right]$$

$$= \frac{(x + y)\ \dfrac{\partial}{\partial y}(x^2 + y^2) - (x^2 + y^2)\ \dfrac{\partial}{\partial y}(x + y)}{(x + y)^2}$$

$$= \frac{(x + y)\ 2y - (x^2 + y^2)\ 1}{+ y)^2}$$

$$= \frac{2xy + 2y^2 - x^2 - y^2}{(x + y)^2} = \frac{2xy + y^2 - x^2}{(x + y)^2}$$

$$\frac{\partial z}{\partial y} = \frac{y^2 + 2xy - x^2}{(x + y)^2} \tag{2}$$

Now $\dfrac{\partial z}{\partial x} - \dfrac{\partial z}{\partial y} = \dfrac{1}{(x + y)^2}\ [x^2 + 2xy - y^2 - y^2 - 2xy + x^2]$

$$= \frac{2x^2 - 2y^2}{(x + y)^2} = \frac{2\ (x^2 - y^2)}{(x + y)^2}$$

$$\frac{\partial z}{\partial x} - \frac{\partial z}{\partial y} = \frac{2\ (x + y)\ (x - y}{(x + y)\ (x + y)} = \frac{2\ (x - y)}{(x + y)}$$

$$\left(\frac{\partial z}{\partial x} - \frac{\partial z}{\partial y}\right) = \frac{4\ (x - y)^2}{(x + y)^2} \tag{3}$$

Again

$$1 - \frac{\partial z}{\partial x} - \frac{\partial z}{\partial y} = 1 - \frac{x^2 + 2xy - y^2}{(x + y)^2} - \frac{y^2 + 2xy - x^2}{(x + y)^2}$$

$$= \frac{(x + y)^2 - (x^2 + 2xy - y^2) - (y^2 + 2xy - y^2)}{(x + y)^2}$$

$$= \frac{x^2 + 2xy + y^2 - x^2 - 2xy + y^2 - y^2 - 2xy + x^2}{(x + y)^2}$$

$$= \frac{x - 2xy + y^2}{(x + y)^2} = \frac{(x - y)^2}{(x + y)^2}$$

$$4\left(1 - \frac{\partial z}{\partial x} + \frac{\partial z}{\partial y}\right) = 4\,\frac{(x - y)^2}{(x + y)^2} \tag{4}$$

From equation (3) and (4) we have

$$\left[\frac{\partial z}{\partial x} - \frac{\partial z}{\theta y}\right]^2 = 4\left[1 - \frac{\partial z}{\partial x} - \frac{\partial z}{\partial y}\right] \qquad \textit{(proved)}$$

Problem 4 If $x = r\cos\theta$, $y = r\sin\theta$, show that

(i) $$\frac{\partial x}{\partial r} = \frac{\partial r}{\partial x}$$

(ii) $$\frac{1}{r}\frac{\partial x}{\partial \theta} = r\frac{\partial \theta}{\partial x}$$

$$x = r\cos\theta = f(r, \theta)$$

$$\frac{\partial x}{\partial r} = \frac{\partial}{\partial r}[r\cos\theta] = \cos\theta \frac{\partial}{\partial r}(r) = \cos\theta \qquad (1)$$

Again $$x^2 + y^2 = r^2\cos^2\theta + r^2\sin^2\theta$$

$$x^2 + y^2 = r^2(\cos^2\theta + \sin^2\theta)$$

$$x^2 + y^2 = r^2 \cdot 1$$

$$r^2 = x^2 + y^2$$

Differentiating partially with respect to x we have

$$2r \cdot \frac{\partial r}{\partial x} = 2x$$

$$\Rightarrow \frac{\partial r}{\partial x} = \frac{x}{r}$$

$$\Rightarrow \frac{\partial r}{\partial x} = \cos\theta \qquad (2)$$

From equation (1) and (2) we have.

$$\frac{\partial x}{\partial r} = \frac{\partial r}{\partial x} \qquad [F. P. P.]$$

$$x = r\cos\theta$$

$$\frac{\partial x}{\partial \theta} = \frac{\partial}{\partial \theta}[r\cos\theta]$$

$$= r\frac{\partial}{\partial \theta}(\cos\theta) = r(-\sin\theta) = -r\sin\theta$$

$$\Rightarrow \frac{1}{r}\frac{\partial x}{\partial \theta} = -\sin\theta \qquad (3)$$

Again $$\frac{r\sin\theta}{r\cos\theta} = \frac{y}{x}$$

$$\tan\theta = \frac{y}{x} \qquad (4)$$

Differentiating (4) partially w.r.t. x we have

$$\sec^2\theta\frac{\partial \theta}{\partial x} = y\left(-\frac{1}{x_2}\right)$$

$$\frac{\partial \theta}{\partial x} = -\frac{y}{x^2\sec^2\theta}$$

$$\frac{\partial \theta}{\partial x} = -\frac{r \sin \theta}{r^2 \cos^2 \theta \cdot \sec^2 \theta}$$

$$\frac{\partial \theta}{\partial x} = -\frac{\sin \theta}{r}$$

$$\Rightarrow r \frac{\varrho \theta}{\delta \theta} = -\sin \theta \tag{5}$$

From equation (3) and (5) we have

$$\frac{1}{r} \frac{\partial x}{\partial x} = r \frac{\partial \theta}{\partial x} \qquad \textit{(Proved)}$$

Problem 5 If $u = \phi\,(y + ax) + \psi\,(y - ax)$ show that

$$\frac{\partial^2 u}{\partial x^2} - a^2 \frac{\partial^2 u}{\partial y^2} = 0$$

Solution We have $u = \phi\,(y + ax) + \psi\,(y - ax)$

Differentiating w.r.t. to x partially we have

$$\frac{\partial u}{\partial x} = \phi'\,(y + ax) \frac{\partial}{\partial x} (y + ax) + \psi'\,(y - ax) \frac{\partial}{\partial x} (y - ax)$$

$$= \phi'\,(y + ax)\,(0 + a) + \psi'\,(y - ax)\,(0 - a)$$

$$= a\phi'\,(y + ax) - a\psi'\,(y - ax)$$

Again differentiating partially with respect to x we have

$$\frac{\partial^2 u}{\partial x^2} = a^2 \phi''\,(y + ax) + a^2 \psi''\,(y - ax)$$

$$\frac{\partial^2 u}{\partial x^2} = a^2 [\phi''\,(y + ax) + \psi''\,(y - ax)] \tag{1}$$

Again $u = \phi\,(y + ax) + \psi\,(y - ax)$

differentiating partially with respect to y we have

$$\frac{\partial u}{\partial y} = \phi'\,(y + ax) \frac{\partial}{\partial y} (y + ax) + \psi'\,(y - ax) \frac{\partial}{\partial y} (y - ax)$$

$$\frac{\partial u}{\partial y} = \phi'\,(y + ax) + \psi'\,(y - ax)$$

Again differentiating partially with respcct to y we have

$$\frac{\partial^2 u}{\partial y^2} = \phi''\,(y + ax) + \psi''\,(y - ax) \tag{2}$$

From equation (1) and (2) it is clear that

$$\frac{\partial^2 u}{\partial x^2} = a^2 \frac{\partial^2 u}{\partial y^2} \qquad \textit{(Proved)}$$

Problem 6 If $\frac{1}{u} = \sqrt{x^2 + y^2 + z^2}$ show that

(i) $x\frac{\partial u}{\partial x} + y\frac{\partial u}{\partial y} + z\frac{\partial u}{\partial z} + u = 0$

(ii) $\frac{\partial^2 u}{\partial x^2} + \frac{\partial^2 u}{\partial y^2} + \frac{\partial^2 u}{\partial z^2} = 0$

Solution

$$\frac{1}{u} = \sqrt{x^2 + y^2 + z^2}$$

$$\frac{1}{u} = (x^2 + y^2 + z^2)^{1/2}$$

$$u = \frac{1}{(x^2 + y^2 + z^2)^{1/2}}$$

$$u = (x^2 + y^2 + z^2)^{-1/2}$$

$$\frac{\partial u}{\partial x} = \frac{\partial}{\partial x}[x^2 + y^2 + z^2)^{-1/2}]$$

$$\frac{\partial u}{\partial x} = -\frac{1}{2}(x^2 + y^2 + z^2)^{-1/2-1}\frac{\partial}{\partial x}(x^2 + y^2 + z^2)$$

$$= -\frac{1}{2}(x^2 + y^2 + z^2)^{-3/2}\, 2x$$

$$\frac{\partial u}{\partial x} = -x(x^2 + y^2 + z^2)^{-3/2} \quad (1)$$

$$\frac{\partial u}{\partial y} = -y\ \ x^2 + y^2 + z^2)^{-3/2} \quad (2)$$

$$\frac{\partial u}{\partial z} = -z(x^2 + y^2 + z^2)^{-3/2} \quad (3)$$

$$x\frac{\partial u}{\partial x} + y\frac{\partial u}{\partial y} + z\frac{\partial u}{\partial z}$$

$$= -x^2(x^2 + y^2 + z^2)^{-3/2} - y^2(x^2 + y^2 + z^2)^{-3/2} - z^2(x^2 + y^2 + z^2)^{-3/2}$$

$$= -(x^2 + y^2 + z^3)^{-3/2}(x^2 + y^2 + z^2)$$

$$= -(x^2 + y^2 + z^2)^{-(3/2)+1} = -(x^2 + y^2 + z^2)^{-(3+2)/2}$$

$$= -(x^2 + y^2 + z^2)^{-1/2} = -\frac{1}{\sqrt{x^2 + y^2 + z^2}}$$

Thus $$x\frac{\partial u}{\partial x}+y\frac{\partial u}{\partial y}+z\frac{\partial u}{\partial z}+u$$

$$=\frac{1}{\sqrt{x^2+y^2+z^2}}-\frac{1}{\sqrt{x^2+y^2+z^2}}=0$$

i.e. $$x\frac{\partial u}{\partial x}+y\frac{\partial u}{\partial y}+z\frac{\partial u}{\partial z}+u=0$$

$$\frac{\partial^2 u}{\partial x^2}=\frac{\partial}{\partial x}\left(\frac{\partial u}{\partial x}\right)=\frac{\partial}{\partial x}[-x(x^2+y^2+z^2)^{-3/2}]$$

$$=-\frac{\partial}{\partial x}[x(x^2+y^2+z^2)^{-3/2}]$$

$$=-\left[x\frac{\partial}{\partial x}\{(x^2+y^2+z^2)^{-3/2}\}+(x^2+y^2+z^2)^{-3/2}\frac{\partial}{\partial x}(x)\right]$$

$$=-[x\times\frac{-3}{2}(x^2+y^2+z^2)^{-(3/2)-1}2x+(x^2+y^2+z^2)^{-3/2}]$$

$$=-[-3x^2(x^2+y^2+z^2)^{-5/2}+(x^2+y^2+z^2)^{-3/2}]$$

$$=-(x^2+y^2+z^2)^{-5/2}[-3x^2+x^2+y^2+z^2]$$

$$=-(x^2+y^2+z^2)^{-5/2}[y^2+z^2-2x^2]$$

$$\frac{\partial^2 u}{\partial x^2}=-\frac{(y^2+z^2-2x^2)}{(x^2+y^2+z^2)^{5/2}}$$

Similarly $$\frac{\partial^2 u}{\partial y^2}=-\frac{(x^2+z^2-2y^2}{(x^2+y^2+z^2)^{5/2}}$$

and $$\frac{\partial^2 u}{\partial z^2}=-\frac{(y^2+x^2-2z^2)}{(x^2+y^2+z^2)^{5/2}}$$

Adding we have $$\frac{\partial^2 u}{\partial x^2}+\frac{\partial^2 u}{\partial y^2}+\frac{\partial^2 u}{\partial z^2}$$

$$=-\left[\frac{x^2+y^2-2z^2+y^2+z^2-2x^2+x^2+z^2-2y^2}{(x^2+y^2+z^2)^{5/2}}\right]$$

$$=-\frac{0}{(x^2+y^2+z^2)^{5/2}}=0$$

$$\frac{\partial^2 u}{\partial x^2}+\frac{\partial^2 u}{\partial y^2}+\frac{\partial^2 u}{\partial z^2}=0$$ *(Proved)*

Problem 7 If $u=\log(x^3+y^3+z^3-3xyz)$ show that

(i) $$\frac{\partial u}{\partial x}+\frac{\partial u}{\partial y}+\frac{\partial u}{\partial z}=\frac{3}{x+y+z}$$

(ii) $$\left(\frac{\partial}{\partial x}+\frac{\partial}{\partial y}+\frac{\partial}{\partial z}\right)^2 u=-\frac{9}{(x+y+z)^2}$$

Solution $$u = \log (x^3 + y^3 + z^3 - 3xyz)$$

$$\frac{\partial u}{\partial x} = \frac{3x^2 - 3yz}{x^3 + y^3 + z^3 - 3xyz}$$

$$\frac{\partial u}{\partial x} = \frac{3(x^2 - yz)}{x^3 + y^3 + z^3 - 3xyz}$$

similarly $$\frac{\partial u}{\partial y} = \frac{3(y^2 - zx)}{x^3 + y^3 + z^3 - 3xyz}$$

$$\frac{\partial u}{\partial z} = \frac{3(z^2 - xy)}{x^3 + y^3 + z^3 - 3xyz}$$

We have $$\frac{\partial u}{\partial x} + \frac{\partial u}{\partial y} + \frac{\partial u}{\partial z} = \frac{3(x^2 - yz + y^2 - zx + z^2 - xy)}{(x^3 + y^3 + z^3) - 3xyz)}$$

$$= \frac{3(x^2 + y^2 + z^2 - xy - yz - zx)}{(x + y + z)(x^2 + y^3 + z^2 - xy - yz - zx)}$$

$$\frac{\partial u}{\partial x} + \frac{\partial y}{\partial y} + \frac{\partial u}{\partial z} = \frac{3}{(x + y + z)}$$ *(Proved)*

(ii) $$\left(\frac{\partial}{\partial x} + \frac{\partial}{\partial y} + \frac{\partial}{\partial z}\right)^2 u$$

$$= \left(\frac{\partial}{\partial x} + \frac{\partial}{\partial y} + \frac{\partial}{\partial z}\right)\left(\frac{\partial}{\partial x} + \frac{\partial}{\partial y} + \frac{\partial}{\partial z}\right) u$$

$$= \left(\frac{\partial}{\partial x} + \frac{\partial}{\partial y} + \frac{\partial}{\partial z}\right)\left(\frac{\partial u}{\partial x} + \frac{\partial u}{\partial y} + \frac{\partial u}{\partial z}\right)$$

$$= \left(\frac{\partial}{\partial x} + \frac{\partial}{\partial y} + \frac{\partial}{\partial z}\right)\left(\frac{3}{x + y + z}\right)$$

$$= 3\left[\frac{\partial}{\partial x}\left(\frac{1}{x + y + z}\right) + \frac{\partial}{\partial y}\left(\frac{1}{x + y + z}\right) + \frac{\partial}{\partial z}\left(\frac{1}{x+y+z}\right)\right]$$

$$= 3\left[-\frac{1}{(x + y + z)^2} - \frac{1}{(x + y + z)^2} - \frac{1}{(x + y + z)^2}\right]$$

$$= \frac{3(-3)}{(x + y + z)^2}$$

$$= -\frac{9}{(x + y + z)^2}$$

i.e. $$\left(\frac{\partial}{\partial x} + \frac{\partial}{\partial y} + \frac{\partial}{\partial z}\right) u = -\frac{9}{(x + y + z)^2}$$ *(Proved)*

Problem 8 If $u = \sin^{-1} \dfrac{x}{y}$, prove that

$$x \frac{\partial u}{\partial x} + y \frac{\partial u}{\partial y} = 0$$

Solution $u = \sin^{-1} \dfrac{x}{y}$

$$\frac{\partial u}{\partial x} = \frac{\partial}{\partial x}\left[\sin^{-1} \frac{x}{y}\right] = \frac{1}{\sqrt{1-x^2/y^2}} \frac{\partial}{\partial x}\left(\frac{x}{y}\right)$$

$$= \frac{y}{\sqrt{y^2-x^2}} \frac{1}{y} = \frac{1}{\sqrt{y^2-x^2}}$$

$$x \frac{\partial u}{\partial x} = \frac{x}{\sqrt{y^2-x^2}}$$

$$\frac{\partial u}{\partial y} = \frac{\partial}{\partial y}\left\{\sin^{-1} \frac{x}{y}\right\} = \frac{1}{\sqrt{1-x^2/y^2}} \cdot \frac{\partial}{\partial y}\left(\frac{x}{y}\right)$$

$$= \frac{y}{\sqrt{y^2-x^2}} \frac{x}{(-y^2)} = -\frac{x}{y\sqrt{y^2-x^2}}$$

$$y \frac{\partial u}{\partial y} = -\frac{x}{\sqrt{y^2-x^2}}$$

Then $x \dfrac{\partial u}{\partial x} + y \dfrac{\partial u}{\partial y} = \dfrac{x}{\sqrt{y^2-x^2}} - \dfrac{x}{\sqrt{y^2-x^2}}$

$$x \frac{\partial u}{\partial x} + x \frac{\partial u}{\partial y} = 0$$ ***(Proved)***

Problem 9 Show that the function $z = \psi\,(x^2 + y^2)$ satisfies the equation

$$y \frac{\partial z}{\partial x} = x \frac{\partial z}{\partial y}$$ *[I.F.S. 88]*

Solution $z = \psi\,(x^2 + y^2)$

$$\frac{\partial z}{\partial x} = \varphi^1\,(x^2 + y^2) \frac{\partial}{\partial x} \psi^1\,(x^2 + y^2)$$

$$\frac{\partial z}{\partial x} = \psi^1\,(x^2 + y^2)\, 2x$$

$$\frac{\partial z}{\partial x} = 2x\, \psi^1\,(x^2 + y^2)$$

$$y \frac{\partial z}{\partial x} = 2xy\, \psi^1\,(x^2 + y^2) \quad (1)$$

Again $\frac{\partial z}{\partial y} = \psi^1 (x^2 + y^2) \frac{\partial}{\partial y}(x^2 + y^2) = (x^2 + y^2)\, 2y$

$$= 2y\, \psi^1 (x^2 + y^2)$$

$$x \frac{\partial z}{\partial y} = 2xy\, \psi^{-1} (x^2 + y^2) \qquad (2)$$

From equation (1) and (2) it is clear that

$$y \frac{\partial z}{\partial x} = x \frac{\partial z}{\partial y} \qquad (proved)$$

Problem 10 If $u = x^2 + y^2 + z^2$, prove that

$$x \frac{\partial u}{\partial x} + y \frac{\partial u}{\partial y} + z \frac{\partial u}{\partial y} = 2u$$

Solution $u = x^2 + y^2 + z^2$

$$\frac{\partial u}{\partial x} = 2x, \frac{\partial u}{\partial y} = 2y \quad \frac{\partial u}{\partial z} = 2z$$

$$x \frac{\partial u}{\partial x} + y \frac{\partial u}{\partial y} + z \frac{\partial u}{\partial z} = 2 (x^2 + y^2 + z^2) = 2u$$

i e. $x \frac{\partial u}{\partial x} + y \frac{\partial u}{\partial z} + z \frac{\partial u}{\partial z} = 2u$ (*proved*)

Problem 11 If $u = \log (x^2 + y^2)$, show that

$$\frac{\partial^2 u}{\partial x^2} + \frac{\partial^2 u}{\partial y^2} = 0$$

Solution $y = \log (x^2 + y^2)$

$$\frac{\partial u}{\partial x} = \frac{\partial}{\partial x} \{\log (x^2 + y^2)\}$$

$$\frac{\partial u}{\partial x} = \frac{2x}{x^2 + y^2} \qquad (1)$$

$$\frac{\partial^2 u}{\partial x^2} = 2 \frac{\partial}{\partial x} \left\{\frac{2x}{x^2 + y^2}\right\}$$

$$= 2 \frac{[(x^2 + y^2) \cdot 1 - x (2x)]}{(x^2 + y^2)^2} = \frac{2 \,\|x^2 + y^2 - 2x^2]}{(x^2 + y^2)^2}$$

$$\frac{\partial^2 u}{\partial x^2} = \frac{2 (y^2 - x^2)}{(x^2 + y^2)^2}$$

similarly $\frac{\partial^2 u}{\partial y^2} = \frac{2 (z^2 - y^2)}{(x^2 + y^2)^2}$

$$\frac{\partial^2 u}{\partial x^2} + \frac{\partial^2 u}{\partial y^2} \equiv 2 \frac{[y^2 - x^2 + x^2 - y^2]}{(x^2 + y^2)^2} = \frac{2 \cdot 0}{(x^2 + y^2)^2} = 0$$

$$\frac{\partial^2 u}{\partial x^2} + \frac{\partial^2 u}{\partial y^2} = 0 \qquad (proved)$$

8

Homogeneous Functions

Let $u = f(x, y)$ be any function of x and y. If the sum of the powers of x and y in each term of $f(x, y)$ be equal, then $f(x, y)$ is called a homogeneous function. If the sum of the powers of x and y in each term of $f(x, y)$ be n, then $f(x, y)$ is called a homogeneous function of order n.

Euler's theorem on Homogeous Function of two variables

Statements: If $n = f(x, y)$ be a homogeneous function in x and y of degree n then

$$u\frac{\partial u}{\partial x} + y\frac{\partial u}{\partial y} = nu$$

Proof. Let

$$u = f(x, y)$$

$$u = A_1 x^{\alpha_1} y^{\beta_1} + A_3 x^{\alpha_2} y^{\beta_2} + A_3 x^{\alpha_3} y^{\beta_3} + \ldots + A_n x^{\alpha_n} y^{\beta_n} \quad (1)$$

where $\alpha_1 + \beta_1 = \alpha_2 + \beta_2 = \alpha_3 + \beta_3 = \ldots = \alpha_n + \beta_n = n$

Differentiating equation (1) with respect to x we have

$$\frac{\partial u}{\partial x} = A_1 \alpha_1 x^{\alpha_1 - 1} y^{\beta_1} + A_2 \alpha_2 x^{\alpha_2 - 1} y^{\beta 2} + \ldots + A_n \alpha_n x^{\alpha_n - 1}$$

Multiplying this with x we have

$$x\frac{\partial u}{\partial x} = \alpha_1 A_1 x^{\alpha_1} y^{\beta_1} + \alpha_2 A_2 x^{\alpha_2} a^{\beta_2} + \ldots + \alpha_n A_n x^{\alpha_n} y^{\beta_n} \quad (2)$$

similarly differentiating equation (1) $w \cdot r$ to y and multiplying with y we have

$$y\frac{\partial n}{\partial y} = \beta_1 A_1 x^{\alpha_1} y^{\beta_1} + \beta_2 A_2 x^{\alpha_2} y^{\beta_2} + \ldots + \beta_n A_n x^{\alpha_n} y^{\beta_n} \quad (3)$$

Adding equation (2) and (3) we have

$$x\frac{\partial n}{\partial x} + y\frac{\partial u}{\partial y} = (\alpha_1 + \beta_1) A_1 x^{\alpha_1} y^{\beta_1} + (\alpha_2 + \beta_2) A_2 x^{\alpha_2} y^{\beta_2}$$

$$+ (\alpha_3 + \beta_3) A_3 x^{\alpha_3} y^{\beta_3} + \ldots + (\alpha_u + \beta_n) A_n x^{\alpha} y^{\beta_n}$$

$$= n[A_1 x^{\alpha_1} y^{\beta_1} + A_2 x^{\alpha_2} y^{\beta_2} + \ldots + A_n x^{\alpha_n} y^{\beta_n}] = nu$$

Thus $$x \frac{\partial u}{\partial x} + y \frac{\partial u}{\partial y} = n u$$

Generalisation If $u = f(x, y, z)$ be a homogeneous function of x, y and z of order n, then

$$x \frac{\partial u}{\partial x} + y \frac{\partial u}{\partial y} + z \frac{\partial u}{\partial z} = nu$$

Proof. $$u = f(x. y, z)$$

$$= A_1 x^{\alpha_1} y^{\beta_1} z^{\gamma_1} + A_2 x^{\alpha_2} y^{\beta_2} z^{\gamma_2} + \ldots + A_n x^{\alpha_n} y^{\beta_n} z^{\gamma_n} \quad (1)$$

where $\alpha_1 + \beta_1 + \gamma_1 = \alpha_2 + \beta_2 + \gamma_3 = \ldots = \alpha_n + \beta_n + \gamma_n = n$

Differentiating eqeation (1) with respect to x i.e. taking y and z as constant

$$\frac{\partial u}{\partial x} = A_1 \alpha_1 x^{\alpha_1 -1} y^{\beta_1} z^{\gamma_1} + A_2 \alpha_2 x^{\alpha_2 - 1} y^{\beta_2} z^{\gamma_2} + \ldots + A_n \alpha_n x^{\alpha_n -1} y^{\beta_n} z^{\gamma_n}$$

$$x \frac{\partial u}{\partial x} = A_1 \alpha_1 x^{\alpha_1} y^{\beta_1} z^{\gamma_1} + A_2 \alpha_2 x^{\alpha_2} y^{\beta_2} z^{\beta_2} + \ldots + A_n \alpha_n x^{\alpha_n} y^{\beta_n} z^{\gamma_n} \quad (2)$$

similarly $$y \frac{\partial u}{\partial y} = A_1 \beta_1 x^{\alpha_1} y^{\beta_1} y^{\gamma_1} + A_2 \beta_2 x^{\alpha_2} y^{\beta_2} z^{\gamma_2} + \ldots + A_n \beta_n x^{\alpha_n} y^{\beta_n} z^{\gamma_n} \quad (3)$$

and $$z \frac{\partial u}{\partial z} = A_1 \gamma_1 x^{\alpha_1} y^{\beta_1} z^{\gamma_1} + A_2 \gamma_2 x^{\alpha_2} y^{\beta_2} z^{\gamma_2} + \ldots + A_n \gamma_n x^{\alpha_n} y^{\beta_n} z^{\gamma_n} \quad (4)$$

Adding equation (2), (3) and (4) we have

$$x \frac{\partial u}{\partial x} + y \frac{\partial u}{\partial y} + z \frac{\partial u}{\partial z} = A_1 (\alpha_1 + \beta_1 + \gamma_1) x^{\alpha_1} y^{\beta_1} z^{\gamma_1}$$

$$+ A_2 (\alpha_2 + \beta_2 + \gamma_2) x^{\alpha_2} y^{\beta_2} z^{\gamma_2} + \ldots + A_n (\alpha_n + \beta_n + \gamma_n) x^{\alpha_n} y^{\beta_n} z^{\gamma_n}$$

$$= n [A_1 x^{\alpha_1} y^{\beta_1} \delta^{\gamma_1} + A_2 x^{\alpha_2} y^{\beta_2} z^{\gamma_2} + \ldots + A_n x^{\alpha_n} y^{\beta_n} z^{\gamma_n}[= nu$$

Thus $$x \frac{\partial u}{\partial x} + y \frac{\partial u}{\partial y} + z \frac{\partial u}{\partial z} = nu$$ *(Proved)*

Problem 1 Euler's theorem when

$$u = x^3 \log \frac{y}{x}$$

Solution From the given relation

$$u = x^3 \log \frac{y}{x}$$

$$u = x^3 [\log y - \log x]$$

$$\frac{\partial u}{\partial x} = x^3 \left[0 - \frac{1}{x}\right] + [\log y - \log x]\, 3x^2$$

$$= -x^2 + 3x^2 \log \frac{y}{x}$$

$$x \frac{\partial u}{\partial y} = -x^3 + 3x^3 \log \frac{y}{x} \tag{1}$$

Again $$\frac{\partial u}{\partial x} = x^3 \left[\frac{1}{y} - 0\right] + \log \frac{y}{x} \cdot 0$$

$$\frac{\partial u}{\partial y} = \frac{x^3}{y}$$

$$\Rightarrow y \frac{\partial u}{\partial u} = x^3 \tag{2}$$

Adding equation (1) and (2) we have

$$x \frac{\partial u}{\partial x} + y \frac{\partial u}{\partial d} = 3\, x^3 \log \frac{y}{x}$$

$$x \frac{\partial u}{\partial u} + y \frac{\partial n}{\partial y} = 3u$$

But here the given function $u = x^3 \log \frac{y}{x}$ is a homogeneous function of 3rd order. Thus the given function satisfies Euler's Theorem.

Problem 2 Verify Euler's Theorem for the expression

$$x^n \sin \frac{y}{x}$$

Solution Let $u = x^n \sin \frac{y}{x}$

which is of the order n

$$\frac{\partial u}{\partial u} = \frac{\partial}{\partial x} \left\{u^n \sin \frac{y}{x}\right\}$$

$$= \frac{\partial}{\partial x} (x^n) \sin \frac{y}{x} + x^n \frac{\partial}{\partial x} \left(\sin \frac{y}{x}\right)$$

$$= nx^{n-1} \sin \frac{y}{x} + x^n \cos \frac{y}{x} \frac{\partial}{\partial x} \left(\frac{y}{x}\right)$$

$$= nx^{n-1} \sin \frac{y}{x} + x^n \cos \frac{y}{x} \left(\frac{y}{-x^2}\right)$$

$$= nx^{n-1} \sin \frac{y}{x} - yx^{n-2} \cos \frac{y}{x}$$

$$\therefore, \qquad x\frac{\partial u}{\partial x} = nx^n \sin\frac{y}{x} - yx^{n-1}\cos\frac{y}{x} \tag{1}$$

Again
$$\frac{\partial u}{\partial y} = \frac{\partial}{\partial y}\left\{x^n \sin\frac{y}{x}\right\}$$

$$= x^n \frac{\partial}{\partial y}\left\{\sin\frac{y}{x}\right\} + \text{ı in}\frac{y}{x}\frac{\partial}{\partial y}(x^n)$$

$$= x^n \cos\frac{y}{x}\cdot\frac{\partial}{\partial y}\left(\frac{y}{x}\right) + \sin\frac{y}{x}\cdot 0$$

$$= x^n \left(\cos\frac{y}{x}\right)\cdot\frac{1}{x} + 0 = x^{n-1}\cos\frac{y}{x}$$

$$y\frac{\partial u}{\partial y} = yx^{n-1}\cos\frac{y}{x} \tag{2}$$

Adding equation (1) and (2) we hove

$$x\frac{\partial u}{\partial x} + y\frac{\partial u}{\partial y} = nx^n \sin\frac{y}{x}$$

$$x\frac{\partial u}{\partial x} + y\frac{\partial u}{\partial x} = nu$$

so Euler's theorem is verified.

Problem 3 Verify Euler's theorem when

$$u = \frac{x(x^3 - y^3)}{x^3 + y^3}$$

Solution Here the given function

$$u = \frac{x\ x^3\left(1 - \frac{y^3}{x^3}\right)}{x^3\left(1 + \left(\frac{y^3}{x^3}\right)\right)} = \frac{x\left(1 - \frac{y^3}{x^3}\right)}{\left(1 + \frac{y^3}{x^3}\right)}$$

$$u = \frac{x\left(1 - \frac{y^3}{x^3}\right)}{\left(1 + \frac{y^3}{x^3}\right)} = x\,\phi\left(\frac{y}{x}\right)$$

which is of the order one

$$u = x\,\frac{(x^3 - y^3)}{(x^3 + y^3)}$$

Taking logarithm on both sides we have

$$\log u = \log x + \log(x^3 - y^3) - \log(x^3 + y^3) \tag{A}$$

Differentiating with respect to x we have

$$\frac{1}{u}\frac{\partial u}{\partial x} = \frac{1}{x} + \frac{1}{x^3 - y^3}\frac{\partial}{\partial x}(x^3 - y^3) - \frac{1}{x^3 + y^3}\frac{\partial}{\partial x}(x^3 + y^3)$$

$$\frac{1}{u}\frac{\partial u}{\partial x} = \frac{1}{x} + \frac{3x^2}{x^3 - y^3} - \frac{3x^2}{x^3 + y^3} \tag{1}$$

Similarly differentiating (A) partially with respect to y we have

$$\frac{1}{u}\frac{\partial u}{\partial y} = 0 + 1\,\frac{1}{x^3 - y^3} \times \frac{\partial}{\partial y}(x^3 - y^3) - \frac{1}{x^3 + y^3}\frac{\partial}{\partial y}(x^3 + y^3)$$

$$\frac{1}{u}\frac{\partial u}{\partial y} = -\frac{3y^2}{(x^3 - y^3)} - \frac{3y^2}{(x^3 + y^3)} \tag{2}$$

Multiplying (1) with x and (2) with y and adding we have

$$\frac{1}{u}\left(x\frac{\partial u}{\partial x} + y\frac{\partial u}{\partial y}\right) = 1 + \frac{3x^3}{x^3 - y^3} - \frac{3x^3}{x^3 + y^3} - \frac{3y^3}{x^2 - y^3} - \frac{3y^3}{x^3 + y^3}$$

$$= 1 + \frac{3}{x^3 - y^3}(x^3 - y^3) - \frac{3}{{}^3 + y^3}(x^3 + y^3) = 1 + 3 - 3) = 1$$

i.e. $$\frac{1}{u}\left(x\frac{\partial u}{\partial x} + y\frac{\partial u}{\partial y}\right) = 1$$

$$\Rightarrow x\frac{\partial u}{\partial x} + y\frac{\partial u}{\partial y} = u$$

Thus Euler's Theorem is satisfied, *(Proved)*

Problem 4 If $u = \log \dfrac{x^2 + y^2}{x + y}$, prove that

$$x\frac{\partial u}{\partial x} + y\frac{\partial n}{\partial y} = 1$$

we have $$u = \log \frac{x^2 + y^2}{x + y}$$

$$u = \log \frac{x^2\left(1 + \frac{y^2}{x^2}\right)}{x\left(1 + \frac{y}{x}\right)}$$

$$u = \log \frac{x\left(1 + \frac{y^2}{x^2}\right)}{x\left(1 + \frac{y}{x}\right)}$$

Thus u is a function of x and y of order one

Now $$u = \log \frac{x^2 + y^2}{x + y}$$

$$u = \log(x^2 + y^2) - \log(x + y) \tag{1}$$

Differentiating equation (1) with respect to x partially we have

$$\frac{\partial u}{\partial x} = \frac{1}{(x^2+y^2)}\frac{\partial}{\partial x}(x^2+y^2) - \frac{1}{x+y}\frac{\partial}{\partial x}(x+y)$$

$$= \frac{2x}{x^2+y^2} - \frac{1}{x+y}$$

$$x\frac{\partial u}{\partial x} = \frac{2x^2}{x^2+y^2} - \frac{x}{x+y} \qquad (2)$$

Again differentiating equation (1) partially with respect to y we have

$$\frac{\partial u}{\partial y} = \frac{1}{x^2+y^2}\frac{\partial}{\partial y}(x^2+y^2) - \frac{1}{x+y}\frac{\partial}{\partial y}(x+y)$$

$$\frac{\partial u}{\partial u} = \frac{2y}{x^2+y^2} - \frac{1}{x+y}$$

$$y\frac{\partial u}{\partial y} = \frac{\partial y^2}{{}_2+yx^2} - \frac{y}{x+y} \qquad (3)$$

Adding equation (2) and (3) we have

$$x\frac{\partial u}{\partial x} + y\frac{\partial u}{\partial y} = \frac{2(x^2+y^2)}{(x^2+y^2)} - \frac{(x+y)}{(x+y)} = 2-1$$

$$x\frac{\partial u}{\partial x} + y\frac{\partial u}{\partial y} = 1 \qquad \textit{(Proved)}$$

Probiem 5 If $u = \cos^{-1}\frac{x-y}{x+y}$, prove that

$$x\frac{\partial u}{\partial x} + y\frac{\partial u}{\partial y} = 0$$

Solutlon $u = \cos^{-1}\frac{x-y}{x+y}$

$$\cos u = \frac{x-y}{x+y}$$

Let $v = \cos u = \frac{x-y}{x+y} = \frac{x\left(-\frac{y}{x}\right)}{x\left(1+\frac{y}{x}\right)}$

Then v is a function of order zero.

Thus from Euler's theorem on Homogenous equation we have

$$x\frac{\partial v}{\partial x} + y\frac{\partial v}{\partial y} = 0$$

$$x(-\sin u)\frac{\partial u}{\partial x} + y(-\sin u)\frac{\partial u}{\partial y} = 0$$

$$-\sin u\left[x\frac{\partial u}{\partial x} + y\frac{\partial u}{\partial y}\right] = 0$$

$$\Rightarrow \frac{\partial u}{\partial v} + y\frac{\partial u}{\partial y} = 0 \text{ since } \sin u \neq 0.$$

Problem 6 $u = \sin^{-1} \dfrac{x^2 + y^2}{x + y}$, show that

$$x \frac{\partial u}{\partial x} + y \frac{\partial u}{\partial y} = \tan u$$

Solution $u = \sin^{-1} \dfrac{x^2 + y^2}{x + y}$

$$\Rightarrow \sin u = \frac{x^2 + y^2}{x + y}$$

$$\Rightarrow \sin u = \frac{x^2\left(1 + \frac{y^2}{x^2}\right)}{x\left(1 + \frac{y}{x}\right)}$$

$$\Rightarrow v = \sin u = \frac{x\left(1 + \frac{y^2}{x^2}\right)}{\left(1 + \frac{y}{x}\right)}$$

Thus v is a function of x and y of osder one since v is a homogeneous function of x and y. So it will satisfy Euler's theorem

i.e. $$x \frac{\partial v}{\partial x} + y \frac{\partial v}{\partial y} = 1v$$

$$x \cos u \frac{\partial u}{\partial x} + y \cos u \frac{\partial u}{\partial y} = v$$

$$x \frac{\partial u}{\partial x} + y \frac{\partial u}{\partial y} = \frac{v}{\cos u}$$

$$x \frac{\partial u}{\partial y} + y \frac{\partial u}{\partial y} = \frac{\sin u}{\cos u}$$

$$x \frac{\partial u}{\partial x} + y \frac{\partial u}{\partial y} = \tan u \qquad \textit{(Proved)}$$

Problem 7 $u \sin^{-1} \dfrac{x + y}{\sqrt{x} + \sqrt{y}}$, prove that

$$x \frac{\partial u}{\partial u} + y \frac{\partial u}{\partial y} = \frac{1}{2} \tan u \qquad \text{(IFS 83)}$$

Solution We have $u = \sin^{-1} \dfrac{x + y}{\sqrt{x} + \sqrt{y}}$

$$\sin u = \frac{x + y}{\sqrt{x} + \sqrt{y}}$$

$$v = \sin u = \frac{x\left(1+\frac{y}{x}\right)}{\sqrt{x}\left(1+\frac{\sqrt{y}}{\sqrt{x}}\right)}$$

$$v=\sin u=x^{1/2}\frac{\left(1+\frac{y}{x}\right)}{\left(1+\frac{\sqrt{y}}{\sqrt{x}}\right)}$$

v is a homogenous function of x and y of order $\frac{1}{2}$. So Euler's theorem is satisfied.

$$x\frac{\partial v}{\partial x}+y\frac{\partial v}{\partial y}=\frac{1}{2}v$$

$$x\cos u\frac{\partial u}{\partial x}+y\cos u\frac{\partial u}{\partial y}=\frac{1}{2}\sin u$$

$$\cos u\left(x\frac{\partial u}{\partial x}+y\frac{\partial u}{\partial y}\right)=\frac{1}{2}\sin u$$

$$x\frac{\partial u}{\partial x}+y\frac{\partial u}{\partial y}=\frac{1}{2}\frac{\sin u}{\cos u}$$

$$x\frac{\partial u}{\partial x}+y\frac{\partial u}{\partial y}=\frac{1}{2}\tan u$$ *(Proved)*

Problam 8 If $u=\tan^{-1}\frac{x^3+y^3}{x-y}$, prove that

$$x\frac{\partial u}{\partial x}+y\frac{\partial u}{\partial y}=\sin 2u$$ (IFS 81)

Solution $$u=\tan^{-1}\frac{x^3+y^3}{x-y}$$

$$\tan u=\frac{x^3+y^3}{x-y}$$

$$\tan u=\frac{x^3\left(1+\frac{y^3}{x^3}\right)}{x\left(1-\frac{y}{x}\right)}$$

$$v=\tan u=\frac{x^2\left(1+\frac{y^3}{x^3}\right)}{\left(1-\frac{y}{x}\right)}$$

which is a homogeneous function of x and y of order 2.

$$v=\tan u$$

so from Euler's theorem we have

$$x\frac{\partial v}{\partial x}+y\frac{\partial v}{\partial y}=2v$$

$$x\sec^2 u\frac{\partial u}{\partial x}+y\sec^2 u\frac{\partial u}{\partial y}=2v$$

$$\left(x\frac{\partial u}{\partial x}+y\frac{\partial u}{\partial y}\right)=2\frac{\tan u}{\sec^2 u}$$

$$\left(x\frac{\partial u}{\partial x}+y\frac{\partial u}{\partial y}\right)=2\sin u\cos u$$

$$\left(x\frac{\partial u}{\partial x}+y\frac{\partial u}{\partial y}\right)=2\sin\cos u$$

$$\left(x\frac{\partial u}{\partial x}+y\frac{\partial u}{\partial y}\right)=\sin 2u$$ *(Proved)*

Problem 9 If $u=\sin^{-1}\left(\frac{x}{y}\right)+\tan^{-1}\left(\frac{y}{x}\right)$; show that

$$x\frac{\partial u}{\partial x}+y\frac{\partial u}{\partial y}=0$$ (IFS 82)

Solution First we transform $\sin^{-1}\frac{x}{y}$ in the form of $\tan^{-1}\frac{x}{v}$

Let $$\theta=\sin^{-1}\frac{x}{y}$$

$$\sin\theta=\frac{x}{y}$$

$$\cos\theta=\sqrt{1-\frac{x^2}{y^2}}=\frac{\sqrt{y^2-x^2}}{y}$$

$$\tan\theta=\frac{\sin\theta}{\cos\theta}=\frac{x}{\sqrt{y^2-x^2}}$$

$$\tan\theta=\frac{x}{\sqrt{y^2-x^2}}$$

$$\theta=\tan^{-1}\frac{x}{\sqrt{y^2-x^2}}$$

o $$u=\tan^{-1}\left(\frac{x}{\sqrt{y^2-x^2}}\right)+\tan^{-1}\left(\frac{y}{x}\right)$$

$$u = \tan^{-1}\frac{\dfrac{x}{\sqrt{y^2-x^2}}+\dfrac{y}{x}}{1-\dfrac{x}{\sqrt{y^2-x^2}}\cdot\dfrac{y}{x}}$$

$$u = \tan^{-1}\frac{\dfrac{x^2+y\sqrt{y^2-x^2}}{x\sqrt{y^2-x^2}}}{\dfrac{x\sqrt{y^2-x^2}-xy}{x\sqrt{y^2-x^2}}}$$

$$u = \tan^{-1}\frac{x^2+y\sqrt{y^2-x^2}}{x\sqrt{y^2-x^2}-xy}$$

$$\tan u = \frac{x^2+y\sqrt{y^2-x^2}}{x\sqrt{y^2-x^2}-xy}$$

$$= \frac{x^2\left[1+\frac{y}{x}\sqrt{\left(\frac{y}{x}\right)^2-1}\right]}{x^2\left[\sqrt{\left(\frac{y}{x}\right)^2-1}-\frac{y}{x}\right]} = \phi\left(\frac{y}{x}\right)$$

$\theta = \tan u$ is a homogeneous function of zero (0) degree $v = \tan u$

According to Euler's theorem we have

$$x\frac{\partial v}{\partial x}+y\frac{\partial v}{\partial y} = 0.v$$

$$x\frac{\partial v}{\partial x}+y\frac{\partial v}{\partial y} = 0$$

$$x\sec^2 u\frac{\partial u}{\partial x}+y\sec^2 u\frac{\partial v}{\partial y} = 0$$

$$\sec^2 u\left\{x\frac{\partial u}{\partial x}+y\frac{\partial v}{\partial y}\right\} = 0$$

$$x\frac{\partial u}{\partial x}+y\frac{\partial v}{\partial y} = 0$$

because $\sec^2 \neq 0$ *(Proved)*

Problem 10 If $\sin u = \dfrac{x^2-y^2}{x^2+y^2}$

Prove that $x\dfrac{\partial u}{\partial x}+y\dfrac{\partial u}{\partial y} = 0$

Solution $$\sin u = \frac{x^2 - y^2}{x^2 + y^2}$$

$$\sin u = \frac{x^2\left(1 - \frac{y^2}{x^2}\right)}{x^2\left(1 + \frac{y^2}{x^2}\right)}$$

$$\sin u = \frac{\left\{1 - \left(\frac{y}{x}\right)^2\right\}}{\left\{1 + \left(\frac{y}{x}\right)^2\right\}} = \phi\left(\frac{y}{x}\right)$$

So sin a is u homogeneous funct'on of x and y of orderz ero so according Euler's theorem

let $$v = \sin u$$

so $$x\frac{\partial v}{\partial x} + y\frac{\partial v}{\partial y} = 0 \cdot v$$

$$x\frac{\partial v}{\partial v} + y\frac{\partial v}{\partial y} = 0$$

$$x \cdot \cos u\frac{\partial v}{\partial x} + y\cos u\frac{\partial v}{\partial y} = 0$$

$$\Rightarrow \cos u\left\{x\frac{\partial u}{\partial y} + y\frac{\partial u}{\partial y}\right\} = 0$$

$$x\frac{\partial u}{\partial x} + y\frac{\partial u}{\delta y} = 0 \qquad \textit{(Proved)}$$

since $$\cos u \neq 0$$

Problem 11 If $u = \tan^{-1}\frac{x^2 + y^2}{x + y}$, show that

$$x\frac{\partial u}{\partial x} + y\frac{\partial u}{\partial y} = \frac{1}{2}\sin 2u$$

Solution $$u = \tan^{-1}\frac{x^2 + y^2}{x + y}$$

$$\Rightarrow \tan u = \frac{x^2 + y^2}{x + y}$$

$$\Rightarrow \tan u = \frac{x^2\left(1 + \frac{y^2}{x^2}\right)}{x\left(1 + \frac{y}{x}\right)}$$

$$\Rightarrow \tan u = \frac{x\left\{1 + \left(\frac{y}{x}\right)^2\right\}}{\left\{1 + \frac{y}{x}\right\}} = x\,\phi\left(\frac{y}{x}\right)$$

$\therefore$ tan u is a homogeneous function of x and y of order one so according to Euler's theorem

Let $$v = \tan u$$

$$x\frac{\partial v}{\partial x} + y\frac{\partial v}{\partial y} = v$$

$$x\sec^2 u\frac{\partial u}{\partial x} + y\sec^2 u\frac{\partial u}{\partial y} = \tan u$$

$$\sec^2 u\left\{x\frac{\partial u}{\partial x} + y\frac{\partial u}{\partial y}\right\} = \tan u$$

$$x\frac{\partial u}{\partial x} + y\frac{\partial u}{\partial y} = \frac{\tan u}{\sec^2 u}$$

$$x\frac{\partial u}{\partial x} + y\frac{\partial u}{\partial y} = \frac{\sin u}{\cos u}\cdot\cos^2 u$$

$$x\frac{\partial u}{\partial x} + y\frac{\partial u}{\partial y} = \sin u\cos u$$

$$x\frac{\partial u}{\partial x} + y\frac{\partial u}{\partial y} = \frac{2\sin u\cos u}{2}$$

$$x\frac{\partial u}{\partial x} + y\frac{\partial u}{\partial y} = \frac{1}{2}\sin 2u$$

Promblem 12 If be a homogeneous fnnction of degree n in x and y and if

$u = (x^2 + y^2)^{-n/2}$, show that

$$\frac{\partial}{\partial x}\left(H\frac{\partial u}{\partial x}\right) + \frac{\partial}{\partial y}\left(H\frac{\partial u}{\partial y}\right) = 0$$

Solution We have $u = (x^2 + y^2)^{-n/2}$

$$\frac{\partial u}{\partial x} = \frac{\partial}{\partial x}\{(x^2 + y^2)^{-n/2}\}$$

$$= -\frac{n}{2}(x^2 + y^2)^{-(n/2)-1}.2x$$

$$= -nx(x^2 + y^2)^{-(n/2)-1}$$

Similarly $$\frac{\partial u}{\partial y} = -ny(x^2 + y^3)^{-(n/2)-1}$$

$$LHS = \frac{\partial}{\partial x}\left(H\frac{\partial u}{\partial x}\right) + \frac{\partial}{\partial y}\left(H\frac{\partial u}{\partial y}\right)$$

$$= \frac{\partial H}{\partial x}\cdot\frac{\partial u}{\partial x} + H\frac{\partial^2 u}{\partial x^2} + \frac{\partial H}{\partial y}\cdot\frac{\partial u}{\partial y} + H\frac{\partial^2 u}{\partial y^2}$$

$$= H\left(\frac{\partial^2 u}{\partial x^2} + \frac{\partial^2 u}{\partial y^2}\right) + \left(\frac{\partial H}{\partial x}\cdot\frac{\partial u}{\partial x} + \frac{\partial H}{\partial y}\cdot\frac{\partial u}{\partial y}\right)$$

$$= H\left(\frac{\partial^2 u}{\partial x^2} + \frac{\partial^2 u}{\partial y^2}\right) + \left\{-nx\,(x^2 + y^2)^{-n/2-1}\frac{\partial H}{\partial x} - ny(x^2+y^2)^{-n/2-1}\frac{\partial H}{\partial y}\right\}$$

$$= H\left(\frac{\partial^2 u}{\partial x^2} + \frac{\partial^2 u}{\partial y^2}\right) - n\,(x^2 + y^2)^{-(n/2)-1}\left(x\frac{\partial H}{\partial x} + y\frac{\partial H}{\partial y}\right)$$

since H is a homogeneous function of degree n in x and y then

$$x\frac{\partial H}{\partial x} + y\frac{\partial H}{\partial y} = nH$$

$$\frac{\partial}{\partial x}\left(H\frac{\partial u}{\partial x}\right) + \frac{\partial}{\partial y}\left(H\frac{\partial u}{\partial y}\right)$$

$$= H\left(\frac{\partial^2 u}{\partial x^2} + \frac{\partial^2 u}{\partial y^2}\right) - n\,(x^2 + y^2)^{-(n/2)-1} \times nH$$

$$= H\left(\frac{\partial^2 u}{\partial x} + \frac{\partial^2 u}{\partial y^2}\right) - n^2\,(x^2 + y^2)^{-(n/2)-1}\,nH$$

$$= H\left[\frac{\partial^2 u}{\partial x^2} + \frac{\partial^2 u}{\partial y^2} - n^2\,(x^2 + y^2)^{-(n/2)-1}\right] \tag{1}$$

$$u = (x^2 + y^2)^{-n/2}$$

$$\Rightarrow \frac{\partial u}{\partial x} = -n/2\,(x^2 + y^2)^{-(n/2)-1}\,2x$$

$$= -nx\,(x^2 + y^2)^{-(n/2)-1}$$

similarly $\frac{\partial u}{\partial y} = -ny\,(x^2 + y^2)^{-(n/2)-1}$

$$\frac{\partial^2 u}{\partial x^2} = \frac{\partial}{\partial x}\left(\frac{\partial u}{\partial x}\right)$$

$$= \frac{\partial}{\partial x}\left[-nx\,(x^2 + y^2)^{-(n/2)-1}\right]$$

$$= -n\left[1\,(x^2 + y^2)^{-(n/2)-1} + x\,(-n/2-1)\,(x^2 + y^2)^{-(n/2)-2}\,2x\right]$$

$$= -n\left[(x^2 + y^2)^{-(n/2)-1} + \frac{(-n-2)}{2}\,(x^2 + y^2)^{-(n/2)-2}\,2x^2\right]$$

$$= -n\,(x^2 + y^2)^{-(n/2)-1} + n\,(n+2)\,(x^2 + y^2)^{-(n/2)-2}\,x^2$$

$$= n\,(x^2 + y^2)^{-(n/2)-1}\left[-1 + (n+2)\frac{x^2}{(x^2 + y^2)}\right]$$

similarly $\dfrac{\partial^2 u}{\partial y^2} = n\ (x^2 + y^2)^{-(n/2)-1}\left[-2 + (n+2)\ \dfrac{y}{x^2+y^2}\right]$

$$\frac{\partial^2 u}{\partial x_2} + \frac{\partial^2 u}{\partial y^2} = n\,(x^2+y^2)^{-(n/2)-1}\left[-2 + (n+2)\,\frac{(x^2+y^2)}{(x^2+y^2)}\right]$$

$$= n\,(x^2+y^2)^{-(n/2)-1}\,[-2+n+2] = n^2\,(x^2+y^2)^{-(n-/2)-1}$$

so we have $\dfrac{\partial}{\partial x}\left(H\dfrac{\partial u}{\partial x}\right) + \dfrac{\partial}{\partial x}\left(H\dfrac{\partial u}{\partial y}\right)$

$$H\,[n^2\,(x^2+y^2)^{(-n/2)-1} - n^2\,(x^2+y^2)^{(-n/2-1)}] = H \times 0 = 0$$

i.e. $\dfrac{\partial}{\partial x}\left(H\dfrac{\partial u}{\partial x}\right) + \dfrac{\partial}{\partial x}\left(H\dfrac{\partial n}{\partial y}\right) = 0$ *(proved)*

Problem 13 If $u = f(x, v)$ is a homogeneous function of degree n, then

(i) $x\dfrac{\partial^2 u}{\partial x^2} + y\dfrac{\partial^2 u}{\partial x \partial y} = (n-1)\dfrac{\partial u}{\partial x}$

(ii) $x\dfrac{\partial^2 u}{\partial x \partial y} + y\dfrac{\partial^2 u}{\partial y^2} = (n-1)\dfrac{\partial u}{\partial y}$

(iii) $x^2\dfrac{\partial^2 u}{\partial x^2} + 2xy\dfrac{\partial^2 u}{\partial x \partial y} + y^2\dfrac{\partial^2 u}{\partial y^2} = n\,(n-1)\,u$

Solution Since $u = f(x, y)$ is a homogeneous function of nth order therefore from Euler's thereom

$$x\frac{\partial u}{\partial x} + y\frac{\partial u}{\partial y} = n\,u \tag{1}$$

Differentiating partially with respect to x on both sides we have [i.e. taking y as constant]

$$\frac{\partial}{\partial x}\left[x\frac{\partial u}{\partial x} + y\frac{\partial u}{\partial y}\right] = \frac{\partial}{\partial x}(n\,u)$$

$$\frac{\partial}{\partial x}\left(x\frac{\partial u}{\partial x}\right) + \frac{\partial}{\partial x}\left(y\frac{\partial u}{\partial y}\right) = n\frac{\partial u}{\partial x} \tag{2}$$

$$\frac{\partial n}{\partial x} + x\frac{\partial^2 u}{\partial x^2} + 0 \cdot \frac{\partial u}{\partial y} + y\frac{\partial^2 u}{\partial x \partial y} = n\frac{\partial u}{\partial x} \tag{3}$$

$$x\frac{\partial^2 u}{\partial x^2} + y\frac{\partial^2 u}{\partial x \partial y} = n\frac{\partial u}{\partial x} - \frac{\partial u}{\partial x}$$

$$\Rightarrow x\frac{\partial^2 u}{\partial x^2} + y\frac{\partial^2 u}{\partial x \partial y} = (u-1)\frac{\partial u}{\partial x} \tag{4}$$ *(proved*

Again differentiating (1) partially with respect to y we have (taking x as constant)

$$\frac{\partial}{\partial x}\left\{x\frac{\partial u}{\partial x} + y\frac{\partial u}{\partial y}\right\} = \frac{\partial}{\partial y}(n\,u)$$

$$\frac{\partial}{\partial y}\left(x\ \frac{\partial u}{\partial x}\right)+\frac{\partial}{\partial y}\left(y\ \frac{\partial u}{\partial y}\right)=n\ \frac{\partial u}{\partial y}$$

$$0\cdot\frac{\partial u}{\partial x}+\ x\cdot\ \frac{\partial^2 u}{\partial y\partial x}+1\cdot\frac{\partial u}{\partial y}+y\ \frac{\partial^2 u}{\partial y^2}=\ n\ \frac{\partial u}{\partial y}$$

$$x\ \frac{\partial^2 u}{\partial y\partial x}+y\ \frac{\partial^2 u}{\partial y^2}=(n-1)\ \frac{\partial u}{\partial y}\quad \text{Since}\ \frac{\partial^2 u}{\partial^2 u}=\frac{\partial^2 u}{\partial x\ \partial y}$$

so
$$x\ \frac{\partial^2 u}{\partial y\ \partial x}+y\frac{\partial^2 u}{\partial y^2}=(n-1)\ \frac{\partial u}{\partial y} \qquad (5) \qquad \textit{(Proved)}$$

Multiplying (4) with x and (5) withy and adding we have

$$x^2\ \frac{\partial^2 u}{\partial x^2}+\ 2xy\ \frac{\partial^2 u}{\partial x\ \partial y}+y^2\ \frac{\partial^2 u}{\partial y^2}=(n-1)\left(x\frac{\partial u}{\partial x}+y\frac{\partial x}{\partial y}\right)$$

$$x^2\ \frac{\partial^2 u}{\partial x^2}+\ 2xy\ \frac{\partial^2 u}{\partial x\ \partial y}+\ y^2\ \frac{\partial^2 u}{\partial x^2}=n\ (n-1)\ u \qquad \textit{(Proved)}$$

Problem 14. If $u=\tan^{-1}\dfrac{x^3+y^3}{x-y}$ prove that

$$x^2\ \frac{\partial^2 u}{\partial x^2}\ +2xy\ \frac{\partial^2 u}{\partial x\ \partial y}+\ y^2\frac{\partial^2 u}{\partial y^2}=\sin\ 2u\ (1-4\ \sin^2 u) \qquad [\textit{I.F.S. 81}]$$

Solution From the given relation

$$u=\tan^{-1}\frac{x^3+y^3}{x-y}$$

$$\Rightarrow \tan u=\frac{x^3+y^3}{x-y}$$

$$\Rightarrow \tan u=\frac{x^3\left(1+\dfrac{y_3}{x^3}\right)}{x\left(1\ -\ \dfrac{y}{x}\right)}$$

$$\Rightarrow \tan u=\frac{x^2\left(1+\dfrac{y^3}{x^3}\right)}{\left(1\ -\ \dfrac{y}{x}\right)}$$

Let $\qquad v=\tan u$

Thus v is a homogeneous function of x and of order 2.

We know that if v is a homogeneous function of x and y of order n then we have.

$$x^2\ \frac{\partial^2 v}{\partial x^2}\ +2xy\ \frac{\partial^2 v}{\partial x\ \partial y}+y^2\ \frac{\partial^2 v}{\partial y^2}\ =n\ (n-1)\ v$$

Here $\quad n = 2$

So $\quad x^2 \frac{\partial^2 v}{\partial x^2} + 2xy \frac{\partial^2 v}{\partial x \partial y} + y^2 \frac{\partial^2 v}{\partial y^2} = 2(2-1)v$

$$x^2 \frac{\partial^2 v}{\partial x^2} + 2xy \frac{\partial^2 v}{\partial x \partial y} + y^2 \frac{\partial^2 v}{\partial y^2} = 2v$$

$$x^2 \frac{\partial^2 v}{\partial x^2} + 2xy \frac{\partial^2 v}{\partial x \partial y} + y^2 \frac{\partial^2 v}{\partial y^2} = 2v$$

$$x^2 \frac{\partial^2 v}{\partial x^2} + 2xy \frac{\partial^2 v}{\partial x \partial y} + y^2 \frac{\partial^2 v}{\partial y^2} = 2 \tan u \quad (1)$$

we have $\quad v = \tan u$ therefore

$$\frac{\partial v}{\partial x} = \sec^2 u \frac{\partial u}{\partial x}$$

$$\frac{\partial^2 v}{\partial x^2} = \frac{\partial}{\partial x}\left(\frac{\partial v}{\partial x}\right) = \frac{\partial}{\partial x}\left\{\sec^2 u \frac{\partial u}{\partial x}\right\}$$

$$= \frac{\partial}{\partial x}(\sec^2 u \frac{\partial u}{\partial x} + \frac{\partial}{\partial x}\left(\frac{\partial u}{\partial x}\right)\sec^2 u$$

$$= 2 \sec u \sec u \tan u \frac{\partial u}{\partial x} \cdot \frac{\partial u}{\partial x} + \frac{\partial^2 u}{\partial x^2} \sec^2 u$$

$$= 2 \sec^2 u \tan u \left(\frac{\partial u}{\partial x}\right)^2 + \frac{\partial^2 u}{\partial x^2} \sec^2 u$$

Similarly $\quad \frac{\partial^2 v}{\partial y^2} = 2 \sec^2 u \tan u \left(\frac{\partial u}{\partial y}\right)^2 + \frac{\partial^2 u}{\partial y^2} \sec^2 u$

Again $\quad \frac{\partial^2 v}{\partial x \partial x} = \frac{\partial^2 v}{\partial y \partial x} = \frac{\partial}{\partial y}\left(\frac{\partial v}{\partial x}\right)$

$$= \frac{\partial}{\partial y}\left(\sec^2 u \frac{\partial u}{\partial x}\right) = \frac{\partial}{\partial y}(\sec^2 u \frac{\partial u}{\partial x} + \frac{\partial}{\partial y}\left(\frac{\partial u}{\partial x}\right) \sec^2 u$$

$$= 2 \sec u \sec u \tan u \frac{\partial u}{\partial y} \frac{\partial u}{\partial x} + \frac{\partial^2 u}{\partial y \partial x}$$

$$= 2 \sec^2 u \tan u \left(\frac{\partial u}{\partial x}\right)\left(\frac{\partial u}{\partial y}\right) + \sec^2 u \frac{\partial^2 u}{\partial y \partial x}$$

$$= \sec^2 u \frac{\partial^2 u}{\partial x \partial y} + 2 \sec^2 u \tan u \left(\frac{\partial u}{\partial x}\right)\left(\frac{\partial u}{\partial y}\right)$$

Hence fron equation (1) we have

$$x^2\left[2\sec^2 u\tan u\left(\frac{\partial u}{\partial x}\right)^2+\frac{\partial^2 u}{\partial x^2}\sec^2 u\right]$$

$$+\,2xy\left[\sec^2 u\,\frac{\partial^2 u}{\partial x\,\partial y}+2\sec^2 u\tan u\left(\frac{\partial u}{\partial x}\right)\left(\frac{\partial u}{\partial y}\right)\right]$$

$$+\;y^2\left[2\sec^2 u\tan u\left(\frac{\partial u}{\partial y}\right)^2+\frac{\partial^2 u}{\partial y^2}\;\sec^2 u\right]=2\tan u$$

or $$2\sec^2 u\tan\left[x^2\left(\frac{\partial u}{\partial x}\right)^2+2xy\left(\frac{\partial u}{\partial x}\right)\left(\frac{\partial u}{\partial y}\right)+y^2\left(\frac{\partial u}{\partial y}\right)^2\right]$$

$$+\sec^2 u\left[x^2\frac{\partial^2 u}{\partial x^2}+2xy\,\frac{\partial^2 u}{\partial x\,\partial y}+y\,\frac{2\partial^2 u}{\partial y^2}\right]=2\tan u$$

or $$2\sec^2 u\tan u\left(x\,\frac{\partial u}{\partial x}+y\,\frac{\partial u}{\partial y}\right)^2$$

$$+\sec^2 u\left[x^2\frac{\partial^2 u}{\partial x^2}+2xy\,\frac{\partial^{\circ} u}{\partial x\,\partial y}+y^2\,\frac{\partial^2 u}{\partial y^2}\right]=2\tan u \qquad (2)$$

since $$u=\tan^2\frac{x^3+y^3}{x-y}$$

$$\tan u=\frac{x^3+y^3}{x-y}$$

$$\tan u=\frac{x^2\left(1+\dfrac{y^3}{x^3}\right)}{x\left(1-\dfrac{y}{x}\right)}=\frac{x^2\left(1+\dfrac{y^3}{x^3}\right)}{\left(1-\dfrac{y}{x}\right)}$$

Let $v=\tan u$ thus v is a homageneus function of x and y of 2nd degree. Then According to Euler is theorem

$$x\,\frac{\partial v}{\partial x}+y\,\frac{\partial v}{\partial y}=2v$$

$$x\sec^2 u\,\frac{\partial u}{\partial x}+y\sec^2 u\,\frac{\partial u}{\partial y}=2\tan u$$

$$\left(x\,\frac{\partial u}{\partial x}+y\,\frac{\partial u}{\partial y}\right)=2\,\frac{\tan u}{\sec^2 u}$$

$$x\,\frac{\partial u}{\partial x}+y\,\frac{\partial u}{\partial y}=\frac{2\tan u}{1}\times\cos^2 u$$

$$x\,\frac{\partial u}{\partial x}+y\,\frac{\partial u}{\partial y}=\frac{2\sin u}{\cos u}\cdot\cos^2 u$$

$$x\,\frac{\partial u}{\partial x}+y\,\frac{\partial u}{\partial y}=2\sin u\cos u$$

$$x\,\frac{\partial u}{\partial x}+y\,\frac{\partial u}{\partial y}=\sin^2 u$$

Hence from equation (2) we have

$$2 \sec u \tan u (\sin 2u)^2 + \sec^2 u \left[x^2 \frac{\partial^2 u}{\partial x^2} + 2xy \frac{\partial^2 u}{\partial x \partial y} + y^2 \frac{\partial^2 u}{\partial y^2} \right] = 2 \tan u$$

$$\sec^2 u \left[x^2 \frac{\partial^2 u}{\partial x^2} + 2xy \frac{\partial^2 u}{\partial x \partial y} + y^2 \frac{\partial^2 u}{\partial y^2} \right]$$
$$= 2 \tan u [1 - \sec^2 u \sin^2 2u]$$

$$x^2 \frac{\partial^2 u}{\partial x^2} + 2xy \frac{\partial^2 u}{\partial x \partial y} + y^2 \frac{\partial^2 u}{\partial y^2}$$
$$= \sin 2u [1 - 4 \sin^2 u \cos^2 u \sec^2 u]$$
$$= \sin 2u [1 - 4 \sin^2 u] \qquad \textit{(proved)}$$

Problem 15 If $u = x\phi\left(\frac{x}{y}\right) + \psi\left(\frac{y}{x}\right)$ prove that

$$x^2 \frac{\partial^2 u}{\partial x^2} + 2xy \frac{\partial^2 u}{\partial x \partial y} + y^2 \frac{\partial^2 u}{\partial y^2} = 0$$

Let $\qquad u = x + \gamma$

where $\qquad x = x\phi\left(\frac{x}{y}\right)$

which is a homogenous function of first (1) order

and $\qquad \gamma = \psi\left(\frac{y}{x}\right)$

which is a homogeneous function of zero order. Then

$$x^2 \frac{\partial^2 X}{\partial x^2} + 2xy \frac{\partial^2 X}{\partial x \partial y} + y^2 \frac{\partial^2 X}{\partial y^2} = 1 (1-1) x = 0$$

$$x^2 \frac{\partial^2 x}{\partial x^2} + 2y \frac{\partial^2 x}{\partial x \partial y} + y^2 \frac{\partial^2 x}{\partial y^2} = 0 \qquad (1)$$

Again $\qquad x^2 \frac{\partial^2 Y}{\partial x^2} + 2xy \frac{\partial^2 Y}{\partial x \partial y} + y^2 \frac{\partial^2 Y}{\partial y^2} = (0-1) Y$

$$x^2 \frac{\partial^2 \gamma}{\partial x^2} + 2xy \frac{\partial^2 \gamma}{\partial x \partial y} + y^2 \frac{\partial^2 \gamma}{\partial y^2} = 0 \qquad (2)$$

Now we have

$$x^2 \frac{\partial^2 u}{\partial x^2} + 2xy \frac{\partial^2 u}{\partial x \partial y} + y^2 \frac{\partial^2 u}{\partial y^2}$$

$$= x^2 \frac{\partial^2}{\partial x^2}(X + Y) + 2xy \frac{\partial^2}{\partial x \partial y}(X + Y) + y^2 \frac{\partial^2}{\partial y^2}(X + Y)$$

$$= \left(x^2 \frac{\partial^2 X}{\partial x^2} + 2xy \frac{\partial^2 X}{\partial y \partial y} + y^2 \frac{\partial^2 x}{\partial y^2} \right)$$
$$+ \left(x^2 \frac{\partial^2 \gamma}{\partial x^2} + 2xy \frac{\partial^2 \gamma}{\partial x \partial y} + y^2 \frac{\partial^2 \gamma}{\partial y^2} \right) = 0 + 0 = 0$$

Thus

$$x^2 \frac{\partial^2 u}{\partial x^2} + 2xy \frac{\partial^2 u}{\partial x \partial y} + y^2 \frac{\partial^2 u}{\partial y^2} = 0 \qquad \textit{(proved)}$$

Problem 16 $u = (x^2 + y^2)^{2/3}$ prove that

$$x^2 \frac{\partial^2 u}{\partial x^2} + 2xy \frac{\partial^2 u}{\partial x \partial y} + y^2 \frac{\partial^2 u}{\partial y^2} = \frac{4}{9} u$$

Solution $u = (x^2 + y^2)^{2/3}$ (1)

Differentiating (1) partially with respect to x [i.e. treating y as constant] we have

$$\frac{\partial u}{\partial x} = \frac{2}{3} (x^2 + y^2)^{2/3-1} \frac{\partial}{\partial x} (x^2 + y^2)$$

$$= \frac{2}{3} (x^2 + y^2)^{-1/3}\, 2x$$

$$= \frac{4}{3}\, x\, (x^2 + y^2)^{-1/3} \qquad (1)$$

Similarly $\frac{\partial u}{\partial y} - \frac{4}{3}\, y\, (x^2 + y^2)^{-1/3}$ (2)

Again differentiating (1) purtially with respect to x we hove

$$\frac{\partial^2 u}{\partial x^2} = \frac{4}{3}\left[(x^2+y^2) - \frac{1}{3} + x\left(-\frac{1}{3}\right)[(x^2 + y^2)^{-1/3-1}\, 2x\right]$$

$$= \frac{4}{3}\left[(x^2 + y^2)^{-1/3} - \frac{2}{3}\, x^2 (x^2 + y^2)^{-4/3}\right]$$

Similarly $\frac{\partial^2 u}{\partial y^2} = \frac{4}{3}\left[(x^2 + y^2)^{-1/3} - \frac{2}{3}\, y^2 (x^2 + y^2)^{-4/3}\right]$

Now $\frac{\partial^2 u}{\partial x\, \partial y} = \frac{\partial}{\partial x}\left[\frac{\partial u}{\partial y}\right]$

$$= \frac{\partial}{\partial x}\left[\frac{4}{3}\, y\, (x^2 + y^2)^{-1/3}\right] \qquad \text{i.e. } y = \text{const}$$

$$= \frac{4}{3}\left[0 \cdot (x^2 + y^2)^{-1/3} + y\left(-\frac{1}{3}\right)(x^2 + y^2)^{-4/3}\, 2x\right]$$

$$= \frac{4}{3}\left[\frac{2}{3}\, xy\, (x^2 + y^2)^{-4/3}\right]$$

$$= -\frac{8}{9}\, xy\, (x^2 + y^2)^{-4/3}$$

Fow we have

$$x^2 \frac{\partial^2 u}{\partial x^2} + 2xy \frac{\partial^2 u}{\partial x \, \partial y} + y^2 \frac{\partial^2 u}{\partial y^2}$$

$$= x^2 \left[\frac{4}{3} (x^2 + y^2)^{-1/3} - \frac{8}{9} (x^2 + y^2)^{-4/3} x^2 \right]$$

$$+ 2xy \left[-\frac{8}{9} xy (x^2 + y^2)^{-4/3} \right]$$

$$+ y^2 \left[\frac{4}{3} (x^2 + y^2)^{-1/3} - \frac{8}{9} (x^2 + y^2)^{-4/3} y^2 \right]$$

$$= \frac{4}{3} (x^2 + y^2)^{-1/3} (x^2) - \frac{8}{9} (x^2 + y^2)^{-4/3} x^4$$

$$- \frac{16}{9} x^2 y^2 (x^2 + y^2)^{-4/3}$$

$$+ \frac{4}{3} (x^2 + y^2)^{-1/3} y^2 - \frac{8}{9} (x^2 + y^2)^{-4/3} y^4$$

$$= \frac{4}{3} (x^2 + y^2)^{-1/3} (x^2 + y^2) - \frac{8}{9} (x^2 + y^2)^{-4/3} (x^4 + y^4 + 2x^2 y^2)$$

$$= \frac{4}{3} (x^2 + y^2)^{2/3} - \frac{8}{9} (x^2 + y^2)^{-4/3} (x^2 + y^2)^2$$

$$= \frac{4}{3} (x^2 + y^2)^{2/3} - \frac{8}{9} (x^2 + y^2)^{2/3}$$

$$= (x^2 + y^2)^{2/3} \left(\frac{4}{3} - \frac{8}{9} \right)$$

$$= (x^2 + y^2)^{2/3} \frac{(12 - 8)}{9}$$

$$= \frac{4}{9} (x^2 + y^2)^{2/3}$$

$$= \frac{4}{9} u$$

i.e. $$x^2 \frac{\partial^2 u}{\partial x^2} + 2xy \frac{\partial^2 u}{\partial x \, \partial y} + y^2 \frac{\partial^2 u}{\partial y^2} = \frac{4}{9} u$$ *(proved)*

Problem 17 $f(x, y, z) = \begin{vmatrix} x^2 & y^2 & z^2 \\ x & y & z \\ 1 & 1 & 1 \end{vmatrix}$ then

prove that $$\frac{\partial f}{\partial x} + \frac{\partial f}{\partial y} + \frac{\partial f}{\partial z} = 0$$

Solution $f(x, y, z) = x^2(y-z) - y^2(x-z) + z^2(x-y)$

$$f(x, y, z) = x^2(y-z) + y^2(z-x) + z^2(x-y)$$

$$\frac{\partial f}{\partial x} = (y-z)\,2x + y^2(0-1) + z^2(1-0)$$

$$= 2xy - 2xz - y^2 + z^2 \qquad (1)$$

$$\frac{\partial f}{\partial y} = x^2(1-0) + 2y(z-x) + z^2(0-1)$$

$$= x^2 + 2yz - 2xy - z^2 \qquad (2)$$

$$\frac{\partial f}{\partial z} = x^2(0-1) + y^2(1-0) + 2z(x-y)$$

$$\frac{\partial f}{\partial z} = -x^2 + y^2 + 2xz - 2yz \qquad (1)$$

Adding equation (1), (2) and (3) we have

$$\frac{\partial f}{\partial x} + \frac{\partial f}{\partial y} + \frac{\partial f}{\partial z} = 0 \qquad \textit{(proved)}$$

INDETERMINATE FORMS

Some Important Functions

$$(1+x)^n = 1 + nx + \frac{n(n-1)}{1\cdot 2}x^2 + \ldots$$

$$e^x = 1 + x + \frac{x^2}{2!} + \frac{x^3}{3!} + \ldots$$

$$\log(1+x) = x - \frac{x^2}{2} + \frac{x^3}{3} - \frac{x^4}{4} + \ldots$$

$$\sin x = x - \frac{x^3}{3!} + \frac{x^5}{5!} \ldots,$$

$$\cos x = 1 - \frac{x^2}{2!} + \frac{x^2}{4!} - \ldots$$

$$\tan x = x + \frac{x^3}{3} + \frac{2x^5}{15} + \ldots \text{ etc}$$

First Form $\frac{0}{0}$; L' Hospital's Rule

et $\phi(x)$ and $\psi(x)$ be functions of x capable of being expanded by Taylor's theorem and if $\phi(a) = 0$ and $\psi(a) = 0$ then

$$\operatorname*{Lt}_{x \to a} \frac{\phi(x)}{\psi(x)} = \operatorname*{lt}_{x \to a} \frac{\phi'(x)}{\psi'(x)}$$

provided the later limit exists (finite or infinite).

Ex. 1 limit of $\frac{\sin \theta}{\theta}$ when $\theta \to 0$

This is of the form $\frac{0}{0}$

$$\text{The given limit} = \lim_{\theta \to 0} \frac{\sin \theta}{\theta}$$

$$= \lim_{\theta \to 0} \frac{\text{differential coefficient of } \sin \theta}{\text{differential coefficient of } \theta}$$

$$= \lim_{\theta \to 0} \frac{\cos \theta}{1}$$

$$= \cos \theta = 1$$

Ex. 2 limit of $\frac{\tan \theta}{\theta}$ when $\theta \to 0$

Solution This it of the form $\frac{0}{0}$

$$\lim_{\theta \to 0} \frac{\tan \theta}{\theta} = \lim_{\theta \to 0} \frac{dc \text{ of } \tan \theta}{dc \text{ of } \theta}$$

$$= \lim_{\theta \to 0} \frac{\sec^2 \theta}{1} = \sec^2 0 = 1$$

Problem 1 Evaluate $\lim_{\theta \to 0} \frac{a^x - 1}{x}$

Solution putting $x = 0$ we have

$$\frac{a^x - 1}{x} = \frac{a^0 - 1}{0} = \frac{1 - 1}{0} = \frac{0}{0} \text{ (form)}$$

i.e. $$\lim_{x \to 0} \frac{a^x - 1}{x} = \lim_{x \to 0} \frac{dc\ (a^x - 1)}{dc \text{ of } (x)}$$

$$dc\ (a^y) = a^x \log a$$

$$= \lim_{x \to 0} \frac{a^x \log a - 0}{1}$$

$$= \lim_{x \to 0} a^x \log a$$

$$= a^0 \log a = \log a$$

i.e. $$\lim_{x \to 0} \frac{a^x - 1}{x} = \log a$$

Problem 2 Evaluate $\lim\limits_{x\to 0} \dfrac{\log(1-x^2)}{\log \cos x}$

Solution Putting $x = 0$ we have

$$\frac{\log(1-x^2)}{\log \cos x} = \frac{\log(1-0)}{\log \cos 0} = \frac{\log 1}{\log 1} = \frac{0}{0} \text{ (form)}$$

So using L' Hospitals rule we have

$$\lim_{x\to 0} \frac{\log(1-x^2)}{\log \cos x} = \lim_{x\to 0} \frac{dc\,\{\log(-x^2)\}}{dc\,\{\log \cos x\}}$$

$$= \lim_{x\to 0} \frac{\frac{1}{1-x^2}\cdot(1-2\dot{x})}{\frac{1}{\cos x}(-\sin x)} = \lim_{x\to 0} \frac{2x}{1-x^2} \times \frac{1}{\tan x}$$

$$= 2 \lim_{x\to 0} \frac{1}{1-x^2} \cdot \frac{1}{\left(\frac{\tan x}{x}\right)}$$

Remember $\lim\limits_{x\to 0} \dfrac{\tan x}{x} = 1$

$$= 2 \lim_{x\to 0} \frac{1}{1-x^2} \cdot \frac{1}{\lim\limits_{x\to 0} \left(\frac{\tan x}{x}\right)}$$

$$= 2 \cdot \frac{1}{1-0} \cdot \frac{1}{1} = 2 \textbf{ Ans}$$

Problem 3 Evaluate $\lim\limits_{x\to 0} \dfrac{\log(1+kx^2)}{1-\cos x}$

Solution Putting $x = 0$ we have

$$\frac{\log(1+kx^2)}{1-\cos x} = \frac{\log(1+k\cdot 0)}{1-\cos 0} = \frac{\log 1}{1-1} = \frac{0}{0} \text{ (form)}$$

Apply L' Hospital's rule

$$\lim_{x\to 0} \frac{\log 1+kx^2)}{1-\cos x} = \lim_{x\to 0} \frac{dc\,\{\log(1+kx^2)\}}{dc\,\{1-\cos x\}}$$

$$= \lim_{x\to 0} \frac{\frac{1}{1+kx^2}\cdot(2kx)}{0-(-\sin x)} = \lim_{x\to 0} \frac{2kx}{1+kx^2} \cdot \frac{1}{\sin x}$$

$$= \lim_{x\to 0} \frac{2k}{1+kx^2} \cdot \frac{1}{\lim\limits_{x\to 0} \frac{\sin x}{x}} = \frac{2k}{1+k\cdot 0} \frac{1}{1} = 2k$$

$\lim\limits_{x\to 0} \dfrac{\sin x}{x} = 1$

i.e. $\lim\limits_{x\to 0} \dfrac{\log(1+kx^2)}{1-\cos x} = 2k$, **Ans.**

Problem 4 Prove that

$$\lim_{x\to 0} \frac{xe^x - \log(1+x)}{x_2} = \frac{3}{2}$$

Solution Putting $x = 0$ we have

$$\frac{xe^x - \log(1+x)}{x^2} = \frac{0\cdot e^0 - \log 1}{0^2} = \frac{0}{0} \text{ (form)}$$

we find out the limit of this expression by using the expansion of e^x and $\log(1+x)$

$$\frac{xe^x - \log(1+x)}{x^2}$$

$$= \frac{x\left\{1 + x + \frac{x^2}{2!} + \frac{x^3}{3!} + \ldots\right\} - \left\{x - \frac{x^2}{2} + \frac{x^3}{3} - \frac{x^4}{4} + \ldots\right\}}{x^2}$$

$$= \frac{x + x^2 + \frac{x^3}{2!} + \frac{x^4}{3!} + \ldots - x + \frac{x^2}{2} - \frac{x^3}{3} + \frac{x^4}{4} - \ldots}{x^2}$$

$$= \frac{\left(x^2 + \frac{x^2}{2}\right) + x^3\left(\frac{1}{2} - \frac{1}{3}\right) + \text{heigher powers of } x}{x^2}$$

$$= \frac{\frac{3x^2}{2} + x^3\frac{1}{6} + \text{heigher powers of } x}{x^2}$$

$$= \frac{3}{2} + x\frac{1}{6} + 0(x)$$

$$\lim_{x\to 0} \frac{xe^x - \log(1+x)}{x^2}$$

$$= \lim_{x\to 0} \frac{3}{2} + \frac{x}{6} + 0(x) = \frac{3}{2} + 0 + 0 = \frac{3}{2} \qquad \textit{(Proved)}$$

Problem 5 Find $\lim_{x\to 1} \frac{\sin \pi x}{\sin 3\pi x}$ [*I.F.S. 88*]

Solution putting $x = 1$ we have

$$\frac{\sin \pi x}{\sin 3\pi x} = \frac{\sin \pi\cdot 1}{\sin 3\pi} = \frac{0}{0} \text{ (form)}$$

so applying L' Hospital's rule we have

$$\lim_{x\to 1} \frac{\sin \pi x}{\sin 3\pi x} = \lim_{x\to 1} \frac{dc\,(\sin \pi x)}{dc\,(\sin 3\pi x)}$$

$$= \lim_{x\to 1} \frac{\pi \cos \pi x}{3\pi \cos 3\pi x} = \frac{1}{3} \lim_{x\to 1} \frac{\cos \pi x}{\cos 3\pi x}$$

$$= \frac{1}{3} \frac{\cos \pi}{\cos 3\pi} = \frac{1}{3} \frac{(-1)}{\cos (2\pi + \pi)}$$

$$= -\frac{1}{3\,(\cos \pi)} = -\frac{1}{3\,(-1)} = \frac{1}{3}$$

i.e. $\lim_{x\to 1} \frac{\sin \pi x}{\sin 3\pi x} = \frac{1}{3}$ **Ans.**

Problem 6 Evaluate $\lim_{x\to 0} \frac{(1+x)^n - 1}{x}$ [*I.F.S. 86*]

Solution putting $x = 0$ we have

$$\frac{(1+x)^n - 1}{x} = \frac{(1+0)^n - 1}{x} = \frac{1-1}{0} = \frac{0}{0} \text{ (form)}$$

We shall solve this problem by using the expansion of $(1 + x)^n$

$$\frac{(1+x)^n - 1}{x} = \frac{1 + {}^nc_1\, x^1 + {}^nc_2\, x^2 + {}^nc_3\, x^3 + \ldots - 1}{x}$$

$$= \frac{{}^nc_1\, x + {}^nc_2\, x^2 + {}^nc_3\, x^2 + \ldots}{x}$$

$$= {}^nc_1 + {}^nc_2\, x^1 + {}^nc_3\, x^2$$

$$\lim_{x\to 0} \frac{(1+x)^n - 1}{x} = {}^nc_1 + {}^nc_2 \lim_{x\to 0} x + \text{etc.}$$

$$\lim_{x\to 0} \frac{(1+x)^n - 1}{x} = {}^nc_1 = \frac{n\,!}{(n-1)\,!\,1\,!} = \frac{n\,(n-)\,!}{(n-1)\,!\,1\,!}$$

$$\lim_{x\to 0} \frac{(1+x)^n - 1}{x} = n$$ **Ans.**

Problem 7 Evaluate

(i) $\lim_{x\to 1} \frac{\log x}{x-1}$

(ii) $\lim_{x\to 1} \frac{\log x}{x^n - 1}$

Solution Putting $x=1$ we have

$$\frac{\log x}{x-1} = \frac{\log 1}{1-1} = \frac{0}{0} \quad \text{(Form)}$$

so using L' Hospital's rule we have

$$\lim_{x\to 1} \frac{de\,(\log x)}{de\,(x-1)}$$

$$= \lim_{x\to 1} \frac{1/x}{1-0} \lim_{x\to 1} \frac{1}{x} = 1$$ **Ans.**

(ii) Putting $x = 1$ we have

$$\frac{\text{iog } x}{x^n - 1} = \frac{\log 1}{1-1} = \frac{0}{0} \qquad \text{(from)}$$

so using L[1] Hospital's rule we have

$$\lim_{x\to 1} \frac{\log x}{x^n - 1} = \lim_{x\to 1} \frac{dc\,(\log x)}{de\,(x^n - 1)} = \lim_{x\to 1} \frac{1/x}{nx^{n-1}}$$

$$\lim_{x\to 1} \frac{\log x}{x^n - 1} = \lim_{x\to 1} \frac{1}{nx^n} = \frac{1}{n\,(1)^n} = \frac{1}{n}$$ **Ans.**

Problem 8 Evaluate

$$\lim_{x\to\pi/4} \frac{1-\tan x}{1-\sqrt{2}\sin x}$$

Solution Putting $x = \frac{\pi}{4}$ we have

$$\lim_{x\to \pi/4} \frac{1-\tan x}{1-\sqrt{2}\sin x} = \frac{1-\tan \pi/4}{1-\sqrt{2}\sin \pi/4} = \frac{1-1}{1-\sqrt{2}\;1/\sqrt{2}}$$

$$= \frac{1-1}{1-1} = \frac{0}{0} \qquad \textit{(from)}$$

so applylng L' Hospitals rule we have

$$\lim_{x\to \pi/4} \frac{1-\tan x}{1-\sqrt{2}\sin x} = \lim_{x\leftarrow \pi/4} \frac{dc\,(1-\tan x)}{dc\,(1-\sqrt{2}\sin x)}$$

$$= \lim_{x\to \pi/4} \frac{0-\sec^2 x}{0-\sqrt{2}\cos x} = \lim_{x\to \pi/4} \frac{\sec^2 x}{\sqrt{2}\cos x}$$

$$= \lim_{x\to\pi/4} \frac{1}{\sqrt{2}\cos^3 x} = \frac{1}{\sqrt{2}\,(\cos \pi/4)^3}$$

$$= \frac{1}{\sqrt{2}\left(\frac{1}{\sqrt{2}}\right)^3} = \frac{1}{\sqrt{2} \times \frac{1}{2\sqrt{2}}}$$

i.e. $$\lim_{x\to \pi/4} \frac{1-\text{ten } x}{1-\sqrt{2}\sin x} = 2$$ **Ans.**

Problem 9 $\lim_{x \to 0} \dfrac{e^x - e^{-x}}{\log(1+x)}$

Solution Puttting $x = 0$, we have

$$\lim_{x \to 0} \frac{e^x - e^{-x}}{\log(1+x)} = \frac{c^0 - e^{-0}}{\log 1} = \frac{1-1}{0} = \frac{0}{0} \quad \text{(form)}$$

we here use expansions of e^x, e^{-x} and $\log(1+x)$ to solve the problem

$$e^x = 1 + x + \frac{x^2}{2!} + \frac{x^3}{3!} + \ldots$$

$$e^{-x} = 1 - x + \frac{x^2}{2!} - \frac{x^3}{3!} + \ldots$$

$$\log(1+x) = x - \frac{x^2}{2} + \frac{x^3}{3} - \frac{x^4}{4} + \ldots$$

$$e^x - e^x = 1 + x + \frac{x^2}{2!} + \frac{x^3}{3!} + \ldots - 1 + x - \frac{x^2}{2!} + \frac{x^3}{3!} \ldots$$

$$e^x - e^{-x} = 2x + 2\frac{x^3}{3!} + \frac{2x^5}{5!} + \ldots$$

$$e^x - e^x = 2x\left(1 + \frac{x^2}{3!} + \frac{x^4}{5!} + \ldots\right)$$

$$\log(1+x) = x - \frac{x^2}{2} + \frac{x^3}{3} - \ldots$$

$$\log(1+x) = x\left[1 - \frac{x}{2} + \frac{x^2}{3} \ldots\right]$$

Then the expression

$$\frac{e^x - e^{-x}}{\log(1+x)} = 2x\frac{\left[1 + \frac{x^2}{3!} + \frac{x^4}{5!} + \ldots\right]}{x\left[1 - \frac{x}{2} + \frac{x^2}{3} - \ldots\right]}$$

$$= \frac{2\left(1 + \frac{x^2}{3!} + \frac{x^4}{5!} + \ldots\right)}{\left(1 - \frac{x}{2} + \frac{x^2}{3} - \ldots\right)}$$

$$\lim_{x \to 0} \frac{e^x - e^{-x}}{\log(1+x)} = 2 \lim_{x \to 0} \frac{\left(1 + \frac{x^2}{3!} + \frac{x^4}{5!} + \ldots\right)}{\left(1 - \frac{x}{2} + \frac{x^2}{3} - \ldots\right)}$$

$$= 2\frac{(1 + 0 + 0 + \ldots)}{(1 - 0 + 0 - \ldots)} = 2 \cdot 1 = 2$$

$$\lim_{x \to 0} \frac{e^x - e^{-x}}{\log(1+x)} = 2 \quad \textbf{Ans.}$$

Probelm 10 Evaluate

$$\lim_{x\to 0} \frac{e^{ax}-e^{-ax}}{\log(1+bx)}$$

Solution Substituting $x=0$ we nave

$$\lim_{x\to 0} \frac{e^{ax}-e^{-ax}}{\log(1+bx)} = \frac{e^0-e^{-0}}{\log 1} = \frac{1-1}{0} = \text{(form)}$$

So applying L' Hospitals rule we have

$$\lim_{x\to 0} \frac{e^{ax}-e^{-ax}}{\log(1+bx)}$$

$$= \lim_{x\to 0} \frac{d\cdot c \text{ of } \{e^{ax} - e^{-ax}\}}{d\cdot c \text{ of } \{\log(1+bx)\}}$$

$$= \lim_{x\to 0} \frac{ae^{ax}+ae^{-ax}}{\frac{b}{1+bx}}$$

$$= \frac{a}{b} \lim_{x\to 0} (1+b.0)(c^{ax}+e^{-ax})$$

$$= \frac{a}{b} (1+b\cdot 0 (e^0+e^{-0})$$

$$= \frac{a}{b}(1+1) = \frac{2a}{b}$$

i.e. $$\lim_{x\to 0} \frac{e^{ax}-e^{-ax}}{\log(1+bx)} = \frac{2a}{b}$$ **Ans.**

Problem 11 $$\lim_{x\to 0} \frac{x-\sin x}{x^3}$$

Solution Putting $x=0$ we have the expression

$$\frac{x-\sin x}{x^3} = \frac{0-0}{0} = \frac{0}{0} \text{ (form)}$$

So applying L' Hospitals rule we have

$$\lim_{x\to 0} \frac{x-\sin x}{x^3} = \lim_{x\to 0} \frac{dc\,(x-\sin x)}{dc\,(x^3)}$$

$$= \lim_{x\to 0} \frac{(1-\cos x)}{3x^2} \qquad \left[\frac{0}{0} \text{ form Again}\right]$$

So Again applying L' Hospitals rule we have

$$\lim_{x\to 0} \frac{(1-\cos x)}{3x^2} = \lim_{x\to 0} \frac{d.c\,(1-\cos x)}{d.c\,(3x^2)}$$

$$= \lim_{x\to 0} \frac{0+\sin x}{6x} = \frac{1}{6} \lim_{x\to 0} \left(\frac{\sin x}{x}\right)$$

$$= \frac{1}{6} \times 1 = \frac{1}{6} \quad \textbf{Ans.}$$

Since $\lim_{x\to 0} \dfrac{\sin x}{x} = 1$

ANOTHER METHOD

We can also solve this problem by using expansion of $\sin x$

$$\sin x = x - \frac{x^3}{3!} + \frac{x^5}{5!} \ldots$$

So $$x - \sin x = x - \left(x - \frac{x^3}{3!}\right) + \frac{x^5}{5!} - \ldots\Big)$$

$$= x - x + \frac{x^3}{3!} - \frac{x^5}{5!} + \ldots = \frac{x^3}{3!} - \frac{x^5}{5!} + \ldots$$

$$= x^3\left(\frac{1}{3!} - \frac{x^2}{5!} + \ldots\right)$$

$$\frac{x-\sin x}{x^3} = \frac{1}{3!} - \frac{x^2}{5!} + \ldots$$

Taking limit as $x \to 0$ on both sides we have,

$$\lim_{x\to 0} \frac{x-\sin x}{x^3} = \frac{1}{3!} - 0 + 0 = \frac{1}{3!} = \frac{1}{3\times 2} = \frac{1}{6}$$

i.e. $$\lim_{x\to 0} \frac{x-\sin x}{x^3} = \frac{1}{6} \quad \textbf{Ans.}$$

Problem 12 Evaluate $\lim_{x\to 0} \dfrac{\tan x - x}{x^2 \tan x}$

Solution Substituting $x = 0$ we have the expression

$$\frac{\tan x - x}{x^2 \tan x} = \frac{0-0}{0} = \frac{0}{0} \text{ (form)}$$

to solve this problem we use the expansion of $\tan x$. We have

$$\tan x = x + \frac{x^3}{3} + \frac{2}{15} x^5 + \ldots \tag{1}$$

$$\Rightarrow \tan x - x = \frac{x^3}{3} + \frac{2}{15}x^5 + \ldots$$

$$\Rightarrow \tan x - x = x^2\left(\frac{x}{3} + \frac{2}{15}x^3 + \ldots\right)$$

$$\Rightarrow \frac{\tan x - x}{x^2} = \frac{x}{3} + \frac{2}{15}x^3 + \ldots \qquad (2)$$

Dividing (2) by (1) we have

$$\frac{\tan x - x}{x^2 \tan x} = \frac{\frac{x}{3} + \frac{2}{15}x^3 + \ldots}{x + \frac{x^3}{3} + \frac{2}{15}x^5 + \ldots}$$

$$\frac{\tan x - x}{x^2 \tan x} = \frac{x\left(\frac{1}{3} + \frac{2}{15}x^2 + \ldots\right)}{x\left(1 + \frac{x^2}{3} + \frac{2}{15}x^4 + \ldots\right)}$$

Taking limit of both sides as $x \to 0$ we have

$$\lim_{x\to 0} \frac{\tan x - x}{x^2 \tan x} = \frac{1}{3} \qquad \textbf{Ans.}$$

Problem 13 Evaluate $\lim\limits_{x\to 0} \frac{\log(1+x^3)}{\sin^3 x}$

Solution Substituting $x = 0$ we have the expression

$$\lim_{x\to 0} \frac{\log(1+x^3)}{\sin^3 x} = \frac{\log(1+0)}{\sin^3 0} = \frac{\log 1}{0} = \frac{0}{0} \text{ (form)}$$

Thus applying L' Hospitals rule we have

$$\lim_{x\to 0} \frac{\log(1+x^3)}{\sin^3 x} = \lim_{x\to 0} \frac{d{\cdot}c\{\log(1+x^3)\}}{d{\cdot}c\,\{\sin^3 x\}}$$

$$= \lim_{x\to 0} \frac{\frac{3x^2}{1+x^3}}{3\sin^2 x \cos x}$$

$$= \lim_{x\to 0} \frac{3x^2}{3(1+x^3)\sin^2 x \cos x}$$

$$\lim_{x\to 0} \frac{\sin x}{x} = 1$$

$$= \frac{1}{\lim\limits_{x\to 0}(1+x^3)} \times \frac{1}{\lim\limits_{x\to 0}\left(\frac{\sin x}{x}\right)^2 \times \lim\limits_{x\to 0} \cos x}$$

$$= \frac{1}{1+0} \times \frac{1}{(1)^2} \times \frac{1}{1}$$

i.e. $$\lim_{x\to 0} \frac{\log(1+x^3)}{\sin^3 x} = 1 \qquad \textbf{Ans.}$$

Problem 14 $\lim_{x\to 0} \frac{x^{1/2}\tan x}{(e^x-1)^{3/2}}$

Solution Putting $x = 0$ we have the expression

$$\frac{x^{1/2}\tan x}{(e^x-1)^{3/2}} = \frac{0}{(1-1)^{3/2}} = \frac{0}{0} \text{ (form)}$$

We solve this problem by using expansion of $\tan x$ and e^x

$$\tan x = x + \frac{x^3}{3} + \frac{2}{15}x^5 + \ldots$$

$$x^{1/2}\tan x = x^{1/2}\left[x + \frac{x^3}{3} + \frac{2}{15}x^5 + \ldots\right]$$

$$= x^{1/2}.x\left[1 + \frac{x^2}{3} + \frac{2}{15}x^4 + \ldots\right]$$

$$= x^{3/2}\left[1 + \frac{x^2}{3} + \frac{2}{15}x^4 + \ldots\right]$$

$$e^x = 1 + x + \frac{x^2}{2!} + \frac{x^3}{3!} + \ldots$$

$$e^x - 1 = x + \frac{x^2}{2!} + \frac{x^3}{3!} + \ldots$$

$$(e^x-1)^{3/2} = \left(x + \frac{x^2}{2!} + \frac{x^3}{3!} + \ldots\right)^{3/2}$$

$$= x^{3/2}\left(1 + \frac{x}{2!} + \frac{x^2}{3!} + \ldots\right)^{3/2}$$

$$\frac{x^{1/2}\tan x}{(e^x-1)^{3/2}} = \frac{x^{3/2}\left[1 + \frac{x^2}{3} + \frac{2x^4}{15} + \ldots\right]}{x^{3/2}\left[1 + \frac{x}{2!} + \frac{x^2}{3!} + \ldots\right]}$$

Taking limit on both sides as $x \to 0$ we have

$$\lim_{x\to 0}\frac{x^{1/2}\tan x}{(e^x-1)^{3/2}} = 1 \quad \textbf{Ans.}$$

Problem 15 $\lim_{x\to 0} \frac{\sin hx - \sin x}{x^3}$

Solution Putting $x = 0$ we have

$$\frac{\sin hx - \sin x}{x^3} = \frac{\sin 0 - \sin 0}{0} = \frac{0}{0} \text{ (form)}$$

So applying L'Hospital's rule we have

$$\lim_{x\to 0} \frac{\sin hx - \sin x}{x^3}$$

Remember dc of $(\sin hx) = \cos hx$

$$dc\ (\cos hx) = \sin hx$$

$$= \lim_{x\to 0} \frac{dc\ \{\sin hx - \sin x\}}{dc\ (x^3)}$$

$$= \lim_{x\to 0} \frac{\cos hx - \cos x}{3x^2} \left(\frac{0}{0} \text{ form}\right)$$

Again applying L' Hospitals rule we have

$$= \lim_{x\to 0} \frac{d.c\ \{\cos h\ x - \cos x\}}{dc \text{ of } (3x^2)}$$

$$= \lim_{x\to 0} \frac{\sin hx + \sin x}{6x} \left(\frac{0}{0}\right) \text{ form}$$

Applying L' Hospitals rule we have

$$= \lim_{x\to 0} \frac{dc\ (\sin hx + \sin x)}{dc\ (6x)} = \lim_{x\to 0} \frac{\cos hx + \cos x}{6}$$

$$= \frac{\cos 0 + \cos 0}{6} = \frac{1+1}{6} = \frac{2}{6} = \frac{1}{3}$$

$$\lim_{x\to 0} \frac{\sin hx - \sin x}{x^3} = \frac{1}{3} \quad \textbf{Ans.}$$

Problem 16 $\lim_{x\to 0} \dfrac{\tan x - \sin x}{\sin^3 x}$

Solution Putting $x = 0$ in the expression

$$\frac{\tan x - \sin x}{\sin^3 x} = \frac{0-0}{(0)^3} = \frac{0}{0} \quad \text{(Form)}$$

So we use the expansion of sin x and tax x.

$$\sin x = x - \frac{x^3}{3!} + \frac{x^5}{5!} - \ldots \tag{1}$$

$$\cos x = 1 - \frac{x^2}{2!} + \frac{x^4}{4!} - \ldots \tag{2}$$

$$\tan x = x + \frac{x^3}{3} + \frac{2}{15}x^5 + \tag{3}$$

$$\tan x - \sin x = \left(x + \frac{x^3}{3} + \frac{2}{15}x^5 + \ldots\right) - \left(x - \frac{x^3}{3\,!} + \frac{x^5}{5\,!} - \ldots.\right)$$

$$= x + \frac{x^3}{3} + \frac{2}{15}x^5 + \ldots - x + \frac{x^3}{3\,!} - \frac{1}{5\,!}x^5 + \ldots$$

$$= x^3\left(\frac{1}{3} + \frac{1}{3\,!}\right) + x^5\left(\frac{2}{15} - \frac{1}{5!}\right) + \ldots.$$

$$= x^3\left(\frac{1}{3} + \frac{1}{6}\right) + x^5\left(\frac{2}{15} - \frac{1}{60}\right) + \ldots$$

$$= x^3\left(\frac{6+3}{18}\right) + x^5\left(\frac{8-1}{60}\right) + \ldots.$$

$$= \frac{x^3}{2} + \frac{7}{60}x^5 + \ldots$$

$$\tan - \sin x = x^3\left(\frac{1}{2} + \frac{7}{60}x^2 + \ldots\right) \tag{4}$$

$$\sin^3 x = (\sin x)^3 = \left[x - \frac{x^3}{3\,!} + \frac{x^5}{5\,!} - \ldots\right]^3$$

$$= x^3\left[1 - \frac{x^2}{3\,!} + \frac{x^4}{5\,!} - \ldots\right]^3 \tag{5}$$

Dividing equation (4) with (5) we have

$$\frac{\tan x - \sin x}{\sin^3 x} = \frac{x^3\left(\frac{1}{2} + \frac{7}{60}x^2 + \ldots.\right)}{x^3\left[1 - \frac{x^2}{3\,!} + \frac{x^4}{5\,!} - \ldots.\right]^3}$$

Taking limit on both sides as $x \to 0$ we have

$$\lim_{x\to 0} \frac{\tan x - \sin x}{\sin^3 x} = \frac{(\frac{1}{2} + 0 + \ldots)}{(1 - 0 + 0)^3}$$

$$\lim_{x\to 0} \frac{\tan - \sin x}{\sin^3 x} = \frac{1}{2} \qquad \textbf{Ans.}$$

Problem 17 $\displaystyle \lim_{x\to 0} \frac{\sin x - \cos x}{x - \sin x}$

Solution Putting $x = 0$ we have

$$\frac{\sin x - x\cos x}{x \sin x} = \frac{\sin 0 - 0 \cdot \cos 0}{0 - \sin 0} = \frac{0}{0} \text{ (form)}$$

We use the expanslon of $\sin x$ and $\cos x$

$$\sin x = x - \frac{x^3}{3\,!} + \frac{x^5}{5\,!} - \frac{x^7}{7\,!} + \ldots$$

$$\cos = 1 - \frac{x^2}{2\,!} + \frac{x^4}{4\,!} - \ldots.$$

$$x \cos x = x\left[1 - \frac{x^2}{2\,!} + \frac{x^4}{4\,!} - \ldots.\right]$$

$$\sin x - x \cos x = x - \frac{x^3}{3\,!} + \frac{x^5}{5\,!} - \ldots - \left(x - \frac{x^3}{2\,!} + \frac{x^5}{4\,!} - \ldots.\right)$$

$$= x - \frac{x^3}{2\,!} + \frac{x^5}{5\,!} + \ldots. - x + \frac{x^3}{2\,!} - \frac{x^5}{4\,!} + \ldots$$

$$= x^3\left(\frac{1}{2\,!} - \frac{1}{3\,!}\right) + x^5\left(\frac{1}{5\,!} - \frac{1}{4\,!}\right) + \ldots$$

$$= x^3\left(\frac{1}{2} - \frac{1}{6}\right) + x^5\left(\frac{1}{60} - \frac{1}{24}\right) + \ldots \quad (1)$$

$$x - \sin x = x - \left[x - \frac{x^3}{3\,!} + \frac{x^5}{5\,!} - \ldots.\right]$$

$$= x - x + \frac{x^3}{3\,!} - \frac{x^5}{5\,!} + \ldots$$

$$= x^3\left(\frac{1}{2\,!}\right) - \frac{x^5}{5\,!} + \ldots$$

$$= \frac{x^3}{6\,!} - \frac{x^3}{5\,!} + , \ldots$$

$$\frac{\sin - x \cos x}{x - \sin x} = \frac{x^3\left[\frac{3-2}{6}\right] + x^5\left(\frac{1}{60} - \frac{1}{24}\right) + \ldots}{x^3\left[\frac{1}{6}\right] - \frac{x^5}{5\,!} + \ldots,}$$

$$= \frac{\frac{x^3}{6} + x^5\left(\frac{1}{60} - \frac{1}{24}\right) + \ldots}{\frac{x^3}{6} - \frac{x^5}{5!} + \ldots}$$

$$= \frac{x^3\left[\frac{1}{6} + x^2\left(\frac{1}{6\theta} - \frac{1}{24}\right) + \ldots\right]}{x^3\left[\frac{1}{6} - \frac{x^2}{5\,!} + \ldots\right]}$$

Taking limit on both sides cos x so we have

$$\lim_{x \to 0} \frac{\sin x - x \cos x}{x - \sin x} = \frac{1}{6} \Big/ \frac{1}{6} = 1$$

$$\lim_{x \to 0} \frac{\sin x - x \cos x}{x - \sin x} = 1 \quad \textbf{Ans.}$$

Problem 16. Evaluate $\lim\limits_{x \to \pi/2} \dfrac{x \sin x - \pi/2}{\cos x}$

Solution Putting $x = \pi/2$ we have

$$\frac{x \sin x - \pi/2}{\cos x}$$

$$= \frac{\pi/2 \sin \pi/2 - \pi/2}{\cos \pi/2} = \frac{\pi/2 - \pi/2}{\cos x} = \frac{0}{0} \text{(form)}$$

So applying L' Hospital's rule we have

$$\lim_{x \to \pi/2} \frac{x \sin x - \pi/2}{\cos x} = \lim_{x \to \pi/2} \frac{dc \cdot \{\sin x - \pi/2\}}{d \cdot c\{\cos x\}}$$

$$= \lim_{\pi \to \pi/2} \frac{x \cos x + \sin x - 0.}{-\sin x}$$

$$= \lim_{x \to \pi/2} \frac{x \cos x + \sin x}{-\sin x}$$

$$= \frac{\pi/2 \cos \pi/2 + \sin \pi/2}{-\sin \pi/2}$$

$$= \frac{\pi/2 \cdot 0 + 1}{-1} = \frac{1}{-1} = -1$$

$$\lim_{x \to \pi/2} \frac{x \sin x - \pi/2}{\cos x} = -1 \quad \textbf{Ans.}$$

Problem 17 Evalute $\lim\limits_{x \to 0} \dfrac{x \cos - \sin x}{x^3}$

Substituting $x = 0$ we have

$$\frac{x \cos x - \sin x}{x^3} = \frac{0 \cdot \cos 0 - \sin 0}{0^3} = \frac{0}{0} \text{ form}$$

i.e. so applying ['Hospitals rule we have

$$\lim_{x \to 0} \frac{x \cos x - \sin x}{x^3}$$

$$= \lim_{x \to 0} \frac{\text{dc } \{x \cos x - \sin x\}}{\text{dc } \{x^3\}}$$

$$= \lim_{x \to 2} \frac{\text{d} \cdot \text{c } \{x \cos x\} - \text{d} \cdot \text{c } \{\sin x\}}{3x^2}$$

$$= \lim_{x \to 0} \frac{x(-\sin x) + \cos x - \cos x}{3x^2}$$

$$= \lim_{x\to 0} \frac{-x \sin x}{3x^2} \left(\frac{0}{0} \text{ form}\right)$$

$$= \frac{-1}{3} \lim_{x\to 0} \frac{x \sin x}{x^2} = -\frac{1}{3} \lim_{x\to 0} \frac{\sin x}{x}$$

$$= -\frac{1}{3} \times 1 = -\frac{1}{3} \text{ since } \lim_{x\to 0} \frac{\sin x}{x} = 1$$

i.e. $$\lim_{x\to 0} \frac{x \cos x - \sin x}{x^3} = -\frac{1}{3} \quad \textbf{Ans.}$$

Problem 18 Evaluate $\lim_{x\to 0} \frac{x \cos x - \log (1+x)}{x^2}$

Putting $x = 0$ we have

$$\frac{x \cos x - \log (1+x)}{x^2} = \frac{0 \cos 0 - \log (1+0)}{x2}$$

$$= \frac{0 \cdot 1 - \log 1}{0} = \frac{0-0}{0} = \frac{0}{0} \text{ (form)}$$

We can solve the limit by using the expansion of $\cos x$ and $\log (1+x)$.

$$\cos x = 1 - \frac{x^2}{2!} + \frac{x^4}{4!} \cdots$$

$$x \cos x = x - \frac{x^3}{2!} + \frac{x^5}{4!} - \cdots \quad (1)$$

$$\log (1+x) = x - \frac{x^2}{2} + \frac{x^3}{3} - \frac{x^4}{4} + \cdots \quad (2)$$

Now $x \cos x - \log (1+x)$

$$= x - \frac{x^3}{2!} + \frac{x^5}{4!} - \cdots - x + \frac{x^2}{2} - \frac{x^3}{2} + \frac{x^4}{4} - \cdots$$

$$= \frac{x^2}{2} - \frac{x^3}{2!} + \frac{x^4}{4} + \frac{x^5}{4!} - \cdots$$

$$\frac{x \cos x - \log (1+x)}{x^2} = \frac{\frac{x^2}{2} - \frac{x^3}{2!} + \frac{x^4}{4} + \frac{x^5}{4!} - \cdots}{x^2}$$

$$= \frac{1}{2} - \frac{x}{2!} + \frac{x^2}{4} + \frac{x^3}{4!} - \cdots$$

Taking limit on both sides as $x \to 0$ we have

$$\lim_{x\to 0} \frac{x \cos x - \log (1+x)}{x^2} = \frac{1}{2} - 0 + 0 + 0$$

$$\Rightarrow \lim_{x\to 0} \frac{x \cos x - \log (1+x)}{x^2} = \frac{1}{2} \quad \textbf{Ans.}$$

Problem 20 $\lim\limits_{x\to 0} \dfrac{e^x - \log(e + ex)}{x^2}$

Solution Putting $x = 0$ we have

$$\lim_{x\to 0} \frac{e^x - \log(e + ex)}{x^2} = \frac{e^0 - \log(e + 0)}{0}$$

$$= \frac{1 - \log e}{0} = \frac{1 - 1}{0} = \frac{0}{0} \text{ (form)}$$

We solve this problem by using the expansion of e^x and $\log(1 + x)$

$$\lim_{x\to 0} \frac{e^x - \log(e + ex)}{x^2} = \lim_{x\to 0} \frac{e^x - \log e(1 + x)}{x^2}$$

$$= \lim_{x\to 0} \frac{e^x - \log e - \log(1 + x)}{x^2}$$

$$e^x = 1 + x + \frac{x^2}{2!} + \frac{x^3}{3!} + \frac{x^4}{4!} + \ldots$$

$$\log(1 + x) = x - \frac{x^2}{2} + \frac{x^3}{3} - \frac{x^4}{4} + \ldots$$

$$e^x - \log(1 + x) = 1 + x + \frac{x^2}{2!} + \frac{x^3}{3!} + \frac{x^4}{4!} + \ldots$$

$$- x + \frac{x^2}{2} - \frac{x^3}{3} + \frac{x^4}{4} \ldots$$

$$= 1 + \frac{x^2}{2} + \frac{x^2}{2!} + \frac{x^3}{3!} - \frac{x^3}{3} + \frac{x^4}{4!} + \frac{x^4}{4} + \ldots$$

$$= 1 + x^2 + \frac{x^3}{6} - \frac{x^3}{3} + \frac{x^4}{24} + \frac{x^4}{4} + \ldots$$

$$= 1 + x^2 + \frac{1}{3} x^3 + x^4 \left(\frac{1}{24} + \frac{1}{4}\right) + \ldots$$

$$e^x - \log(1 + x) - \log e = 1 + x^2 + \frac{x^3}{3} + x^4 \left(\frac{1}{24} + \frac{1}{4}\right) + \ldots - \log e$$

$$= x^2 + \frac{x^3}{3} + x^4 \left(\frac{1}{24} + \frac{1}{4}\right) + \ldots$$

$$\frac{e^x - \log(1 + x) - \log e}{x^2} = 1 + \frac{x}{3} + x^2 \left(\frac{1}{24} + \frac{1}{4}\right) + \ldots$$

Taking limit on both sides as $x \to 0$ we have

$$\lim_{x\to 0} \frac{e^x - \log(e + ex)}{x^2} = 1 + 0 + 0$$

i.e. $\lim\limits_{x\to 0} \dfrac{e^x - \log(e + ex)}{x^2} = 1$ **Ans.**

Problem 21 Evaluate $\lim_{x\to 0} \dfrac{xe^x - \log(1+x)}{x^2}$

Solution Putting $x = 0$ we have

$$\frac{xe^x - \log(1+x)}{x^2} = \frac{0\cdot e^0 - \log(1+0)}{0}$$

$$= \frac{0\cdot 1 - \log 1}{0} = \frac{0-0}{0} = \frac{0}{0} \text{ (form)}$$

We can solve this problem by using the expansion of e^x and $\log(1+x)$

$$e^x = 1 + x + \frac{x^2}{2!} + \frac{x^3}{3!} + \ldots$$

$$\log(1+x) = x - \frac{x^2}{2} + \frac{x^3}{3} - \ldots$$

$$xe^x - \log(1+x) = x + x^2 + \frac{x^3}{2!} + \frac{x^4}{3!} + \ldots$$

$$- x + \frac{x^2}{2} - \frac{x^3}{3} + \ldots$$

$$= \frac{3}{2}x^2 + \frac{x^3}{2!} - \frac{x^3}{3} + \ldots$$

$$\frac{xe^x - \log(1+x)}{x^2} = \frac{3}{2} + 0(x)$$

Taking limit on both sides as $x \to 0$ we have

$$\lim_{x\to 0} \frac{xe^x - \log(1+x)}{x^2} = \frac{3}{2} \qquad \textbf{Ans.}$$

Problem 22 Evaluate $\lim_{x\to 0} \dfrac{e^x - e^{-x} - 2x}{x - \sin x}$

Solution Putting $x = 0$ we have

$$\frac{e^x - e^{-x} - 2x}{x - \sin x} = \frac{e^0 - e^{-0} - 2\cdot 0}{0 - \sin 0}$$

$$= \frac{1 - 1 - 0}{0 - 0} = \frac{0}{0} \text{ (form)}$$

so applying L'Hospitals rule we have

$$= \lim_{x\leftarrow 0} \frac{e^x - e^{-x} - 2x}{x - \sin x} = \lim_{x\to 0} \frac{d\cdot c\,\{e^x - e^x - 2x\}}{d\cdot c\,\{x - \sin x\}}$$

$$= \lim_{x\to 0} \frac{e^x + e^{-x} - 2}{1 - \cos x}$$

Problem 7 Evaluate $\lim_{x\to 0} \log_x (\tan x)$

Solution substituting $x = 0$ we have

$$\log_x (\tan x) = \frac{\log_e (\tan x)}{\log_e x} = \frac{\log_e (\tan 0)}{\log_e (0)} = \frac{\log_e 0}{\log_e 0} = \frac{\infty}{\infty} \text{ form}$$

Applying L'Hospitals rule we have

$$\lim_{x\to 0} \log_x (\tan x) = \lim_{x\to\infty} \frac{\log_e \tan x)}{\log_e x)} = \lim_{x\to 0} \frac{dc\,\{\log_e (\tan x)\}}{dc\,\{\log_e (x)\}}$$

$$= \lim_{x\to 0} \frac{\frac{1}{\tan x}}{\frac{1}{x}} = \lim_{x\to\infty} \frac{x}{\tan x} = \left(\frac{\infty}{\infty}\right) \text{ form}$$

$$= \lim_{x\to 0} \frac{dc\,(x)}{dc\,(\tan x)} = \lim_{x\to 0} \frac{1}{\sec^2 x} = \frac{1}{\sec^2 0} = \frac{1}{1} = 1$$

i.e. $\lim_{x\to 0} \log_x (\tan x) = 1$ **Ans.**

Problem 8 Evaluate $\lim_{x\to 0} \log_{\sin x} (\sin 2x)$

Solution By the change of rule of base we have

$$\log_{(\sin x)} \sin 2x = \frac{\log_e (\sin 2x)}{\log_e (\sin x)}$$

putting $x = 0$ in the expression we have

$$\lim_{x\to 0} \log_{\sin x} (\sin x) = \lim_{x\to 0} \frac{\log_e (\sin 2x)}{\log_e (\sin x)}$$

$$= \frac{\log_e (0)}{\log_e (0)} = \frac{\infty}{\infty} \text{ form}$$

so applying L'Hospitals rule we have

$$\lim_{x\to 0} \log_{\sin x} (\sin 2x) = \lim_{x\to 0} \frac{dc\,\{\log_e (\sin 2x)\}}{dc\,\{\log_e (\sin x)\}}$$

$$= \lim_{x\to 0} \frac{\frac{2\,(\cos 2x)}{\sin 2x}}{\frac{\cos x}{\sin x}} = \lim_{x\to 0} \frac{2 \sin x}{\cos x} \cdot \frac{\cos 2x}{\sin 2x}$$

$$= 2 \lim_{x\to 0} \frac{\sin x \cos 2x}{\cos x \cdot 2 \sin x \cos x} = \lim_{x\to 0} \frac{\cos 2x}{\cos^2 x}$$

$$= \frac{\cos 0}{\cos 0} = 1$$

$\lim_{x\to 0} \log_{\sin x} (\sin 2x) = 1$ **Ans.**

Form $0 \times \infty$

let $$u = \phi(x) \times \psi(x)$$

where $\phi(x) \to 0$ and $\psi(x) \to \infty$ when $x \to a$

then $\phi(x) \times \psi(x) \to 0 \times \infty$ when $x \to a$

In order to bring it to the form $\frac{0}{0}$ we write $\phi(x) \times \psi(x)$ in the following

$$u = \phi(x) \times \psi(x)$$

$$u = \frac{\phi(x)}{\frac{1}{\psi(x)}}$$

when it is reduced to the form $\left(\frac{0}{0}\right)\left(\text{or } \frac{\infty}{\infty}\right)$ then we find out its limit by the method given in the form I or (in form II) [*Must revise*]

Problem 1 Evaluate $\lim_{x \to \infty} 2x \tan \frac{a}{2x}$ (*IFS 86*)

Solution This is of the form $\infty \times 0$

let $$\frac{1}{2x} = \theta$$

when $$x \to \infty \; \frac{1}{2\infty} = \theta \text{ i.e. } \theta \to 0$$

$$\lim_{x \to 0} 2x \tan \frac{a}{2x} = \lim_{x \to \infty} \frac{1}{\theta} \tan a\theta = \lim_{\theta \to 0} \frac{\tan a\theta}{\theta}$$

$$= \lim_{\theta \to 0} \frac{\tan a\theta}{a\theta} \times a = a \lim_{\theta \to 0} \frac{\tan a\theta}{a\theta} = a \times 1 = a$$

$$\lim_{x \to \infty} 2x \tan \frac{a}{2x} = a$$ **Ans.**

Problem 2 Evaluate $\lim_{x \to 0} \sin x \log x$

Solution Putting $x = 0$ we have

$$\sin x \log x = \sin 0 \times \log 0 = 0 \times \infty$$

Thus $\lim_{x \to 0} \sin x \log x$ is of the form $0 \times \infty$

$$\lim_{x \to 0} \sin x \log x = \lim_{x \to 0} \frac{\log x}{\operatorname{cosec} x}$$ which is of the form $\frac{\infty}{\infty}$

$$\lim_{x\to\infty} \frac{x^n}{e^x} = \lim_{x\to\infty} \frac{d\cdot c\,(x^n)}{d\cdot c\,(e^x)}$$

$$= \lim_{n\to\infty} \frac{nx^{n-1}}{e^x} = n \lim_{x\to\infty} \frac{x^{n-1}}{e^x}$$

$$= n \lim_{x\to\infty} \frac{d\cdot c\,(x^{n-1})}{d\cdot c\,(e^x)} = n \lim_{x\to\infty} \frac{(n-1)\,x^{n-2}}{e^x}$$

$$= n\,(n-1) \lim_{x\to\infty} \frac{x^{n-2}}{e^x}\left(\frac{\infty}{\infty} \text{ form}\right)$$

$$= n\,(n-1) \lim_{x\to\infty} \frac{dc\,(x^{n-2})}{dc\,(e^x)}$$

$$= n\,(n-1) \lim_{x\to\infty} \frac{(n-2)\,x^{n-3}}{e^x}$$

$$= n\,(n-1)\,(n-2) \lim_{x\to\infty} \frac{x^{n-3}}{e^x}\left[\frac{\infty}{\infty} \text{ form}\right]$$

$$= n\,(n-1)\,(n-2) \lim_{x\to\infty} \frac{d\cdot c\,(x^{n-3})}{d\cdot c\,(e^x)}$$

$$= n\,(n-1)\,(n-2) \lim_{x\to\infty} \frac{(n-3)\,x^{n-4}}{e^x}$$

$$= n\,(n-1)\,(n-2)(n-3) \lim_{x\to\infty} \frac{x^{n-4}}{e^x}\left[\frac{\infty}{\infty}\right] \text{form}$$

$$= n\,(n-1)\,(n-2)\,(n-3)\ldots 3\cdot 2\cdot 1 \lim_{x\to\infty} \frac{1}{e^x}$$

$$= \underline{/n} \lim_{x\to\infty} \frac{1}{e^x} = \underline{/n}\,\frac{1}{e^\infty} = \frac{/n}{\infty} = 0$$

Problem 2 $\lim_{x\to a} \dfrac{\log (x-a)}{\log (e^x-e^a)}$

Solution Substituting $x = a$ we have the expression

$$\lim_{x\to a} \frac{\log (x-a)}{\log (e^x-e^a)} = \frac{\log (a-a)}{\log (e^a-e^a)} = \frac{\log 0}{\log 0} = \frac{\infty}{\infty} \text{ (form)}$$

Applying L' Hospitals rule we have

$$\lim_{x\to a} \frac{\log (x-a)}{\log (e^x-e^a)} = \lim_{x\to a} \frac{dc\,\{\log (x-a)\}}{dc\,\{\log (e^x-e^a)\}}$$

$$= \lim_{x\to a} \frac{\dfrac{1}{x-a}}{\dfrac{e^x}{e^x-e^a}} = \lim_{x\to a} \frac{e^x-e^a}{e^x\,(x-a)} = \frac{0}{0} \text{ (form)}$$

So applying L'Hospitals rule we have

$$\lim_{x\to a} \frac{e^x - e^a}{e^x (x-a)} = \lim_{x\to a} \frac{d\cdot c\,\{c^x - e^a\}}{d\cdot c\,\{e^x(x-a)\}} = \lim_{x\to a} \frac{e^x - 0}{e^x \cdot 1 + (x-a)\, e^x}$$

$$= \lim_{x\to a} \frac{e^x}{e^x + (x-a)\, e^x}$$

$$= \frac{e^a}{e^a + (a-a)\, e^a} = \frac{e^a}{e^a} = 1$$

i.e. $\lim_{x\to 0} \dfrac{\log (x-a)}{\log (e^x - e^a} = 1$ **Ans.**

Problem 3 Evaluate $\lim_{x\to 0} \log_{tan\, x} (\tan 2x)$ *(Must Revise)*

Solution We know by the change of base formula

$$\log_a m = \frac{\log_e m}{\log_e a}$$

Hence we can express $\log_{\tan x} (\tan 2x)$

as $\log_{\tan x} (\tan 2x) = \dfrac{\log_e (\tan 2x)}{\log_e (\tan x)}$

substituting $x = 0$ we have the expression

$$\frac{\log_e (\tan 2x)}{\log_e (\tan x)} = \frac{\log_e (0)}{\log_e (0)} = \frac{\infty}{\infty} \text{ (form)}$$

$$1.\ e^{-\infty} = \frac{1}{e^{\infty}} = 0 \qquad 2.\ -\infty = \log 0$$

so applying L' Hospital's rule we have the given limit

$$= \lim_{x\to 0} \log_{(\tan x)} (\tan 2x) = \lim_{x\to 0} \frac{\log_e (\tan 2x)}{\log_e (\tan x)}$$

$$= \lim_{x\to 0} \frac{d\cdot c\{\log_e (\tan 2x)\}}{d\cdot c\,\{\log_e (\tan x)\}} = \lim_{x\to 0} \frac{\dfrac{1}{\tan 2x} \sec^2 2x \cdot 2}{\dfrac{\sec^2 x}{\tan x}}$$

$$= \lim_{x\to 0} \frac{2 \tan x \sec^2 2x}{\tan\ 2x \sec^2 x} \left[\frac{0}{0}\right] \text{form}$$

Again applying L'Hospitals rule we

$$= \lim_{x\to 0} \frac{\frac{2\sin x}{\cos x} \; \frac{1}{\cos^2 2x}}{\frac{\sin 2x}{\cos 2x} \times \frac{1}{\cos^2 x}} = \lim_{x\to 0} \frac{2\sin x}{\cos x} \times \frac{\cos 2x}{\sin 2x} \; \frac{\cos^2 x}{\cos^2 2x}$$

$$= \lim_{x\to 0} \frac{2\sin x \times \cos 2x}{\cos x \times 2\sin x\cos x} \; \frac{\cos^2 x}{\cos^2 2x} = \lim_{x\to 0} \frac{\cos x}{\cos x\cos 2x}$$

$$= \lim_{x\to 0} \frac{1}{\cos 2x} = \frac{1}{\cos 0} = 1 \Rightarrow \lim_{x\to 0} \log_{\tan x} (\tan 2x) = 1 \qquad \textbf{Ans.}$$

Problem 4 Evaluate $\lim\limits_{x\to\infty} \dfrac{\log n}{n}$

Solution Substituting $n = \infty$ in the given expression we have

$$\lim_{n\to\infty} \frac{\log n}{n} = \frac{\log \infty}{\infty} = \frac{\infty}{\infty} \text{ (form)}$$

so applying L'Hospitals rule we have

$$\lim_{n\to\infty} \frac{\log n}{n} = \lim_{n\infty\infty} \frac{dc\,(\log n)}{dc\,(n)}$$

$$= \lim_{n\to\infty} \frac{1/n}{1} = \lim_{n\to\infty} \frac{1}{n} = \frac{1}{\infty} = 0$$

Problem 5 Evaluate $\lim\limits_{x\to\pi/2} \dfrac{\tan x}{\tan 3x}$

Solution Putting $x = \frac{\pi}{2}$ we have the expression

$$\lim_{x\to\pi/2} \frac{\tan x}{\tan 3x} = \frac{\tan \pi/2}{\tan 3\pi/2} = \frac{\infty}{\infty} \text{ (form)}$$

so applying L'Hospital's rule we have

$$\lim_{x\to\pi/2} \frac{\tan x}{\tan 3x} = \lim_{x\to\pi/2} \frac{dc\,(\tan x)}{dc\,(\tan 3x)}$$

$$= \lim_{x\to\pi/2} \frac{\sec^2 x}{3\sec^2 3x} = \frac{1}{3}$$

$$= \frac{1}{3} \lim_{x\to\pi/2} \frac{\cos^2 3x}{\cos^2 x} \left[\frac{0}{0} \text{ form}\right]$$

so applying L'Hospitals rule we have

$$=\frac{1}{3}\lim_{x\to\pi/2}\frac{dc\,(\cos^2 3x)}{dc\,(\cos^2 x)}=\frac{1}{3}\lim_{x\to\pi/2}\frac{2\cos 3x\,(-\sin 3x)\cdot 3}{2\cos x\,(-\sin x)}$$

$$=\frac{1}{3}\cdot 3\lim_{x\to\pi/2}\frac{\sin 3x\cos 3x}{\sin x\cos x}=\lim_{x\to\pi/2}\frac{2\sin 3x\cos 3x}{2\sin x\cos x}$$

$$=\lim_{x\to\pi/2}\frac{\sin 6x}{\sin 2x}=\frac{\sin 6\pi/2}{\sin 2\pi/2}=\frac{\sin 3\pi}{\sin\pi}\left[\frac{0}{0}\text{ form}\right]$$

Again applying L'Hospitals rule we have

$$\lim_{x\to\pi/2}\frac{dc\,\{\sin 6x\}}{dc\,\{\sin 2x\}}=\lim_{x\to\pi/2}\frac{6\cos 6x}{2\cos 2x}$$

$$=3\lim_{x\to\pi/2}\frac{\cos 6x}{\cos 2x}=3x\frac{\cos 6\pi/2}{\cos 2\pi/2}$$

$$=3\frac{\cos 3\pi}{\cos\pi}=\frac{3\cos(\pi+2\pi)}{\cos\pi}=3\frac{\cos\pi}{\cos\pi}=3$$

i.e. $\lim_{x\to\pi/2}\frac{\tan x}{\tan 3x}=3$ **Ans.**

Problem 6 $\lim_{x\to 0}\frac{\log x}{\cot x}$

Solution Putting $x=0$ we have

$$\frac{\log x}{\cot x}=\frac{\log 0}{\cot 0}=\frac{\infty}{\infty}\text{ (form)}$$

so applying L'Hospitals rule we have

$$\lim_{x\to 0}\frac{\log x}{\cot x}=\lim_{x\to 0}\frac{dc\,(\log x)}{dc\,(\cot x)}$$

$$=\lim_{\pi\to 0}\frac{\frac{1}{x}}{-\operatorname{cosec}^2 x}=-\lim_{x\to 0}\frac{\sin^2 x}{x}$$

which is of the form $\left[\frac{0}{0}\right]$ so applying L'Hospitals rule we have

$$\lim_{x\to 0}\frac{\log x}{\cot x}=-\lim_{x\to 0}\frac{d.c\sin^2 x)}{d.c\,(x)}=-\lim_{x\to 0}\frac{2\sin x\cdot\cos x}{1}$$

$$=-\lim_{x\to 0}\sin 2x=-\sin 0=0$$

$$\Rightarrow\lim_{x\to 0}\frac{\log x}{\cot x}=0 \qquad \textbf{Ans.}$$

$$\text{Cor} \lim_{x\to 0} \frac{1}{x}\left(\frac{1}{x} - \cot x\right) = \lim_{x\to 0} \frac{\frac{1}{x}\left[\frac{x}{3} + \frac{2}{15}x^3 + \ldots\right]}{\left[1 + \frac{x^2}{3} + \ldots\right]}$$

$$= \lim_{x\to 0} \frac{\left[\frac{1}{3} + \frac{2}{15}x^2 + \ldots\right]}{\left[1 + \frac{x^2}{3} + \ldots\right]}$$

$$= \frac{\frac{1}{3} + 0 + \ldots}{1 + 0 + 0\ldots} = \frac{1}{3}$$

i.e. $\lim_{x\to 0}\left(\frac{1}{x^2} - \frac{1}{x\tan x}\right) = \frac{1}{3}$

Problem 2 Evaluate $\lim_{x\to 0}\left(\frac{1}{x^2} - \frac{1}{\sin^2 x}\right)$ [*IFS 88*]

Solution Putting $x = 0$ we have the expression

$$\frac{1}{x^2} - \frac{1}{\sin^2 x} = \frac{1}{0} - \frac{1}{0} = \infty - \infty \qquad (\textit{indeterminate})$$

$$\lim_{x\to 0}\left(\frac{1}{x^2} - \frac{1}{\sin^2 x}\right) = \lim_{x\to 0}\left[\frac{\sin^2 x - x^2}{x^2 \sin^2 x}\right]$$

which is of the form $\left(\frac{0}{0}\right)$

$$= \lim_{x\to 0} \frac{\left[x - \frac{x^3}{3!} + \frac{x^5}{5!}\ldots\right]^2 - x^2}{x^2\left(x - \frac{x^3}{3!} + \frac{x^5}{5!} - \ldots\right)^2}$$

$$= \lim_{x\to 0} \frac{x^2 - \frac{2}{3!}x^4 + \text{higher powers of } x \text{ starting from } x^6 - x^2}{x^2\left[x^2 - \frac{2x^4}{3!} + \text{higher powers of } x \text{ starting form } x^6\right]}$$

$$= \lim_{x\to 0} \frac{-\frac{2}{6}x^4 + \text{higher powers of } x \text{ starting from } x^6}{x^4 - \frac{2}{6}2x^4 + \text{heigher powers of } x \text{ starting from } x^6}$$

$$= \lim_{x\to 0} \frac{x^4(-\frac{1}{3} + \text{higher powers of } x)}{x^4(1 - \text{heigher powers of } x)} = -\frac{1}{3}$$

i.e. $\lim_{x\to 0}\left(\frac{1}{x^2} - \frac{1}{\sin^2 x}\right) = -\frac{1}{3}$ **Ans.**

Problem 3 Evaluate $\lim_{x \to \pi/2} (\sec x - \tan x)$

Solution Putting $x = \frac{\pi}{2}$ in the expression $\sec x - \tan x$

we have $\sec \frac{\pi}{2} - \tan \frac{\pi}{2}$ which is of the form $\infty - \infty$ (indeterminate).

So we want to change this limit to the form $\frac{0}{0}$

$$\lim_{x \to \pi/2} (\sec x - \tan x) = \lim_{x \to \pi/2} \left[\frac{1}{\cos x} - \frac{\sin x}{\cos x}\right]$$

$$= \lim_{x \to \pi/2} \frac{(1 - \sin x)}{\cos x}$$

which is of the form $\frac{0}{0}$. Hence using L'Hospitals rule we have

$$\lim_{x \to \pi/2} \frac{d.c \{1 - \sin x\}}{d.c (\cos x)} = \lim_{x \to \pi/2} \frac{0 - \cos x}{-\sin x} = \lim_{x \to \pi/2} \frac{\cos x}{\sin x}$$

$$= \frac{\cos \pi/2}{\sin \pi/2} = \frac{0}{1} = 0$$

i.e. $\lim_{x \to \pi/2} (\sec x - \tan x) = 0$ **Ans.**

Problem 4 Evaluate $\lim_{x \to \pi/2} \left[x \tan x - \frac{\pi}{2} \sec x\right]$

Solution Substituting $x = \frac{\pi}{2}$ we have

$$\lim_{x \pi/2} x \tan x - \frac{\pi}{2} \sec x = \frac{\pi}{2} \tan \frac{\pi}{2} - \frac{\pi}{2} \sec \frac{\pi}{2} = \infty - \infty$$

Thus the given limit is of the form $\infty - \infty$. We have to change it to the form $\frac{0}{0}$

$$\lim_{x \to \pi/2} \left[x \tan x - \frac{\pi}{2} \sec x\right] = \lim_{x \to \pi/2} \left[x \frac{\sin x}{\cos x} - \frac{\pi}{2} \frac{1}{\text{oos } x}\right]$$

$$= \lim_{x \to \pi/2} \left[\frac{2x \sin x - \pi}{2 \cos x}\right]$$

which is of the form $\frac{0}{0}$. So using L'Hospitals rule we have

$$\lim_{x\to\pi/2}\left[x\tan x-\frac{\pi}{2}\sec x\right]$$

$$=\lim_{x\to\pi/2}\frac{2x\sin x-\pi}{2\cos x}=\lim_{x\to\pi/2}\frac{d\cdot c\,\{2x\sin x-\pi\}}{d\cdot c\,\{2\cos x\}}$$

$$=\lim_{x\to\pi/2}\frac{d\cdot c\,(2x\sin x)-0}{d\cdot c\,(2\cos x)}=\lim_{x\to\pi/2}\frac{2\,[x\cos x+\sin x\cdot 1]}{-2\sin x}$$

$$=\frac{\pi/2\cos\pi/2+\sin\pi/2}{-\sin\pi/2}=\frac{\pi/2\times 0+1}{-1}=-\frac{1}{1}=-1$$

i.e. $\lim_{x\to\pi/2}\left[x\tan x-\frac{\pi}{2}\right]=-1$ **Ans.**

Problem 5 $\lim_{x\to 0}\left\{\frac{1}{2x^2}-\frac{1}{2x\tan x}\right\}$

Solution putting $x=0$ the expression

$$\frac{1}{2x^2}-\frac{1}{2x\tan x}=\frac{1}{0}-\frac{1}{0}=\infty-\infty$$

i.e. the given limit is of the form $\infty-\infty$

$$\lim_{x\to 0}\left\{\frac{1}{2x^2}-\frac{1}{2x\tan x}\right\}$$

$$=\frac{1}{2}\lim_{x\to 0}\left[\frac{1}{x^2}-\frac{1}{x\tan x}\right]=\frac{1}{2}\lim_{x\to 0}\left[\frac{1}{x^2}-\frac{1}{x\sin x/\cos x}\right]$$

$$=\frac{1}{2}\lim_{x\to 0}\left[\frac{1}{x^2}-\frac{\cos x}{x\sin x}\right]=\frac{1}{2}\lim_{x\to 0}\left[\frac{\sin x-x\cos x}{x^2\sin x}\right]$$

which is of the form $\frac{0}{0}$ so applying L[1] Hospitals rule we have

$$\frac{1}{2}\lim_{x\to 0}\left[\frac{\sin x-x\cos x}{x^2\sin x}\right]$$

$$=\frac{1}{2}\lim_{x\to 0}\frac{d\cdot c\,[\sin x-x\cos x]}{d\cdot c\,[x^2\sin x]}$$

$$=\frac{1}{2}\lim_{x\to 0}\frac{[\cos x-\{x(-\sin x)+\cos x\cdot 1\}]}{x^2\cos x+\sin x\,2x}$$

$$=\frac{1}{2}\lim_{x\to 0}\frac{\cos x+x\sin x-\cos x}{x^2\cos x+2x\sin x}$$

$$=\frac{1}{2}\lim_{x\to 0}\frac{x\sin x}{x\,(2\sin x+x\cos x)}=\lim_{x\to 0}\frac{\sin x}{2\sin+x\cos x}$$

which is again of the form $\frac{0}{0}$

$$=\frac{1}{2}\lim_{x\to 0}\frac{\cos x}{2\cos x + x\,(-\sin x) + \cos x\cdot 1}$$

$$=\frac{1}{2}\lim_{x\to 0}\frac{\cos x}{3\cos x - x\sin x}=\frac{1}{2}\times\frac{\cos 0}{3\cos 0}=\frac{1}{2}\times\frac{1}{3}=\frac{1}{6}$$

i.e. $\lim_{x\to 0}\left\{\frac{1}{2x^2}-\frac{1}{2x\tan x}\right\}=\frac{1}{6}$ **Ans.**

Problem 6 Evaluate $\lim_{x\to 0}\left(\frac{1}{x^2}-\cot^2 x\right)$

Solution Substituting $x = 0$ we have the expression

$$\frac{1}{x^2}-\cot^2 x$$

$$=\frac{1}{0}-\frac{1}{\tan^2 0}=\frac{1}{0}-\frac{1}{0}=\infty-\infty$$

Thus the given limit is of the form $\infty - \infty$ we can solve this problem by using the expansions of $\sin x$ and $\cos x$.

$$\lim_{x\to 0}\left(\frac{1}{x^2}-\cot^2 x\right)=\lim_{x\to 0}\left(\frac{1}{x^2}-\frac{\cos^2 x}{\sin^2 x}\right)$$

$$=\lim_{x\to 0}\frac{\sin^2 x - x^2\cos^2 x}{x^2\sin^2 x}=\lim_{x\to 0}\frac{(\sin x^2)-(x\cos x^2)}{(x\sin x)^2}$$

which is of the form $\left(\frac{0}{0}\right)$

we have $\sin x = x - \frac{x^3}{3!}+\frac{x^5}{5!}-\ldots$ (1)

$$x\sin x = x\left(x-\frac{x^3}{3!}+\frac{x^5}{5!}\right)-\ldots \quad (2)$$

$$x\sin x = \left(x^2-\frac{x^4}{3!}+\frac{x^6}{5!}-\ldots\right) \quad (3)$$

$$\cos x = 1-\frac{x^2}{2i}+\frac{x^4}{4!}-\frac{x^6}{6!}+\ldots$$

$$x\cos x = x\left(1-\frac{x^2}{2!}+\frac{x^4}{4!}-\frac{x^6}{6!}+\ldots\right)$$

$$= x-\frac{x^3}{2!}+\frac{x^5}{4!}-\frac{x^7}{6!}+\ldots \quad (4)$$

squaring equation (2) we have

$$x^2 \sin^2 x = \left(x^2 - \frac{x^4}{3!} + \frac{x^6}{5!} - \ldots \right)^2$$

$$= x^4 + \frac{x^8}{36!} - \frac{2x^6}{3!} + \ldots \qquad (5)$$

squaring equation (4) we have

$$x^2 \cos^2 x$$

$$= \left(x - \frac{x^3}{2!} + \frac{x^5}{4!} - \frac{x^7}{6!} + \ldots \right)^2$$

$$= x^2 + \frac{x^6}{4} - \frac{2x^4}{2!} + \ldots \qquad (6)$$

squaring equation (1) we have

$$\sin^2 x = \left(x - \frac{x^3}{3!} + \frac{x^5}{5!} - \ldots \right)^2$$

$$= x^2 + \frac{x^6}{36} - \frac{2x^4}{3!} + \ldots \qquad (7)$$

Now we have $\lim_{x \to 0} \left(\frac{1}{x^2} - \cot^2 x \right)$

$$= \lim_{x \to 0} \frac{(\sin x)^2 - (x \cos x)^2}{(x \sin x)^2}$$

$$= \lim_{x \to 0} \frac{x^2 + \frac{x^6}{36} - \frac{2x^4}{3 \times 2} + \ldots - x^2 - \frac{x^6}{4} + x^4 - - \ldots}{x^4 + \frac{x^8}{36} - \frac{2x^6}{3 \times 2} + \ldots}$$

$$= \lim_{x \to 0} \frac{x^4 \left[\left(1 - \frac{1}{3} \right) + \text{higher powers of } x \right]}{x^4 \left[1 + \frac{x^4}{36} - \frac{x^2}{3} + \ldots \right]}$$

$$\lim_{x \to 0} \frac{\frac{2}{3} + \text{higher powers of } x}{1 + \text{higher powers of } x} = \frac{\frac{2}{3} + 0}{1 + 0} = \frac{2}{3}$$

i.e. $\lim_{x \to 0} \left(\frac{1}{x^2} - \cot^2 x \right) = \frac{2}{3}$ **Ans.**

Form 0^0, ∞^0 and 1^α

Let $y = u^v$ (1)

Where u and v are functions of x

Now taking logarithm of equation (1) we have

$$\log y = v \log u$$

Then three cases may arise

Case I If $u = 0$ and $v = 0$ and $x = a$ then $y = 0^0$

Case II If $u = \infty$ and $v = 0$ and $x = a$ then $y = \infty^0$

Case III If $u = 1$ and $v = \infty$ and $x = a$ then $y = 1^\infty$

According to case I

If $u = 0$ $v = 0$ then

$$\log y = 0 \log 0 = 0 \times \infty$$

According to case (II) if $u = \infty$ $v = 0$ then

$$\log y = 0 \log \infty$$

$$\log y = 0 \times \infty$$

If $u = 1$ and $v = \infty$ then according to case (iii) we have

$$\log y = \infty \log 1$$

$$\log y = \infty \times 0$$

That is in all the three situations $\log y$ is reduced to indeterminate form $0 \times \infty$

Hence in these cases, we shall first take the logarithm of the given function and then proceed according to the form III ($0 \times \infty$) form.

Problem 1 Find the limit of $\left(1 + \frac{a}{x}\right)^x$ as $x \to \infty$

$$\log y = \lim_{x \to \infty} \left(1 + \frac{a}{x}\right)^x$$

Taking logarithm on both sides we have

$$\log y = \log\left[\lim_{x \to \infty} \left(1 + \frac{a}{x}\right)^x\right]$$

$$\log y = \lim_{x \to \infty} \log \left(1 + \frac{a}{x}\right)^x$$

Since logarithm and limit operations are interchangible

$$\log y = \lim_{x \to 0} x \cdot \log\left(1 + \frac{a}{x}\right)$$

$$\log y = \infty \times \log(1 + 0)$$

$$\log y = \infty \times \log 1$$

$$\log y = \infty \times 0$$

i.e. here log y is of the form $\infty \times 0$ so ɔhanging it to the form $\frac{0}{0}$

we have

$$\log y = \lim_{x\to\infty} \frac{\log\left(1+\frac{a}{x}\right)}{1/x} \left[\frac{0}{0}\text{ farm}\right]$$

So applying L' Hospitals rule we have

$$\log y = \lim_{x\to 0} \frac{\log\left(1+\frac{a}{x}\right)}{\frac{1}{x}}$$

$$\text{loe } y = \lim \frac{d\cdot c\left\{\log\left(1+\frac{a}{x}\right)\right\}}{d\cdot c\left(\frac{1}{x}\right)}$$

$$\log y = \lim_{x\to 0} \frac{1/1+\frac{a}{x}\, d\cdot c\left(1+\frac{a}{x}\right)}{-1/x^2}$$

$$\log y = \lim_{x\to 0} \frac{1/1+\frac{a}{x}\left(0-\frac{a}{x^2}\right)}{-\frac{1}{x^2}} = \lim_{x\to\infty} \frac{\frac{x}{x+u}\cdot\frac{(-a)}{x^2}}{-\frac{1}{x^2}}$$

$$= \lim_{x\to\infty} \frac{-\frac{ax}{(x+a)x^2}}{-\frac{1}{x^2}} = \lim_{x\to\infty} \frac{ax}{(x+a)}$$

$$= \lim_{x\to\infty} \frac{\frac{ax}{x}}{\frac{x+a}{x}}$$ dividing the N^r and

D^r by x

$$\log y = \lim_{x\to\infty} \frac{a}{1+\frac{a}{x}}$$

$$\log y = \frac{a}{1+\frac{a}{\infty}}$$

$$\log y = \frac{a}{1+0} = \frac{a}{1} = a$$

Since $\qquad \log y = a$

$$y = e^a$$

i.e. $\qquad \lim_{x\to\infty}\left(1+\frac{a}{x}\right)^x = e^a \qquad$ **Ans.**

IInd Method $\qquad y = \lim_{x\to\infty}\left(1+\frac{a}{x}\right)^x$

$$\log y = \lim_{x\to\infty} x\log\left(1+\frac{a}{x}\right)$$

$$\log y = \text{iim}_{x\to\infty} x\left[\frac{a}{x} - \frac{\left(\frac{a}{x}\right)^2}{2} + \frac{\left(\frac{a}{x}\right)^3}{3} \ldots\right]$$

$$\log y = \lim_{x\to\propto} x\left[\frac{a}{x} - \frac{a^2}{2x^2} + \frac{a}{3x^3} - \ldots\right]$$

$$\log y = \lim_{x\to\infty}\left[a - \frac{a^2}{2x} + \frac{a^3}{3x^2} - \ldots\right]$$

$$\log y = a - 0 + 0\ldots$$

$$\log y = a$$

$$\Rightarrow y = e^a$$

i.e. $\qquad \lim_{x\to a}\left(1+\frac{a}{x}\right)^x = e^a \qquad$ **Ans.**

Note $\qquad \left(1+\frac{a}{x}\right)^x$ is of the form or 1^∞ as $x\to\infty$

Problem 2 Evaluate $\lim_{x\to 1} x^{\frac{1}{1-x}}$

Solution The given limit is of the form (1^∞)

$$(x^{1/(1-x)}) = 1\,(1)^{1/(1-1)} = 1^{1/0} = 1^\infty$$

Let $\qquad y = \lim_{x\to 1} x^{1/1-x}$

Taking logarithm on both sides we have

$$\log y = \log \lim_{x\to 1} x^{1/1-x}$$

$$\log y = \lim_{x\to 1} \log x^{1/1-x}$$

$$\log y = \lim_{x\to 1}\left(\frac{1}{1-x}\right)\log x$$

$$\log y = \lim_{x\to 1}\frac{\log x}{1-x}$$

Which is of the form $\frac{0}{0}$. Hence applying L' Hospitals rule we have

$$\log y = \lim_{x\to 1}\frac{\log x}{1-x}$$

$$\log y = \lim_{x\to 1}\frac{d\cdot c\,(\log x)}{d\cdot c\,(1-x)}$$

$$\log y = \lim_{x\to 1}\frac{1/x}{0-1}$$

$$\log y = \lim_{x\to 1} -\frac{1}{x}$$

$$\log y = -1$$

i.e. $$y = e^{-1} = \frac{1}{e}$$

i.e. $$\lim_{x\to 1} x^{1/1-x} = \frac{1}{e} \qquad \textbf{Ans.}$$

Problem 3 Evaluate $\lim_{x\to 0}\left(\frac{\tan x}{x}\right)^{1/x^2}$

Solution Let $y = \left(\frac{\tan x}{x}\right)^{1/x^2}$

$$\log y = \frac{1}{x^2}\log\left(\frac{\tan x}{x}\right)$$

$$\tan x = x + \frac{x^3}{3} + \frac{2}{15}x^5 + \ldots$$

$$\frac{\tan x}{x} = 1 + \frac{x^2}{3} + \frac{2}{15}x^4 + \ldots$$

$$\log\left(\frac{\tan x}{x}\right) = \log\left\{1 + \left(\frac{x^2}{3} + \frac{2}{15}x^4 + \ldots\right)\right\}$$

$$= \left(\frac{x^2}{3} + \frac{2}{15}x^4 + \ldots\right) - \frac{\left(\frac{x^2}{3} + \frac{2}{15}x^4 + \ldots\right)^2}{2}$$

$$+ \frac{1}{3}\left(\frac{x^2}{3} + \frac{2}{15}x^4 + \ldots\right)^3 - \ldots$$

$$= \frac{x^2}{3} + x^4\left(\frac{2}{15} - \frac{1}{2\cdot 9}\right) + \text{higher powers of } x^2$$

$$= \frac{x^2}{3} + x^4\left(\frac{2}{15} - \frac{1}{18}\right) + \text{higher powers of } x^2$$

$$= \frac{x^2}{3} + x^4\left(\frac{12-5}{90}\right) + \text{higher powers of } x^2$$

$$= \frac{x^2}{3} + \frac{7}{90}x^4 + \text{higher powers of } x^2$$

$$\frac{1}{x^2}\log\left(\frac{\tan x}{x}\right) = \frac{1}{x^2}\left[\frac{x^2}{3} + \frac{7}{90}x^4 + \text{higher powers of } x^2\right]$$

$$= \frac{1}{3} + \frac{7}{90}x^2 + \text{higher powers of } x^2$$

$$\log y = \frac{1}{3} + \frac{7}{90}x^2 + \text{higher powers of } x^2$$

Taking limit on both sides as $x \to 0$ we have

$$\lim_{x\to 0} \log y = \frac{1}{3} \quad \log \lim_{x\to 0} y = \frac{1}{3} \lim_{x\to 0}\left(\frac{\tan x}{x}\right)^{1/x^2} = e^{1/3}$$ **Ans.**

Problem 4 Evaluate $\lim_{x\to 0}\left(\frac{\tan x}{x}\right)^{1/x}$

Solution let $y = \lim_{x\to 0}\left(\frac{\tan x}{x}\right)^{1/x}$

Taking logarithm on both sides we have

$$\log y = \lim_{x\to 0}\frac{1}{x}\log\left(\frac{\tan x}{x}\right) \text{ we have}$$

$$\tan x = x + \frac{x^3}{3} + \frac{2}{15}x^5 + \ldots$$

$$\frac{\tan x}{x} = 1 + \frac{x^2}{3} + \frac{2}{15}x^4 + \ldots$$

$$\log\left(\frac{\tan x}{x}\right) = \log\left\{1 + \left(\frac{x^2}{3} + \frac{2}{15}x^4 + \ldots\right)\right\}$$

$$= \left(\frac{x^2}{3} + \frac{2}{15}x^4 + \ldots\right) - \frac{1}{2}\left(\frac{x^2}{3} + \frac{2}{15}x^4 + \ldots\right)^2$$

$$+ \frac{1}{3}\left(\frac{x^2}{3} + \frac{2}{15}x^4 + \ldots\right) - \ldots$$

$$= \frac{x^2}{3} + \frac{2}{15}x^4 - \frac{1}{2}\left(\frac{x^4}{9} + \ldots\right)$$

$$= \frac{x^2}{3} + x^4\left(\frac{2}{15} - \frac{1}{18}\right) + \text{higher powers of } x^2$$

$$= \frac{x^2}{3} + x^4\left(\frac{12-5}{90}\right) + \text{higher powers of } x^2$$

$$= \frac{x^2}{3} + \frac{7}{90}x^4 + \text{higher powers of } x^2$$

$$\frac{1}{x}\log\left(\frac{\tan x}{x}\right) = \frac{1}{x}\left[\frac{x^2}{3} + \frac{7}{90}x^4 + \text{higher powers of } x^2\right]$$

$$= \frac{x}{3} + \frac{7}{90}x^3 + \text{higher powers of } x^2$$

Taking limit as $x \to 0$

$$\lim_{x\to 0} \frac{1}{x}\log\left(\frac{\tan x}{x}\right) = 0$$

i.e. $\log y = 0$

$$y = e^0 = 1$$

i.e. $\lim_{x\to 0}\left(\frac{\tan x}{x}\right)^{1/x} = 1$ **Ans.**

Problem 5 Evalnate $\lim_{x\to 0}\left(\frac{\sin x}{x}\right)^{1/x^2}$

Solution let $y = \lim_{x\to 0}\left(\frac{\sin x}{x}\right)^{1/x^2}$.

Taking logarithm on both sides we have

$$\log y = \log\left\{\lim_{x\to 0}\left(\frac{\sin x}{x}\right)^{1/x^2}\right\}$$

$$\log y = \lim_{x\to 0} \log\left\{\left(\frac{\sin x}{x}\right)^{11x^2}\right\}$$

$$\log y = \lim_{x\to 0}\frac{1}{x^2}\log\frac{\sin x}{x} \qquad (1)$$

we have the expansion

$$\sin x = x - \frac{x^3}{3!} + \frac{x^5}{5!} - \ldots$$

$$\sin x = x - \frac{x^3}{3\times 2} + \frac{x^5}{5\times 4\times 3\times 2\times 1} - \ldots$$

$$\sin x = x - \frac{x^3}{6} + \frac{x^5}{120} - \ldots$$

$$\frac{\sin x}{x} = 1 - \frac{x^2}{6} + \frac{x^4}{120} - \ldots$$

$$\log \frac{\sin x}{x} = \text{iog} \left\{1 - \frac{x^2}{6} + \frac{x^4}{120} - \ldots\right\}$$

$$\log \frac{\sin x}{x} = \log \left\{1 - \left(\frac{x^2}{6} - \frac{x^4}{120} + \ldots,\right)\right\}$$

Remember $\log(1-x) = -x - \frac{x^2}{2} - \frac{x_3}{3} - \ldots$

$$\log \frac{\sin x}{x} = -\left(\frac{x^2}{6} - \frac{x^4}{120} \ldots\right) - \frac{1}{2}\left(\frac{x^2}{6} - \frac{x^4}{120} + , \ldots\right)^2 + \frac{1}{3}\left(\frac{x^2}{6} - \frac{x^4}{120} + , \ldots\right)^3 - \ldots$$

$$= -\frac{x^2}{6} + \frac{x^4}{120} - \frac{x^4}{72} + \text{higher powers of } x^2$$

$$= -\frac{x^2}{6} + x^4\left(\frac{1}{120} - \frac{1}{72}\right) + \text{higher powers of } x^2$$

$$= -\frac{x^2}{6} + x^4\left(\frac{3-5}{360}\right) + \text{higher powers of } x^2$$

$$= -\frac{x^2}{6} - \frac{2}{360} x^4 + \text{higher powers of } x^2$$

$$\frac{1}{x^2} \log \frac{\sin x}{x} = -\frac{1}{6} - \frac{1}{180} x^2 + \text{higher powers of } x^2$$

Taking limit as $x \to 0$ on both sides we have

$$\lim_{x \to 0} \frac{1}{x^2} \log \frac{\sin x}{x} = -\frac{1}{6}$$

$$\log y = -\frac{1}{6}$$

$$y = e^{-1/6}$$

i.e. $\lim_{x \to 0} \left(\frac{\sin x}{x}\right)^{1|2} = e^{-1/6}$

Problem 6 Evaluate $\lim_{x \to 0} \left(\frac{\sin x}{x}\right)^{1/x}$

Solution In the previous example we have just find out the value of

$$\log \frac{\sin x}{x} = -\frac{x^2}{6} - \frac{1}{180} x^4 + \text{higher powers of } x^2 \quad (1)$$

let $y = \lim_{x \to 0} \left(\frac{\sin x}{x}\right)^{1/x}$

Taking logarithm on both sides we have

$$\log y = \log \left\{ \lim_{x\to 0} \left(\frac{\sin x}{x}\right)^{1/x} \right\}$$

$$\log y = \lim_{x\to 0} \log \left\{ \left(\frac{\sin x}{x}\right)^{1/x} \right\}$$

$$\text{iog } y = \lim_{x\to 0} \frac{1}{x} \log \left(\frac{\sin x}{x}\right)$$

$$\frac{1}{x} \log \frac{\sin x}{x} = \frac{1}{x}\left[-\frac{x^2}{6} - \frac{1}{180} x^4 + \text{higher powers of } x^2 \right]$$

$$= -\frac{x}{6} - \frac{x^3}{180} + \text{higher powers of } x^2$$

Taking limit on both sides we have

$$\lim_{x\to 0} \frac{1}{x} \log \frac{\sin x}{x} = 0$$

i.e. $\log y = 0$

i.e. $y = e^0 = 1$

i.e. $\lim_{x\to 0} \left(\frac{\sin x}{x}\right)^{1/x} = e^0 = 1$ **Ans.**

Problem 7 Evaluate $\lim_{x\to\pi/2} (\sin x)^{\tan x}$.

Solution Putting $x = \frac{\pi}{2}$ in the expression we have

$$(\sin x)^{\tan x} = \left(\sin \frac{\pi}{2}\right)^{\tan \pi/2}$$

$$= 1^{\infty} \quad \text{which is indeterminate}$$

let $y = \lim_{x\to\pi/2} (\sin x)^{\tan x}$

Taking logarithm on both sides we have

$$\log y = \lim_{x\to\pi/2} \tan x \log \sin x$$

$$\log y = \lim_{x\to\pi/2} \frac{\log \sin x}{\cot x}$$

which is of the form $\left(\frac{\infty}{\infty}\right)$. So applying L'Hospital's rule we have

$$\log y = \lim_{x\to\pi/2} \frac{d.c\,\{\log \sin x\}}{d\cdot c\,(\cot x)}$$

$$\log y = \lim_{x\pi\to/2} \frac{\frac{1}{\sin x}\cos x}{-\operatorname{cosec}^2 x}$$

$$\log y = -\lim_{x\to x/2} \frac{\cos x}{\sin x} \times \frac{1}{\operatorname{cosec}^2 x}$$

$$\log y = -\lim_{x\to\pi/2} \frac{\cos x}{\sin x} \times \sin^2 x$$

$$\log y = \lim_{x\to x/2} \cos x \cdot \sin x$$

$$\log y = \cos\frac{\pi}{2} \sin\frac{\pi}{2}$$

$$\log y = 0 \times 1 = 0$$

$$\log y = 0$$

i.e. $$y = e^o = 1$$

i.e. $$\lim_{x\to\pi/2} (\sin x)^{\tan x} = 1 \qquad \textbf{Ans.}$$

Problem 8 Evaluate $\lim\limits_{x\to 0} (\cos x) \cot^{2,x}$

Solution When $x = 0$ then the given expression is

$$(\cos x)^{\cot 2x} = (\cos 0)^{\cot 2\, 0} = 1^\infty$$

which is interminate form

let $$y = \lim_{x\to 0} (\cos x)^{\cot 2\, x}$$

Taking logarithm on both side we have

$$\log y = \log \{\lim_{x\to 0} (\cos x)^{\cot 3\, x}\}$$

$$\log y = \{\lim_{x\to 0} \log (\cos x)^{\cot 2\, x}\}$$

$$\log y = \lim_{x\to 0} \cot^2 x \log (\cos x)$$

$$\log y = \lim_{x\to 0} \frac{\log\cos x}{\tan^2 x} \left[\frac{0}{0} \text{ form}\right]$$

So applying L'Hospitals rule we have

$$\log y = \lim_{x\to 0} \frac{d.c\,\{\log(\cos x)\}}{d.c\,\{\tan^2 x\}}$$

$$\log y = \lim_{x\to 0} \frac{\frac{1}{\cos x}(-\sin x)}{2\tan x \sec^2 x}$$

$$\log y = \lim_{x\to 0} -\frac{\tan x}{2\tan x \sec^2 x}$$

$$\log y = -\frac{1}{2} \lim_{\pi\to 0} \cos^2 x$$

$$\log y = -\frac{1}{2} \times (\cos 0)^2$$

$$\log y = -\frac{1}{2} \times 1$$

$$\log y = -\frac{1}{2}$$

$$y = e^{-1/2} = \frac{1}{\sqrt{e}}$$

i.e. $\lim_{x\to 0} (\cos x)^{\cot 2x} = \frac{1}{\sqrt{e}}$

Problem 9 Evaluate $\lim_{x\to a} \left(2-\frac{x}{a}\right)^{\tan(\pi x/2a)}$

Solution Putting $x=a$ in the given expression it reduces to the form 1^∞ which is indeterminate

let $$y = \lim_{x\to a} \left(2-\frac{x}{a}\right)^{\tan \pi x/2a}$$

Taking logarithm on both sides we have

$$\log y = \lim_{x\to a} \log \left\{\left(2-\frac{x}{a}\right)^{\tan \pi x/2a}\right\}$$

$$\log y = \lim_{x\to a} \tan\frac{\pi x}{2a}\left[\log\left(2-\frac{x}{a}\right)\right]$$

$$\log y = \lim_{x\to a} \frac{\log\left(2-\frac{x}{a}\right)}{\cot\frac{\pi x}{2a}} \quad \left[\frac{0}{0} \text{ form}\right]$$

So applying L' Hospitals rule we have

$$\log y = \lim_{x \to a} \frac{d.c\left\{\log\left(2-\frac{x}{a}\right)\right\}}{d.c\left\{\cot\frac{\pi x}{2a}\right\}}$$

$$\log y = \lim_{x\to a} \frac{1/2-\frac{x}{a}\cdot\left(-\frac{1}{a}\right)}{-\text{cosce}^2\frac{\pi x}{2a}\cdot\frac{\pi}{2a}}$$

$$\log y = \lim_{x\to a} \frac{2a}{\pi}\frac{1}{a\left(2-\frac{x}{a}\right)\text{cosce}^2\frac{\pi x}{2a}}$$

$$\log y = \frac{2}{\pi}\lim_{x\to a} \frac{\sin^2\frac{\pi x}{2a}}{\left(2-\frac{x}{a}\right)}$$

$$\log y = \frac{2}{\pi} \times \frac{\sin^2 \pi/2}{(2-1)}$$

$$\log y = \frac{2}{\pi} \times 1$$

$$\log y = \frac{2}{\pi}$$

$$y = e^{2|\pi}$$

$$\therefore \lim_{x\to a}\left(2-\frac{x}{a}\right)^{\tan x|2x} = e^{2'\pi} \quad \textbf{Ans.}$$

Problem 10 Evaluate

$$\lim_{x\to 0} (\cot x)^{1/\text{lgg } x}$$

Solution Putting $x = 0$ in the given expression we have

$$(\cot x)^{1/\log x} = (\cot 0)^{1/\log x}$$

$$= (\infty)^{1/\infty} = (\infty)^0 \text{ which is indeterminate.}$$

Let $\quad y = \lim_{x\to 0} (\cot x)^{1/\log x}$

Taking logadithm on both side we have

$$\log y = \left\{\lim_{x\to 0} (\cot x)^{1/\log x}\right\}$$

$$\log y = \lim_{x\to 0} \log (\cot x)^{1/\log x}$$

$$\log y = \lim_{x\to 0} {}^{1/\log x}\cdot \log \cot x$$

$$\log y = \lim_{x\to 0} \frac{\log \cot x}{\log x}\left[\text{form } \frac{\infty}{\infty}\right]$$

So applying L' Hospitals rule we have

$$\log y = \lim_{x\to 0} \frac{d.c \{\log \cot x\}}{d.c \{\log x\}}$$

$$\log y = \lim_{x\to 0} \frac{\frac{1\ (-\text{cosce}^2 x)}{\cot x}}{1/x}$$

$$\log y = \lim_{x\to 0} -\frac{\text{cosce}^2 x}{\cot x}\cdot \frac{x}{1}$$

$$\log y = -\lim_{x\to 0} \frac{x}{\sin^2 x \cdot \frac{\cos x}{\sin x}}$$

$$\log y = -\lim_{x\to 0} \frac{x}{\sin x \cos x}$$

$$\log y = -\lim_{x\to 0} \frac{1}{\left(\frac{\sin x}{x}\right)\times \cos x}$$

$$\log y = -\lim_{x\to 0} \frac{1}{\cos x} \times \frac{1}{\lim_{x\to 0}\left(\frac{\sin x}{x}\right)}$$

$$\log y = -\frac{1}{\lim_{x\to 0} \cos x} \times \frac{1}{\lim_{x\to 0}\left(\frac{\sin x}{x}\right)}$$

$$\log y = -\frac{1}{1} \times \frac{1}{1}$$

$$\log y = -1$$

$$y = e^{-1} = \frac{1}{e}$$

i.e. $$\lim_{x\to 0} (\cot x)^{1/\log x} = \frac{1}{e}$$ **Ans.**

Problem 11 Evaluate

$$\lim_{x\to 0} (\sin x)^{\tan x}$$

Solution Putting $x = 0$ in the given expression we have

$$(\sin x)^{\tan x} = (\sin\ 0)^{\tan 0} = 0^0$$

Thus the given limit is of the form $\frac{0}{0}$

$$\text{let } y = \lim_{x\to 0} (\sin x)^{\tan x}$$

Taking logarithm on both side we have

$$\log y = \log \lim_{x\to 0} (\sin x)^{\tan x}$$

$$\log y = \lim_{x\to 0} \log \{(\sin x^{\tan x}\}$$

$$\log y = \lim_{x\to 0} \tan x \log \sin x$$

$$\log y = \lim_{x\to 0} \frac{\log \sin x}{\cot x} \left[\frac{\infty}{\infty} \text{ form}\right]$$

So applying L' Hospitals rule we have

$$\log y = \lim_{x\to 0} \frac{d.c \{\log \sin x\}}{d.c (\cot x)}$$

$$\log y = \lim_{x\to 0} \frac{\frac{\cos x}{\sin x}}{-\text{cosce}^2 x}$$

$$\log y = \lim_{x\to 0} -\frac{\cos x}{\sin x} \times \sin^2 x$$

$$\log y = -\lim_{x\to 0} \cos\cdot\text{sln } x$$

$$\log y = -\cos 0 \sin 0$$

$$\log y = -1 \times 0 = 0$$

$$y = e^0 = 1$$

i.e. $$\lim_{x\to 0} (\sin x)^{\tan x} = 1 \qquad \textbf{Ans.}$$

[*IFS 84*]

Problem 12 Evaluate $\lim_{x\to 0} (\cos x)^{1/x2}$

Solution Putting $x = 0$ in the expression we have

$$\cos x)^{1/x2} = (\cos 0)^{1/0} = 1^\infty \qquad (\textit{indeterminate})$$

Thus the given limit is off the form 1^∞

$$\text{let } y = \lim_{x\to 0} (\cos x)^{1/x2}$$

Taking logarithm on both sides we have

$$\log y = \left\{\lim_{x\to 0} (\cos x)^{1/x2}\right\}$$

$$\log y = \log_{x\to 0} \{\log \cos x)^{1/2}\}$$

$$\log y = \lim_{x\to 0} \frac{1}{x^2} \log \cos x$$

$$\log y = \lim_{x\to 0} \frac{\log \cos x}{x^2} \left[\text{from } \frac{0}{0}\right]$$

So applying L' Hospitals rue we have

$$\log y = \lim_{x\to 0} \frac{d.c \{\log (\cos x)\}}{d.c\,(x^2)}$$

$$\log y = \frac{\frac{1}{\cos x}(-\sin x)}{2x}$$

$$\log y = \lim_{x\to 0} -\frac{1}{2} \times \frac{\tan x}{x}$$

$$\log y = -\frac{1}{2} \lim_{x\to 0} \left(\frac{\tan x}{x}\right)$$

$$\log y = -\frac{1}{2} \times 1 \quad \Big| \quad \lim_{x\to 0} \frac{\tan x}{x} = 1$$

$$\log y = -\tfrac{1}{2}$$

$$y = e^{-1/2} \quad \frac{1}{\sqrt{e}}$$

i.e. $$\lim_{x\to 0} (\cos x)^{1/x2} = \frac{1}{\sqrt{e}}$$ **Ans.**

Problem 13 Evaluate

$$\lim_{x\to 0} \left(\frac{1}{x}\right)^{\tan x}$$

Solution Substituting $x = 0$ in the given expression we have

$$\left(\frac{1}{x}\right)^{\tan x} = \left(\frac{1}{0}\right)^{\tan 0} = \infty^0$$ ***(indeterminate)***

Let us suppose that $y = \lim_{x \to 0} \left(\frac{1}{x}\right)^{\tan x}$

Taking logarithm on both sides we have

$$\log y = \log \left\{\lim_{x \to 0} \left(\frac{1}{x}\right)^{\tan x}\right\}$$

$$\log y = \lim_{x \to 0} \log \left(\frac{1}{x}\right)^{\tan x}$$

$$\log y = \lim_{x \to 0} \tan x \log \left(\frac{1}{x}\right) [0 \times \infty]$$

$$\log y = \lim_{x \to 0} \frac{\log^{(1/x)}}{\cot x} \left[\frac{\infty}{\infty}\right]$$

So applying L' Hospitals rule we have

$$\log y = \lim_{x \to 0} \frac{\log^{(1/x)}}{\cot x}$$

$$\log y = \lim_{x \to 0} \frac{d.c \{\log^{(1/x)}\}}{d.c \{\cot x\}}$$

$$\log y = \lim_{x \to 0} \frac{\frac{1}{x} \cdot \left(-\frac{1}{x^2}\right)}{-\text{cosce}^2 x}$$

$$\log y = \lim_{x \to 0} \frac{x/x^2}{\text{cosce}^2 x}$$

$$\log y = \lim_{x \to 0} \frac{1}{x \text{ cosce}^2 x}$$

$$\log y = \lim_{x \to 0} \frac{\sin^2 x}{x} \text{ which is the form } \frac{0}{0}$$

So applying L' Hospitals rule we have

$$\log y = \lim_{x \to 0} \frac{d.c \{\sin^2 x\}}{d.c (x)}$$

$$\log y = \lim_{x \to 0} \frac{2 \sin x \cos x}{1}$$

$$\log y = \lim_{x \to 0} \sin 2x$$

$$\log y = 0$$

$$y = e^0 = 1$$

i.e. $\lim_{x \to 0} \left(\frac{1}{x}\right)^{\tan x} = 1$ **Ans.**

Problem 14 $\lim_{x \to \pi/2} (\sec x)^{\cot x}$

Solution Let $y = \lim_{x \to \pi/2} (\sec x)^{\cot} \; [\infty^0 \text{ form}]$

Taking logarithm on both sides we have

$$\log y = \log \{ \lim_{x \to \pi/2} (\sec x)^{\cot x} \}$$

$$\log y = \lim_{x \to \pi/2} \log (\sec x)^{\cot x}$$

$$\log y = \lim_{x \to \pi/2} \cot x \,(\log \sec x)$$

$$\log y = \lim_{x \to \pi/2} \frac{\log \sec x}{\tan x} \left[\frac{\infty}{\infty} \text{ form} \right]$$

So applying L' Hospitals rule we have

$$\log y = \lim_{x \to \pi/2} \frac{d.c \,\{\log \sec x\}}{d.c \; d.c \,\{\tan x\}}$$

$$\log y = \lim_{x \to \pi/2} \frac{\frac{1}{\sec x} \sec x \tan x}{\sec^2 x}$$

$$\log y = \lim_{x \to \pi/2} \frac{\tan x}{\sec^2 x}$$

$$\log y = \lim_{x \to \pi/2} \frac{\frac{\sin x}{\cos x}}{\frac{1}{\cos^2 x}}$$

$$\log y = \lim_{x \to \pi/2} \sin x \cos x$$

$$\log y = \sin \frac{\pi}{2} \cos \frac{\pi}{2}$$

$$\log y = 1 \times 0 = 0$$

$$\log y = 0 \Rightarrow y = e^0 = 1$$

$$\lim_{x \to \pi/2} (\sec x)^{\cot x} = 1 \qquad \textbf{Ans.}$$

Problem 15 Evaluate $\lim_{x \to 0} (\cos x)^{1/x}$

Puttining $x = 0$ the given expression is of the form 1^∞.

$$\text{let } y = \lim_{x \to 0} (\cos)^{1/x}$$

Taking logarithm on both sides we have

$$\log y = \log \left\{ \lim_{x\to 0} (\cos x)^{1/x} \right\}$$

$$\log y = \lim_{x\to 0} \log (\cos x)^{1/x}$$

$$\log y = \lim_{x\to 0} \frac{1}{x} \log \cos x$$

$$\log y = \lim_{x\to 0} \frac{\log \cos x}{x}$$

Which is of the form $\left(\frac{0}{0}\right)$ so applying L' Hospitals rule we have

$$\log y = \lim_{x\to 0} \frac{d.c \{\log \cos x\}}{d.c\,(x)}$$

$$\log y = \lim_{x\to 0} \frac{\frac{1}{\cos x}(-\sin x)}{x^1}$$

$$\log y = \lim_{x\to 0} -\tan x$$

$$\log y = 0$$

$$y = e^0 = 1$$

i.e $$\lim_{x\to 0} (\cos x)^{1/x} = 1$$ **Ans.**

9

Maxima and Minima of a Function of a Single Variable

Problem 1 Find the maximum and minimum values of y

where $$y = 2x^3 - 21x^2 + 36x - 20$$

Solution Here $y = 2x^3 - 21x^2 + 36x - 20$

$$\therefore \quad \frac{dy}{dx} = 6x^2 - 42x^2 + 36$$

Now for maxima or minima $\frac{dy}{dx} = 0$

i e.
$$6x^2 - 42x + 36 = 0$$
$$6(x^2 - 7x + 6) = 0$$
$$\Rightarrow x^2 - 7x + 6 = 0$$
$$\Rightarrow x^2 - 6x - x + 6 = 0$$
$$\Rightarrow x(x - 6) - 1(x - 6) = 0$$
$$\Rightarrow (x - 1)(x - 6) = 0$$

Then either $x - 1 = 0$ or $x - 6 = 0$

i.e. $x = 1$ or $x = 6$

Now
$$\frac{d^2 y}{dx^2} = 12x - 42$$

$$\left[\frac{d^2 y}{dx^2}\right]_{x=1} = [12x - 42]_{x=1} = 12 \times 1 - 42$$
$$= 12 - 42 = -30 \ (-\text{ve})$$

Thus y is maximum at $x = 1$

$$\left[\frac{d^2 y}{dx^2}\right]_{x=1} = 12x - 42 = 12 \times 6 - 42$$
$$= 72 - 42 = 30 \ (+\text{ ve})$$

y has a minimum value at $x = 6$.

Maximum vallue of $y = [2x^3 - 21x^2 + 36x - 20]_{x=1}$

$$= 2(1)^3 - 21(1)^2 + 36(1) - 20$$

$$= 2 \times 1 - 21 + 36 - 20$$

$$= 2 + 36 - 41 = 38 - 41$$

Maximum value of $y = -3$

Minimum value $y = [2x^3 - 21x^2 + 36x - 20]_{x=6}$

$$= 2(6)^3 - 21(6)^2 + 36(6) - 20$$

$$= 2 \times 216 - 21(36) + 216 - 20$$

$$= 432 - 756 + 216 - 20$$

$$= 648 - 776 = -128$$

Minimum value of $y = -128.$

Problem 2 Find the maximum value of $\dfrac{\log x}{x}$

Sloution Let $y = \dfrac{\log x}{x}$

$$\therefore \quad \frac{dy}{dx} = \frac{x(1/x) - \log x \cdot 1}{x^2}$$

$$\frac{dy}{dx} = \frac{1 - \log x}{x^2} \qquad (1$$

Now for maxima or minima, $\dfrac{dy}{dx} = 0$

Therefore $\dfrac{1 - \log x}{x^2} = 0$

i.e. $1 - \log x = 0$

$$\Rightarrow \log x = 1$$

$$\Rightarrow \log x = \log e$$

$$\Rightarrow \quad x = e$$

Thus at $x = e$ the function $\dfrac{\log x}{x}$ may have maxima or minima.

Now $$\frac{d^2 y}{dx^2} = \frac{d}{dx}\left(\frac{dy}{dx}\right)$$

$$\frac{d^2 y}{dx^2} = \frac{d}{dx}\left[\frac{1 - \log x}{x^2}\right] = \frac{x^2(0 - 1/x) - (1 - \log x)\,2x}{x^4}$$

$$= \frac{-x - 2x + 2x \log x}{x^4}$$

$$\left[\frac{d^2 y}{dx^2}\right]_{x=e} = \frac{-e-2e+2e \log e}{e^4}$$

$$\left[\frac{d^2 y}{dx^2}\right]_{x=e} = \frac{-3e+2e}{e^4}$$

$$\left[\frac{d^2 y}{dx^2}\right]_{x=e} = \frac{-e}{e^4} = -\frac{1}{e^3} \ (-\text{ve})$$

Thus y has maximum value at $x = e$

Maximum value of y i.e. of $\frac{\log x}{x}$ is

$$\frac{\log e}{e} = \frac{1}{e}$$

Maximum value of $y = \frac{1}{e}$

Problem 3 Show that $\sin x\,(1 + \cos x)$ is a maximum when $x = \frac{\pi}{3}$.

Solution Let $y = \sin x\,(1 + \cos x)$

$$\frac{dy}{dx} = \sin x \, d{\cdot}c\,(1 + \cos x) + (1 + \cos x)\, d{\cdot}c\,(\sin x)$$

$$\frac{dy}{dx} = \sin x\,(0 - \sin x) + (1 + \cos x) \cos x$$

$$\frac{dy}{dx} = -\sin^2 x + \cos x + \cos^2 x$$

Formula $\cos^2 x - \sin^2 x = \cos 2x$ (Remember)

$$\frac{dy}{dx} = \cos x + \cos^2 x - \sin^2 x$$

$$\frac{dy}{dx} = \cos x + \cos 2x \qquad (1)$$

Now for maxima or minima, $\frac{dy}{dx} = 0$

$$\therefore \quad \cos x + \cos 2x = 0$$

$$\Rightarrow \quad \cos 2x = -\cos x = \cos(\pi - x)$$

$$\Rightarrow \quad 2x = \pi - x$$

$$\Rightarrow \quad 3x = \pi$$

$$\Rightarrow \quad x = \frac{\pi}{3}$$

i.e. the given function $y = \sin x\,(1 + \cos x)$ is maximum or minimum at $x = \frac{\pi}{3}$

Again differentiating equation (1) we have

$$\frac{d^2 y}{dx^2} = - \sin x - 2 \sin 2x$$

$$\left[\frac{d^2 y}{dx^2}\right] x = \frac{\pi}{3} = - \sin \frac{\pi}{3} - 2 \sin 2 \frac{\pi}{3}$$

$$= - \sin \frac{\pi}{3} - 2 \sin \left(\pi - \frac{\pi}{3}\right) = - \frac{\sqrt{3}}{2} - \sin \frac{\pi}{3}$$

$$= - \frac{\sqrt{3}}{2} - 2 \frac{\sqrt{3}}{2} = - \frac{\sqrt{3}}{2} \text{ (– ve)}$$

$$= - \frac{\sqrt{3}}{2} - 2 \sin \frac{\pi}{3}$$

Thus the value of $y = \sin x (1 + \cos x)$ is maximum at $x = \frac{\pi}{3}$

Maximum value of $y = \sin x (1 + \cos x)$ is

$$\sin \frac{\pi}{3} \left(1 + \cos \frac{\pi}{3}\right) = \frac{\sqrt{3}}{2} \left(1 + \frac{1}{2}\right)$$

Maximum value of $y = \frac{\sqrt{3}}{2} \frac{3}{2} = \frac{3\sqrt{3}}{4}$ **Ans.**

Problem 4 Examine whether $x^{1/x}$ possesses a maximum or a minimum value and determine the same.

Solution Let $y = x^{1/x}$

Taking logarithm of both sides, we get

$$\log y = \frac{1}{x} \log x$$

$$\log y = \frac{\log x}{x}$$

differentiating we have

$$\frac{1}{y} \frac{dy}{dx} = \frac{x \cdot 1/x - \log x \cdot 1}{x^2}$$

$$\frac{1}{y} \frac{dy}{dx} = \frac{1 - \log x}{x^2} \qquad (1)$$

$$\frac{dy}{dx} = \frac{y (1 - \log x)}{x^2} \qquad (2)$$

Now for maxima or minima $\frac{dy}{dx} = 0$

i.e. $$\frac{y(1 - \log x)}{x^2} = 0$$

i.e. $$1 - \log x = 0$$

$$\log x = 1 = \log e$$

$$\Rightarrow \quad x = e$$

Again differentiating equation (1) we have

$$\frac{1}{y}\frac{d^2y}{dx^2} + \frac{dy}{dx}\left(-\frac{1}{y^2}\right) = \frac{x^2(0 - 1/x) - (1 - \log x)\,2x}{x^4}$$

$$= \frac{-x - 2x + 2x\log x}{x^4} = \frac{-3x + 2x\log x}{x^4}$$

$$= \frac{(-3 + 2\log x)\,x}{x^4} = \frac{-3 + 2\log x}{x^3} \qquad (3)$$

For maxima or minima $\frac{dy}{dx} = 0$ and $x = e$

$$\frac{1}{y}\frac{d^2y}{dx^2} + 0 = \frac{-3 + 2\log e}{e^3}$$

$$\frac{1}{y}\frac{d^2y}{dx^2} = \frac{-3 + 2}{e^3} = -\frac{1}{e^3}$$

$$\frac{d^2y}{dx^2} = \frac{-1}{e^3}\cdot y \Rightarrow \frac{d^2y}{dx^2} = -x^{1/x}\frac{1}{e^3} = -\frac{e^{1/e}}{e^3}$$

$$\frac{d^2y}{dx^2} = -\text{ve}$$

Hence the function has got a maximum value at $x = e$ and its maximum value is

$$y_{\max} = [x^{1/x}]\ x = e$$
$$y_{\max} = e^{1/e}$$

Problem 5 Determine p and q such that $x^2 + px + q$ has maximum value where $x = 1$. *(IFS 88)*

Solution Let $y = x^2 + px + q$

For maxima or minima of y the first derivative of y i.e. $\frac{dy}{dx}$ vanishes

$$\frac{dy}{dx} = 0$$

i.e. $$\frac{d}{dx}(x^2 + px + q) = 0$$

i.e. $$2x + p = 0$$

$$\Rightarrow \quad 2x = -p$$

$$\Rightarrow \quad x = -\frac{p}{2}$$

Again $$\frac{d^2y}{dx^2} = 2 \; (+\text{ ve})$$

So the function y has a minimum value at $x = 1$

so $$\frac{-p}{2} = 1 \quad \Rightarrow \quad p = -2$$

Again $$y_{\min} = [x^2 + px + q]_{x=1}$$
$$= (1)^2 + p \cdot 1 + q = 1 + p + q$$

Given that at $x = 1$ the minimum value of y is 3

so $$1 + p + q = 3$$
$$1 - 2 + q = 3$$
$$-1 + q = 3$$
$$\Rightarrow \quad q = 3 + 1 = 4$$

Thus the value of p and q such that $x^2 + px + q$ has minimum value 3 when $x = 1$ is -2 and 4. **Ans.**

Problem 6 show taht $\sin^p \theta \cos^q \theta$ attains a maximum when $\tan \theta = \dfrac{\sqrt{p}}{q}$

Solution Let $y = \sin^p\theta \cos^q \theta$

Taking logarithm on both sides we have

$$\log y = \log \{\sin^p \theta \cos^q \theta\}$$

$$\log y = \log \{(\sin \theta)^p (\cos \theta)^q\}$$

$$\log y = \log \{(\sin \theta)^p\} + \log \{(\cos \theta \, 1^q\}$$

$$\log y = p \log \sin \theta + q \log \cos \theta$$

Differentiating with respect to θ we have

$$\frac{1}{y}\frac{dy}{d\theta} = \frac{p}{\sin \theta}\cos \theta + \frac{q}{\cos \theta} \times (-\sin \theta)$$

$$\frac{1}{y}\frac{dy}{d\theta} = p \cot \theta - q \tan \theta \tag{1}$$

$$\frac{dy}{d\theta} = y\,(p \cot \theta - q \tan \theta) \tag{2}$$

For maxima or minima of a function $\frac{dy}{d\theta} = 0$

i.e. $$y\,(p \cot \theta - q \tan \theta) = 0$$

i.e. $$p \cot \theta - q \tan \theta = 0$$

$$p \cot \theta = q \tan \theta$$

$$\frac{p}{\tan \theta} = q \tan \theta$$

$$\tan \theta = \frac{p}{q}$$

$$\Rightarrow \tan \theta = \sqrt{\frac{p}{q}}$$

Again differentiating (1) with respect to θ we have

$$\frac{1}{y}\frac{d^2 y}{d\theta^2} + \frac{dy}{d\theta}\left(-\frac{1}{y^2}\right) = -\,p \operatorname{cosec}^2 \theta - q \sec^2 \theta$$

$$\frac{1}{y}\frac{d^2 y}{d\theta^2} - \frac{1}{y^2}\frac{dy}{d\theta} = -\,(p \operatorname{cosec}^2 \theta + q \operatorname{scc}^2 \theta)$$

sinee $\frac{dy}{d\theta} = 0$

Therefore $$\frac{1}{y}\frac{d^2 y}{d\theta^2} = -\,[p\,(\operatorname{cosec}^2 \theta + q \sec^2 \theta]$$

$$\frac{d^2 y}{d\theta^2} = -y\,[p \operatorname{cosec}^2 \theta + q \sec^2 \theta] \qquad (3)$$

Since $$\tan \theta = \sqrt{\frac{p}{q}}$$

$$\tan^2 \theta = \frac{p}{q}$$

$$1 + \tan^2 \theta = 1 + \frac{p}{q}$$

$$\sec^2 \theta = \frac{p+q}{q}$$

$$\cot^2 \theta = \frac{q}{p}$$

$$1 + \cot^2 \theta = 1 + \frac{q}{p} = \frac{p+q}{p}$$

$$\operatorname{cosec}^2 \theta = \frac{p+q}{p}$$

$$\left[\frac{d^2 y}{d\theta^2}\right]_{\tan\theta=\sqrt{p/q}} = -y\left[p\frac{p+q}{p} + q\frac{p+q}{q}\right]$$

$$\left[\frac{d^2 y}{d\theta^2}\right]_{\tan\theta=\sqrt{p/q}} = -y\,[2p + 2q]$$

$$\left[\frac{d^2 y}{d\theta^2}\right]_{\tan\theta=\sqrt{p/q}} = -2y\,(p + q)\,(-\text{ve})$$

Hence the given function $y = \sin^p\theta\cos^q\theta$ has a maximum value when $\tan\theta = \sqrt{\frac{p}{q}}$ *(Proved)*

Problem 7 Find the maximum value of $x^p y^q$ having given $x + y = a$

Solution The given function consists of two variables x and y so at first we change it to a function containing only one variable.

let $$u = x^p y^q \tag{1}$$

given that $x + y = a$

$$\Rightarrow y = (a-x) \tag{2}$$

From equation (2) equation (1) reduces to

$$u = x^p (a-x)^q$$

Taking logarithm on both sides we have

$$\log u = \log\{x^p (a-x)^q\}$$

$$\log u = \log x^p + \log (a-x)^q$$

$$\log u = p\log x + q\log(a-x) \tag{3}$$

Differentiating with respect to x we have

$$\frac{1}{u}\frac{du}{dx} = \frac{p}{x} + \frac{q}{a-x}\cdot(-1)$$

$$\frac{1}{u}\frac{du}{dx} = \frac{p}{x} - \frac{q}{a-x} \tag{3a}$$

For maxima or minima of the function

i.e. $$\frac{du}{dx} = 0$$

so $$\frac{p}{x} - \frac{q}{a-x} = 0$$

$$\Rightarrow \quad \frac{p(a-x)-qx}{x(a-x)} = 0$$

$$\Rightarrow \quad p(a-x) - qx = 0$$

$$\Rightarrow \quad ap - px - qx = 0$$

$$\Rightarrow \quad ap - x(q + p) = 0$$

$$\Rightarrow \quad x(q + p) = ap$$

$$\Rightarrow \quad x = \frac{ap}{q + p} = \frac{ap}{p + q} \tag{4}$$

Since $\quad x + y = a$

$$\Rightarrow \quad \frac{ap}{p + q} + y = a$$

$$\Rightarrow \quad y = a - \frac{ap}{p + q}$$

$$\Rightarrow \quad y = \frac{a(p + q) - ap}{p + q}$$

$$\Rightarrow \quad y = \frac{ap + aq - ap}{p + q}$$

$$\Rightarrow \quad y = \frac{aq}{p + q} \tag{5}$$

The function $u = x^p y^q$ has maximum or minimum value

at $$x = \frac{ap}{p + q}, \; y = \frac{aq}{p + q}$$

Again differentiating equation 3 (a) with respect to x we have

$$\frac{1}{u} \frac{d^2 u}{dx^2} - \frac{1}{u^2} \frac{du}{dx} = -\frac{p}{x^2} - (-1) \frac{q}{(a - x)^2}(-1)$$

$$\frac{1}{u} \frac{d^2 u}{dx^2} - \frac{1}{u^2} \frac{du}{dx} = -\frac{p}{x^2} - \frac{q}{(a - x)^2}$$

Since for maxima or minima $\frac{du}{dx} = 0$

so $$\frac{1}{u} \frac{d^2 u}{dx^2} = -\frac{p}{x^2} - \frac{q}{(a - x)^2}$$

so $$\frac{1}{u} \frac{d^2 u}{dx^2} = -\left[\frac{p}{x^2} + \frac{q}{(a - x)^2}\right]$$

$$\frac{d^2 u}{dx^2} = -u\left[\frac{p}{x^2} + \frac{q}{(a - x)^2}\right]$$

$$\frac{d^2 u}{dx^2} = -\text{ ve}$$

Thus the given function $u = x^p y^q$ has a maximum value at

$$u = \frac{ap}{p + q} \quad \text{and} \quad y = \frac{aq}{p + q}$$

Maximum value of $u = x^p y^q$ is

$$u_{max} = \left[\frac{ap}{p+q}\right]^p \left[\frac{aq}{p+q}\right]^q$$

$$u_{max} = \frac{a^p p^p}{(p+q)} \frac{a^q q^q}{(p+q)^q}$$

$$u_{max} = a^{p+q} \frac{p^q q^q}{(p+q)^{p+q}}$$ **Ans.**

Problem 8 What point on the curve $xy^2 = 1$ is nearest to the origin.

Solution Let the co-ordinates of any point on the curve be (x, y)

Let the distance of the point (x, y) from the origin $= z$ then

$$z^2 = (x-0)^2 + (y-0)^2$$

i.e.

$$z^2 = x^2 + y^2 \tag{1}$$

we have to find minimum value of z, subject to the condition

$$xy^2 = 1 \tag{2}$$

$$y^2 = \frac{1}{x} \tag{3}$$

Then from equation (1) we have

$$z^2 = x^2 + y^2$$

$$z^2 = x^2 + \frac{1}{x} \tag{4}$$

Differentiating with respect to z we have

$$2z \frac{dz}{dx} = 2x - \frac{1}{x^2} \tag{4a}$$

$$2z \frac{dz}{dx} = \frac{2x^3 - 1}{x^2} \tag{5}$$

Now for maxima or minima $\frac{dz}{dx} = 0$. therefore

$$\frac{2x^3 - 1}{x^2} = 0$$

$$2x^3 - 1 = 0$$

$$2x^3 = 1$$

$$\Rightarrow \quad x^3 = \frac{1}{2}$$

$$\Rightarrow \quad x = \left(\frac{1}{2}\right)^{1/3}$$

Again differentiating equation (4a) we have

$$2\left[z\frac{d^2z}{dx^2}+\frac{dz}{dx}\right]=2\cdot 1+\frac{2}{x^3}$$

$$2\left[z\frac{d^2z}{dx^2}+0\right]=2\left(1+\frac{1}{x^3}\right)$$

$$2z\frac{d^2z}{dx^2}=2+\frac{2}{x^3}$$

$$2z\frac{d^2z}{dx^2}=2+\frac{2}{\frac{1}{2}}$$

$$2z\frac{d^2z}{dx^2}=2+4$$

$$2z\frac{d^2z}{dx^2}=6$$

$$z\frac{d^2z}{dx^2}=3\ (+\text{ve})$$

z is minimum at $x=(\frac{1}{2})^{1/3}$

Now we shall solve the problems involving Geometry.

In this connection it is necessary to remember the following formulae for the area and the volume of some important figures.

(I) Sphere. whose radius is $= r$

Volume $= \frac{4}{3}\pi r^3$

Surface $= 4\pi r^2$

(II) Cylinder whose hight $= h$ and radius of the base is r

Volume $= \pi r^2 h$

Curved surface $= 2\pi rh$

Whole surface $= 2\pi rh + 2\pi r^2$

(III) Cone whose height $= h$, radius of the base $= r$ and slant height $= l$

slant height

$$l=\sqrt{h^2+r^2}$$

Volume $= \frac{1}{3}\pi r^2 h$

Curved surface

$$=\pi rl$$

$$=\pi r\sqrt{h^2+r^2}$$

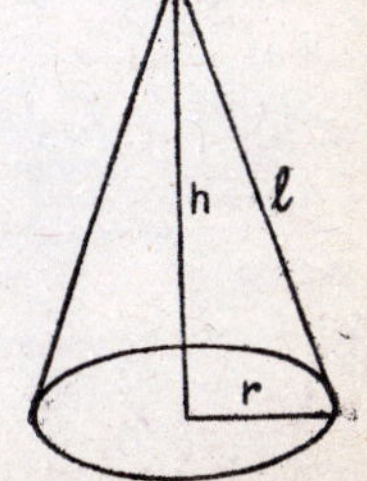

whole surface

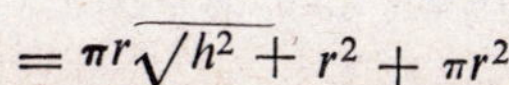

$$=\pi r\sqrt{h^2+r^2}+\pi r^2$$

Problem 9 The sum of parameters of a circlc and a spquare is l show that when the sum of the areas is least, the side of the square is double the radius of the circle.

Solution Let the radius of the circle is r and a side of the square is a

Perimeter of the square $= 4a$

Perimeter of the circle $= 2\pi r$

Given that the sum of perimeters of a circle and a square is l

i.e. $$l = 2\pi r + 4a \tag{1}$$

Area of the square $= a^2$

Area of the circle $= \pi r^2$

Let the sum of the areas of the square and the circle is A then

$$A = \pi r^2 + a^2 \tag{2}$$

From cquation (1) we havc

$$4a = l - 2\pi r$$

$$a = \frac{(l-2\pi r)}{4} \tag{3}$$

with the help of this relation equation (2) reduces to

$$A = \pi r^2 + \frac{(l-2\pi r)^2}{16} \tag{4}$$

Differentiating equation with respect to r we have

$$\frac{dA}{dr} = 2\pi r + \frac{1}{16} \cdot 2\,(l-2\pi r)\,(-2\pi) \tag{5}$$

$$\frac{dA}{dr} = 2\pi r - \frac{\pi}{4}\,(l-2\pi r) \tag{6}$$

For maxima or minima we have $\dfrac{dA}{dr} = 0$

i.e. $$2\pi r - \frac{\pi}{4}\,(l-2\pi r) = 0$$

i.e. $$2\pi r = \frac{\pi}{4}\,(l-2\pi r)$$

i.e. $$2\pi r = \pi \times \left(\frac{l-2\pi r)}{4}\right)$$

i.e. $$2\pi r = \pi a$$

i.e. $$a = 2r$$

we have now to show that sum of the areas is least for this value.

Again differentiating equation (5) with respect to r we have

$$\frac{d^2A}{dr^2} = 2\pi - \frac{\pi}{4}\ (0 - 2\pi)$$

$$\frac{d^2\ A}{dr^2} = 2\pi + \frac{\pi^2}{2} = +\ \text{ve}$$

Hence the sum of their areas will be minimum when $a = 2r$ (*Proved*)

Problem 10 Show that the maximum rectangle inscribed in a circle is *a* square.

Solution Let the radius of the circle is a. Let $ABCD$ be a maximum ractangle inscribed in the circle whose radius is a. We have to show that the rectangle $ABCD$ is a square.

Let $\qquad \angle QOB = \theta . OB = a$

$$OQ = a \cos \theta$$

$$QB = a \sin \theta$$

Thus the co-ordinates of the point B is $(a \cos \theta,\ a \sin \theta)$

$$AB = pQ = 2OQ = 2\ a \cos \theta$$

$$AB = 2\ a \cos \theta$$

$$BD = 2\ Q\ B$$

$$BD = 2 \cdot a \sin \theta$$

Let S be the area of the rect angle then

$$S = AB \times BD$$

$$S = 2a \cos \theta \times 2a \sin \theta$$

$$S = 4a^2 \sin \theta \cos \theta$$

$$S = 2a^2\ 2 \sin \theta \cos \theta$$

$$S = 2a^2 \sin^2 \theta$$

For maximum or minimum values of S we must have

$$\frac{ds}{d\theta} = 0$$

$$\frac{ds}{d\theta} = 2a^2\ (\cos 2\theta) \cdot 2 = 0$$

$$\frac{ds}{d\theta} = 4a^2 \cos^2 \theta = 0 \qquad (3)$$

i.e. $\qquad \cos 2\theta = 0$

$$\Rightarrow \cos 2\theta = \cos\frac{\pi}{2}$$

$$\Rightarrow 2\theta = \frac{\pi}{2}$$

$$\Rightarrow \theta = \frac{\pi}{4}$$

Again differentiating equation (1) we have

$$\frac{d^2 s}{d\theta^2} = 4a^2 (-2 \sin 2\theta)$$

$$\frac{d^2 s}{d\theta^2} = -8a^2 \sin 2\theta$$

$$\left[\frac{d^2 s}{d\theta}\right]_{\theta=\frac{\pi}{4}} = -8a^2 \sin 2 \cdot \frac{\pi}{2}$$

$$\left[\frac{d^2 s}{d\theta^2}\right]_{\theta=\frac{\pi}{4}} = -8a^2 \sin \frac{\pi}{2}$$

$$= -8a^2 \times 1 = -8a^2 = -\text{Ve}$$

So S has a maximum value at $\theta = \frac{\pi}{4}$ at $\theta = \frac{\pi}{4}$ the value of the sides of the rectangle are given by

$$AB = 2a \cos \theta$$

$$AB = 2a \cos \frac{\pi}{4}$$

$$AB = 2a \frac{1}{\sqrt{2}}$$

$$AB = \sqrt{2}a$$

$$CD = 2a \sin \theta$$

$$CD = 2a \sin \frac{\pi}{4}$$

$$CD = 2a \frac{1}{\sqrt{2}}$$

$$CD = \sqrt{2a}$$

Thus $AB = CD = \sqrt{2a}$

Hence the maximum rectangle inscribed in a circle is a square. *(Proved)*

Problem 11 Show that the right circular cylinder of given surface and maximum volume is such that its height is equal to the diameter of the base.

Solution Let $ABCD$ be a right circular cylinder whose height is h and the radius of the base is r. Let S be the surface of the right circular cylinder and V is the volume of the right circular cylinder

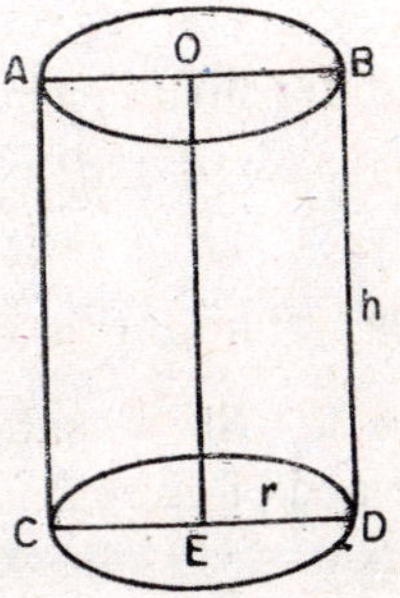

$$S = 2\pi r^2 + 2\pi rh \tag{1}$$

$$V = \pi r^2 h \tag{2}$$

Since the surface of the cylender is given so $S =$ (constant)

$$2\pi r^2 + 2\pi rh = l$$

$$2\pi rh = l - 2\pi r^2$$

$$h = \frac{l - 2\pi r^2}{2\pi r} \tag{3}$$

Putting the value of h from equation (3) in (2) we have

$$V = \pi r^2 h$$

$$V = \pi r^2 \left[\frac{l - 2\pi r^2}{2\pi r}\right]$$

$$V = \frac{r}{2}\left[l - 2\pi r^2\right]$$

$$V = \frac{rl}{2} - \pi r^3 \tag{4}$$

Differentiating equation (4) with respect to r we have

$$\frac{dv}{dr} = \frac{l}{2} - 3\pi r^2 \tag{4(a)}$$

For maxim or minima of V, $\frac{dv}{dr} = 0$

i.e.

$$\frac{l}{2} - \pi r^2 = 0$$

$$3\pi r^2 = \frac{l}{2}$$

$$r^2 = \frac{r}{6\pi}$$

$$l = 6\pi r^2$$

$$2\pi r^2 + 2\pi rh = 6\pi r^2$$
$$2\pi rh = 6\pi r^2 - 2\pi r^2$$
$$2\pi rh = 4\,\pi r^2$$
$$h = 2r \qquad (5)$$

Again differentiating equation 4(*a*) we have

$$\frac{d^2 v}{dr^2} = 0 - 6\pi r = \text{ve}$$

Thus the volume of the cylinder is maximum when $h = 2r$. (*Proved*)

Problem 12 Show that the semi-vertical angle of the cone of maximum volume and of given slant height is $\tan^{-1}(\sqrt{2}$

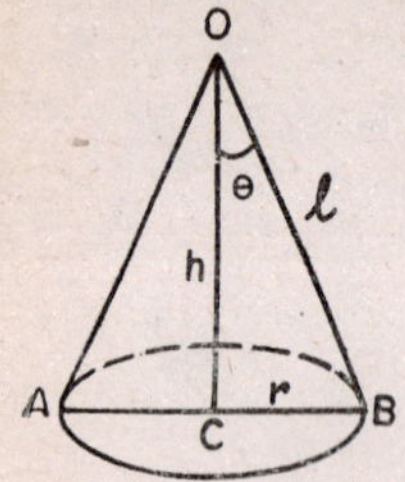

Solution Let 0 be the vertex of the one. *AB* be the diameter of the base. Let $BC = r$ be the radius of the base let h be the height of the cone and l is the slant height of the cone. Let $\angle BOC = \theta$

Slant height

$$\text{(Given) } l = \sqrt{h^2 + r^2} \qquad (1)$$

Volume of the cone

$$V = \frac{1}{3}\pi r^2 h \qquad (2)$$

Squaring equation (1) we have

$$h^2 + r^2 = l^2 \text{ (constant)}$$
$$r^2 = l^2 - h^2$$

Hence
$$V = \frac{1}{3}\pi r^2 h$$
$$V = \frac{1}{3}\pi (l^2 - h^2) h$$
$$V = \frac{1}{3}\pi l^2 h - \frac{1}{3}\pi h^3$$

Differentiating with respects to h we have

$$\frac{dV}{dh} = \frac{1}{3}\pi l^2 - \frac{1}{3}\cdot 3\pi h^2$$
$$\frac{dV}{dh} = \frac{1}{3}\pi l^2 - \pi h^2 \qquad (3)$$

For maxima or minima $\dfrac{dv}{dh} = 0$

i.e. $$\frac{1}{3}\pi l^2 - \pi h^2 = 0$$

i.e. $$\frac{\pi l^2}{3} = \pi h^2$$

$$l^2 = 3h^2$$

$$h^2 + r^2 = 3h^2$$

$$r^2 = 2h^2$$

$$r = \sqrt{2}h$$

Again differentiating equation (3) we have

$$\frac{d^2 r}{dh^2} = 0 - 2\pi h$$

$$\frac{d^2 V}{dh^2} = -2\pi h \ (-\text{ve})$$

Therefore V is maximum at $r = \sqrt{2}h$

New Let semi vertical angle be θ then

$$\frac{r}{h} = \sqrt{2}$$

$$\tan\theta = \frac{r}{h} = \sqrt{2}$$

i.e. $$\theta = \tan^{-1}\sqrt{2}$$

Hence the semivertical angle of the cone of maximum volume and of given slant height is $\tan^{-1}\sqrt{2}$. *(Proved)*

Problem 13 Show that the semivertical angle of a right circular cone of a given surface and maximum volume is $\sin^{-1}\left(\frac{1}{3}\right)$.

Solution Let α be the semivertical angle and 0 be the vertex of a right circular cone. Let r be the radius of the base of the cone, h the height and l the slant height. Let S be the surface of the right circular cone.

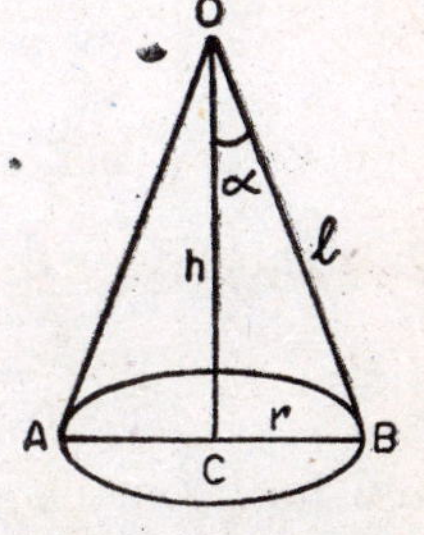

$$S = \pi r^2 + \pi r l$$

$$l = \sqrt{h^2 + r^2} \qquad \Rightarrow l^2 = h^2 + r^2$$

$$S = \pi r^2 + \pi r\sqrt{h^2 + r^2} \qquad \Rightarrow h^2 = (l^2 - r^2)$$

Since the surface of the right circular cone is given so

$$\pi r^2 + \pi r l = k \tag{1}$$

Volume of the right circular cone is given by

$$V = \frac{1}{3}\pi r^2 h \qquad (1)\,(a)$$

From equation (1) we have

$$\pi r l = k - \pi r^2$$

$$l = \frac{k - \pi r^2}{\pi r} \tag{2}$$

Squaring equation (1)(*a*) we have

$$V = \left[\frac{1}{3}\,\pi r^2\, h\right]^2$$

$$V^2 = \frac{1}{9}\,\pi^2\, r^4\, h^2$$

$$V^2 = \frac{1}{9}\,\pi^2\, r^4\, [l^2 - r^2]$$

$$V^2 = \frac{1}{9}\,\pi^2\, r^4 \left[\left(\frac{k - \pi r^2}{\pi r}\right)^2 - r^2\right]$$

$$V^2 = \frac{1}{9}\,\pi^2\, r^4 \left[\left(\frac{k}{\pi r} - r\right)^2 - r^2\right]$$

$$V^2 = \frac{1}{9}\,\pi^2\, r^4 \left[\frac{k^2}{\pi^2\, r^2} - \frac{2k}{\pi r}\cdot r + r^2 - r^2\right]$$

$$V^2 = \frac{1}{9}\,\pi^2\, r^4 \left[\frac{k^2}{\pi^2\, r^2} - \frac{2k}{\pi}\right]$$

$$V^2 = \frac{1}{9}\,\pi^2 \left[\frac{k^2\, r^2}{\pi^2} - \frac{2kr^4}{\pi}\right]$$

$$V^2 = \frac{1}{9}\,\pi^2\, \frac{[k^2\, r^2 - 2k\,\pi r^4]}{\pi^2}$$

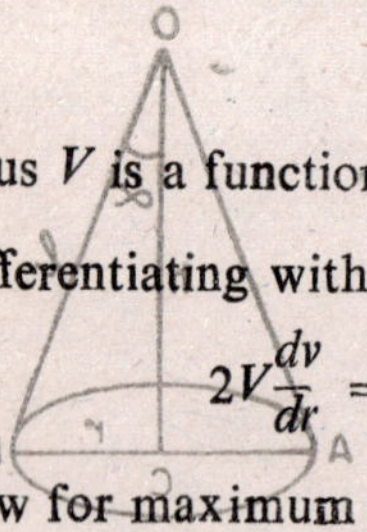

$$V^2 = \frac{1}{9}\, k\, [kr^2 - 2\pi r^4] \tag{3}$$

Thus V is a function of r only

Differentiating with respect to r the equation (3) we have

$$2V\frac{dv}{dr} = \frac{1k}{9}\,[2kr - 8\pi r^3] \tag{4}$$

Now for maximum or minimum value of V we have

$$\frac{dv}{dr} = 0$$

i.e. $$\frac{1}{9}\, k\, [2kr - 8\pi r^3] = 0$$

i.e. $$2kr - 8\pi r^3 = 0$$

$$2kr = 8\pi r^3$$

$$k = 4\pi r^2$$

$$4\pi r^2 = k$$

$$4\pi r^2 = \pi r^2 + \pi r l$$

$$3\pi r^2 = \pi r l$$

$$l = 3r$$

Again differentiating equation (4) with respect for we have

$$2V\frac{d^2 v}{dr^2} + 2\frac{dv}{dr} = \frac{1k}{9}[2k - 16\pi r^2]$$

For maxima or minima $\dfrac{dv}{dr} = 0$

$$2V\frac{d^2 v}{dr^2} = \frac{k}{9}[2k - 16\pi r^2]$$

$$2V\frac{d^2 v}{dr^2} = \frac{k}{9}[2\cdot 4\pi r^2 - 16\pi r^2]$$

$$2V\frac{d^2 v}{dr^2} = \frac{k}{9}[8\pi r^2 - 16\pi r^2]$$

$$2V\frac{d^2 v}{dr^2} = \frac{k}{9}[-8\pi r^2]$$

$$2v\frac{d^2 v}{dr^2} = \frac{4}{9}\pi r^2(-8\pi r^2)$$

$$2v\frac{d^2 v}{dr^2} = -\frac{32}{9}\pi^2 r^4 \; (-\text{ve})$$

$\therefore$ Thus the volume of the cone will be maximum when $l = 3r$

Now from triangle OCB

$$\sin\alpha = \frac{r}{l} = \frac{1}{3}$$

$$\sin\alpha = \tfrac{1}{3}$$

$$\Rightarrow \alpha = \sin^{-1}\left(\frac{1}{3}\right)$$

Hence the semivertical angle of a right circular cone of a given surface and maximum volume is $\sin^{-1}(\tfrac{1}{3})$ *(Proved)*

Problem 14 Show that the radius of the right circular cylinder of greatest curved surface which can be inscribed in a given cone is half that of the cone. *[I.F.S. 85]*

Solution Let h be the height of the cone and r to be the radius of the base of the cone let x be the radius of the base of the right circular cylinder and y be the height of the right circular cylinder curved surface of the right circular cylinder is given by $2\pi xy$

$$2\pi xy = S$$

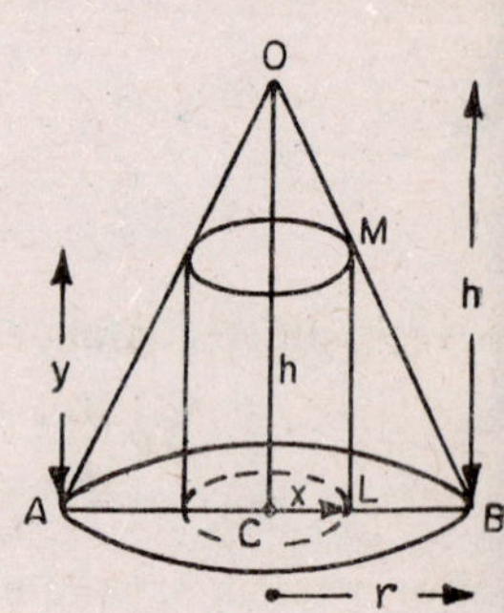

The two triangles BML and OCB are similar

$$\frac{ML}{OC} = \frac{BL}{BC}$$

$$\frac{y}{h} = \frac{r-x}{r}$$

$$y = \frac{(r-x)}{r} h$$

Hence the surface (curved)

$$S = 2\pi xy$$

$$S = \left(\frac{r-x}{r}\right) h$$

$$S = \frac{2\pi h}{r} (rx - x^2) \quad (1)$$

Differentiating equation (1) with to x we have

$$\frac{ds}{dx} = \frac{2\pi h}{r} (r-2x) \quad (2)$$

For maxima of minima of

$$S \text{ we have } \frac{ds}{dx} = 0$$

i.e. $$\frac{2\pi h}{r} (r-2x) = 0$$

$$\Rightarrow r - 2x = 0$$

$$\Rightarrow \quad 2x = r$$

$$\Rightarrow \quad x = \frac{r}{2}$$

Again differentiating equation (2) with respect to x we have.

$$\frac{d^2 s}{dx^2} = \frac{2\pi h}{r} (0-2)$$

$$\frac{d^2 s}{dx^2} = -\frac{4\pi h}{r} \; (-\text{ve})$$

Thus the curved surface of a right circular cylinder inscribed in a cone is maximum if the radius of the cylinder is half of *the cone*. (*Proved*)

Problem 15 Show that the height of the cylinder of maximum vloume that can be inscribed in a sphere of radius r is $\dfrac{2r}{\sqrt{3}}$. [*I.F.S. 83*]

Solution Let r be the radius of the circle let $BPO = \theta$ let a cylinder of maximum volume is inscribed in it.

$$OP = r\cos\theta \quad \text{and } BO = r\sin\theta$$

$$CD = 2r\sin\theta$$

Let h be the height of the cylinder then

$$h = 2r\sin\theta$$

Radius of the base of the circular cylinder

$$= r\cos\theta$$

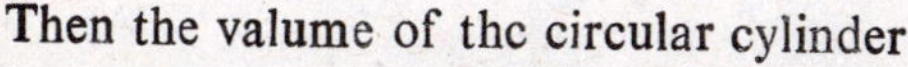

Then the valume of thc circular cylinder

$$= \pi\,(\text{radius of the base of the circular cylinder})^2 \times \text{height}$$
$$= \pi\,(r\cos\theta)^2 \times 2r\sin\theta$$
$$= \pi r^2\cos^2\theta \times 2r\sin\theta$$
$$= \pi r^3\, 2\cos\theta\sin\theta\cos\theta$$
$$= \pi r^3\sin 2\theta\cos\theta \qquad (1)$$

For maximum or minimum volume we have

$$\frac{dv}{d\theta} = 0 \quad [\text{Here } \theta \text{ is variable and } r \text{ is constant}]$$

$$\frac{dv}{d\theta} = \pi r^3\,[2\cos 2\theta\cos\theta + \sin 2\theta\,(-\sin\theta)]$$

$$\frac{dv}{d\theta} = \pi r^3\,[2\cos 2\theta\cos\theta - \sin 2\theta\sin\theta] \qquad (2)$$

For maximum or minimum

$$\pi r^3\,[2\cos 2\theta\cos\theta - \sin 2\theta\sin\theta] = 0$$
$$2\cos 2\theta\cos\theta - \sin 2\theta\sin\theta = 0$$
$$2\cos 2\theta\cos\theta = \sin 2\theta\sin\theta$$
$$2\cos 2\theta\cos\theta = 2\sin\theta\cos\theta\sin\theta$$
$$\Rightarrow \quad \cos 2\theta = \sin^2\theta$$
$$\Rightarrow \quad 1 - 2\sin^2\theta = \sin^2\theta$$
$$\Rightarrow \quad 3\sin^2\theta = 1$$
$$\Rightarrow \quad \sin^2\theta = \tfrac{1}{3}$$

$$\Rightarrow \qquad \sin\theta = \frac{1}{\sqrt{3}}$$

$$\cos\theta = \sqrt{1-\frac{1}{3}}$$

$$\cos\theta = \sqrt{\frac{3-1}{3}}$$

$$\cos\theta = \sqrt{\frac{2}{3}}$$

$$\sin 2\theta = 2\sin\theta\cos\theta = 2\,\frac{1}{\sqrt{3}} \times \frac{\sqrt{2}}{\sqrt{3}}$$

$$\sin 2\theta = \frac{2\sqrt{2}}{3}$$

$$\cos^2\theta = \cos^2\theta - \sin^2\theta = \frac{2}{3} - \frac{1}{3} = \frac{1}{3}$$

Again diflerentiating equation (2) we have

$$\frac{d^2 v}{d\theta^2} = \pi r^3 [2\{\cos 2\theta(-\sin\theta) + \cos\theta(-2)\sin 2\theta\}] - \pi r^3 [\sin 2\theta\cos\theta + \sin\theta\, 2\cos 2\theta]$$

$$\frac{d^2 v}{d\theta^2} = \pi r^3 [-2\sin\theta\cos 2\theta - 4\sin 2\theta\cos\theta] - \pi r^3 [\sin 2\theta\cos\theta + 2\sin\theta\cos 2\theta]$$

$$\frac{d^2 v}{d\theta^2} = \pi r^3 [-2\sin\theta\cos 2\theta - 4\sin 2\theta\cos\theta - \sin 2\theta\cos\theta - 2\sin\theta\cos 2\theta]$$

$$\frac{d^2 v}{d\theta^2} = \pi r^3 [-4\sin\theta\cos 2\theta - 5\sin 2\theta\cos\theta]$$

$$\left[\frac{d^2 v}{d\theta^2}\right]_{\sin\theta = 1/\sqrt{3}} = \pi r^3 \left[-4\,\frac{1}{\sqrt{3}}\,\frac{1}{3} - 52\,\frac{\sqrt{2}}{3}\,\frac{\sqrt{2}}{\sqrt{3}}\right]$$

$$\left[\frac{d^2 v}{d\theta^2}\right]_{\sin\theta = 1/\sqrt{3}} = \pi r^3 \left[-\frac{4}{3\sqrt{3}} - \frac{20}{3\sqrt{3}}\right]$$

$$\left[\frac{d^2 v}{d\theta^2}\right]_{\sin\theta = 1/\sqrt{3}} = \pi r^3\,\frac{(-24)}{3\sqrt{3}}\ (-\text{ve})$$

So volume is maximum at

$$\sin\theta = \frac{1}{\sqrt{3}}$$

Now we have to prove that the height of the circular cylinder is $\frac{2r}{\sqrt{3}}$

$$h = 2r \sin \theta$$

$$h = 2r \frac{1}{\sqrt{3}}$$

$$h = \frac{2r}{\sqrt{3}}$$

i.e. the height of the circular cylinder of maximum volume that can be in scribed in a sphere of radius r is $\frac{2r}{\sqrt{3}}$ (*Proved*)

Prblem 16 A wire of length a is cut into two parts which are bent respectively in the form of a square and a circle. Show that the least value of the sum of the area so formed is $\frac{a^2}{4(\pi + 4}$ [*I.F.S. 82*]

Solution Let the wire of length a is cut into two parts whose lengths are x and y respeetively. Then $x + y = a$ (1)

The wire of whose length is x is bent to form a square and the wire whose length is y is bent to form a circle.

Then the perimeter of the square $= x$

i.e. 4 side = perimeter $= x$

$\Rightarrow$ one side of a square $= \frac{x}{4}$

Thus the area A_1 of the square

$$A_1 = \left(\frac{x}{4}\right)^2 = \frac{x^2}{16} \tag{2}$$

Perimeter of the circle $= y$

2π (radius of the circle) $= y$

$\Rightarrow$ radius of the circle $= \frac{y}{2\pi}$

Thus the area A_2 of the circle $= A_2 = \left(\frac{y}{2\pi}\right)^2$

$$A_2 = \pi \frac{y^2}{4\pi^2} = \frac{y^2}{4\pi} \tag{3}$$

Let A denotes the total (i.e. the sum of) the are of the square and the circle.

$$A = A_1 + A_2$$

$$= \frac{x^2}{16} + \frac{y^2}{4\pi^2} \tag{4}$$

From equation (1) $\quad y = a - x$

Hence $$A = \frac{x^2}{16} + \frac{(a-x)^2}{4\pi} \tag{5}$$

For maxima or minima of A

$$\frac{dA}{dx} = 0$$

Differentiating equation (5) we have

$$\frac{dA}{dx} = \frac{2x}{16} + \frac{2(a-x)}{4\pi}(-1)$$

$$\frac{dA}{dx} = \frac{x}{8} - \frac{(a-x)}{2\pi} \tag{6}$$

For maxima or minima

$$\frac{x}{8} - \frac{(a-x)}{2\pi} = 0$$

$$\frac{x}{8} = \frac{a-x}{2\pi}$$

$$\pi x = 4a - 4x$$

$$\pi x + 4x = 4a$$

$$\Rightarrow (\pi + 4)x = 4a$$

$$\Rightarrow \quad x = \frac{4a}{\pi + 4}$$

and $$y = a - x$$

$$y = a - \frac{4a}{\pi + 4}$$

$$\Rightarrow y = \frac{\pi a + 4a - 4a}{\pi + 4}$$

$$\Rightarrow y = \frac{\pi a}{\pi + 4}$$

Thus A has maximum or minimum value at

$$x = \frac{4a}{\pi + 4}; \; y = \frac{\pi a}{\pi + 4}$$

Again differentiating equation (5) we have

$$\frac{d^2A}{dx^2} = \frac{1}{8} - \frac{(0-1)}{2\pi}$$

$$\frac{d^2A}{dx^2} = \frac{1}{8} + \frac{1}{2\pi} \; (+\text{ve})$$

So A has minimum value at

$$\pi = \frac{4a}{\pi + 4} \quad \text{and} \quad y = \frac{\pi a}{\pi + 4}$$

Minimum value of A

$$A_{\min} = \frac{x^2}{16} + \frac{y^2}{4\pi} = \frac{16a^2}{16\,(\pi + 4)^2} + \frac{a^2\,\pi^2}{(\pi + 4)^{\prime 2}\,4\pi}$$

$$= \frac{a^2}{(\pi^2 + 4)^2} + \frac{\pi a^2}{4\,(\pi^2 + 4)^2}$$

$$= \frac{a^2\,[4 + \pi]}{4\,(\pi + 4)^2} = \frac{a^2}{4\,(\pi + 4)}$$

Minimum Area $$= \frac{a}{4\,(\pi + 4)}$$

least value of the area so formed is

$$= \frac{a^2}{4\,(\pi + 4)}$$ *(Proved)*

Problem 17 Show that the curved surface of a right cone of a given volume is least when its semi-vertical angle is $\tan^{-1}(1/\sqrt{2})$ [*IFS 85*]

Solution Let OAB is a right cone of height h, Let C be the centre of the base of the cone and r is the radius of the base of the cone. Let l is the slant height of the cone.

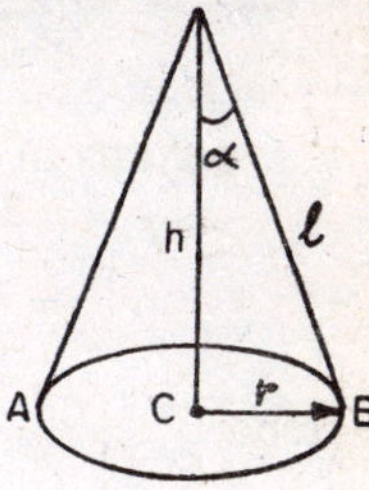

Then the curved surface is given by

$$\pi r l \tag{1}$$

where $$l = \sqrt{h^2 + r^2} \tag{2}$$

Thus the curved surface is given by

$$S = \pi r \sqrt{h^2 + r^2} \tag{3}$$

The volume of the right cone is given by

$$V = \frac{1}{3}\pi r^2 h \tag{4}$$

since the volume of the cone is given so

$$\frac{1}{3}\,\pi r^2 h = k$$

$$h = \frac{3k}{\pi r^2} \tag{5}$$

Now squaring equation (3) we have

$$S^2 = \pi^2 r^2 (h^2 + r^2)$$

$$S^2 = \pi^2 r^2 \left(\frac{9k^2}{\pi^2 r^4} + r^2\right)$$

$$S^2 = \pi^2 r^2 \left(\frac{9k^2 + \pi^2 r^6}{\pi^2 r^4}\right)$$

$$S^2 = \frac{9k^2 + \pi^2 r^6}{r^2}$$

$$S^2 = \frac{9k^2}{r^2} + \pi^2 r^4 \tag{6}$$

Differentiating equation (6) with respect to r we have

$$2S \frac{ds}{dr} = \frac{9k^2 (-2)}{r^3} + \pi^2 4r^3$$

$$2S \frac{ds}{dr} = -\frac{18k^2}{r^3} + 4\pi^2 r^3$$

$$2\left(s \frac{ds}{dr}\right) = 2\left(-\frac{9k^2}{r^3} + 2\pi^2 r^3\right)$$

$$S \frac{ds}{dr} = -\frac{9k^2}{r^3} + 2\pi^2 r^3 \tag{7}$$

For maxima or minima of S we have

$$\frac{ds}{dr} = 0$$

Hence $$-\frac{9k^2}{r^3} + 2\pi^2 r^3 = 0$$

i.e. $$\frac{9k^2}{r^3} = 2\pi^2 r^3$$

i.e. $$9k^2 = 2\pi^2 r^6 \tag{8}$$

Putting the values of k^2 in (8) we have

$$9\left(\frac{1}{9} \pi^2 r^4 h^2\right) = 2\pi^2 r^6$$

$$\pi^2 r^4 h^2 = 2\pi^2 r^6$$

$$h^2 = 2r^2$$

Taking square root on both sides we have

$$h = \sqrt{2}\ r \tag{9}$$

Again differentiating equation (7) we have

$$S\frac{d^2 s}{dr^2}+\frac{ds}{dr}=\frac{27 k^2}{r^4}+2\pi^2 3r^2$$

$$S\frac{d^2 s}{dr^2}+0=\frac{27 k^2}{r^4}+6\pi^2 r^2$$

$$S\frac{d^2 s}{dr^2}=\frac{27}{r^4}\times\frac{1}{9}\pi^2 r^4 h^2+6\pi^2 r^2$$

$$S\frac{d^2 s}{dr^2}=3\pi^2 h^2+6\pi^2 r^2$$

$$S\frac{d^2 s}{dr^2}=3\pi^2(\sqrt{2}r)^2+6\pi^2 r^2$$

$$S\frac{d^2 s}{dr^2}=3\pi^2 2r^2+6\pi^2 r^2$$

$$S\frac{d^2 s}{dr^2}=6\pi^2 r^2+6\pi^2 r^2$$

$$S\frac{d^2 s}{dr^2}=12\pi^2 r^2$$

$$\frac{d^2 s}{dr^2}=\frac{12\pi^2 r^2}{S}$$

$$\frac{d^2 s}{dr^2}=\frac{12\pi^2 r^2}{\pi r\sqrt{h^2+r^2}}$$

$$\left[\frac{d^2 s}{dr^2}\right]_{h=\sqrt{2}r}=\frac{12\pi^2 r^2}{\pi r\sqrt{2r^2+r^2}}$$

$$\left[\frac{d^2 s}{dr^2}\right]_{h=\sqrt{2}r}=\frac{12\pi^2 r^2}{\pi r\sqrt{3}r}$$

$$\left[\frac{d^2 s}{dr^2}\right]_{h=\sqrt{2}r}=4\sqrt{3}\,\pi\ (+\text{ve})$$

so the curved surface is minimum for

$$h=\sqrt{2}\,r$$

i.e. for $\quad \dfrac{r}{h}=\dfrac{1}{\sqrt{2}}$

let α be the semivertical angle

then $\quad \tan\alpha=\dfrac{r}{h}=\dfrac{1}{\sqrt{2}}$

$$\alpha=\tan^{-1}\left(\frac{1}{\sqrt{2}}\right)$$

so curved surface is minimum for semi-vertical angle

$$\alpha=\tan^{-1}\left(\frac{1}{\sqrt{2}}\right)$$

(Proved)

Problem 18 Show that the right circular cylinder of a given suɹface and maximum volume is such that its height is equal to its diameter.

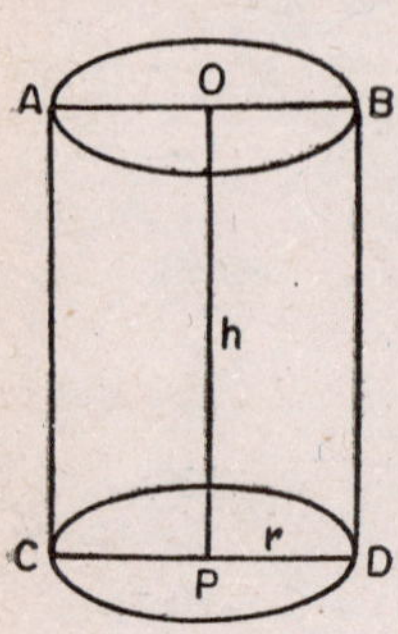

Solution Let $ABCD$ be a right circular cylinder of height hand, r as the radius of the base. Let V and S be the volume and the surface of the right circular cylinder. Then we have to show that for given surface S and maximum volume V

$$h = 2r$$

$$\begin{pmatrix}\text{Constant}\\ \text{source given}\end{pmatrix} \qquad S = 2\pi r^2 + 2\pi rh \tag{1}$$

$$V = \pi r^2 h \tag{2}$$

From equation (1) we have

$$2\pi r^2 + 2\pi rh = s$$

$$2\pi rh = s - 2\pi r^2$$

$$h = \left[\frac{s - 2\pi r^2}{2\pi r}\right] \tag{3}$$

Putting the value of h from (3) in equation (2) we have

$$V = \pi r^2 \left[\frac{s - 2\pi r^2}{2\pi r}\right]$$

$$V = \frac{sr}{2} - \frac{2\pi r^3}{2}$$

$$V = \frac{sr}{2} - \pi r^3 \tag{4}$$

Differentiating with respect to r we have

$$\frac{dv}{dr} = \frac{s}{2} - 3\pi r^2 \tag{5}$$

Again differentiating with respect to r we have

$$\frac{d^2 v}{dr^2} = -6\pi r \ (-\text{ve}) \tag{6}$$

So v is maximum

For maxima or minima of v

$$\frac{dv}{dr} = 0$$

i.e. $$\frac{s}{2} - 3\pi r^2 = 0$$

i.e.
$$\frac{s}{2} = 3\pi r^2$$
$$s = 6\pi r^2$$
$$2\pi r^2 + 2\pi rh = 6\,\pi r^2$$
$$2\pi rh = 4\pi r^2$$
$$h = 2r = d \qquad \text{(diameter of the right circular cylinder)}$$

Thus for a given surface and maximum volume the height of the right circular cylinder is equal to the diameter.

(*Proved*)

Problem 19 A cone is circumscribed to a sphere of radius r; show that the volume of the cone is a minimum, its altitude is $4r$ and its semi-vertical angle α is given by $\sin\alpha = \frac{1}{3}$

[*I.F.S. 84*]

Solution Let ABC be cone which is circumscribed to a sphere whose radius is r. Let OC be the radius of the base of the cone and OA be its altitude. Let α be the semi-vertical angle then we have to show that

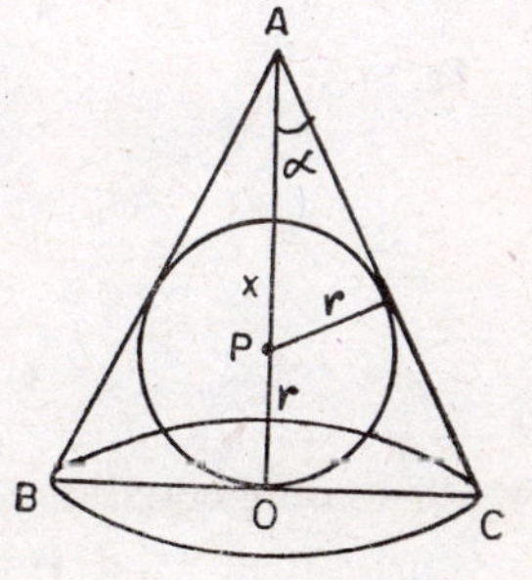

$$OA = 4r \text{ and } \sin\alpha = \tfrac{1}{3}$$

Volume of the right circular cone is given by

$$= \tfrac{1}{3}\,\pi\,(OC)^2\,OA \tag{1}$$
$$OA = AP + PO$$
$$OA = x + r$$

where P is the centre of the circle whose radius is r

Again from the triangle OAC

$$\tan\alpha = \frac{OC}{OA}$$

$$\tan\alpha = \frac{OC}{x + r}$$

$$\Rightarrow OA = (x + r)\tan\alpha$$

So the volume of the right circular cone is given by

$$V = \tfrac{1}{3}\,\pi\,(x + r)^2 \tan^2\alpha\,(x + r)$$
$$V = \tfrac{1}{3}\,\pi\,(x + r)^3 \tan^2\alpha \tag{2}$$

Since r is constant so here there are two variables viz x and α changing the variable α to the form x

$$\sin\alpha = \frac{r}{x}$$

$$\cos\alpha = \sqrt{1 - \sin^2\alpha}$$

$$\cos \alpha = \sqrt{1 - \frac{r^2}{x^2}}$$

$$\cos \alpha = \sqrt{\frac{x^2 - r^2}{x^2}}$$

$$\cos \alpha = \frac{\sqrt{x^2 - r^2}}{x}$$

$$\tan \alpha = \frac{r}{\sqrt{x^2 - r^2}} \qquad (3)$$

with the help of equation (3) (2) reduces to

$$V = \frac{1}{3} \pi (x + r)^3 \left[\frac{r}{\sqrt{x^2 - r^2}}\right]^2$$

$$V = \frac{1}{3} \pi (x + r)^3 \frac{r^2}{(x^2 - r^2)}$$

$$V = \frac{1}{3} \pi (x + r)^3 \frac{r^2}{(x + r)(x - r)}$$

$$V = \frac{1}{3} \pi \frac{(x + r)^2}{(x - r)} r^2$$

$$V = \frac{1}{3} \pi r^2 \frac{(x + r)^2}{(x - r)} \qquad (4)$$

Differentiating equation (4) with respect to x we have

$$\frac{dv}{dx} = \frac{1}{3} \pi r^2 \frac{d}{dx}\left\{\frac{(x + r)^2}{(x - r)}\right\}$$

$$\frac{dv}{dx} = \frac{\frac{1}{3} \pi r^2 \left[(x - r) \frac{d}{dx}(x + r)^2 - (x + r)^2 \frac{d}{dx}(x - r)\right]}{(x - r)^2}$$

$$\frac{dv}{dx} = \frac{1}{3} \pi r^2 \frac{[(x - r)\, 2\,(x + r) - (x + r)^2 . 1]}{(x - r)^2}$$

$$\frac{dv}{dx} = \frac{1}{3} \pi r^2 \frac{[2\,(x + r)(x - r) - (x + r)^2]}{(x - r)^2}$$

$$\frac{dv}{dx} = \frac{1}{3} \pi r^2 \frac{(x + r)\,[2x - 2r - x - r]}{(x - r)^2}$$

$$\frac{dv}{dx} = \frac{1}{3} \pi r^2 \frac{(x + r)(x - 3r)}{(x - r)^2}$$

For maxima or minima of the volume of cone

$$\frac{dv}{dx} = 0$$

$$\Rightarrow \qquad (x + r)\,(x - 3r) = 0$$

$$\Rightarrow \quad \text{either } x + r = 0 \text{ or } x - 3r = 0$$

$$\Rightarrow \qquad x = -r \quad \text{or} \quad x = 3r$$

But $\quad x = -r$ is in admissible

$\therefore \quad x = 3r$

when the value of x is slightly less than $3r$, $\frac{dv}{dx} = -$ve and when the value x is slightly greater than $3r$, then

$$\frac{dv}{dx} = +\text{ve}$$

Since the sign changes from negative to positive, therefore volume is minimum when $x = 3r$ in this case the altitude of the cone $= OC$

$$= x + r$$
$$= 3r + r = 4r$$

α can be given by

$$\sin \alpha = \frac{r}{x} = \frac{r}{3r} = \frac{1}{3}$$

$$\sin \alpha = \frac{1}{3}$$

$$\Rightarrow \alpha = \sin^{-1}\left(\frac{1}{3}\right)$$

Thus for minimum volume the semivertical angle is given by

$$\sin \alpha = \frac{1}{3} \qquad \textit{(Proved)}$$

roblem 20 Show that the volume of the greatest cylinder which can be inscribed in a cone of height h and semivertical angle α is

$$\frac{4}{27} \pi h^3 \tan^2 \alpha \qquad \text{[IFS 83]}$$

Solution Let 0 AB be a cone of height h i.e. $OC = h$

Let r be the radius of the base of the cone. Let greatest cylinder is drawn within cone whose height is y and the radius of the base is x

$$MN = y$$
$$CN = x$$

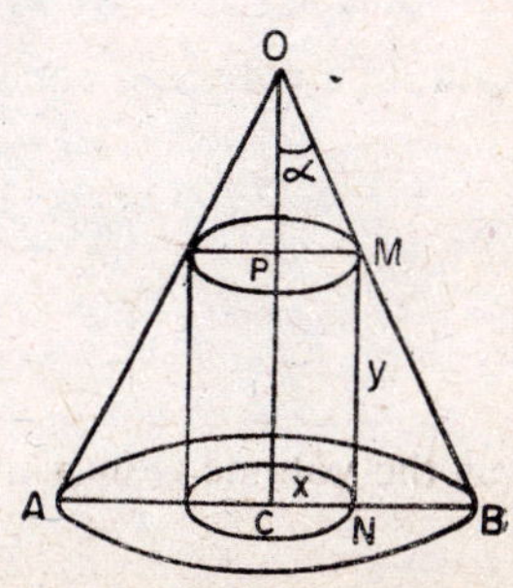

Volume of the cylinder is given by

$$V = \pi x^2 \cdot y \qquad (1)$$

Let α be the semivertical angle of the cone

$$\text{then } \tan \alpha = \frac{BC}{OC}$$

$$\tan \alpha = \frac{r}{h}$$

V is a function of two variables x and y. We have to change it is only one function.

Since the triangle MBN and OBC are similar so

$$\frac{BN}{CB} = \frac{MN}{OC}$$

$$\frac{r-x}{r} = \frac{y}{h}$$

$$y = \frac{h\,(r-x)}{r} \tag{3}$$

Putting the value of y from (3) in equation (2), we have

$$V = \pi x^2 \frac{h\,(r-x)}{r} \tag{4}$$

Differentiating equation (4) with respect to x we have

$$\frac{dv}{dx} = \frac{\pi h}{r} \frac{d}{dx} [rx^2 - x^3]$$

$$\frac{dv}{dx} = \frac{\pi h}{r} [2rx - 3x^2] \tag{5}$$

For maxima or minima of $V \dfrac{dv}{dx} = 0$

$$\frac{\pi h}{r} [2rx - 3x^2] = 0$$

$$\Rightarrow \quad 2rx - 3x^2 = 0$$

$$\Rightarrow \quad 2rx = 3x^2$$

$$\Rightarrow \quad 2r = 3x$$

$$\Rightarrow \quad x = \frac{2r}{3}$$

Again differentiating equation (5) we have

$$\frac{d^2 v}{dx^2} = \frac{\pi h}{r} [2r - 6x]$$

$$\left[\frac{d^2 v}{dx^2}\right]_{x=2r/3} = \frac{\pi h}{r} [2r - 4r] = \frac{\pi h}{r} [-2r] = -\text{ve}$$

Thus the volume is maximum at

$$x = \frac{2}{3} r$$

Maximum volume V is given by

$$V = \pi x^2 h \frac{(r-x)}{r}$$

$$V = \pi \left(\frac{2}{3} r\right)^2 h \frac{(r-2/3r)}{r}$$

$$V = \pi \frac{4}{9} r^2 h \frac{(r)}{3r}$$

$$V = \frac{4}{27} \pi r^2 h$$

Putting $r = h \tan \alpha$ we have

$$V = \frac{4}{27} \pi (h \tan \alpha)^2 h$$

$$V = \frac{4}{27} \pi h^2 \tan^2 \alpha \cdot h$$

$$V = \frac{4}{27} \pi h^3 \tan^2 \alpha$$

(Proved)

10

Successive Differentiation

We denote the derivative $\frac{dy}{dx}$ by y_1

Second derivative $\frac{d^2 y}{dx^2}$ by y_2

Third derivative $\frac{d^3 y}{dx^2}$ by y_3

... ...

... ...

nth derivative $\frac{d^n y}{dx^n}$ by y_n.

Article I nth differential coefficient of x^m

Let $y = x^m$

Then $y_1 = mx^{m-1}$

$y_2 = m(m-1)x^{m-2}$

$y^3 = m(m-1)(m-2)x^{m-3}$

... ...

$y_n = m(m-1)(m-2)(m-3)\ldots(m-n+1)x^{m-n}$

Remember

Cor. If $m = n$ then

$y_n = n(n-1)(n-2)(n-3)\ldots(n-n+1)$

$y_n = n(n-1)(n-2)\ldots 3.2.1.$

Remember $y_n = L_n$

Hence if $y = x^n$ then $y_n = L_n$

and $y_{n+1} = 0,\ y_{n+2} = 0$ etc.

As aparticular case if $y = x^3$ then

$y_3 = L_3,\ y_4 = 0,\ y_5 = 0$ etc.

Article II *n*th differential coefficient of $\frac{1}{ax+b}$

Let $$y = \frac{1}{ax+b} = (ax+b)^{-1}$$

Differentiating with respect to x we have

$$\frac{dy}{dx} = (-1)(ax+b)^{-1-1}\frac{d}{dx}(ax+b)$$

$$\frac{dy}{dx} = (-1)(ax+b)^{-2}a$$

$$y_1 = (-1)(ax+b)^{-2}a$$

Again differentiating we have

$$y_2 = (-1)(-2)(ax+b)^{-3}a \times a$$

$$y_2 = (-1)(-2)a^2(ax+b)^{-3}$$

Similarly $$y_3 = (-1)(-2)(-3)a^3(ax+b)^{-4}$$

$$\ldots \qquad \ldots \qquad \ldots$$

$$y_n = a^n(-1)(-2)(-3)\ldots \text{ to } n \text{ factors } (ax+b)^{(n+1)}$$

$$= \frac{a^n(-1)^n 1\cdot 2\cdot 3 \ldots n}{(ax+b)^{n+1}}$$

Remember $$y_n = \frac{a^n(-1)^n Ln}{(ax+b)^{n+1}}$$

Article III *n*th differential coefficient of e^{mx}

Let $$y = e^{mx}$$

$$y_1 = me^{mx}$$

$$y^2 = m\cdot me^{mx} = m^2 e^{mx}$$

$$y^2 = m^3 e^{mx}$$

Thus $$y_n = m^n e^{mx}$$ Remember

Cor I Putting $m = 1$ above, we get $y = e^x$

$$y_n = e^x$$

(R)

Cor II Let $$y = a^{mx}$$

Them $$y = e^{\log a^{mx}}$$

$$y = e^{mx \log a}$$

Let $$m \log a = k$$

Then $y = e^{kx}$

$$y_n = k^n e^{kx}$$

$$y_n = (m \log a)^n e^{(m \log a) \cdot x}$$

$$y_n = (m \log a)^n e^{\log a^{mx}}$$

$$y_n = m^n (\log a)^n a^{mx} \qquad (R)$$

If Then $m = 1$

$$y = a^x$$

$$y_n = (\log a)^n a^x \qquad (R)$$

Article V I nth differential coefficient of log $(ax + b)$

Let $y = \log (ax + b)$

Then
$$y_1 = \frac{a}{ax + b}$$

$$y_1 = a (ax + b)^{-1}$$

$$y_2 = a (-1) (ax + b)^{-2} \cdot a$$

$$= a^2 (-1) (ax + b)^{-2}$$

$$y_3 = a^2 (-1) (-2) (ax + b)^{-3} \cdot a$$

$$y_3 = a^3 (-1) (-2) (ax + b)^{-3}$$

Similarly $y_n = a^n (-1)(-2) \ldots$ to $(n-1)$ factors $X (ax + b)^{-n}$

$$y_n = \frac{a^n (-1)^{n-1} 1 \cdot 2 \cdot 3 \ldots (n-1)}{(ax + b)^n} \qquad (R)$$

VI nth differential coefficient of sin $(ax + b)$

Let $y = \sin (ax + b)$

$$y_1 = a \cos (ax + b) = a \sin \left(ax + b + \frac{\pi}{2}\right)$$

Since $\sin \left(\frac{\pi}{2} + \theta\right) = \cos \theta$

$$y_1 = a \sin \left(ax + b + \frac{\pi}{2}\right)$$

$$y_2 = a^2 \cos \left(ax + b + \frac{\pi}{2}\right)$$

$$= a^2 \sin \left(ax + b + \frac{\pi}{2} + \frac{\pi}{2}\right)$$

$$= a^2 \sin \left(ax + b + 2 \cdot \frac{\pi}{2}\right)$$

Similarly $$y_3 = a^3 \cos\left(ax + b + \frac{2\pi}{2}\right)$$

$$= a^3 \sin\left(ax + b + \frac{2\pi}{2} + \frac{\pi}{2}\right)$$

$$y_3 = a^3 \sin\left(ax + b + \frac{3\pi}{2}\right)$$

$$\cdots \qquad \cdots$$

$$\cdots \qquad \cdots$$

Similarly $$y_n = a^n \sin\left(ax+b + n\ \frac{\pi}{2}\right) \qquad (R)$$

VI *n*th differential coefficient of $\cos(ax + b)$

Let $$y = \cos(ax + b)$$

Then $$y_1 = -\sin(ax + b)\, a$$

$$y_1 = -a \sin(ax + b)$$

$$y_1 = a \cos\left((ax + b + \frac{\pi}{2}\right)$$

Since $$\cos\left(\frac{\pi}{2} + \theta\right) = -\sin\theta$$

$$y_2 = -a \sin\left(ax + b + \frac{\pi}{2}\right) a$$

$$= -a^2 \sin\left(ax + b + \frac{\pi}{2}\right)$$

$$= a^2 \cos\left(ax + b + \frac{\pi}{2} + \frac{\pi}{2}\right)$$

$$= a^2 \cos\left(ax + b + \frac{2\pi}{2}\right)$$

$$y_3 = -a^2 \sin\left(ax + b + \frac{2\pi}{2}\right) a$$

$$= -a^3 \sin\left(ax + b + \frac{2\pi}{2}\right)$$

$$= a^3 \cos\left(ax + b + \frac{2\pi}{2} + \frac{\pi}{2}\right)$$

$$= + a^3\left(\cos ax + b + \frac{3\pi}{2}\right)$$

$$\cdots \qquad \cdots$$

$$\cdots \qquad \cdots$$

$$y_n = a^n \cos\left(ax + b + \frac{n\pi}{2}\right) \qquad (R)$$

VII nth differential coefficient of $e^{ax} \sin (bx + c)$

Solution Let $y = e^{ax} \sin (bx + c)$

Then

$$y_1 = e^{ax} \cdot dc \{\sin (bx + c)\} + \sin (bx + c)\, d{\cdot}c\, (e^{ax})$$

$$y_1 = e^{ax} \cos (bx + c)\, b + \sin (bx + c)\, e^{ax} \cdot a$$

$$y_1 = e^{ax}\, b \cos (bx + c) + \sin (bx + c)\, ae^{ax}$$

$$y_1 = e^{ax} \{a \sin (bx + c) + b \cos (bx + c)\}$$

Let $a = r \cos \theta \qquad b = r \sin \theta$

So that $r^2 = a^2 + b^2$ and $\tan \theta = \dfrac{b}{a}$

Thus

$$y_1 = e^{ax} \{r \cos \theta \sin (bx + c) + r \sin \theta \cos (bx + c)\}$$

$$y_1 = e^{ax}\, r \sin (bx + c + \theta)$$

Similarly differentiating twice, thrice, we get

$$y_2 = r \times re^{ax} \sin (bx + c + \theta + \theta)$$

$$y_2 = r^2 e^{ax} \sin (bx + c + 2\theta)$$

$$y_3 = r^3 e^{ax} \sin (bx + c + 3\theta)$$

And generally

$$y_n = r^n e^{ax} \sin (bx + c + n\theta) \qquad (R)$$

Where $r = \sqrt{a^2 + b^2)}$ and $\theta = \tan^{-1} \left(\dfrac{b}{a}\right)$

VIII Find the nth differential coefficient of

$$e^{ax} \cos (bx + c)$$

Let $y = e^{ax} \cos (bx + c)$

Differentiating y with respect to x we have

$$\frac{dy}{dx} = \frac{d}{dx} \{e^{ax} \cos (bx + c)\}$$

$$y_1 = e^{ax} \cdot \frac{d}{dx} [\cos (bx + c)] + \cos (bx + c) \frac{d}{dx} (e^{ax})$$

$$y_1 = e^{ax} [-\sin (bx + c)]\, b + \cos (bx + c)\, e^{ax} \cdot a$$

$$y_1 = -be^{ax} \sin (bx + c) + ae^{ax} \cos (bx + c)$$

$$y_1 = e^{ax} [a \cos (bx + c) - b \sin (bx + c)]$$

Putting $a = r \cos \theta$ and $b = r \sin \theta$ we have

$$y_1 = e^{ax} [r \cos \theta \cos (bx + c) - r \sin \theta \sin (bx + c)]$$

$$y_1 = re^{ax} [\cos (bx + c + \theta)]$$

$$y_1 = re^{ax} \cos (bx + c + \theta) \qquad (1)$$

Where r and θ and θ are given by the relation

$$r^2 = a^2 + b^2 \tan\theta = \frac{b}{a}$$

Similarly differentiating equation (1) in the similar manner we have

$$y_2 = r^2 e^{ax} \cos(bx + c + 2\theta)$$

Similarly $\quad y_n = r^n e^{ax} \cos(bx + c + n\theta) \qquad (R)$

Where $\quad r = \sqrt{a^2 + b^2}$ and $\theta = \tan^{-1}\left(\frac{b}{a}\right)$

Problem 1 If $\quad ax^2 + 2hxy + by^2 = 1$, prove that

$$\frac{d^2 y}{dx^2} = \frac{h^2 - ab}{(hx + by)^3}$$

Solution Given $\quad ax^2 + 2bxy + by^2 = 1$

Differentiating with respect to x we have

$$2ax + 2h\left[x\frac{dy}{dx} + y\cdot 1\right] + 2by\frac{dy}{dx} = 0$$

$$2ax + 2hx\frac{dy}{dx} + 2hy + 2by\frac{dy}{dx} = 0$$

$$2(hx + by)\frac{dy}{dx} = -2(ax + hy)$$

$$\frac{dy}{dx} = -\frac{(ax + hy)}{(hx + hy)}$$

Again differentiating with respect to x we have

$$\frac{d^2 y}{dx^2} = -\frac{[(hx + by)d\cdot c(ax + hy) - (ax + hy)d\cdot c(hx + by)]}{[(h + by)^2]}$$

$$\frac{d^2 y}{dx^2} = -\frac{[(hx + by)(a + hy_1) - (ax + by)(h + by_1)]}{[(hx + by)^2]}$$

$$\frac{d^2 y}{dx^2} = -\frac{[ahx + h^2 xy_1 + aby + bhyy_1 - (ahx + abxy_1 + h^2 y + bhyy_1)]}{(hx + by)^2}$$

$$\frac{d^2 y}{dx^2} = -\frac{[ahx + h^2 xy_1 + aby + bhyy_1 - ahx - abxy - h^2 y - bhyy_1]}{(hx + by)^2}$$

$$\frac{d^2 y}{dx^2} = -\frac{[h^2 xy_1 + aby - abxy_1 - h^2 y]}{(hx + by)^2}$$

$$\frac{d^2 y}{dx^2} = -\frac{[(h^2 - ab)xy_1 + (ab - h^2)y]}{(hx + by)^2}$$

$$\frac{d^2 y}{dx^2} = -\frac{[(h^2-ab)\, xy_1-(h^2-ab)\, y]}{(hx-by)^2}$$

$$\frac{d^2 y}{dx^2} = -\frac{[h^2-ab)\,(xy_1-y)]}{(hy+bx)^2}$$

$$\frac{d^2 y}{x^2} = -\frac{(h^2-ab)}{(hx+by)^2}\,(y-xy_1) \quad (1)$$

We have given that

$$ax^2+2hxy+by^2=1$$

From this $\quad \dfrac{dy}{dx} = -\dfrac{(ax+hy)}{(hx+by)}$

i.e. $\quad y_1 = -\dfrac{(ax+hy)}{(hx+by)}$

$$\Rightarrow \quad xy_1 = -\frac{x\,(ax+hy)}{(hx+by)}$$

$$\Rightarrow \quad y-xy_1 = y+\frac{x\,(ax+hy)}{(hx+by)}$$

$$\Rightarrow \quad y-xy_1 = \frac{hyx+by^2+ax^2+bxy}{(hx+by)}$$

$$\Rightarrow \quad y-xy_1 = \frac{ax^2+2hxy+by^2}{(hx+by)}$$

$$y-xy_1 = \frac{1}{hx+by} \text{ since } \quad ax^2+2hxy+by^2=1 \quad (1)$$

Putting the value of $y-xy_1$ from equation (2) inequation (1) we have

$$\frac{d^2 y}{dx^2} = \frac{(h^2-ab)}{(hx+by)^2}\cdot\frac{1}{(hx+by)}$$

$$\frac{d^2 y}{dx^2} = \frac{(h^2-ab)}{(hx+by)^3} \quad (Provea)$$

Problem 2 If $y = A\sin mx + B\cos mx$, prove that $y_2 = -m^2 y$

Solution Let $\quad y = A\sin mx + B\cos mx$

Differentiating with respect to x we have

$$\frac{dy}{dx} = A\cos mx\, m - B\sin mx.m$$

$$\frac{dy}{dx} = m\,(A\cos mx\cdot m - B\sin mx\cdot m)$$

Again differentiating with respect to x we have

$$\frac{d^2 y}{dy^2} = m\,[-A \sin mxm\cdot - B \cos m\cdot xm]$$

$$\frac{d^2 y}{dx^2} = -m^2\,[A \sin mx + B \cos m x]$$

$$\frac{d^2 y}{dx^2} = -m^2 y$$

Thus $\quad y_2 = -m^2 y$ (Proved)

Problem 3 If $y = Ae^{mx} + Be^{-mx}$, prove that $y_2 = m^2 y$.

Solution Since $y = Ae^{mx} + Be^{-mx}$ (1)

Differentiating equation (1) with respect to x we have

$$\frac{dy}{dx} = Ae^{mx}\cdot m + Be^{-mx}(-m)$$

$$\frac{dy}{dx} = m\,[Ae^{mx} - Be^{-mx}]$$

Again differentiating with respect to x we have

$$\frac{d^2 y}{dx^2} = m^2\,[Ae^{mx}\cdot m - Be^{-mx}(-m)]$$

$$\frac{d^2 y}{dx^2} = m^2\,[Ae^{mx} + Be^{-mx}]$$

i.e. $\quad \dfrac{d^2 y}{dx^2} = m^2 y$

i.e. $\quad y_2 = m^2 y$ (Proved)

Problem 4 If $y = \sin mx + \cos mx$, prove that

$$y_n = m^n\,[1 + (-1)^n \sin 2mx]^{1/2}$$

Solution Let $y = \sin mx + \cos mx$

$$y_n = m^n \sin\left(mx + \frac{n\pi}{2}\right) + m^n \cos\left(mx + \frac{n\pi}{2}\right)$$

$$y_n = m^n\left[\sin\left(mx + \frac{n\pi}{2}\right) + \cos\left(mx + \frac{n\pi}{2}\right)\right]$$

$$y_n = m^n\left[\left\{\sin\left(mx + \frac{n\pi}{2}\right) + \cos\left(mx + \frac{n\pi}{2}\right)\right\}^2\right]^{1/2}$$

$$y_n = m^n\left[\sin^2\left(mx + \frac{n\pi}{2}\right) + \cos^2\left(mx + \frac{n\pi}{2}\right) + 2\sin\left(mx + \frac{n\pi}{2}\right)\cos\left(mx + \frac{n\pi}{2}\right)\right]^{1/2}$$

$$y_n = m^n [1 + \sin (2mx + n\pi)]^{1/2}$$
$$y_n = m^n [1 + \sin 2\, mx \cdot \cos n\pi + \cos 2\, mx \sin n\pi]^{1/2}$$
$$y_n = m^n [1 + \sin 2\, mx\, (-1)^n + \cos 2mx \cdot 0]^{1/2}$$

Since $\cos n\pi = -1$ if n is even

$= +1$ if n is odd.

So $\cos n\pi = (-1)^n$ for n even or odd, and $\sin n\pi = 0$

$$y_n = m^n [1 + \sin 2mx\, (-1)^n]^{1/2}$$ *(Proved)*

Problem 5 If $\sqrt{x+y} + \sqrt{y-x} = c$, prove tnat

$$y_2 = \frac{2}{c^2}$$

We have $\sqrt{x+y} + \sqrt{y-x} = c$

Squaring both sides we have

$$x + y + y - x + 2\sqrt{(y+x)(y-x)} = c^2$$
$$2y + 2\sqrt{(y^2 - x^2} = c^2$$
$$\Rightarrow \quad 2\sqrt{y^2 - x^2} = c^2 - 2y$$

Squaring both sides we have

$$4(y^2 - x^2) = c^4 - 4c^2 y + 4y^2$$
$$4y^2 - 4x^2 = c^4 - 4c^2 y + 4y^2$$
$$c^4 + 4x^2 - 4c^2 y = 0$$

Differentiating with respect to x we have

$$0 + 8x - 4c^2 \frac{dy}{dx} = 0$$
$$8x - 4c^2 y_1 = 0$$

Again differentiating with respect to x we have

$$8 - 4c^2 y_2 = 0$$
$$\Rightarrow 4c^2 y_2 = 8$$
$$\Rightarrow y_2 = \frac{8}{4c^2}$$
$$\Rightarrow y_2 = \frac{2}{c^2}$$ *(Proved)*

Problem 6 Find the nth differential of coefficient $\frac{1}{x+a}$

Solution Let $y = \frac{1}{(x+a)} = (x+a)^{-1}$

Then
$$y_1 = -1)(x + a)^{-2}$$
$$y_2 = (-1)(-2)(x + a)^{-3}$$
$$y_3 = (-1)(-2)(-3)(x + a)^{-4}$$
$$\ldots \qquad \ldots$$
$$\ldots \qquad \ldots$$
$$y_n = (-1)(-2)(-3)\ldots(-n)(x + a)^{-(n+1)}$$
$$y_n = (-1)^n \, 1\cdot 2\cdot 3 \ldots n \, (x + a)^{-(n+1)}$$
$$y_n = \frac{(-1)^n \, n!}{(x + a)^{n+1}} \qquad \textbf{Ans.}$$

Problem 7 Find the nth differential coefficient of log $(1 + x)$.

Solution Let $\quad y = \log(1 + x)$

Differentiating with respect to x we have
$$\frac{dy}{dx} = \frac{1}{(1 + x)}$$

i.e.
$$y_1 = \frac{1}{1 + x}$$

Again differentiating with respect to x we have
$$y_2 = \frac{d}{dx}[(1 + x)^{-1}]$$
$$y_2 = (-1)(1 + x)^{-2}$$

Similarly
$$y_3 = (-1)(-2)(1 + x)^{-3}$$
$$\ldots \qquad \ldots$$
$$\ldots \qquad \ldots$$
$$y_n = (-1)(-2)(-3)\ldots \text{ to } (n-1) \text{ factors } (1 + x)^{-n}$$
$$y_n = (-1)^{n-1} \, 1\cdot 2\cdot 3 \ldots (n-1)(1 + x)^{-n}$$
$$y_n = \frac{\lfloor n-1 \, (-1)^{n-1}}{(1 + x)^n} \qquad \textbf{Ans.}$$

Problem 8 Find the nth differential coefficient of sin $2x$ cos $3x$,

Solution Let $\quad y = \sin 2x \cos 3x$
$$y = \frac{2}{2}[\sin 2x \cos 3x]$$
$$y = \tfrac{1}{2}[2 \sin 2x \cos 3x]$$
$$y = \tfrac{1}{2}[\sin(2x + 3x) + \sin(2x - 3x)]$$
$$y = \tfrac{1}{2}[\sin 5x + \sin(-x)] = \tfrac{1}{2}[\sin 5x - \sin x]$$
$$y_n = \frac{1}{2}\left[5^n \sin\left(5x + n\frac{\pi}{2}\right) - \sin\left(x + n\frac{\pi}{2}\right)\right] \qquad \textbf{Ans.}$$

Problem 9 Find the nth derivation of $ex \cos x$.

Solution Let $y = e^x \cos x$

If $y = e^{ax} \cos (ax + b)$ then

$$y_n = r^n e^{an} [\cos (ax + b + n\theta)]$$

where $r^2 = a^2 + b^2$

and $\tan \theta = \frac{b}{a}$

Here $a = 1, b = 1$

So $r^2 = a^2 + b^2$

i.e. $r^2 = 1 + 1 = 2$

i.e. $r = \sqrt{2}$

and $\tan \theta = \frac{1}{1} = 1$

i.e. $\theta = \frac{\pi}{4}$

So if $y = e^x \cos x$

$$y_n = \sqrt{2})^n e^x \cos \left(x + \frac{n\pi}{4}\right)$$

$$y_n = 2^{n/2} e^x \cos \left(x + \frac{n\pi}{4}\right) \quad \textbf{Ans.}$$

Problem 10 Find the nth differential coefficient of $e^x \sin^2 x$.

$$y = e^x \sin 2\, x$$

$$y = e^x \frac{1 - \cos 2x}{2}$$

$$y = \frac{e^x}{2} - \frac{e^x \cos 2x}{2}$$

$$y_n = \frac{d^n}{dx^n}\left(\frac{e^x}{2}\right) - \frac{d^n}{dx^n}\left\{\frac{e^x \cos 2x}{2}\right\}$$

$$y_n = \frac{e^x}{2}$$

$$a = 1, b = 2$$

then $r^2 = u^2 + b^2$

$$r^2 = 1 + 4 = 5$$

$$r = (5)^{1/2}$$

$$\tan\theta = \frac{2}{1} \Rightarrow \theta = \tan^{-1}(2)$$

$$y_n = \frac{e^x}{2} - \frac{r^n e^{ax} \cos(2x + n\theta)}{2}$$

$$y_n = \frac{e^x}{2} - \frac{(5)^{1/2} e^x \cos(2x + n\tan^{-1} 2)}{2}$$

$$y_n = \tfrac{1}{2} e^x [1-(5)^{1/2} \cos(2x + n\tan^{-1/2})]$$ **Ans.**

Promblem 11 Find the nth differential coefficient of $e^{3x} \sin 2x \cos x$.

Solution We have $y = e^{3x} \sin 2x \cos x$

$$y = \tfrac{1}{2}[e^{3x}\, 2 \sin 2x \cos x]$$

$$y = \tfrac{1}{2} e^{3x} [\sin(2x + x) + \sin(2x - x)]$$

$$y = \frac{e^{3x}}{2}\left[\sin 3x + \sin x\right]$$

$$y = \tfrac{1}{2}[e^{3x} \sin 3x + e^{3x} \sin x] \quad (1)$$

Differentiating equation (1) to n times we have

$$y_n = \frac{1}{2}\frac{d^n}{dx^n}[e^{3x} \sin 3x] + \frac{1}{2}\frac{d^n}{dx^n}[e^{3x} \sin x] \quad (2)$$

If we have $y = e^{ax} \sin(bx + c)$

then $y_n = r^n e^{ax} \sin(bx + c + n\theta)$

where $r = \sqrt{a^2 + b^2},\ \theta = \tan^{-1}\frac{b}{a}$

Then we have $\frac{d^n}{dx^n}[e^{3x} \sin 3x]$

Here $a = 3\ b = 3$

$$r^2 = a^2 + b^2$$

$$r^2 = 9 + 9 = 18$$

$$r = \sqrt{18} = (18)^{1/2}$$

$$\text{ten}\,\theta = \frac{3}{3} = 1 \Rightarrow \theta = \frac{\pi}{4}$$

$$\frac{d^n}{dx^n}[e^{3x} \sin 3x] = (18)^{n/2} e^{3x} \sin\left(3x + \frac{n\pi}{4}\right) \quad (3)$$

Aagain $\frac{d^n}{dx^n}[e^{3x} \sin x]$

Here $$a = 3\ b = 1$$
$$r^2 = a^2 + b^2$$
$$r^2 = 9 + 1 = 10$$
$$r = (10)^{1/2}$$
$$\tan\theta = \tfrac{1}{3}$$
$$\theta = \tan^{-1}\tfrac{1}{3}$$

$$\frac{d^n}{dx^n}[e^{3x}\sin x] = (10)^{n/2}\sin e^{3x}\sin(x + n\theta)$$
$$= 10^{n/2} e^{3x}\sin(x + n\ \text{ten}^{-1}\tfrac{1}{3})$$
$$y_n = \frac{1}{2}\left[(18)^{n/2} e^{3x}\sin\left(3x + \frac{n\pi}{4}\right)\right.$$
$$\left. + (10)^{n/2} e^{3x}\sin(x + n\tan^{-1}\tfrac{1}{3})\right]$$
$$y_n = \frac{1}{2} e^{3x}\ [(18)^{n/2}\sin\left(3x + \frac{n\pi}{4}\right)$$
$$+ (10)^{n/2}\sin(x + \tan^{-1}\tfrac{1}{3})$$ **Ans.**

Problem 12 Prove that

$$\frac{d^3x}{dy^3} = -\frac{\dfrac{d^3y}{dx^3}\cdot\dfrac{dy}{dx} - 3\left(\dfrac{d^2y}{dx^2}\right)^2}{(dy/dx)^5}$$

Solution We have

$$\frac{dx}{dy} = \frac{1}{dy/dx}$$

Differentiating equation (1) with to y we have

$$\frac{d}{dy}\left(\frac{dx}{dy}\right) = \frac{d}{dy}\left[\frac{1}{dy/dx}\right]$$

$$\frac{d^2x}{dy^2} = \frac{d}{dx}\left[\frac{1}{(dy/dx)}\right]\cdot\frac{dx}{dy}$$

$$\frac{d^2x}{dy^2} = \frac{\left[\dfrac{dy}{dx}\cdot\dfrac{d}{dx}(1) - 1\dfrac{d}{dx}\left(\dfrac{dy}{dx}\right)\right]}{(dy/dx)^2}\cdot\frac{1}{(dydx/)}$$

$$\frac{d^2x}{dy^2} = \frac{\dfrac{dy}{dx}.0 - \dfrac{d^2y}{dx^2}}{(dy/dx)^3}$$

$$\frac{d^2x}{dy^2} = -\frac{d^2y/dx^2}{(dy/dx)^3} \qquad (2)$$

Again differentiating equation (2) with respect to y we have

$$\frac{d}{dy}\left(\frac{d^2 x}{dy^2}\right) = -\frac{d}{dy}\left[\frac{d^2 y}{dx^2} \Big/ \left(\frac{dy}{dx}\right)^3\right]$$

$$\frac{d^3 x}{dy^3} = -\frac{d}{dx}\left[\frac{d^2 y}{dx^2} \Big/ \left(\frac{dy}{dx}\right)^3\right]\frac{dx}{dy}$$

$$\frac{d^3 x}{dy^3} = -\frac{\left(\frac{dy}{dx}\right)^3 \frac{d}{dx}\left(\frac{d^2 y}{dx^2}\right) - \frac{d^2 y}{dx^2} \cdot \frac{d}{dx}\left[\left(\frac{dy}{dx}\right)^3\right]}{\left(\frac{dy}{dx}\right)^6} \frac{1}{\left(\frac{dy}{dx}\right)}$$

$$\frac{d^3 x}{dy^2} = -\frac{\left[\left(\frac{dy}{dx}\right)^3 \cdot \frac{d^3 y}{dx^3} - \frac{d^2 y}{dx^2} \cdot 3\left(\frac{dy}{dx}\right)^2 \frac{d^2 y}{dx^2}\right]}{\left(\frac{dy}{dx}\right)^7}$$

$$\frac{d^3 x}{dy^3} = -\frac{\left(\frac{dy}{dx}\right)^2\left[\frac{dy}{dx} \cdot \frac{d^3 y}{dx^3} - 3\left(\frac{d^2 y}{dx^2}\right)^2\right]}{\left(\frac{dy}{dx}\right)^7}$$

$$\frac{d^3 x}{dy^3} = -\frac{\left[\frac{d^3 y}{dy^3} \cdot \frac{dy}{ax} - 3\left(\frac{d^2 y}{dx^2}\right)^2\right]}{\left(\frac{dy}{dx}\right)^5}$$ **Ans.** *(Proved)*

Problom 13 If $y = \log(\sin x)$, prove that

$$y_3 = \frac{2\cos x}{\sin^3 x}$$

Solution $y = \log(\sin x)$

Differentiating with respect to x we have

$$\frac{dy}{dx} = \frac{d}{dx}[\log(\sin x)]$$

$$\frac{dy}{dx} = \frac{\cos x}{\sin x}$$

$$y_1 = \frac{\cos x}{\sin x}$$

Again differentiating with respect to x we have

$$y_2 = \frac{\sin x \frac{d}{dx}(\cos x) - \cos x \frac{d}{dx}(\sin x)}{(\sin x)^2}$$

$$y_2 = \frac{\sin x(-\sin x) - \cos x \cos x}{\sin^2 x}$$

$$y_2 = \frac{-\sin^2 x - \cos^2 x}{\sin^2 x}$$

$$y_2 = \frac{-(\sin^2 x + \cos^2 x)}{\sin^2 x}$$

$$y_2 = -\frac{1}{\sin^2 x}$$

Differentiating with respect to x we have

$$y_3 = -\left[\frac{\sin^3 x \cdot 0 - 1 \cdot 2 \sin x \cos x}{\sin^4 x}\right.$$

$$y_3 = -\frac{(-2 \sin x \cos x)}{\sin^4 x}$$

$$y_3 = \frac{2 \sin x \cos x}{\sin^4 x}$$

$$y_3 = \frac{2 \cos x}{\sin^3 x}$$ (*Proved*)

Problem 14 Prove that

$$\frac{d^3 y}{dx^3} = \frac{\frac{d^3 x}{dy^3} \frac{dx}{dy} - 3\left(\frac{d^2 x}{dy^2}\right)^2}{(dx/dy)^5}$$

Solution We have

$$\frac{dy}{dx} = \frac{1}{dx/dy}$$

Differentiating both sines with respect to x we have

$$\frac{d}{dx}\left(\frac{dy}{dx}\right) = \frac{d}{dx}\left[\frac{1}{\frac{dx}{dy}}\right]$$

$$\frac{d^2 y}{dx^2} = \frac{d}{dy}\left[\frac{1}{\frac{dx}{dy}}\right] \cdot \frac{dy}{dx}$$

$$\frac{d^2 y}{dx^2} = \frac{\frac{dx}{dy} \frac{d}{dy}(1) - 1 \frac{d}{dy}\left(\frac{dx}{dy}\right)}{(dx/dy)^2} \cdot \frac{1}{dx/dy}$$

$$\frac{d^2 y}{dx^2} = \frac{\frac{dx}{dy} \cdot 0 - \frac{d^2 x}{dy^2}}{(dx/dy)^3}$$

$$\frac{d^2 y}{dx^2} = -\frac{d^2 x}{dy^2} \bigg/ \left(\frac{dx}{dy}\right)^3$$

ifferenntiating again both sides with respect to x we have

$$\frac{d}{dx}\left[\frac{d^2 y}{dx^2}\right] = -\frac{d}{dx}\left[\frac{d^2 x}{dy^2}\Big/\left(\frac{dx}{dy}\right)^2\right]$$

e. $$\frac{d^3 y}{dx^3} = -\frac{d}{dy}\left[\frac{d^2 x}{dy^2}\Big/\left(\frac{dx}{dy}\right)^3\right]\frac{dy}{dx}$$

e. $$\frac{d^3 y}{dx^3} = -\frac{\left[\left(\frac{dx}{dy}\right)^3 \frac{d}{dy}\left(\frac{d^2 x}{dy^2}\right) - \frac{d^2 x}{dy^2}\frac{d}{dy}\left\{\left(\frac{dx}{dy}\right)^3\right\}\right]}{(dx/dy)^6}\frac{dy}{dx}$$

e. $$\frac{d^3 y}{dx^3} = -\frac{\left[\left(\frac{dx}{dy}\right)^3 \cdot \frac{d^3 x}{dy^3} - \frac{d^2 x}{dy^2}\cdot 3\left(\frac{dx}{dy}\right)^2 \cdot \frac{d^2 x}{dy^2}\right]}{\left(\frac{dx}{dy}\right)^6} \frac{1}{\frac{dx}{dy}}$$

e. $$\frac{d^3 y}{dx^2} = -\frac{\left[\left(\frac{dx}{dy}\right)^3 \cdot \frac{d^3 x}{dy^3} - 3\left(\frac{dx}{dy}\right)^2\left(\frac{d^2 x}{dy^2}\right)^2\right]}{\left(\frac{dx}{dy}\right)^7}$$

e. $$\frac{d^3 y}{dx^3} = -\frac{\left(\frac{dx}{dy}\right)^2\left[\frac{dx}{dy}\cdot\frac{d^3 x}{dy^3} - 3\left(\frac{d^2 x}{dy^2}\right)^2\right]}{\left(\frac{dx}{dy}\right)^7}$$

e. $$\frac{d^3 y}{dx^3} = -\frac{\left[\frac{dx}{dy}\cdot\frac{d^3 x}{dy^3} - 3\left(\frac{d^2 x}{dy^2}\right)^2\right]}{(dx/dy)^5}$$ *(Proved)*

roblem 15 Find nth derivative of

$$y = e^x \sin 2x$$

olution If $y = e^{ax} \sin(bx + c)$ then we know that

$$y_n = r^n e^{ax} \sin(bx + c + n\theta)$$

here $r^2 = a^2 + b^2$ and $\tan\theta = \frac{b}{a}$ in the present example

$$a = 1,\ b = 2 \text{ and } c = 0$$

$$r^2 = a^2 + b^2$$

$$r^2 = 1^2 + 2^2$$

$$r^2 = 1 + 4 = 5$$

$$r = 5^{\frac{1}{2}}$$

$$\tan\theta = \frac{2}{1} \quad \text{i.e.} \quad \theta = \tan^{-1} 2$$

Now $y_n = r^n e^{ax} \sin(2x + n\theta)$

e. $y_n = 5^{n/2} e^x \sin(2x + n \tan^{-2})$ **Ans.**

Problem 16 Find the nth derivative of $y = e^x \cos 2x$

Solution We know that if

$$y = e^{ax} \cos (bx + c) \text{ then}$$
$$y_n = r^n e^{ax} \cos (bx + c + n\theta)$$

where $r^2 = a^2 + b^2$

and $\tan \theta = \dfrac{b}{a}$

If $y = e^x \cos 2x$

then $a = 1, b = 2$ and $c = 0$

$$r^2 = a^2 + b^2 \text{ and } \tan \theta = \frac{b}{a}$$
$$r^2 = 1 + 4 = 5$$
$$r = 5\frac{1}{2} \text{ and } \tan \theta = \frac{2}{1}$$

i.e. $\theta = \tan^{-1} 2$

$$y = e^x \cos 2x$$

then $y_n = r^n e^x \cos (2x + n\theta)$

$$y_n = (5)^{n/2} e^x \cos (2x + n \tan^{-1} 2)$$
$$y_n = (5)^{n/2} e^x \cos (2x + n \tan^{-2} 2) \qquad \textbf{Ans.}$$

Problem 17 If $y = \dfrac{1}{(ax + b)^m}$ then find the nth derivative

Solution Let $y = \dfrac{1}{(ax+b)^{-m}}$

Differentiating with respect to x we have

$$\frac{dy}{dx} = \frac{d}{dx}\left[\frac{1}{(ax + b)^m}\right]$$
$$\frac{dy}{dx} = \frac{d}{dx} [ax + b)^m]$$
$$\frac{dy}{dx} = -m (ax + b)^{-m-1} \frac{d}{dx} (ax + b)$$
$$\frac{dy}{dx} = -m (ax + b)^{-m-1} a$$
$$\frac{dy}{dx} = -ma (ax + b)^{-m-1}$$

i.e. $y_1 = -ma (ax + b)^{-m-1}$

gain differentiating with respect to x we have

$$y_2 = -am(-m-1)(ax+b)^{-m-1-1}\frac{d}{dx}(ax+b)$$

$$y_2 = -m(-m-1)\,a\,(ax+b)^{-m-2}\,a$$

$$y_2 = -m(-m-1)\,a^2(ax+b)^{-m-2}$$

imilarly $\quad y_3 = -a^3 m(-m-1)(-m-2)(ax+b)^{-m-3}$

$$\ldots \qquad \ldots \qquad \ldots \qquad \ldots,$$

$$y_n = -a^n m(-m-1)(-m-2)\ldots(-m-n+1)(ax+b)^{-m-n}$$

$$y_n = -a^n m(-m-1)(-m-2)\ldots \text{ to } n \text{ terms } (ax+b)^{-m-n}$$

e. $\quad y_n = a^n(-1)^n m(m+1)(m+2)\ldots(m+n-1)(ax-b)^{m-n}$

e. $\quad y_n = \dfrac{a^n(-1)^n m(m+1)(m+2)\ldots(m+n-1)}{(ax+b)^{m+n}}$ **Ans.**

roblem 18 Find the nth derivative of $y = \sin^2 x$.

olution We have $y = \sin^2 x$

$$y = \frac{2\sin^2 x}{2}$$

e. $\quad y = \dfrac{1-\cos 2x}{2}$

$$y = \frac{1}{2} - \frac{1}{2}\cos 2x$$

aking the nth derivative with respect to x

$$y_n = \frac{d^n}{dx^n}\left(\frac{1}{2}\right) - \frac{1}{2}\frac{d^n}{dx^n}(\cos 2x)$$

$$y_n = 0 - \frac{1}{2}\frac{d^n}{dx^n}(\cos 2x) \tag{1}$$

e know that if $\quad y = \cos(ax+b)$

ien $\quad y_n = a^n \cos(ax+b+n\pi/2)$

ence from equation (1) we have

$$y_n = 0 - \frac{1}{2}(2)^n \cos\left(2x + \frac{n\pi}{2}\right)$$

$$y_n = -(2)^{n-1}\cos\left(2x + \frac{n\pi}{2}\right)$$

oblem 19 Find the nth derivative of $y = \cos^2 x$

lution Try yourself $(2)^{n-1}\cos\left(2x + \dfrac{n\pi}{2}\right)$ **Ans.**

Problem 20 $y = e^x \sin x \sin 2x$

Solution Find the nth derivative of y

$$y = e^x \sin x \sin 2x$$

$$y = \tfrac{1}{2}\,[e^x\, 2 \sin x \sin x]$$

$$y = \frac{e^x}{2}\,[\cos(x-2x) - \cos(x+2x)]$$

$$2 \sin A \sin B = \cos(A-B) - \cos(A+B)$$

$$y = \frac{e^x}{2}\,[\cos(-x) - \cos 3x]$$

$$y = \frac{e^x}{2}\,[\cos x - \cos 3x]$$

$$y = \frac{e^x}{2}\cos x - \frac{e^x}{2}\cos 3x$$

when $y = e^{ax}\cos(bx + c)$

Then $y_n = r^n e^{ax}\cos(bx + c + n\theta)$

where $r^2 = a^2 + b^2$

$$r = (a^2 + b^2)^{1/2} \qquad \tan\theta = \frac{b}{a}$$

$$y = \frac{e^x \cos x}{2} - \frac{e^x}{2}\cos 3x$$

$$y_n = \frac{d^n}{dx^n}\left[\frac{e^x \cos x}{2}\right] - \frac{d^n}{dx^n}\,[e^x \cos 3x]$$

For first term $a = 1 \quad b = 1$

$$r^2 = 1^2 + 1^2 = 1 + 1 = 2$$

$$r = 2^{\frac{1}{2}}$$

and $\tan\theta = \dfrac{b}{a} = \dfrac{1}{1} = 1$

$$\theta = \frac{\pi}{4}$$

For second term $a = 1, b = 3$

$$r^2 = a^2 + b^2$$

$$r^2 = 1^2 + 3^2 \qquad \tan\theta = \frac{b}{a}$$

$$r^2 = 1 + 9 = 10 \qquad \tan\theta = 3$$

$$r = (10)^{1/2} \qquad \theta = \tan^{-1} 3$$

$$y_n = \frac{1}{2} 2^{1/2} e^x \cos\left(x + n\frac{\pi}{4}\right) - \tfrac{1}{2}(10)^{1/2} e^x \cos(3x + \tan^{-1} 3)$$

$$= \frac{1}{2}\left[2^{n/2} e^x \cos\left(x + \frac{n\pi}{4}\right) - 10^{n/2} e^x \cos(3x + n\tan^{-1} 3)\right] \quad \textbf{Ans.}$$

Now we shall consider to form an equation by combining the second derivative, first derivative and the given function.

Problem 21 If $y = \frac{ax-b}{a-bx}$, prove that

$$2y, y_3 = 3y_2^2$$

Solution We have $y = \frac{(ax-b)}{(a-bx)}$

$$\Rightarrow y(a-bx) = (ax-b)$$

Differentiating both sides with respect to x we have

$$y(0-b\cdot 1) + (a-bx)y_1 = (a\cdot 1-0)$$

$$-by + (a-bx)y_1 = a$$

$$(a-bx)y_1 - by = a$$

Again differentiating with respect to x on both sides

$$(a-bx)y_2 + y_1(0-b) - by_1 = 0$$

$$(a-bx)y_2 - by_1 - by_1 = 0$$

$$(a-bx)y_2 - 2by_1 = 0 \quad (1)$$

$$(a-bx)y_2 = 2by_1$$

$$(a-bx)y_2 = 2by_1 \quad (2)$$

Again differentiating equation (2) we have

$$(a-bx)y_3 + y_2(0-b) = 2by_2$$

$$(a-bx)y_3 - by_2 = 2by_2$$

$$\Rightarrow (a-bx)y_3 = 3by_2 \quad (3)$$

Now dividing equation (2) by (3) we have

$$\frac{y_2}{y_3} = \frac{2by_1}{3by_2}$$

$$\Rightarrow 3y_2^2 = 2y_1 y_3$$

i.e. $2y_1 y_3 = 3y_2^2$ *(Proved)* (4)

Problem 22 If $\quad y = e^{a \sin^{-1} x}$, prove that

$$(1-x^2)\, y_2 - xy_1 = a^2 y$$

Solution We have $y = e^{a \sin^{-1} x}$

Differentiating with respect to x we have

$$\frac{dy}{dx} = e^{a\sin^{-1} x} \cdot \frac{d}{dx} (a \sin^{-1} x)$$

$$y_1 = e^{a\sin^{-1} x} \; a \frac{1}{\sqrt{1-x^2}}$$

$$y_1 \sqrt{1-x^2} = ae^{a \sin^{-1} x}$$

$$y_1 \sqrt{1-x^2} = ay$$

Squaring both sides we have

$$y_1^2 (1-x^2) = a^2 y^2$$

Now again differentiating with respect to x we have

$$2y_1 y_2 (1-x^2) + y_1^2 (0-2x) = a^2\, 2y\, y_1$$

$$2y_1 y_2 (1-x^2) - 2xy_1^2 = 2a^2 y\, y_1$$

$$2y_1 [y_2 (1-x^2) - xy_1] = 2a^2 y\, y_1$$

$$y_2 (1-x^2) - xy_1 = a^2 y$$

i.e. $\quad (1-x^2)\, y_2 - xy_1 = a^2 y$ *(Proved)*

Problem 23 If $y = \sin (m \sin^{-1} x)$, prove that

$$(1-x^2)\, y_2 - xy + m^2 y) = 0$$

Solution We have

$$y = \sin (m \sin^{-1} x)$$

Differentiating both sides with respect to x we have

$$\frac{dy}{dx} = \cos (m \sin^{-1} x) \frac{d}{dx} [m \sin^{-1} x]$$

$$\frac{dy}{dx} = \cos (m \sin^{-1} x)\, m \frac{d}{dx} [\sin^{-1} x]$$

$$\frac{dy}{dx} = \cos (m \sin^{-1} x)\, m \frac{1}{\sqrt{1-x^2}}$$

$$y_1 = m \frac{\cos (m \sin^{-1} x)}{\sqrt{1-x^2}}$$

or $\quad y_1 \sqrt{1-x^2} = m (\cos m \sin^{-1} x)$

or $\quad y_1 \sqrt{1-x^2} = m \sqrt{1-\sin^2 (m \sin^{-1} x)}$

Squaring both sides we have

$$y_1^2 (1-x^2) = m^2 [1-\sin^2 (m \sin^{-1} x)]$$

$$y_1^2 (1-x^2) = m^2 [1-y^2]$$

Again differentiating both sides with respect to x we have

$$(1-x^2)\, 2y_1 y_2 + y_1^2 (0-2x) = m^2 [0-2yy_1]$$

$$2(1-x^2)\, y_1 y_2 - 2xy_1^2 = -2m^2 yy_1$$

$$2y_1 [(1-x^2)\, y_2 - xy_1] = -2m^2 yy_1$$

$$(1-x^2)\, y_2 - xy_1 = -m^2 y$$

i.e. $$(1-x^2)\, y_2 - xy_1 + m^2 y = 0$$

Problem 24 If $y = (\tan^{-1} x)^2$; prove that

$$(1+x^2)^2 \frac{d^2y}{dx^2} + 2x(1+x^2) \frac{dy}{dx} = 2$$

Solution We have $y = (\tan^{-1} x)^2$

Differentiating both sides with respect to x we have

$$y_1 = 2 \tan^{-1} x \cdot \frac{d}{dx} [\tan^{-1} x]$$

i.e. $$y_1 = 2 \tan^{-1} x \frac{1}{1+x^2}$$

i.e. $$y_1 = 2 \frac{\tan^{-1} x}{1+x^2} \tag{1}$$

Again differntiating with respect to x both sides we have

$$y_2 = 2 \frac{d}{dx} \left[\frac{\tan^{-1} x}{1+x^2}\right]$$

$$y_2 = 2 \frac{\left[(1+x^2) \frac{d}{dx} (\tan^{-1} x) - \tan^{-1} x \frac{d}{dx} (1+x^2)\right]}{1+x^2)^2}$$

$$y_2 = 2 \frac{\left[(1+x^2) \frac{1}{(1+x^2)} - \tan^{-1} x\, (2x)\right]}{(1+x^2)^2}$$

i.e. $$y_2 = \frac{2[1-2x \tan^{-1} x]}{(1+x^2)^2}$$

i.e. $$y_2 = \frac{2 - 4x \tan^{-1} x}{(1+x^2)^2}$$

$$(1+x^2)^2 y_2 = 2 - 4x \tan^{-1} x$$

i.e. $$(1+x^2)^2 y_2 + 4x \tan^{-1} x = 2 \tag{2}$$

From equation (1) we have

$$y_1 = \frac{2\tan^{-1} x}{1+x^2}$$

$$y_1(1+x^2) = 2\tan^{-1} x$$

$$\Rightarrow 4\tan^{-1} x = 2y_1(1+x^2) \qquad (3)$$

Putting the value of $4\tan^{-1} x$ from equation (3) in equation (1) we have

$$(1+x^2)^2 y_2 + 2(1+x^2) y_1 = 2$$

Replacing y_1 from $\frac{dy}{dx}$ and y_2 from $\frac{d^2y}{dx^2}$ we have

$$(1+x^2)^2 \frac{d^2y}{dx^2} + 2(1+x^2)\frac{dy}{dx} = 2 \qquad \textit{(Proved)}$$

Problem 25 If $x = \cos(\log y)$, show that $(1-x^2)y_2 - xy_1 = y$

Solution Here $\cos(\log y) = x$

$$\Rightarrow \log y = \cos^{-1} x$$

Differentiating both sides with respect to x we have

$$\frac{1}{y}\frac{dy}{dx} = -\frac{1}{\sqrt{1-x^2}}$$

$$\frac{1}{y} = -\frac{1}{\sqrt{1-x^2}}$$

$$\sqrt{1-x^2}\, y_1 = -y$$

squaring both sides we have

$$(1-x^2)y_1^2 = y^2$$

| $y = \cos^{-1} x \quad \frac{dy}{dx} = -\frac{1}{\sqrt{1-x^2}}$ |

Again differenting both sides with respecr to x we have,

$$(1-x^2)\,2y_1y_2 + y_1^2(0-2x) = 2yy_1$$

$$(1-x^2)\,2y_1y_2 - 2xy_1^2 = 2yy_1$$

$$2y_1[1-x^2)y_2 - 2xy_1] = 2yy_1$$

i.e.

$$(1-x^2)y_2 - xy_1 = y \qquad \textit{(Proved)}$$

Problem 26 If $y = a\cos(\log x) + b\sin(\log x)$

Prove that $x^2y_2 + xy_1 + y = 0$

Solution $y = a\cos(\log x) + b\sin(\log x)$

differentiating both sides with respect to x we have

$$\frac{dy}{dx} = -\mathrm{a}\sin(\log x)\frac{d}{dx}(\log x) + b\cos(\log x)\frac{d}{dx}(\log x)$$

$$\frac{dy}{dx} = -a\sin(\log x)\frac{1}{x} + b\cos(\log x)\frac{1}{x}$$

i.e. $$x \cdot \frac{dy}{dx} = -a \sin(\log x) + b \cos(\log x)$$

$$xy_1 = -a \sin(\log x) + b \cos(\log x)$$

Again differentiating with respect to x we have

$$xy_2 + y_2 \cdot 1 = -a \cos(\log x) \frac{1}{x} - b \sin(\log x) \frac{1}{2}$$

$$xy_2 + y_1 = -\frac{1}{x} [a \cos(\log x) + b \sin(\log x)]$$

$$x(xy_2 + y_1) = -[a \cos(\log x) + b \sin(\log x)]$$

$$x^2 y_2 + xy_1 = -y$$

$$x^2 y_2 + xy_1 + y = 0$$ *(proved)*

Problem 25 If $y = A(x + \sqrt{x^2-1})^n + B(x - \sqrt{x^2-1})^n$, prove that $(x^2-1) y_2 + xy_1 = n^2 y$

Solution Here $y = A(x + \sqrt{x^2-1})^n + B(x - \sqrt{x^2-1})^n$

Differentiating with respect to x both sides we have

$$\frac{dy}{dx} = A\, n\, (x + \sqrt{x^2-1})^{n-1} \left\{1 + \frac{1\,(2x)}{2\sqrt{x^2-1}}\right\} + Bn\,(x - \sqrt{x^2-1})^{n-1} \left\{1 - \frac{2x}{2\sqrt{x^2-1}}\right\}$$

$$\frac{dy}{dx} = An\,(x + \sqrt{x^2-1})^{n-1} \frac{(\sqrt{x^2-1} + x)}{\sqrt{x^2-1}} + Bn\,(x - \sqrt{x^2-1})^{n-1} \frac{(\sqrt{x^2-1} - x)}{\sqrt{x^2-1}}$$

$$y_1 = \frac{An\,(x + \sqrt{x^2-1})^n}{\sqrt{x^2-1}} - \frac{Bn\,(x - \sqrt{x^2-1})^n}{\sqrt{x^2-1}}$$

i.e. $$(\sqrt{x^2-1})\, y_1 = An\,(x + \sqrt{x^2-1})^n - Bn\,(x - \sqrt{x^2-1})^n \quad (1)$$

Again differentiating (1) with respect to x we have

$$(\sqrt{x^2-1})\, y_2 + y_1 \frac{(2x-0)}{2\sqrt{x^2-1}} = An\, n\,(x + \sqrt{x^2-1})^{n-1} \left\{1 + \frac{2x}{2\sqrt{x^2-1}}\right\} - Bn\, n\,(x - \sqrt{x^2-1})^{n-1} \left\{1 - \frac{2x}{2\sqrt{x^2-1}}\right\}$$

$$= An^2 (x + \sqrt{x^2-1})^{n-1} \frac{(x + \sqrt{x^2-1})}{\sqrt{x^2-1}}$$

$$- Bn^2 (x - \sqrt{x^2-1})^{n-1} \frac{(\sqrt{x^2-1}-x)}{\sqrt{x^2-1}}$$

$$= An^2 \frac{(x + \sqrt{x^2-1})^n}{\sqrt{x^2-1}} + Bn^2 \frac{(x-\sqrt{x^2-1})^{n-1}}{\sqrt{x^2-1}} (x-\sqrt{x^2-1})$$

Therefore $\sqrt{(x^2-1)}\, y_2 + \frac{xy_1}{\sqrt{x^2-1}}$

$$= An^2 \frac{(x + \sqrt{x^2-1})^n}{\sqrt{x^2-1}} + \frac{Bn^2 (x-\sqrt{x^2-1})^n}{\sqrt{x^2-1}}$$

$$\frac{(x^2-1)\, y_2 + xy_1}{\sqrt{x^2-1}} = n^2 \frac{[A\,(x + \sqrt{x^2-1})^n + B\,(x-\sqrt{x^2-1})^n]}{\sqrt{x^2-1}}$$

i.e. $(x^2-1)\, y_2 + xy_1 = n^2\, [A\,(x + \sqrt{x^2-1})^n + B\,(x-\sqrt{x^2-1})^n]$

i.e. $(x^2-1)\, y_2 + xy_1 = n^2\, y$ *(Proved)*

where $y = A\,(x + \sqrt{x^2-1})^n + B\,(x-\sqrt{x^2-1})^n$

Problem 26 If $y = (a + bx)\, e^{-nx}$ prove that

$$\frac{d^2 y}{dx^2} + 2n \frac{dy}{dx} + n^2 y = 0$$

Solution Let $y = (a + bx)\, e^{-nx}$

Differentiating both sides with respect to x we have

$$\frac{dy}{dx} = (a + bx) \frac{d}{dx} (e^{-nx}) + e^{-nx} \frac{d}{dx} (a + bx)$$

$$y_1 = (a + bx)\,(-n)\, e^{-nx} + e^{-nx}\, (0 + b)$$

$$y_1 = -ne^{-nx}\, (a + bx) + be^{-nx}$$

$$y_1 = -n\, (a + bx)\, e^{-nx} + be^{-nx}$$

$$y_1 = -ny + be^{-nx} \quad (1)$$

Again differentiating with respect to x we have

$$y_2 = -ny_1 + be^{-nx}\, (-n)$$

$$y_2 = -ny_1 - nbe^{-nx} \quad (2)$$

From equation (1) we have

$$y_1 + ny = be^{-nx} \quad (3)$$

Putting the value of be^{-nx} from equation (3) inequation (2) we have

$$y_2 = -ny_1 - n(y_1 + ny)$$

$$y_2 = -ny_1 - ny_1 - n^2 y$$

$$\Rightarrow \quad y_2 = -2ny_1 - n^2 y$$

$$\Rightarrow \quad y_2 + 2ny_1 + n^2 y = 0$$

Replacing y_1 and y_2 by $\frac{dy}{dx}$ and $\frac{d^2y}{dx^2}$ we have

$$\frac{d^2y}{dx^2} + 2n\frac{dy}{dx} + n^2 y = 0 \qquad \textit{(Proved)}$$

Problem 27 If $y = \log\left(\frac{x}{a+bx}\right)^x$ then prove that

$$x^3 y_2 = (y - xy_1)^2$$

Solution $\quad y = \log\left(\frac{x}{a+bx}\right)^x$

$$y = x\log\left(\frac{x}{a+bx}\right)$$

$$y = x[\log x - \log(a+bx)]$$

Differentiating both sides with respect to x we have

$$y_1 = x\left[\frac{1}{x} - \frac{b}{a+bx}\right] + [\log x - \log(a+bx)]\,1$$

$$y_1 = x\left(\frac{1}{x} - \frac{b}{a+bx}\right) + \log\frac{x}{a+bx}$$

$$y_1 = x\left[\frac{a+bx-bx}{x(a+bx)}\right] + \log\frac{x}{a+bx}$$

$$y_1 = \frac{ax}{x(a+bx)} + \log\frac{x}{(a+bx)}$$

$$y_1 = \frac{a}{(a+bx)} + \log\frac{x}{(a+bx)} \qquad (1)$$

Since $\quad y = x\log\frac{x}{a+bx}$

$$\Rightarrow \quad \frac{y}{x} = \log\frac{x}{a+bx} \qquad (2)$$

From equation (1) and (2) we have

$$y_1 = \frac{a}{(a+bx)} + \frac{y}{x}$$

$$y_1 - \frac{y}{x} = \frac{a}{(a+bx)}$$

$$\Rightarrow \qquad xy_1 - y = \frac{ax}{(a+bx)}$$

Again differentiating both sides

With respect to x we have

$$xy_2 + y_1 - y_1 = \frac{(a+bx)\, a - ax\,(0 + b.1)}{(a+bx)^2}$$

$$xy_2 = \frac{(a+bx)\, a - axb}{(a+bx)^2}$$

$$xy_2 = \frac{a\,[a + bx - bx]}{(a+bx)^2}$$

$$xy_2 = \frac{a^2}{(a+bx)^2}$$

Multiplying both sides with x^2

$$x^3\, y_2 = \frac{a^2\, x^2}{(a+bx)^2}$$

$$x^3\, y_2 = \left[\frac{ax}{a+bx}\right]^2$$

$$x^3\, y_2 = (xy_1 - y)^2$$

i.e. $$x^3\, y_2 = (y - xy_1)^2$$ (*Proved*)

Problem 28 If $y = (\sin^{-1} x)^2$, prove that $(1-x^2)\, y_2 - xy_1 = 2$ [*IFS 84*]

Solution $y = (\sin^{-1} x)^2$

Differentiating both sides with respect to x we have

$$\frac{dy}{dx} = 2 \sin^{-1} x \cdot \frac{d}{dx} [\sin^{-1} x]$$

$$y_1 = 2 \sin^{-1} x \; \frac{1}{\sqrt{1-x^2}}$$

$$y_1 \sqrt{1-x^2} = 2 \sin^{-1} x$$

Squaring both sides we have

$$y_1^2\, (1-x^2) = 4\, (\sin^{-1} x)^2$$

$$y_1^2\, (1-x)^2 = 4y$$

Again differentiating both sides we have

$$y_1^2(0-2x)+(1-x^2)\,2y_1\,y_2 = 4y_1$$

$$-2xy_1^2+(1-x^2)\,2y_1\,y_2 = 4y_1$$

$$2y_1\,[(1-x^2)\,y_2-xy_1] = 4y_1$$

$$(1-x^2)\,y_2-xy_1 = 2$$ [P·oved)

Problem 29 If $x = \sin(\log y)$, prove that $(1-x^2)\,y_2-xy_1 = y$

Solution We have $x = \sin(\log y)$

$\Rightarrow$ $\log y = \sin^{-1} x$

Differentiating both sides with respect to x we have

$$\frac{1}{y}\frac{dy}{dx} = \frac{1}{\sqrt{1-x^2}}$$

$$\frac{y_1}{y} = \frac{1}{\sqrt{1-x^2}}$$

$$y_1\sqrt{1-x^2} = y$$

Squaring both sides we have

$$y_1^2(1-x^2) = y^2$$

Again differentiating both sides with respect to x we have

$$y_1^2(0-2x)+(1-x^2)\,2y_1\,y_2 = 2y\,y_1$$

$$-2xy_1^2+(1-x^2)\,2y_1\,y_2 = 2y\,y_1$$

$$2y_1\,[(1-x^2)\,y_2-xy_1] = 2y\,y_1$$

i.e. $$(1-x^2)\,y_2-xy_1 = y$$ *(Proved)*

Problem 30 If $x = \cosh\left(\frac{\log y}{m}\right)$, prove that

$$(x^2-1)\,y_2+xy_1-m^2\,y = 0$$

Solution We have the following differential coefficient of inverse hyperbolic function

$$\frac{d}{dx}(\sin h^{-1} x) = \frac{1}{\sqrt{1+x^2}}$$

$$\frac{d}{dx}(\cos h^{-1} x) = \frac{1}{\sqrt{x^2-1}}$$

$$\frac{d}{dx}(\tan h^{-1} x) = \frac{1}{1-x^2}\ (x < 1)$$

$$\frac{d}{dx}(\cot h^{-1} x) = -\frac{1}{x^2-1}\ (x > 1)$$

$$\frac{d}{dx}(\sec h^{-1} x) = -\frac{1}{x\sqrt{1-x^2}}\quad \frac{d}{dx}(\text{cosec}\, h^{-1} x)] = -\frac{1}{x\sqrt{x^2+1}}$$

Since $$x = \cos h \left(\frac{\log y}{m}\right)$$

$$\Rightarrow \qquad \frac{\log y}{m} = \cos h^{-1} x$$

$$\Rightarrow \qquad \log y = m \cos h^{-1} x$$

Differentiating with respect to x we have

$$\frac{1}{y}\frac{dy}{dx} = m \frac{1}{\sqrt{x^2-1}}$$

$$\frac{y_1}{y} = \frac{m}{\sqrt{x^2-1}} \Rightarrow y_1\sqrt{x^2-1} = my$$

Squaring both sides we have

$$y_1^2 (x^2-1) = m^2 y^2$$

Differentiating both sides with respect to x we have

$$y_1^2 (2x) + (x^2-1) 2y_1 y_2 = m^2 2y y_1$$

$$2xy_1^2 + (x^2-1) 2y_1 y_2 = 2m^2 y y_1$$

$$2y_1 [xy_1 + (x^2-1) y_2] = 2 m^2 y y_1$$

$$xy_1 + (x^2-1) y_2 = m^2 y$$

i.e. $$(x^2-1) y_2 + xy_1 - m^2y = 0$$ *(Proved)*

Problem 31 If $x = \sin h \left(\frac{\log y}{m}\right)$, prove that

$$(x^2 + 1) y_2 + xy_1 = m^2 y$$

Solution We have $x = \sin h \left(\frac{\log y}{m}\right)$

$$\Rightarrow \qquad \frac{\log y}{m} = \sin h^{-1} x$$

$$\Rightarrow \log y = m \sin h^{-1x}$$

Differentiating both sides with respect to x we have

$$\frac{1}{y}\frac{dy}{dx} = \frac{m}{\sqrt{1 + x^2}}$$

$$\frac{y_1}{y} = \frac{m}{\sqrt{1 + x^2}}$$

$$y_1\sqrt{1 + x^2} = my$$

Squaring both sides we have

$$y_1^2 (1 + x^2) = m^2 y^2$$

Differentiating again with respect to x we have

$$y_1^2 (2x) + (1 + x^2) 2y_1 y_2 = m^2 2yy_1$$

$$2y_1 [xy_1 + (1 + x^2) y_2] = 2y_1 m^2 y$$

$$(1 + x^2) y_2 + xy_1 = m^2 y \qquad (Proved)$$

Leibnitz Theorem (*Remember*)

Statement If u and v are any two functions of x which possess derivatives of nth order then

$$y_n = u_n v + {}^n c_1 u_{n-1} v_1 + {}^n c_2 u_{n-2} v_2 + \ldots {}^n c_r u_{n-r} v_r + \ldots + {}^n c_n uv$$

FORMULA

Remember $\qquad D^n [e^{ax} f(x)] = e^{ax} (D + a)^n f(x)$

Where $\qquad D \equiv \frac{d}{dx}$

Problem 32 If $y = x^2 e^{ax}$, find y_n.

Here we take $v = x^2$, $u = e^{ax}$

$$\therefore \quad v_1 = 2x \quad u_2 = 2 \quad v_3 = 0$$

$$v_4 = 0, \quad v_5 = 0 \text{ etc} \ldots$$

$$u = e^{ax}, \quad u_1 = ae^{ax} \quad u_2 = a^2 e^{ax} \quad u_3 = a^3 e^{ax} \ldots \quad u_n = a^n e^{ax}$$

According to Leibnitz theorem.

$$y_n = u_n v + {}^n c_1 u_{n-1} v_1 + {}^n c_2 u_{n-2} v_2 + {}^n c_3 u_{n-3} v_3 + \ldots + \ldots {}^n c_n uv_n$$

$$y_n = a^n e^{ax} \cdot x^2 + n a^{n-1} e^{ax} 2x + \frac{n(n-1)}{2 \cdot 1} a^{n-2} e^{ax} 2 + 0 + 0 + \ldots$$

$$y_n = a^n e^{ax} x^2 + 2n a^{n-1} x e^{ax} + n(n-1) a^{n-2} e^{ax}$$

$$y_n = a^{n-2} e^{ax} [a^2 x^2 + 2n ax + n(n-1)] \qquad \textbf{Ans.}$$

Problem 33 If $y = x^2 \cos x$ find y.

Solution Here we take $v = x^2$ $u = \cos x$ so that

$$u_1 = 2\text{-}x, v_2 = 2, v_3 = 0, v_4 = 0 \ldots$$

$$u = \cos x$$

$$u_n = (1)^n \cos\left(x + \frac{n\pi}{2}\right)$$

i.e. $\qquad u_n = \cos\left[x + \frac{n\pi}{2}\right]$

According to Leibnitz theorem we have

$$y_n = u_n v + {}^n c_1 u_{n-1} v_1 + {}^n c_2 u_{n-2} v + {}^n c^3 u_{2-3} v_3 + \ldots$$

But here $v_3 = 0, v_4 = 0$ so

$$y_n = u_n v + {}^nc_1 u_{n-1} v_1 + {}^nc_2 u_{u-2} v_2$$

$$u_n = \cos\left(x + \frac{n\pi}{2}\right)$$

$$u_{n-1} = \cos\left[x + \frac{(n-1)}{2}\pi\right]$$

$$u_{n-2} = \cos\left[x + \frac{(n-2)}{2}\pi\right]$$

So
$$y_n = \cos\left(x + \frac{n\pi}{2}\right)\cdot x^2 + {}^nc_1 \cos\left\{x + \frac{(n-1)}{2}\pi\right\}2x$$
$$+ {}^nc_2 \cos\left\{x + \frac{(n-2)}{2}\pi\right\}2\cdot$$

$$y_n = \cos\left(x + \frac{n\pi}{2}\right)x^2 + 2xn \cos\left\{x + \left(\frac{n-1}{2}\right)\pi\right\}$$
$$+ n(n-1)\cos\left\{x + \frac{(n-2)}{2}\pi\right\} \quad \textbf{Ans.}$$

Problem 34 If $y = x^2 \log x$, find $y_n, n \geqslant 3$

Solution Here we take

$$v = x^2 \text{ and } u = \log x \text{ so that}$$
$$v_1 = 2x,\ v_2 = 2\ v_3 = 0,\ v_4 = 0 \text{ etc,}$$
$$u = \log x,\ u_1 = \frac{1}{x},\ u_2 = -\frac{1}{x^2}$$
$$u_3 = (-1)(-2)\frac{1}{x^3}\ldots$$
$$\ldots \qquad \ldots \qquad \ldots$$
$$u_n = \frac{(-1)(-2)(-3)\ldots(-(n-1)}{x^n}$$
$$= \frac{(-1)^{n-1}(n-1)!}{x^n}$$

According to Leibnitz theorem

$$y_n = u_n v + {}^nc_1 u_{n-1} v_1 + {}^nc_2 u_{n-2} v_2 + \ldots$$

$$y_n = \frac{(-1)^{n-1}(n-1)!}{x^n} x^2 + n\frac{(-1)^{n-2}(n-2)!}{x^{n-1}}(2x)$$
$$+ \frac{n(n-1)}{2!}\frac{(-1)^{n-3}(n-3)!}{x^{n-2}}\cdot 2 + 0 + 0$$

$$y_n = \frac{(-1)^{n-1} \underline{|n-1}}{x^{n-2}} + \frac{(-1)^{n-2} \underline{|n-2}}{x^{n-2}} 2n$$

$$+ \frac{n(n-1)(-1)^{n-3}}{x^{n-2}} \underline{|n-3}$$

$$y_n = \frac{(-1)^{n-3} \underline{|n-3}}{x^{n-2}} [(-1)^2 (n-1)(n-2) + (-1)(n-2) 2n + n(n-1)]$$

$$y_n = \frac{(-1)^{n-3} \underline{|n-3}}{x^{n-2}} [n-1)(n-2) - 2n(n-2) + n(n-1)]$$

$$y_n = \frac{(-1)^{n-3} \underline{|n-3}}{x^{n-2}} [n^2 - 2n - n + 2 - (2n^2 - 4n) + n^2 - n]$$

$$y_n = \frac{(-1)^{n-3} \underline{|n-3}}{x^{n-2}} [n^2 - 2n - n + 2 - 2n^2 + 4n + n^2 - n]$$

$$y_n = \frac{(-1)^{n-3} \underline{|n-3}}{x^{n-2}} [2]$$

$$y_v = \frac{2(-1)^{n-3} \underline{|n-3}}{x^{n-2}}$$

Problem 35 If $y = e^{a \sin^{-1} x}$, prove that

(i) $(1-x^2) y_2 - xy_1 - a^2 y = 0$

(ii) $(1-x^2) y_{n+2} - (2n+1) x y_{u+1} - (n^2 + a^2) y_n = 0$

Solution Here $y = e^{a \sin^{-1} x}$

Differentiating both sides with respect to x we have

$$\frac{dx}{dx} = \frac{d}{dx} [e^{a \sin^{-1} x}]$$

i.e. $\frac{dy}{dx} = e^{a \sin-1x} \frac{d}{dx} [a \sin^{-1} x]$

i.e. $\frac{dy}{dx} = e^{\sin-1x} a \frac{1}{\sqrt{1-x^2}}$

i.e. $y_1 = e^{a \sin-1x} \frac{a}{\sqrt{1-x^2}}$

i.e. $(\sqrt{1-x^2}) y_1 = ae^{a \sin^{-1} x}$

i.e. $(\sqrt{1-x^2}) y_1 = ay$

Squaring both sides with respect to x we have

$$(1-x^2) y_1^2 = a^2 y^2$$

Differentiating both sides with respect to x we have

$$(1-x^2)\,2y_1\,y_2 + y_1^2\,(0-2x) = a^2\,2y\,y_1$$

$$(1-x^2)\,2y_1\,y_2 - 2x\,y_1^2 = a^2\,2y\,y_1$$

$$2y_1\,[(1-x^2)\,y_2 - xy_1] = 2y_1\,(a^2\,y)$$

i.e. $$(1-x^2)\,y_2 - xy_1 = a^2\,y$$

i.e. $$(1-x^2)\,y_2 - xy_1 - a^2\,y = 0 \qquad (1)$$

[*First part proved*]

Differentiating equation (1) with respect to x n times we have.

$$\frac{d^n}{dx^n}[(1-x^2)\,y_2] - \frac{d^n}{dx^n}[xy_1] - \frac{d^n}{dx^n}[a^2\,y] = 0 \qquad (2)$$

Applying Leibnitz theorem let us consider the first term

$$\frac{d^n}{dx^n}[(1-x^2)\,y_2]$$

Let $$u = y_2\ \ v = (1-x^2)$$

$$u_n = y_{n+2}$$

$$u_{n-1} = y_{n-1+2} = y_{n+1}$$

$$n_{n-2} = y_{n-2+2} = y_n$$

$$v_1 = -2x$$

$$v_2 = -2, \qquad v_3 = 0, \qquad v_4 = 0,$$

we know that $$\frac{d^n}{dx^n}(nv)$$

$$= u_n\,v + {}^nc_1\,u_{n-1}\,v_1 + {}^nc_2\,u_{n-2}\,v_2 + {}^nc_3\,u_{n-3}\,v_3 + \ldots$$

$$\frac{d^n}{dx_n}[(1-x^2)\,y_2] = y_{n+2}\,(1-x^2) + n\,y_{n+1}\,(-2x)$$

$$+ \frac{n\,(n-1)}{2!}\,y_n\,(-2) + 0 + 0$$

i.e. $$\frac{d^n}{dx^n}[1-x^2)\,y_2] = (1-x^2)\,y_{n+2} - 2nx\,y_{n+1} - n(n-1)\,y_n \qquad (3)$$

Let us consider the second term $\dfrac{d^n}{dx^n}[xy_1]$

Here $$v = x\ \ u = y_1$$

$$u_n = y_{n+1}$$

$$u_{n-1} = y_{n-1+1} = y_n$$

$$v_1 = 1 \qquad v_2 = 0$$

Then $$\frac{d^n}{dx^n}(xy_1) = y_{n+1}\, x + y_n\, 1 + 0 + 0$$

$$\frac{d^n}{dx^n}(xy_1) = x\, y_{n+1} + y_n \qquad (4)$$

From equation (2), (3) and (4) we have

$$(1-x^2)\, y_{n+2} - 2nx\, y_{n+1} - n\,(n-1)\, y_n - xy_{n+1} - ny_n - a^2\, y_n = 0$$

i.e. $$(1-x^2)\, y_{n+2} - 2nx\, y_{n+1} - n^2]y_n + ny_n - xy_{n+1} - ny_n - a^2\, y_n = 0$$

i.e. $$(1-x^2)\, y_{n+2} - (2n+1)\, xy_{n+1} - (n^2 + a^2)\, y_n = 0$$

Problem 36 If $y = (\sin^{-1} x)^2$ prove that

(i) $(1 + x^2)\, y_2 - xy_1 = 2$

(ii) $(1-x^2)\, y_{n+2} - (2n+1)\, xy_{n+1} - n^2\, y_n = 0$ [*IFS 84*]

Solution We have $y = (\sin^{-1} x)^2$

Differentiating both sides with respect to x we have

$$\frac{dy}{dx} = 2\sin^{-1} x\, \frac{d}{dx}[\sin^{-1} x]$$

$$\frac{dy}{dx} = 2\sin^{-1} x\, \frac{1}{\sqrt{1-x^2}}$$

$$y_1 = 2\sin^{-1} x\, \frac{1}{\sqrt{1-x^2}}$$

i.e. $$y_1\sqrt{1-x^2} = 2\sin^{-1} x$$

Squaring both sides we have

$$(y_1\sqrt{1-x})^2 = (2\sin^{-1} x)^2$$

$$y_1^2\,(1-x^2) = 4\,(\sin^{-1} x)^2$$

$$y_1^2\,(1-x^2) = 4y \qquad (1)$$

Now differentiating equation (1) with respect to x we have

$$2y_1\,(1-x^2)\, y_2 + y_1^2\,(0-2x) = 4y_1$$

$$2y_1\,[1-x^2)\, y_2 - xy_1] = 4y_1$$

i.e. $$(1-x^2)\, y_2 - xy_1 = 2 \qquad (2)$$

(*First part proved*)

Again differentiating n times (2) with respect to x we have.

$$\frac{d^n}{dx^n}[(1-x^2)\, y_2 - xy_1] = 0$$

$$\frac{d^n}{dx^n}[(1-x^2)\, y_2] - \frac{d^n}{dx^n}[xy_1] = 0 \qquad (3)$$

Considering the first term we have

$$u = y_2 \qquad v = 1-x^2$$
$$u_n = y_n + 2 \qquad v_1 = -2x$$
$$u_{n-1} = y_{n-1+2} = y_{n+1} \quad v_2 = -2$$
$$u_{n-2} = y_{n+2-2} = y_n \quad v_3 = 0$$

thus $$\frac{d^n}{dx_n}[(1-x^2)\,y_2] = y_{n+2}\,(1-x^2) + {}^nc_1\,y_{n+1}\,(-2x)$$
$$+ {}^nc_2\,y_n\,(-2) + 0 + 0$$

i.e. $$\frac{d^n}{dx^n}[(1-x^2)\,y_2] = y_{n+2}\,(1-x^2) - 2nx\ y_{n+1} + \frac{n\,(n-1)}{2!}\,y_n\,(-2)$$

$$\frac{d^n}{dx^n}[(1-x^2)\,y_2] = y_{n+2}\,(1-x^2) - 2nx\ y_{n+1} - n\,(n-1)\,y_n \tag{4}$$

Again consider $\frac{d^n}{dx^n}[xy_1]$.

Here
$$u = y_1 \qquad v = x$$
$$u_n = y_{n+1}, \quad v_1 = 1$$
$$u_{n-1} = y_n \qquad v_2 = 0$$

so $$\frac{d^n}{dx^n}[xy_1] = y_{n+1}\,x + {}^nc_1\,y_n\cdot 1 + 0$$

i.e. $$\frac{d^n}{dx^n}[xy_1] = y_{n+1}\,x + ny_n \tag{5}$$

From equation (3), (4) and (5) we have

$$(1-x^2)\,y_{n+2} - 2nx\,y_{n+1} - n\,(n-1)\,y_n - xy_{n+1} - ny_n = 0$$
$$(1-x^2)\,y_{n+2} - (2n+1)\,xy_{n+1} - n^2\,y_n + {}^ny_n - ny_n + ny_n = 0$$

i.e. $$(1-x^2)\,y_{n+2} - (2n+1)\,xy_{n+1} - n^2\,y_n = 0 \qquad \textit{Proved)}$$

Problem 37 If $y = \sin\,(m \sin^{-1} x)$ prove that

(i) $(1-x^2)\,y_2 - xy_1 + m^2\,y = 0$

(ii) $(1-x^2)\,y_{n+2} - (2n+1)\,xy_{n+1} + (m^2 - n^2)\,y_n = 0$

(iii) $\lim\limits_{x\to 0} \dfrac{y_n + 2}{y_n} = n^2 - m^2$

Solution We have $y = \sin\,(m \sin^{-1} x)$ (1)

Differentiating (1) both sides with respect to x we have

$$\frac{dy}{dx} = \cos\,(m \sin^{-1} x)\,\frac{d}{dx}\,(m \sin^{-1} x)$$

$$\frac{dy}{dx} = \cos\,(m \sin^{-1} x)\; m\,\frac{1}{\sqrt{1-x^2}}$$

$$\frac{dy}{dx} = \sqrt{1-\sin^2 (m \sin^{-}t\ x)}\frac{m}{\sqrt{1-x^2}}$$

$$\frac{dy}{dx} = \sqrt{1-y^2}\frac{m}{\sqrt{1-x^2}}$$

$$y_1 \sqrt{1-x^2} = m \sqrt{1-y^2}$$

Squaring both sides we have

$$y_1^2 (1-x^2) = m^2 (1-y^2)$$

Differentiating with respect to x we have

$$2y_1\, y_2 (1-x^2) + y^2 (0-2x) = m^2 (0-2yy_1)$$

$$2y_1\, y_2 (1-x^2) - 2xy_1^2 ==2m\, ^2y\, y_1$$

i.e. $$(1-x^2)\, y_2 - xy_1 = -m^2\, y$$

i.e. $$(1-x^2)\, y_2 - xy_1 + m^2\, y = 0 \qquad (2)$$

(*First part proved*)

Now again differentiating equation (2) n times we have

$$\frac{d^n}{dx^n} [(1-x^2)\, y_2 - xy_1 + m^2\, y] = 0$$

$$\frac{d^n}{dx^n} [(1-x^2)\, y_2] - \frac{d^n}{dx^n} [xy_1] + \frac{d^n}{dx^n} [m^2\, y] = 0 \qquad (3)$$

Consider the first term $\frac{d^n}{dx^n} (1-x^2)\, y_2]$

Here
$$u = y_2 \qquad v = (1-x^2)$$
$$u_n = y_{n+2} \qquad v_1 = -2x$$
$$u_{n-1} = y_{n-1+2} = y_{n+1} \quad v_2 = -2$$
$$u_{n-2} = y_{n-2+2} \qquad v_3 = 0$$
$$u_{n-2} = y_n \qquad v_4 = 0 \text{ etc.}$$

$$\frac{d^n}{xd^n} [(1-x^2)\, y_2] = u_n\, v + {}^nc_1\, u_{n-1}\, v_1 + {}^nc_2\, u_{u-2}\, v_{21} + {}^nc_3\, u_{n-3}\, v_3 + \ldots$$

$$= y_{n+2} (1-x^2) + ny_{n+1} (-2x) + \frac{n(n-1)}{2!} y_n (-2)$$

$$+ 0 + 0$$

i.e. $$\frac{d^n}{dx^n} [(1-x^2)\, y_2] = y_{n+2} (1-x^2) - 2nx\, y_{n+1} - n\,(n-1)\, y_n \qquad (4)$$

Let us consider the second term $\frac{d^n}{dx^n}[xy_1]$

Here
$$u_u = y_1 \qquad v = x$$
$$u_n = y_{n+1} \qquad v_1 = 1$$
$$u_{n-1} = y_n \qquad v_2 = 0$$

Thus
$$\frac{d^n}{dx^n} = [ny_1] = y_{n+1} \cdot x + ny_n \cdot 1 + 0$$
$$= xy_{n+1} + ny_n \tag{5}$$

From equation (3) (4) and (5) we have
$$(1-x^2)\, y_{n+2} - 2nx\, y_{n+1} - n(n-1)\, y_n - xy_{n+1} - ny_n + m^2\, y_n = 0$$

i.e. $$(1-x^2)\, y_{n+2} - (2n+1)\, xy_{n+1} - n^2\, y_n + ny_n - ny_n + m^2\, y_n = 0$$

i.e. $$(1-x^2)\, y_{n+2} - (2n+1)\, xy_{n+1} + (m^2 - n^2)\, y_n = 0$$

(Second part proved

Dividing throughout with $(1-x^2)$ we have
$$y_{n+2} - \frac{(2n+1)\, x\, y_{n+1}}{(1-x^2)} + \frac{(m^2-n^2)}{(1-x^2)}\, y_n = 0$$

Taking limit on both sides as $x \to 0$we have
$$\lim_{x\to 0} y_{n+2} - 0 + (m^2 - n^2) \lim_{x\to 0} y_n = 0$$

i.e. $$\lim_{x\to 0} y_{n+2} = -(m^2-n^2) \lim_{x\to 0} y_n\, x = 0$$

i.e. $$\lim_{x\to 0} \frac{y_{n+2}}{y_n} = -(m^2-n^2) = n^2 - m^2$$

i.e. $$\lim_{x\to 0} \frac{y_{n+2}}{y_n} = n^2 - m^2$$ *(Third part proved)*

Problem 38 If $y = x^n \log x$, prove that
$$y_n = \underline{|n}\left[\log x + 1 + \frac{1}{2} + \frac{1}{3} + \ldots + \frac{1}{n}\right]$$
[*I.F.S. 86, 82*]

Solution We have $y = x^n \log x$

Taking nth derivative we have
$$\frac{d^n}{dx^n}(y) = \frac{d^n}{dx^n}[x^n \log x]$$

i.e. $$y_n = \frac{d^{n-1}}{dx^{n-1}}\left[\frac{d}{ax}(x^n \log x)\right]$$

i.e. $$y_n = \frac{d^{n-1}}{dx^{n-1}}\left[\frac{d}{dx}(x^n)\log x + \frac{d}{dx}(\log x)(x^n)\right]$$

$$y_n = \frac{d^{n-1}}{dx^{n-1}}\left[nx^{n-1}\log x + \frac{x^n}{x}\right]$$

$$y_n = \frac{d^{n-1}}{dx^{n-1}}[nx^{n-1}\log x + x^{n-1}]$$

$$y_n = n\frac{a^{n-1}}{dx^{n-1}}(x^{n-1}\log x) + \frac{d^{n-1}}{dx^{n-1}}(x^{n-1}) \tag{1}$$

since $\frac{d^n}{dx^n}(x^n) = n!$

$\Rightarrow \frac{d^{n-1}}{dx^{n-1}}(x^{n-1}) = (n-1)!$

since $y = x^n \log x$

$\Rightarrow \frac{d^n}{dx^n}(y) = \frac{d^n}{dx^n}(x^n \log x)$

i.e. $$y_n = \frac{d^n}{dx^n}[x^n \log x]$$

Thus $$y_{n-1} = \frac{d^{n-1}}{dx^{n-1}}(x^{n-1}\log x)$$

Thus equation (1) reduces to

$$y^n = n\, y_{n-1}\,(n-1)! \tag{2}$$

Dividing both sides with $n!$ we have

$$\frac{y_n}{n!} = \frac{n\, y_{n-1}}{n!} + \frac{(n-1)}{n!}$$

$$\frac{y_n}{n!} = \frac{n\, y_{n-1}}{n\,(n-1)!} + \frac{(n-1)!}{n\,(n-1)!}$$

$$\frac{y_n}{n!} = \frac{y_{n-1}}{(n-1)!} + \frac{1}{n} \tag{3}$$

Substituting $(n-1)\,(n-2)\,\ldots\,2$ for n we have

$$\frac{y_{n-1}}{(n-1)!} = \frac{y_{n-3}}{(n-2)!} + \frac{1}{n-1} \tag{4}$$

$$\frac{y_{n-2}}{(n-2)!} = \frac{y_{n-3}}{(n-3)!} + \frac{1}{n-2} \tag{5}$$

$\ldots \qquad \ldots$

$\ldots \qquad \ldots$

$$\frac{y_2}{2!} = \frac{y_1}{1} + \frac{1}{2} \tag{6}$$

Adding all these equations we haxe

$$\frac{y_n}{n!} = \left[y_1 + \frac{1}{2} + \frac{1}{3} + \frac{1}{4} + \frac{1}{5} + \frac{1}{6} = \dots \frac{1}{n-2} + \frac{1}{n-1} + \frac{1}{n}\right]$$

$$y_n = n!\left[y_1 + \frac{1}{2} + \frac{1}{3} + \frac{1}{4} + \dots \frac{1}{n-1} + \frac{1}{n}\right] \qquad (7)$$

We have $y_1 = \frac{d}{dx}[x \log x] = \left[x\frac{1}{x} + \log x \cdot 1\right] = (1 + \log x)$

$$y_1 = 1 + \log x$$

Therefore $y_n = n!\left[1 + \log x + \frac{1}{2} + \frac{1}{3} \dots + \frac{1}{n-1} + \frac{1}{n}\right]$

$$y_n = n!\left[\log x + 1 + \frac{1}{2} + \frac{1}{3} + \dots + \frac{1}{n-1} + \frac{1}{n}\right] \quad \textit{(Proved)}$$

Problem 39 Show that

$$\frac{d^n}{dx^n}\left(\frac{\log x}{x}\right) = \frac{(-1)^n /n}{x^{n+1}}\left[\log x - 1 - \frac{1}{2} - \frac{1}{3} - \dots - \frac{1}{n}\right] \text{[\textit{IFS} 85]}$$

Solution Let $u = \frac{1}{x}$ $v = \log x$

$$u = \frac{1}{x} = x^{-1}$$

$$u_1 = (-1)x^{-2}$$

$$u_2 = (-1)(-2)\,x^{-3}$$

$$u_3 = (-1)(-2)(-3)\,x^{-4}$$

$$\dots \qquad \dots$$

$$u_n = (-1)(-2)(-3)\dots(-n)\,x^{-(n+1)}$$

i.e. $u_n = \frac{(-1)^n\, n!}{x^{n+1}}$

$$u_{n-1} = \frac{(-1)^{n-1}\,(n-1)\,!}{x^n}$$

$$v_1 = \frac{1}{x}$$

$$v_2 = -\frac{1}{x^2}$$

$$v_3 = \frac{(-1)(-2)}{x^3}$$

$$v_n = \frac{(-1)(-2)\dots(n-1)}{x^n}$$

$$v_n = \frac{(-1)^{n-1}\,(n-1)!}{x^n}$$

Hence by leibnitz theorem we have.

$$\frac{d^n}{dx^n}\left[\frac{\log x}{x}\right] = u_n\, v + {}^n c_1\, u_{n-1}\, v_1 + {}^n c_2\, u_{n-2}\, v_2 + \ldots + {}^n c_n\, uv_n$$

$$\frac{d^n}{dx^n}\left[\frac{\log x}{x}\right] = \frac{(-1)^n\, n!}{x^{n+1}} \log x + {}^n \frac{(-1)^{n-1}\,(n-1)!}{x^n}\, \frac{1}{x}$$

$$+ \frac{n\,(n-1}{1\cdot 2}\,(-1)^{n-2}\, \frac{(n-2)!}{x^{n-1}} \left(-\frac{1}{x^2}\right) + \ldots$$

$$\frac{d^n}{dx^n}\left[\frac{\log x}{x}\right] = \frac{(-1)^n\, n!}{x^{n+1}}\left[\log x - \frac{1}{1} - \frac{1}{2} - \frac{1}{3} \ldots \frac{1}{n}\right]$$

i.e. $$\frac{d^n}{dx^n}\left[\frac{\log x}{x}\right] = \frac{(-1)^n\, n!}{x^{n+1}}\left[\log x - 1 - \frac{1}{2} - \frac{1}{3} - \ldots - \frac{1}{n}\right]$$ *(Proved)*

Problem 40 If $p = \frac{d^n}{dx^n}\{(x^2-1)^n\}$, show that

$$\frac{d}{dx}\left[(1-x^2)\,\frac{dp}{dx}\right] + n\,(n+1)\,P = 0$$

Solution Let $y = (x^2-1)^n$ (1)

Then $$p = \frac{d^n y}{dx^n}$$

Differentiating equation (1) with respect to x we have

$$\frac{dy}{dx} = n\,(x^2-1)^{n-1}\,\frac{d}{dx}\,(x^2-1)$$

$$\frac{dy}{dx} = n\,(x^2-1)^{n-1}\,(2x-0)$$

i.e. $$y_1 = n\,(x^2-1)^{n-1}\,2x$$

Multiplying both sides with (x^2-1) we have

$$y_1\,(x^2-1) = 2nx\,(x^2-1)^n$$

i.e. $$(x^2-1)\frac{dy}{dx} = 2nxy$$ (2)

Now differentiating equation (2) $(n+1)$ number of times

$$(x^2-1)\,\frac{d^{n+2}\,y}{dx^{n+2}} + {}^{n+1}c_1\,\frac{d^{n+1}\,y}{dx^{n+1}}\,(2x) + {}^{n+1}c_2\,\frac{d^u\,y}{dx^n}\,(2)$$

$$= 2n\left[\frac{d^{n+1}\,y}{dx^{n+1}}\cdot x + {}^{n+1}c_1\,\frac{d^n\,y}{dx^n}\cdot 1\right]$$

i.e. $$(x^2-1)\frac{d^{n+2}\,y}{dx^{n+2}} + (n+1)\,2x\,\frac{d^{n+1}\,y}{dx^{n+1}} + \frac{(n+1)\,n}{2}\,\frac{d^n\,y}{dx^n}\cdot 2$$

$$= 2n\,\frac{d^{n+1}\,y}{dx^{n+1}}\,x + 2n\,(n+1)\,\frac{d^n\,y}{dx^n}$$

i.e. $(x^2-1)\frac{d^{n+2}y}{dx^{n+2}}+2x\frac{d^{n+1}y}{dx^{n+1}}+n^2\frac{d^n y}{dx^n}+n\frac{d^n y}{dx^n}-2n^2\frac{d^n y}{dx^n}$

$$-2n\frac{d^n y}{dx^n}=0$$

i.e. $$(x^2-1)\frac{d^{n+2}y}{dx^{n+2}}+2x\frac{d^{n+1}y}{dx^{n+1}}-n^2\frac{d^n y}{dx^n}-n\frac{d^n y}{dx^n}=0$$

i.e. $$(x^2-1)\frac{d^{n+2}y}{dx^{n+2}}+2x\frac{d^{n+1}y}{dx^{n+1}}-n(n+1)\frac{d^n y}{dx^n}=0$$

If we put $p=\frac{d^n y}{dx^n}$ then, $(x^2-1)\frac{d^2p}{dx^2}+2x\frac{dp}{dx}-n(n+1)p=0$

Then $$\frac{d}{dx}\left[(x^2-1)\frac{dp}{dx}\right]-n(n+1)p=0$$

$\Rightarrow$ $$\frac{d}{dx}\left[(1-x^2)\frac{dP}{dx}\right]+n(n+1)p=0 \text{ (Proved)}$$

Problem 41 If $y=\tan^{-1}x$, then prove that

$$(1+x^2)y_{n+1}+2nxy_n+n(n-1)y_{n-1}=0$$

Solution We have $y=\tan^{-1}x$

Differentiating with respect to x we have

$$\frac{dy}{dx}=\frac{1}{1+x^2}$$

$$y_1=\frac{1}{(1+x^2)}$$

i.e. $(1+x^2)y_1=1$

Differentiating with respect to x n times

$$\frac{d^n}{dx^n}[(1+x^2)y_1]=\frac{d^n}{dx^n}[1]$$

Here $u=y_1\quad v=1+x^2$

Then $u_n=y_{n+1}$ and $v=1+x^2$

$u_{n-1}=y_n \qquad v_1=2x$

$u_{n-2}=y_{n-1} \qquad v_2=2$

$u_{n-3}=y_{n-2} \qquad v_3=0$

then applying Leibnitz theorem we have

$$u_n v+{}^nc_1 u_{n-1}v_1+{}^nc_2 u_{n-2}v_2+0=0$$

$$y_{n+1}(1+x^2)+ny_n\cdot 2x+\frac{n(n-1)}{2}y_{n-1}2=0$$

$$(1+x^2)y_{n+1}+2nxy_n+n(n-1)y_{n-1}=0 \qquad \text{(Proved)}$$

Problem 42 If $y = a\cos(\log x) + b\sin(\log x)$ then prove that

$$x^2 y_{n+2} + (2n+1)xy_{n+1} + (n^2+1)y_n = 0$$

Solution We have $y = a\cos(\log x) + b\sin(\log x)$ (1)

Differentiating with respect to x we have

$$\frac{dy}{dx} = -a\sin(\log x)\frac{1}{x} + b\cos(\log x)\frac{1}{x}$$

$$xy_1 = -a\sin(\log x) + b\cos(\log x) \quad (2)$$

Again differentiating equation (2) with respect to x we have

$$xy_2 + y_1 = -a\cos(\log x)\frac{1}{x} - b\sin(\log x)\frac{1}{x}$$

i.e. $x^2 y_2 + xy_1 = -[a\cos(\log x) + b\sin(\log x)]$

i.e. $x^2 y_2 + xy_1 = -y$

i.e. $x^2 y_2 + xy_1 + y = 0$

Differentiating with respect to x n times we have

$$\frac{d^n}{dx^n}[x^2 y_2] + \frac{d^n}{dx^n}[xy_1] + \frac{d^n}{dx^n}[y] = 0$$

Applying Leibnitz theorem we have

$$y_{n+2}\,x^2 + ny_{n+1}\,2x + n\frac{(n-1)}{2}\cdot y_n\,2 - + y_{n+1}\,x + ny_n\cdot 1 + y_n = 0$$

i.e. $x^2 y_{n+2} + 2x^n y_{n+1} + n^2 y_n - ny_n + xy_{n+1} + ny_n + y_n = 0$

i.e. $x^2 x_{n+2} + (2n+1)xy_{n+1} + (n^2+1)y_n = 0$ (*Proved*)

Problem 43 If $y = x^{n-1}\log x$, prove that

$$y_n = \frac{\lfloor n-1}{x}$$

Solution $y = x^{n-1}(\log x)$

Differentiating both sides n times we have

$$\frac{d^n}{dx^n}(y) = \frac{d^n}{dx^n}[x^{n-1}(\log x)]$$

$$y_n = \frac{d^n}{dx^n}[x^{n-1}(\log x)]$$

Using Leibnitz theorem we have

$$v = x^{n-1} \qquad u = \log x$$

we can easily solve the problem

Problem 44 Find y_n if $y = \dfrac{1}{x^2 + a^2}$

Solution Here $$y = \frac{1}{x^2 + a^2} = \frac{1}{(x + ia)(x - ia)}$$

Using partial fraction we have

$$\frac{1}{(x + ia)(x - ia)} = \frac{A}{(x + ia)} + \frac{B}{(x - ia)} \quad (1)$$

i.e. $$\frac{1}{(x + ia)(x - ia)} = \frac{A(x - ia) + B(x + ia)}{(x + ia)(x - ia)}$$

i.e. $$A(x - ia) + B(x + ia) = 1$$

Now substituting $x = ia$ we have

$$B(ia + ia) = 1$$

$$2\,aiB = 1$$

i.e. $$B = \frac{1}{2ai}$$

Again substituting $x = -ia$ we have

$$A(-ia - ia) + B(-ia + ia) = 1$$

i.e. $$-2aiA = 1$$

i.e. $$A = -\frac{1}{2ai}$$

Putting the values of A and B in equation (1) we have

$$\frac{1}{(x + ia)(x - ia)} = -\frac{1}{2ai(x + ia)} + \frac{1}{2ai}\frac{1}{(x - ia)}$$

$$\frac{1}{(x + ia)(x - ia)} = \frac{1}{2ai}\left[\frac{1}{(x - ia)} - \frac{1}{(x + ia)}\right]$$

Thus $$y = \frac{1}{x^2 + a^2} = \frac{1}{2ai}\left[\frac{1}{(x - ia)} - \frac{1}{(x + ia)}\right]$$

Consider $$\frac{1}{(x - ia)} = (x - ia)^{-1}$$

Differentiating once with respect to x we have $-1\,(x - ia)^{-2}$

Differentiating twice we have $(-1)(-2)(x - ai)^{-3}$

Differentiating n times $(-1)(-2)\ldots n$ time $(x - ia)^{-(n+1)}$

i.e. nth derivative $$= \frac{(-1)^n \underline{|n}}{(x - ia)^{n+1}}$$

Similarly the nth derivative of

$$\frac{1}{(x+ia)} = \frac{(-1)^n |\underline{n}}{(x+ia)^{n+1}}$$

i.e.
$$y_n = \frac{1}{2ai}\left[\frac{(-1)^n |\underline{n}}{(x-ia)^{n+1}} - \frac{(-1)^n |\underline{n}}{(x+ia)^{n+1}}\right]$$

i.e.
$$y_n = \frac{(-1)^n |\underline{n}}{2ai}\left[\frac{1}{(x-ia)^{n+1}} - \frac{1}{(x+ia)^{n+1}}\right]$$

To simplify this we use De Moivre's theorem. For this we put

$$x = r\cos\theta$$
$$a = r\sin\theta$$

So that
$$r^2 = x^2 + a^2 \text{ and } \tan\theta = \frac{a}{x}$$

Hence
$$y_n = \frac{(-1)^n |\underline{n}}{2ai}\left[\frac{1}{\{r\cos\theta - ir\sin\theta\}^{n+1}} - \frac{1}{\{r\cos\theta + ir\sin\theta\}^{n+1}}\right]$$

i.e.
$$y_n = \frac{(-1)^n |\underline{n}}{2ai}\left[\frac{1}{r^{n+1}(\cos\theta - i\sin\theta)^{n+1}} - \frac{1}{r^{n+1}(\cos\theta + i\sin\theta)^{n+1}}\right]$$

i.e.
$$y^n = \frac{(-1)^n |\underline{n}}{2a^i\, r^{n+1}}\left[\frac{1}{e^{-I(n+1)\theta}} - \frac{1}{e^{i(n+1)\theta}}\right]$$

$$y_n = \frac{(-1)^n |\underline{n}}{2ai\, r^{n+1}}\left(e^{i(n+1)\theta} - e^{-i(n+1)\theta}\right)$$

$$y_n = \frac{(-1)^n |\underline{n}}{2ai\, r^{n+2}}\,[2i\sin(n+1)\,\theta]$$

$$y_n = \frac{(-1)^n |\underline{n}}{2ai\,(x^2+a^2)^{(n+1)/2}}\,2i\sin(n+1)\,\theta$$

i.e.
$$y_n = \frac{(-1)^n |\underline{n}\,\sin(n+1)\,\theta}{a\,(x^2+a^2)^{(n+1)/2}} \qquad \textbf{Ans.}$$

We can also write equation (2) in other form

since $r\sin\theta = a$

$$\Rightarrow r = \frac{a}{\sin\theta}$$

$$\Rightarrow r^{n+1} = \frac{a^{n+1}}{\sin^{n+1}\theta}$$

i.e.
$$y_n = \frac{(-1)^n |\underline{n}}{2^{ai}/a^{n+1}/\sin^{n+1}\theta}\,2i\sin(n+1)\,\theta$$

i.e. $$y_n = \frac{(-1)^n \lfloor n}{a^{n+2}} \sin^{n+1}\theta \sin(n+1)\theta$$

i.e. If $$y = \frac{1}{a^2 + x^2}$$

then $$y_n = \frac{(-1)^n \lfloor n}{a^{n+2}} \sin^{n+1}\theta \sin(n+1)\theta \qquad \text{[Remember]}$$

where $\tan\theta = \frac{a}{x}$ i.e. $\theta = \tan^{-1}\left(\frac{a}{x}\right)$

Problem 45 If $y = \tan^{-1} x$ find y_n.

Solution Here $y = \tan^{-1} x$

$$\therefore \quad y_1 = \frac{1}{1 + x^2} \tag{1}$$

Differentiating equation (1) to $n-1$ times we have

$$y_n = \frac{(-1^{\,n-1} \lfloor n-1}{a^{n+1}} \sin^n\theta \sin n\theta$$

where $a = 1 = r\sin\theta$ and $x = r\cos\theta$

$$\tan\theta = \frac{1}{x} \quad \text{i.e.} \quad \theta = \tan^{-1}\frac{1}{x} = \cot^{-1} x$$

i.e. $$y_n = \frac{(-1)^{n-1} \lfloor n-1}{1)^{n+1}} \sin^n\theta \sin n\theta$$

$$y_n = (-1)^{n-1} \lfloor n-1 \ \sin^n\theta \sin n\theta \quad \textbf{Ans.}$$

Problem 46 If $y = \tan^{-1}\frac{2x}{1-x^2}$ find y_n

Solution $$y = \tan^{-1}\frac{2x}{1-x^2} = 2\tan^{-1} x$$

i,e. $$y = 2\tan^{-1} x$$

Differentiating both sides with respect to x we have

$$y_1 = \frac{2}{1+x^2}$$

$$y_1 = 2\frac{1}{1 + x^2}$$

Here $a = 1$

So differentiating $(n-1)$ times we have

$$y_n = 2\,\frac{(-1)^{n-1}\,\underline{|n-1}\,\sin^n\theta\,\sin n\theta}{(1)^{n+1}}$$

i.e.
$$y_n = \frac{2\,(-1)^{n-1}\,\underline{|n-1}\,\sin^n\theta\,\sin n\theta}{(1)^{n+1}}$$

i.e.
$$y_n = 2\,(-1)^{n-1}\,\underline{|n-1}\,\sin^n\theta\,\sin n\theta \qquad \textbf{Ans.}$$

where
$$\tan\theta = \frac{1}{x}$$

$$\theta = \tan^{-1}\frac{1}{x} \qquad \text{i.e.} \qquad \theta = \cot^{-1} x$$

Problem 47 If $y = \dfrac{x}{x^2 + a^2}$, find y_n

Solution
$$y = \frac{x}{(x^2 + a^2)}$$

$$y = \frac{x}{x^2 - a^2\,i^2}$$

$$y = \frac{x}{(x+ai)\,(x-ia)}$$

Using partial fraction we have

$$\frac{x}{(x+ai)\,(x-ia)} = \frac{A}{(x+ai)} + \frac{B}{(x-ai)}$$

where A and B are constant to be determined

$$\frac{x}{(x+ai)\,(x-ai)} = \frac{A\,(x-ai) + B\,(x+ai)}{(x+ai)\,(x-ai)}$$

i.e. $A\,(x-ai) + B\,(x+ai) = x$

Substituting $x = ai$ on both sides we have

$$A\,(ai-ai) + B\,(ai+ai) = ai$$

i.e.
$$2ai\,B = ai$$

$$B = \tfrac{1}{2}$$

Again substituting $x = -ai$ we have

$$A\,(-ai-ai) + B\,(-ai+ai) = -ai$$

$$A = \tfrac{1}{3}$$

Thus $$\frac{x}{(x+ai)(x-ia)} = \frac{1}{2(x+ai)} + \frac{1}{2(x-ai)}$$

i.e. $$\frac{x}{(x+ai)(x-ai)} = \frac{1}{2}\left[\frac{1}{(x+ai)} + \frac{1}{(x-ai)}\right]$$

i.e, $$y = \frac{1}{2}\left[\frac{1}{(x+ai)} + \frac{1}{(x-ai)}\right]$$

Consider the first term *i.e.* $\frac{1}{x+ai}$

Differentiating once with respect to x we have $(-1)(x+ai)^{-2}$

Differentiating twice we have $(-1)(-2)(x+ai)^{-3}$

Differentiating n times we have

$$(-1)(-2)(-3)\ldots(-n)(x+ai)^{-(n+1)}$$

i.e. $$\frac{(-1)^n \underline{/n}}{(x+ai)^{n+1}}$$

Similarly the n th derivative of $\frac{1}{(x-ai)}$ is given by $\frac{(-1)^n \underline{/n}}{(x-ai)^{n+1}}$

Thus $$y_n = \frac{1}{2}\left[\frac{(-1)^n \underline{/n}}{(x+ai)^{n+1}} + \frac{(-1)^n \underline{/n}}{(x-ai)^{n+1}}\right]$$

$$y_n = \frac{(-1)^n \underline{/n}}{2}\left[\frac{1}{(x+ai)^{n+1}} + \frac{1}{(x-ai)^{n+1}}\right]$$

To solve this we have to put

$$x = r\cos\theta \quad a = r \text{ in } \theta$$

$$x^2 + a^2 = r^2 \quad \text{and} \quad \tan\theta = \frac{a}{x}$$

$$y_n = \frac{(-)^n \underline{/n}}{2}\left[\frac{1}{r^{n+1}e^{\,i(n+1)\theta}} + \frac{1}{r^{n+1}\,e^{-i(n+)\theta}}\right]$$

Therefore $$y_n = \frac{(-1)^n \underline{/n}}{2r^{n+1}}\left[e^{-(ni+1)\theta} + e^{i(n+1)\theta}\right]$$

$$y_n = \frac{(-)^n \underline{/n}}{2r^{n+1}}\left[2\cos(n+1)\theta\right]$$

i.e $$y_n = \frac{(-1)^n \underline{/n}\cos(n+1)\theta}{r^{n+1}}$$

since $$a = r\sin\theta$$

$$\Rightarrow r = \frac{a}{\sin\theta}$$

$$\Rightarrow r^{n+1} = \frac{a^{n+1}}{\sin^{n+1}\theta}$$

i.e. $$y_n = \frac{(-1)^n \underline{/n} \cos (n+1)\theta}{a^{n+1}/\sin^{n+1}\theta}$$

$$y_n = \frac{(-1)^n \underline{/n}}{a^{n+1}} \sin^{(n+1)}\theta \cos (n+1)\theta$$

where $\tan \theta = \frac{a}{x}$

$$\Rightarrow \theta = \tan^{-1}\left(\frac{a}{x}\right) \qquad \textbf{(Remember)}$$

$$\theta = \cot^{-1}\left(\frac{x}{a}\right) \qquad \textbf{Ans.}$$

Problem 48 If $p^2 = a^2 \cos^2 \theta + b^2 \sin^2 \theta$, prove that

$$p + \frac{d^2 p}{d\theta^2} = \frac{a^2 b^2}{p^3} \qquad [I.E.S. 92]$$

Solution $$P^2 = a^2 \cos^2 \theta + b^2 \sin^2 \theta$$

Differentiating both sides with respect to θ we have

$$2p \frac{dp}{d\theta} = a^2\, 2 \cos \theta\, (-\sin \theta) + b^2\, 2 \sin \theta\, (\cos \theta)$$

$$2P \frac{dp}{d\theta} = -a^2 \sin 2\theta + b^2 \sin 2\theta$$

i.e. $$2p \frac{dp}{d\theta} = (b^2 - a^2) \sin 2\theta$$

$$p \frac{dp}{d\theta} = \left(\frac{b^2 - a^2}{2}\right) \sin 2\theta \qquad (1)$$

Differentiating equation (1) with respect to θ we nave

$$p \frac{d^2 p}{d\theta^2} + \frac{dp}{d\theta} \cdot \frac{dp}{d\theta} = 2\left(\frac{b^2 - a^2}{2}\right) \cos 2\theta$$

i.e. $$P \frac{d^2 p}{d\theta^2} + \left(\frac{dp}{d\theta}\right)^2 = (b^2 - a^2) \cos 2\theta \qquad (2)$$

Multiplying equation (2) with p^2 we have

$$p^3 \left(\frac{d^2 p}{d\theta^2}\right) + P^2 \left(\frac{dp}{d\theta}\right)^2 = p^2 (b^2 - a^2) \cos 2\theta$$

$$P^3 \left(\frac{d^2 p}{d\theta^2}\right) + \frac{(b^2 - a^2)^2 \sin^2 2\theta}{4} = p^2 (b^2 - a^2) \cos 2\theta$$

$$p^3 \left(\frac{d^2 p}{d\theta^2}\right) = p^2 (b^2 - a^2) \cos 2\theta - \frac{(b^2 - a^2)^2}{4} \sin^2 2\theta$$

$$p^3 \left(\frac{d^2 p}{d\theta^2}\right) = p^2 (b^2 - a^2)(\cos^2 \theta - \sin^9 \theta) - \left(\frac{b^2 - a^2}{4}\right)^2 4\sin^2 \theta \cos^2 \theta$$

Adding both sides p^4 we have

$$p^4 + P^3\left(\frac{d^2 p}{d\theta^2}\right) = p^4 + p^2 (b^2-a^2)(\cos^2\theta - \sin^2\theta)$$
$$-(b^2-a^2)^2 \sin^2\theta \cos{}^2\theta$$

$$p^4 + P^3\left(\frac{d^2 p}{d\theta^2}\right) = p^2 [p^2 + (b^2-a^2)(\cos^2\theta - \sin^2\theta)]$$
$$-(b^2-a^2)^2 \sin^2\theta \cos^2\theta$$

$$p^4 + P^3\left(\frac{d^2 p}{d\theta^2}\right) = p^2 [p^2 + (b^2-a^2)(1-2\sin^2\theta)]$$
$$-(b^2-a^2)^2 \sin^2\theta (1-\sin^2\theta)$$

$$p^4 + p^3\left(\frac{d^2 p}{d\theta^2}\right) = p^2 [p^2 + (b^2-a^2) - 2(b^2-a^2)\sin{}^2\theta$$
$$-(b^2-a^2)^2 \sin^2\theta + (b^2-a^2)^2 \sin^4\theta] \quad (3)$$

Now we have $\quad p^2 = a^2\cos^2\theta + b^2 \sin^2\theta$

$$p^2 = a^2(1-\sin^2\theta) + b^2\sin^2\theta$$
$$p^2 = a^2 - a^2\sin^2\theta + b^2\sin^2\theta$$
$$p^2 = a^2 + (b^2-a^2)\sin^2\theta$$
$$p^2 - a^2 = (b^2-a^2)\sin^2\theta \quad (4)$$

With the help of equation (4) equation (3) reduces to

$$p^4 + p^3\left(\frac{d^2 p}{d\theta^2}\right) = p^2 [p^2 + (b^2-a^2) - 2(p^2-a^2)]$$
$$-(b^2-a^2)(p^2-a^2) + (p^2-a^2)]$$

i.e. $\quad p^4 + p^3\left(\frac{d^2 p}{d\theta^2}\right) = [p^2 + b^2 - a^2 - 2p^2 + 2a^2]$

$$(-p^2-a^2)\{(b^2-a^2)-(p^2-a^2)\}$$

i.e. $\quad p^4 + p^3\left(\frac{d^2 p}{d\theta^2}\right) = p^2(-p^2 + b^2 + a^2) - (p^2-a^2)(b^2-a^2-p^2+a^2)$

i.e. $\quad p^4 + p^3\left(\frac{d^2 p}{d\theta^2}\right) = p^2(b^2-p^2-a^2) - (p^2-a^2)(b^2-p^2)$

$$= p^2b^2 - p^4 + a^2p^2 - p^2b^2 + p^4 + a^2b^2 - a^2p^2$$

i.e. $\quad p^4 + p^3\left(\frac{d^2 p}{d\theta^2}\right) = a^2b^2$

i.e. $\quad p^3\left[p + \frac{d^2 p}{d\theta^2}\right] = a^2 b^2$

i.e. $\quad p + \frac{d^2 p}{d\theta^2} = \frac{a^2 b^2}{p^3}$ *(Provea*

Problem 49 If $y^{-1/m} + y^{1/m} = 2x$ prove that

$$(x^2-1)\,y_2 + xy_1 - m^2\,y = 0$$

Solution Let us consider that

$$y^{1/m} = u$$

$$\Rightarrow \quad \frac{1}{y^{1\cdot/m}} = \frac{1}{u}$$

$$\Rightarrow \quad y^{-1/m} = \frac{1}{u}$$

Therefore we have

$$u + \frac{1}{u} = 2x$$

$$\Rightarrow u^2 + 1 = 2xu$$

$$\Rightarrow u^2 - 2xu + 1 = 0$$

$$\Rightarrow u = \frac{2x \pm \sqrt{4x^2 - 4\cdot 1\cdot 1}}{2\cdot 1}$$

$$\Rightarrow u = \frac{2(x \pm \sqrt{x^2-1}}{2}$$

i.e. $$u = x \pm \sqrt{x^2-1}$$

Thus $$y^{1/m} = x \pm \sqrt{x^2-1}$$

$$\Rightarrow \quad y = [x \pm \sqrt{x^{\cdot}-1}]^m \qquad (1)$$

Now differentiating equation (1) with respect to x we have

i.e. $$y_1 = m\,[x \pm \sqrt{x^2-1}]^{m-1}\left[1 \pm \frac{2x}{2\sqrt{x^2-1}}\right]$$

i.e. $$y_1 = m\,[x \pm \sqrt{x^2-1}]^{m-1}\,\frac{[\sqrt{x^2-1} \pm x]}{\sqrt{x^2-1}}$$

i.e. $$y_1\sqrt{x^2-1} = m\,[x \pm \sqrt{x^2-1}]^{m-1}\,[\sqrt{x^2} \pm x]$$

i.e. $$y_1\sqrt{x^2-1} = m\,[x \pm \sqrt{x^2-1}]^{m-1}\,(\pm)\,(x \pm \sqrt{x^2-1}]$$

$$y_1\sqrt{x^2-1} = (\pm)\,m\,[x \pm \sqrt{x^2-1}]^m$$

i.e. $$y_1\sqrt{x_2-1} = \pm\,my$$

Squaring both sides we have

$$y_1^2\,(x^2-1) = m^2\,y^2$$

Differentiating both sides with respect to x we have

$$2y_1\, y_2\, (x^2-1) + y_1^2\, (2x-0) = m^2\, 2yy_1$$

$$2y_1\, y_2\, (x^2-1) + 2xy_1^2 = 2y_1\, m^2\, y$$

$$2y_1\, [x^2-1)\, y_2 + xy_1] = 2y_1\, m^2\, y$$

i.e. $$(x^2-1)\, y_2 + xy_1 = m^2\, y$$

$$\Rightarrow (x^2-1)\, y_1 + xy_1 - m^2\, y = 0$$ (*Proved*)

Problem 50 **If** $\cos^{-1}\left(\frac{y}{b}\right) = \log\left(\frac{x}{n}\right)^n$ prove that

$$x^2\, y_{n+2} + (2n+1)\, xy_{n+1} + 2n^2\, y_n = 0$$

Solution Here use the formula

$$\frac{d}{dx}[\cos^{-1} x] = -\frac{1}{\sqrt{1-x^2}}$$

we have $$\cos^{-1}\left(\frac{y}{b}\right) = \log\left(\frac{x}{n}\right)^n$$

ie $$\cos^{-1}\left(\frac{y}{b}\right) = n \log\left(\frac{x}{n}\right)$$

Differentiating both sides with respect to x we have

$$-\frac{1}{\sqrt{-y^2/b^2}} \cdot \frac{d}{dx}\left(\frac{y}{b}\right) = n\, \frac{1}{x/n} \cdot \frac{d}{dx}\left(\frac{x}{n}\right)$$

i.e. $$-\frac{y_1}{b\sqrt{b^2-y^2}} = \frac{n^2}{x} \cdot \frac{1}{n}$$

i.e. $$-\frac{y_1}{\sqrt{b^2-y^2}} = \frac{n}{x}$$

i.e. $$n\sqrt{b^2-y^2} = -y_1\, x$$

Squaring both sides we have

$$x^2\, y_1^2 = n^2\, (b^2-y^2)$$

$$x^2\, y_1^2 = n^2\, (b^2-y^2)$$

Differentiating this equation with respect to x we have

$$x^2\, 2y_1\, y_2 + y_1^2\, 2x = n^2\, (0-2yy_1)$$

i.e. $$2y_1\, [x^2\, y_2 + xy_1] = -2y_1\, n^2\, y$$

i.e. $$x^2\, y_2 + xy_1 + n^2\, y = 0 \qquad (1)$$

Differentiating equation (1) with respect to x n times we have

$$\frac{d^n}{dx^n}[x^2\, y_2] + \frac{d^n}{dx^n}[xy_1] + \frac{d^n}{dx^n}(n^2\, y) = 0$$

Applying Leibnitz theorem we have

$$x^2\, y_{n+2} + ny_{n+1} \cdot 2x + \frac{n\,(n-1)}{21} y_n \cdot 2\, 0 + xy_{n+1} + n\, y_n \cdot 1 + 0 + n^2\, y_n = 0$$

i.e. $$x^2\, y_{n+2} + 2nx\, y_{n+1} + n\,(n-1)\, y_n + xy_{n+1} + ny_n + n^2\, y_n = 0$$

i.e. $$x^2\, y_{n+2} + (2n+1)\, xy_{n+1} - ny_n + ny_n + n^2\, y_n = 0$$

i.e. $$x^2\, y_{n+2} + (2n+1]\, xy_{n+1} + n^2\, y_n = 0$$ (*Proved*)

11

Envelope

Let us consider the equation

$$x \cos \alpha + y \sin \alpha = a \tag{1}$$

This represents a straight line by giving different values to a, we shall obtain the equations of different straight lines but all these different straight lines have one charteristic feature common to each of them viz, each straight line is at the same distance a from the origin. On account of this property these straight lines are said to constitute a family and α, which is constant for one lines but different for different lines, and whose different values give different members of the family, is called the parameter of the family. If should be noted that the position of the line varies with a.

As we have a family of straight lines, we have a family of curves thus the equation $\quad (x-a)^2 + y^2 = r^2$

represents a family of circles for different values of a, all the individual members of the family having the common characteristic viz, they are of equal radii 'r' and their centres lie on x-axis. Here α is the parameter.

Def^n of Envelop

If each of the members of the family of curves

$$C \equiv F(x, y, \alpha) = 0 \text{ touches}$$

a fixed curve E, then E is called the envelop of the family of curves C. The curve E also at each point, is touched by some member of the family C.

Envelop of straight lines

Remember The equation of the envelop of the family of straight lines

$F(x, y, \alpha) = y - f(\alpha) \cdot x - \phi(d) = 0$ (α being parameter) is the eliminate

of $F = 0$ and $\quad \dfrac{\partial F}{\partial \alpha} = 0$.

Problem 1 Find the envelop of the straight line

$$y = mx + \frac{a}{m}$$

m being the variable parameter ($m \neq 0$)

Here $$mx + \frac{a}{m} - y = 0$$

Multiplying both sides by $-$ve sign

$$y - mx = \frac{a}{m} = 0 \tag{1}$$

Which is of the form

$$y - f(m)x - \phi(m) = 0$$

Where m is the parameter

Then equation of the envelop is gieven by eliminating m from

$$F = 0 \text{ i.e. (1) and from } \frac{\partial F}{\partial m} = 0$$

$$\frac{\partial F}{\partial m} = \frac{\partial}{\partial m}\{y - mx - \frac{a}{m} = 0$$

$$\frac{\partial F}{\partial m} = -x + \frac{a}{m^2} = 0$$

i.e. $$\frac{a}{m^2} - x = 0$$

$$\frac{a}{m^2} = x$$

$$\Rightarrow m^2 = \frac{a}{x}$$

$$\Rightarrow m = \pm\sqrt{\frac{a}{x}}$$

Putting value of m in equation (1) we have

$$y - mx - \frac{a}{m} = 0$$

i.e. $$y - x\left(\pm\sqrt{\frac{a}{x}}\right) - \frac{a}{\pm\sqrt{a/x}}$$

i.e. $$y = \pm(\sqrt{ax} + \sqrt{ax})$$

$$y = \pm\, 2\sqrt{ax}$$

Squaring both sides we have

$$y^2 = 4ax$$

i.e. $y^2 = 4ax$ i.e. parabola) is the required envelop of the straight line $y = mx + \frac{a}{m}$ m being a parameter.

Problem 2 Find the envelop of the straight lines

$$\frac{x}{a} + \frac{y}{b} = 1$$

Where a and b are variable parameters, connected by the relation $a + b = c$, c being a non zero constant

Solution Differentiating the equation of the line and the given relation with respect to a we get

$$-\frac{x}{a^2} - \frac{y}{b^2}\frac{db}{da} = 0 \tag{1}$$

$$1 + \frac{db}{da} = 0 \tag{2}$$

$$\frac{db}{da} = 1 \tag{3}$$

Putting the value of $\frac{db}{da}$ from (3) in (1) we have

$$-\frac{x}{a^2} - \frac{y}{b^2}(-1) = 0$$

$$-\frac{x}{a^2} + \frac{y}{b^2} = 0$$

$$\Rightarrow \qquad \frac{y}{b^2} = \frac{x}{a^2}$$

$$\Rightarrow \qquad \frac{a^2}{x} = \frac{b^2}{y}$$

$$\Rightarrow \qquad \frac{a}{\sqrt{x}} = \frac{b}{\sqrt{y}}$$

$$\Rightarrow \qquad \frac{a}{\sqrt{x}} + \frac{b}{\sqrt{y}} = \frac{a+b}{\sqrt{x}+\sqrt{y}}$$

$$\Rightarrow \qquad \frac{a}{\sqrt{x}} + \frac{b}{\sqrt{y}} = \frac{c}{\sqrt{x}+\sqrt{y}}$$

$$\Rightarrow \qquad a = \frac{c\sqrt{x}}{\sqrt{x}+\sqrt{y}} \qquad b = \frac{c\sqrt{y}}{\sqrt{x}+\sqrt{y}}$$

Substituting the values of a and b in equation of the line we have

$$\frac{x}{\sqrt{x}/\sqrt{x}+\sqrt{y}} + \frac{y}{c\sqrt{y}/\sqrt{x}+\sqrt{y}} = 1$$

$$\frac{x(\sqrt{x}+\sqrt{y})}{c\sqrt{x}} + \frac{(\sqrt{x}+\sqrt{y})y}{c\sqrt{y}} = 1$$

i.e. $$\sqrt{x}(\sqrt{x}+\sqrt{y})+(\sqrt{x}+\sqrt{y})\sqrt{y}=c$$

$$\Rightarrow \quad x+y+2\sqrt{x}\sqrt{y}=c$$

i.e. $$(\sqrt{x}+\sqrt{y})^2=c$$

i.e. $$\sqrt{x}+\sqrt{y}=\sqrt{c} \tag{4}$$

Equation (4) is the required envelop of the straight line

$$\frac{x}{a}+\frac{y}{b}=1 \quad \textbf{Ans.}$$

Problem 3 Find the envelop of the family of straight lines

$$A\alpha^2+B\alpha+C=0$$

where α is the variable parameter, and A, B, C are linear functions of x, y.

Solution We have $A\alpha^2+B\alpha+C=0$

Differentiating with respect to α we have

$$2A\alpha+B=0$$

$$\alpha=-\frac{B}{2A}$$

Substituting this value in

$$A\alpha^2+B\alpha+C=0 \text{ we get}$$

$$A\left(-\frac{B}{2A}\right)^2+B\left(-\frac{B}{2A}\right)+C=0$$

$$A\frac{B^2}{4A^2}-\frac{B^2}{2A}+C=0$$

$$\frac{B^2}{4A}-\frac{B^2}{2A}+C=0$$

$$-\frac{B^2}{4A}+C=0$$

$$\frac{B^2}{4A}=C$$

$$\Rightarrow \quad B^2=4AC$$

Thus the envelop of the family of straight lines $A\alpha^2+B\alpha+C=0$ is the curve $B^2=4AC$.

Note. When thc parameter ocurs is a quadratic in any equation

The above result is sometimes used in determining the envelope.

Problem 4 Find the envelop of the family of straight lines given by

$$y = mx + \sqrt{a^2 m^2 + b^2}, \text{ parameter } m.$$

Solution $$y = mx + \sqrt{a^2 m^2 + b^2}$$

$$\Rightarrow \quad y - mx = \sqrt{a^2 m^2 + t^2}$$

Squaring both sides we have

$$(y - mx)^2 = a^2 m^2 + b^2$$

$$\Rightarrow y^2 - 2mxy + m^2x^2 = a^2 m^2 + b^2$$

$$\Rightarrow a^2 m^2 + b^2 + 2mxy - m^2 x^2 - y^2 = 0$$

$$\Rightarrow m^2 (a^2 - x^2) + m(2xy) + (b^2 - y^2) = 0 \qquad (2)$$

This is a quadratic in m *parameter*

$$A = a^2 - x^2$$

$$B = 2xy$$

$$C = (b^2 - y^2)$$

Then the envelop of (1) is given by the relation

$$B^2 = 4AC$$

i.e. $$4x^2 y^2 = 4(a^2 - x^2)(x^2 - y^2)$$

i.e. $$x^2 y^2 = a^2 b^2 - a^2 y^2 - b^2 x^2 + x^2 y^2$$

i.e. $a^2 y^2 + b^2x^2 = a^2 b^2$

Dividing both sides with $a^2 b^2$ we have

$$\frac{a^2 y^2 + b^2 x^2}{a^2 b^2} = \frac{a^2 b^2}{a^2 b^2}$$

$$\frac{y^2}{b^2} + \frac{x^2}{a^2} = 1$$

Thus $\dfrac{x^2}{a^2} + \dfrac{y^2}{b^2} = 1$ is the rcquired envelop of the family of straight line

$$y = mx + \sqrt{a^2 m^2 + b^2}$$

Problem 5 Find the cnvelop of the family of straight lines

$$x \cos \alpha + y \sin x = a \cos \alpha \sin \alpha \quad \text{parameter } \alpha,$$

Solution The family of straight lines

$$x \cos \alpha + y \sin \alpha = a \cos \alpha \sin \alpha$$

Dividing both sides with sin α cos α we have

$$\frac{x \cos \alpha}{\sin \alpha \cos \alpha} + \frac{y \sin \alpha}{\cos \alpha \sin \alpha} = a$$

$$\frac{x}{\sin \alpha} + \frac{y}{\cos \alpha} = a$$

$$x \operatorname{cosec} \alpha + \sec \alpha y = a \qquad \text{(A)}$$

Differentiating this equation with respect to α we have

$$-x (\operatorname{cosec} \alpha \cot \alpha) + (\sec \alpha \tan \alpha) y = 0$$

$$-\frac{x}{\sin \alpha} \times \frac{\cos \alpha}{\sin \alpha} + y \frac{1}{\cos \alpha} \cdot \frac{\sin \alpha}{\cos \alpha} = 0$$

$$y \frac{\sin \alpha}{\cos^2 \alpha} = x \frac{\cos \alpha}{\sin^2 \alpha}$$

$$\frac{\sin^3 \alpha}{\cos^3 \alpha} = \frac{x}{y}$$

i.e. $$\tan^3 \alpha = \frac{x}{y}$$

$$\Rightarrow \quad \tan \alpha = \left(\frac{x}{y}\right)^{1/3}$$

$$\Rightarrow \quad \tan^2 \alpha = \left(\frac{x}{y}\right)^{2/3}$$

$$\Rightarrow \quad 1 + \tan^2 \alpha = + \frac{x^{2/3}}{y^{2/3}}$$

$$\Rightarrow \quad 1 + \tan^2 \alpha = \frac{x^{2/3} + y^{2/3}}{y^{2/3}}$$

$$\Rightarrow \quad \sec^2 \alpha = \frac{x^{2/3} + y^{2/3}}{y^{2/3}}$$

$$\Rightarrow \quad \sec \alpha = \frac{\sqrt{x^{2/3} + y^{2/3}}}{y^{1/3}} \qquad (1)$$

Again $$\tan \alpha = \left(\frac{x}{y}\right)^{1/3}$$

$$\Rightarrow \quad \cot \alpha = \left(\frac{y}{x}\right)^{1/3}$$

$$\Rightarrow \quad \cot^2 \alpha = \left(\frac{y}{x}\right)^{2/3}$$

$$\Rightarrow \quad 1 + \cot^2 \alpha = 1 + \left(\frac{y}{x}\right)^{2/3}$$

$$\Rightarrow \qquad \operatorname{cosec}^2 \alpha = \frac{x^{2/3} + y^{2/3}}{x^{2/3}}$$

$$\Rightarrow \qquad \operatorname{cosec} \alpha = \frac{\sqrt{x^{2/3} + y^{2/3}}}{x^{1/3}}$$

Putting the value of sec α and cosec α inequation (A) we have

$$x \frac{\sqrt{x^{2/3} + y^{2/3}}}{x^{1/3}} + y \frac{\sqrt{x^{2/3} + y^{2/3}}}{y^{1/3}} = a$$

$$x^{2/3} \sqrt{x^{2/3} + y^{2/3}} + y^{2/3} \sqrt{x^{2/3} + y^{2/3}} = a$$

$$\sqrt{x^{2/3}+y^{2/3}}\,(x^{2/3} + {}^{2/3}) = a$$

$$\Rightarrow \qquad (x^{2/3} + y^{2/3})^{3/2} = a$$

$$\Rightarrow \qquad x^{2/3} + y^{2/3} = a^{2/3} \tag{2}$$

Equation (2) is the required envelop of the family of lines

$$x \cos \alpha + y \sin \alpha = a \sin \alpha \cos \alpha.$$

Problem 6 Find the envelopes of the straigt line

$$\frac{x}{a} + \frac{y}{b} = 1$$

where the parameters a and b are connected by the relation

(i) $a^2 + b^2 = c^2$ (ii) $ab = c^2$, being a constant.

Solution We have the equation of the family of straight lines

$$\frac{x}{a} + \frac{y}{b} = 1 \tag{A}$$

Differentiating with respect to a we have

$$-\frac{x}{a^2} - \frac{y}{b^2} \cdot \frac{db}{da} = 0 \tag{1}$$

We have given the condition

$$a^2 + b^2 = c^2 \tag{2}$$

Differentiating equation (2) with respect to a we have

$$2a + 2b \frac{db}{da} = 0$$

$$\Rightarrow \qquad 2b \frac{db}{da} = -2a$$

$$\Rightarrow \qquad \frac{db}{da} = -\frac{a}{b}. \tag{3}$$

Putting the value of $\frac{db}{da}$ from equation (3) in (1) we have

$$-\frac{x}{a^2}-\frac{y}{b^2}\left(-\frac{a}{b}\right)=0$$

$$-\frac{x}{a^2}+\frac{ay}{b^3}=0$$

$$\frac{ay}{b^3}=\frac{x}{a^2}$$

$$\frac{x}{a^3}=\frac{y}{b^3}$$

$$\Rightarrow \quad \frac{x^{1/3}}{a}=\frac{y^{1/3}}{b}$$

$$\Rightarrow \quad \frac{(x^{1/3})^2}{a^2}=\frac{(y^{1/3})^2}{b^2}$$

$$\Rightarrow \quad \frac{x^{2/3}}{a^2}=\frac{y^{2/3}}{b^2}$$

$$\Rightarrow \quad \frac{a^2}{x^{2/3}}=\frac{b^2}{y^{2/3}}=\frac{a^2+b^2}{x^{2/3}+y^{2/3}}$$

$$\Rightarrow \quad \frac{a^2}{x^{2/3}}=\frac{b^2}{y^{7/3}}=\frac{c^2}{x^{2/3}+y^{2/3}}$$

$$\Rightarrow \quad \frac{a^2}{x^{2/3}}=\frac{c^2}{x^{2/3}+y^{2/3}}$$

$$\Rightarrow \quad \frac{a}{x^{1/3}}=\frac{c}{\sqrt{x^{2/3}+y^{2/3}}}$$

$$\Rightarrow \quad a=\frac{x^{1/3}c}{\sqrt{x^{2/3}+y^{2/3}}}$$

Similarly $$b=\frac{y^{1/3}c}{\sqrt{x^{2/3}+y^{2/3}}}$$

Putting the values of *a* and *b* in equation (A) we have

$$\frac{x}{\frac{x^{1/3}c/}{\sqrt{x^{2/3}+y^{2/3}}}}+\frac{y}{\frac{y^{1/3}c}{\sqrt{x^{2/3}+y^{2/3}}}}=1$$

$$\frac{x^{2/3}(\sqrt{x^{2/3}+y^{2/3}})}{c}+\frac{y^{2/3}\sqrt{x^{2/3}+y^{2/3}}}{c}=1$$

i.e. $$\sqrt{x^{2/3}+y^{2/3}}\,(x^{2/3}+y^{2/3})=c$$

$$\Rightarrow \quad (x^{2/3}+y^{2/3})^{3/2}=c$$

i.e. $$x^{2/3}+y^{2/3}=c^{2/3}$$

which is the required envelop of the given family of straight lines

Another method

Since
$$ab = c^2$$
$$\Rightarrow \quad b = \frac{c^2}{a}$$

Putting the value of b In equation $\frac{x}{a} + \frac{y}{b} = 1$ we have

$$\frac{x}{a} + \frac{y}{c^2/a} = 1$$
$$\frac{x}{a} + \frac{ay}{c^2} = 1$$
$$\frac{c^2 x + a^2 y}{ac^2} = 1$$

i e.
$$a^2 y + c^2 x - ac^2 = 0$$
$$\Rightarrow \quad \frac{ya^2}{A} - \frac{c^2 a}{B} + \frac{c^2 x}{C} = 0$$

This is quadratic in the parameter a so we have
$$B^2 = 4AC$$
$$(-C^2)^2 = 4 \cdot y\, c^2\, x$$

i.e.
$$c^4 = 4xyc^2$$

i.e.
$$4xy = c^2$$

This is the required envelop of the family of straight lines
$$\frac{x}{a} + \frac{y}{b} = 1$$

subject to the condition $\quad ab = c^2 \quad$ **Ans.**

Problem 7 Find the envelop of the family of ellipses
$$\frac{x^2}{\alpha^2} + \frac{y^2}{(a-\alpha^2)} = 1$$

α being a parameter

Solution Differentiating equation
$$\frac{x^2}{\alpha^2} + \frac{y^2}{(a-\alpha)^2} = 1 \tag{1}$$

with respect to α we have
$$\frac{d}{d\alpha}\,[x^2\, \alpha^2 + y^2\, (a-\alpha)^{-2}] = 0$$

$$x^2 \frac{(-2)}{\alpha^3} + \frac{y^2(-2)}{(a-\alpha)^3} = 0$$

$$\frac{x^2}{\alpha^3} - \frac{y^2}{(a-\alpha)^3} = 0$$

i.e. $$\frac{x^2}{\alpha^3} = \frac{y^2}{(a-\alpha)^3}$$

i.e. $$\frac{x^2}{\alpha^2/\alpha} = \frac{y^2}{(a-\alpha)^2/(a-\alpha)}$$

i.e. $$\frac{x^2/\alpha^2}{\alpha/1} = \frac{y^2/(a-\alpha)^2}{(a-\alpha)/1}$$

i.e. $$\frac{x^2/\alpha^2}{\alpha/1} = \frac{y^2/(a-\alpha)^2}{(a-\alpha)/1} = \frac{x^2/\alpha^2 + y^2/(a-\alpha)^2}{\alpha/1 + a-\alpha/1}$$

$$= \frac{x^2/\alpha^2 + y^2/(a-\alpha)^2}{a} = \frac{1}{a}$$

i.e. Again $$\frac{x^2}{\alpha^3} = \frac{y^2}{(a-\alpha)^3} = \frac{1}{a}$$

$$\frac{x^{2/3}}{\alpha} = \frac{y^{2/3}}{a-\alpha} = \frac{1}{a^{1/3}} = \frac{x^{2/3} + y^{2/3}}{a}$$

$$x^{2/3} + y^{2/3} = a^{2/3}$$

which is the required α eliminate between (1) and (2) and hence is the equation of the required envelop.

Problem 8 Find the envelop of the circle

$$(x-\alpha)^2 + y^2 - 4\alpha = 0$$

where α being the parameter

Solution We have $$(x-\alpha)^2 + y^2 - 4\alpha = 0$$

$$\Rightarrow \quad x^2 - 2x\alpha + \alpha^2 + y^2 - 4\alpha = 0$$

$$\Rightarrow \quad \alpha^2 - \alpha(2x+4) + (x^2 + y^2) = 0$$

$$\Rightarrow \quad \alpha^2 - 2(x+2)\alpha + (x^2 + y^2) = 0$$

Since this is a quadraratic equation in α so equation of envelop may be obtain by the condition $B^2 = 4Ac$]

i.e. $$[-2(x+2)]^2 = 4 \cdot 1 (x^2 + y^2)$$

i.e. $$4(x+2)^2 = 4(x^2 + y^2)$$

$$x^2 + 4x + 4 = x^2 + y^2$$

i.e. $$x^2 + y^2 - x^2 - 4x - 4 = 0$$

i.e. $$y^2 - 4x - 4 = 0$$

which is the required envelop of the family of circles

Problem 9 Find the envelop of the family of circles

$$(x-a)^2 + y^2 = \frac{a^2}{2}$$

where a is a parameter *[I.F.S. 88]*

Solution The equation of the family of circles is

$$(x-a)^2 + y^2 = \frac{a^2}{2}$$

i.e. $$x^2 - 2ax + a^2 + y^2 = \frac{a^2}{2}$$

i e. $$x^2 - 2ax + \frac{a^2}{2} + y^2 = 0$$

i.e. $$2x^2 - 4ax + a^2 + 2y^2 = 0$$

i.e. $$a^2 - 4ax + 2(x^2 + y^2) = 0$$

which is a quadratic equation in a so envelop may be obtained using the relation $$B = 4\ Ac$$

i.e. $$(4x)^2 = 4 \cdot 1 \cdot 2 (x^2 + y^2)$$

i.e. $$216\, x^2 = 8\,(x^2 + y^2)$$

i.e $$x^2 + y^2 - 2x^2 = 0$$

i.e. $$y^2 - x^2 = 0$$

This is the required equation of envelop of the family of circles

$$(x-a)^2 + y^2 = \frac{a^2}{2}$$ **Ans.**

Problem 10 Find the evolute of the parabola $y^2 = 4ax$ (evolute being regarded as the envelop of its normals).

Solution The equation of the parabola is $y^2 = 4ax$
The equation of the normal at the point $(am^2, -2am)$ is given by

$$y = mx - 2am - am^3 \tag{1}$$

where m is the parameter
Differentiating equation (1) with respect to m we have

$$0 = x - 2a - 3am^2$$

$$3am^2 = x - 2a$$

$\Rightarrow$ $$m^2 = \frac{x-2a}{3a}$$

Again we have from equation (1)

$$y = m\,(x-2a-am^2)$$

$$y = m\left[x-2a-a\,\frac{(x-2a)}{3a}\right]$$

$$y = m\left[\frac{3ax-6a^2-ax+2a^2}{3a}\right]$$

$$y = m\left[\frac{2ax-4a^2}{3a}\right]$$

$$y = m\,\frac{2a\,[x-2a]}{3a}$$

$$y = m\cdot 2a\,m^2$$

i.e $$y = 2a\,m^3$$

$$y^2 = 4a^2\,m^6 = 4a^2\,(m^2)^3$$

$$y^2 = 4a^2\left(\frac{x-2a}{3a}\right)^3$$

$$y^2 = 4a^2\,\frac{(x-2a)^3}{27a^3}$$

i.e. $$27y^2 = \frac{4\,(x-2a)^3}{a}$$

i.e. $$27ay^2 = 4\,(x-2a)^3$$

which is the envelop of the normals

i.e. the required evolute of the parabola $y^2 = 4ax$.

Problem 11 Find the envelop of circles whose centre lie on the rectangular hyperbola $xy = c^2$ and which pass through its centre.

Solution Let the equation of a circle having centre at (α, β) is given by

$$(x-\alpha)^2 + (y-\beta)^2 = (\text{radius})^2$$

$$x^2-2x\alpha + \alpha^2 + y^2-2\beta y + \beta^2 = (\text{radius})^2$$

i.e. $$x^2 + y^2-2x\alpha-2y\beta + \alpha^2 + \beta^2 = a^2\ (\text{radius} = a) \qquad (1)$$

Since it passes through the centre of the rectangular hyperbola $xy = c^2$ which is the origin (0, 0) here

$$0 + 0-0-0 + \alpha^2 + \beta^2 = a^2$$

i.e. $$a^2 = \alpha^2 + \beta^2$$

Thus the required equation of the circle is

$$x^2 + y^2-2x\alpha-2y\beta + a^2 = a^2$$

i.e. $$x^2 + y^2-2x\alpha-2y\beta = 0 \qquad (2)$$

ince centre (α, β) lies on the rectangular hyperbola

$$xy = c^2$$

o $$\alpha\beta = c^2$$

This is the case of two parameter family connected by a relation given by equation (3)

From equation (3)

$$\beta = \frac{c^2}{\alpha}$$

.e. $$x^2 - 2x\alpha + y^2 - 2y\beta = 0$$

i.e. $$x^2 - 2x\alpha + y^2 - 2y\frac{c^2}{\alpha} = 0$$

i.e. $$x^2\alpha - 2x\alpha^2 + \alpha y^2 - 2yc^2 = 0$$

i.e. $$2x\alpha^2 - \alpha(x^2 + y^2) + 2yc^2 = 0$$

which is a quadratic in α so applying the formula $B^2 = 4Ac$ we have

$$[-(x^2 + y^2)]^2 = 4 \cdot 2x \cdot 2yc^2$$

$$(x^2 + y^2)^2 = 16\,xyc^2$$

which is the required equation of the circles whose centre lie on the rectangular hyperbola $xy = c^2$ and which passes through its centre.

Problem 12 Obtain the envelop of the family of curves

$$\frac{x^2}{\alpha} + \frac{y^2}{k^2 - \alpha^2} = 1$$

where α is the parameter interpret the result

Solution The equation of the family of curves

$$\frac{x^2}{\alpha^2} + \frac{y^2}{k^2 - \alpha^2} = 1$$

Here α is the parameter of this family

i.e. $$\frac{x^2(k^2 - \alpha^2) + \alpha^2 y^2}{\alpha^2(k^2 - \alpha^2)} = 1$$

i.e. $$x^2(k^2 - \alpha^2) + \alpha^2 y^2 = \alpha^2(k^2 - \alpha^2)$$

i,e. $$x^2 k^2 - x^2\alpha^2 + \alpha^2 y^2 = \alpha^2 k^2 - \alpha^4$$

i.e. $$\alpha^4 - \alpha^2 k^2 + x^2 k^2 - x^2\alpha^2 + \alpha^2 y^2 = 0$$

i.e. $$\alpha^4 - \alpha^2(k^2 + x^2 - y^2) + x^2 k^2 = 0$$

.e. $$(\alpha^2)^2 - (x^2 + k^2 - y^2)\alpha^2 + x^2 k^2 = 0$$

Putting $\alpha^2 = t$

i.e. $$t^2 - (x^2 + k^2 - y^2)\,t + x^2 k^2 = 0$$
$$A\,(=1) \qquad (B) \qquad (C)$$

This is a quadratic in t, the envelop is given by the relation

$$B^2 = 4\,Ac$$

$$[-(x^2 + k^2 - y^2)]^2 = 41 \cdot x^2 k^2$$

$$(x^2 + k^2 - y^2)^2 = 4x^2 k^2$$

i.e. $$(x^2 + k^2 - y^2)^2 - 4x^2 k^2 = 0$$

i.e. $$(x^2 + k^2 - y^2)^2 - (2xk)^2 = 0$$

i.e. $$(x^2 + k^2 - y^2 + 2xk)\,(x^2 + k^2 - y^2 - 2xk) = 0$$

i.e. $$[(x + k)^2 - y^2]\,[(x - k)^2 - y^2] = 0$$

i.e. $$(x + k + y)\,(x + k - y)\,(x - k + y)\,(x - k - y) = 0$$

This is the required equation of the envelop which represents the four straight lines

$$x + k + y = 0, \quad x + k - y = 0\; x - k + y = 0$$
$$x - k - y = 0 \text{ which form a square.}$$

Problem 13 Find the envelop of the circle, whose centre is on the parabola $y^2 = 4ax$ and which passes through the vertex. *[IAS 85]*

Solution Any point on the parabola $y^2 = 4ax$ is $(at^2, 2at)$. The circle passes through the vertex of the parabola $y^2 = 4ax$. The vertex is on (0, 0).

The equation of the circle passing through (0, 0) and whose centre is at $(at^2, 2\,at)$ where t is a parameter

Equation of the circle passing through at^2, 2at) is given by

$$(x - at^2)^2 + (y - 2at)^2 = (\text{radius})^2 \tag{1}$$

Since (1) passes through (0, 0) so

$$(0 - \text{at}^2) + (0 - 2\text{ at}) = r^2$$

$$a^2 + 4 + 4a^2 t^2 = r^2 \tag{2}$$

So the equation of the circle is

$$(x - at^2)^2 + (y - 2\,at)^2 = a^2 t^4 + 4a^2 t^2$$

$$x^2 - 2ax\,t^2 + a^2 t^4 + y^2 - 4y\,(at) + 4a^2 t^2 = a^2 t^4 + 4a^2 t^2$$

i.e. $$x^2 - 2axt^2 + y^2 - 4ayt = 0$$

i.e. $$(-2ax)\,t^2 - (4ay)\,t + (x^2 + y^2) = 0$$

This is a quadratic in t so applying the formula

$$B^2 = 4\ Ac \text{ we have}$$

$$[-(4ay)]^2 = 4\,(-2ax)\,(x^2 + y^2)$$

$$216a^2\, y^2 = -8ax\,(x^2 + y^2)$$

$$2ay^2 + x\,(x^2 + y^2) = 0$$

i.e. $$2ay^2 + x^3 + xy^2 = 0$$

i.e. $$x^3 + x^2\,(2a + x) = 0$$

Which is the required equation of the envelop of the circle whose centre is on the parabola $y^2 = 4ax$ and which passes through the vertex of the parabola. **Ans.**

Problem 14 From any point on the elipse

$\dfrac{x^2}{a^2} + \dfrac{y^2}{b^2} = 1$, perpendiculars are drawn to the axes show that the line joining the feet of perpendiculars always touches the curve

$$\left(\frac{x}{a}\right)^{2/3} + \left(\frac{y}{b}\right)^{2/3} = 1$$

Let $p\ (a \cos \theta,\ b \sin \theta)$ be any point on the ellipse

$$\frac{x^2}{a^2} + \frac{y^2}{b^2} = 1$$

Solution Let PM and PN be $-r$ on the axis of x and y respectively. Then the co-ordinates of M are $(a \cos \theta, 0)$ and the co-ordinates of N are $(0, b \sin \theta)$

Now we have the equation of MN passing through two points $(a \cos \theta, 0)$ and $(0, b \sin \theta)$

$$y - 0 = \frac{0 - b \sin \theta}{a \cos \theta - 0}\,(x - a \cos \theta)$$

i.e. $$y = \frac{-b \sin \theta}{a \cos \theta}\,(x - a \cos \theta)$$

$$-\frac{y}{b \sin \theta} = \frac{x - a \cos \theta}{a \cos \theta}$$

$$\Rightarrow -\frac{y}{b \sin \theta} = \frac{x}{a \cos \theta} - 1$$

i.e. $$\frac{x}{a \cos \theta} + \frac{y}{b \sin \theta} = 1 \qquad (1)$$

Now we have to find the envelop of this family where θ is a parameter Differentiating equation (1) with respect to θ we have

$$\frac{x\,(-\sin \theta)}{-a \cos^2 \theta} + \frac{y \cos \theta}{b\,(-\sin^2 \theta)} = 0$$

i.e. $$\frac{x \sin\theta}{a\cos^2\theta} = \frac{y\cos\theta}{b\sin^2\theta}$$

i.e. $$\frac{x}{a\cos^3\theta} = \frac{y}{b\sin^3\theta}$$

$$\frac{a\cos^3\theta}{x} = \frac{b\sin^3\theta}{y}$$

i.e. $$\frac{\cos^3\theta}{x/a} = \frac{\sin^8\theta}{y/b}$$

i.e. $$\frac{\cos\theta}{(x/a)^{1/3}} = \frac{\sin\theta}{(y/b)^{1/3}} = \frac{\sqrt{\cos^2\theta+\sin^2\theta}}{\sqrt{(x/a^{2/3}+(y/b)^{2/3}}}$$

$$= \frac{1}{\sqrt{(x/a)^{2/3}+(y/b)^{2/3}}}$$

i.e. $$\cos = \frac{(x/a)^{1/3}}{\sqrt{(x/a)^{2/3}+(y/b)^{2/3}}}$$

and $$\sin\theta = \frac{(y/b)^{1/3}}{\sqrt{(x/a)^{2/3}+(y/b)^{2/3}}}$$

Putting the values of sin θ and cos θ in equation (1) we have

$$\frac{\dfrac{x}{a\,(x/a)^{1/3}}}{\sqrt{(x/a)^{2/3}+(y/b)^{2|3}}} + \frac{\dfrac{y}{b\,(y/b)^{1/3}}}{\sqrt{(x/a)^{2/3}+(y/b)^{2/3}}}$$

$$\frac{x}{a}\cdot\frac{\sqrt{(x/a)^{2/3}+(y/b)^{2/3}}}{(x/a)^{1/3}} + \frac{y}{b}\cdot\frac{\sqrt{(x/a)^{2/z}+(y/b)^{2/3}}}{(y/b)^{1/3}} = 1$$

$$\sqrt{\left(\frac{x}{a}\right)^{2/3}+\left(\frac{y}{b}\right)^{2/3}}\left[\left(\frac{x}{a}\right)^{2/3}+\left(\frac{y}{b}\right)^{2/3}\right] = 1$$

i.e. $$\left[\left(\frac{x}{a}\right)^{2/3}+\left(\frac{y}{b}\right)^{2/3}\right]^{3/2} = 1$$

i.e. $$\left(\frac{x}{a}\right)^{2/3}+\left(\frac{y}{b}\right)^{2/3} = 1^{2/3}$$

i.e. the required equation of envelop is $\left(\frac{x}{a}\right)^{2/3}+\left(\frac{y}{b}\right)^{2/3} = 1$

Problem 15 Find the envelop of the circle which pass through the centre of the ellipse $\frac{x^2}{a^2}+\frac{y^2}{b^2} = 1$ and their centres are upon its circumference.

Solutlon The equation of the circle is given by

$$(x-\alpha)^2 + (y-\beta)^2 = r^2 \tag{1}$$

Where (α, β) is the centre of the circle and a is the radius of the circle

Let $(a \cos \theta, b \sin \theta)$ be any point on the ellipse. Since the centre of the family circles are upon its circumfrrence so

$$\alpha = a \cos \theta$$

$$\beta = b \sin \theta$$

i.e. $(a \cos \theta, b \sin \theta)$ are the co-ordinates of the centre where θ is the parameter.

So the equation of the family of circles are given by

$$(x-a \cos \theta)^2 + (y-b \sin \theta)^2 = r^2 \tag{2}$$

Again the circles are passing through the centre of the ellipse

$$\frac{x^2}{a^2} + \frac{y^2}{b^2} = 1$$

i.e, through (0, 0) so we have

$$(0-a \cos \theta)^2 + (0-b \sin \theta)^2 = r^2$$

i.e. $$a^2 \cos^2 \theta + b^2 \sin^2 \theta = r^2 \tag{3}$$

Thus the equation of the circle is given by

$$(x-a \cos \theta)^2 + (y-b \sin \theta)^2 = r^2$$

$$(x-a \cos \theta)^2 + (y-b \sin \theta)^2 = a^2 \cos^2 \theta + b^2 \sin^2 \theta$$

i.e. $$x^2-2ax \cos \theta + a^2 \cos^2 \theta + y^2-2by \sin \theta + b^2 \sin^2 \theta$$

$$= a^2 \cos^2 \theta + b^2 \sin^2 \theta$$

i.e. $$x^2 + y^2-2ax \cos \theta-2by \sin \theta = 0 \tag{4}$$

Now differentiating equation (4) with respect to θ (θ is the parameter of the family of circles) we have

$$0 + 0 + 2ax \sin \theta-2by \cos \theta = 0$$

i.e. $$2ax \cos \theta-2by \sin \theta = 0 \tag{5}$$

From equation (4) we have

$$x^2 + y^2 = 2ax \cos \theta + 2by \sin \theta \tag{6}$$

Now squaring (5) and (6) and adding thereby we have

$$(x^2 + y^2)^2 = 4a^2 x^2 + 4b^2 y^2$$

i.e. $$(x^2 + y^2)^2 = 4 (a^2 x^2 + b^2 y^2)$$ **Ans.**

Which is the required equation of the envelop of the circle passing through the centre of the ellipse $\frac{x^2}{a^2} + \frac{y^2}{b^2} = 1$ and whose centre lie on the circumferrence of the ellipse. **Ans.**

Problem 16 Show that the envelop of the family of circles whose diameters are the double ordinates of the parabola $y^2 = 4ax$ is the parabola

$$y^2 = 4a(x + a)$$

Solution Let one end of the double ordinate of the parabola is $(at^2, 2at)$. Then the co-ordinate of the other end is $at^2, -2at)$.

Now we have to find the equation of the circle whose diameter is the line joining two points $(at^2, 2at)$ and $at^2, -2at)$. We know that the equation of a circle whose diameters is the line joining two points (x_1, y_1) and $(x_2; y_2)$ is given by

$$(x - x_1)(x - x_2) + (y - y_1)(y - y_2) = 0$$

i.e. $$(x - at^2)(x - at^2) + (y - 2at)(y - 2at) = 0$$

Where t is the parameter here

i.e. $$x^2 - xat^2 + a^2 t^4 + y^2 + 2aty - 2aty - 4a^2 t^2 = 0$$

i.e. $$x^2 + y^2 - 2axt^2 + a^2 t^4 - 4a^2 t^2 = 0$$

i.e. $$a^2 t^4 - (2ax + 4a^2) t^2 + (x^2 + y^2) = 0$$

Which is aquadratic in t so applying the formula

$$B^2 = 4Ac$$

i.e. $$[-(2ax + 4a^2)]^2 = 4 \cdot a^2 (x^2 + y^2)$$

$$[-2a(x + 2a)]^2 = 4a^2 (x^2 + y^2)$$

i.e. $$4a^2 (x + 2a)^2 = 4a^2 (x^2 + y^2)$$

i.e. $$(x + 2a)^2 = x^2 + y^2$$

i.e. $$x^2 + 4ax + 4a^2 = x^2 + y^2$$

i.e. $$y^2 = 4ax + 4a^2$$

i.e. $$y^2 = 4a(x + a) \qquad \textbf{Ans.}$$

Which is the required envelop. *(Proved)*

Problem 17 Find the envelop of family of ellipse

$$\frac{x^2}{a^2} + \frac{y^2}{b^2} = 1 \text{ such that } a^2 + b^2 = c$$

OR

Find the envelop of the ellipse of having the axis of co-ordinates as principal axis and the sum of the squares of their semi axes as constant.

Solntion The equation of the family of ellipse is

$$\frac{x^2}{a^2} + \frac{y^2}{b^2} = 1 \qquad (1)$$

With the condition

$$a^2 + b^2 = c \tag{2}$$

Differentiating equation (1) with respect to a we have

$$-\frac{2x^2}{a^3} - \frac{2y^2}{b^3}\frac{db}{da} = 0$$

$$\frac{x^2}{x^3} + \frac{y^2}{b^3}\left(\frac{db}{da}\right) = 0 \tag{3}$$

Differentiating equation (2) we have

$$2a + 2b\frac{db}{da} = 0$$

i.e. $$a + b\frac{db}{da} = 0$$

i.e. $$b\frac{db}{da} = -a$$

$$\Rightarrow \quad \frac{db}{da} = -\frac{a}{b} \tag{4}$$

Putting the value of $\frac{db}{da} = -\frac{a}{b}$ from (4) in equation (3) we have

$$\frac{x^2}{a^3} + \frac{y^2}{b^3}\left(-\frac{a}{b}\right) = 0$$

i.e. $$\frac{x^2}{a^3} = \frac{y^2}{b^4}$$

i.e. $$\frac{x^2}{a^4} = \frac{ay^2}{b^4}$$

i.e. $$\frac{x^2/a^2}{a^2} = \frac{y^2/b^2}{b^2}$$

$$\frac{x^2/a^2}{a^2} = \frac{y^2/b^2}{b^2} = \frac{x^2/a^2 + y^2/b^2}{a^2 + b^2}$$

i.e. $$\frac{y^2}{b^4} = \frac{x^2/a^2 + y^2/b^2}{c} = \frac{x^2}{a^4}$$

i.e. $$\frac{x^2}{a^4} = \frac{y}{b^4} = \frac{1}{c}$$

i.e $$\frac{a^4}{x^2} = \frac{b^4}{y^2} = \frac{c}{1}$$

i.e. $$\frac{a^2}{x} = \frac{b^2}{y} = \sqrt{c}$$

$$\Rightarrow a^2 = \sqrt{cx}$$

$$b^2 = \sqrt{cy}$$

Putting the values of a^2 and b^2 in equation $\frac{x^2}{a^2} + \frac{y^2}{b^2} = 1$ we have

$$\frac{x^2}{(\sqrt{c})\, x} + \frac{y^2}{(\sqrt{c})\, y} = 1$$

i.e. $$\frac{x}{\sqrt{c}} + \frac{y}{\sqrt{c}} = 1$$

i.e. $$x + y = \sqrt{c}$$

Which is the required envelop of the ellipse $\frac{x^2}{a^2} + \frac{y^2}{b^2} = 1$ subjected with the condition $a^2 + b^2 = c$. **Ans.**

12

Analytical Geometry of Two Dimensions

Straight lines, pair of straight lines, circles, system of cirles, Ellipse, parabola, hyperbola, (referred to principal axis) Reduction of a second degree equation to standard form. Tangents *and normals.*

Previous years questions

Q. 1 (a) If $ax^2 + 2h\,xy + by^2 + 2gx + 2fy + c = 0$ represents a pair of intersecting straight lines, prove that the lines $ax + hy + g = 0$, $bx + by + f = 0$ and $gx + fy + c = 0$ are concurrent.

(b) Find the condition that $lx + my + n = 3$ is normal to the parabola $y^2 = 4ax$.

(c) P, Q, R, S are four coplanar points on the sides AB, BC, CD, DA of a skew quadraliteral; prove that

$$\frac{AP}{PB}\cdot\frac{BQ}{QC}\cdot\frac{CR}{RD}\cdot\frac{DS}{SA} = 1$$

Q. 2 (a) Find the circles passing through the points of intersection of the circle $x^2 + y^2 = 4$ and $x^2 + y^2 - 2x - 4y + 4 = 0$ and having radius $2\sqrt{2}$.

(b) Find the tangents to the elipse $\frac{x^2}{a^2} + \frac{y^2}{b^2} = 1$ which make angle $\frac{\pi}{4}$ with the x axis.

Q. 3 (a) Find the equation to the sphere having the join of (a, b, c) and (α, β, γ) as a diameter.

(b) If e and e^1 are the eccentricities of a hyperbola and its conjugate, prove that $\frac{1}{e^2} + \frac{1}{e^{12}} = 1$.

(c) Prove that the equation $9x^2 - 24xy + 16y^2 - 50x - 100y + 225 = 0$ represents a parabola and find its axis. *[I.F.S. 88]*

Q. 4 (a) The straight line $lx + my = 1$ meets the circle $x^2 + y^2 = 1$ in P and Q. If O is the centre of the circle, show that

$$\cos\left(\frac{1}{2} < POQ\right) = \frac{1}{(l^2 + m^2)^{1/2}}$$

(b) Show that if r_1, r_2 are the radii of the circles

$$S_1 \equiv x^2 + y^2 + 2g_1 x + 2f_1 y + c_1 = 0$$

and $S_2 \equiv x^2 + y^2 + 2g_2 x + 2f_2 y + c_2 = 0$, then the points at which the circles subtend equal angles lie on the circle $\frac{S_1}{r_1^2} = \frac{S_2}{r_2^2}$.

Q. 5 (a) The normal at a point on the line $x = c$. Prove that the sides of the triangle PQR touch the parabola $y^2 = 16a(x + 2a - c)$.

(b) The straight line $2x - y - 4 = 0$ touches a hyperbola whose foci are $(-3, 0)$ and $(3, 0)$. Find the equation to the hyperbola.

Q. 6 (a) The straight line $x - y = 5$ touches the ellipse with foci at $(-3, 0)$ and $(3, 0)$. Find the equation to the ellipse.

(b) Two conics have a common focus and directrix. If any tangent to one intersects the other in P, Q show that $\left(\frac{1}{2} \; P\hat{s}\, Q\right) = \frac{e}{e^1} \cdot e_1\ e^1$ being their eccentricities. [I.F.S. 87]

Q. 7 (a) Prove that if the equation

$$ax^2 + 2h\,xy + by^2 + 2gx + 2fy + c = 0$$

represents a pair of paralles straight lines, then $h^2 = ab$ and $af^2 = bg^2$ and that the distance between them is $2\,[(g^2 - ac)/a\,(a + b)]^{1/2}$.

(b) Consider the chords of the circle $x^2 + y^2 + 2gx + 2fy + 2c = 0$ which subtend a right angle at the origin-show that the locus of the feet of perpendiculars from the origin on these chords is the circle

$$x^4 + y^2 + gx + fy + e = 0$$

Q .8 (a) Show that the circle described on any focal chard of a parabolic as diameter, touches the directrix.

(b) Prove that the portion of a tangent to a hyerbola intercepted between the asymptotes is bisected as the point of contact and the area of the triangle formed by the tangent and the two asymptotes is constant.

Q. 9 (a) Show that the locus of the poles of the normal chords of the ellipse $\frac{x^2}{a^2} + \frac{y^2}{b^2} = 1$ is $\frac{a^6}{x^2} + \frac{b^6}{y^2} = (a^2 - b^2)^2$

If the conics $ax^2 + 2h\,xy + by^2 + 2gx + 2fy + c = 0$

and $a^1 x^2 + 2h^1 xy + b^1 y^2 + 2g^1 x + 2f^1 y + c^1 = 0$

intersect in concyclic points, show that $\frac{a - b}{b} = \frac{a^1 - b^1}{b^1}$ and that the co-ordinates of the circle are

$$\left(\frac{hg^1 - h^1 g}{ab^1 - a^1 b}, \frac{bf^2 - b^1 f}{ab^1 - a^1 b}\right)$$

[I.F.S. 86]

Q. 10 Prove that the equation

$$3y^2-8xy-3x^2-29x+3y-18=0$$

represents a pair of straight lines. Find their point of intersection and also the angle between them.

(b) Prove that the chords of the parabola $y^2 = 4ax$ whose equation is $y-x\sqrt{2}+4a\sqrt{2}=0$ is normal to the curve and its length is $6\sqrt{3}\,a$.

Q. 11(a) Prove that the radical axis of two circles is the straight line passing through the common points of the two circles and it is at right angles to the line joining their centres.

(b) Tangents are drawn from any point on the ellipse $\frac{x^2}{a^2}+\frac{y^2}{b^2}=$ to the circle $x^2+y^2=r^2$ prove that the chords of contact are tangents to the ellipse $a^2x^2+b^2y^2=r^4$.

Q. 12 (a) Find the assymptotes of the hyperbola

$$3x^2-5xy-2y^2+5x+11y-8=0$$

(b) Find the equations to the tangents to the conic which are parallel to the straight line $x+4y=0$, *[I.F.S. 85]*

Q. 13 (a) Find the equation to the pair of straight lines joining the origin to the intersections of the straight $y=mx+c$ and the circle $x^2+y^2=a^2$. Prove that they are at right angles if $2c^2=a^2(1+m^2)$.

(b) Find the radical centre of the circles

$$x^2+y^2+x+y+3=0$$

$$x^2+y^2+2x+4y+5=0$$

$$x^2+y^2-7x-8y-9=0$$

Q. 14 (a) Find whether the straight line $x+y=2+\sqrt{2}$ touches the circle $x^2+y^2-2x-2y+1=0$.

(b) Prove that, in general, three normals can be drawn from a point to the parabola $y^2=4ax$ and that the algebraic sum of the ordinates of the feet of these normals is zero.

Q. 15 (a) Determine the nature of the conic represented by the equation $12x^2-23xy+10y^2-25x+26y=14$ and find its centre.

(b) If *a* rectangular hyperabola circumscribes a triangle, show that it also passes through the orthocentre of the triangle. *[I.F.S. 84]*

Q. 16 (a) If $ax^2+2hxy+by^2+2gx+2fy+c=0$ represents apair of straight lines equidistant from the origin, prove that

$$f^4-g^4=c(bf^2-ag^2)$$

(*b*) Prove that the length of the chord of the rectangular hyperbola $ny=c^2$ with its middle point at (α, β) is

$$2\sqrt{\frac{(\alpha^2+\beta^2)(\alpha\beta-c^2)}{\alpha\beta}}$$

Q. 17 (a) Prove that the area of the trangle formed by the tangents from (α, β) to the circle $x^2 + y^2 = a^2$ and their chord of contact is

$$\left|\frac{a(\alpha^2 + \beta^2 - a^2)^{3/2}}{\alpha^2 + \beta^2}\right|.$$

(b) If the normal to an ellipse of ecentricity e at one end of a latus rectum passes through an end of its minor axis, prove that $e^2 + e^4 = 1$

Q. 18 If the ordinates of three points A_1 B_1 C on the parabola $y^2 = 4ax$ are in geometric progression, prove that the tangents at A and C interest on the vertical through B.

(b) Prove that the length of the common chord of the circles $x^2 + y^2 + 2\lambda x + c = 0$ and $x^2 + y^2 + 2\mu y - c = 0$ is

$$2\sqrt{\frac{(\lambda^2 - c)(u^2 + c)}{\lambda^2 + \mu^2}}$$ [I.F.S. 83]

Q. 19 (a) Find the co-ordinates of the orthocentre of the angle whose vertices are $(-5, -7)$; $(13, 2)$ and $(-5, 6)$

(b) If $ax^2 + 2hxy + by^2 + 2fx + 2fy + c = 0$ represents apair of parallel straight lines, prove that the distance between these lines is

$$2\sqrt{\frac{g^2 - ac}{a(a+b)}}$$

Q. 20 (a) The combined equation of two sides of a triangle whose orthocentres is (c, d) is

$$ax^2 + 2hxy + by^2 = 0$$

Where $a + b \neq 0$ prove that the remaining side is given by the equation

$$(a + b)(cx + dy) = ad^2 - 2hcd + bc^2$$

(b) If the straight line $x \cos \alpha + y \sin \alpha = p$ interset the circle $x^2 + y^2 = a^2$ in two distinct points A and B prove that the equation to the circle, with AB as diameter is

$$(x^2 + y^2 - a^2) - 2p(x \cos \alpha + y \sin \alpha - p) = 0$$

(c) If e and f are the eccentricities of a pair of conjugate hyperbolas, prove that

$$\frac{1}{e^2} + \frac{1}{f^2} = 1$$

Q. 21 (a) If $lx + my + n = 0$ is normal to the parabola $y^2 = 4ax$, prove that $al^3 + 2alm^2 = -m^2 n$

(b) A sphere whose centre lies in the positive octant passes through the origin and cuts the plane $x = 0$; $y = 0$, $z = 0$ in circles of radii $\sqrt{a}$, $\sqrt{2b}$, $\sqrt{2c}$ respectively. Show that the equation is

$$x^2 + y^2 + z^2 - 2\{\sqrt{(b^2 + c^2 - a^2}\}x - 2\{\sqrt{c^2 + a^2 - b^2}\}y$$
$$-2\sqrt{\{a^2 + b^2 - c^2\}}\, z = 0$$ [I.F.S. 82]

Q. 22 (a) Show that the lines joining the origin to the interscction of

$$3x^2 + 5xy - 3y^2 + 2x + 3y = 0 \text{ and } 3x - 2y = 1$$

are at right angles.

(b) Show that the latus rectum of the parabola

$$(a^2 + b^2)(x^2 + y^2) = (bx + ay - ab)^2 \text{ is}$$

$$\frac{2ab}{\sqrt{a^2 + b^2}}$$

(c) Find the co-ordinates of the limiting points of the co-axial system to whtch the circles

$$x^2 + y^2 + 4x + 2y + 5 = 0 \text{ and}$$

$$x^2 + y^2 + 2x + 4x + 7 = 0 \text{ belong}$$

Q. 23 (a) Chords of a hyperbola whose equation is

$$\frac{x^2}{a^2} - \frac{y^2}{b^2} = 1$$

are drawn, all passing through the fixed point (h, k); prove that the locus of their middle points is a hyperbola whose centre is the point $\left(\frac{h}{2}, \frac{k}{2}\right)$ and which is similar to either the hyperbola or its conjugate.

(b) prove that the line $x \cos \alpha + y \sin \alpha = p$ will touch the ellipse

$$\frac{x^2}{a^2} + \frac{y^2}{b^2} = 1, \text{ if } a^2 \cos^2 \alpha + b^2 \sin^2 \alpha = p^2$$

(c) Prove that the three normals can be drawn to a parabola from a given point and that the sum of the ordinates of the feet of the normal is zero.

[*I.F.S. 81*]

13

Pair of Straight Lines

Equation

$$ax^2 + 2hxy + by^2 + 2gx + 2fy + c = 0$$

is called the general equation of the second degree

Problem 1 To show that the equation of the form $ax^2 + 2hxy + by^2 = 0$ represents a pair of straight lines both passing through the origin.

Solution we have $ax^2 + 2hxy + by^2 = by^2 + 2hxy + ax^2$

$$= b\left(y^2 + \frac{2h}{b}xy + \frac{a}{b}x^2\right) = b(y - m_1 x)(y - m_2 x)$$

$$= b[y^2 - (m_1 + m_2)xy + m_1 m_2 x^2]$$

Equating the coefficients of xy and x^2 we get

$$m_1 + m_2 = -\frac{2h}{b} \text{ and } m_1 m_2 = \frac{a}{b}$$

m_1, m_2 are the roots of the quadratic

$$z^2 + \frac{2h}{b}z + \frac{a}{b} = 0$$

i.e. $$m_1, m_2 = -\frac{2h/b \pm \sqrt{4h^2/b^2 - 4 \cdot a/b}}{2}$$

$$m_1, m_2 = -\frac{2h/b \pm 2\sqrt{h^2 - ab}/b}{2}$$

i.e. $$m_1 = -h/b + \frac{\sqrt{h^2 - ab}/b}{b}$$

$$m_1 = \frac{[-h + \sqrt{h^2 - ab}]}{b}$$

and $$m_2 = \frac{[-h - \sqrt{h^2 - ab}]}{b}$$

Hence the given equation represents the lines

$$y = m_1 x \tag{1}$$

$$y = m_2 x \tag{2}$$

The two lines given by (1) and (2) will be real and different if m_1 and m_2 are real ie if $h^2 > ab$ real and concident if $h^2 = ab$ and imaginary if $h^2 < ab$.

Problem 2 Find the angle between the lines

$$ax^2 + 2hxy + by^2 = 0$$

Solution Let the equation of pair of lines be

$$ax^2 + 2hxy + by^2 = 0$$

Let this represents two lines

$$y - m_1 x = 0 \text{ and } y - m_2 x = 0$$

both passing through the origin.

Then $$ax^2 + 2hxy + by^2 = b(y - m_1 x)(y - m_2 x)$$

$$ax^2 + 2hxy + by^2 = b[y^2 - (m_1 m_2) xy + m_1 m_2 x^2]$$

Equating the coefficients of x^2 and xy on both sides we have

$$(m_1 + m_2) = -\frac{2h}{b}$$

$$m_1 m_2 = \frac{a}{b}$$

If θ be the angle between the lines, we have

$$\tan\theta = \pm\frac{m_1 - m_2}{1 + m_1 m_2}$$

$$= \pm\frac{[(m_1 + m_2)^2 - 4 m_1 m_2]}{1 + m_1 m_2}$$

$$\tan\theta = \pm\frac{\sqrt{-(2h/b)^2 - 4 \cdot a/b}}{1 + a/b}$$

$$\tan\theta = \pm\frac{\sqrt{4h^2/b^2 - 4a/b}}{1 + a/b}$$

i.e. $$\tan\theta = \pm\frac{2\sqrt{h^2 - ab}}{a + b}$$

the +or—ve sign being take n according as θ is accute or θ is *obtuse.*

Cor. (1) if $h^2 - ab > 0$, the lines are real

(ii) if $h^2 - ab = 0$, the lines are coincidet.

(iii) if $h^2 - ab < 0$, the lines are imaginary, but pass through the real point (0, 0)

Let the lines given by the equation $ax^2 + 2hxy + by^2 = 0$ will be at right angles to one another i.e. $\theta = 90°$

$$\tan 90° = \pm\frac{2\sqrt{h^2 - ab}}{a + b}$$

$$\infty = \pm\frac{2\sqrt{h^2 - ab}}{a + b}$$

$$\Rightarrow \frac{1}{0} = \pm\frac{2\sqrt{h^2 - ab}}{a + b}$$

i.e. $a + b = 0$ Remember

The lines represented by

i.e. $ab^2 + 2hxy + by^2 = 0$

will be at right angles if the sum of the coefficients of x^2 and y^2 is zero.

Problem 3 Find the bisecrors of angles between the lines

$$ax^2 + 2hxy + by^2 = 0$$

To obtain the equation of the straight lines bisecting the angles between the lines $ax^2 + 2hxy + by^2 = 0$, the axis being rectangular.

Solution We know that the equation $ax^2 + 2hxy + by^2 = 0$ represents a pair of straight lines $y - m_1 x = 0$ and $y - m_2 x = 0$ passing through the origin. Let OX and OY be the rectangular co-ordinate axis let the line OL and OL_2 makes angles θ_1 an θ_2 with the + ve direction of x – axis i.e. with the line OX. Let the bisector of the angle between the two lines makes an angle θ with the x axis

Then $m_1 + m_2 = -\frac{2h}{b}$

$$m_1 m_2 = \frac{a}{b}$$

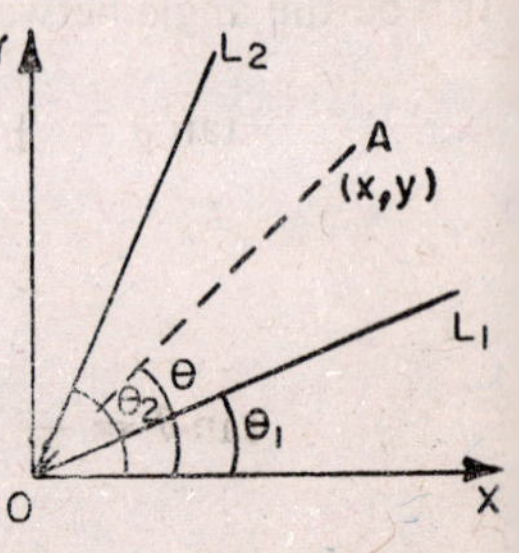

From the geometry of the figure for since OA is the bisector of the angles between the lines OL_1 and OL_2 so

$$\theta - \theta_1 = \theta_2 - \theta$$

i.e. $2\theta = \theta_1 + \theta_2$

Where $m_1 = \tan \theta_1,\ m_2 = \tan \theta_2$

Now $\tan 2\theta = \tan(\theta_1 + \theta_2)$

$$\tan 2\theta = \frac{\tan \theta_1 + \tan \theta_2}{1 - \tan \theta_1 \tan \theta_2}$$

$$\frac{2 \tan \theta}{1 - \tan^2 \theta} = \frac{\tan \theta_1 + \tan \theta_2}{1 - \tan \theta_1 \tan \theta_2} \quad (1$$

Let $A\ (x, y)$ be any point on the bisector of the lines

$$ax^2 + 2hxy + by^2 = 0$$

Then $$\tan\theta = \frac{y}{x}$$

Now from equation (1) we have

$$\frac{2 \cdot y/x}{1 - y^2/x^2} = \frac{m_1 + m_2}{1 - m_1 m_2}$$

i.e. $$\frac{2y/x}{(x^2 - y^2)/x^2} = \frac{-2h/b}{1 - a/b}$$

i.e. $$\frac{2y}{x} \cdot \frac{x^2}{(x^2 - y^2)} = \frac{-2h/b}{(b-a)/b}$$

i.e. $$\frac{xy}{x^2 - y^2} = -\frac{h}{(a-b)}$$

i.e. $$\frac{xy}{x^2 - y^2} = \frac{h}{b-a}$$

i.e. $$\boxed{\frac{x^2 - y^2}{a - b} = \frac{xy}{h}}$$ **Remember**

which is the required equation of the bisector of the angle between the straight lines

$$ax^2 + 2hxy + by^2 = 0$$

Problem 4 To find the condition that the general equation of second degree

$$ax^2 + 2hxy + by^2 + 2gx + 2fy + c = 0$$

may represent two straight lines.

Solution Let us treat the equation

$$ax^2 + 2hxy + by^2 + 2gx + 2fy + c = 0 \qquad (1)$$

as quadratic in x we have

$$ax^2 + 2x\,(hy + g) + (by^2 + 2fy + c) = 0$$

$$\therefore \quad x = \frac{-2(hy+g) \pm \sqrt{4(hy \pm g)^2 - 4 \cdot a\,(by^2 + 2fy + cy)}}{2 \cdot a}$$

$$\therefore \quad x = \frac{2\,[-(hy + g) \pm \sqrt{(hy + g)^2 - a\,(by^2 + 2fy + c)}}{2a}$$

i.e. $$ax + hy + g = \pm\sqrt{(hy + g)^2 - a\,(by^2 + 2fy + c)} \qquad (2)$$

The equation (1) will be resolved into linear factor if the expression under the radical sign of (2) viz $(hy+g)^2 - a\,(xy^2+2fy+c)$ be a perfect square.

i.e. if $\quad h^2y^2 + g^2 + 2hgy - aby^2 - 2afy - ac = 0$

be a perfect square i.e. if

$$y^2\,(h^2-ab) + 2y\,(hg-af) + (g^2-ac) = 0 \tag{3}$$

be a perfect square,

If equation (3) be a perfect square then the discrimant of this equation must be zero

i.e. $$4\,(hg-af)^2 - 4\,(h^2-ab)\,(g^2-ac) = 0$$

i.e. $$(hg-af)^2 - (h^2-ab)\,(g^2-ac) = 0$$

i.e. $$h^2 g^2 + a^2 f^2 - 2ahgf - (h^2 g^2 - h^2 ac - abg^2 + a^2 bc) = 0$$

i.e. $$h^2 g^2 + a^2 f^2 - 2ahgf - h^2 g^2 + h^2 ac + abg^2 - a^2 bc = 0$$

i.e. $$a^2 f^2 - 2ahgf + ah^2c + abg^2 - a^2bc = 0$$

i.e. $$a\,[af^2 - 2fgh + ch^2 + bg^2 - abc] = 0$$

Since $a \neq 0$

$$\Rightarrow \quad af^2 + bg^2 + ch^2 - 2fgh - abc = 0$$

Remember $$\Rightarrow \quad \boxed{abc + 2fgh - af^2 - bg^2 - ch^2 = 0} \tag{4}$$

The expression on the L.H.S. of equation (4) is called the discriminant of the general equation of second degree i.e. of

$$ax^2 + 2hxy + by^2 + 2gx + 2fy + c = 0$$

Problem 1 Find the condition that one of the lines $ax^2 + 2hxy + by^2 = 0$ may coincide with one of the line $a_1\,x^2 + 2h_1\,xy + b_1\,y^2 = 0$

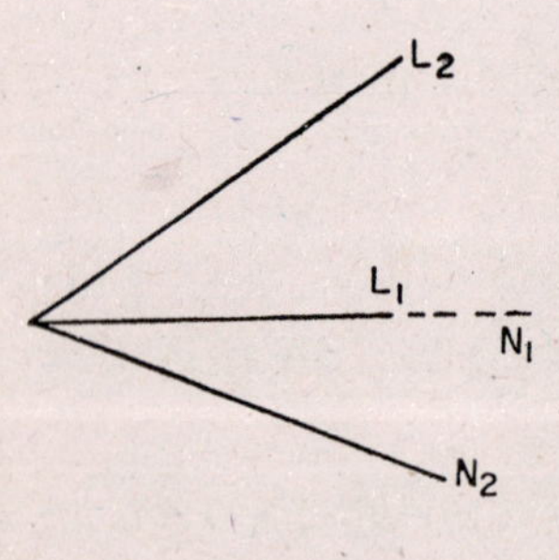

Solution Let one of the lines of the two pair of straight lines $ax^2 + 2hxy + by^2 = 0$ (1)

and $\quad a_1\,x^2 + 2h_1\,xy + b_1\,y^2 = 0$ (2)

coincides. Let (1) represents the lines OL_1 and OL_2 equation (2) represents the line ON_1 and ON_2. The lines OL_1 and ON coincides. All the lines passes through the origin $O\,(0, 0)$.

Let the equation to the common straight lines be $\quad y - mx = 0$ (2)

i.e. $\quad y = mx$

So $(y-mx)$ must be a factor of L.H.S. of both the equation (1) and (2)

i,e. $\quad y = mx$ satisfies both the equation (1) and (2)

Putting $y = mx$ in both the equation (1) and (2) we have

$$ax^2 + 2\,hx\,(mx) + b\,(mx)^2 = 0$$

i.e. $$x^2\,[a + 2hm + m^2\,b] = 0$$

i.e. $$bm^2 + 2hm + a = 0 \quad (4)$$

and $$a_1\,x^2 + 2h_1\,x\,(mx) + b_1\,(mx)^2 = 0$$

i.e. $$a_1\,x^2 + (2h_1)\,m\cdot x^2 + b_1\,m^2\,x^2 = 0$$

$$x^2\,[b_1\,m^2 + 2h_1\,m + a_1] = 0$$

Since $x \neq 0$

i.e. $$b_1\,m^2 + 2h_1\,m + a_1 = 0 \quad (5)$$

Solving equation (4) and (5) we have

$$\frac{m^2}{2ha_1 - 2ah_1} = \frac{m}{ab_1 - a_1b} = \frac{1}{2bh_1 - 2hb_1}$$

$$m^2 = \frac{ha_1 - ah_1}{bh_1 - hb_1} \quad m = \frac{ab_1 - a_1b}{2(bh_1 - hb_1)}$$

So $$\frac{ha_1 - ah_1}{(bh_1 - hb_1)} = \frac{(ab_1 - a_1b)^2}{4\,(bh_1 - hb_1)^2}$$

Try to Remember

i.e. $$\boxed{(ab_1 - a_1b)^2 = 4\,(ha_1 - ah_1)\,(bh_1 - hb_1)}$$

which is the required condition.

Problem 2 Obtain the equation of a pair of straight lines through the origin which are at right angles to the pair of lines given by the equation

$$ax^2 + 2hxy + by^2 = 0$$

Solution $ax^2 + 2hxy + by^2 = 0$ represents two st. lines $(y - m_1\,x) = 0$ and $(y - m_2\,x) = 0$ both passing through the origin (0, 0).

i.e. $$(ax^2 + 2hxy + by^2) = b\,(y - m_1\,x)\,(y - m_2\,x)$$

i.e. $$ax^2 + 2hxy + by^2 = b\,[y^2 - (m_1 + m_2)\,xy + m_1\,m_2\,x^2]$$

Equating the coefficients of x^2 and xy on both sides we have

$$2h = -(m_1 + m_2)\,b$$

i.e. $$m_1 + m_2 = -\frac{2h}{b} \text{ (always remember)}$$

$$b\,m_1\,m_2 = a$$

i.e. $$m_1\,m_2 = \frac{a}{b} \text{ (always remember)}$$

Let the slope of the lines which are $\perp r$ to the lines $ax^2 + 2hxy + by^2 = 0$ and passing through origin is m_3 and m_4 so the equations are

$$(y - m_3\,x) \equiv 0 \quad \text{and} \quad y - m_4\,x = 0$$

So $\qquad m_1 m_3 = -1 \qquad\qquad m_2 m_4 = -1$

$$m_3 = -\frac{1}{m_1} \qquad \Rightarrow m_4 = -\frac{1}{m_2}$$

So the equations of the iines are

$$\left(y + \frac{1}{m_1} x\right) = 0 \qquad \text{and} \left(y + \frac{1}{m_2} x\right) = 0$$

i.e. $\qquad (m_1 y + x) = 0 \qquad \text{and} \qquad (m_2 y + x) = 0$

So the equation of pair of lines are given by

$$(m_1 y + x)(m_2 y + x) = 0$$

i.e. $\qquad m_1 m_2 y^2 + (m_1 + m_2) xy + x^2 = 0$

i.e. $\qquad \frac{a}{b} y^2 - \frac{2h}{b} xy + x^2 = 0$

i.e. $\qquad \boxed{ay^2 - 2hxy + bx^2 = 0}$ **Remember** Ans.

which is the required equation of pair of straight lines passing through origin and $\perp r$ to the lines

$$ax^2 + 2hxy + by^2 = 0$$

Problem 3 Prove that the pair of lines

$$a^2 x^2 + 2h (a + b) xy + b^2 y^2 = 0$$

is equally inclined to the pair

$$ax^2 + 2hxy + by^2 = 0$$

Solution The first pair is equally inclined to the second pair if the bisector of the first is the same as the bisector of the second. The bisector of the first pair of lines are given by

$$\frac{x^2 - y^2}{a^2 - b^2} = \frac{xy}{h(a + b)}$$

$$\Rightarrow \frac{x^2 - y^2}{(a+b)(a-b)} = \frac{xy}{h(a + b)}$$

$$\frac{x^2 - y^2}{a - b} = \frac{xy}{h}$$

which is also the equation of the bisector of the second pair. Hence the result.

Problem 4 If pairs of straight lines

$$x^2 - 2pxy - y^2 = 0 \text{ and } x^2 - 2qxy - y^2 = 0$$

be such that each bisects the angles between the other pair, prove that $pq = -1$.

Solution Bisector of $x^2-2pxy-y^2=0$ is given by

$$\frac{x^2-y^2}{1-(-1)}=\frac{xy}{-p}$$

i.e. $$\frac{x^2-y^2}{2}=\frac{xy}{-p} \tag{1}$$

i.e. $$-p(x^2-y^2)=2xy$$

i.e. $$-px^2+py^2=2xy$$

i.e. $$px^2+2xy-py^2=0$$

i.e. $$x^2+\frac{2}{p}xy-y^2=0 \tag{2}$$

Again since $x^2-2qxy-y^2=0$ is the bisector of $x^2-2pxy-y^2=0$

So the equation (2) and $x^2-2qxy-y^2=0$ must be identical. Thus equating of the coefficients of xy we have

$$\frac{2}{p}=-2q$$

i.e. $$\boxed{pq=-1}$$ *(Proved)*

Problem 5 Prove that the equation

$$x^2-5xy+4y^2+x+2y-2=0$$

represents two straight lines, find their point of intersection and the angle between them.

Solution The given equation can be written as

$$x^2-5xy+4y^2+x+2y-2=0$$

i.e. $$x^2-(5y-1)x+(4y^2+2y-2)=0$$

i.e. $$x^2-(5y-1)x+2(2y^2+y-1)=0$$

Since this is a quadratic in x so

$$x=\frac{(5y-1)\pm\sqrt{(5y-1)^2-4.2(2y^2+y-1)}}{2}$$

i.e. $$x=\frac{(5y-1)\pm\sqrt{25y^2-10y+1-1(16y^2+8y-8)}}{2}$$

i.e. $$x=\frac{(5y-1)\pm\sqrt{25y^2-10y+1-16y^2-8y+8}}{2}$$

i.e. $$x=\frac{(5x-1)\pm\sqrt{(9y^2-18y+9)}}{2}$$

i.e. $$x=\frac{(5y-1)\pm\sqrt{9(y^2-2y+1)}}{2}$$

i.e. $x = \dfrac{(5y-1) \pm 3\sqrt{(y-1)^2}}{2}$

i.e. $x = \dfrac{(5y-1) \pm 3\,(y-1)}{2}$

i.e. $x = \dfrac{5y-1 + 3y-3}{2}$ (Taking + ve sign)

i.e. $x = \dfrac{8y-4}{2}$

i.e. $x = 4y-2$ i.e. $x-4y + 2 = 0$ (1)

and $x = \dfrac{5y-1-3\,(y-1)}{2}$ (Taking −ve sign)

i.e. $x = \dfrac{5y-1-3y + 3}{2}$

i.e. $x = \dfrac{2y + 2}{2}$

i.e. $x = y + 1$

i.e. $x-y-1 = 0$ (2)

The given equation, therefore, represents the two straight lines

$$x-4y + 2 = 0 \text{ and } x-y-1 = 0 \quad (3)$$

Solving the equation (3) simultaneously we have

$$\frac{x}{4+2} = \frac{y}{2+1} = \frac{1}{-1+4}$$

i.e. $\dfrac{x}{6} = \dfrac{y}{3} = \dfrac{1}{3}$

i.e. $x = 2,\ y = 1$

That is the point of intersection is (2, 1).

The slope of the two lines are $\frac{1}{4}$ and 1.

So the angle between the two lines is given by

$$\tan\theta = \frac{m_1 - m_2}{1 + m_1 \times m_2}$$

i.e. $\tan\theta = \dfrac{1-\frac{1}{4}}{1 + 1\frac{1}{4}}$

$\tan\theta = \dfrac{3/4}{5/4}$ i.e. $\tan\theta = \dfrac{3}{4} \times \dfrac{4}{5}$

i.e. $\tan\theta = \dfrac{3}{5}$

$\therefore$ $\theta = \tan^{-1}\left(\dfrac{3}{5}\right)$ **Ans.**

Ptoblem 6 Find the value of k so that the equation

$$x^2 + kxy + y^2 - 5x - 7y + 6 = 0$$

may represent two straight lines.

Solution The general equation of second degree i.e.

$$ax^2 + 2hxy + by^2 + 2gx + 2fy + c = 0$$

represents a pair of straight lines if

$$abc + 2fgh - af^2 - bg^2 - ch^2 = 0$$

In the given equation

$$a = 1, \quad 2h = k, \quad b = 1$$

$$2g = -5, 2f = -7, c = 6$$

Then $\quad 1\cdot 1\cdot 6 + (-7)\left(-\frac{5}{2}\right)\frac{k}{2} - 1\left(-\frac{7}{2}\right)^2 - 1\cdot\left(-\frac{5}{2}\right) - 6\left(\frac{k}{2}\right)^2 = 0$

i.e. $\quad 6 + \frac{35k}{4} - \frac{49}{4} - \frac{25}{4} - 6\frac{k^2}{4} = 0$

i.e. $\quad 6 + \frac{35k}{4} - \frac{74}{4} - \frac{6k^2}{4} = 0$

i.e. $\quad 24 + 35k - 74 - 6k^2 = 0$

i.e. $\quad -6k^2 + 35k - 50 = 0$

i.e. $\quad 6k^2 - 35k + 50 = 0$

i.e. $\quad 6k^2 - 20k - 15k + 50 = 0$

i.e. $\quad 2k(3k - 10) - 5(3k - 10) = 0$

i.e. $\quad (2k - 5)(3k - 10) = 0$

so either $\quad 2k - 5 = 0 \Rightarrow k = \frac{5}{2}$

or $\quad 3k - 10 = 0 \Rightarrow k = \frac{10}{3}$

i.e. $\quad k = \frac{5}{2}, \frac{10}{3}$ **Ans.**

Problem 7 If the equation $ax^2 + 2hxy + by^2 + 2gx + 2fy + c = 0$ represents a pair of parallel lines prove that

(i) $\quad \frac{a}{h} = \frac{h}{b} = \frac{g}{f}$ and

(ii) the distance between them is

$$= 2\sqrt{\frac{g^2 - ca}{a(a + b)}}$$ [*I.F.S. 82*]

Solution $ax^2 + 2hxy + by^2 + 2gx + 2fy + c = 0$
represents the parallel straight lines given by

$$lx + my + n = 0 \text{ and}$$
$$lx + my + n_1 = 0$$

Then we have $ax^2 + 2hxy + by^2 + 2gx + 2fy + c$

$$\equiv (lx + my + n)(lx + my + n_1)$$

i.e.
$$ax^2 + 2hxy + by^2 + 2gx + 2fy + c$$
$$\equiv l^2 x^2 + lmxy + ln_1 x + lm xy + m^2 y^2 + mn_1 y + nlx + mny + nn_1$$

i.e.
$$ax^2 + 2hxy + by^2 + 2gx + 2fy + c$$
$$\equiv l^2 x^2 + m^2 y^2 + 2 lmxy + l(n + n_1)x + m(n + n_1)y + nn_1$$

Equating the coefficient of x^2, y^2, axy and the constant term on both sides we have

$$l^2 = a \qquad\qquad 2g = l(n + n_1)$$
$$m^2 = b \qquad\qquad 2f = m(n + n_1)$$
$$lm = h \qquad\qquad c = nn_1$$

Now
$$\frac{a}{h} = \frac{l^2}{lm} = \frac{l}{m} \tag{1}$$
$$\frac{h}{b} = \frac{lm}{m^2} = \frac{l}{m} \tag{2}$$
$$\frac{g}{f} = \frac{2l(n + n_1)}{2m(n + n_1)} = \frac{l}{m} \tag{3}$$

From equation (1), (2) and (3) we have

$$\frac{a}{h} = \frac{h}{h} = \frac{g}{f} \qquad [F.P.P.]$$

The perpendicular distance between

$$lx + my + n = 0 \text{ and}$$
$$lx + my + n_1 = 0$$

is given by
$$= \frac{n - n_1}{\sqrt{l^2 + m_2}}$$

we have
$$(n - n_1)^2 = (n + n_1)^2 - 4nn_1$$
$$= \left(\frac{2g}{l}\right)^2 - 4c$$
$$= \frac{4g^2}{l^2} - 4e = 4\left(\frac{g^2}{l^2} - c\right) = 4\frac{g^2 - cl^2}{l^2}$$
$$n - n_1 = \frac{2\sqrt{g^2 - cl^2}}{l}$$

So the distance between them ($\perp r$ in the sense that they are parallel to each other)

$$= \frac{2\sqrt{g^2 - cl^2}}{l\sqrt{l^2 + m^2}} = \frac{2\sqrt{g^2 - ca}}{\sqrt{a}\ \sqrt{a+b}}$$

$$= \frac{2\sqrt{g^2 - ca}}{\sqrt{(a + b)\, a}} \qquad \text{[Second Part Proved]}$$

$$l^2 = a \Rightarrow l = \sqrt{a}$$

Problem 8 Prove that the angle between the straight lines joining the origin to the intersection of the straight line $y = 3x + 2$ with the curve $x^2 + 2xy + 3y^2 + 4x + 8y - 11 = 0$ is

$$\tan^{-1} \frac{2\sqrt{2}}{3}$$

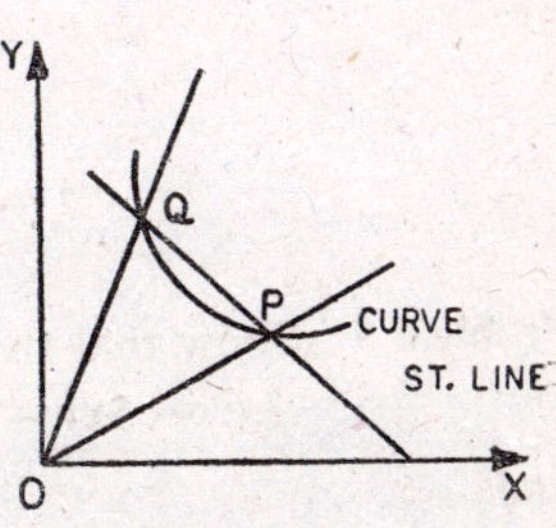

Note To obtain the equation to the lines joining the origin to the points of intersection of a given line and a given curve, make the equation of the curve, homogeneous with the help of the equation to the given straight line

Remember this fact and apply this to the above type of problems.

Solution The equation of the lines joining the origin to the intersection of the given line with the curve is

$$x^2 + 2xy + 3y^2 + (4x + 8y)\left(\frac{y - 3x}{2}\right) - 11\left(\frac{y - 3x}{2}\right)^2 = 0$$

$$x^2 + 2xy + 3y^2 + \frac{(4x + 8y)(y - 3x)}{2} - 11\frac{(y - 3x)^2}{4} = 0$$

i.e. $$4x^2 + 8xy + 12y^2 + 2(4x + 8y)(y - 3x) - 11(y - 3x)^2 = 0$$

$$4x^2 + 8xy + 12y^2 + 8xy + 16y^2 - 24x^2 - 48xy - (11y^2 - 66xy + 99x^2) = 0$$

i.e. $$4x^2 + 8xy + 12y^2 + 8xy + 16y^2 - 24x^2 - 48xy - 11y^2 + 66xy - 99x^2 = 0$$

$\Rightarrow$ $$-119x^2 + 17y^2 + 34xy = 0$$

i.e. $$119x^2 - 34xy - 17y^2 = 0$$

$$17(7x^2 - 2xy - y^2) = 0$$

i.e. $$7x^2 - 2xy - y^2 = 0$$

Here $a = 7 \quad b = -1 \quad 2h = -2 \quad h = -1$

If θ be the angle between the lines, then

$$\tan\theta = \frac{2\sqrt{h^2 - ab}}{a + b}$$

i.e. $$\tan\theta = \frac{2\sqrt{(-1)^2-7(-1)}}{7-1}$$

i.e. $$\tan\theta = \frac{2\sqrt{1+7}}{6}$$

i.e. $$\tan\theta = \frac{2\sqrt{8}}{6}$$

$$\tan\theta = \frac{\sqrt{8}}{3}$$

$$\tan\theta = \frac{\sqrt{4\times 2}}{3}$$

i.e. $$\tan\theta = \frac{2\sqrt{2}}{3}$$

$$\theta = \tan^{-1}\left(\frac{2\sqrt{2}}{3}\right)$$ **Ans.**

Problem 9 Show that the lines joining the origin to the intersection of

$$3x^2 + 5xy - 3y^2 + 2x + 3y = 0$$

and

$$3x - 2y = 1 \text{ at right angles}$$ [*I.F.S. 81*]

Solution The equation of the lines joining the origin and the intersection of curve and straight line can be obtained by making the equation of the curve of homogeneous with the help of equation of straight line.

$$3x^2 + 5xy - 3y^2 + 2x + 3y = 0$$

$$3x^2 + 5xy - 3y^2 + (2x + 3y)\cdot 1 = 0$$

i.e. $$3x^2 + 5xy - 3y^2 + (2x + 3y)(3x - 2y) = 0$$

i.e. $$3x^2 + 5xy - 3y^2 + 6x^2 - 4xy + 9xy - 6y^2 = 0$$

i.e. $$9x^2 + 10xy - 9y^2 = 0$$

Here $$a = 9,\quad b = -9$$

$$a + b = 9 - 9 = 0$$

So the lines are at right angles. *(Proved)*

Problem 10 Find the value of k so that the lines which join the origin to points of intersection of the line $y - x = k$ and the curve $x^2 + y^2 + 4x - 6y - 36 = 0$ may be at right angles.

Solution The equation of line joining the origin to the intersection of the given line with the curve is

$$x^2 + y^2 + (4x - 6y)\left(\frac{y-x}{k}\right) - 36\left(\frac{y-x}{k}\right)^2 = 0$$

i.e. $$x^2 + y^2 + \frac{(4x-6y)(y-x)}{k} - 36\frac{(y-x)^2}{k^2} = 0$$

i.e. $$k^2[(x^2 + y^2)] + k(4x-6y)(y-x) - 36(y^2-2xy + x^2) = 0$$

i.e. $$k^2x^2 + k^2y^2 + k(10xy-4x^2-6y^2) - 36(y^2-2xy + x^2$$

i.e. $$k^2x^2 + k^2y^2 + 10kxy - 4kx^2 - 6ky^2 - 36y^2 + 72xy - 36x^2 = 0$$

i.e. $$x^2(k^2-4k-36) + y^2(k^2-6k-36) + xy(10k + 72) = 0$$

i.e. $$x^2(k^2-4k-36) + y^2(k^2-6k-36) + 2xy(5k + 36) = 0$$

If the lines are at right angles the coefficient of x^2 + coefficient of $y^2 = 0$

$$\Rightarrow k^2-4k-36 + k^2-6k-36 = 0$$

i.e. $$2k^2-10k-72 = 0$$

i.e. $$k^2-5k-36 = 0$$

$$k^2-9k + 4k - 36 = 0$$

i.e. $$k(k-9) + 4(k-9) = 0$$

i.e. $$(k + 4)(k-9) = 0$$

i.e. $k = 9$ or -4 **Ans.**

Problem 11 Show that the product of the perpendiculars from any point $(\alpha_1 \beta)$ on the lines $ax^2 + 2b\,xy + by^2 = 0$ is

$$\frac{ae^2 + 2h\alpha\beta + b\beta^2}{\sqrt{(a-b)^2 + 4h^2}}$$

Solution Let the two lines be represented by the equation $ax^2 + 2h\,xy + by^2 = 0$ be

$$y-m_1x = 0 \quad \text{and} \quad y-m_2x = 0 \tag{1}$$

Then $$m_1 + m_2 = -\frac{2h}{b} \quad \text{and} \quad m_1m_2 = \frac{a}{b}$$

Now if p_1 and p_2 be the lengths of the perpendicnlar from the point $(\alpha_1 \beta)$ on the lines (1), then

$$p_1 = \frac{\beta - m_1\alpha}{\sqrt{1 + m_1^2}} \quad \text{and} \quad p_2 = \frac{\beta - m_2\alpha}{\sqrt{1 + m_2^2}}$$

$$\therefore \quad p_1p_2 = \frac{(\beta - m_1\alpha)(\beta - m_2\alpha)}{\sqrt{1 + m_1^2}\sqrt{1 + m_2^2}}$$

$$= \frac{\beta^2 - (m_1 + m_2)\alpha_1\beta + m_1m_2\alpha^2}{\sqrt{1 + m_1^2 + m_2^2 + m_1^2m_2^2}}$$

$$= \frac{\beta^2 - (-2h/b)\alpha\beta + a/b\,\alpha^2}{\sqrt{1 + (m_1 + m_2)^2 - 2m_1m_2 + (m_1m_2)^2}}$$

$$p_1 p_2 = \frac{\beta^2 + 2h/b\, \alpha\beta + a/b\, \alpha^2}{\sqrt{1 + 4h^2/b^2 - 2a/b + a^2/b^2}}$$

$$p_1 p_2 = \frac{b\, \beta^2 + 2h\alpha\beta + a\alpha^2}{\sqrt{b^2 + 4h^2 - 2ab + a^2}}$$

$$p_1 p_2 = \frac{a\alpha^2 + 2h\alpha\beta + b\beta^2}{\sqrt{(a-b)^2 + 4h^2}}$$

Problem 12. Find the equation to the pair of straight lines joining the origin to the intersections of the straight line $y = mx + c$ and the circle $x^2 + y^2 = a^2$. Prove that they are at right angles if

$$ac^2 = a^2 (1 + m^2) \qquad \text{[I.F.S. 84]}$$

Solution The equation of the pair of straight lines joining the origin to the intersections of the straight line $y = mx + c$ (1) and the circle $x^2 + y^2 = a^2$ (2) can be obtained by making the equation (2) homogenous with tne help of equation (1)

$$x^2 + y^2 = a^2 \cdot 1$$

$$x^2 + y^2 = a^2 \left(\frac{y-x}{c}\right)^2 \qquad \left| \quad \frac{y-mx}{c} = 1 \right.$$

$$x^2 + y^2 = \frac{a^2}{c^2} (y-mx)^2$$

$$c^2 (x^2 + y^2) = a^2 (y^2 - 2\, mxy + m^2 x^2)$$

i.e. $$c^2 x^2 + c^2 y^2 = a^2 y^2 - 2ma^2 xy + a^2 m^2 x^2$$

i.e. $$c^2 x^2 + c^2 y^2 - a^2 y^2 + 2m\, a^2 xy - a^2 m^2 x^2 = 0$$

i.e. $$(c^2 - a^2 m^2)\, x^2 + (c^2 - a^2)\, y^2 + 2m\, a^2 xy = 0 \qquad (3)$$

If the two lines represente d by (3) are at right angles then coefficient of x^2 + coefficient of $y^2 = 0$

i.e. $$c^2 - a^2 m^2 + c^2 - a^2 = 0$$

$$2c^2 = a^2 + a^2 m^2$$

i.e $$2c^2 = a^2 (1 + m^2)$$

Problem 13 If the equation

$$ax^2 + 2h\, xy + by^2 + 2gx + 2fy + c = 0$$

represents a pair of straight lines equidistant from the origin show that

$$f^4 - g^4 = c\, (bf^2 - ag^2) \qquad \text{[I.F.S. 83]}$$

Solution The general equation of 2nd degree is

$$ax^2 + 2hxy + by^2 + 2gx + 2fy + c = 0$$

Let this represents a pair of straight lines given by

$$l_1 x + m_1 y + n_1 \quad \text{and} \quad l_2 x + m_2 y + n_2 = 0$$

$$ax^2 + 2hxy + by^2 + 2gx + 2fy + c$$
$$\equiv (l_1 x + m_1 y + n_1)(l_2 x + m_2 y + n_2)$$

$$ax^2 + 2hxy + by^2 + 2gx + 2fy + c$$
$$= l_1 l_2 x^2 + l_1 m_2 xy + l_1 n_2 x$$
$$+ m_1 l_2 xy + m_1 m_2 y^2 + m_1 n_2 y$$
$$+ n_1 l_2 x + n_1 m_2 y + n_1 n_2$$

$$ax^2 + 2hxy + by^2 + 2gx + 2fy + c$$
$$\equiv l_1 l_2 x^2 + (l_1 m_2 + m_1 l_2) xy + m_1 m_2 y^2$$
$$+ (l_1 n_2 + n_1 t_2) x + (m_1 n_2 + n_1 m_2) y + n_1 n_2$$

Equation the coefficient of x^2, y^1, xy x, y and the constant term we have

$$l_1 l_2 = a \qquad l_1 n_2 + n_1 l_2 = 2g$$
$$l_1 m_2 + m_1 l_2 = 2h \qquad m_1 n_2 + n_1 m_2 = 2f$$
$$m_1 m_2 = b \qquad n_1 n_2 = c$$

The distances of the straight lines from the origin is given by

$$\frac{0 + 0 + n_1}{\sqrt{i_1^2 + m_2^1}} \quad \text{and} \quad \frac{0 + 0 + n_2}{\sqrt{l_2^2 + m_2^2}}$$

i.e. $$\frac{n_1}{\sqrt{l_1^2 + m_1^2}} \quad \text{and} \quad \frac{n_2}{\sqrt{l_2^2 + m_2^2}}$$

Since the straight lines are equidistant from the origin so

$$\frac{n_1}{\sqrt{l_1^2 + m_1^2}} = \frac{n_2}{\sqrt{l_2^2 + m_2^2}}$$

$$\Rightarrow \quad \frac{n_1^2}{l_1^2 + m_1^1} = \frac{n_2^2}{l_2^2 + m_2^2}$$

$$\Rightarrow \quad n_1^2 (l_2^2 + m_2^2) = n_2^2 (l_1^2 + m_1^2)$$

$$\Rightarrow \quad n_1^2 l_2^2 + n_1^2 m_2^2) = n_2^2 l_1^2 + n_2^2 m_1^2$$

$$\Rightarrow \quad n_1^2 l_2^2 - n_2^2 l_1^2 = n_2^2 m_1^2 - n_1^2 m^2$$

$$\Rightarrow (n_1 l_2 + n_2 l_1)(n_1 l_2 - n_2 l_1)$$
$$= (n_2 m_1 + n_1 m_2)(n_2 m_1 - n_1 m_2)$$

squaring both sides we have

$$(n_1 l_2 + n_2 l_1)^2 (n_1 l_2 - n_2 l_1)^2$$
$$= (n_2 m_1 + n_1 m_2)^2 (n_2 m_1 - n_1 m_2)^2$$

$$(n_1 l_2 + n_2 l_1)^2 [n_1 l_2 + n_2 l_1)^2 - 4 l_1 l_2 n_1 n_2]$$
$$= (n_2 m_1 + n_1 m_2)^2 [(n_2 m_1 + n_1 m_2)^2 - 4 n_1 n_2 m_1 m_2]$$

$$(2g)^2\,[(2g)^2-4ac] = (2f)^2)\,[2f^2-4cb]$$
$$4g^2\,[4g^2-4ac] = 4f^2\,[4f^2-4bc]$$
$$16g^2\,(g^2-ac) = 16f^2\,(f^2-bc)$$
$$g^4-g^2\,ac = f^4-f^2\,bc$$
$$f^4-g^4 = f^2\,bc-\;g^2\,ac$$
$$f^4-g^4 = c\,[bf^2-ag^2]$$

(*Proved*)

Problem 14 Find the length of the intercept made on the line made on the line $lx+my+n=0$ by the pair of lines $ax^2+2hxy+by^2=0$ and find the area of the triangle thus formed.

Solution Let the equation of the two straight lines represented by the equation

$ax^2+2hxy+by^2=0$ be

$$y-m_1\,x=0$$

and
$$y-m_2\,x=0$$

$$m_1+m_2=-\frac{2h}{b}\,m_1\,m_2=\frac{a}{b}$$

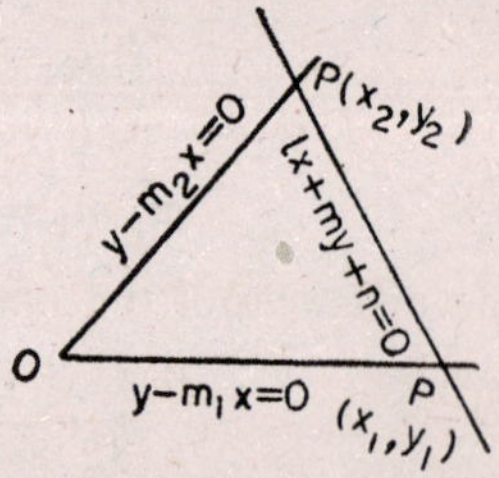

let $p\,(x_1, y_1)$ be the point of intersection of the line $y-m_1\,x=0$ and $lx+my+n=0$ sincc (x_1, y_1) lies on both the lines $y-m_1\,x=0$ and $lx+my+n=0$. Thus it will satisfy both the equation

$$y_1-m_1\,x_1=0$$

i.e.
$$y_1=m_1\,x_1$$

and
$$lx_1+my_1+n=0$$

i.e.
$$lx_1+mm_1\,x_1+n=0$$
$$x_1\,(l+mm_1)=-n$$
$$\Rightarrow x_1=-\frac{n}{(l+mm_1)}$$

and
$$y_1=-\frac{m_1\,n}{l+mm_1}$$

Similarly if $\theta\,(x_2, y_2)$ be the point of intersection of the line $y-m_2\,x=0$ and $lx+my+n=0$ then

$$y_2-m_2\,x_2=0 \qquad \Rightarrow y_2=m_2\,x_2$$
$$lx_2+my_2+n=0$$
$$lx_2+mm_2\,x_2+n=0$$
$$\Rightarrow x_2\,(l+mm_2)=-n$$
$$\Rightarrow x_2=-\frac{n}{l+mm_2} \quad \text{and} \quad y_2=-\frac{m_2\,n}{l+mm_2}$$

Thus the co-ordinates of the point of intersection

$$P\left[-\frac{n}{l+mm_2}, \quad \frac{-m_1 n}{l+mm_1}\right]$$

$$\text{and } Q\left[-\frac{n}{l+mm_2}, -\frac{m_2 n}{l+mm_2}\right]$$

The Co-ordinate of the point 0 (0, 0)

Let the length of the intercept $pQ = d$

Then, $$d^2 = [x_1-x_2]^2 + [y_1-y_2]^2$$

$$d^2 = \left[\frac{-n}{l+mm_1} + \frac{n}{l+mm_2}\right]^2 + \left[\frac{-m_1 n}{l+mm_1} + \frac{m_2 n}{l+mm_2}\right]^2$$

i.e. $$d^2 = \frac{[-n(l+mm_2)+n(l+mm_1)]^2}{[(l+mm_1)(l+mm_2)]^2} + \frac{[-m_1 n(l+mm_2)+m_2 n(l+mm_1)]^2}{(l+mm_1)(l+mm_2)]^2}$$

$$d^2 = \frac{[-mn(m_1-m_2]^2}{[l^2+lm(m_1+m_2)+m^2m_1m_2]}$$

$$+\frac{[-m_1nl-m_1m_2mn+m_2nl+m_1m_2mn}{[l^2+lm(m_1+m_2)+m^2m_1m_2]^2}$$

$$d^2 = \frac{m^2n^2(m_1-m_2)^2}{[l^2+lm(m_1+m_2)+m^2m_1m_2]^2} + \frac{n^2l^2(m_2-m_1)^2}{[l^2+lm(m_1+m_2)+m^2m_1m_2]^2}$$

$$d^2 = \frac{m^2n^2(m_1-m_2)^2}{l^2+lm(m_1+m_2)+m^2m_1m]^2} + \frac{n^2l^2(m_1-m_2^2)}{[l+lm(m_1+m_2)+m^2m_1m_2]}$$

$$d^2 = \frac{n^2(l^2+m^2)(m_1-m_2)^2}{[l^2+lm(m_1+m_2)+m^2m_1m_2]^2}$$

Now $$(m_1-m_2) = (m_1+m_2)^2-4m_1m_2$$

$$(m_1-m_2)^2 = \frac{4h^2}{b^2} - 4\frac{a}{b}$$

i.e. $$(m_1-m_2)^2 = \frac{4(h^2-ab)}{b^2}$$

i.e. $$m_1-m_2 = \frac{2\sqrt{h^2-ba}}{b}$$

Hence $$d^2 = \frac{n^2(l^2+m^2)4(h-ab)/b^2}{[l^2+lm(-2h/b)+m^2a/b]^2}$$

i.e. $$d^2 = \frac{n^2(l^2+m^2)4(h^2-ab)}{(bl^2-2hlm+am^2)^2}$$

$$d = \frac{2n\sqrt{l^2+m^2}\sqrt{h^2-ab}}{(am^2-2hlm+bl^2)}$$

$$d = \frac{2n\sqrt{l^2+m^2}\sqrt{h^2-ab}}{am^2-2hlm+bl^2}$$ **Ans.**

Area of a triangle whose vertics are (x_1, y_1); $(x_2\ y_2)$ and (x_3, y_3) is given b

$$\tfrac{1}{2}[x_1(y_2-y_3)+x_2(y_3-y_1)+x_3(y_1-y_2)]$$

If the co-ordinate of one vertices is (0, 0) i.e. $(x_1, y_1) = (0, 0)$ then

Area of the triangle is$= \frac{1}{2}[x_2 y_3 - x_3 y_2]$

Here
$$x_2 = -\frac{n}{l+mm_1}$$

$$y_2 = \frac{-m_1 n}{l+mm_1}$$

$$x_3 = -\frac{n}{l+mm_2}$$

$$y_3 = -\frac{m_2 n}{l+mm_2}$$

$$\text{Area} = \frac{1}{2}\left[-\frac{a}{l+mm_1} - \frac{m_2 n}{l+mm_2} - \frac{-n}{l+mm_2} - \frac{-m_1 n}{l+mm_1}\right.$$

$$= \frac{1}{2}\left[\frac{m_2 n^2}{(l+mm_1)(l+mm_2)} - \frac{m_1 n^2}{(l+mm_1)(l+mm_2)}\right]$$

$$= \frac{1}{2}\frac{n^2(m_2-m_1)}{(l+mm_1)(l+mm_2)} = \frac{1}{2}\frac{n^2(m_2-m_1)}{l^2+lm(m_1+m_2)+m^2 m_1 m_2}$$

$$\text{Area} = \frac{1}{2}\frac{n^2(m_2-m_1)}{l^2+lm(m_1+m_2)+m^2 m_1 m_2}$$

We have $m_1 + m_2 = -\frac{2h}{b}$

$$m_1 m_2 = \frac{a}{b}$$

Then $(m_2-m_1)^2 = (m_2+m_1)^2 - 4m_1 m_2$

$$= \left(-\frac{2h}{b}\right)^2 - \frac{4a}{b} = \frac{4h^2}{b^2} - \frac{4a}{b} = \frac{4(h^2-ab)}{b^2}$$

i.e. $\quad m_2 - m_1 = \frac{2\sqrt{h^2-ab}}{b}$

$$\text{Area} = \frac{1}{2}\frac{n^2\, 2\sqrt{h^2-ab}}{b\,[\cdot l^2 + lm(-2h(/b) + m^2 a/b]}$$

$$\text{Area} = \frac{n^2\sqrt{h^2-ab}}{b\,[l^2 - 2lmh/b + m^2 a/b]}$$

$$\text{Area} = \frac{n^2\sqrt{h^2-ab}}{b\,[am^2 + bl^2 - 2lmh]}$$

$$\text{Area} = \frac{n^2\sqrt{h^2-ab}}{am^2 - 2lmh + bl^2} \qquad \textbf{Ans.}$$

Problem 15 Show that the straight lines joining the origin to the points of intersectien of the curves

$$ax^2 + 2hxy + by^2 + 2gx = 0$$

and
$$a_1 x^2 + 2h_1 xy + b_1 y^2 + 2g_1 x = 0$$

will be at right angles if $\dfrac{a+b}{b} = \dfrac{a_1 + b_1}{g_1}$

Solution The equation of the straight lines joining the origin to the points of intesection of the curves

$$ax^2 + 2hxy + by^2 + 2gx = 0 \quad (1)$$

and
$$a_1 x^2 + 2h_1 xy + b_1 y^2 + 2g_1 x = 0 \quad (2)$$

Can be obtained by obtaining a homogeneous equation of 2nd degree with the help of equation (1) and (2) multiplying equation (1) by g_1 and (2) by g we have

$$ag_1 x^2 + 2hg_1 xy + bg_1 y^2 + 2gg_1 x = 0 \quad (3)$$

$$a_1 g^2 + 2h_1 gxy + bigy^2 + 2gg_1 x = 0 \quad (4)$$

subtrating (4) by (3) we have

$$(ag_1 - a_1 g)\, x^2 + 2xy\, 2xy\, (hg_1 - h_1 g) + g^2\, (bg_1 - b_1 g)$$

The two straight lines represented by this are at right angles if cofficient of x^2 + coefficient of $y^2 = 0$

i.e.
$$ag_1 - a_1 g + bg_1 - b_1 g = 0$$

i.e.
$$ag_1 + bg_1 = a_1 g + b_1 g$$

$$\Rightarrow \quad (a+b)\, g_1 = (a_1 + b_1)\, g$$

$$\Rightarrow \quad \frac{a+b}{g} = \frac{a_1 + b_1}{g_1}$$

(Proved)

Problem 16 If the equation $ax^2 + 2hxy + by^2 + 2gx + 2fy + c = 0$ represents a pair of straight lines equidistant from the origin show that

$$h\,(g^2 - f^2) = fg\,(a-b)$$

[*Similar as in I.F.S. 237*]

Solution Let $ax^2 + 2hxy + by^2 + 2gx + 2fy + c = 0$ represents a pair of straight lines given by

$$l_1 x + m_1 y + n_1 = 0 \text{ and } l_2 x + m_2 y + n_2 = 0$$

Then we have the identity.

$$ax^2 + 2hxy + by^2 + 2gx + 2fy + c$$
$$\equiv (l_1 x + m_1 y + n_1)(l_2 x + m_2 y + n_2)$$
$$\equiv l_1 l_2 x^2 + l_1 m_2 xy + l_1 n_2 x + l_2 m_1 xy + m_1 m_2 y^2 + m_1 n_2 y + l_2 n_1 x + m_2 n_1 y + n_1 n_2$$
$$= l_1 l_2 x^2 + xy\,(l_1 m_2 + l_2 m_1) + m_1 m_2 y^2 + (l_1 n_2 + l_2 n_1) + (m_1 n_2 + m_2 n_1)\, y + n_1 n_2$$

Since $ax^2 + 2hxy + by^2 + 2gx + 2fy + c$

$$\equiv l_1 l_2 x^2 + xy(l_1 m_2 + l_2 m_1) + m_1 m_2 y^2 + (l_1 n_2 + l_2 n_1)x + (m_1 n_2 + m_2 n_1)y + n_1 n_2$$

is an identity

So equating the coefficient of x^2, y^2, xy, x, y and the constant term on both sides we have

$$l_1 l_2 = a \qquad l_1 n_2 + l_2 n_1 = 2g$$
$$l_1 m_2 + l_2 m_1 = 2h \qquad m_1 n_2 + m_2 n_1 = 2f$$
$$m_1 m_2 = b \qquad n_1 n_2 = c$$

$\perp r$ distance of $l_1 x + m_1 y + n_1 = 0$ from (0, 0 is given by

$$\frac{n_1}{\sqrt{l_1^2 + m_1^2}}$$

and the $\perp r$ distance $l_2 x + m_2 y + n_2 = 0$ from (0, 0) is given by

$$\frac{n_2}{\sqrt{l_2^2 + m_2^2}}$$

From question they are equidistant

$$\frac{n_1}{\sqrt{l_1^2 + m_1^2}} = \frac{n_2}{\sqrt{l_2^2 + m_2^2}}$$

Squaring both sides we have

$$\frac{n_2^1}{l_1^2 + m_1^2} = \frac{n_2^2}{l_2^2 + m_2^2}$$

$$\Rightarrow \qquad n_1^2 (l_2^2 + m_2^2) = n_2^2 (l_2^2 + m_1^2)$$

$$\Rightarrow \qquad n_1' l_2^2 - n_2^2 l_2^2 = m_1^2 n_2^2 - m_2^2 n_1^2$$

$$\Rightarrow (n_1 l_2 - n_2 l_1)(n_1 l_2 + n_2 l_1) = (m_1 m_2 - m_2 n_1)(m_1 n_2 + m_2 n_1)$$

same question as S. No. 13] soproceed after this.

Problem 17 If the equation $ax^2 + 2hxy + by^2 + 2gx + 2fy + c$ represents two straight lines, prove that the product of the length of the $1r$ from the origin on these lines is

$$\frac{c}{\sqrt{(a-b)^2 + 4h^2}}$$

Solution Let the lines are

$$l_1 x + m_1 y + n_1 = 0$$

And $\qquad l_2 x + m_2 y + n_2 = 0$

i.e. $\qquad ax^2 + 2hxy + by^2 + 2gx + 2fy + c$

$$\equiv (l_1 x + m_1 y + n_1)(l_2 x + m_2 y + n_2)$$

where the relation are

$$l_1 l_2 = a \qquad l_1 n_2 + l_2 n_1 = 2g$$

$$l_1 m_2 + l_2 m_1 = 2h \qquad m_1 n_2 + m_2 n_1 = 2f$$

$$m_1 m_2 = b \qquad n_1 n_2 = c$$

Let lengths of the perpendicular to the the line $l_1 x + m_1 y + n_1 = 0$ and $l_2 x + m_2 y + n_2 = 0$ are P_1 and P_2 then

$$P_1 = \frac{n_1}{\sqrt{l_1^2 + m_1^2}}$$

$$P_2 = \frac{n_2}{\sqrt{l_2^2 + m_2^2}}$$

We have to show that

$$p_1 p_2 = \frac{n_1 n_2}{\sqrt{(i_1^2 + m_1^2)(l_2^2 + m_2^2)}} \tag{1}$$

we have $(l_1^2 + m_1^2)(l_2^2 + m_2^2)$

$$= l_1^2 l_2^2 + + m_1^2 m_2^2 + l_2^2 m_1^2 + l_1^2 m_2^2$$

$$= (l_1 l_2)^2 + (m_1 m_2)^2 + (l_2 m_1)^2 + (l_1 m_2)^2$$

$$= (l_1 l_2)^2 + (m_1 m_2)^2 + (l_2 m_1 + l_1 m_2)^2 - 2l_2 m_1 l_1 m_2$$

$$= (l_1 l_2)^2 + (m_1 m_2)^2 + (l_2 m_1 + l_1 m_2)^2 - 2l_1 l_2 m_1 m_2$$

$$= a^2 + b^2 + (2h)^2 - 2ab$$

$$= a^2 - 2ab + b^2 + 4h^2 = (a-b)^2 + 4h^2$$

i.e. product of the length of perpendiculars is

i.e. $$p_1 p_2 = \frac{c}{\sqrt{(a-b)^2 + 4b^2}}$$ *(Proved)*

Problem 1 (i) Find the angle between the lines joining the origin to the points common to $x - y = 2$ and $5x^2 + 12xy - 8y^2 + 8x - 4y + 12 = 0$.

(ii) If the angle between the lines joining the origin to the points of intersection of $lx + my = 1$ and $x^2 + y^2 = a^2$ be 45^a show that

$$4[a^2(l^2 + m^2) - 1] = [a^2(l^2 + m^2) - 2]^2$$

Solution (i) At firs we shall obtain the equation of the line joining the origin to the points common to $x - y = 2$ (1)

and $5x^2 + 12xy - 8y^2 + 8x - 4y + 12 = 0$ (2)

For this we shall make equation (2) homogenous with the hep of equation

$$x - y = 2$$

$$\Rightarrow \left(\frac{x-y}{2}\right) = 1$$

We have $$5x^2 + 12xy - 8y^2 + 8x - 4y + 12 = 0$$

i.e. $$5x^2 + 12xy - 8y^2 + (8x - 4y)\,1 + 12.1^2 = 0$$

i.e. $$5x^2 + 12xy - 8y^2 + (8x - 4y)\left(\frac{x-y}{2}\right) + 12\left(\frac{x-y}{2}\right)^2 = 1$$

i.e. $$(5x^2 + 12xy - 8y^2) + \frac{(8x - 4y)(x - y)}{2} + 12\left(\frac{x^2 - 2xy + y^2}{4} = 1\right)$$

i.e. $$(5x^2 + 12xy - 8y^2) + (4x - 2y)(x - y) + 3(x^2 - 2xy + y^2) = 1$$

$$5x^2 + 12xy - 8y^2 + 4x^2 - 4xy - 2xy + 2y^2 + 3x^2 - 6xy + 3y^2 = 1$$

$$12x^2 - 0 \cdot xy - 3y^2 = 0$$

Here $$a = 12 \qquad 2h = 0 \qquad \Rightarrow h = 0$$

$$b = -3$$

Let θ is the angle between them $\theta = \dfrac{2\sqrt{h^2 - ab}}{a + b}$

i.e. $$\tan\theta = \frac{2\sqrt{(0)^2 - (12)(-3)}}{12 - 3}$$

$$\tan\theta = \frac{2\sqrt{36}}{9}$$

$$\tan\theta = \frac{2 \times 6}{9}$$

$$\tan\theta = \frac{4}{3}$$

$$\Rightarrow \theta = \tan^{-1}\left(\frac{4}{3}\right)$$

(ii) The equation of the line joining the origin to the point of intersection of $lx + my = 1$ and $x^2 + y^2 = a^2$ can be obtained by making the equation $x^2 + y^2 = a^2$ homogeneous with the help of the equation

$$lx + my = 1$$

$$x^2 + y^2 = a^2 \cdot 1^2$$

i.e. $$x^2 + y^2 = a^2 (lx + my)^2$$

i.e. $$x^2 + y = a^2 [l^2 x^2 + m^2 y^2 + 2lx\, m^2]$$

i.e. $$x^2 + y^2 = a^2 l^2 x^2 + a^2 m^2 y^2 + 2lma^2 xy$$

i.e. $$x^2 \left(\frac{1 - a^2 l^2}{A}\right) + y^2 \left(\frac{1 - a^2 m^2}{B}\right) - 2\, lma^2\, xy = 0$$

Which is a hormogeneous form of second dergree of the form

$$Ax^2 + By^2 + 2hxy = 0 \qquad (1)$$

where

$$A = (1 - a^2 l^2)$$

$$B = (1 - a^2 m^2)$$

$$H = -a^2 lm$$

Since the angle between the lines (1) 45°

So

$$\tan 45^\circ = \frac{2\sqrt{H^2 - AB}}{A + B}$$

$$1 = \frac{2\sqrt{H^2 - AB}}{A + B}$$

i.e.

$$(A + B)^2 = 4 (H^2 - AB)$$

i.e.

$$4 [(-a^2 lm)^2 - (1 - a^2 l^2) (1 - a^2 m^2)] = [1 - a^2 l^2 + 1 - a^2 m^2]^2$$

i.e.

$$4 [a^4 l^2 m^2 - (1 - a^2 m^2 - a^2 l^2 + a^4 l^2 m^2)] = [2 - a^2 (l^2 + m^2)]^2$$

$$4 [a^4 l^2 m^2 - 1 + a^2 (l^2 + m^2)] - a^4 l^2 m^2] = [2 - a^2 (l^2 + m^2)]$$

i.e.

$$4 [a^2 [l^2 + m^2) - 1] = [a^2 (l^2 + m^2) - 2] \text{ [Proved]}$$

Problem 2 If the equation $ax^2 + 2hxy + by^2 + 2gx + 2fy + c = 0$ represents two straiget lines, prove that the square of the distance of their point of intersection from the origin

$$\frac{c(a + b) - f^2 - g^2}{ab - h^2}$$

Solution If the straight lines are at right angles, then the above distance

$$= \frac{f^2 + g^2}{b^2 + h^2}$$

To solve this equation At first Remember the following facts.

The pair of straight line

$$ax^2 + 2hxy + by^2 + 2gx + 2fy + c = 0 \qquad (1)$$

Is parallel to the pair of straight line

$$ax^2 + 2hxy + by^2 = 0 \qquad (2)$$

Since we know that the angle between the pair of straight line (2) is given by

$$\tan \theta = \frac{2\sqrt{h^2 - ab}}{a + b}$$

Hence the angle between the line (1) is also given by

$$\tan \theta = \frac{2\sqrt{h^2 - ab}}{a + b}$$

Let $ax^2 + 2hxy + by^2 + 2gx + 2fy + c = 0$ represents two straight lines given by $l_1 x + m_1 y + n_1 = 0$ (1)

and $l_2 x + m_2 y + n_2 = 0$ (2)

then we have the identify

$$ax^2 + 2hxy + by^2 + 2gx + 2fy + c$$
$$\in (l_1 x + m_1 y + n_1)(l_2 x + m_2 y + n_2)$$
$$ax^2 + 2hxy + by^2 + 2gx + 2fy + c$$
$$\equiv l_1 l_2 x^2 + (l_1 m_2 + l_2 m_1) xy + (l_1 n_2 + l_2 n_1) x$$
$$+ m_1 m_2 y^2 + (m_1 n_2 + m_2 n_1) y + n_1 n_2 \quad (3)$$

Since (3) is an identify so equating the coefficients of x^2, xy, x, y and the constant terms on both sides we have

$$l_1 l_2 = a$$
$$l_1 m_2 + l_2 m_1 = 2h$$
$$l_1 n_2 + l_2 n_1 = 2g$$
$$m_1 n_2 + m_2 n_1 = 2f$$

and

$$n_1 n_2 = c$$
$$m_1 m_2 = b$$

The co-ordinate of the point of intersection $(x_1 y)$ is obtained by solving equation (1) and 2

$$\frac{x}{m_1 n_2 - m_2 n_1} = \frac{y}{l_2 n_1 - l_1 n_2} = \frac{1}{l_1 m_2 - l_2 m_1}$$

i.e.

$$x = \frac{m_1 n_2 - m_2 n_1}{l_1 m_2 - l_2 m_1}, \; y = \frac{l_2 n_1 - l_1 n_2}{l_1 m_2 - l_2 m_1}$$

we have

$$(l_1 m, - l_2 m_1)^2$$
$$= (l_1 m_2 + l_2 m_2)^2 - 4l_1 l_2 m_1 m_2$$
$$= (2h)^2 - 4ab = 4h^2 - 4ab = 4(h^2 - ab)$$
$$\Rightarrow (l_2 m_2 - l_2 m_1) = 2\sqrt{h^2 - ab}$$

and

$$(m_1 n_2 - m_2 n_1)^2 = (m_1 n_2 + m_2 n_1)^2 - 4m_1 m_2 n_1 n_2$$
$$= (2f)^2 - 4bc = 4f^2 - 4bc = 4(f^2 - bc)$$

i.e.

$$(m_1 n_2 - m_2 n_1) = 2\sqrt{f^2 - bc}$$
$$(l_2 n_1 - l_1 n_2)^2 = (l_2 n_1 + l_1 n_2)^2 - 4l_1 l_2 n_1 n_2$$
$$= (2g)^2 - 4ac = 4g^2 - 4ac = 4(g^2 - ac)$$

i.e.

$$(l_2 n_1 - l_1 n) = 2\sqrt{g^2 - ac}$$

Thus the the co-ordinates of the point of intersection is

$$x = \frac{\sqrt{f^2-bc}}{\sqrt{h^2-ab}}$$

$$y = \frac{\sqrt{g^2-ac}}{\sqrt{h^2-ab}}$$

The point of intersection is

$$\left(\sqrt{\frac{f^2-bc}{h^2-ab}}, \sqrt{\frac{g^2-ha}{h^2-ab}}\right)$$

The square of the distance of (x, y) from origin we have

$$(x-0)^2 + (y-0)^2 = x^2 + y^2$$

$$= \frac{f^2-bc}{h^2-ab} + \frac{g^2-ac}{h^2-ab} = \frac{f^2-bc+g^2-ac}{h^2-ab}$$

$$= \frac{f^2+g^2-c(a+b)}{h^2-ab}$$

In case if the straight lines are at right angles to each other then

$$a + b = 0 \qquad \Rightarrow a = -b \quad \text{or} \quad b = -a$$

Then square the distance from origin

$$= \frac{f^2+g^2-c \times 0}{h^2-b(-b)} = \frac{f^2+g^2}{h^2+b^2} \qquad \textit{(Proved)}$$

Problem 30 Show that the length of the straight line joining the fect of the $\perp r$ let fall from the point (f, g) on the pair of lines

$$ax^2 + 2hxy + by^2 = 0 \text{ is}$$

$$2\sqrt{\frac{(h^2-ab)(f^2+g^2)}{(a-b)^2+4h^2}}$$

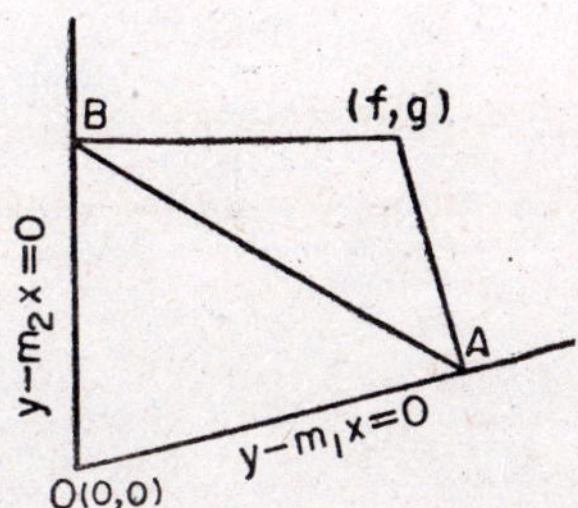

Problem 4 Find the condition so that two of the lines given by $ax^3 + 3bx^2y + 3cxy^2 + dy^3 = 0$ may be at right angless.

Theory Form of the equation of two perpendiculars straight lines through the origin.

We know that the equation of two straight lines passing through origin is given by $ax^2 + by^2 + 2hxy = 0$

Since they are right angles to each other so

$$a + b = 0$$

$$\Rightarrow \quad b = -a$$

So the equation of the straight line becomes

$$ax^2 + 2hxy - a^2y = 0$$

$$\left[x^2 + \frac{2h}{a}xy - y^2\right] = 0$$

i.e. $$x^2 + \frac{2h}{a}xy - y^2 = 0$$

Since $$a \neq 0$$

Which is of the form $$x^2 + pxy - y^2 = 0$$

Where $$p = \frac{2h}{a} \text{ is a constant}$$

The given equation being homogeneous of 3rd degree represents three straight lines passing through the origin. Since two of these lines are to be at right angles, as such one factor giving these two lines will be of the form

$$x^2 + pxy - y^2 = 0$$

The other factor will be linear homogeneous and let it be

$$ax - dy = 0$$

$$\therefore \quad ax^3 + 3bx^2y + 3cxy^2 + dy^3 = (x^2 + pxy - y^2)(ax - dy)$$

$$\therefore \quad ax^3 + 3bx^2y + 3cxy^2 + dy^3 = ax^3 - dx^2y + apx^2y - pdxy^2 - y^2ax + dy^3$$

$$\therefore \quad ax^3 + 3bx^2y + 3cxy^2 + dy^3 = ax^3 + (ap - d)x^2y - (pd + a)xy^2 + dy^3$$

Compairing the coefficient of similar terms, we get

$$3b = ap - d \qquad (1)$$

$$3c = -a - pd \qquad (2)$$

The required condition is obtained by eliminating the unknown quantity p from (3) and (4)

$$3b + d = ap$$

$$\Rightarrow \frac{3b + d}{a} = p$$

And $$3c + a = -pd$$

$$p = -\frac{(3c + a)}{d}$$

Thus
$$\frac{3b+d}{a} = -\frac{(3c+a)}{d}$$

i.e.
$$(3b+d)\,d + a\,(3c+a) = 0$$

i.e.
$$3bd + d^2 + 3ac + a^2 = 0$$

i.e.
$$a^2 + 3ac + 3bd + d^2 = 0$$

Problem 5 The distance of a point (x_1, y_1) from each of two straight lines which pass through origin is δ prove that the lines are given by

$$(yx_1 - xy_1)^2 = \delta^2\,(x^2 + y^2)$$

Let any line through origin be

$$y - mx = 0 \text{ or } m = \frac{y}{x}$$

$\therefore$
$$\delta = \frac{y_1 - mx_1}{\sqrt{1+m^2}}$$

or
$$\delta^2\,(1+m^2) = (y_1 - mx_1)^2 \qquad (1)$$

Now putting $y = mx$ i.e. $m = \frac{y}{x}$ inequation (1) we have

$$\delta^2\left(1 + \frac{y^2}{x^2}\right) = \left(y_1 - \frac{y}{x}\,x_1\right)^2$$

i.e.
$$\delta^2\,\frac{(x^2+y^2)}{x^2} = \frac{(xy_1 - x_1y)^2}{x^2}$$

i.e.
$$\delta^2\,(x^2+y^2) = (xy_1 - x_1y)^2$$

Which is the required equation.

Problem 6 Prove that the two of the straight lines given by

$$ay^4 + bxy^3 + cx^2y^2 + dx^3y + ex^4 = 0$$

Will be at right angles if $(b+d)\,(ad+be) + (a-e)^2\,(a+c+e)$

Solution Since the given equation

$$ay^4 + bxy^3 + cx^2y^2 + dx^3y + ex^4 = 0 \qquad (1)$$

is a homogeneous equation of 4th degree. So this equation represents four straight lines passing through the origin (0, 0)

Since the two straight lines are perpendicular to each other so one of the factor of (1) is of the form

$$x^2 + pxy - y^2 = 0$$

So equation (1) is identical with

$$ay^4 + bxy^3 + cx^2y^2 + dx^3y + ex^4 \equiv (x^2 + pxy - y^2)\,ex^2 + qxy - ay^2)$$
$$\equiv ex^4 + qx^3y - ax^2y^2 + pex^3y + pqx^2y^2 - apxy^3 - ex^2y^2 - qxy^3 + ay^4$$
$$\equiv ex^4 + (pe+q)\,x^3y + (pq-e-a)\,x^2y^2 - (ap+q)\,xy^3 + ay^4$$

Now compairing the coefficient of similar powers on both sides we have

$$pe + q = d, \text{ (2) } pq - e - a = c \text{ (3) } ap + q = -b, \tag{4}$$

From equation (2) we have $\quad pq = a + c + e$

From (2) and (3) $\quad pe + q = d$

$$ap + q = -b \Rightarrow -ap - q = b$$

Adding we have $\quad pe - ap = b + d$

$$p(e-a) = b + d$$

$$\Rightarrow \quad p = \frac{b + d}{e - a} \tag{5}$$

Now $\quad \dfrac{(b+d)e}{e-a} + q = d$

$$\Rightarrow \quad d - \frac{(b+d)e}{e-a} = q$$

$$\Rightarrow \frac{d(e-a) - (b+d)e}{(e-a)} = q$$

$$\Rightarrow \frac{de - ad - be - de}{e-a} = q$$

$$\Rightarrow q = -\frac{(ad + be)}{e - a} \tag{6}$$

Now putting the values of p and q from (5) and (6) in

$pq = a + c + e$ we have

$$\frac{(b+d)}{(e-a)} \times -\frac{(ad+be)}{(e-a)} = (a + c + e)$$

$$-(b+d)(ad+be) = (a+c+e)^2 (e-a)^2$$

i.e. $\quad (b+d)(ad+be) + (e-a)^2 (a+c+e) = 0$

i.e. $\quad (b+d)(ad+be) + (a+e)^2 + (a+c+e) = 0$

Which is the required condition.

Problem 7 Prove that the two of the straight lines given by

$ax^3 + bx^2y + cxy^2 + dy = 0$ will be at right angles if

$$a^2 + ae + bd + d^2 = 0$$

Solution Given equation

$$ax^3 + bx^2y + cxy^2 + dy^3 = 0 \tag{1}$$

is a homogeneous equation of 3rd degree so it represents three lines passing through the origin. Since the two straight lines are at right angles equation of the pair of straight lines is of the form

$$x^2 + pxy - y^2 = 0 \tag{2}$$

So $x^2 + pxy - y^2 = 0$ must be a factor of the equation (1)

The other tactor is of the form $ax - dy$ 0

So $$ax^3 + bx^2 y + cxy^2 + dy^3 \equiv (x^2 + pxy - y^2)(ax - dy)$$

i.e. $$ax^3 + bx^2 y + cxy^2 + dy^3 = ax^3 - dx^2 y + apx^2 y - pdxy^2 - axy^2 + dy^3$$

i.e. $$ax^3 + bx^2 y + cxy^2 + dy^3 \equiv ax^3 + (ap - d) x^2 y - (pd + a) xy^2 + dy^3$$

Compaining the coefficient of similar powers on both sides we have

$$ap - d = b \Rightarrow ap = b + d \Rightarrow p = \frac{b + d}{a} \quad (3)$$

$$-(pd + a) = c; \quad -pd = c + a \Rightarrow p = -\frac{(a - c)}{d} \quad (4)$$

From equation (2) and (4) we have

$$\frac{b + d}{a} = -\frac{(a + c)}{d}$$

$$\Rightarrow \quad (b + d) d + a(a + c) = 0$$

$$\Rightarrow \quad bd + d^2 + a^2 + ac = 0$$

$$\Rightarrow \quad a^2 + ac + bd + d^2 = 0$$

which is the required equation *(Proved)*

Problem 8 If the lines $ax^2 + 2hxy + by^2 = 0$ be the two sides of a parallelogram and the line $px + qy = 1$ is one of the diagonals, show that the other diagonal is $y(bp - hq) = x(aq - hb)$

Solution Let the equation

$$ax^2 + 2hxy + by^2 = 0$$

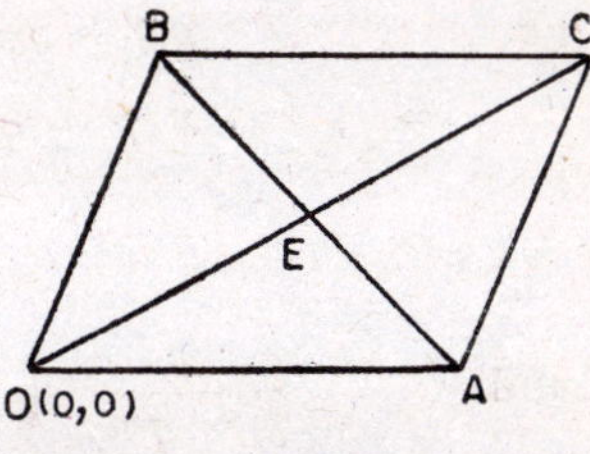

represents two straight lines $y = m_1 x$ and $y = m_2 x$ both passing through origin. Let these two lines intersecting at (0, 0) makes a parallelogram $OACB$. Let OC and AB be two diameters of it. Let $px + qy = 1$ is the equation of the diameter AB. Because we can it take this as the equation of OC because $px + qy = 1$ does not passes through 0(0, 0) is the origin. We have to find the equation of OC.

[**Note** The intersecting point of the diagonals of a parallelogram divides them into two equal parts i.e. $BE = EA$, $OE = EC$]

Hence E is the middle point of the line AB. To find the co-ordinates of E we have to find the co-ordinates of A and B. Since A is the intersection of the line OA and AB

i.e. intersection of $\quad y = m_1 x$. (1)

and $\quad px + qy = 1$ (2)

So co-ordinates of A may be obtained by solving (1) and (2)

$$px + qy = 1$$

$$\Rightarrow \quad px + qm_1 x = 1$$

$$\Rightarrow \quad x(p + qm_1) = 1$$

$$\Rightarrow \quad x = \frac{1}{p + qm_1}$$

Again $$\frac{p}{p + qm_1} + qy = 1$$

$$\Rightarrow \quad qy = 1 - \frac{p}{p + qm_1}$$

$$\Rightarrow \quad qy = \frac{p + qm_1 - p}{p + qm_1}$$

$$\Rightarrow \quad qy = \frac{qm_1}{p + qm_1}$$

$$\Rightarrow \quad y = \frac{m_1}{p + qm_1}$$

The co-ordinates of A is $\left[\frac{1}{p + qm_1}, \frac{m_1}{p + qm_1}\right]$

Again the co-ordinates of B can be obtained by solving

$$y = m_2 x \text{ and } px + qy = 1$$

i.e. $$px + qm_2 x = 1$$

$$\Rightarrow \quad x(p + qm_2) = 1$$

$$\Rightarrow \quad x = \frac{1}{p + qm_2}$$

and $$\frac{p}{p + qm_2} + qy = 1$$

$$\Rightarrow \quad qy = 1 - \frac{p}{p + qm_2}$$

$$\Rightarrow \quad qy = \frac{p + qm_2 - p}{p + qm_2}$$

$$\Rightarrow \quad y = \frac{m_2}{p + qm_2}$$

The co-ordinates of B is $\left[\frac{1}{p + qm_2}, \frac{m_2}{p + qm_2}\right]$

E is the middle point of AB so the co-ordinates of E is given by

$$x = \frac{1}{2}\left[\frac{1}{p + qm_1} + \frac{1}{p + qm_2}\right]$$

$$x = \frac{1}{2}\left[\frac{p + qm_2 + p + qm_1}{(p + qm_1)(p + qm_2)}\right]$$

$$x = \frac{1}{2}\left[\frac{2p + q(m_1 + m_2}{p^2 + pq(m_1 + m_2) + q^2 m_1 m_2}\right]$$

where the relation

$$m_1 + m_2 = -\frac{2h}{b}$$

$$m_1 m_2 = \frac{a}{b}$$

$$x = \frac{1}{2}\left[\frac{2p + q\left(-\frac{2h}{b}\right)}{p^2 + pq\left(\frac{-2h}{b}\right) + q\frac{a}{b}}\right]$$

$$x = \frac{1}{2}\left[\frac{2p - \frac{2hq}{b}}{p^2 - \frac{2hqp}{b} + \frac{aq^2}{b}}\right]$$

$$x = \frac{pb - hq}{bp^2 - 2hqp + aq^2}$$

$$x = \frac{pb - hq}{aq^2 - 2hpq + bp^2}$$

$$y = \frac{1}{2}\left[\frac{m_1}{p + qm_1} + \frac{m_2}{p + qm_2}\right]$$

$$y = \frac{1}{2}\left[\frac{pm_1 + qm_1 m_2 + pm_2 + qm_1 m_2}{(p + qm_1)(p + qm_2)}\right]$$

$$y = \frac{1}{2}\left[\frac{p(m_1 + m_2) + (m_1 m_2 2q)}{p^2 + pq(m_1 + m_2) + q^2 m_1 m_2}\right]$$

$$y = \frac{1}{2}\left[\frac{p\left(-\frac{2h}{b}\right) + \frac{a}{b} 2q}{\frac{a^2 - 2hpq + bp^2}{b}}\right]$$

$$y = \frac{1}{2}\left[\frac{-2ph + 2aq}{aq^2 - 2hpq + bp^2}\right]$$

$$y = \frac{(ap - ph)}{aq^2 - 2hpq + bp^2}$$

So the co-ordinates of E is

$$\left[\frac{pb-hq}{aq^2-2hpq+bp^2}, \quad \frac{aq-ph}{aq^2-2phq+bp^2}\right]$$

The equation of the line passing through two points

$$0\ (0, 0) \text{ and } E\left[\frac{pb-hq}{aq^2-2hpq+bp^2}, \quad \frac{aq-ph}{aq^2-2hpq+bp^2}\right]$$

is given by

$$y-0=\frac{\left(\dfrac{aq-ph}{aq^2-2hpq+bp^2}-0\right)}{\left(\dfrac{pb-hq}{aq^2-2hpq+bp^2}-0\right)}(x-0)$$

$$\Rightarrow \qquad y=\frac{(aq-ph)}{(pb-hq)}x$$

$$\Rightarrow (pb-hq)\,y=(aq-ph)\,x$$ *(Proved)*

Problem 9 If one of the straight lines given by the equation

$$ax^2+2hxy+by^2=0$$

coincide with one of those given by

$$a_1\,x^2+2h_1\,xy+b_1\,y^2=0$$

and the other line represented by them be $\perp$. prove that

$$\frac{ha_1\,b_1}{b_1-a_1}=\frac{h_1\,ab}{b-a}=\frac{1}{2}\sqrt{-aa_1\,bb_1}$$

Solution Let the lines represented by the first pair be

$$y=m_1\,x \quad \text{and} \quad y=m_2\,x$$

then $$m_1+m_2=-\frac{2h}{b} \tag{1}$$

$$m_1\,m_2=\frac{a}{b} \tag{2}$$

then by the given condition of the question the lines represented by the second pair are

$$y=m_1\,x \text{ and } y=-\frac{1}{m_2}x$$

So that $$m_1+\left(-\frac{1}{m_2}\right)=-\frac{2h^1}{b^1} \tag{3}$$

and $$m_1\left(-\frac{1}{m_2}\right)=\frac{a^1}{b^1} \tag{4}$$

Multiplying equation (2) and (4) we have

$$-m_1^2 = \frac{aa'}{bb'}$$

or $$m_1^2 = \frac{-aa_1\,bb_1}{b^2\,b'^2}$$

$\therefore$ $$m_1 = \frac{\sqrt{-aa_1\,bb_1}}{bb_1}$$

Substituting the value of m_1 in equation (2) we have

$$\frac{\sqrt{-aa_1'\,bb_1'}}{bb'}m_2 = \frac{a}{b}$$

i.e. $$m_2 = \frac{ab_1'}{\sqrt{-aa_1^1\,bb_1^1}}$$

$\Rightarrow$ $$m_2 = \frac{ab^1\sqrt{-aa_1^1/bb_1}}{-aa/bb^1} = -\frac{\sqrt{-aa'/bb_1^1}}{a/b}$$

Substituting the values of m_1 and m_2 in (1) we have

$$\frac{\sqrt{-aa_1'\,bb_1'}}{bb_1} - \frac{\sqrt{-aa_1\,bb_1}}{ab_1} = -\frac{2h}{b}$$

$\Rightarrow$ $$\frac{\sqrt{-aa_1\,bb_1}}{b}\left[\frac{1}{b_1} - \frac{1}{a_1}\right] = -\frac{2b}{b}$$

$\Rightarrow$ $$\sqrt{-aa_1\,bb_1}\,\frac{a_1-b_1}{a_1\,b_1} = -2h$$

$\Leftarrow$ $$\frac{ha_1\,b_1}{b_1-a_1} = \frac{1}{2}\sqrt{-aa_1\,bb_1} \qquad (5)$$

Again putting the values of m_1, m_2 in equation (3) we have

$$\frac{\sqrt{-aa_1\,bb_1}}{bb_1} - \frac{\sqrt{-aa_1\,bb_1}}{ab_1} = -\frac{2h_1}{b_1}$$

$$\frac{\sqrt{-aa_1\,bb_1}}{b_1}\left[\frac{1}{b} - \frac{1}{a}\right] = -\frac{2h_1}{b_1}$$

$$\sqrt{-aa_1\,bb_1}\left[\frac{a-b}{ab}\right] = -2h_1$$

$\Rightarrow$ $$\frac{h_1\,ab}{b-a} = \frac{1}{2}\sqrt{-aa_1\,bb_1} \qquad (6)$$

From equation (5) and (6) we have

$$\frac{ha_1\,b_1}{b_1-a_1} = \frac{h_1\,ab}{b-a} = \frac{1}{2}\sqrt{-aa_1\,bb_1} \qquad \textit{(Proved)}$$

Problem 10 Prove that the equation $x^3 + 3x^2y - 3xy^2 - y^3 = 0$ represents three straight lines equally inclined to one another.

Solution Changing to polar coordinates, the equation becomes

$$r^3 \cos^3\theta + 3r^2 \cos^2\theta \, r \sin\theta$$

$$-3r \cos\theta \, r^2 \sin^2\theta - r^3 \sin^3\theta = 0$$

$$r^3 [\cos^3\theta + 3\cos^2\theta \sin\theta - 3\cos^2\theta \sin\theta - \sin^3\theta] = 0$$

Since $r \neq 0$ so

$$\cos^3\theta + 3\cos^2\theta \sin\theta - 3\sin^2\theta \cos\theta - \sin^3\theta = 0$$

Dividing both sides with $\cos^3\theta$ we have

$$1 + 3\tan\theta - 3\tan^2\theta - \tan^3\theta = 0$$

$$\Rightarrow \quad 3\tan\theta - \tan^3\theta = -(1 - 3\tan^2\theta)$$

$$\Rightarrow \quad \frac{3\tan\theta - \tan^3\theta}{1 - 3\tan^2\theta} = -1$$

$$\Rightarrow \quad \tan 3\theta = -\tan\frac{\pi}{4}$$

$$\Rightarrow \quad \tan 3\theta = \tan\left(-\frac{\pi}{4}\right)$$

$$\Rightarrow \quad 3\theta = n\pi - \frac{\pi}{4}$$

$$\Rightarrow \quad \theta = \left[n\pi - \frac{\pi}{4}\right]\frac{1}{3}$$

$$n = 0, 1, 2$$

$$\theta = \frac{1}{3}\left[\pi - \frac{\pi}{4}\right] = \frac{1}{3}, \frac{7\pi}{4} = \frac{\pi}{12}$$

Putting $n = 2$

$$\theta = \frac{1}{3}\left(2\pi - \frac{\pi}{4}\right)$$

$$= \frac{1}{3} \cdot \frac{7\pi}{4} = \frac{7\pi}{12}$$

Putting $n = 3$

$$\theta = \frac{1}{3}\left(3\pi - \frac{\pi}{4}\right) = \frac{11\pi}{12}$$

The locus is therefore three straight lines through the origin at angles $\frac{\pi}{4}$, $\frac{7\pi}{12}$, $\frac{11\pi}{12}$ to the axis of x and thus they are equally inclined to the *ax* is of x

(*Proved*)

Problem 28 Prove that the line $ax + by + c = 0$ and the two lines

$$(ax + by)^2 - 3(ay - bx)^2 = 0$$

rom an equilateral triangle and find its area

Solution The equation

$$(ax + by)^2 - 3(ay - bx)^2 = 0$$

can be written in the following form

$$ax + by = \pm\sqrt{3}(ay - bx)$$

$$\Rightarrow \quad (ax + by) \mp \sqrt{3}(ay - bx) = 0$$

$$\Rightarrow \quad (ax + by) - \sqrt{3}(ay - bx) = 0$$

and $$(ax + by) + \sqrt{3}(ay - bx) = 0$$

$$\Rightarrow \quad x(a + \sqrt{3}b) + (b - \sqrt{3}a)y = 0 \qquad (1)$$

and $$x(a - \sqrt{3}b) + y(b + \sqrt{3}a) = 0 \qquad (ii)$$

Also the third side of the triangle is

$$ax + by + c = 0 \qquad (iii)$$

If θ is the angle between

From equation (1) we have

$$y(b - \sqrt{3}a) = -x(a + \sqrt{3}b)$$

$$\Rightarrow \quad y = -\frac{(a + \sqrt{3}b)}{(b - \sqrt{3}a)}x$$

Thus the slope of this line i.e.

$$m_1 = -\frac{a + \sqrt{3}b}{b - \sqrt{3}a}$$

Again from equation (2)

$$y(b + \sqrt{3}a) = -(a - \sqrt{3}b)x$$

$$\Rightarrow \quad y = -\frac{(a - \sqrt{3}b)}{b + \sqrt{3}a)}x$$

Thus the slope of this line is

$$m_2 = -\frac{(a - \sqrt{3}b)}{(b + \sqrt{3}a)}$$

From the line $ax + by + c = 0$

$$\Rightarrow \quad by = -ax - c$$

$$\Rightarrow \quad y = -\frac{a}{b}x - \frac{c}{a}$$

Thus the slope of this line is

$$m_3 = -\frac{a}{b}$$

Let θ be the angle between (i) and (iii) then

$$\tan\theta = \pm\frac{m_1 - m_3}{1 + m_1 m_3}$$

$$\tan\theta = \pm\frac{-\dfrac{(a+\sqrt{3}b)}{(b-\sqrt{3}a)} + \dfrac{a}{b}}{1 + \dfrac{a+\sqrt{3}b}{b-\sqrt{3}a}\cdot\dfrac{a}{b}}$$

$$\tan\theta = \pm\frac{a(b-\sqrt{3}a) - b(a+\sqrt{3}b)}{b(b-\sqrt{3}a) + a(a+\sqrt{3}b)}$$

$$\tan\theta = \pm\frac{-\sqrt{3}a^2 - \sqrt{3}b^2}{(a^2+b^2)}$$

$$\tan\theta = \pm(-)\sqrt{3}\frac{(a^2+b^2)}{(a^2+b^2)}$$

$$\tan = \mp\sqrt{3}$$

$\therefore$ the acute angle between (i) and (ii) $= 60°$.

14

Circles, System of Circles

Equation of the circle whose centre is h_1 k) and radius is a is given by

$$(x-h)^2 + (y-k)^2 = a^2 \quad (1)$$

The equation of the circle whose cenrre is at (0, 0) and radius is a is given by

$$x^2 + y^2 = a^2 \quad (2)$$

Circle passing through the origin of co-ordinates and having its centre at h_1 k).

In this case radius $a = \sqrt{h^2 + k^2}$ and hence equation of the circle is

$$(x-h)^2 + (y-k)^2 = a^2$$

e

$$x^2 + y^2 - 2hx - 2ky = 0 \quad (3)$$

a) Circle whose centre is (h_1 k) and which touches the axis of x:

$$x^2 + y^2 - 2hx - 2ky + h^2 = 0$$

b) Circle whose centre is (h_1 k) and which touches the ax is of y is given by

$$x^2 + y^2 - 2hx - 2ky + k^2 = 0$$

c) Circle touching both the axis

In this case if h is the radius of the circle, then its centre will be (h_1 h) and hence its equation is

$$(x-h)^2 + (y-h)^2 = h^2$$

$$x^2 + y^2 - 2hx - 2hy + h^2 = 0$$

General equation of the circle

$$x^2 + y^2 + 2gx + 2fy + c = 0$$

is the required general equation of a circle.

If the circle passes through origin then $c = 0$ and its equation is

$$x^2 + y^2 + 2gx + 2fy = 0$$

Condition for the general equation of 2nd degree to represent a circle.

The general equation of 2nd degree is

$$ax^2 + by^2 + 2hxy + 2gx + 2fy + c = 0 \quad (1)$$

Equation (1) represents a circle if the coefficients of x^2 and y^2 are equa and if the coefficient of xy is zero.

i.e. If $$a = b$$

and $$h = 0$$

Again the general equation of the circle contains three independent con stants $g_1 f$ and c. Therefore a circle can be made to pass through any thre given points.

Centre and radius of the circle whose general equation is given

$$x^2 + y^2 + 2gx + 2fy + c = 0$$

Above equation can be written as

$$x^2 + y^2 + 2gx + g^2 + 2fy + f^2 + c = g^2 + f^2$$

$$(x + g)^2 + (y + f)^2 = g^2 + f^2 - c$$

Then the co-ordinate of the centre is $(-g, -f)$ and the radius is

$$\sqrt{g^2 + f^2 - c}$$

Problem 1 Find the co-ordinates of the centre and radius of the circl passing through the points (3, 4), (3, −6), (−1, 2).

Solution Let the circle be

$$x^2 + y^2 + 2gx + 2fy + c = 0 \quad (1$$

Since (1) passes through three points (3, 4); (3, −6), (−1, 2) so substitu ting these co-ordinates in (1) we have.

$$25 + 6g + 8f + c = 0 \quad (2$$

$$45 + 6g - 12f + c = 0 \quad (3$$

$$5 - 2g + 4f + c = 0 \quad (4$$

from (2) and (3)

$$-20f + 20 = 0$$

$$\Rightarrow 20f = 20$$

$$\Rightarrow f = 1$$

Again $$45 + 6g - 12f + c = 0$$

$$\frac{15 - 6g + 12f + 3c = 0}{60 + 4c = 0}$$

$$4c = -60$$

$$\Rightarrow c = -15$$

Putting the value of f and c in (2) we have

$$25 + 6g + 8.1 + (-15) = 0$$

i.e.

$$25 + 8 - 15 + 6g = 0$$

$$\Rightarrow \quad 33 - 15 + 6g = 0$$

$$\Rightarrow \quad 18 + 6g = 0$$

$$\Rightarrow \quad 6g = -18$$

$$\Rightarrow \quad g = -\frac{18}{6} = -3$$

Thus $\quad g = -3 \quad f = 1, \quad c = -15$

Then the equation of the circles given by

$$x^2 + y^2 - 6x + 2y - 15 = 0$$

Co-ordinates of centre are $(-g, -f)$

i.e. $\quad (3, -1)$

Raduis of the circles

$$\sqrt{g^2 + f^2 - c} = \sqrt{9 + 1 + 15} = \sqrt{25} = 5 \qquad \textbf{Ans.}$$

Equation of a circle on the line AB joining (x_1, y_1) and (x_2, y_2) as diameter is given by

$$\boxed{(x - x_1)(x - x_2) + (y - y_1)(y - y_2) = 0}$$

Article Equation of tangent and normal at any point (x_1, y_1) on the general circle.

The normal at any point on the circle passes through the centre. The tangent at any point $p\,(x_1, y_1)$ to a circle is perpendicular to the normal at p which passes through the centre $c\,(-g, -f)$.

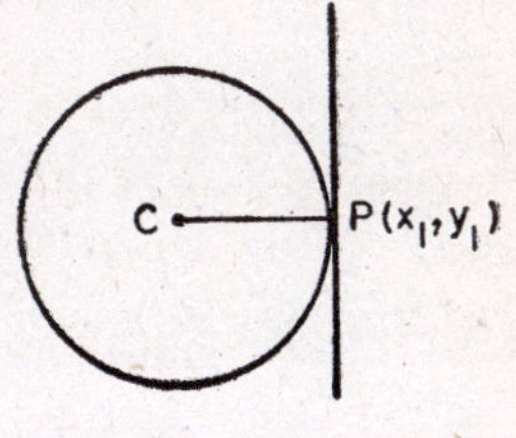

Now siope of the line Cp is $\dfrac{y_1 + f}{x_1 + g}$ and hence the slope of the tangent at p is $-\dfrac{x_1 + g}{y_1 + f}$ and thus the equation of the tangent is

$$y - y_1 = -\frac{x_1 + g}{y_1 + f}(x - x_1)$$

$$\Rightarrow \quad (y - y_1)(y_1 + f) = -(x_1 + g)(x - x)_1$$

$$\Rightarrow \quad yy_1 + yf - y_1 f - y_1^2 = -[xx_1 - x_1^2 + xg - x_1 g]$$

$$\Rightarrow \quad yy_1 + yf - y_1 f - y_1^2 = -xx_1 + x_1^2 - xg + x_1 g$$

$$\Rightarrow \quad xx_1 + yy_1 + gx + fy = x_1^2 + y_1^2 + x_1 g + y_1 f \qquad (1)$$

But since the point (x_1, y_1) lies on the circle

$$x^2 + y^2 + 2gx + 2fy + c = 0$$

so it will satisfy this

$$x_1^2 + y_1^2 + 2gx_1 + 2fy_1 + c = 0$$

i.e.
$$x_1^2 + y_2^1 + gx_1 + fy_1 = -(gx_1 + fy_1 + c) \qquad (2)$$

Putting the values of $x_1^2 + y_1^2 + gx_1 + fy_1$ from (2) in equation (1) we have

$$xx_1 + yy_1 + gx + fy = -(gx_1 + fy_1 + c)$$

$$\Rightarrow \quad xx_1 + yy_1 + g(x + x_1) + f(y + y_1) + c = 0 \qquad (3)$$

Equation (3) is the required equation for the tangent at any point (x_1, y_1).

Remember Equation of circle is

$$x^2 + y^2 + 2gx + 2fy + c = 0$$

For finding the equation of tangent at point (x_1, y_1) replace x^2 by xx_1, y^2 by yy_1, $2x$ by $x + x_1$; $2y$ by $y + y_1$

i.e. equation of the tangent is

$$\boxed{xx_1 + yy_1 + g(x + x_1) + f(y + y_1) + c = 0}$$

Equation of Normal Slope of the normal as it passes through $(-g, -f)$ and (x_1, y_1) is $\dfrac{y_1 + f}{x_1 + g}$. So the equation of the normal is passing through (x_1, y_1) is

$$y - y_1 = \frac{y_1 + f}{x_1 + g}(x - x_1)$$

$$(y - y_1)(x_1 + g) = (y_1 + f)(x - x_1)$$

$$y(x_1 + g) - y_1(x_1 + g) = (y_1 + f)x - (y_1 + f)x_1$$

i.e. $x(y_1 + f) - y(x_1 + g) - (fx_1 - gy_1) = 0$

Tangent interms of *m* Let $x^2 + y^2 = a^2$ and let $y = mx + c$ be the tangent. a is the radius of the circle. Then in this case. The length of $\perp r$ from the point (0, 0) to the line $y = mx + c$ must be equal to the radius

y=mx+C

C
(0,0)

i.e.
$$\frac{C}{\pm\sqrt{1 + m^2}} = a$$

or
$$C = \pm a\sqrt{1 + m^2}$$

$\therefore$
$$y = mx \pm a\sqrt{1 + m^2}$$

is always tangent to the circle $x^2 + y^2 = a^2$

Therefore parallel to any given direction m we can find two lines

$$y = mx \pm a\sqrt{1 + m^2}$$

both of which will touch the circle

$$x^2 + y^2 = a^2$$

Cor 1 Condition that the line $lx + my + n = 0$ may touch the circle

$$x^2 + y^2 + 2gx + 2fy + c = 0$$

The general equation of 2nd degree $x^2 + y^2 + 2gx + 2fy + c = 0$ represents *a* circle whose centre is $(-g, -f)$ and radius is $\sqrt{g^2 + f^2 - c}$.

In this case the length of $\perp r$ from the point $(-g_2 - f)$ to the line $lx + my + n = 0$ must be equal to the radius

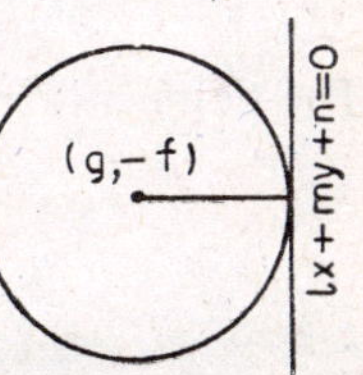

i.e.
$$\frac{-lg - mf + n}{\sqrt{l^2 + m^2}} = \sqrt{g^2 + f^2 - c}$$

Squaring both sides we have

$$[-lg - mf + n]^2 = (l^2 + m^2)(g^2 + f^2 - c)\, l^2 g^2 + m^2 f^2 + n^2$$
$$-2\, lmgf - 2mfn - 2lgn$$
$$= (l^2 + m^2)(g^2 + f^2) - c\,(l^2 + m^2)$$
$$n^2 + 2lmgf - 2mfn - 2lgn = lf^2 + m^2 g^2 - c\,(l^2 + m^2)$$
$$C\,(l^2 + m^2) + n^2 - l^2 f^2 - m^2 g^2 + 2lmgf - 2mfn - 2lgn = 0$$
$$\Rightarrow \quad C\,(l^2 + m^2) + n^2 - [l^2 f^2 - 2lmgf + m^2 g^2] - 2mfn - 2lgn = 0$$

i.e.
$$(l^2 + m^2)\, c + n^2 - (fl - gm)^2 - 2fmn - 2gnl = 0$$

This is the required condition.

Cor 2 To find the point of contact in case the line $y = mx + c$ touches the circle $x^2 + y^2 = a^2$

Let equation of the circles $x^2 + y^2 = a^2$ (1)

The straight line $y = mx + c$ touches circle (1) at the point (x_1, y_1). Then (x_1, y_1) is the point of contact.

Since $y = mx + c$ touches the circle $x^2 + y^2 = a^2$.
So $y = mx + c$ must be a tangent then

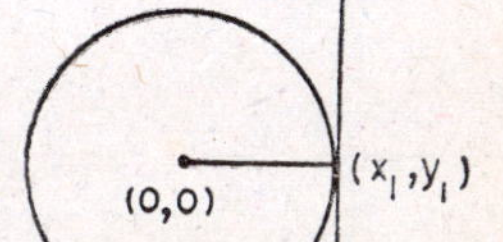

$$C^2 = a^2(1 + m^2)$$

i.e.
$$C = a\sqrt{1 + m^2}$$

Thus the equation of tangent is

$$y = mx + a\sqrt{1 + m^2} \quad (1)$$

Then it must be identical with the tangent at the point (x_1, y_1) to the circle $x^2 + y^2 = a^2$

Equation of the tangent at the point (x_1, y_1) on the circle (x_1, y_1) is given by

$$xx_1 + yy_1 - a^2 = 0 \quad (2)$$

Then comparing (1) and (2) we have

$$\frac{x}{m} = \frac{y_1}{-1} = \frac{-a^2}{a\sqrt{1+m^2}}$$

i.e.
$$x_1 = -\frac{am}{\sqrt{1+m^2}}$$

$$y_1 = \frac{a}{\sqrt{1+m^2}}$$

The point of contact is given by

$$\left(-\frac{am}{\sqrt{1+m^2}}, \frac{a}{\sqrt{1+m^2}}\right)$$

Theorom Length and the mid point of the chord intercepted by the circle $x^2 + y^2 = a^2$ on the line $y = mx + c$

Solution Let the equation of the circle is

$$x^2 + y^2 = a^2 \tag{1}$$

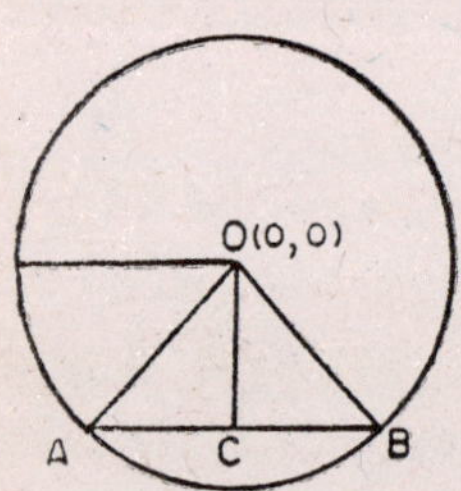

Let 0 (0, 0) be the origin of the circle

Let AB be a chord the equation of AB is

$$y = mx + C$$

From 0 (0, 0)$\perp r$ is drawn to AB. Then this perpendicular cuts the point C which ist he middle point of AB. Then we have to find the co-ordinate of the point C and the length of the intercept AB.

Equation of the line AB is $y = mx + c$ (2)

where m is the slope of AB

Since the line OC is $\perp r$ to AB so the slope of the line OC is $-\dfrac{1}{m}$

Again since OC passes through (0, 0) so equation of the line OC is given by

$$y - 0 = -\frac{1}{m}(x - 0)$$

i.e.
$$y = -\frac{1}{m}x$$

i.e.
$$my + x = 0 \tag{3}$$

Solving equation (2) and (3) we can find the co-ordinate of c

Putting the value of y from equation (2) in equation (3)

$$m(mx + c) + x = 0$$

$$m^2 x + mc + x = 0$$

$$(m^2 + 1)x + mc = 0$$

$$\Rightarrow x = -\frac{mc}{m^2 + 1}$$

Putting the value of x in equation (2) we have

$$y = m\cdot\left(-\frac{mc}{m^2+1}\right) + c = -\frac{m^2 c}{m^2+1} + c$$

$$= c\left[-\frac{m^2}{m^2+1} + 1\right] = c\left[-\frac{m^2 + m^2 + 1}{m^2+1}\right]$$

$$y = \frac{c}{m^2+1}$$

Hence the co-ordinate of the mid point c is given by

$$\left[-\frac{mc}{m^2+1}, \frac{c}{m^2+1}\right].$$

OC = perpendicular distance of (0, 0) from AB

i.e. $y = mx + c = \dfrac{c}{\sqrt{1+m^2}}$

OA = radius of the circle $= a$

$$AC = \sqrt{OA^2 - OC^2} = \sqrt{a^2 - \frac{c^2}{(1+m^2)}}$$

$$AC = \sqrt{\frac{a^2(1+m^2)-c^2}{(1+m^2)}}, \quad \text{then} \quad AB = 2\,AC$$

i.e. $$AB - 2\sqrt{\frac{a^2(1+m^2)-c^2}{(1+m^2)}}$$

i.e. $$AB = 2\left[\frac{a^2(1+m^2)-c^2}{(1+m^2)}\right]^{1/2}$$

Article Lengths of the chords intercepted by the circle

$$x^2 + y^2 + 2gx + 2fy + c = 0$$

from the axes of x and y are

$2\sqrt{g^2 - c}$ and $2\sqrt{f^2 - c}$ respectively

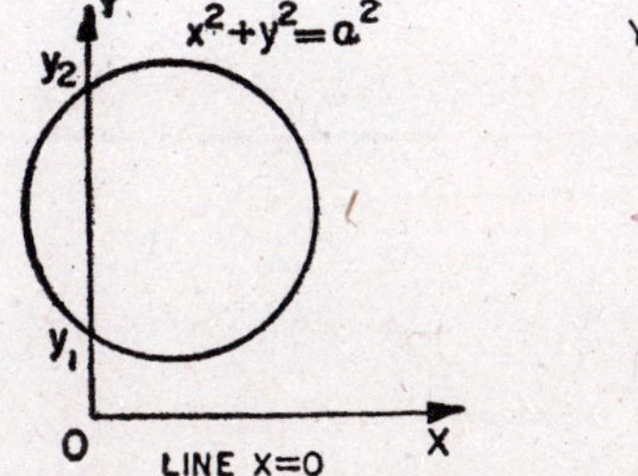

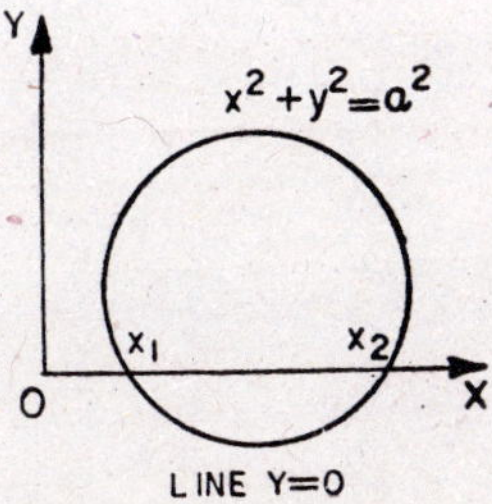

Let us suppose that the circle $x^2 + y^2 + 2gx + 2fy + c = 0$ cuts the x-axis, in two points x_1 and x_2. Then we have to find the value of $x_1 - x_2$.

The equation of the line x-axis is given by $y = 0$. Then the length of the chord can be obtained by solving equation

$$x^2 + y^2 + 2gx + 2fy + c = 0$$

and $\qquad y = 0$

Then $\qquad x^2 + 0^2 + 2gx + 2f0 + c = 0$

i.e. $\qquad x^2 + 2gx + c = 0$

Then sum of the roots $\qquad x_1 + x_2 = -2g$

Product of roots $\qquad x_1 x_2 = c$

Then $\qquad (x_1 - x_2)^2 = (x_1 + x_2)^2 - 4x_1 x_2$

$$= (-2g)^2 - 4c = 4g^2 - 4c = 4(g^2 - c)$$

i.e. $\qquad x_1 - x_2 = 2\sqrt{g^2 - c}$

Again let the circle $x^2 + y^2 + 2gx + 2fy + c = 0$ cuts the y axis at the points y_1 and y_2 then we have to find the value of $y_1 - y_2$

This value can be obtained by solving

$$x^2 + y^2 + 2gx + 2fy + c = 0$$

and $\qquad x = 0$

i.e. $\qquad y^2 + 2fy + c = 0$

which is a quadratic equation in y

Let y_1 and y^2 are its roots then

$$y_1 + y_2 = -2f$$

$$y_1 y_2 = c$$

$$(y_1 - y_2)^2 = (y_1 + y_2)^2 - 4y_1 y_2$$

$$= (-2f)^2 - 4c = 4f^2 - 4c$$

$$= 4(f^2 - c)$$

$$y_1 - y_2 = 2\sqrt{f^2 - c}$$

Problem 1 Find the equation of the circle described on the line joining (2, 3) and (4, 5) as diameter. Also find the equations of the tangents which are perpendicular to this diameter.

Solution Circle described on (2, 3) and 4, 5) as diameter is

$$(x-2)(x-4) + (y-3)(y-5) = 0$$

$$x^2 - 4x - 2x + 8 + y^2 - 3y - 5y + 15 = 0$$

i.e. $\qquad x^2 - 6x + 8 + y^2 - 8y + 15 = 0$

i.e. $\qquad x^2 + y^2 - 6x - 8y + 23 = 0$

i.e. $\qquad x^2 - 2 \cdot 3x + 3^2 + y^2 - 2 \cdot 4y + 4^2 + 23 = 9 + 16$

i.e. $\qquad (x-3)^2 + (y-4)^2 = 25 - 23$

i.e. $\qquad (x-3)^2 + (y-4)^2 = 2$

Thus the centre is (3, 4) and the radius is $\sqrt{2}$

Slop of the line joining the diameter is

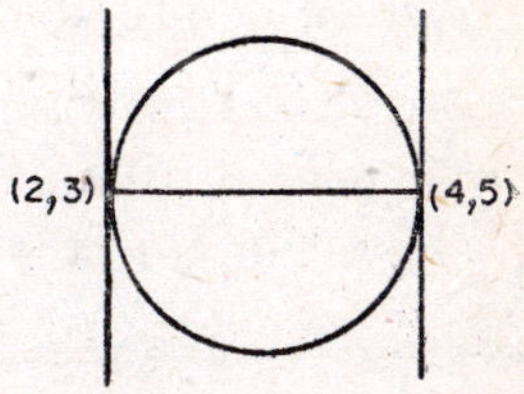

$$\frac{5-3}{4-2} = 1$$

(2,3) (4,5)

Any line parallel to the diameter is

$$y = x + k$$

or $$x - y + k = 0$$

If it is a tangent to the circle then perpendicular from the centre (3, 4) should be equal to the radius $\sqrt{2}$

$$\therefore \quad \frac{3-4+k}{\pm\sqrt{1+1}} = \sqrt{2}$$

or $$\frac{-1+k}{\pm\sqrt{2}} = \sqrt{2}$$

i.e. $$k - 1 = \pm 2$$

$$\Rightarrow \quad k = 1 \pm 2$$

i.e. $$k = 3, -1$$

So equation of the tangent parallel to the diameter are given by

$$x - y + 3 = 0 \quad \text{and} \quad x - y - 1 = 0$$

The tangents which will be perpendicular to this diameter will clearly be tangents at the extremities of the diameter whose cquation are

$$xx_1 + yy_1 - 3(x + x_1) - 4(y + y_1) + 23 = 0$$

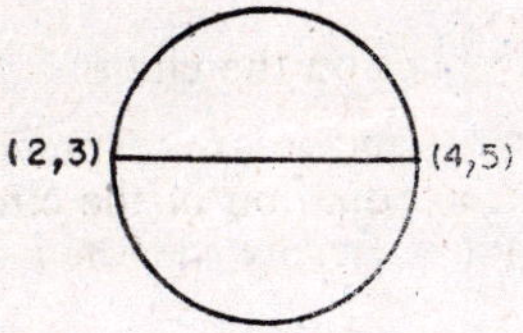

(2,3) (4,5)

where $(x_1\ y_1)$ will be (2, 3) and (4, 5) the extremities of diameter. Equation of these tangents are

$$x\cdot 2 + y3 - 3(x + 2) - 4(y + 3) + 23 = 0$$

$$2x + 3y - 3x - 6 - 4y - 12 + 23 = 0$$

$$\Rightarrow \quad -x - y + 5 = 0$$

i.e. $$x + y - 5 = 0 \quad (1)$$

$$x\cdot 4 + y\cdot 5 - 3(x + 4) - 4(y + 5) + 23 = 0$$

i.e. $$4x + 5y - 3x - 12 - 4y - 20 + 23 = 0$$

$$x + y - 9 = 0$$

Problem 2 If the two circles $x^2 + y^2 + 2gx + 2fy = 0$

and $$x^2 + y^2 + 2g'x + 2f'y = 0$$

touch each other show that $fg_1 = f_1 g$

Solution Since both the circle has no constant terms so they passes through the origin. Since they touch each other so the co-ordinate of the point of (contact is (0, 0) i.e. they must touch each other at the point (0, 0).

In this case the tangent at (0, 0) to both the circle must be identical.

Tangent to the circle

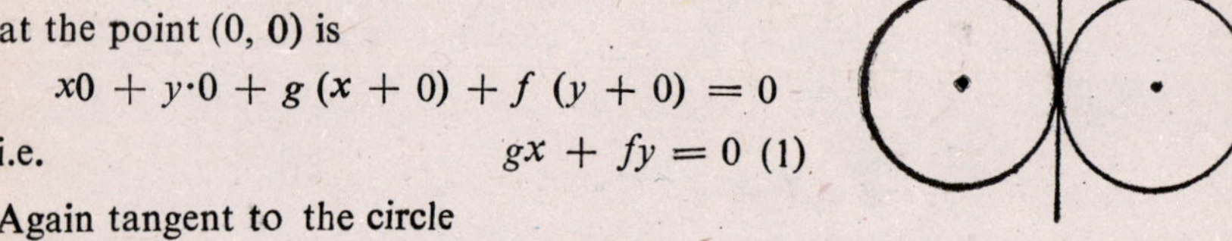

$$x^2 + y^2 + 2gx + 2fy = 0$$

at the point (0, 0) is

$$x0 + y\cdot 0 + g(x + 0) + f(y + 0) = 0$$

i.e. $$gx + fy = 0 \quad (1)$$

Again tangent to the circle

$$x^2 + y^2 + 2g_1 x + 2f_1 y = 0$$

at the point (0, 0) is

$$x\cdot 0 + y\cdot 0 + g_1(x + 0) + f_1(y + 0) = 0$$

i.e. $$xg_1 + f_1 y = 0 \quad (2)$$

Now equation (1) and (2) must be identical, Compairing equation (1) and (2). we have $$\frac{g}{g_1} = \frac{f}{f_1}$$

$$\Rightarrow \quad gf_1 = g_1 f \qquad \textit{(Proved)}$$

Parametric representation

It is often convenient to express the co-ordinates of any point on the curve interms of one variable. It is clear that the values

$$x = a\cos\theta,\ y = a\sin\theta \quad (1)$$

always satisfies the equation of the circle

$$x^2 + y^2 = a^2.$$

Hence for all values of θ, the point $(a\cos\theta, a\sin\theta)$ lies on the circle.

θ is called a parameter and equation (1) in which x and y are expressed interms of a single variable θ is called a parametric equation of the circle $x^2 + y^2 = a^2$ and the co-ordinates of any point is briefly denoted by θ i.e. $(a\cos\theta, a\sin\theta)$.

If the circle has the equation $(x-\alpha)^2 + (y-\beta)^2 = r^2$ the co-ordinates of any point on the circle are

$$x = \alpha + r\cos\theta \qquad y = \alpha + r\sin\theta$$

Theorem To find the equation of the chord joining the points θ_1 and θ_2 on the circle $x^2 + y^2 = a^2$.

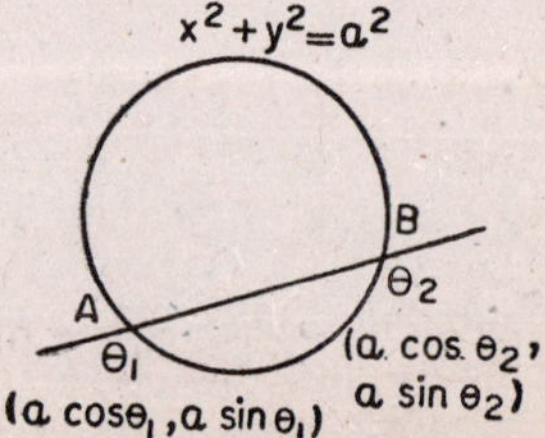

Proof. Equation of the circle is $x^2 + y^2 = a^2$. Let A and B be two points whose co-ordinates are θ_1 and θ_2. The chord AB is jointed. We have to find the equation of the chord AB. The co-ordinates of the poits A and B are given by

$$(a\cos\theta_1, a\sin\theta_1) \text{ and } (a\cos\theta_2, a\sin\theta_2)$$

where a is the radius of the circle

Equation of AB is the equation of the line passing through two points $(a \cos \theta_1, a \sin \theta_1)$ and $(a \cos \theta_2, a \sin \theta_2)$

Equation may be written as

$$y - a \sin \theta_1 = \frac{a \sin \theta_1 - a \sin \theta_2}{a \cos \theta_1 - a \cos \theta_2} (x - a \cos \theta_1)$$

$$\Rightarrow \quad y - a \sin \theta_1 = \frac{2 \cos \frac{\theta_1 + \theta_2}{2} \sin \frac{\theta_1 - \theta_2}{2}}{2 \sin \frac{\theta_1 + \theta_2}{2} \sin \frac{\theta_2 - \theta_1}{2}} (x - a \cos \theta_1)$$

$$\Rightarrow \quad y - a \sin \theta_1 = -\frac{\cos \frac{\theta_1 + \theta_2}{2}}{\sin \frac{\theta_1 + \theta_2}{2}} (x - a \cos \theta_1)$$

$$\Rightarrow \quad y \sin \frac{\theta_1 + \theta_2}{2} - a \sin \theta_1 \sin \frac{\theta_1 + \theta_2}{2}$$

$$= -x \cos \frac{\theta_1 + \theta_2}{2} + a \cos \theta_1 \cos \frac{\theta_1 + \theta_2}{2}$$

$$\Rightarrow \quad x \cos \frac{\theta_1 + \theta_2}{2} + y \sin \frac{\theta_1 + \theta_2}{2}$$

$$= a \cos \theta_1 \cos \frac{\theta_1 + \theta_2}{2} + a \sin \theta_1 \sin \frac{\theta_1 + \theta_2}{2}$$

$$\Rightarrow \quad x \cos \frac{\theta_1 + \theta_2}{2} + y \sin \frac{\theta_1 + \theta_2}{2} = a \cos \left(\theta_1 - \frac{\theta_1 + \theta_2}{2} \right)$$

$$= a \cos \left[\frac{2\theta_1 - \theta_1 - \theta_2}{2} \right] = a \cos \frac{(\theta_1 - \theta_2)}{2}$$

Thus the equation of the chord is given by

$$\boxed{x \cos \frac{\theta_1 + \theta_2}{2} + y \sin \frac{\theta_1 + \theta_2}{2} = a \cos \frac{\theta_1 - \theta_2}{2}} \quad \textbf{Remember}$$

Problem 3 Find the equation to the circle which touches the axis of y at a distance 4 from the origin and cuts off an intercept 6 from the axis of x.

Solution Let the general equation of the circle is

$$x^2 + y^2 + 2gx + 2fy + c = 0 \quad (1)$$

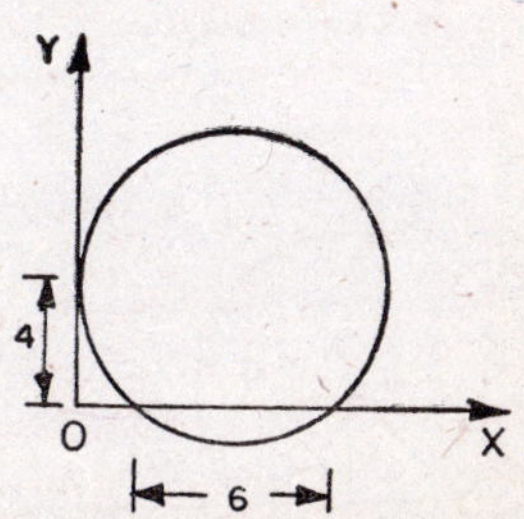

This circle meets the axis of y in points given by $0^2 + y^2 + 2g \cdot 0 + 2f \cdot y + c = 0$

i.e.

$$y^2 + 2fy + c = 0 \quad (2)$$

which is obtained by putting $x = 0$ in equation (1)

Since the circle touches the axis of y at the point distant 4 from the origin. Thus the equation (2) must be equivalent to $(y-4)^2 = 0$

i.e. $y^2 + 2fy + c \equiv (y-4)^2$

i.e. $y^2 + 2fy + c \equiv y^2 - 8y + 16$

i.e. $2fy = -8y$ and $c = 16$

i.e. $f = -4$ and $c = 16$ (3)

Again the circle (1) cuts the axis of x in two points. These points may be obtained by putting $y = 0$ in equation (1)

i.e. $x^2 + 0 + 2gx + 2f \cdot 0 + 16 = 0$

i.e. $x^2 + 2gx + 16 = 0$

Then sum of two roots

i.e. $x_1 + x_2 = -2g$

$$x_1 x_2 = 16$$

From question it is given that

$$x_1 - x_2 = 6$$

$$(x_1 - x_2)^2 = (x_1 + x_2)^2 - 4x_1 x_2 = (-2g)^2 - 4 \cdot 16 = 4g^2 - 64$$

i.e. $36 = 4g^2 - 64$

i.e. $4g^2 = 36 + 64$

$$4g^2 = 100$$

$$g^2 = \frac{100}{4}$$

$\therefore$ $g = \pm 5$

i.e. $2g = \pm 10$

Hence the equation of the circle is given by

$$x^2 + y^2 \pm 10x + (-8)y + 16 = 0$$

i.e. $x^2 + y^2 \pm 10x - 8y + 16 = 0$ **Ans.**

Problem 2 A circle touches one given straight line and cuts off a constant length $2a$ from another straight line $\perp r$ to the former. Find the locus of its centre.

Solution In the given question $c(\alpha, \beta)$ is the centre of the circle Equation. Let the two perpendicular lines are the x axis and the y-axis. Circle touches Y axis at P and cuts intercept $2a$ from X axis

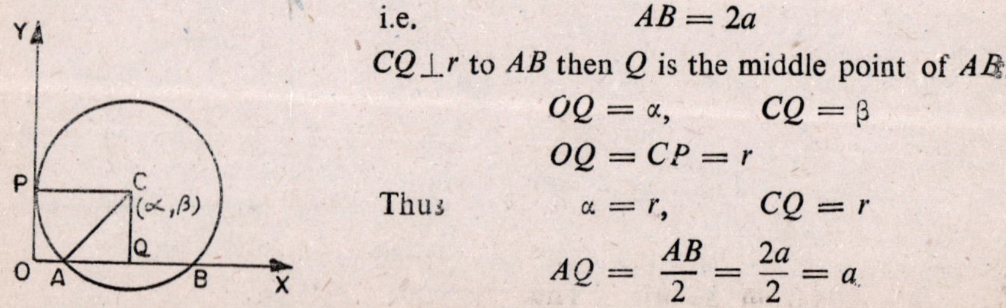

i.e. $AB = 2a$

$CQ \perp r$ to AB then Q is the middle point of AB.

$OQ = \alpha$, $CQ = \beta$

$OQ = CP = r$

Thus $\alpha = r$, $CQ = r$

$$AQ = \frac{AB}{2} = \frac{2a}{2} = a$$

Now from triangle CAQ we have,

$$CA^2 = AQ^2 + CQ^2$$

$$r^2 = a^2 + \beta^2$$

$$\Rightarrow \quad \alpha^2 = a^2 + \beta^2 \qquad \text{[since } \alpha = r\text{]}$$

$$\Rightarrow \quad \alpha^2 - \beta^2 = a^2 \qquad (1)$$

So the locus of the centre (α, β) is obtained by putting $\alpha = x$ and $\beta = y$ in equation (1)

$$\boxed{x^2 - y^2 = a^2} \qquad (2)$$

Equation (2) is the required locus of the centre (α, β) **Ans.**

Problem 3 Find the equation of the circle which touches the two co-ordinate axes at a distance a from the origin.

Solution Let (α, β) be the centre of the circle and r the radius

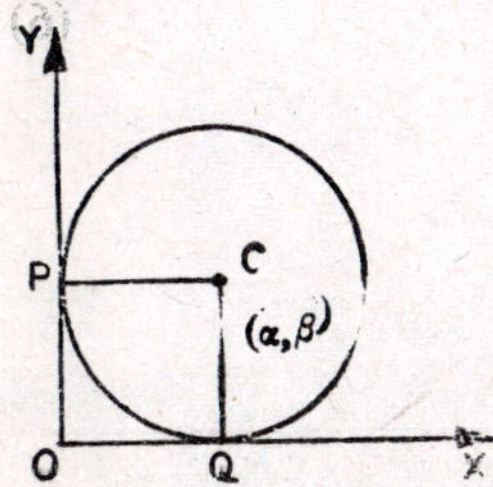

Then equation of the circle is given by

$$(x-\alpha)^2 + (y-\beta)^2 = a^2 \qquad (1)$$

The circle touches the axis of X and Y at the points Q and P respectively

$$CP = \alpha \; CQ = \beta \; ; CP = a, CQ = a$$

(ξ question)

Again $CP = r$ (radius) $CQ = r$ (radius)

So $\qquad r = a$

Thus the equation of the circle raduces to

$$(x-a^2) + (y-a)^2 = a^2$$

$$x^2 - 2ax + a^2 + y^2 - 2ay + a^2 = a^2$$

Thus $\qquad x^2 + y^2 - 2ax - 2ay + a^2 = 0$

Which is the required equation of the circle.

Problem 4 Find the equation to the circle through the points (2, −3) and (−3, 5) and having its centre on the line $2x - 3y + 5 = 0$

Solution The general equation of circle is

$$x^2 + y^2 + 2gx + 2fy + c = 0 \qquad (1)$$

Equation (1) passes through points (2, 3) and (−3, 5) so these will satisfy equation (1) i.e.

$$(2)^2 + (-3)^2 + 2g \cdot 2 + 2f(-3) + c = 0$$

.i.e $\qquad 4 + 9 + 4g - 6f + c = 0$

i.e. $$4g - 6f + 13 + c = 0 \quad (2)$$

and $$(-3)^2 + (5)^2 + 2g \cdot (-3) + 2f(5) + c = 0$$

i.e. $$9 + 25 - 6g + 10f + c = 0$$

i.e. $$34 - 6g + 10f + c = 0 \quad (3)$$

The centre of the circle (1) is the point $(-g, -f)$. Since this point lies on the side

$$2x - 3y + 5 = 0$$

so $$-2g + 3f + 5 = 0 \quad (1)$$

Subtracting equation (2) from equation (3) we have

$$34 - 6g + 10f + c - 4g + 6f - 13 - c = 0$$

$$21 - 10g + 16f = 0$$

i.e. $$10g - 16f - 21 = 0 \quad (5)$$

Multiyly (4) by (5) we have

$$-10g + 15f + 25 = 0 \quad (6)$$

Adding equation (5) and (6) we have

$$-f + 4 = 0$$

$$\Rightarrow \quad f = 4 \qquad 2f = 8$$

Then $$10g - 16 \times 4 - 21 = 0$$

$$10g - 64 - 21 = 0$$

$$10g - 85 = 0$$

$$10g = 85$$

$$2g = \frac{85}{5} = 17$$

Again from (3) we have

$$34 - 51 + 10 \times 4 + c = 0$$

i.e. $$34 - 51 + 40 + c = 0$$

$$74 - 51 + c = 0$$

i.e. $$23 + c = 0$$

i.e. $$c = -23$$

Putting the values of g, f and c in equation (1)

$$x^2 + y^2 + 17x + 8y - 23 = 0$$

This is the required equation of the circle. **Ans.**

Problem 5 A circle passes through a fixed point O and cuts two fixed perpendicular straight lines through O in P and Q. If the straight line PQ always passes through a fixed point, find the locus of the centre of the circle.

Solution Let circle passes through a fixed point O and let centre of the circle is (α, β). CL and CM are drawn $\perp$ to OP and OQ then

$$OL = \alpha, \qquad OM = \beta$$

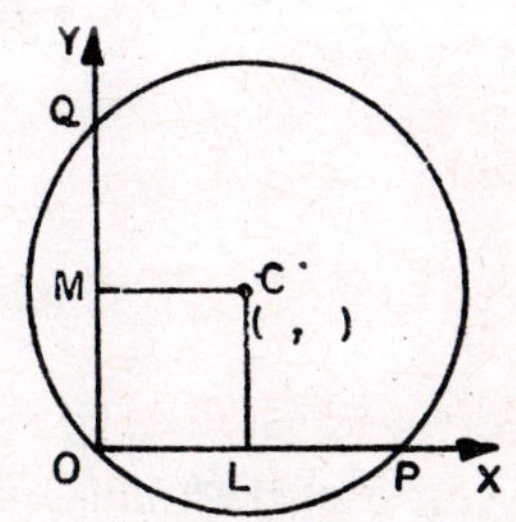

Let take the point O as origin (0, 0)

Then $\qquad OP = 2 \cdot OL = 2\alpha$

$$OQ = 2 \cdot OM = 2\beta$$

Equation of the line PQ is given by

$$\frac{x}{2\alpha} + \frac{y}{2\beta} = 0 \qquad (1)$$

because this lines cuts intercepts 2α and 2β from the co-ordinates axis.

Again equation (1) passes through a fixed point (h, k) so

$$\frac{h}{2\alpha} + \frac{k}{2\beta} = 1 \qquad (2)$$

Locus of the centre (α, β) can be obtained by replacing α by x and β by y in equation (2). Thus the locus of the centre (α, β) is glven by

$$\boxed{\frac{h}{2x} + \frac{k}{2y} = 1}$$

i.e. $\qquad \dfrac{h}{x} + \dfrac{k}{y} = 2 \qquad$ **Ans.**

Problem 6 Find the area of an equilateral triangle inscribed in the circle $x^2 + y^2 + 2gx + 2fy + c = 0$.

Solution Let equation of the circle is

$$x^2 + y^2 + 2gx + 2fy + c = 0$$

Let an equilateral triangle is inscribed in the circle ABC be the equilateral triangle. We have to find the area of the equilateral triangle

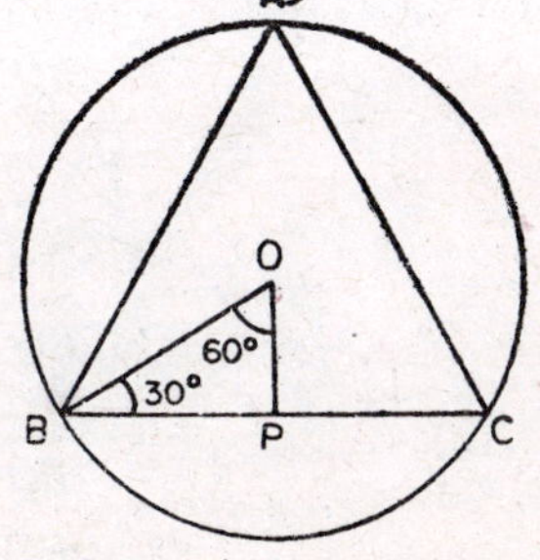

Area of $\Delta\, ABC = \dfrac{\sqrt{3}}{4} \times (\text{side})^2$

$$= \frac{\sqrt{3}}{4}\,(BC)^2 \qquad (2)$$

$(-g, -f)$ is the centre of the circle and $\sqrt{g^2 + f^2 - c}$ is the radius of the circle. From centre O draw $OP \perp BC$. Then P is the mid point of BC

$$\angle BOP = 60°$$

Then from $\Delta\ OBP$

$$\sin 60^\circ = \frac{BP}{OB}$$

$$BP = OP \sin 60$$

$$= \frac{\sqrt{3}}{2}\ OB = \frac{\sqrt{3}}{2}\sqrt{g^2 + f^2 - c}$$

$$BC = 2 \cdot BP = 2 \cdot \frac{\sqrt{3}}{2}\sqrt{g^2 + f^2 - c}$$

$$= \sqrt{3\,(g^2 + f^2 - c)}$$

Now area of the triangle ABC

$$= \frac{\sqrt{3}}{4}(BC)^2 = \frac{\sqrt{3}}{4}\left[\sqrt{3\,(g^2 + f^2 - c)}\right]^2$$

$$= \frac{\sqrt{3}}{4} \cdot 3\,(g^2 + f^2 - c) = \frac{3\sqrt{3}}{4}(g^2 + f^2 - c)$$

Problem 7 Some chords of a circle subtend a right angle at the point $(\alpha, 0)$. Find the locus of their middle point.

Solution Let us suppose that the equation of the circle is

$$x^2 + y^2 = a^2$$

where the co-ordinate of the centre of the circle is (0, 0) and the radius of the circle is a. $O(0, 0)$ is the centre of the circle. At point $P(\alpha, 0)$ the chord AB makes right angle. Let $Q(h, k)$ is the middle point of AB.

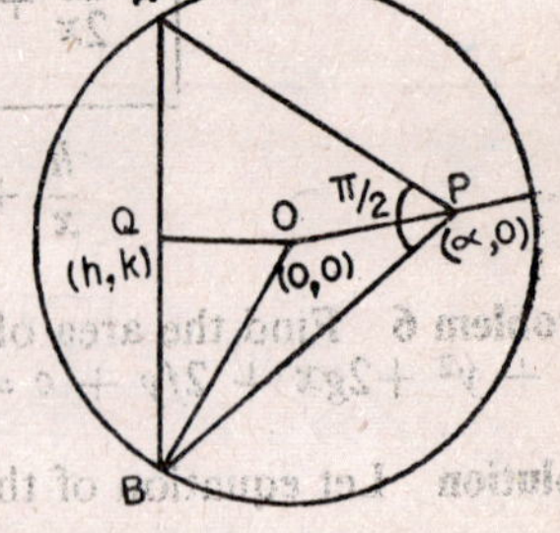

$$OB = \text{radius of the circle} = a$$

Since $Q\ (h_1\ k)$ is the middle point of the chord AB so

$$AQ = QB$$

Again since $APB = \pi/2$ (right angle) and Q is the middle point of AB so it is clear from the Geometry that

$$BQ = PQ = AQ$$

Since $\qquad OQ$ is $\perp r\ AB$

So $\qquad \angle OQB = \frac{\pi}{2}$

So $\qquad BQ^2 = OB^2 - OQ^2$

$$BQ^2 = a^2 - [(h-0)^2 + (k-0)^2]$$

$$BQ^2 = a^2 - (h^2 + k^2) \qquad (1)$$

$$PQ^2 = (h-\alpha)^2 + (k-0)^2$$

(2)

Since $BQ = PQ$

$$\Rightarrow \quad BQ^2 = PQ^2$$

$$\Rightarrow \quad a^2 - h^2 - k^9 = (h - \alpha)^2 + k^2$$

$$\Rightarrow \quad a^2 - h^2 - k^2 = h^2 + \alpha^2 - 2h\alpha + k^2$$

$$\Rightarrow \quad 2h^2 + 2k^2 - 2h\alpha + \alpha^2 - a^2 = 0 \quad (3)$$

Locus of the middle point is obtained by replacing $(h_1\ k)$ by $(x_1\ y)$ locus is given by

$$2x^2 + 2y^2 - 2x\alpha + \alpha^2 - a^2 = 0$$

which represents a circle. **Ans.**

Problem 8 Find the equation of the circle which touches both axis and has a radius 5.

Solution Centre of the circcle is (5, 5) and the radius is 5 then equation of the circle is written as

$$(x-5)^2 + (y-5)^2 = (5)^2$$

i.e. $x^2 - 10x + 25 + y^2 - 10y + 25 = 25$

i.e. $\quad x^2 + y^2 - 10x - 10y + 25 = 0$

which is the required equation of the circle.

Problem 9 Prove that the straight line $x + y = 2 + \sqrt{2}$ touches the cirele $x^2 + y^2 - 2x - 2y + 1 = 0$ and find the point contact. [*I.F.S. 84*]

Solution $\quad x^2 + y^2 - 2x - 2y + 1 = 4$

Equation of the circle is

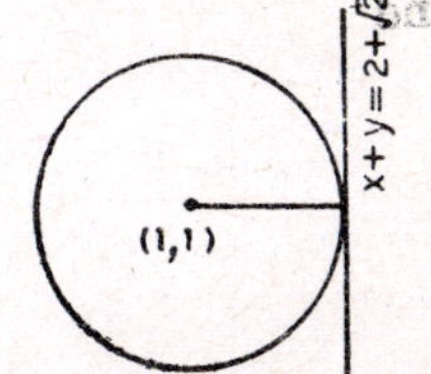

$$x^2 + y^2 - 2x - 2y + 1 = 0$$

$$x^2 - 2x + 1 + y^2 - 2y + 1 = 1$$

i.e. $\quad (x-1)^2 + (y-1)^2 = 1$

Thus the centre of the circles (1, 1) and the radius is 1.

Length of perpendicular from (1, 1) to the line $x + y = 2 + \sqrt{2}$ is

$$\frac{1 + 1 - 2 - \sqrt{2}}{\sqrt{1^2 + 1^2}} = \frac{2 - 2 - \sqrt{2}}{\pm\sqrt{2}} = 1$$

Which is equal to the radius. Thus the given line touches the circle whose equation is

$$y^2 + y^2 - 2x - 2y + 1 = 0$$

To get the point of contact we may proceed as follows.

From the equation of the straight line we have

$$y + x = 2 + \sqrt{2}$$

i.e. $$y = -x + 2 + \sqrt{2}$$

Now putting the value of y in equation (1) we have

$$(x-1)^2 + (-x + 2 + \sqrt{2} - 1)^2 = 1$$

$$(x-1)^2 + (1 + \sqrt{2} - x)^2 = 1$$

$$x^2 - 2x + 1 + (1 + \sqrt{2})^2 + x^2 - 2x(\sqrt{2} + 1) = 1$$

$$x^2 - 2x + 1 (1 + \sqrt{2})^2 + x^2 - 2\sqrt{2}x - 2x = 1$$

$$2x^2 - 4x - 2\sqrt{2}x + (\sqrt{2} + 1)^2 = 0$$

$$2x^2 - (2 + \sqrt{2})x + (\sqrt{2} + 1)^2 = 0$$

Multiplying both sides by 2

$$4x^2 - 4(2 + \sqrt{2})x + [\sqrt{2}(\sqrt{2} + 1)]^2 = 0$$

$$4x^2 - 4(2 + \sqrt{2})x + (2 + \sqrt{2})^2 = 0$$

$$(2x)^2 - 2\,2x(2 + \sqrt{2}) + (2 + \sqrt{2})^2 = 0$$

i.e. $$[2x - (2 + \sqrt{2})]^2 = 0$$

$\Rightarrow$ $$2x - (2 + \sqrt{2}) = 0$$

$\Rightarrow$ $$x = \frac{2 + \sqrt{2}}{2}$$

and $$y = 2 + \sqrt{2} - x$$

$$y = 2 + \sqrt{2} - \left(\frac{2 + \sqrt{2}}{2}\right)$$

$$= \frac{4 + 2\sqrt{2} - 2 - \sqrt{2}}{2} = \frac{2 + \sqrt{2}}{2}$$

Hence the co-ordinates of the point of contact are

$$\tfrac{1}{2}(2 + \sqrt{2}), \tfrac{1}{2}(2 + \sqrt{2})$$ **Ans.**

Problem 1 Find the co-ordinates of the points where the straight line $y + x = 5$ intersects the circle

$$x^2 + y^2 - 4x + 2y - 11 = 0$$

Find also the length of the chord intercepted.

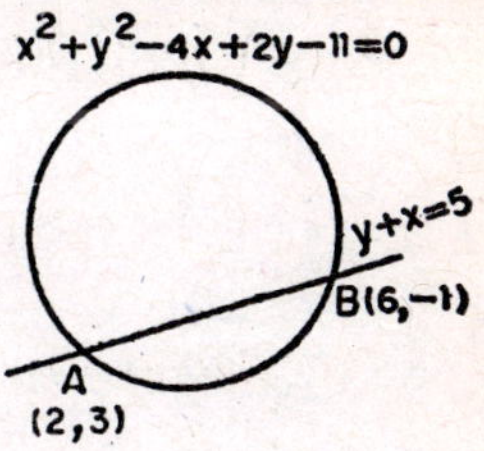

Solution The co-ordinate of the point of contact A and B can be obtained by solving the equations.

$$x^2 + y^2 - 4x + 2y - 11 = 0 \qquad (1)$$

and

$$y + x = 5 \qquad (2)$$

From equation (2) we have

$$y = 5 - x$$

Putting the value of y from equation (3) in equation (1) we have

$$x^2 + (5-x)^2 - 4x + 2(5-x) - 11 = 0$$

i.e. $\quad x^2 + 25 - 10x + x^2 - 4x + 10 - 2x - 11 = 0$

i.e. $\quad 2x^2 - 16x + 24 = 0$

i.e. $\quad 2(x^2 - 8x + 12) = 0$

i.e. $\quad x^2 - 8x + 12 = 0$

i.e. $\quad x^2 - 6x - 2x + 12 = 0$

i.e. $\quad x(x-6) - 2(x-6)$

i.e. $\quad (x-2)(x-6) = 0$

If $\quad x - 2 = 0; \quad x - 6 = 0$

$$x = 2; \quad x = 6$$

Putting $\quad x = 2, \quad 6$ in $y = -x + 5$

$$y = -2 + 5 = 3$$

$$y = -6 + 5 = -1$$

Thus the point of intersection are (2, 3) and (6, −1)

The length of the chord intercepted

$$= \sqrt{(6-2)^2 + (3+1)^2} = \sqrt{4^2 + 4^2}$$

$$= \sqrt{16 + 16} = \sqrt{16 \times 2} = 4\sqrt{2}$$

Problem 2 Find the co-ordinates of the points of intersection of the circles

$$x^2 + y^2 - 8x - 2y + 12 = 0$$

$$x^2 + y^2 - 5x - y - 6 = 0$$

Solution The equation of the circles are

$$x^2 + y^2 - 8x - 2y + 12 = 0 \qquad (1)$$

$$x^2 + y^2 - 5x - y - 6 = 0$$

Subtracting (2) from (1) we have

$$x^2 + y^2 - 8x - 2y + 12 - x^2 - y^2 + 5x + y + 6 = 0$$

$$-3x - y + 18 = 0$$

$$y = 18 - 3x$$

$$y = 3(6 - x) \qquad (3)$$

Substituting the value of y from equation (3) in equation (2) we have

$$x^2 + 9(6-x)^2 - 5x - 3(6-x) - 6 = 0$$

$$x^2 + 9(36 - 12x + x^2) - 5x - 18 + 3x - 6 = 0$$

i.e. $\quad x^2 + 324 - 108x + 9x^2 - 5x - 18 + 3x - 6 = 0$

i.e. $\quad 10x^2 - 110x + 300 = 0$

$\Rightarrow \quad 10(x^2 - 11x + 30) = 0$

$\Rightarrow \quad x^2 - 11x + 30 = 0$

$\Rightarrow \quad x^2 - 6x - 5x + 30 = 0$

i.e. $\quad x(x-6) - 5(x-6) = 0$

$\Rightarrow \quad (x-5)(x-6) = 0$

$\Rightarrow \quad x = 5$ or 6

Putting $\quad x = 5$

$$y = 3(6 - x)$$

$$y = 3(6 - 5)$$

$$y = 3 \times 1 = 3$$

For $\quad x = 6$

$$y = 3(6-6) = 3 \times 0 = 0$$

Thus the points of intersection are (5, 3) and (6, 0).

Problem 3 The straight line $3x - 4y + k = 0$ touches the circle

$$x^2 + y^2 - 4x + 8y - 5 = 0$$

find the value of k.

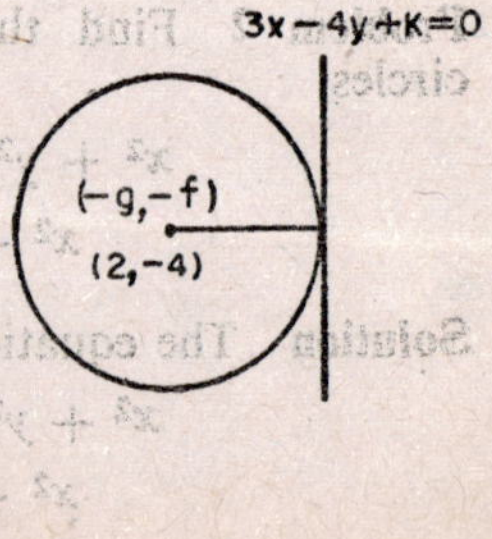

Solution Equation of the circle is

$$x^2 + y^2 - 4x + 8y - 5 = 0$$

3x−4y+K=0

(−g,−f)

(2,−4)

Here $\quad 2g = -4 \qquad 2f = 8$

$\Rightarrow \quad g = -2 \quad \Rightarrow f = 4$

Thus the co-ordinate of the centre is $(2, -4)$

The line $3x-4y+k=0$ be atangent if the $\perp'$ distance from $(2, -4)$ to the line $3x-4y+k=0$ must be equal to the radius of the circle

$$\text{Radius of the circle} = \sqrt{g^2+f^2-c} \qquad c=-5$$

$$= \sqrt{2^2+(-4)^2-c} = \sqrt{4+16-c}$$

$$= \sqrt{20-c} = \sqrt{20+5} = \sqrt{25} = 5$$

Length of perpendicular from $(2, -4)$ to the line $3x-4y+k=0$ is given by

$$= \frac{3.2-4(-4)+k}{\sqrt{3^2+(-4^2)}}$$

$$= \frac{6+16+k}{\sqrt{9+16}} = \frac{22+k}{\pm 5}$$

If the line touches the circle, then

$$\pm\frac{22+k}{5} = 5$$

$$\Rightarrow \qquad 22+k = \pm 25$$

$$k = 3 \text{ or } 47 \qquad \textbf{Ans.}$$

Problem 5 Find the equation to the circle which has its centre be at the point (3, 4) and touches the straight line

$$5x+12y=11$$

Solution The perpendicular distance from the centre of the circle upon the given line which is tangent is equal to the radius of the circle

i.e. $$\frac{5.3+12.4-11}{\sqrt{5^2+12^2}} = r$$

$$\Rightarrow \qquad \frac{15+48-11}{\sqrt{25+144}} = \frac{52}{13} = 4 = r$$

Thus the centre of the circle is (3, 4) and radius equal to 4. Then the equation of the circle is given by

$$(x-3)^2+(y-4)^2 = 4^2$$

$$x^2-6x+9+y^2-8y+16 = 16$$

i.e. $$x^2+y^2-6x-8y+9=0$$

Problem 6 Find the equation of the tangent to the circle $x^2 + y^2 = 9$ which is parallel to the line $2x + 2y + 3 = 0$.

Solution Equation of the line parallel to

$$2x + 2y + 3 = 0$$

is given by $$2x + 2y + 3 = 0$$

Equation of the circle is $$x^2 + y^2 = 9$$

$$\Rightarrow \quad x^2 + y^2 = 3^2$$

i.e. $$(x-0)^2 + (y-0)^2 = 3^2$$

Thus the centre of the circle is (0, 0) and the radius is 3. Since the line $2x + 2y + c = 0$ is the tangent on the circle so length of $\perp r$ (from (0, 0) to the line $2x + 2y + c = 0$ must be equal to the radius 3

$$\frac{2.0 + 2.0 + c}{\sqrt{2^2 + 2^2}} = 3$$

$$\frac{c}{\sqrt{8}} = 3$$

$$\frac{c}{\pm 2\sqrt{2}} = 3$$

$$\Rightarrow \quad c = \pm 6\sqrt{2}$$

Therefore the equations to the tangent are

$$2x + 2y \pm 6\sqrt{2} = 0$$

i.e. $$x + y \pm 3\sqrt{2} = 0 \qquad \textbf{Ans.}$$

Problem 6 Find the condition that the line $x \cos \alpha + y \sin \alpha = p$ should touch the circle $x^2 + y^2 = 2ax$. Hence prove that the locus of the foot of the perpendicular from the origin upon the tangent to the circle has for its equation in polar co-ordinates. $r = a(1 + \cos \theta)$.

Solution Equation of the circle can be written in the form

$$x^2 + y^2 - 2ax = 0$$

$$x^2 - 2ax + a^2 + y^2 = a^2$$

i.e. $$(x-a)^2 + y^2 = a^2$$

i.e. $$(x-a)^2 + (y-0)^2 = a^2$$

Thus the co-ordinates of the centre are $(a, 0)$ and its radius $= a$.

If the line $x \cos \alpha + y \sin \alpha = p$ touches the circle then the length of perpendicular from $(a, 0)$ to the line must be equal to the radius of the circle

i.e.
$$\frac{a \cos \alpha + 0 \sin \alpha - p}{\sqrt{\cos^2 \alpha + \sin^2 \alpha}} = a$$

i.e.
$$\frac{a \cos \alpha - p}{\pm 1} = a$$

The locus of the foot of the perpendicular from the origin on the tangent to the circle will be obtained by putting

$$p = r \qquad \text{and } \alpha = \theta$$

i.e. the required locus is

$$-(a \cos \theta - r) = a$$

i.e.
$$r = a + a \cos \theta$$

$$r = a\,(1 + \cos \theta) \qquad \textit{(Proved)}$$

Problem 7 Find the locus of the foot of the perpendicular let fall on any tangent to a circle from a fixed point on the circle.

Solution Let equation of the circle be

$$x^2 + y^2 = a^2$$

Let P $(a \cos \alpha, a \sin \alpha)$ be a fixed point on the circle, so that α is costant

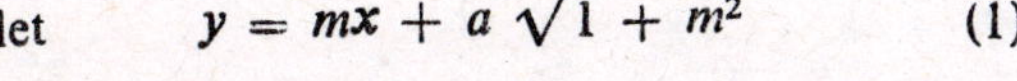

let
$$y = mx + a\sqrt{1 + m^2} \qquad (1)$$

be any tangent to the circle.

Equation (1) can be written as

$$mx - y + a\sqrt{1 + m^2} = 0 \qquad (2)$$

Equation of any line $\perp^r$ to equation (2) is given by

$$x + my + k = 0 \qquad (3)$$

line (3) passes through the point P $(a \cos \alpha, a \sin \alpha)$ so

$$a \cos \alpha + ma \sin \alpha + k = 0$$

$$k = -(m \sin \alpha + \cos \alpha)\, a$$

Hence equation of any line $\perp$ to (1) and passing through the point P is

$$my + x = a\,(m \sin \alpha + \cos \alpha) \qquad (4)$$

Required locus is obtained by eliminating m between (1) and (4)

From equation (4) we have

$$my + x = (m \sin \alpha + \cos \alpha)\, a$$

$$\Rightarrow \quad my - am \sin \alpha = a \cos \alpha - x$$

$$\Rightarrow \quad m\,(y - a \sin \alpha) = (a \cos \alpha - x)$$

$$\Rightarrow \quad m = \frac{a \cos \alpha - x}{y - a \sin \alpha} \qquad (5)$$

Putting the value of m from (5 i.e. n (1)) we have

$$(y - mx)^2 = a^2 (1 + m^2)$$

$$\left[y - \frac{(a \cos \alpha - x)}{y - a \sin \alpha}\, x\right]^2 = a^2 \left[1 + \left(\frac{a \cos \alpha - x}{y - a \sin \alpha}\right)^2\right]$$

$$\frac{[y\,(y - a \sin \alpha) - x\,(a \cos \alpha - x)]^2}{(y - a \sin \alpha)^2} = a^2 \left[1 + \frac{(y - a \sin \alpha)^2 + (a \cos \alpha - x)^2}{(y - a \sin \alpha)^2}\right]$$

$$[y^2 - ay \sin \alpha - ax \cos \alpha + x^2]^2 = a^2[(a \sin \alpha)^2 + (\cos \alpha - x)^2]$$

$$\Rightarrow \quad [x^2 + y^2 - ax \cos \alpha - ay \sin \alpha]^2 = a^2\, [(a \cos \alpha - x) + (y - a \sin \alpha)^2)]$$

which is the required locus.

Problem 8 A line moves such that the sum of the perpendiculars drawn to it from two fixed points is constant prove that it always touches a fixed circle. Find the equation of the circle.

Solution Let the equation of the line be $ax + by - 1 = 0$. Let the two fixed points be (x_1, y_1) and (x_2, y_2). From question

$$\frac{ax_1 + by_1 - 1}{\sqrt{a^2 + b^2}} + \frac{ax_2 + by_2 - 1}{\sqrt{a^2 + b^2}} = k$$

$$\frac{a\,(x_1 + a_2) + b\,(y_1 + y_2) - 2}{\sqrt{a^2 + b^2}} = k$$

$$\frac{a\,\dfrac{(x + x_2)}{2} + b\,\dfrac{(y_1 + y_2}{2} - 1}{\sqrt{a^2 + b^2}} = \frac{k}{2} \qquad (1)$$

Which shows that the line $ax + by - 1 = 0$ touches the circule whose centre is

$$\frac{x_1 + x_2}{2},\ \frac{y_1 + y_2}{2} \text{ and radius is } \left(\frac{k}{2}\right)^2$$

Thus the equation of the circle is

$$\left[x - \frac{x_1 + x_1}{2}\right]^2 + \left[y - \frac{y_1 + y_2}{2}\right]^2 = \left(\frac{k}{2}\right)^2$$

Since the length of the perpendicular from $\dfrac{x_1 + x_2}{2}, \dfrac{y_1 + y_2}{2}$ on the line $ax + by - 1 = 0$ satisfies (1). **Ans.**

Problem 9 Find the condition that the line $lx + my + n = 0$ should touch the circle $x^2 + y^2 = a^2$.

Solution The equation of the circle is

$$x^2 + y^2 = a^2$$

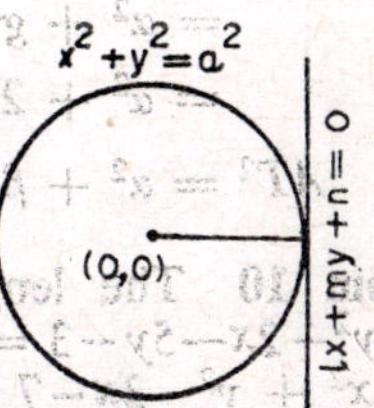

The co-ordinate of the centre is (0, 0) and the radius is a. The line $lx + my + n = 0$ touches the circle if the length of ⊥r drawn from (0, 0) to be line $lx + my + n = 0$ is equal to the radius of the circle i.e.

$$\frac{l \cdot 0 + m \cdot 0 + n}{\sqrt{l^2 + m^2}} = a$$

i.e. $$\frac{n}{\sqrt{l^2 + m^2}} = a$$

i.e. $$\frac{n^2}{l^2 + m^2} = a^2$$

i.e. $$n^2 = a^2 (l^2 + m^2)$$

Which is the required equation that the line $lx + my + n - 0$ touches circle $x^2 + y^2 = a^2$ **Ans.**

Article Length of the tangent from a given point (α, β).

Let A be the point $(\alpha_1 \beta)$. If the line through A is a tangent to the circle, the point P and Q concide at T and

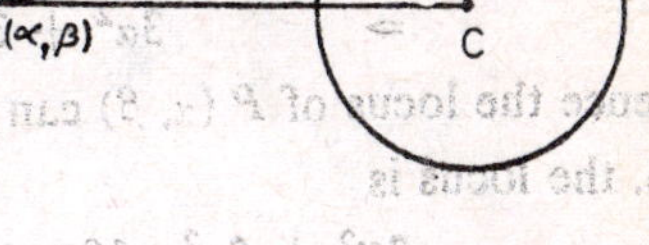

$$AP \cdot AQ = AT^2$$

Consequently the square of the length of the tangent from the point $(\alpha_1 \beta)$ to the circle $x^2 + y^2 + 2g\alpha + 2f\beta + C = 0$ is

$$= AP \cdot AQ = \alpha^2 + \beta^2 + 2g\alpha + 2f\beta + C. \qquad \textit{(Remember)}$$

Another Method

Let from the point (α, β) tangent AT is drawn to the circle $\Delta\ ACT$ is a right angled triangle. Then

$$AC^2 = AT^2 + CT^2 \qquad (1$$

Since the equation of the circle is $x^2 + y^2 + 2gx + 2fy + c = 0$. The co-ordinate of the centre is $(-g, -f)$ and the radius is $\sqrt{g^2 + f^2 - c}$.

$$AC^2 = (\alpha + g)^2 + (\beta + f)^2$$

$$CT^2 = (\text{radius})^2$$

$$= (\sqrt{g^2 + f^2 - c})^2 = g^2 + f^2 - c$$

Now from relation (1) we have

$$AT^2 = AC^2 - CT^2 = (\alpha + g)^2 + (\beta + f)^2 - (g^2 + f^2 - c)$$

$$= \alpha^2 + g^2 + 2\alpha g + \beta^2 + f^2 + 2\beta f - g^2 - f^2 + c$$

$$= \alpha^2 + 2g\alpha + \beta^2 + \beta^2 + 2f\beta + c$$

$$AT^2 = \alpha^2 + \beta^1 + 2g\alpha + 2f\beta + c$$

Problom 10 The length of the tangent from a point P to the circle $x^2 + y^2 - 2x - 5y - 3 = 0$ is double the length of the tangent from it to circle $x^2 + y^2 - 3x - 7 = 0$. Show that the locus of P is a circle of radius

$$\frac{5\sqrt{17}}{6}$$

Solution Let the co-ordinate of the point P is (α, β). Length of tangent from the point $P(\alpha, B)$ to the cirele $x^2 + y^2 + 2x - 5y - 3 = 0$ is PR and is given by

$$PR^2 = \alpha^2 + \beta^2 - 2\alpha - 5\beta - 3 \qquad (1)$$

Let the length of the tangent from $(\alpha_1 \beta)$ to the circle $x^2 + y^2 - 3x - 7$ is PQ and is given by

$$PQ^2 = \alpha^2 + \beta^2 - 3\alpha - 7 \qquad (2)$$

It is given by the question that

$$PR = 2PQ$$

$$\Rightarrow \quad PR^2 = 4PQ^2$$

$$\Rightarrow \quad \alpha^2 + \beta^2 - 2\alpha - 5\beta - 3 = 4(\alpha^2 + \beta^2 - 3\alpha - 7)$$

$$\Rightarrow \quad \alpha^2 + \beta^2 + 2\alpha - 5\beta - 3 = 4\alpha^2 + 4\beta^2 - 12\alpha - 28$$

$$\Rightarrow \quad 3\alpha^2 + 3\beta^2 - 10\alpha + 5\beta - 25 = 0$$

Hence the locus of $P(\alpha, \beta)$ can be obtained by replacing α, β by x and y i.e. the locus is

$$3x^2 + 3y^2 - 10x + 5y - 25 = 0$$

$$x^2 + y^2 - \frac{10}{3}x + \frac{5}{3}y - \frac{25}{3} = 0$$

Here

$$2g = -\frac{10}{3} \quad 2f = \frac{5}{3}$$

$$g = -\frac{5}{3} \quad f = \frac{5}{6}$$

The radius of this circle is $\sqrt{g^2 + f^2 - c}$

$$= \sqrt{\frac{25}{9} + \frac{25}{36} + \frac{25}{3}} = \sqrt{\frac{100 + 25 + 300}{36}}$$

$$= \sqrt{\frac{425}{36}} = \sqrt{\frac{25 \times 17}{36}} = \frac{5\sqrt{17}}{6}$$

(Proved)

Problem 11 Show that the length of the tangent from any point on the circle

$$x^2 + y^2 + 2gx + 2fy + c = 0 \text{ to the circle}$$
$$x^2 + y^2 + 2gx + 2fy + c_1 = 0 \text{ is } \sqrt{c_1 - c}$$

Solution Let the equation of two circles be

$$x^2 + y^2 + 2gx + 2fy + c = 0 \quad (1)$$
$$x^2 + y^2 + 2gx + 2fy + c_1 = 0 \quad (2)$$

The co-ordinate of the centre of both the circle is $(-g, -f)$ and the radius of the circle (1) is $\sqrt{g^2 + f^2 - c}$ and the radius of the circle (2) is
$$\sqrt{g^2 + f^2 - c_1}$$

Since the centre of both the circle is $(-g, -f)$ so the two circles (1) and (2) are concentric. Without loss of any generality let us suppose that (1) represents the larger circle and (2) represents the smaller circle.

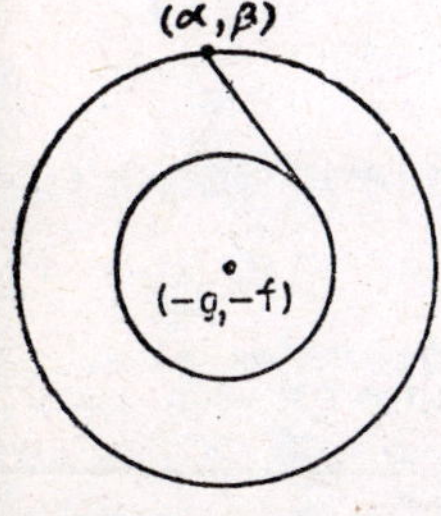

Let (α, β) is a point on the circle (1) from (α, β) a tangent is drawn to the circle (2).

Length of the tangent from (α, β) to the circle

$$x^2 + y^2 + 2gx + 2fy + c_1 \text{ is given by}$$

$$\sqrt{\alpha^2 + \beta^2 + 2g\alpha + 2f\beta + c_1} \quad (3)$$

Again since (α, β) lies on the circle (1) i.e. it will satisfy (1) so

$$\alpha^2 + \beta^2 + 2g\alpha + 2f\beta + c = 0 \quad (4)$$

From equation (4)

$$\alpha^2 + \beta^2 + 2g\alpha + 2f\beta = -c \quad (5)$$

From equation (3) and (5) the length of the tangent is

$$\sqrt{-c + c_1} = \sqrt{c_1 - c}$$

length of tangent $= \sqrt{c_1 - c}$ (*Proved*)

Condition for contact of two circles

(i) If the two circles touch each other externally, then the sum of their radii will be equal to the distance between their centres.

(ii) If they touch internally, then the difference of their radii will be equal to the distance between their centres.

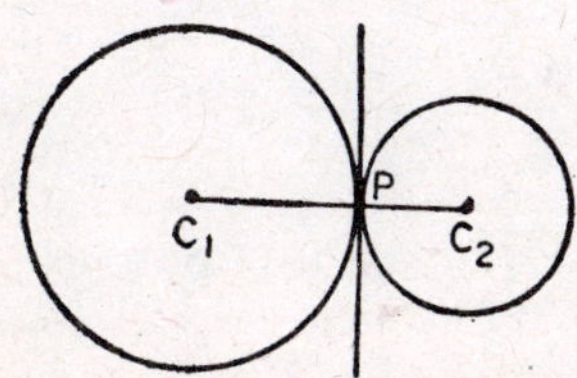

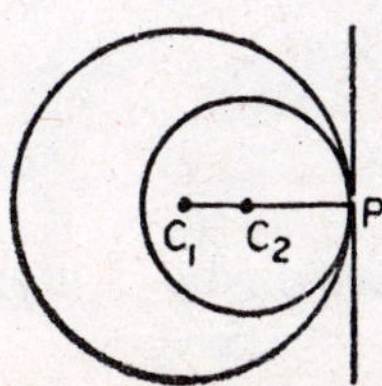

Problem 12 Prove that the two circles

$$x^2 + y^2 + 2ax + c^2 = 0$$

$$x^2 + y^2 + 2by + c^2 = 0$$

touch each of her if

$$\frac{1}{a^2} + \frac{1}{b^2} = \frac{1}{c^2}$$

Solution Equation of the circles are

$$x^2 + y^2 + 2ax + c^2 = 0 \qquad (1)$$

$$x^2 + 2ax + a^2 + y^2 + c^2 = a^2$$

i.e. $$(x + a)^2 + (y + 0)^2 = a^2 - c^2$$

Thus the centre of this circle is $(-a, 0)$ and the radius is $\sqrt{a^2 - c^2}$

Again equation of another circle can be written as

$$x^2 + y^2 + 2by + c^2 = 0$$

$$x^2 + y^2 + 2by + b^2 + c^2 = b^2$$

i.e. $$(x + 0)^2 + (y + b)^2 + c^2 = b^2$$

i.e. $$(x + 0)^2 + (y + b)^2 = b^2 - c^2$$

The centre of this circle is $(0, -b)$ and radius is $\sqrt{b^2 - c^2}$

Circles (1) and (2) will touch each other if the distance between the centres is equal to the sum of the radius of the two circles

i.e. $$\sqrt{a^2 - c^2} + \sqrt{b^2 - c^2} = \sqrt{(-a-0)^2 + (a + b)^2}$$

$$\sqrt{a^2 - c^2} + \sqrt{b^2 - c^2} = \sqrt{a^2 + b^2}$$

Squaring both sides we have

$$a^2 - c^2 + b^2 - c^2 + 2\sqrt{(a^2 - c^2)(b^2 - c^2)} = a^2 + b^2$$

$$-2c^2 + 2\sqrt{(a^2 - c^4)(b^2 - c^2)} = 1$$

i.e. $$2\sqrt{(a^2 - c^2)(b^2 - c^2)} = 2c^2$$

Again squaring both sides, we have

$$(a^2 - c^2)(b^2 - c^2) = c^4$$

$$a^2 b^2 - a^2 c^2 - b^2 c^2 + c^4 = c^4$$

i.e. $$a^2 b^2 = a^2 c^2 + b^2 c^2$$

i.e. $$\frac{1}{c^2} = \frac{a^2 + b^2}{a^2 b^2}$$

i.e. $$\frac{1}{a^2} + \frac{1}{b} = \frac{1}{c^2}$$

which is the required condition for the circle (1) and (2) to touch each other.

(Proved)

Problem 13 Find the equation of the circle whose radius is 3 and which touches the circle $x^2 + y^2 - 4x - 6y - 12 = 0$ internally at the point $(-1, -1)$

Solution Let the equation of the circle is

$$x^2 + y^2 - 4x - 6y - 12 = 0$$

$$x^2 - 2.2.x + 2^2 + y^2 - 2 \cdot 3y + 3^2 - 12 = 2^2 + 3^2$$

i.e. $$(x-2)^2 + (y-3)^2 = 13 + 12$$

i.e. $$(x-2)^2 + (y-3)^2 = 25$$

i.e. $$(x-2)^2 + (y-3)^2 = 5^2$$

Thus the centre of the circle is (2, 3) and radius is 5 $\Rightarrow c_1 p = 5$

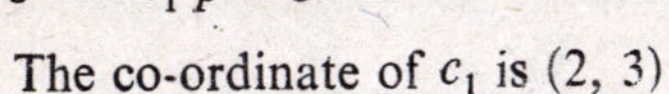

The co-ordinate of c_1 is (2, 3)

Let the point of contact is $(-1, -1)$

i.e. the co-ordinate of point p is $(-1, -1)$

and it it is given that $c_2 \ p = 3$

Then $$c_1 c_2 = 5 - 3 = 2$$

i.e. c_2 cuts the line joining points (2, 3) and $(-1, -1)$ in the ratio 2 : 3

Let the co-ordinates of c_2 be (x, y) then

$$x = \frac{2(-1) + 3 \cdot 2}{2 + 3} = \frac{-2 + 6}{5} = \frac{4}{5}$$

$$y = \frac{2(-1) + 3 \cdot 3}{2 + 3} = \frac{-2 + 9}{5} = \frac{7}{5}$$

$$\alpha = \frac{4}{5}, \ \beta = \frac{7}{5}$$

Hence equation of the circle whose centre is $\left(\frac{4}{5}, \frac{7}{5}\right)$ and radius is 3 is

given by $\left(x - \frac{4}{5}\right)^2 + \left(y - \frac{7}{5}\right)^2 = 3^2$

i.e. $$\frac{(5x-4)^2}{25} + \frac{(5y-7)^2}{25} = 9$$

$$25x^2 - 40x + 16 + 25y^2 - 70y + 49 = 25 \times 9$$

$$25x^2 + 25y^2 - 40x - 70y + 65 - 225 = 0$$

i.e $$25x^2 + 25y^2 - 40x - 70y - 160 = 0$$

i.e. $$5(5x^2 + 5y^2 - 8x - 14y - 32) = 0$$

i.e. $$5x^2 + 5y^2 - 8x - 14y - 32 = 0$$

which is the required equation of the circle

Problem 14 If two circles

$$x^2 + y^2 + 2gx + 2fy = 0$$
$$x^2 + y^2 + 2g_1 x + 2f_1 y = 0$$

touch each other, show that

$$\frac{g}{g_1} = \frac{f}{f_1}$$

Solution The equation of two circles are

$$x^2 + y^2 + 2gx + 2fy = 0 \quad (1)$$
$$x^2 + y^2 + 2g_1 x + 2f_1 y = 0 \quad (2)$$

The co-ordinate of the centres are $(-g, -f)$ and $(-g_1, -f_1)$

Radius of the circle (1) is $\sqrt{g^2 + f^2}$

Radius of the circle (2) is $\sqrt{g_1^2 + f_1^2}$

Since (1) and (2) touches each other so the sum of radius must be equal to the distance between $(-g, -f)$ and $(-g_1, -f_1)$

i.e. $\sqrt{(g-g_1)^2 + (f-f_1)^2} = \sqrt{g^2 + f^2} + \sqrt{g_1^2 + f_1^2}$

Squaring both sides we have

$$(g-g_1)^2 + (f-f_1)^2 = g^2 + f^2 + g_1^2 + f_1^2 + 2\sqrt{(g^2 + f^2)(g_1^2 + f_1^2)}$$

i.e. $-2gg_1 - 2ff_1 = 2\sqrt{(g^2 + f^2)(g_1^2 + f_1^2)}$

$$-(gg_1 + ff_1) = \sqrt{(g^2 + f^2)(g_1^2 + f_1^2)}$$

Squaring both sides we have

$$g^2 g_1^2 + f^2 f_1^2 + 2gf g_1 f_1 = g^2 g_1^2 + g^2 f_1^2 + f^2 g_1^2 + f_1^2$$

i.e. $g^2 f_1^2 + f^2 g_1^2 = 2gf g_1 f_1$

i.e. $g^2 f_1^2 - gf g_1 f_1 = gf g_1 f_1 - f^2 g_1^2$

i.e. $gf_1 [gf_1 - fg_1] = fg_1 [gf_1 - fg_1]$

i.e. $gf_1 = fg_1$

i.e. $\frac{g}{g_1} = \frac{f}{f_1}$ *(Proved)*

Theorem Show that from any point there can be drawn two tangents real or imaginary to a circle.

The equation to any tangent is

$$y = mx + a\sqrt{1 + m^2}$$

If this passes through the given point (α, β) we have

$$\beta = m\alpha + a\sqrt{1 + m^2}$$

$$\beta - m\alpha = a\sqrt{1 + m^2}$$

Squaring both sides we have

$$(\beta - m\alpha)^2 = a^2 (1 + m^2)$$

$$\beta^2 + m^2 \alpha^2 - 2m\alpha\beta = a^2 + a^2 m^2$$

$$m^2 (\alpha^2 - a^2) - 2m\alpha\beta + (\beta^2 - a^2) = 0 \qquad (1)$$

The equation (1) is a quadratic equation which gives the direction of those tangents to the circle which pass through the point (α, β). Since a quadratic equation has two roots, two tangents will pass through any point (α, β).

Evidently, the two tangents from (α, β) will be real, coincident or imaginary according as the roots of (1) are real, coincident or imaginary.

According as $\quad (-2\alpha\beta)^2 - 4(\alpha^2 - a^2)(\beta^2 - a^2) > = < 0$

i.e. $\quad 4\alpha^2 \beta^2 - 4[\alpha^2 \beta^2 - a^2 \beta^2 - a^2 \alpha^2 + a^4] > = < 0$

i.e. $\quad 4\alpha^2 \beta^2 - 4\alpha^2 \beta^2 + 4a^2 \beta^2 + 4a^2 \alpha^2 - 4a^4 > = < 0$

i.e. $\quad 4a^2 (\alpha^2 + \beta^2 - a^2) > = < 0$

i.e. $\quad \alpha^2 \beta^2 - a^2 > = < 0$

i.e. $\quad \alpha^2 + \beta^2 > = < a^2$

i.e. according as the point $(\alpha_1 \beta)$ is out side on or inside the circle.

Article Remember This equation to the pair of tangents from a given point to the circle.

Let equation of the circle is

$$x^2 + y^2 + 2gx + 2fy + c = 0$$

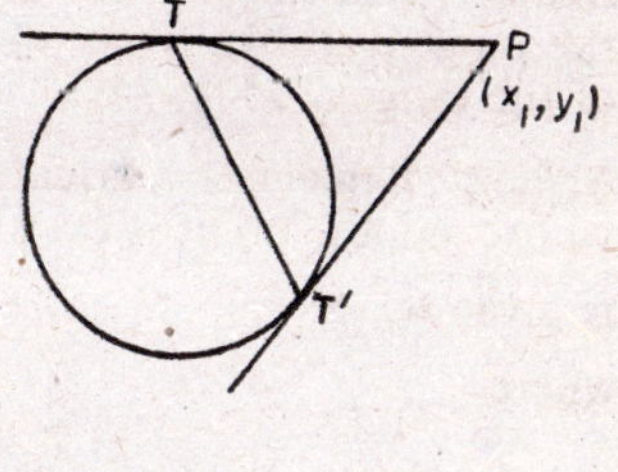

The equation of the pair of tangents drawn from the point (x_1, y_1) is given by

$$SS_1 = T^2$$

where $\quad S \equiv x^2 + y^2 + 2gx + 2fy + c$

$$S_1 \equiv x_1^2 + y_1^2 + 2gx_1 + 2fy_1 + c$$

$$T = xx_1 + yy_1 + g(x + x_1) + f(y + y_1) + c$$

Article Chord of contact.

Defination If from any point A without a circle two tangents AP, AQ be drawn to the circle, the straight line PQ joining the points of contact is called the chord of contact of tangents from A.

Article To find the equation of the chord of contact of tangents from (α, β) to the circle $x^2 + y^2 = a^2$.

Let equation of the cirele is

$$x^2 + y^2 = a^2 \qquad (1)$$

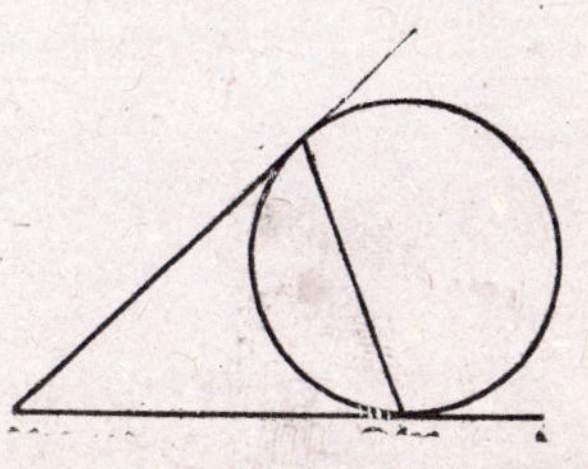

From the point $A(\alpha, \beta)$ two tangents AP and AQ are drawn. The co-ordinates of the point P and Q are (α_1, β_1) and (α_2, β_2)

where $A(\alpha, \beta)$, $B(\alpha_2, \beta_2)$ and $P(\alpha_1, \beta_1)$

Equation of the tangent at point (α_1, β_1) is given by

$$x\alpha_1 + y\beta_1 = u^2 \quad (2)$$

Equation of the tangent at point (α_2, β_2) is given by

$$x\alpha_2 + y\beta_2 = a^2 \quad (3)$$

Equation (2) and (3) passes through the point $(\alpha. \beta)$ so it will satisfy equation (2) and (3)

i.e. $$\alpha\alpha_1 + \beta\beta_1 = a^2 \quad (4)$$

and $$\alpha\alpha_2 + \beta\beta_2 = a^2 \quad (5)$$

Therefore (α_1, β_1) and (α_2, β_2) both satisfy the equation

$$\alpha x + \beta y = a^2$$

Therefore the equation of the chord of contact is

$$\boxed{\alpha x + \beta y = a^2}$$

which represents a straight line.

Note Remember Equation of the chord of contact of the tangents drawn from the point (α, β) to the circle

$$x^2 + y^2 + 2gx + 2fy + c = 0 \text{ is}$$

$$x\alpha + y\beta + g(x + \alpha) + f(y + \beta) + c = 0$$

Article Remember The form of the equation of the chord of contact of the tangent drawn from the point (α, β) is the same as that of the equation of the tangent at (α, β).

Article Remember Equation of the chord of the circle $x^2 + y^2 = a^2$ whose middle point is (α, β)

is given by $$S_1 = T$$

where $$S_1 = \alpha^2 + \beta^2 - a^2$$

$$T = x\alpha + y\beta - a^2$$

Article Remember Locus of the middle points of a system of parallel chords of a circle is the diameter of the circle $\perp$ to the chords.

Problem 15 Find the locus of the point of intersection of two tangents to a circle $x^2 + y^2 = a^2$ which are at right angles to one another.

Solution Let PT and PR be two tangents which meet at the point (α, β) at right angles. Then the equation of pair of tangents drawn from $(\alpha. \beta)$ to the circle $x^2 + y^2 = a^2$ is given by

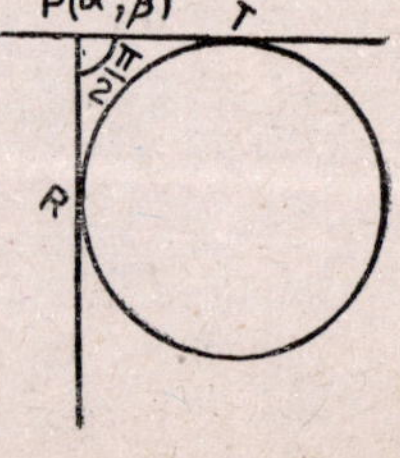

$$SS_1 = T^2$$

where $S = x^2 + y^2 - a^2$

$$S_1 = \alpha^2 + \beta^2 - a^2$$

$$T = x\alpha + y\beta - a^2$$

i.e. $$(x^2 + y^2 - a^2)(\alpha^2 + \beta^2 - a^2) = (x\alpha + y\beta - a^2)^2 \quad (1)$$

The pair of straight lices are $\perp'$ to each other if

$$\text{coefficient of } x^2 + \text{coefficient of } y^2 = 0$$

i.e. $$[\alpha^2 + \beta^2 - a^2 - \alpha^2 + \beta^2 - a^2 - \beta^2] = 0$$

$$\alpha^2 + \beta^2 - 2a^2 = 0$$

i.e. $$\alpha^2 + \beta^2 = 2a^2$$

locus of the point of intersection (α, β) is therefore a circle and is given by $$x^2 + y^2 = 2a^2 \qquad \textbf{Ans.}$$

Problem 16 Find the condition that the chord of contact of tangents from the point (α, β) to the circle $x^2 + y^2 = a^2$ should subtend a right angle at the centre. [*Must prepare*]

Solution Let the equation of the circle is

$$x^2 + y^2 = a^2 \qquad (1)$$

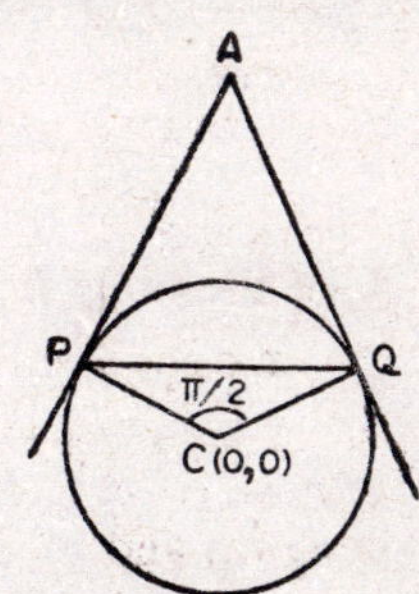

Let from the point A (α, β) AP and AQ (tangents) are drawn to the circle. PQ is the chord of contact. Then the equation of the chord of contact is $x\alpha + yB = a^2$ (2)

Let the chord of contact PQ makes angle $\pi/2$ at the centre C.

Equation of the pair of lines (CP and CQ) can be obtained by making equation (1) homogeneous with the help of (2)

i.e. Equation of pair of lines CP and CQ is given by

$$x^2 + y^2 = a^2 \, 1$$

$$x^2 + y^2 = a^2 \left[\frac{x\alpha + y\beta}{a^2}\right]^2$$

i.e. $$x^2 + y^2 = a^2 \frac{(x\alpha + y\beta)^2}{a^2}$$

i.e. $$a^2 (x^2 + y^2) = (x\alpha + y\beta)^2$$

If these lines are $\perp$ 'to each other then

co-efficient of x^2 + co-efficient of $y^2 = 0$

i.e. $$a^2 - \alpha^2 + a^2 - \beta^2 = 0$$

i.e. $$2a^2 - \alpha^2 - \beta^2 = 0$$

i.e. $$\boxed{\alpha^2 + \beta^2 = 2a^2} \qquad \textbf{Ans.}$$

Which is other required condition.

Problem 4 The chord of contact of the tangent drawn from any point on the circle $x^2 + y^2 = a^2$ to the circle $x^2 + y^2 = b^2$ touches the circle $x^2 + y^2 = c^2$ show that a,b c are in GP [*Must Prepare*]

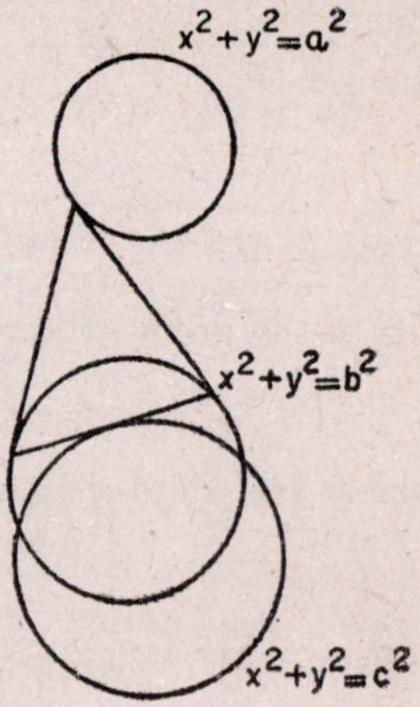

Solution Let the point on the circle

$$x^2 + y^2 = a^2 \qquad (1)$$

is $(a \cos \theta, a \sin \theta)$

From this point tangent are drawn to the circle

$$x^2 + y^2 = b^2$$

Then the equation of the chord of contact is

$$x\, a \cos \theta + y\, a \sin \theta = b^2$$

i.e. $$x \cos \theta + y \sin \theta = \frac{b^2}{a} \qquad (2)$$

this line touches the circle

$$x^2 + y^2 = c^2 \qquad (3)$$

x²+y²=a²

x²+y²=b²

x²+y²=c²

Then tangent at this cirsle must concide with (2).

Equation of the tangent at $(c \cos\theta \;\; c \sin \theta)$ is given by

$$x\, c \cos \theta + y \cdot c \sin \theta = 0$$

i.e. $$x \cos \theta + y \sin \theta = c \qquad (4)$$

Compaining (2) and (4) we have $c = \frac{b^2}{a}$ i.e. $b = \sqrt{ac}$

i.e. a, b, C are in Geometric progression.

Problem 4 Find the equation of the chord of the circle

$$x^2 + y^2 + 6x + 8y + 9 = 0$$

whose middle point is $(-2, -3)$.

Solution The equation of the chord whose middle point is known say (x_1, y_1) is given in the form

$$S_1 = T$$

Here $$S = x^2 + y^2 + 6x + 8y + 9$$

$\therefore$ $$S_1 = x_1^2 + y_1^2 + 6x_1 + 8y_1 + 9$$

$$S_1 \equiv (-2)^2 + (-3)^2 + 6(-2) + 8(-3) + 9$$

$$S_1 \equiv 4 + 9 - 12 - 24 + 9$$

$$S_1 \equiv 22 - 12 - 24$$

$$S_1 = -14$$

and $$T = xx_1 + yy_1 + 3(x + x_1) + 4(y + y_1) + 9 = 0$$

i.e. $$T = x(-2) + y(-3) + (x - 2) + 4(y - 3) + 9 = 0$$

$$T \equiv -2x - 3y + 3x - 6 + 4y - 12 + 9$$

$$T \equiv x + y - 9$$

Therefore the required equation of the chord is

$$x + y - 9 = -14 \quad \Rightarrow x + y + 5 = 0$$

Problem 5 Find the locus of the middle points fo chards of the circle $x^2 + y^2 = a^2$ which

(i) Passes through a fixed point (h, k).

(ii) Which subtend a right angle at the centre.

Solution Let the co-ordinates of the middle point of the circle

$$x^2 + y^2 = a^2 \text{ is } (\alpha, \beta)$$

Equation of the chord is given by

$$S_1 = T$$

where

$$S = x^2 + y^2 - a^2$$

$$S_1 = \alpha^2 + \beta^2 - a^2$$

$$T = x\alpha + y\beta - \beta a^2$$

Equation of the chard is

$$S_1 = T$$

i.e.

$$\alpha^2 + \beta^2 - a^2 = x\alpha + y\beta - a^2$$

i.e.

$$x\alpha + y\beta = \alpha^2 + \beta^2 \quad (1)$$

Since equation (1) passes through the fixed (h, k) so $(h_1 k)$ will satisfy equation (1)

i.e.

$$h\alpha + k\beta = \alpha^2 + \beta^2$$

Locus of (α, β) is obtained by replacing α by x and β by y. i.e. the locus is

$$hx + ky = x^2 + y^2$$

which is the equation of a circle.

(ii) Sinee equation of the circle is $x^2 + y^2 = a^2$ so the co-ordinate of the centre is $(0, 0)$. (α, β) is the moddle point of the chord AB.

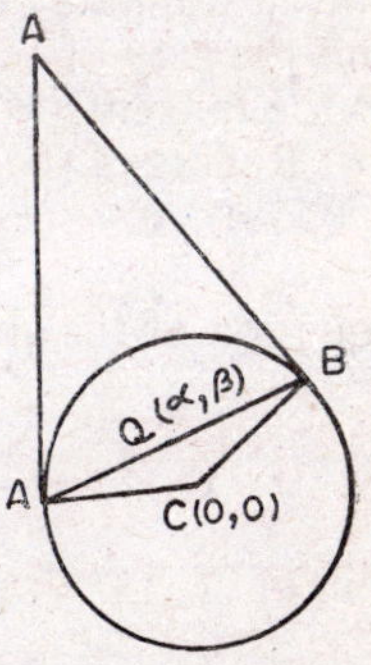

Equation of the chord of contact whose middle point is (α, β) is given by

$$x\alpha + y\beta = \alpha^2 + \beta^2 \quad (1)$$

Equation of the pair of lines passing through the origin and meeting the points C and A; and C and A can be obtained by making equation of the circle $x^2 + y^2 = a^2$ with the help of $x\alpha + y\beta = \alpha^2 + \beta^2$

$$x^2 + y^2 = a^2\, 1^2$$

$$x^2 + y^2 = a^2 \left(\frac{x\alpha + y\beta}{\alpha^2 + \beta^2}\right)^2$$

$$(x^2 + y^2)(\alpha^2 + \beta^2)^2 = \alpha^2 (x\alpha + y\beta)^2$$

$$x^2 (\alpha^2 + \beta^2)^2 + y^2 (\alpha^2 + \beta^2)^2 = a^2 [x^2 \alpha^2 + y^2 \beta^2 + 2xy\, \alpha\beta]$$

i.e. $x^2 [(\alpha^2 + \beta^2)^2 - a^2 \alpha^2] + y^2 [\alpha^2 + \beta^2)^2 - a^2 \beta^2] - 2a^2 \alpha\beta\, xy = 0$

If the angle between the two lines be at right angle, then the co-efficient of x^2 + co-efficient of $y^2 = 0$

i.e. $$(\alpha^2 + \beta^2)^2 - a^2 \alpha^2 + (\alpha^2 + \beta^2)^2 - a^2 \beta^2 = 0$$

$$2(\alpha^2 + \beta^2) - a^2(\alpha^2 + \beta^2) = 0$$

i.e. $$(\alpha^2 + \beta^2)[2(\alpha^2 + \beta^2) - a^2] = 0$$

$$\alpha^2 + \beta^2 \neq 0$$

So $$2\alpha^2 + \beta^2) - a^2 = 0$$

$$\Rightarrow \quad \alpha^2 + \beta^2 = \frac{a^2}{2}$$

So the locus of α, β) is

$$x^2 + y^2 = \frac{a^2}{2} \quad \textbf{Ans.}$$

Problem 19 Tangents are drawn form the point (α, β) to the circle $x^2 + y^2 = a^2$; prove that the area of the triangle formed by them and the straight line joining their point of contaet is

$$\frac{a(\alpha^2 + \beta^2 - a^2)^{3/2}}{\alpha^2 + \beta^2} \quad (I.F.S.\ 83)$$

Solution Let $P(\alpha, \beta)$ be any point from where two tangents PA and PB are drawn. AB is the chard of contact. Let the equation of the circle is

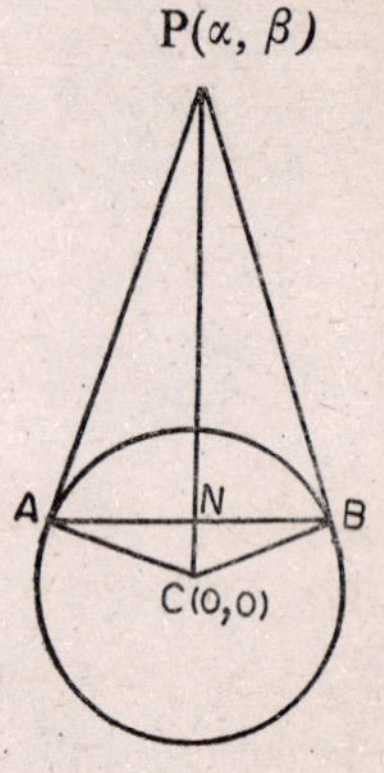

$$x^3 + y^2 = a^2$$

Tne co-ordinate of the centre C is $(0, 0)$ we have to find the area of the triangle PAB which is formed by the tangent PA and PB and the chard of contact AB. Radius of thc circle is a i.e.

$$BC = a$$

Equation of the chord of contact is given by

$$x\alpha + y\beta = 0$$

i.e. $$x\alpha + y\beta - a^2 = 0$$

Length of $\perp r$ drawn from $C(0, 0)$ to the line AB is given by

$$\frac{2 \cdot 0 + \beta \cdot 0 - a^2}{\sqrt{\alpha^2 + \beta^2}}$$

i.e. $$- \pm \frac{-a^2}{\sqrt{\alpha^2 + \beta^2}} = \frac{a^2}{\sqrt{\alpha^2 + \beta^2}}$$

$$CN = + \frac{a^2}{\sqrt{\alpha^2 + \beta^2}}$$

Again from the right angled triangle BNC we have

$$BN^2 = BC^2 - CN^2$$

$$BN^2 = a^2 - \frac{a^4}{(\alpha^2 + \beta^2)}$$

i.e.
$$BN^2 = a^2\left[1 - \frac{a^2}{\alpha^2 + \beta^2}\right]$$

$$BN^2 = a^2 \frac{[\alpha^2 + \beta^2 - a^2]}{\alpha^2 + \beta^2}$$

i.e.
$$BN = a\sqrt{\frac{\alpha^2 + \beta^2 - a^2}{\alpha^2 + \beta^2}}$$

Thus
$$2\,BN = AB$$

Again the length of perpendicular from the point (α, β) to the line

$x\alpha + y\beta - a^2 = 0$ is given by

$$PN = \frac{\alpha\alpha + \beta\beta - a^2}{\sqrt{\alpha^2 + \beta^2}}$$

$$PN = \frac{\alpha^2 + \beta^2 - a^2}{\sqrt{\alpha^2 + \beta^2}}$$

Area of triangle $\Delta\, PAB$ is given by

$$\Delta\, PAB - \tfrac{1}{2} \times \text{Base} \times \text{height}$$

$$\Delta\, PAB = \tfrac{1}{2} \times 2a\sqrt{\frac{\alpha^2 + \beta^2 - a^2}{\alpha^2 + \beta^2}}\ \frac{\alpha^2 + \beta^2 - a^2}{\sqrt{\alpha^2 + \beta^2}}$$

$$\Delta\, PAB = a\,\frac{[\alpha^2 + \beta^2 - a^2]^{3/2}}{\alpha^2 + \beta^2}$$ *(Proved)*

Problem 7 Find the locus of the centre of a circle

$$x^2 + y^2 + 2gx + 2fy + c = 0$$

which is such that the tangents drawn to the circle from the origin are always at right angles.

Solution Equation of the circle is

$$x^2 + y^2 + 2gx + 2fy + c = 0$$

So the centre of this circle's $(-g, f)$

Eqution of the pair of tangents drawn from any point (α, β) to the circle (1) is given by

$$SS_1 = T^2$$

where
$$S = x^2 + y^2 + 2gx + 2fy + c$$
$$S_1 = \alpha^2 + \beta^2 + 2g\alpha + 2f\beta + c$$
$$T = x\alpha + y\beta + g(x + \alpha) + f(y + \beta) + c$$

Since the pair of tangents are drawn from the origin (0, 0) so the equation of the pair of tangent is

$$SS_1 = T^2$$

where $S = x^2 + y^2 + 2gx + 2fy + c$

$$S_1 = 0 + 0 + 0 + 0 + c = c$$

$$T = 3 + 0 + gx + fy + c$$

i.e. the equation of the pair of lines is

$$(x^2 + y^2 + 2gx + 2fy + c)\, c = (gx + fy + c)^2 \qquad (1)$$

If the two taneents representcd by the equation (1) are at right angles then co-efficient of x^2 + the co-efficient of $y^2 = 0$

i.e. $(c-g^2) + (c-f^2) = 0$

$$2c - g^2 - f^2 = 0$$

i.e. $f^2 + g^2 = 2c$

Thus the locus of the centre is

$$x^2 + y^2 = 2c$$

Problem 21 From any point on the circle $x^2 + y^2 + 2gx + 2fy + c = 0$ tangents are drawn to the circle

$$x^2 + y^2 + 2gx + 2fy + (g^2 + f^2)\cos^2\alpha + c\sin^2\alpha = 0,$$

show that the angle between them is 2α.

Solution Equation of the first circle is

$$x^2 + y^2 + 2gx + 2fy + c = 0 \qquad (1)$$

Then the centre of the circle is $(-g. -f)$ and the radius is

$$\sqrt{g^2 + f^2 - c}$$

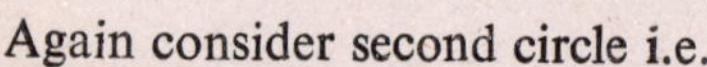

Again consider second circle i.e.

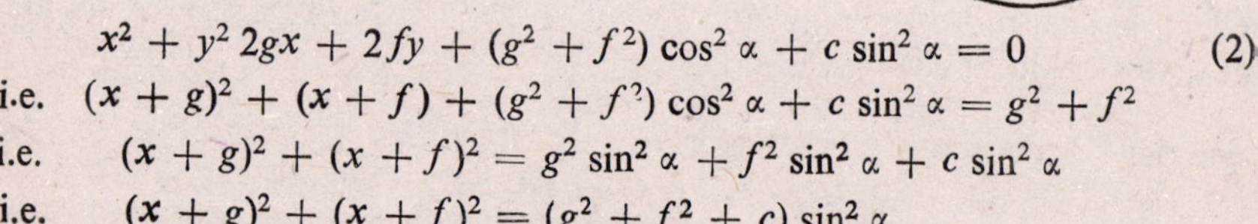

$$x^2 + y^2\, 2gx + 2fy + (g^2 + f^2)\cos^2\alpha + c\sin^2\alpha = 0 \qquad (2)$$

i.e. $(x + g)^2 + (x + f) + (g^2 + f^2)\cos^2\alpha + c\sin^2\alpha = g^2 + f^2$

i.e. $(x + g)^2 + (x + f)^2 = g^2\sin^2\alpha + f^2\sin^2\alpha + c\sin^2\alpha$

i.e. $(x + g)^2 + (x + f)^2 = (g^2 + f^2 + c)\sin^2\alpha$

Thus the co-ordinate of the centre is $(-g, -f)$ and the radius is

$$\sqrt{g^2 + f^2 - c}\,\sin\alpha$$

Since $\sin\alpha < 2$

So $\sqrt{g^2 + f^2 - c}\,\sin\alpha < \sqrt{g^2 + f^2 - c}$

Thus both the circles are concentric i.e. having the same centre $(-g, -f)$. The circle (1) is the greater circle and the circle (2) is the smallar circie.

Let p is the point on the greater circle from where two tangents PT and PR are drawn.

CT is f^r to PT and CT is the radius of the smaller circle CP is the radius of the larger cicrle

$$CT = \sqrt{g^2 + f^2 - c} \sin \alpha$$

$$CP = \sqrt{g^2 + f^2 - c}$$

Let $\quad < CPT = \theta$

Then $\quad TPR = 2\theta$

We have to show that

$$2\theta = 2\alpha$$

From the right angled triangle CPT

$$\sin \theta = \frac{CT}{CP}$$

$$\sin \theta = \frac{\sqrt{g^2 + f^2 - c}}{\sqrt{g^2 + f^2 - c}} \sin \alpha$$

$$\Rightarrow \quad \sin \theta = \sin \alpha$$

$$\Rightarrow \quad \theta = \alpha$$

So the angle between the tangents is 2θ i.e. 2α *(Proved)*

Problem 22 Find the locus of the middle points of the chord of the circle $x^2 + y^2 = a^2$ which subtend a right angle at the point $(c, 0)$.

Solution (α, β) is the mtddle point of the chord. The equation of the chord is given as $\quad S_1 = T$

Where $\quad S_1 = \alpha^2 + \beta^2 - a^2$

$$T = x\alpha + y\beta - a^2$$

i.e. the equation of the chord is given as

$$\alpha^2 + \beta^2 - a^2 = x\alpha + y\beta - a^2$$

i.e. $\quad x\alpha + y\beta = \alpha^2 + \beta^2$

Transfer the origin to $(c, 0)$ so that the equation of the circle becomes

$$(x + 0^2 + y^2 = a^2 \tag{1}$$

And the equation of the chord becomes

$$(x + c)\alpha + y\beta = \alpha^2 + \beta^2$$

$$\Rightarrow \quad x\alpha + y\beta = \alpha^2 + \beta^2 - \alpha c$$

$$\Rightarrow \quad \frac{x\alpha + y\beta}{\alpha^2 + \beta^2 - \alpha c} = 1$$

$$\Rightarrow \quad \frac{x\alpha}{\alpha^2 + \beta^2 - \alpha c} + \frac{y\beta}{\alpha^2 + \beta^2 - \alpha c} = 1$$

i.e. $\quad lx + my = 1 \qquad (2)$

Where $l = \dfrac{\alpha}{\alpha^2 + \beta^2 - \alpha c}$ and $m = \dfrac{\beta}{\alpha^2 + \beta^2 - \alpha c}$

The equation of the pair of lines joining the origin viz., $(c, 0)$ to the points of intersection of (1) with (2) is

$$x^2 + y^2 + 2xe\,(lx + my) + (c^2 - a^2)\,(lx + my)^2 = 0$$

If these lines be at right angle then, as before

$$1 + 2lc + (c^2 - a^2)\,l^2 + 1 + (c^2 - a^2)\,m^2 = 0$$

$$\Rightarrow \quad 2 + 2lc + (c^2 - a)\,l^2 + m^2) = 0$$

$$\Rightarrow \quad 2\,[1 + lc] + (c^2 - a^2)\,(l + m^2) = 0$$

$$\Rightarrow 2\left[1 + \frac{\alpha c}{\alpha^2 + \beta^2 - \alpha c}\right] + (c^2 - a^2)\left[\frac{(\alpha^2)}{(\alpha^2 + \beta^2 - \alpha c)^2} + \frac{\beta^2}{(\alpha^2 + \beta^2 - \alpha c)^2}\right] = 0$$

$$\Rightarrow 2\,\frac{(\alpha^2 + \beta^2)}{\alpha^2 + \beta^2 - \alpha c} + (c^2 - a^2)\,\frac{(\alpha^2 + \beta^2)}{(\alpha^2 + \beta^2 - \alpha c)^2} = 0$$

$$\Rightarrow \quad 2\,(\alpha^2 + \beta^2)\,(\alpha^2 + \beta^2 - \alpha c) + (c^2 - a^2)\,(\alpha^2 + \beta^2) = 0$$

$$\Rightarrow \quad (\alpha^2 + \beta^2)\,[2\alpha^2 + 2\beta^2 - 2\alpha c + (c^2 - a^2)] = 0$$

i.e. $\Rightarrow \quad 2(\alpha^2 + \beta^2 - \alpha c) + c^2 - a^2 = 0$

Hence the locus of (α, β) w.r.t. the new origin is

$$2\,(x^2 + y^2 - xc) + (c^2 - a^2) = 0$$

Transferring back to the old origin, the locus has the equation

$$2\,\{(x - c)^2 + y^2 - (x - c)\,c\} + c^2 - a^2 = 0$$

$$\Rightarrow \quad 2\,(x^2 + y^2) - 6xc + 5c^2 - a^2 = 0$$

which is the required locus. **Ans.**

15

Pole and Polar

If through a point A (within or without a circle) there be drawn any straight line to meet the circle in P and Q the the lucas of the point of intersection of the tangents at P and Q is called the polar of A with respect to the circle and the given point A is called to the pole of its polar

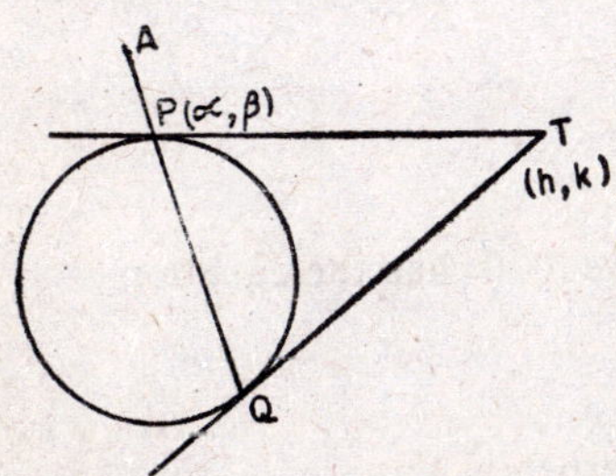

Equation of Polar

Article (R) Equation of the polar of the point (α, β) with respect to the circle

$$x^2 + y^2 = a^2$$

is $$x\alpha + y\alpha = a^2$$

Article (R) Equation of the polar of the point (α, β) with respect to the circle $$x^2 + y^2 + 2gx + 2fy + c = 0 \text{ is}$$

$$x\alpha + y\beta + g(x + \alpha) + f(y + \beta) + c = 0$$

Article Pole of the line

$lx + my + n = 0$ with respect to the circle $x^2 + y^2 = a^2$

Solution Let (α, β) be the pole of the line

$$lx + my + n = 0$$

i.e. $$lx + my + n = 0 \quad (1)$$

is the polar of the point with respect to the circle

$$x^2 + y^2 = a^2$$

Again polar of the point (α, β) with respect to the circle $x^2 + y^2 = a^2$ is given by $$x\alpha + y\beta - a^2 \quad (2)$$

Since equation (1) and (2) are identical so comparing equation (1) and (2) we have

$$\frac{\alpha}{l} = \frac{\beta}{m} = \frac{-a^2}{n}$$

i.e. $$\varepsilon = -\frac{a^2 l}{n}$$

$$\beta = -\frac{a^2 m}{n}$$

Hence the co-ordinates of the pole are

$$\left(-\frac{a^2 l}{n}, -\frac{a^2 m}{n}\right)$$

Properties of Pole and Polar

(1) The polar of a point with respect to a circle is $\perp$ to the radius drawn through the point.

Let the equation of the circle be $$x^2 + y^2 = a^2 \quad (1)$$

Polar of any point (α, β) with respect to (1) is

$$x\alpha + y\beta = a^2$$

$$\Rightarrow \quad y = -x\frac{\alpha}{\beta} + a^2 \quad (2)$$

The line joining the point (α, β) with the centre (0, 0) has the equation

$$y = \frac{\beta}{\alpha} x$$

Product of their scopes $= -1$, the lines are perpendicular.

(ii) If the line joining the centre 0 of a circle to a given point A meets the polar of A in R, then $OA \cdot OR = (\text{radius})^2$

Here $$OA = \sqrt{\alpha^2 + \beta^2}$$

and OR = length of $\perp$ from (0, 0) on polar of A

i.e. $$x\alpha + y\beta - a^2 = 0$$

$$\frac{-a^2}{\pm\sqrt{\alpha^2 + \beta^2}} = \frac{a^2}{\sqrt{\alpha^2 + \beta^2}}$$

$$OA \cdot OR = \sqrt{\alpha^2 + \beta^2} \frac{a^2}{\sqrt{\alpha^2 + \beta^2}}$$

i.e. $$OA \cdot OR = a^2$$

i.e. $$OA \cdot OR = (\text{radius})^2$$

(iii) If the polar of a point A passes through B, then the polar of B shall pass through A.

Let the equation of the circle be $x^2 + y^2 = a^2$

Let (α_1, β_1) be the co-ordinates of A and (α_2, β_2) be the co-ordinates of B.

The polar of A is then $x\alpha_1 + y\beta_1 = a^2$

Since it passes through the poit (α_2, β_2) we have

$$\alpha_2 \alpha_1 + \beta_2 \beta_1 = a^2$$

Which is the condition also that (α_1, β_1) lie on the line

$$\alpha_2 x + \beta_2 y = a^2 \text{ which is the polar of } B(\alpha_2, \beta_2) \qquad \textit{(Proved)}$$

Two points such that each lies on the polar of other are called *Conjugate points.*

Remember Hence the condition that (α_1, β_1) and (α_2, β_2) should be conjugate points for the circle $x^2 + y^2 = a^2$ is

$$\boxed{\alpha_1 \alpha_2 + \beta_1 \beta_2 = a^2}$$

Similarly condition that $(\alpha_1\ \beta_1)$ and (α_2, β_2) should be conjugate point for the circle $x^2 + y^2 + 2gx + 2fy + c = 0$ is

Remember $\alpha_1 \alpha_2 + \beta_1 \beta_2 + g(\alpha_1 + \alpha_2) + f(\beta_1 + \beta_2) + c = 0$

(iv) If the pole of a line L_1 lies on the line L_2, then the pole of L_2 lie on L_1.

Let
$$L_1 = l_1 x + m_1 y + n_1 = 0 \qquad (1)$$
$$L_2 = l_2 x + m_2 y + n_2 = 0 \qquad (2)$$

Let (α_1, β_1) be the pole of the line (1) then the polar of $(\alpha_1\ \beta_1)$ with respect to a circle $x^2 + y^2 = a^2$ is

$$x\alpha_1 + y\beta_1 - a^2 = 0 \qquad (1)$$

Then compairing (1) and (3) we have

$$\frac{\alpha_1}{l_1} = \frac{\beta_1}{m_1} = -\frac{\alpha^2}{n_1}$$

$$\alpha_1 = -\frac{a^2 l_1}{n_1}$$

$$\beta_1 = -\frac{a^2 m_1}{n_1}$$

Since $(\alpha_1\ \beta_1)$ lies on the line (2)

So
$$l_2 \alpha_1 + m_2 \beta_1 + n_2 = 0$$

i e.
$$l_2\left(-\frac{a^2 l_1}{n_1}\right) + m_2\left(-\frac{a^2 m_1}{n_1}\right) + n_2 = 0$$

i.e.
$$-a^2 l_1 l_2 - a^2 m_1 m_2 + n_1 n_2 = 0$$

i.e.
$$a^2 (l_1 l_2 + m_1 m_2) = n_1 n_2$$

This is also the pole of L_2 will lie on L_1

Two lines such that each contains the pole of the other are called *Conjngate Lines.*

Problem 23 Find the pole of $2x-3y+10=0$ with respect to the circle

$$x^2+y^2\,4x-6y+7=0$$

Solution Let (α, β) be the pole so that the equation of polar with respect to the circle $x^2+y^2+4x-6y+7=0$ is

$$x\alpha+y\beta+2(x+\alpha)-3(y+\beta)+7=0 \tag{1}$$

Then (1) must be identical with

$$2x-3y+10=0$$

i.e.
$$\frac{\alpha+2}{2}=\frac{(\beta-3)}{-3}=\frac{2+\alpha-3\beta+7}{10}$$

From first and last equality

$$10(\alpha+2)=2(2\alpha-3\beta+7)$$

i.e.
$$10\alpha+20=4\alpha-6\beta+14$$

$$6\alpha+6\beta+6=0$$

$\Rightarrow$
$$\alpha+\beta+1=0$$

From the first and the second equality

$$-3\alpha-6=2\beta-6$$

i.e.
$$2\beta=-3\alpha$$

i.e.
$$\beta=-\frac{3}{2}\alpha$$

$\Rightarrow$
$$\alpha-\frac{3}{2}\alpha+1=0$$

$\Rightarrow$
$$2\alpha-3\alpha+2=0$$

$\Rightarrow$
$$-\alpha+2=0$$

$\Rightarrow$
$$\alpha=2$$

$$\beta=-3$$

The co-ordinate of the pole is (α, β)

i.e. $(2, -3)$

Problem 24 Find the locus of P which is such that its polar with respect to the circle $x^2+y^2=a^2$ touches another circle

$$(x-h)^2+(y-k)^2=r^2$$

Solution Let the co-ordinate of the pole is (α, β) and its polar with respect to the circle $x^2+y^2=a^2$ is given by

$$x\alpha+y\beta=a^2 \tag{1}$$

Again since (1) touches the circle

$$(x-h)^2+(y-k)^2=r^2$$

Hence length of perpendicular from (h, k) to the line $x\alpha + y\beta = a^2$ must be equal to the radius of the circle

Thus
$$\frac{h\alpha + k\beta - a^2}{\sqrt{\alpha^2 + \beta^2}} = r$$

i.e.
$$(h\alpha + k\beta - a^2)^2 = r^2 (\alpha^2 + \beta^2)$$

Hence the locus of the point (α, β) is
$$(hx + ky - a^2)^2 = r^2 (x^2 + y^2) \qquad \textbf{Ans.}$$

Problem 25 Prove that the polar of a given point with respect to any of the circles $x^2 + y^2 + 2px + c = 0$, where p is a variable, always passes through a fixed point.

Solution Let the given point be (h, k). The polar of the point (h, k) with respect to the circles $x^2 + y^2 + 2px + c = 0$, is
$$xh + yk + p(x + h) + c = 0$$

Clearly the polar always passes through a fixed point

If the coefficient of the variable point is equal to zero

i.e.
$$x + h = 0$$

i.e.
$$x = -h$$

Putting the value of x in
$$xh + yk + c = 0 \qquad \text{Since} \qquad p = 0$$

Again
$$-h \cdot h + y.k + c = 0$$

i.e.
$$-h^2 + yk + c = 0$$
$$yk = h^2 - c$$
$$y = \frac{h^2 - c}{k}$$

Thus the polar always passes through a fixed point
$$\left(-h, \frac{h^2 - c}{k}\right) \qquad \textit{(Proved)}$$

Problem 6 If the polar of the point (α, β) with respect to the circle $x^2 + y^2 = a^2$ touches the circle $(x+a)^2 + y^2 = a^2$; show that (α, β) is on the curve given by $y^2 + 2ax = a^2$ [*Must preoare*]

Solution Polar of the point (α, β) with respect to the circle
$$x^2 + y^2 = a^2 \text{ is given by}$$
$$x\alpha + y\beta = a^2 \qquad (1)$$

Since (1) touches the circle $(x-a)^2 + y^2 = a^2$ – (2) so the length of perpendicular from $(a, 0)$ [centre] to line (1) must be equal to the radius of the circle.

i.e. $$\frac{a\alpha + 0\cdot\beta - a^2}{\pm\sqrt{\alpha^2+\beta^2}} = a$$

i.e. $$\frac{a\alpha - a^2}{\pm\sqrt{\alpha^2+\beta^2}} = a$$

i.e. $$\frac{a\alpha - a^2}{+\sqrt{\alpha^2+\beta^2}} = a$$

i.e. $$\frac{a(\alpha - a)}{\pm\sqrt{\alpha^2+\beta^2}} = a$$

$$(\alpha - a)^2 = \alpha^2 + \beta^2$$

On squaring both sides

$$\alpha^2 - 2a\alpha + o^2 = a^2 + \beta^2$$

$$\beta^2 + 2a\alpha = a^2$$

Thus the locus of the point (α, β) is given by

$$y^2 + 2ax = a^2$$

(Proved)

Problem 27 Prove that the three points (α_1, β_1), (α_2, β_2) and (α_3, β_3) will be collinear if and only if their polars w.r.t. the circles $x^2 + y^2 = a^2$ are concurrent.

Solution The polars of the three points (α_1, β_1); (α_2, β_2) and (α_3, β_3) with respect to the given circle $x^2 + y^2 = a^2$ are given by

$$x\alpha_1 + y\beta_1 - a^2 = 0 \quad (1)$$

$$x\alpha_2 + y\beta_2 - a^2 = 0 \quad (2)$$

$$x\alpha_3 + y\beta_3 - a^2 = 0 \quad (3)$$

If the three lines are concurrent

Then

$$\begin{vmatrix} \alpha_1 & \beta_1 & -a^2 \\ \alpha_2 & \beta_2 & -a^2 \\ \alpha_3 & \beta_3 & -u^2 \end{vmatrix} = 0$$

or

$$-a^2 \begin{vmatrix} \alpha_1 & \beta_1 & 1 \\ \alpha_2 & \beta_2 & 1 \\ \alpha_3 & \beta_3 & 1 \end{vmatrix} = 0$$

i.e.

$$\begin{vmatrix} 1 & \alpha_1 & \beta_1 \\ 1 & \alpha_2 & \beta_2 \\ 1 & \alpha_3 & \beta_3 \end{vmatrix} = 0 \quad (4)$$

But equation (4) represents twice the area of the triangle formed by the given points and it is equal to zero as such the points are collinear.

Problem 28 Show that if two points are conjugate w.r.t. a circle the square of the distance between them is equal to the sum of the squares of the tangents from them to the circle,

Solution Let the equation of the circle is

$$x^2 + y^2 = a^2$$

Let the two points are $A(\alpha_1, \beta_1)$ and $\beta(\alpha_2, \beta_2)$. These two points are conjugate to each other so the condition is

$$\alpha_1 \alpha_2 + \beta_1 \beta_2 - a^2 = 0$$

i.e. $$\alpha_1 \alpha_2 + \beta_1 \beta_2 = a^2 \tag{1}$$

Again length of tangent from (α_1, β_1) to the circle

$$x^2 + y^2 = a^2 \text{ is}$$

$$t_1^2 = \alpha_1^2 + \beta_1^2 - a^2$$

and the length of tangent from (α_2, β_2) to the circle

$$x^2 + y^2 = a^2 \text{ is}$$

$$t_2^2 = \alpha_2^2 + \beta_2^2 - a^2$$

Then $$AB = (\alpha_1 - \alpha_2)^2 + (\beta_1 - \beta_2)^2$$

$$= \alpha_1^2 + \alpha_2^2 - 2\alpha_1 \alpha_2^2 + \beta_1^2 + \beta_2^2 - 2\beta_1 \beta_2$$

$$= \alpha_1^2 + \beta_1^2 + \alpha_2^2 + \beta_2^2 - 2(\alpha_1 \alpha_2 + \beta_1 \beta_2)$$

$$= \alpha_1^2 + \beta_1^2 + \alpha_2^2 + \beta_2^2 - 2a^2$$

$$= (\alpha_1^2 + \beta_1^2 - a^2) + (\alpha_2^2 + \beta_2^2 - a^2)$$

$$= t_1^2 + t_2^2$$

i,e. $$AB = t_1^2 + t_2^2$$ **(*Proved*)**

Common tangents of two circles

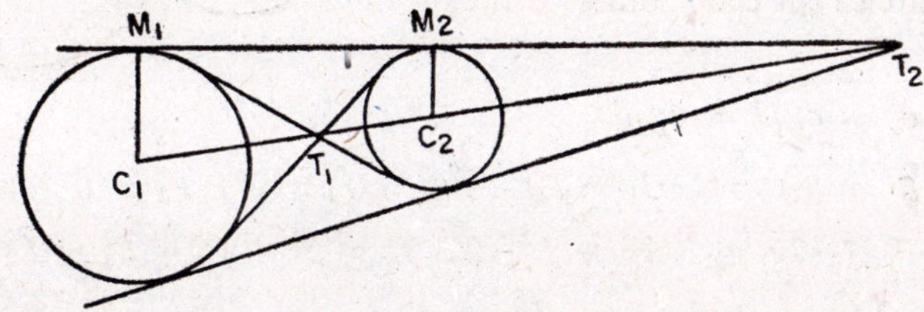

Remember Two pairs of common tangents can be drawn to two circles and the point of intersection of each pair lies on the line joining the centres of the two circles.

The point where transverse tangents cuts each other eat T_1 divides the line the point joining the centres internally in the ratio of the radii i.e. T_1 divides c_1 c_2 in the ratio of radii of the two circles.

And the point where the direct tangents cuts each other divides the line joining the centre externally.

16

System of Circles

When the two circles intersect each other at right angles, the circies are said to be orthogonal.

Article Orthogonal Circles

Find the condition that the circles

$$x^2 + y^2 + 2g_1x + 2f_1y + c_1 = 0$$

and $$x^2 + y^2 + 2g_2x + 2f_2y + c_2 = 0$$

should be orthogonal.

Let C_1 and C_2 be the centres of two circles which intersect at P. The co-ordinates of C_1 are $(-g_1, -f_1)$ and of c_2 $(-g_2, -f_2)$

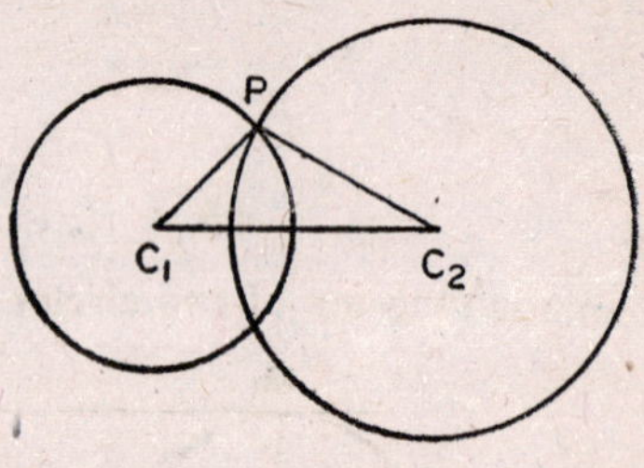

$$c_1 p^2 = g_1^2 + f_1^2 - c_1$$

$$c_2 p^2 = g_2^2 + f_2^2 - c_2$$

Since the circles cut each other orthogonally

So $\quad c_1 c_2^2 = c_1 p^2 + c_2 p^2$

i.e. $\quad (-g_1 + g_2)^2 + (-f_1 + f_2)^2 = g_1^2 + f_1^2 - c_1 + g_2^2 + f^{\cdot} - c_2$

i.e. $\quad g_1^2 + g_2^2 - 2g_1 g_2 + f_1^2 + f_2^2 - 2f_1 f_2 = g_1^2 + g_2^2 + f_1^2 + f_2^2 - c_1 - c_2$

i.e. $\quad -2(g_1 g_2 + f_1 f_2) = -(c_1 + c_2)$

i.e. $\quad 2(g_1 g_2 + f_1 f_2) = c_1 + c_2$

which is the required condition

i.e. two circles $\quad x^2 + y^2 + 2g_1 x + 2f_1 y + c_1 = 0$

and $\quad x^2 + y^2 + 2g_2 x + 2f_2 y + c_2 = 0$

$$\boxed{2(g_1 g_2 + f_1 f_2) = c_1 + c_2} \qquad \textbf{Remember} \qquad (1)$$

Problem 1 Find the value of p such that the circles

$$x^2 + y^2 + px + 3y - 5 = 0$$

and $$x^2 + y^2 + 5x + py + 7 = 0$$ cut orthogonally

Solution We have here

$$g_1 = \frac{p}{2} \qquad f_1 = \frac{3}{2} \qquad c_1 = -5$$

$$g_2 = \frac{5}{2} \qquad f_2 = \frac{p}{2} \qquad c_2 = 7$$

we know that the condition that the two circles

$$x^2 + y^2 + 2g_1 x + 2f_1 y + c_1 = 0$$

and $$x^3 + y^2 + 2g_2 x + 2f_2 y + c_2 = 0$$ cut orthogonally

if $$2(g_1 g_2 + f_1 f_2) = c_1 + c_2$$

i.e. $$2\left(\frac{p}{2} \cdot \frac{5}{2} + \frac{3}{2} \cdot \frac{p}{2}\right) = -5 + 7$$

i.e. $$2\left(\frac{5p}{4} + \frac{3p}{4}\right) = 2$$

i.e. $$\frac{8p}{4} = 1 \text{ i.e. } \quad 2p = 1$$

$\Rightarrow$ $$p = \tfrac{1}{2}$$ **Ans.**

Problem 2 Find the equation of the circle whose centre is (1, 2) and which cuts orthogonally the circles

$$x^2 + y^2 - 3x + 4y + 5 = 0$$

Solution If these circles cut each other orthogonaliy then

$$\angle c_1 p c_2 = \pi/2$$

i.e. $c_1 p \perp^r$ to $c_2 p$

i.e. $c_1 p$ is the length of tangent

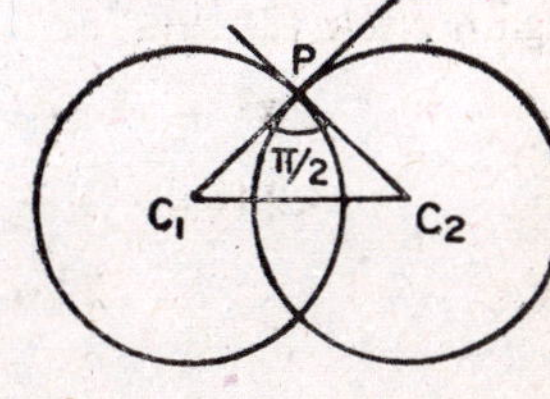

Drawn from the centre c_1 to the circle

$$x^2 + y^2 - 3x + 4y + 5 = 0$$

$c_1 p$ is also the radius of the circle whose centre is (1, 2)

$c_1 p^2$ = square of the length of tangent from c_1 to the circle

$$x^2 + y^2 - 3x + 4y + 5 = 0$$

$$c_1 p^2 = (1)^2 + (2)^2 - 3 \cdot (1) + 4(\cdot 2) + 5$$

$$= 1 + 4 - 3 + 8 + 5 = 15$$

Thus the equation of the circle whose centre is (1, 2) and radius is $\sqrt{15}$ is given by the equation

$$(x-1)^2 + (y-2)^2 = 15$$

i.e. $$x^2 - 2x + 1 + y^2 - 4y + 4 = 15$$

i,e. $$x^2 + y^2 - 2x - 4y - 10 = 0 \qquad \textbf{Ans.}$$

Problem 3 Find the equation of a circle which passes through the origin and cuts orthogonally the circles.

$$x^2 + y^2 - 8y + 12 = 0$$

and $$x^2 + y^2 - 4y - 6y - 3 = 0$$

Solution Let the equation of the circle is

$$x^2 + y^2 + 2gx + 2fy + c = 0 \qquad (1)$$

Since it passes through the origin i.e. from the point (0, 0)

So $$0 + 0 + 0 + 0 + c = 0$$

Thus the equation of the circle passing through the origin (0, 0) is given by

$$x^2 + y^2 + 2gx + 2fy = 0 \qquad (2)$$

The circle cuts the circle

$$x^2 + y^2 - 0\cdot x - 8y + 12 = 0$$

orthogonally so

$$2\,(g\cdot 0 + f_x - 4) = 0 + 12$$

i.e. $$-8f = 12$$

$$2f = \frac{12}{-4}$$

$$2f = -4$$

Again circle (2) cuts the circle

$$x^2 + y^2 - 4x - 6y - 3 = 0 \text{ orthogonally}$$

So $$2\,[g\,(-2) + f\,(-3)] = -3$$

i.e. $$2\,[-2g - 3f] = -3$$

$$-2g - 3f = -\frac{3}{2}$$

i.e. $$2g - 3\left(-\frac{3}{2}\right) = -\frac{3}{2}$$

i.e. $$-2g + \frac{9}{2} = -\frac{3}{2}$$

i.e. $$-2g = -\frac{3}{2} - \frac{9}{2}$$

i.e. $$-2g = \frac{-12}{2}$$

i.e. $$-2g = -6, \text{ i.e. } 2g = 6$$

Thus the equation of the circle becomes

$$x^2 + y^2 + 6x - 3y = 0 \qquad \textbf{Ans.}$$

Problem 4 Prove that the two circles which pass through the points $(0, a)$ and $(0, -a)$ and touch the line $y = mx + c$ will cut orthogonally if

$$c^2 = a^2 (2 + m^2)$$

Solution Let the equation of the circle is

$$x^2 + y^2 + 2gx + 2fy + k = 0 \qquad \text{(n)}$$

Since circle (1) passes through the points $(0, a)$ and $(0, -a)$ so the (1) is satisfied by these two points

i.e. $$(0)^2 + (a)^2 + 2 \cdot 0\, x + 2af + k = 0$$

i.e. $$a^2 + 2af + k = 0 \qquad (2)$$

and $$(0)^2 + (-a)^2 + 2 \cdot 0\, x + 2(-a)f + k = 0$$

i.c. $$a^2 - 2af + k - 0 \qquad (3)$$

Adding equation (2) and (3) we have

$$2a^2 + 2k = 0$$

i.e. $$2a^2 = 2k$$

i.e. $$k = -a^2 \qquad (4)$$

Putting the value of k from equation (2) in equation (1) we have

$$a^2 + 2af - a^2 = 0$$

i.e. $$2af = 0$$

i.e. $$f = 0 \qquad (5)$$

Therefore the equation of the circle becomes

$$x^2 + y^2 + 2gx - a^2 = 0 \qquad (6)$$

If the line $y = mx + c$ touches the circle (6) then length of $\perp r$ drawn from the circle of (6) to the line $y = mx + c$ must be equol to the radius of the circle (6).

Radius of the circle (6) is

$$\sqrt{g^2 + 0 + a^2} = \sqrt{g^2 + a^2}$$

Centre of the circle (6) is $(-g, 0)$

Length of $\perp r$ from $(-g, 0)$ to the line $y = mx + c$ is given by i.e. on $y - mx - c$

$$\frac{0 - m(-g) - c}{\sqrt{1^2 + (-m)^2}} = \frac{mg - c}{\sqrt{1 + m^2}}$$

Thus $$\frac{mg - c}{\sqrt{1 + m^2}} = \sqrt{g^2 + a^2}$$

squaring both sides we have

$$(mg - c)^2 = (g^2 + a^2)(1 + m^2)$$

i.e. $$m^2 g^2 - 2mgc + c^2 = g^2(1 + m^2) + a^2(1 + m^2)$$

i.e. $$g^2(m^2 - 1 - m^2) - 2mgc + c^2 - a^2(1 + m^2) = 0$$

i.e. $$-g^2 - 2mgc + (c^2 - a^2 - a^2 m^2) = 0$$

i.e $$g^2 + 2mcg + (a^2 m^2 + a^2 - c^2) = 0 \quad (7)$$

This gives two values of g corresponding to the two circles.

Let thc two values be g_1 and g_2, so that the equations of the two circles are

$$x^2 + y^2 + 2g_1 x - a^2 = 0 \quad (8)$$

$$x^2 + y^2 + 2g_2 x - a^2 = 0 \quad (9)$$

Two circles (8) and (9) will intersect each other orthogonally if

$$2(g_1 g_2 + 0) = -a^2 - a^2$$

i.e. $$2g_1 g_2 = -2a^2$$

i.e. $$g_1 g_2 = -a^2$$

Again from equation (7) we have

$$g_1 g_2 = a_2 + a^2 m^2 - c^2$$

So $$a^2 + a^2 m^2 - c^2 = -a^2$$

i.e. $$2a^2 + a^2 m^2 = c^2$$

i.e. $$a^2(2 + m^2) = c^2$$

i.e. $$\boxed{c^2 = a^2(2 + m^2)} \quad \textit{(Proved)}$$

Problem 5 If the equations of two circles whose radii are a and a_1 be respectively $S = 0$ and $S_1 = 0$, show that the circles

$$\frac{S}{a} \pm \frac{S_1}{a_1} = 0 \text{ intersect at right angles.}$$

Solution Let the equations of two circles are

$$S = x^2 + y^2 + 2gx + 2fy + c = 0 \quad (1)$$

$$S_1 = x^2 + y^2 2g_1 x + 2f_1 y + c_1 = 0 \quad (2)$$

Radii of the two circles are a and a_1 then

$$a^2 = (\sqrt{g^2 + f^2 - c})^2 = g^2 + f^2 - c$$

$$a_1^2 = (\sqrt{g_1^2 + f_1^2 - c_1})^2 = g_1^2 + f_1^2 - c_1$$

$$\frac{s}{a} = (x^2 + y^2)\frac{1}{a} + 2x\frac{g}{a} + 2y\frac{f}{a} + \frac{c}{a} = 0$$

$$\frac{s_1}{a_1} = (x^2\ y^2)\frac{1}{a_1} + 2x\frac{g_1}{a_1} + 2y\frac{f_1}{a_1} + \frac{c_1}{a_1} = 0$$

Now $\frac{s}{a} + \frac{s_1}{a_1} = (x^2 + y^2)\left(\frac{1}{a} + \frac{1}{a_1}\right) + 2x\left(\frac{g}{a_1} + \frac{g_1}{a_1}\right)$

$$+ 2y\left(\frac{f}{a} + \frac{f_1}{a_1}\right) + \left(\frac{c}{a} + \frac{c_1}{a_1}\right) = 0 \qquad (3)$$

and $\frac{s}{a} - \frac{s_1}{a_1} = (x^2 + y^2)\left(\frac{1}{a} - \frac{1}{a_1}\right) + 2x\left(\frac{g}{a} - \frac{g_1}{a_1}\right)$

$$+ 2y\left(\frac{f}{a} - \frac{f_1}{a_1}\right) + \left(\frac{c}{a} - \frac{c_1}{a_i}\right) \equiv 0 \qquad (4)$$

Let $\frac{1}{a} + \frac{1}{a_1} = k$ and $\frac{1}{a} - \frac{1}{a_1} = k_1$

Then (3) and (4) can be written as

$$\frac{s}{a} + \frac{s_1}{a_1} \equiv (x^2 + y^2) + 2x\frac{\left(\frac{g}{a} + \frac{g_1}{a_1}\right)}{k} + 2y\frac{\left(\frac{f}{a} + \frac{f_1}{a_1}\right)}{k} + \frac{\left(\frac{c}{a} + \frac{c_1}{a_1}\right)}{k} = 0 \qquad (5)$$

and $$\frac{s}{a} - \frac{s_1}{a_1} = (x^2 + y^2) + 2x\frac{\left(\frac{g}{a} - \frac{g_1}{a_1}\right)}{k_1} + 2y\frac{\left(\frac{f}{a} - \frac{f_1}{a_1}\right)}{k_1} + \frac{\left(\frac{c}{a} - \frac{c_1}{a_1}\right)}{k_1} = 0 \qquad (6)$$

Circles (5) and (6) will cut each other orthogonally if

$$2\left[\frac{\left(\frac{g}{a} + \frac{g_1}{a_1}\right)}{k} + \frac{\left(\frac{g}{a} - \frac{g_1}{a_1}\right)}{k_1} + \frac{\left(\frac{f}{a} + \frac{f_1}{a_1}\right)\left(\frac{f}{a} - \frac{f_1}{a_1}\right)}{k\qquad k_1}\right] = \frac{\left(\frac{c}{a} + \frac{c_1}{a_1}\right)}{k} + \frac{\left(\frac{c}{a} - \frac{c_1}{a_1}\right)}{k_1}$$

$$\Rightarrow 2\left[\frac{g^2}{a^2} - \frac{g_1^2}{a_1^2} + \frac{f_2}{a_2} - \frac{f_1^2}{a_1^2}\right] = k_1\left(\frac{c}{a} + \frac{c_1}{a_1}\right) + k\left(\frac{c}{a} - \frac{c_1}{a_1}\right)$$

i.e. $$2\left[\frac{g^2+f^2}{a^2}-\frac{g_1^2+f_1^2}{a_1^2}\right]=\frac{c}{a}(k+k_1)-\frac{c_1}{a_1}(k-k_1)$$

i.e. $$2\left[\frac{g^2+f^2}{a^2}-\frac{g_1^2+f_1^2}{a_1^2}\right]=\frac{c}{a}\cdot\frac{2}{a}-\frac{c_1}{a_1}\cdot\frac{2}{a_1}$$

i.e. we have to prove

$$2\left[\frac{a^2+c}{a^2}-\frac{a_1^2+c_1}{a_1^2}\right]=2\left[\frac{c}{a^2}-\frac{c_1}{a_1^2}\right]$$

i.e. we have to prove

$$\frac{a^2+c}{a^2}-\frac{a_1^2+c_1}{a_1^2}=\frac{c}{a^2}-\frac{c_1}{a_1^2}$$

We have $$LHS\ \frac{\alpha^2+c}{a^2}-\frac{a_1^2+c_1}{a_1^2}=\left(1+\frac{c}{a^2}\right)-\left(1+\frac{c_1}{a_1^2}\right)$$

$$=1+\frac{c}{a^2}-1-\frac{c_1}{a_1^2}=\frac{c}{a^2}-\frac{c_1}{a_1^2}\quad RHS$$ *(Proved)*

Hence the Problem

17

Radical Axis

Definition The radical axis of two circles is the locus of a point which moves so that the lengths of the tangents, drawn from it to the two circles are equal.

Let the equations to the two circles be

$$x^2 + y^2 + 2gx + 2fy + c = 0 \quad (1)$$

and $$x^2 + y^2 + 2g_1 x + 2 f_1 y + c_1 = 0 \quad (2)$$

Let $p(x_1. y_1)$ be a point from which the tangents to (1) and (2) are equal

Therefore $$x_1^2 + y_1^2 + 2gx_1 + 2fy_i + c$$
$$= x_1^2 + y_1^2 + 2g_1 x_1 + 2 f_1 y_1 + c_1$$

i.e. $2(g-g_1)x_1 + 2(-f-f_1) + (c-c_1) = 0$ (3)

Therefore the locus of the point (x_1, y_1) is a straight line

$$2(g-g_1)x + 2(f-f_1)y + c-c_1 = 0 \quad (4)$$

Which is the equation of the radical axis.

If the equations to the circlcs be written in the form $s = 0$ and $s_1 = 0$, the equation of the radical axis may be written as $s - s_1 = 0$

Article 1 The radical axis of two circles is a straight line $\perp^r$ to the line joining the centres.

Let the equation of the first circles

$$s \equiv x^2 + y^2 + 2gx + 2fy + c = 0 \quad (1)$$

$$s_1 \equiv x^2 + y^2 + 2g_1 x + 2f_1 y + c = 0 \quad (2)$$

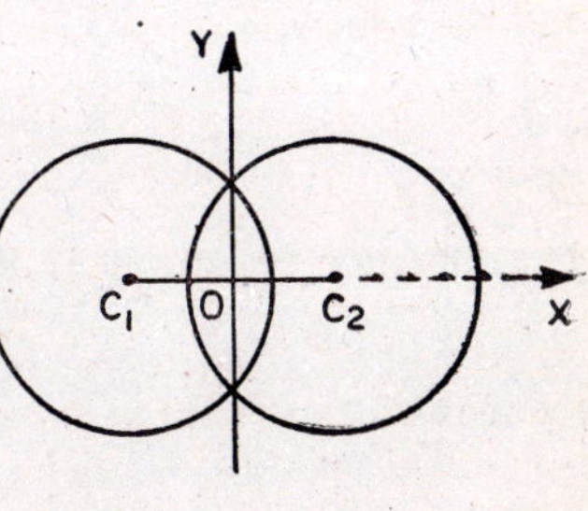

Equation of the radical axis is given by

$$2(g-g_1)x + 2(f-f_1)y + c-c_1 = 0 \quad (3)$$

Slope of the radical axis is $-\dfrac{(g-g_1)}{(f-f_1)}$

Again centres of the circles (1) and (2) are $(-g, -f)$ and $(-g_1, -f_1)$ slope of the line joining centres $c\ (-g, -f)$ and $c_1\ (-g_1\ -f_1)$ is given by

$$\frac{-f_1+f}{-g_1+g}=\frac{f-f_1}{g-g_1}$$

Product of the slopes of the line joining the centres of two circles and the radical axis is

$$-\frac{(g-g_1}{(f-f_1)}\times\frac{(f-f_1)}{(g-g_1)}=-1$$

Hence the radical axis of two circles is a straight line $\perp$ to the line joining their centres. *(Proved)*

Artiele 2 The radical axis of three circles taken in pairs are concurrent.

Let the equations of three circles be

$$S_1=0 \tag{1}$$

$$S_2=0 \tag{2}$$

$$S_3=0 \tag{3}$$

The radical axis of (2) and (3) is

$$S_2-S_3=0 \tag{4}$$

The radical axis of (3) and (1) is

$$S_3-S_1=0 \tag{5}$$

The radical axis of (1) and (2) is

$$S_1-S_2=0 \tag{6}$$

Adding equations (4), (5) and (6) the sum identically vasnhes. Therefore the equations (4), (5) and (6) hold simultaneously that is the radical axis meet in a point.

This point is called the radical centre of the three circles

Article 3 To find the locus of the centre of a circle cutting two circles orthogonally.

Let the equation of two circles be

$$x^2+y^2+2g_1x+2f_1y+c_1=0 \tag{1}$$

And
$$x^2+y^2+2g_2x+2f_2y+c_2=0 \tag{2}$$

Let the equation of the circles which cuts (1) and (2) orthogenally be

$$x^2+y^2+2gx+2fy+c=0 \tag{3}$$

So that its centre is $(-g, -f)$, (3) intersects (1) orthogenally therefore

$$2(gg_1+ff_1)=c+c_1 \tag{4}$$

Again circle (3) intersect (2) orthogenally therefore

$$2(gg_2+ff_2)=c+c_2 \tag{5}$$

Subtracting (5) from (4) we have

$$2g(g_1-g_2) + 2f(f_1-f_2) = c_1-c_2$$

Therefore the locus of the centre $(-g_1, -f)$ is

$$2(-x)(g_1-g_2) + 2(-y)(f_1-f_2) = c_1-c_2$$

i.e. $$2x(g_1-g_2) + 2y(f_1-f_2) + c_1-c_2 = 0$$

Which is the radical axis of the two circles'

Note Remember If a circle cuts two circles orthogenally, the radical axis of the two circles passes through the centre of the circle.

Remember The general equation of circles passing through the common points of two given circles

Let $$S = x^2 + y^2 + 2gx + 2fy + c = 0$$

And $$S_2 = x^2 + y^2 + 2g_1x + 2f_1y + c_1 = 0$$

be the two given circles then for different value of k, $S + kS_2 = 0$ represents a system of circles passing through the common points of $S = 0$ and $S_1 = 0$ and hence (having the same redical axis) c_0 axal with the circles $S = 0$, $S_1 = 0$

Remember Equation of the system determined by a circle and a given line

Let $S \equiv x^2 + y^2 + 2gx + 2fy + c = 0$ be given circle

And $L = lx + my + n = 0$ be the given straight line.

Then for different value of k, $S + kL = 0$ represents a system of circles of which $L = 0$ is the radical axis and $S = 0$ is the one of the members.

For different value of k it represents different circles each passing through the common points of $S = 0$ and, $L = 0$

Problem 1 Find the equation of the circle which passes through (1, 2) and through the points of intersection of the circles.

$$x^2 + y^2 - 5x - 2y + 8 = 0, \; x^2 + y^2 - 3x - y + 6 = 0$$

Solution The equa tion of the cirle passing through the intersection of

$$x^2 + y^2 - 5x - 2y + 8 = 0 \qquad (1)$$

And $$x^2 + y^2 - 3x - y + 6 = 0$$

is given by $x^2 + y^2 - 5x - 2y + 8 + k(x^2 + y^2 - 3x - y + 6) = 0$ (3)

Circle (3) passes through the point (1, 2) so

$$1^2 + 2^2 - 5\cdot1 - 2\cdot2 + 8 + k(1^2 + 2^2 - 3\cdot1 - 2 + 6) = 0$$

i.e. $$1 + 4 - 5 - 4 + 8 + k(1 + 4 - 3 - 2 + 6) = 0$$

i.e. $$4 + k6 = 6$$

i.e. $$6k = -4$$

i.e. $$k = -\frac{2}{3}$$

Putting value of k in equation (3) we have the equation of circle

$$x^2 + y^2 - 5x - 2y + 8 - \tfrac{2}{3}(x^2 + y^2 - 3x - y + 6) = 0$$

$$3(x^2 + y^2 - 5x - 2y + 8) - 2(x^2 + y^2 - 3x - y + 6) = 0$$

i.e. $$x^2 + y^2 - 9x - 4y + 12 = 0$$

Which is the required equation. *(Proved)*

Problem 2 Find the equation of the circle whose diameter is the common chord of the circles.

$$x^2 + y^2 + 2x + 3y + 1 = 0$$

and $$x^2 + y^2 + 4x + 3y + 2 = 0$$

Solution Equation of common chord of both circle is given by

$$x^2 + y^2 + 2x + 3y + 1 = x^2 + y^2 + 4x + 3y + 2$$

i.e. $$2x + 1 = 0 \qquad (1)$$

Equation of the circle passing through the intersection of circle

$$x^2 + y + 2x + 3y + 1 = 0 \text{ and}$$

line [chord (common)] $2x + 1 = 0$ is given by

$$(x^2 + y^2 + 2x + 3y + 1) + k(2x + 1) = 0 \qquad (2)$$

i.e. $$x^2 + y^2 2x + 3y + 1 + 2k\,x + k = 0$$

i.e. $$x^2 + y^2 + 2x(1 + k) + 3y + (1 + k) = 0$$

centre of this circle is

$$\left[-(k + 1), -\frac{3}{2}\right]$$

centre will lie on (1) if it satisfies equation of the common chord $2x + 1$

i.e. $$-2(k + 1) + 1 = 0$$

$$-2k - 2 + 1 = 0$$

i.e. $$-2k - 1 = 0$$

i.e. $$k = -\tfrac{1}{2}$$

Therefore equation of the circle is

$$(x^2 + y^2 + 2x + 3y + 1) - \tfrac{1}{2}(2x + 1) = 0$$

i.e. $$2(x^2 + y^2 + 2x + 3y + 1) - (2x + 1) = 0$$

i.e. $$2x^2 + 2y^2 + 4x + 6y + 2 - 2x - 1 = 0$$

i.e. $$2x^2 + 2y^2 + 2x + 6y + 1 = 0$$ **Ans.**

Problem 3 If OP, OQ are the tangents from the origin to the circle

$$x^2 + y^2 + 2gx + 2fy + c = 0,$$

Show that the equation of the circum circle ofthe $\Delta\ OPQ$ is

$$x^2 + y^2 + gx + fy = 0$$

Solution We know that the equalion of the chord of contact drawn to a circle $x^2 + y^2 + 2gx + 2fy + c = 0$ from the point (x_1, y_1) is given by

$$xx_1 + yy_1 + g(x + x_1) + f(y+y_1)\ c = 0$$

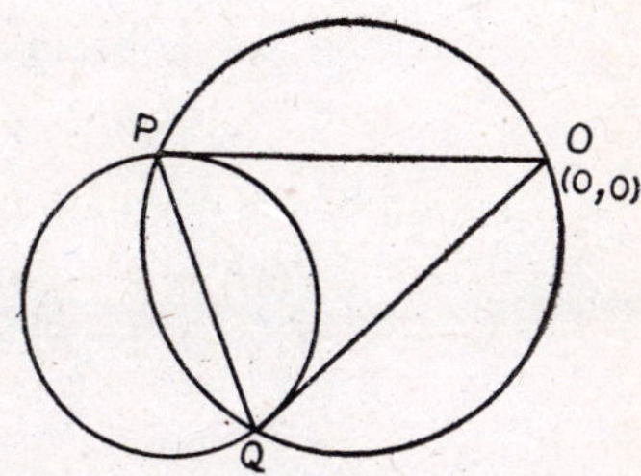

So the equation of the chord of contact to the circle

$$x^2 + y^2 + 2gx + 2fy + c = 0$$

from (0, 0) is given by

$$x\cdot 0 + y\cdot 0 + g(x + 0) + f(y + 0) + c = 0$$

i.e.
$$gx + fy + c = 0$$

The equation of a circle passing through the intersection of the circle

$$x^2 + y^2 + 2gx + 2fy + c = 0$$

and the chord of contact $gx + fy + c = 0$ is given by

$$x^2 + y^2\ 2gx + 2fy + c + \lambda(gx + fy + c) = 0 \qquad (1)$$

Circle also passes through the point (0, 0) i.e. origin. So it will satisfy the equation (1) i.e.

$$c + \lambda c = 0$$

i.e.
$$\lambda c = -c$$

i.e.
$$\lambda = -1$$

Putting the value of λ in equation (1). The equation of the circle circumscribing $\Delta\ OPQ$ is given by

$$x^2 + y^2 + 2gx + 2fy + c - 1\ (gx + fy + c) = 0$$

i.e.
$$x^2 + y^2 + 2gx + 2fy + c - gx - fy - c = 0$$

i.e.
$$x^2 + y^2 + gx + fy + c - c = 0$$

i.e.
$$x^2 + y^2 + gx + fy = 0$$

Problem 4 Find the length of the common chord of the circles whose equations are $(x-a)^2 + y^2 = a^2$ and $x^2 + (y-b)^2 = b^2$ and prove that the equation of the circle whose diameter is the common chord is

$$(a^2 + b^2)(x^2 + y^2) = 2ab\,(bx + ay)$$

Solution The equations of two circles can be written as

$$(x-a)^2 + y^2 = a^2$$

i.e. $$x^2 + a^2 - 2ax + y^2 = a^2$$

i.e. $$x^2 + y^2 - 2ax = 0 \quad (1)$$

And $$x^2 + (y-b)^2 = b^2$$

i.e. $$x^2 + y^2 - 2by + b^2 = b^2$$

i.e. $$x^2 + y^2 - 2by = 0 \quad (2)$$

The equation of the common chord of two circles (1) and (2) is given by

$$(x^2 + y^2 - 2ax) - (x^2 + y^2 - 2by) = 0$$

i.e. $$x^2 + y^2 - 2ax - x^2 - y^2 + 2by = 0$$

i.e. $$bv - ax = 0$$

i.e. $$ax - by = 0 \quad (3)$$

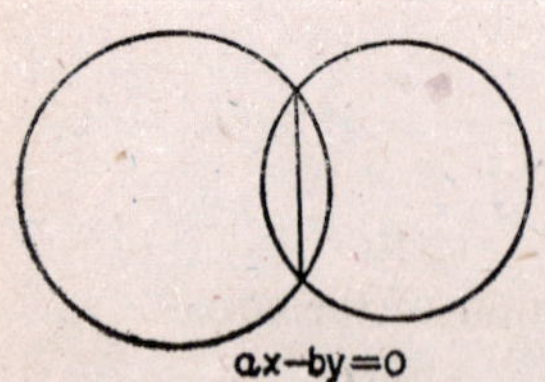

The equation of the circle passing through the intersection of (1) and (3) is given by

$$x^2 + y^2 - 2ax + \lambda\,(ax - by) = 0$$

i.e. $$x^2 + y^2 - 2ax + \lambda ax - \lambda by = 0$$

i.e. $$x^2 + y^2 + x\,(\lambda a - 2a) - \lambda by = 0 \quad (4)$$

If the chord $ax - by = 0$ is the diameter of the circle (4) then the centre of circle (4) must lie on the line $ax - by = 0$

The centre of the circle (4) is

$$\left(\frac{2a - \lambda a}{2}, \frac{\lambda b}{2}\right)$$

Since it lies on the line (3) so it will satisfy (3) so

$$\left(\frac{2a - \lambda a}{2} - b\left(\frac{\lambda b}{2}\right)\right) = 0$$

i.e. $$2a^2 - \lambda a^2 - b^2\,\lambda = 0$$

$$2a^2 = \lambda\,(a^2 + b^2)$$

i.e. $$\lambda = \frac{2a^2}{a^2 + b^2}$$

So the equation of the circle passing through the intersection of (1) and the common chord $ax - by = 0$ is given by

Problem 5 Find the radical axis of the circles $x^2 + y^2 + 2by + c^2 = 0$ and $x^2 + y^2 + 2by + c^2 = 0$ and hence deduce that the condition that they touch each other is

$$\frac{1}{a^2} + \frac{1}{b^2} = \frac{1}{c^2}$$

olution We have

$$S_1 = 0 = x^2 + y^2 + 2ax + c^2 \tag{1}$$

nd

$$S_2 = x^2 + y^2 + 2by + c^2 = 0 \tag{2}$$

quation of the radical axis is given by

$$S_1 - S_2 = 0$$

e. $$x^2 + y^2 + 2ax + c^2 - x^2 - y^2 - 2bx - c^2 = 0$$

e. $$2(ax - by) = 0$$

e. $$ax - by = 0 \tag{3}$$

emember The two circles touches each other if the radical axis of the wo circles touches one cercle

e. $$a\dot{x} - by = 0 \text{ touches}$$

$$x^2 + y^2 + 2ax + c^2 = 0$$

hen solving (3) and (1) we have

$$x^2 + \left(\frac{a}{b}\ x\right)^2 + 2ax + c^2 = 0$$

$$x^2 + \frac{a^2}{b^2} x^2 + 2ax + c^2 = 0$$

.e. $$x^2\left(\frac{a^2 + b^2}{b^2}\right) + 2ax + c^2 = 0 \tag{4}$$

ince the line (3) touches the circle (1) so the equation (4) have equal roots o

$$B^2 - 4\ Ac = 0$$

$$(2a)^2 - 4\ \frac{a^2 + b^2}{b^2} \cdot c^2 = 0$$

$$4a^2 - \frac{4(a^2 + b^2)}{b^2} c^2 = 0$$

.e. $$4[a^2 b^2 - (a^2 + b^2) c^2] = 0$$

.e. $$a^2 b^2 - (a^2 + b^2) c = 0$$

.e. $$(a^2 + b^2) c^2 = a^2 b^2$$

.e. $$\frac{a^2 + b^2}{a^2 b^2} = \frac{1}{c^2}$$

.e. $$\frac{1}{c^2} + \frac{1}{b^2} = \frac{1}{c^2}$$

Problem 6 The polars of a point w.r.t. two given circles meet i show that the radical axis of the circles bisect the line PQ.

Let the point P be $(\bar{\alpha}, \beta)$ and the equations of two circles be

$$x^2 + y^2 + 2g_1 x + c = 0$$

And

$$x^2 + y^2 + 2g_2 x + c = 0$$

The polars of the point P w.r.t. the two given circles (1) and (2) are therefore

$$x\alpha + y\beta + g_1(x + \alpha) + c = 0 \quad (3)$$

And

$$x\alpha + y\beta + g_2(x + \alpha) + c = 0 \quad (4)$$

Lines (3) and (4) let each other at the point Q. x and y which can be obtained by solving equation (3) and (4) subtracting (4) from (3) we have

$$x(g_1 - g_2) + \alpha(g_1 - g_2) = 0$$

i.e.

$$(g_1 - g_2)(x + \alpha) = 0$$

Since

$$g_1 \neq g_2$$

So

$$x + \alpha = 0$$

$$\Rightarrow \quad x = -\alpha$$

Putting the value of $x = -\alpha$ in equation (3) we have

$$-\alpha \cdot \alpha + y\beta + g_1(0) + c = 0$$

$$-\alpha^2 + c + y\beta = 0$$

i.e.

$$y\beta = -c + \alpha^2$$

$$y = \frac{-c + \alpha^2}{\beta} = \frac{\alpha^2 - c}{\beta}$$

The co-ordinate of the point Q is

$$\left(-\alpha, \frac{\alpha^2 - c}{\beta}\right)$$

The co-ordinate of middle point of PQ is

$$\frac{\alpha - \alpha}{2}, \frac{\beta + \alpha^2 - c}{2}$$

i.e.

$$\left(0, \frac{\alpha^2 + \beta - c}{2}\right)$$

The middle point of PQ is on the line $x = 0$ i.e. on the y axis

Again equation of the radical axis of the two circles is

$$(g_2 - g_2)x = 0$$

Since

$$g_1 - g_2 \neq 0$$

$$\Rightarrow \quad x = 0$$

i.e. the y axis

Thus the radical axis of both the circle bisect the line joining the points. P and Q.

Problem 6 Find the equation of the circle circumscribing the triangle formed by the axis and the line $ax + by = 1$

Solution The equation of a conic passing throygh the points of intersection of the lines $x = 0, y = 0$ and $ax + by - 1 = 0$ taken in pairs is

Remember $xy + \lambda x\,(ax + by - 1) + uy\,(ax + by - 1) = 0$

This will represents a circle if the coefficient of x^2 = the coefficient of y^2 and the coefficient of $xy = 0$

The coefficient of $x^2 = \lambda a$

The coefficient of $y^2 = \mu b$

The coefficient of $xy = \lambda b + \mu a + 1$

Hence $\lambda a = \mu a$ (2)

And $1 + \lambda b + \mu a = 0$ (3)

From (2) and (3)

$$1 + \lambda b + \frac{\lambda a}{b} \cdot a = 0$$

i.e. $$\lambda\left(b + \frac{a^2}{b}\right) = -1$$

i.e. $$\lambda\left(\frac{b^2 + a^2}{b}\right) = -1$$

i.e. $$\lambda = -\frac{b}{a^2 + b^2}$$

$$\mu = \frac{\lambda a}{b}$$

$$\mu = -\frac{ab}{(a^2+b^2)b}$$

i.e. $$\mu = -\frac{a}{a^2 + b^2}$$

Substituting the values of λ and μ in equation (1) we have

$$xy + \frac{(-b)}{(a^2 + b^2)}\,x\,(ax + by - 1) + \frac{(-a)}{a^2 + b^2}\,y\,(ax + by - 1) = 0$$

i.e. $$(a^2 + b^2)\,xy + (ax + by - 1)\,(bx + ay) = 0$$

$$(ax + by - 1)\,(bx + ay) = (a^2 + b^2)\,xy$$

$$abx^2 + a^2\,xy + b^2\,xy + aby^2 - bx - ay - (a^2 + b^2)\,xy = 0$$

i.e. $$abx^2 + aby^2 - bx - ay + xy\,(a^2 + b^2 - b^2 - a^2 - b^2) = 0$$

i.e. $$abx^2 + aby^2 - bx - ay = 0$$

i.e. $$x^2 + y^2 - \frac{x}{a} - \frac{y}{b} = 0$$

Which is the required equation of the circle

Problem 8 Obtain the equation of the circle which cuts orthogenally each of the three circles

$$x^2 + y^2 = 16 \qquad (1)$$

$$x^2 + y^2 - 14x + 40 = 0 \qquad (2)$$

And

$$x^2 + y^2 - 12y + 32 = 0 \qquad (3)$$

Solution The radical axis of circle (1) and (2) is given by

$$S_1 - S_2 = 0$$

where $S_1 = x^2 + y^2 - 16x = 0$

and $S_2 = x^2 + y^2 - 14x + 40 = 0$

i.e. $x^2 + y^2 - 16 - x^2 - y^2 + 14x - 40 = 0$

i.e. $14x - 56 = 0$

i,e. $14(x - 4) = 0$

i.e. $x - 4 = 0 \qquad (4)$

The radical axis of the circles (1) and (3) is given by

$$S_1 - S_3 = 0$$

$$S_3 = x^2 + y^2 - 12y + 32 = 0$$

$$x^2 + y^2 - 16 - x^2 - y^2 + 12y - 32 = 0$$

$$12y - 48 = 0$$

i.e. $y - 4 = 0 \qquad (5)$

These two lines meet in point (4, 4) which is therefore the radical centre the square of the length of the tangent from the point (4, 4) to each of the given circle

$$(\sqrt{(4)^2 + (4)^2 - 16}) = (\sqrt{16})^2 = 16$$

The required equation of the circle is therefore

$$(x - 4)^2 + (y - 4)^2 = 16$$

i.e. $x^2 - 8x + 16 + y^2 - 8y + 16 = 16$

i.e. $x^2 + y^2 - 8x - 8y + 16 = 0$

Problem 9 Tangents are drawn to the circle $x^2 + y^2 = 12$ at the points where it met by the circle $x^2 + y^2 - 5x + 3y - 2 = 0$; find the point of intersection of these tangents.

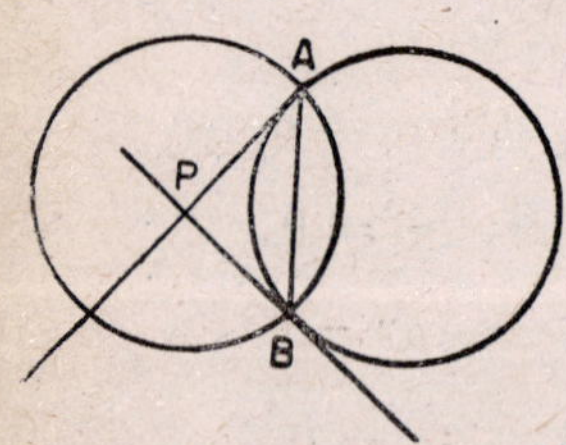

Let the equation of two circles be

$$S_1 = x^2 + y^2 - 12 = 0$$

$$S_2 = x^2 + y^2 - 5x + 3y - 2 = 0 \qquad (1)$$

Let these two circles cuts each other at the points A and B i.e. AB is the common chord of the two circles. Let the tangent at the two points A and B cut each other at the point $P(\alpha, \beta)$ Then AB is the chord of contact.

(α, β) is the point of intersection of these tangents so that the radical axis of the two circles is the chord of contact of the tangents drawn from (α, β) to the circles $x^2 + y^2 = 12$

The equation of the radical axis is

$$s_1 - s_2 = 0$$

i.e. $x^2 + y^2 - 5x + 3y - 2 - x^2 - y^2 + 12 = 0$

i.e. $$-5x + 3y + 10 = 0$$

i.e. $$5x - 3y - 10 = 0$$

$$5x - 3y = 10 \tag{1}$$

Also the equation of chord of contact of the tangents from (α, β) to the circle $x^2 + y^2 = 12$ is

$$x\alpha + y\beta = 12 \tag{2}$$

Since (1) and (2) are identical so

$$\frac{5}{\alpha} = \frac{-3}{\beta} = \frac{10}{12}$$

i.e. $$\frac{\alpha}{5} = \frac{\beta}{-3} = \frac{12}{10}$$

$$\alpha = \frac{12 \times 5}{10 \times 5}, \ \alpha = 6$$

And $$\beta = \frac{12 \times (-3}{10} = \frac{-18}{5} = -3\frac{3}{5}$$

Therefore the co-ordinates of the point of intersection are

$$\left(6, -3\frac{3}{5}\right)$$

Problem 10 Prove that the locus of the centre of a circle cutting three given circles at the same angle is a straight line through the radical centre.

Solution Let the equation of the three circles be

$$S_1 \equiv (x - \alpha_1)^2 + (y - \beta_1)^2 - r_1 = 0 \tag{1}$$

$$S_2 \equiv (x - \alpha_2)^2 + (y - \beta_2) - r_2^2 = 0 \tag{2}$$

$$S_3 \equiv (x - \alpha_3)^2 + (y - \beta_3)^2 - r_3 = 0 \tag{3}$$

Let (h, k) be the centre and a be the radius of the cutting circles so that its equation is $(x - h)^2 + (y - k)^2 = a^2$ (4)

Let θ be the constant angle of intersection since (1) and (4) intersect at an angle θ therefore we have

$$(h - \alpha_1)^2 + (k - \beta_1)^2 = r_1^2 + a^2 - 2r_1 a \cos\theta$$

Similary $$(h - \alpha_2)^2 + (k - \beta_2)^2 = r_2^2 + a^2 - 2r_2 a \cos\theta$$

$$(h - \alpha_3)^2 + (k - \beta_3)^2 = r_3^2 + a^2 - 2r_3 a \cos\theta$$

Eliminating a^2 and $a \cos \theta$ from these equations we get

$$\begin{vmatrix} (h-\alpha_1)^2 + (k-\beta_1)^2 - r_1^2 & 1 & r_1 \\ (h-\alpha_2)^2 + (k-\beta_3)^2 - r_2^2 & 1 & r_2 \\ (h-\alpha_3)^2 + (k-\beta_3)^2 - r_3^2 & 1 & r_3 \end{vmatrix} = 0$$

Hence the locus of (h, k) is given by

$$\begin{vmatrix} (x-\alpha_1)^2 + (y-\beta_1)^2 - r_1^2 & 1 & r_1 \\ (x-\alpha_2)^2 + (y-\beta_2)^2 - r_2^2 & 1 & r_2 \\ (x-\alpha_3)^2 + (y-\beta_3)^2 - r_3^2 & 1 & r_3 \end{vmatrix} = 0$$

$$\begin{vmatrix} s_1 & 1 & r_1 \\ s_2 & 1 & r_2 \\ s_3 & 1 & r_3 \end{vmatrix} = 0$$

i.e.
$$\begin{vmatrix} r_1 & s_2 & 1 \\ r_2 & s_2 & 1 \\ r_3 & s_3 & 1 \end{vmatrix} = 0$$

i.e. $\quad r_1 (s_2 - s_3) + r_2 (s_3 - s_1) + r_3 (s_1 - s_2) = 0 \qquad (3)$

This is the equation of a straight line because it is of the first degree

Since $\quad r_1 \neq 0 \neq r_2 \neq r_3 \neq 0$

So $\quad s_2 - s_3 = 0 \quad$ i.e. $\quad s_2 = s_3$

$\quad s_3 - s_1 = 0 \quad\quad s_3 = s_1$

and $\quad s_1 - s_2 = 0 \quad\quad s_1 = s_2$

i.e. $\quad s_1 = s_2 = s_3$

(radical centre of the three circles)

So the straight line passes through the radical centre of the three circles.

Problem 11 Prove that the two circles

$$x^2 + y^2 - 2ax + 2by + c = 0$$

and $\quad x^2 + y^2 + 2bx + 2ay - c = 0$ are orthogonal

Solution We know that the two circles

$$x^2 + y^2 + 2g_1 x + 2f_1 y + c_1 = 0$$

and $\quad x^2 + y^2 + 2g_2 x + 2f_2 y + c_2 = 0$

Cut each other orthogonally

if $\quad 2(g_1 g_2 + f_1 f_2) = c_1 + c_2$

Here $\quad g_1 = -a, \quad g_2 = b \quad c_1 = c$

$\quad f_1 = b, \quad f_2 = a \quad c_2 = c$

We see that $2(g_1 g_2 + f_1 f_2) = 2(-ab + ab) = 0 = c - c$

So the given two circles are orthogonal.

Problem 12 Show that the circles

$$x^2 + y^2 + 2x - 8y + 8 = 0$$

and
$$x^2 + y^2 + 10x - 2y + 22 = 0$$

touch each other and find thc point of contact

Solution Equation of the first circle is

$$s_1 \equiv x^2 + y^2 + 2x - 8y + 8 = 0$$

i.e. $s_1 \equiv x^2 + 2x + 1^2 + y^2 - 2\cdot 4y + 4^2 + 8$
$$= 1^2 + 4^2$$

$$s_1 \equiv (x + 1^2) + (y-4)^2 + 8 = 17$$

i.e.
$$(x + 1)^2 + (y-4)^2 = 17 - 8$$

i.e.
$$(x + 1)^2 + (y-4)^2 = 9$$

i.e.
$$(x + 1)^2 + (y-4)^2 = 3^2$$

Thus the centre of this circle is $(-1, 4)$ and the radius is 3

Again equation of the 2nd circle is

$$x^2 + y^2 + 10x - 2y + 22 = 0$$

i.e. $x^2 + 2\cdot 5x + 5^2 + y^2 - 2y + 1^2 + 22 = 5^2 + 1^2$

i.e.
$$(x + 5)^2 + (y-1)^2 = 26 - 22 = 4$$

i.e.
$$(x + 5)^2 + (y-1)^2 = 2^2$$

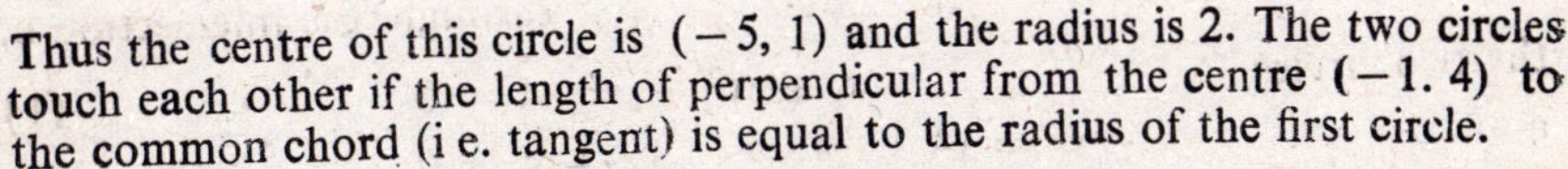

Thus the centre of this circle is $(-5, 1)$ and the radius is 2. The two circles touch each other if the length of perpendicular from the centre $(-1. 4)$ to the common chord (i e. tangent) is equal to the radius of the first circle.

Equation of the chord of contact (i.e. tangent) is

$$s_1 - s_2 = 0$$

$$x^2 + y^2 + 10x - 2y + 22 - x^2 - y^2 - 2x + 8y - 8 = 0$$

i.e.
$$8x + 6y + 14 = 0$$

i.e.
$$4x + 3y + 7 = 0$$

length of $\perp r$ from $(-1, 4)$ to the line

$$4x + 3y + 7 = 0 \text{ is}$$

$$\frac{4(-1) + 3\cdot 4 + 7}{\sqrt{4^2 + 3^2}} = \frac{-4 + 12 + 7}{\sqrt{25}}$$

$$= \frac{19-4}{\sqrt{25}} = \frac{15}{5} = 3$$

which is the radius of the first circle. So the two circles touch each other.

Let they touch each other at the point (α, β) then we have to find th value of α_1 and β, (α, β) intersect the line joining of the centres $(-1, 4$ and $(-5, 1)$ internally in the ratio of their centres i.e. in 3:2

$$\alpha = \frac{3(-5) + 2(-1)}{3 + 2} = \frac{-15-2}{5} = -\frac{17}{5}$$

$$\beta = \frac{3(1) + 2(4)}{3 + 2} = \frac{3 + 8}{5} = \frac{11}{5}$$

Thus the point of contact is $\left(\frac{17}{5}, \frac{11}{5}\right)$ **Ans.**

Problem 13 Find the equation of the circle which passes through the points of intersection of the circle.

(1) $$x^2 + y^2 - 6x - 6y + 8 = 0$$

and $$x^2 + y^2 - 10y - 40 = 0$$

and passes through the point (2, 3)

Solution Easy

Problem 14 Find the equation of the circle which passes through the point of intersection of the circle

$$x^2 + y^2 = 4$$

and $$x^2 + y^2 - 2x - 4y + 4 = 0$$

and touching the line $$x + 2y = 0$$

Solution The equation of the circle passing through the intersection of the two circles

$$s_1 \equiv x^2 + y^2 - 4 = 0 \qquad (1)$$

and

$$s_2 \equiv x^2 + y^2 - 2x - 4y + 4 = 0 \qquad (2)$$

is given by

$$s_2 + \lambda s_1 = 0$$

$$x^2 + y^2 - 2x - 4y + 4 + \lambda(x^2 + y^2 - 4) = 0$$

i.e. $$x^2 + y^2 - 2x - 4y + 4 + \lambda x^2 + \lambda y^2 - 4\lambda = 0$$

i.e. $$x^2(1 + \lambda) + y^2(1 + \lambda) - 2x - 4y + 4(1 - \lambda) = 0 \qquad (3)$$

Since the line $x + 2y = 0$ touches the circle (3)

So putting $x = -2y$ in (3) we have

$$(-2y)^2 (1+\lambda)+y^2 (1+\lambda)-2 (-2y)-4y+4 (1-\lambda) = 0$$

i.e. $4y^2 (1+\lambda)+y^2 (1 + \lambda) + 4y-4y + 4 (1-\lambda) = 0$

i.e. $$5y^2 (1 + \lambda) + 4 (1-\lambda) = 0 \quad (4)$$

Line $x + 2y = 0$ touches the circle (3) if equation (4) have equal roots

i.e. if $$B^2-4 AC = 0$$

i.e. $$0-45 (1 + \lambda).4 (1-\lambda) = 0$$

i.e. $$1-\lambda^2 = 1$$

i.e. $$\lambda^2 = 1$$

i.e. $$\lambda = \pm 1$$

Putting the value of $\lambda = 1$ we have the equation of circle is

$$x^2 (1 + 1) + y^2 (1 + 1)-2x-4y + 4 (1-1) = 0$$

i.e. $$2x^2 + 2y^2-2x-4y = 0$$

i.e. $$2 (x^2 + y^2-x-2y) = 0$$

i.e. $$x^2 + y^2-x-2y = 0$$

which is the required equation of the circle.

Problem 15 Find the equation of the circle which passes through the points of intersection of the circle

$$x^2 + y^2-4 = 0$$

and $$x^2 + y^2 + 2x-3 = 0$$

and has radius equal to 4.

Solution Let the equation of the two circles are

$$s_1 \equiv x^2 + y^2-4 = 0$$

$$s_2 \equiv x^2 + y^2 + 2x-3 = 0$$

The equation of the circle passing through the intersection of the two circles $s_1 = 0$ and $s_2 = 0$ is given by the relation $s_2 + \lambda s_1 = 0$

i.e. $$x^2 + y^2 + 2x-3 + \lambda (x^2 + y^2-4) = 0$$

$$x^2 + y^2 + 2x-3 + \lambda x^2 + \lambda y^2-4\lambda = 0$$

$$x^2 (1 + \lambda) + y^2 (1 + \lambda) + 2x-(3 + 4\lambda) = 0$$

i.e. $$x^2 + y^2 + \frac{2x}{1 + \lambda} - \frac{(3 + 4\lambda)}{1 + \lambda} = 0$$

Here $$g = -\frac{1}{1 + \lambda} \qquad f = 0 \qquad c = -\frac{(3 + 4\lambda)}{(1 + \lambda)}$$

Radius of the circle $= \sqrt{g^2 + f^2 - c}$

$$= \sqrt{\frac{1}{(1+\lambda)^2} + \frac{(3+4\lambda)}{(1+\lambda)}} = \sqrt{\frac{1+(3+4\lambda)(1+\lambda)}{(1+\lambda)^2}}$$

$$= \sqrt{\frac{1+3+3\lambda+4\lambda+4\lambda^2}{(1+\lambda)^2}} = \sqrt{\frac{4\lambda^2+7\lambda+4}{(1+\lambda)^2}}.$$

i.e. square of the radius of the circle

$$\equiv \frac{4\lambda^2+7\lambda+4}{(1+\lambda)^2} = 16$$

$$4\lambda^2 + 7\lambda + 4 = 16(1 + 2\lambda + \lambda^2)$$

$$4\lambda^2 + 7\lambda + 4 = 16 + 32\lambda + 16\lambda^2$$

i.e. $\quad 12\lambda^2 + 25\lambda + 12 = 0$

$$\lambda = \frac{-25 \pm \sqrt{(25)^2 - 4\cdot 12\cdot 12}}{2\cdot 12}$$

$$\lambda = \frac{-25 \pm \sqrt{625-576}}{24}$$

$$\lambda = \frac{-25 \pm \sqrt{49}}{24}$$

$$\lambda = \frac{-25 \pm 7}{24} = \frac{-32}{24} \text{ or } \frac{-18}{24}$$

So the equation of the circle is given by

$$x^2 + y^2 + 2x - 3 - \frac{4}{3}(x^2 + y^2 - 4) = 0$$

i.e. $\quad 3x^2 + 3y^2 + 6x - 9 - 4x^2 - 4y^2 + 16 = 0$

i.e. $\quad -x^2 - y^2 + 6x + 7 = 0$

i.e. $\quad x^2 + y^2 - 6x - 7 = 0$

and $\quad x^2 + y^2 + 2x - 3 - \frac{3}{4}(x^2 + y^2 - 4) = 0$

i.e. $\quad 4x^2 + 4y^2 + 8x - 12 - 3x^2 - 3x^2 - 3y^2 + 12 = 0$

i.e. $\quad x^2 + y^2 + 8x = 0$

Problem 16 Find the radical axis of the pair of circles

$$x^2 + y^2 = 144$$

and $\quad x^2 + y^2 - 15x + 11y = 0$

The equation of the two circles are

$$s_1 \equiv x^2 + y^2 - 144 = 0 \qquad (1)$$

$$s_2 \equiv x^2 + y^2 - 15x + 11y = 0 \qquad (2)$$

Radical axis of the two circles $s_1 = 0$ and $s_2 = 0$ is given by

$$s_1 - s_2 = 0$$

i.e. $x^2 + y^2 - 144 - x^2 - y^2 + 15x - 11y = 0$

i.e. $$15x - 11y - 144 = 0 \quad \textbf{Ans.}$$

Problem 17 Find the radical axis of the pair of circles

$$x^2 + y^2 + 2x + 3y - 7 = 0$$

and $$x^2 + y^2 - 2x - y + 1 = 0$$

and find the length of their common chord.

Solution The equation of the two circle are

$$s_1 = x^2 + y^2 + 2x + 3y - 7 = 0$$

$$s_2 = x^2 + y^2 - 2x - y + 1 = 0$$

The equation of the radical axis is given by

$$s_1 - s_2 = 0$$

i.e. $x^2 + y^2 + 2x + 3y - 7 - x^2 - y^2 + 2x + y - 1 = 0$

$$4x + 4y - 8 = 0$$

i.e. $$4(x + y - 2) = 0$$

i.e. $$x + y = 2$$

i.e. $$x - y - 2 = 0$$

Now we have to find the equation of a circle whose diameter is the common chord of the two circles. Then the diameter of the circle is the length of the common chord.

Equation of the circle which passes through the intersection of the circle (1) and the line $x + y - 2 = 0$ is given by

$$s_1 + k(x + y - 2) = 0$$

i.e. $$x^2 + y^2 + 2x + 3y - 7 + k(x + y - 2) = 0$$

i.e. $$x^2 + y^2 + 2x + 3y - 7 + kx + ky - 2k = 0$$

i.e. $$x^2 + y^2 + x(k + 2) + y(k + 3) - (7 + 2k) = 0 \qquad (3)$$

The centre of this circle is

$$\left(-\frac{k+2}{2} - \frac{k+3}{2}\right)$$

Equation (3) represents the equation of a circle whose diameter is the common chord if the centre $\left(-\frac{k+2}{2}, -\frac{k+3}{2}\right)$ lies on the line

$$x + y - 2 = 0$$

i.e. $$-\frac{(k+2)}{2}+(-1)\frac{(k+3)}{2}-2=0$$

$$-k-2-k-3=4$$

$$-2k=9$$

$\Rightarrow$ $$k=-\frac{9}{2}$$

So the equation of the circle is

$$x^2+y^2+2x+3y-7-\frac{9}{2}(x+y-2)=0$$

i.e. $$2x^2+2y^2+4x+6y-14-9x-9y+18=0$$

i.e. $$2x^2+2y^2-5x-3y+4=0$$

i.e. $$x^2+y^2-\frac{5}{2}x-\frac{3}{2}y+2=0$$

Here $$g=-\frac{5}{4},\ f=-\frac{3}{4},\ c=2$$

radius of the circle $$=\sqrt{g^2+f^2-c}$$

$$=\sqrt{\frac{25}{16}+\frac{9}{16}-2}$$

$$=\sqrt{\frac{34-32}{16}}=\frac{\sqrt{2}}{16}=\frac{\sqrt{2}}{4}$$

Length of the common chard

Diameter of the axit $2x$ Radius of the circle

$$=2\frac{\sqrt{2}}{4}=\frac{\sqrt{2}}{2}$$

Length of the common chard $=\dfrac{\sqrt{2}}{2}$ **Ans.**

Problem 18 Prove that the length of the common chord of the circle

$$x^2\div y^2+2\lambda x+c=0$$

and $$x^2+y^2-2\mu y-c=0 \text{ is}$$

$$2\sqrt{\frac{(\lambda^2-c)(u^2+c)}{\lambda^2+\mu^2}}$$

Solution Equations of the two circles is

$$s_1\equiv x^2+y^3+2\lambda x+c=0 \tag{1}$$

$$s_2\equiv x^2+y^2+2\mu y-c=0 \tag{2}$$

The equation of the radical axis is given by

$$s_1 - s_2 = 0$$

i.e. $$2(\lambda x - 2\mu y + 2c) = 0$$

i.e. $$\lambda x - \mu y + c = 0$$

i.e. equation of the line AB is

$$\lambda x - \mu y + c = 0$$

Radius of the circle (1) is given by $\sqrt{\lambda^2 - c}$

Centre of the circle (1) is $(-\lambda, 0)$

Length of the perpendicular from $(-\lambda, 0)$ to the line

$\lambda x - by + b = 0$ is given by

$$OP = \frac{\lambda(-\lambda) + \mu \cdot 0 + c}{\sqrt{\lambda^2 + u^2}}$$

$$OP = \frac{-\lambda^2 + c}{\sqrt{\lambda^2 + u^2}} = -\frac{(\lambda^2 - c)}{\sqrt{\lambda^2 + u^2}}$$

$$OA^2 = (\sqrt{\lambda^2 - c})^2 = \lambda^2 - c$$

$$AP^2 = OA^2 - OP^2$$

$$AP =^2 (\lambda^2 - c) - \frac{\{-(\lambda^2 - c)\}^2}{\lambda^2 + \mu^2}$$

$$AP^2 = (\lambda^2 + u^2)\frac{(\lambda^2 - c) - (\lambda^2 - c)^2}{(\lambda^2 + u^2)}$$

$$AP^2 = \sqrt{\frac{\lambda^2 - c)(\lambda^2 + \mu^2) - (y^2 - c)^2}{\lambda^2 + \mu^2}}$$

$$= \sqrt{\frac{\lambda^4 + \lambda^2 u^2 - c\lambda^2 - cu^2 - (\lambda^4 - 2c\lambda^2 + c^2)}{(\lambda^2 + u^2)}}$$

$$= \sqrt{\frac{\lambda^4 + \lambda^2 \mu^2 - c\lambda^2 - c\mu^2 - \lambda^4 + 2c\lambda^2 - c^2}{(\lambda^2 + \mu^2)}}$$

$$= \sqrt{\frac{\lambda^2 \mu^2 + c\lambda^2 - c\mu^2 - c^2}{(\lambda^2 + \mu^2)}}$$

$$= \sqrt{\frac{u^2(\lambda^2 - c) + c(\lambda^2 - c}{(\lambda^2 + \mu^2)}}$$

$$= \sqrt{\frac{(\lambda^2 - c)(\mu^2 + c)}{(\lambda^2 + \mu^2)}}$$

Length of the cemmon coord

$$AB = 2AP$$

$$= 2\sqrt{\frac{(\lambda^2 - c)(\mu^2 + c)}{(\lambda^2 + \mu^2)}}$$

(*Proved*)

Problem 19 Find the radical centres of the circles

$$x^2 + y^2 = 9,\ x^2 + y^2 - 2x - 2y = 5$$

and $\quad x^2 + y^2 + 4x + 6y = 19$

Solution We have the three circles given by

$$s_1 \equiv x^2 + y^2 - 9 = 0 \qquad (1)$$

$$s_2 \equiv x^2 + y^2 - 2x - 2y - 5 = 0 \qquad (2)$$

$$s_3 = x^2 + y^2 + 4x + 6y - 19 = 3 \qquad (3)$$

The radical centre of (1) and (2) is given by

$$s_1 - s_2 = 0$$

i.e. $\quad x^2 + y^2 - 9 - x^2 - y^2 + 2x + 2y + 5 = 0$

i.e. $\quad 2x + 2y - 4 = 0$

i.e. $\quad x + y - 2 = 0 \qquad (4)$

Radical centre of (2) and (3) is given by

$s_2 - s_3 = 0 \quad$ i.e. $x^2 + y^2 - 2x = 2y - 5 - x^2 - y^2 - 4x - 6y + 19 = 0$

i.e. $\quad -6x - 8y + 14 = 0$

$$3x + 4x - 7 = 0 \qquad (5)$$

The co-ordinate of the radical centre is obtained by solving equations (4) and (5).

$$x - y - 2 = 0$$

ond $\quad 3x + 4y - 7 = 0$

$$3x + 3y = 6 = 0$$

$$3x + 4y - 7 = 0$$

$$0 - y + 1 = 0$$

i.e. $\quad y = 1$

Then $\quad 1 + x - 2 = 0$

$$x - 1 = 3$$

i.e. $\quad x = 1$

Thus the co-ordinate of the radical centre is (1, 1).

18

Coaxial Circles

A system of circles is said to be coaxial when they have a common radical axis, that is, the radical axis of each pair of circles of the system is the same.

The equation to a coaxial system can be writtcn as

$$x^2 + y^2 + 2gx + c = 0$$

Where g isa parameter and c is a constant.

Radical axis meets the circle in the points

$$(0, \sqrt{-c}) \text{ and } (0, -\sqrt{-c})$$

Limiting points of a coaxal system

Definition The centres of the circles of a coaxel system which are of zero radius are called the limiting points of the coaxial system.

The equation of circles of the coaxal system be

$$x^2 + y^2 + 2gx + c = 0$$

It can be written as

$$(x + g)^2 + y^2 = g^2 - c$$

If this circle has a zero radius, then

$$g^2 - c = 0$$

$$\Rightarrow \qquad g^2 = c$$

$$\Rightarrow \qquad g = \pm \sqrt{c}$$

i.e. The centres of such circles are $(\sqrt{c}, 0)$ and $(-\sqrt{c}, 0)$ which are the two limiting points of the coaxal system.

Remember

The limiting points are real if the circles of the system intersect in imaginary points and the limiting points are imaginary if they intersect in real points.

Remember

(1) If L and L_1 be the liming points of a system of coaxial circles, the polar of either of these points with respect to any circle of the system passes through the other.

(2) If $x^2 + y^2 + 2gx + c = 0$ be the coaxal system of circles then

$$x^2 + y^2 + 2fy - c = 0$$

represent a coaxal system of circles whose member cuts the members of the first system orthogonally.

Where the value of f will be different for different members of the system and c will be same for all of them or

We can say that equations of the orthogonal coaxal system can be written

as $$x^2 + y^2 + 2gx + c = 0$$

and $$x^2 + y^2 + 2fy - c = 0$$

R Properties of orthogonal systems

(i) If one system of two orthogonal systems is of intersecting species, the other is of non-intersecting species; in other words, if one possesses limiting points, the other does not.

(ii) Every circle of one system passes through the limiting points, of the other system.

(iii) The centres of the circles of one system lie on the radical axis of the other system.

(iv) The length of the tangent from the centre of any circle of one system to circle of another system is equal to the radius of the first circle.

Remember all the properties

Problem 1 Find the limiting points of the system of circles of which two members are

$$x^2 + y^2 - 6x - 6y + 4 = 0$$

and $$x^2 + y^2 - 2x - 4y + 3 = 0$$

Solution The radical axis of the system is

$$x^2 + y^2 - 6x - 6y + 4 - x^2 - y^2 + 2x + 4y - 3 = 0$$

i.e. $$-4x - 2y + 1 = 2$$

i.e. $$4x + 2y - 1 = 0$$

Therefore the equation to the system of circles coaxal with the given circle is

$$x^2 + y^2 - 2x - 4y + 3 + k\,(4x + 2y - 1) = 0$$

i.e $$x^2 + y^2 - 2x - 4y + 3 + 4kx + 2ky - k = 0$$

i.e. $$x^2 + y^2 - 2x\,(1 - 2k) - 2y\,(2 - k) + (3 - k) = 0 \quad (1)$$

The centre of the circle is

$$[(1-2k), (2-k)] \quad (2)$$

Radius of the circle $= \sqrt{(1-2k)^2 + (2-k)^2-(3-k)}$

$$= \sqrt{1 + 4k^2-4k + 4-4k + k^2-3 + k}$$

$$= \sqrt{5k^2-7k + 2}$$

If radius becomes zero then

$$\sqrt{5k^2-7k + 2 = 0}$$

i.e. $5k^2-7k + 2 = 0$

i.e. $5k^2-5k-2k + 2 = 0$

i.e. $5k(k-1)-2(k-1) = 0$

i.e. $(k-1)(5k-2) = 0$

i.e. either $k = 1$ or $k = \frac{2}{5}$

Putting the values of k in (2) we have the co-ordinate of the centre

$$(-1, 1) \quad \text{and} \quad \left(\frac{1}{5}, \frac{8}{5}\right)$$

Thus the limiting point are

$$(-1, 1) \quad \text{and} \quad \left(\frac{1}{5}, \frac{8}{5}\right)$$

Problem 2 Find the limiting points of the system

$$x^2 + y^2 + 2x + 4y + 7 = 0$$

and $x^2 + y^2 + 5x + y + 4 = 0$

Solution The members of the coaxal circles are

$$s_1 \equiv x^2 + y^2 + 2x + 4y + 7 = 0 \quad (1)$$

$$s_2 \equiv x^2 + y^2 + 5x + y + 4 = 0 \quad (2)$$

The equation of the coaxal circle is given by

$$s_1-s_2 = 0$$

i.e. $x^2 + y^2 + 2x + 4y + 7-x^2-y^2-5x-y-4 = 0$

iie. $-3x + 3y + 3 = 0$

i.e. $x-y=3 = 0$

Now equation of the coaxal circle is the circle passing through the intersection of the circle $x^2 + y^2 + 2x + 4y + 7 = 0$ and the line $x-y-3 = 0$ is

$$(x^2 + y^2 + 2x + 4y + 7) + k(x-y-3) = 0 \quad (2)$$

i.e. $x^2 + y^2 + 2x + 4y + 7 + kx-ky-3k = 0$

i.e. $x^2 + y^2 + x(k + 2) + y(4-k) + 7-3k = 0$

Centre of the circle is

$$-\frac{(k+2)}{2}, -\frac{4-k)}{2}$$

and the radius is

$$\sqrt{\left(\frac{k+2}{2}\right)^2+\left(\frac{4-k}{2}\right)^2-(7-3k)}$$

$$=\sqrt{\frac{k^2+4k+4}{4}-\frac{16-8k+k^2}{4}-(7-3k)}$$

$$=\sqrt{\frac{k^2+4k+4+16-8k+k^2-(7-3k)\,4}{4}}$$

$$=\sqrt{\frac{k^2+4k+4+16-8k+k^2-28+12k}{4}}$$

$$=\sqrt{\frac{2k^2-8}{4}}$$

If radius of the circle is zero

$$\sqrt{\frac{2k^2-8}{4}}=0$$

i.e. $2k^2-8=8$

i.e. $2k^2=4$

$$k=\pm 2$$

Thus the centre of the circle is zero radius is $(-2, 1)$ and $(0; -3)$ **Ans.**

Problem 3 Find the equation of the circle which passes through the origin and belongs to the coaxal system whose limiting points are (1, 2) and (3, 4).

Solution The limiting points are the Point circles with zero radius) of the coaxial system and hence their equations are

$$(x-1)^2+(y-2)^2=0$$

And $(x-3)^2+(y-4)^2=0$

The equations of any circle belonging to this sytem is

$$(x-1)^2+(y-2)^2+k\,[x-3)^2+(y-4)^2]=0$$

This will pass through the origin if

$$1^2+2^2+k\,[3^2+4^2]=0$$

$$1+4+k\,(9+16)=0$$

$$5+25\,k=0$$

i.e. $$25k = -5$$

i.e. $$k = -\frac{5}{25}$$

i.e. $$k = -\frac{1}{5}$$

Hence the equation of the required circle is

$$(x-1)^2 + (y-2)^2 + \left(-\frac{1}{5}\right)[(x-3)^2 + (y-4)^2] = 0$$

i.e. $$(x^2-2x+1) + (y^2-4y+4) - \frac{1}{5}[x^2-6x+9+y^2-8y+16] = 0$$

i.e. $$5x^2-10x+5+5y^2-20y+20-x^2+6x-9-y^2+8y-16 = 0$$

i.e. $$4x^2+4y^2-4x-12y = 0$$

i.e. $$4(x^2+y^2-x-3y) = 0$$

i.e. $$x^2+y^2-x-3y = 0$$

Which is the required equation of the co axal circles.

Problem 4 Prove that the limiting points of the system

$$x^2 + y^2 + 2gx + c + \lambda(x^2 + y^2 + 2fy + k) = 0$$

Subtend a right angle at the origin if

$$\frac{c}{g^2} + \frac{k}{f^2} = 2$$

Solution The equation of the circle can be written as

$$x^2 + y^2 + 2gx + c + \lambda x^2 + \lambda y^2 + 2f\lambda y + 2f\lambda y + \lambda k = 0$$

i.e. $$x^2(1+\lambda) + y^2(1+\lambda) + 2gx + 2f\lambda y + (c+\lambda k) = 0$$

i.e. $$x^2 + y^2 + \frac{2g}{(1+\lambda)}x + \frac{2f\lambda}{(1+\lambda)}y + \frac{(c+\lambda k)}{(1+\lambda)} = 0$$

Radius of the circle is given by

$$r = \sqrt{\frac{(-g)^2}{(1+\lambda)^2} + \frac{(-f\lambda)^2}{(1+\lambda)^2} - \frac{(c+\lambda k)}{(1+\lambda)}}$$

$$r^2 = \frac{g^2}{(1+\lambda)^2} + \frac{f^2\lambda^2}{(1+\lambda)^2} - \frac{c+\lambda k}{(1+\lambda)}$$

$$r^2 = \frac{g^2 + f^2\lambda^2 - (c+\lambda k)(1+\lambda)}{(1+\lambda)^2}$$

For the limiting points we should have

$$r = 0$$

i.e. $$r^2 = 0$$

i.e. $$g^2 + f^2 \lambda^2 - (c + \lambda k)(1 + \lambda) = 0$$

i.e. $$(c + \lambda k)(1 + \lambda) - g^2 - f^2\lambda^2 = 0$$

$$c + \lambda k + c\lambda + \lambda^2 k - g^2 - f^2 \lambda^2 = 0$$

$$\lambda^2 (k - f^2) + \lambda(c + \lambda)1 + (c - g^2) = 0 \tag{2}$$

This is a quadratic equation in λ Hence there will be two limiting points, corresponding to the two roots this equation

Let the two roots be λ_1 and λ_2

The centre of the circle (1) is given by $\left(\frac{-g}{1 + \lambda}, \frac{-f\lambda}{1 + \lambda}\right.$

Hence the co-ordinates of the two limiting points are

$$\left(-\frac{g}{1 + \lambda_1}, -\frac{f\lambda_1}{1 + \lambda_1}\right) \text{ and } \left(-\frac{g}{1 + \lambda_2}, -\frac{\lambda_2 f}{1 + \lambda_2}\right)$$

Let 0 (0, 0) be the origin and the two limiting points are A and B. Given that

$$< AOB = 90^\circ$$

i.e. $$OA \perp OB$$

Slope of the line OA is

$$\frac{O - x - \frac{f\lambda_1}{1 + \lambda_1}}{O - x - \frac{g}{1 + \lambda_1}} = \frac{\frac{f\lambda_1}{1 + \lambda_1}}{\frac{g}{1 + \lambda_1}}$$

i.e. $$\frac{f\lambda_1}{1 + \lambda_1} \cdot \frac{1 + \lambda_1}{g}$$

Slope of the line OB is

$$= \frac{O - X - \frac{\lambda_2 f}{1 + \lambda_2}}{O - X - \frac{g}{1 + \lambda_2}}$$

$$= \frac{\lambda_2 f}{1 + \lambda_2} \times \frac{1 + \lambda_2}{g}$$

Since $OA \perp r\ OB$

$$\frac{f\lambda_1}{g} \times \frac{\lambda_2 f}{g} = -1$$

$$f^2 \lambda_1 \lambda_2 + g^2 = 0$$

But from equation (2)

$$\lambda_1 \lambda_2 = \frac{c-g^2}{k-f^2}$$

So
$$f^2 \frac{(c-g^2)}{(k-f^2)} + g^2 = 0$$

i.e.
$$f^2 (c-g^2) + g^2 (k-f^2) = 0$$

i.e.
$$cf^2 - f^2g^2 + kg^2 - f^2g^2 = 0$$

$$cf^2 + kg^2 = 2f^2g^2$$

Dividing both sides with f^2g^2 we have

$$\frac{c}{g^2} + \frac{k}{f^2} + 2$$

Which is the required condition that the limiting points of the system

$$x^2 + y^2 + 2gx + c + \lambda (x^2 + y^2 + 2fy + k) = 0$$

Subtend a right angle at the origin. *(Proved)*

Problem 5 Find the general equation of the system of co axal cirles containing the circles $x^2 + y^2 = 9$ and the limiting point (2, 3). Find also the other liming point.

The limiting point is a circle of zero radius

Limiting point (2, 3) is given by

$$(x-2)^2 + (y-3)^2 = 0$$

i.e.
$$x^2 - 4x + 4 + y^2 - 6y + 9 = 0$$

Equation of the system of co axal circles containing the circle $x^2 + y^2 - 9 = 0$ and the limiting point (2, 3) is given by

$$(x-2)^2 + (y-3)^2 + k (x^2 + y^2 - 9) = 0$$

$$x^2 - 4x + 4 + y^2 - 6y + 9 + kx^2 + ky^2 - 9k = 0$$

i.e.
$$x^2 (1 + k) + y^2 (1 + k) - 4x - 6y + (13 - 9k) = 0$$

$$x^2 + y^2 - \frac{4}{(1 + k)} x - \frac{6y}{1 + k} + \frac{13-9k}{(1 + k)} = 0$$

Centre of this circle is

$$\left(-\frac{2}{1 + k}, -\frac{3}{1 + k}\right)$$

The radius of this circle is

$$\sqrt{\left(-\frac{2}{1 + k}\right)^2 + \left(-\frac{3}{1 + k}\right)^2 - \left(\frac{13-9k}{1 + k}\right)}$$

$$= \sqrt{\frac{4}{(1 + k)^2} + \frac{9}{(1 + k)^2} - \frac{(13-9k)}{1 + k}}$$

$$\sqrt{\frac{13}{((1+k)^2} - \frac{(13-9k)}{(1+k)}} = \sqrt{\frac{13-(13-9.)(1+k)}{(1+k)^2}}$$

$$= \sqrt{13-\left\{\frac{13+13k-9k-9k^2}{(1+k)^2}\right\}}$$

$$= \sqrt{\frac{13-(13+4k-9k^2)}{(1+k)^2}}$$

i.e. $$= \sqrt{\frac{9k-4k}{(1+k)^2}}$$

If the radius is zero then

$$9k^2-4k = 0$$

$$9k = 4$$

$$k = \frac{4}{9}$$

Putting the values of $k = \frac{4}{9}$ in (1) the equation of the system of co-axal circle is given by

$$x^2+y^2-4x-6y+13+\frac{4}{9}(x^2+y^2-9) = 0$$

i.e. $$9x^2+9y^2-36x-54y+117+4x^2+4y^2-36$$

i.e. $$13x^2+13y^2-36x-54y+81 = 0$$

i.e. $$x^2+y^2-\frac{36}{13}x-\frac{54}{13}y+\frac{81}{13} = 0$$

Which is the required equation of the system of coaxal circles. **Ans.**

Problem 6 The origin is a limiting point of a system of co-axal circles of which $x^2+y^2+2gx+2fy+c=0$ is a member. Find the co-ordinates of the other limiting point.

Solution The limiting point (0, 0) is a circle of radius zero and the centre at the point (0, 0).

The equation of the limiting point is given by

$$(x-0)^2+(y-0)^2 = 0$$

i.e. $$x^2+y^2 = 0 \qquad (1)$$

Now the equation of the co-axal system of circles is given by

$$x^2+y^2+2gx+2fy+k(x^2+y^2)+c = 0$$

i.e. $$x^2+y^2+2gx+2fy+kx^2+ky^2+c = 0$$

$$x^2+(1+k)+y^2(1+k)+2gx+2fy+c = 0$$

$$x^2+y^2+\frac{2gx}{1+k}x+\frac{2f}{1+k}y+\frac{c}{1+k}$$

Centre of this system of co-axal circles is

$$\left(-\frac{g}{1+k},-\frac{f}{1+k}\right).$$

The radius of this circle is

$$\sqrt{\frac{g^2}{(1+k)^2}+\frac{f^2}{(1+k)^2}-\frac{c}{(1+k^2)}}=\sqrt{\frac{g^2+f^2-c(1+k)}{(1+k)^2}}$$

If the radius of the circle is zero then

$$\frac{g^2+f^2-c(1+k)}{(1+k)^2}=0$$

i.e. $\quad g^2+f^2-c(1+k)=0$

i.e. $\quad g^2+f^2-c-ck=0$

i.e. $\quad ck=g^2+f^2-c$

$$k=\frac{g^2+f^2-c}{c}$$

Thus the cente of the co-axal circle of zero radius is

$$\left(-\frac{g}{1+k},-\frac{f}{1+k}\right)$$

i.e. $$\left(-\frac{g}{1+\frac{g^2+f^2-c}{c}},-\frac{f}{1+\frac{g^2+f^2-c}{c}}\right)$$

i.e. $$\left(-\frac{cg}{g^2+f^2},-\frac{cf}{g^2+f^2}\right)$$ **Ans.**

Problem 7 The lengths of the tangents from a fixed point to three circles of a coaxal system are t_1, t_2, t_3 respectively. If P, Q, R be the centres of the three circles, where Q lies between P and R on the line of centres, show that

$$QRt_1^2+RPt_2^2+PQt_3^2=0$$

Solution Let the lines of centres of the given coaxal system be the $x-$axis and the radicai axis be the y axis.

Then the equation of the three circles can be written as

$$x^2+y^2+2g_1x+c=0 \qquad (1)$$

$$x^2+y^2+2g_2x+c=0 \qquad (2)$$

$$x^2+y^2+2g_3x+c=0 \qquad (3)$$

Let (α, β) be the fixed point. By hypothesis

$$t_1^2=\alpha^2+\beta^2+2g_1\alpha+c$$

$$t_2^2=\alpha^2+\beta^2+2g_2\alpha+c$$

$$t_3^2=\alpha^2+\beta^2+2g_3\alpha+c$$

$$\underset{(-g_1,\,0)}{P}\qquad \underset{(-g_2\,0)}{Q}\qquad \underset{(-g_3\,0)}{R}$$

Then $QR = -g_3-(-g_2)$

$QR = -g_3 + g_2 = g_2-g_3$

$RP = g_3-g_1$ and $PQ = g_1-g_2$

Now $QRt_1^2 + RPt_2^2 + PQt_3^2$

$$= (g_2-g_3)(\alpha^2 + \beta^2 + 2g_1\alpha + c) + (g_3-g_1)(\alpha^2 + \beta^2 + 2g_2\alpha + c)$$
$$+ (g_1-g_2)(\alpha^2 + \beta^2 + 2g_3\alpha + c) = 0$$ *(Proved)*

Problem 8 If the circle $x^2 + y^2-2\alpha x-2\beta y + c = 0$ is the circle of a coaxal system having the origin as a limiting point, find the other limiting point.

Solution The limiting point (0, 0) is the point circle of the coaxal system having the radius equal to zero

i.e. $$(x-0)^2 + (y-0)^2 = 0$$

i.e. $$x^2 + y^2 = 0$$

The equation of the coaxal circle is given by

$$x^2 + y^2-2\alpha x-2\beta y + c + k(x^2 + y^2) = 0$$

i.e. $$x^2 + y^2-2\alpha x-2\beta y + c + kx^2 + ky^2 = 0$$

i.e. $$x^2(1 + k) + y^2(1 + k)-2\alpha x-2\beta y + c = 0$$

$$x^2 + y^2-\frac{2\alpha}{1 + k}x-\frac{2\beta}{1 + k}y + \frac{c}{1 + k} = 0$$

Centre of this circle is $\left(\frac{\alpha}{1 + k}, \frac{\beta}{1 + k}\right)$

The radius of this circle is

$$\sqrt{\frac{\alpha^2}{(1 + k)^2} + \frac{\beta^2}{(1 + k)^2}-\frac{c}{(1 + k)^2}} = \sqrt{\frac{\alpha^2 + \beta^2-c(1 + k)}{(1 + k)^2}}$$

If the radius of the circle is zero

Then $$\alpha^2 + \beta^2-c(1 + k) = 0$$

i.e. $$\alpha^2 + \beta^2-c = ck$$

i.e. $$k = \frac{\alpha^2 + \beta^2-c}{c}$$

Then the centre of the coaxal system of circle is

$$\left(\frac{\alpha c}{\alpha^2 + \beta^2}, \frac{\beta c}{\alpha^2 + \beta^2}\right)$$

Which the other limiting point of the coaxal system of circles. **Ans.**

Problem 9 Show that the equation of the coaxal system whose limiting points are (0, 0) and (a, b) is

$$x^2 + y^2 + k(2ax + 2by - a^2 - b^2) = 0$$

Solution Limiting points (0, 0) and (a, b) are the point circles of radius 0 and centres at the two points. Their equations are given by

$$(x-0) + (y-0)^2 = 0$$

i.e. $$S_1 \equiv x^2 + y^2 = 0 \qquad (1)$$

And $$(x-a)^2 + (y-b)^2 = 0$$

i.e. $$x^2 + a^2 + y^2 + b^2 - 2ax - 2by = 0$$

i.e. $$S_2 \equiv x^2 + y^2 - 2ax - 2by + a^2 + b^2 = 0 \qquad (2)$$

Equation of radical axis is given by $S_1 - S_2 = 0$

i.e. $$2ax + 2by - a^2 - b^2 = 0 \qquad (3)$$

Equation of the system of coaxal circles is given by

$$x^2 + y^2 + k(2ax + 2by - a^2 - b^2) = 0 \qquad \textit{(Proved)}$$

Problem 10 The origin is a limiting point of a system of coaxal circles of which $x^2 + y^2 + 2gx + 2fy + c = 0$ is a member. Show that the eqations of the circles of the orthogonal system are

$$(x^2 + y^2)(g + k) + c(x + ky) = 0$$

For different value of k.

Solution Since origin is a limiting point of a system of coaxal circles hence the equation of the circle of the system is a circle of zero radius and having its centre at (0, 0) and is therefore given by

$$(x-0)^2 + (y-0)^2 = 0$$

i.e, $$x^2 + y^2 = 0$$

The equation of the system of coaxial circles is given by

$$(x^2 + y^2 + 2gx + 2fy + c) + k(x^2 + y^2) = 0$$

i.e. $$y^2 + y^2 + 2gx + 2fy + c + k_1 x^2 + k_1 y^2 = 0$$

$$x^2(1 + k_1) + y^2(1 + k_1) + 2gx + 2fy + c = 0$$

i.e. $$x^2 + y^2 + \frac{2g}{1 + k_1}x + \frac{2f}{1 + k_1}y + \frac{c}{1 + k} = 0 \qquad (1)$$

Let the circle $x^2 + y^2 + 2px + 2qy + r = 0$
cut every circle given by (1) for different values of orthogenally then applying the condition of ortho-gonality, we have

$$2p\frac{g}{1 + k_1} + 2q\frac{f}{1 + k_1} = \frac{c}{1 + k_1} + r$$

i.e. $$2pg + 2qf = c + (1 + k_1)r$$

i.e. $$(2pg + 2qf - c - r) - k_1 r = 0$$

Since this relation holds for all values of k_1 so

$$2pg + 2qf - c = 0$$

And

$$r = 0$$

i.e.

$$2pg + 2qf - c = 0$$

$$2qf = c - 2pg$$

$$q = \frac{c-2pg}{2f}$$

Putting the value q and r the equation of the system of circles orthogenal to (1) is given by

$$x^2 + y^2 + 2px + 2\left(\frac{c-2pg}{2f}\right)y = 0$$

i.e.

$$x^2 + y^2 + 2px + \left(\frac{c-2pg}{2f}\right) = 0$$

$$x^2 + y^2 + 2p\left[x + \left(\frac{c-2pg}{2pf}\right)y\right] = 0$$

Now let

$$\frac{c-2pg}{2pf} = k$$

So that

$$c - 2pg = 2pkf$$

$$2p(g + kf) = c$$

i.e.

$$2p = \frac{c}{g+kf}$$

Equation of the sytem of circle is

$$x^2 + y^2 + \frac{c}{g+kf}(x + ky) = 0$$

i.e.

$$(x^2 + y^2)(g + kf) + c(x + ky) = 0$$

For different values of k. *(Proved)*

19

Parabola

Standard equation of the parabola is

$$y^2 = 4ax$$

Where $2a$ is the distance of focus from the directrix.

Theorem Find the condition that the line $y = mx + c$ may touch the parabola $y^2 = 4ax$.

Solution The parabola is

$$y^2 = 4ax \qquad (1)$$

And the straight line is

$$y = mx + c \qquad (2)$$

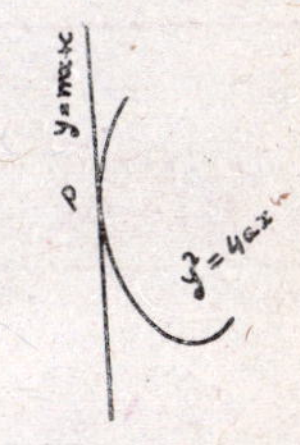

From (1) and (2) we have

$$(mx + c) = 4ax$$

i.e. $$m^2 x^2 + c^2 + 2mxc = 4ax$$

or $$m^2 x^2 + 2x(mc - 2a) + c^2 = 0$$

If the given line touches the parabola then the values of x given by (3) must be equal i.e.

$$[-2(mc - 2a)^2 = 4m^2 c^2$$

i.e. $$4(mc - 2a)^2 = 4m^2 c^2$$

i.e. $$m^2 c^2 + 4a^2 - 4acm = m^2 c^2$$

i.e. $$4a^2 = 4ac\, m$$

i.e. $$c = \frac{a}{m}$$

This is the required condition of tangency.

Putting the values of $c = \dfrac{a}{m}$ in the equation of the line

$$y = mx + c$$

$$y = mx + \frac{a}{m}$$

Thus $$y = mx + \frac{a}{m} \quad (1)$$

touches the parabola $y^2 = 4ax$ (1)

The co-ordinates of the point of contact can be obtained by solving (2) and (2)

$$\left(mx + \frac{a}{m}\right)^2 = 4ax$$

$$m^2 x^2 + \frac{a^2}{m^2} + 2x a \frac{a}{m} = ax$$

$$m^2 x^2 + \frac{a^2}{m^2} = 2ax$$

$$m^2 x^2 - 2ax + \frac{a^2}{m^2} = 0$$

i.e. $$\left((mx - \frac{a}{m}\right)^2 = 0$$

i.e. $$mx - \frac{a}{m} = 0$$

i,e. $$mx = \frac{a}{m}$$

i.e. $$x = \frac{a}{m^2}$$

Again $$y = m \cdot \frac{a}{m^2} + \frac{a}{m}$$

$$y = \frac{a}{m} + \frac{a}{m} = 2\frac{a}{m}$$

Remember (1) The point of contact is $\left(\frac{a}{m^2}, \frac{2a}{m}\right)$

Remember (2) The equation of the tangent at any point at^2, $2at$) of the parabola $y^2 = 4ax$ is

$$y \cdot 2at = 2a(x + at^2)$$

$$\text{or } yt = x + at^2$$

(3) The equation of the tangent at any point (x_1, y_1) of the parabola $y^2 = 4ax$ i.e. given by

$$\boxed{y\, y_1 = 2a\,(x + x_1)}$$

To find the equation of normal to the parabola $y^2 = 4ax$ at the point (x_1, y_1).

Equation of the parabola is

$$y^2 = 4ax$$

Then the equation of the tangent at the point (x_1, y_1) is given by

$$y\,y_1 = 2a\,(x + x_1)$$

$$y\,y_1 = 2ax + 2ax_1$$

$$y = \frac{2ax}{y_1} + \frac{2ax_1}{y_1}$$

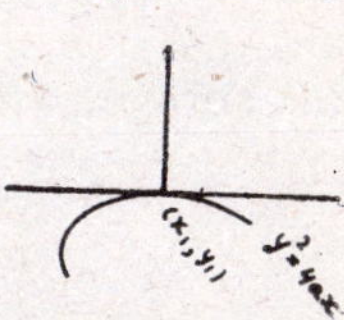

Which is of the form $y = mx + c$ where m is the slope of the line
The slope of the tangent

$$= \frac{2g}{y_1}$$

The normal at (x_1, y_1) is perpendicular to the tangent at (x_1, y_1)
So slope of the tangent x slope of the normal $= -1$
i.e. slope of the normal

$$= -\frac{1}{2a/y_1} = -\frac{y_1}{2a}$$

Hence the equation of the normal at the point $(x_1 + y_1)$ is given by

$$(y - y_1) = -\frac{y_1}{2a}(x - x_1)$$

Note (*i*) The equation of the normal at $(am^2, -2am)$ is

$$y + 2am = -\left(\frac{-2am}{2g}\right)(x - am^2)$$

$$y + 2am = mx - am^3$$

i.e. $$\boxed{y = mx - 2am - am^3}$$

Equation of the normal at the point $(am^2, -2am)$ is given by

$$\boxed{y = mx - 2am - am^3} \rightarrow \textbf{Remember}$$

Equation of the normal at thc point $(at^2, 2at)$ is

$$y - 2at = -\frac{2at}{2a}(x - at^2)$$

$$y - 2at = -tx + at^3$$

i.e. $$\boxed{y + tx = 2at + at^3} \rightarrow \textbf{Remember}$$

Theorem Show that three normals can in general, be drawn to a parabola from any point and these normals are such that

(i) The sum of their slopes = 0

(ii) The sum of the ordinates of their feet = 0 [*I.F.S.* 81, 84]

Let the equation of the parabola be

$$y^2 = 4ax \qquad (1)$$

Then the equation of the normal *at* $(am^2) - 2am)$ is

$$y = mx - 2am - am^3 \qquad (2)$$

If the normal passes through a fixed point $Q\ (x_1, y_1)$ then

$$y_1 - mx_1 - 2am - am^3$$

or
$$am^3 + (2a - x_1)\ x_1 + y_1 = 0 \qquad (3)$$

This equation is a cubic equation in m; hence if gives three values of m_1 say m_1, m_2, m_3. Corresponding to each of these scopes we get a normal passing through the point (x_1, y_1).

Hence from any point three normals can in general be drawn to a parabola. Since m_1, m_2, m_3 are the roots of equation (3)

So
$$m_1 + m_2 + m_3 = -\frac{\text{coefficient of } m^2}{\text{coefficient of } m^3}$$

$$m_1 + m_2 + m_3 = -\frac{0}{a} = 0$$

Hence the sum of the slopes of the normals of the parabola $y^2 = 4ax$ drawn from any point is zero.

(ii) The sum of ordinates of the feet of the three normals

$$= -2am_1 - 2am_2 - 2am_3$$

$$= -2a\ (m_1 + m_2 + m_3)$$

$$= -2a \times 0 = 0$$

Hence the sum of the ordinates of the three normals is zero.

Theorem Find the locus of the point of intersection of two perpendicular tangents to the parabola $y^2 = 4ax$

Equation of the parabola is

$$y^2 = 4ax \qquad (1)$$

Equation of any tangent to the parabola is (1)

$$y = mx + \frac{a}{m} \qquad (2)$$

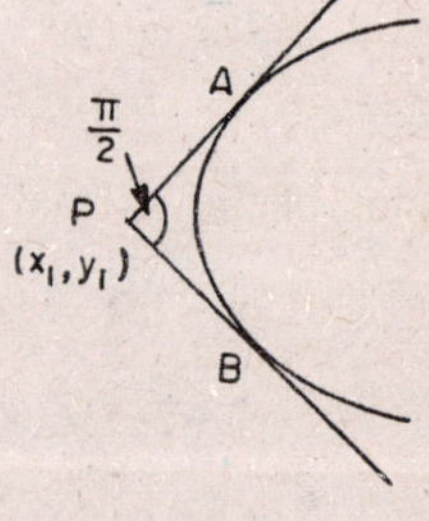

If it passes through the point (x_1, y_1) then

$$y_1 = mx_1 + \frac{a}{m}$$

$$my_1 = m^2\ x_1 + a$$

$$m^2\ x_1 - my_1 + a = 0$$

This is a quadratic equation in m. So it will give two values of $m \cdot m_1$, and m_2
$$m_1 m_2 = \frac{a}{x_1}$$

Since the two tangents are at right angles to each other

Therefore $$m_1 m_2 = -1$$

i.e. $$\frac{a}{x_1} = -1$$

i.e. $$a = -x_1$$

i.e. $$x_1 + a = 0$$

Locus of the point (x_1, y_1) is $x + a = 0$

which is the directrix of the parabola, hence the perpendicular tangents to a parabola always meet on the directrix of the parabola.

Remember Equation of the chord of contact of the tangents drawn from a point (x_1, y_1) to the parabola $y^2 = 4ax$ is given by

$$\boxed{yy_1 = 2a(x + x_1)}$$

Remember Polar of the point (x_1, y_1) with respect to the parabola

$y^2 = 4ax$ is given by

$$\boxed{yy_1 = 2a(x + x_1)}$$

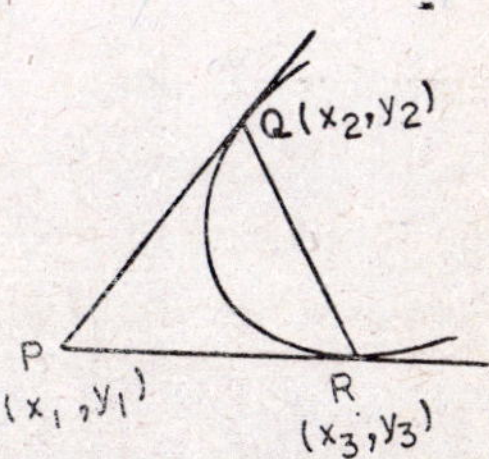

Remember (1) Equation of the chord of a parabola $y^2 = 4ax$ whose middle point is (x_1, y_1) is

$$\boxed{(y - y_1)\, y_1 = 2a(x - x_1)}$$

Remember (2) The equation of the pair of tangents from a point (x_1, y_1) to the parabola

$$y^2 = 4ax \text{ is}$$

$$ss_1 = T^2$$

i.e. $$[y^2 - 4ax][y_1^2 - 4ax_1] = [yy_1 - 2a(x + x_1)]^2$$

Remember (3) The equation of a chord of the parabola interms of its middle point (x_1, y_1) is $T = s_1$.

Theorem Prove that in a parabola the subnormal is of constant length.

Proof Let P be the point $(at^2, 2at)$ and PN be the ordinate $2at$ and PG the normal meeting the axis in G

$$ON = at^2,\ PN = 2at$$

Then NG = subnormal of the point P

The equation of the normal at P to the parabola is

$$y + tx = 2at + at^3 \qquad (1)$$

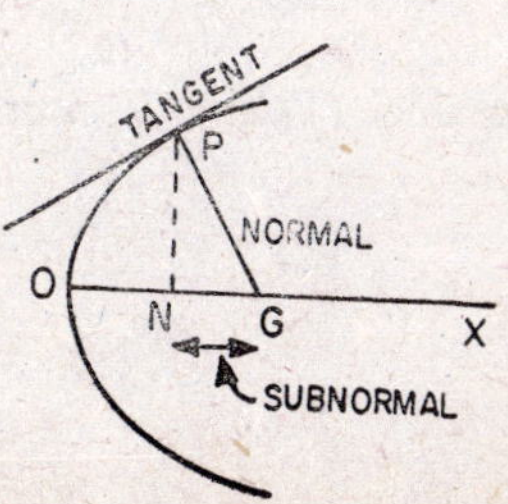

If meets the axis *at* G_1 whose equation is $y = 0$

From (1) for G $\quad tx = 2at + at^3$

$$x = \frac{2at + at^3}{t}$$

$$x = 2a + at^2$$

i.e. $\quad OG = 2a + at^2$

$$ON = at^2$$

Then $\quad NG = OG - ON$

$$NG = 2a + at^2 - at^2$$

$$NG = 2a \text{ which is constant}$$

Remember Equation of thc directrix

$$= x + a = 0.$$

The coordinate of s = (a, 0 [focus]

A is the vertex (0, 0) when equation of parabola is $\quad y^2 = 4ax$

A is the mid point of sz. parabola is the locus of a point which moves. So that its distance from the fixed point, called the focus is equal to its distance from the fixed straight llne, called the directr ix.

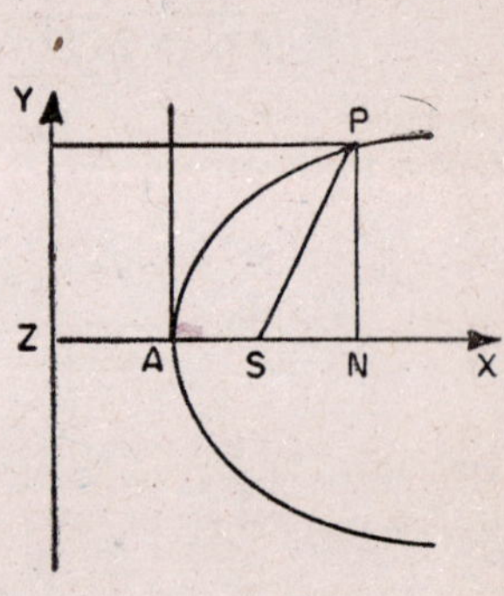

Problem 1 Show that the line $x \cos \alpha + y \sin \alpha = p$ touches the parabola $y^2 = 4ax$ if $p \cos \alpha + a \sin^2 \alpha = 0$ and that the point of contact is

$$(a \tan^2 \alpha, -2a \tan \alpha)$$

Let $\quad x \cos \alpha + y \sin \alpha = p \quad (1)$

touches the parabola.

Equation of the tangent to the parabola at the point (x_1, y_1) is given by

$$yy_1 = 2a(x + x_1)$$

i.e. $\quad yy_1 = 2ax + 2ax_1 \quad (2)$

Now since (1) and (2) represent the same line so

$$\frac{y_1}{\sin \alpha} = \frac{-2a}{\cos \alpha} = \frac{2ax_1}{p}$$

$$y_1 = -2a \tan \alpha$$

and $\quad x_1 = \dfrac{-p}{\cos \alpha}$

But (x_1, y_1) is on the parabola $y^2 = 4ax$

So it will satisfy this $\quad y_1^2 = 4ax_1$

$$4a^2 \tan^2 x = 4a\left(\frac{-p}{\cos \alpha}\right)$$

$$4a^2 \tan^2 \alpha = \frac{-4ap}{\cos \alpha}$$

$$p = -a \tan^2 \alpha \cos \alpha$$

$$p = -a \frac{\sin^2 \alpha}{\cos^2 \alpha} \cos \alpha$$

$$p \equiv -\frac{a \sin^2 \alpha}{\cos^2 \alpha} \tag{3}$$

Thus

$$x_1 = -\frac{p}{\cos \alpha}$$

$$x_1 = -\frac{\frac{(-a) \sin^2 \alpha}{\cos \alpha}}{\cos \alpha}$$

$$x_1 = a \frac{\sin^2 \alpha}{\cos^2 \alpha}$$

$$x_1 = a \tan^2 \alpha$$

Thus the point of contact is (x_1, y_1)

i.e. $\quad (a \tan^2 \alpha, -2a \tan \alpha)$

From the relation (3) we have

$$\boxed{p \cos \alpha + a \sin^2 \alpha = 0}$$

which is the required condition that the line

$$x \cos \alpha + y \sin \alpha = p$$

touches the parabola $y^2 = 4ax$ *(Proved)*

Problem 2 Prove that the straight line $y = m + c$ touches the parabola $y^2 = 4a(x + a)$ if

$$c = ma + \frac{a}{m}$$

Solution $\quad y^2 = 4a(x + a) \quad (1)$

is the equation of the parabola and let

$$y = mx + c \tag{2}$$

touches the parabola then solving equation (1) and (2) we have

$$(mx + c)^2 = 4a(x + a)$$

$$m^2 x^2 + c^2 + 2mxc = 4a(x + a)$$

$$m^2 x^2 + c^2 + 2mxc = 4ax + 4a^2$$

$$m^2 x^2 + 2mxc - 4ax + c^2 - 4a^2 = 0$$

$$m^2 x^2 + 2x(mc - 2a) + (c^2 - 4a^2) = 0$$

Since this is aquadratic equation in x and since $y = mx + c$ touches the parabola so the two values of x must be equal ann in ths case

$$4(mc - 2a)^2 - 4 \cdot m^2 (c^2 - 4a^2)^2 = 0$$

i.e.

$$(mc - 2a)^2 = m^2 (c^2 - 4a^2)$$

i.e.

$$m^2 c^2 + 4a^2 - 4amc = m^2 c^2 - 4a^2 m^2$$

$$4amc = 4a^2 + 4a^2 m^2$$

$$4amc = 4a^2 (1 + m^2)$$

$$mc = a(1 + m^2)$$

$$c = \frac{a}{m} + am$$

i.e.

$$\boxed{c = ma + \frac{a}{m}} \qquad \textit{(Proved)}$$

Which is the required condition that the line $y = mx + c$ touches the parabola

$$y^2 = 4a(x + a)$$

Problem 3 If the line $2x + 3y = 1$ touches the parabola $y^2 = 4ax$, find the length of the lakes rectum.

Solution Equation of the parabola is

$$y^2 = 4ax \qquad (1)$$

Equation of the tangent to (1) is

$$y = mx + \frac{a}{m} \qquad (3)$$

Since the line $2x + 3y = 1$ (4)

Touches the parabola

Camparing $y^2 = 4ax$

So (3) and (4) we have

$$\frac{1}{3} = \frac{m}{-2} = \frac{a/m}{1}$$

$$m = -\frac{2}{3}$$

and

$$\frac{a}{m} = \frac{1}{3}$$

$$ma = \frac{m}{3}$$

$$a = -\frac{2}{3} \times \frac{1}{3} = -\frac{2}{9}$$

$$a = -\frac{2}{9}$$

length of the latus rectum $= 4a$

$$= 4 \times \left(-\frac{2}{9}\right) = -\frac{8}{9}$$

Length of the latus rectium $= \frac{8}{9}$ in magnitude.

Problem 4 A straight line touches both $x^2 y^2 = 2a^2$ and $y^2 = 8ax$ show that its equation is $\quad y = \pm (x + 2a)$

Solution Let the line $\quad y = mx + c$

touches both the circles

$$x^2 + y^2 = 2a^2 \qquad (1)$$

and $\qquad y^2 = 8ax$

Equation (1) can be written as

$$x^2 + y^2 = (\sqrt{29})^2$$

So this represents a circle having centre at (0, 0) and radius actual to $\sqrt{2}\,a$
We know that the line $y = my + c$ touches the circle

$$x^2 + y^2 = a^2 \text{ if}$$

$$c = \pm a\sqrt{1 + m^2}$$

In this case $\qquad c = \pm \sqrt{2}\,a\sqrt{1 + m^2} \qquad$ **(3)**

Again the line $y = mx + c$ touches the parabola $y^2 = 4a\,x$ if

$$c = \frac{a}{m}$$

Here $\qquad c = \frac{2a}{m} \qquad (4)$

Hence from (3) and (4) we have

$$\pm \sqrt{2}\,a\sqrt{1 + m^2} = \frac{2a}{m}.$$

Squaring both sides

$$2a^2 (1 + m^2) = \frac{4a^2}{m^2}$$

$$m^4 + m^2 = 2$$

$$m^4 + m^2 - 2 = 0$$

i.e. $\quad m^4 + 2m^2 - m^2 - 2 = 0$

i.e. $m^2 (m^2 + 2) - 1 (m^2 + 2) = 0$

i.e. $\quad (m^2 - 1)(m^2 + 2) = 0$

Since $\quad m^2 + 2 \neq 0$

$$m^2 - 1 = 0$$

$$\Rightarrow \quad m^2 = 1$$

$$\Rightarrow \quad m^2 = \pm 1$$

So the equation of the line touching both the curves is given by

$$y = mx + c$$

$$y = \pm x \pm \frac{2a}{m}$$

$$y = \pm x \pm \frac{2a}{\pm 1}$$

$$y = \pm x \pm 2a$$

$$x = \pm (x + 2a) \qquad \textit{(Proved)}$$

Problem 5 Find the locus of the point of intersection of tangents to the parabola $y^2 = 4ax$, the angle between them being always a given α.

Solution Equation of the parabola is

$$y^2 = 4ax \qquad (1)$$

Then the equation of the tangent touching this parabola is

$$y = mx + \frac{a}{m}$$

$$\Rightarrow \quad y = \frac{m^2 x + a}{m}$$

$$\Rightarrow \quad my = m^2 x + 9$$

Let the $\quad \Rightarrow m^2 x - my + a = 0 \qquad (2)$

Which is a quadratic equation m

Thus m have two values say m_1 and m^2.

For the two values of m i.e. m_1 and m_2 (i.e. two different slopes) there are two tangents let the two tangents cut each other at a point $p\ (h, k)$.

Then (h, k) will satisfy the equation (2)

So $\quad m^2 h - mk + a = 0$

$$m_1 + m_2 = \frac{k}{h}$$

$$m_1 m_2 = \frac{a}{h}$$

Let θ be the angle between them then

$$\tan\theta = \pm\frac{m_1 - m_2}{1 + m_1 m_2}$$

$$\tan\theta = \pm\frac{\sqrt{(m_1 + m_2)^2 - 4m_1 m_2}}{1 + m_1 m_2}$$

$$\tan\alpha = \pm\frac{\sqrt{\frac{k^2}{h^2} - 4\frac{a}{h}}}{1 + m_1 m_2}$$

$$\tan\alpha = \frac{\sqrt{\frac{k^2}{h^2} - 4\frac{a}{h}}}{1 + a/h}$$

$$\tan\alpha = \pm\sqrt{\frac{k^2 - 4ah}{a + h}}$$

$$(a + h)\tan\alpha = \pm\sqrt{\frac{k^2 - 4ah}{a}}$$

squaring both sides we have

$$(a + h)^2\tan^2\alpha = k^2 - 4ah$$

Locus of the point (h, k) is given by

$$\boxed{(a + x)^2\tan^2\alpha = y^2 - 4ax} \qquad \textbf{Ans.}$$

Problem 6 Two tangents to a parabola $y^2 = 4ax$ meet at an angle of 45°, prove that the locus of the point of interscetion of the tangents is the curve

$$y^2 - 4ax = (x + a)^2$$

Solution Let the equation of the parabola is

$$y^2 = 4ax \qquad (1)$$

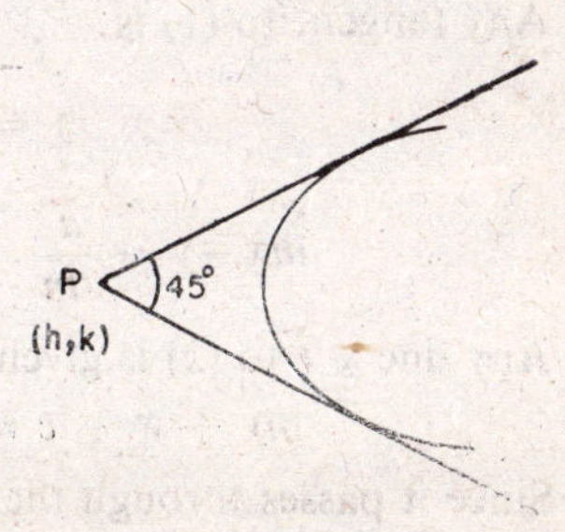

$y\ mx + \frac{a}{m}$ touches the parabola (1)

$$y = mx + \frac{a}{m}$$

i.e. $\quad my = m^2 x + a$

i.e. $\quad m^2 x - my + a = 0$

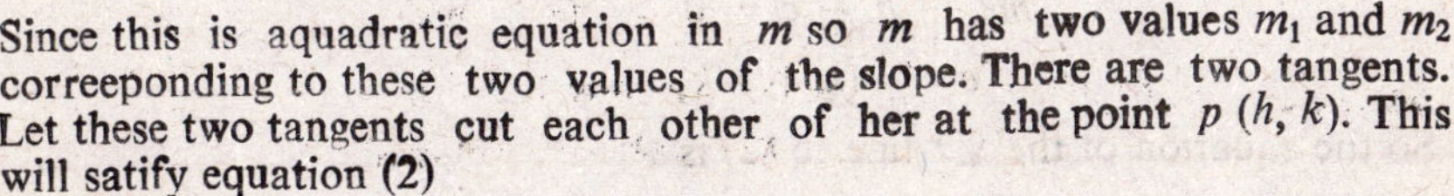
Since this is aquadratic equation in m so m has two values m_1 and m_2 correeponding to these two values of the slope. There are two tangents. Let these two tangents cut each other of her at the point $p\ (h, k)$. This will satify equation (2)

$$m^2 h - mk + a = 0$$

$$m_1 + m_2 = \frac{k}{h}$$

$$m_1 m_2 = \frac{a}{h}$$

Thc angle between the two tangents is 45°

$$\tan 45 = \pm \frac{m_1 - m_2}{1 + m_1 m_2}$$

i.e.

$$\tan 45 = \pm \frac{\sqrt{(m_1 + m_2)^2 - 4m_1 m_2}}{1 + m_1 m_2}$$

$$1 = \pm \frac{\sqrt{\frac{k^2}{h^2} - \frac{4a}{h}}}{1 + a/h}$$

$$1 = \pm \frac{\sqrt{k^2 - 4ah}}{a + h}$$

$$(a + h = \sqrt{k^2 - 4ah}$$

Squaring both sides we have

$$a + h)^2 = k^2 - ah \quad (3)$$

Locus of (h, k) is obtained by replacing h by x and k by y in (3)

$$(a + x)^2 = y^2 - 4ax \qquad \textbf{Ans.}$$

Problem 7 Find the locus of the foot of the perpendicular drawn from a fixed point to any tangent to a parabola.

Solution Equation of the parabola is

$$y^2 = 4ax \quad (1)$$

and the fixed point is (h, k).

Any tangent to (1) is

$$y = mx + \frac{a}{m}$$

$$mx - y + \frac{a}{m} = 0 \quad (2)$$

Any line ⊥r to (2) is given by

$$my + x + c = 0 \quad (3)$$

Since it passes through the point $(h_1 k)$ so

$$mk + h + c = 0$$

$$c = -(h + mk)$$

So the equation of the ⊥r line to (2) is

$$x + my - h - mk = 0$$

$$m(y - k) = h - x$$

$$m = \frac{h - x}{y - k}$$

Substituting the value of m in equation (2) we have

$$\left(\frac{h-x}{y-k}\right) x-y+\frac{(y-k)\, a}{(h-x)}=0$$

i.e. $x\,(h-x)^2-y\,(h-y)\,(y-k)+(y-k)^2\,a=0$

This is the required locus of the foot of the perpendicular.

Problem 8 Find the locus of the foot of the perpendicular drawn from the vertex of the parabola $y^2=4ax$ on any tangent to the parabola.

Solution Let A be the vertex of the parabola

$$y^2=4ax$$

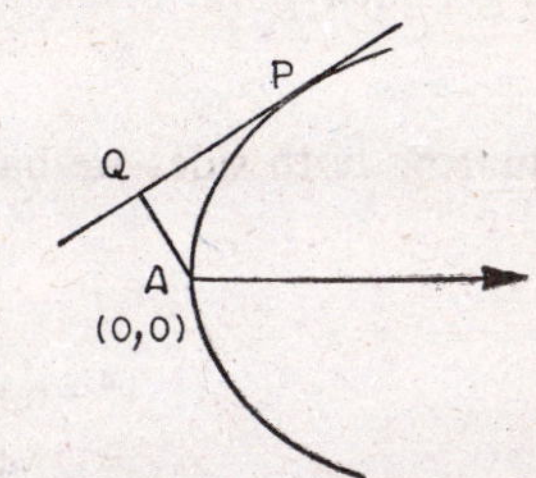

Then the co-ordinates of A is (0, 0)

Equation of any tangent to the parabola

$y^2=4ax$ is given by

$$y=mx+\frac{a}{m} \qquad (1)$$

Slope of the tangent is m

Slope of any line perpendicular to the tangent is $-\frac{1}{m}$

Then equation of the perpendicular line to the tangent is the equation of a straight line passing through (0, 0) and having slope $-\frac{1}{m}$

i.e. $$y-0=-\frac{1}{m}\,(x-0)$$

$$y=-\frac{x}{m}$$

$$m=-\frac{x}{y}$$

Putting the value of m in equation (1) we have

$$y=\frac{-x}{y}\cdot x+\frac{a}{-x/y}$$

$$y=\frac{-x^2}{y}-\frac{ay}{x}$$

$$xy^2=-x^3-ay^2$$

$$xy^2+x^3+ay^2=0 \qquad (2)$$

Equation (2) is the required locus of the point Q

Problem 9 Prove that the two parabolas $y^2 = 4ax$ and $x^2 = 4by$ by will cut one another at an angle

$$\tan^{-1} \frac{3a^{1/3}\, b^{1/3}}{2(a^{2/3} + b^{2/3})}$$

Solution Solving the equations of the two parabolas

$$y^2 = 4ax \tag{1}$$

and

$$x^2 = 4by \tag{2}$$

we get their point of inter section

$$y^2 = 4ax$$

Squaring both sides we have

$$y^4 = 16a^2\, x^2$$

$$y^2 = 16a^2\,(4by)$$

$$y^4 - 64a^2\, by = 0$$

$$y\,(y^3 - 64a^2\, b) = 0$$

$$y\,(y^3 - 4^3\, a^2\, b) = 0$$

So either $\qquad y = 0$

or $\qquad y^3 - 4^3\, a^2\, b = 0$

$$y^3 = 4^3\, a^2\, b$$

$$y = 4a^{2/3}\, b^{1/3}$$

So $\qquad y = 0$ and $y = 4a^{2/3}\, b^{1/5}$

Putting these two values in

$$y^2 = 4ax$$

$$0 = 4ax \text{ (if } y = 0)$$

$$\Rightarrow \qquad x = 0$$

$$16\, a^{4/3}\, b^{2/3} = 4ax$$

$$x = 4a^{4/3-1}\, b^{2/3}$$

$$x = 4a^{1/3}\, b^{2/3}$$

So their point of Intersection are (0,0) and $(4a^{1/3}\, b^{2/3}, 4a^{2/3}\, b^{1/3})$

Now the tangents to the parabola $y^2 = 4ax$ and $x^2 = 4by$ at the point $(4a^{1/3}\, b^{2/3}, 4a^{2/3}\, b^{1/3})$ are respectively.

$$y.4^{2/3}\, b^{1/3} = 2a\,(x + 4a^{1/3}\, b^{2/3})$$

Slope of this line

$$= \frac{2a}{4a^{2/3}\, b^{1/3}} = \frac{1}{2}\, \frac{a^{1/3}}{b^{1/3}} = \frac{1}{2} \left(\frac{a}{b}\right)^{1/3}$$

$$x \cdot 4a^{1/3}\, b^{2/3} = 2b\,(y + 4a^{2/3}\, b^{1/3})$$

Slope of this line

$$= \frac{4a^{1/3} b^{2/3}}{2b} = 2\frac{a^{1/3}}{b^{1/3}} = 2\left(\frac{a}{b}\right)^{1/3}$$

If θ be the angle between these tangents then

$$\tan\theta = \pm \frac{m_1 - m_2}{1 + m_1 m_2}$$

$$\tan\theta = \frac{\pm \frac{1}{2}\left(\frac{a}{b}\right)^{1/3} - 2\left(\frac{a}{b}\right)^{1/3}}{1 + \frac{1}{2}\left(\frac{a}{b}\right)^{1/3} 2\left(\frac{a}{b}\right)^{1/3}}$$

$$\tan\theta = \frac{\pm \frac{1}{2} a^{1/3} b^{-1/3} - 2a^{1/3} b^{-1/3}}{1 + a^{1/3} b^{-1/3} a^{1/3} b^{-1/3}}$$

$$\tan\theta = \pm \frac{-3a^{1/3} b^{-1/3}}{2(1 + a^{2/3} b^{-2/3})}$$

$$\tan\theta = \pm \frac{-3a^{1/3} b^{-1/3}}{2\left(1 + \frac{a^{2/3}}{b^{2/3}}\right)}$$

$$\tan\theta = \frac{3a^{1/3}/b^{1/3}}{2(a^{2/3} + b^{2/3})/b^{2/3}}$$

$$\tan\theta = \frac{3a^{1/3} b^{2/3}/b^{1/3}}{2(a^{2/3} + b^{2/3})} = \frac{3a^{1/3} b^{1/3}}{2(a^{2/3} + b^{2/3})}$$

$$\theta = \tan^{-1} \frac{3a^{1/3} b^{1/3}}{2(a^{2/3} + b^{2/3})}$$

Hence the two parabolas $y^2 = (4ax$ and $x^2 = 4by$ will cut one another at an angle

$$\tan^{-1} \frac{3a^{1/3} b^{1/3}}{2(a^{2/3} + b^{2/3})} \qquad \textit{(Proved)}$$

Problem 10 Prove that the locus of the middle points of all tangents drawn from points on the directrix to the parabola

$$y^2 = 4ax \text{ is}$$

$$y^2 (2x + a) = a(3x + a)^2$$

Solution Equation of the parabola is

$$y^2 = 4ax$$

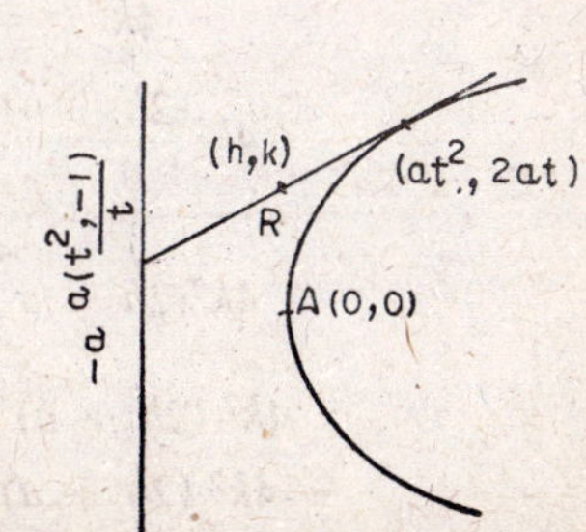

Equation of tangent at the point $(at^2, 2at)$ is given by

$$yt = x + at^2 \qquad (1)$$

Equation of the directrix is

$$x + a = 0 \qquad (2)$$

The co-ordinate of the point of intersection can be obtained by solving equation (1) and (2)

From equation (2) we have

$$x = -a$$

$$yt = -a + at^2$$

$$y = -\frac{a(1-t^2)}{t} = \frac{(at^2-a)}{t} = \frac{a(t^2-1)}{t}$$

Thus the co-ordinate of the point of intersection is

$$\left(-a, \frac{a(t^2-1)}{t}\right)$$

Let the co-ordinate of the middle point of the line intercepted between the directrix and the tangent at $(at^2, 2at)$ is (h, k)

then $$h = \frac{at^2-a}{2}$$

$$2h = at^2 - a$$

i.e. $$2h + a = at^2$$

$$t^2 = \frac{2h+a}{a} \qquad (3)$$

and $$k = \frac{\frac{a(t^2-1)}{t} + 2at}{2}$$

$$k = \frac{a(t^2-1)}{2t^2} + \frac{2at}{2}$$

$$k = \frac{at^2 - a + 2at^2}{2t}$$

$$2kt = 3at^2 - a$$

$$2kt = a(3t^2-1)$$

Squaring both sides we have

$$4k^2 t^2 = a^2(3t^2-1)^2$$

$$4k^2\frac{(2h+a)}{a} = a^2\left[\frac{3(2h+a)}{a} - 1\right]^2$$

$$4k^2(2h + a = a^3\left[\frac{6h+3a-a}{a}\right]^2$$

$$4k^2(2h+a) = a(6h+2a)^2$$

$$4k^2(2h+a) = 4a(3h+a)^2$$

Locus of the point $R(h, k)$ is given by

$$4y^2(2x + a) = 4a(3x + a)^2$$

i.e. $$y^2(2x + a) = 4a(3x + a)^2$$

Locus of point (h_1, k) is

$$\boxed{y^2(2x + a) = a(3x + a)^2} \qquad \textit{(Proved)}$$

Problem 11 If P, Q and R be three points on a parabola whose ordinates are in geometric progression. Prove that the tangents at P and R meets on the ordinate of Q. [*I.F.S. 83*]

Solution Let the three points P. Q and R are on the parabola

$$y^2 = 4ax$$

Let the co-ordinates of the points P, Q and R are

$$(at_1^2, 2at_1);\ at_2^2, 2at_2);\ (at_3^2, 3at)$$

From question

$$2at_1,\ 2at_2, \text{ and } 2at_3 \text{ are in } AP$$

$$(2at_2)^2 = 2at_1 \cdot 2at_3$$

$$4a^2\, t_2^2 = 4a_1^2\, t_1\, t_3$$

$$t_2^2 = t_1\, t_3 \qquad (1)$$

The equation of the tangents to the parabola $y^2 = 4ax$ at P and R is given by

$$yt_1 = x + at_1^2$$

$$yt_3 = x + at_3^2$$

$$y = \frac{x + at_1^2}{t_1} \qquad (2)$$

$$y = \frac{x + at_2^3}{t_3} \qquad (2)$$

From equation (2) and (4) we have

$$\frac{x + at_1^2}{t_1} = \frac{x + at_3^3}{t_3}$$

$$at_3 + at_1^2\, t_3 = xt_1 + at_1\, t_3^2$$

$$x(t_3 - t_1) = at_1\, t_3^3 - at_1^2\, t_3$$

$$x(t_3 - t_1) = at_1\, t_3\, (t_3 - t_1)$$

$$x = at_1\, t_3 \frac{(t_3 - t_1)}{(t_3 - t_1)}$$

$$x = at^2_2$$

But $x = at_2^2$ is is the equation of the ordinate of Q. [*Hence the results*]

Problem 12 Prove analytically, that the locus of a the foot of the perpendicular from the focus of aparabola on the tangent at any point is the tangent at the vertex.

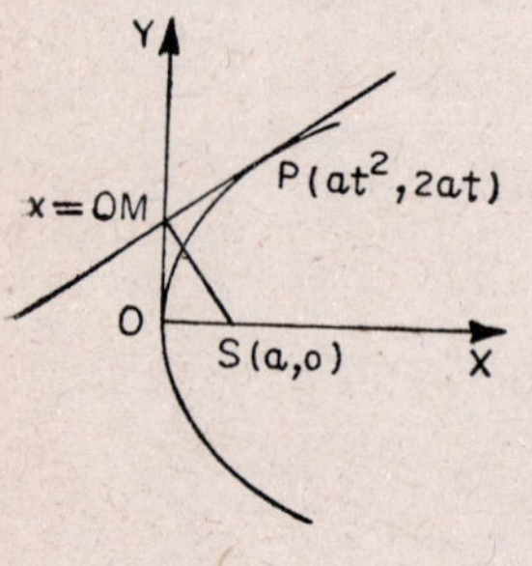

Solution Let the equation of the parabola is

$$y^2 = 4ax$$

$S\ (a, 0)$ be the co-ordinate of the focus. At the point $P\ (at^2, 2gt)$ tangent is drawn. Tangent at any point $(at^2, 2at)$ is given by

$$yt = x + at^2$$

$$y = \frac{x}{t} + at \qquad (1)$$

Then slope of this line is $\frac{1}{t}$ slope of the line perpendicular to this line is t

Now equation of the line whose slope is $-t$ and passes through the point $(a, 0)$ is given by

$$y-0 = -t\,(x-a)$$

$$y = -tx + at$$

$$y + tx = at \qquad (2)$$

The co-ordinate of the foot of the perpendicular SM can be obtained by solving equation (1) and (2)

$$\frac{x}{t} + at = -tx + at$$

$$\frac{x}{t} + tx = 0$$

i.e. $$x\,(1 + t^2) = 0$$

$$1 + t^2 \neq 0 \quad \therefore \quad x = 0 \text{ and } \quad y = at$$

Evidently $M\ (0, at)$ satisfies the equation $x = 0$

Hence the locus of M is a tangent at the vertex i.e. $x = 0$ i.e. y axis.

(Proved)

Problem 13 Prove that the orthocentre of the triangle formed by any three tangents to a parabola lies on the directrix.

Solution The three tangents to the parabola $y^2 = 4ax$ at (t_1), (t_2) and t_3 are

$$yt_1 = x + at_1^2 \qquad (1)$$

$$yt_2 = x + at_2^2 \qquad (2)$$

$$yt_3 = x + x + at_3^2 \qquad (3)$$

Let A, B, C be the points of intersection of (2), (3): (3) (1) and (1), (2) respectively

Subtracting (3) from equation (2) we have

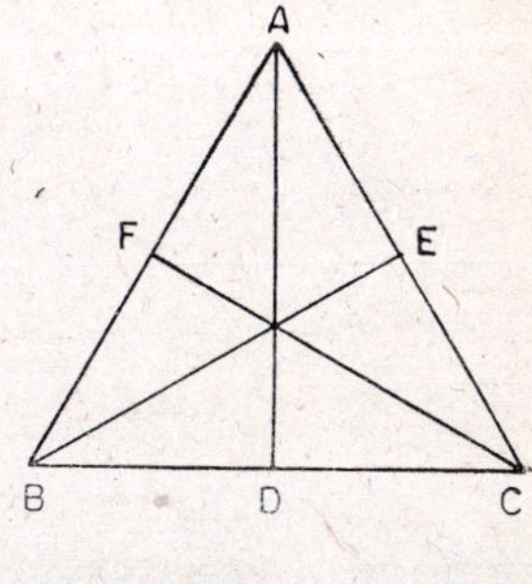

$$y(t_2-t_3) = a(t_2^2-t_3^2)$$

i.e.
$$y(t_2-t_3) = a(t_2-t_3)(t_2+t_3)$$

or
$$y = a(t_2+t_3)$$

From equation (2)

$$x = yt_2-at_2^2$$
$$x = a(t_2+t_3)t_2-at^2$$
$$x = a(t^2+t_2 t_3)-at^2$$
$$x = at_2 t_3$$

Hence the co-ordinates of A is

$$(at_2 t_3, a(t_2+t_3))$$

Similarly the co-ordinates of the point B and C are

$$(at_3 t_1, a(t_3+t_1))$$

and
$$(at_1 t_2, a(t_1+t_2))$$

From A, B, C drawn perpendiculars AD, BE, CF on their opposite sides.

slope of (1) we of the line is BC is $\frac{1}{t_1}$

$\therefore$
$$AD \perp^r BC$$

so the slope of $AD = -t_1$

Equation of AD passing through A is

$$y-a(t_2+t_3) = -t_1(x-at_2 t_3) \quad (4)$$

Similarly the equations of BC and CF are respectively

$$y-a(t_8+t_1) = -t_2(x-at_3 t_1) \quad (5)$$

and
$$y-a(t_1+t_2) = -t_3(x-a t_1 t_2) \quad (6)$$

Solving (4) and (5), we get the orthocentre, their point of intersection.

$$a(t_1-t_2) = x(t_2-t_1)$$

or
$$x = -a$$
$$y = a(t_2+t_3)-t_1(-a-at_2 t_3)$$
$$y = a(t_1+t_2+t_3+t_1 t_2 t_3)$$

Hence the orthocentre is

$$[-a, a(t_1+t_2+t_3+t_1 t_2 t_3)]$$

it also satisfies (6) clearly the orthocentre satisfies the equation of the directrix $x+a=0$

Hence the orthocentre lies on the directrix. *(Proved)*

Problem 14 Prove that the area of the triangle formed by the tangents from the point (x_1, y_1) to the parabola $y^2 = 4ax$ and their chord of contact is

$$\frac{1}{2a}(y^2-ax_1)^{3/2}$$

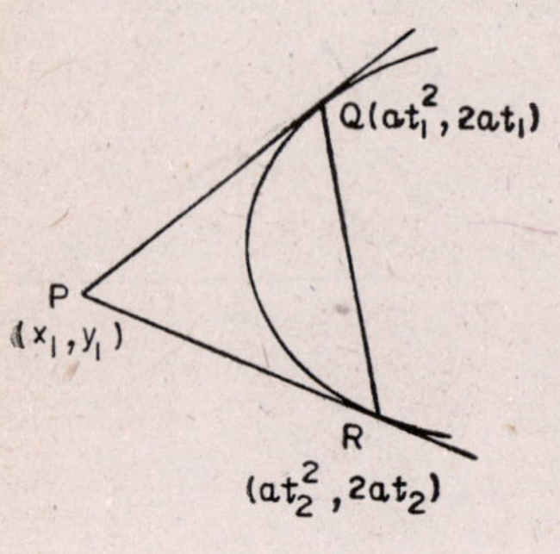

Solution Let $y^2 = 4ax$ be the equation of the parabola from the point $p\ (x_1, y_1)$ tangents PQ and PR are drawn. The co-ordinates of the point Q and R are

$$(at_1^2, 2at_1): (at_2^2, 2at_2)$$

QR is the chord of contact, Then PQR is the triangle formed by the points P $(x_1. x_1)$; $Q\ (at_1^2, 2at_1)$ and $R\ (at_2^2. 2at_2)$

Area of the triange $\Delta\ PQR$

$$= \tfrac{1}{2}[x_1(2at_2-2at_1) + at_2^2(2at-y_1) + at_1^2(y_1-2at_2)$$
$$= \tfrac{1}{2}[2ax_1 t_2-2ax_1(t_2-t_1)-2a^2 t_1 t_2^2-y_1 at^2+y_1 at^2-2a^2 t^2 t_2]$$
$$= \tfrac{1}{2}[2ax_1(t_2-t_1) + 2a^2 t_1 t_1(t_2-t_1)-ay_1(t_2^2-t_1^2)]$$
$$= \tfrac{1}{2}[(t_2-t_1)\{2ax_1 + 2a^2 t_1 t_2-ay_1(t_2+t_1)\}]$$
$$= \frac{t_2-t_1}{2}\{2ax_1 + 2a^2 t_1 t_2-ay_1(t_2+t_1)\}$$

Tangent at Q is

$$yt_1 = x + at_1^2 \tag{1}$$

Tangent at R is

$$yt_2 = x + at_2^2 \tag{2}$$

The tangents at Q and R passes through the point (x_1, y_1) so

$$y_1 t_1 = x_1 + at_1^2 \tag{3}$$
$$y_1 t_2 = x_1 + at_2^2 \tag{4}$$

From (3) and (4) we have

$$y_1(t_1-t_2) = a(t_1^2-t_2^2)$$
$$y_1(t_1-t_2) = a(t_1-t_2)(t_1+t_2)$$
$$t_1 + t_2 = \frac{y_1}{a} \Rightarrow y_1 = a(t_1+t_2) \quad 5)$$

Area of the triangle PQR Is

$$= \frac{(t_2-t_1)}{2}\{2ax_1 + 2a^2 t_1 t_2-ay_1(t_2+t_1)\}-5\ (a)$$

From equation (3)

$$y_1 t_1 = x_1 + at_1^2 \tag{6}$$

Putting the value of y_1 from (5) in (6) we have

$$a(t_1 + t_2)t_1 = x_1 + at_1^2$$

$$at_1^2 + at_1 t_2 = x_1 + at_1^2$$

$$x_1 = at_1 t_2$$

$$t_1 t_2 = \frac{x_1}{a}$$

Putting the values of $t_1 + t_1$ and $t_1 t_2$ in 5 (a) we have

Area of ΔPQR

$$= \frac{(t_2 - t_1)}{2}\{2ax_1 + 2a^2 t_1 t_2 - ay_1(t_2 + t_1)\}$$

$$t_2 - t_1 = \sqrt{(t_1 + t_2)^2 - 4t_1 t_2}$$

$$= \sqrt{\frac{y_1^2}{a^2} - 4\frac{x_1}{a}} = \sqrt{\frac{y_1^2 - 4x_1 a}{a^2}}$$

$$= \sqrt{\frac{y_1^2 - 4x_1 a}{a}}$$

$$\Delta PQR = \frac{\sqrt{y_1^2 - 4x_1 a}}{2a}\left\{2a x_1 + 2a^2 \frac{x_1}{a} - ay_1 \frac{y_1}{a}\right\}$$

$$= \frac{\sqrt{y_1^2 - 4x_1 a}}{2a}\{2ax_1 + 2x_1 a - y_1^2\}$$

$$= \frac{\sqrt{y_1^2 - 4x_1 a}}{2a}\{4ax_1 - y_1^2\}$$

$$= \frac{\sqrt{y_1^2 - 4x_1 a}}{2a}(-)(y_1^2 - 4ax_1)$$

$$= -\frac{[y_1^2 - 4x_1 a]^{3/2}}{2a}$$

$$\Delta PQR = -\frac{[y_1^2 - 4x_1 a]^{3/2}}{2a}$$

$$= \frac{(y_1^2 - 4ax_1)^{3/2}}{2a} \text{ numerically}$$

Problem 15 Prove that the area of the triangle formed by three points on a parabola is twice the area of the triangle formed by the tangenrs at those points.

Solution Let the equation of the parabola is $y^2 = 4ax$.

Let the co-ordinates of the points AB and C are

$$(at_1^2, 2at_1)\ (at^2, 2at_2)\ (at_3^2, 2at_3)$$

Then ΔABC is the triangle formed by the three points A, B and C on the parabola and PQR is the triangle formed by the intersection of the three tangents drawn at the points A, B and C

Then we have to prove that $\quad \Delta ABC$

$$= \tfrac{1}{2}\,[at_1^2\,(2t_2-2at_3) + at_2^2\,(2at_3-2at_1) + at_3^2\,(2at_1-2at_2)]$$
$$= \tfrac{1}{2}\,[2a^2\,t_1^2\,(t_2-t_3) + 2at_2^2\,(t_3-t_1) + 2a^2\,(t_1-t_3)\,\tfrac{1}{3}^2]$$
$$= a^2\,[t_1^2\,(t_3-t_3) + t_2^2\,(t_3-t_1) + t_3^2\,(t_1-t_3)] \quad (1)$$

Equations of the tangents at the point t_1, t_2 and t_3 is given by

$$yt_1 = x + at_1^2 \quad (2)$$
$$yt_2 = x + at^2 \quad (3)$$
$$yt_3 = x + at_3^2 \quad (4)$$

Co-ordinate of the point Q can be obtained by the [interseetion of (2) and (3)

$$\frac{x + at_1^2}{t_1} = \frac{x + at^2}{t_2}$$
$$x\,t_2 + at_2^2\,t_2 = xt_1 + at_1\,t^2$$
$$x\,(t_2-t_1) = at_1\,t_2^2 - at_1\,t_2$$
$$x\,(t_2-t_1) = at_1\,t_2\,(t_2-t_1)$$
$$x = at_1\,t_2$$

Again
$$yt_1 = at_1t_2 + at_1^2$$
$$yt_1 = at_1\,(t_2 + t_1)$$
$$y = a\,(t_1 + t_2)$$

Thus the co-ordinate of the point Q is $(at_1\,t_2,\ a\,(t_1 + t_2))$

The co-ordinate of the point R is $\quad (at_2\,t_3.\ a\,(t_1 + t_3))$

The Co-ordinate of the point P is $(a\,t_1\,t_3,\ a\,t_1 + t_3)$

Area of the triangle PQR

$$= \tfrac{1}{2}\,[at_1\,t_2\,\{a\,(t_1 + t_3) - a\,(t_1 + t_3)]$$
$$+ at_2\,t_3\,\{a\,(t_1 + t_3) - a\,(t_1 + t_2)\}$$
$$+ at_1\,t_3\,\{a\,(t_1 + t_2) - a\,(t_2 + t_3)\}]$$
$$= \tfrac{1}{2}\,[at_1\,t_2\,\{a\,(t_2-t_1)\} + at_2\,t_3\,\{a\,(t_3-t_2) + at_1t_3\,\{a.(t_1-t_3\}]$$
$$= \tfrac{1}{2}a^2\,[t_1\,t_2\,(t_2-t_1) + t_2\,t_3\,(t_3-t_2) + t_1\,t_3\,(t_1-t_3)]$$
$$= \tfrac{1}{2}\,a^2\,[t_1\,t_2^2 - t_1^2\,t_2 + t_2\,t - t_2^2\,t_3 + t_1^2\,t_3 - t_2^2 - t_1]$$
$$= \tfrac{1}{2}\,a^2\,[t_1^2\,(t_2-t_3) + t^2\,(t_3-t_1) + t_1^2\,(t_1-t_2)]$$
$$= \tfrac{1}{2}\,a^2\,[t_1^2\,[t_2-t_3) + t^2\,(t_3-t_1) + t_3^2\,(t_1-t_2)]$$

[Taking magnitude only]

$$\Delta PQR = \tfrac{1}{2}\,\Delta ABC$$

i.e.
$$2\,\Delta PQR = \Delta ABC \qquad \textit{(Proved)}$$

Problem 16 Find the common tangent of the two parabolas.

$$y^2 = 4ax \quad \text{and} \quad x^2 = 4by$$

Solution Let $\quad y^2 = 4ax \quad (1)$

and $\quad x^2 = 4by \quad (2)$

be equation of any two parabolas.

Let $y = mx + c$ be the common tangent to both the parabolas.

Since $y = mx + c$ be the tangent to the parabola

$$y^2 = 4ax$$

$$\text{then } c = \frac{m}{a}$$

Equation of the tangent to the parabola

$$y^2 = 4ax \text{ is}$$

$$y = mx + \frac{a}{m} \quad (3)$$

Again this is the tangent to the parabola

$$x^2 = 4by$$

$$\frac{x^2}{4b} = mx + \frac{a}{m}$$

$$mx^2 = (m^2 x + a)\, 4b$$

$$mx^2 - 4bm^2 x - 4ab = 0 \quad (4)$$

Since (3) is tangent to the parabola so two values of x of equation (4) must be equal.

$$(-4bm^2)^2 - 4\, m\, (-4ab) = 0$$

i.e. $\quad 16b^2\, m^4 + 16\, mab = 0$

$$b^2\, m^4 = -mab$$

$$m^3 = -\frac{a}{b} = (-1)^3\, \frac{a}{b}$$

$$m = -\left(\frac{a}{b}\right)^{1/3}$$

Putting the value of m in equation (2) we have the equation of common tangent

$$y = -\left(\frac{a}{b}\right)^{1/3} x + \frac{a}{-(a/b)^{1/3}}$$

$$y = -\left(\frac{a}{b}\right)^{1/3} x - a\left(\frac{b}{a}\right)^{1/3}$$

$$y = -\frac{a^{1/3}}{b^{1/3}}\, x - a\, \frac{b^{\frac{1}{3}}}{a^{\frac{1}{3}}}$$

$$y = -\frac{a^{1/3}\, x}{b^{1/3}} - \frac{a^{2/3}\, b^{1/3}}{1}$$

$$yb^{1/3} = -xa^{1/3} - a^{2/3}\, b^{2/3}$$

or $$xa^{1/3} + yb^{1/3} + a^{2/3}\, b^{2/3} = 0$$

This is the required common tangent.

Problem 17 Find the condition that the line $y = mx + c$ *may* be normal to the parabola $y^2 = 4ax$

Solution Equation of the normal at the point $(am^2 - 2am)$ is given by

$$y = mx - 2am - am^3 \tag{1}$$

If the line $y = mx + c$ is normal (2)

to the parabola $y^2 = 4ax$ then (2) and (3) are the same.

Hence comparing their coefficients

We get $$c = -2\, am - am^3$$

This is the required condition.

Problem 18 Find the condition that $lx + my + n = 0$ is normal to the paraboloa $y^2 = 4ax$. [*IFS 88, 82*]

Equation of the normal at the point $(at^2, 2at)$ is given by

$$y + tx = 2at + at\ 3$$

$$y = -tx + 2at + at^3 \tag{1}$$

Since $lx + my + n = 0$ (2)

is also normal to the parabola $y^2 = 4ax$

So (1) and (2) will represent the same straight line. So comparing equation (1) and (2) we have

$$\frac{y}{m} = \frac{t}{l} = \frac{2at + at^3}{-n}$$

$$t = \frac{l}{m}$$

and $$2at + at^3 = -\frac{n}{m}$$

$$2a\, \frac{l}{m} + a\, \frac{l^3}{m^3} = -\frac{n}{m}$$

$$2alm^2 + al^3 = -nm^2$$

$$al^3 + 2alm^2 = -m^2\, n$$

Another form of the equation

If $lx + my + n = 0$ is normal to the parabola $y^2 = 4ax$, prove that

$$al^3 + 2alm^2 = -m^2\, n$$ [*I.F.S. 82*]

Problem 18 If the normal at $(at_1^2)\ 2at_1)$ meets the parabola $y^2, = 4ax$ again at $(at^2, 2at_2)$ prove that

$$t_2 = -t_1 - \frac{2}{t_1}$$

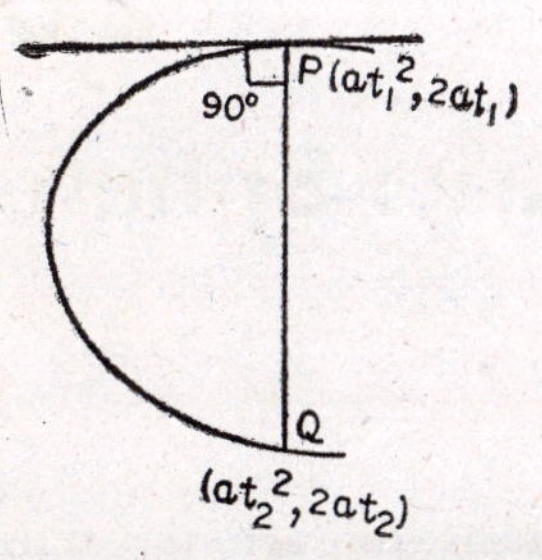

Solution Let the equation of the parabola is

$$y^2 = 4ax$$

Normal at the point $(at_1^2, 2at_1)$ is given by

$$y + t_1 x = 2at_1 + at_1^3 \tag{1}$$

PQ is the normal whose equation is given by (1)

Since (1) again passes through $Q\ (at^2, 2at_2)$

So $Q\ (at^2, 2at_2)$ will satisfy equation (1)

i.e.

$$2at_2 + t_1\, at_2^2 = 2at_1 + at_1^3$$

$$at_1\, t_2^2 - at_1^3 = 2at_1 - 2at_2$$

$$at_1\, (t_2^2 - t_1^2) = 2a\, (t_1 - t_2)$$

$$t_1\, (t_2 - t_1)\, (t_2 + t_1) = 2\, (t_1 - t_2)$$

$$-t_1\, (t_2 + t_1) = 2$$

$$t_2 + t_1 = -\frac{2}{t_1}$$

i.e.

$$t_2 = -t_1 - \frac{2}{t_1} \qquad \textit{(Proved)}$$

20

Solid Geometry : Sphere

Problem 1 Find the equation of the sphere passing through the three points (3, 0, 2), (−1, 1. 1), (2, −5, 4) and having its centre in the plane

$$2x + 3y + 4z = 6$$

Solution Let the equation of the sphere be

$$x^2 + y^2 + z^2 + 2gx + 2fy + 2wz + d = 0 \qquad (1)$$

As the sphere passes through (3. 0, 2); (−1, 1, 1) (2, −5, 4). So these points satisfy equation (1)

$$9 + 0 + 4 + 6g + 4w + d = 0$$

$$6g + 4w + 13 + d = 0 \qquad (2)$$

$$1 + 1 + 1 - 2g + 2f + 2w + d = 0$$

$$\Rightarrow \quad 3 - 2g + 2f + 2w + d = 0$$

$$\Rightarrow \quad -2g + 2f + 2w + 3 + d = 0 \qquad (3)$$

$$4 + 25 + 16 + 4g - 10f + 8w + d = 0$$

i.e. $$4g - 10f + 8w + 45 + d = 0 \qquad (4)$$

We know that the centre of the sphere

$$x^2 + y^2 + z^2 + 2gx + 2fy + 2wz + d = 0$$

has the co-ordinates $(-g, -f, -w)$

But it is given that the centre lies in the plane

$$2x + 3y + 4z = 6$$

i.e. $$-2g - 3f - 4w - 6 = 0$$

i.e. $$2g + 3f + 4w + 6 = 0 \qquad (5)$$

Adding (3) and (5) we have

$$5f + 6w + 9 + d = 0 \qquad (6)$$

(3) × 2 + (4) give

$$-4g + 4f + 4w + 6 + 2d + 4g - 10f + 8w + 45 + d = 0$$

$$-6f + 12w + 51 + 3d = 0 \qquad (7)$$

(2) + (3) × 2

$$6g + 4w + 13 + d - 6g + 6f + 6w + 9 + 3d = 0$$

$$6f + 10w + 22 + 4d = 0 \qquad (8)$$

Now (8) −4 × (6)

$$6f + 10w + 22 + 4d - 20f - 24w - 36 - 4d = 0$$

$$-14f - 14w - 14 = 0$$

$$-f - w - 1 = 0 \qquad (9)$$

Again (7) − 3 × (6)

$$-6f + 12w + 51 + 3d - 15f - 18w - 27 - 3d = 0$$

$$-21f - 6w + 24 = 0 \qquad (10)$$

Now (10) − 6 × (9)

$$-21f - 6w + 24 + 6f + 6w + 6 = 0$$

$$-15f + 30 = 0$$

$$15f = 30$$

$$f = 2$$

Putting the value of $f = 2$ in equation

$$\left.\begin{aligned} -21 \times 2 - 6w + 24 &= 0 \\ -42 - 6w + 24 &= 0 \\ -6w - 18 &= 0 \\ 6w &= -18 \\ w &= -3 \end{aligned}\right\} f = 2,\ w = -3$$

Now putting the value of f and w in (6) we have

$$10 - 18 + 9 + d = 0$$

$$-8 + 9 + d = 0$$

$$\Rightarrow \qquad d + 1 = 0$$

$$\Rightarrow \qquad d = -1$$

Putting the value of f_1 w in (5) we have

$$2g + 6 - 12 + 6 = 0$$

$$2g = 0$$

$$\Rightarrow \qquad g = 0$$

$$f = 2,\ g = 0,\ w = -3,\ d = 0$$

Putting the values of these in equation (1) we have

$$x^2 + y^2 + z^2 + 4y - 6z - 1 = 0$$

which is the required equation of the sphere

21
Plane

Equation of the plane in the intercept form

1. $$\frac{x}{a}+\frac{y}{b}+\frac{z}{c}=1$$

2. Normal form $\quad lx + my + nz = p$

3. General form $ax + by + cz + d = 0$

4. (i) Angle between

$$ax + by + cz + d = 0$$

and
$$a_1 x + b_1 y + c_1 z + d_1 = 0$$

i.e.
$$\cos^{-1}\left\{\frac{aa_1 + bb_1 + cc_1}{\sqrt{(a^2 + b^2 + c^2)(a_1^2 + b_1^2 + c_2^2)}}\right\}$$

(ii) Planes are $\perp'$ if

$$aa_1 + bb_1 + cc_1 = 0$$

(iii) Planes are parallel if

$$\frac{a}{a_1}=\frac{b}{b_1}=\frac{c}{c_1}$$

(iv) Bisector of the angles between the planes are

$$\frac{ax + by + cz + d}{\sqrt{a^2 + b^2 + c^2}} = \pm\frac{a_1 x + b_1 y + c_1 z + d_1}{\sqrt{a_1^2 + b_1^2 + c_1^2}}$$

Problem 1 Find the intercepts made on the co-ordinate axes by the plane

$$x + 2y - 2z = 9$$

Find the length of the normal from the origin to the plane

$$x + 2y - 2z = 9$$

and also the direction cosine of the normal.

Solution The given plane is

$$x + 2y - 2z = 9$$

$$\frac{x}{9} + \frac{2y}{9} - \frac{2z}{9} = 1$$

i.e. $$\frac{x}{9} + \frac{y}{9/2} + \frac{z}{-9/2} = 1$$

Hence the intercepts on the axis are

$$9, \frac{9}{2}, -\frac{9}{2}$$

The given plane is $x + 2y - 2z = 9$

Evidently the proportional direction cosines of the normal to the given plane are $1, 2, -2$

The actual direction-cosines of the normal are

$$\frac{1}{\sqrt{1^2 + 2^2 + (-2)^2}}, \frac{2}{\sqrt{1^2 + 2^2 + (-2)^2}}, \frac{-2}{\sqrt{1^2 + 2^2 + (-2)^2}}$$

i.e. $\frac{1}{3}, \frac{2}{3}, -2/3,$

Let us now write the equation of the given plane in the normal form

$$lx + my + nz = p$$

$\therefore$ The equation of the given plane

$$x + 2y - 2z = 9$$

can be written as

$$\frac{x}{3} + \frac{2y}{3} - \frac{2z}{3} = \frac{9}{3}$$

i.e. $$\frac{x}{3} + \frac{2}{3}y - \frac{2}{3}z = 3$$

Hence the length of the normal from the origin to the plane is 3.

Problem 2 O is the origin and A is the point (a, b, c). Find the direction cosines of the join OA and deduce the equation of the plane through A at right angles to OA.

Solution The proportion direction-cosines of OA are a, b, c

$\therefore$ Actual d.c.s of OA are

$$\frac{a}{\sqrt{a^2 + b^2 + c^2}}, \frac{b}{\sqrt{a^2 + b^2 + c^2}}, \frac{c}{\sqrt{a^2 + b^2 + c^2}}$$

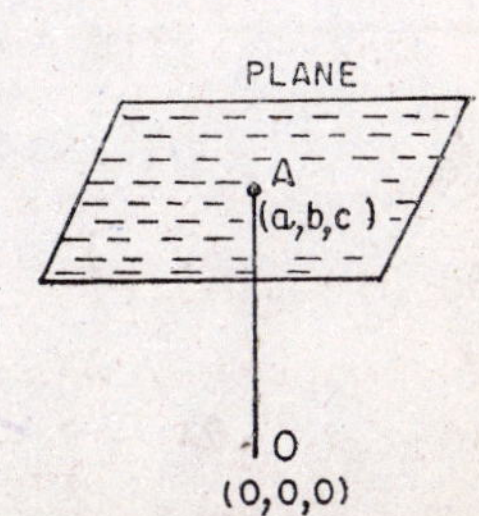

$\therefore$ Any plane perpendicular to OA is

$$\frac{a}{\sqrt{a^2 + b^2 + c^2}}x + \frac{b}{\sqrt{a^2 + b^2 + c^2}}y + \frac{c}{\sqrt{a^2 + b^2 + c^2}}z = k \quad (1)$$

Now the equation (1) passes through the point (a, b, c) so

$$\frac{a^2}{\sqrt{a^2+b^2+c^2}}+\frac{b^2}{\sqrt{a^2+b^2+c^2}}+\frac{c^2}{\sqrt{a^2+b^2+c^2}}=k$$

$$\Rightarrow \qquad k=\sqrt{a^2+b^2+c^2}$$

Thus the equation of the plane is

$$\frac{ax+by+cz}{\sqrt{a^2+b^2+c^2}}\equiv\sqrt{a^2+b^2+c^2}$$

$$\Rightarrow \qquad ax+by+cz=a^2+b^2+c^2 \qquad \textbf{Ans.}$$

Problem 3 Find the equation of the plane through $p(2, 3, -1)$ at right angles to OP. O being the origin.

Solution Since $O(0, 0, 0)$ is the origin and $p(2, 3, -1)$ is *a* point. So the proportional direction cosines of the line OP are $2-0, 3-0, -1-0=2, +3, -1$

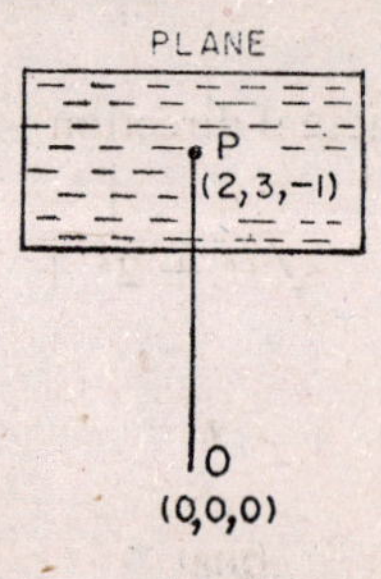

The actual direction cosine of the line OP are

$$\frac{2}{\sqrt{2^2+3^2+(-1)^2}}, \frac{3}{\sqrt{2^2+3^2+(-1)^2}}, \frac{-1}{\sqrt{2^2+3^2+(-1)^2}}$$

i.e. $$\frac{2}{\sqrt{14}}, \frac{3}{\sqrt{14}}, \frac{-1}{\sqrt{14}}$$

We know that the equation of a plane is given by

$$lx+my+nz=p$$

where l, m, n are the *d*.c. *s* of the normal to the plane.

So the equation of the plane perpendicular to OP is given by

$$\frac{2}{\sqrt{14}}x+\frac{3}{\sqrt{14}}y-\frac{z}{\sqrt{14}}=p \qquad (1)$$

Since this plane passes through the point $(2, 3, -1)$ so

$$\frac{4}{\sqrt{14}}+\frac{9}{\sqrt{14}}+\frac{1}{\sqrt{14}}=p$$

i.e. $$p=\frac{14}{\sqrt{14}}=\sqrt{14}$$

So the equation of the plane becomes

$$2x+3y-z=14$$

i.e. $$2x+3y-z-14=0 \qquad \textbf{Ans.}$$

Problem 4 Find the equation of the plane that passes through (2, −3, 1) and is perpendicular to the line joining the points (3, 4, −1) and (2, −1, 5)

Solution The proportional direction cosine of the line joining the points (3, 4, −1) and (2, −1, 5) is given by

$$3-2, 4-(-1), -1-5$$

i.e. $\perp, 5, -6$

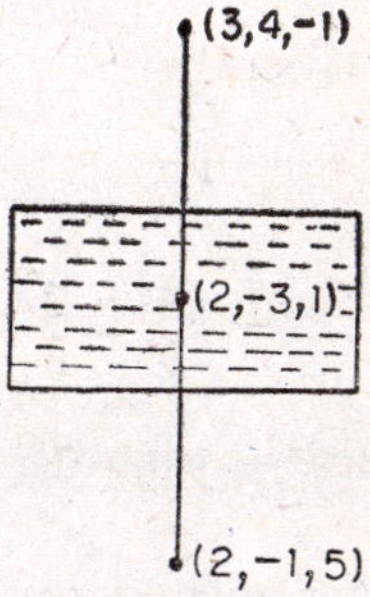

(3,4,−1)

(2,−3,1)

(2,−1,5)

The actual direction cosines of the line joining the points (3, 4, −1)

and (2, −1, 5) is given by

$$\frac{1}{\sqrt{1^2+5^2+(-6)^2}}, \frac{5}{\sqrt{1^2+5^2+(-6)^2}},$$

$$\frac{-6}{\sqrt{1^2+5^2+(-6)^2}}$$

i.e. $$\frac{1}{\sqrt{62}}, \frac{5}{\sqrt{62}}, -\frac{6}{\sqrt{62}}$$

Now the equation of the plane $\perp r$ to this line is given by

$$\frac{1}{\sqrt{62}}x + \frac{5}{\sqrt{62}}y - \frac{6z}{\sqrt{62}} = p$$

But this plane passes through the point (2, −3, 1) so

$$\frac{2}{\sqrt{62}} - \frac{15}{\sqrt{62}} - \frac{6}{\sqrt{62}} = p \qquad (1)$$

$$\frac{-19}{\sqrt{62}} = p$$

Thus the equation of the plane becomes

$$\frac{x}{\sqrt{62}} + \frac{5y}{\sqrt{62}} - \frac{6z}{\sqrt{62}} = -\frac{19}{\sqrt{62}}$$

i.e. $$x - 5y - 6z = -19$$

i.e. $$\boxed{x + 5y - 6z + 19 = 0}$$

Which is the required equation of the plane,

Problem 5 Find the equation of the two planes through the points (0, 4, −3); (6, −4, 3) other than the plane through the origin, which cut off from the axes intercepts whose sum is zero.

Solution Equation of the plane which cuts off intercepts a, b and c from the co-ordinate axes is given by

$$\frac{x}{a} + \frac{y}{b} + \frac{z}{c} = 1$$

It is given that

$$a + b + c = 0 \tag{2}$$

Since equation (1) pesses through the point (0, 4, −3) and (6, −4, 3) we have

$$\frac{4}{b} - \frac{3}{c} = 1 \tag{3}$$

$$\text{and } \frac{6}{a} - \frac{4}{b} + \frac{3}{c} = 1 \tag{4}$$

Adding equation (3) and (4) we have

$$\frac{6}{a} = 2 \quad \Rightarrow \quad a = \frac{6}{2} = 3$$

Now from equation (2) we have

$$3 + (b + c) = 0$$

$$\Rightarrow \quad b + c = -3$$

$$\Rightarrow \quad c = -3 - b$$

$$\Rightarrow \quad c = -(3 + b)$$

Putting the value of c in equation (3) we have

$$\frac{4}{b} + \frac{3}{3 + b} = 1$$

i.e. $$\frac{4\,(3 + b) + 3\,b}{b\,(3 + b)} = 1$$

i.e. $$\frac{12 + 4b + 3b}{b\,(3 + b)} = 1$$

i.e. $$7b + 12 = 3b + b^2$$

i.e. $$b^2 + 3b - 7b - 12 = 0$$

$$\Rightarrow \quad b^2 - 4b - 12 = 0$$

$$\Rightarrow \quad b^2 - 6b + 2b - 12 = 0$$

$$\Rightarrow \quad b\,(b - 6) + 2\,(b - 6) = 0$$

$$\Rightarrow \quad (b + 2)\,(b - 6) = 0$$

either $$b + 2 = 0 \quad \text{or} \quad b - 6 = 0$$

$$\Rightarrow \quad b = -2 \quad \text{or} \quad b = 6$$

When $\qquad b = -2$ then $\qquad c = -(3 + b)$

f $\qquad c = -(3-2)$

$$c = -1$$

if $\qquad b = 6 \qquad c = -(3 + b) = -(3 + 6) = -1$

So there are two sets of solution

$$\left.\begin{array}{l} a = 3 \\ b = -2 \\ c = -1 \end{array}\right\} \quad \text{and} \quad \left\{\begin{array}{l} a = 3 \\ b = 6 \\ c = -9. \end{array}\right.$$

So the equation of the planes are

$$\frac{x}{3} + \frac{y}{-2} + \frac{z}{-1} = 1$$

i.e. $$\frac{x}{3} - \frac{y}{2} - \frac{z}{1} = 1 \qquad (5)$$

And $$\frac{x}{3} + \frac{y}{6} + \frac{z}{-9} = 1$$

$$\Rightarrow \quad \frac{x}{3} + \frac{y}{6} - \frac{z}{9} = 1 \qquad (6)$$

Equation (5) and are eqn. (6) the required equations of the planes. **Ans.**

Problem 6 Show that the four points $(0, -1, -1)$, $(4, 5, 1)$, $(3, 9, 4)$ and $(-4, 4, 4)$ lie in a plane and find also the **equation of the plane.**

Solution Let the equation of the plane can be written as.

$$Ax + By + Cz + D = 0 \qquad (1)$$

Since equation (1) passes through $(0, -1, -1)$

So $$-B - C + D = 0 \qquad (2)$$

Since plane passes through $(4, 5, 1)$ $(3, 9, 4)$ so

$$4A + 5B + C + D = 0 \qquad (3)$$

$$3A + 9B + 4C + D = 0 \qquad (4)$$

(3) $-$(2) and (3) $-$(4) give

$$4A + 5B + C + D + B + C - D = 0$$

$$4A + 6B + 2C = 0 \qquad (5)$$

And $$A - 4B - 3C = 0 \qquad (6)$$

By cross multiplication we get

$$\frac{A}{-18+8} = \frac{B}{2+12} = \frac{C}{-16-6}$$

$$\frac{A}{-10} = \frac{B}{14} = \frac{C}{-22}$$

$$\frac{A}{-5} = \frac{B}{7} = \frac{C}{-11} = k \text{ (say)}$$

Then

$$A = -5k$$

$$B = 7k$$

$$C = -11k$$

From (2)

$$-7k + 11k + D = 0$$

$$4k + D = 0$$

$$\Rightarrow \quad D = -4k$$

Hence from equation (1) the equation of the plane beeomes

$$-5kx + 7ky - 11kz - 4k = 0$$

i.e.

$$5x - 7y + 11z + 4 = 0 \qquad (7)$$

The fourth point $(-4, 4, 4)$ lies on the plane (7) because if satisfies the equation

$$5(-4) - 7(4) + 11 \times 4 + 4$$

$$= -20 - 28 + 44 + 4$$

$$= -48 + 48 = 0$$

Hence the four given points are coplanar.

Problem 7 Find the equation to the plane through the points $P(1, 1, 1)$; $Q(3, -1, 2)$ and $R(-3, 5, -4)$

Solution The general equation of the plane is given by

$$ax + by + cz + d = 0 \qquad (1)$$

Since this plane passes through the point $(1, 1, 1)$; $(3, -1, 2)$ and $(-3, 5, 4)$ so

$$a + b + c + d = 0 \qquad (2)$$

$$3a - b + 2c + d = 0 \qquad (3)$$

$$-3a + 5b - 4c + d = 0 \qquad (4)$$

(3) – (2) gives

$$2a - 2b + c = 0 \qquad (5)$$

(3) – (4) given

$$6a - 6b + 6c = 0$$

i.e.

$$a - b + c = 0 \qquad (6)$$

Then from (5) and (6) [By cross Multiplication] we have

$$\frac{a}{-2+1} = \frac{b}{1-2} = \frac{c}{-2+2} = k$$

i.e.
$$\frac{a}{-1} = \frac{b}{-1} = \frac{c}{0} = k$$

$$\Rightarrow \left.\begin{aligned} a &= -k \\ b &= -k \\ c &= 0 \end{aligned}\right\}$$

Putting the value of a, b, c in (2)

$$-k-k+0+d = 0$$
$$d = 2k$$

Putting the value of a, b and c in equation (1) we have

$$-kx-ky+0+2k = 0$$

i.e. $$-x-y+2 = 0$$

i.e. $$x+y-2 = 0$$

i.e. $$x+y = 2$$

Which is the required equation of the plane.

Problem 8 From the point $P(1, 2, 1)$, perpendiculars PL and PM be drawn to Yz and Zx planes. Find the equation of the plane OLM, where 0 is the origin.

Solution Here P is $(1, 2, 1)$

PL is $\perp r$ to Yz plane

i.e. $x = 0$

i.e. L is $(0, 2, 1)$

PM is $\perp^r$ to Zx plane

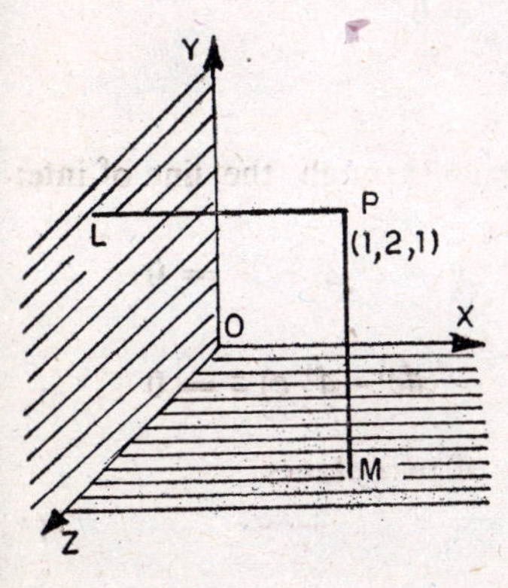

i.e. $y = 0$

i.e. M is $(1, 0, 1)$

Let the equation of the plane OLM is

$$ax+by+cz+d = 0 \quad (1)$$

Since equation (1) passes through the origin $(0, 0, 0)$ so

$$a \cdot 0 + b \cdot 0 + c \cdot 0 + d = 0$$

i.e. $$d = 0$$

Again equation (1) passes through the points $L(0, 2, 1)$ and $M(1, 0\ 1)$ so

$$a \cdot 0 + b \cdot 2 + c \cdot 1 = 0$$
$$2b + c = 0$$
$$b = -\frac{c}{2}$$

And $$a + b\cdot 0 + c\cdot 1 = 0$$

i.e. $$a + c = 0 \qquad (3$$

i.e. $$a = -c$$

Thus the equation of the plane is given as

$$-cx - \frac{c}{2}y + cz = 0$$

i.e. $$-2cx - cy + 2cz = 0$$

i.e. $$2x + y - 2z = 0$$

Which is the required equation of the plane OLM. **Ans.**

Formulas: (5) The distance of (x_1, y_1, z_1) from $ax + by + cz + d = 0$ is

$$\pm \frac{ax_1 + by_1 + cz_1 + d}{\sqrt{a^2 + b^2 + c^2}}$$

(6) $$ax^2 + by^2 + cz^2 + 2fyz + 2gzx + 2hxy = 0$$

will represent a pair of planes if

$$abc + 2fgh - af^2 - bg^2 - ch^2 = 0$$

(7) plane through the line of intersection of

And $S_1 = 0$ and $S_2 = 0$ is

$$S_1 + k\,S_2 = 0$$

Plane through $(x_1, y_1\ z_1)$, (x_2, y_2, z_2) and (x_3, y_3, z_3) is

$$\begin{vmatrix} x & y & z & 1 \\ x_1 & y_1 & z_1 & 1 \\ x_2 & y_2 & z_2 & 1 \\ x_3 & y_3 & z_3 & 1 \end{vmatrix} = 0$$

Problem 9 Show that the equation of the plane through the line of intersection of the planes

$$ax + by + cz + d = 0 \text{ and } a^1 x + b^1 y + c^1 z + d^1 = 0$$

and the again is

$$(da^1 - d^1 a)\,x + (db^1 - d^1 b)\,y + (dc^1 - d^1 c)\,z = 0$$

Solution Any plane through the intersection of two planes

$$ax + by + cz + d = 0 \qquad (1)$$

and $$a^1 x + b^1 y + c^1 z + d^1 = 0 \qquad (2)$$

is given by

$$(ax + by) + (cz + d) + k\,(a^1 x + b^1 y + c^1 z + d^1) = 0 \qquad (3)$$

Since the equation (3) passes through origin (0, 0, 0) so

$$d + kd^1 = 0$$

$$\Rightarrow \qquad k = -\frac{d}{d^1}$$

Putting the value of k in equation (3) we have

$$(ax + by + cz + d) - \frac{d}{d^1}(a^1 x + b^1 y + c^1 z) + d^1 = 0$$

i.e. $$d^1(ax + by + cz + d) - (a^1 x + b^1 y + c^1 z + d^1) d = 0$$

i.e. $$ad^1 x + bd^1 y + cd^1 z + dd^1 - a^1 dx - b^1 dy - c^1 dz - dd^1 = 0$$

i.e. $$(ad^1 - a^1 d) x + (bd^1 - b^1 d) y + (cd^1 - c^1 d) z = 0$$

i.e. $$(a^1 d - ad^1) x + (db^1 - bd^1) y + (dc^1 - cd) z = 0$$

Which is the required equation of the plane, **Ans.**

Problem 10 Find the equation of the plane through the point (2, −1, 1) and the line $4x - 3y + 5 = 0 = y - 2z - 5$

Solution The equation of the plane through the intersection of the planes

$$4x - 3y + 5 = 0 \qquad (1)$$

and $$y - 2z - 5 = 0 \qquad (2)$$

is given by

$$(4x - 3y + 5) + k(y - 2z - 5) = 0 \qquad (3)$$

Since this plane passes through the point (2, −1, 1) so

$$[4.2 - 3(-1) + 5] + k[-1 - 2(1) - 5] = 0$$

i.e. $$(8 + 3 + 5) + k(-1 - 2 - 5) = 0$$

i.e. $$16 - 8k = 0$$

i.e $$8k = 16$$

$$\Rightarrow \qquad k = 2$$

Thus the equation of the plane is given by

$$(4x - 3y + 5) + 2(y - 2z - 5) = 0$$

i.e. $$4x - 3y + 5 + 2y - 4z - 10 = 0$$

i.e. $$4x - y - 4z - 5 = 0$$

Which is the required equation of the plane.

Problem 11 Prove that the equation of the plane through (α, β, γ) and parallel to

$$ax + by + cz = 0 \text{ is } ax + by + cz = a\alpha + b\beta + c\gamma$$

Solution The equation of the given plane is

$$ax + by + cz = 0 \qquad (1)$$

We know that the equation of the plane parallel to (1) is given by

$$ax + by + cz = k \tag{2}$$

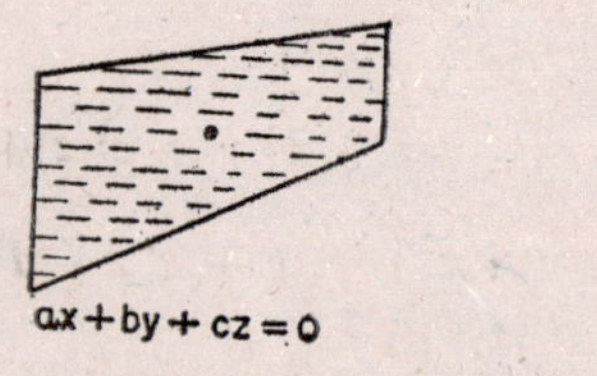

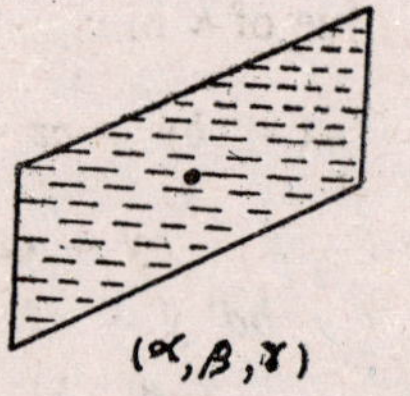

Since equation (2) passes through the point (α, β, γ) so we have

$$a\alpha + b\beta + c\gamma = k$$

Thus the required equation of the plane is

$$ax + by + cz = a\alpha\ b\beta + c\gamma \quad \textit{(Proved)}$$

Problem 12 Find the equation of the plane through (2, 3, −4) and (1, −1, 3) and parallel to x axis.

Solution Let the equation of the plane be

$$ax + by + cz + d = 0 \tag{1}$$

It passes through (2, 3, −4) and (1, −1, 3)

∴ $$2a + 3b - 4c + d = 0 \tag{2}$$

$$a - b + 3c + d = 0 \tag{3}$$

From (2)−(3)

$$a + 4b - 7c = 0 \tag{4}$$

Since plane (1) is parallel to the x-aaxis whose direction casines are (1, 0, 0)

∴ $$a.1 + b \cdot 0 + c \cdot 0 = 0$$

i.e. $$a = 0$$

Putting this value in (4) we have

$$0 + 4b - 7c = 0$$

$$\Rightarrow \quad 4b = 7c$$

$$b = \frac{7}{4}\ c$$

Now putting this value in (3)

$$0 - \frac{7}{4}\ c + 3c + d = 0$$

i.e. $$-7c + 12c + 4d = 0$$

i.e. $$5c + 4d = 0$$

i.e. $$4d = -5c$$

$$\Rightarrow \quad d = -\frac{5}{4} c$$

Hence the equation of the plane is

$$\frac{7}{4} cy + cz - \frac{5}{4} c = 0$$

$$7y + 4z - 5 = 0$$

Which is the required equation of the plane. **Ans.**

Problem 13 Find the equation of the plane through the line of intersection of the planes $ax + by + cz + d = 0$

$$a^1 x + b^1 y + c^1 z + d^1 = 0$$

and parallel to the x-axcis.

Solution The equation of the plane through the intersection of the planes

$$ax + by + cz + d = 0$$

and $$a^1 x + b^1 y + c^1 z + d^1 = 0$$

is given by

$$(ax + by + cz + d) + k(a^1 x + b^1 y + c^1 z + d^1) = 0 \quad (1)$$

$$(a + ka^1) x + (b + kb^1) y + (c + kc^1) z + (d + kd^1) = 0 \quad (2)$$

Plane (2) is parallel to the x-axis.

The direction cosines of the x-axis is are $(1, 0, 0)$

So $$(a + ka^1) \cdot 1 + (b + kb^1) \cdot 0 + (c + kc^1) 0 = 0$$

i.e. $$a + ka^1 = 0$$

i.e. $$k = -\frac{a}{a^1}$$

So the required eqnation of the plane is given as

$$(a^1 b - ab^1) y + (a^1 c - ac^1) z + (a^1 d - ad^1) = 0 \quad \textbf{Ans.}$$

Problem 14 Find the distance between the planes

$$ax + by + cz + d = 0 \quad \text{and} \quad ax + by + cz + e = 0$$

Solution The given planes are parallel as

$$\frac{a}{a} = \frac{b}{b} = \frac{c}{c}$$

Let $\qquad P$ *be* (x_1, y_1, z_1)

PQ is $\perp^r$ to $ax + by + cz + d = 0$

$$PQ = \pm \frac{ax_1 + by_1 + cz_1 + d}{\sqrt{a^2 + b^2 + c^2}}$$

PR is $\perp$ to $ax + by + cz + e = 0$

$$\therefore \quad PR = \pm \frac{ax_1 + by_1 + cz_1 + e}{\sqrt{a^2 + b^2 + c^2}}$$

Hence the required distance

$$= QR = PR - PQ$$

$$= \pm \left[\frac{ax_1 + by_1 + cz_1 + e}{\sqrt{a^2 + b^2 + c^2}} - \frac{ax_1 + by_1 + cz_1 + d}{\sqrt{a^2 + b^2 + c^2}} \right]$$

$$= \pm \frac{e - d}{\sqrt{a^2 + b^2 + c^2}}$$

Problem 15 Find the equation of the plane through the points (2, 2, 1) and (9, 3, 6) and perpendicular to the plane

$$2x + 6y + 6z = 9$$

Solution The equation of the given plane is

$$2x + 6y + 6z = 9 \tag{1}$$

Let the equation of the plane perpendicular to (1) can be written as

$$ax + by + cz + d = 0 \tag{2}$$

Since the plane (2) is perpendicular to (1) so

$$2a + 6b + 6c = 0 \tag{3}$$

Since plane (2) passes through points (2, 2, 1) and (9, 3, 6) so

$$2a + 2b + c + d = 0 \tag{4}$$

and
$$9a + 3b + 6c + d = 0 \tag{5}$$

From (5) – (4) we have

$$7a + b + 5c = 0 \tag{6}$$

From (3) we have $\quad a + 3b + 3c = 0 \qquad (7)$

By cross multiplication we have

$$\frac{a}{3-15} = \frac{b}{5-21} = \frac{c}{21-1}$$

$$\frac{a}{-12} = \frac{b}{-16} = \frac{c}{20}$$

$$\frac{a}{3} = \frac{b}{4}\ \frac{c}{-5} = k \text{ (say)}$$

So $\qquad a = 3k, \quad b = 4k, \quad c = -5k$

Putting the value of a, b and c in equation (3) we have

$$6k + 8k - 5k + d = 0$$

i.e. $$9k + d = 0$$

$$\Rightarrow d = -9k$$

Putting the value of a, b, c and d in (2) the required equation of the plane can be written as

$$3kx + 4ky - 5kz - 9k = 0$$

i.e. $$3x + 4y - 5z - 9 = 0$$

i.e, $$3x + 4y - 5z = 0 \quad \textbf{Ans.}$$

Problem 16 Find the equation of the plane through the points $(1, -2, 4)$ and $(3, -4, 5)$ and perpendicular to the yz plane,

Solution The equation of the given yz, plane is

$$x = 0 \tag{1}$$

Let the equation of the plane perpendicular to (1) be

$$ax + by + cz + d = 0 \tag{2}$$

Then $$a \cdot 1 + b \cdot 0 + c \cdot 0 = 0 \quad \text{i.e.} \quad a = 0 \tag{3}$$

By the question, (2) passes through the points

$$(1, -2, 4) \quad \text{and} \quad (3, -4, 5)$$

$\therefore$ $$a - 2b + 4c + d = 0$$

i.e. $$-2b + 4c + d = 0 \quad [\therefore \; a = 0] \tag{4}$$

and $$3a - 4b + 5c + d = 0$$

i.e. $$-4b + 5c + d = 0 \quad [\because \; a = 0] \tag{5}$$

By cross multiplication of (4) and (5) we have

$$\frac{b}{4-5} = \frac{c}{-4+2} = \frac{d}{-10+16}$$

i.e. $$\frac{b}{-1} = \frac{c}{-2} = \frac{d}{6} = k \text{ (say)}$$

Then $$b = -k, \quad c = -2k, \quad d = 6k$$

Putting the values of a, b, c, d in equation (2) the required equation of the plane is

$$-ky - 2kz + 6k = 0$$

i.e. $$\boxed{y + 2z - 6 = 0}$$

Problem 17 Find the equation of the plane through the point $(-1, 3, 2)$ and perpendicular to the planes

$$x + 2y + 2z = 5$$

and $$3x + 3y + 2z = 8$$

Solution Let the equation of the plane is

$$ax + by + cz + d = 0 \qquad (1)$$

Since it passes through the point $(-1, 3, 2)$ so

$$-a + 3b + 2c + d = 0 \qquad (2)$$

Subtracting equation (2) from equation (1) we have

$$a(x + 1) + b(y-3) + c(z-2) = 0 \qquad (3)$$

Since the plane (1) is perpendicular to the plane

$$x + 2y + 2z = 5$$

and $$3x + 3y + 2z = 8$$

So $$a + 2b + 2c = 0 \qquad (4)$$

and $$3a + 3b + 2c = 0 \qquad (5)$$

From cross multiplication of equation (4) and (5) we have

$$\frac{a}{4-6} = \frac{b}{6-2} = \frac{c}{3-6}$$

i.e. $$\frac{a}{-2} = \frac{b}{4} = \frac{c}{-3} = k$$

$$\Rightarrow \quad a = -2k, \quad b = 4k, \quad c = -3k$$

Putting the value of a, b, c in equation (3) wc have the required equation of the plane as

$$-2k(x + 1) + 4k(y-3) + (-3k)(z-2) = 0$$

i.e. $$k[-2x-2 + 4y-12-3z + 6] = 0$$

i.e. $$-2x + 4y-3z-8 = 0$$

i.e. $$\boxed{2x-4y + 3z + 8 = 0}$$ **Ans.**

Problem 18 Find the equation of the plane through the intersection of the planes

$$x + 2y + 3z = 4 \quad \text{and} \quad 2x + y-z + 5 = 0$$

and perpendicular to the plane $5x + 3y + 6z + 8 = 0$

Solution The equation of the plane through the intersection of the planes

$$x + 2y + 3z = 4 \quad \text{and} \quad 2x + y-z + 5 = 0$$

is given by $(x + 2y + 3z-4) + k(2x + y-z + 5) = 0$

i.e. $$x(1 + 2k) + y(2 + k) + z(3-k)-(4-5k) = 0 \qquad (1)$$

Since the plane (1) is perpendicular to

$$5x + 3y + 6z + 8 = 0$$

$$\Rightarrow \quad 5(1 + 2k) + 3(2 + k) + 6(3 - k) = 0$$

i e, $\quad 5 + 10k + 6 + 3k + 18 - 6k = 0$

ii.e. $\quad 29 + 7k = 0$

i.e. $\quad k = -\dfrac{29}{7}$

Putting the value of $k = -\dfrac{29}{7}$ we have the equation of plane as

$$(x + 2y + 3z - 4) - \frac{29}{7}(2x + y - z + 5) = 0$$

i.e. $\quad 7x + 14y + 21z - 28 - 58x - 29y + 29z - 145 = 0$

i.e. $\quad -51x - 15y + 50z - 173 = 0$

i.e. $\quad 51x + 15y - 50z + 173 = 0$

Which is the required equation of the plane.

Problem 19 Find the equation of the plane containing the line

$$x - 2y + z + 3 = 0 \quad \text{and} \quad x + 2y + 2z = 5$$

and perpendicular to the xy-plane.

Solution Equation of the plane containing the line

$$x - 2y + z + 3 = 0 \quad \text{and} \quad x + 2y + 2z - 5 = 0$$

is given by

$$x - 2y + z + 3) + k(x + 2y + 2z - 5) = 0$$

i.e. $\quad x(1 + k) - 2y(1 - k) + z(1 + 2k) + (3 - 5k) = 0 \qquad (1)$

Now since plane (1) is perpendicular to xy plane

i.e. $\quad z = 0$

So $\quad (1 + k)\cdot 0 + (-2)(1 - k)\cdot 0 + (1 + 2k)\cdot 1 = 0$

i.e. $\quad 1 + 2k = 0$

$$\Rightarrow \quad 2k = -1$$

$$\Rightarrow \quad k = -\tfrac{1}{2}$$

Putting the value of $k = -\frac{1}{2}$ in the equation of the plane

$$(x - 2y + z + 3) - \tfrac{1}{2}(x + 2y + 2z - 5) = 0$$

i.e. $\quad 2x - 4y + 2z + 6 - x - 2y - 2z + 5 = 0$

i.e. $\quad x - 6y + 11 = 0$

Which is the required equation of the plane. **Ans.**

Problem 20 Show that the planes $2x + 5y + 3z = 0$, $7y - 5z + 4 = 0$ and $x - y + 4z = 2$ intersect in a straight line.

Solution Any plane through the line of intersection of the planes

$$2x + 5y + 3z = 0$$

and

$$7y - 5z + 4 = 0$$

is

$$2x + 5y + 3z + \lambda(7y - 5z + 4) = 0$$

If for some value of λ, this is the same plane as $x - y + 4z = 2$ then the three planes will intersect in a straight line

For $\lambda = -1$

We have $2x + 5y + 3z + \lambda(7y - 5z + 4) = 0$

$$\Rightarrow \quad 2x + 5y + 3z - 1(7y - 5z + 4 = 0$$

$$\Rightarrow \quad 2x + 5y + 3z - 7y + 5z - 4 = 0$$

$$\Rightarrow \quad 2x - 2y + 8z - 4 = 0$$

i.e.

$$x - y + 4z - 2 = 0$$

$$\Rightarrow \quad x - y + 4z = 2$$

Hence the three given planes intersect in a straight line. *(Proved)*

Problem 21 Find the angle between the planes

$$x + 2y + 3z = 5 \quad \text{and} \quad 3x - 3y + z = 1$$

Solution θ is given by

$$\cos\theta = \frac{aa_1 + bb_1 + cc_1}{\sqrt{a^2 + b^2 + c^2}\sqrt{a_1^2 + b_1^2 + c_1^2}}$$

$$\cos\theta = \frac{1 \cdot 3 + 2(-3) + 3 \cdot 1}{\sqrt{1^2 + 2^2 + 3^2}\sqrt{3^2 + (-3)^2 + 1^2}}$$

$$\cos\theta = \frac{3 - 6 + 3}{\sqrt{14}\sqrt{19}} = 0$$

So

$$\theta = \frac{\pi}{2}$$

i.e. the two planes are at right angles

Problem 22 Find the planes bisecting the angles between the planes

$$x + 2y + 2z = 9 \quad \text{and} \quad 4x - 3y + 12z + 13 = 0$$

and point out which bisects the aucte angle.

Solution The given planes are

$$x + 2y + 2z = 9$$

i.e.

$$-x - 2y - 2z + 9 = 0 \qquad (1)$$

and

$$4x - 3y + 12z + 13 = 0 \qquad (2)$$

The equations of the bisecting planes are given by

$$\frac{-x-2y-2z+9}{\sqrt{1+4+4}} = \pm \frac{4x-3y+12z+13}{\sqrt{16+9+144}}$$

i.e. $\quad 13(-x-2y-2z+9) = \pm\, 3\,(4x-3y+12z+13)$

i.e. $\quad -13x-26y-26z+117 = \pm\,(12x-9y+36z+39)$

Taking +ve sign

$$-13x-26y-26z+117 = 12x-9y+36z+39$$

i.e. $\quad -25x-17y-62z+78=0$

i.e. $\quad 25x+17y+62z-78=0 \qquad (3)$

and $\quad -13x-26y-26z+117 = -(12x-9y+36z+39)$

[*Taking − ve sign*]

i.e. $\quad -13x-26y-26z+117 = -12x+9y-36z-39$

$$-x-35y+10z+156=0$$

i.e. $\quad x+35y-10z-156=0 \qquad (4)$

If θ is the angle between (1) and (3)

$$\cos\theta = \frac{25.1+17\cdot 2+62\times 2}{\sqrt{4+4+1}\,\sqrt{25^2+17^2+62^2}} = \frac{183}{3\times 68}$$

$$\cos\theta = \frac{61}{68} > \frac{1}{\sqrt{2}}$$

i.e. $\quad \theta < 45^\circ$

Heace the plane

$25x+17y+62z-78=0$ bisects the acute angle.

Problem 23 Show that the equation

$$2x^2-6y^2-12z^2+18yz+2zx+xy=0$$

represents a pair of planes and find the angle between them.

Solution We know that the equation

$$ax^2+by^2+by^2+cz^2+2fyz+2gzx+2hxy=0$$

Will represent *a* pair of planes if

$$abc+2fgh-af^2-bg^2-ch^2=0$$

Here $\quad a=2.\ b=-6,\ c=-12$

$$2f=18,\ 2g=2,\ 2h=1$$

So $\quad abc+2fgh-af^2-bg^2-ch^2 = 2\times(-6)\times(-12)+18\times 1\times \frac{1}{2}$
$-2\times 81-(-6)\,1-(-12)\times\frac{1}{4}$

i.e. $\quad 144+9-162+6+3$

i.e. $\quad 144+18-162 = 162-162 = 0$

The angle θ between the pair of planes is given by

$$\tan\theta = 2\,\frac{\sqrt{f^2 + g^2 + h^2 - bc - ca - ab}}{a + b + c}$$

$$\tan\theta = 2\,\frac{\sqrt{81 + 1 + \frac{1}{4} - 72 + 24 + 12}}{-16}$$

$$\tan\theta = 2\,\frac{\sqrt{\dfrac{1 + 40 + 96 + 48}{4}}}{-16}$$

$$\tan\theta = -2\,\frac{\sqrt{175}}{32} \qquad \textbf{Ans.}$$

$$\tan\theta = -2\,\frac{\sqrt{25 \times 7}}{32}$$

$$\tan\theta = -\frac{2 \times 5\sqrt{7}}{32}$$

$$\tan\theta = -\frac{5\sqrt{7}}{16}$$

Remember Formula The angle between the pair of planes

$ax^2 + by^2 + cz^2 + 2fyz + 2gzx + 2hxy = 0$ is given

$$\tan\theta = \frac{2\sqrt{f^2 + g^2 + h^2 - bc - ca - ab}}{a + b + c}$$

And they are $\perp^r$ to each other if

$$\boxed{a + b + c = 0}$$

Problem 24 The plane $ax + by = 0$ is rotated about its line of intersection with the plane $z = 0$ through an angle θ. Prove that the equation of the plane in its new position is

$$ax + by \pm z\sqrt{a^2 + b^2}\tan\theta = 0$$

Solution As the plane $ax + by = 0$ is rotated about its line of intersection with the plane $z = 0$ so that the plane will pass through the intersection of the planes $ax + by = 0$, $z = 0$

Let the plane after rotation be

$$ax + by + kz = 0 \tag{1}$$

(1) makes an angle θ with the given plane $ax + by = 0$

$$\therefore \qquad \cos\theta = \frac{a\cdot a + b\cdot b + k\cdot 0}{\sqrt{a^2 + b^2 + k^2}\sqrt{a^2 + b^2}}$$

$$\cos\theta = \frac{\sqrt{a^2 + b^2}}{\sqrt{a^2 + b^2 + k^2}}$$

i.e. $$(a^2 + b^2 + k^2) \cos^2 \theta = (a^2 + b^2)$$

$$k^2 \cos^2 \theta = (a^2 + b^2)(1 - \cos^2 \theta)$$

$$k^2 \cos^2 \theta = (a^2 + b^2) \sin^2 \theta$$

$$\Rightarrow \quad k^2 = (a^2 + b^2) \tan^2 \theta$$

$$k = \pm \sqrt{a^2 + b^2} \tan \theta$$

Hence the required planes are

$$ax + by \pm z \sqrt{a^2 + b^2} \tan \theta = 0 \qquad \textit{(Proved)}$$

Problem 25 Show that

$$\frac{a}{y-z} + \frac{b}{z-x} + \frac{c}{x-y} = 0 \text{ represent of pair of Planes}$$

we know that $ax^2 + by^2 + cz^2 + 2fyz + 2gzx + 2hxy = 0$
will rspresent a pair of planes if

$$abc + 2fgh - af^2 - bg^2 - ch^2 = 0$$

Given equation is

$$\frac{a}{y-z} + \frac{b}{z-x} + \frac{c}{x-y} = 0$$

i.e. $$\frac{a(z-x)(x-y) + b(y-z)(x-y) + c(y-z)(z-x)}{(y-z)(z-x)(x-y)} = 0$$

i.e. $$a(xz - x^2 + xy - yz) + b(yx - y^2 - zx + yz) + c(yz - yx - z^2 - xz) = 0$$

i.e. $$ax^2 + by^2 + cz^2 + (a-b-c)yz + (b+c-a)zx + (c-a-b)xy = 0$$

i.e. $$ax^2 + by^2 + cz^2 - (b+c-a)yz - (c+a-b)zx - (a+b-c)xy = 0 \qquad (1)$$

Equation (1) will represent a of pair planes if

$$\begin{vmatrix} a & -\frac{1}{2}(a+b-c) & -\frac{1}{2}(c+a-b) \\ -\frac{1}{2}(a+b-c) & b & -\frac{1}{2}(b+c-a) \\ -\frac{1}{2}(c+a-b) & -\frac{1}{2}(b+c-a) & c \end{vmatrix} = 0$$

Adding all the rows to the first row

$$\begin{vmatrix} 0 & 0 & 0 \\ -\frac{1}{2}(a+b-c & b & -\frac{1}{2}(b+c-a) \\ -\frac{1}{2}(c+a-b) & -\frac{1}{2}(b+c-a) & c \end{vmatrix}$$

Which is clearly zero

Hence the given equation represents two planes. *(Proved)*

Problem 29 A plane meets the co-ordinate axes in A, B, C such that the controid of the triangle ABC is the point (a, b, c) show that the equation of the plane is

$$\frac{x}{a} + \frac{y}{b} + \frac{z}{c} = 3$$

Solution Let the equation of the plane be

$$\frac{x}{\alpha} + \frac{y}{\beta} + \frac{z}{\gamma} = 1$$

Then A, B, C are $(\alpha, 0, 0)$, $(0, \beta, 0)$ and $(0, 0, \gamma)$

$$\therefore \quad a = \frac{\alpha + 0 + 0}{3}$$

$$b = \frac{0 + \beta + 0}{3}$$

$$c = \frac{0 + 0 + \gamma}{3}$$

i.e.

$$\left.\begin{aligned} \alpha &= 3a \\ \beta &= 3b \\ \gamma &= 3c \end{aligned}\right\}$$

Then the equation of the plane becomes

$$\frac{x}{3a} + \frac{y}{3b} + \frac{z}{3c} = 1$$

i.e.

$$\frac{x}{a} + \frac{y}{b} + \frac{z}{c} = 3 \qquad (Proved)$$

Problem 27 Two systems of the rectangular axis have the same origin. If a plane cuts them at a distances a, b, c and a^1, b^1, c_1 respectively from tne origin, prove that

$$\frac{1}{a^2} + \frac{1}{b^2} + \frac{1}{c^2} = \frac{1}{a^{12}} + \frac{1}{b^{12}} + \frac{1}{c^{12}}$$

Solution Let the equation of the plane with respect to the two system of the rectangular axes be

$$\frac{x}{a} + \frac{y}{b} + \frac{z}{c} = 0 \qquad (1)$$

$$\frac{x}{a^1} + \frac{x}{b^1} + \frac{z}{c^1} - 1 = 0$$

From the origin (0, 0, 0) draw perpendicular to the plane. Since (1) and (2) represent the same plane, therefore

$$\frac{1}{\sqrt{\frac{1}{a^2} + \frac{1}{b^2} + \frac{1}{c^2}}} = \frac{1}{\sqrt{\frac{1}{a^{12}} + \frac{1}{b^{12}} + \frac{1}{c^{12}}}}$$

Thus

$$\frac{1}{a^2} + \frac{1}{b^2} + \frac{1}{c^2} + = \frac{1}{a^{12}} + \frac{1}{b^{12}} + \frac{1}{c^{12}}$$

Problem 28 A variable plane is at a constant distance p from the origin and meets the axes at PQR. Find the locus of the centroid of the triangle PQR.

Solution Let the plane be $lx + my + nz = p$ where

p is a constant given and $\quad l^2 + m^2 + n^2 = 1 \qquad (1)$

$$\frac{x}{p/l} + \frac{y}{p/m} + \frac{z}{p/n} = 1$$

The co-ordinate of the point P, Q, and R are given by

$$\left(\frac{p}{l}, 0, 0\right), \left(0, \frac{p}{m}, 0\right), \left(0, 0, \frac{p}{n}\right)$$

If (α, β, γ) be the centroid of the triangle PQR then

$$\alpha = \frac{p/l + 0 + 0}{3} \quad l = \frac{p}{3\alpha}$$

$$\beta = \frac{0 + p/m + 0}{3} \quad \Rightarrow m = \frac{p}{3\beta}$$

$$\gamma = \frac{0 + 0 + p/n}{3} \quad \Rightarrow n = \frac{p}{3\gamma}$$

Putting the value of l, m and n in (1) we have

$$\frac{p^2}{9\alpha^2} + \frac{p^2}{9\beta^2} + \frac{p^2}{9\gamma^2} = 1$$

i.e.

$$\frac{1}{\alpha^2} + \frac{1}{\beta^2} + \frac{1}{\gamma^2} + = \frac{9}{p^2}$$

$\therefore$ Locus of (α, β, γ) is given by

$$\frac{1}{x^2} + \frac{1}{y^2} + \frac{1}{z^2} = \frac{9}{p^2}$$

Problem 29 Find the locus of the point whose distance from (1, 2, 3) is half distance from $2x + y - 2z = 7$

Solution Let the point be (α, β, γ) the distance of (α, β, γ) from (1, 2, 3) is given by

$$\sqrt{(\alpha-1)^2 + (\beta-2)^2 + (\gamma-3)^2}$$

The distance of (1, 2, 3) from

$$2x + y - 2z = 7 \text{ is}$$

$$\frac{2\cdot 1 + 2 - 2\cdot 3 - 7}{\sqrt{4 + 1 + 4}} = -\frac{9}{3} = -3$$

From the problem $\sqrt{(\alpha-1)^2 + (\beta-1)^2 + (\gamma-1)^2} = -3/2$

i.e. $$(\alpha-1)^2 + (\beta-1)^2 + (\gamma-1)^2 = \frac{9}{4}$$

The locus of (α, β, γ) has the equation

$$(x-1)^2 + (y-1)^2 + (z-1)^2 = \frac{9}{4} \qquad \textbf{Ans.}$$

Problem 30 The axis are rectangular and a point p moves on a fixed plane

$$\frac{x}{a} + \frac{y}{b} + \frac{z}{c} = 1$$

The plane through P perpendicular to OP meets the axes in A, B, C. The plane through A, B, C parallel to YOZ, ZOX, XOY respectively intersect in Q. Show that the locus of Q is

$$\frac{1}{x^2} + \frac{1}{y^2} + \frac{1}{z^2} = \frac{1}{ax} + \frac{1}{by} + \frac{1}{cz}$$

Solution Let p be (x_1, y_1, z_1) and $0\ (0, 0, 0)$

$\therefore$ p is on

$$\frac{x}{a} + \frac{y}{b} + \frac{z}{c} = 1$$

$\therefore$ $$\frac{x_1}{a} + \frac{y_1}{b} + \frac{z_1}{c} = 1 \qquad (1)$$

Direction ratios of op are

$$x_1 - 0, y_1 - 0, z_1 - 0 \text{ i.e. } x_1, y_1, z_1$$

The equation of the plane through $p\ (x_1, y_1, z_1)$ and $\perp^r$ to OP is

$$lx + my + nz = p$$

Where l, m, n are the actual direction cosines of the line OP

$$\frac{x_1\, x}{\sqrt{x_1^2 + y_1^2 + z_1^2}} + \frac{y_1\, y}{\sqrt{x_1^2 + y_1^2 + z_1^2}} + \frac{z_1\, z}{\sqrt{x_1^2 + y_1^2 + z_1^2}}$$

Since this passes through (x_1, y_1, z_1) so

$$\frac{x_1^2 + y_1^2 + z_1^2}{\sqrt{x_1^2 + y_1^2 + z_1^2}} = p$$

So the equation of the plane becomes

$$xx_1 + yy_1 + zz_1 = x_1^2 + y_1^2 + z_1^2$$

i.e. $$\frac{x}{\dfrac{x_1^2 + y_1^2 + z_1^2}{x_1}} + \frac{y}{\dfrac{x_1^2 + y_1^2 + z_1^2}{y_1}} + \frac{z}{\dfrac{x_1^2 + y_1^2 + z_1^2}{z_1}} = 1$$

Thus this plane meets the axes in A, B, C

$$A \text{ is } \left(\frac{x_1^2 + y_1^2 + z_1}{x_1}, 0, 0\right)$$

$$B \text{ is } \left(0, \frac{x_1^2 + y_1^2 + z_1^2}{y_1}, 0\right)$$

$$C \text{ is } \left(0, 0 \frac{x_1^2 + y_1^2 + z_1^2}{z_1}\right)$$

The equation of the plane through A and parallel to $Y\,0\,Z$ plane is

$$x = \frac{x_1^2 + y_1^2 + z_1^2}{x_1} \tag{2}$$

The equation of the plane through B and parallel to $Z\,0\,X$ plane

$$y = \frac{x_1^2 + y_1^2 + z_1^2}{y_1} \tag{3}$$

The equation of the plane through C and parallel to $X\,0\,Y$ plane

$$z = \frac{x_1^2 + y_1^2 + z_1^2}{z_1} \tag{4}$$

Eliminating $x_1\ y_1, z_1$ from (2), (3). (4) we get the locus of Q

$$\frac{1}{x^2} + \frac{1}{y^2} + \frac{1}{z^2} = \frac{x_1^2 + y_1^2 + z_1^2}{(x_1^2 + y_1^2 + z_1^2)^2} = \frac{1}{x_1^2 + y_1^2 + z_1^2}$$

Also $$\frac{1}{ax} + \frac{1}{by} + \frac{1}{cz} = \frac{\frac{x_1}{a} + \frac{y_1}{b} + \frac{z_1}{c}}{x_1^2 + y_1^2 + z_1^2} = \frac{1}{x_1^2 + y_1^2 + z_1^2}$$

i.e. $$\frac{1}{ax} + \frac{1}{by} + \frac{1}{cz} = \frac{1}{x^2} + \frac{1}{y^2} + \frac{1}{z^2}$$

Thus locus of Q is $\dfrac{1}{x^2} + \dfrac{1}{y^2} + \dfrac{1}{z^2} = \dfrac{1}{ax} + \dfrac{1}{by} + \dfrac{1}{cz}$

22

Straight Lines

Remember Formula (1) Equation of a line through (x_1, y_1, z_1) and having direction cosines l, m, n are

$$\frac{x-x_1}{l}=\frac{y-y_1}{m}=\frac{z-z_1}{n}=r\ (say)$$

(2) The plane $ax+by+cz+d=0$ is parallel to the line

$$\frac{x-x_1}{l}=\frac{y-y_1}{m}=\frac{z-z_1}{n} \quad \text{if } al+bm+cn=0$$

(3) line $\dfrac{x-x_1}{l}=\dfrac{y-y_1}{m}=\dfrac{z-z_1}{n}$

lies wholly in the plane

$$ax+by+cz+d=0$$

if

$$al+bm+cn=0$$

and

$$ax_1+by_1+cz_1+d=0$$

(4) Distance of (x_1, y_1, z_1) from

$$\frac{x-\alpha}{l}=\frac{y-\beta}{m}=\frac{z-\gamma}{n} \text{ is}$$

$$\sum \{(y_1-\beta)\,n-(z_1-\gamma)\,m\}^2$$

(5) Two straight lines

$$\frac{x-x_1}{l_1}=\frac{y-y_1}{m_1}=\frac{z-z_1}{n_1} \text{ and}$$

$$\frac{x-x_2}{l_2}=\frac{y-y_2}{m_2}=\frac{z-z_2}{n_2} \text{ are coplanar if}$$

$$\begin{vmatrix} x_2-x_1 & y_2-y_1 & z_2-z_1 \\ l_1 & m_1 & n_1 \\ l_2 & m_2 & n_2 \end{vmatrix}=0$$

The equation of the plane containing these lines is

$$\begin{vmatrix} x-x_1 & y-y_1 & z-z_1 \\ l_1 & m_1 & n_i \\ l_2 & m_2 & n_2 \end{vmatrix} = 0$$

Problem 1 Show that the line

$4x = 3y = -z$ is perpendicular to $3x = -y = -4z$

Solution We know that two straight lines whose direction cosines are l_1, m_1, n_1 are l_2, m_2, n_2 are perpendicular to each other if

$$l_1 l_2 + m_1 m_2 + n_1 n_2 = 0 \tag{1}$$

The straight line $4x = 3y = -z$ can be written as

$$\frac{4x}{12} = \frac{3y}{12} = \frac{z}{-12}$$

i.e. $$\frac{x}{3} = \frac{y}{4} = \frac{z}{-12}$$

i.e. the direction cosines of this line is 3, 4 and -12

Again the 2nd straight line can be written as

$$3x = -y = -4z$$

$$\frac{3x}{12} = \frac{y}{-12} = \frac{-4z}{12} \quad \text{i.e.} \quad \frac{x}{4} = \frac{y}{-12} = \frac{z}{-3}$$

i.e. the direction co sines of this line is 4. -12. -3

Now we have $l_1 l_2 + m_1 m_2 + n_1 n_2$

$$= 3 \times 4 + (-12)\, 4 + (-12) \times (-3)$$

$$= 12 - 48 + 36 = 48 - 48 = 0 \text{ (verified)}$$

So the two straight lines are perpendicular to each other.

Problem 2 Find the direction cosines of the line whose equation is

$$x + y - z + 1 = 0,\ 4x + y - 2z + 2 = 0$$

Solution Two planes $x + y - z + 1 = 0$ and $4x + y - 2z + 2 = 0$ will cut in a straight line say AB. We have to find the direction cosines of this line.

Let the direction cosines of this line AB is

l, m and n

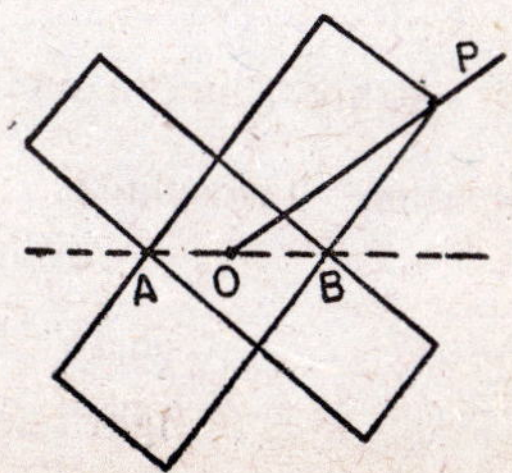

Equation of the planes are

$$x + y - z + 1 = 0$$

i.e. the direction cosines of the normal to this planes is

1, 1 and -1

Again the equation of the 2nd plane is

$$4x + y - 2z + 2 = 0$$

So the direction cosines of the normal to this plane is

$$4,\ 1,\ -2$$

So the line whose d.c.'s are l, m, n is perpendicular to both the normals whose d.c.'s are

$$1,\ 1 \quad \text{and} \quad -1$$

and $$4,\ 1 \quad \text{and} \quad -2$$

So $$1l + 1m - n = 0 \tag{1}$$

And $$4l + m - 2n = 0 \tag{2}$$

By cross multiplication of (1) and (2) we have

$$\frac{l}{-2+1} = \frac{m}{-4+2} = \frac{n}{1-4}$$

i.e. $$\frac{l}{-1} = \frac{m}{-2} = \frac{n}{-3}$$

i.e. $$\frac{l}{1} = \frac{m}{2} = \frac{n}{3} = \frac{\sqrt{l^2 + m^2 + n^2}}{\sqrt{1^2 + 2^2 + 3^2}}$$

$$\frac{l}{1} = \frac{m}{2} = \frac{n}{3} = \frac{1}{\sqrt{14}}$$

Thus $$l = \frac{1}{\sqrt{14}}$$

$$m = \frac{2}{\sqrt{14}}$$

And $$n = \frac{3}{\sqrt{14}}$$

Thus the d.c.'s of the line AB is

$$\frac{1}{\sqrt{14}},\ \frac{2}{\sqrt{14}} \text{ and } \frac{3}{\sqrt{14}}$$ **Ans.**

Problem 3 Put the equations $4x + 4y - 5z = 12$,
$8x + 12y - 13z = 32$

of a straight line in symmetrical form.

Solution Two planes

$$4x + 4y - 5z = 12 \tag{1}$$

And $$8x + 12y - 13z = 32 \tag{2}$$

will cut in a straight line. Let the d.c.'s of the straight line is lm and n

Then $$4l + 4m - 5n = 0 \qquad (3)$$

And $$8l + 12m - 13n = 0 \qquad (4)$$

By the cross multiplication of (3) and (4) we have

$$\frac{l}{-52 + 60} = \frac{m}{-40 + 52} = \frac{n}{48 - 32}$$

i.e. $$\frac{l}{8} = \frac{m}{12} = \frac{n}{16}$$

i.e. $$\frac{l}{2} = \frac{m}{3} = \frac{n}{4}$$

Thus the direction cosines of the line are proportional to 2, 3 and 4

Put $$z = 0$$

we have $$4x + 4y - 12 = 0$$

$$8x + 12y - 32 = 0$$

i.e. $$x + y - 3 = 0 \qquad (5)$$

And $$2x + 3y - 8 = 0 \qquad (6)$$

Solving (5) and (6) we have

$$\frac{x}{-8 + 9} = \frac{y}{-6 + 8} = \frac{1}{3 - 2}$$

i.e. $$\frac{x}{1} = \frac{y}{2} = \frac{1}{1}$$

i.e. $$x = 1, y = 2$$

Thus the straight line passes through the point (1, 2, 0)

Thus the equation of the straight line passing through (1, 2, 0) and whose d.c.'s are

$$\frac{2}{\sqrt{29}}, \frac{3}{\sqrt{29}}, \frac{4}{\sqrt{29}}$$

is given in the symmetrical form as

$$\frac{x-1}{\frac{2}{\sqrt{29}}} = \frac{y-2}{\frac{3}{\sqrt{29}}} = \frac{z-0}{\frac{4}{\sqrt{29}}}$$

i.e. $$\frac{x-1}{2} = \frac{y-2}{3} = \frac{z}{4}$$

which is the required equation of the straight line **Ans.**

Problem 4 Find the equations to the straight line drawn from the origin to intersect the line

$$3x + 2y + 4z - 5 = 0 = 2x - 3y + 4z + 1$$

and
$$2x - 4y + z + 6 = 0 = 3x - 4y + z - 3$$

Solution The equations of the required line are

$$3x + 2y + 4z - 5 + k(2x - 3y + 4z + 1) = 0 \quad (1)$$

and
$$2x - 4y + z + 6 + k_1(3x - 4y + z - 3) \quad (2)$$

If the above line passes through the origin (0, 0, 0) then

$$-5 + k = 0 \Rightarrow k = 5$$

and
$$6 - 3k_1 = 0 \Rightarrow k_1 = 2$$

Putting the value of k and k_1 we get

$$3x + 2y + 4z - 5 + 10x - 15y + 20z + 5 = 0$$

i.e.
$$13x - 13y + 24z = 0$$

and
$$2x - 4y + z + 6 + 2(3x - 4y + z - 3) = 0$$

$$\Rightarrow \quad 2x - 4y + z + 6 + 6x - 8y + 2z - 6 = 0$$

$$\Rightarrow \quad 8x - 12y + 3z = 0$$

Hence the required equation to the line are

$$13x - 13y + 24z = 0 = 8x - 12y + 3z$$

Problem 5 Find the equation to the line passing through (−1, 3, 2) and perpendicular to the plane $x + 2y + 2z = 3$. Also find the length of the perpendicular from the given point to the given plane.

Solution The direction cosine of the normal to the plane

$$x + 2y + 2z = 3$$

are proportional to (1, 2, 2). So the line which is perpendicular to the plane

$$x + 2y + 2z = 3$$

has the direction cosine proportional to (1, 2, 2). Now the equations of a line through (−1, 3, 2) and having d-cosines proportional to (1, 2, 2) are

$$\frac{x+1}{1} = \frac{y-3}{2} = \frac{z-2}{2}$$

Now the length of the perpendicular from (−1, 3, 2) to

$x + 2y + 2z = 3$ is given by

$$\frac{-1 + 2\cdot 3 + 2\cdot 2 - 3}{\sqrt{1^2 + 2^2 + 2^2}}$$

$$= \frac{-1+6+4-3}{3} = 2 \qquad \textbf{Ans.}$$

Problem 6 Show that the equations of the perpendicular from (α, β, γ) to the plane $ax + by + cz + d = 0$ are

$$\frac{x-\alpha}{a} = \frac{y-\beta}{b} = \frac{z-\gamma}{c}$$

and deduce the distance of the point from the plane.

Solution $$ax + by + cz + d = 0 \qquad (1)$$

is the equation of the plane where a, b, c are the proportional direction ratios of the normal to this plane. Any line perpendicular to this plane have the direction cosines proportional to a, b and c.

Thus the equation of the straight line passing through (α, β, γ) and whose $d \cdot cs$ are proportional to a, b, c are given by

$$\frac{x-\alpha}{a} = \frac{y-\beta}{b} = \frac{z-\gamma}{c}$$

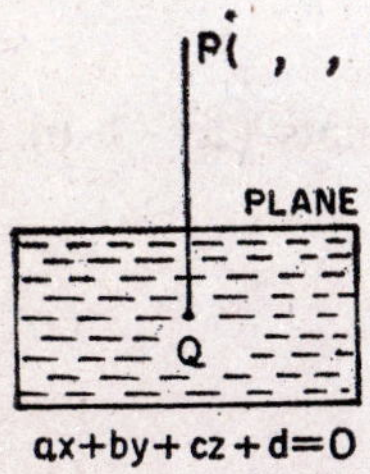

P(, ,)

PLANE

Q

ax+by+cz+d=0

Any point on this line is given by

$$(ar + \alpha, br + \beta, cr + \gamma)$$

If this point lies on plane (1) then

$$a(ar + \alpha) + b(br + \beta) + c(cr + \gamma) + d = 0$$

$$(a^2 + b^2 + c^2) r + a\alpha + b\beta + c\gamma + d = 0$$

$$\Rightarrow r = -\frac{(a\alpha + b\beta + c\gamma + d)}{(a^2 + b^2 + c^2}$$

Now perpendicular distance from the point (α, β, γ) from the plane (1)

$$p^2 = \text{distance between } (\alpha, \beta, \gamma) \text{ and } (\alpha r + \alpha, br + \beta, cr + \gamma)$$

$$= (ar + \alpha - \alpha)^2 + (br + \beta - \beta)^2 + (cr + \gamma - \gamma)^2$$

$$= a^2 r^2 + b^2 r^2 + c^2 r^2$$

$$= r^2 (a^2 + b^2 + c^2)$$

$$= \frac{(a\alpha + b\theta + c\gamma - d)^2}{(a^2 + b^2 + c)^2} \cdot (a^2 + b^2 + c^2)$$

$$p^2 = \frac{(a\alpha + b\beta + c\gamma + d)^2}{(a^2 + b^2 + c^2)}$$

$$p = \frac{a\alpha + b\beta + c\gamma + d}{\sqrt{a^2 + b^2 + c^2}} \text{ in magnitude.} \qquad \textbf{Ans.}$$

Problem 7 Find the equations of the line through the point (3. 2, 1) and parallel to the line $\dfrac{x-4}{2} = \dfrac{y+1}{3} = \dfrac{z-2}{5}$

Solution Let the equations to the line through (3, 2, 1) be

$$\frac{x-3}{l} = \frac{y-2}{m} = \frac{z-1}{n} \qquad (1)$$

The line (1) is parallel to

$$\frac{x-4}{2}=\frac{y+1}{3}=\frac{z-2}{-5} \tag{2}$$

$$\therefore \quad \frac{l}{2}=\frac{m}{3}=\frac{n}{-5}=k \text{ (say)}$$

$$l=2k,\ m=3k,\ n=-5k$$

Putting the values of l, m, n in (1) we obtain

$$\frac{x-3}{2k}=\frac{y-2}{3k}=\frac{z-1}{-5k}$$

i.e.

$$\frac{x-3}{2}=\frac{y-2}{3}=\frac{z-1}{-5}$$

Which is required equation of the straight line.

Problem 8 Find the equation to the plane through the points (2, −1. 0), (3, −4, 5) and parallel to the straight line

$$2x=3y=4z$$

Solution Let the equation of the plane be

$$ax+by+cz+d=0 \tag{1}$$

It passes through two points (2, −1, 0) and (3, −4, 5)

So

$$2a-b+d=0 \quad (2)$$

$$3a-4b+5c+d=0 \quad (3)$$

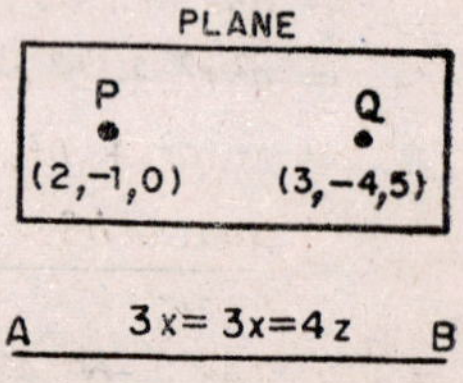

Subtracting (2) by (3) we have

$$a-3b+5c=0 \quad (4)$$

PLANE

P (2,−1,0)

Q (3,−4,5)

A 3x= 3x=4 z B

Equation of the straight line is

$$2x=3y=4z$$

Which can be written in the symmentric form as

$$\frac{x}{6}=\frac{y}{4}=\frac{z}{3}$$

The direction consine of this line is proportional to 6, 4, 3. The direction cosine of the normal to the plane (1) is given by a, b, c. Then normal to the plane (1) in perpendicular to the straight line then in this case

$$6a+4b+3c=0 \tag{4}$$

$$a-3b+5c=0 \tag{5}$$

Then by cross multiplication we have

$$\frac{a}{20+9}=\frac{b}{3-30}=\frac{c}{-18-4}$$

$$\frac{a}{29}=\frac{b}{-27}=\frac{c}{-22}$$

$$\frac{a}{-29}=\frac{b}{27}=\frac{c}{22}=k \text{ (say)}$$

$$a=-29k$$
$$b=27k$$
$$c=22k$$

Putting the value of a, b and c in equation (2) we have

$$-58k-27k+d=0$$
$$d=85k$$

Putting the value of a, b, c and d in equation (1)

$$-29xk+27yk+22zk+85k=0$$

i.e.
$$29x-27y-22z-85=0$$

Which is the required equation of the plane. **Ans.**

Problem 9 Find the equations to the line through the point (1, 2, 3) parallel to the line
$$x-y+2z=5,$$
$$3x+y+z=6$$

Solution Equation to the line through (1, 2, 3) is given by

$$\frac{x-1}{l}=\frac{y-2}{m}=\frac{z-3}{n} \qquad (1)$$

Where l, m and n are the direction cosines of the line

$$\left.\begin{aligned} x-y+2z&=5\\ 3x+y+z&=6\end{aligned}\right\}$$

and

are the equations of the plane

Where 1, -1, 2 and 3, 1, 1 are the $d{\cdot}cs$ of the normal to them.

Since the line (1) is parallel to the line (2) so

$$l-m+2n=0 \qquad (3)$$
$$3l+m+n=0$$

$$\frac{l}{-1-2}=\frac{m}{6-1}=\frac{n}{1+3}$$

$$\frac{l}{-3}=\frac{m}{5}=\frac{n}{4}=k \text{ (say)}$$

$$l=-3k$$
$$m=5k$$
$$n=4k$$

So the equation of the straight line is

$$\frac{x-1}{-3k}=\frac{y-2}{5k}=\frac{z-3}{4k}$$

$$\frac{x-1}{-3}=\frac{y-2}{5}=\frac{z-3}{4}$$

Which is the required equation of the **straight line.**

Problem 10 Find the point where the line joining (2, −3, 1) and (3, −4, −5) cuts the plane $2x + y + z = 7$

Solution The equations of the line joining (2, −3, 1) and (3, −4, −5) are.

$$\frac{x-2}{2-3}=\frac{y+3}{-3+4}=\frac{z-1}{1+5}$$

or
$$\frac{x-2}{-1}=\frac{y+3}{1}=\frac{z-1}{6}=\lambda$$

i.e.
$$x=2-\lambda : y = \lambda-3$$
$$z = 6\lambda+1$$

Any point on the line has the co-ordinates $(2-\lambda, \lambda-3, 6\lambda + 1)$ If the line cuts the plane at this point, then

$$2(2-\lambda) + (\lambda-3) + (6\lambda + 1) = 7$$

i.e.
$$4-2\lambda + \lambda-3 + 6\lambda + 1 = 7$$
$$5\lambda = 5$$
$$\Rightarrow \qquad \lambda = 1$$

Hence the required point is (1, —2, 7)

Problem 11 If the axes are rectangular, find the distance from the point (3, 4, 5) to the point where the line

$$\frac{x-3}{1}=\frac{y-4}{2}=\frac{z-5}{2}$$

meets theplane $x + y + z = 17$

Solution Any point on the line

$$\frac{x-3}{1}=\frac{y-4}{2}=\frac{z-5}{2}$$

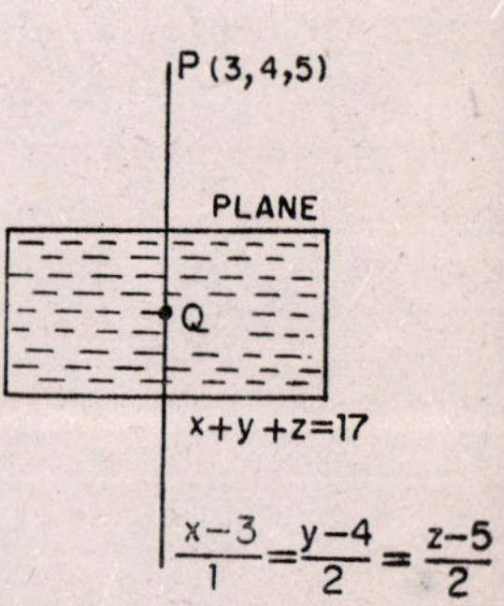

is given by

$$x = r + 3, y = 2r + 4, z = 2r + 5$$

i.e. by $(r + 3, 2r + 4, 2r + 5)$

If this point lies on the plane

$$x + y + z = 17 \text{ then}$$

$$r + 3 + 2r + 4 + 2r + 5 = 17$$

$$5r + 12 = 17 \quad 5r = 5 \quad r = 1$$

Thus the co-ordinate of the point Q is

$R(4, 6, 7)$

Thus $$QP = \sqrt{(4-3)^2 + (6-4)^2 + (7-5)^2}$$

$$QP = \sqrt{1 + 4 + 4}$$

$$QP = 3 \quad \textbf{Ans.}$$

Problem 12 Find the equations of the perpendicular from the point $(3, -1, 11)$ to the line

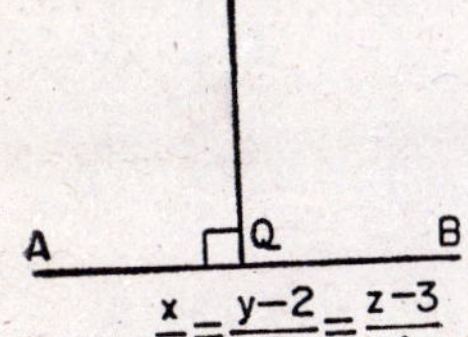

$$\frac{x}{2} = \frac{y-2}{3} = \frac{z-3}{4}$$

Solution The equation of the given line AB is

$$\frac{x}{2} = \frac{y-2}{3} = \frac{z-3}{4}$$

Any point on this lines is given by

$$(2r, 3r + 2, 4r + 3)$$

Then the direction ratios of the line PQ is given by

$$2r-3, 3r + 3, 4r-7$$

Again since PQ is $\perp'$ to AB and hence

$$(2r-3)\cdot 2 + (3r + 3)\cdot 3 + (4r-8)\cdot 4 = 0$$

i.e. $$4r-6 + 8r + 9 + 16r-32 = 0$$

i.e. $$29 r-28 = 0 \quad \Rightarrow \quad r = 1$$

Thus direction cosines of the line PQ are preportional to $-1, 6, -4$

Hence the equation of the st line which passes through $(3, -1, 11)$ and whose d ratios are $-1, 6, -4$ are given by

$$\frac{x-3}{-1} = \frac{y+1}{6} = \frac{z-11}{-4} \quad \textbf{Ans,}$$

Problem 13 Find the equatian of the line through the point $(1, 2, 4)$ and perpendicular to the line

$$3x + 2y-z-4 = 0 = x-2y-2z-5$$

Solution The equation of any plane through AB, the line of intersection of

$$3x + 2y-z-4 = 0 \qquad (1)$$

and $$x-2y-2z-5 = 0 \qquad (2)$$

is $$(3x + 2y-z-4) + k\,(x-2y-2z-5) = 0 \qquad (3)$$

If the plane passes through the point p (1, 2, 4) then

$$(3\cdot 1 + 2.2 - 4 - 4) + k\,(1 - 2.2 - 2.4 - 5) = 0$$

i.e. $(3 + 4 - 8) + k\,(1 - 4 - 8 - 5) = 0$

i.e. $-1 + k\,(-16) = 0$

i.e. $-16\,k = 1$

$\Rightarrow \quad k = -\dfrac{1}{16}$

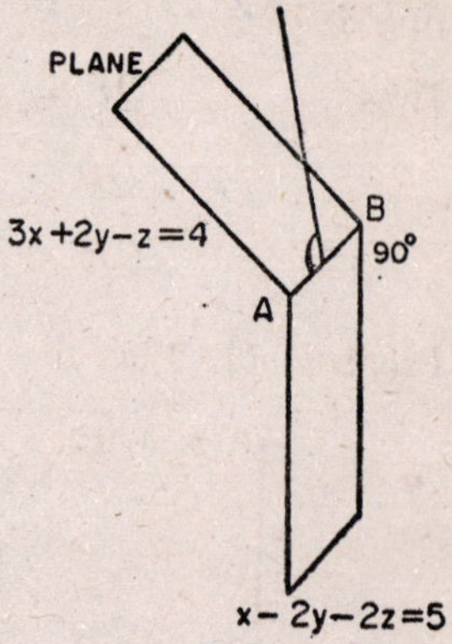

Substituting the value of k in equation of the plane passing through AB and P is given by

$$(3x + 2y - z - 4) - \frac{1}{16}(x - 2y - 2z - 5) = 0$$

i.e. $48x + 32y - 16z - 64 - x + 2y + 2z + 5 = 0$

i.e. $47x + 34y - 14z - 59 = 0$ (4)

We know that the general equation of a plane is

$$ax + by + cz + d = 0 \tag{5}$$

Since it passes through the point (1, 2, 4) so

$$a + 2b + 4c + d = 0 \tag{6}$$

Subtracting (6) by (5) we have

$$a\,(x - 1) + b\,(y - 2) + c\,(z - 4) = 0 \tag{7}$$

If the plane (7) is perpendicular to the line

$$3x + 2y - z - 4 = 0 = x - 2y - 2z - 5$$

Then $3a + 2b - c = 0$ (8)

$a - 2b - 2c = 0$ (9)

By the cross multiplication of equation (8) and (9) we have

$$\frac{a}{-4-2} = \frac{b}{-1+6} = \frac{c}{-6-2}$$

i.e. $\dfrac{a}{-6} = \dfrac{b}{5} = \dfrac{c}{-8} = k$ (say)

Therefore $a = -6k,\ b = 5k,\ c = -8k$

Thus the equation of the plane $\perp r$ to the given line is

$$-6\,(x - 1) + 5)\,(y - 2) - 8\,(z - 4) = 0$$

i.e. $6x - 6 - 5y + 10 + 8z - 32 = 0$

i.e. $6x - 5y + 8z - 28 = 0$

Hence the required line is

$$47x + 34y - 14z - 59 = 0 = 6x - 5y + 8z - 28$$

Ans.

Problem 14 Find the equations to the perpendicular from the origin to the line

$$x + 4y + 4z - 27 = 0$$
$$2x + 2y + 52 - 21 = 0$$

and also obtain the co-ordinates of the foot of the perpendicular.

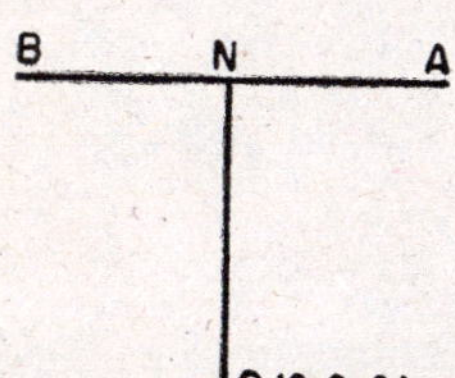

Solution Let (l, m, n) be the direction ratios of AB, the line of intersection of the given planes.

Then
$$l + 4m + 4n = 0 \quad (1)$$
$$2l + 2m + 5n = 0 \quad (2)$$

By cross multiplication we have

$$\frac{l}{20-8} = \frac{m}{8-5} = \frac{n}{2-8}$$

i.e:
$$\frac{l}{12} = \frac{m}{3} = \frac{n}{-6}$$

i.e.
$$\frac{l}{4} = \frac{m}{1} = \frac{n}{-2}$$

i.e. the direction ratios of the line AB are $4, 1, -2$

Putting $z = 0$ in the given equations of the two planes then.

$$\boxed{x + 4y - 27 = 0} \quad (3)$$
$$2x + 2y + 5.0 - 21 = 0$$

i.e.
$$\boxed{2x + 2y - 21 = 0} \quad (4)$$

$$\frac{x}{-84 + 54} = \frac{y}{-54 + 21} = \frac{1}{2-8}$$
$$\frac{x}{-30} = \frac{y}{-33} = \frac{1}{-6}$$

i.e.
$$x = 5, \ y = \frac{33}{6}$$

i.e.
$$x = 5 \quad \text{and} \quad y = \frac{11}{2}$$

$\therefore$ The equations to AB are

$$\frac{x-5}{4} = \frac{y-11/2}{1} = \frac{z-0}{-2} = r \text{ (say)} \quad (5)$$

Any point on the line AB are gven by

$$\left(4r + 5, r + \frac{11}{2}, -2r\right)$$

Let the co-ordinates of N is $\left(4r+5, r+\frac{11}{2}, -2r\right)$

Then the $d.c.$ of the line $O\,N$ are proportional to

$$4r+5-0=4r+5$$

$$r+\frac{11}{2}-0=r+\frac{11}{2}$$

$$-2r-0=-2r$$

Since $0N$ is $\perp r$ to AB so

$$4\,(4r+5)+1\left(r+\frac{11}{2}\right)-2\,(-2r)=0$$

i.e.
$$16r+20+r+\frac{11}{2}+4r=0$$

$$\Rightarrow \quad 2\cdot 1r+\frac{51}{2}=0$$

$$\Rightarrow \quad r=-\frac{51}{2\times 21}$$

$$\Rightarrow \quad r=-\frac{17}{14}$$

Thus the foot of perpendicular is

$$\left(\frac{1}{7}, \frac{30}{7}, \frac{17}{7}\right)$$

Hence the equation ON (the *st* line passing through $(0, 0, 0)$ and have $d.c.$ proportional to $\frac{1}{7}, \frac{30}{7}, \frac{17}{7}\Big)$ is given by

$$\frac{x}{1/7}=\frac{y}{30/7}=\frac{z}{17/7} \quad \text{i.e.} \quad \frac{x}{1}=\frac{y}{30}=\frac{z}{17}$$

Problem 15 Prove that the lines

$$\frac{x+1}{2}=\frac{y+2}{3}=\frac{z+3}{4};$$

$$\frac{x-3}{3}=\frac{y-2}{4}=\frac{z-1}{5}$$

are coplanar, find their common point and the equation of the plane in whichthey lie.

Solution The first line is

$$\frac{x+1}{2}=\frac{y+2}{3}=\frac{z+3}{4}=r \text{ (say)}$$

$\therefore$ $$x = 2r-1$$
$$y = 3r-2$$
$$z = 4r-3$$

$\therefore$ Any point on the first line is $(2r-1, 3r-2, 4r-3)$

The second line is

$$\frac{x-3}{3}=\frac{y-2}{4}=\frac{z-1}{5} = r_1 \text{ (say)}$$

$\therefore$ $$x = 3r_1 + 3, y = 4r_1 + 2 \; z = 5r_1 + 1$$

Any point on the second line is $(3r_1 + 3, 4r_1 + 2, 5r_1 + 1)$

If the two lines are coplanar, then these points should coincide for same values of r and r_1 and hence we get

$2r-1 = 3r_1 + 3$ i.e. $2r-3r_1-4 = 0$ (1)

$3r-2 = 4r_1 + 2$ i.e. $3r-4r_1-4 = 0$ (2)

$4r-3 = 5r_1 + 1$ i.e. $4r-5r_1-4 = 0$ (3)

From (1) and (2) we have

$$\frac{r}{12-16} = \frac{r_1}{-12 + 8} = \frac{1}{-8 + 9}$$

i.e. $$\frac{r}{-4}=\frac{r_1}{-4}=\frac{1}{1}$$

i.e. $$r = -4 \quad r_1 = -4$$

Putting the values of r and r_1 in equation (3) we have

$4(-4) -5(-4)-4=-16 + 20-4 = 20-20 = 0$

i.e. $0 = 0$ is true

Hence the lines are coplanar their common point is $(2r-1, 3r-2, 4r-3)$

i.e. $(-9, -14, -19)$

The equation of the plane containing the two given lines is

$$\begin{vmatrix} x+1 & y+2 & z+3 \\ 2 & 3 & 4 \\ 3 & 4 & 5 \end{vmatrix} = 0$$

i.e. $(x + 1)(15-16)-(y + 2)(10-12) + (z + 3)(8-9) = 0$

i.e. $$(x + 1)(-1)-(y + 2)(-2) + (z + 3)(-1) = 0$$

i.e. $$-x-1 + 2y + 4-z-3 = 0$$

i.e. $$-x + 2y-z = 0$$
$$x-2y + z = 0$$

which is the required equation of the plane containing the two straight lines

Problem 16 Prove that the equation of the plane through the origin containing the line

$$\frac{x-a}{l}=\frac{y-b}{m}=\frac{z-c}{n} \text{ is}$$

$$x(bn-cm)+y(cl-an)+z(am-bl)=0$$

Solution The general equation of plane is given by

$$\alpha x+\beta y+\gamma z+\delta=0 \tag{1}$$

Since it passes through the origin

So $$\alpha\cdot 0+\beta\cdot 0+\gamma\cdot 0+\delta=0$$

i.e. $$\delta=0$$

So the equation of the plane becomes

$$\alpha x+\beta y+\gamma z=0 \tag{2}$$

As the given line is on the plane and (a, b, c) is *a* point on the line,

$$a\alpha+b\beta+c\gamma=0 \tag{3}$$

Now the d.c.'s of the normal to the plane are proportional to α, β, γ. But this normal is perpendicular to the line

So $$\alpha l+\beta\cdot m+\gamma\cdot n=0 \tag{4}$$

By cross-multiplication of (1) and (2) we have

$$\frac{\alpha}{bn-cm}=\frac{\beta}{cl-an}=\frac{\gamma}{am-bl}$$

$\therefore$ The required plane has the equation

$$(bn-cm)x+(cl-an)y+(am-bl)z=0$$

Problem 17 Find the equation of the plane through the point (α, β, γ) and through the straight line

$$\frac{x-a}{l}=\frac{y-b}{m}=\frac{z-c}{n}$$

Solution The general equation of any plane is given by

$$Ax+By+Cz+D=0 \tag{1}$$

Since (α, β, γ) is a point on this plane

So $$A\alpha+B\beta+C\gamma+D=0 \tag{2}$$

Substracting (2) from (1) we have

$$A(x-\alpha)+B(y-\beta)+C(z-\gamma)=0 \tag{3}$$

Again since the plane contains the line

$$\frac{x-a}{l}=\frac{y-b}{m}=\frac{z-c}{n}$$

So the plane (2) consists of the point (a, b, c)

So $$A(a-\alpha) + B(b-\beta) + C(c-\gamma) = 0 \quad (4)$$

A, B and C are the direction ratios of the normal to the plane (3)

So the normal to the plane is perpendicular to the line

$$\frac{x-a}{l} = \frac{y-b}{m} = \frac{z-c}{n}$$

where l, m and n are the direction ratios of the line

Hence $$Al + Bm + Cn = 0 \quad (5)$$

Elimination A, B and C from (3), (4) and (5) the required equation of the plane is

$$\begin{vmatrix} x-\alpha & y-\beta & z-\gamma \\ a-\alpha & b-\beta & c-\gamma \\ l & m & n \end{vmatrix} = 0$$ **Ans.**

Problem 18 Find the equation of the plane through the line

$$\frac{x-\alpha}{l} = \frac{y-\beta}{m} = \frac{z-y}{n} \text{ parallel to}$$

$$\frac{x-\alpha^1}{l^1} = \frac{y-\beta^1}{m^1} = \frac{z-y^1}{n^1}$$

Solution Let the equation of the plane is

$$Ax + By + Cz + D = 0 \quad (1)$$

Since this plane contains the line

$$\frac{x-\alpha}{l} = \frac{y-\beta}{m} = \frac{z-\gamma}{n}$$

So $$A\alpha + B\beta + C\gamma + D = 0 \quad (2)$$

Substracting (2) from (1) we have

$$A(x-\alpha) + B(y-\beta) + C(z-\gamma) = 0 \quad (3)$$

A, B and C are the direction ratios of the normal to the plane (3) and l, m, n be the d ratios of the line and since the normal is $\perp^r$ to the line

$$\frac{x-\alpha^1}{l} = \frac{y-\beta}{m} = \frac{z-\gamma}{n}$$

So $$Al + Bm + Cn = 0 \quad (4)$$

Again since plane (2) is parallel to

$$\frac{x-\alpha}{l^1} = \frac{y-\beta^1}{m^1} = \frac{z-\gamma^1}{n^1}$$

So $$Al^1 + Bm^1 + Cn^1 = 0 \quad (5)$$

So eliminating A, B and C from (3), (4) and (5) we can obtain the equation of the plane

$$\begin{vmatrix} x-\alpha & y-\beta & z-\gamma \\ l & m & n \\ l^1 & m^1 & n^1 \end{vmatrix} = 0$$

$\Rightarrow (x-\alpha)(mn^1-m^1n)+(y-\beta)(nl^1-n^1l)+(lm^1-l^1m)(z-\gamma)=0$ **Ans.**

Problem 19 Obtain the equation of the plane which contains the tine

$$\frac{x-1}{2}=-y-1=\frac{z-3}{4}$$

and is perpendicular to the plane

$$x+2y+z=12$$

Solution Let the equation of the plane be

$$Ax+By+Cz+D=0 \tag{1}$$

Equation of the straight line can be written in a symmetrical form as

$$\frac{x-1}{2}=\frac{y+1}{-1}=\frac{z-3}{4} \tag{2}$$

Since the plane (1) contains the line (2) hence

$$A(1)+B(-1)+C(3)+D=0 \tag{3}$$

Substracting (3) from (1) we have

$$A(x-1)+B(y+1)+C(z-3)=0 \tag{4}$$

where A, B and C are the direction ratios of the normal to the plane (4) and direction ratios of the line (2) is 2, -1, 4

So $$2A-B+4C=0 \tag{5}$$

Again since the plane (4) is perpendicular to the plane

$$x+2y+z=12$$

So $$A\cdot 1+2B+C=0 \tag{6}$$

$$2A-B+4C=0 \tag{5}$$

By cross multiplication we have

$$\frac{A}{8+1}=\frac{B}{2-4}=\frac{C}{-1-4}$$

$$\frac{A}{9}=\frac{B}{-2}=\frac{C}{-5}=k \text{ (say)}$$

$\therefore$ $$A=2k \qquad B=4k \qquad C=-5k$$

So equation of the plane becomes

$$9(x-1)-2(y+1)+(-5)(z-3)=0$$

$$9x-9-2y-2-5z+15=0$$

i.e. $$9x-2y-5z+4=0$$

which is the required equation of the plane **Ans.**

Problem 20 Find the equation of the plane passing through

$$\frac{x}{l}=\frac{y}{m}=\frac{z}{n}$$

and perpendicular to the plane containing

$$\frac{x}{m}=\frac{y}{n}=\frac{z}{l} \text{ and } \frac{x}{n}=\frac{y}{l}=\frac{z}{m}$$

Solution Equation of the plane containing the lines

$$\frac{x}{m}=\frac{y}{n}=\frac{z}{l}$$

and $\frac{x}{n}=\frac{y}{l}=\frac{z}{m}$ is given by

$$\begin{vmatrix} x & y & z \\ m & n & l \\ n & l & m \end{vmatrix}=0$$

i.e. $$x(mn-l^2)+y(ln-m^2)+z(ml-n^2)=0 \qquad (1)$$

Let the equation of the plane which we have to find is

$$Ax+By+Cz+D=0 \qquad (2)$$

Since this plane passes through the line

$$\frac{x-0}{l}=\frac{y-0}{m}=\frac{z-0}{n}$$

i.e. (0, 0, 0) is on the plane

i.e. $A.O+B.O+C\cdot O+D=0$

i.e. $D=0$

Thus the equation of the plane reduces from (2) to

$$Ax+By+Cz=0 \qquad (3)$$

and since A, B, C are the d ratios of the normal to the plane (3). Thus normal is perpendicular to the straight line

$$\frac{x}{l}=\frac{y}{m}=\frac{z}{n}$$

i.e. $$Al+Bm+Cn=0 \qquad (4)$$

Again since plane (4) is perpendicular to (1)

Hence $\quad A\,(mn-l^2) + B\,(ln-m^2) + C\,(ml-n^2) = 0 \qquad (5)$

So eliminating A, B and C from equation (3), (4) and (5) the equation of the plane becomes

$$\begin{vmatrix} x & y & z \\ l & m & n \\ mn-l^2 & nl-m^2 & lm-n^2 \end{vmatrix} - 0 \quad \textbf{Anr.}$$

Problem 21 Find the equation of the plane through the point (1, 1, 1) and perpendicular to the line

$$x-2y + z = 2;\ 4x + 3y-z + 1 = 0$$

Solution Let (l, m, n) be the direction ratios of the given line

Then
$$l-2m + n = 0$$
$$4l + 3m-n = 0$$

Solving by cross multiplication we have

$$\frac{l}{2-3} = \frac{m}{4+1} = \frac{n}{3+8}$$

$$\frac{l}{-1} = \frac{m}{5} = \frac{n}{11}$$

The direction ratios of the given line is

$$-1,.5, 11$$

Then the equation of the plane $\perp$ to the given line is

$$-1x + 5y + 11z + k = 0 \qquad (1)$$

Since it passes through the point (1, 1, 1) so

$$-1 + 5 + 11 + k = 0$$

i,e.
$$15 + k = 0$$

i.e.
$$k = -15$$

Hence the equation of the plane becomes

$$-x + 5y + 11z - 15 = 0$$

i.e.
$$x-5y-11z + 15 = 0 \qquad \textbf{Ans.}$$

Problem 22 Find the equation of the plane which passes through the line $\quad 3x + 5y + 7z-5 = 0 = x + y + z-3$

and is parallel to the line

$$4x + y + z = 0 = 2x-3y-5z$$

Solution

Let (l, m, n) be the direction cosines of CD, the line of intersection of the planes

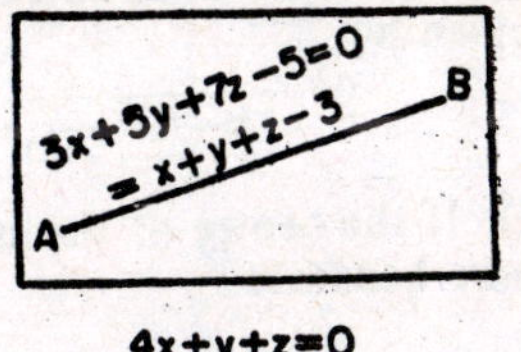

$$4x + y + z = 0 \quad (1)$$

and $$2x - 3y - 5z = 0 \quad (2)$$

Then $$4l + m + n = 0$$

$$2l - 3m - 5n = 0$$

$$\frac{l}{-5+3} = \frac{m}{2+20} = \frac{n}{-12-2}$$

$$\frac{l}{-2} = \frac{m}{22} = \frac{n}{-14}$$

$$\frac{l}{1} = \frac{m}{-11} = \frac{n}{7}$$

∴ Direction ratios of CD is $(1, -11, 7)$

Equation of the plane through the intersection of

$$3x + 5y + 7z - 5 = 0$$

And $$x + y + z - 3 = 0$$

is given by $$3x + 5y + 7z - 5 + k(x + y + z - 3) = 0$$

i.e. $$x(3 + k) + y(5 + k) + z(7 + k) - (5 + 3k) = 0 \quad (3)$$

Since this plane is parallel to the line whose d.c.'s are (l, m, n)

i.e. $$(1, -11, 7)$$

So $$(3 + k) \times 1 - 11(5 + k) + 7(7 + k) = 0$$

i.e. $$3 + k - 55 - 11k + 49 + 7k = 0$$

i.e. $$-3k - 3 = 0$$

i.e. $$3k = -3$$

$$k = -1$$

Putting the value of k in (3) the required equation of the plane is given by

$$x(3-1) + y(5-1) + z(7-1) - (5-3) = 0$$

$$2x + 4y + 6z - 2 = 0$$ **Ans.**

Formulas of Sphere

Remember (1) Equation of a sphere whose centre is (α, β, γ) and radius$=r$ is given by

$$\boxed{(x-\alpha)^2 + (y-\beta)^2 + z-\gamma)^2 = r^2} \quad (1)$$

(2) If the centre of the sphere be origin (0, 0, 0), the equation of the sphere becomes

$$\boxed{x^2 + y^2\ z^2 = r^2} \quad (2)$$

(3) General form of the equation of the sphere be

$$x^2 + y^2 + z^2 + 2ux + 2vy + 2wz + d = 0 \quad (3)$$

Centre of the sphere is $-u, -v, -w$ and radius is $\sqrt{u^2+v^2+w^2-d}$

(4) The equation of *a* sphere through four points (x_1, y_1, z_1); (x_2, y_2, z_2); (x_3, y_3, z_3) and $(x_4, y_4, z_4,)$ is given by

$$\begin{vmatrix} x^2+y^2+z^2 & x & y & z & 1 \\ x_1^2+y_1^2+z_1^2 & x_1 & y_1 & z_1 & 1 \\ x_2^2+y_2^2+z_2^2 & x_2 & y_2 & z_2 & 1 \\ x_3^2+y_3^2+z_3^2 & x_3 & y_3 & z_3 & 1 \end{vmatrix} = 0$$

(5) The equation of a sphere whose diameter is the line joining two points (x_1, y_1, z_1) and (x_2, y_2, z_2).

Remember

$$\boxed{(x-x_1)(x-x_2) + (y-y_1)(y-y_2) + (z-z_1)(z-z_2) = 0}$$

(6) Equation of the targent plane to a sphere $x^2 + y^2 + z^2 = a^2$ at any point (x_1, y_1, z_1) is given by

$$\boxed{xx_1 + yy_1 + zz_1 = a^2}$$

23

Determinants

If x, y be eliminated from the equation

$$a_1 x + b_1 y = 0$$

and
$$a_2 x + b_2 y = 0$$

we get
$$a_1 b_2 - a_2 b_1 = 0$$

This result is usually written in the form

$$\begin{vmatrix} a_1 & b_1 \\ a_2 & b_2 \end{vmatrix} = 0$$

In other words we write symbolically

$$\begin{vmatrix} a_1 & b_1 \\ a_2 & b_2 \end{vmatrix} = a_1 b_2 - a_2 b_1$$

Thus 2^2 quantities viz. a_1, b_1, a_2 b_2 are, arranged in the form of a square with two rows (horizontal lines) and two columns (vertical lines) enclosed between two vertical lines as

$$\begin{vmatrix} a_1 & b_1 \\ a_2 & b_2 \end{vmatrix}$$

are said to form of determinant of second order. The quantities a_1, a_2, b_1 b_2 are called the consituents of the determinant and the term a_1 b_2, a_2 b_1 called the element similarly, if x y, z be eliminated from the equations

$$a_1 x + b_1 y + c_1 z = 0$$
$$a_2 x + b_2 y + c_2 z = 0$$

and
$$a_3 x + b_3 y + c_3 z = 0$$

We obtain
$$a_1 (b_2 c_3 - b_3 c_2) - b_1 (a_2 c_3 - a_3 c_2) + c_1 (a_2 b_3 - a_3 b_2) = 0$$

The expression on the left is written in the compact form

$$\begin{vmatrix} a_1 & b_1 & c_1 \\ a_2 & b_2 & c_2 \\ a_3 & b_3 & c_3 \end{vmatrix}$$

Thus 3^2 quantities are arranged in the form of a square, with three rows and three columns and, therefore form a determinant of the third order.

Properties of determinants

Theorem 1 The value of a determinant remains unaltered it is column be changed into rows and the rows into columns.

Proof Let

$$\Delta = \begin{vmatrix} a_1 & b_1 & c_1 \\ a_2 & b_2 & c_2 \\ a_3 & b_3 & c_3 \end{vmatrix}$$

and
$$\Delta^1 = \begin{vmatrix} a_1 & a_2 & a_3 \\ b_1 & b_2 & b_3 \\ c_1 & c_2 & c_3 \end{vmatrix}$$

Now

$$\Delta = a_1 \begin{vmatrix} b_2 & c_2 \\ b_3 & c_3 \end{vmatrix} - b_1 \begin{vmatrix} a_2 & c_2 \\ a_3 & c_3 \end{vmatrix} + c_1 \begin{vmatrix} a_2 & b_2 \\ a_3 & b_3 \end{vmatrix}$$

$$\Delta = a_1 (b_2 c_3 - b_3 c_2) - b_1 (a_2 c_3 - a_3 c_2) + c_1 (a_2 b_3 - a_3 b_2)$$
$$\Delta = a_1 (b_2 c_3 - b_3 c_2) + b_1 (a_3 c_2 - a_2 c_3) + c_1 (a_2 b_3 - a_3 b_2)$$
$$\Delta = a_1 (b_2 c_3 - b_3 c_2) + a_2 (b_3 c_1 - b_1 c_3) + a_3 (b_1 c_2 - b_2 c_1)$$

i.e. $\Delta = \Delta$ *(Proved)*

Theorem 2 If two adjacent rows or columns of a determinant are interchanged, the sign of the determinant is changed, but the value remains unaltered.

Proof Let

$$\Delta = \begin{vmatrix} a_1 & b_1 & c_1 \\ a_2 & b_2 & c_2 \\ a_3 & b_3 & c_3 \end{vmatrix}$$

$$\therefore \quad \Delta = a_1 (b_2 c_3 - b_3 c_2) - b_1 (a_2 c_3 - a_3 c_2) + c_1 (a_2 b_3 - a_3 b_2) \tag{1}$$

Again let
$$\Delta^1 = \begin{vmatrix} b_1 & a_1 & c_1 \\ b_2 & a_2 & c_2 \\ b_3 & a_3 & c_3 \end{vmatrix}$$

$$\Delta^1 = b_1 (a_2 c_3 - a_3 c_2) - b_2 (a_1 c_3 - a_3 c_1) + b_3 (a_1 c_2 - a_2 c_1)$$
$$\Delta^1 = a_1 (b_3 c_2 - b_2 c_3) + b_1 (a_2 c_3 - a_3 c_2) + c_1 (a_3 b_2 - a_2 b_3)$$
$$\Delta^1 = -a_1 (b_2 c_3 - b_3 c_2) + b_1 (a_2 c_3 - a_3 c_2) - c_1 (a_2 b_3 - a_3 b_2)$$
$$\Delta^1 = -[a_1 (b_2 c_3 - b_3 c_2) - b_1 (a_2 c_3 - a_3 c_2) + c_1 (a_2 b_3 - a_3 b_2)]$$
$$\Rightarrow \Delta^1 = -\Delta$$

Thus we see that

If the parallel lines of a determinant are interchanged the determinant retains its absolute value but changes in sign.

$$\begin{vmatrix} a_1 & b_1 & c_1 \\ a_2 & b_2 & c_2 \\ a_3 & b_3 & c_3 \end{vmatrix} = - \begin{vmatrix} b_1 & a_1 & c_1 \\ b_2 & a_2 & c_2 \\ b_3 & a_3 & c_3 \end{vmatrix}$$

Theorem 3 A determinant, of which any two rows or columns are identical, vanishes.

Let the determinant be

$$\Delta = \begin{vmatrix} a_1 & a_1 & c_1 \\ a_2 & a_2 & c_2 \\ a_3 & a_3 & c_3 \end{vmatrix} \tag{1}$$

$$= - \begin{vmatrix} a_1 & a_1 & c_1 \\ a_2 & a_2 & c_2 \\ a_3 & a_3 & c_3 \end{vmatrix}$$

interchange two of its column

i.e.
$$\Delta = -\Delta$$
$$\Rightarrow 2\Delta = 0$$
$$\Rightarrow \Delta = 0$$

Theorem 4 If every constituent of a row or a column be multiplied by a constant, the determinant is then multiplied by the same constant.

Proof Let

$$\Delta = \begin{vmatrix} a_1 & b_1 & c_1 \\ a_2 & b_2 & c_2 \\ a_3 & b_3 & c_3 \end{vmatrix}$$

Let each constituent of first column be multiplied by m and

$$\Delta^1 = \begin{vmatrix} ma_1 & b_1 & c_1 \\ ma_2 & b_2 & c_2 \\ ma_3 & b_3 & c_3 \end{vmatrix}$$

$$\Delta^1 = ma_1 \begin{vmatrix} b_2 & c_2 \\ b_3 & c_3 \end{vmatrix} - ma_2 \begin{vmatrix} b_1 & c_1 \\ b_3 & c_3 \end{vmatrix} + ma_3 \begin{vmatrix} b_1 & c_1 \\ b_2 & c_2 \end{vmatrix}$$

$$\Delta^1 = m \left[a_1 \begin{vmatrix} b_2 & c_2 \\ b_3 & c_3 \end{vmatrix} - a_2 \begin{vmatrix} b_1 & c_1 \\ b_3 & c_3 \end{vmatrix} + a_3 \begin{vmatrix} b_1 & c_1 \\ b_2 & c_2 \end{vmatrix} \right]$$

$$\Delta^1 = m\,\Delta$$

Similarly

$$\begin{vmatrix} ma_1 & nb_1 & pc_1 \\ ma_2 & nb_2 & pc_2 \\ ma_3 & nb_3 & pc_3 \end{vmatrix} = mnp \begin{vmatrix} a_1 & b_1 & c_1 \\ a_2 & b_2 & c_2 \\ a_3 & b_3 & c_3 \end{vmatrix}$$

Theorem 5 If each constituent of any row or any column be the sum of two or more than two quantities, the determinant can be expressed as the sum of the two or more than two determinants of the same order.

$$\Delta^1 = \begin{vmatrix} a_1 + l_1 + m_1 + n_1 & b_1 & c_1 \\ a_2 + l_2 + m_2 + n_2 & b_2 & c_2 \\ a_3 + l_3 + m_3 + n_3 & b_3 & c_3 \end{vmatrix}$$

Proof Let

Expanding Δ^1 in terms of the constituents of the first column we get

$$\Delta^1 = (a_1 + l_1 + m_1 + n_1) A_1 - (a_2 + l_2 + m_2 + n_2) A_2 + a(_3 + l_3 + m_3 + n_3) A_3$$

$$\Delta^1 = (a_1 A_1 - a_2 A_2 + a_3 A_3) + (l_1 A_1 - l_2 A_2 + l_3 A_3) + (m_1 A_1 - m_2 A_2 + m_3 A_3) + (n_1 A_1 - n_2 A_2 + n_3 A_3)$$

$$\Delta^1 = \begin{vmatrix} a_1 & b_1 & c_1 \\ a_2 & b_2 & c_2 \\ a_3 & b_3 & c_3 \end{vmatrix} + \begin{vmatrix} l_1 & b_1 & c_1 \\ i_2 & b_2 & c_2 \\ l_3 & b_3 & c_3 \end{vmatrix} + \begin{vmatrix} m_1 & b_1 & c_1 \\ m_2 & b_2 & c_2 \\ m_3 & b_3 & c_3 \end{vmatrix} + \begin{vmatrix} n_1 & b_1 & c_1 \\ n_2 & b_2 & c_2 \\ n_3 & b_3 & c_3 \end{vmatrix}$$

Hence the result.

Theorcm 6 If the constituent of any row or column, be increased or diminished by any equimultiple of the corresponding constituents of one or more of the other rows or columns, the value of the determinants remains unaltered.

Proof Let

$$\Delta = \begin{vmatrix} a_1 & b_1 & c_1 \\ a_2 & b_2 & c_2 \\ a_3 & b_3 & c_3 \end{vmatrix} \qquad (1)$$

Now adding to the first column the sum of m timcs the second column and $-n$ times the third column, the determinant (1) becames, a new determinant

$$\Delta^1 = \begin{vmatrix} a_1 + mb_1 - nc_1 & b_1 & c_1 \\ a_2 + mb_2 - nc_2 & b_2 & c_2 \\ a_3 + mb_3 - nc_3 & b_3 & c_3 \end{vmatrix}$$

We have to prove that the determinants (1) and (2) are identical.

i.e. to prove that

$$\Delta^1 = \Delta$$

Now

$$\Delta^1 = \begin{vmatrix} a_1 + mb_1 - nc_1 & b_1 & c_1 \\ a_2 + mb_2 - nc_2 & b_2 & c_2 \\ a_3 + mb_3 - nc_3 & b_3 & c_3 \end{vmatrix}$$

$$= \begin{vmatrix} a_1 & b_1 & c_1 \\ a_2 & b_2 & c_2 \\ a_3 & b_3 & c_3 \end{vmatrix} + \begin{vmatrix} mb_1 & b_1 & c_1 \\ mb_2 & b_2 & c_2 \\ mb_3 & b_3 & c_3 \end{vmatrix} + \begin{vmatrix} -nc_1 & b_1 & c_1 \\ -nc_2 & b_2 & c_2 \\ -nc_3 & b_3 & c_3 \end{vmatrix}$$

$$= \begin{vmatrix} a_1 & b_1 & c_1 \\ a_2 & b_2 & c_2 \\ a_3 & b_3 & c_3 \end{vmatrix} + m \begin{vmatrix} b_1 & b_1 & c_1 \\ b_2 & b_2 & c_2 \\ b_3 & b_3 & c_3 \end{vmatrix} - n \begin{vmatrix} c_1 & b_2 & c_1 \\ c_2 & b_2 & c_2 \\ c_3 & b_3 & c_3 \end{vmatrix}$$

$$= \Delta + m \cdot 0 - n \cdot 0 = \Delta$$

i.e. $\Delta^1 = \Delta$

because, the last two determinants vanish, since their two columns are identical.

(Proved)

Problem 1 Evaluate.

$$\begin{vmatrix} b+c & a & a \\ b & c+a & b \\ c & c & a+b \end{vmatrix}$$

Solution After subtrac:ing the sum of the constituents of the second and the third row to the corresponding constituents of the first row we have.

$$\begin{vmatrix} 0 & -2c & -2b \\ b & c+a & b \\ c & c & a+b \end{vmatrix} = 2\begin{vmatrix} 0 & -c & -b \\ b & c+a & b \\ c & c & a+b \end{vmatrix}$$

$$= 2\begin{vmatrix} 0 & -c & -b \\ b & a & 0 \\ c & 0 & a \end{vmatrix}$$

[After adding the constituent of the first row to the corresponding constituent of the second and third row.]

$$= 2\left[0\begin{vmatrix} a & 0 \\ a & a \end{vmatrix} + c\begin{vmatrix} b & 0 \\ c & a \end{vmatrix} - b\begin{vmatrix} b & a \\ c & 0 \end{vmatrix}\right]$$

$$= 2\,[abc + abc] = 2\cdot 2abc = 4abc$$

Problem 2 Factorise

$$\begin{vmatrix} 1 & 1 & 1 \\ \alpha & \beta & \gamma \\ \alpha^3 & \beta^3 & \gamma^3 \end{vmatrix}$$

Solution Let $\Delta = \begin{vmatrix} 1 & 1 & 1 \\ \alpha & \beta & \gamma \\ \alpha^3 & \beta^3 & \gamma^3 \end{vmatrix}$

Substracting the first column from second column and the third column we have

$$\Delta = \begin{vmatrix} 0 & 0 & 0 \\ \alpha & \beta-\alpha & \gamma-\alpha \\ \alpha^3 & \beta^3-\alpha^3 & \gamma^3-\alpha^3 \end{vmatrix}$$

$$\Delta = (\beta-\alpha)(\gamma-\alpha)\begin{vmatrix} 1 & 0 & 0 \\ \alpha & 1 & 1 \\ \alpha^3 & \beta^2+\alpha\beta+\alpha^2 & \gamma^2+\gamma\alpha+\alpha^2 \end{vmatrix}$$

$$\Delta = (\beta-\alpha)(\gamma-\alpha)\left[1\begin{vmatrix} 1 & 1 \\ \beta^2+\alpha\beta+\alpha^2 & \gamma^2+\gamma\alpha+\alpha^2 \end{vmatrix}\right]$$

$$\Delta = (\beta-\alpha)(\gamma-\alpha)[\gamma^2+\gamma\alpha+\alpha^2-\beta^2-\alpha\beta-\alpha^2]$$

$$\Delta = (\beta-\alpha)(\gamma-\alpha)[(\gamma+\beta)(\gamma-\beta)+\alpha(\gamma-\beta)]$$

$$\Delta = (\beta-\alpha)(\gamma-\alpha)(\gamma-\beta)(\alpha+\beta+\gamma)$$

i.e. $\Delta = (\alpha-\beta)(\beta-\gamma)(\gamma-\alpha)(\alpha+\beta+\gamma)$ **Ans.**

Problem 3 Evaluate $\begin{vmatrix} a-b-c & 2a & 2a \\ 2b & b-c-a & 2b \\ 2c & 2c & c-a-b \end{vmatrix}$

Solution Adding the second and third rows to the first row

$$\Delta = \begin{vmatrix} a+b+c & a+b+c & a+b+c \\ 2b & b-c-a & 2b \\ 2c & 2c & c-a-b \end{vmatrix}$$

$$\Delta = (a+b+c)\begin{vmatrix} 1 & 1 & 1 \\ 2b & b-c-a & c-a-b \\ 2c & 2c & c-a-b \end{vmatrix}$$

Substracting the third column to the first column we have

$$\Delta = (a+b+c)\begin{vmatrix} 0 & 1 & 1 \\ 0 & b-c-a & 2b \\ a+b+c & 2c & c-a-b \end{vmatrix}$$

$$\Delta = (a+b+c)^2\begin{vmatrix} 0 & 1 & 1 \\ 0 & b-c-a & 2b \\ 1 & 2c & c-a-b \end{vmatrix}$$

$$\Delta = (a+b+c)^2\begin{vmatrix} 1 & 1 \\ b-c-a & 2b \end{vmatrix}$$

$$\Delta = (a+b+c)^2(2b-b+c+a)$$

$$\Delta = (a+b+c)^2(a+b+c)$$

$$\Delta = (a+b+c)^3$$ **Ans.**

Problem 4 Evaluate $\begin{vmatrix} x & y & z \\ x^2 & y^2 & z^2 \\ y^2 & zx & xy \end{vmatrix}$

Solution Multiplying the first column by x, the second column by y and the third column by z and dividing the determinant by xyz

$$\Delta = \frac{1}{xyz}\begin{vmatrix} x^2 & y^2 & z^2 \\ x^3 & y^3 & z^3 \\ xyz & xyz & xyz \end{vmatrix}$$

$$\Delta = \frac{xyz}{xyz}\begin{vmatrix} x^2 & y^2 & z^2 \\ x^3 & y^3 & z^3 \\ 1 & 1 & 1 \end{vmatrix}$$

Substracting the last column from the first and second column

$$\Delta = \begin{vmatrix} x^2-z^2 & y^2-z^2 & z^2 \\ x^3-z^3 & y^3-z^3 & z^3 \\ 0 & 0 & 1 \end{vmatrix}$$

$$\Delta = (x-z)(y-z)\begin{vmatrix} x+z & y+z & z^2 \\ x^2+xz+z^2 & y^2+yz+z^2 & z^3 \\ 0 & 0 & 1 \end{vmatrix}$$

$$\Delta = (x-z)(y-z)\begin{vmatrix} 0 & 0 & 1 \\ x+z & y+z & z^2 \\ x^2+xz+z^2 & y^2+yz+z^2 & z^3 \end{vmatrix}$$

Interchanging for two times so there is no change in sign

$$\Delta = (x-z)(y-z)\begin{vmatrix} x+z & y+z \\ x^2+xz+z^2 & y^2+yz+z^2 \end{vmatrix}$$

$$\Delta = (x-z)(y-z)[(x+z)(y^2+yz+z^2)-(y+z)(x^2+xz+z^2)]$$

$$\Delta = (x-z)(y-z)[xy^2+xyz+xz^2+y^2z+yz^2+z^3-yx^2-xyz-yz^2-x^2z-xz^2-z^3]$$

$$\Delta = (x-z)(y-z)(xy^2+y^2z-yx^2-x^2z)$$

$$\Delta = (x-z)(y-z)[xy(y-x)+z(y^2-x^2)]$$

$$\Delta = (x-z)(y-z)[xy(y-z)+z(y+x)(y-x)]$$

$$\Delta = (x-z)(y-z)[(y-x)(xy+yz+zx)]$$

$$\Delta = (x-z)(y-z)(y-x)(xy+yz+zx)$$

$$\Rightarrow \Delta = (x-y)(y-z)(z-x)(xy+yz+zx)$$ **Ans.**

Problem 5 Evaluate

$$\begin{vmatrix} 1 & a & a^2-bc \\ 1 & b & b^2-ca \\ 1 & c & c^2-ab \end{vmatrix}$$

$$\Delta = \begin{vmatrix} 1 & a & a^2-bc \\ 1 & b & b^2-ca \\ 1 & c & c^2-ab \end{vmatrix} = \begin{vmatrix} 1 & a & a^2 \\ 1 & b & b^2 \\ 1 & c & c^2 \end{vmatrix} + \begin{vmatrix} 1 & a & -bc \\ 1 & b & -ca \\ 1 & c & -ab \end{vmatrix}$$

$$= \begin{vmatrix} 1 & a & a^2 \\ 1 & b & b^2 \\ 1 & c & c^2 \end{vmatrix} - \begin{vmatrix} 1 & a & bc \\ 1 & b & ca \\ 1 & c & ab \end{vmatrix}$$

$$= \begin{vmatrix} 1 & a & a^2 \\ 1 & b & b^2 \\ 1 & c & c^2 \end{vmatrix} - \frac{1}{abc}\begin{vmatrix} a & a^2 & abc \\ b & b^2 & abc \\ e & c^2 & abc \end{vmatrix}$$

Multiplying first, second and third row by a, b and c respectively

$$= \begin{vmatrix} 1 & a & a^2 \\ 1 & b & b^2 \\ 1 & c & c^2 \end{vmatrix} - \frac{abc}{abc}\begin{vmatrix} a & a^2 & 1 \\ b & b^2 & 1 \\ c & c^2 & 1 \end{vmatrix}$$

$$= \begin{vmatrix} 1 & a & a^2 \\ 1 & b & b^2 \\ 1 & c & c^2 \end{vmatrix} + \begin{vmatrix} a & 1 & a^2 \\ b & 1 & b^2 \\ c & 1 & c^2 \end{vmatrix}$$

Interchanging second and third column

$$= \begin{vmatrix} 1 & a & a^2 \\ 1 & b & b^2 \\ 1 & c & c^2 \end{vmatrix} - \begin{vmatrix} 1 & a & a^2 \\ 1 & b & b^2 \\ 1 & c & c^2 \end{vmatrix}$$

Interchanging first and second column $= 0$

i.e.
$$\begin{vmatrix} 1 & a & a^2-bc \\ 1 & b & b^2-ca \\ 1 & c & c^2-ab \end{vmatrix} = 0$$

Problem 6 Prove that

$$\begin{vmatrix} (b+c)^2 & a^2 & a^2 \\ b^2 & (c+a)^2 & b^2 \\ c^2 & c^2 & (a+b)^2 \end{vmatrix} = 2abc\,(a+b+c)^3$$

Solution Substracting the third column from the first and the second we have

$$\Delta = \begin{vmatrix} (b+c)^2-a^2 & 0 & a^2 \\ 0 & (c+a)^2-b^2 & b^2 \\ c^2-(a+b)^2 & c^2-(a+b)^2 & a+b)^2 \end{vmatrix}$$

$$= (a+b+c)^2 \begin{vmatrix} b+c-a & 0 & a^2 \\ 0 & c+a-b & b^2 \\ c-a-b & c-a-b & (a+b)^2 \end{vmatrix}$$

Now adding the first and second row and subtracting from the third we have

$$\Delta = (a+b+c)^2 \begin{vmatrix} b+c-a & 0 & a^2 \\ 0 & c+a-b & b^2 \\ -2b & -2a & 2ab \end{vmatrix}$$

Now multiplying first column by a and second column by b we have

$$\Delta = \frac{(a+b+c)^2}{ab} \begin{vmatrix} (b+c-a)\,a & 0 & a^2 \\ 0 & (c+a-b)\,b & b^2 \\ -2ab & -2ab & 2ab \end{vmatrix}$$

Adding last column to the other two columns we have

$$\Delta = \frac{(a+b+c)^2}{ab} \begin{vmatrix} a\,(b+c) & a^2 & a^2 \\ b^2 & b\,(c+a) & b^2 \\ 0 & 0 & 2ab \end{vmatrix}$$

$$\Delta = \frac{(a+b+c)^2}{ab} \begin{vmatrix} 0 & 0 & 2ab \\ a\,(b+c) & a^2 & a^2 \\ b^2 & b\,(c+a) & b^2 \end{vmatrix}$$

$$\Delta \equiv \frac{(a+b+c)^2}{ab}\,2ab \begin{vmatrix} a\,(b+c) & a^2 \\ b^2 & b\,(c+a) \end{vmatrix}$$

$$\Delta = 2ab\,\frac{(a+b+c)^2}{ab} \begin{vmatrix} ab+ac & a^2 \\ b^2 & bc+ab \end{vmatrix}$$

$$\Delta = 2ab \left|\frac{(a+b+c)^2}{ab}\right. \{(ab+ac)(bc+ab)—a^2b^2\}$$

$$\Delta = 2ab\,\frac{(a+b+c)^2}{ab}\,\{ab^2c + a^2b^2 + abc^2 + a^2bc - a^2b^2\}$$

$$\Delta = 2ab\,\frac{(a+b+c)^2}{ab}\,abc\,(a+b+c)$$

$$\Delta = 2abc\,(a+b+c)^3 \qquad \textit{(Proved)}$$

Problem 7 Solve

$$\begin{vmatrix} x+a & b & c \\ a & x+b & c \\ a & b & x+c \end{vmatrix} = 0$$

$$\text{L.H.S.} = \begin{vmatrix} x+a & b & c \\ a & x+b & c \\ a & b & x+c \end{vmatrix}$$

Solution Adding the second and third column and adding it to first column we have

$$\text{L.H.S.} = \begin{vmatrix} x+a+b+c & b & c \\ x+a+b+c & x+b & c \\ x+a+b+c & b & x+c \end{vmatrix}$$

$$= (x+a+b+c)\begin{vmatrix} 1 & b & c \\ 1 & x+b & c \\ 1 & b & x+c \end{vmatrix}$$

Now subtracting third row with first and the second row we have

$$\text{L.H.S.} = (x+a+b+c)\begin{vmatrix} 0 & 0 & -x \\ 0 & x & -x \\ 1 & b & x+c \end{vmatrix}$$

$$\text{L.H.S.} = (x+a+b+c)(-x)\begin{vmatrix} 0 & x \\ 1 & b \end{vmatrix}$$

$$\text{L.H.S.} = (x+a+b+c)(-x)(-x)$$

$$= x^2\,(x+a+b+c)$$

Then

$$\begin{vmatrix} x+a & b & c \\ a & x+b & c \\ a & b & x+c \end{vmatrix} = 0$$

$$\Rightarrow \quad x^2 (x + a + b + c) = 0$$

$$\Rightarrow \quad \text{either } x^2 = 0 \quad \Rightarrow \quad x = 0$$

or $\quad x + a + b + c = 0$

$$\Rightarrow \quad x = -(a + b + c) \qquad \textbf{Ans.}$$

Problem 8 Prove that

$$\begin{vmatrix} x & a & a & a \\ a & x & a & a \\ a & a & x & a \\ a & a & a & x \end{vmatrix} = (3a + x)(a-x)^3$$

Adding all the three columns in the first column we have

Solution

$$\Delta = \begin{vmatrix} x+3a & a & a & a \\ x+3a & x & a & a \\ x+3a & a & x & a \\ x+3a & a & a & x \end{vmatrix}$$

$$\Delta = (x + 3a) \begin{vmatrix} 1 & a & a & a \\ 1 & x & a & a \\ 1 & a & x & a \\ 1 & a & a & x \end{vmatrix}$$

Now subtracting the fourth row from the three rows we have

$$\Delta = (x + 3a) \begin{vmatrix} 0 & 0 & 0 & a-x \\ 0 & x-a & 0 & 0 \\ 0 & 0 & x-a & a-x \\ 1 & a & a & x \end{vmatrix}$$

$$\Delta = (x + 3a)(x-a)^3 \begin{vmatrix} 0 & 0 & 0 & 1 \\ 0 & 1 & 0 & 0 \\ 0 & 0 & 1 & -1 \\ 1 & a & a & x \end{vmatrix}$$

$$\Delta = (x + 3a)(x-a)^3(-1) \begin{vmatrix} 0 & 0 & 1 \\ 1 & 0 & 0 \\ 0 & 1 & -1 \end{vmatrix}$$

$$\Delta = (x + 3a)(x-a)^3(-1)1 \begin{vmatrix} 1 & 0 \\ 0 & 1 \end{vmatrix}$$

$$\Delta = (x + 3a)(x-a)^3(-1)(1-0)$$

$$\Delta = (x + 3a)(x-a)^2(-1)(x-a)$$

$$\Delta = (x + 3a)(a-x)^2(a-x)$$

$$\Rightarrow \Delta = (x + 3a)\, a-x)^3$$ *(Proved)*

Problem 9 Prove that

$$\begin{vmatrix} a & b & c & d \\ -a & b & c & d \\ -a & -b & c & d \\ -a & -b, & -c & d \end{vmatrix} = 8abcd$$

Solution Let

$$\Delta = \begin{vmatrix} a & b & c & d \\ -a & b & c & d \\ -a & -b & c & d \\ -a & -b & -c & d \end{vmatrix}$$

Taking a, b, c, d from the four columns respectively we have

$$\Delta = abcd \begin{vmatrix} 1 & 1 & 1 & 1 \\ -1 & 1 & 1 & 1 \\ -1 & -1 & 1 & 1 \\ -1 & -1 & -1 & 1 \end{vmatrix}$$

Now adding first row to the three rows we have

$$\Delta = abcd \begin{vmatrix} 1 & 1 & 1 & 1 \\ 0 & 2 & 2 & 2 \\ 0 & 0 & 2 & 2 \\ 0 & 0 & 0 & 2 \end{vmatrix}$$

$$\Rightarrow \quad \Delta = abcd \times 1 \begin{vmatrix} 2 & 2 & 2 \\ 0 & 2 & 2 \\ 0 & 0 & 2 \end{vmatrix}$$

$$\Rightarrow \quad \Delta = abcd \begin{vmatrix} 2 & 2 \\ 0 & 2 \end{vmatrix}$$

$$\Rightarrow \quad \Delta = 2abcd\ (4-0)$$

$$\Rightarrow \quad \Delta = 8abcd$$

i.e.

$$\begin{vmatrix} a & b & c & d \\ -a & b & c & d \\ -a & -b & c & d \\ -a & -b & -c & d \end{vmatrix} = 8abcd$$

(*Proved*)

Problem 10 Prove that

$$\begin{vmatrix} a^3 & 3a^2 & 3a & 1 \\ a^2 & a^2+2a & 2a+1 & 1 \\ a & 2a+1 & a+2 & 1 \\ 1 & 3 & 3 & 1 \end{vmatrix} = (a-1)^6$$

Operating $c_1 - c_2 + c_3 - c_4$ we have

$$\Delta = \begin{vmatrix} a^3 - 3a^2 + 3a - 1 & 3a^2 & 3a & 1 \\ 0 & a^2+2a & 2a+1 & 1 \\ 0 & aa+1 & a+2 & 1 \\ 0 & 3 & 3 & 1 \end{vmatrix}$$

$$\Delta = (a-1)^3 \begin{vmatrix} 1 & 3a^2 & 3a & 1 \\ 0 & a^2+2a & 2a+1 & 1 \\ 0 & 2a+1 & a+2 & 1 \\ 0 & 3 & 3 & 1 \end{vmatrix}$$

$$\Delta = (a-1)^3 \begin{vmatrix} a^2+2a & 2a+1 & 1 \\ 2a+1 & a+2 & 1 \\ 3 & 3 & 1 \end{vmatrix}$$

Now operating $R_1 - R_2$, $R_2 - R_3$ we have

$$\Delta = (a-1)^3 \begin{vmatrix} a^2-1 & a-1 & 0 \\ 2a-2 & a-1 & 0 \\ 3 & 3 & 1 \end{vmatrix}$$

$$\Delta = (a-1)^3\,(a-1)(a-1) \begin{vmatrix} a+1 & 1 & 0 \\ 2 & 1 & 0 \\ 3 & 3 & 1 \end{vmatrix}$$

$c_1 - c_2$ gives

$$\Delta = (a-1)^5 \begin{vmatrix} a & 1 & 0 \\ 1 & 1 & 0 \\ 0 & 3 & 1 \end{vmatrix}$$

$$\Delta = (a-1)^5\,\{a\,(1-0)\; -1\,(1-0)\}$$
$$\Delta = (a-1)^5\,(a-1)$$
$$\Delta = (a-1)^6$$

Thus

$$\begin{vmatrix} a^3 & 3a^2 & 3a & 1 \\ a^2 & a^2+2a & 2a+1 & 1 \\ a & a2+1 & a+2 & 1 \\ 1 & 3 & 3 & 1 \end{vmatrix} = (a-1)^6$$

Problem 11 Evaluate

$$\begin{vmatrix} a+x & b & c & d \\ a & b+x & c & d \\ a & b & c+x & d \\ a & b & c & d+x \end{vmatrix}$$

Adding all the columns to the first columns we have

$$\Delta = \begin{vmatrix} a+x+b+c+d & b & c & d \\ x+a+b+c+d & b+x & c & d \\ x+a+b+c+d & b & c+x & d \\ x+a+b+c+d & b & c & d+x \end{vmatrix}$$

$$\Delta = (x + a + b + c + d \begin{vmatrix} 1 & b & c & d \\ 1 & b+x & c & d \\ 1 & b & c+x & d \\ 1 & b & c & d+x \end{vmatrix}$$

Now operating $R_1 - R_2$, $R_2 - R_3$ $R_3 - R_4$ we have

$$\Delta = (x + a + b + c + d) \begin{vmatrix} 0 & -x & 0 & 0 \\ 0 & x & -x & 0 \\ 0 & 0 & x & -x \\ 1 & b & c & d+x \end{vmatrix}$$

$$\Delta = (x + a + b + c + d(-1) \begin{vmatrix} -x & 0 & 0 \\ x & -x & 0 \\ 0 & x & -x \end{vmatrix}$$

$$\Delta = (x + a + b + c + d)(-1)(-x) \begin{vmatrix} -x & 0 \\ x & -x \end{vmatrix}$$

$$\Delta = (x + a + b + c + d)\, x\, (x^2 - 0)$$

$$\Delta = (x + a + b + c + d)\, x^3$$

Thus

$$\begin{vmatrix} a+x & b & c & d \\ a & b+x & c & d \\ a & b & c+x & d \\ a & b & c & d+x \end{vmatrix} = (x^3 x + b + a + c + d)$$

Problem 12 Evaluate

$$\begin{vmatrix} 1 & 1 & 1 & 1 \\ a & b & c & d \\ a^2 & b^2 & c^2 & d^2 \\ a^3 & b^3 & c^3 & d^3 \end{vmatrix}$$

Solution From the operation $c_1 - c_2$, $c_2 - c_3$, and $c_3 - c_4$ we have

$$\Delta = \begin{vmatrix} 0 & 0 & 0 & 1 \\ a-b & b-c & c-d & d \\ a^2-b^2 & b^2-c^2 & c^2-d^2 & d^2 \\ a^3-b^3 & b^3-c^3 & c^3-d^3 & d^3 \end{vmatrix}$$

$$\Delta = (a-b)(b-c)(c-d)\begin{vmatrix} 0 & 0 & 0 & 1 \\ 1 & 1 & 1 & d \\ a+b & b+c & c+d & d^2 \\ a^2+ab+b^2 & b^2+bc+c^2 & c^2+cd+d^2 & d^3 \end{vmatrix}$$

$$\Delta = (a-b)(b-c)(c-d)(-1)\begin{vmatrix} 1 & 1 & 1 \\ a+b & b+c & c+d \\ a^2+ab+b^2 & b^2+bc+c^2 & c^2+cd+d^2 \end{vmatrix}$$

Operating $c_1 - c_2$, $c_2 - c_3$ we have

$$\Delta = (a-b)(b-c)(c-d)(-1)\begin{vmatrix} 0 & 0 \\ a-c & b-d \\ ab+a^2-bc-c^2 & b^2+bc-d^2--cd \end{vmatrix}$$

$$\Delta = (a-b)(b-c)(c-d)(-1)\begin{vmatrix} a-c & b-d \\ b(a-c)+(a^2-c^2) & (b^2-d^2)+c(b-d) \end{vmatrix}$$

$$\Delta = (a-b)(b-c)(c-d)(-1)\begin{vmatrix} (a-c) & b-d \\ (a-c)(a+b+c) & (b-d)(b+c+d) \end{vmatrix},$$

$$\Delta = (a-b)(b-c)(c-d)(a-c)(b-d)(-1)\begin{vmatrix} 1 & 1 \\ a+b+c & b+cd \end{vmatrix}$$

$$\Delta = (a-b)(b-c)(c-d)(a-c)(b-d)(-1)\{b+c+d-a-b-c\}$$

$$\Delta = (a-b)(b-c)(c-d)(a-c)(b-d)(a-d) \qquad \textbf{Ans.}$$

Problem 13 Evaluate

$$\begin{vmatrix} 1+a & 1 & 1 & 1 \\ 1 & 1+b & 1 & 1 \\ 1 & 1 & 1+c & 1 \\ 1 & 1 & 1 & 1+d \end{vmatrix}$$

Solution we have

$$\Delta = \begin{vmatrix} 1+a & 1 & 1 & 1 \\ 1 & 1+b & 1 & 1 \\ 1 & 1 & 1+c & 1 \\ 1 & 1 & 1 & 1+d \end{vmatrix}$$

$$= \frac{abcd}{abcd}\begin{vmatrix} 1+a & 1 & 1 & 1 \\ 1 & 1+b & 1 & 1 \\ 1 & 1 & 1+c & 1 \\ 1 & 1 & 1 & 1+d \end{vmatrix}$$

$$= abcd\begin{vmatrix} \frac{1+a}{a} & \frac{1}{b} & \frac{1}{c} & \frac{1}{d} \\ \frac{1}{a} & \frac{1+b}{b} & \frac{1}{c} & \frac{1}{d} \\ \frac{1}{a} & \frac{1}{b} & \frac{1+c}{c} & \frac{1}{d} \\ \frac{1}{a} & \frac{1}{b} & \frac{1}{c} & \frac{1+d}{d} \end{vmatrix}$$

$$\Delta = abcd\begin{vmatrix} 1+\frac{1}{a} & \frac{1}{b} & \frac{1}{c} & \frac{1}{a} \\ \frac{1}{a} & 1+\frac{1}{b} & \frac{1}{c} & \frac{1}{d} \\ \frac{1}{a} & \frac{1}{b} & 1+\frac{1}{c} & \frac{1}{d} \\ \frac{1}{a} & \frac{1}{b} & \frac{1}{c} & 1+\frac{1}{d} \end{vmatrix}$$

Now adding all the three columns to the first column we have.

$$\Delta = abcd\begin{vmatrix} 1+\frac{1}{a}+\frac{1}{b}+\frac{1}{c}+\frac{1}{d} & \frac{1}{b} & \frac{1}{c} & \frac{1}{d} \\ 1+\frac{1}{a}+\frac{1}{b}+\frac{1}{c}+\frac{1}{d} & 1+\frac{1}{b} & \frac{1}{c} & \frac{1}{d} \\ 1+\frac{a}{a}+\frac{1}{b}+\frac{1}{c}+\frac{1}{d} & \frac{1}{b} & 1+\frac{1}{c} & \frac{1}{d} \\ 1+\frac{1}{a}+\frac{1}{b}+\frac{1}{c}+\frac{1}{d} & \frac{1}{b} & \frac{1}{c} & 1+\frac{1}{d} \end{vmatrix}$$

$$\Delta = abcd\left(1+\frac{1}{a}+\frac{1}{b}+\frac{1}{c}+\frac{1}{d}\right)\begin{vmatrix} 1 & \frac{1}{b} & \frac{1}{c} & \frac{1}{d} \\ 1 & 1+\frac{1}{b} & \frac{1}{c} & \frac{1}{d} \\ 1 & \frac{1}{b} & 1+\frac{1}{c} & \frac{1}{d} \\ 1 & \frac{1}{b} & \frac{1}{c} & +\frac{1}{d} \end{vmatrix}$$

Now operating $R_1 - R_2$, $R_2 - R_3$, $R_3 - R_4$ we have

$$\Delta = abcd\left(1 + \frac{1}{a} + \frac{1}{b} + \frac{1}{c} + \frac{1}{d}\right)\begin{vmatrix} 0 & -1 & 0 & 0 \\ 0 & 1 & -1 & 0 \\ 0 & 0 & 1 & -1 \\ 1 & \frac{1}{b} & \frac{1}{c} & 1+\frac{1}{d} \end{vmatrix}$$

$$\Delta = abcd\left(1 + \frac{1}{a} + \frac{1}{b} + \frac{1}{c} + \frac{1}{d}\right)(-1)+\begin{vmatrix} -1 & 0 & 0 \\ 1 & -1 & 0 \\ 0 & 1 & -1 \end{vmatrix}$$

$$\Delta = -abcd\left(1 + \frac{1}{a} + \frac{1}{b} + \frac{1}{c} + \frac{1}{d}\right)(-1)\begin{vmatrix} -1 & 0 \\ 1 & -1 \end{vmatrix}$$

$$\Delta = -abcd\left(1 + \frac{1}{a} + \frac{1}{b} + \frac{1}{c} + \frac{1}{d}\right.(-1)(1-0)$$

$$\Delta = abcd\left(1 + \frac{1}{a} + \frac{1}{b} + \frac{1}{c} + \frac{1}{d}\right) \qquad \textbf{Ans.}$$

Problem 14 Show that

$$\begin{vmatrix} 1 & a & a^2 & a^3 + bcd \\ 1 & b & b^2 & b^3 + adc \\ 1 & c & c^2 & c^3 + dab \\ 1 & d & d^2 & d^3 + abc \end{vmatrix} = 0$$

Solution Let

$$\Delta = \begin{vmatrix} 1 & a & a^2 & a^3 + bcd \\ 1 & b & b^2 & b^3 + cda \\ 1 & c & c^2 & c^3 + dab \\ 1 & d & d^2 & d^3 + abc \end{vmatrix}$$

$$\Rightarrow \qquad \Delta = \begin{vmatrix} 1 & a & a^2 & a^3 \\ 1 & b & b^2 & b^3 \\ 1 & c & c^2 & c^3 \\ 1 & d & d^2 & d^3 \end{vmatrix} + \begin{vmatrix} 1 & a & a^2 & bcd \\ 1 & b & b^2 & cda \\ 1 & c & c^2 & dab \\ 1 & d & d^2 & abc \end{vmatrix}$$

$$\Rightarrow \qquad \Delta = \Delta_1 + \Delta_2$$

$$\text{Where} \qquad \Delta_1 = \begin{vmatrix} 1 & a & a^2 & a^3 \\ 1 & b & b^2 & b^3 \\ 1 & c & c^2 & c^3 \\ 1 & d & d^2 & d^3 \end{vmatrix}$$

$$\Delta = \begin{vmatrix} 1 & a & a^2 & bcd \\ 1 & b & b^2 & cda \\ 1 & c & c^2 & dab \\ 1 & d & d^2 & abc \end{vmatrix}$$

$$\Delta_2 = \frac{abcd}{abcd} \begin{vmatrix} 1 & a & a^2 & bcd \\ 1 & b & b^2 & cda \\ 1 & c & c^2 & dab \\ 1 & d & d^2 & abc \end{vmatrix}$$

$$\Delta = 1/abcd \begin{vmatrix} a & a^2 & a^3 & abcd \\ b & b^2 & b^3 & abcd \\ c & c^2 & c^3 & abcd \\ d & d^2 & d^3 & abcd \end{vmatrix}$$

$$\neq \frac{1}{abcd} \times abcd \begin{vmatrix} a & a^2 & a^3 & 1 \\ b & b^2 & b^2 & 1 \\ c & c^2 & c^3 & 1 \\ d & d^2 & d^3 & 1 \end{vmatrix}$$

$$= - \begin{vmatrix} 1 & a & a^2 & a^3 \\ 1 & b & b^2 & b^3 \\ 1 & c & c^2 & c^3 \\ 1 & d & d^2 & d^3 \end{vmatrix}$$

$$= - \Delta_1$$

$$\text{Thus} \qquad \Delta = - \Delta_1 + \Delta_2$$

$$\Delta = \Delta_1 - \Delta_1 = 0$$

Hence the result

Problem 15 Show that

$$\begin{vmatrix} a^2+x & ab & ac & ad \\ ba & b^2+x & bc & bd \\ ca & cb & c^2+x & cd \\ da & db & dc & d^2+x \end{vmatrix} = x^3(a^2+b^2+c^2+d^2+x)$$

Solution We have

$$\Delta = \begin{vmatrix} a^2+x & ab & ac & ad \\ ba & b^2+x & bc & bd \\ ca & cb & c^2+x & cd \\ da & db & dx & d^2+x \end{vmatrix}$$

Multiplying first column by a, second by b, third by c, and the fourth by d wehave

$$\Delta = \frac{1}{abcd}\begin{vmatrix} a(a^2+x) & ab^2 & ac^2 & ad^2 \\ ba^2 & b(b^2+x) & bc^2 & bd^2 \\ ca^2 & cb^2 & c(c^2+x) & cd^2 \\ du^2 & db^2 & dc^2 & d(d^2+x \end{vmatrix}$$

$$\Delta \frac{1}{abcd} \times abcd \begin{vmatrix} a^2+x & b^2 & c^2 & d^2 \\ a^2 & b^2+x & c^2 & d^2 \\ a^2 & b^2 & c^2+x & d^2 \\ a^2 & b^2 & c^2 & d^2+x \end{vmatrix}$$

$$\Delta = 1 \begin{vmatrix} a^2+x & b^2 & c^2 & d^2 \\ a^2 & b^2+x & c^2 & d^2 \\ a & b^2 & c^2+x & d^2 \\ a^2 & b^2 & c^2 & d^2+x \end{vmatrix}$$

Adding the three columns to the first column we have

$$\Delta = \begin{vmatrix} a^2+b^2+c^2+d^2+x & b^2 & c^2 & d^2 \\ a^2+b^2+c'+d^2+x & b^2+x & c^2 & d^2 \\ a^2+b^2+c^2+d^2+x & b^2 & c^2+x & d^2 \\ a^2+b^2+c^2+d^2+x & b^2 & c^2 & d^2+x \end{vmatrix}$$

$$\Delta = (a^2+b^2+c^2+d^2+x)\begin{vmatrix} 1 & b^2 & c^2 & d^2 \\ 1 & b^2+x & c^2 & d^2 \\ 1 & b^2 & c^2+x & d^2 \\ 1 & c^2 & c^2 & d^2+x \end{vmatrix}$$

Now operating R_1-R_2, R_2-R_3, R_3-R_4 we have

$$\Delta = (a^2+b^2+c^2+d^2+x)\begin{vmatrix} 0 & -x & 0 & 0 \\ 0 & x & -x & 0 \\ 0 & 0 & x & -x \\ 1 & b^2 & c^2 & d^2+x \end{vmatrix}$$

$$\Delta = (a^2+b^2+c^2+d^2+(-1)\begin{vmatrix} -x & 0 & 0 \\ x & -x & 0 \\ 0 & x & -x \end{vmatrix}$$

$$\Delta = (a^2+b^2+c^2+d^2+x)\, x \begin{vmatrix} -x & 0 \\ x & -x \end{vmatrix}$$

$$\Delta = (a^2+b^2+c^2+d^2+x)\, x\, (x^2-0)$$

$$\Delta = x^3 (a^2+b^2+c^2+d^2+x) \qquad \textbf{Ans.}$$

Problem 16 Prove that

$$\begin{vmatrix} a & b & c & d \\ -b & a & -d & c \\ -c & d & a & -b \\ -d & -c & b & a \end{vmatrix} = (a^2+b^2+c^2+d^2)^2$$

Solution We have

$$\Delta = \begin{vmatrix} a & b & c & d \\ -b & a & -d & c \\ -c & d & a & b \\ -d & -c & b & a \end{vmatrix}$$

$$\Delta = \frac{abcd}{abcd}\begin{vmatrix} a & b & c & d \\ -b & a & -d & c \\ -c & d & a & -b \\ -d & -c & b & a \end{vmatrix}$$

$$\Delta = \frac{1}{abcd}\begin{vmatrix} a^2 & ab & ac & ad \\ -b^2 & ab & -ad & bc \\ -c^2 & cd & ac & -bc \\ -d^2 & cd & bd & ad \end{vmatrix}$$

Now operating $R_1 + R_1 - R_2 - R_3 - R_4$

$$\Delta = \frac{1}{abcd}\begin{vmatrix} a^2+b^2+c^2+d^2 & 0 & 0 & 0 \\ -b^2 & ad & -bd & bc \\ -c^2 & cd & ac & -bc \\ -d^2 & -cd & bd & ad \end{vmatrix}$$

$$\Delta = \frac{(a^2+b^2+c^2+d^2)}{abcd}\begin{vmatrix} ab & -bd & bc \\ cd & ac & -bc \\ -cd & bd & ad \end{vmatrix}$$

$$\Delta = \frac{(a^2+b^2+c^2+d^2)}{(abcd)}\cdot bcd\begin{vmatrix} a & -d & c \\ d & a & -b \\ -c & b & a \end{vmatrix}$$

$$\Delta = \frac{(a^2+b^2+c^2+d^2)}{a}\left[a\begin{vmatrix} a & -b \\ b & a \end{vmatrix} + d\begin{vmatrix} d & -b \\ -c & a \end{vmatrix} + c\begin{vmatrix} d & a \\ -c & b \end{vmatrix}\right]$$

$$\Delta = \frac{(a+b^2+c^2+d^2)}{a}[a(a^2+b^2) + d(ad-bc) + c(bd+ac)]$$

$$\Delta = \frac{(a^2+b^2+c^2+d^2)}{a}[a(a^2+b^2) + ad^2+bcd - bcd + ac^2$$

$$\Delta = \frac{(a^2+b^2+c^2+d^2)}{a}\cdot a(a^2+b^2+c^2+d^2)$$

$\Delta = (a^2+b^2+c^2+d^2)^2$ RHS *(Proved)*

Problem 17 Factorise $\begin{vmatrix} a & b & c & d \\ b & a & d & c \\ c & d & a & b \\ d & c & b & a \end{vmatrix}$

Solution Adding the second, third and the fourth columns in the first column

$$\Delta = \begin{vmatrix} a+b+c+d & b & c & d \\ a+b+c+d & a & d & c \\ a+b+c+d & d & a & b \\ a+b+c+d & c & b & a \end{vmatrix}$$

$$\Delta = (a+b+c+d) \begin{vmatrix} 1 & b & c & d \\ 1 & a & d & c \\ 1 & d & a & b \\ 1 & c & b & a \end{vmatrix}$$

i.e. $a+b+c+d$ is one of the factors of the given determinant.

Similarly subtracting the sum of the third and the fourth columns from the first and second columns

$$\Delta = \begin{vmatrix} a+b-c-d & b & c & d \\ b+a-d-c & a & a & c \\ c+d-a-b & d & a & b \\ d+c-b-a & c & b & a \end{vmatrix}$$

$$= (a+b-c-d) \begin{vmatrix} 1 & b & c & d \\ 1 & a & d & c \\ -1 & d & a & b \\ -1 & c & b & a \end{vmatrix}$$

i.e, $a+b-c-d$, is ths other factor of the determinant

Similarly it can be shown that $a+c-b-d$ and $a+d-b-c$ are the other factor of the determinant.

Since the determinant is of fourth degree hence the other will be a constant.

Hence $\Delta = k\,(a+b+c+d)\,(a+b-c-d)\,(a+c-b-d)\,(a+d-b-c)$

Now equating the coefficient of a^4 we ket k^{-1}

$\therefore \quad \Delta = (a+b+c+d)\,(a+b-c-d)\,(a+d-b-c)$

Problem 18 Factorise

$$\begin{vmatrix} 0 & x & y & z \\ x & 0 & z & y \\ y & z & 0 & x \\ z & y & x & 0 \end{vmatrix}$$

Solution Adding the second, third and the fourth column in the first column

$$\Delta = \begin{vmatrix} x+y+z & x & y & z \\ x+y+z & 0 & z & y \\ x+y+z & z & 0 & x \\ x+y+z & y & x & 0 \end{vmatrix}$$

$$= (x+y+z \begin{vmatrix} 1 & x & y & z \\ 1 & 0 & z & y \\ 1 & z & 0 & x \\ 1 & y & x & 0 \end{vmatrix}$$

Now from $R_2 - R_1$, $R_3 - R_2$, $R_4 - R_3$ we get

$$\Delta = (x+y+z) \begin{vmatrix} 1 & x & y & z \\ 0 & -x & z-y & y-z \\ 0 & z & -z & x-y \\ 0 & y-z & x & -x \end{vmatrix}$$

$$\Delta = (x+y+z) \begin{vmatrix} -x & z-y & y-z \\ z & -z & x-y \\ y-z & x & -x \end{vmatrix}$$

Again from $c_1 + c_2$, $c_2 + c_3$

$$\Delta = (x+y+z) \begin{vmatrix} -x+z-y & 0 & y-x \\ 0 & -z+x-y & x-y \\ y+x-z & 0 & -x \end{vmatrix}$$

$$\Delta = (x+y+z)\,(x+y-z)\,(x-y-z \begin{vmatrix} -1 & 0 & y-z \\ 0 & 1 & x-y \\ 1 & 0 & -x \end{vmatrix}$$

Now operating $R_1 + R_3$ we have

$$\Delta = (x + y + z)(x + y - z)(x - y - z)\begin{vmatrix} 0 & 0 & y-z-x \\ 0 & 1 & x-y \\ 1 & 0 & -x \end{vmatrix}$$

$$\Delta = (x + y + z)(x + y - z)(x - y - z)(+1)\begin{vmatrix} 0 & y-z-x \\ 1 & x-y \end{vmatrix}$$

$$\Delta = (x + y + z)(x + y - z)(x - y - z)(+1)(z + x - y)$$

$$\Delta = (x + y + z)(x + y - z)(x - y - z)(y - x - z)(-1)$$

$$\Delta = -(x + y + z)(x + y - z)(y + z - x)(x + z - y)$$

Problem 19 If $2s = a + b + c$, prove that

$$\begin{vmatrix} a^2 & (s-a)^2 & (s-a)^2 \\ (s-b)^2 & b^2 & (s-b)^2 \\ (s-c)^2 & (s-c)^2 & c^2 \end{vmatrix} = 2s^2 (s-a)(s-b)(s-c)$$

Solution Let $s - a = x : s - b = y ; s - c = z$

Then $3s - (a + b + c) = x + y + z$

i.e. $3s - 2s = x + y + z$

$\Rightarrow$ $s = x + y + z$ (1)

Again $y + z = 2s - (b + c)$

$y + z = a + b + c - (b + c)$

$y + z = a$ (2)

$x + z = 2s - (a + c)$

i.e. $x + z = a + b + c - (a + c)$

i.e. $x + z = b$

and $x + y = 2s - (a + b)$

i.e. $x + y = a + b + c - (a + b)$

i.e. $x + y = c$ (4)

Now the determinant becomes

$$\Delta = \begin{vmatrix} (y+z)^2 & x^2 & x^2 \\ y^2 & (x+z)^2 & y^2 \\ z^2 & z^2 & (x+y)^2 \end{vmatrix}$$

Subtracting the last column from the first and second column respectively

$$\Delta = \begin{vmatrix} (y+z)^2-x^2 & 0 & x^2 \\ 0 & (x+z)^2-y^2 & y^2 \\ z^2-(x+y)^2 & (z^2-(x+y)^2 & (x+y)^2 \end{vmatrix}$$

$$\Delta = (x+y+z)^2 \begin{vmatrix} y+z-x & 0 & x^2 \\ 0 & x+z-y & y^2 \\ z-x-y & z-x-y & (x+y)^2 \end{vmatrix}$$

Now adding first row and second row and subtracting it from the third row we have

$$\Delta = (x+y+z)^2 \begin{vmatrix} y+z-x & 0 & x^2 \\ 0 & x+z-y & y^2 \\ -2y & -2x & 2xy \end{vmatrix}$$

$$\Delta = 2\,(x+y+z)^2 \begin{vmatrix} y+z+x & 0 & x^2 \\ 0 & x+z-y & y^2 \\ -y & -x & xy \end{vmatrix}$$

Multiplying column and the second column with x and y respectively we have

$$\Delta = \frac{2(x+y+z)^2}{xy} \begin{vmatrix} (y+z-x)\,x & 0 & -x^2 \\ 0 & y(x+z-y) & y^2 \\ -xy & -xy & xy \end{vmatrix}$$

$$\Delta = 2\,\frac{(x+y+z)^2}{xy}\,xy \begin{vmatrix} y+z-x & 0 & x \\ 0 & x+z-z & y \\ -xy & -xy & xy \end{vmatrix}$$

Adding last column to the first two columns we have

$$\Delta = 2\,(x+y+z)^2 \begin{vmatrix} y+z & x & y \\ y & x+z & y \\ 0 & 0 & xy \end{vmatrix}$$

$$\Delta = 2\,(x+y+z)^2 \begin{vmatrix} 0 & 0 & xy \\ y+z & x & x \\ y & x+z & y \end{vmatrix}$$

$$\Delta = 2(x+y+z)^2 xy \begin{vmatrix} y+z & x \\ y & x+z \end{vmatrix}$$

$$\Delta = 2(x+y+z)\, xy\, [(y+z)(x+z)-xy]$$

$$\Delta = 2(x+y+z)\, xy\, [xy+yz+xz+z^2-xy]$$

$$\Delta = 2(x+y+z)\, xyz\, (x+y+z)$$

$$\Delta = 2xyz\,(x+y+z)^3$$

Putting the values of x, y, z the value of the determinant becomes.

$$\Delta = 2(s-a)(s-b)(s-c)\, s^3$$

Thus $\begin{vmatrix} a^2 & (s-a)^2 & (s-a)^2 \\ (s-b)^2 & b^2 & (s-b)^2 \\ (s-c)^2 & (s-c)^2 & c^2 \end{vmatrix} = 2s^3 (s-a)(s-b)(s-c)$

(Proved)

Problem 20 If ω is a complex cube root of unity, proove that

$$\begin{vmatrix} 1 & \omega & \omega^2 \\ \omega & \omega^2 & 1 \\ \omega^2 & 1 & \omega \end{vmatrix} = 0$$

[*IFS 88*]

Solution Since ω is a complex cube root of unity

i e. $\omega = 3\sqrt{1}$

i.e. $\omega^3 = 1$

$$\Delta = \begin{vmatrix} 1 & \omega & \omega^2 \\ \omega & \omega^2 & 1 \\ \omega^2 & 1 & \omega \end{vmatrix}$$

Adding second and third column to the first column we hava

$$\Delta = \begin{vmatrix} 1+\omega+\omega^2 & \omega & \omega^2 \\ 1+\omega+\omega^2 & \omega^2 & 1 \\ 1+\omega+\omega^2 & 1 & \omega \end{vmatrix}$$

Since $1+\omega+\omega^2 = 0$

$$\Delta = \begin{vmatrix} 0 & \omega & \omega^2 \\ 0 & \omega^2 & 1 \\ 0 & 1 & \omega \end{vmatrix}$$

$\Delta = 0$ [expanding by columns] *(Proved)*

Problem 21 If a, b, c are distinctant

$$\begin{vmatrix} a & a^3 & a^4-1 \\ b & b^3 & b^4-1 \\ c & c^3 & c^4-1 \end{vmatrix} = 0 \qquad [I.F.S.\ 83)$$

Prove that $abc\,(ab + bc + ca) = a + b + c$

Solution $LHS = \begin{vmatrix} a & a^3 & a^4-1 \\ b & b^3 & b^4-1 \\ c & c^3 & c^4-1 \end{vmatrix}$

$$= \begin{vmatrix} a & a^3 & a^4 \\ b & b^3 & b^4 \\ c & c^3 & c^4 \end{vmatrix} + \begin{vmatrix} a & a^3 & -1 \\ b & b^3 & -1 \\ c & c^3 & -1 \end{vmatrix}$$

$$= \begin{vmatrix} a & a^3 & a^4 \\ b & b^3 & b^4 \\ c & c^3 & c^4 \end{vmatrix} - \begin{vmatrix} a & a^3 & 1 \\ b & b^3 & 1 \\ c & c^3 & 1 \end{vmatrix}$$

$= \Delta_1 - \Delta_2$

where $\quad \Delta_1 = \begin{vmatrix} a & a^3 & a^4 \\ b & b & b^4 \\ c & c^3 & c^4 \end{vmatrix}$

and $\quad \Delta_2 = \begin{vmatrix} a & a^3 & 1 \\ b & b^3 & 1 \\ c & c^3 & 1 \end{vmatrix}$

Now at first we find the value of the two determinants Δ_1 and Δ_2

$$\Delta_1 = \begin{vmatrix} a & a^3 & a^4 \\ b & b^3 & b^4 \\ c & c^3 & c^4 \end{vmatrix}$$

$$\Delta_1 = abc \begin{vmatrix} 1 & a^2 & a^3 \\ 1 & b^2 & b^3 \\ 1 & c^2 & c^3 \end{vmatrix}$$

Operating $R_1 - R_2$ and $R_2 - R_3$ wc have

$$\Delta_1 = abc \begin{vmatrix} 0 & a^2-b^2 & a^3-b^3 \\ 0 & b^2-e^2 & b^3-c^3 \\ 1 & c^2 & c^3 \end{vmatrix}$$

$$\Delta_1 = abc\,(a-b)\,(b-c) \begin{vmatrix} 0 & a+b & a^2+ab+b^2 \\ 0 & b+c & b^2+bc+c^2 \\ 1 & c^2 & c^3 \end{vmatrix}$$

Again operating $R_1 - R_2$ we have

$$\Delta_1 = abc\,(a-b)\,(b-c) \begin{vmatrix} 0 & a-c & a^2+ab-bc-c^2 \\ 0 & b+c & b^2+bc+c^2 \\ 1 & c^2 & c^3 \end{vmatrix}$$

$$\Delta_1 = abc\,(a-b)\,(b-c) \begin{vmatrix} 0 & a-c & (a-c)\,(a+c)+b\,(a-c) \\ 0 & b+c & b^2+bc+c^2 \\ 1 & c^2 & c^2 \end{vmatrix}$$

$$= abc\,(a-b)\,(b-c)\,(a-c) \begin{vmatrix} 0 & 1 & a+b+c \\ 0 & b+c & b^2+bc+c^2 \\ 1 & c^2 & c^3 \end{vmatrix}$$

$$= abc\,(a-b)\,(b-c)\,(a-c) \begin{vmatrix} 1 & a+b+c \\ b+c & b^2+bc+c^2 \end{vmatrix}$$

$$= abc\,(a-b)\,(b-c)\,(a-c)\,(b^2+bc+c^2-ab-b^2-bc \\ -ac-bc-c^2)$$

$$= abc\,(a-b)\,(b-c)\,(a-c)\,(-)\,(ab+bc+ca)$$

$$= abc\,(a-b)\,(b-c)\,(c-a)\,(ab+bc+ca) \qquad (1)$$

and $\Delta_2 = \begin{vmatrix} a & a^3 & 1 \\ b & b^3 & 1 \\ c & c^3 & 1 \end{vmatrix} = \begin{vmatrix} 1 & a & a^3 \\ 1 & b & b^3 \\ 1 & c & c^3 \end{vmatrix}$

Operating $R_1 - R_2$ and $R_2 - R_3$ we have

$$\Delta_2 = \begin{vmatrix} 0 & a-b & a^3-b^3 \\ 0 & b-c & b^3-c^3 \\ 1 & c & c^3 \end{vmatrix}$$

$$= (a-b)(b-c)\begin{vmatrix} 0 & 1 & a^2+ab+b^2 \\ 0 & 1 & b^2+bc+c^2 \\ 1 & c & c^3 \end{vmatrix}$$

$$= (a-b)(b-c)\begin{vmatrix} 1 & a^2+ab+b^2 \\ 1 & b^2+bc+c^2 \end{vmatrix}$$

$$= (a-b)(b-c)(b^2+bc+c^2-a^2-ab-b^2)$$

$$= (a-b)(b-c)\{b(c-a)+(c-a)(c+a)\}$$

$$= (a-b)(b-c)(c-a)(a+b+c) \qquad \textbf{(2)}$$

Hence from question we have

$$\Delta_1 - \Delta_2 = 0$$

$$\Rightarrow \quad abc\,(a-b)(b-c)(c-a)(ab+bc+ca) - (a-b)(b-c)(c-a)(a+b+c) = 0$$

Since a, b, c are distinct so

$$abc\,(ab+bc+ca) = (a+b+c) \qquad \textit{(Proved)}$$

Problem 22 Prove that

$$\begin{vmatrix} 1+a_1 & a_2 & a_3 & a_4 \\ a_1 & 1+a_2 & a_3 & a_4 \\ a_1 & a_2 & 1+a_3 & a_4 \\ a_1 & a_2 & a_3 & 1+a_4 \end{vmatrix} = 1+a_1+a_2+a_3+a_4$$

Solution Adding to the first column, the rest of the columns we get

$$\Delta = \begin{vmatrix} 1+a_1+a_2+a_3+a_4 & a_2 & a_3 & a_4 \\ 1+a_1+a_2+a_3+a_4 & 1+a_2 & a_3 & a_4 \\ 1+a_1+a_2+a_3+a_4 & a_2 & 1+a_3 & a_4 \\ 1+a_1+a_2+a_3+a_4 & a_2 & a_3 & 1+a_4 \end{vmatrix}$$

$$\Delta = 1+a_1+a_2+a_3+a_4 \begin{vmatrix} 1 & a_2 & a_3 & a_4 \\ 1 & 1+a_2 & a_3 & a_4 \\ 1 & a_2 & 1+a_3 & a_4 \\ 1 & a_2 & a_3 & 1+a_4 \end{vmatrix}$$

Again subtract the first column from all the remaining columns after multiplying respectively by $a_2\ a_3\ a_4$ Then

$$\Delta = (1 + a_1 + a_2 + a_3 + a_4)\begin{vmatrix} 1 & 0 & 0 & 0 \\ 1 & 1 & 0 & 0 \\ 1 & 0 & 1 & 0 \\ 1 & 0 & 0 & 1 \end{vmatrix}$$

Now consider the determinant

$$\begin{vmatrix} 1 & 0 & 0 & 0 \\ 1 & 1 & 0 & 0 \\ 1 & 0 & 1 & 0 \\ 1 & 0 & 0 & 1 \end{vmatrix}$$

In which there are four (4) rows and 4 columns. Let this determinant is denoted by D_4.

Then expanding by the top element at the left

$$D_4 = \begin{vmatrix} 1 & 0 & 0 \\ 0 & 1 & 0 \\ 0 & 0 & 1 \end{vmatrix} ; \ \overline{4-1} \text{ rows and } \overline{4-1} \text{ columns}$$

$$= D_3$$

Similarly $D_3 = D_2$

Thus $D_4 = D_2 = \begin{vmatrix} 1 & 0 \\ 0 & 1 \end{vmatrix} = 1$

Hence $\Delta = (1 + a_1 + a_2 + a_3 + a_4)$ *(Proved)*

Problem 23 Prove that

$$\begin{vmatrix} a^2 & bc & ac + c^2 \\ a^2 + ab & b^2 & ac \\ ab & b^2 + cb & c^2 \end{vmatrix} = 4a^2\, b^2\, c^2$$

Solution

$$\Delta = \begin{vmatrix} a^2 & bc & ac + c^2 \\ a^2 + ab & b^2 & ac \\ ab & b^2 + cb & c^2 \end{vmatrix}$$

$$\Delta = abc \begin{vmatrix} a & c & a+c \\ a+b & b & a \\ b & b+c & c \end{vmatrix}$$

Taking out a, b, c from c_1, c_2, c_3 respectively.

Now operating $c_1 \to c_1 + c_2$

$$\Delta = abc \begin{vmatrix} a+c & c & a+c \\ a+2b & b & a \\ 2b+c & b+c & c \end{vmatrix}$$

Operating $c_1 \to c_1 - c_3$

$$\Delta = abc \begin{vmatrix} 0 & c & a+c \\ 2b & b & a \\ 2b & b+c & c \end{vmatrix}$$

$$\Delta = abc \begin{vmatrix} 0 & c & a+c \\ 2b & b & a \\ 0 & c & c-a \end{vmatrix} \text{ Replacing } R_3 \to R_3 - R_2$$

$$\Delta = abc\,(-2b) \begin{vmatrix} c & a+c \\ c & c-a \end{vmatrix}$$

$$\Delta = abc\,(-2b) \begin{vmatrix} 0 & 2a \\ c & c-a \end{vmatrix}$$

By $\quad R_1 \to R_1 - R_2$

$\Delta = abc\,(-2b)\,a(-2ac)$ Expanding the determinant

$\Delta = 4a^2\,b^2\,c^2$

i.e. $$\begin{vmatrix} a^2 & bc & ac+c^2 \\ a^2+ab & b^2 & ac \\ ab & b^2+bc & c^2 \end{vmatrix} = 4a^2\,b^2\,c^2 \qquad (\textit{Proved})$$

Problem 24 Evaluate the determinant

$$\begin{vmatrix} (b+c) & (a+b) & a \\ (c+a) & (b+c) & b \\ (a+b) & (c+a) & c \end{vmatrix} = a^3 + b^3 + c^3 - 3abc$$

Solution Let $\Delta = \begin{vmatrix} b+c & a+b & a \\ c+a & b+c & b \\ a+b & c+a & c \end{vmatrix}$

By operating $c \to c_1 + c_3$

$$\Delta = \begin{vmatrix} a+b+c & a+b & a \\ a+b+c & b+c & b \\ a+b+c & c+a & c \end{vmatrix}$$

$$\Delta = (a+b+c) \begin{vmatrix} 1 & a+b & a \\ 1 & b+c & b \\ 1 & c+a & c \end{vmatrix}$$

$$\Delta = (a+b+c) \begin{vmatrix} 1 & a & a \\ 1 & b & b \\ 1 & c & c \end{vmatrix} + (a+b+c) \begin{vmatrix} 1 & b & a \\ 1 & c & b \\ 1 & a & c \end{vmatrix}$$

First term vanishes since two columns of this are identical

$$\Delta = (a+b+c) \begin{vmatrix} 1 & b & a \\ 1 & c & b \\ 1 & a & c \end{vmatrix}$$

$$\Delta = (a+b+c) \begin{vmatrix} 0 & b-c & a-b \\ 0 & c-a & b-c \\ 1 & a & c \end{vmatrix}$$

Operating $R_1 - R_2$ and $R_2 - R_3$

$$\Delta = (a+b+c) \begin{vmatrix} b-c & a-b \\ c-a & b-c) \end{vmatrix}$$

expanding by column we have

$$\Delta = (a+b+c)\{b^2 - 2bc + c^2 - (a-b)(c-a)\}$$
$$\Delta = (a+b+c)\{b^2 - 2bc + c^2 - (ac - a^2 - bc + ab)\}$$
$$\Delta = (a+b+c)(b^2 - 2bc + c^2 - ac + a^2 + bc - ab)$$
$$\Delta = (a+b+c)(a^2 + b^2 + c^2 - ab - bc - ca)$$
$$\Delta = a^3 + b^3 + c^3 - 3abc$$

(*Proved*)

Problem 25 Prove that

$$\begin{vmatrix} a^2 & a^2-(b-c)^2 & bc \\ b^2 & b^2-(c-a)^2 & ca \\ c^2 & c^2-(a-b)^2 & ab \end{vmatrix}$$

$$= (b-c)(c-a)(a-b)(a+b+c)(a^2+b^2+c^2) \qquad (I.F.S.\ 87)$$

Solution Applying $c_2 \to c_2 - c_1$ we get

$$\Delta = \begin{vmatrix} a^2 & -(b-c)^2 & bc \\ b^2 & -(c-a)^2 & ca \\ c^2 & -(a-b)^2 & ab \end{vmatrix}$$

$$\Delta = -\begin{vmatrix} a^2 & b^2+c^2 & bc \\ b^2 & c^2+a^2 & ca \\ c^2 & a^2+b^2 & ab \end{vmatrix} \text{ applying } c_2 \to c_2 + c_1$$

$$\Delta = -\begin{vmatrix} a^2 & a^2+b^2+c^2 & bc \\ b^2 & a^2+b^2+c^2 & ca \\ c^2 & a^2+b^2+c^2 & ab \end{vmatrix} \text{ applying } c_2 \to c_2 + c_1$$

$$\Delta = -(a^2+b^2+c^2)\begin{vmatrix} a^2 & 1 & bc \\ b^2 & 1 & ca \\ c^2 & 1 & ab \end{vmatrix} \text{ taking } a^2+b^2+c^2 \text{ common from the second column}$$

$$\Delta = (a^2+b^2+c^2)\begin{vmatrix} 1 & a^2 & bc \\ 1 & b^2 & ca \\ 1 & c^2 & ab \end{vmatrix} \text{ interchanging first and second column}$$

$$\Delta = (a^2+b^2+c^2)\begin{vmatrix} 1 & a^2 & bc \\ 0 & b^2-a^2 & ca-bc \\ 0 & c^2-a^2 & ab-bc \end{vmatrix} \text{ by } \begin{matrix} R_2 \to R_2 - R_1 \\ R_3 \to R_3 - R_1 \end{matrix}$$

$$\Delta = (a^2+b^2+c)^2\begin{vmatrix} 1 & a^2 & bc \\ 0 & (b-a)(b+a) & c(a-b) \\ 0 & (c-a)(c+a) & b(a-c) \end{vmatrix}$$

$$\Delta = (a^2+b^2+c^2)(a-b)(c-a)\begin{vmatrix} 1 & a^2 & bc \\ 0 & -(b+a) & c \\ 0 & +(c+a) & -b \end{vmatrix}$$

$$\Delta = (a^2 + b^2 + c^2)(a-b)(c-a)\begin{vmatrix} -(b+a) & c \\ (c+a) & -b \end{vmatrix}$$

Operating $c_2 \to c_2 - c_1$ we have

$$\Delta = (a^2 + b^2 + c^2)(a-b)(c-a)\begin{vmatrix} -(b+a) & (a+b+c) \\ (c+a) & -(a+b+c) \end{vmatrix}$$

$$\Delta = (a^2 + b^2 + c^2)(a-b)(c-a)(a+b+c)\begin{vmatrix} -(b+a) & 1 \\ (c+a) & -1 \end{vmatrix}$$

$$\Delta = (a^2 + b^2 + c^2)(a-b)(c-a)(a+b+c)(a+b-c-a)$$

$$\Delta = (a^2 + b^2 + c^2)(a-b)(b-c)(c-a)(a+b+c) \quad \textit{(Proved)}$$

Problem 26 Prove that

$$\begin{vmatrix} 1+a^2-b^2 & 2ab & -2b \\ 2ab & 1-a^2+b^2 & 2a \\ 2b & -2a & 1-a^2-b^2 \end{vmatrix} = (1+a^2+b^2)^3$$

Solution Let us denote the given determinant by

$$\Delta = \begin{vmatrix} 1+a^2-b^2 & 2ab & -2b \\ 2ab & 1-a^2+b^2 & 2a \\ 2b & -2a & 1-a^2-b^2 \end{vmatrix}$$

Now operating $c_1 - bc_3$

$$\Delta = \begin{vmatrix} 1+a^2+b^2 & 2ab & -2b \\ 0 & 1-a^2+b^2 & 2a \\ 2b-b(1-a^2-b^2) & -2a & 1-a^2-b^2 \end{vmatrix}$$

$$\Delta = \begin{vmatrix} 1+a^2+b^2 & 2ab & -2b \\ 0 & 1-a^2+b^2 & 2a \\ b(1+a^2+b^2) & -2a & 1-a^2-b^2 \end{vmatrix}$$

Now operating $R_3 \to R_3 - bR_1$

$$\Delta = \begin{vmatrix} 1+a^2+b^2 & 2ab & -2b \\ 0 & 1-a^2+b^2 & 2a \\ 0 & -2a-2ab^2 & 1-a^2+b^2 \end{vmatrix}$$

$$\Delta = (1+a^2+b^2)\begin{vmatrix} 1-a^2+b^2 & 2a \\ -2a(1+b^2) & 1-a^2+b^2 \end{vmatrix}$$

$$\Delta = (1 + a^2 + b^2)\,[(1 - a^2 + b^2)^2 + 4a^2(1 + b^2)]$$
$$\Delta = (1 + a^2 + b^2)\,[(1 + b^2)^2 + a^4 - 2a^2(1 + b^2) + 4a^2(1 + b^2)]$$
$$\Delta = (1 + a^2 + b^2)\,[(1 + b^2)^2 + (a^2)^2 + 2a^2(1 + b^2)]$$
$$\Delta = (1 + a^2 + b^2)\,[(1 + b^2 + a^2)^2]$$
$$\Delta = (1 + a^2 + b^2)^3 \qquad \textit{(Proved)}$$

Problem 27 Prove that

$$\begin{vmatrix} b+c & c+a & a+b \\ b_1+c_1 & c_1+a_1 & a_1+b_1 \\ b_2+c_2 & c_2+a_2 & a_2+b_2 \end{vmatrix} = 2\begin{vmatrix} a & b & c \\ a_1 & b_1 & c_1 \\ a_2 & b_2 & c_2 \end{vmatrix}$$

$$\text{LHS}\begin{vmatrix} b+c & c+a & a+b \\ b_1+c_1 & c_1+a_1 & a_1+b_1 \\ b_2+c_2 & c_2+a_2 & a_2+b_2 \end{vmatrix}$$

$$= \begin{vmatrix} b & c+a & a+b \\ b_1 & c_1+a_1 & a_1+b_1 \\ b_2 & c_2+a_2 & a_2+b_2 \end{vmatrix} + \begin{vmatrix} c & c+a & a+b \\ c_1 & c_1+a_1 & a_1+b_1 \\ c_2 & c_2+a_2 & a_2+b_2 \end{vmatrix}$$

[Expressing the determinant into sum of two determinants]

$$\Delta = \begin{vmatrix} b & c & a+b \\ b_1 & c_1 & a_1+b_1 \\ b_2 & c_2 & a_2+b_2 \end{vmatrix} + \begin{vmatrix} b & a & a+b \\ b_1 & a_1 & a_1+b_1 \\ b_2 & a_2 & a_2+b_2 \end{vmatrix}$$

$$+ \begin{vmatrix} c & c & a+b \\ c_1 & c_1 & a_1+b_1 \\ c_2 & c_2 & a_2+b_2 \end{vmatrix} + \begin{vmatrix} c & a & a+b \\ c_1 & a_1 & a_1+b_1 \\ c_2 & a_2 & b_2+b_2 \end{vmatrix}$$

$$\Delta = \begin{vmatrix} b & c & a \\ b_1 & c_1 & a_1 \\ b_2 & c_2 & a_2 \end{vmatrix} + \begin{vmatrix} c & a & b \\ c_1 & a_1 & b_1 \\ c_2 & a_2 & b_2 \end{vmatrix}$$

All the other determinants vanishes since two columns are identical

$$\Delta = -\begin{vmatrix} b & a & c \\ b_1 & a_1 & c_1 \\ b_2 & a_2 & c_2 \end{vmatrix} - \begin{vmatrix} a & c & b \\ a_1 & c_1 & b_1 \\ a_2 & c_2 & b_2 \end{vmatrix}$$

$$\Delta = + \begin{vmatrix} a & b & c \\ a_1 & c_1 & c_1 \\ a_2 & b_2 & c_2 \end{vmatrix} + \begin{vmatrix} a & b & c \\ a_1 & b_1 & c_1 \\ a_2 & b_2 & c_2 \end{vmatrix}$$

$$\Delta = 2 \begin{vmatrix} a & b & c \\ a_1 & b_1 & c_1 \\ a_2 & b_2 & c_2 \end{vmatrix} \text{(RHS)}$$

(Proved)

Problem 28 Prove that

$$\begin{vmatrix} -2a & a+b & a+c \\ b+a & -2b & b+c \\ c+a & c+b & -2c \end{vmatrix} = 4\,(b+c)\,(c+a)\,(a+b)^2$$

Solution Let

$$\Delta = \begin{vmatrix} -2a & a+b & a+c \\ b+a & -2b & b+c \\ c+a & c+b & -2c \end{vmatrix}$$

Putting $b = -c$ in the given determinant

$$\Delta = \begin{vmatrix} -2a & a-c & a+c \\ -c+a & +2c & 0 \\ c+a & 0 & -2c \end{vmatrix}$$

Now adding all the columns to the first column we have

$$\Delta = \begin{vmatrix} 0 & a-c & a+c \\ c+a & 2c & 0 \\ a-c & 0 & -2b \end{vmatrix}$$

Now subtracting second column from third we have.

$$\Delta = \begin{vmatrix} 0 & a-c & 2c \\ c+a & 2c & -2c \\ a-c & 0 & -2c \end{vmatrix}$$

Now adding first row to the second and the third row we have

$$\Delta = \begin{vmatrix} 0 & a-c & 2c \\ c+a & a+c & 0 \\ a-c & a-c & 0 \end{vmatrix}$$

$$\Delta = (a + c)(a-c)\begin{vmatrix} 0 & a-c & 2c \\ 1 & 1 & 0 \\ 1 & 1 & 0 \end{vmatrix}$$

= 0 since the last two rows are identical

Hence putting $b = -c$ in the given determinant vanishes. Therefore $b+c$ is a factor of the given determinant similarly we can show that $c + a$ and $a + b$ are also the factors of the given determinant.

Now, the given determinant is of third degree as is clear from the diagonal terms $(-2a) \times (-2b) \times (-2c) = -8abc$. Hence the remaining factor, if any, must be constant say k

Therefore $\Delta\ k (b + c)(c + a)(a + b)$

Where k is a constant to be determined.

$$\begin{vmatrix} -2a & a+b & a+c \\ b+a & -2b & b+c \\ c+a & c+b & -2c \end{vmatrix} = k(b+c)(c+a)(a+b)$$

Putting $a = 0$, $b = 1$ and $c = 2$ we have

$$\begin{vmatrix} 0 & 1 & 2 \\ 1 & -2 & 3 \\ 2 & 3 & -4 \end{vmatrix} = k \times 3 \times 2 \times 1$$

$$6k = -1\begin{vmatrix} 1 & 0 \\ 2 & -4 \end{vmatrix} + 2\begin{vmatrix} 1 & -2 \\ 2 & 3 \end{vmatrix}$$

$$6k = -1(-4-6) + 2(3+4)$$

$$6k = 10 + 14$$

$$6k = 24$$

So $\quad k = 4$

So
$$\begin{vmatrix} -2a & a+b & a+c \\ b+a & -2b & b+c \\ c+a & c+b & -2c \end{vmatrix} = 4(a+b)(b+c)(c+a) \text{ Ans.}$$

Problem 29 Prove that

$$\begin{vmatrix} a+b+2c & a & b \\ c & b+c+2a & b \\ c & a & c+a+2b \end{vmatrix} = 2\,(a+b+c)^3$$

Adding the second and third column to the first column we have

$$\Delta = \begin{vmatrix} 2a+2b+2c & a & b \\ 2a+2b+2c & b+c+2a & b \\ 2a+2b+2c & a & c+a+2b \end{vmatrix}$$

$$\Delta = 2\,(a+b+c) \begin{vmatrix} 1 & b & a \\ 1 & b+c+2a & b \\ 1 & a & c+a+2b \end{vmatrix}$$

Subtracting first row from the second and third row we have

$$\Delta = 2\,(a+b+c) \begin{vmatrix} 1 & a & b \\ 0 & a+b+c & 0 \\ 0 & 0 & a+b+c \end{vmatrix}$$

$$\Delta = 2\,(a+b+c)\,(a+b+c)\,(a+b+c) \begin{vmatrix} 1 & a & b \\ 0 & 1 & 0 \\ 0 & 0 & 1 \end{vmatrix}$$

Taking $(a+b+c)$ common from the second and third row.

$$\Delta = 2(a+b+c)\,(a+b+c)\,(a+b+c) \begin{vmatrix} 1 & 0 \\ 0 & 1 \end{vmatrix}$$

$$\Delta = (a+b+c)^3.$$

So $\Delta = 2\,(a+b+c)^3$ *(Proved)*

Problem 30 Prove that

$$\begin{vmatrix} a & b+c & a^2 \\ b & c+a & b^2 \\ c & a+b & c^2 \end{vmatrix} = -(b-c)\,(c-a)\,(a-b)\,(a+b+c)$$

Let

$$\Delta = \begin{vmatrix} a & b+c & a^2 \\ b & c+a & b^2 \\ c & a+b & c^2 \end{vmatrix}$$

Adding the second column to the first column we have.

$$\Delta = \begin{vmatrix} a+b+c & b+c & a^2 \\ a+b+c & c+a & b^2 \\ a+b+c & a+b & c^2 \end{vmatrix}$$

$$\Delta = (a+b+c)\begin{vmatrix} 1 & b+c & a^2 \\ 1 & c+a & b^2 \\ 1 & a+b & c^2 \end{vmatrix}$$

Now applying $R_1 - R_2$, and $R_2 - R_3$ we have.

$$\Delta = 2\,(a+b+c)\begin{vmatrix} 0 & b-a & a^2-b^2 \\ 0 & c-b & b^2-c^2 \\ 1 & a+b & c^2 \end{vmatrix}$$

$$\Delta = 2(a+b+c)\,(a-b)\,(b-c)\begin{vmatrix} 0 & -1 & a+b \\ 0 & -1 & b+c \\ 1 & a+b & c^2 \end{vmatrix}$$

$$\Delta = 2\,(a+b+c)\,(a-b)\,(b-c)\begin{vmatrix} -1 & a+b \\ -1 & b+c \end{vmatrix}$$

$$\Delta = 2\,(a+b+c)\,(a-b)\,(b-c)\,(-b-c+a+b)$$

$$\Delta = 2\,(a+b+c)\,(a-b)\,(b-c)\,(a-c)$$

$$\Delta = -2\,(a+b+c)\,(a-b)\,(b-c)\,(c-a) \text{ RHS.}$$ *(Proved)*

Problem 31 Prove that

$$\begin{vmatrix} x & y & z \\ x^2 & y^2 & z^2 \\ y^2 & zx & xy \end{vmatrix} = \begin{vmatrix} 1 & 1 & 1 \\ x^2 & y^2 & z^2 \\ x^3 & y^3 & c^3 \end{vmatrix}$$

$$= (y-z)\,(z-x)\,(x-y)\,(xy+yz+zx)$$

Let the determinant is denoted by

$$\Delta = \begin{vmatrix} x & y & z \\ x^2 & y^2 & z^2 \\ yz & zx & xy \end{vmatrix}$$

$$\Delta = \frac{1}{xyz}\begin{vmatrix} x^2 & y^2 & z^2 \\ x^3 & y^3 & z^3 \\ xyz & xyz & xyz \end{vmatrix}$$

$$\Delta = \frac{xyz}{xyz}\begin{vmatrix} x^2 & y^2 & z^2 \\ x^3 & y^3 & z^3 \\ 1 & 1 & 1 \end{vmatrix}$$

$$\Delta = \begin{vmatrix} 1 & 1 & 1 \\ x^2 & y^2 & z^2 \\ x^3 & y^3 & z^3 \end{vmatrix}$$

Now operating $c_2 - c_1$ and $c_3 - c_1$ we have

$$\Delta = \begin{vmatrix} 1 & 0 & 0 \\ x^2 & y^2 - x^2 & z^2 - x^2 \\ x^3 & y^3 - x^3 & z^3 - x^3 \end{vmatrix}$$

$$\Delta = \begin{vmatrix} 1 & 0 & 0 \\ x^2 & (y-x)(y+x) & (z-x)(z+x) \\ x^3 & (y-x)(y^2+xy+x^2) & (z-x)(z^2+xy+x^2) \end{vmatrix}$$

$$\Delta = \begin{vmatrix} 1 & 0 & 0 \\ x^2 & y+x & z+x \\ x^3 & y^2+xy+x^2 & z^2+xz+x^2 \end{vmatrix}(y-z)(z-x)$$

Operating we have $c_3 \rightarrow c_3 - c_2$

$$\Delta = (y-x)(z-x)\begin{vmatrix} 1 & 0 & 0 \\ x^2 & y+x & z-y \\ x^3 & y^2+x^2+xy & z^2+xz-y^2-xy \end{vmatrix}$$

$$\Delta = (y-x)(z-x)\begin{vmatrix} 1 & 0 & 0 \\ x^2 & y+x & z-y \\ x^3 & y^2+x^2+xy & (z-y)(z+y)+x(z-y) \end{vmatrix}$$

$$\Delta = (y-x)(z-x)(z-y)\begin{vmatrix} 1 & 0 & 0 \\ x^2 & y+x & 1 \\ x^3 & x^2+y^2+xy & x+y+z \end{vmatrix}$$

$$\Delta = (y-x)(z-x)(z-y)\begin{vmatrix} y+x & 1 \\ x^2+y^2+xy & x+y+z \end{vmatrix}$$

$$\Delta = (x-y)(z-x)(z-y)(xy+y^2+yz+x^2+xy+xz - x^2-y^2-xy)$$

$$\Delta = (x-y)(y\times z)(z-x)(xy+yz+zx) \qquad \textit{(Proved)}$$

Product of Determinants

Problem 32 show that

$$\begin{vmatrix} 0 & c & b \\ c & 0 & a \\ b & a & 0 \end{vmatrix}^2 = \begin{vmatrix} b^2+c^2 & ab & ac \\ ab & c^2+a^2 & bc \\ ac & bc & a^2+b^2 \end{vmatrix}$$

Solution $LHS = \begin{vmatrix} 0 & c & b \\ c & 0 & a \\ b & a & 0 \end{vmatrix}^2$

$$= \begin{vmatrix} 0 & c & b \\ c & 0 & a \\ b & a & 0 \end{vmatrix} \times \begin{vmatrix} 0 & c & b \\ c & 0 & a \\ b & a & 0 \end{vmatrix}$$

$$= \begin{vmatrix} 0\cdot 0 + c\cdot c + b\cdot b & 0\cdot c + c\cdot 0 + ba & 0\cdot b + c\cdot a + b\cdot 0 \\ c.0 + 0\cdot c + a\cdot b & c\cdot c + 0\cdot 0 + a\cdot a & c\cdot b + 0\, a + a\cdot 0 \\ b\cdot 0 + a\cdot c + 0\cdot b & b\cdot c + a\cdot 0 + 0\cdot a & b\cdot b + a\cdot a + 0\cdot 0 \end{vmatrix}$$

$$= \begin{vmatrix} b^2+c^2 & ab & ac \\ ab & a^2+c^2 & bc \\ ac & bc & a^2+b^2 \end{vmatrix}$$

$$= \begin{vmatrix} b^2+c^2 & ab & ac \\ ab & c^2+a^2 & bc \\ ac & bc & a^2+b^2 \end{vmatrix} = RHS \qquad \textit{(Proved)}$$

Proclem 33 $\begin{vmatrix} 2bc-a^2 & c^2 & b^2 \\ c^2 & 2ac-b^2 & a^2 \\ b^2 & a^2 & 2ab-c^2 \end{vmatrix} = \begin{vmatrix} a & b & c \\ b & c & a \\ c & a & b \end{vmatrix}$

$$= (a^3+b^3+c^3-3abc)^2$$

Solution we have

$$=\begin{vmatrix} a & b & c \\ b & c & a \\ c & a & b \end{vmatrix}^2$$

$$=\begin{vmatrix} a & b & c \\ b & c & a \\ c & a & b \end{vmatrix} \times \begin{vmatrix} a & b & c \\ b & c & a \\ c & a & b \end{vmatrix}$$

$$=\begin{vmatrix} a & b & c \\ b & c & a \\ c & a & b \end{vmatrix} \times (-1) \begin{vmatrix} a & c & b \\ b & a & c \\ c & b & a \end{vmatrix}$$

$$=\begin{vmatrix} a & b & c \\ b & c & a \\ c & a & b \end{vmatrix} \times \begin{vmatrix} -a & c & b \\ -b & a & c \\ -c & b & a \end{vmatrix}$$

$$=\begin{vmatrix} 2bc-a^2 & c^2 & b^2 \\ c^2 & 2ac-b^2 & a^2 \\ b^2 & a^2 & 2ab-c^2 \end{vmatrix} = LHS \qquad \textit{(Proved)}$$

Again $\begin{vmatrix} a & b & c \\ b & c & a \\ c & a & b \end{vmatrix}^2$

$$= [a\,(bc-a^2)-b\,(b^2-ca) + c\,(ab-c^2)]^2$$

$$= [(abc-a^3-b^3 + abc + abc-c^3]^2$$

$$= (a^3 + b^3 + c3-3abc)^2 \qquad \textit{(Proved)}$$

Problem 34 Prove that the determinant

$$\begin{vmatrix} -a^2 & ab & ac \\ ab & -b^2 & bc \\ ac & bc & -c^2 \end{vmatrix}$$

is a perfect square of a determinant and find its value.

Solution Let us find the co-factors of all the elements of the determinant

$$\begin{vmatrix} 0 & c & b \\ c & 0 & a \\ b & a & 0 \end{vmatrix}$$

The co-factor of 0 $= \begin{vmatrix} 0 & a \\ a & 0 \end{vmatrix} = 0-a^2 = -a^2$

The co-factor of $c = -\begin{vmatrix} c & a \\ b & 0 \end{vmatrix} = -(0-ab) = ab$

The co-factor of $b = \begin{vmatrix} c & 0 \\ b & a \end{vmatrix} = (ac-0) = ac$

The co-factor of $c = -\begin{vmatrix} c & b \\ a & 0 \end{vmatrix} = -(0-ab) = ab$

The co-factor of 0 $= \begin{vmatrix} 0 & b \\ b & 0 \end{vmatrix} = 0-b^2 = -b^2$

The co-factor of $a = -\begin{vmatrix} 0 & c \\ b & a \end{vmatrix} = -(0-bc) = bc$

The co-factor of $b = \begin{vmatrix} c & b \\ 0 & a \end{vmatrix} = (ac-0) = ac$

The factor of $a = -\begin{vmatrix} 0 & b \\ c & a \end{vmatrix} = -(0-bc) = bc$

The co-factor 0 $= \begin{vmatrix} 0 & c \\ c & 0 \end{vmatrix} = (0-c^2) = -c^2$

Hence
$$\begin{vmatrix} -a^2 & ab & ac \\ ab & -b^2 & bc \\ ac & bc & -c^2 \end{vmatrix} = \begin{vmatrix} 0 & c & b \\ c & 0 & a \\ b & a & 0 \end{vmatrix}^2$$

Thus the given determinant is a perfect square of the determinant

$$\begin{vmatrix} 0 & c & b \\ c & 0 & a \\ b & a & 0 \end{vmatrix}$$

Value of the given determenant

$$= \begin{vmatrix} 0 & c & b \\ c & 0 & a \\ b & a & 0 \end{vmatrix}^2 = [-c\,(0-ab)+b\,(ac-0)]^2 = (2abc)^2 = 4a^2\,b^2\,c^2$$

Problem 35 Find the value of

$$\begin{vmatrix} a^2+\lambda^2 & ab+c\lambda & ca-b\lambda \\ ab-c\lambda & b^2+\lambda^2 & bc+a\lambda \\ ca+b\lambda & bc-a\lambda & c^2+\lambda^2 \end{vmatrix} \times \begin{vmatrix} \lambda & c & -b \\ -c & \lambda & a \\ b & -a & \lambda \end{vmatrix}$$

Solution Let us find the co-factors of the elements of

$$\begin{vmatrix} \lambda & c & -b \\ -c & \lambda & a \\ b & -a & \lambda \end{vmatrix}$$

The co-factors of $\lambda = \begin{vmatrix} \lambda & a \\ -a & \lambda \end{vmatrix} = \lambda^2 + a^2$

The co-factors of $c = -\begin{vmatrix} -c & a \\ b & \lambda \end{vmatrix} = -(-c\lambda - ab) = ab + c\lambda$

The co-factor of $-b = \begin{vmatrix} -c & \lambda \\ b & -a \end{vmatrix} = (ac - b\lambda)$

The co-factor of $-c = -\begin{vmatrix} c & -b \\ -a & \lambda \end{vmatrix} = -(c\lambda - ab) = ab - c\lambda$

The co-factor of $\lambda = \begin{vmatrix} \lambda & -b \\ b & \lambda \end{vmatrix} = \lambda^2 + b^2$

The co-factor of $a = -\begin{vmatrix} \lambda & c \\ b & -a \end{vmatrix} = -(-a\lambda - bc) = a\lambda + bc$

The co-factor of $b = \begin{vmatrix} c & -b \\ \lambda & a \end{vmatrix} = ac + b\lambda$

The co-factor of $-a = -\begin{vmatrix} \lambda & -b \\ -c & a \end{vmatrix} = (bc - a\lambda)$

The co-factor of $\lambda = \begin{vmatrix} \lambda & c \\ -c & \lambda \end{vmatrix} = \lambda^2 + c^2$

Therefore $\begin{vmatrix} \lambda & c & -b \\ -c & \lambda & a \\ b & -a & \lambda \end{vmatrix}^2 = \begin{vmatrix} a^2+\lambda^2 & ab+c\lambda & ca-b\lambda \\ ab-c\lambda & b^2+\lambda^2 & bc+a\lambda \\ ca+b\lambda & bc-a\lambda & c^2+\lambda^2 \end{vmatrix}$

$$\text{Thus} \quad \begin{vmatrix} a^2+\lambda^2 & ab+c\lambda & ca-b\lambda \\ ab-c\lambda & b^2+\lambda^2 & bc+a\lambda \\ ca+b\lambda & bc-a\lambda & c^2+\lambda^2 \end{vmatrix} \times \begin{vmatrix} \lambda & c & -b \\ -c & \lambda & a \\ b & -a & \lambda \end{vmatrix}$$

$$= \begin{vmatrix} \lambda & c & -b \\ -c & \lambda & a \\ b & -a & \lambda \end{vmatrix}^2 \times \begin{vmatrix} \lambda & c & -b \\ -c & \lambda & a \\ b & -a & \lambda \end{vmatrix}$$

$$= \begin{vmatrix} \lambda & c & -b \\ -c & \lambda & a \\ b & -a & \lambda \end{vmatrix}^3 \quad \textbf{Ans.}$$

$$= \lambda(\lambda^2+a^2) - c(-c\lambda - ab) - b(ac - b\lambda)]^3$$
$$= [\lambda^3 + a^2\lambda + c^2\lambda + abc - abc + b\lambda^2]^3$$
$$= [\lambda^3 + \lambda(a^2+b^2+c^2)]^3 \quad \textbf{Ans.}$$

Problem 36 Show that

$$\begin{vmatrix} yz-x^2 & zx-y^2 & xy-z^2 \\ zx-y^2 & xy-z^2 & yz-x^2 \\ xy-z^2 & yz-x^2 & zx-y^2 \end{vmatrix} = \begin{vmatrix} x & y & z \\ y & z & x \\ z & x & y \end{vmatrix}^2 = \begin{vmatrix} r^2 & u^2 & u^2 \\ u^2 & r^2 & u^2 \\ u^2 & u^2 & r^2 \end{vmatrix}$$

where $r^2 = x^2 + y^2 + z^2$ and $u^2 = yz + zx + xy$

Solution Let us find the co-factors of the elements of the determinant

$$\begin{vmatrix} x & y & z \\ y & z & x \\ z & x & y \end{vmatrix}$$

The co-factor of $x = \begin{vmatrix} z & x \\ x & y \end{vmatrix} = yz - x^2$

The co-factor of $y = -\begin{vmatrix} y & x \\ z & y \end{vmatrix} = zx - y^2$

The co-factor of $z = \begin{vmatrix} y & z \\ z & x \end{vmatrix} = xy - z^2$

The co-factor of $y = -\begin{vmatrix} y & z \\ x & y \end{vmatrix} = xz - y^2$

The co-factor of $z = \begin{vmatrix} y & z \\ z & x \end{vmatrix} = xy - z^{-}$

The co-factor of $x = -\begin{vmatrix} x & z \\ y & x \end{vmatrix} = (yz - x^2)$

The co-factor of $y = \begin{vmatrix} x & y \\ y & z \end{vmatrix} = xz - y^2$

Co-factor of $z = \begin{vmatrix} x & z \\ z & y \end{vmatrix} = xy - z^2,$

Co-factor $x = -\begin{vmatrix} x & y \\ z & x \end{vmatrix} = yz - x^2$

This shows that $\begin{vmatrix} x & y & z \\ y & z & x \\ z & x & y \end{vmatrix}^2 = \begin{vmatrix} yz-x^2 & zx-y^2 & xy-z^2 \\ zx-y^2 & xy-z^2 & yz-x^2 \\ xy-z^2 & yz-x^2 & zx-y^2 \end{vmatrix}$

(*First part proved*)

For the second part

$$\begin{vmatrix} x & y & z \\ y & z & x \\ z & x & y \end{vmatrix}^2 = \begin{vmatrix} x & y & z \\ y & z & x \\ z & x & y \end{vmatrix} \times \begin{vmatrix} x & y & z \\ y & z & x \\ z & x & y \end{vmatrix}$$

$$= \begin{vmatrix} x\cdot x + y\cdot y + z\cdot z & x\cdot y + y\cdot z + z\cdot x & x\cdot z + y\cdot x + z\cdot y \\ x\cdot y + z\cdot y + x\cdot z & y\cdot y + z\cdot z + x\cdot x & y\cdot z + z\cdot x + x\cdot y \\ z\cdot x + x\cdot y + y\cdot z & z\cdot y + x\cdot z + y\cdot x & z\cdot z + x\cdot x + y\cdot y \end{vmatrix}$$

$$= \begin{vmatrix} x^2+y^2+z^2 & xy+yz+zx & xy+yz+zx \\ xy+yz+zx & x^2+y^2+z^2 & xy+yz+zx \\ xy+yz+zx & xy+yz+zx & x^2+y^2+z^2 \end{vmatrix}$$

$$= \begin{vmatrix} r^2 & u^2 & u^2 \\ u^2 & r^2 & u^2 \\ u^2 & u^2 & r^2 \end{vmatrix}$$

(*Proved*)

Problem 37 If $u = ax + by + cz, \quad v = ay + bz + cx$
and $w = az + bx + cy,$ prove that

$$\begin{vmatrix} a & b & c \\ b & c & a \\ c & a & b \end{vmatrix} \times \begin{vmatrix} x & y & z \\ y & z & x \\ z & x & y \end{vmatrix} = u^3 + v^3 + w^3 - 3uvw$$

Proof. $\text{LHS} = \begin{vmatrix} a & b & c \\ b & c & a \\ c & a & b \end{vmatrix} \times \begin{vmatrix} x & y & z \\ y & z & x \\ z & x & y \end{vmatrix}$

$$= \begin{vmatrix} a\cdot x + b\cdot y + c\cdot z & a\cdot y + b\cdot z + c\cdot x & az + bx + cy \\ bx + cy + az & by + cz + ax & bz + cx + ay \\ cx + ay + bz & cy + az + bx & cz + ax + by \end{vmatrix}$$

$$= \begin{vmatrix} ax + by + cz & ay + bz + cx & az + bx + cy \\ bx + cy + az & by + cz + ax & bz + cx + ay \\ cx + ay + bz & cy + az + bx & cz + ax + by \end{vmatrix}$$

$$= \begin{vmatrix} u & v & w \\ w & u & v \\ v & w & u \end{vmatrix}$$

Now expanding the determinant by rows we have

$$u \begin{vmatrix} u & v \\ w & u \end{vmatrix} - v \begin{vmatrix} w & v \\ v & u \end{vmatrix} + w \begin{vmatrix} w & u \\ v & w \end{vmatrix}$$

$= u\,(u^2 - vw) - v\,(uw - v^2) + w\,(w^2 - uv),$

$= u^3 - uvw - uvw + v^3 + w^3 - uvw$

$= u^3 + v^3 + w^3 - 3uvw$ R. H. S. *(Proved)*

Problem 38 Prove that

$$\begin{vmatrix} 3 & a + b + c & a^2 + b^4 + c^2 \\ u + b + c & a^2 + b^2 + c^2 & a^3 + b^3 + c^3 \\ a^2 + b^2 + c^2 & a^3 + b^3 + c^3 & a^4 + b^4 + c^4 \end{vmatrix} = \begin{vmatrix} 1 & 1 & 1 \\ a & b & c \\ a^2 & h^2 & c^2 \end{vmatrix}$$

Solution R.H.S. $= \begin{vmatrix} 1 & 1 & 1 \\ a & b & c \\ a^2 & b^2 & c^2 \end{vmatrix}^2$

$$= \begin{vmatrix} 1 & 1 & 1 \\ a & b & c \\ a^2 & b^2 & c^2 \end{vmatrix} \times \begin{vmatrix} 1 & 1 & 1 \\ a & b & c \\ a^2 & b^2 & b^2 \end{vmatrix}$$

$$= \begin{vmatrix} 1\cdot1+1\cdot1+1\cdot1 & 1\cdot a+1\cdot b+1\cdot c & 1\cdot a+1\cdot b+c^2 \\ a\cdot1+b\cdot1+c\cdot1 & a\cdot a+b\cdot b+c\cdot c & a\cdot a^2+b\cdot b^2+c\cdot c^2 \\ a^2\times1+b^2\times1+c^2\times1 & a^2\times a+b^2\times b+c^2\cdot c & a^2\times a^2+b^2b^2+c^2\times c^2 \end{vmatrix}$$

$$= \begin{vmatrix} 3 & a+b+c & a^2+b^2+c^2 \\ a+b+c & a^2+b^2+c^2 & a^3+b^3+c^3 \\ a^2+b^2+c^2 & a^3+b^3+c^3 & a^4+b^4+c^4 \end{vmatrix} \text{ L.H.S. (Proved)}$$

Problem 39 Express

$$\begin{vmatrix} (1+ax)^2 & (1+ay)^2 & (1+az) \\ (1+bx)^2 & (1+by)^2 & (1+cz)^2 \\ (1+cx)^2 & (1+cy)^2 & (1+ay)^2 \end{vmatrix}$$

as a product of the two determinants.

Proof. We have the determinant

$$\Delta = \begin{vmatrix} (1+ax)^2 & (1+ay)^2 & (1+az)^2 \\ (1+bx)^2 & (1+by)^2 & (1+bz)^2 \\ (1+cx)^2 & (1+cy)^2 & (1+cz)^2 \end{vmatrix}$$

$$= \begin{vmatrix} 1+2a\cdot x+a^2\cdot x^2 & 1+2a\cdot y+a^2\cdot y^2 & 1+2a\cdot z+a^2\cdot z^2 \\ 1+2bx+b^2\cdot x^2 & 1+2b\cdot y+b^2 y^2 & 1+2b\cdot z+b^2 z^2 \\ 1+2cx+c^2 x^2 & 1+2c\cdot y+c^2 y^2 & 1+2c\cdot z+c^2 z^2 \end{vmatrix}$$

$$= \begin{vmatrix} 1 & 2a & a^2 \\ 1 & 2b & b^2 \\ 1 & 2c & c^2 \end{vmatrix} \times \begin{vmatrix} 1 & x & x^2 \\ 1 & y & y^2 \\ 1 & z & z^2 \end{vmatrix} \text{ by raw multiplication} \quad \textbf{Ans.}$$

Problem 40 Express

$$\begin{vmatrix} (a-x)^2 & (b-x)^2 & (c-x)^2 \\ (a-y)^2 & (b-y)^2 & (c-y)^2 \\ (a-z)^2 & (b-z)^2 & (c-z)^2 \end{vmatrix}$$

as product of two determinants and find its value.

Solution The given determinant is

$$\Delta = \begin{vmatrix} (a-x)^2 & (b-x)^2 & (c-x)^2 \\ (a-y)^2 & (b-y)^2 & (c-y)^2 \\ (a-z)^2 & (b-z)^2 & (c-z)^2 \end{vmatrix}$$

$$\Delta = \begin{vmatrix} 1\cdot a^2-2ax+x^2 & 1\cdot b^2-2b\cdot x+x^2 & 1\cdot c^2-2cx+x^2 \\ 1\cdot a^2-2ay+y^2 & 1\cdot b^2-2by+y^2 & 1\cdot c^2-2cy+y^2 \\ 1\cdot a^2-2az+z^2 & 1\cdot b^2-2b\cdot z+z^2 & 1\cdot c^2-2cz+z^2 \end{vmatrix}$$

$$= \begin{vmatrix} 1 & x & x^2 \\ 1 & y & y^2 \\ 1 & z & z^2 \end{vmatrix} \times \begin{vmatrix} a^2 & -2a & 1 \\ b^2 & -2b & 1 \\ c^2 & -2c & 1 \end{vmatrix}$$

Thus the given determinant is expressed as the product of two determi nants say Δ_1 and Δ_2

Where $$\Delta_1 = \begin{vmatrix} x & x & x^2 \\ 1 & y & y^2 \\ 1 & z & z^2 \end{vmatrix}$$

$$\Delta_2 = \begin{vmatrix} a^2 & -2a & 1 \\ b^2 & -2b & 1 \\ c^2 & -2c & 1 \end{vmatrix}$$

Now we have to find the value of the determinants. For this we will find value of Δ_1 and Δ_2

$$\Delta_1 = \begin{vmatrix} 1 & x & x^2 \\ 1 & y & y^2 \\ 1 & z & z^2 \end{vmatrix}$$

Operating R_1-R_2 and R_2-R_3 we have

$$\Delta_1 = \begin{vmatrix} 0 & x-y & x^2-y^2 \\ 0 & y-z & y^2-z^2 \\ 1 & z & z^2 \end{vmatrix}$$

$$\Delta_1 = (x-y)\,(y-z) \begin{vmatrix} 0 & 1 & x+y \\ 0 & 1 & y+z \\ 1 & z & z^2 \end{vmatrix}$$

$$\Delta_1 = (x-y)\,(y-z)1 \begin{vmatrix} 1 & x+y \\ 1 & y+z \end{vmatrix}$$

$$\Delta_1 = (x-y)(y-z)(y+z-x-y)$$

$$\Delta_1 = (x-y)(y-z)(z-x) \qquad (1)$$

and $$\Delta_2 = \begin{vmatrix} a^2 & -2a & 1 \\ b^2 & -2b & 1 \\ c^2 & -2c & 1 \end{vmatrix}$$

$$\Delta_2 = -2\begin{vmatrix} a^2 & a & 1 \\ b^2 & b & 1 \\ c^2 & c & 1 \end{vmatrix} = -2(-1)\begin{vmatrix} a & a^2 & 1 \\ b & b^2 & 1 \\ c & c^2 & 1 \end{vmatrix}$$

$$= 2(-1)\begin{vmatrix} a & 1 & a^2 \\ b & 1 & b^2 \\ c & 1 & c^2 \end{vmatrix} = -2(-1)\begin{vmatrix} 1 & a & a^2 \\ 1 & b & b^2 \\ 1 & c & c^2 \end{vmatrix}$$

$$= 2\begin{vmatrix} 1 & a & a^2 \\ 1 & b & b^2 \\ 1 & c & c^2 \end{vmatrix}$$

Now operating $R_1 - R_2$ and $R_2 - R_3$ we have

$$\Delta_2 = 2\begin{vmatrix} 0 & a-b & a^2-b^2 \\ 0 & b-c & b^2-c^2 \\ 1 & c & c^2 \end{vmatrix}$$

$$\Delta_2 = 2\begin{vmatrix} 0 & a-b & (a+b)(a-b) \\ 0 & b-c & (b+c)(b-c) \\ 1 & c & c^2 \end{vmatrix}$$

$$\Delta_2 = 2(a-b)(b-c)\begin{vmatrix} 0 & 1 & a+b \\ 0 & 1 & b+c \\ 1 & c & c^2 \end{vmatrix}$$

$$\Delta_2 = 2(a-b)(b-c)\begin{vmatrix} 1 & a+b \\ 1 & b+c \end{vmatrix}$$

$$= 2(a-b)(b-c)(b+c-a-b)$$

$$= 2(a-b)(b-c)(c-a) \qquad (2)$$

Since $\Delta = \Delta_1 \Delta_2$

So $\Delta = 2(x-y)(y-z)(z-x)(a-b)(c-c)(c-a)$ **Ans.**

Matrices; Algebra of matrices, adjoint of a matrix, inversion of matrices, rank of a matrix, Application of matrices to the solution of linear equations (*in three unknown*)

Adjoint of matrix:

Problem 1 Find the adjoint of the matrix

$$\begin{bmatrix} 1 & -2 & 3 \\ 0 & 2 & -1 \\ -4 & 5 & 2 \end{bmatrix}$$

Solution Let $A = \begin{bmatrix} 1 & -2 & 3 \\ 0 & 2 & -1 \\ -4 & 5 & 2 \end{bmatrix}$

∴ The co-factors of the elements of the first row of $|A|$

$$= \begin{vmatrix} 2 & -1 \\ 1 & 2 \end{vmatrix}, -\begin{vmatrix} 0 & -1 \\ -4 & 2 \end{vmatrix}, \begin{vmatrix} 0 & 2 \\ -4 & 5 \end{vmatrix}$$

$= 4 + 5, -(0-4)\ (0 + 8)$

i.e. 9, 4, 8

The co-factor of the elements of the second row of $|A|$

$$= -\begin{vmatrix} -2 & 3 \\ 5 & 2 \end{vmatrix}, \begin{vmatrix} 1 & 3 \\ -4 & 2 \end{vmatrix}, -\begin{vmatrix} 1 & -2 \\ -4 & 5 \end{vmatrix} = 19, 14, 3$$

The co-factors of the elements of the third row of $|A|$

$$\begin{vmatrix} -2 & 3 \\ 2 & 1 \end{vmatrix}, -\begin{vmatrix} 1 & 3 \\ 0 & -1 \end{vmatrix}, \begin{vmatrix} 1 & -2 \\ 0 & 2 \end{vmatrix}$$

i.e. $\quad -4, 1, 2$

The matrix B whose elements are the co-factors of the corresponding elements of $|A|$ is

$$B = \begin{bmatrix} 9 & 4 & 8 \\ 19 & 14 & 3 \\ -4 & 1 & 2 \end{bmatrix}$$

Hence adjoint of

$$A = B^1 = \begin{bmatrix} 9 & 19 & -4 \\ 4 & 14 & 1 \\ 8 & 3 & 2 \end{bmatrix}$$

Problem 2 If
$$A = \begin{bmatrix} 1 & 0 & -4 \\ 0 & -1 & 2 \\ -1 & 2 & 1 \end{bmatrix}$$

and
$$B = \begin{bmatrix} 0 & 0 & 1 \\ 0 & 1 & 0 \\ 1 & 0 & 0 \end{bmatrix}$$

then find X such that $AX = B$

Solution $A = \begin{bmatrix} 1 & 0 & -4 \\ 0 & -1 & 2 \\ -1 & 2 & 1 \end{bmatrix}$

$$|A| = \begin{vmatrix} 1 & 0 & -4 \\ 0 & -1 & 2 \\ -1 & 2 & 1 \end{vmatrix}$$

$|A| = 1\,(-1-4)-4\,(0-1)$

$|A| = -5 + 4 = -1$

The cofactors of the elements 1, 0, -4

are $\begin{vmatrix} -1 & 2 \\ 2 & 1 \end{vmatrix}, -\begin{vmatrix} 0 & 2 \\ -1 & 1 \end{vmatrix} \quad \begin{vmatrix} 0 & -1 \\ -1 & 2 \end{vmatrix}$

i.e. $\quad -1-4, \quad -(0+2) \quad (0-1)$

i.e. $\quad -5 \quad -2 \quad -1$

The cofactors of the elements 0. -1, 2

are $-\begin{vmatrix} 0 & -4 \\ 2 & 1 \end{vmatrix}, \begin{vmatrix} 1 & -4 \\ -1 & 1 \end{vmatrix} - \begin{vmatrix} 1 & 0 \\ -1 & 2 \end{vmatrix}$

i.e. $\quad -8, \quad -3, \quad -2$

The cofactors of the elements -1, 2, 1 are

$\begin{vmatrix} 0 & -4 \\ -1 & 2 \end{vmatrix}, \begin{vmatrix} 1 & -4 \\ 0 & 2 \end{vmatrix}, \begin{vmatrix} 1 & 0 \\ 0 & -1 \end{vmatrix}$

i.e. $\quad -4, \quad -2 \quad -1$

Le. $C = \begin{bmatrix} -5 & -2 & -1 \\ -8 & -3 & -2 \\ -4 & -2 & -1 \end{bmatrix}$

$\therefore \quad C^1 = $ Adjoint of A

$$\text{Adjoint of } A = C^1 = \begin{bmatrix} -5 & -8 & -4 \\ -2 & -3 & -2 \\ -1 & -2 & -1 \end{bmatrix}$$

$$\therefore \quad A^{-1} = \frac{\text{Adjoint } A}{|A|}$$

$$A^{-1} = \frac{1}{-1}\begin{bmatrix} -5 & -8 & -4 \\ -2 & -3 & -2 \\ -1 & -2 & -1 \end{bmatrix}$$

$$A^{-1} = \begin{bmatrix} 5 & 8 & 4 \\ 2 & 3 & 2 \\ 1 & 2 & 1 \end{bmatrix}$$

$$\because \quad AX = B$$

Operating both sides with A^{-1} we have

$$A^{-1}(AX) = A^{-1}B$$

$$\Rightarrow \quad (A^{-1}A)X = A^{-1}B$$

$$\Rightarrow \quad IX = A^{-1}B$$

$$\Rightarrow \quad X = A^{-1}B$$

i.e.
$$X = \begin{bmatrix} 5 & 8 & 4 \\ 2 & 3 & 2 \\ 1 & 2 & 1 \end{bmatrix} \times \begin{bmatrix} 0 & 0 & 1 \\ 0 & 1 & 0 \\ 1 & 0 & 0 \end{bmatrix}$$

$$X = \begin{bmatrix} 4 & 8 & 5 \\ 2 & 3 & 2 \\ 1 & 2 & 1 \end{bmatrix}$$

Inverse of a Matrix If the matrices A and B are so related that

$$AB = BA = I$$

then B is called the inverse of A and is written as A^{-1}

Adjoint Matrix The transposed matrix

$$\begin{bmatrix} A_1 & A_2 & A_3 \\ B_1 & B_2 & B_3 \\ C_1 & C_2 & C_3 \end{bmatrix} \text{ of the matrix } \begin{bmatrix} A_1 & B_1 & C_1 \\ A_2 & B_2 & C_2 \\ A_3 & B_3 & C_3 \end{bmatrix}$$

where $A_1, B_1, C_1 \ldots$ are the cofactors of the elements $a_1, b_1, c_1, \ldots$ of the determinant

$$\begin{bmatrix} a_1 & b_1 & c_1 \\ a_2 & b_2 & c_2 \\ a_3 & b_3 & c_3 \end{bmatrix}$$

is called the adjoint matrix of the square matrix

$$\begin{bmatrix} a_1 & b_1 & c_1 \\ a_2 & b_2 & c_2 \\ a_3 & b_3 & c_3 \end{bmatrix}$$

Theorem If A and B be two n rowed square matrices, then prove that

$$adj\,(AB) = adj\,B\;adj\,A$$

Proof We know that

$$(AB)\,\{adj\,(AB)\} = |AB|\,I = \{adj\,(AB)\}\,AB$$

Now $AB\,(adj\,B)\,(adj\,A)$

$$= A\,(B\;adj\,B)\,(adj\,A) = A\,(|B|\,I)\,(adj\,A)$$

$$= |B|\,AI\,(adj\,A) = |B|\,A\,(adj\,A)$$

$$= |B|\;|A|\,I = |A|\;|B|\,I = |AB|\,I$$

$$= AB\,\{adj\,(AB)\} \qquad (1)$$

Again $\{(adj\,B)\,(adj\,A)\}\,AB$

$$= (adj\,B)\,\{(adj\,A)\,A\}\,B = (adj\,B)\,(|A|\,I)\,B$$

$$= \{(adj\,B)\,B\}\,|A|\,I = |B|\,I\;|A|\,I$$

$$= |B|\;|A|\,I = |AB|\,I$$

$$= \{adj\,(AB)\}\,AB \qquad (2)$$

Relation (1) and (2) shows that $adj\,(AB) = adj\,(B)\,adj\,(A)$ *(Proved)*

Theorem 2 Prove that the necessary and sufficient condition for the existence of the inverse of a square matrix is that it must be non-singular.

Proof (1) The condition is necessary

Let A be an $n \times n$ matrix and B be its inverse

Then by the definition of inverse

$$AB = BA = I$$

$\therefore$ $|AB| = |I|$

Hence $|A|\;|B| = 1$

Hence $|A| \neq 0$

i.e. the matrix A must be non-singular

(ii) The condition is sufficient i.e. $|A| \neq 0$

Let A be a non singular $n \times n$ matrix

Let the matrix $$B = \frac{adj\ A}{|A|}$$

Then $$AB = A \cdot \frac{adj\ A}{|A|}$$

$$= \frac{A\,(adj\ A)}{|A|} = \frac{|A|\ I}{|A|} = I$$

$$AB = I$$

again $$BA = \frac{adj\ A}{|A|} = \frac{(adj\ A)\ A}{|A|}$$

$$= \frac{|A|\ I}{|A|}$$

i.e. $$BA = I$$

Thus we see that $AB = BA = I$

Hence $$B = \frac{adj\ A}{|A|}$$

is the inverse of A and it exists *(Proved)*

Theorem 3 Prove that the inverse of a non-singular matrix is unique

Proof Let A be a non-singular $n \times n$ matrix. If possible, let B and C be two inverses of A

Then $$AB = BA = I$$
$$AC = CA = I$$

Now we have by associative property of the matrix product

$$C\,(AB) = (CA)\,B$$

R.H.S. $(CA)\,B = IB = B$ (1)

Again L.HS. $= C\,(AB) = C\,(I) = C$ (2)

From (1) and (2) we have

$$C\,(AB) = (CA)\,B$$

$\Rightarrow$ $$B = C$$

Thus the inverse is unique

Theorem 4 If A and B be two non-singular matrices of the same order then prove that $(AB)^{-1} = B^{-1} A^{-1}$

i.e. the inverse of the product of two non-singular matrices is equal to the product of their inverses in reverse order.

Proof Let A and B be two n-square non-singular matricesthen

$$|AB| = |A|\,|B|$$

Since $|AB| \neq 0, |B| \neq 0 \quad \Rightarrow \quad |AB| \neq 0$

Hence the non-singular matrix AB must possess an inverse

Now $(AB)(B^{-1}A^{-1}) = A(BB^{-1})A^{-1}$

$$= AIA^{-1} = AA^{-1}$$

$$(AB)(B^{-1}A^{-1} = I \qquad (1)$$

Again $(B^{-1}A^{-1})(AB) = B^{-1}(A^{-1}A)B$

$$= B^{-1}IB = B^{-1}B = I \qquad (2)$$

From relation (1) and (2) we see that

$$(AB)(B^{-1}A^{-1}) = (B^{-1}A^{-1})(AB) = I$$

Thus $B^{-1}A^{-1}$ is the inverse of AB

i.e. $(AB)^{-1} = B^{-1}A^{-1}$ ***(Proved)***

Problem 3 Find the adjoint and inverse of the matrix

$$A = \begin{bmatrix} 1 & 2 & 3 \\ 3 & 4 & 5 \\ 6 & 7 & 9 \end{bmatrix}$$

Solution Let $A = \begin{bmatrix} 1 & 2 & 3 \\ 3 & 4 & 5 \\ 6 & 7 & 9 \end{bmatrix}$

$$|A| = \begin{bmatrix} 1 & 2 & 3 \\ 3 & 4 & 5 \\ 6 & 7 & 9 \end{bmatrix}$$

$$= 1\begin{vmatrix} 4 & 5 \\ 7 & 9 \end{vmatrix} - 2\begin{vmatrix} 3 & 5 \\ 6 & 9 \end{vmatrix} + 3\cdot\begin{vmatrix} 3 & 4 \\ 6 & 7 \end{vmatrix}$$

$$= (36-35) - 2(27-30) + 3(21-24)$$

$$= 1 - 2 \times (-3) + 3 \times (-3) = 1 + 6 - 9 = -2$$

$$|A| = -2$$

Now the cofactors of the elements of the first row i.e. of 1, 2 and 3 are

$$\begin{vmatrix} 4 & 5 \\ 7 & 9 \end{vmatrix}, \; -\begin{vmatrix} 3 & 5 \\ 6 & 9 \end{vmatrix}, \; \begin{vmatrix} 3 & 4 \\ 6 & 7 \end{vmatrix}$$

i.e, $(36-35) \quad -(27-30) \quad (21-24)$

i.e. $1 \quad 3 \quad -3$

The cofactors of the elements of the 2nd row i.e. of 3, 4, 5 are

$$-\begin{vmatrix} 2 & 3 \\ 7 & 9 \end{vmatrix}, \begin{vmatrix} 1 & 3 \\ 6 & 9 \end{vmatrix}, -\begin{vmatrix} 1 & 2 \\ 6 & 7 \end{vmatrix}$$

i.e. $\quad -(18-21), \quad (9-18) \quad -(7-12)$

i.e. $\quad 3 \quad -9 \quad 5$

The cofactors of the elements of the third row i.e. of 6, 7, 9 are

$$\begin{vmatrix} 2 & 3 \\ 4 & 5 \end{vmatrix}, -\begin{vmatrix} 1 & 3 \\ 3 & 5 \end{vmatrix}, \begin{vmatrix} 1 & 2 \\ 3 & 4 \end{vmatrix}$$

$$= (10-12), \quad -(5-9), \quad (4-6)$$

i.e. $\quad -2 \quad 4 \quad -2$

Let
$$B = \begin{bmatrix} 1 & 3 & -3 \\ 3 & -9 & 5 \\ -2 & 4 & -2 \end{bmatrix}$$

Hence Adjoint $A = B^1 = \begin{bmatrix} 1 & 3 & -2 \\ 3 & -9 & 4 \\ -3 & 5 & -2 \end{bmatrix}$

Hence, the inverse of $A = \dfrac{adj\ A}{|A|}$

$$A^{-1} = \begin{bmatrix} -\frac{1}{2} & -\frac{3}{2} & 1 \\ -\frac{3}{2} & +\frac{9}{2} & -2 \\ \frac{3}{2} & -\frac{5}{2} & 1 \end{bmatrix} \textbf{ Ans.}$$

Problem 4 If $A = \begin{bmatrix} 1 & -2 & 3 \\ -4 & 2 & 5 \end{bmatrix}$

and
$$B = \begin{bmatrix} 1 & 3 \\ -1 & 0 \\ 2 & 4 \end{bmatrix}$$

Prove that $(AB)^1 = B^1 A^1$

Where A^1, B^1 denote the transpose of the matrices A and B.

Solution The number of columns in $A = 3$

The number of rows in $B = 3$

$\therefore$ A and B are conformed for the product AB

$$AB = \begin{bmatrix} 1 & -2 & 3 \\ -4 & 2 & 5 \end{bmatrix} \times \begin{bmatrix} 1 & 3 \\ -1 & 0 \\ 2 & 4 \end{bmatrix}$$

$$= \begin{bmatrix} 1+2+6 & 3+0+12 \\ -4-2+10 & -12+0+20 \end{bmatrix} = \begin{bmatrix} 9 & 15 \\ 4 & 8 \end{bmatrix}$$

$$\Rightarrow (AB)^1 = \begin{bmatrix} 9 & 4 \\ 15 & 8 \end{bmatrix} \quad (1)$$

$$B^1 = \begin{bmatrix} 1 & -1 & 2 \\ 3 & 0 & 4 \end{bmatrix}$$

$$A^1 = \begin{bmatrix} 1 & -4 \\ -2 & 2 \\ 2 & 5 \end{bmatrix}$$

$$\text{Now } B^1 A^1 = \begin{bmatrix} 1 & -1 & 2 \\ 3 & 0 & 4 \end{bmatrix} \begin{bmatrix} 1 & -4 \\ -2 & 2 \\ 3 & 5 \end{bmatrix}$$

Since the no of columns in $B^1 = 3$ the no of rows in $A^1 = 3$

Thus B^1 and A^1 are conformable for the product B^1A^1

$$B^1 A^1 = \begin{bmatrix} 1\cdot 1+2+6 & -4-2+10 \\ 3+0+12 & -12+0+20 \end{bmatrix} = \begin{bmatrix} 9 & 4 \\ 15 & 8 \end{bmatrix} \quad (2)$$

From equation (1) and (2) it is clear that $(AB)^1 = B^1A^1$ *(Proved)*

Rank of a Matrix

A matrix is said to be of rank r when it contains at least one non-zero determinant of order r and no such determinant of order $r + 1$. The rank of a non-singular matrix A of order n is n, as its one minor of order n, that is $|A|$ does not vanish.

Problem 1 Find the rank of the matrix

$$\begin{bmatrix} 1 & 2 & 3 \\ 4 & 5 & 6 \\ 2 & 1 & 2 \end{bmatrix}$$

Solution Since the given matrix is of order 3×3, therefore there can be only one minor of almost order 3×3, of the given matrix, that

$$\begin{vmatrix} 1 & 2 & 3 \\ 4 & 5 & 6 \\ 2 & 1 & 2 \end{vmatrix} = 1\begin{vmatrix} 5 & 6 \\ 1 & 2 \end{vmatrix} - 2\begin{vmatrix} 4 & 6 \\ 2 & 2 \end{vmatrix} + 3\begin{vmatrix} 4 & 5 \\ 2 & 1 \end{vmatrix}$$

$$= 1\,(10-6)-2\,(8-12)+3\,(4-10)$$

$$= 4+8-18 = 12-18 = -6 \neq 0$$

Hence the rank of the given matrix is 3.

Problem 2 Find the rank of the matrix

$$\begin{bmatrix} 1 & 2 & 3 \\ 2 & 4 & 7 \\ 3 & 6 & 10 \end{bmatrix}$$

Let $\quad A = \begin{bmatrix} 1 & 2 & 3 \\ 2 & 4 & 7 \\ 3 & 6 & 10 \end{bmatrix}$ of order 3×3

There can be only one minor of A at almost order 3×3, i.e.

$$\begin{vmatrix} 1 & 2 & 3 \\ 2 & 4 & 7 \\ 3 & 6 & 10 \end{vmatrix} = 1\cdot\begin{vmatrix} 4 & 7 \\ 6 & 10 \end{vmatrix} - 2\begin{vmatrix} 2 & 7 \\ 3 & 10 \end{vmatrix} + 3\begin{vmatrix} 2 & 4 \\ 3 & 2 \end{vmatrix}$$

$$= 1\,(40-42)-2(20-21)+4\,(12-12)$$

$$= -2+2 = 0$$

This shows that $p\,(A) < 3$

Now let us consider any one such minor of A of order 2×2 i.e.

$$\begin{vmatrix} 2 & 3 \\ 4 & 7 \end{vmatrix} = 14-12 = 2 \neq 0$$

Hence $p\,(A) = 2$ **Ans.**

Problem 3 Find the rank of the matrix

$$A = \begin{bmatrix} 1 & 1 & 1 \\ a & b & c \\ a^2 & b^2 & c^2 \end{bmatrix}, \ a, b, c \text{ being real}$$

Solution $A = \begin{bmatrix} 1 & 1 & 1 \\ a & b & c \\ a^2 & b^2 & c^2 \end{bmatrix}$

Let us at first find the determinant

$$\Delta = \begin{vmatrix} 1 & 1 & 1 \\ a & b & c \\ a^2 & b^2 & c^2 \end{vmatrix}$$

Operating $c_1 - c_2$ and $c_2 - c_3$ we have

$$\Delta = \begin{vmatrix} 0 & 0 & 1 \\ a-b & b-c & c \\ a^2-b^2 & b^2-c^2 & c^2 \end{vmatrix}$$

$$\Delta = (a-b)(b-c) \begin{vmatrix} 0 & 0 & 1 \\ 1 & 1 & c \\ a+b & b+c & c^2 \end{vmatrix}$$

$$\Delta = (a-b)(b-c) \begin{vmatrix} 1 & 1 \\ a+b & b+c \end{vmatrix} \begin{matrix} = (a-b)(b-c)(b+c-a-b) \\ = (a-b)(b-c)(c-a) \end{matrix}$$

Since the given matrix is of crder 3×3, therefore there can be only one minor of order 3×3 of i.e.

$$\begin{vmatrix} 1 & 1 & 1 \\ a & b & c \\ a^2 & b^2 & c^2 \end{vmatrix} = (a-b)(b-c)(c-a)$$

Now three cases may arise.

Cases Let $a \neq b \neq c$

Then $|A| \neq 0$

i.e. $\begin{vmatrix} 1 & 1 & 1 \\ a & b & c \\ a^2 & b^2 & c^2 \end{vmatrix} \neq 0$

Hence $p(A) = 3$

Case II Let $a = b \neq c$

Then in this case

$$|A| = \begin{vmatrix} 1 & 1 & 1 \\ a & b & c \\ a^2 & b^2 & c^2 \end{vmatrix} = 0 \quad \text{as } a-b=0$$

So $p(A) < 3$

Now let us consider any minor of order 2×2 of A which does not vanish and u

$$\begin{vmatrix} 1 & 1 \\ b & c \end{vmatrix} \text{ which does not vanish.}$$

Since
$$\begin{vmatrix} 1 & 1 \\ b & c \end{vmatrix} = c - b \neq 0 \text{ as } b \neq c$$

Hence $f(A) = 2$ **Ans.**

Case III Let $a = b = c$ then in this case

$$|A| = \begin{vmatrix} 1 & 1 & 1 \\ a & b & c \\ a^2 & b^2 & c^2 \end{vmatrix} = (a-b)(b-c)(c-a) = 0 \text{ as } a = b = c$$

Hence $P(A) < 3$

Now consider the minor of order 2×2 which does not vanish. The minors of A are

$$\begin{vmatrix} 1 & 1 \\ a & b \end{vmatrix}, \begin{vmatrix} 1 & 1 \\ b & c \end{vmatrix}, \begin{vmatrix} 1 & 1 \\ a & c \end{vmatrix} \begin{vmatrix} a & b \\ a^2 & b^2 \end{vmatrix}$$

$$\begin{vmatrix} b & c \\ b^2 & c^2 \end{vmatrix}, \begin{vmatrix} a & c \\ a^2 & c^2 \end{vmatrix}, \begin{vmatrix} 1 & 1 \\ a^2 & b^2 \end{vmatrix}, \begin{vmatrix} 1 & 1 \\ b^2 & c^2 \end{vmatrix}$$

$$\begin{vmatrix} 1 & 1 \\ a^2 & c^2 \end{vmatrix} \text{ all of which vanish}$$

$\therefore \quad f(A) < 2$

Let us consider any one minor say $|1|$ of order $|x|$ of A. Evidently $|1| \neq 0$.

Hence $f(A) = 1$ **Ans.**

Problem 4 Prove that the three points (x_1, y_1) (x_2, y_2) and (x_3, y_3) are collinear if the rank of the matrix

$$\begin{bmatrix} x_1 & y_1 & 1 \\ x_2 & y_2 & 1 \\ x_3 & y_3 & 1 \end{bmatrix} \text{ is less than 3.}$$

Solution Since the three points (x_1, y_1); (x_2, y_2) and (x_3, y_3) are collinear. So they lie on a straight line

$$ax + by + c = 0 \text{ say} \tag{1}$$

The points (x_1, y_1); (x_2, y_2); (x_3, y_3) lie one so they will satisfy (1)

Hence
$$ax_1 + by_1 + c = 0 \quad (2)$$
$$ax_2 + by_2 + c = 0 \quad (3)$$
$$ax_3 + by_3 + c = 0 \quad (4)$$

Now eliminating a, b and c from (2), (3) and (4) we have

$$\begin{vmatrix} x_1 & y_1 & 1 \\ x_2 & y_2 & 1 \\ x_3 & y_3 & 1 \end{vmatrix} = 0$$

Now let us consider the matrix

$$A = \begin{bmatrix} x_1 & y_1 & 1 \\ x_2 & y_2 & 1 \\ x_3 & y_3 & 1 \end{bmatrix}$$

Since if has a minor of order 3×3 which vanishes i.e.

$$\begin{vmatrix} x_1 & y_1 & 1 \\ x_2 & y_2 & 1 \\ x_3 & y_3 & 1 \end{vmatrix} = 0$$

Hence $\quad P(A) < 3$ *(Proved)*

Preblem 5 Find the rank of the matrix

$$\begin{bmatrix} 1 & 2 & 3 & 4 \\ 2 & 4 & 6 & 8 \\ -1 & -2 & -2 & -4 \end{bmatrix}$$

Solution Let us suppose that

$$A = \begin{bmatrix} 1 & 2 & 3 & 4 \\ 2 & 4 & 6 & 8 \\ -1 & -2 & -2 & -4 \end{bmatrix}$$

Since this is a matrix of the type 3×4 so there is no any minor of the type 4×4.

Hence $\quad P(A) < 4$.

Now let us consider all the possible minors of order 3×3 and that are

$$\begin{vmatrix} 1 & 2 & 3 \\ 2 & 4 & 6 \\ -1 & -2 & -2 \end{vmatrix}, \begin{vmatrix} 2 & 3 & 4 \\ 4 & 6 & 8 \\ -2 & -2 & -4 \end{vmatrix}, \begin{vmatrix} 1 & 3 & 4 \\ 2 & 6 & 8 \\ -1 & -2 & 4 \end{vmatrix}, \begin{vmatrix} 1 & 2 & 4 \\ 2 & 4 & 8 \\ -1 & -2 & 4 \end{vmatrix}$$

The value of the minors are

$$\begin{vmatrix} 1 & 2 & 3 \\ 2 & 4 & 6 \\ -1 & -2 & -2 \end{vmatrix} = 1(-8+12) - 2(-4+6) + 3(-4+4) \\ = -4 + 4 = 0$$

$$\begin{vmatrix} 2 & 3 & 4 \\ 4 & 6 & 8 \\ -2 & -2 & -4 \end{vmatrix} = 2(-24+16) - 3(-16+16) + 4(-8+12) \\ = -16 + 16 = 0$$

$$\begin{vmatrix} 1 & 3 & 4 \\ 2 & 6 & 8 \\ -1 & -2 & 4 \end{vmatrix} = 1(24+16) - 3(8+8) + 4(-4+6) \\ = 40 - 48 + 8 = 48 - 48 = 0$$

and $$\begin{vmatrix} 1 & 2 & 4 \\ 2 & 4 & 8 \\ -1 & -2 & 4 \end{vmatrix} = 1(16+16) - 2(8+8) + 4(-4+4) \\ = 32 - 32 = 0$$

Thus we see that all the minors of A of order 3×3 vanishes.

So $$P(A) < 3$$

Let the minor of A of order 2×2 is $\begin{vmatrix} 2 & 3 \\ -2 & 2 \end{vmatrix}$

where $$\begin{vmatrix} 2 & 3 \\ -2 & -2 \end{vmatrix} = -4 + 6 = 2 \neq 0$$

Thus $$P(A) = 2$$ **Ans.**

Problem 6 Find the rank of matrix

$$\begin{vmatrix} 0 & 1 & 2 & 3 \\ 0 & 0 & 1 & -1 \\ 0 & 0 & 0 & 0 \end{vmatrix}$$

Solution Let $A = \begin{vmatrix} 0 & 1 & 2 & 3 \\ 0 & 0 & 1 & -1 \\ 0 & 0 & 0 & 0 \end{vmatrix}$

This matrix is of the form 3×4 so there cannot be a minor of order 4×4. Hence

$$P(A) < 4$$

Now consider of the minors of order 3 × 3 of the matrix A.
and they are

$$\begin{vmatrix} 0 & 1 & 2 \\ 0 & 0 & 1 \\ 0 & 0 & 0 \end{vmatrix}, \begin{vmatrix} 0 & 1 & 3 \\ 0 & 0 & -1 \\ 0 & 0 & 0 \end{vmatrix} \text{and} \begin{vmatrix} 0 & 2 & 3 \\ 0 & 1 & -1 \\ 0 & 0 & 0 \end{vmatrix}, \begin{vmatrix} 1 & 2 & 3 \\ 0 & 1 & -1 \\ 0 & 0 & 0 \end{vmatrix}$$

All of which vanish.

Hence $$P(A) < 3$$

Now consider the minor of order 2 × 2 which does not vanish and that is

$$\begin{vmatrix} 2 & 3 \\ 1 & -1 \end{vmatrix} = (-1-3) = -4 \neq 0$$

Hence $$P(A) = 2$$

i.e. the rank of the matrix is (wo). **Ans.**

Problem 7 Find the rank of the matrix A defined by

$$A = \begin{bmatrix} 1 & 3 & 4 & 3 \\ 3 & 9 & 12 & 9 \\ -1 & -3 & -4 & -3 \end{bmatrix}$$

Solution Since the given matrix A is of order 3 × 4, therefore no minor of order 4 × 4 of A can be formed.

Let us consider all the minors of order 3 × 3 of A and that are

$$\begin{vmatrix} 1 & 3 & 4 \\ 3 & 9 & 12 \\ -1 & -3 & -4 \end{vmatrix}, \begin{vmatrix} 1 & 3 & 3 \\ 3 & 9 & 9 \\ -1 & -3 & -3 \end{vmatrix},$$

$$\begin{vmatrix} 1 & 4 & 3 \\ 3 & 12 & 9 \\ -1 & -4 & -3 \end{vmatrix}, \begin{vmatrix} 3 & 4 & 3 \\ 9 & 12 & 9 \\ -3 & -4 & -3 \end{vmatrix}$$

all of which vanish, so

$$P(A) < 3$$

Now consider the minor of order 2 × 2 we see that all the minors of order 2 × 2 vanish i.e. $P(A) < 2$. Now only the minor of order 1 does not vanish.

Hence $P(A) = 1$ **Ans.**

Problem 8 Find the rank of $\begin{bmatrix} 2 & 1 & 4 & 7 \\ 3 & 6 & 2 & 1 \\ 0 & 0 & 1 & 5 \end{bmatrix}$

Solution Let $A = \begin{bmatrix} 2 & 1 & 4 & 7 \\ 3 & 6 & 2 & 1 \\ 0 & 0 & 1 & 5 \end{bmatrix}_{3 \times 4}$

This matrix is of the form 3×4.

Hence we cannot find any non-vanishing minor of order 4×4.

So $$P(A) < 4$$

Now consider the minors of order 3×3

$$\begin{vmatrix} 2 & 1 & 4 \\ 3 & 6 & 2 \\ 0 & 0 & 1 \end{vmatrix} = 2(6-0) - 1(3-0) + 4(0-0) = 12 - 3 = 9 \neq 0$$

Hence $P(A) = 3$ **Ans.**

Solution of linear Equations (three unknowns)

Problem 1 Solve the equations

$$3x + y + 2z = 3$$
$$2x - 3y - z = -3$$
and $$x + 2y + z = 4$$
with the help of matrices

Solution Here $A = \begin{bmatrix} 3 & 1 & 2 \\ 2 & -3 & -1 \\ 1 & 2 & 1 \end{bmatrix}$

$$X = \begin{bmatrix} x \\ y \\ z \end{bmatrix} \quad B = \begin{bmatrix} 3 \\ -3 \\ 4 \end{bmatrix}$$

The given system of equations may be written in a matrix form

$$AX = B \tag{1}$$

Since $|A| \neq 0$, so A^{-1} exists operating both sides of (1) with A^{-1} we have

$$A^{-1}(AX) = A^{-1}B$$
$$\Rightarrow (A^{-1}A)X = A^{-1}B$$
$$\Rightarrow IX = A^{-1}B$$
$$\Rightarrow X = A^{-1}B$$

So we have at first to find the value of A^{-1}

$$A = \begin{bmatrix} 3 & 1 & 2 \\ 2 & -3 & -1 \\ 1 & 2 & 1 \end{bmatrix}$$

$$|A| = \begin{vmatrix} 3 & 1 & 2 \\ 2 & -3 & -1 \\ 1 & 2 & 1 \end{vmatrix}$$

$$= 3 \begin{vmatrix} -3 & -1 \\ 2 & 1 \end{vmatrix} - 1 \begin{vmatrix} 2 & -1 \\ 1 & 1 \end{vmatrix} + 2 \begin{vmatrix} 2 & -3 \\ 1 & 2 \end{vmatrix}$$

$$= 3(-3+2) - 1(2+1) + 2(4+3)$$

$$= 3(-1) - 1(3) + 2(7) = -3 - 3 + 14$$

$$= -6 + 14 = 8$$

Now the co-factors of the elements of the first row i.e. of 3, 1, 2 are

$$\begin{vmatrix} -3 & -1 \\ 2 & 1 \end{vmatrix}, \; - \begin{vmatrix} 2 & -1 \\ 1 & 1 \end{vmatrix}, \; \begin{vmatrix} 2 & -3 \\ 1 & 2 \end{vmatrix}$$

i.e. $\quad -3 + 2, \quad -(2+1), (4+3)$

i.e. $\quad -1 - 3, 7$

The co-factors of the elements of the 2nd row i.e. of 2, -3, -1 are

$$- \begin{vmatrix} 1 & 2 \\ 2 & 1 \end{vmatrix}, \; \begin{vmatrix} 3 & 2 \\ 1 & 1 \end{vmatrix} - \begin{vmatrix} 3 & 1 \\ 1 & 2 \end{vmatrix}$$

i.e. $\quad -(1-4), (3-2), -(6-1)$

i.e. $\quad 3, 1, -5$

and the co-factors of the elements of the 3rd row i.e. of 1, 2, 1 are

$$\begin{vmatrix} 1 & 2 \\ -3 & -1 \end{vmatrix} - \begin{vmatrix} 3 & 2 \\ 2 & -1 \end{vmatrix}, \; \begin{vmatrix} 3 & 1 \\ 2 & -3 \end{vmatrix}$$

i.e. $\quad (-1+6), -(-3-4)\,(-9-2)$

$\quad 5, 7, -11$

$$B = \begin{bmatrix} -1 & -3 & 7 \\ 3 & 1 & -5 \\ 5 & 7 & -11 \end{bmatrix}$$

$$B^1 = \begin{bmatrix} -1 & 3 & 5 \\ -3 & 1 & 7 \\ 7 & -5 & -11 \end{bmatrix}$$

$$A^{-1} = \frac{1}{|A|}\begin{bmatrix} -1 & 3 & 5 \\ -3 & 1 & 7 \\ 7 & -5 & -11 \end{bmatrix}$$

$$A^{-1} = \frac{1}{8}\begin{bmatrix} -1 & 3 & 5 \\ -3 & 1 & 7 \\ 7 & -5 & -11 \end{bmatrix}$$

$$X = A^{-1} B$$

$$X = \frac{1}{8}\begin{bmatrix} -1 & 3 & 5 \\ -3 & 1 & 7 \\ 7 & -5 & -11 \end{bmatrix}\begin{bmatrix} 3 \\ -3 \\ 4 \end{bmatrix}$$

$$X = \frac{1}{8}\begin{bmatrix} -3 & -9 & +20 \\ -9 & -3 & +28 \\ 21 + 15 & & -44 \end{bmatrix} = \frac{1}{8}\begin{bmatrix} 8 \\ 16 \\ -8 \end{bmatrix} = \begin{bmatrix} 1 \\ 2 \\ -1 \end{bmatrix}$$

$$\Rightarrow \quad X = \begin{bmatrix} 1 \\ 2 \\ -1 \end{bmatrix}$$

i.e.

$$\begin{bmatrix} x \\ y \\ z \end{bmatrix} = \begin{bmatrix} 1 \\ 2 \\ -1 \end{bmatrix}$$

$\Rightarrow \quad x = 1 \quad y = 2 \quad z = -1$ **Ans.**

Problem 2 Solve with the help of matrices, the following simultaneous equations

$$x + y + z = 6$$
$$2x + y - 3z = -5$$
$$3x - 2y + z = 2$$

Solution Here $\Delta = \begin{vmatrix} 1 & 1 & 1 \\ 2 & 1 & -3 \\ 3 & -2 & 1 \end{vmatrix}$

$$= 1 \begin{vmatrix} 1 & -3 \\ -2 & 1 \end{vmatrix} - 1 \begin{vmatrix} 2 & -3 \\ 3 & 1 \end{vmatrix} + 1 \begin{vmatrix} 2 & 1 \\ 3 & -2 \end{vmatrix}$$

$$= 1\,(1-6) - 1\,(2+9) + 1\,(-4-3)$$

$$= -5 - 11 - 7 = -23$$

We can write the system of equations in matrix form as

$$Ax = B \text{ where}$$

$$A = \begin{bmatrix} 1 & 1 & 1 \\ 2 & 1 & -3 \\ 3 & -2 & 1 \end{bmatrix}$$

$$X = \begin{bmatrix} x \\ y \\ z \end{bmatrix} \qquad B = \begin{bmatrix} 6 \\ -5 \\ 2 \end{bmatrix}$$

Then the solution is given by

$$X = A^{-1} B$$

Now we have to find the value of A^{-1}.

The co-factors of the elements 1, 1, 1 of the first row is

$$\begin{vmatrix} 1 & -3 \\ -2 & 1 \end{vmatrix} \quad - \begin{vmatrix} 2 & -3 \\ 3 & 1 \end{vmatrix} \quad \begin{vmatrix} 2 & 1 \\ 3 & -2 \end{vmatrix}$$

$$1-6, \; -(2+9), \; (-4-3)$$

i.e $\quad -5, \quad -11 \quad -7$

The co-factors of the elements 2, 1, -3 of the 2nd row are given by

$$-\begin{vmatrix} 1 & 1 \\ -2 & 1 \end{vmatrix} . \begin{vmatrix} 1 & 1 \\ 3 & 1 \end{vmatrix}, \begin{vmatrix} 1 & 1 \\ 3 & -2 \end{vmatrix}$$

$$= -(1+2) \; ; \; (1-3), \quad -(-2-3)$$

$$= -3, \quad -2, \quad 5$$

The cofactors of the elements 3, -2, 1 of the third row are given by

$$\begin{vmatrix} 1 & 1 \\ 1 & -3 \end{vmatrix} - \begin{vmatrix} 1 & 1 \\ 2 & -3 \end{vmatrix}, + \begin{vmatrix} 1 & 1 \\ 2 & 1 \end{vmatrix}$$

$$-3-1, \; -(-3-2), \; (1-2)$$

i.e. $\quad -4, \quad 5 \quad -1$

Le t $C = \begin{bmatrix} -5 & -11 & -7 \\ -3 & -2 & 5 \\ -4 & 5 & -1 \end{bmatrix}$

$$C^1 = \begin{bmatrix} -5 & -3 & -4 \\ -11 & -2 & 5 \\ -7 & 5 & -1 \end{bmatrix}$$

$$A^{-1} = \frac{1}{|A|} \text{ ad joint of } A$$

$$A^{-1} = \frac{c^1}{|A|} = -\frac{1}{23}\begin{bmatrix} -5 & -3 & -4 \\ -11 & -2 & 5 \\ -7 & 5 & -1 \end{bmatrix}$$

Then $X = A^{-1} B$

$$\Rightarrow \quad X = -\frac{1}{23}\begin{bmatrix} -5 & -3 & -4 \\ -11 & -2 & 5 \\ -7 & 5 & -1 \end{bmatrix}\begin{bmatrix} 6 \\ -5 \\ 2 \end{bmatrix}$$

$$\Rightarrow \quad X = -\frac{1}{23}\begin{bmatrix} -30 + 15 - 8 \\ -66 + 10 + 10 \\ -42 - 25 - 2 \end{bmatrix}$$

$$\Rightarrow \quad X = -\frac{1}{23}\begin{bmatrix} -23 \\ -46 \\ -69 \end{bmatrix} \quad \Rightarrow \quad X = \begin{bmatrix} 1 \\ 2 \\ 3 \end{bmatrix}$$

where $X = \begin{bmatrix} x \\ y \\ z \end{bmatrix}$ x, y, z are unknowns

So $\begin{bmatrix} x \\ y \\ z \end{bmatrix} = \begin{bmatrix} 1 \\ 2 \\ 3 \end{bmatrix}$

$\Rightarrow \quad x = 1, y = 2, z = 3$ **Ans.**

Problem 3 In *a* given electrical network the equation for the current i_1, i_2, i_3 are

$$3i_1 + i_2 + i_3 = 8,\ 2i_1 - 3i_2 - 2i_3 = -5,\ 7i_1 + 2i_2 - 5i_3 = 0$$

Solve these equations by matrix method

Solution Let $X = \begin{bmatrix} i_1 \\ i_2 \\ i_3 \end{bmatrix}$

where i_1, i_2 and i_3 are to be determined. The system of equations may be written in the form of a matrix $AX = B$

where $$A = \begin{bmatrix} 3 & 1 & 1 \\ 2 & -3 & -2 \\ 7 & 2 & -5 \end{bmatrix} \quad B = \begin{bmatrix} 8 \\ -5 \\ 0 \end{bmatrix}$$

The determinant of A

$$|A| = \begin{vmatrix} 3 & 1 & 1 \\ 2 & -3 & -2 \\ 7 & 2 & -5 \end{vmatrix}$$

$$|A| = 3\begin{vmatrix} -3 & -2 \\ 2 & -5 \end{vmatrix} - 1\begin{vmatrix} 2 & -2 \\ 7 & -5 \end{vmatrix} + 1\begin{vmatrix} 2 & -3 \\ 7 & 2 \end{vmatrix}$$

$$|A| = 3\,(15 + 4) - 1\,(-10 + 14) + 1\,(4 + 21)$$

$$|A| = 57 - 4 + 25$$

$$|A| = 82 - 4 = 78$$

$$A = \begin{bmatrix} 3 & 1 & 1 \\ 2 & -3 & -2 \\ 7 & 2 & -5 \end{bmatrix}$$

The cofactors of the elements 3, 1, 1 of the first row are given by

$$\begin{vmatrix} -3 & -2 \\ 2 & -5 \end{vmatrix}, -\begin{vmatrix} 2 & -2 \\ 7 & -5 \end{vmatrix}, \begin{vmatrix} 2 & -3 \\ 7 & 2 \end{vmatrix}$$

i.e. $$15 + 4,\ -(-10 + 14),\ 4 + 21$$

$$19, \quad -4, \quad 25,$$

The cofactor of the elements 2, -3, -2 of the 2nd row we have

$$-\begin{vmatrix} 1 & 1 \\ 2 & -5 \end{vmatrix}, \begin{vmatrix} 3 & 1 \\ 7 & -5 \end{vmatrix}, - \Big|, - \begin{vmatrix} 3 & 1 \\ 7 & 2 \end{vmatrix}$$

i.e. $\quad -(-5-2), (-15-7) - (6-7)$

$$7, -22, 1,$$

The cofactors of the elements 7, 2, -5 of the third row, are

$$\begin{vmatrix} 1 & 1 \\ -3 & -2 \end{vmatrix}, - \begin{vmatrix} 3 & 1 \\ 2 & 2 \end{vmatrix}, \begin{vmatrix} 3 & 1 \\ 7 & 2 \end{vmatrix}$$

i.e. $\quad -2+3, -(6-2),(6-7)$

i.e. $\quad 1, -4, -1$

Let $\quad C = \begin{bmatrix} 19 & -4 & 25 \\ 7 & -22 & 1 \\ 1 & -4 & -1 \end{bmatrix}$

$$C^1 = \begin{bmatrix} 19 & 7 & 1 \\ -4 & -22 & -4 \\ 25 & 1 & -1 \end{bmatrix}$$

$$Adj\,(A) = \begin{bmatrix} 19 & 7 & 1 \\ -4 & -22 & -4 \\ 25 & 1 & -1 \end{bmatrix}$$

$$A^{-1} = \frac{adj}{|A|} = \frac{1}{78}\begin{bmatrix} 19 & 7 & 1 \\ -4 & -22 & -4 \\ 25 & 1 & -1 \end{bmatrix}$$

$$X = A^{-1}B$$

$\Rightarrow$ $$X = \frac{1}{78}\begin{bmatrix} 19 & 7 & 1 \\ -4 & -22 & -4 \\ 25 & 1 & -1 \end{bmatrix}\begin{bmatrix} 8 \\ -5 \\ 0 \end{bmatrix}$$

$\Rightarrow$ $$X = \frac{1}{78}\begin{bmatrix} 19.8 + 7 \times -5 + 1\cdot 0 \\ -4 \times 8 + 22 \times 5 + (-4) \times 0 \\ 25 \times 8 - 5 \times 1 - 1 \times 0 \end{bmatrix}$$

$$\Rightarrow \qquad X = \frac{1}{78}\begin{bmatrix} 152 - 35 \\ -32 + 110 \\ 200 - 5 \end{bmatrix} \qquad \Rightarrow \qquad X = \frac{1}{78}\begin{bmatrix} 117 \\ 78 \\ 195 \end{bmatrix}$$

$$\Rightarrow \qquad X = \begin{bmatrix} \frac{3}{2} \\ 1 \\ \frac{5}{2} \end{bmatrix}$$

$$\Rightarrow \qquad \begin{bmatrix} i_1 \\ i_2 \\ i_3 \end{bmatrix} = \begin{bmatrix} \frac{3}{2} \\ 1 \\ \frac{5}{2} \end{bmatrix}$$

$$i_1 = \frac{3}{2}, \quad i_2 = 1, i_3 = \frac{5}{2} \qquad \textbf{Ans.}$$

Problem Solve the following linear equation with the help of matrix method: $x + y + z = 1, x + 2y + z = 2, x + y + 2z = 0$

Solution The system of linear equation may be written in a matrix form

$$AX = B \tag{1}$$

where

$$A = \begin{bmatrix} 1 & 1 & 1 \\ 1 & 2 & 1 \\ 1 & 1 & 2 \end{bmatrix}$$

$$X = \begin{bmatrix} x \\ y \\ z \end{bmatrix} \qquad B = \begin{bmatrix} 1 \\ 2 \\ 0 \end{bmatrix}$$

$$|A| = \begin{vmatrix} 1 & 1 & 1 \\ 1 & 2 & 1 \\ 1 & 1 & 2 \end{vmatrix}$$

$$= 1\ (4-1) - 1\ (2-1) + 1\ (1-2)$$

$$= 3 - 1 - 1 = 3 - 2 = 1$$

Since $|A| = 1 \neq 0$ so A^{-1} exists

So premultiplying equation (1) with A^{-1}, we have

$$A^{-1}(AX) = A^{-1}B$$

$$\Rightarrow \quad (A^{-1}A)X = A^{-1}B$$

$$\Rightarrow \quad IX = A^{-1}B$$

$$\Rightarrow \quad X = A^{-1}B$$

Let us find A^{-1}

The cofactors of the elements 1, 1, 1 of the first row, we have

$$\begin{vmatrix} 2 & 1 \\ 1 & 2 \end{vmatrix}, -\begin{vmatrix} 1 & 1 \\ 1 & 2 \end{vmatrix}, \begin{vmatrix} 1 & 2 \\ 1 & 1 \end{vmatrix}$$

i.e. $4-1,\ -(2-1),\ (1-2)$

i.e. $3,\quad -1,\quad -1.$

The cofactors of the elements 1, 2, 1 of the 2nd row, we have

$$-\begin{vmatrix} 1 & 1 \\ 1 & 1 \end{vmatrix}, \begin{vmatrix} 1 & 1 \\ 1 & 2 \end{vmatrix} - \begin{vmatrix} 1 & 1 \\ 1 & 1 \end{vmatrix}$$

i.e. $-(2-1),\ (2-1),\ -0$

i.e. $-1,\ 1,\ 0$

The cofactors of the elements 1, 1, 2 of the third row we have

$$\begin{vmatrix} 1 & 1 \\ 2 & 1 \end{vmatrix}, -\begin{vmatrix} 1 & 1 \\ 1 & 1 \end{vmatrix}, \begin{vmatrix} 1 & 1 \\ 1 & 2 \end{vmatrix}$$

i.e. $(1-2),\ -(1-1),\ (2-1)$

i.e. $-1,\ 0,\ 1$

Let $$C = \begin{bmatrix} -3 & -1 & -1 \\ -1 & 1 & 0 \\ -1 & 0. & 1 \end{bmatrix}$$

$$C^1 = \begin{bmatrix} 3 & -1 & -1 \\ -1 & 1 & 0 \\ -1 & 0 & 1 \end{bmatrix}$$

Adjoint of $$A = C^1 = \begin{bmatrix} 3 & -1 & -1 \\ -1 & 1 & 0 \\ -1 & 0 & 1 \end{bmatrix}$$

$$A^{-1} = \frac{adj\,(A)}{|A|}$$

$$A^{-1} = \begin{bmatrix} 3 & -1 & -1 \\ -1 & 1 & 0 \\ -1 & 0 & 1 \end{bmatrix}$$

$$X = A^{-1}B = \begin{bmatrix} 3 & -1 & -1 \\ -1 & 1 & 0 \\ -1 & 0 & 1 \end{bmatrix} \begin{bmatrix} 1 \\ 2 \\ 0 \end{bmatrix} = \begin{bmatrix} 3 & -2 & -0 \\ -1 & +2 & +0 \\ -1 & +0 & +0 \end{bmatrix}$$

$$X = \begin{bmatrix} 1 \\ 1 \\ -1 \end{bmatrix}$$

i.e. $$\begin{bmatrix} x \\ y \\ z \end{bmatrix} = \begin{bmatrix} 1 \\ 1 \\ -1 \end{bmatrix}$$

$\Rightarrow x = 1, y = 1, z = -1$

Problem 5 Solve $2x + 3y + 5z = 6$

$$3x - 2y + 4z = 3$$

$$2x + y - z = 1$$

Solution The system of equation may be written in a matrix form

$$Ax = B,$$

where $$A = \begin{bmatrix} 2 & 3 & 5 \\ 3 & -2 & 4 \\ 2 & 1 & -1 \end{bmatrix}$$

$$X = \begin{bmatrix} x \\ y \\ z \end{bmatrix} \qquad B = \begin{bmatrix} 6 \\ 3 \\ 1 \end{bmatrix}$$

$$|A| = \begin{vmatrix} 2 & 3 & 5 \\ 3 & -2 & 4 \\ 2 & 1 & -1 \end{vmatrix}$$

$$= 2\begin{vmatrix} -2 & 4 \\ 1 & -1 \end{vmatrix} - 3\begin{vmatrix} 3 & 4 \\ 2 & -1 \end{vmatrix} + 5\begin{vmatrix} 3 & -2 \\ 2 & 1 \end{vmatrix}$$

$$= 2\,(2-4) - 3\,(-3-8) + 5\,(3+4)$$

$$= 2x\,(-2) - 3\,(-11) + 5 \times 7$$

$$= -4 + 33 + 35 = 68 - 4 = 64$$

since $|A| \neq 0$ so A^{-1} exists

$$AX = B$$

$$\Rightarrow \quad A^{-1}(AX) = A^{-1} B$$

$$\Rightarrow \quad IX = A^{-1} B$$

$$\Rightarrow \quad X = A^{-1} B$$

so we have to find the value of A^{-1}

The co-factors of the elements 2, 3, 5 of the first row are

$$\begin{vmatrix} -2 & 4 \\ 1 & -1 \end{vmatrix}, -\begin{vmatrix} 3 & 4 \\ 2 & -1 \end{vmatrix}, \begin{vmatrix} 3 & -2 \\ 2 & 1 \end{vmatrix}$$

$(2-4);\ -(3-8)\ (3+4) = -2;\ 11;\ 7$

The co-factors of the elements 3, -2, 4 of the 2nd row are

$$-\begin{vmatrix} 3 & 5 \\ 1 & -1 \end{vmatrix} = -(-3-5) = -(-8) = 8$$

$$\begin{vmatrix} 2 & 5 \\ 2 & -1 \end{vmatrix} = -2 - 10 = -12$$

$$-\begin{vmatrix} 2 & 3 \\ 2 & 1 \end{vmatrix} = -(2-6) = -(-4) = 4$$

The co-factor of the elements 2, $1-1$ of the third row are

$$\begin{vmatrix} 3 & 5 \\ -2 & 4 \end{vmatrix}, -\begin{vmatrix} 2 & 5 \\ 3 & 4 \end{vmatrix}, \begin{vmatrix} 2 & 3 \\ 3 & -2 \end{vmatrix}$$

i.e. $\quad 12 + 10 - (8-15)\ (-4-9)$

i.e. $\quad 22 \quad 7, -13$

$$\text{Let} \quad C = \begin{bmatrix} -2 & 11 & 7 \\ 8 & -12 & 4 \\ 22 & 7 & -13 \end{bmatrix}$$

$$C^1 = \begin{bmatrix} -2 & 8 & 22 \\ 11 & -12 & 7 \\ 7 & 4 & -13 \end{bmatrix}$$

$$Adj\,(A) = \begin{bmatrix} -2 & 8 & 22 \\ 11 & -12 & 7 \\ 7 & 4 & -13 \end{bmatrix}$$

$$A^{-1} = \frac{Adj\,(A)}{|A|} = \frac{1}{64}\begin{bmatrix} -2 & 8 & 22 \\ 11 & -12 & 7 \\ 7 & 4 & -13 \end{bmatrix}$$

$$X = A^{-1}\,B$$

$$X = \frac{1}{64}\begin{bmatrix} -2 & 8 & 22 \\ 11 & -12 & 7 \\ 7 & 4 & -13 \end{bmatrix}\begin{bmatrix} 6 \\ 3 \\ 1 \end{bmatrix}$$

$$X = \frac{1}{64}\begin{bmatrix} -12 + 24 + 22 \\ 66 - 36 + 7 \\ 42 + 12 - 13 \end{bmatrix}$$

$$X = \frac{1}{64}\begin{bmatrix} 34 \\ 37 \\ 41 \end{bmatrix}$$

$$\begin{bmatrix} x \\ y \\ z \end{bmatrix} = \begin{bmatrix} 34/64 \\ 37/64 \\ 41/64 \end{bmatrix}$$

$$\Rightarrow x = \frac{34}{64} \quad y = \frac{37}{64} \quad z = \frac{41}{64}$$ **Ans.**

Problem 1 Find the rank

$$\begin{bmatrix} 0 & -1 & -2 \\ 8 & 9 & 10 \\ 8 & 8 & 8 \end{bmatrix}$$

Solution We know that the elementary transformation do not alter the rank of the matrix.

$$\begin{bmatrix} 0 & -1 & -2 \\ 8 & 9 & 10 \\ 8 & 8 & 8 \end{bmatrix} \sim \begin{bmatrix} 8 & 8 & 8 \\ 8 & 9 & 10 \\ 0 & -1 & -2 \end{bmatrix}$$

By operoting $R_1 \longleftrightarrow R_3$

$$\sim \begin{bmatrix} 1 & 1 & 1 \\ 8 & 9 & 10 \\ 0 & -1 & -2 \end{bmatrix} \text{ By operating } R_1 \rightarrow \frac{1}{8} R_1$$

$$\sim \begin{bmatrix} 1 & 1 & 1 \\ 0 & 1 & 2 \\ 0 & -1 & -2 \end{bmatrix} \text{ By operating } R_1 \rightarrow R_2 - 8 R_1$$

$$\sim \begin{bmatrix} 1 & 0 & 0 \\ 0 & 1 & 2 \\ 0 & -1 & -2 \end{bmatrix} \text{ By operating } c_2 \rightarrow c_2 - c_1, \; c_3 \rightarrow c_3 - c_1$$

$$\sim \begin{bmatrix} 1 & 0 & 0 \\ 0 & 1 & 2 \\ 0 & 0 & 0 \end{bmatrix} \text{ By operating } R_3 \rightarrow R_3 + R_2$$

$$\sim \begin{bmatrix} 1 & 0 & 0 \\ 0 & 1 & 0 \\ 0 & 0 & 0 \end{bmatrix} \text{ By operating } c_3 \rightarrow c_3 - c_2$$

$$= \begin{bmatrix} I_2 & 0 \\ 0 & 0 \end{bmatrix}$$

Hence the rank of the given matrix is 2.

Problem 40 Show that

$$\begin{vmatrix} y^2+z^2 & xy & zx \\ xy & z^2+x^2 & yz \\ zx & yz & z^2+y^2 \end{vmatrix} = 4x^2\, y^2\, z^2$$

Solution Let us suppose that

$$\Delta = \begin{vmatrix} y^2+z^2 & xy & yz \\ xy & z^2+x^2 & yz \\ zx & yz & x^2+y^2 \end{vmatrix}$$

$$\Delta = \frac{1}{yz\ zx\ xy}\begin{vmatrix} yz\,(y^2+z^2) & xy\cdot yz & zx\ yz \\ xy\ zx & (z^2+x^2)\ zx & yz\cdot zx \\ zx\cdot xy & yz\cdot xy & (x^2+y^2)\ xy \end{vmatrix}$$

Now taking yz from first column, zx from second column and xy from the third column, we have

$$\Delta = \frac{yz\ zx\ xy}{yz\ zx\ xy}\begin{vmatrix} y^2+z^2 & y^2 & z^2 \\ x^2 & z^2+x^2 & z^2 \\ x^2 & y^2 & x^2+y^2 \end{vmatrix}$$

$$\Delta = \begin{vmatrix} y^2+z^2 & y^2 & z^2 \\ x^2 & z^2+x^2 & z^2 \\ x^2 & y^2 & x^2+y^2 \end{vmatrix}$$

Putting $x^2 = 0$

Then $$\Delta = \begin{vmatrix} y^2+z^2 & y^2 & z^2 \\ 0 & z^2 & z^2 \\ 0 & y^2 & y^2 \end{vmatrix}$$

$$\Delta = y^2\, z^2 \begin{vmatrix} y^2+z^2 & y^2 & z^2 \\ 0 & 1 & 1 \\ 0 & 1 & 1 \end{vmatrix}$$

$\Delta = 0$, since two rows are identical

$\therefore$ x^2 is factor of Δ. Similarly y^2 and z^2 are factors

Again, Δ is of the sixth degree in x, y and z, and we know already the factors x^2, y^2 and z^2. If there is another factor, it must be a nubmer.

$$\begin{vmatrix} y^2+z^2 & y^2 & z^2 \\ x^2 & z^2+x^2 & z^2 \\ x^2 & y^2 & x^2+y^2 \end{vmatrix} = N\, x^2\, y^2\, z^2,$$

where N is a number

Put $x = y = 1 = z$

$$\text{Then} \quad \begin{vmatrix} 2 & 1 & 1 \\ 1 & 2 & 1 \\ 1 & 1 & 2 \end{vmatrix} = N$$

$$\therefore \quad N = 2\begin{vmatrix} 2 & 1 \\ 1 & 2 \end{vmatrix} - 1\begin{vmatrix} 1 & 1 \\ 1 & 2 \end{vmatrix} + 1\begin{vmatrix} 1 & 2 \\ 1 & 1 \end{vmatrix}$$

$$N = 2\,(4-1) - 1\,(2-1+1)\,(1-2)$$

$$N = 2 \times 3 - 1 - 1$$

$$N = 6 - 2 = 4$$

Thus the given determinant

$$\Delta = \begin{vmatrix} y^2+z^2 & y^2 & z^2 \\ x^2 & z^2+x^2 & z^2 \\ x^2 & y^2 & x^2+y^2 \end{vmatrix} = 4\, x^2\, y^2\, z^2 \qquad \textit{(Proved)}$$

24

Concept of Limit: Continuity and Differentiability of a Function of one Variable

By the expression the variable x opproaches the constant number a' or simply x tends to the value a' we mean that x assumes successively values whose numerical difference frcm a i.e. $|X-a|$ is gradually less and less, and can ultimately be taken to be less than any small quantity we can imagine we denote this by the symbol $x \to a$.

If the variable x, remaining always greater than a, approaches a, such that ultimately $x-a$ is less than any preassigned positive quantity, however small (but $x \neq a$ actually) then we say that x approches or tends to 'a' from the right, and denote it by the symbol $x \to a+0$ or simply by $x \to a^+$

similarly when x is less than a alloays, and $a-x$ is ultimately less than any preassigned positive quantity, however small, we say x tends to 'a' from the left and we denofe it by $x \to a-0$, or simply by $x \to \bar{a}^-$.

Limit of a function

$\lim\limits_{x \to a} f(x)$: When x approaches a constant quantity a from either side if there exists a definite finite number l towards which $f(x)$ approaches, such that the numerical difference of $f(x)$ and l can be made as small as we pleased i.e. less than any preassigned positive quantity, however small) by taking x sufficiently close to a, then l is defined as the limit of $f(x)$ as tends to a. This is symbolically written as

$$\operatorname*{Lt}_{x \to a} f(x) = l$$

Mathematically speaking

$\lim\limits_{x \to a} f(x) = l$ provided, given any preassigned positive quantity ϵ, however small, we can determine another positive quantity δ (depending on ϵ such that $$|f(x)-l| < \epsilon$$

for all values of x satisfying

$$0 < |x-a| \leqslant \delta$$

Some Important Limits

(1) $\lim_{n\to\infty}\left(1+\frac{1}{n}\right)^n = e$ (2) $\lim_{x\to 0}(1+x)^{1/x} = e$

(3) $\lim_{x\to 0}\frac{(1+x)^n-1}{x} = n$ (4) $\lim_{x\to 0}\frac{x^n-a^n}{x-a} = na^{n-1}$

where n is an integer $n \neq 0$

(5) $\lim_{x\to 0}\frac{e^x-1}{x} = 1$ (6) $\lim_{x\to 0}\frac{\sin x}{x} = 1$

(7) $\lim_{x\to 0}\cos x = 1$ (8) $\lim_{x\to 0}\frac{\log(1+x)}{x} = 1$

(9) $\lim_{x\to 0}\frac{\tan x}{x} = 1$ (10) $\lim_{x\to 0}\frac{a^x-1}{x} = \log_e a$

Remember

Problem 1 Evaluate $\lim_{x\to 0}\frac{\tan 2x - x}{3x - \sin x}$

Solution $\lim_{x\to 0}\left[\frac{\tan 2x - x}{3x - \sin x}\right]$

Dividing the numerator and denominator with x we have.

$$= \lim_{x\to 0}\frac{\left[\frac{\tan 2x - x}{x}\right]}{\left[\frac{3x - \sin x}{x}\right]} = \lim_{x\to 0}\frac{\left[\frac{\tan 2x}{x} - \frac{x}{x}\right]}{\left[\frac{3x}{x} - \frac{\sin x}{x}\right]}$$

$$= \frac{\lim_{x\to 0}\frac{\tan 2x}{2x}2 - 1}{\lim_{x\to 0}3\cdot - \lim_{x\to 0}\frac{\sin x}{x}} = \frac{2-1}{3-1} = \frac{1}{2}$$

i.e. $\lim_{x\to 0}\frac{\tan 2x - x}{3x - \sin x} = \frac{1}{2}$ **Ans.**

Problem 2 Evaluate $\lim_{x\to\infty}\frac{\sin x}{x}$

Solution Let $x = \frac{1}{y}$

So that when $x \to \infty$ then $y \to 0$

$$\therefore \quad \lim_{x\to\infty}\frac{\sin x}{x} = \lim_{y\to 0} y\left(\sin\frac{1}{y}\right) = 0$$

Since sin $\left(\frac{1}{y}\right)$ oscillates between -1 and 1 for all values of y.

Problem 3 $\lim_{\theta \to \pi/2} (\sec \theta - \tan \theta)$

Here for $\theta = \frac{\pi}{2}$ $\sec \theta - \tan \theta = \infty - \infty$ which is an indeterminate form

Solution We have $\sec \theta - \tan \theta = \sec \theta - \tan \theta$

$$= \frac{1}{\cos \theta} - \frac{\sin \theta}{\cos \theta} = \frac{1 - \sin \theta}{\cos \theta}$$

$$\lim_{\theta \to \pi/2} \sec \theta - \tan \theta = \lim_{\theta \to \pi/2} \frac{1 - \sin \theta}{\cos \theta}$$

which is of the form $\frac{1 - \sin \pi/2}{\cos \pi/2} = \frac{1-1}{0} = \frac{0}{0}$

So applying L' Hospitals rule, we have

$$\lim_{\theta \to \pi/2} (\sec \theta - \tan \theta) = \lim_{\theta \to \pi/2} \frac{(1 - \sin \theta)}{\cos \theta}$$

$$= \lim_{\theta \to \pi/2} \frac{d \cdot c\,[1 - \sin \theta]}{d \cdot c\,[\cos \theta]} = \lim_{\theta \to \pi/2} \frac{0 - \cos \theta}{-\sin \theta}$$

$$= \lim_{\theta \to \pi/2} \frac{\cos \theta}{\sin \theta} = \frac{\cos \pi/2}{\sin \pi/2} = \frac{0}{1} = 0 \quad \textbf{Ans.}$$

i.e. $\lim_{\theta \to \pi/2} (\sec \theta - \tan \theta) = 0$

Problem 4 $\lim_{x \to a} \frac{\sqrt{a + 2x} - \sqrt{3x}}{\sqrt{3a + x} - 2\sqrt{x}}$

Solution Now we have the numerator

$$= \sqrt{a + 2x} - \sqrt{3x} = \frac{\sqrt{a + 2x} - \sqrt{3x}}{\sqrt{a + 2x} + \sqrt{3x}} \times (\sqrt{a + 2x} + \sqrt{3x})$$

$$= \frac{a + 2x - 3x}{\sqrt{a + 2x} + \sqrt{3x}} = \frac{a - x}{\sqrt{a + 2x} + \sqrt{3x}} \quad (1)$$

and the Dedominator

$$= \sqrt{3a + x} - 2\sqrt{x} = \frac{\sqrt{3a + x} - 2\sqrt{x}}{\sqrt{3a + x} + 2\sqrt{x}} \times \sqrt{3a + x} + 2\sqrt{x}$$

$$= \frac{3a + x - 4x}{\sqrt{3a + x} + 2\sqrt{x}} = \frac{3a - 3x}{\sqrt{3a + x} + 2\sqrt{x}}$$

$$= \frac{3\,(a - x)}{\sqrt{3a + x} + 2\sqrt{x}}$$

Thus $\dfrac{\sqrt{a+2x}-\sqrt{3x}}{\sqrt{3a+x}-2\sqrt{x}} = \dfrac{(a-x)}{\sqrt{a+2x}+\sqrt{3x}} \times \dfrac{\sqrt{3a+x}+2\sqrt{x}}{3(a-x)}$

$$= \frac{1}{3} \cdot \frac{\sqrt{3a+x}+2\sqrt{x}}{\sqrt{a+2x}+\sqrt{3x}}$$

Taking limit on both sides as $x \to a$ we have

$$\lim_{x\to a} \frac{\sqrt{a+x\,2x}-\sqrt{3x}}{\sqrt{3a+x}-2\sqrt{x}} = \frac{1}{3} \lim_{x\to a} \frac{\sqrt{3a+x}+2\sqrt{x}}{\sqrt{a+2x}+\sqrt{3x}}$$

$$= \frac{1}{3} \frac{\sqrt{3a+a}+2\sqrt{a}}{\sqrt{a+2a}+\sqrt{3a}} = \frac{1}{3} \frac{\sqrt{4a}+2\sqrt{a}}{\sqrt{3a}+\sqrt{3a}}$$

$$= \frac{1}{3} \frac{2\sqrt{a}+2\sqrt{a}}{2\sqrt{3a}} = \frac{1}{3} \cdot \frac{4\sqrt{a}}{2\sqrt{3}\sqrt{a}} = \frac{2}{3\sqrt{3}}$$

i.e. $\displaystyle\lim_{x\to a} \frac{\sqrt{a+2x}-\sqrt{3x}}{\sqrt{3a+x}-2\sqrt{x}} = \frac{2}{3\sqrt{3}}$ **Ans.**

Problem 5 Use the formula

$\displaystyle\lim_{x\to 0} \left(\frac{a^x-1}{x}\right) = \log a$ to show that

$$\lim_{x\to 0} \left[\frac{2^x-1}{\sqrt{1+x}-1}\right] = 2\log 2$$

Solution $\dfrac{2^x-1}{\sqrt{1+x}-1} = \dfrac{2^x-1}{\sqrt{1+x}-1} \times \dfrac{\sqrt{1+x}+1}{\sqrt{1+x}+1}$

$$= \frac{(2^x-1)\times(\sqrt{1+x}+1)}{(1+1x-1)}$$

$$= \left(\frac{2^x-1}{x}\right) \times (\sqrt{1+x}+1)$$

Taking limit on both sides as $x \to 0$ we haue

$$\lim_{x\to 0} \frac{2^x-1}{\sqrt{1+x}-1} = \lim_{x\to 0} \frac{(2^x-1)}{x} \times (\sqrt{1+x}+1)$$

i.e. $\displaystyle\lim_{x\to 0} \frac{2^x-1}{\sqrt{1+x}-1} = \lim_{x\to 0} \frac{(2^x-1)}{x} \times \lim_{x\to 0} (\sqrt{1+x}+1)$

i.e. $\displaystyle\lim_{x\to 0} \frac{2^x-1}{\sqrt{1+x}-1} = \log 2\,(\sqrt{1}+1)$

$$= \log 2\,(1+1) = 2\log 2$$

Problem 6 Evaluate $\lim\limits_{x\to a}\left[\dfrac{xe^{-x}-ae^{-a}}{x-a}\right]=(1-a)\,e^{-a}$

Solution Let $x=a+h$ so that $x\to a$ $h\to 0$

$$\lim_{x\to a}\left[\frac{xe^{-x}-ae^{-a}}{x-a}\right]$$

$$=\lim_{h\to 0}\frac{[(a+h)\,e^{-(a+h)}-ae^{-a}]}{h}$$

$$=\lim_{h\to 0}\frac{[ae^{-(a+h)}+he^{-(a+h)}-ae^{-a}}{h}$$

$$=\lim_{h\to 0}\left[\frac{ae^{-(a+b)}}{h}+e^{-(a+b)}-\frac{ae^{-a}}{h}\right]$$

$$=\lim_{h\to 0}\left[\frac{ae^{-a}\cdot e^{-h}}{h}+e^{-a}\cdot e^{-h}-\frac{ae^{-a}}{h}\right]$$

$$=\lim_{h\to 0}\left[\frac{ae^{-a}}{h}(e^{-h}-1)+e^{-(a+h)}\right]$$

$$=\lim_{h\to 0} ae^{-a}\left(\frac{e^{-h}-1}{h}\right)+e^{-a}$$

$$=ae^{-a}\lim_{h\to 0}\left[1-h+\frac{h^2}{2!}-\frac{h^3}{3!}+\frac{h^4}{4!}\ldots-1\right]+e^{-a}$$

$$=ae^{-a}(-1)+e^{-a}$$

$$=-ae^{-a}+e^{-a}$$

$$=e^{-a}(1-a)$$

Remembe

$$\lim_{h\to 0}\frac{e^{-h}-1}{(-h)}=1$$

Problem 7 Evaluate $\lim\limits_{x\to 0}\left(\dfrac{1-\cos x}{x^2}\right)$

Solutiou $\lim\limits_{x\to 0}\left(\dfrac{1-\cos x}{x^2}\right)=\lim\limits_{x\to 0}\dfrac{2\sin^2 x/2}{x^2}$

$$=2\lim_{x\to 0}\frac{(\sin x/2)^2}{x^2/4\times 4}=\frac{2}{4}\lim_{x\to 0}\frac{(\sin x/2)^2}{(x/2)^2}$$

$$=\frac{1}{2}\times\lim_{x\to 0}\left[\frac{\sin x/2}{x/2}\right]^2=\frac{1}{2}\times 1=\frac{1}{2}$$ **Ans.**

Limit

Problem 8 Evaluate $\lim\limits_{x\to a} \dfrac{x \sin a - a \sin x}{x-a}$

Putting $x = a + h \quad \Rightarrow \quad x - a = h$

If $\quad x \to a \quad \Rightarrow \quad h \to 0$

Thus the given expression becomes

$$\lim_{x\to 0} \frac{(a+h)\sin a - a \sin (a+h)}{h}$$

$$= \lim_{h\to 0} \frac{a \sin a + h \sin a - a [\sin a \cos h + \cos a \sin h]}{h}$$

$$= \lim_{h\to 0} \frac{a \sin a + h \sin a - a \sin a \cos h - a \cos a \sin h}{h}$$

$$= \lim_{h\to 0} \frac{a \sin a (1-\cos h)}{h} + \sin a - a \cos a \left(\frac{\sin h}{h}\right)$$

$$= a \sin a \lim_{h\to 0} \frac{2\sin^2 h/2}{h} + \sin a - a \cos a \lim_{h\to 0} \frac{\sin h}{h}$$

$$= 2a \sin a \lim_{h\to 0} \frac{\sin^2 h/2h}{h^2/4\times 4} + \sin a - a \cos a\cdot 1$$

$$= 2a \sin a \lim_{h\to 0} \left(\frac{\sin h/2}{h/2}\right)^2 \frac{h}{4} + \sin a - a \cos a$$

$$= 0 + \sin a - a \cos a$$

i.e. $\quad \lim\limits_{x\to a} \dfrac{x \sin a - a \sin x}{x-a} = \sin a - a \cos a$

Problem 9 Evaluate $\lim\limits_{x\to 0} \dfrac{e^{\sin x}-1}{x}$

Solution $\lim\limits_{x\to 0} \dfrac{e^{\sin x}-1}{\sin x} \times \dfrac{\sin x}{x} = \lim\limits_{x\to 0} \dfrac{e^{\sin x}-1}{\sin x} \times \lim\limits_{x\to 0} \dfrac{\sin x}{x}$

$$= \lim_{x\to 0} \frac{1 + \sin x + \left(\frac{\sin x}{2!}\right)^2 + \frac{\sin^3 x}{3!} + \ldots - 1}{\sin x} \times 1$$

$$= \lim_{x\to 0} 1 + \frac{1}{2!} \sin x + \frac{1}{3!} \sin^2 x + \ldots$$

$$= 1 + 0 + 0 = 1$$

i.e. $\quad \lim\limits_{x\to 0} \dfrac{e^{\sin x}-1}{x} = 1 \quad$ **Ans.**

Problem 10 Evaluate $\lim\limits_{x \to 0} \dfrac{a^x - 1}{x}$

Putting $a^x - 1 = y$

when $x = 0 \quad a^0 - 1 = y \quad$ i.e. $1 - 1 = 0 = y$

i.e. if $x \to 0 \qquad y \to 0$

$$\lim_{x \to 0} \frac{a^x - 1}{x} \qquad a^x - 1 = y$$

$$\Rightarrow a^x = 1 + y$$

$$= \lim_{y \to 0} \frac{y}{\dfrac{\log(1 + y)}{\log a}} \qquad \Rightarrow x \log a = \log(1 + y)$$

$$\Rightarrow \qquad x = \frac{\log(1 + y)}{\log a}$$

$$= \lim_{y \to 0} \log a \frac{y}{\log(1 + y)}$$

$$= \log a \times \lim_{y \to 0} \frac{y}{\log(1 + y)} \quad \left[\frac{0}{0}\right] \text{form}$$

So applying *l* Hospitals rule we have

$$\lim_{x \to 0} \frac{a^x - 1}{x} = \log a \lim_{y \to 0} \frac{y}{\log(1 + y)}$$

$$= \log a \lim_{y \to 0} \frac{\text{d.c. } (y)}{\text{d.c. } \{\log(1 + y)\}}$$

$$= \log a \times \lim_{y \to 0} \frac{1}{\dfrac{1}{(1 + y)}(0 + 1)} = \log a \times \lim_{y \to 0} (1 + y)$$

$$= (\log a) \times 1 = \log a$$

Thus $\lim\limits_{x \to 0} \dfrac{a^x - 1}{x} = \log a$ [Base e is not mentioned]

25

Continuity and Dfferentiability

Continuity at a point

The function $f(x)$ is said to be continuous when $x = a$ if $f(x)$ possesses a definite limit as x tends to the value a from either side and each of these limits is equal to $f(a)$

i.e. $\lim_{x \to a-0} f(x) = f(a) = \lim_{x \to a+0} f(x)$

Continuity in an interval

A function $f(x)$ is said to be continuous in the closed interval $[a, b]$ if it is continuous at every point of the open interval (a, b)

Differentiability

A function $f(x)$ defined at a point a in a certain neighbourhood of a is said to be differentiable at a if the limits

$$\lim_{h \to 0} \frac{f(a+h) - f(a)}{h} \quad \text{and} \quad \lim_{h \to 0} \frac{f(a-h) - f(a)}{-h}$$

both exist and have the same value.

The value is called the differential coefficient of $f(x)$ at a and h is denoted by $f^1(a)$.

Problem 1 Prove that $\lim_{x \to a} \frac{x^2 - a^2}{x - a}$ exists. Find its value.

Solution Here $f(x) = \frac{x^2 - a^2}{x - a}$

Then *R.H.S.* limit

$$f(a+0) = \lim_{h \to 0} f(a+h)$$

$$= \lim_{h \to 0} \frac{(a+h)^2 - a^2}{a + h - a} = \lim_{h \to 0} \frac{a^2 + 2ah + h^2 - a^2}{h}$$

$$= \lim_{b \to 0} \frac{2ah + h^2}{h} = \lim_{h \to 0} (2a + h) = 2a$$

i.e. *R.H.S.* limit $= 2a$

$$L.H.S.\text{ limit} = f(a-0) = \lim_{h\to 0} f(a-h)$$

$$= \lim_{h\to 0} \frac{(a-h)^2 - a^2}{a-h-a} = \lim_{h\to 0} \frac{a^2 - 2ah + h^2 - a^2}{-h}$$

$$= \lim_{h\to 0} \frac{h^2 - 2ah}{-h} = \lim_{h\to 0} (-h) + \lim_{h\to 0} 2a$$

$$= 0 + 2a = 2a$$

$L.H.S.$ limit $= 2a$

Since $f(a+0) = f(a-0)$ therefore the given limit exists and its value is $2a$.

Problem 2 Prove that $\lim_{x\to a} \frac{1}{1 - e^{1/x-a}}$ does not exist.

Solution For this we have to check that $R.H.S.$ and $L.H.S.$ limits are equal or not

$R.H.S.$ limit

$$f(a+0) = \lim_{h\to 0} f(a+h)$$

$$= \lim_{h\to 0} \frac{1}{1 - e^{1/a+h-a}} = \lim_{h\to 0} \frac{1}{1 - e^{1/h}}$$

$$= \frac{1}{1 - e^{\infty}} = \frac{1}{1-\infty} = \frac{1}{\infty} = 0$$

Again $L.H.S.$ limit

$$= f(a-h) = \lim_{h\to 0} \frac{1}{1 - e^{1/-h}} = \frac{1}{1 - e^{-1/0}} = \frac{1}{1 - e^{-\infty}}$$

$$= \frac{1}{1 - \frac{1}{e^{\infty}}} = \frac{1}{1-0} = 1$$

We find that $\lim_{h\to 0} f(a+h) \neq \lim_{h\to 0} f(a-h)$

Hence the given limit does not exist.

Problem 3 Prove that the function $f(x) = x^3 - 3x$ is continuous for all real values of x.

Solution Let us examine the continuity of the given function at $x = a$, wher a is any finite real quantity

Now $\quad f(a) = a^3 - 3a$

R.H.S. limit $f(a+0)$

$$= \lim_{h\to 0} f(a+h) = \lim_{h\to 0} (a+h)^3 - 3(a+h)$$

$$= \lim_{h\to 0} a^3 + 3ah^2 + 3a^2h - 3a - 3h + h^3 = a^3 - 3a$$

L.H.S. limit $= f(a-0)$

$$= \lim_{h\to 0} f(a-h) = \lim_{h\to 0} (a-h)^3 - 3(a-h)$$

$$= \lim_{h\to 0} a^3 - 3ah(a-h) - h^3 - 3a + 3h = a^3 - 3a$$

Since $f(a+0) = f(a) = f(a-0)$.

Therefore, the given function is continuous for all real values of x, since a is an arbitrary point of the real line.

Problem 4 Prove that $2^{1/x}$ is discontinuous at $x = 0$.

Solution Let $f(x) = 2^{1/x}$

Now $R.H.S. f(0+0) = \lim_{h\to 0} f(0+h) = \lim_{h\to 0} f(h)$

$$= \lim_{h\to 0} 2^{1/h} = 2^{1/0} = 2^{\infty} = \infty$$

L.H.S. limit $= f(0-0) = \lim_{h\to 0} f(0-h) = \lim_{h\to 0} f(-h)$

$$= \lim_{h\to 0} 2^{-1/h} = \lim_{h\to 0} \frac{1}{2^{1/h}} = \frac{1}{2^{1/0}} = \frac{1}{2^{\infty}} = \frac{1}{\infty} = 0$$

Since *L.H.S.* limit $\neq$ *R.H.S.* limit so the limit does not exist so there is no question of continuity. Thus the function $2^{1/x}$ is discontinuous at the point $x = 0$ **Ans.**

Problem 5 A function $f(x)$ is defined as follows

$f(x) = 1 + x$, if $x \leqslant 2$;

$f(x) = 5 - x$ if $x \geqslant 2$

Is the function continuous at $x = 2$

Solution *RHS* limit $= f(2+0)$

$$= \lim_{h\to 0} f(2+h) = \lim_{h\to 0} 5 - (2+h) = \lim_{h\to 0} 3 - h$$

$= 3 - 0 = 3$

RHS limit $= 3$

LHS limit $= f(2-0)$

$$= \lim_{h\to 0} f(2-h) = \lim_{h\to 0} 1 + 2 - h = \lim_{h\to 0} 3 - h = 3 - 0 = 3$$

The value of the function at the point $x = 2$

$$f(2) = 1 + 2 \quad \text{or } 5-2 = 3$$

Here we see that

LHS limit = *RHS* = value of the function.

Thus the given function is continuous at the point $x = 2$.

Problem 6 Given that

$$f(x) = \begin{cases} \dfrac{\sin x}{x}, x \neq 0; 2, x = 0 \end{cases}$$

Test the continuity of $f(x)$ at $x = 0$

Solution *RHS* limit

$$f(0+0) = \lim_{h\to 0} f(0+h) = \lim_{h\to 0} f(h)$$

$$= \lim_{h\to 0} \frac{\sin h}{h} = 1$$

LHS limit $= f(0-0)$

$$= \lim_{h\to 0} f(0-h) = \lim_{h\to 0} f(-h)$$

$$= \lim_{h\to 0} \frac{\sin(-h)}{-h} = \lim_{h\to 0} \frac{-\sin h}{-h} = \lim_{h\to 0} \frac{\sin h}{h} = 1$$

$$f(0) = 2$$

Here *RHS* limit

= *LHS* limit ≠ value of the function.

Thus the function is discontinuous at the point $x = 0$.

Problem 7 Examine the function defined below for continuity at $x = 0$

$$f(x) = \frac{\sin^2 ax}{x^2}, \text{ for } x \neq 0 .$$

$$f(x) = 1, \text{ for } x = 0$$

Solution *RHS* limit

$$f(0+0) = \lim_{h\to 0} f(0+h) = \lim_{h\to 0} f(h)$$

$$= \lim_{h\to 0} \frac{\sin^2 ah}{h^2} = \lim_{h=0} \frac{\sin^2 ah}{a^2 h^2} \times a^2$$

$$= a^2 \times \lim_{h\to 0} \left(\frac{\sin ah}{ah}\right)^2 = a^2 \times \lim_{ah\to 0} \left(\frac{\sin a h}{ah}\right)^2$$

$$= a^2 \times 1 = a^2$$

Since $h \to 0 \Rightarrow an \to 0$

RHS limit $= a$

LHS limit $= f(0-0) = \lim\limits_{h \to 0} f(a-h)$

$$= \lim_{h \to 0} f(-h) = \lim_{h \to 0} \frac{[\sin a(-h)]^2}{(-h)^2}$$

$$= \lim_{h \to 0} \frac{[\sin(-ah)]^2}{+h^2} = \lim_{h \to 0} \frac{(-\sin ah)^2}{h^2}$$

$$= \lim_{h \to 0} \frac{\sin^2 ah}{h^2} = \lim_{h \to 0} \frac{(\sin ah)^2}{a^2 h^2} \times a^2$$

$$= \lim_{h \to 0} \left(\frac{\sin ah}{ah}\right)^2 \times a^2 = \lim_{ah \to 0} \left(\frac{\sin ah}{ah}\right)^2 \times a^2$$

Since $h \to 0$ $a^{*}h \to 0 = a^2 \times 1 = a^2$

value of the function $f(0) = 1$

Here *LHS* limit $=$ *RHS* limit $\neq$ value of the function

Thus the given function in discontinuous at $x = 0$

Problem 8 Prove that the function

$$f(x) = \frac{x^2}{a} - a, \quad \text{for } 0 < x < a$$

$$f(x) = 0 \text{ for } x = a$$

$$f(x) = a - \frac{a^2}{x^2}, \text{ for } x > a$$

is continuous at $x = a$.

Solution *RHS* limit $= f(a + 0)$

$$= \lim_{h \to 0} f(a+h) = \lim_{h \to 0} a - \frac{a^3}{(a+h)^2}$$

$$= \lim_{h \to 0} a - \lim_{h \to 0} \frac{a^3}{a^2} = a - a = 0$$

LHS limit $= f(a-0)$

$$= \lim_{h \to 0} f(a-h)$$

$$= \lim_{h \to 0} \frac{(a+h)^2}{a} - a$$

$$= \lim a - \lim a = a - a = 0$$

Value of the function i.e. $f(a) = 0$

Thus the given function is continuous at $x = a$.

Problem 9 If $f(x) = x \sin \frac{1}{x}$, for $x \neq 0$, and $f(0) = 0$,

Show that $f(x)$ is continuous at $x = 0$.

Solution *RHS* limit $= f(0+0) = \lim_{h \to 0} f(0+h)$

$$= \lim_{h \to 0} f(h) = \lim_{h \to 0} h \sin \frac{1}{h} = 0$$

$=$ because value of $\sin \frac{1}{h}$ oscillates between -1 and 1

i.e. $\left| \sin \frac{1}{h} \right| \leqslant 1$

LHS limit $= f(0-0) = \lim_{h \to 0} f(0-h) = \lim_{h \to 0} f(-h)$

$$= \lim_{h \to 0} -h \sin \left(-\frac{1}{h} \right)$$

$$= \lim -h(-1) \sin \frac{1}{h} = \lim_{h \to 0} h \sin \frac{1}{h}$$

$$= 0 \left| \sin \frac{1}{h} \right| \leqslant 1$$

Value of the function at $x = 0$

$$f(0) = 0$$

We have *RHS* limit = *LHS* limit = Value of the function

So the given function is continuous at the point $x = 0$. *(Proved)*

Problem 10 Prove that the function $f(x) = \frac{e^{1/x}}{1 + e^{1/x}}$ $f(0) = 0$

is discontinuous at $x = 0$

Solution Here $f(x) = \frac{e^{1/x}}{1 + e^{1/x}}$

We have to check the continuity of the function at $x = 0$

RHS limit $= f(0+0) = \lim_{h \to 0} f(0+h) = \lim_{h \to 0} f(h)$

$$= \lim_{h \to 0} \frac{e^{1/h}}{1 + e^{1/h}} = \lim_{h \to 0} \frac{1}{\frac{1 + e^{1/h}}{e^{1/h}}}$$

$$= \lim_{h \to 0} \frac{1}{e^{-1/h} + 1} = \frac{1}{e^{-1/0} + 1}$$

$$= \frac{1}{e^{-\infty} + 1} = \frac{1}{e^{-1/\infty} + 1} = \frac{1}{1/\infty + 1} = \frac{1}{0+1} = 1$$

RHS limit $= 1$

LHS limit $= f(0-h) = \lim_{h\to 0} f(-h)$

$$= \lim_{h\to 0} \frac{e^{-1/h}}{1+e^{-1/h}} = \lim_{h\to 0} \frac{1}{\frac{1}{e^{-1/h}}+1}$$

$$= \lim_{h\to 0} \frac{1}{e^{1/h}+1} = \frac{1}{e^{1/0}+1} = \frac{1}{e^{\infty}+1}$$

$$= \frac{1}{\infty} = 0$$

It is given that $f(0) = 0$

So we find that $f(0+0) \neq f(0-0) = f(0)$

Hence the given function is discontinuous at the point.

Problem 11 Discuss the continuity of $f(x)$: $\dfrac{x-1}{1+e^{1/x-1}}$ if $x \neq 1$

at $x = 1$ if $x = 1$

Solution We have

RHS limit $= f(1+0) = \lim_{h\to 0} f(1+h)$

$$= \lim_{h\to 0} \frac{(1+h)-1}{1+e^{1/1+h-1}} = \lim_{h\to 0} \frac{h}{1+e^{1/h}}$$

$$= \lim_{h\to 0} \frac{h/e^{1/h}}{(1/e^{1/h})} = \lim_{h\to 0} \frac{he^{-1/h}}{e^{-1/h}+1}$$

$$= \frac{0}{0+1} = 0$$

Again *LHS* limit $f(1-0) = \lim_{h\to 0} f(1-h)$

$$= \lim_{h\to 0} \frac{1-h-1}{1+e^{1/1-h-1}} = \lim_{h\to 0} \frac{-h}{1+e^{-1/h}}$$

$$= \lim_{h\to 0} \frac{-h}{1+1/e^{1/h}} = -\frac{0}{1+1} = 0$$

By question, $f(1) = 0$ we find that

$$\lim_{h\to 0} f(1+h) = f(1) = \lim_{0\leftarrow h} f(1-h)$$

Hence the given function $f(x)$ is continuous at $x = 1$.

Problem 12 A function is defined as follows

$$f(x) = 1 + \sin x, \text{ for } 0 < x < \frac{\pi}{2}$$

$$f(x) = 2 + \left(x - \frac{\pi}{2}\right)^2, \text{ for } \frac{\pi}{2} \leqslant x < \infty$$

Discuss differentiability at $x = \dfrac{\pi}{2}$.

Solution For the differentiability we have to prove that

$$\lim_{h \to 0} \frac{f\left(\frac{\pi}{2} + h\right) - f(\pi/2)}{h} = \lim_{h \to 0} \frac{f\left(\frac{\pi}{2} - h\right) - f\left(\frac{\pi}{2}\right)}{-h}$$

Right hand side derivative

$$= \lim_{h \to 0} \frac{f\left(\frac{\pi}{2} + h\right) - f\left(\frac{\pi}{2}\right)}{h}$$

$$= \lim_{h \to 0} \frac{2 + \left(\frac{\pi}{2} + h - \frac{\pi}{2}\right)^2 - \left\{2 + \left(\frac{\pi}{2} - \frac{\pi}{2}\right)^2\right\}}{h}$$

$$= \lim_{h \to 0} \frac{2 + h^2 - 2}{h} = \lim_{h \to 0} \frac{h^2}{h} = \lim_{h \to 0} = 0$$

LHS derivative

$$= \lim_{h \to 0} \frac{f\left(\frac{\pi}{2} - h\right) - f\left(\frac{\pi}{2}\right)}{-h}$$

$$= \lim_{h \to 0} \frac{1 + \sin\left(\frac{\pi}{2} - h\right) - \left\{2 + \left(\frac{\pi}{2} - \frac{\pi}{2}\right)^2\right\}}{h}$$

$$= \lim_{h \to 0} \frac{1 + \cos h - 2}{-h} = \lim_{h \to 0} \frac{\cos h - 1}{-h} = \lim_{h \to 0} \frac{(\cos h - 1)}{h}$$

$$= \lim_{h \to 0} \frac{2 \sin^2 h/2}{h} = 2 \lim_{h \to 0} \frac{(\sin h/2)^2}{h^2/4 \times 4/h}$$

$$= \lim_{h \to 2} \frac{2h}{4} \left[\frac{\sin h/2}{h/2}\right]^2 = \tfrac{1}{2} \lim_{h \to 0} h = \tfrac{1}{2} \times 0 = 0$$

Thus we see that *RHS* limit = *LHS* limit

Hence the given function is differentiable at $\dfrac{\pi}{2}$.

Problem 13 If $f(x) = x^2 \sin \frac{1}{x}$, for $x \neq 0$ and $f(0) = 0$ show that $f(x)$ is continuous and differentiable at $x = 0$

Solution We know that a function $f(x)$ is continuous at a point $x = 0$ then we have

$$f(x + 0) = f(0) = f(x-0)$$

i.e. the *RHS* limit *LHS* limit and the value of the function at that point are same.

RHS limit $= f(0 + 0)$

$$= \lim_{h \to 0} f(0 + h) = \lim_{h \to 0} f(h)$$

$$= \lim_{h \to 0} h^2 \sin \frac{1}{h} \quad \text{Since} \quad h \to 0 \text{ and } h \neq 0$$

$$= 0 \quad \text{Since} \quad \left| \sin \frac{1}{h} \right| \leqslant 1$$

$$RHS \text{ limit} = 0 \qquad (1)$$

LHS limit $= f(0-0)$

$$= \lim_{h \to 0} f(0-h) = \lim_{h \to 0} f(-h)$$

$$= \lim_{h \to 0} (-h)^2 \sin \left(- \frac{1}{h} \right)$$

$$= \lim_{h \to 0} h^2 \sin\left(- \frac{1}{h} \right) = \lim_{h \to 0} -h^2 \sin \frac{1}{h}$$

$$= - \lim_{h \to 0} h^2 \sin\left(\frac{1}{h} \right)$$

$$= 0 \text{ since } \left| \sin \frac{1}{h} \right| \leqslant 1$$

value of the function at the point $x = 0$ we have

$$f(0) = 0$$

Thus we see that

$$f(0 + 0) = f(0) = f(0-0)$$

Hence the given function is continuous at the point $x = 0$

Now we have to check the differentiability of the function at the point $x = 0$.

RHS derivative $= \lim_{h\to 0} \dfrac{f(0+h)-f(0)}{h}$

$= \lim_{h\to 0} \dfrac{f(h)-f(0)}{h} = \lim_{h\to 0} \dfrac{h^2 \sin 1/h - 0}{h}$

$= \lim_{h\to 0} h \sin \dfrac{1}{h} = 0$ since $\left|\sin\dfrac{1}{h}\right| \leqslant 1$

LHS derivative $= \lim_{h\to 0} \dfrac{f(0-h)-f(0)}{-h} = \lim_{h\to 0} \dfrac{f(-h)-f(0)}{-h}$

$= \lim_{h\to 0} - \dfrac{[f(-h)-f(0)]}{h}$

$= \lim_{h\to 0} \dfrac{(-h)^2 \sin(-1/h)-0}{-h}$

$= \lim_{h\to 0} \dfrac{h^2 \sin(-1/h)-0}{-h} = \lim_{h\to 0} \dfrac{-h^2 \sin 1/h}{-h}$

$= \lim_{h\to 0} h \sin 1/h = 0$

Here we see that

$$\lim_{h\to 0} \frac{f(0+h)-f(0)}{h} = \lim_{h\to 0} \frac{f(0-h)-f(0)}{-h}$$

Thus the given function is differentiable at the point $x = 0$. ***(Proved)***

Problem 14 Is the following function continuous and differentiable at $x = \frac{1}{2}$?

$$f(x) = \begin{cases} x, & 0 \leqslant x < \frac{1}{2} \\ 1-x & \frac{1}{2} \leqslant x < 1 \end{cases}$$

Solution We have to check the continuity of the function $f(x)$ at the point $x = \frac{1}{2}$. For this we have to prove tnat

$$f(\tfrac{1}{2}+0) = f(\tfrac{1}{2}) = f(\tfrac{1}{2}-0)$$

i.e. *RHS* limit = value of the function = *LHS* limit

RHS limit $= f(\frac{1}{2}+0)$

$= \lim_{h\to 0} f(\frac{1}{2}+h) = \lim_{h\to 0} 1-(\frac{1}{2}+h)$

$= \lim_{h\to 0} 1-\frac{1}{2}-h = \lim_{h\to 0} \frac{1}{2}-h = \frac{1}{2}-0 = \frac{1}{2}$

LHS limit $= f(\frac{1}{2}-0)$

$= \lim_{h\to 0} f(\frac{1}{2}-h) = \lim_{h\to 0} \frac{1}{2}-h = \frac{1}{2}-0 = \frac{1}{2}$

Now $\qquad f(\tfrac{1}{2}) = 1 - \tfrac{1}{2} = \tfrac{1}{2}$

Thus we see that $f(\tfrac{1}{2} + 0) = f(\tfrac{1}{2}) = f(\tfrac{1}{2} - 0)$

Hence the given function is differentiable at the point $x = \tfrac{1}{2}$.

Now we have to check for the differentiability of the function at the point $x = \tfrac{1}{2}$. For this we have to show that

$$\lim_{h\to 0} \frac{f(\tfrac{1}{2}+h) - f(\tfrac{1}{2})}{h} = \lim_{h\to 0} \frac{f(\tfrac{1}{2}-h) - f(\tfrac{1}{2})}{-h}$$

$$RHS \text{ derivative} = \lim_{h\to 0} \frac{f(\tfrac{1}{2}+h) - f(\tfrac{1}{2})}{h} = \lim_{h\to 0} \frac{[1-(\tfrac{1}{2}+h)] - [1-\tfrac{1}{2}]}{h}$$

$$= \lim_{h\to 0} \frac{(\tfrac{1}{2}-h) - \tfrac{1}{2}}{h} = \lim_{h\to 0} \frac{-h}{h} = \lim_{h\to 0} (-1)$$

$$RHS \text{ derivative} = -1 \qquad (1)$$

$$LHS \text{ derivative} = \lim_{h\to 0} \frac{f(\tfrac{1}{2}-h) - f(\tfrac{1}{2})}{-h} = \lim_{h\to 0} \frac{\tfrac{1}{2} - h - \tfrac{1}{2}}{-h}$$

$$= \lim_{h\to 0} \frac{-h}{-h} = \lim_{h\to 0} 1 = 1$$

Here we see that

$$\lim_{h\to 0} \frac{f(\tfrac{1}{2}+h) - f(\tfrac{1}{2})}{h} \neq \lim_{h\to 0} \frac{f(\tfrac{1}{2}-h) - f(\tfrac{1}{2})}{-h}$$

Hence the given function is not differentiable at the point $x = \tfrac{1}{2}$.

Problem 15 A function is defined on the real line R as follows :

$$f(x) = x \sin \frac{1}{x}, \; x \neq 0$$

$$f(0) = 0$$

Show that f is not differentiable at $x = 0$

Solution For this we have to prove that the RHS derivative and the left hand side derivative of the function at the point $x = 0$ are not equal

$$RHS \text{ derivative} = \lim_{h\to 0} \frac{f(0+h) - f(0)}{h} = \lim_{h\to 0} \frac{f(h) - f(0)}{h}$$

$$= \lim_{h\to x} \frac{h \sin 1/h - 0}{h} = \lim_{h\to 0} \sin 1/h$$

The limit does not exist because the value of $\sin 1/h$ oscillates between $+1$ and -1

LHS derivative $= \lim_{h\to 0} \frac{f(0-h)-f(0)}{-h} = \lim_{h\to 0} \frac{f(-h)-f(0)}{-h}$.

$$= \lim_{n\to 0} \frac{-h \sin(-1/h)-0}{-h} = \lim_{h\to 0} \frac{h \sin 1/h}{-h}$$

$= -\lim_{h\to 0} \sin 1/h$ which does not exist as $\sin 1/h$ cscil-lates between $+1$ and -1

Since both the limit do not exist. So we cannot say for the equality of two i.e.

$$\lim_{h\to 0} \frac{f(0+a)-f(0)}{h} \neq \lim_{h\to 0} \frac{f(0-h)-f(0)}{h}$$

Thus the given function is not differentiable at the point $x = 0$

Problem 16 Let $f(x) = e^{-1/x^2} \sin 1/x$ for $x \neq 0, f(0) = 0$

Test the differentiability of the function at $x = 0$

Solution For the differentiability of $f(x)$ at the point $x = 0$ we have to check that

$$\lim_{h\to 0} \frac{f(0+h)-f(0)}{h} \quad \text{and} \quad \lim_{h\to 0} \frac{f(0-h)-f(0)}{-h}$$

are equal or not.

If the two limits are equal then we say that the given function is differentiable at $x = 0$ otherwise not differentiable at $x = 0$

R.H.S. derivative

$$\lim_{h\to 0} \frac{f(0+h)-f(0)}{h} = \lim_{h\to 0} \frac{f(h)-f(0)}{h}$$

$$= \lim_{h\to 0} \frac{e^{-1/h^2} \sin 1/h - 0}{h} = \lim_{h\to 0} \frac{\sin 1/h}{h \cdot e^{1/h^2}}$$

$$= \lim_{h\to 0} \frac{\sin 1/h}{h \times \left[\frac{1}{h^2} + \frac{1}{2!\, h^4} + \frac{1}{3!\, h^6} + \dots\right]}$$

$$= \lim_{h\to 0} \frac{\sin 1/h}{h + \frac{1}{h} + \frac{1}{2!\, h^3} + \dots}$$

$$= \frac{\text{a finite quantity}}{0 + \infty} \quad \text{i.e. } |\sin 1/h| < 1 = 0$$

$$L.H.S. \text{ derivative} = \lim_{h\to 0} \frac{f(0-h)-f(0)}{-h} = \lim_{h\to 0} \frac{f(-h)-f(0)}{-h}$$

$$= \lim_{h\to 0} \frac{f(-h)-0}{-h} = \lim_{h\to 0} \frac{f(-h)}{-h}$$

$$= \lim_{h\to 0} \frac{e^{-1/(-h)^2} \sin(-1/h)}{-h} = \lim_{h\to 0} \frac{e^{-1/h^2}(-\sin 1/h)}{-h}$$

$$= \lim_{h\to 0} \frac{e^{-1/h^2} \sin 1/h}{h} = \lim_{h\to 0} \frac{\sin 1/h}{h\, e^{1/h^2}}$$

$$= \lim_{h\to 0} \frac{\sin 1/h}{h\,[1 + 1/h^2 + 1/2!\, h^4 + 1/3!\, h^6 + \ldots]}$$

$$= \lim_{h\to 0} \frac{\sin 1/h}{h + 1/h + 1/2\, h^3 + \ldots}$$

$$= \frac{\text{a finite quantity}}{0 + \infty} = 0$$

i.e. $\quad R.H.S.$ derivative $= L.H.S.$ derivative

Thus the given function is differentiable at the point $x = 0$

Problem 17 Examine the function defined by

$$f(x) = x^2 \cos(e^{1/x}), \quad x \neq 0 \qquad f(0) = 0$$

with regard to differentiability at $x = 0$

Solution Here $\lim_{h\to 0} \dfrac{f(0+h) - f(0)}{h}$

$$= \lim_{h\to 0} \frac{(0+h)^2 \cos(e^{1/0+h}) - 0}{h} = \lim_{h\to 0} \frac{h^2 \cos(e^{1/h})}{h}$$

$$= \lim h \cos(e^{1/h}) = 0 \times \text{a finite quantity} = 0$$

Since $\cos(e^{1/h})$ oscillates between -1 and $+1$ as $h\to 0$ and hence finite

and $\lim_{h\to 0} \dfrac{f(0-h) - f(0)}{-h} = \lim_{h\to 0} \dfrac{f(-h) - f(0)}{-h}$

$$= \lim_{h\to 0} \frac{f(-h)}{-h} = \lim_{h\to 0} (-h)^2 \cos(e^{-1/h})$$

$$= \lim_{h\to 0} \frac{h^2 \cos(e^{-1/h})}{-h} = \lim_{h\to 0} -h \cos(e^{-1/h})$$

$$= -\lim_{h\to 0} h \times \lim_{h\to 0} \cos(e^{-1/h})$$

$$= -\lim_{h\to 0} h \times \cos(e^{-1/0}) = 0 \times \cos(e^{-\infty})$$

$$= 0 \times \cos(1/e^{\infty}) = 0 \times \cos(0) = 0 \times 1 = 0$$

Here we see that at the point $x = 0$

$R.H.S.$ derivative $0 = L.H.S.$ derivative at the point 0

Hence the given function is differentiable at $x = 0$

Problem 18 If $f(x) = \dfrac{x}{1 + e^{1/x}}$, $x \neq 0$ and $f(0) = 0$

show that $f(x)$ is not differentiable at $x = 0$

Solution To check the differentiability
we have to check either

$$\lim_{h\to 0} \frac{f(0+h)-f(0)}{h} \quad \text{and} \quad \lim_{h\to 0} \frac{f(0-h)-f(0)}{-h}$$

are equal at the point $x = 0$ or not. If they are equal then we say that the function is differentiable at $x = 0$ or not

$$f(0+h) = f(h)$$

$$f(0+h) = \frac{h}{1+e^{1/h}} \tag{1}$$

and $$f(0-h) = f(-h) = \frac{-h}{1+{}^{-}e^{1/h}}$$

$$f(0-h) = \frac{-h}{1+e^{-1/h}} \tag{2}$$

Now we have *R.H.S.* derivative

$$= \lim_{h\to 0} \frac{f(0+h)-f(0)}{h} = \lim_{h\to 0} \frac{f(h)-f(0)}{h}$$

$$= \lim_{h\to 0} \frac{h}{1+e^{1/h}/h} - 0 = \lim_{h\to 0} \frac{h}{h(1+e^{1/h})}$$

$$= \lim_{h\to 0} \frac{1}{1+e^{1/h}} = \frac{1}{1+e^{1/0}} = \frac{1}{1+e^{\infty}}$$

$$= \frac{1}{1+\infty} = 0$$

i.e. $$\lim_{h\to 0} \frac{f(0+h)-f(0)}{h} = 0 \tag{3}$$

Again $$\lim_{h\to 0} \frac{f(0-h)-f(0)}{-h} = \lim_{h\to 0} \frac{f(-h)-f(0)}{-h}$$

$$= \lim_{h\to 0} \frac{-h(1+e^{-1/h})}{-h} = \lim_{h\to 0} \frac{-h}{-h(1+e^{-1/h})}$$

$$= \lim_{h\to 0} \frac{1}{1+e^{-1/h}} = \frac{1}{1+e^{-\infty}} = \frac{1}{1+1/e^{\infty}}$$

$$= \frac{1}{1+0} = 1$$

Thus we have

$$\lim_{h\to 0} \frac{f(0+h)-f(0)}{h} \neq \lim_{h\to 0} \frac{f(0-h)-f(0)}{-h}$$

Hence the given function is not differentiable at the point $x = 0$.

Problem 19 If $f(x) = x \dfrac{e^{1/x}-e^{-1/x}}{e^{1/x}+e^{-1/x}}$, $x \neq 0$, $f(0) = 0$,

show that $f(x)$ is not differentiable at $x = 0$

Solution Here $\lim\limits_{h\to 0} \dfrac{f(0+h)-f(0)}{h}$

$$= \lim_{h\to 0} \frac{f(h)-f(0)}{h} = \lim_{h\to 0} h \frac{e^{1/h}-e^{-1/h}}{(e^{1/h}+e^{-1/h})/h}$$

$$= \lim_{h\to 0} \frac{h(e^{1/h}-e^{-1/h})}{h(e^{1/h}+e^{-1/h})} = \lim_{h\to 0} \frac{e^{1/h}-e^{-1/h}}{e^{1/h}+e^{-1/h}}$$

$$= \lim_{h\to 0} \frac{1-e^{-2/h}}{1+e^{-2/h}}$$

Dividing the numerator and the denominator by $e^{1/h}$

$$= \frac{1-e^{-2/0}}{1+e^{-2/0}} = \frac{1-e^{-\infty}}{1+e^{-\infty}} = \frac{1-1/e^{\infty}}{1+1/e^{\infty}}$$

$$= \frac{1-1/\infty}{1+1/\infty} = \frac{1-0}{1+0} = \frac{1}{1} = 1$$

$$L.H.S. \text{ derivative} = \lim_{h\to 0} \frac{f(0-h)-f(0)}{-h} = \lim_{h\to 0} \frac{f(-h)-f(0)}{-h}$$

$$= \lim_{h\to 0} \frac{-h\,[e^{-1/h}-e^{-1/h}]}{-h\,[e^{-1/h}+e^{-1/-h}]} = \lim_{h\to 0} \frac{-h\,[e^{-1/h}-e^{1/h}]}{-h\,[e^{-1/h}-e^{1/h}]}$$

$$= \lim_{h\to 0} \frac{-h\,[e^{-2/h}-1]}{-h\,[e^{-2/h}+1]} = \frac{[e^{-\infty}-1]}{[e^{-\infty}+1]}$$

$$= \frac{[1/e^{\infty}-1]}{1/e^{\infty}+1]} = \frac{[0-1]}{[0+1]} = \frac{-1}{1} = -1$$

Since $\lim\limits_{h\to 0} \dfrac{f(0+h)-f(0)}{h} \neq \lim\limits_{h\to 0} \dfrac{f(0-h)-f(0)}{-h}$

So the given function is not continuous at the point $x = 0$ **Ans.**

Problem 20 Prove that the function $f(x) = |x|$ is continuous at $x = 0$ but not differentiable at $x = 0$.

Solution *R.H.S.* limit $= f(0+0) = \lim_{h \to 0} f(0+h)$

$$= \lim_{h \to 0} f(h) = \lim_{h \to 0} |h| = 0$$

L.H.S. limit $= f(0-0) = \lim_{h \to 0} f(0-h) = \lim_{h \to 0} f(-h)$

$$= \lim_{h \to 0} |-h| = \lim_{h \to 0} |h| = 0$$

$$f(0) = |0| = 0$$

Here we see that *R.H.S.* limit $=$ *L.H.S.* limit

$=$ value of the function at the point $x = 0$

Thus the given function is continuous at $x = 0$

For differentiability *R.H.S.* derivative

$$= \lim_{h \to 0} \frac{f(0+h) - f(0)}{h} = \lim_{h \to 0} \frac{f(h) - f(0)}{h}$$

$$= \lim_{h \to 0} \frac{|h|}{h} = \cdot 1$$

and *L.H.S.* derivative

$$\lim_{h \to 0} \frac{f(0-h) - f(0)}{-h} = \lim_{h \to 0} \frac{|-h| - 0}{-h} = - \lim_{h \to 0} \frac{|h|}{h} = -1$$

Here $\lim_{h \to 0} \frac{f(0+h) - f(0)}{h} \neq \lim_{h \to 0} \frac{f(0-h) - f(0)}{-h}$

Thus the given function is continuous at the point $x = 0$ but not differentiable at that point.

26

DE (Differential Equation)

To solve any diffeerential quation we mean to find the relation between x, y and *constant*.

We have different methods for solving any *DE*.

(1) By trial (2) By variable seperable

(3) Homogeneous equation (4) linear equation

Verification of the solution of differential equation

Problem 1 Verify that $y = ce^{-x}$ is the solution of the differential equation

$$y' + y = 0$$

Solution

$$y' = \frac{dy}{dx}$$

$$\frac{dy}{dx} + y = 0$$

$$L.H.S. = \frac{dy}{dx} + y = \frac{d}{dx}(ce^{-x}) + ce^{-x}$$

$$= ce^{-x}(-1) + ce^{-x} = -ce^{-x} + ee^{-x} = 0$$

Therefore $y = ce^{-x}$ is the solution of the given differential equation $y' + y = 0$

Problem 2 Verify that $y = A \cos 2x + B \sin 2x$

$$\left[\text{Where} \qquad y' = \frac{d^2y}{dx^2}\right]$$

is the solution $y'' + 4y = 0$

Solution $y'' + 4y = \frac{d^2y}{dx^2} + 4y = \frac{d}{dx}\left(\frac{dy}{dx}\right) + 4y$

$$= \frac{d}{dx}[-2A \sin 2x + 2B \cos 2x] + 4y$$

$$= -2A\, 2 \cos 2x + 2B(-2) \sin 2x + 4y$$

$$= -4A \cos 2x - 4B \sin 2x + 4y$$

$$= -4(A \cos 2x + B \sin 2x) + 4y = -4y + 4y = 0$$

i.e. $y = A \cos 2x + B \sin 2x$ is the solution of $y'' + 4y = 0$

Variable separable method

If x and y are two variabies and a equation is of the form

$$\frac{dy}{dx} = \frac{f(y)}{f(x)}$$

then taking the variable of x on one side and variable of y on other side is known as seperation of the variables and then integrating we find the solution.

Problem 3 Solve $(1 + y^2)\, dy = x^2\, dx$

Solution Integrating both sides

$$\int (1 + y^2)\, dy = \int x^2\, dx$$

$$y + \frac{y^3}{3} = \frac{x^3}{3} + C \qquad \textbf{Ans.}$$

Problem 4 Solve $(1 + \cos x)\, dy = (1 - \cos x)\, dx$

$$2 \cos^2 x/2\, dy = 2 \sin^2 x^2/2\, dx$$

$$dy = \frac{\sin^2 x/2}{\cos^2 x/2}\, dx$$

$$dy = \tan^2 x/2\, dx$$

$$dy = (\sec^2 x/2 - 1)\, dx$$

$$\int dy = \int \sec^2 x/2\, dx - \int dx$$

$$y = 2 \tan x/2 - x + c$$

$$\boxed{y = 2 \tan x/2 - x + c} \qquad \textbf{Ans.}$$

Problem 4 $(x^2 - yx^2)\, dy + (y^2 + x^2 y^2)\, dy = 0$

Solution $x^2 (1 - y)\, dy + y^2 (1 + x^2)\, dx = 0$

$$x^2 (1 - y)\, dy = -y^2 (1 + x^2)\, dx$$

$$\frac{(1 - y)\, dy}{y^2} = -\left(\frac{1 + x^2}{x^2}\right) dx$$

$$\left(\frac{1}{y^2} - \frac{1}{y}\right) dy = -\frac{1}{x^2}\, dx - dx$$

We have $\int y^{-2}\, dy - \int \frac{dy}{y} = \int x^{-2}\, dx - \int dx$

$$\frac{y^{-2}+1}{-2+1} - \log y = -\frac{x^{-2}+1}{-2+1} - x$$

$$c + \frac{y^{-1}}{-1} - \log y = -\frac{x^{-1}}{-1} - x$$

$$c - \frac{1}{y} - \log y = \frac{1}{x} - x$$

$$c = \frac{1}{x} + \frac{1}{y} + \log y - x \qquad \textbf{Ans.}$$

Problem 6 Solve: $\sec^2 x \tan y\, dx + \sec^2 y \tan x dy = 0$

Solution Dividing throughout by $\tan x \tan y$ we have

$$\frac{\sec^2 x \tan y dx}{\tan x \tan y} + \frac{\sec^3 y \tan x dy}{\tan x \tan y} = 0.$$

$$\frac{\sec^2 x dx}{\tan x} + \frac{\sec^2 y dx}{\tan y} = 0$$

Integrating both sides $\int \frac{\sec^2 x dx}{\tan x} + \int \frac{\sec^2 y}{\tan y}\, dy = \int 0$

$$I_1 + I_2 = \int 0$$

$$I_1 = \int \frac{\sec^2 x dx}{\tan x}$$

Let $\tan x = t$

$$\sec^2 x dx = di$$

$$I_1 = \int \frac{dt}{t} = \log t$$

$$= \log \tan x$$

$$I_2 = \log \tan y$$

$$\log \tan x + \log \tan y = \log c$$

$$\log \tan x \tan y = \log c$$

$$\boxed{\tan x \tan y = c}$$

which is the required solution

Problem 7 Solve $\frac{dy}{dx} + \sqrt{\frac{1-y^2}{1-x^2}} = 0$

$$\frac{dy}{dx} = -\frac{\sqrt{1-y^2}}{\sqrt{1-x^2}}$$

$$\int \frac{dx}{\sqrt{1-x^2}} = \sin^{-1} x$$

$$\frac{dy}{\sqrt{1-y^2}} = - \frac{dx}{\sqrt{1-x^2}}$$

$$\int \frac{dy}{\sqrt{1-y^2}} + \int \frac{dx}{\sqrt{1-x^2}} = \int 0$$

$$\boxed{\sin^{-1} y + \sin^{-1} x = c}$$

Required solution of the given differential equation.

Problem 7 Solve $y^1 = (1 + x)(1 + y^2)$

Solution $$\frac{dy}{dx} = (1 + x)(1 + y^2)$$

$$\frac{dy}{1 + y^2} = (1 + x)\, dx$$

$$\int \frac{dy}{1 + y^2} = \int (1 + x)\, dx$$

$$\tan^{-1} y = x + \frac{x^2}{2} + c \qquad \textbf{Ans.}$$

Problem 8 Solve $\left(y - x\frac{dy}{dx}\right) = a\left(y^2 + \frac{dy}{dx}\right)$

Solution $$y - x\frac{dy}{dx} = ay^2 + a\frac{dy}{dx}$$

$$y - ay^2 = a\frac{dy}{dx} + x\frac{dy}{dx}$$

$$y(1 - ay) = \frac{dy}{dx}(a + x)$$

$$\frac{dx}{a + x} = \frac{dy}{y(1 - ay)}$$

Integrating both sides

$$\int \frac{dx}{a + x} = \int \frac{dy}{y(1 - ay)}$$

$$\log (a + x) = I + c \qquad (1)$$

$$I = \int \frac{dy}{y(1 - ay)}$$

$$\frac{1}{y(1 - y)} \equiv \frac{A}{y} + \frac{B}{(1 - ay)}$$

$$\frac{1}{y(1 - ay)} = \frac{A(1 - ay) + By}{y(1 - ay)}$$

$$A(1 - ay) + By \equiv 1$$

Putting $$y = \frac{1}{a}$$

$$A\left(1-a\cdot\frac{1}{a}\right)+\frac{B1}{a} = 1$$

$$B\cdot\frac{1}{a} = 1$$

$$\Rightarrow \quad B = a \qquad A = 1$$

$$B = a$$

Put $$y = 0$$

$$A(1-0) + B\cdot 0 = 1$$

$$A = 1$$

$$\frac{1}{y\,(1-ay)} = \frac{1}{y} + \frac{a}{(1-ay)}$$

$$\int\frac{dy}{y\,(1-a)} = \int\frac{dy}{y} + \int\frac{ady}{(1-ay)}$$

$$I = \log y + a\,\frac{\log(1-ay)}{-a}$$

$$I = \log y - \log(1-ay) \tag{2}$$

Substituting the value of I from (2) in (1)

$$\log(a+x) = \log y - \log(1-ay) + \log c$$

$$\log(a+x) - \log y + \log(1-ay) = \log c$$

$$\log\frac{(a+x)(1-ay)}{y} = \log c$$

$$\frac{(a+x)(1-ay)}{y} = c$$

$$[\log m + \log n = \log m\cdot n,\ \log m - \log n = \log m/n]$$

$$\Rightarrow \quad \boxed{(a+x)(1-ay) = cy}$$

Which is the required solution

Homogeneous equation

If the power of N^r and D^r are same then we say that differential equation is Homgeneous

$$\frac{dy}{dx} = \frac{2xy}{x^2+y^2} \text{ (Homogeneous)}$$

$$\frac{dy}{dx} = \frac{2x}{x^2+y^2} \text{ (non Homogeneous)}$$

$$\frac{dy}{dx} = \frac{x^3}{x^3+3x^2y+y^3} \text{(Homogeneous)}$$

Method for solving Homogeneous equation

Put $$y = vx$$

$$\left.\frac{dy}{dx} = v + x\frac{dv}{dx}\right]$$

Problem 10 Solve $x^2 y^1 = x^2 + xy + y^2$

$$x^2 \frac{dy}{dx} = x^2 + xy + y^2$$

$$\frac{dy}{dx} = \frac{x^2 + xy + y^2}{x^2}$$

Solution So the given differential equation is a Homogeneous equation. Therefore substituting

$$y = v\,x \text{ and}$$

$$\frac{dy}{dx} = v + x\frac{dv}{dx} \quad \text{we have}$$

$$v + x\frac{dv}{dx} = \frac{x^2 + x \cdot vx + v^2 x^2}{x^2}$$

$$v + x\frac{dv}{dx} = \frac{x^2 + vx^2 + v^2 x^2}{x^2}$$

$$v + x\frac{dv}{dx} = \frac{x^2(1 + v + v^2)}{x^2}$$

$$v + x\frac{dv}{dx} = 1 + v + v^2$$

$$x\frac{dv}{dx} = 1 + v^2$$

$$x\frac{dv}{dx} = 1 + v^2$$

$$\frac{dv}{1 + v^2} = \frac{dx}{x}$$

$$\int \frac{dv}{1 + v^2} = \int \frac{dx}{x}$$

$$y = vx$$

$$\frac{y}{x} = v$$

$$\tan^{-1} v = \log x + c$$

$$\tan^{-1}\frac{y}{x} = \log x + c \qquad \textbf{Ans.}$$

Linear differential equation

Any equation of the form

$$\frac{dy}{dx} + Py = Q \tag{1}$$

Where P and Q are either constants or functions of x.

$$\frac{dy}{dx} + 2y = 3 \text{ (linear)}$$

$$\frac{dy}{dx} + 2y = x \text{ (linear)}$$

$$\frac{dy}{dx} + 3x\,y = x \text{ (linear)}$$

$$\frac{dy}{dx} + x^2\,y = 1 \text{ (linear)}$$

Equation (1) is said to be a linear equation in y

$$\frac{dx}{dy} + Px = Q$$

Where P and Q are either constant or function of y (linear in x).

Example

$$\frac{dy}{dx} + (\sin x)\,y = 2 \text{ linear)}$$

$$\frac{dy}{dx} + (\sin x)\,y = \cos x \text{ (linear)}$$

Method of Solution

At first we find Integrating factor (I.F)

$$\text{IF} = e^{\int p \cdot dx}$$ (Remember)

Solution is $\boxed{y\,IF = \int Q \cdot IF \cdot dx}$

Problem 1 Solve $\frac{dy}{dx} + 1\,y = \sin x$

Solution $P = 1 \qquad Q = \sin x$

$$IF = e^{\int p\,dx} = e^{\int 1\,dx} = e^{\int dx} = e^x$$

$$y \cdot IF = \int QIF\, dx$$

$$y \cdot e^x = \int \sin x \cdot e^x\, dx$$

$$ye^x = I \qquad (1)$$

$$I = \int \sin x \cdot e^x\, dx$$

$$= e^x \cdot (-\cos x) - \int e^x (-\cos x)\, dx$$

$$= -e^x \cos x + \int e^x \cos x\, dx$$

$$I = -e^x \cos x + e^x \cdot \sin x - \int e^x \sin x\, dx$$

$$2I = e^x (\sin x - \cos x) \Rightarrow I = e^x \frac{(\sin x - \cos x)}{2}$$

$$y \cdot e^x = \frac{e^x}{2} (\sin x - \cos x) + c$$

$$y = \frac{\sin x - \cos y}{2} + ce^{-x} \qquad \textbf{Ans.}$$

Problem 11 Solve

$$(3xy + y^2)\, dx + (x^2 + xy)\, dy = 0$$

$$(x^2 + xy)\, dy = -(3xy + y^2)\, dx$$

$$\frac{dy}{dx} = -\frac{(3xy + y^2)}{(x^2 + xy)} \text{ (Homogeneous equation)}$$

Now putting $\quad y = vx$

and $\quad \frac{dy}{dx} = v + x\left|\frac{dv}{dx}\right|$

$$v + x\frac{dv}{dx} = -\frac{[3 \cdot x \cdot vx + v^2 x^2]}{[x^2 + x \cdot vx]}$$

$$v + x\frac{dv}{dx} = -\frac{x^2 [3v + v^2]}{x^2 [1 + v]}$$

$$v + x\frac{dv}{dx} = -\frac{(3v + v^2)}{(1 + v)}$$

$$v + x\frac{dv}{dx} = -\frac{v(3 + v)}{(1 + v)}$$

$$x\frac{dv}{dx} = -\frac{v(3 + v)}{(1 + v)} - v$$

$$x\frac{dv}{dx} = -v\left[\frac{v + 3}{1 + v} + 1\right]$$

$$x\frac{dv}{dx} = -v\left[\frac{3 + v + 1 + v}{1 + v}\right]$$

$$x\frac{dv}{dx} = -v\left[\frac{4+2v}{(1+v)}\right]$$

$$x\frac{dv}{dx} = -\frac{2\cdot v\,[2+v]}{1+v)}$$

$$\frac{(1+v)\,dv}{v\,(v+2)} = -\frac{2dx}{x}$$

Integrating both sides

$$\int\frac{(1+v)}{v(v+2)}\,dv = -\int 2\,\frac{dx}{x}$$

$$I = -2\int\frac{dx}{x} = -2\log x + c$$

Where $\qquad I = \int\frac{1+v}{v\,(v+2)}\,dv$

$$\frac{1+v}{v\,(v+2)} = \frac{1}{v\,(v+2)} + \frac{v}{v\,(v+2)}$$

$$\int\frac{1+v}{v\,(v+2)}\,dv = \int\frac{1}{(v\,(v+2)}\,dv + \int\frac{1}{v+2}\,dv \qquad (1)$$

$$\frac{1}{v\,(v+2)} = \frac{A}{v} + \frac{B}{v+2} = \frac{A\,(v+2) + Bv}{v\,(v+2)}$$

$$\frac{1}{v\,(v+2)} = \frac{A\,(v+2) + Bv}{v\,(v+2)}$$

$$A\,(v+2) + Bv = 1$$

Put $\qquad v = 0$

$$2A = 1 \quad \Rightarrow \quad A = \tfrac{1}{2}$$

$$\Rightarrow \qquad B = -\tfrac{1}{2}$$

$$\frac{1}{v\,(v+2)} = \frac{1}{2v} + \left(-\frac{1}{2}\right)\frac{1}{(v+2)}$$

$$= \frac{1}{2v} - \frac{1}{2\,(v+2)}$$

$$\int\frac{1+v}{v\,(v+2)}\,dv = \int\frac{1}{2v}\,dv - \int\frac{1}{2\,(v+2)}\,dv + \int\frac{1}{v+2}\,dv$$

$$I = \tfrac{1}{2}\log v - \tfrac{1}{2}\log(v+2) + \log(v+2)$$

$$= \tfrac{1}{2}\log v + \tfrac{1}{2}\log(v+2)$$

$$= \tfrac{1}{2}[\log v + \log(v+2)] = \tfrac{1}{2}\log v\,(v+2)$$

$$\tfrac{1}{2}\log v\,(v+2) = -\,2\log x + c$$

$$\frac{1}{2}\ \log\ \frac{y}{x}\left(\frac{y}{x}+2\right) = -\,2\log x + c$$

$$\frac{1}{2}\log\frac{y}{x}\left(\frac{y+2x}{x}\right) = -\,2\log x + c$$

$$\frac{1}{2}\log\left(\frac{y^2+2xy}{x^2}\right) = -\,2\log x + c \qquad \textbf{Ans.}$$

Problem 12 Solve

$$\frac{dy}{dx} + 2y = 6e^x.$$

$$P = 2,\ Q = 6e^x$$

The given equations is a linear equation

$$IF = e^{\int P\cdot dx} = e^{\int 2\cdot dx} = e^{2x}$$

Solution

$$\boxed{y\ IF = \int Q\cdot IF\cdot dx}$$

$$y\cdot e^{2x} = \int 6e^x\cdot e^{2x}\,dx$$

$$ye^{2x} = 6\int e^{3x}\,dx$$

$$ye^{2x} = 6\,\frac{e^{3x}}{3} + c$$

$$ye^{2x} = 2e^{3x} + c \qquad \textbf{Ans.}$$

27

Integral Calculas

Integration is the opposite process of differentiation:

(1) $\frac{d}{dx}(\sin x) = \cos x$

(2) $\frac{d}{dx}(\cos x) = -\sin x$

(1) $\int \cos x \, dx = \sin x + c$

(2) $\int \sin x = -\cos x + c$

(3) $\int \sec^2 x \, dx = \tan x + c$

(4) $\int \text{cosec}^2 x \, dx = -\cot x + c$

(5) $\int e^x = e^x + c$

(6) $\int \sec x \tan x \, dx = \sec x + c$

(7) $\int \frac{1}{x} dx = \log x$

(8) $\int x^n \, dx = \frac{x^{n+1}}{n+1} + c$

(9) $\int e^{3x} \, dx = \frac{e^{3x}}{3} + c$

(10) $\int \sin 3x \, dx = -\frac{\cos 3x}{3} + c$

(11) $\int (ax + b)^n \, dx = \frac{(ax + b)^{n+1}}{a(n + 1)} + c$

(12) $\int e^{(3x+4)} \, dx = \frac{e^{3x+4}}{3} + c$

Methods of Integrating the functions

(1) Integrating **by substitution**

(2) Integration by parts

(3) Integration by partial fraction

(4) Definite Integral

Integration by substitution

(1) $$I = \int \frac{\log x}{x} dx$$

Let $\log x = t.$

Taking differential we have

$$\frac{1}{x} dx = dt$$

$$I = \int t \, dt$$

$$\boxed{\int x^n \, dx = \frac{x^{n+1}}{n+1}}$$

$$I = \frac{t^{1+1}}{1+1} + c$$

$$I = \frac{(\log x)^2}{2} + c \text{ **Ans.**}$$

(2) $$\int \sqrt{ax+b} \, dx = \int (ax+b)^{(1/2)+1} \, dx$$

$$= \frac{(ax+b)^{1/2+1}}{a\left(\frac{1}{2}+1\right)} + c = \frac{(ax+b)^{3/2}}{a \, 3/2} + c$$

$$= \frac{2}{3a}(ax+b)^{3/2} + c$$

(3) $$\int \frac{\sin(\tan^{-1} x)}{1+x^2} dx$$

let $\tan^{-1} x = t$

$$\frac{1}{(1+x^2)} dx = dt$$

$$I = \int \sin t \, dt$$

$$= -\cos t + c = -\cos(\tan^{-1} x) + c$$ **Ans.**

(4) $$\int \frac{1}{1-\tan x} dx$$ *[Typical Problem]*

$$I = \int \frac{1}{1-\tan x} dx$$

$$I = \int \frac{1}{1 - \frac{\sin x}{\cos x}} dx$$

$$I = \int \frac{\cos x}{\cos - \sin x} dx = \int \frac{\cos x}{\cos x - \sin x} dx$$

$$= \frac{2 \cos x}{2 (\cos x - \sin x)} dx$$ *Note*

$$I = \frac{1}{2} \int \frac{(\cos x - \sin x) + (\cos x + \sin x)}{(\cos x - \sin x)} dx$$

$$I = \frac{1}{2} \int \left[1 + \frac{\cos x + \sin x}{\cos x - \sin x} \right] dx$$

$$I = \frac{1}{2} \left[\int 1\, dx + \int \frac{\cos x + \sin x}{\cos x - \sin x} \right] dx$$

$$I = \frac{1}{2} x + \frac{1}{2} \int \frac{\cos x + \sin x}{\cos x - \sin x} dx$$

$$I = \frac{x}{2} + \frac{1}{2} I_1$$

Where $I_1 = \int \frac{\cos x + \sin x}{\cos x - \sin x} dx$

Let $\cos x - \sin x = t$

$$(-\sin x - \cos x)\, dv = dt$$

$$(\cos x + \sin x)\, dv = dt$$

$$I_1 = \int \frac{-dt}{t} = -\log t$$

$$= -\log (\cos x - \sin x) + c$$

$$I = \frac{x}{2} + \frac{1}{2} \left[-\log (\cos x - \sin x) + c \right]$$

$$I = \frac{x}{2} - \frac{1}{2} \log (\cos x - \sin x) + c$$ **Ans.**

(5) $\int \frac{1}{1 + \tan x} dx$ *[Try yourself]*

Problem 1 $\int x \sqrt{x + 2}\, dx$ *Imp.*

Solution Let $x + 2 = t^2$

$$(1 + 0)\, dx = 2tdt \qquad dx = 2tdt$$

$$\sqrt{x+2} = t$$
$$x + 2 = t^2,\ x = t^2 - 2,\ x + 2 = t^2,\ (x+2)^{1/2} = t,$$
$$t^5 = (x+2)^{5/2},\ t^3 = (x+2)^{3/2}$$

$$I = \int (t^2 - 2)\, t\, 2t dt$$
$$I = 2\int (t^2 - 2)\ \ t^2\, dt$$
$$I = 2\int (t^4 - 2t^2)\, dt$$
$$I = 2\int t^4\, dt - 4\int t^2\, dt$$
$$I = \frac{2t^5}{5} - \frac{4t^3}{3} + c$$
$$I = \frac{2\,(x+2)^{5/2}}{5} - \frac{4}{3}\ (x+2)^{3/2} + c \qquad \textbf{Ans.}$$

Problem 2 $$I = \int \frac{\tan x}{\sec x + \cos x}\, dx$$

Solution $$I = \int \frac{(\sin x)/\cos x}{(1/\cos x) + \cos x}\, dx$$

$$I = \int \frac{(\sin x)/\cos x}{(1 + \cos^2 x)/\cos x}\, dx$$

$$I = \int \frac{\sin x dx}{1 + \cos^2 x}$$

$$\int \frac{dx}{x^2 + a^2} = \frac{1}{a}\ \tan^{-1}\frac{x}{a} + c$$

Let $\cos x = t$

diff $-\sin x dx = dt \qquad \sin x dx = -dt$

$$I = \int \frac{-dt}{1 + t^2} = -\int \frac{dt}{1 + t^2}$$
$$= \int \frac{dt}{1^2 + t^2} = -\frac{1}{1}\ \tan^{-1}\frac{t}{1}\ + c$$
$$= -\tan^{-1}(\cos x) + c \qquad \textbf{Ans.}$$

Problem 3 $\int \frac{1}{(2x-7)^3}\, dx\ \ I = \int (2x-7)^{-3}\, dx$

$$= \frac{(2x-7)^{-3+1}}{2(-3+1)} + c = \frac{(2x-7)^{-2}}{2\,(-2)} + c$$
$$= -\ \frac{(2x-7)^{-2}}{4} + c = -\ \frac{1}{4\,(2x-7)^2} + c \qquad \textbf{Ans.}$$

Problem 4 $$I=\int\frac{dx}{(a\sin x+b\cos x)^2}$$

Solution $$I=\int\frac{dx}{\left[\cos x\left(a\dfrac{\sin x}{\cos x}+b\right)\right]^2}$$

$$I=\int\frac{1\,dx}{\cos^2 x\,(a\tan x+b)^2}$$

$$I=\int\frac{\sec^2 x dx}{(a\tan x+b)^2}$$

Let $a\tan x+b=t$

$$a\sec^2 x dx=dt$$

$$\sec^2 x dx=\frac{dt}{a}$$

$$I=\int\frac{dt}{at^2}=\frac{1}{a}\int t^{-2}\,dt$$

$$=\frac{1}{a}\,\frac{t^{-2+1}}{-2+1}+c=\frac{1}{a}\,\frac{t^{-1}}{-1}+c$$

$$=-\frac{1}{a}\,\frac{1}{(a\tan x+b)}+c \qquad \textbf{Ans.}$$

Problem 5 $$\int\frac{\sec^2 x}{\sqrt{16+\tan^2 x}}\,dx$$

Solution $$I=\int\frac{\sec^2 x dx}{\sqrt{4^2+\tan^2 x}}$$

Let $\tan x=4\tan\theta$

$$\sec^2 x dx=4\sec^2\theta d\theta$$

$$I=\int\frac{4\sec^2\theta d\theta}{\sqrt{4^2+4^2\tan^2\theta}}$$

$$I=\int\frac{4\sec^2\theta\,d\theta}{\sqrt{4^2(1+\tan^2\theta)}}$$

$$I=\int\frac{4\sec^2\theta d\theta}{4\sec\theta}$$

$$I=\int\sec\theta d\theta$$

$$I=\log(\sec\theta+\tan\theta)+c$$

$$\tan x=4\tan\theta$$

$$\Rightarrow \qquad \tan\theta = \frac{\tan x}{}$$

$$\Rightarrow \qquad \tan^2\theta = \frac{\tan^2 x}{16}$$

$$\Rightarrow \qquad 1 + \tan^2\theta = 1 + \frac{\tan^2 x}{16}$$

$$\sec^2\theta = \frac{16 + \tan^2 x}{16}$$

$$\sec\theta = \frac{\sqrt{16 + \tan^2 x}}{4}$$

$$\tan\theta = \frac{\tan x}{4}$$

$$I = \log\left(\frac{\sqrt{16 + \tan^2 x}}{4} + \frac{\tan x}{4}\right) + c \qquad \textbf{Ans.}$$

$$I = \log\left[\frac{\sqrt{16 + \tan^2 x} + \tan x}{4}\right] + c \qquad \textbf{Ans.}$$

Problem 6 $\int \sqrt{a^2 - x^2}\, dx$

Solution Let $x = a\sin\theta$

$$\frac{x}{a} = \sin\theta \quad \Rightarrow \quad \theta = \sin^{-1}\frac{x}{a}$$

$$dx = a\cos\theta d\theta$$

$$I = \int \sqrt{a^2 - a^2\sin^2\theta}\, a\cos\theta d\theta$$

$$I = \int a\cos\theta a\cos\theta d\theta$$

$$I = a^2 \int \cos^2\theta d\theta$$

$$I = \frac{a^2}{2}\int 2\cos^2\theta\, d\theta$$

$$[\sin\theta = x/a,\ \sin^2\theta = x^2/a^2,\ \cos^2\theta = 1 - \sin^2\theta]$$

$$= 1 - x^2/a^2$$

$$2\cos^2\theta = 1 + \cos 2\theta$$

$$I = \frac{a^2}{2}\int (1 + \cos 2\theta)\, d\theta$$

$$I = \frac{a^2}{2}\left[\theta + \frac{\sin 2\theta}{2}\right] + c$$

$$I = \frac{a^2}{2}\left[\sin^{-1}\frac{x}{a} + \frac{2\sin\theta\cos\theta}{2}\right] + c$$

$$I = \frac{a^2}{2}\left[\sin^{-1}\frac{x}{a} + \frac{x}{a}\frac{\sqrt{a^2 - x^2}}{a}\right] + c$$

Problem 7 $\int \frac{dx}{a + b \cos x}$ [*Typical*]

Solution Let $t = \frac{\tan x}{2}$ (1)

$$dt = \sec^2 \frac{x}{2} \; \frac{1}{2} \; dx$$

$\int \frac{dx}{a + b \sin x}$, $\int \frac{\cos x}{1 + \cos^2 x + \tan x} dx$
$dt = \frac{1}{2} \sin^2 \frac{x}{2} dx$

$$\int \frac{\cos x}{1 + \cos^2 x}, \quad \cos 2\theta = \frac{1 - \tan^2 \theta}{1 + \tan^2 \theta}$$

$$dt = \frac{1}{2} \left(1 + \tan^2 \frac{x}{2}\right) dx$$

$$dt = \frac{1}{2} (1 + t^2) \, dx$$

$$\frac{2dt}{1 + t^2} = dx \tag{2}$$

We know $\cos x = \frac{1 - \tan^2 x/2}{1 + \tan^2 x/2}$ [*Formula*]

$$\cos x = \frac{1 - t^2}{1 + t^2}$$

Now the form of Integration changes to

$$I = \int \frac{2dt}{(1 + t^2) \left[a + b \frac{1 - t^2}{1 + t^2} \right]}$$

$$I = \int \frac{2dt}{a (1 + t^2) + b (1 - t^2)}$$

$$I = \int \frac{2dt}{(a + at^2) + b - b + 2}$$

$$I = 2 \int \frac{dt}{(a + b) + \{(a - b) \, t^2\}}$$

$$I = 2 \int \frac{dt}{(\sqrt{a + b})^2 + \{\sqrt{a - bt}\}^2}$$

$$I = 2 \cdot \frac{1}{\sqrt{a+b}\,\sqrt{a-b}} \tan^{-1} \frac{(\sqrt{a-b})\,t}{\sqrt{a+b}} + c$$

$$I = \frac{2}{\sqrt{a^2-b^2}} \tan^{-1} \sqrt{\frac{a-b}{a+b}}\, t + c$$

$$I = \frac{2}{\sqrt{a^2-b^2}} \tan^{-1} \sqrt{\frac{a-b}{a+b}} \tan \frac{x}{2} + c \qquad \textbf{Ans.}$$

$$\boxed{\sin x = \frac{2 \tan x/2}{1+\tan^2 x/2} = \frac{2t}{1+t^2}}$$

Define Integral, we deflnite

$$\int_a^b f(x)\, dx = \Big[F(x) \Big]_a^b = F(b) - F(a)$$

If a and b are *finite* definite then integral is known as finite *integral.*

Evaluate $\displaystyle \int_0^{\pi} \frac{dx}{5 + 4 \cos x} \Big]$

Let $\displaystyle t = \tan \frac{x}{2}\; dt \Rightarrow \sec \frac{2x}{2} \cdot \frac{1}{2}\, dx = dt$

$$dt = \left(1 + \tan^2 \frac{x}{2}\right) \frac{1}{2}\, dx$$

$$dt = (1 + t^2) \frac{1}{2}\, dx$$

$$\frac{2dt}{1+t^2} = dx$$

Limits

when	$x = 0$	$x = \pi$
	$t = \tan \frac{x}{2}$	$t = \tan \frac{\pi}{2}$
	$t = \tan \frac{0}{2}$	$t = \tan 90$
	$= 0$	$t = \infty$

lower $lt = 0$ upper $lt = \infty$

Integration $\displaystyle I = \int_0^{\infty} \frac{2dt}{(1+t^2)\left[5 + 4\,\dfrac{1-t^2}{1+t^2}\right]}$

$$\cos x = \frac{1-\tan^2 x/2}{1+\tan^2 x/2} = \frac{1-t^2}{1+t^2}$$

$$= \int_0^\infty \frac{2dt}{5(1+t^2)+4(1-t^2)}$$

$$= \int_0^\infty \frac{2dt}{5+5t^2+4-4t^2} = \int_0^\infty \frac{2dt}{9+t^2}$$

$$= \int_0^\infty \frac{dt}{3^2+t^2} = 2\frac{1}{3}\left[\tan^{-1}\frac{t}{3}\right]_0^\infty$$

$$\tan\frac{\pi}{2} = \infty, \frac{\pi}{2} = \tan^{-1}\infty, \tan = 0 \tan^{-1} 0 = 0$$

$$= \frac{2}{3}\left[\tan^{-1}\frac{\infty}{3} - \tan^{-1}\frac{0}{3}\right] = \frac{2}{3}[\tan^{-1}\infty - \tan^{-1} 0]$$

$$= \frac{2}{3}\left[\frac{\pi}{2} - 0\right] = \frac{2}{3} \times \frac{\pi}{2} = \frac{\pi}{3}$$ **Ans.**

Problem 8 $\int_0^1 \frac{dx}{1+x^2} = \left[\tan^{-1} x\right]_0^1$

Solution $\int \frac{dx}{1+x^2} = \tan^{-1} x$

$$= \tan^{-1} 1 - \tan^{-1} 0 = \frac{\pi}{4} - 0 = \frac{\pi}{4}$$ **Ans.**

$$\tan\frac{\pi}{4} = 1 \tan 0 = 0$$

when $x = 1 \quad \tan\theta = 1$

Problem 9 Evaluate $\int_0^1 \frac{dx}{1+x^2}$

$x = 0$

Solution Let $x = \tan\theta$

$$dx = \sec^2\theta \, d\theta$$

$$x = \tan\theta$$

$$I = \int_0^{\pi/4} \tan x \, dx$$

$$I = \left[\log \sec x\right]_0^{\pi/4} = \log\sec\frac{\pi}{4} - \log\sec 0$$

$$= \log\sqrt{2} - \log 1 = \log\sqrt{2} - 0$$

$$\log 1 = 0$$

$$= \log(2)^{1/2} = \frac{1}{2}\log 2$$

$$\log m^n = n \log m$$

Properties of Definite Integral

(1) $$\int_a^b f(x)\,dx = -\int_b^a f(x)\,dx$$

(2) $$\int_a^b f(x)\,dx = \int_a^c f(x)\,dx + \int_c^b f(x)\,dx$$

if $a < c < b$

(3) $$\int_a^a f(x)\,dx = 0$$

(4) $$\int_0^a f(x)\,dx = \int_0^a f(a-x)\,dx$$

(5) $$\int_{-a}^{+a} f(x)\,dx = 2\int_0^a f(x)\,dx \quad \text{if } f(x) \text{ is even}$$

$f(x) = x^2 \quad f(-x) = (-x)^2 = x^2 \quad f(-x) = f(x) \rightarrow f$ is even

$f(-x) = -f(x) - f$ is odd

Problem 10 $\int_0^{\pi/2} \frac{\sin x}{\sin x\ x + \cos x}\,dx = \frac{\pi}{4}$

Solution

$$I = \int_0^{\pi/2} \frac{\sin x}{\sin x + \cos x}\,dx \tag{1}$$

$$I = \int_0^{\pi/2} \frac{\sin(\pi/2-x)}{\sin(\pi/2-x) + \cos(\pi/2-x)}\,dx$$

$$I = \int_0^{\pi/2} \frac{\cos x}{\cos x + \sin x}\,dx = \int_0^{\pi/2} \frac{\cos x}{\sin x + \cos x} \tag{2}$$

adding (1) and (2)

$$2I = \int_0^{\pi/2} \left[\frac{\sin x}{\sin x + \cos x} + \frac{\cos x}{\sin x + \cos x}\right] dx$$

$$2I = \int_0^{\pi/2} \left[\frac{\sin x + \cos x}{\sin x + \cos x}\right] dx$$

$$2I = \int_0^{\pi/2} dx$$

$$2I = \Big[\,x\,\Big]_0^{\pi/2}$$

$$\Rightarrow \quad 2I = \frac{\pi}{2} - 0 = \frac{\pi}{2}$$

$$2I = \frac{\pi}{2} \quad \Rightarrow \quad I = \frac{\pi}{4}$$

Problem 11 Prove that $\int_0^{\pi/2} \log \tan x \, dx = 0$

$$I = \int_0^{\pi/2} \log \tan x \, dx \qquad (1)$$

$$I = \int_0^{\pi/2} \log \tan (\pi/2 - x) \, dx$$

$$I = \int_0^{\pi/2} \log \cot x \, dx \qquad (2)$$

Adding (1) and (2)

$$2I = \int_0^{\pi/2} [\log \tan x + \log \cot x] \, dx$$

$$2I = \int_0^{\pi/2} \log (\tan x \cdot \cot x) \, dx$$

| $\log 1 = 0$ |

$$2I = \int_0^{\pi/2} \log \left(\frac{\sin x}{\cos x} \cdot \frac{\cot x}{\sin x} \right) dx$$

$$2I = \int_0^{\pi\ 2} \log 1 \, dx$$

$$2I = 0 \quad \Rightarrow \quad I = 0 \qquad \textit{(Proved)}$$

Problem 12 $I = \int_0^{\pi/4} \log (1 + \tan x) \, dx$

Solution $I = \int_0^{\pi/4} \log \left[1 + \tan \left(\frac{\pi}{4} - x \right) \right] dx$

$$I = \int_0^{\pi/4} \log [1 + \tan (45 - x)] \, dx$$

$$I = \int_0^{\pi/4} \log \left[1 + \frac{\tan 45 - \tan x}{1 + \text{ton } 45 \tan x} \right] dx$$

| $\tan (A - B) = \frac{\tan A - \tan B}{1 + \tan A \tan B}$ |

$$I = \int_0^{\pi/4} \log \left[1 + \frac{1 - \tan x}{1 + \tan x} \right] dx$$

$$I = \int_0^{\pi/4} \text{iog} \left[\frac{1 + \tan x + 1 - \tan x}{1 + \tan x} \right] dx$$

$$I = \int_0^{\pi/4} \log \left[\frac{2}{1 + \tan x} \right] dx$$

$$I = \int_0^{\pi/4} \log 2 - \log (1 + \tan x)]\, dx$$

$$I = \int_0^{\pi/4} \log 2\, dx - \int_0^{\pi/4} \log (1 + \tan x)\, dx$$

$$I = \log 2 \int_0^{\pi/4} dx - I$$

$$2I = \log 2 \left(x \right)_0^{\pi/4}$$

$$2I = \log 2 \left(\frac{\pi}{4} - 0\right)$$

$$2I = \frac{\pi}{4} \log 2$$

$$I = \frac{\pi}{8} \log 2 \qquad \textbf{Ans.}$$

Problem 13 $\int_{-\pi/2}^{\pi/\pi} \sin^2 x\, dx$

Solution $f(x) = \sin^2 x \quad f(-x) = [\sin (-x)]^2 = [-\sin x]^2$

$= \sin^2 x = f(x) \quad f(x)$ is even function

$$\int_{-\pi/2}^{\pi/2} \sin^2 x\, dx = 2 \int_0^{\pi/2} \sin^2 x\, dx \qquad \textbf{Prop. (5)}$$

$$= \int_0^{\pi/2} 2 \sin^2 x\, dx = \int_0^{\pi/2} (1 - \cos 2x)\, dx$$

$$= \left[x - \frac{\sin 2x}{2} \right]_0^{\pi/2}$$

$$\sin \pi = 0 = \left(\frac{\pi}{2} - \frac{\sin 2 \cdot \pi/2}{2}\right) - \left(0 - \frac{\sin 0}{2}\right)$$

$$= \left(\frac{\pi}{2} - \frac{0}{2}\right) = \frac{\pi}{2}$$

$$\int_{-\pi/2}^{\pi/2} \sin^2 x\, dx = \frac{\pi}{2} \qquad \textbf{Ans.}$$

Special Integrals

(1) $$\int \frac{dx}{x^2 - a^2}$$

$$I = \int \frac{dx}{(x-a)(x+a)} \tag{1}$$

$$\int \frac{dx}{x} = \log x \quad \int \frac{dx}{x+a} = \log (x+a), \int \frac{dx}{x-a} = \log (x-a)$$

$$\frac{1}{(x-a)(x+a} \equiv \frac{A}{(x-a)} + \frac{B}{(x+a)} \text{ (Rule)}$$

$$\frac{1}{(x-a)(x+a)} \equiv \frac{A(x+a) + B(x-a)}{(x-a)(x+a)}$$

$$A(x+a) + B(x-a) \equiv 1$$

Put $x = a$

$$2a\,A = 1$$

$$\Rightarrow A = \frac{1}{2a}$$

Put $x = -a$

$$B(-a-a) = 1$$

$$-2a\,B = 1$$

$$\Rightarrow B = -\frac{1}{2a}$$

$$\frac{1}{(x-a)(x+a)} = \frac{1}{2a(x-a)} - \frac{1}{2a(x+a)}$$

$$I = \int \left[\frac{1}{2a(x-a)} - \frac{1}{2a(x+a)}\right] dx$$

$$= \frac{1}{2a}\left[\int \frac{dx}{x-a} - \int \frac{dx}{x+a}\right]$$

$$= \frac{1}{2a}[\log(x-a) - \log(x+a)] + c$$

$$= \frac{1}{2a} \log \left|\frac{x-a}{x+a}\right| + c$$

$$\log m - \log n = \log \frac{m}{n}$$

$$\int \frac{dx}{x^2 - a^2} = \frac{1}{2a} \log \left|\frac{x-a}{x+a}\right| + c$$

(2) $$\int \frac{dx}{a^2 - x^2} = \int \frac{dx}{(a-x)(a+x)}$$

$$\frac{1}{(a-x)(a+x)} = \frac{A}{(a-x)} + \frac{B}{(a+x)}$$

$$= \frac{1}{2a} \log \left|\frac{a+x}{a-x}\right| + c$$

(3) $$\int \frac{dx}{\sqrt{x^2-a^2}} = \log|x+\sqrt{x^2-a^2}| + c$$

Let $$x = a \sec\theta$$

$$dx = a\sec\theta\tan\theta\, d\theta$$

$$I = \int \frac{a\sec\theta\tan\theta\, d\theta}{\sqrt{a^2(\sec^2\theta-1)}}$$

$$I = \int \frac{a\sec\theta\tan\theta\, d\theta}{a\tan\theta}$$

$$I = \int \sec\theta\, d\theta$$

$$I = \log(\sec\theta + \tan\theta) + c$$

$$I = \log\left[\frac{x}{a} + \frac{\sqrt{x^2-a^2}}{a}\right] + c$$

$$I = \log\left[\frac{x+\sqrt{x^2-a^2}}{a}\right] + c$$

$$I = \log|x+\sqrt{x^2-a^2}| - \log a + c$$

$$I = \log|x+\sqrt{x^2-a^2}| + c$$ (*Proved*)

$x = a\sec\theta \quad \frac{x}{a} = \sec\theta \quad \frac{x^2}{a^2} = \sec^2\theta$
$\frac{x^2}{a^2} - 1 = \sec^2\theta - 1 \quad \frac{\sqrt{x^2-a^2}}{a} = \tan\theta$
$\frac{x^2-a^2}{a^2} = \tan^2\theta$

(4) $$\int \frac{dx}{\sqrt{x^2+a^2}} = \log|x+\sqrt{x^2+a^2}| + c$$

$$x = a\cot\theta$$

$$dx = -a\,\text{cosec}^2\theta\, d\theta$$

$$I = \int \frac{-a\,\text{cosec}^2\theta\, d\theta}{\sqrt{a^2(\cot^2\theta+1)}}$$

$$I = -\int \frac{a\,\text{cosec}^2\theta\, d\theta}{a\,\text{cosec}\,\theta}$$

$$I = -\int \text{cosec}\,\theta\, d\theta$$

$$I = +\log(\text{cosec}\,\theta + \cot\theta) + c$$

$$x = a \cot \theta$$

$$\Rightarrow \frac{x^2}{a^2} = \cot^2 \theta \qquad \Rightarrow \qquad 1 + \frac{x^2}{a^2} = 1 + \cot^2 \theta$$

$$\Rightarrow \frac{x^2 + a^2}{a^2} = \operatorname{cosec}^2 \theta$$

$$\frac{\sqrt{x^2 + a^2}}{a} = \operatorname{cosec} \theta$$

$$= \log \left(\frac{\sqrt{x^2 + a^2}}{a} + \frac{x}{a} \right) + c$$

$$= \log (x + \sqrt{x^2 + a^2}) + c$$

Problem 14 Evaluate

$$= \int \frac{dx}{\sqrt{4 + x^2}}$$

$$I = \int \frac{dx}{\sqrt{2^2 + x^2}}$$

$$x = 2 \tan \theta$$

$$dx = 2 \sec^2 \theta \, d\theta$$

$$I = \int \frac{2 \sec^2 \theta \, d\theta}{\sqrt{2^2 + 2^2 \tan^2 \theta}}$$

$$I = \int \frac{2 \sec^2 \theta \, d\theta}{\sqrt{2^2 (1 + \tan^2 \theta)}}$$

$$I = \int \frac{\sec^2 \theta \, d\theta}{\sec \theta}$$

$$I = \int \sec \theta \, d\theta$$

$$I = \log (\sec \theta + \tan \theta) + c$$

$$I = \log \left(\frac{\sqrt{x^2 + 2^2}}{2} + \frac{x}{2} \right) + c$$

$$I = \log (\sqrt{x^2 + 4} + x) + c \qquad \textbf{Ans.}$$

Problem 15 $\int \frac{1}{x^2 + 4x + 7} \, dx$

$$x^2 + 4x + 7 = x^2 + 2 \cdot 2x + (2)^2 + 3 = (x + 2)^2 + 3$$

$$= (x + 2)^2 + (\sqrt{3})^2$$

$$\int \frac{dx}{a^2+x^2} = \frac{1}{a} \tan^{-1} \frac{x}{a}$$

$$\int \frac{dx}{(x+2)^2 + (\sqrt{3})^2} = \frac{1}{\sqrt{3}} \tan^{-1} \frac{x+2}{\sqrt{3}} + c$$

$$= \frac{1}{\sqrt{3}} \tan^{-1} \frac{x+2}{\sqrt{3}} + c \qquad \textbf{Ans.}$$

Problem 16 $\int \frac{1}{9x^2 + 6x + 2}$

$$9x^2 + 6x + 1 = (3x)^2 + 2 \cdot 3x + 1^2 = (3x+1)^2$$

$$\int \frac{dx}{a^2 + x^2} = \frac{1}{a} \tan^{-1} \frac{x}{a}$$

$$\int \frac{dx}{3x+1)^2} = \int (3x+1)^{-2}\, dx$$

$$= \frac{(3x+1)^{-2+1}}{3(-2+1)} + c \qquad \int x^n = \frac{x^{n+1}}{n+1}$$

$$= \frac{(3x+1)^{-1}}{3(-1)} = -\frac{1}{3(3x+1)} + c \qquad \textbf{Ans.}$$

Problem 17 $\int \frac{dx}{3x^2 + 13x - 10} = 3\left(x^2 + \frac{13x}{3} - \frac{10}{3}\right)$

$$= 3\left[x^2 + \frac{2 \cdot 13}{6} x + \left(\frac{13}{6}\right)^2 - \left(\frac{13}{6}\right)^2 - \frac{10}{3}\right]$$

$$= 3\left[\left(x + \frac{13}{6}\right)^2 - \frac{169}{36} - \frac{10}{3}\right]$$

$$3\left[\left(x + \frac{13}{6}\right)^2 - \frac{289}{36}\right] = 3\left[\left(x + \frac{13}{6}\right)^2 - \left(\frac{14}{6}\right)^2\right]$$

(1) $\int \cos^3 x dx$
(2) $\int \sin^3 x dx$] *same type* *(Try yourself*

$$\int \sin ax\, dx = -\frac{\cos ax}{a}$$

Let $I = \int \cos^3 x dx$

we have $\cos 3x = 4\cos^3 x - 3\cos x$

$$\cos 3x + 3\cos x = 4\cos^3 x$$

$$\frac{\cos 3x + 3\cos x}{4} = \cos^3 x$$

$$I = \int \frac{(\cos 3x + 3\cos x)\,dx}{4}$$

$$= \frac{1}{4}\left[\int \cos\ 3x dx + 3\int \cos\ x dx\right]$$

$$= \frac{1}{4}\left[\frac{\sin 3x}{3} + 3\sin x\right] + c$$

$$= \frac{1}{4}\left[\frac{\sin 3x + 9\sin x}{3}\right] + c$$

$$= \frac{\sin 3x + 9\sin x}{12} + c \qquad \textbf{Ans.}$$

Problem 18 $\int \sin^3 x dx$

$$\sin 3x = 3\sin x - 4\sin^3 x$$

$$4\sin^3 x = 3\sin x - \sin 3x$$

$$\sin^3 x = \frac{3\sin x - \sin 3x}{4}$$

[*Same approach*]

Problem 19 $\int \sin^3 x \cos^3 x dx$

$$I = \int \sin^3 x \cdot \cos^2 x \cdot \cos x dx$$

$$I = \int \sin^3 x\,(1 - \sin^2 x)\cos x dx$$

Solution Let $\sin x = t$

$$\cos x dx = dt$$

$$I = \int t^3 (1 - t^2)\,dt$$

$$= \int t^3\,dt - \int t^5 dt = \frac{t^4}{4} - \frac{t^6}{6} + c$$

$$= \frac{\sin^4 x}{4} - \frac{\sin^6 x}{6} + c$$

Problem 20 $\int \cos 2x \cos 4x \cos 6\, x dx$

$$= \frac{1}{2}\int 2\cos 2x \cos 4x \cos 6\, x dx$$

Solution $2\cos A \cos B = \cos(A + B) + \cos(A - B)$

$$= \frac{1}{2}\int [\cos 6x + \cos 2x]\cos 6x\,dx$$

$$= \frac{1}{2}\int \cos^2 6x dx + \frac{1}{2}\int \cos 2x \cdot \cos 6\, x dx$$

$\boxed{2\cos^2 A = 1 + \cos 2A}$

$$= \frac{1}{2 \times 2}\int 2\cos^2 6x\,dx + \frac{1}{2 \times 2}\int 2\cos 2x \cos 6x\,dx$$

$$= \frac{1}{4}\int [1 + \cos 12x]\,dx + \frac{1}{4}\int [\cos 8x + \cos 4x]\,dx$$

$$= \frac{1}{4}\left[x + \frac{\sin 12x}{12}\right] + \frac{1}{4}\left[\frac{\sin 8x}{8} + \frac{\sin 4x}{4}\right] + c$$

Problem 21 $= \int \frac{(1-\cos x)}{(1+\cos x)}\,dx = \int \frac{2\sin^2 x/2}{2\cos^2 x/2}\,dx$

Solution $\boxed{1 - \cos x = 2\sin^2 x/2,\ 1 + \cos x = 2\cos^2 x/2}$

$$I = \int \tan^2 x/2\,dx$$

$$I = \int (\sec^2 x/2 - 1)\,dx,\ (\tan^2\theta = \sec^2\theta - 1)$$

$$I = \int \sec^2 x/2\,dx - \int dx$$

$$I = \frac{\tan x/2}{1/2} - x + c$$

$$I = 2\tan x/2 - x + c \quad \textbf{Ans.}$$

Problem 22 $I = \int \frac{\cos x}{1 + \cos x}\,dx$

Solution $I = \int \frac{\cos x}{1 + \cos x}\,dx$

$$I = \int \frac{(2\cos^2 x/2 - 1)}{2\cos^2 x/2}\,dx$$

$\boxed{1 + \cos x = 2\cos^2 x/2,\ \cos 2x = 2\cos^2 x - 1,\ \cos x = 2\cos^2 x/2 - 1}$

$$I = \int \left(1 - \frac{1}{2}\sec^2 x/2\right) dx$$

$$I = \int dx - \frac{1}{2}\int \sec^2 x/2\,dx$$

$$I = x - \frac{1}{2}\,\frac{\tan x/2}{1/2} + c$$

$$I = (x - \tan x/2) + c \quad \textbf{Ans.}$$

Problem 23 $\int \frac{\sin^2 x}{1 + \cos x}\,dx = \int \frac{1 - \cos^2 x}{1 + \cos x}\,dx$

$$= \int \frac{(1 + \cos x)(1 - \cos x)}{(1 + \cos x)}\,dx$$

$$= \int dx - \int \cos x\,dx = x - \sin x + c$$

Problem 24 $\int \frac{1}{(1 + \sin x)} dx$

$$I = \int \frac{(1 - \sin x)}{(1 + \sin x)(1 - \sin x)} dx$$

Solution $I = \int \frac{1 - \sin x}{\cos^2 x} dx$

$$I = \int \frac{1}{\cos^2 x} dx - \int \frac{\sin x}{\cos x} \cdot \frac{1}{\cos x} dx$$

$$I = \int \sec^2 x dx - \int \sec x \tan x dx$$

$$I = (\tan x - \sec x) + c \quad \text{Ans.}$$

Standard Integral

Problem 25 $\int \frac{dx}{x^2 + a^2} = \frac{1}{a} \tan^{-1} \frac{x}{a} + c$

Solution $I = \int \frac{dx}{x^2 + a^2}$

Let $x = a \tan \theta$

$\Rightarrow$ $\frac{x}{a} = \tan \theta$

$$dx = a \sec^2 \theta dx$$

$$\tan^{-1} \frac{x}{a} = \theta$$

$$I = \int \frac{a \sec^2 \theta d\theta}{a^2 \tan^2 \theta + a^2}$$

$$I = \int \frac{a \sec^2 \theta \cdot dx}{a^2 (\tan^2 \theta + 1)}$$

$$I = \frac{1}{a} \int \frac{\sec^2 \theta d\theta}{\sec^2 \theta}$$

$$\boxed{\frac{x}{a} = \tan \theta \quad \tan^{-1} \frac{x}{a} = \theta}$$

$$I = \frac{1}{a} \int d\theta$$

$$I = \frac{\theta}{a} + c$$

$$\boxed{I = \frac{1}{a} \tan^{-1} \frac{x}{a} + c} \quad \textbf{Ans.}$$

Problem 26 $\int \frac{dx}{\sqrt{a^2-x^2}} = \sin^{-1}\frac{x}{a} + c$

Solution Let

$$x = a\sin\theta$$

$$dx = a\cos\theta d\theta$$

$$I = \int \frac{a\cos\theta d\theta}{\sqrt{a^2-a^2\sin^2\theta}}$$

$$I = \int \frac{a\cos\theta dx}{\sqrt{a^2(1-\sin^2\theta)}}$$

$$I = \int \frac{a\cos\theta d\theta}{a\cos\theta}$$

$$I = \int d\theta = \theta + c$$

$$\boxed{x = a\sin\theta,\ \frac{x}{a} = \sin\theta,\ \sin^{-1}\left(\frac{x}{a}\right) = \theta}$$

$$\boxed{I = \sin^{-1}\frac{x}{a} + c}$$ **Ans.**

Integration as a limit of a sum

Problem `7 (1) $\int_1^2 x dx$ as the limit of sum

(2) $\int_0^2 e^x dx$ as the limit of sum

Solution Any integral

$$\int_a^b f(x)\,dx = (b-a) \lim_{n\to\infty} \frac{1}{n} [f(a) + f(a+h) + f(a+2h) + f(a+3h) + \ldots + f\{a+(n-1)h\}]$$

where $h = \frac{b-a}{n}$

Problem 26 $\int_1^2 x dx \quad f(x) = x \qquad a = 1, b = 2$

Solution $\int_a^b f(x)\,dx = (b-a) \lim_{n\to\infty} \frac{1}{n}[f(a) + \ldots + f(a+n-1)h\}]$

$$h = \frac{2-1}{n} = \frac{1}{n}$$

$$\int_0^2 x dx = (2-1) \lim_{n\to\infty} \frac{1}{n}\left[f(1) + f\left(1+\frac{1}{n}\right) + f\left(1+\frac{2}{n}\right) + \ldots + f\left(1+\frac{n-1}{n}\right)\right]$$

$$= \lim_{n\to\infty} \frac{1}{n}\left[1 + 1 + \frac{1}{n} + 1 + \frac{2}{n} + \ldots + 1 + \frac{n-1}{n}\right]$$

$$\boxed{f(x) = x \quad f(1) = 1}$$

$$= \lim_{n\to\infty} \frac{1}{n}\left[n + \left\{\frac{1}{n} + \frac{2}{n} + \ldots + \frac{n-1}{n}\right\}\right]$$

$$= \lim_{n\to\infty} \frac{1}{n}\left[n + \frac{(1+2+\ldots+n-1)}{n}\right]$$

$$= \lim_{n\to\infty} \frac{1}{n}\left[n + \frac{(n-1)\,n}{2n}\right] = \lim_{n\to\infty}\left[\frac{n}{n} + \frac{(n-1)n}{2n}\right]$$

$$\boxed{1 + 2 + 3 + \ldots + n = \frac{n(n+1)}{2}}$$

$$= \lim_{n\to\infty}\left[1 + \frac{n-1}{2n}\right] = \lim_{n\to\infty}\left[1 + \frac{1}{2} - \frac{1}{2n}\right] = \frac{3}{2} - 0 = \frac{3}{2}$$

Problem 28 $\int_0^2 (x^2+1)\,dx$ as the limit of sum

$$f(x) = x^2 + 1 \qquad a = 0, b = 2$$

$$h = \frac{b-a}{n} = \frac{2}{n}$$

Solution $\int_0^2 (x^2+1)\,dx = 2 \lim_{n\to\infty} \frac{1}{n}\left[f(0) + f\left(0+\frac{2}{n}\right) + f\left(0+\frac{4}{n}\right) + \ldots + f\left\{0 + (n-1)\frac{2}{n}\right\}\right]$

$$\boxed{\begin{array}{ll} f\left(\frac{2}{n}\right) = \left(\frac{2}{n}\right)^2 + 1 & 0 + \frac{2}{n} = f\left(\frac{2}{n}\right) \\ = \left(\frac{2}{n}\right)^2 + 1 = \frac{2^2}{n^2} + 1 & f\frac{(2n-2)}{n} = \frac{(2n-2)^2}{n^2} + 1 \end{array}}$$

$$= 2\lim_{n\to\infty} \frac{1}{n}\left[1 + \left(\frac{2^2}{n^2} + 1\right) + \left(\frac{4^2}{n^2} + 1\right) + \ldots + \left\{\frac{(2n-2)^2}{n^2} + 1\right\}\right]$$

$$= 2 \lim_{n\to\infty} \frac{1}{n}\left[\{1 + 1 + \ldots n \text{ terms}\} + \left\{\frac{2^2}{n^2} + \frac{4^2}{n^2} + \ldots + \frac{(2n-2)^2}{n^2}\right\}\right]$$

$$= 2 \lim_{n\to\infty} \frac{1}{n}\left[n + \frac{1}{n^2}\{2^2 + 4^2 + \ldots + (2n-2)^2\}\right]$$

$$= 2 \lim_{n\to\infty} \frac{1}{n}\left[n + \frac{2^2}{n^2}\{1^2 + 2^2 + 3^2 + \ldots (n-1)^2\}\right]$$

(1) $1 + 2 + 3 + \ldots + n = \dfrac{n(n+1)}{2}$

(2) $1^2 + 2^2 + 3^2 + \ldots + n^2 = \dfrac{n(n+1)(2n+1)}{6}$

(3) $1^3 + 2^3 + \ldots + n^3 = \left[\dfrac{n(n+1)}{2}\right]^2$

$$= 2 \lim_{n\to\infty} \frac{1}{n}\left[n + \frac{2^2}{n^2}(n-1)\ \frac{n\{2(n-1)+1\}}{6}\right]$$

$$= 2 \lim_{n\to\infty} \frac{1}{n}\left[n + \frac{2^2}{n^2}\frac{(n-1)\,n\,(2n-1)}{6}\right]$$

$$= 2 \lim_{n\to\infty} \frac{1}{n}\left[n + \frac{2}{3}\frac{(n-1)(2n-1)}{n}\right]$$

$$= 2 \lim_{n\to\infty} \left[1 + \frac{2}{3}\frac{(n-1)}{n}\frac{(2n-1)}{n}\right]$$

$$= 2 \lim_{n\to\infty} \left[1 + \frac{2}{3}\left(1-\frac{1}{n}\right)\left(2-\frac{1}{n}\right)\right]$$

$$= 2\left[1 + \frac{2}{3}\left(1-\frac{1}{\infty}\right)\left(2-\frac{1}{\infty}\right)\right]$$

$$= 2\left[1 + \frac{2}{3}(1-0)(2-0)\right] = 2\left[1 + \frac{2}{3} \times 1 \times 2\right]$$

$$= 2\left[1 + \frac{4}{3}\right] = 2\left[\frac{7}{3}\right] = \frac{14}{3} \quad \textbf{Ans.}$$

Problem 29 $\int_0^2 e^x\, dx \qquad f(x) = e^x \qquad a = 0,\ b = 2$

$$h = \frac{b-a}{n} = \frac{2}{n}$$

Solution $\int_0^2 e^x\,dx = 2 \lim_{n\to\infty} \frac{1}{n}\Big[f(0) + f\left(0+\frac{2}{n}\right)$

$+ \ldots + f\left\{0 + (n-1)\frac{2}{n}\right\}\Big]$

$$= 2 \lim_{n\to\infty} \frac{1}{n}\left[f(0) + f\left(\frac{2}{n}\right) + \ldots + f\left\{\frac{2(n-1)}{n}\right\}\right]$$

$$= 2 \lim_{n\to\infty} \frac{1}{n}\left[e^0 + e^{2/n} + e^{4/n} + \ldots + e^{2(n-1)/n}\right]$$

$$= 2 \lim_{n\to\infty} \frac{1}{n}\left[e^0 + e^{2/n} + e^{4/n} + e^{6/n} + \ldots + e^{(2n-2)/n}\right]$$

$(a) + a(r^2) + ar^2 + ar^3 + \ldots + ar^n$

$r =$ common ratio

Sum of n terms of G.P. $= \frac{a(r^n-1)}{r-1}$

$$= 2 \lim_{n\to\infty} \frac{1}{n} \cdot \left[\frac{1\{(e^{2/n})^n - 1\}}{e^{2/n}-1}\right]$$

$c \cdot r = e^{2/n} \qquad a = e^0 = 1$

$$= 2 \lim_{n\leftarrow\infty} \frac{1}{n}\left[\frac{e^{2n/n}-1}{e^{2/n}-1}\right]$$

$$= 2 \lim_{n\to\infty} \frac{1}{n} \frac{(e^2-1)}{(e^{2/n}-1)} = \lim_{n\to\infty} \frac{(e^2-1)}{n(e^{2/n}-1)}$$

$$= 2(e^2-1) \lim_{n\to\infty} \frac{1}{n(e^2/n-1)}$$

$$= 2(e^2-1) \frac{1}{\lim_{n\to\infty} n(e^{2/n}-1)} \qquad (1)$$

$e^x = 1 + x + \frac{x^2}{2!} + \frac{x^3}{3!} + \ldots + \frac{x^n}{n!}$

Now let us calculate $\lim_{n\to\infty} n(e^{2/n}-1)$

$$= \lim_{n\to\infty} n\left[1 + \frac{2}{n} + \frac{(2/n)^2}{2!} + \frac{(2/n)^3}{3!} + \ldots -1\right]$$

$$= \lim_{n\to\infty} n\left[\frac{2}{n} + \frac{4}{2n^2} + \frac{8}{6n^3} + \ldots\right]$$

$$= \lim_{n\to\infty} \left[2 + \frac{4}{2n} + \frac{8}{6n^2} + 0\left(\frac{1}{n}\right)\right]$$

$$= 2 + \frac{4}{\infty} + \frac{8}{\infty} + 0 + 0 + 0$$

$$= 2 + 0 + 0 = 2$$

$$\boxed{0\left(\frac{1}{n}\right) = \text{ord. of } \frac{1}{n}}$$

$$\int_6^2 e^x\, dx = \frac{2(e^2 - 1)}{2} = (e^2 - 1)$$

Problem 30 Prove that $\int_0^\pi \frac{dx}{(1 + \sin x)} = 2$

Solution Let $I = \int_0^\pi \frac{dx}{(1 + \sin x)}$

$$I = \int_0^\pi \frac{dx\,(1 - \sin x)}{(1 + \sin x))1 - \sin x)} = \int_0^\pi \frac{(1 - \sin x)\,dx}{\cos^2 x}$$

$$I = \int_0^\pi \frac{(1 - \sin x)}{\cos^2 x}\, dx$$

$$I = \int_0^\pi \left[\frac{1}{\cos^2 x} - \frac{\sin x}{\cos x} \cdot \frac{1}{\cos x}\right] dx$$

$$I = \int_0^\pi [\sec^2 x - \sec x \cdot \tan x]\, dx$$

$$I = \Big[\tan x - \sec x\Big]_0^\pi$$

$$I = (\tan \pi - \sec \pi) - (\tan 0 - \sec 0)$$

$$I = (0 + 1) - (0 - 1)$$

$$\boxed{\cos \pi = -1 \qquad \sec \pi = -1}$$

$$I = 1 + 1 \qquad I = 2$$

$$\int_0^\pi \frac{dx}{(1 + \sin x)} = 2$$

28

Appendix

(1) Find the area bounded by $y^2 = 4ax$, $\frac{x}{b} + \frac{y}{c} = 1$ and the x-axis in the positive quadrant of the xoy plane (a, b, c are real positive) [*I.F.S.* 89]

(2) Find the area of the ellipse

$$\frac{x^2}{a^3} + \frac{y^2}{b^2} = 1$$ [*I.F.S.* 88]

(3) Find the length of the complete arc of the cycloid

$$x = a\,(\theta - \sin\theta),\ y = a\,(1 - \cos\theta)$$ [*I.F.S.* 87]

(4) Find the entrinsic equation of the curve

$$r = 2a\,(1 - \cos\theta)$$ [*I.F.S.* 85]

(5) Show that the area cut off a parabola by any double ordinate is two thirds of the corresponding rectangle contained by that double ordinate and its distance from the vertex. [*I.F.S.* 85]

(6) A circular arc revolves about its chord; prove that the area of the surface generated is $4\pi a^2 (\sin\alpha - \alpha\cos\alpha)$ where a is the radius of the circle and 2α is the angle subtended by the arc at the centre.

(7) Find the length of the arc of the ceycloid whose equations are

$$x = a\,(t - \sin t),\ y = a\,(1 - \cos t)$$

(8) Show that the volume of a spherical segment of height h, the radius of whose base is c is

$$\frac{\pi h}{6}(3c^2 + h)$$

9. Determine the area of the surface of a paraboloid generated by revolution about the x-axis of an arc of the parabola $y^2 = 2px$ which corresponds to the variation of x from $x = 0$ to $x = a$.

10. Find the area, lying above x-axis and included between the circle $x^2 + y^2 = 2ax$, and the parabola $y^2 = ax$.

11. Show that the area bounded by the cissoid

$$x = a \sin^2 t \qquad y = \frac{a \sin^3 t}{\cos t}$$

and its assymple is $\frac{3}{4} \pi a^2$

12. Find the volume of a frustum of a righ circular cone by integration.

13. Find the area lying between the two loops of the limacon

$$r = 1 + 2 \sin \theta$$

Rectification

Formula for the rectification

(i) $$S = \int \sqrt{\left\{1 + \left(\frac{dy}{dx}\right)^2\right\}}\, dx$$

(ii) $$S = \int \left\{\sqrt{1 + \left(\frac{dx}{dy}\right)^2}\right\} dy$$

(iii) $$S = \int \left\{\sqrt{r^2 + \left(\frac{dr}{d\theta}\right)^2}\right\} d\theta$$

(iv) $$S = \int \left\{\sqrt{1 + r^2 \left(\frac{d\theta}{dr}\right)^2}\right\} dr$$

(v) $$S = \int \left\{\sqrt{\left(\frac{dx}{dt}\right)^2 + \left(\frac{dy}{dt}\right)^2}\right\} dt$$

Problem 1 Rectify the curve or find the length of an arch of the curve

$$x = a\,(t + \sin t)$$

$$y = a\,(1 - \cos t)$$ *[I.F.S. 84, 87]*

Solution $x = a\,(t + \sin t)$

$$\frac{dx}{dt} = a\,(1 + \cos t)$$

$$y = (1 - \cos t)$$

$$\frac{dy}{dt} = a\,(0 + \sin t) = a \sin t$$

$$\frac{dy}{dt} = a \sin t \qquad (2)$$

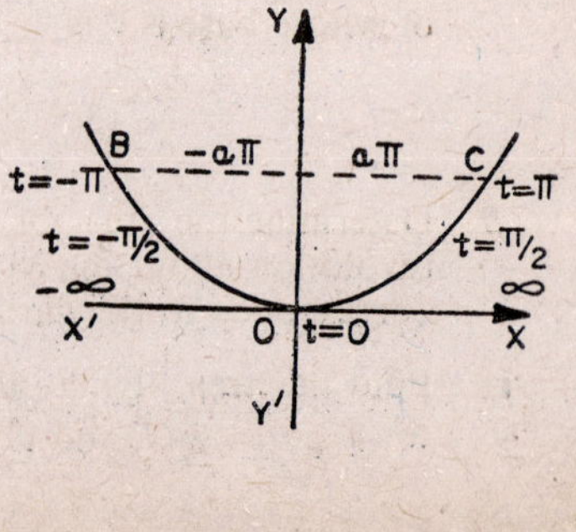

The length of an arch of the curve

= length of the curve lying between two successive cusps.

$$= \text{Arc } BOC = 2 \times \text{arc } OC$$

$$= 2 \times \int_0^{\pi} \left[\left(\frac{dx}{dt}\right)^2 + \left(\frac{dy}{dt}\right)^2\right]^{1/2} dt$$

$$= 2 \times \int_0^{\pi} [\{a(1 + \cos t)^2 + (a \sin t)^2]^{1/2} dt$$

$$= 2 \times \int_0^{\pi} a^2 \{1 + \cos^2 t\ 2 \cos t + \sin^2 t\}]^{1/2} dt$$

$$= 2 \times a \int_0^{\pi} \sqrt{2 + 2 \cos t}\, dt$$

$$= 2\sqrt{2}a \int_0^{\pi} \sqrt{2 \cos^2 t/2}\, dt$$

$$= 2\sqrt{2}a\sqrt{2} \int_0^{\pi} \cos t/2\, dt = 4a\left[2\sin t/2\right]_0^{\pi}$$

$$= 8a \times \left[\sin \frac{\pi}{2} - \sin 0\right] = 8a[1 - 0] = 8a$$ **Ans.**

Problem 2 Find the whole length of the astroid $x^{2/3} + y^{2/3} = a^{2/3}$

Solution The curve is symmetrical about both the axes and crosses the x-axis at

$(\pm a, 0)$ and $(0, \pm a)$

Equation is $x^{2/3} + y^{2/3} = a^{2/3}$

differentiating we have

$$\tfrac{2}{3} x^{-1/3} + \tfrac{2}{3} y^{-1/3} = 0$$

$$\Rightarrow \quad \frac{dy}{dx} = -\left(\frac{y}{x}\right)^{1/3}$$

$$1 + \left(\frac{dy}{dx}\right)^2 = 1 + \left(\frac{y}{x}\right)^{2/3} = \frac{x^{2/3} + y^{2/3}}{x^{2/3}} = \frac{a^{2/3}}{x^{2/3}}$$

As clear from the figure required length of the curve

$$= 4\int_0^a \sqrt{1 + \left(\frac{dy}{dx}\right)^2}\, dx = 4\int_0^a \sqrt{\frac{a^{2/3}}{x^{2/3}}}\, dx$$

$$= 4\int_0^a a^{1/3} x^{-1/3}\, dx = 4a^{1/3} \int_0^a x^{-1/3}\, dx$$

$$= 4a^{1/3} \left[\frac{x^{(-1/3)+1}}{-\frac{1}{3}+1}\right]_0^a = 4a^{1/3} \left[\frac{x^{2/3}}{\frac{2}{3}}\right]_0^a$$

$$= 4a^{1/3}\, \frac{a^{2/3}}{2/3} = \frac{4 \times 3}{2}\, a = 6a$$ **Ans.**

Problem 3 Find the entire length of the cardiod

$$r = a\,(1 + \cos\theta)$$

Solution The shape of the curve is shown in the figure. The equation of the curve

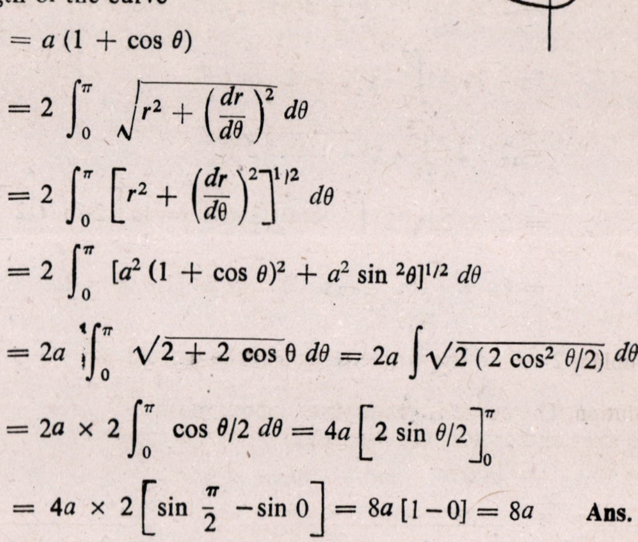

$$r = a\,(1 + \cos\theta)$$

$$\frac{dr}{d\theta} = -a\sin\theta$$

Required length of the curve

$$r = a\,(1 + \cos\theta)$$

$$= 2\int_0^{\pi} \sqrt{r^2 + \left(\frac{dr}{d\theta}\right)^2}\,d\theta$$

$$= 2\int_0^{\pi} \left[r^2 + \left(\frac{dr}{d\theta}\right)^2\right]^{1/2} d\theta$$

$$= 2\int_0^{\pi} [a^2\,(1 + \cos\theta)^2 + a^2 \sin^2\theta]^{1/2}\,d\theta$$

$$= 2a\int_0^{\pi} \sqrt{2 + 2\cos\theta}\,d\theta = 2a\int\sqrt{2\,(2\cos^2\theta/2)}\,d\theta$$

$$= 2a \times 2\int_0^{\pi} \cos\theta/2\,d\theta = 4a\left[2\sin\theta/2\right]_0^{\pi}$$

$$= 4a \times 2\left[\sin\frac{\pi}{2} - \sin 0\right] = 8a\,[1-0] = 8a$$ **Ans.**

Problem 4 Find the whole length of the curve

$$x = a\cos^3 t$$

$$y = a\sin^3 t$$

Solution The shape of the curve is like

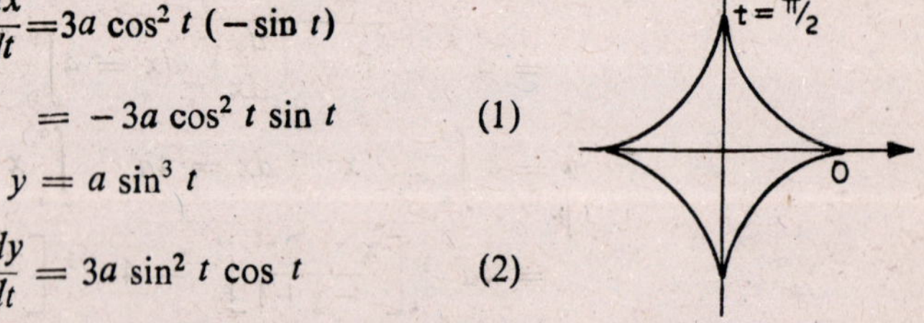

Here $x = a\cos^3 t$

$$\frac{dx}{dt} = 3a\cos^2 t\,(-\sin t)$$

$$= -3a\cos^2 t\sin t \qquad (1)$$

$$y = a\sin^3 t$$

$$\frac{dy}{dt} = 3a\sin^2 t\cos t \qquad (2)$$

t varies from 0 to $\pi/2$ for the first quadrant.

The whole length of the curve

$$= 4 \times \text{length of are in first quadrant}$$

$$= 4 \times \int_0^{\pi/2} \sqrt{\left(\frac{dx}{dt}\right)^2 + \left(\frac{dy}{dt}\right)^2}\, dt$$

$$= 4 \times \int_0^{\pi/2} \sqrt{(9a^2\cos^4 t \sin^2 t + 9a^2 \sin^4 t \cos^2 t)}\, dt$$

$$= 12a \int_0^{\pi/2} \cos t \sin t\, dt$$

$$= 12\, a \int_0^{\pi/2} \frac{2 \sin t \cos t}{2} = 6a \int_0^{\pi/2} \sin 2t\, dt$$

$$= 6a \left[-\frac{\cos 2t}{2}\right]_0^{\pi/2} = \frac{6a}{2} \{-[\cos \pi - \cos 0]\}$$

$$= 3a \{-(-1-1)\} = 3a \times 2 = 6a \qquad \textbf{Ans.}$$

Intrinsic equation

(a) Intrinsic equation from the cartesian equation.

$$y = f(x)$$

$$\tan \psi = \frac{dy}{dx} \tag{1}$$

$$S = \int_0^x \sqrt{1 + \left(\frac{dy}{dx}\right)^2}\, dx$$

$$S = \psi(x) \text{ (say)} \tag{ii}$$

Eliminate x between (i) and (ii) we obtain a relation between sand ψ which is the required intrinsic equation of the curve.

(b) To obtain the intrinsic equation from the polar equation.

$$r = f(\theta)$$

$$\psi = \theta + \phi \tag{i}$$

$$\tan \phi = r \frac{d\theta}{dr} \tag{ii}$$

$$S = \int_\alpha^\theta \sqrt{r^2 + \left(\frac{dr}{d\theta}\right)^2}\, d\theta$$

$$S = \phi(\theta) \tag{iii}$$

Eliminating θ and ϕ form (i), (ii) and (iii) we obtain a relation between s and ψ which is the required intinsic equation of the curve.

(c) To obtain the intrinsic equation from parametric equations.

$x = f_1(t), y = f_2(t)$ be the parametric equation of the curve.

$$S = \int_{t1}^{t2} \left[\left(\frac{dx}{dt}\right)^2 + \left(\frac{dy}{dt}\right)^2\right]^{1/2} dt$$

$$S = F(t) \text{ say} \qquad \text{(i)}$$

$$\tan\psi = \frac{dy/dt}{dx/dt} = \phi(t) \text{ (say)} \qquad \text{(iii)}$$

Eliminating t between (i) and (ii) we obtain a relation between s and ψ which is required intrinsic equation of the curve.

Problem 11 Find the intrinsic equation of

$$r = a(1 - \cos\theta)$$

Solution

$$r = a(1 - \cos\theta)$$

$$\frac{dr}{d\theta} = a\sin\theta$$

$$\tan\phi = r\frac{d\theta}{dr}$$

$$\tan\phi = \frac{r}{a\sin\theta}$$

$$\tan\phi = \frac{a(1-\cos\theta)}{a\sin\theta}$$

$$\tan\phi = \frac{2a\sin^2\theta/2}{2a\sin\theta/2\cos\theta/2}$$

$$\tan\phi = \tan\theta/2$$

$$\Rightarrow \quad \phi = \frac{\theta}{2}$$

$$\psi = \theta + \phi = \theta + \theta/2 = 3\theta/2 \Rightarrow \theta = 2/3\,\psi$$

$$S = \int_0^\theta \sqrt{r^2 + \left(\frac{dr}{d\theta}\right)^2}\, d\theta$$

$$S = \int_0^\theta \sqrt{a^2(1-\cos\theta)^2 + a^2\sin^2\theta\, d\theta}$$

$$S = a\int_0^\theta \sqrt{1 - 2\cos\theta + \cos^2\theta + \sin^2\theta}\, d\theta$$

$$S = a\int_0^\theta \sqrt{2(1-\cos\theta)}\, d\theta$$

$$S = a\int_0^\theta \sqrt{2\cdot 2\sin^2\theta/2}\,d\theta$$

$$S = 2a\int_0^\theta \sin\theta/2\,d\theta$$

$$S = 2a\left(-2\cos\theta/2\right)_0^\theta$$

$$S = 4a\,(1-\cos\theta/2)$$

$$S = 4a\,(1-\cos\psi/3)$$

$$S = 4a\times 2\sin^2\psi/6$$

$$S = 8a\sin^2\psi/6$$

which is the required intirisic equation.

Problem 2 Prove that the intrinsic equation of the cycloid

$$x = a\,(\theta + \sin\theta)$$

$$y = a\,(1-\cos\theta)$$

is $s = 4a\sin\psi$

Solution

$$\frac{dx}{d\theta} = a\,(1+\cos\theta)$$

$$\frac{dy}{d\theta} = a\sin\theta$$

$$\frac{dy}{dx} = \frac{a\sin\theta}{(1+\cos\theta)\,a}$$

$$\frac{dy}{dx} = \frac{2a\sin\theta/2\cos\theta/2}{2\cos^2\theta/2}$$

$$\tan\psi = \tan\theta/2$$

$$\psi = \theta/2$$

$$S = \int_0^\theta \sqrt{\left(\frac{dx}{d\theta}\right)^2 + \left(\frac{dy}{d\theta}\right)^2}\,d\theta$$

$$S = \int_0^\theta \sqrt{a^2(1+\cos\theta)^2 + a^2\sin^2\theta}\,d\theta$$

$$S = a\int_0^\theta \sqrt{2+2\cos\theta}\,d\theta$$

$$S = 2a\int_0^\theta -\cos\theta/2\,d\theta$$

$$S = 2a\times 2\sin\theta/2$$

$$S = 4a\sin\theta/2$$

$$S = 4a\sin\psi$$

29

Volumes of Solids of Revolution

Problem 1 Find the volume of a spherical segment of height h, the radius of whose base is c [*IFS 82*]

Solution Here the required. Volume is generated by the revolution of the area $ABCA$ of the circle $x^2 + y^2 = a^2$ about x axis and for the arc BA

$$BC = C \qquad CA = h$$

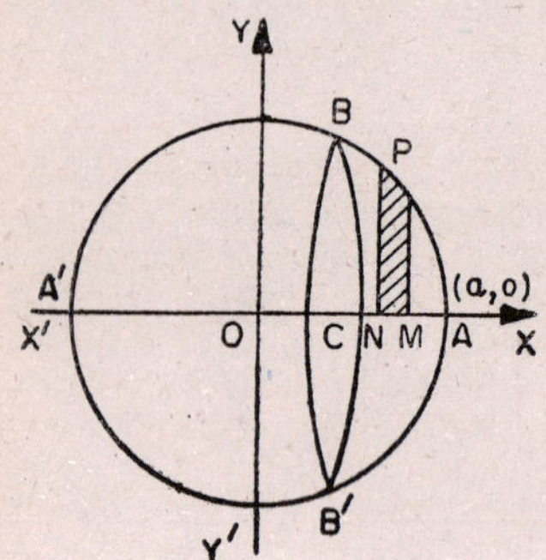

x varies from OC to a

Where $OC = a-h$, $BC = C$

Also if we join O and B we have

$$OB^2 = OC^2 + BC^2$$

$$a^2 = (a-h)^2 + c^2$$

$$a^2 = a^2 - 2ah + h^2 + c^2$$

$$2ah = h^2 + c^2$$

$$a = \frac{h^2 + c^2}{2h} \tag{1}$$

For the arc BA, x varies from $(a-h)$ to a where a is given by (1)
The required volume

$$= \int_{a-h}^{a} \pi y^2 \, dx \text{ where } x^2 + y^2 = a^2$$

$$= \pi \int_{a-h}^{a} (a^2 - x^2) \, dx = \pi \left[a^2 x - \frac{x^3}{3} \right]_{a-h}^{a}$$

$$= \pi \left[\left(a^3 - \frac{a^3}{3} \right) - \left\{ a^2 (a-h) - \frac{1}{3} (a-h)^3 \right\} \right]$$

$$= \pi \left[\frac{2}{3} a^3 - \left\{ a^3 - a^2 h \left(\frac{a^3 - h^3 + 3ah^2 - 3ha^2}{3} \right) \right\} \right]$$

$$= \pi \left[\frac{2}{3} a^2 - \left\{ a^3 - a^2 h - \frac{a^3}{3} + \frac{h^2}{3} - ah^2 + ha^2 \right\} \right]$$

$$= \pi \left\{ a^2 h - \frac{h^3}{3} + ah^2 - ha^2 \right\} = \pi \left[ah^2 - \frac{h^3}{3} \right]$$

$$= \pi h^2 \left[a - \frac{h}{3} \right] = \pi h^2 \left[\frac{c^2 + h^2}{2h} - \frac{h}{3} \right]$$

$$= \frac{\pi h}{6} [3(c^2 + h^2) - 2h^2] = \frac{1}{6} \pi h [3c^2 + h^2] \quad \textbf{Ans.}$$

Formula 1 The volume of the solid generated by the revolution of the area bounded by the curve $y = f(x)$, x axis and the ordinates $x = a$, $x = b$ about the x axis is

$$\boxed{\int_a^b \pi y^2 \, dx}$$

Formula 2 The volume of the solid generated by the revolution of the area bounded by the curve $x = f(y)$, the y axis and the lines $y = a$ and $y = b$ is given by

$$\boxed{\int_a^b \pi x^2 \, dy}$$

Formula 3 If the equations of the generating curve be given by

$$x = f_1(t) \text{ and } y = f_2(t)$$

and it is revolved about x axis then the formula corresponding to

$$\int_a^b \pi y^2 \, dx \qquad \text{becames}$$

$$\int_{t1}^{t_2} \pi \left\{ f_2(t) \right\}^2 \frac{d}{dt} \left\{ f_1(t) \right\}$$

Where t_1 and t_2 are the values of t corresponding to $x = a$ and $x = b$.

Problem 1 Find the volume of the solid generated by revolving the ellipse

$$\frac{x^2}{a^2} + \frac{y^2}{b^2} = 1 \text{ about } x \text{ axis}$$

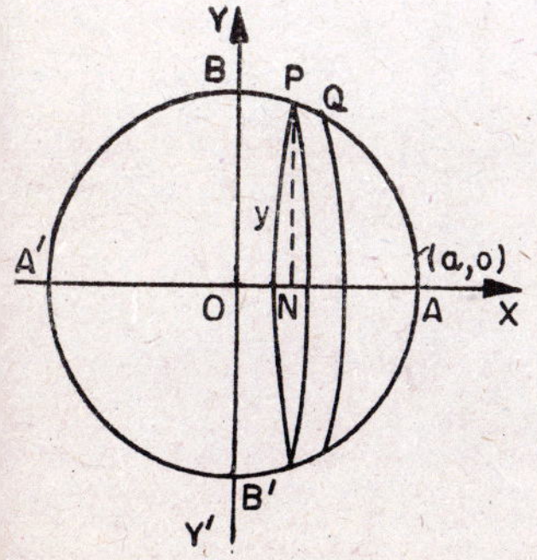

Solution The solid is generated by revolving the upper half of the area of the ellipse about x – axis.

∴ The required volume

$$= \int_{-a}^{a} \pi y^2 \, dx$$

$$\text{Where } \frac{x^2}{a^2} + \frac{y^2}{b^2} = 1$$

$$\Rightarrow \frac{y^2}{b^2} = 1 - \frac{x^2}{a^2}$$

$$\Rightarrow \frac{y^2}{b^2} = \frac{a^2 - x^2}{a^2}$$

$$\Rightarrow y^2 = \frac{b^2}{a^2}(a^2 - x^2)$$

The required volume

$$= \int_{-a}^{a} \pi \frac{b^2}{a^2}(a^2 - x^2)\, dx = \pi \frac{b^2}{a^2}\int_{-a}^{a} (a^2 - x^2)\, dx$$

$$= \pi \frac{b^2}{a^2}\left[a^2 x - \frac{x^3}{3}\right]_{-a}^{a} = \pi \frac{b^2}{a^2}\left[\frac{4}{3} a^3\right] = \frac{4}{3}\pi ab^2$$

Problem 2 Find the volume of the solid generated by the revolution of the curve $y = \dfrac{a^3}{(a^2+x^2)}$ about its *assymptote.*

Solution $\quad y = \dfrac{a^3}{a^2 + x^2}$

or $\quad x^2 y = a^2 (a - y)$

$\therefore$ The equation of its assyptote is $y = 0$ i.e. x-axis (equating the coefficient of highest degree term of x to zero)

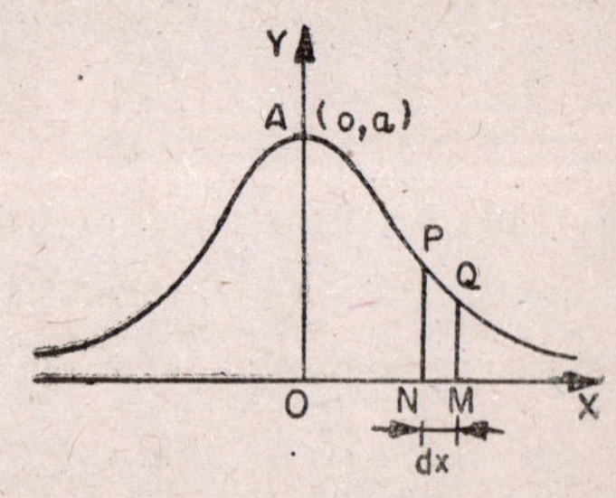

Then the elementry strip $PNMQ$, which when revolved about $y = 0$ generates a volume

$$= \pi y^2 \,\delta x \text{ and also}$$

for the whole curve x varies from $-\infty$ to ∞

Required volume $\quad = \displaystyle\int_{-\infty}^{\infty} \pi y^2\, dx = \int_{-\infty}^{\infty} \pi \frac{a^6}{(a^2 + x^2)^2}\, dx$

$$= \pi a^6 \int_{-\infty}^{\infty} \frac{dx}{(a^2 + x^2)^2} = 2\pi a^6 \int_0^{\infty} \frac{dx}{(a^2 + x^2)^2}$$

Since the function is an even function

Put $\quad x = a \tan\theta$

$\quad dx = a \sec^2\theta\, d\theta$

Required volume $\quad = \displaystyle 2\pi a^6 \int_0^{\infty} \frac{dx}{(a^2 + x^2)^2} = 2\pi a^6 \int_0^{\pi/2} \frac{a \sec^2\theta\, d\theta}{(a^2 + a^2 \tan^2\theta)^2}$

$$= \frac{2\pi a^6 \cdot a}{a^4} \int_0^{\pi/2} \cos^2\theta\, d\theta$$

$$= 2\pi a^3 \int_0^{\pi/2} \cos^2\theta\, d\theta = 2\pi a^3 \frac{1}{2}\,\frac{1}{2}\,\pi$$

$$= \frac{1}{2}\pi^2 a^3 \qquad \textbf{Ans.}$$

Problem 3 Show that the differential equation of all parabolas having their axis of symmetry coincident with the x axis is

$$y\frac{d^2y}{dx^2}+\left(\frac{dy}{dx}\right)^2=0$$

[*IFS 87*]

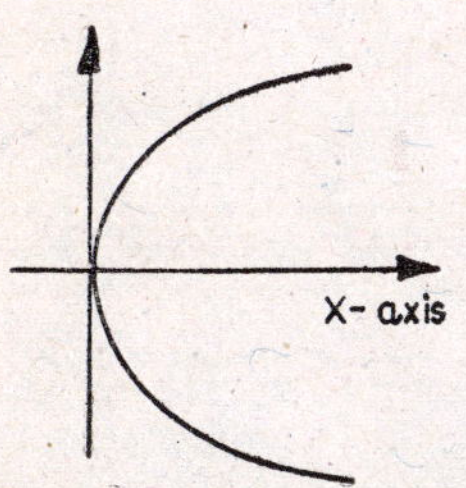

Solution Equation of the parabola

$$y^2=4ax$$

Differentiating we have

$$2y\frac{dy}{dx}=4a$$

$$\frac{dy}{dx}=\frac{2a}{y}$$

$$y\frac{dy}{dx}=2a$$

Again differentiating we have

$$y\frac{d^2y}{dx^2}+\left(\frac{dy}{dx}\right)\left(\frac{dy}{dx}\right)=0$$

$$y\frac{d^2y}{dx^2}+\left(\frac{dy}{dx}\right)^2=0$$

Which is the required differential equation of the parabola.

Problem 4 A particle whose mass is m is acted upon by a force

$m\mu\left(x+\frac{a^4}{x^3}\right)$ towards the origin; if it starts from rest at a distance a, show that it will arrive at the origin in time $\frac{\pi}{4\sqrt{\mu}}$

Solution Since the force $m\mu\left(x+\frac{a^4}{x^3}\right)$ is towards the origin 0 and the force $m\frac{d^2x}{dt^2}$ is in the direction of x increasing therefore the equation of motion is

$$m\frac{d^2x}{dt^2}=-m\mu\left(x+\frac{a^4}{x^3}\right)$$

$$\frac{d^2x}{dx}=-\mu\left(x+\frac{a^4}{x^3}\right)$$

$$v\frac{dv}{dx}=-\mu\left(x+\frac{a^4}{x^3}\right)$$

$$v\frac{dv}{dx}=-\mu\left(x+\frac{a^4}{x^3}\right)$$

$$v\,dv=-\mu\left(x+\frac{a^4}{x^3}\right)dx$$

Integrating we have

$$\frac{v^2}{2}=-\mu\left(\frac{x^2}{2}-\frac{a^4}{2x^2}\right)+\frac{c}{2}$$

$$v^2=-\mu\left(x^2-\frac{a^4}{x^2}\right)+c$$

Initially $\quad x=a,\ v=0$

$$0=-\mu\left(a^2-\frac{a^4}{a^2}\right)+c$$

$$\Rightarrow c=0$$

$$v^2=\left(\frac{dx}{dt}\right)=-\mu\left(x^2-\frac{a^4}{x^2}\right)$$

$$\frac{dx}{dt}=\sqrt{\mu}\sqrt{\left(\frac{a^4}{x^2}-x^2\right)}$$

$$\frac{dx}{dt}=\sqrt{\mu}\,\frac{\sqrt{a^4-x^4}}{x^2}$$

$$\frac{dx}{dt}=\sqrt{\mu}\sqrt{\frac{a^4-x^4}{x^2}}$$

$$\sqrt{\mu}\,dt=\frac{x\,dx}{\sqrt{a^4-x^4}}$$

Integrating both sides we have

$$\sqrt{\mu}t=\frac{1}{2}\cos^{-1}\frac{x^2}{a^2}+c_1$$

Initially $\quad x=a,\ t=0$

$$0=\frac{1}{2}\cos^{-1}\frac{a^2}{a^2}+c_1$$

$$c_1=0$$

$$\sqrt{\mu}\,t=\frac{1}{2}\cos^{-1}\frac{x^2}{a^2}$$

$$\frac{x^2}{a^2}=\cos(2\sqrt{\mu}\,t)$$

$$x^2=a^2\cos(2\sqrt{\mu}\,t)$$

By putting $x = 0$ we get the time to reach the origin

$$0 = a^2 \cos (2 \sqrt{\mu}\, t)$$

$$\cos (2 \sqrt{\mu}\, t = 0 = \cos \pi/2$$

$$2 \sqrt{\mu}\, t = \pi/2$$

$$t = \frac{\pi}{4\sqrt{\mu}} \qquad \textit{(Proved)}$$

Problem 4 A particle moves in a straight line OA, starting from rest at A, with an acceleration towards 0 equal to μ times the distance of the particle from O Find the time it will take to reach the point. *[I.F.S. 85]*

Solution
$$\frac{d^2 x}{dt^2} = -\mu x$$

$$v \frac{dv}{dx} = -\mu x$$

$$vdv = -\mu x dx$$

Integrating we have

$$\frac{v^2}{2} = -\mu \frac{x^2}{2} + c \qquad (1)$$

When
$$x = a \qquad v = 0$$

$$\Rightarrow O = -\mu \frac{a^2}{2} + c$$

$$\Rightarrow c = \mu \frac{a^2}{2} \qquad (2)$$

Putting the value of c from (2) in (1) we have.

$$\frac{v^2}{2} = -\frac{\mu x^2}{2} + \frac{\mu a^2}{2}$$

$$\Rightarrow v^2 = \mu (a^2 - x^2)$$

$$\Rightarrow \left(\frac{dx}{dt}\right)^2 = \mu (a^2 - x^2)$$

$$\Rightarrow \frac{dx}{dt} = \sqrt{u} \sqrt{a^2 - x^2}$$

$$\Rightarrow \frac{dx}{\sqrt{a^2 - x^2}} = \sqrt{\mu}\, dt$$

Integrating both sides we have

$$\sin^{-1} \frac{x}{a} = \sqrt{u}\, t + c$$

If
$$x = a \qquad t = 0$$

$$\frac{\pi}{2} = c$$

$$\Rightarrow \qquad \sin^{-1}\frac{x}{a} = \sqrt{\mu}t + \frac{\pi}{2}$$

for $x = 0$ the time is t then

$$\sin^{-1}(0) = \sqrt{\mu}\, t + \pi/2$$

$$\sqrt{\mu}\, t = -\pi/2$$

$$\Rightarrow \qquad t = -\frac{\pi}{2\sqrt{\mu}}$$

Taking time as +ve we have

$$t = \frac{\pi}{2\sqrt{\mu}} \qquad \textbf{Ans.}$$

Problem 5 Find the surface of the solid formed by the revolution of the cardiod $r = a(1 + \cos\theta)$ about the initial line.

[I.F.S. 86]

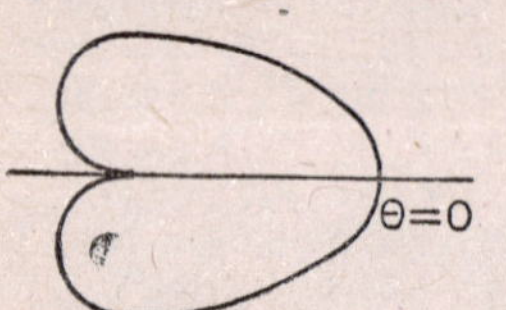

Solution For the upper half of the curve θ varies from 0 to π $\quad r = a(1 + \cos\theta)$

we get $\quad \dfrac{dr}{d\theta} = a(-\sin\theta)$

$$\therefore \qquad \frac{ds}{d\theta} = \sqrt{r^2 + \left(\frac{dr}{d\theta}\right)^2}$$

$$\frac{ds}{d\theta} = \sqrt{a^2(1 + \cos\theta)^2 + a^2\sin^2\theta}$$

$$\frac{ds}{d\theta} = \sqrt{a^2(2 + 2\cos\theta)}$$

$$\frac{ds}{d\theta} = 2a\cos\theta/2$$

The required surface

$$= 2\pi\int_{\theta-0}^{\pi} y\,ds \quad = 2\pi\int_0^{\pi} r\sin\theta\,\frac{ds}{d\theta}\cdot d\theta$$

$$= 2\pi\int_0^{\pi} a(1 + \cos\theta)\sin\theta\; 2a\cos\theta/2\; d\theta$$

$$= 2\pi\int_0^{\pi} a\,2\cos^2\theta/2 \cdot 2\sin\theta/2\; 2\cos\theta/2\; a\cos\theta/2\; d\theta$$

$$= 16\pi a^2\int_0^{\pi}\sin\theta/2\cos^4\left(\frac{\theta}{2}\right)d\theta$$

$$= 32\pi a^2\int_0^{\pi/2}\sin t\cos^4 t\, dt$$

$$= 32\pi a^2\left[-\cos^5 t\right]_0^{\pi/2} = \frac{32\pi a^2}{5} \qquad \textbf{Ans.}$$

30

Volumes and Surface of Revolution

Volume of a solid of revolution:

The volume obtained by revolving about x-axis the arc of the curve $y = f(x)$ intercepted between the points whose abscissae are a, b is

$$\int_a^b \pi y^2\, dx \qquad \text{i.e.} \qquad \pi \int_a^b [f(x)]^2\, dx$$

From obove we conclude that the volume obtained by revolving about y-axis, the arc of the curve $x = f(y)$ intercepted between the points whose ordinates are, a, b is $\int_a^b \pi x^2\, dy$.

Volume of any axis of revolution:

Let AD be a curve and OX be the line. Let PM be the length of perpendicular from P to the line and OM is the distance of the foot of the perpendicular from origin. Then the volume is given by

$$V = \int_{OA}^{OB} \pi\, (MP)^2\, d\,(OM).$$

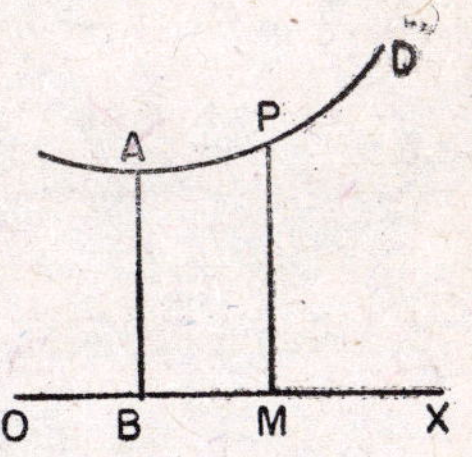

Surface of revolution:

The area of the surface of the solid obtained on revolving about x-axis, the arc of the curve whose abscissae are a and b is given by

$$\int_a^b 2\pi\, y \frac{ds}{dx} \cdot dx$$

In case of the polar curve $r = f(\theta)$ it changes to

$$\int_a^b 2\pi\, y \frac{ds}{d\theta} \cdot d\theta$$

4. Important Relation.

(i) $$\frac{ds}{dy} = \sqrt{1 + \left(\frac{dx}{dy}\right)^2}$$

(ii) $$\frac{ds}{dt} = \sqrt{\left(\frac{dx^2}{dt}\right) + \left(\frac{dy}{dt}\right)^2}$$

(iii) $$\frac{ds}{d\theta} = \sqrt{r^2 + \left(\frac{dr}{d\theta}\right)^2}$$

Problem 1 The loop of the curve $2ay^2 = x(x-a)^2$ revolves about X-axis. Find the volume of the solid so generated.

Solution $$2\,ay^2 = x\,(x-a)^2$$

$\therefore$ $$y^2 = \frac{x(x-a)^2}{2a}$$

The volume is to be find about the revolution of the x-axis.

The abscissae are $x = 0, a$

Required volume $$= \int_0^a \pi y^2\, dx$$

$$= \int_0^a \frac{\pi}{2a} x\,(x-a)^2\, dx = \frac{\pi}{2a}\int_0^a (x^3 + xa^2 - 2ax^2)\, dx$$

$$= \frac{\pi}{2a}\left[\frac{a^4}{4} + \frac{a^2 x^2}{2} - \frac{2ax^3}{3}\right]_0^a = \frac{\pi}{2a}\left[\frac{a^4}{4} + \frac{a^4}{2} - \frac{2a^4}{3}\right]$$

$$= \frac{\pi}{2a} \times \frac{2a^4}{24} = \frac{\pi a^3}{24}$$ **Ans.**

Problem 2 Find the volume of the solid obtained by revolving the loop of the curve $a^2 y^2 = x^2 (2a-x)(x-a)$ about x-axis.

Solution $$y^2 = \frac{x^2}{a^2}(2a-x)(x-a)$$

The abscissae are $x = a, 2a$.

Reqd. volume is therefore

$$= \int_a^{2a} \pi^2 y^2\, dx = \pi \int_a^{2a} \frac{x^2}{a^2}(2ax - 2a^2 - x^2 + ax)\, dx$$

$$= \frac{\pi}{a^2}\int_a^{2a} (3ax^3 - 2a^2 x^2 - x^4)\, dx = \frac{\pi}{a^2}\left[\frac{3a\,x^4}{4} - \frac{2a^2 x^3}{3} - \frac{x^5}{5}\right]_a^{2a}$$

$$= \frac{\pi}{a^2}\left[\left(12a^5 - \frac{16}{3}a^5 - \frac{32}{5}a^5\right) - \left(\frac{3a^5}{4} - \frac{2a^5}{3} - \frac{a^5}{5}\right)\right]$$

$$= \frac{\pi}{a^2}\left[\frac{4a^5}{15} + \frac{7a^5}{60}\right] = \frac{\pi}{a^2}\left[\frac{16a^5 + 7a^5}{60}\right]$$

$$= \frac{\pi}{a^2} \times \frac{23a^5}{60} = \frac{23\pi a^3}{60}$$ **Ans.**

Problem 4 Prove that the volume of the solid generated by the revolution of an ellipse round its minor axis is a mean proportional between that generated by the revolution of the ellipse and of its auxiliary circle round the major axis.

Solution Let the eqn. of the ellipse be

$$\frac{x^2}{a^2} + \frac{y^2}{b^2} = 1$$

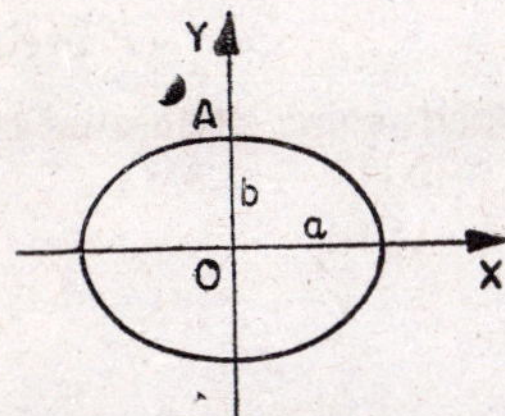

and the auxiliary circle about the major axis be $x^2 + y^2 = a^2$

Let v_1 be the volume of the solid revolving the minor axis i.e. y axis.

$$\therefore \qquad v_1 = \int \pi\, x^2\, dy$$

the ordinates are 0, to b.

$$= 2 \int_0^b \pi \frac{a^2}{b^2} (b^2 - y^2)\, dy$$

[$\because$ The function is symmetrical]

$$= \frac{2a^2\pi}{b^2}\left[\int_0^b b^2\, dy - \int_0^b y^2\, dy\right]$$

$$= \frac{2a^2\pi}{b^2}\left[b^2 y - \frac{y^3}{3}\right]_0^b = \frac{2a^2\pi}{b^2}\left[b^3 - \frac{b^3}{3}\right]$$

$$= \frac{a^2\pi}{b^2} \times 2 \cdot \frac{2b^3}{3} = \frac{4}{3}\pi a^2 b$$

$$v_1 = \frac{4}{3}\pi a^2 b \ldots 1$$

v_2 be the volume of the solid about major a is i.e. x axis.

$$v_2 = 2\int_0^a \pi \frac{b^2}{a^2}(a^2 - x^2)\, dx \qquad [\because \text{ they are symmetrical}]$$

$$= \frac{2\pi b^2}{a^2}\left[a^2 x - \frac{x^3}{3}\right]_0^a$$

$$= \frac{2\pi b^2}{a^2}\left[a^3 - \frac{a^3}{3}\right] = \frac{4}{3}\pi ab^2 \ldots 2$$

v_3 be the volume of solid generated by circle revolving about its major axis. i.e. x-axis.

$$\therefore \quad v_3 = 2\int_0^a \pi y^2\,dx \qquad \text{[since the function is symmetrical]}$$

$$= 2\pi \int_0^a (a^2 - x^2)\,dx$$

$$= 3\pi \left[a^2 x - \frac{x^3}{3}\right]_0^a = 2\pi \left[a^3 - \frac{a^3}{3}\right] = \frac{4}{3}\pi a^3 \quad \ldots 3$$

Here from all the three eqn.

$$v_1 = \sqrt{v_2 v_3}$$

$$\text{i.e. } v_1 \propto v_2 v_3 \qquad \textit{(Proved)}$$

Problem 5 Find the volume of the spindle shaped solid generated by revolving the hypocycloid $x^{2/3} + y^{2/3} = a^{2/3}$ about x-axis,

Solution The eqn. of the hypocycloid is $x^{2/3} + y^{2/3} = a^{2/3}$.

Required volume about axis of x is $= 2\int_0^a \pi y^2\,dx$

[$\because$ The function is symmetrical]

$$= 2\pi \int_0^a (a^{2/3} - x^{2/3})^3\,dx$$

$$= 2\pi \int_0^a [(a^2 - x^2 - 3a^{2/3} x^{2/3} (a^{2/3} - x^{2/3})]\,dx$$

$$= 2\pi \int_0^a [a^2 - x^2 - 3a^{4/3} x^{2/3} + 3a^{2/3} x^{4/3}]\,dx$$

$$= 2\pi \left[a^2 x - \frac{x^3}{3} - \frac{3 \times 3a^{4/3}}{5} x^{5/3} + \frac{3 \times 3}{7} a^{2/3} x^{7/3}\right]_0^a$$

$$= 2\pi \left[a^3 - \frac{a^3}{3} - \frac{9}{5} a^{4/3} \cdot a^{5/3} + \frac{9}{7} a^{2/3} \cdot a^{7/3}\right]$$

$$= 2\pi \left[a^3 - \frac{a^3}{3} - \frac{9}{5} a^3 + \frac{9}{7} a^3\right]$$

$$= 2\pi \left[\frac{105a^3 - 35a^3 - 189a^3 + 135a^3}{105}\right] = \frac{2\pi}{105} \times 16a^3 = \frac{32\pi a^3}{105}$$

Problem 6 Prove that the volume of the solid generated by the revolution of the curve $y = \dfrac{a^3}{a^2 + x^2}$ about its asymptote is $\dfrac{\pi^2 a^3}{2}$.

Solution The curve is $\qquad y = \dfrac{a^3}{a^2 + x^2}$

$$y^2 = \frac{a^6}{(a^2 + x^2)^2}$$

the asymptote of this curve is $y = 0$ i e. x-axis i.e. volume is to be determined of the solid generated by the revolution of x-axis.

Req. volume is therefore

$$= 2\pi \int_0^\infty y^2\, dx = 2\pi \int_0^\infty \frac{a^b}{(a^2 + x^2)^2}\, dx$$

Let $\qquad x = a \tan \theta$

$$dx = a \sec^2 \theta\, d\theta$$

when $\qquad x \to 0, \theta \to 0$

and $\qquad x \to \infty, \theta \to \frac{\pi}{2} = 2\pi\, a^6 \int_0^{\pi/2} \frac{a \sec^2 \theta\, d\theta}{a^4 \sec^2 \theta \sec^2 \theta}$

$$= 2\pi a^3 \int_0^{\pi/2} \cos^2 d\theta = \pi a^3 \int_0^{\pi/2} (1 + \cos 2\theta)\, d\theta$$

$$= \pi a^3 \left[\int_0^{\pi/2} d\theta + \int_0^{\pi/2} \cos\ 2\theta\, d\theta\right]$$

$$= \pi a^3 \left[\theta + \frac{\sin 2\theta}{2}\right]_0^{\pi/2}$$

$$= \pi \times \frac{\pi}{2}\, a^3 = \frac{\pi^2\, a^3}{2} \qquad \textit{(Proved)}$$

Problem 7 Show that the volume of the solid generated by revolving the area included between the curves $y^2 = x^3$ and $x^2 = y^3$ about x-axis is $\frac{5\pi}{28}$.

Solution Let V_1 be volume generated by the x-axis to the curve $y^2 = x^3$ while V_2 be the volume generated by x-axis to the curve $x^2 = y^3$. Therefore the volume of the solid between the area of these curves are

$$V = V_1 - V_2$$

The abscissae are given as

$$y^2 = x^3 \qquad \Rightarrow \qquad y = x^{3/2}$$

and $\qquad x^2 = y^3 \qquad \Rightarrow \qquad y = x^{2/3}$

$\Rightarrow \qquad x^{3/2} - x^{2/3} = 0$

$\Rightarrow \qquad x^{3/2}\,(1 - x^{-5/6}) = 0$

$\Rightarrow \qquad x = 0, 1$

Required volume $= \int_0^1 \pi y_1^2\, dx - \Big]_0^1 \pi y_2^2\, dx = \pi \Big]_0^1 x^3\, dx - \pi \int_0^1 x^{4/3}\, dx$

$$= \pi \frac{x^4}{4}\int_0^1 - \frac{3}{7}\,\pi\, x^{7/3} \int_0^1 = \frac{1}{4}\,\pi - \frac{3}{7}\,\pi$$

$$= \pi \left|\frac{3}{7} - \frac{1}{4}\right| = \frac{5\pi}{28} \qquad \textit{(Proved)}$$

Problem 8 Find the volume formed by the revolution of the loop of the curve $y^2 = x^2(a-x)/(a+x)$ about the x-axis.

Solution The volume is to be determined by revolving x-axis the abscissae are 0 to a.

Reqd. volume is therefore $= \int_0^a \pi y^2\, dx = \pi \int_0^a x^2 \frac{(a-x)}{a+x}\, dx$

$$= \pi \int_0^a x^2 \frac{(a+x-2x)}{a+x}\, dx$$

$$= \pi \left[\int_0^a x^2\, dx - \int_0^a \frac{2x^3}{a+x}\, dx\right] = \pi\left[\frac{x^3}{3} - I_1\right]$$

Let $$I_1 = \int_0^a \frac{2x^3}{a+x}\, dx$$

Let $$a + x = z \qquad dx = dz$$

$$\Rightarrow \quad x = z - a$$

$$\Rightarrow \quad x^3 = z^3 - a^3 - 3az^2 + 3a^2 z$$

When $x \to 0,\ z \to a$ and $x \to a,\ z \to 2a$.

$$I_1 = 2\int_a^{2a} \left(\frac{z^3 - a^3 - 3az^2 + 3a^2 z}{z}\right) dz$$

$$= 2\int_a^{2a} \left(z^2 - \frac{a^3}{z} - 3az + 3a^2\right) dz$$

$$= 2\left[\frac{z^3}{3} - a^3 \log z - \frac{3az^2}{2} + 3a^2 z\right]_a^{2a}$$

$$= 2\left[\left(\frac{8a^3}{3} - \frac{a^3}{3}\right) - \left(a^2 \log \frac{2a}{a}\right) - \left(\frac{3az^2\, a^2}{2} - \frac{3a}{2} \cdot a^2\right) + 3a^2 \cdot (2a - a)\right]$$

$$= 2\left[\frac{7a^3}{3} - a^3 \log 2 - \frac{9a^3}{2} + 3a^3\right]$$

$$\therefore \quad V = \pi\left[\frac{a^3}{3} - \frac{14a^3}{3} + 2a^3 \log 2 + 9a^3 - 6a^3\right]$$

$$= \pi\left[\frac{a^3 - 14a^3 + 6a^3 \log 2 + 9a^3}{3}\right]$$

$$= \frac{\pi}{3}[6a^3 \log 2 - 4] = \frac{2a^3\pi}{3}[\log 2^3 - 2\log e]$$

$[\because \log e = 1]$

$$= \frac{2}{3}\pi a^3 [\log 8/e^2]$$

Problem 12 Trace the curve $y = e^x \sin x$ as x varies from 0 to π and show that the volume of the solid obtained by revolving it about x-axis is $\pi\,(e^{2\pi} - 1)/8$.

Solution The volume of the solid generated by revolving the curve about x-axis is given as

$$V = \pi \int_0^\pi (e^x \sin x)^2\, dx$$

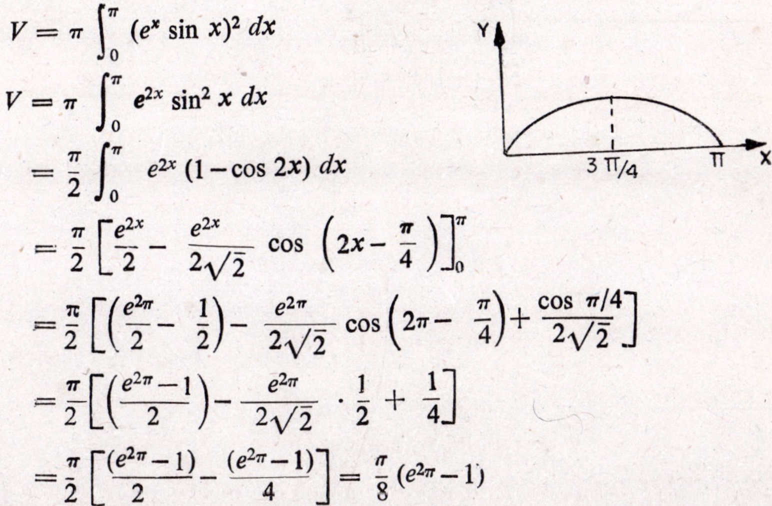

$$V = \pi \int_0^\pi e^{2x} \sin^2 x\, dx$$

$$= \frac{\pi}{2} \int_0^\pi e^{2x}(1 - \cos 2x)\, dx$$

$$= \frac{\pi}{2}\left[\frac{e^{2x}}{2} - \frac{e^{2x}}{2\sqrt{2}} \cos\left(2x - \frac{\pi}{4}\right)\right]_0^\pi$$

$$= \frac{\pi}{2}\left[\left(\frac{e^{2\pi}}{2} - \frac{1}{2}\right) - \frac{e^{2\pi}}{2\sqrt{2}} \cos\left(2\pi - \frac{\pi}{4}\right) + \frac{\cos \pi/4}{2\sqrt{2}}\right]$$

$$= \frac{\pi}{2}\left[\left(\frac{e^{2\pi} - 1}{2}\right) - \frac{e^{2\pi}}{2\sqrt{2}} \cdot \frac{1}{2} + \frac{1}{4}\right]$$

$$= \frac{\pi}{2}\left[\frac{(e^{2\pi} - 1)}{2} - \frac{(e^{2\pi} - 1)}{4}\right] = \frac{\pi}{8}(e^{2\pi} - 1)$$

Problem 13 Trace the curves $y = \sin x$ and $y = \cos x$ as x varies from 0 to $\pi/2$ and show the volume obtained by revolving about x-axis then region enclosed by them and the x axis is $\pi\,(\pi - 2)/4$.

Solution The curves of $\sin x$ and $\cos x$ as x varies from 0 to $\pi/2$.

Here the function are intersecting at the point $\pi = \pi/4$. The region under which the function is integratable is contineous i.e. 0 to $\pi/4$ and $\pi/4$ to $\pi/2$.

Reqd. volume

$$= \pi \int_0^{\pi/4} \sin^2 x dx + \pi \int_{\pi/4}^{\pi/2} \cos^2 x dx$$

$$= \pi \int_0^{\pi/4} \frac{(1 - \cos 2x}{2} dx + \pi \int_{\pi/4}^{\pi/2} \frac{(1 + \cos 2x)}{2} dx$$

$$= \frac{\pi}{2}\left[x - \frac{\sin 2\pi}{2}\right]_0^{\pi/4} + \frac{\pi}{2}\left[\pi + \frac{\sin 2x}{2}\right]_{\pi/4}^{\pi/2}$$

$$= \frac{\pi}{2}\left[\frac{\pi}{4} - \frac{1}{2}\right] + \frac{\pi}{2}\left[\frac{\pi}{2} - \frac{\pi}{4} - \frac{1}{2}\right]$$

$$= \frac{\pi}{2}\left[\frac{\pi}{2} - 1\right] = \frac{\pi}{4}(\pi - 2) \qquad \textit{(Proved)}$$

Problem 14 Find the volume of the solid generated by rotating completely about x-axis the area enclosed between $y^2 = x^3 + 5x$ and the lines $x = 2$ and $x = 4$.

Solution Volume $= \int_2^4 \pi y^2\, dx = \pi \int_2^4 (x^3 + 5x)\, dx$

$$= \pi \left[\frac{x^4}{4} + 5\frac{x^2}{2}\right]_2^4 = \pi \left[64 + \frac{80}{2} - (4 + 10)\right]$$

$$= \pi\,[104 - 14] = 90\,\pi$$

Problem 15 Find the volume generated by the revolution of an arc of the catenary.

$y = c \cos h\, x/c$ about the axis of x between $x = a$ and $x = b$

Solution $y = c \cos h \dfrac{x}{c}$

The volume $= \int_a^b \pi y^2\, dx = \pi \int_a^b c^2 \cos h^2 \dfrac{x}{c}\, dx$

we know that $\cos h^2 x + \sin h^2 x = \cos h\, 2x$

and $\cos h^2 x - \sin h^2 x = 1$

Hence $\cos h\, 2x = 2 \cos h^2 x - 1$

$$= \pi \int_a^b c^2 \left(2 \cos h^2 \frac{x}{c}\right) dx$$

$$= \pi c^2 \int_a^b \frac{1}{2}\left(1 + \cos h \frac{2x}{c}\right) dx$$

$$= \frac{\pi c^2}{2}\left[\int_a^b dx + \int_a^b \cos h \frac{2x}{c}\, dx\right]$$

$$= \frac{\pi c^2}{2}\left[x + \frac{c \sin h\, 2x}{2c}\right]_a^b$$

$$= \frac{\pi c^2}{4}\left[2x + c \sin h \frac{2x}{c}\right]_a^b$$

Problem 16 Show that the volume of the solid obtained by revolving about x-axis the area enclosed by the parabola $y^2 = 4ax$ and its evolute $27\, ay^2 = 4\,(x - 2a)^3$ is $80\,\pi\, a^3$.

Solution The volume of the curve is given by

$$V = \int_a^b \pi y^2\, dx \text{ about axis of } x$$

a and b is to be find out

$$y^2 = 4\,ax \text{ and } y^2 = \frac{4}{27a}\,(x - 2a)^3$$

$$\Rightarrow \quad 4ax = \frac{4}{27a}(x-2a)^3$$

$$\Rightarrow \quad 27a^2 x = x^3 - 8a^3 - 6ax(x-2a)$$

$$\Rightarrow \quad x^3 - 6ax^2 + 12a^2 x - 27a^2 x - 8a^3 = 0$$

$$\Rightarrow \quad x^3 - 6x^2 a - 15a^2 x - 8a^3 = 0$$

$$\Rightarrow \quad (x-8a)(x+a)^2 = 0$$

Hence we get the abscissae as $8a$ and $2a$.

Reqd. volume is therefore = volume of the parabola from 0 to $8a$ – volume of the evolute from $2a$ to $8a$

$$= \pi \int_0^{8a} 4ax\,dx - \int_{2a}^{8a} \frac{4}{27a}(x-2a)^3\,dx$$

$$= \pi 4a \frac{x^2}{2}\Big]_0^{8a} - \frac{4\pi}{27a}\left[\frac{x^4}{4} - 8a^3 x - \frac{6}{3}ax^3 + 12a^2\frac{x^2}{2}\right]_{2a}^{8a}$$

$$= \pi\, 2a \times 64a^2 - \frac{4\pi}{27a}[(1024a^4 - 4a^4) - (64a^4 - 16a^4)$$

$$-1024a^4 + 16a^4 + (384a^4 - 24a^4)]$$

$$= 128a^3\pi - \frac{4}{27a} \times 324a^4\pi$$

$$= 128a^3\pi - 48a^3\pi = 80\pi a^3 \qquad (Proved)$$

Problem 18 Find the valume generated by $y = x \sin mx$ as the area lying between $x = 0$ and $x = 2\pi/m$ revolves about x-axis.

Solution Required volume is therefore

$$= \int_0^{2\pi/m} \pi y^2\,dx = \pi \int_0^{2\pi/m} x^2 \sin^2 mx\,dx$$

$$= \frac{\pi}{2}\int_0^{2\pi/m} x^2(1-\cos 2mx)\,dx$$

$$= \frac{\pi}{2}\left[\int_0^{2\pi/m} x^2\,dx - \int_0^{2\pi/m} x^2 \cos 2mx\,dx\right]$$

$$= \frac{\pi}{2}\left[\frac{x^3}{3}\right]_0^{2\pi/m} - \frac{\pi}{2}\left[\frac{x^2 \cdot \sin 2mx}{2m}\right]_0^{2\pi/m} + \frac{\pi}{2}\int_0^{2\pi/m} 2x\frac{\sin 2mx}{2m}\,dx$$

$$= \frac{\pi}{2}\left[\frac{8\pi^3}{3m^3}\right] - \frac{\pi}{2m}\int_0^{2\pi/m} - x \sin 2mx\,dx$$

$$= \frac{4\pi^4}{3m^3} - \frac{\pi}{2m}\left[\frac{-x\cos 2mx}{2m}\right]_0^{2\pi/m} + \int_0^{2\pi/m} \frac{-\cos 2mx}{2m}\,dx$$

$$= \frac{4\pi^4}{3m^3} - \frac{\pi}{2m}\left[\frac{-x\cos 2mx}{2m}\right]_0^{2\pi/m} - \frac{\sin 2mx}{8m^3}\Big]_0^{\pi}$$

$$= \frac{8\pi^4}{3m^3} - \frac{\pi}{2}\left[\frac{\pi}{m^3}\right] = \frac{4}{3}\frac{\pi^4}{m^3} - \frac{\pi^2}{2m^3} = \frac{\pi^2}{6m^3}(8\pi^2 - 3) \ (Proved)$$

Problem 19 The loop of the curve $r = a \cos 3\theta$ lying between $\theta = -\frac{\pi}{6}$ and $\theta = \frac{\pi}{6}$ revolves about the initial line. Show that the volume of the solid thus obtained is $\frac{19\pi a^3}{960}$

Solution The volume of the solid revolving about the initial line with the two lines

$$y = \theta_1 \quad \text{and} \quad y = \theta_2.$$

Volume $= \int_{\theta_1}^{\theta_2} \frac{2}{3} \pi r^3 \sin \theta \, d\theta$

The angle lies from 0 to $\pi/6$

$$V = \frac{2}{3} \int_0^{\pi/6} \pi a^3 \cos^3 3\theta \sin \theta d\theta$$

$$= \frac{2}{3} \pi a^3 \int_0^{\pi/6} a^3 (4 \cos^3 \theta - 3 \cos \theta)^3 \sin \theta \, d\theta$$

$= \text{Let} \quad \cos \theta = z \quad$ when $\theta \to 0, z = 1$

$-\sin \theta d\theta = dz \qquad \theta \to \frac{\pi}{6}, \; z_1 = \sqrt{\frac{3}{2}}$

$\sin \theta d\theta = -dz$

$$V = \frac{2}{3} \pi a^3 \int_{\sqrt{3/2}}^{1} (4t^3 - 3t)^3 \, dt$$

$$= \frac{2}{3} \pi a^3 \int_{\sqrt{3/2}}^{1} (64t^9 - 27t^3 - 144t^7 + 108t^5) \, dt$$

$$= \frac{2}{3} \pi a^3 \left[\frac{64t^{10}}{10} - \frac{27t^4}{4} - \frac{144t^8}{8} + \frac{108t^6}{6} \right]_{\sqrt{3/2}}^{1}$$

$$= \frac{2}{3} \pi a^3 \left[\frac{64}{10}\left(1 - \frac{243}{1024}\right) - 18\left(1 - \frac{81}{256}\right) + 18\left(1 - \frac{27}{64}\right) - \frac{27}{4}\left(1 - \frac{9}{16}\right) \right]$$

$$= \frac{2}{3} \pi a^3 \left[\frac{32}{5} \cdot \frac{781}{1024} - 18 \cdot \frac{175}{256} + 18 \cdot \frac{37}{64} - \frac{27}{4} \times \frac{7}{16} \right]$$

$$= \frac{2}{3} \pi a^3 \left[\frac{781}{160} - \frac{1575}{12} + \frac{333}{32} - \frac{189}{64} \right]$$

$$= \frac{2}{3} \pi a^3 \cdot \frac{19}{640} = \frac{19}{640} \pi a^3 \qquad \textbf{Ans.}$$

Problem 20 Prove that the volume generated by the revolution about the initial line of the limacon $r = a + b \cos \theta$, $a > b$ is $4\pi a \dfrac{(a^2 + b^2)}{3}$.

Solution Volume

$$= \frac{2}{3}\pi \int_0^{\pi} r^3 \sin \theta \, d\theta$$

$$= \frac{2}{3}\pi \int_0^{\pi} (a + b \cos \theta)^3 \sin \theta \, d\theta$$

Let $a + b \cos \theta = z$, $b \sin \theta d\theta = dz$

$$\sin \theta d\theta = -dz/b$$

when $\theta \to 0$, $z \to a + b$

$\theta \to \pi$, $z \to a - b$

$$= \frac{2}{3}\frac{\pi}{b}\int_{a-b}^{a+b} z^3 \, dz = \frac{2\pi}{3b}\left[\frac{z^4}{4}\right]_{a-b}^{a+b}$$

$$= \frac{\pi}{6b}[(a + b)^4 - (a - b)^4]$$

$$= \frac{\pi}{6b}[a^4 + b^4 + 4a^3 b + 6a^2 b^2 + 4ab^2 - a^4 + 4a^3 b - 6a^2 b^2 + 4ab^2 - b^4]$$

$$= \frac{\pi}{6b} \cdot [8ab^3 + 8a^3 b]$$

$$= \frac{\pi}{6b} \cdot 8ab\,(a^2 + b^2)$$

$$= \frac{4a\pi}{3}(a^2 + b^2)$$ **Ans.**

31
Any Axis of Revolution

Problem 1 A figure is bound by the axis of y and the arc of the ellipse $b^2 x^2 + a^2 y^2 = a^2 b^2$ on which x is negative. A solid is generated by the revolution of this figure about the line $x = -2a$ prove that its volume is

$$2\pi\left(\pi - \frac{2}{3}\right)a^2 b$$

Solution The equation of the ellipse is given to be

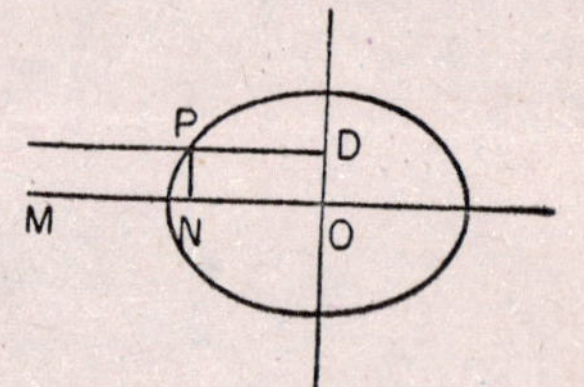

$$b^2 x^2 + a^2 y^2 = a^2 b^2$$

$$\Rightarrow \qquad \frac{x^2}{a^2} + \frac{y^2}{b^2} = 1$$

Since the function is symmetrical hence volume is given by

$$= 2\pi \int_0^b (MD)^2\, d(OD) - 2\pi \int_0^b (PM)^2\, d(PN)$$

The limits are 0 to b, since the curve is bounded by the y-axis

$$PM^2 = (MD - PD)^2 = (2a - x)^2$$

$$= 2\pi \int_0^b (2a)^2\, dy - 2\pi \int_a^b (2a - x)^2\, dy$$

$$= 2\pi \int 4a^2\, dy - 2\pi \int_0^b (2a - x)^2\, dy$$

$$= 2\pi \cdot 4a^2 \cdot b - 2\pi \int_a^b (2a - x)^2\, dy$$

Let $\qquad I = 2\pi \int_a^b (2a - x)^2\, dy$

Let $\qquad x = a\cos\theta,\ y = b\sin\theta,\ dy = b\cos\theta\, d\theta$

when $\qquad y \to 0, \qquad \theta \to 0$

$y \to b. \qquad \theta = \pi/2$

$$= 2\pi \int_0^{\pi/2} b\,(2a - a\cos\theta)^2 \cos\theta\, d\theta$$

$$= 2\pi a^2 b \int_0^{\pi/2} (2 - \cos\theta)^2 \cos\theta\, d\theta$$

$$= 2\pi a^2 b \int_0^{\pi/2} (4 + \cos^2\theta - 4\cos\theta)\cos\theta\, d\theta$$

$$= 2\pi a^2 b \left[4\sin\theta \Big|_0^{\pi/2} + \frac{2}{3\cdot 1} - 4\cdot\frac{1}{2}\cdot\frac{\pi}{2} \right]$$

$$= 2\pi a^2 b \left[4 + \frac{2}{3} - \pi \right] = 2\pi a^2 b \left(\frac{14}{3} - \pi \right)$$

Reqd. volume is given by,

$$= 8\pi a^2 b - 2\pi a^2 b \left(\frac{14}{3} - \pi \right) = 8\pi a^2 b + 2\pi a^2 b \left[\pi - \frac{14}{3} \right]$$

$$= 2\pi a^2 b \left[4 + \pi - \frac{14}{3} \right] = 2\pi a^2 b \left(\pi - \frac{2}{3} \right)$$

$$= 2\pi a^2 b \left(\pi - \frac{2}{3} \right) \quad \textbf{Ans.}$$

Problem 2 The ellipse $b^2 x^2 + a^2 y^2 = a^2 b^2$ is divided into two parts by the line $x = 1/2a$ and the smaller part is rotated through four right angles about this line. Prove that the volume generated is

$$\pi a^2 b \left(\frac{3}{4}\sqrt{3} - \frac{\pi}{3} \right)$$

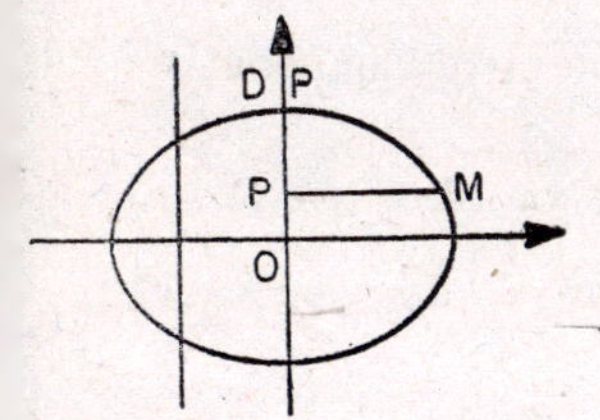

Solution Since the line $x = a/2$ and parabola is intersecting at point D.

We can find then the coordinate of D solving these two, so that we can find the distance we have

$$b^2 \cdot a^2/4 + a^2 y^2 = a^2 b^2$$

$$\Rightarrow \qquad a^2 y^2 = \tfrac{3}{4} a^4 b^2$$

$$\Rightarrow \qquad y^2 = \tfrac{3}{4} b^2$$

$$\Rightarrow \qquad y = \frac{\sqrt{3}}{2} b$$

$$\therefore \qquad D\left(\frac{1}{2}, \frac{\sqrt{3}}{2} b \right)$$

Reqd. volume $= 2\pi \int_0^{\sqrt{3}/2b} (PM)^2\, dy$

here $\qquad PM = x - a/2$

$$= \int_0^{\sqrt{3}/2\, b} \left(x - \frac{a}{2}\right)^2 dy = 2\pi \int_0^{\sqrt{3}/2\, b} \left(x^2 + \frac{a^2}{4} - ax\right) dy$$

$$= 2\pi \int_0^{\sqrt{3}/2\, b} \left\{\frac{a^2}{b^2}\left((b^2 - y^2) - a \cdot \frac{a}{b}\sqrt{(b^2 - y^2)} + \frac{a^2}{4}\right\} dy$$

$$= 2\pi \left[\frac{a^2}{b^2}\left(b^2 y - \frac{y^3}{3}\right)\right]_0^{b\sqrt{3}/2} - \frac{a^2}{b}\left\{\sqrt{b^2 - y^2} \cdot y/2\right.$$

$$\left. + \frac{b^2}{2}\sin^{-1}\frac{y}{b}\left\{_0^{b\sqrt{3}/2} + \left\{\frac{a^2}{4} y\left\{_0^{b\sqrt{3}/2}\right]\right.\right.\right.$$

$$= 2\pi \left[\frac{a^2}{b^2}\left(\frac{\sqrt{3}}{2} b^3 - b^3 \frac{\sqrt{3}}{8}\right) - \frac{a^2}{b}\left\{\frac{b\sqrt{3}}{4}\sqrt{\left(b^2 - \frac{3b^2}{4}\right)}\right.\right.$$

$$\left. + \frac{b^2}{2}\frac{\pi}{3}\left\{ + a^2 b \frac{\sqrt{3}}{8}\right]\right.$$

$$= 2\pi \left[\frac{3}{8}\frac{a^2}{b^2}\sqrt{3}\, b^3 - \frac{a^2}{b}\left\{\frac{b^2\sqrt{3}}{8} + \frac{\pi b^2}{6}\left\{ + a^2 b \frac{\sqrt{3}}{8}\right]\right.\right.$$

$$= 2\pi \left[\frac{3\sqrt{3}}{8} a^2 b - \frac{a^2}{b}\left\{\frac{\sqrt{3} b^2}{8} + \frac{\pi b^2}{6}\left\{ + \frac{\sqrt{3}}{8} a^2 b\right]\right.\right.$$

$$= 2\pi\, a^2 b \left[\frac{3\sqrt{3} - \sqrt{3} + \sqrt{3}}{8} - \frac{\pi}{6}\right]$$

$$= 2\pi\, a^2 b \left[\frac{3\sqrt{3}}{8} - \frac{\pi}{6}\right] = \pi\, a^2 b \left[\frac{3\sqrt{3}}{4} - \frac{\pi}{3}\right]$$

$$= \pi\, a^2 b \left[\frac{3\sqrt{3}}{4} - \frac{\pi}{3}\right]$$

Problem 3 Show that the volume obtained on revolving about $x = a/$. the area enclosed between the curves

$$xy^2 = a^2(a - x),\ (a - x) y^2 = a^2 x \text{ is } \pi a^3 (4 - \pi)/4.$$

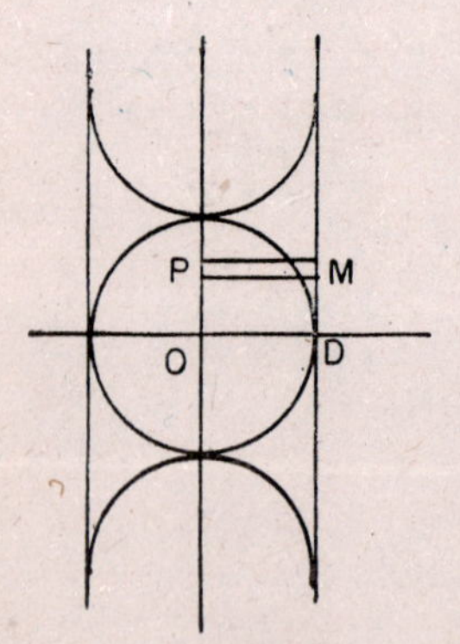

Solution $\qquad x = \dfrac{a^3}{a^2 + y^2}$

and $\qquad y = \dfrac{ay^2}{a^2 + y^2}$

$\therefore$ volume $\qquad = 2\displaystyle\int_a^b (PM)^2\, d(MD)$

$a \cdot b$ is to be determined

$$\frac{a^3}{a^2 + y^2} = \frac{ay^2}{a^2 + y^2}$$

$$a^2(a^2 - y^2) = 0$$

$$\Rightarrow \quad y = \pm a$$

The curve is symmetrical hence the limit is from 0 to a

$$(PM) = (x-a/2)^2$$

$$= 2\pi \int_0^a \left(x - \frac{a}{2} \right)^2 dy$$

$$= 2\pi \int_0^a \left[\frac{a}{a^2+y^2} - \frac{a}{2} \right]^2 dy$$

Let $\quad y = a \tan \theta$

$$dy = a \sec^2 \theta \, d\theta$$

When $\quad y = 0, \quad \theta = 0$

When $\quad y \to a, \quad \theta = \pi/4$

$$= \frac{2\pi}{4} \int_0^{\pi/4} \left[\frac{a^3}{a^2 \sec^2 \theta} - \frac{a}{2} \right]^2 a \sec^2 \theta \, d\theta$$

$$= \frac{\pi a^3}{2} \int_0^{\pi/4} \left(2 - \frac{1}{\cos^2 \theta} \right)^2 \cos^2 \theta \, d\theta$$

$$= \frac{\pi a^3}{2} \int_0^{\pi/4} \left[4 + \frac{1}{\cos^4 \theta} - \frac{4}{\cos^2 \theta} \right] \cos^2 \theta \, d\theta$$

$$= \frac{\pi a^3}{2} \int_0^{\pi/4} \left[\frac{4 \cos^4 \theta + 1 - 4 \operatorname{ces}^2 \theta}{\cos^4 \theta} \right] \cos^2 \theta \, d\theta$$

$$= \frac{\pi a^3}{2} \int_0^{\pi/4} \left[4 \cos^2 \theta + \sec^2 \theta - 4 \right] d\theta$$

$$= \frac{\pi a^3}{2} \left[2 \left(\theta + \frac{\sin^2 \theta}{2} \right)_0^{\pi/4} + \tan \theta \Big|_0^{\pi/4} - 4\theta \Big|_0^{\pi/4} \right]$$

$$= \frac{\pi a^3}{2} \left[2 \left(\frac{\pi}{4} + \frac{1}{2} \right) + 1 - \pi \right]$$

$$= \frac{\pi a^3}{2} \left[\frac{\pi}{2} - \pi + 2 \right]$$

$$= \frac{\pi a^3}{2} \left[2 - \frac{\pi}{2} \right] = \frac{\pi a^3}{4} (4 - \pi)$$

$$= \frac{\pi a^3}{4} (4 - \pi)$$

Problem 4 The area enclosed by the parabolas $x^2 = 4ay$ and $x^2 = 4a\,(2a-y)$ revolves about the line $y = a$, find the volume of the solid so generated

Solution The two eqns. of the parabola's are

$$x^2 = 4\,ay \text{ and } y^2 = 4a\,(2a-y)$$

The pt. of intersection is now,

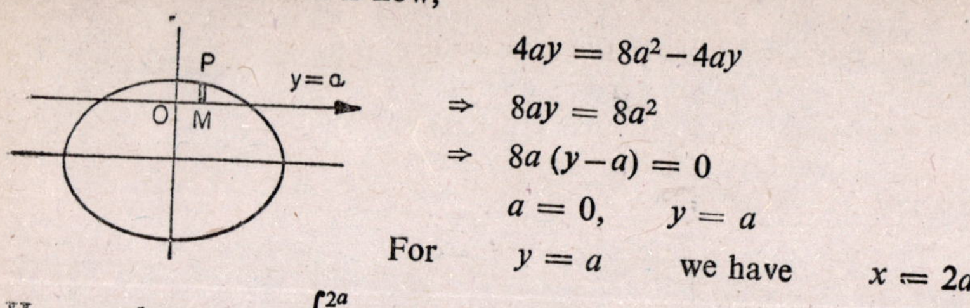

$$4ay = 8a^2 - 4ay$$

$$\Rightarrow \quad 8ay = 8a^2$$

$$\Rightarrow \quad 8a(y-a) = 0$$

$$a = 0, \qquad y = a$$

For $y = a$ we have $x = 2a$

Hence volume $= 2\pi \int_0^{2a} (PM)^2 \, dx$

$$(PM)^2 = (y-a)^2$$

$$= 2\pi \int_0^{2a} (y-a)^2 \, dx = 2\pi \int_0^{2a} \left(\frac{x^2}{4a} - a\right)^2 dx$$

$$= 2\pi \int_0^{2a} \left[\frac{x^4}{16a^2} + a^2 - \frac{x^2}{a}\right] dx$$

$$= 2\pi \left[\frac{x^5}{80a^2} + a^2 x - \frac{x^3}{6}\right]_0^{2a}$$

$$= 2\pi \left[\frac{32a^5}{80a^2} + 2a^3 - \frac{8a^3}{6}\right]$$

$$= 2\pi \left[\frac{2a^3}{5} + 2a^3 - \frac{4a^3}{3}\right] = \frac{2\pi}{15} [6a^3 + 30a^3 - 20a^3]$$

$$= \frac{32\pi a^3}{15}$$

Problem 5 A quadrant of a circle of radius a, revolves about its chord show that the volume of the spindle thus generated is $\pi/6\sqrt{2}\,(10-3\pi)a^3$.

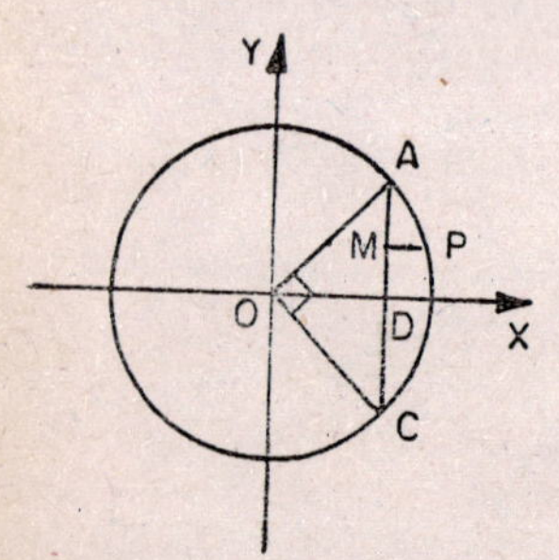

Solution Let the circle be $x^2 + y^2 = a^2$

In $\Delta\, OAC$,

$$OA^2 + OC^2 = AC^2$$

$$\Rightarrow \quad a^2 + a^2 = AC^2$$

$$\Rightarrow \quad 2a^2 = AC^2$$

$$\Rightarrow \quad AD = \frac{AC}{2} = a/\sqrt{2}$$

Therefore $\qquad OD = \sqrt{a^2 - a^2/2}$

$$= \sqrt{a^2/2} = a/\sqrt{2}$$

The limits are from 0 to $a/\sqrt{2}$

Reqd. volume $= 2\int_0^{a/\sqrt{2}} \pi\,(PM)^2\,d\,(MD)$

$$= 2\pi\int_0^{a/\sqrt{2}} \left(x - \frac{a}{\sqrt{2}}\right)^2 dy$$

But $x = \sqrt{a^2-y^2}$

$$= 2\pi\int_0^{a/\sqrt{2}} \left(\sqrt{a^2-y^2} - \frac{a}{\sqrt{2}}\right)^2 dy$$

$$= 2\pi\int_0^{a/\sqrt{2}} \left(a^2-y^2+\frac{a^2}{2} - \sqrt{2}a\sqrt{a^2-y^2}\right) dy$$

$$= 2\pi\int_0^{a/\sqrt{2}} \left(\frac{3a^2}{2} - y^2 - \sqrt{2}a\sqrt{a^2-y^2}\right) dy$$

$$= 2\pi\left[\frac{3a^2}{2}\cdot\frac{a}{\sqrt{2}} - \frac{a^3}{6\sqrt{2}} - a\sqrt{2}\left(y\,\frac{\sqrt{a^2-y^2}}{2} + \frac{a^2}{2}\sin^{-1}\frac{y}{a}\right)_0^{a/\sqrt{2}}\right]$$

$$= 2\pi\left[\frac{4}{3}\frac{a^3}{\sqrt{2}} - a\sqrt{2}\left(\frac{a/\sqrt{2}\cdot a\sqrt{2}}{2} + \frac{a^2}{2}\sin^{-1}\frac{a}{\sqrt{2}\cdot a}\right)\right]$$

$$= 2\pi\left[\frac{4a^3}{3\sqrt{2}} - a\sqrt{2}\left(\frac{a^2}{4} + \frac{\pi a^2}{8}\right)\right]$$

$$= 2\pi\left[\frac{4a^3}{3\sqrt{2}} - a\sqrt{2}\,\frac{a^2}{4}\left(1+\frac{\pi}{2}\right)\right]$$

$$= 2\pi\left[\frac{4a^3}{3\sqrt{2}} - \frac{a^3}{2\sqrt{2}}\left(1+\frac{\pi}{2}\right)\right]$$

$$= 2\pi a^3\left[\frac{8-3-3\pi/2}{6\sqrt{2}}\right] = \frac{2\pi a^3}{6\sqrt{2}}\,[5-3\pi/2]$$

$$= \frac{\pi a^3}{6\sqrt{2}}(10-3\pi)$$

Problem 6 The ellipse $x^2/a^2 + y^2/b^2 = 1$ $(a > b)$ revolves about the tangent at one extremity of its minor axis. Show that the volume of the solid obtained is $2\pi^2 ab^2$

Solution Minor axis is y axis. The tangent is the line BD

Redq. volume is therefore

$$= 2\int_0^a \pi\,(QP)^2\,dx - 2\int_0^a \pi\,(PM)^2\,dx$$

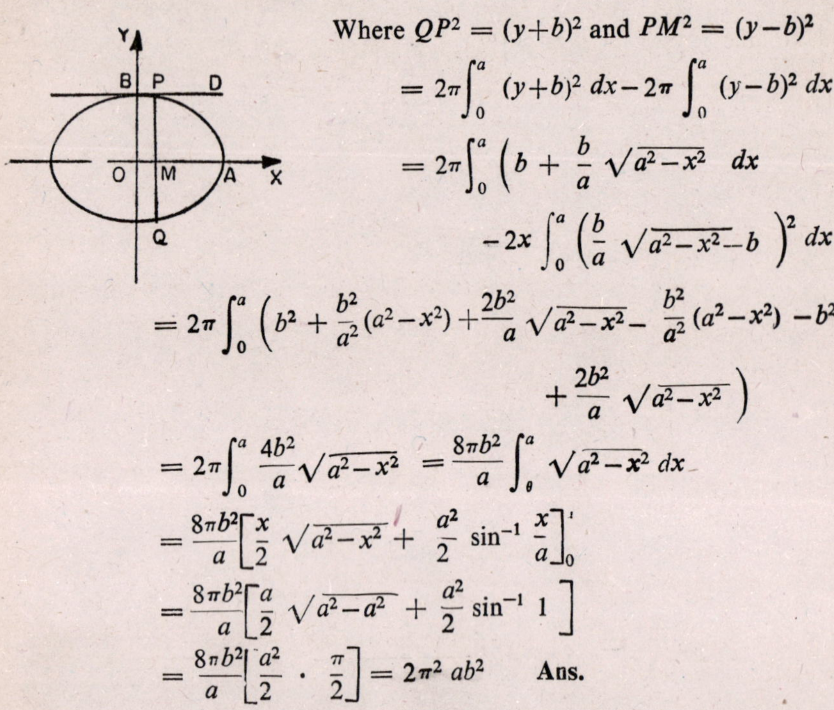

Where $QP^2 = (y+b)^2$ and $PM^2 = (y-b)^2$

$$= 2\pi\int_0^a (y+b)^2\,dx - 2\pi\int_0^a (y-b)^2\,dx$$

$$= 2\pi\int_0^a \left(b + \frac{b}{a}\sqrt{a^2-x^2}\right.\ dx$$

$$-2x\int_0^a \left(\frac{b}{a}\sqrt{a^2-x^2}-b\right)^2 dx$$

$$= 2\pi\int_0^a \left(b^2 + \frac{b^2}{a^2}(a^2-x^2) + \frac{2b^2}{a}\sqrt{a^2-x^2} - \frac{b^2}{a^2}(a^2-x^2) - b^2 + \frac{2b^2}{a}\sqrt{a^2-x^2}\right)$$

$$= 2\pi\int_0^a \frac{4b^2}{a}\sqrt{a^2-x^2} = \frac{8\pi b^2}{a}\int_\theta^a \sqrt{a^2-x^2}\,dx$$

$$= \frac{8\pi b^2}{a}\left[\frac{x}{2}\sqrt{a^2-x^2} + \frac{a^2}{2}\sin^{-1}\frac{x}{a}\right]_0^1$$

$$= \frac{8\pi b^2}{a}\left[\frac{a}{2}\sqrt{a^2-a^2} + \frac{a^2}{2}\sin^{-1} 1\right]$$

$$= \frac{8\pi b^2}{a}\left[\frac{a^2}{2}\cdot\frac{\pi}{2}\right] = 2\pi^2 ab^2 \qquad \textbf{Ans.}$$

Problem 8 Find the volume of the solid generated by the revolution of the curve $(a-x)\,y^2 = a^2 x$ about is asymptote.

Solution The asymptote of its curve is given as $x = a$

The volume is therefore

$$= 2\pi\int_0^\infty (PM^2)\cdot dy)$$

$$PM^2 = (x-a)^2$$

But since $\quad (a-x)\,y^2 = a^2 x$

$$\Rightarrow \quad x = \frac{ay^2}{a^2+y^2} = 2\pi\int_0^\infty \left[\frac{ay^2}{a^2+y^2} - a\right]^2 dy$$

$$= 2\pi\int_0^\infty \left[\frac{ay^2 - a^3 - a^2y^2}{a^2+y^2}\right]^2 dy = 2\pi a^6 \int_0^\infty \frac{1}{(a^2+y^2)^2}\,dy$$

Let $\quad y = a\tan\theta \quad$ when $y \to 0, \quad \theta \to 0$

$dy = a\sec^2\theta\,d\theta$ and when $y \to \infty$, $\theta \to \pi/2$

$$= 2\pi a^6 \int_0^{\pi/2} \frac{a\sec^2\theta\,d\theta}{a^4\sec^4\theta}$$

$$= 2\pi a^3 \int_0^{\pi/2} \cos^2\theta\,d\theta = \pi a^3 \int_0^{\pi/0} (1+\cos^2\theta)\,d\theta$$

$$= \pi a^3 \left[\theta + \frac{\sin 2\theta}{2}\right]_0^{\pi/2} = \pi a^3 \times \frac{\pi}{2} = \frac{\pi^2 a^3}{2} \qquad \textbf{Ans.}$$

Problem 9 A surface is formed by the revolution of the curve $y = x^2 e^{-x}$ about the axis of x, show that the volume enclosed by the part of the surface which corresponds to the positive values of x is $3/4\pi$

Solution The eqn. of the curve is $y = x^2 e^{-x}$. The limit for exponential series is upto infinity, hence

$$\text{Volume} = \pi \int_0^\infty y^2\, dx = \pi \int_0^\infty x^4 e^{-2x}\, dx$$

$$= \pi \left[\frac{x^4 e^{-2x}}{-2}\right]_0^\infty - \pi \int_0^\infty \frac{4x^3 e^{-2x}}{-2}\, dx$$

$$= 2\pi \int_0^\infty x^3 e^{-2x}\, dx$$

$$= 2\pi \left[\frac{x^3 e^{-2x}}{-2}\right]_0^\infty - 2\pi \int_0^\infty \frac{3x^2 e^{-2x}}{-2}\, dx$$

$$= 3\pi \int_0^\infty x^2 e^{-2x}\, dx$$

$$= 3\pi \left[\frac{x^2 e^{-2x}}{-2}\right]_0^\infty - 3\pi \int_0^\infty \frac{2x\, e^{-2x}}{-2}\, dx$$

$$= 3\pi \int_0^\infty x e^{-2x}\, dx$$

$$= 3\pi \left\{\frac{xe^{-2x}}{-2}\right\}_0^\infty + \frac{1}{2} \int e^{-2x}\, dx$$

$$= 3\pi \left[\frac{1}{2}\, \frac{e^{-2x}}{-2}\right]_0^\infty = 3\pi\left(\frac{1}{4}\right) = \frac{3}{4}\pi.$$

Problem 10 Show that the volume of the solid generated by the revolution of the curve $r = a + b \sec\theta$ about its asymptote is

$$2\pi a^2 \left(\frac{2}{3}a + \frac{\pi b}{2}\right)$$

Solution Asymptote of the curve $r = a + b\sec\theta$ is $x = b$

Reqd. volume is therefore

$$\text{Volume} = 2 \int_0^\infty \pi\, (PM)^2\, dy$$

$$= 2 \int_0^\infty \pi\, (x - b)^2\, dy/d\theta\; d\theta$$

$$y = r \sin\theta = (a + b\sec\theta)\sin\theta$$

$$y = a\sin\theta + b\tan\theta$$

$$\frac{dy}{} = a\cos\theta + b\sec^2\theta$$

$\therefore \quad \frac{dy}{d\theta}\cdot d\theta = (a \cos \theta + \sec^2 \theta)\, d\theta$

$$= 2\pi \int_0^{\pi/2} a^2 \cos^2 \theta\, (a \cos \theta + b \sec^2 \theta)\, d\theta$$

$$= 2a^2\pi \left[\int_0^{\pi/2} a \cos^3 \theta\, d\theta + \int_0^{\pi/2} b\, d\theta \right]$$

$$= 2a^2\pi \left[a\cdot \frac{2}{3} + b\, \theta \right]_0^{\pi/2}$$

$$= 2a^2\pi \left[\frac{2a}{3} + \frac{b}{2}\, \pi \right]$$

$$= 2\pi a^2 \left[\frac{2a}{3} + \frac{\pi b}{2} \right] \quad \text{Ans.}$$

Problem 1 Find the surface of the sphere of radius a.

Solution The eqn. of the sphere is given by $x^2 + y^2 = a^2$ differentiating both sides we haves,

$$2x + 2y \frac{dy}{dx} = 0 \quad \Rightarrow \quad \frac{dy}{dx} = -\frac{x}{y}$$

Therefore $\quad \frac{ds}{dx} = \sqrt{1 + \left(\frac{dy}{dx}\right)^2} = \sqrt{1 + \frac{x^2}{y^2}}$

$$\frac{ds}{dx} = \frac{a}{y}$$

Required volume is therefore,

$$= 2 \int_0^a 2\pi y\, \frac{a}{y}\, dx \qquad [\because \text{ The function is symmetrical}]$$

$$= 4\pi a x \Big]_0^a = 4\pi a \cdot a = 4\pi a^2$$

Problem 2 Find the surface of the solid generated by revolving the arc of the parabola $y^2 = 4ax$ bounded by its latus rectum about x-axis.

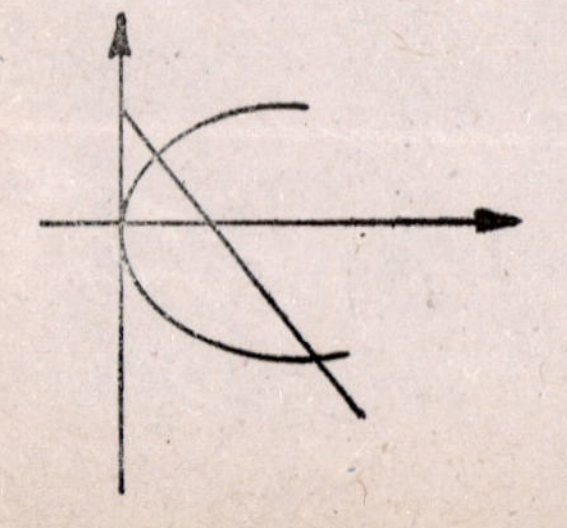

Solution Eqn. of the parabola

$$y^2 = 4ax$$

diff. on both sides.

$$2y \frac{dy}{dx} = 4a$$

$$\frac{dy}{dx} = \frac{2a}{y}$$

$$\therefore \quad \frac{ds}{dx} = \sqrt{1 + \left(\frac{dy}{dx}\right)^2} = \sqrt{1 + \frac{4a^2}{y^2}} = \sqrt{\frac{y^2 + 4a^2}{y^2}}$$

$$= \frac{\sqrt{4ax + 4a^2}}{y} = \frac{2\sqrt{a}\sqrt{x + a}}{y}$$

Required surface

$$= 2\int_0^a 2\pi y \, \frac{2\sqrt{a}\ \sqrt{x + a}}{y}\, dx = 4\pi\sqrt{a}\ \frac{2}{3}\ (x + a)^{\frac{3}{2}}\Big]_0^a$$

$$= \frac{8}{3}\pi\sqrt{a}\left[2\sqrt{2}\ a^{3/2} - a^{3/2}\right]$$

$$= \frac{8}{3}\pi\sqrt{a}\ (2\sqrt{2} - 1)\ a^{3/2} = \frac{8}{3}\pi a^2 (2\sqrt{2} - 1)$$

Problem 3 The part of the parabola $y^2 = 4ax$ bounded by the latus rectum revolves about the tangent at the vertex, find the area of the curved surface of the reel thus generated.

Solution The parabola revolves about the tangent at its vertex i.e. about y-axis.

$$\text{Reqr. surface} = 2\int_0^{2a} 2\pi x \cdot \frac{ds}{dy}\ dy$$

$$\frac{ds}{dy} = \sqrt{1 + \left(\frac{dx}{dy}\right)^2} = 1 + \sqrt{\left(\frac{y}{2a}\right)^2} = \frac{\sqrt{y^2 + 4a^2}}{2a}$$

[∴ The co-ordinate of the latues rectum when intersect the parabola of type $y^2 = ax$ is $(a \cdot 2a)$ and its vertex is $(0, 0)$)

$$\text{Reqd. surface,} = 4\pi \int_0^{2a} \frac{y^2}{4a} \cdot \frac{\sqrt{y^2 + 4a^2}}{2a}\ dy$$

$$= \frac{\pi}{2a^2}\int_0^{2a} y^2\ \sqrt{y^2 + 4a^2}\ dy$$

Let $\quad y = 2a \tan\theta$

$dy = 2a \sec^2\theta\ d\theta \qquad$ when $\quad y \to 0,\ \theta \to 0$

and $y \to 2a,\ \theta \to \frac{\pi}{4}$

$$= \frac{\pi}{2a^2}\int_0^{\pi/4} 4a^2 \tan^2\theta\ 2a \sec\theta \,.\, 2a \sec^2\theta\ d\theta$$

$$= \frac{\pi}{2a^2} \times 16a^4 \int_0^{\pi/4} \tan^2\theta \sec^3\theta\ d\theta$$

$$= 8\pi a^2 \int_0^{\pi/4} (\sec^2\theta - 1) \sec^3\theta\ d\theta$$

$$= 8\pi a^2 \left[\int_0^{\pi/4} \sec^5\theta\ d\theta - \int_0^{\pi/4} \sec^3\theta\ d\theta\right]$$

Applying the Reduction formula for $\int \sec^n x\, dx$

$$= 8\pi a^2 \left[\left\{\tan\theta \sec^2\theta\right\}_0^{\pi/4} + \frac{3}{4}\int_0^{\pi/4} \sec^3\theta\, d\theta\right]$$

$$- 8\pi a^2 \int_0^{\pi/4} \sec^3\theta\, d\theta$$

$$= 8\pi a^2 \left[\frac{\sqrt{2}}{2} - \frac{1}{4}\int_0^{\pi/4} \sec^3\theta\, d\theta\right]$$

$$= \pi a^2 \left[4\sqrt{2} - 2\left\{\tan\theta\sec\theta\left\{_0^{\pi/4} \frac{\pi}{4} - \frac{2}{2}\int_0^{\pi/4} \sec\theta\, d\theta\right]$$

$$= \pi a^2 \left[4\sqrt{2} - \sqrt{2} - \left\{\log(\sec\theta \;\tan\theta)\right\}_0^{\pi/4}\right]$$

$$= \pi a^2 [4\sqrt{2} - \sqrt{2} - \log(\sqrt{2} + 1)]$$

$$= \pi a^2 [5\sqrt{2} - \log(\sqrt{2} + 1)]$$

Problem 4 Find the surface of the solid generated by the revolution of the astroid

$$x = a\cos^3 t,\; y = a\sin^3 t$$

about the axis of x.

Solution $x = a\cos^3 t,\; y = a\sin^3 t$

$$\text{Surface area} = 2\int_0^{\pi/2} 2\pi y \,.\, \frac{ds}{dt} \,.\, dt$$

$$\frac{dx}{dt} = -3a\cos^2 t \sin t$$

$$\frac{dy}{dt} = 3a\sin^2 t\cos t \qquad \sqrt{\left(\frac{dx}{dt}\right)^2 + \left(\frac{dy}{dt}\right)^2}$$

$$\therefore \qquad \frac{ds}{dt} = \sqrt{9a^2\cos^4 t\sin^2 t + 9a^2\sin^4 t\cos^2 t}$$

$$= 3a\sin t\cos t$$

$$\text{Reqd. surface} = 6a\int_0^{\pi/2} 2\pi a\sin^3 t\sin t\cos t\, dt$$

$$= 12\pi a^2 \int_0^{\pi/2} \sin^4 t\cos t\, dt$$

$$= 12\pi a^2 \left.\frac{\sin^5 t}{5}\right]_0^{\pi/2} = 12\pi a^2\,\frac{1}{5} = \frac{}{5}$$

Problem 5 Find the surface of the solid generated by revolving the lemniscate $r^2 = a^2 \cos 2\theta$ about the initial time.

Solution The eqn. of lemniscate, $r^2 = a^2 \cos 2\theta$.

$$2r \frac{dr}{d\theta} = -2a^2 \sin 2\theta$$

$$\Rightarrow \frac{dr}{d\theta} = -a^2 \sin 2\theta$$

Therefore $$\frac{dr}{d\theta} = -\frac{a^2 \sin 2\theta}{r}$$

Then $$\frac{ds}{d\theta} = \sqrt{r^2 + \left(\frac{dr}{d\theta}\right)^2}$$

$$= \sqrt{a^2 \cos 2\theta + \frac{a^4 \sin^2 2\theta}{r^2}}$$

$$= \sqrt{a^2 \cos 2\theta + \frac{a^4 \sin^2 2\theta}{a^2 \cos 2\theta}} = \frac{a}{\sqrt{\cos 2\theta}}$$

[about initial line means about x-axis in polar co-ordinate its eqn. is $\theta = 0$]

Surface area $$= 2\int_0^{\pi/4} 2\pi y \frac{ds}{d\theta} \cdot d\theta$$

$\therefore$ The function is symmetrical

$$= 4\pi \int_0^{\pi/4} r \sin\theta \frac{a}{\sqrt{\cos 2\theta}} d\theta$$

$$= 4\pi a^2 \int_0^{\pi/4} \sqrt{\cos 2\theta} \frac{\sin\theta}{\sqrt{\cos 2\theta}}$$

$$= 4\pi a^2 \Big[-\cos\theta\Big]_0^{\pi/4}$$

$$= 4\pi a^2 \left[1 - \frac{1}{\sqrt{2}}\right] = 4\pi a^2 \frac{\sqrt{2} - 1)}{\sqrt{2}}$$

$$= 2\sqrt{2}\, \pi a^2 (\sqrt{2} -)$$

Problem 6 Find the surface of the solid obtained by revolving the cordiode $r = a(1 - \cos\theta)$ about the initial line

Solution $$r = a(1 - \cos\theta)$$

$$\frac{dr}{d\theta} = a \sin\theta$$

$$\frac{ds}{d\theta} = \sqrt{a^2 (1-\cos\theta)^2 + a^2 \sin^2\theta}$$

$$= a\sqrt{1 + \cos^2\theta + -2\sin\theta + \sin^2\theta}$$

$$= a\sqrt{2(1-\cos\theta)} = a\sqrt{2\times 2\sin^2\theta/2}$$

$$= 2a \sin\frac{\theta}{2}$$

Surface $\displaystyle\int_0^{\pi/2} 2\pi y \frac{ds}{d\theta} \cdot d\theta$

$$= 2\pi\int_0^{\pi/2} r\sin\theta \times 2a\sin\theta/2\, d\theta$$

$$= 4a\pi \int_0^{\pi/2} a\times 2\sin^2\theta/2 \sin\theta/2 \sin\theta/2\, d\theta$$

$$= 8a^2\pi \int 2\sin\theta/2\cos\theta/2\sin^3\theta/2\, d\theta$$

$$= 16a^2\pi\int_0^{\pi/2} \sin^4\theta/2\cdot\cos\theta/2\, d\theta$$

$$= 16\pi a^2 \left.\frac{2\sin^5\theta/2}{5}\right]_0^{\pi/2} = \frac{32\pi a^2}{5}$$

Problem 7 Find the area of the surface of revolution formed by revolving the curve $r = 2a\cos\theta$ about the initial line.

Solution $r = 2a\cos\theta$

$$\frac{dr}{d\theta} = -2a\sin\theta$$

$$\frac{ds}{d\theta} = \sqrt{r^2 + \left(\frac{dr}{d\theta}\right)^2} = \sqrt{4a^2\cos^2\theta + 4a^2\sin^2\theta} = 2a$$

Requiredarea $\displaystyle = \int_0^{\pi/2} 2\pi y\frac{ds}{d\theta} . d\theta$

$$= 2\pi\int_0^{\pi/2} r\sin\theta \frac{ds}{d\theta}\, d\theta$$

$$= 2\pi\int_0^{\pi/2} 2a\cos\theta . \sin\theta\, 2a\, d\theta$$

$$= 8a^2\pi\int_0^{\pi/2} \sin\theta\cos\theta\, d\theta$$

$$= 8\pi a^2 \sin\left.\frac{\pi}{2}\right]_0^{\pi/2} = 8\pi a^2\times\frac{1}{2} = 4\pi a^2$$

Problem 8 Show that the ratio of the area S of the surface formed by the rotation of the arc of the cycloid $x = a(\theta + \sin\theta)$, $y = a(1 + \cos\theta)$ between two consecutive. Cusps about the axis of x to the area enclosed by the cycloid and the axis of x is 64/9.

Solution $x = a(\theta + \sin\theta),\ y = a(1 + \cos\theta)$

$$\frac{dx}{d\theta} = a(1 + \cos\theta)$$

$$\frac{dy}{d\theta} = -a\sin\theta$$

$$\frac{ds}{d\theta} = \sqrt{\left(\frac{dx}{d\theta}\right)^2 + \left(\frac{dy}{d\theta}\right)^2}$$

$$= \sqrt{a^2(1 + \cos\theta)^2 + a^2\sin^2\theta}$$

$$= a\sqrt{1 + \cos^2\theta + 2\cos\theta + \sin^2\theta}$$

$$= a \times 2\cos\theta/2 = 2a\cos\theta/2$$

Required surface is therefore,

$$= 2\int_0^{\pi} 2\pi y \cdot \frac{ds}{d\theta} \cdot d\theta$$

$$= 2\int_0^{\pi} 2\pi a(1 + \cos\theta)\, 2a\cos\theta/2\, d\theta$$

$$= 8a^2\pi \int_0^{\pi} \cos^3\theta/2\, d\theta = 16a^2\pi \int_0^{\pi} \cos^2\theta/2\, d\theta$$

where $\theta \to 0, t \to 0$ Let $\theta/2 = t$

and $\theta \to \pi, t \to \pi/2$ $d\theta = 2dt$

$$= 16a^2\pi \times 2\int_0^{\pi/2} \cos^3 t\, dt$$

[Applying Reduction formulae]

$$= 32a^2\pi \times \frac{2}{3} = \frac{64}{4}\pi a^2$$

Area $$= 2\int_0^{\pi} y \cdot \frac{dx}{d\theta} \cdot d\theta = 2\int_0^{\pi} a(1+\cos\theta)\, a(1+\cos\theta)\, d\theta$$

$$= 2a^2 \int_0^{\pi} (1 + \cos\theta)^2\, d\theta = 2a^2 \int_0^{\pi} 4\cos^4\theta/2\, d\theta$$

$$= 8a^2 \int_0^{\pi} \cos^4\frac{\theta}{2}\, d\theta$$

when $\theta \to 0, z \to 0$ Let $\theta/2 = z$

and $\theta \to \pi, z \to \pi/2$ $d\theta = 2dz$

$$= 8a^2 \cdot 2 \int_0^{\pi/2} \cos^4 z\, dz$$

$$= 16a^2 \frac{3}{4}\frac{1}{2}\frac{a}{2} = 3\pi a^2$$

Required Ratio is ttherefore,

$$= \frac{64}{4}\frac{\pi a^2}{3\pi\, a^2} = \frac{64}{9}$$

Problem 10. Prove that the surface of the solid obtained by revolving the ellipse $b^2 x^2 + a^2 y^2 = a^2 b^2$ about the axis of x is

$$2\pi ab\, [\sqrt{(1-e^2)} + 1/e \sin^{-1} e]$$

e being the eccentricity of the ellipse,

Solution The relation of the eccentricity to a and b is

$$b^2 = a^2\,(1-e^2) \qquad \textit{(Remember)}$$

Let the eqn. of ellipse is $\frac{x^2}{a^2} + \frac{y^2}{b^2} = 1$. Differentiating on both sides,

$$\frac{2x}{a^2} + \frac{2y}{b^2}\frac{dy}{dx} = 0$$

$$\Rightarrow \quad \frac{dy}{dx} = -\frac{b^2}{a^2}\frac{x}{y}$$

Therefore, $$\frac{ds}{dx} = \sqrt{1 + \left(\frac{dy}{dx}\right)^2} = \sqrt{1 + \frac{b^4 x^2}{a^4 y^2}}$$

$$= \sqrt{\frac{a^4 y^2 + b^4 x^2}{a^4 y^2}} = \frac{\sqrt{a^4 y^2 + b^4 x^2}}{a^2 y}$$

We have $a^2 y^2 = a^2 b^2 - b^2 x^2 = b^2 (x^2 - x^2)$

From the given eqn. of the ellipse

$$\therefore \quad a^4 y^2 = a^2 b^2 (a^2 - x^2)$$

hence $a^4 y^2 + b^4 x^2 = a^2 b^2 (a^2 - x^2) + b^4 x^2$

$$= b^2 [a^4 - (a^2 - b^2)\, x^2]$$

$$\therefore \quad \frac{\sqrt{a^4 y^2 + b^4 x^2}}{a^2 y} = b\,\frac{\sqrt{a^4 - (a^2 - b^2)\, x^2}}{a^2 y}$$

Required surface area

$$=2\int_0^a 2\pi\, y\, \frac{ds}{dx}\cdot dx$$

$$=4\pi\int_0^a y\cdot b\,\frac{\sqrt{a^4-(a^2-b^2)\,x^2}}{a^2\, y}\,dx$$

Now using the result $b^2 = a^2\,(1-e^2)$

$$\Rightarrow \quad a^2 e^2 = a^2 - b^2$$

$$=\frac{4\pi b}{a^2}\int_0^a \sqrt{a^4 - a^2 e^2 x^2}\,dx$$

$$=\frac{4\pi b}{a^2}\,ae\int_0^a \sqrt{\left(\frac{a^2}{e^2}-x^2\right)}\,dx$$

$$=\frac{4\pi be}{a}\left[\frac{x}{2}\sqrt{\frac{a^2}{e^2}-x^2}+\frac{a^2}{2e^2}\sin^{-1}\frac{ex}{a}\right]_0^a$$

$$=\frac{4\pi be}{a}\left[\frac{a}{2}\sqrt{\frac{a^2}{e^2}-a^2}+\frac{a^2}{2e^2}\sin^{-1}e\right]$$

$$=\frac{4\pi be}{a}\left[\frac{a}{2}\cdot\frac{a\sqrt{1-e^2}}{e}+\frac{a^2}{2e^2}\sin^{-1}e\right]$$

$$=\frac{4\pi be}{a}\left[\frac{a^2}{2e}\sqrt{1-e^2}+\frac{a^2}{2e^2}\sin^{-1}e\right]$$

$$=2\pi ab\left[\sqrt{1-e^2}+\frac{1}{e}\sin^{-1}e\right]$$

Problem 11 An arc of a circle of radius a revolves about its chord. If the length of the arc is $2a\alpha$ ($\alpha < \pi/2$). Show that the area of the surface generated is $4\pi a^2\,(\sin\alpha-\alpha\cos\alpha)$.

Solution We have the circle with equation

$$x^2+y^2=a^2$$

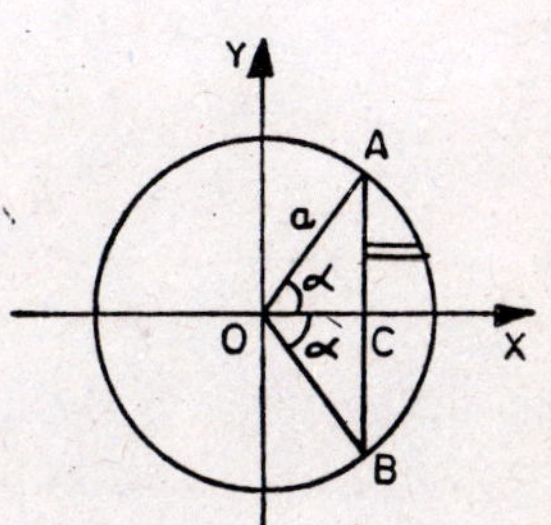

Required surface area

$$=2\int_a^b 2\pi\, PM\,\frac{ds}{dy}\cdot dy$$

a and b is to be determined

We have from the figure

$$OC = a\cos\alpha \qquad \frac{ds}{dy} = \sqrt{1+\left(\frac{dx}{dy}\right)^2}$$

$$AC = a\sin\alpha \qquad = \sqrt{1+\frac{y^2}{x^2}} = \frac{a}{x}$$

$$PM = (x - a\cos\alpha)$$

here $\quad a = 0 \quad$ and $\quad b = a\sin\alpha$

$$= 4\pi \int_0^{a\sin\alpha} (x - a\cos\alpha)\frac{a}{x}\,dy$$

$$= 4\pi\int_0^{a\sin\alpha} a\,dy - 4\pi\int_0^{a\sin\alpha} \frac{a^2\cos\alpha}{\sqrt{a^2-y^2}}\,dy$$

$$= 4\pi\int_0^{a\sin\alpha} dy - 4\pi a^2\cos\alpha\,\sin^{-1}\frac{y}{a}\int_0^{a\sin\alpha}$$

$$= 4\pi a\cdot a\sin\alpha - 4\pi a^2\cos\alpha\,(\sin^{-1}\sin\alpha)$$

$$= 4\pi a^2(\sin\alpha - \alpha\cos\alpha)$$ **(*Proved*)**

Problem 12 Show that the surface of the solid obtained by revolving the arc of the curve $y = \sin x$ from $x = 0$ to $x = \pi$ about x-axis is

$$2\pi\,[\sqrt{2} + \log(1 + \sqrt{2}]$$

Solution Surface of the solid is given

$$= \int_0^{\pi} 2xy\,\frac{ds}{dx}\cdot dx$$

$$\frac{ds}{dx} = \sqrt{1+\left(\frac{dy}{dx}\right)^2} = \sqrt{1+\cos^2 x}$$

$$= 2\pi\int_0^{\pi} \sin x\sqrt{1+\cos^2 x}\,dx$$

Let $\qquad \cos x = t \qquad$ when $x \to 0,\ t = 1$

$-\sin x\,dx = dt \qquad$ and $\quad x \to \pi,\ t = -1$

$\sin x\,dx = -dt$

$$= -2\pi\int_1^{-1} \sqrt{1+t^2}\,dt$$

$$= 2\pi\int_{-1}^{1} \sqrt{1+t^2}\,dt \quad [\because \text{ The functions is even}]$$

$$= 2\times 2\pi\int_0^1 \sqrt{1+t^2}\,dt$$

$$= 4\pi\left[t\,\frac{\sqrt{1+t^2}}{2} + \frac{t^2}{2}\log\left(t + \sqrt{1+t^2}\right)\right]_0^1$$

$$= 4\pi\left[\frac{1}{\sqrt{2}} + \frac{1}{2}\log(1+\sqrt{2})\right]$$

$$= \frac{4\pi}{2}\left[\sqrt{2} + \log(1+\sqrt{2})\right] \qquad \textit{(Proved)}$$

Problem 13 Prove that the surface generated by the revolution of the tractrix

$$x = a\cos t + \frac{a}{2}\log\tan^2\frac{t}{2},\ y = a\sin t$$

about its asymptote is equal to the surface of a sphere of radius a.

Solution The asymptote is about x-axis.

The surface of the tractrix will be then given as

$$= 2\int_0^{\pi} 2\pi y\,\frac{ds}{dt}\,.\,dt$$

$$\frac{ds}{dt} = \sqrt{\left(\frac{dx}{dt}\right)^2 + \left(\frac{dy}{dt}\right)^2}$$

$$= \sqrt{\left(\frac{a\cos^2 t}{\sin t}\right)^2 + a\cos t}$$

$$= \sqrt{\frac{a^2\cos^4 t}{\sin^2 t} + a^2\cos^2 t}$$

$$= a\sqrt{\frac{\cos^4 t + \sin^2 t\cos^2 t}{\sin^2 t}}$$

$$= a\cos t\,\frac{\sqrt{(\sin^2 t + \cos^2 t)}}{\sin t}$$

$$\frac{ds}{dt} = a\cot t$$

Reqd. surface

$$= 2\int_0^{\pi/2} 2\pi y\cdot a\cot t\,dt$$

$$= 4\pi\int_0^{\pi/2} a\sin t\,a\,\frac{\cos t}{\sin t}\,dt$$

$$= 4\pi a^2\int_0^{\pi/2}\cos t\,dt$$

$$= 4\pi a^2\sin t\,\Big]_0^{\pi/2} = 4\pi a^2$$

which is equal to the surface of a sphere of radius a. **(Proved)**

Problem 14 Prove that the surface and the volume of the solid generated by the revolution, about the x-axis of the loop of the curve

$$x = t^2,\ y = t - \frac{t^3}{3}$$

are respectively 3π and $\frac{3\pi}{4}$

Solution We have $x = t^2$ and $y = t - \frac{t^3}{3}$

$$\Rightarrow \quad y = t - \frac{t}{3} \cdot t^2$$

$$\Rightarrow \quad y = t - \frac{tx}{3}$$

$$\Rightarrow \quad 3y = t\,(3 - x)$$

Squaring on both sides we have,

$$9y^2 = t^2 (3-x)^2 \qquad [\because\ x = t^2]$$

$$\Rightarrow \quad 9y^2 = x\,(3-x)^2$$

$$\Rightarrow 9y^2 = x\,[9 + x^2 - 6x]$$

$$x \to 3 \quad \text{when} \quad y \to 0$$

and when $x \to 0,\ t \to 0$ when $x \to 3,\ t \to \sqrt{3}$

Registered surface $= \int_0^{\sqrt{3}} 2\pi y \cdot \frac{ds}{dt} \cdot dt$

$$\frac{ds}{dt} = \sqrt{\left(\frac{dx}{dt}\right)^2 + \left(\frac{dy}{dt}\right)^2}$$

$$= \sqrt{4t^2 + (1-t^2)^2} = \sqrt{(1+t^2)^2} = 1 + t^2$$

Therefore,

$$s = 2\pi \int_0^{\sqrt{3}} \left(t - \frac{1}{3} t^3\right)(1 + t^2)\,dt$$

$$= 2\pi \int_0^{\sqrt{3}} \left(t + t^3 - \frac{t^3}{3} - \frac{t^5}{3}\right) dt$$

$$= 2\pi \left[\frac{t^2}{2} + \frac{t^4}{4} - \frac{t^4}{12} - \frac{t^6}{18}\right]_0^{\sqrt{3}}$$

$$= 2\pi \left[\frac{3}{2} + \frac{9}{4} - \frac{9}{12} - \frac{27}{18}\right]$$

$$= 2\pi \left[\frac{3}{2} + \frac{9}{4} - \frac{3}{4} - \frac{3}{2}\right] = 2\pi \times \frac{6}{4} = 3\pi \qquad \textit{(Proved)}$$

and volume $= \int_0^{\sqrt{3}} \pi y^2 \frac{dx}{dt} \cdot dt = \pi \int_0^{\sqrt{3}} \left(t - \frac{t^3}{3}\right)^2 2t\, dt$

$$= 2\pi \int_0^{\sqrt{3}} \left(t^2 + \frac{t^6}{9} - \frac{2t^4}{3}\right) t\, dt$$

$$= 2\pi \int_0^{\sqrt{3}} \left(t^3 + \frac{t^7}{9} - \frac{2t^5}{3}\right) dt$$

$$= 2\pi \left[\frac{t^4}{4} + \frac{t^8}{72} - \frac{2t^6}{18}\right]_0^{\sqrt{3}}$$

$$= 2\pi \left[\frac{9}{4} + \frac{9}{8} - 3\right] = 2\pi \left[\frac{18 + 9 - 24}{8}\right]$$

$$= 2\pi \times \frac{3}{84} = \frac{3\pi}{4} \qquad \textit{(Proved)}$$

Problem 15 **The figure bounded by a quadrant of circle of radius a and the tangents at its extremities revolves about one of these tangents, prove that**

(i) The volume of the solid thus generated is $(10 - 3\pi)\, \pi a^3/6$

(ii) the area of the curved surface so generated is $\pi\, (\pi - 2)\, a^2$.

Solution (i) The equation of circle is

$$x^2 + y^2 = a^2$$

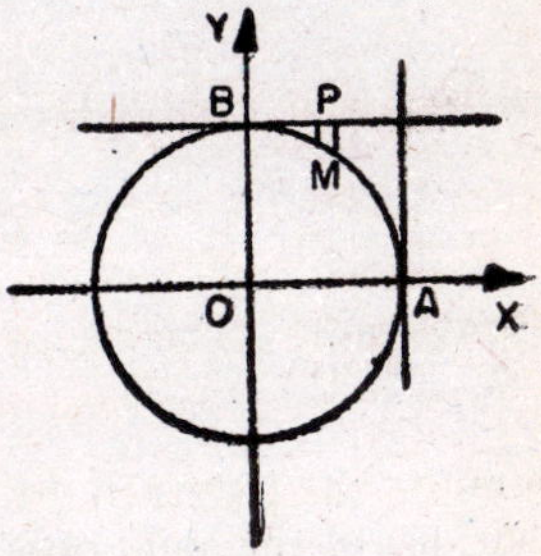

Required volume $= \pi \int_0^a PM^2\, dx$

$$PM^2 = (a - y)^2$$

$$= \pi \int_0^a (a - y)^2\, dx$$

$$= \pi \int_0^a (a^2 + y^2 - 2ay)\, dx$$

$$= \pi \int_0^a [a^2 + a^2 - x^2 - 2a\sqrt{a^2 - x^2}]\, dx$$

$$= \pi \int_0^a [2a^2 - x^2 - 2a\sqrt{a^2 - x^2}]\, dx$$

$$= \pi \left[2a^2 x - \frac{x^3}{3} - 2a \left\{\frac{x}{2}\sqrt{a^2 - x^2} + \frac{a^2}{2} \sin^{-1} \frac{x}{a}\right\}\right]$$

$$= \pi \left[2a^3 - \frac{a^3}{3} - 2a \left\{\frac{a}{2} \sqrt{a^2 - a^2} + \frac{a^2}{2} \sin^{-1} \frac{a}{a}\right\}\right]$$

$$= \pi \left[\frac{5a^3}{3} - 2a \left\{\frac{a^2}{2} \frac{\pi}{2}\right\}\right] = \pi \left[\frac{5a^3}{3} - 2a \cdot \frac{\pi a^2}{4}\right]$$

$$= \pi \left[\frac{5a^3}{3} - \frac{\pi a^3}{2}\right] = \pi \left[\frac{10a^3 - 3\pi a^3}{6}\right]$$

$$= \frac{\pi a^3}{6} (10 - 3\pi) \qquad \textit{(Proved)}$$

(ii) Area $$= \int_0^a 2\pi \, PM \frac{ds}{dx} \cdot dx$$

$$= 2\pi \int_0^a (a - y) \frac{a}{y} dx$$

$$\left[\frac{ds}{dx} = \sqrt{1 + \left(\frac{dy}{dx}\right)^2} = \sqrt{1 + \frac{x^2}{y^2}} = \frac{a}{y}\right]$$

$$= 2\pi \int_0^a \frac{(a - \sqrt{a^2 - x^2})}{\sqrt{a^2 - x^2}} dx$$

$$= 2\pi \int_0^a \frac{a}{\sqrt{a^2 - x^2}} dx - 2\pi \int_0^a dx$$

$$= 2\pi a \sin^{-1} \frac{x}{a}\Big]_0^a - 2\pi x\Big]_0^a$$

$$= 2\pi a \frac{\pi}{2} - 2\pi a = \pi^2 a - 2\pi a$$

$$= \pi a (\pi - 2) \qquad \textit{(Proved)}$$

Problem 16 The arc of the cycloid

$$x = a(\theta - \sin\theta), \; y = a(1 - \cos\theta)$$

joining the points (0, 0) $(a\pi, 2a)$ revolves about its chord, show that the surface of the solid obtained is

$$\frac{32\pi a^2 (\pi - 2)}{3\sqrt{\pi^2 + 4}}$$

Solution $x = a(\theta - \sin\theta)$, $y = a(1 - \cos\theta)$

Surface of the solid is given as

$$= \int_0^\pi 2\pi . PM \frac{ds}{d\theta} d\theta$$

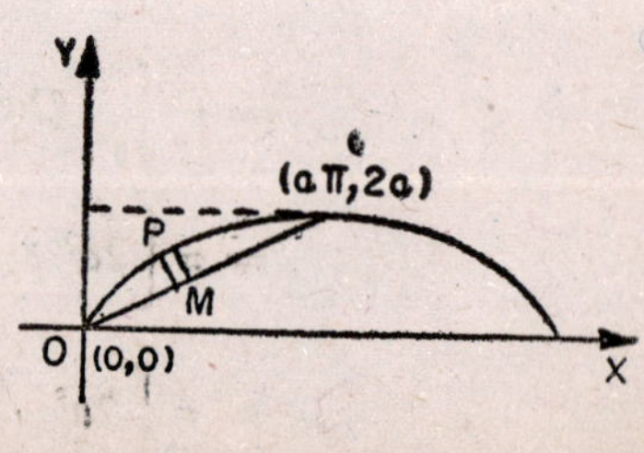

The equation of the line joining points (0, 0) and $(a \cdot \pi \cdot 2a)$ i.e.

$$y = \frac{2a}{a\pi}(x)$$

$$\Rightarrow \quad y = \frac{2x}{\pi} \quad \Rightarrow \quad \pi y - 2x = 0 \qquad (1)$$

Now the perpendicular distance from $P(x, y)$ to line (i) is given by

$$PM = \frac{\pi y - 2x}{\sqrt{\pi^2 + 4}} = 2\pi \int_0^{\pi} \frac{\pi y - 2x}{\sqrt{\pi^2 + 4}} \frac{ds}{d\theta} \cdot d\theta$$

$$\frac{ds}{d\theta} = \sqrt{\left(\frac{dx}{d\theta}\right)^2 + \left(\frac{dy}{d\theta}\right)^2}$$

$$\frac{dx}{d\theta} = a\,(1 - \cos\theta)$$

$$\frac{dy}{d\theta} = a \sin\theta$$

$$\therefore \quad \frac{ds}{d\theta} = \sqrt{a^2 (1 - \cos\theta)^2 + a^2 \sin^2\theta}$$

$$= a\sqrt{1 + \cos^2\theta - 2\cos\theta + \sin^2\theta}$$

$$= a \times 2 \sin\frac{\theta}{2} = 2a \sin\frac{\theta}{2}$$

Required Area $= 2\pi \int_0^{\pi} \frac{\pi y - 2x}{\sqrt{\pi^2 + 4}} \times 2a \sin\frac{\theta}{2}\, d\theta$

$$= \frac{4a\pi}{\sqrt{4 + \pi^2}} \int_0^{\pi} [\pi\,(1 - \cos\theta) - 2\,(\theta - \sin\theta)] \sin\frac{\theta}{2}\, d\theta$$

$$= \frac{4\pi a^2}{\sqrt{\pi^2 + 4}} \int_0^{\pi} \left(2\pi \sin^3\frac{\theta}{2} - 2\theta \sin\frac{\theta}{2} + 4\sin^2\frac{\theta}{2}\cos\frac{\theta}{2}\right) d\theta$$

$$= \frac{8\pi a^2}{\sqrt{\pi^2 + 4}} \int_0^{\pi} \left(\pi \sin^3\frac{\theta}{2} - \theta \sin\frac{\theta}{2} + 2\sin^2\frac{\theta}{2}\cos\frac{\theta}{2}\right) d\theta$$

Let $\theta/2 = t$ when $\theta \to 0,\ t \to 0$

$d\theta = 2dt$ and $\theta \to \pi,\ t \to \theta/2$

$$= \frac{16\pi a^2}{\sqrt{\pi^2 + 4}} \int_0^{\pi/2} (\pi \sin^3 t - 2t \sin t + 2\sin^2 t \cos t)\, dt$$

$$= \frac{16\,\pi a^2}{\sqrt{\pi^2+4}}\left[\frac{2\pi}{3} - 2\left\{-t\cos t + \sin t\Big|_0^{\pi/2} + \frac{2}{3}\right\}\right]$$

$$= \frac{16\pi a^2}{\sqrt{\pi^2+4}}\left[\frac{2\pi}{3} - 2 + \frac{2}{3}\right]$$

$$= \frac{32\pi a^2}{\sqrt{\pi^2+4}}\left[\frac{\pi}{3} - 1 + \frac{1}{3}\right]$$

$$= \frac{32\pi a^2}{3\sqrt{4+\pi^2}}(\pi - 2) \qquad (Proved)$$

Problem 17 Show that the volume generated by the revolution of the loop of the curve $x^2 y^2 = a(x-a)(\pi-b)^2$ about the x-axis is

$$\pi a\,[1/2\,a^2 + 2ab - 5/2\,b^2 + b(2a+b)\log b/a\}$$

Solution $x^2 y^2 = a(x-a)(x-b)^2$

$$y^2 = \frac{a(x-a)(x-b)^2}{x^2}$$

The volume generated

$$= \int_a^b \pi y^2\,dx = \pi a\int_a^b \frac{(x-a)(x-b)^2}{x^2}dx$$

$$= \pi a\int_a^b \frac{(x-a)(x^2+b^2-2xb)}{x^2}dx$$

$$= \pi a\int_a^b \frac{[x^3 + b^2x - 2x^2b - ax^2 - ab^2 + 2axb]}{x^2}dx$$

$$= \pi a\int_a^b \left[x + \frac{b^2}{x} - (2b+a) - \frac{ab^2}{x^2} + \frac{2ab}{x}\right]$$

$$= \pi a\left[\frac{x^2}{2} + b^2\log x - (2b+a)x + \frac{ab^2}{x} + 2ab\log x\right]_a^b$$

$$= \pi a\left[\frac{b^2-a^2}{2} + \log\frac{b}{a}\,b(2a+b) - (2b+a)(b-a) + ab^2\left(\frac{1}{b} - \frac{1}{a}\right)\right]$$

$$= \pi a\left[b(2a+b)\log\frac{b}{a} + \frac{b^2}{a} - \frac{a^2}{2} - 2b^2 + ab + a^2 + ab^2\left(\frac{a-b}{ab}\right)\right]$$

$$= \pi a\left[b(2a+b)\log\frac{b}{a} + \frac{a^2}{2} - \frac{3b^2}{2} + ab + ab - b^2\right]$$

$$= \pi\left[b(2a+b)\log\frac{b}{a} + \frac{a^2}{2} - \frac{5}{2}b^2 + 2ab\right] \qquad (Proved)$$

Problem 18 Show that the surface of the solid obtained by revolving the arc of the curve $y = c \cos h\,(x/c)$ joining $(0, c)$ to (x, y) about x-axis is

$$\pi c\,(x + c \sin h\, x/c \cos h\, x/c)$$

Solution The surface of the solid generated is given by

$$\int_0^x 2\pi y \frac{ds}{dx}\,dx$$

Where
$$\frac{ds}{ax} = \sqrt{1 + \left(\frac{dy}{dx}\right)^2}$$

$$y = c \cos h\,(x/c)$$

$$\frac{dy}{dx} = \frac{c \sin h\, x/c}{c} = \sin h \frac{x}{c}$$

$$\therefore \quad \frac{ds}{dx} = \sqrt{1 + \sin h^2\, x/c} = \cos h \frac{x}{c}$$

$$= \int_0^{\pi} 2\pi c \cos h \left(\frac{x}{c}\right) \cos h \left(\frac{x}{c}\right) dx$$

$$= 2\pi c \int_0^x \cos h^2 \left(\frac{x}{c}\right) dx$$

$$= \pi c \int_0^x \left(1 + \cos h \frac{2x}{c}\right) dx$$

$$= \pi c \left[x + \frac{c}{2} \sin h \frac{2x}{c}\right]_0^x$$

$$= \pi c \left[x + \frac{c}{2} \sin h \frac{2x}{c}\right]$$

$$= \pi c \left[x + \frac{c}{2} \times 2 \sin h \frac{x}{c} \cos h \frac{x}{c}\right]$$

$$= \pi c \left(x + c \sin h \frac{x}{c} \cos h \frac{x}{c}\right)$$

Problem 19 The arc of the ellipse $x^2/a^2 + y^2/b^2 = 1$ lying in the first quadrant revolves about the line $y = b$ show that the volume of the solid thus obtained $(5/2 - \pi/2)\,\pi a b^2$.

Solution Volume is given as

$$= \int_0^a \pi\,(PM)^2\,dx$$

$$PM^2 = (b - y)^2$$

[Since the volume is to be find in the first quadrant hence 2 is not multiplied]

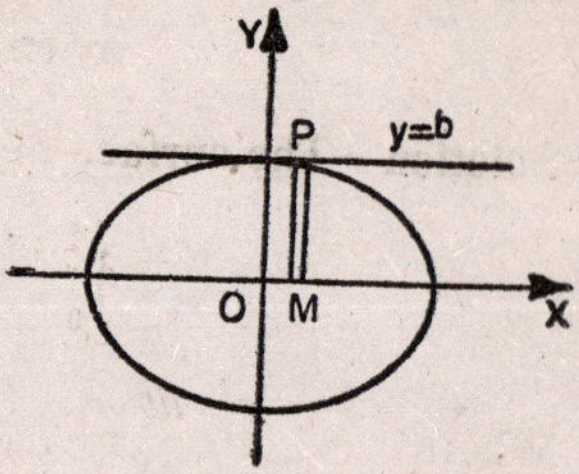

$$= \pi \int_0^a (b-y)^2\, dx$$

$$= \pi \int_0^a (b^2 + y^2 - 2by)\, dx$$

$$= \pi \int_0^a \left[b^2 + \frac{b^2}{a^2}(a^2-x^2) - \frac{2b^2}{a}\sqrt{a^2-x^2} \right] dx$$

$$= \pi \left[b^2 x + \frac{b^2}{a^2}\left(a^2 x - \frac{x^3}{3}\right) - \frac{2b^2}{a}\left\{\frac{x}{2}\sqrt{a^2-x^2} + \frac{a^2}{2}\sin^{-1}\frac{x}{a}\right\}\right]_0^a$$

$$= \pi \left[ab^2 + \frac{b^2}{a^2}\left(a^3 - \frac{a^3}{3}\right) - \frac{2b^2}{a}\left\{\frac{a}{2} \times 0 + \frac{a^2}{2}\frac{\pi}{2}\right\}\right.$$

$$= \pi ab^2 \left[1 + 1 - \frac{1}{3} - \frac{2}{a^4} \times \frac{\pi a^2}{4} \right]$$

$$= \pi ab^2\, [5/3 - \pi/2].$$

(Proved)

Problem 20 Determine the volume generated by revolving the curve $y^2 = b^2 \log(a/x)$ lying between $x = a$ and $x = b$ about the axis of x where $b < a < 0$

Solution Required volume is given by

$$= \int_b^a \pi y^2\, dx = \pi \int_b^a b^2 \log\left(\frac{a}{x}\right) dx$$

$$= \pi b^2 \int_b^a \log\left(\frac{a}{x}\right) dx$$

$$= \pi b^2 \left[x \log\frac{a}{x} - \int_b^a -\frac{x}{a}\frac{1}{x}\, x\, dx \right]$$

$$= \pi b^2 \left[x \log\frac{a}{x} + x \right]_b^a$$

$$= \pi b^2 \left[a \log\frac{a}{a} + a - b \log\frac{a}{b} - b \right]$$

$$= \pi b^2 \left[a - b - b\log\frac{a}{b} \right]$$

(Proved)

Problem 21 Show that if the area lying within the cardiode $r = 2a(1 + \cos\theta)$ and without the parabola $2a = r(1 + \cos\theta)$ revolves about the initial line, the volume generated is $18\pi a^3$.

Solution $r = 2a\,(1 + \cos\theta)$

$$2a = r\,(1 + \cos\theta)$$

The pt. of intersection is given as

$$2a = 2a\,(1 + \cos\theta)^2$$

$$\theta = \pi/2$$

Then Required volume is then given as

$$= \int_0^{\pi/2} \frac{2}{3}\,\pi r^3 \sin\theta\, d\theta - \int_0^{\pi/2} \frac{2}{3}\,\pi r^3 \sin\theta\, d\theta$$

$$= \frac{2}{3}\,\pi \int_0^{\pi/2} (2a)^3\,(1 + \cos\theta)^3 \sin\theta\, d\theta$$

$$-\frac{2}{3}\,\pi \int_0^{\pi/2} \frac{8a^3}{(1 + \cos\theta)^3}\, \sin\theta\, d\theta$$

$$= \frac{2}{3}\,\pi 8a^3 \left[-\frac{(1 + \cos\theta)^4}{4}\right]_0^{\pi/2} - \frac{2}{3}\cdot\pi 8a^3 \int_0^{\pi/2} \frac{\sin\theta\, d\theta}{(1 + \cos\theta)^3}$$

$$= \frac{16}{3}\,\pi a^3 \left[4 - \frac{1}{4}\right] - \frac{16}{3}\,\pi a^3 \left[\frac{1 + \cos\theta)^{-2}}{2}\right]_0^{\pi/2}$$

$$= \frac{16}{3}\,\pi a^3 \left[4 - \frac{1}{4}\right] - \frac{16}{3}\,\pi a^3 \left[\frac{1}{2} - \frac{1}{8}\right]$$

$$= \frac{16}{3}\,\pi a^3 \left[4 - \frac{1}{4} - \frac{1}{2} + \frac{1}{8}\right] - \frac{16}{3}\,\pi a^3 \left[\frac{32 - 2 - 4 + 1}{8}\right]$$

$$= \frac{16}{3}\,\pi a^3 \times \frac{27}{8} = 18\pi a^3$$ *(Proved)*

Problem 22 Show that the volume of the solid formed by revolving one loop of the curve $r^2 = a^2 \cos^2\theta$ about the line $\theta = \pi/2$ is $\pi^2 a^3/4\sqrt{2}$.

Solution $r^2 = a^2 \cos^2\theta.$

Required volume

$$= \int_0^{\pi/4} \frac{2}{3}\,\pi\, r^3 \cos\theta\, d\theta$$

[∴ The revolution is about the line] $\theta = \pi/2$

$$= \frac{4}{3}\,\pi \int_0^{\pi/4} a^3 \cos^{3/2} 2\theta\, d\theta \cos\theta$$

$$= \frac{4}{3}\,\pi a^3 \int_0^{\pi/4} (1 - 2\sin^2\theta)^{3/2} \cos\theta\, d\theta$$

$$= \frac{4}{3}\,\pi a^3 \int_0^{\pi/4} (1 - 2\sin^2\theta)^{3/2} \cos\theta\, d\theta$$

Let $\sqrt{2}\sin\theta = \sin t$ when $\theta \to 0$, $t \to 0$

$$\sqrt{2}\cos\theta\, d\theta = \cos t\, dt \qquad \theta \to \pi/4, \quad t \to \pi/2$$

$$\cos\theta\, d\theta = \frac{\cos t\, dt}{\sqrt{2}}$$

$$= \frac{4}{3}\frac{\pi a^3}{\sqrt{2}}\int_0^{\pi/2} \cos^3 t \cos t\, dt$$

$$= \frac{4}{3}\frac{\pi a^3}{\sqrt{2}}\int_0^{\pi/2} \cos^4 t\, dt = \frac{4}{3}\frac{\pi a^3}{\sqrt{2}}\frac{3}{4}\cdot\frac{1}{2}\cdot\frac{\pi}{2}\frac{\pi^2 a^3}{4\sqrt{2}}$$

Problem 23 Prove that the volume generated by revolving the tractrix

$x = a\,[\cos t + \frac{1}{2}\log\tan^2 t/2]$

$y = a\sin t$ about its asymptote is $2/3\, \pi a^3$.

Solution Asymptote is about x axis

when $x \to 0$ $\quad t \to \pi/2$

and when $x \to \infty$ 0 $\quad t \to 0$

Required volume

$$= 2\int_0^{\pi/2} \pi y^2\, dx = 2\pi a^2 \int_0^{\pi/2} \sin^2 t \frac{dx}{dt}\, dt$$

$$\frac{dx}{dt} = a\left[-\sin t + \frac{1}{2}\cdot\frac{2}{2}\frac{\tan t/2 \sec^2 t/2}{\tan^2 t/2}\right]$$

$$= a\left[-\sin t + \frac{1}{2}\frac{1}{\cos t/2 \sin t/2}\right]$$

$$= a\left[-\sin t + \frac{1}{\sin t}\right] = a\left[\frac{1-\sin^2 t}{\sin t}\right]$$

$$\frac{dx}{dt} = \frac{a\cos^2 t}{\sin t}$$

Therefore volume is given by

$$= 2\pi a^3 \int_0^{\pi/2} \sin^2 t\, \frac{\cos^2 t}{\sin t}\, dt$$

$$= 2\pi a^3\left[-\frac{\cos^3 t}{3}\right]_0^{\pi/2} = \frac{2}{3}\pi a^3.$$

Problem 24 Show that the area of the surface of solid generated by revolving the tractrix $x = a\,(u - \tan hu)$, $y = a$ sechu about ox is equal to the area of the surface of the sphere of radius a.

Solution Area of the surface of the solid is given by

$$2\int_0^\infty 2\pi y\frac{ds}{du}\,du$$

Where $\dfrac{ds}{du}=\sqrt{\left(\dfrac{dx}{du}\right)^2+\left(\dfrac{dy}{du}\right)^2}$

$$\frac{dx}{du}=a\,(1-\sec h^2 u)=a\tan h^2 u$$

$$\frac{dy}{du}=-a\tan hu\sec hu$$

$\therefore$ $\dfrac{ds}{du}=\sqrt{a^2\tan h^4 u+a\tan h^2 u\sec h^2 u}$

$$=a\tan hu\sqrt{\sec h^2 u+\tan h^2 u}$$

$$=a\tan hu \qquad [\because \sec h^2 u+\tan h^2 u=1]$$

$\therefore$ Area $=2\displaystyle\int_0^\infty 2\pi a\tan hu\,du$

$$=4\pi a^2\Big[-\sec hu\Big]_0^\infty=-4\pi a^2\left[\lim_{u\to\infty}\frac{2}{e^u+e^{-u}}-\lim_{u\to\infty}\frac{2}{e^u+c^{-u}}\right]$$

$$=-4\pi a^2\,[0-1]=4\pi a^2$$

Which is equal to the surface area of the sphere of radius a. *(Proved)*

Problem 25 The region enclosed by the curve $y=\tan hx$ its asymptote $y=1$ if axis revolves about the asymptote. Show that the volume of the solid generated is $\pi\log 4/e$.

Solution The curve is $y=\tan hx$. Its asymptote is $y=1$ and the axis is revolving about its asymptote. Required volume is therefore

$$=\int_0^\infty \pi\,(PM)^2\,dx=\int_0^\infty \pi\,(\tan h\,x-1)^2\,dx$$

$$=\pi\int_0^\infty\left\{\frac{e^x-e^{-x}}{e^x+e^{-x}}-1\right\}^2dx$$

$$=\pi\int_0^\infty\left\{\frac{e^x-e^{-x}-e^x-e^{-x}}{e^x+e^{-x}}\right\}^2dx$$

$$=4\pi\int\frac{e^{-2x}}{(e^x+e^{-x})^2}\,dx$$

Let $I = \int \frac{e^{-2x}}{(e^x + e^{-x})^2} = \int \frac{dx}{(e^{2x}+1)^2}$

Let $e^{2x} + 1 = z$

$2e^{2x}\,dx = dz$

$dx = \frac{dz}{2e^{2x}} = \frac{dz}{2(z-1)}$

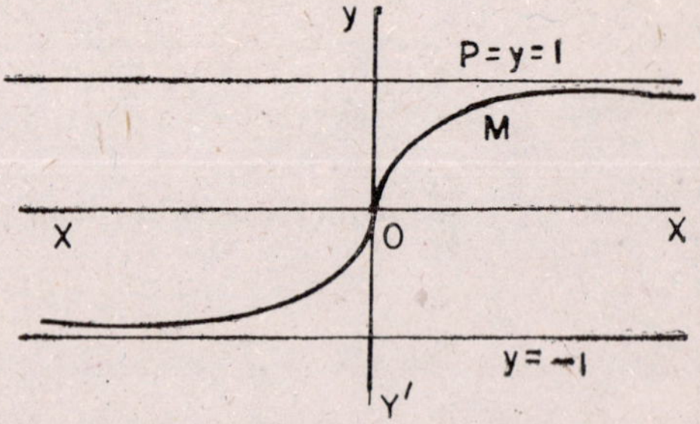

y

P = y = 1

M

X O X

y = −1

Y′

Required integral is therefore,

$= \frac{1}{2} \int \frac{dz}{z^2(z-1)}$

Which is reduced to

$1 = \frac{A}{z} + \frac{B}{z^2} + \frac{C}{z-1}$

$1 = A \cdot z\,(z-1) + B\,(z-1) + Cz^2$

Let $z = 1$ when $z = 0$, and $z = -1$

$C = 1$ $B = -1$ $A = -1$

$= \frac{1}{2}\int \frac{-dz}{z} - \int \frac{dz}{z^2} + \int \frac{dz}{(z-1)}$

$= -\frac{1}{2}\log z + 1/2z + \log(z-1)$

Putting back $z = e^{2x} + 1$

$= \frac{1}{2}\log \frac{z-1}{z} + \frac{1}{2z}$

$= \frac{1}{2}\log \frac{e^{2x}}{e^{2x}+1} + \frac{1}{2\,(e^{2x}+1)}$

Hence the volume is given as

$4\pi\left[-\frac{1}{2}\log \frac{e^{2x}}{e^{2x}+1} + \frac{1}{2\,(e^{2x}+1)}\right]_0^\infty$

$= 4\pi\left[-\frac{1}{2}\log \frac{e^0}{e^0+1} - \frac{1}{2\times 2}\right]$

$= 4\pi\left[-\frac{1}{2}\log \frac{1}{2} - \frac{1}{4}\right]$

$= 4\pi\left[-\frac{1}{2}\log 2 - \frac{1}{4}\log e\right]$

$= \pi\left[2\log 2 - \frac{4}{4}\log e\right]$

$= \pi\left[\log 4 - \log e\right] = \pi\left[\log \frac{4}{e}\right]$ *(Proved)*

Problem 26 Show that the curve $r = a(1 + 2\cos\theta)$ consists of an outer and inter loop. If the area of the inner loop is rotated through two right angles about the initial line show that the volume of the solid so formed is $\pi a^3/12$.

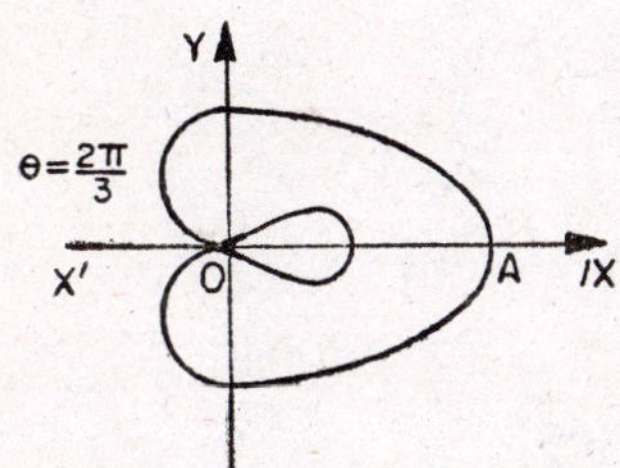

Solution Equation of the curve is

$$r = a(1 + 2\cos\theta)$$

The curve consists of two loops. For the upper half of the larget loop θ varies from 0 to $2\pi/3$ and for the lower half of the smaller loop θ from $2\pi/3$ to π.

Required volume = volume generated by the inner loop by the revolution about the initial line

$$= \frac{2}{3}\pi \int_{2\pi/3}^{\pi} r^3 \sin\theta \, d\theta$$

$$= \frac{2}{3}\pi \int_{2\pi/3}^{\pi} a^3 (1 + 2\cos\theta)^3 \sin\theta \, d\theta$$

Let $1 + 2\cos\theta = z$

when $\theta \to 2\pi/3$, $z = 0$ $\quad\Big|\; -2\sin\theta \, d\theta = dz$

$\theta \to \pi$, $z = -1$ $\quad\Big|\; \sin\theta \, d\theta = -dz/2$

$$= \frac{2\pi}{3}\int_0^{-1} -a^3 z^3 \frac{dz}{2}$$

$$= \frac{\pi a^3}{3}\int_{-1}^{0} z^3 \, dz = \frac{\pi a^3}{3}\left[\frac{z^4}{4}\right]_1^0 = \frac{\pi a^3}{12} \qquad \textit{(Proved)}$$

Problem 27 The arc of the cordiode $r = a(1 + \cos\theta)$ specified by $-x/2 \leqslant \theta \leqslant \pi/2$ is rotated about the $\theta = 0$ prove that the volume and the area of the surface of revolution generated are respectively $5/2\ \pi a^3$ and

$4/5\,(8 - \sqrt{2})\, a^2 \pi$

Solution The volume

$$= \int_0^{\pi/2} \frac{2}{3}\pi r^3 \sin\theta \, d\theta$$

$$= \frac{2}{3}\pi \int_0^{\pi/2} a^3 (1 + \cos\theta)^3 \sin\theta \, d\theta$$

$$= \frac{2}{3}\pi a^3 - \left.\frac{(1 + \cos\theta)^4}{4}\right]_0^{\pi/2}$$

$$= \frac{2}{3}\pi a^3\left[4 - \frac{1}{4}\right] = \frac{2}{3}\pi a^3 \times \frac{15}{4} = \frac{5}{2}\pi a^3 \qquad \textit{(Proved)}$$

Area $= \int_0^{v/2} 2\pi y \dfrac{ds}{d\theta} \cdot d\theta$

$$\frac{ds}{d\theta} = \sqrt{r^2 + \left(\frac{dr}{d\theta}\right)^2}$$

$$\frac{dr}{d\theta} = -a \sin \theta$$

$$\therefore \quad \frac{ds}{d\theta} = \sqrt{a^2 (1+\cos \theta^2) + a^2 \sin^2 \theta}$$

$$= a \sqrt{2 (1+\cos\theta)} = 2a \cos \theta/2$$

Required Area $= \int_0^{\pi/2} 2\pi \times 2a^2\, 2 \cos^2 \dfrac{\theta}{2}\, 2 \sin \dfrac{\theta}{2} \cos^2 \dfrac{\theta}{2} d\theta$

$$= 16\pi a^2 \int_0^{\pi/2} \cos^4 \frac{\theta}{2} \sin \frac{\theta}{2}\, d\theta$$

$$= 16\pi a^2 \left[-2 \frac{\cos^5 \theta/2}{5}\right]_0^{\pi/2}$$

$$= \frac{32\pi a^2}{5}\left[-\cos^5 \frac{\theta}{2}\right]_0^{\pi/2}$$

$$= \frac{32\pi a^2}{5}\left[1 - \left(\frac{1}{\sqrt{2}}\right)^5\right] = \frac{32\pi a^2}{5}\left[1 - \frac{1}{4\sqrt{2}}\right]$$

$$= \frac{32\pi a^2}{5} \frac{(4\sqrt{2}-1)}{4\sqrt{2}} \times \frac{\sqrt{2}}{\sqrt{2}}$$

$$= 4/5\, \pi a^2 (8 - \sqrt{2})$$

(Proved)

Problem 28 The arc of the cardiode $r = a(1 + \cos \theta)$ included between $-\pi/2 \leqslant \theta \leqslant \pi/2$ is rotated about the line $\theta = \pi/2$ find the area of the surface generated

Solution The arc of the cardiode is rotated about $\theta = \pi/2$ i.e. we will be using for area

$$= 2\int_0^{\pi/2} 2\pi x \cdot \frac{ds}{d\theta} \cdot d\theta$$

[about y axis] for $\theta = \pi/2$

$$\frac{ds}{d\theta} = \sqrt{r^2 + \left(\frac{dr}{d\theta}\right)^2} = 2a \cos \frac{\theta}{2}$$

$$= 2 \cdot 2\pi \int_0^{\pi/2} r \cos \theta \, 2a \cos \frac{\theta}{2} \, d\theta$$

$$= 2 \cdot 2\pi \int_0^{\pi/2} 2a^2 (1 + \cos \theta) \cos \theta \cos \frac{\theta}{2} d\theta$$

$$= 8\pi a^2 \int_0^{\pi/2} 2 \cos^2 \frac{\theta}{2} \cos \frac{\theta}{2} \cos \theta \, d\theta$$

$$= 16\pi a^2 \int_0^{\pi/2} \cos^3 \frac{\theta}{2} \cos \theta \, d\theta$$

$$= 16 \pi a^2 \int_0^{\pi/2} \left(1 - \sin^2 \frac{\theta}{2}\right)\left(1 - 2 \sin^2 \frac{\theta}{2}\right) \cos \frac{\theta}{2} d\theta$$

Let $\sin \theta/2 = t$

$$\cos \theta/2 \, d\theta = 2dt$$

When $\theta \to 0, \quad t \to 0$

$$\theta \to \pi/2, \quad t \to 1/\sqrt{2}$$

$$= 32\pi a^2 \int_0^{\sqrt{1/2}} (1 - t^2)(1 - 2t^2) \, dt$$

$$= 32\pi a^2 \int_0^{1/\sqrt{2}} [1 - 3t^2 + + 2t^4] \, dt$$

$$= 32\pi a^2 \left[t - \frac{3t^3}{3} + 2 \frac{t^5}{5}\right]_0^{1/\sqrt{2}}$$

$$= 32\pi a^2 \left[\frac{1}{\sqrt{2}} - \frac{1}{2\sqrt{2}} + \frac{2}{5} \frac{1}{4\sqrt{2}}\right]$$

$$= 32\pi a^2 \left[\frac{20 - 10 + 2}{20\sqrt{2}}\right]$$

$$= \frac{32\pi a^2}{20\sqrt{2}} \times 12 \times \frac{\sqrt{2}}{\sqrt{2}} = \frac{48\sqrt{2} \, \pi a^2}{5} \qquad \textbf{Ans.}$$

32

Statistics

Bivariate Distribution

Correlation, linear-regression involving two variables fitting the straight line, parabolic and exponential curves, properties of correlation co-efficient.

If the change in one variable affects a change in the other variable, the variables are said to be correlated. If the two variables deviate in the same direction i.e. if the increase (or decrease) in one results in a corresponding increase (or decrease) in other, correlation is said to be direct or positive. But if they constantly deviate in the opposite direction i.e. if increase (or decrease) in one results in corresponding decrease (or increase) in the other correlation is said to be inverse or negative.

Correlation Coefficient

Correlation coefficient between two randam variables X and Y, usualy denoted by $r\ (x, y)$ or simply rxy is a numerical measure of linear relationship between them and is defined as

$$r\ (X, Y) = \frac{\text{Cov}\ (X, Y)}{\sigma x\ \sigma y} \tag{1}$$

and is known as Karl pearson corr-coeff.

If $(x_i, y_i)\ i = 1, 2, \ldots n$ is the bivariable distribution then

$$\text{Cov}\ (X, Y) = E\ [\{x - E(X)\}\ \{y - E(Y)\}]$$

$$= \frac{1}{n} \Sigma(x_i - \bar{x})\ (y_i - \bar{y}) = \mu_{11}$$

$$\sigma x^2 = E[\{x - E(x)\}]^2 = \frac{1}{n} \Sigma\ (x_i - \bar{x})^2$$

$$\sigma y^2 = E[\{Y - E(Y)\}]^2 = \frac{1}{n} \Sigma\ (y_i - \bar{y})^2$$

The summation extending over i from 1 to n

Limits for Correlation Coefficient

we have $r\,(X, Y) = \dfrac{\text{Cov}\,(X, Y)}{\sigma X\, \sigma Y}$

then remember that $-1 \leqslant r\,(X, Y) \leqslant 1$.

Remember

Correlation is independent of change of origin and scale.

Remember

Two independent variables are uncorrelated.

Proof. If X and Y are independent variables then Cov $(X, Y) = 0$

$$r\,(X, Y) = \frac{\text{Cov}\,(X, Y)}{\sigma x\, \sigma y} = 0$$

Problem 1 Show that if X^1, Y^1 are the deviations of the randam variables X and Y from their respective means then

(i) $r = 1 - \dfrac{1}{2N} \sum\limits_{i=1} \left(\dfrac{X_i^1}{\sigma x} - \dfrac{Y_i^1}{\sigma y}\right)^2$

(ii) $r = -1 + \dfrac{1}{2N} \sum\limits_{i=1} \left(\dfrac{X_i^1}{\sigma x} + \dfrac{Y_i}{\sigma y}\right)^2$

Deduce that $-1 \leqslant r \leqslant +1$.

Solution Let X and Y be the random variables, X_1^1, Y_i^1 are the deviations of the random variables X and Y from their respected means i.e.

$$X^1 = (X_i - \bar{X})$$
$$Y^1 = (Y_i - \bar{Y})$$

(1) R.H.S. $1 - \dfrac{1}{2N} \sum\limits_{i=1} \left(\dfrac{X_i'}{\sigma x} - \dfrac{Y_i'}{\sigma y}\right)^2$

$$= 1 - \frac{1}{2N}\left[\sum_{i=1} \left\{\frac{X'^2}{\sigma x^2} + \frac{Y_i'^2}{\sigma y^2} - 2\,\frac{X_i'\, Y_i'}{\sigma x\, \sigma y}\right\}\right]$$

$$= 1 - \frac{1}{2N}\left[\frac{1}{\sigma x^2} \sum X_i'^2 + \frac{1}{\sigma y^2} \sum Y_i'^2 - \frac{1}{\sigma X \sigma Y} \sum X_i'\, Y_i'\right]$$

$$= 1 - \frac{1}{2N}\left[\frac{1}{\sigma x^2} \sum (X_i - \bar{X})^2 + \frac{1}{\sigma y^2} \sum (Y_i - \bar{Y})^2 - \frac{2}{\sigma X \sigma Y} \sum (X - \bar{X})\,(Y - \bar{Y})\right.$$

$$= 1 - \frac{1}{2}\left[\frac{1}{\sigma x^2} \cdot \sigma x^2 + \frac{1}{\sigma y^2} \cdot \sigma Y^2 - \frac{2r}{\sigma x\, \sigma y}\; \sigma x\, \sigma y\right]$$

$$= 1 - \tfrac{1}{2}\,[1 + 1 - 2r] = \tfrac{1}{2}\,[2 - 2r]$$

$$= 1 - 1 + r = r \qquad (L.H.S.)$$

(ii) *R.H.S.* $-1+\dfrac{1}{2N}\sum_{i=1}\left(\dfrac{X_i'}{\sigma x}+\dfrac{Y_i'}{\sigma x}\right)^2$

$$=-1+\frac{1}{2N}\sum\left[\left\{\frac{X_i'^2}{\sigma x^2}+\frac{Y_i'^2}{\sigma y^2}+\frac{2X_i'\,Y_i'}{\sigma x\;\sigma y}\right\}\right]$$

$$=-1+\frac{1}{2N}\left[\frac{1}{\sigma x^2}\sum X_i'^2+\frac{1}{\sigma y^2}\sum Y_i'^2+\frac{2}{\sigma x\;\sigma y}\sum X'\,Y'\right]$$

$$=-1+\frac{1}{2N}\left[\frac{1}{\sigma X^2}\sum(X_i-\bar{X})^2+\frac{1}{\sigma Y^2}\sum(Y_i-\bar{Y})^2+\frac{2}{\sigma x\;\sigma y}\sum(X_i-\bar{X})(Y_i-\bar{Y})\right]$$

$$=-1+\frac{1}{2}\left(\frac{1}{\sigma x^2}\frac{1}{N}\sum(X_i-\bar{X})^2+\frac{1}{\sigma Y^2}\frac{1}{N}\sum(Y-\bar{Y})^2+\frac{2}{\sigma X\sigma Y}\frac{1}{N}\sum(X_i-\bar{X})(Y_i-\bar{Y})\right)$$

$$=-1+\frac{1}{2}\left[\frac{1}{\sigma x^2}\,\sigma x^2+\frac{1}{\sigma y^2}\cdot\sigma Y^2+\frac{2}{\sigma x\;\sigma y}\,\text{CoV}\,(X,Y)\right)$$

$$=-1+\left[1+1+\frac{2}{\sigma x\sigma y}\cdot r\cdot\sigma x\;\sigma y\right]$$

$$=-1+1+r=r\qquad(LHS)$$

(*Proved*)

Deduction $\left(\dfrac{X_i'}{\sigma x}-\dfrac{Y_i'}{\sigma y}\right)^2\geqslant 0$ (+ve quantity)

$\Rightarrow$ $\sum\left(\dfrac{X_i'}{\sigma x}-\dfrac{Y_i'}{\sigma y}\right)^2\geqslant 0$

$\Rightarrow$ $\dfrac{1}{2N}\sum\left(\dfrac{X_i'}{\sigma x}-\dfrac{Y_i'}{\sigma y}\right)^2\geqslant 0$

$r=1-$(same +ve quantity)

$\Rightarrow$ $r\leqslant 1$

Equality sign holds when

$$\frac{X_i'}{\sigma x}-\frac{Y_i'}{\sigma y}=0$$

Again $\left(\dfrac{X_i'}{\sigma x}+\dfrac{Y_i'}{\sigma y}\right)^2\geqslant 0$

$$\sum\left(\frac{X_i'}{\sigma x}+\frac{Y_i'}{\sigma y}\right)^2\geqslant 0$$

$$\Rightarrow \quad \frac{1}{2N}\Sigma\left(\frac{X_i'}{\sigma x}+\frac{Y_i'}{\sigma y}\right)^2 \geqslant 0$$

$$r = -1 + \text{some positive quantity}$$

$$\Rightarrow \quad -1 \leqslant r \tag{2}$$

Equality sign holds when

$$\frac{X_i'}{\sigma x}+\frac{Y_i'}{\sigma y}=0$$

From relation (1) and (2) we have $-1 \leqslant r \leqslant 1$ *(Proved)*

Problem 2 The variables X and Y are connected by the equation $ax + by + c = 0$ show that the correlation between them is -1 if the sign of a and b are all alike and $+1$ if they are different. [*IAS 83, 87*]

Solution

$$ax + by + c = 0$$

$$E\{ax + by + c\} = 0$$

$$E(aX) + E(bY) + E(c) = 0$$

$$aE(X) + bE(Y) + c = 0$$

$$\Rightarrow \quad aE(X) + bE(Y) - ax - by = 0$$

$$\Rightarrow \quad a[X - E(X)] + b[Y - E(Y)] = 0$$

$$\Rightarrow \quad \{X - E(X)\} = -\frac{b}{a}[Y - E(Y)] \tag{1}$$

we have to find the value of rxy

we know that $r = \dfrac{\text{Cov}(X, Y)}{\sigma x\, \sigma y}$

where $\text{Cov}(X, Y) = E[\{X - E(X)\}\{Y - E(Y)\}]$

and $\sigma X^2 = E[X - E(X)]^2$

$$\sigma Y^2 = E[Y - E(Y)]^2$$

$$\text{Cov}(X, Y) = E\left[-\frac{b}{a}\{Y - E(Y)\}\{Y - E(Y)\}\right]$$

$$\text{Cov}(X, Y) = E\left[-\frac{b}{a}\{Y - E(Y)\}^2\right]$$

$$\text{Cov}(X, Y) = -\frac{b}{a}E[Y - E(Y)]^2 = -\frac{b}{a}\sigma y^2$$

$$\sigma x^2 = E[X - E(X)]^2$$

$$\sigma x^2 = E\left[\frac{b^2}{a^2}\{Y - E(Y)\}^2\right]$$

$$\sigma x^2 = \frac{b^2}{a^2} E[Y-E(Y)]^2$$

$$\sigma x^2 = \frac{b^2}{a^2} \sigma y^2$$

$$r = \frac{\text{Cov}(X, Y)}{\sqrt{\sigma x^2}\sqrt{\sigma y^2}}$$

$$r = \frac{-\frac{b}{a}\ \sigma y^2}{\sqrt{\sigma y^2}\cdot\sqrt{\frac{b^2}{a^2}\sigma y^2}}$$

$$r = \frac{-\frac{b}{a}\ \sigma y^2}{\left|\frac{b}{a}\right| \sigma y^2}$$

$$= \begin{cases} +1 & \text{if } b \text{ and } a \text{ are of opposite signs} \\ -1 & \text{if } b \text{ and } a \text{ are of same signs} \end{cases}$$

Problem 3 (a) If $z = aX + bY$ and r is the correlation coefficient between X and Y, show that

$$\sigma z^2 = a^2\,\sigma x^2 + b^2\,\sigma y^2 + 2ab\ r\ \sigma x\ \sigma y$$

(b) Show that the correlation coefficient r between two random variables X and Y is given by

$$r = (\sigma x^2 + \sigma y^2 - \sigma^2_{x-y})/2\sigma x\ \sigma y$$

where σx; σy and σ_{x-y} are the standard deviations of X, Y and $X-Y$ respectively.

Solution We have given that

$$Z = aX + bY \tag{1}$$

Taking expectations on both sides

$$E(Z) = E(aX + bY)$$

$$E(Z) = aE(X) + bE(Y) \tag{2}$$

Subtracting (2) from (1) we have

$$[Z-E(Z)] = a[X-E(X)] + b[Y-E(Y)]^2$$

Squaring both sides we have

$$[Z-E(Z)]^2 = a^2[X-E(X)]^2 + b^2[Y-E(Y)] + 2ab[X-E(X)][Y-E(Y)]$$

$$[Z-E(Z)]^2 = a^2[X-E(X)]^2 + b^2[Y-E(Y)]^2 + 2ab[\{X-E(X)\}\{Y-E(Y)\}]$$

Taking expectations on both sides we have

$$E[Z-E(Z)]^2 = a^2 E[X-E(X)]^2 + b^2 E[Y-E(Y)]^2 + 2ab\, E[\{X-E(X)\}\{Y-E(Y)\}]$$

$$\sigma z^2 = a^2 \sigma x^2 + b^2 \sigma y^2 + 2ab \text{ Cov } (X, Y)$$

$$\sigma z^2 = a^2 \sigma x^2 + b^2 \sigma y^2 + 2abr\, \sigma x\, \sigma y$$

(b) For the second part let $a = 1$, $b = -1$

Then $\quad z = x - y$

$$\sigma z^2 = a^2 \sigma x^2 + b^2 \sigma y^2 + 2abr\, \sigma x\, \sigma y$$

$$\sigma^2_{X-Y} = \sigma x^2 + \sigma y^2 - 2r\, \sigma x\, \sigma y$$

$$\Rightarrow 2r\, \sigma x\, \sigma y = \sigma x^2 + \sigma y^2 - \sigma^2_{X-Y}$$

$$\Rightarrow \quad z = \frac{\sigma x^2 + \sigma y^2 - \sigma^2_{X-Y}}{2\sigma x\, \sigma y}$$

where σx, σy and $\sigma x - y$ are the standard deviation of X, Y and $X-Y$ respectively. *(Proved)*

Problem 4 If X and Y are two randem variables with variances σx^2 and σy^2 respectively and r is the coefficient of correlation between them.

If $U = X + KY$ and $V = X + \dfrac{\sigma x}{\sigma y} Y$ find the value of K so that U and V are uncorrelated.

Solution We have

$$U = X + KY \,!\, V = X + \frac{\sigma x}{\sigma y} Y$$

Taking expectations of u and v we have

$$E(U) = E(X) + K(E(Y)$$

$$E(V) = E(X) - \frac{\sigma x}{\sigma y} E(Y)$$

$$U - E(U) = X - E(X) + K[Y - E(Y)] \tag{1}$$

$$V - E(V) = X - E(X - E(x)) + \frac{\sigma x}{\sigma Y}\{Y - E(Y)\} \tag{2}$$

We know that

$$r = \frac{\text{Cov}(X, Y)}{\sigma x\, \sigma y} = E\, \frac{[\{X - E(X)\}\{y - E(X)\}]}{\sigma x\, \sigma y}$$

$$\sigma x^2 = E(X - E(X)]$$

$$\sigma y^2 = E[Y - E(Y)]$$

Again U and V are un-correlated if $r(U, V) = 0$

$\Rightarrow \quad \text{Cov}(U, V) = 0$

i.e. If $$r = \frac{\text{Cov}(U, V)}{\sigma u \; \sigma v} = \frac{E[\{U - E(V)\}\{V - E(V)\}]}{\sigma u \; \sigma v} = 0$$

i.e. If $$E[\{U - E(U)\}\{V - E(V)\}] = 0$$

Now $$\text{LHS} = [\{U - E(U)\}\{V - E(V)\}]$$

$$= E\left[[\{X - E(X)\} + K\{Y - E(Y)\}][\{X - E(X)\} + \frac{\sigma x}{\sigma y}\{Y - E(Y)\right]$$

$$= E\{X - E(X)\}^2 + \frac{\sigma x}{\sigma y} K\{Y - E(Y)\}^2 + \{X - E(X)\}\{Y - E(Y)\}\left(K + \frac{\sigma x}{\sigma y}\right)\Bigg]$$

$$= E[X - E(X)]^2 + K\frac{\sigma x}{\sigma y}[Y - E(Y)]^2 + \left(K + \frac{\sigma x}{\sigma y}\right) E[\{X - E(x)\}\{Y - E(y)\}]$$

$$= \sigma x^2 + K\frac{\sigma x}{\sigma y}\sigma y^2 + \left(K + \frac{\sigma x}{\sigma x}\right)\text{Cov}(X, Y)$$

$$= \sigma x(\sigma x + K\sigma y) + \frac{(\sigma x + K\sigma y)}{\sigma y}\text{Cov}(X, Y)$$

$$= (\sigma x + k\,\sigma y)\left[1 + \frac{\text{Cov}(x, y)}{\sigma y}\right]$$

$$= (\sigma x + k\sigma y)\,\pi x\left[1 + \frac{\text{Cov}(x, y)}{\sigma x\,\sigma y}\right]$$

$$= (\sigma x + k\sigma y)\,\sigma x\,[1 + r]$$

U and V are un-correrlated if

$$(\sigma x + k\sigma y)\,\sigma x\,(1 + r) = 0$$

i.e, $$\sigma x + k\sigma y = 0$$

i.e. $$\sigma x + k\sigma y = 0$$

since $\sigma x \neq 0 \qquad 1 + r \neq 0$

$$K = -\frac{\sigma x}{\sigma y}$$ **Ans.**

Problem 5 If X and Y are un-correlated random variables with means zero and variances σ_1^2 and σ_2^2 respectively, show that

$$U = X \cos \alpha + Y \sin \alpha$$
$$V = X \sin \alpha - y \cos \alpha$$

have a correlation coefficient α is given by

$$\alpha = \frac{\sigma_1^2 - \sigma_2^2}{[(\sigma_1^2 - \sigma_2^2) + 4\sigma_1^2 \sigma_2^2 \operatorname{cosec}^2 2\alpha]^{1/2}} \qquad [I.F.S.\ 82]$$

Solution We are given that

$$r(X, Y) = 0$$
$$\Rightarrow \quad \text{Cov}(X, Y) = 0$$

and
$$\left.\begin{aligned} V(X) &= \sigma x^2 = \sigma_1^2 \\ V(Y) &= \sigma y^2 = \sigma_2^2 \end{aligned}\right\} \qquad (1)$$

given that
$$E(X) = 0$$
$$E(Y) = 0$$

Now
$$P^2(U, V) = \frac{[\text{Cov}(U, \bar{V})]^2}{\sigma u^2 \, \sigma v^2} \qquad (2)$$

$$\begin{aligned}
\sigma u^2 &= V(U) \\
&= E[U - E(U)]^2 \\
&= E[(X \cos \alpha + Y \sin \alpha) - E(X \cos \alpha + Y \sin \alpha)]^2 \\
&= E[(X \cos \alpha + Y \sin \alpha) - \{\cos \alpha\, E(X) + \sin \alpha\, E(Y)]^2\} \\
&= E[\cos \alpha\, (X - E(X)) + \sin \alpha\, (Y - E(Y)]^2 \\
&= E[\cos^2 \alpha \{X - E(X)\}^2 + \sin^2 \alpha \{Y - E(Y)\}^2 \\
&\qquad + 2 \cos \alpha \sin \alpha \{X - E(X)\}\{Y - E(Y)]\} \\
&= \cos^2 \alpha\, E[X - E(X)]^2 + \sin^2 \alpha\, E[Y - E(Y)]^2 \\
&\qquad + 2 \cos \alpha \sin \alpha\, E[\{X - E(x)\}\{Y - E(Y)\}] \\
&= \cos^2 \alpha\, V(X) + \sin^2 \alpha\, V(Y) \\
&\qquad + 2 \sin \alpha \cos \alpha\, \text{Cov}(X, X) \\
&= \cos^2 \alpha\, \sigma x^2 + \sin^2 \alpha\, \sigma y^2 + 2 \sin \alpha \cos \alpha\, \text{Cov}(X, Y) \\
&= \cos^2 \alpha\, \sigma_1^2 + \sin^2 \alpha\, \sigma^2 + 2 \sin \cos \alpha\, 0
\end{aligned}$$

$$\sigma u^2 = \cos^2 \alpha \sigma_1^2 + \sin^2 \alpha\, \sigma_2^2 \qquad (2)$$

Again
$$\begin{aligned}
\sigma v^2 &= E[V - E(V)]^2 \\
\sigma v^2 &= E[\{X \sin \alpha - Y \cos \alpha\} - E\{X \sin \alpha - Y \cos \alpha\}]^2 \\
\sigma v^2 &= E[\sin \alpha \{X - E(X)\} - \cos \alpha \{Y - E(Y)\}]^2 \\
\sigma v^2 &= E[\sin^2 \alpha \{X - E(X)\}^2 + \cos^2 \alpha \{Y - E(Y)\}^2 \\
&\qquad - 2 \sin \alpha \cos \alpha \{X - E(X)\}\{Y - E(Y)\}]
\end{aligned}$$

$$\sigma v^2 = \sin^2 \alpha\, E[X-E(X)]^2 + \cos^2 \alpha\, E[Y-E(Y)]^2 - 2\sin\alpha\cos\alpha\, E[\{X-E(X)\}\{Y-E(Y)\}]$$

$$\sigma v^2 = \sin^2 \alpha\, V(X) + \cos^2 \alpha\, V(X, Y) - 2\sin\alpha\cos\alpha\, \text{Cov}(X, Y)$$

$$\sigma v^2 = \sin^2 \alpha\, \sigma x^2 + \cos^2 \alpha\, \sigma y^2 - 2\sin\alpha\cos\alpha 0$$

$$\sigma v^2 = \sin^2 \alpha\, \sigma_1^2 + \cos^2 \alpha\, \sigma_2^2 \qquad (4)$$

$$\text{Cov}(U, V) = E[\{U-E(U)(V-E(V)\}]$$

$$= E[\{X-E(X)\}\cos\alpha + \sin\alpha\{Y-E(Y)\} \{(X-E(X))\sin\alpha - (Y-E(Y))\cos\alpha\}]$$

$$= E[\sin\alpha\cos\alpha\{X-E(X)\}^2 - \sin\alpha\cos\alpha\{Y-E(Y)\}^2 - \{X-E(X)\}\{Y-E(Y)\}\cos^2\alpha + \{X-E(X)\}\{Y-E(Y)\}\sin^2\alpha\}$$

$$= \sin\alpha\cos\alpha\, E[X-E(X)]^2 - \sin\alpha\cos\alpha\, E[Y-E(Y)]^2 - E[\{X-E(X)\}\{Y-E(Y)\}](\cos^2\alpha - \sin^2\alpha)$$

$$= \sin\alpha\cos\alpha\, V(X) - \sin\alpha\cos\alpha\, V(Y) - \text{Cov}(X, Y)(\cos^2\alpha - \sin^2\alpha)$$

$$= \sin\alpha\cos\alpha\, \sigma x^2 - \sin\alpha\cos\alpha\, \sigma y^2 - 0$$

$$= \sin\alpha\cos\alpha\, \sigma_1^2 - \sin\alpha\cos\alpha\, \sigma_2^2 = \sin\alpha\cos\alpha(\sigma_1^2 - \sigma_2^2)$$

Multiplying (3) and (4) we have

$$\sigma u^2 \sigma v^3 = (\cos^2\alpha\, \sigma_1^2 + \sin^2\alpha\sigma_2^2)(\sin^2\alpha\sigma_1^2 + \cos^2\alpha\, \sigma_2^2)$$

$$= \sin^2 x \cos^2\alpha\, \sigma_1^4 + \cos^4\alpha\, \sigma_1^2\sigma_2^2 + \sin^4\alpha\, \sigma_1^2\sigma_2^2 + \sin^2\alpha\cos^2\alpha\, \sigma_2^4$$

$$= \sin^2\alpha\cos^2\alpha(\sigma_1^4 + \sigma_2^4) + \sigma_1\, \sigma_2^2(\sin^4\alpha + \cos^4\alpha)$$

$$= \sin^2\alpha\cos^2\alpha(\sigma_1^4 + \sigma_2^4) + \sigma_1^2\sigma_2^2[(\sin^2\alpha)^2 + (\cos^2\alpha)^2]$$

$$= \sin^2\alpha\cos^2\alpha(\sigma_1^4 + \sigma_1^4) + \sigma_1^2\sigma_2^2[\sin^2\alpha + \cos^2\alpha)^2 - 2\sin^2\alpha\cos^2\alpha]$$

$$= \sin^2\alpha\cos^2\alpha(\sigma_1^4 + \sigma_2^4) - \sigma_1^2\sigma_2^2) + \sigma_1^2\sigma_2^2$$

$$= \sin^2\alpha\cos^2\alpha(\sigma_1^2 - \sigma\ )^2 + \sigma_1^2\sigma_2^2$$

$$P^2 = \frac{\sin^2\alpha\cos^2\alpha(\sigma_1^2 - \sigma_2^2)^2}{\sin^2\alpha\cos^2\alpha(\sigma_1^2 - \sigma_2^2)^2 + \sigma_1^2\sigma_2^2}$$

$$P^2 = \frac{\frac{1}{4}(\sigma_1^2 - \sigma_2^2)^2 \sin^2 2x}{\sigma_1^2\sigma_2^2 + \sin^2 2\alpha/4\, (\sigma_1^2 - \sigma_2^2)^2}$$

$$P^2 = \frac{(\sigma_1^2 - \sigma_2^2)^2 \sin^2 2\alpha}{4\sigma_1^2\sigma_2^2 + \sin^2 2\alpha\, (\sigma_1^2 - \sigma^2)^2}$$

$$P^2 = \frac{(\sigma_1^2 - \sigma_2^2)^2}{4\alpha_1^2\sigma_2^2 \operatorname{cosec}^2 2\alpha + (\sigma_1^2 - \sigma_2^2)^2}$$

$$P = \frac{(\sigma_1^2 - \sigma_2^2)}{[(\sigma_1^2 - \sigma_2^2)^2 + 4\sigma_1^2\sigma_2^2 \operatorname{cosec}^2 2\alpha]^{1/2}}$$

Problem 6 The random variables X and Y are jointly normally distributed and U and V are defined by

$$U = X \cos \alpha + Y \sin \alpha$$

$$V = Y \cos \alpha - X \sin \alpha$$

Show that U and V will be un-correlated if

$$\tan 2\alpha = \frac{2r\sigma \times \sigma Y}{\sigma X^2 - \sigma Y^2}$$

where $\qquad r = \text{Corr}\,(X, Y);\ \sigma x^2 = \text{Var}\,(X)$

and $\qquad \sigma y^2 = \text{var}\,(Y)$ [*I.F.S. 88*]

Solution U and V will be uncorrelated if

$$r\,(U, V) = \frac{\text{corr}\,(U, V)}{\sigma u\ \sigma v} = 0$$

$$\Rightarrow \text{Corr}\,(U, V) = 0$$

$$\begin{aligned}
\text{Corr}\,(U, V) &= E\,[\{U - E\,(U)\}\ \{V - E\,(V)\}\\
&= E\,[\{X - E\,(X)\}\cos\alpha + (Y - E\,(Y)]\sin\alpha]\\
&\qquad\qquad X\,[(Y - E\,(Y)\}\cos\alpha - \{X - E\,(X)\}\sin\alpha]\\
&= E\,[\{X - E\,(X)\}\ \{Y - E\,(Y)\}\cos^2\alpha - \{X - E\,(X)\}^2\sin\alpha\cos\alpha\\
&\qquad - \{X - E\,(x)\}\ \{Y - E\,(Y)\}\sin^2\alpha + [Y - E\,(Y)]^2\sin\alpha\cos\alpha]\\
&= E[X - E\,(X)].\ [Y - E\,(Y)]\cos^2\alpha - E\,[X - E\,(X)]^2\sin\alpha\cos\alpha\\
&= E\,[\{X - E\,(X)\}\ \{Y - E\,(Y)\}\sin^2\alpha + E\,[Y - E\,(Y))^2\sin\alpha\cos\alpha\\
&= \text{Cov}\,(X, Y)\cos^2\alpha - \sigma x^3\sin\alpha\cos\alpha\\
&\qquad\qquad - \text{Cov.}\,(X, Y)\sin^2\alpha + \sigma y^2\sin\alpha\cos\alpha\\
&= \text{Cov}\,(X, Y)\,\{\cos^2\alpha - \sin^2\alpha\} - \sin\alpha\cos\alpha\,(\sigma x^2 - \sigma y^2)
\end{aligned}$$

U and V are uncorrelated if

$$r\,(U, V) = 0$$

$$\Rightarrow \qquad \text{Cov}\,(U, V) = 0$$

$$\text{Cov}\,(X, Y)\cos 2\alpha - \frac{\sin 2\alpha}{2}\,(\sigma x^2 - \sigma y^2) = 0$$

$$\frac{\sin 2\alpha}{2}\,(\sigma x^2 - \sigma y^2) = \cos 2\alpha\ \text{Cov}\,(X, Y) \qquad (1)$$

we know that $r\,(X, Y) = \dfrac{\text{Cov}\,(X, Y)}{\sigma x\ \sigma y}$

$$\Rightarrow \qquad \text{Cov}\,(X, Y) = r\,\sigma x\ \sigma y$$

So from (1) $\dfrac{\sin 2\alpha}{\cos 2\alpha} = \dfrac{2\,\text{Cov}\,(X, Y)}{\sigma x^2 - \sigma y^2}$

$$\tan 2\alpha = \frac{2r\,\sigma x\,\sigma y}{\sigma x^2 - \sigma y^2}$$

$$\therefore \qquad \tan 2\alpha = \frac{2r\,\sigma x\,\sigma y}{\sigma x^2 - \sigma y^2} \qquad \textit{(Proved)}$$

Problem 7 X and Y are two independent random variables with variances σx^2 and σy^2 respectively. Find the correlation coefficient between X and $X + Y$. [*I.F.S. 85*]

Solution $V(X) = \sigma x^2 = E\,[X - E\,(X)]^2$

$V(Y) = \sigma y^2 = E\,[Y - E\,(Y)]^2$

Since X and Y are independent random variables

$\Rightarrow$ X and Y are uncorrelated

$\Rightarrow$ $\text{Corr}\,(X, Y) = 0$

$\Rightarrow$ $\text{Cov}\,(X, Y) = 0$

$\text{Cov}\,(X, Y) = E\,[\{X - E\,(X)\}\,\{Y - E\,(Y)]= 0$

$$\text{Now} \quad \text{Corr}\,(X, X + Y) = \frac{\text{Cov}\,(X, X + Y)}{\sigma x\,\sigma_{X+Y}} \qquad (1)$$

$$\begin{aligned}
\text{Cov}\,(X, X + Y) &= E\,[\{X - E\,(X)\}.\{X + Y - E\,(X + Y)\}] \\
&= E\,[\{X - E\,(X)\}.\{X + Y - E\,(X) - E\,(Y)\}] \\
&= E\,[\{X - E\,(X)\}\,\{X - E\,(X) + Y - E\,(Y)\}] \\
&= E\,[X - E(X)\}^2 + \{X - E\,(X)\}\,\{Y - E\,(Y)\}] \\
&= E\,[X - E\,(X)]^2 + E\,[\{X - E\,(X)\}\,\{Y - E\,(Y)\}] \\
&= \sigma x^2 + 0
\end{aligned}$$

$$\begin{aligned}
\text{Cov}\,(X, X + Y) &= \sigma x^2 \\
\sigma^2_{X+Y} &= V\,(X + Y) = E\,[\{x + y\} - E\,[\{X + Y\}]^2 \\
&= E\,[X + Y - E\,(Y) - E\,(Y)]^2 \\
&= E\,[\{X - E\,(X)\} + \{Y - E\,(Y)\}]^2 \\
&= E\,[\{X - E\,(X)\}^2 + \{Y - E\,(Y)\}^2 \\
&\qquad + 2\,\{X - E\,(X)\}\,\{Y - E\,(Y)\}] \\
&= E\,[X - E\,(X)]^2 + E\,[Y - E\,(Y)]^2 \\
&\qquad + 2E\,[\{X - E\,(X)\}\,\{Y - E\,(Y)\}] \\
&= \sigma x^2 + \sigma y^2 + 0 = \sigma x^2 + \sigma y^2
\end{aligned}$$

$$\sigma^2_{X+Y} = \sigma x^2 + \sigma y^2 \qquad \Rightarrow \qquad \sigma x + y = \sqrt{\sigma x^2 + \sigma y^2}$$

Now $\text{Corr}(X, X+Y) = \frac{\text{Cov}(x_z, x+y)}{\sigma x\ \sigma y + y}$

$$= \frac{\sigma x^2}{\sigma x \cdot \sqrt{\sigma x^2 + \sigma y^2}}$$

$$r(X, X+Y) = \text{Corr} = \frac{\sigma x}{\sqrt{\sigma x^2 + \sigma y^2}} \qquad \textbf{Ans.}$$

Problem 8 If X, Y are standardised random variables and

$$r(aX + bY, bX + aY) = \frac{1 + 2ab}{a^2 + b^2}$$

find $r(X, Y)$, the coefficient of correlation between X and Y

Solution Since X and Y are standardised random variables we have

$$\left.\begin{array}{l} E(X) = 0 = E(Y) \\ V(X) = 1 = \text{Var}(Y) \end{array}\right\} \qquad (1)$$

$$V(X) = E[X - E(X)]^2 = E[X-0]^2 = E(X^2) = 1 \quad (2)$$

and $\quad V(Y) = E[Y - E(Y)]^2 = E(Y-0]^2 = E(Y^2) = 1 \quad (3)$

Thus $\quad V(X) = V(Y) = E(Y^2) = E(X^2)$

$$\text{Cov}(X, Y) = E[\{X - E(X)\}\{Y - E(Y)\}]$$

$$= E[\{X-0)(Y-0)] = E(XY)$$

$$\text{Cov}(X, Y) = E(XY) \qquad (4)$$

$$r(X, Y) = \frac{\text{Cov}(X. Y)}{\sigma x\ \sigma y}$$

$$\text{Cov}(X, Y) = r(X, Y)\ \sigma x\ \sigma y$$

$\Rightarrow \quad E(x, y) = r(x, y)\ \sigma x\ \sigma y$

Since $\quad \sigma X^2 = V(X) = 1 \qquad \sigma Y^2 = V(Y) = 1$

$\Rightarrow \quad \sigma X = 1 \qquad \Rightarrow \qquad \sigma Y = 1$

Thus $\quad E(X, Y) = r(X, Y) \qquad (5)$

We have $r(aX + bY, bX + aY)$

$$= \frac{\text{Cov}[aX + bX), (bX + aY)]}{[\text{Var}(aX + bY)]^{112} [\text{Var}(bX + aY)]^{1/2}}$$

$$= \frac{\text{Cov}[(aX + bY), (bX + aY)]}{[\text{Var}(aX + bY) \cdot \text{Var}(bX + aY)]^{1/2}}$$

Cov $[aX + bY, bX + aY]$

$$= E[(aX + bY)(bX + aY) - E\{(aX + bY)(bX + aY)\}]$$
$$= E[(aX + bY)(bX + aY) - E(aX + bY)\,E(bX + aY)]$$
$$= E[(aX + bY)(bX + aY) - \{aE(X) + bE(Y)\}\{bE(X) + aE(Y)\}]$$
$$= E[(aX + bY)(bX + aY)]$$
$$= E[abX^2 + a^2XY + b^2XY + abY^2]$$
$$= abE(X^2) + a^2E(X, Y) + b^2E(X, Y) + abE(Y^2)$$
$$= ab\,1 + a^2 r(X, Y) + b^2 r(X, Y) + ab\cdot 1$$
$$= 2ab + (a^2 + b^2)\,r(X, Y) \qquad (6)$$

$$\text{Var}(aX + bY) = E(aX + bY) - E(aX + bY)]$$
$$= E[aX + bY - aE(X) - bE(Y)]^2$$
$$= E[a\{X - E(X)\} + b(Y - E(Y)\}]^2$$
$$= E[a^2\{X - E(X)\}^2 + b^2\{Y - E(Y)\}^2 + 2ab\{X - E(X)\}\{Y - E(Y)\}]$$
$$= a^2E[X - E(X)]^2 + b^2E[Y - E(Y)]^2 + 2ab\,E[\{X - E(X)\}\{Y - E(Y)\}]$$
$$= a^2V(X) + b^2V(Y) + 2ab\,\text{Cov}(X, Y)$$
$$= a^2\cdot 1 + b^2\cdot 1 + 2ab\,E(X, Y)$$
$$= a^2 + b^2 + 2abr(X, Y) \qquad (7)$$

and $\text{Var}(bX + aY) = E[(bX + aY) - E(bX + aY)]^2$

$$= E[bX + aY - bE(X) - a\,E(Y)]^2$$
$$= E[b\{X - E(X)\} + a(Y - E(Y)\}]^2$$
$$= E[b^2\{X - E(X)\}^2 + a^2\{Y - E(Y)\}^2 + 2ab\{X - E(X)\}\{Y - E(Y)\}]$$
$$= b^2E[X - E(X)]^2 + a^2[Y - E(Y)]^2 + 2ab\,E[\{X - E(X)\}\{Y - E(Y)\}]$$
$$= b^2V(X) + a^2V(X) + 2ab\,\text{Cov}(X, Y)$$
$$= b^2\cdot 1 + a^2\cdot 1 + 2ab\cdot E(X, Y)$$
$$= b^2 + a^2 + 2abr(X, Y) \qquad (8)$$

$r(aX + bY, bX + aY)$

$$= \frac{2\,ab + (a^2 + b^2)\,r(X, Y)}{[\{a^2 + b^2 + 2abr(X, Y)\}\{a^2 + b^2 + 2abr(X, Y)\}]^{1/2}}$$
$$= \frac{2ab + (a^2 + b^2)\,r(X, Y)}{a^2 + b^2 + 2abr(X, Y)}$$

Then given that $\frac{1 + 2ab}{a^2 + b^2} = \frac{(a^2 + b^2)\, r\,(X, Y) + 2ab}{a^2 + b^2 + 2abr\,(X, Y)}$

$$(1 + 2ab)(a^2 + b^2) + 2ab\,(1 + 2ab)\;r\,(X, Y)$$
$$= (a^2 + b^2)^2\, r\,(X, Y) + 2ab\,(a^2 + b^2)$$
$$(1 + 2ab)(a^2 + b^2) - 2ab\,(a^2 + b^2)$$
$$= [(a^2 + b^2)^2 - 2ab\,(1 + 2ab)]\; r\,(X, Y)$$
$$= [a^4 + b^4 + 2a^2b^2 - 2ab - 4a^2b^2]\; r\,(X, Y)$$
$$(a^2 + b^2)\,[1 + 2ab - 2ab] = [(a^2 - b^2)^2 - 2ab]\; r\,(X, Y)$$
$$(a^2 + b^2) = [(a^2 - b^2)^2 - 2ab]\; r\,(X, Y)$$
$$\Rightarrow r\;(X, Y) = \frac{a^2 + b^2}{(a^2 - b^2)^2 - 2ab} \qquad \textit{(Proved)}$$

Problem 9 Let X and Y be uncorrelated random variables. If $U = X + Y$ and $V = X - Y$, prove that the coefficient of correlation between U and V is $\frac{\sigma x^2 - \sigma y^2}{\sigma x^2 + \sigma y^2}$. Where σx^2 and σy^2 are variance of X and Y respectively.

Solution Since X and Y are uncorrelated random variables

$$\Rightarrow \text{Corr}\,(X, Y) = 0$$
$$\Rightarrow \text{Cov}\,(X, Y) = 0 \qquad (1)$$
$$r\,(U, V) = r\,(X + Y, X - Y)$$
$$= \frac{\text{Cov}\,(U, V)}{\sigma u\;\sigma v} \qquad (2)$$
$$\text{Cov}\,(U, V) = E\,[\{U - E\,(U)\}\,\{V - E\,(V)]$$
$$= E\,[\{X - E\,(X)\} + (Y - E\,(Y))\}\cdot\{(X - E\,(X)) - (Y - E\,(Y))\}]$$
$$= E\,[X + Y - E(X + Y)\}\,\{X - Y - E\,(X - Y)\}]$$
$$= E\,[X - E\,(X)]^2 - E\,[Y - E\,(Y)]^2$$
$$= V\,(X) - V\,(Y) = \sigma x^2 - \sigma y^2 \qquad (3)$$

Again
$$\sigma u^2 = E\,[(X + Y) - E\,(X + Y)]^2$$
$$= E\,[\{X - E\,(X)\} + \{Y - E\,(Y)\}]^2$$
$$= E\,[\{X - E\,(X)\}^2 + \{Y - E\,(Y)\}^2 + 2\,\{X - E\,(X)]\,\{Y - E\,(Y)\}]$$
$$= E\,[X - E\,(X)]^2 + E\,[Y - E\,(Y)]^2 + 2\,E\,[\{X - E\,(X)\}\,\{Y - E\,(Y)\}]$$
$$= \sigma x^2 + \sigma y^2 + 2\;\text{Cov}\,(X, Y)$$
$$= \sigma x^2 + \sigma y^2 + 0$$

$$\sigma U^2 = \sigma x^2 + \sigma y^2$$

$$\sigma U = \sqrt{\sigma x^2 + \sigma y^2}$$

and $\sigma v^2 = \sigma x - y^2$

$$= E[(X-Y)-E(X-Y)]^2$$

$$= E[X-Y-E(X)+E(Y)]^2$$

$$= E[\{X-E(X)\}-\{Y-E(Y)\}]^2$$

$$= E[\{X-E(X)\}^2 + \{Y-E(Y)\}^2 - 2\{X-E(X)\}\{Y-E(Y)\}]$$

$$= E[X-E(X)]^2 + E[Y-E(Y)]^2 - 2E[\{X-E(X)\}\{Y-E(Y)\}]$$

$$= \sigma x^2 + \sigma y^2 - 2\,\text{Cov}(X, Y)$$

$$= \sigma x^2 + \sigma y^2 - 0$$

$$\sigma v^2 = \sigma x^2 + \sigma y^2$$

$$\Rightarrow \quad \sigma v = \sqrt{\sigma x^2 + \sigma y^2} \tag{5}$$

$$\text{So } r(U, V) = \frac{\sigma X^2 - \sigma Y^2}{\sqrt{\sigma x^2 + \sigma y^2}\sqrt{\sigma x^2 + \sigma y^2}}$$

$$r(U, V) = \frac{\sigma X^2 - \sigma Y^2}{\sigma X^2 + \sigma Y^2}$$

i.e. $\text{Cor } r(X+Y, X-Y) = \dfrac{\sigma x^2 - \sigma y^2}{\sigma x^2 + \sigma y^2}$ (*Proved*)

Problem 10 Two independent random variables X and Y have the following variances:

$\sigma x^2 = 36$, $\sigma x^2 = 16$ calculate the coefficient of correlation between

$$(U = X + Y, V = (X - Y)$$

Solution We know that

$$r(U, V) = \frac{\sigma x^2 - \sigma y^2}{\sigma x^2 + \sigma y^2} \qquad \textit{Remember}$$

$$\text{Then} \quad r(U, V) = \frac{36-16}{36+16} = \frac{20}{52} = \frac{10}{26}$$

$$\text{Cor } r(U, V) = r(U, V) = \frac{5}{12}$$

Where $U = X + Y$, $V = X - Y$ **Ans.**

Problem 11 If X and Y are independent random variables and $V(X) = \sigma x^2$ and $\text{Var}(Y) = \sigma Y^2$

Then show that correlation coefficient between Y and $X-Y$ is

$$\frac{\sigma Y}{\sqrt{\sigma x^2 + \sigma y^2}}$$

Solution Since X and Y are independent random variables so

$$\text{Cor } r(X, Y) = 0$$

$$\Rightarrow \quad \frac{\text{Cov}(X, Y)}{\sigma x \, \sigma y} = 0$$

$$\Rightarrow \quad \text{Cov}(X, Y) = 0$$

$$V(X) = \sigma x^2$$

$$V(Y) = \sigma y^2$$

$$\text{Cor } r(Y, X-Y) = \frac{\text{Co } V(Y, X-Y)}{\sigma x \, \sigma x-y}$$

Where Cov $(X, X-Y)$ is the covariance of X and $X-Y$ σx, $\sigma x-y$ denote the variance of X and $X-Y$ respectively.

Now we have

$$\begin{aligned}
\text{Co } V(Y, X-Y) &= E[\{Y-E(Y)\}\{X-Y-E(X-Y)\}] \\
&= E[\{Y-E(Y)\}\{X-Y-E(X)+E(Y)\}] \\
&= E[\{Y-E(Y)\}\{X-E(X)-(Y-E(Y))\}] \\
&= E[\{Y-E(Y)\}^2-\{X-E(X)\}\{Y-E(Y)\}] \\
&= E[Y-E(Y)]^2-E[\{X-E(X)\}\{Y-E(Y)\}] \\
&= \sigma y^2-\text{Cov}(X, Y) \\
&= \sigma y^2-0 = \sigma Y^2
\end{aligned}$$

Again

$$\begin{aligned}
\sigma X-Y &= V(X-Y) \\
&= E[X-Y-E(X-Y)]^2 \\
&= E[X-Y-E(X)+E(Y)]^2 \\
&= E[\{X-E(X)\}-\{Y-E(Y)\}]^2 \\
&= E[\{X-E(X)]^2+\{Y-E(Y)\}^2 \\
&\qquad -2\{X-E(X)\}\{Y-E(Y\}] \\
&= E[X-E(X)]^2+E[Y-E(Y)]^2 \\
&\qquad -2E[\{X-E(X)\}\{Y-E(Y)\}] \\
&= \sigma^2 x+\sigma y^2-2\,\text{Cov}(X, Y) \\
&= \sigma x^2+\sigma y^2-0 = \sigma x^2+\sigma y^2
\end{aligned}$$

$$\sigma^2_{X-Y} = \sigma x^2 + \sigma y^2$$

$$\Rightarrow \quad \sigma x - y = \sqrt{\sigma x^2 + \sigma y^2}$$

$$\text{Cor } r\,(Y, X-Y) = \frac{\sigma^2 y}{\sigma y\ \sigma x - y}$$

$$\text{Cor } r\,(Y, X-Y) = \frac{\sigma y}{\sqrt{\sigma x^2 + \sigma y^2}} \qquad \textit{(Proved)}$$

Problem 13 Prove that

$$V\,(ax \pm by) = a^2\, V\,(X) + b^2\, V\,(Y) \pm 2ba \text{ Cov } (X, Y)$$

Hence deduce that if X and Y are independent then

$$V\,(X \pm Y) = V\,(X) + V\,(Y)$$

Where $V\,(X)$, $V\,(Y)$, $V\,(X + Y)$ denote the variances of X, Y and $X + Y$ respectively

Solution $V\,(ax \pm by)$

$$= E\,[(aX \pm bY) - E\,(aX \pm by]^2$$
$$= E\,[aX \pm bY - a\,E\,(X) \pm b\,E\,(Y)]^2$$
$$= E\,[a\,\{X - E\,(X)\} \pm b\,\{Y - E\,(Y)\}^2$$
$$= E\,[a^2\,\{X - E\,(X)\}^2 + b^2\,\{Y - E\,(Y)\}^2$$
$$\pm\, 2ab\,\{X - E\,(X)\}\,\{Y - E\,(Y)\}]$$
$$= a^2\,E\,[X - E\,(X)]^2 + b^2\,E\,[Y - E\,(Y)]^2$$
$$\pm\, 2ab\,E\,[\{X - E\,(X)\}\,\{Y - E\,(Y)\}]$$
$$= a^2\,\sigma X^2 + b^2\,\sigma Y^2 \pm 2ab \text{ Cov } (X, Y)$$
$$= a^2\,V\,(X) + b^2\,V\,(Y) \pm 2ab \text{ Cov } (X, Y)$$

Thus $V\,(aX \pm bY)$

$$= a^2\,V\,(X) + b^2\,V\,(Y) \pm 2ab \text{ Cov } (X, Y)$$

Deduction Since X and Y are independent then $\text{Cor } (X, Y) = 0$

$$\Rightarrow \quad \text{Cov } (X, Y) = 0$$

So $\qquad V\,(aX \pm bY)$

$$= a^2\,V\,(X) + b^2\,V\,(Y) \pm 2ab.0$$
$$= a^2\,V\,(X) + b^2\,V\,(Y)$$

putting $\quad a = 1 \quad$ and $\quad b = 1$ we have

$$V\,(X \pm Y) = 1V\,(X) + 1\,(Y)$$

$$\Rightarrow \quad V\,(X \pm Y) = V\,(X) + V\,(Y) \qquad \textbf{(Proved)}$$

Formula for the correlation coefficient for computational work.

We know that $r = \frac{\text{Cov}(X, Y)}{\sigma x \, \sigma y}$

$$\text{Cov}(X, Y) = E[\{X - E(X)\}\{Y - E(Y)\}]$$

$$= \frac{1}{n}\sum_{1=t}^{n}(X_i - \bar{X})(Y_i - \bar{Y})$$

$$= \frac{1}{n}\sum\{X_i Y_i - X_i \bar{Y} - \bar{X} Y_i + \bar{Y}\bar{X})$$

$$= \frac{1}{n}\sum X_i Y_t - \frac{1}{n}\sum X_i \bar{Y} - \frac{1}{n}\sum \bar{X} Y_i + \bar{X}\bar{Y}$$

$$= \frac{1}{n}\sum X_i Y_i - \bar{Y}\frac{1}{n}\sum x_1 - \bar{X}\frac{1}{n}\sum Y_l + \bar{X}\bar{Y}$$

$$= \frac{1}{n}\sum X_i Y_i - \bar{X}\bar{Y} - \bar{X}\bar{Y} + \bar{X}\bar{Y}$$

$$= \frac{1}{n}\sum X_i Y_i - \bar{X}\bar{Y}$$

$$\sigma x^2 = \frac{1}{n}\sum(X_l - \bar{X})^2 = \frac{1}{n}\sum(X_i^2 - 2X_i\bar{X} + \bar{X}^2)$$

$$= \frac{1}{n}\sum X_i^2 - \frac{2\bar{X}}{n}\sum X_i + \bar{X}_1^2$$

$$= \frac{1}{n}\sum X_i^2 - 2\bar{X}\cdot\bar{X} + X^2$$

$$= \frac{1}{n}\sum X_i^2 - 2\bar{X}^2 + \bar{X}^2 = \frac{1}{n}\sum X_i^2 - \bar{X}^2$$

$$\sigma y^2 = \frac{1}{n}\sum(Y_i - \bar{Y})^2$$

$$= \frac{1}{n}\sum(Y_i - 2Y_l\bar{Y} + \bar{Y}^2)$$

$$= \frac{1}{n}\sum Y_i^2 - 2\bar{Y}\bar{Y} + \bar{Y}$$

$$= \frac{1}{n}\sum Y_i^2 - 2\bar{Y}^2 + \bar{Y}^2$$

$$= \frac{1}{n}\sum Y_{i,}^2 - \bar{Y}^2$$

Again since we know that

$$r(X, Y) = \text{Cor}(X, X)$$

$$= \frac{\text{Cov}(\bar{X}, Y)}{\sigma x \ \sigma y}$$

$$= \frac{\frac{1}{n}\Sigma (X_i - \bar{X})(Y_i - \bar{Y})}{\left[\frac{1}{n}\Sigma (X_i - \bar{X})^2 \frac{1}{n}\Sigma (Y_i - \bar{Y})^2\right]^{1/2}}$$

$$= \frac{\Sigma (X_i - \bar{X})(Y_i - \bar{Y})}{[\Sigma (X_i - \bar{X})^2 \Sigma (Y_i - \bar{Y})^2]^{1/2}}$$

Putting $dX = X_i - \bar{X}$

$$dX^2 = (Xi - \bar{X})^2$$

$$dY^2 = (Y_i - \bar{Y})^2$$

$$dY = (Y_i - \bar{Y})$$

So the correlation of X and Y is given by

$$\text{Corr}(X, Y) = r(X, Y) = \frac{\Sigma \, dX \, dY}{\sqrt{\Sigma \, dX^2 \, \Sigma \, dY^2}} \quad (1)$$

Remember Equation (1)

From equation (1) correlation coefficient between X and Y can be obtained by Direct Method.

Working Rule for computing correlation constant by Direct Method.

The coefficient of correlatien is calculated by the following steps.

Step I Denote the one series by X and the other by Y.

Step II Calculate $\bar{X}$ and $\bar{Y}$ of the X and Y series respectively.

Step III Take the deviation of the observation in X series from $\bar{X}$ and write it in a column headed by $dX = X - \bar{X}$. Take the deviations of the observations in Y series from $\bar{Y}$ and write if in a column headed by $dY = Y - \bar{Y}$.

Step IV Square these deviations and write them in a column headed by dX^2 and dY^2.

Step V Multiply the respective dX and dY and write it in column headed by $dX \, dY$.

Step VI Apply the following formula to calculate r or $r(X, Y)$ the coefficient of correlation

$$r = \frac{\Sigma \, dX \, dY}{[\Sigma \, dX^2 \, \Sigma \, dY^2]^{1/2}}$$

where n is the number of observations in X or Y series, σx and σy are the standard deviation of X and Y.

[Remember square of standard deviation is the variance].

i.e. $\sigma x^2 = V(X)$

and $\sigma y^2 = V(Y)$

Problem 1 Find the coefficient of correlation between the heights of fathers and sons from the following data:

Heights of fathers in inches (X)	65	66	67	68	69	70	71
Heights of sons in inches (X)	67	68	66	69	72	72	69

Solution Let the heights of fathers be denoted by X and that of sons by Y

Then
$$\bar{X} = \frac{65 + 66 + 67 + 68 + 69 + 70 + 71}{7} = 68$$

$$\bar{Y} = \frac{67 + 68 + 66 + 69 + 72 + 72 + 69}{7} = 69$$

Let us prepare the following table.

x	dx $x-68$	dx^2 $(x-68)^2$	y	dy $Y-69$	$dy^2 =$ $(Y-69)^2$	$dx\,dy$
65	−3	9	67	−2	4	6
66	−2	4	68	−1	1	2
67	−1	1	66	−3	9	3
68	0	0	69	0	0	0
69	1	1	72	3	9	3
70	2	4	72	3	9	6
71	3	9	69	0	0	0
	$\sum dX$ $= 0$	$\sum dX^2$ $= 28$		$\sum dY$ 0	$\sum dY^2$ $= 32$	$\sum dx\,dy$ $= 20$

Now
$$r(X, Y) = \text{Corr}(X, Y)$$

$$= \frac{\sum dX\,dY}{[\sum dX^2 \sum dY^2]^{1/2}}$$

$$= \frac{20}{[28 \times 32]^{1/2}} = \frac{20}{\sqrt{28 \times 32}}$$

$$= \frac{20}{\sqrt{4 \times 7 \times 16 \times 2}} = \frac{20}{4 \times 2\sqrt{14}}$$

$$= \frac{5}{2\sqrt{14}} = \frac{5}{7.5} = 0.67 \qquad \textit{(Approx)}$$

Regression

Regression analysis is a mathematical measure of the average relationship between two or more variables in terms of the original units of the data.

In regression analysis there are two types of variables. The variable whose value is influenced or is to be predicted is called dependent variable and the variable which influences the values or is used for prediction, is called independent variables. In regression analysis independent variable is also known as regressor or predictor or explanator while the dependent variable is also known as regressed or explained variable.

Lines of Regression

If the variables in a bivariate distribution are related we will find that the points in the scatter diagram will cluster round some curve called the "curve of regression". If the curve is straight line it is called the line of regression and there is said to be linear regression between the variables, otherwise regression is said to be curvi linear. The line of regression is the line which gives the best estimate to the value of one variable for any specific value of the variable. Thus the line of regression is the line of 'best fit' and is obtained by the principles of least squares.

Let us suppose that in the bivariate distribution (X_i, Y_i): $i = 1, 2 \ldots n$ Y is dependent and X is independent variable.

Remember

The equation of the line of regression of Y on X is given by

$$Y - \bar{Y} = r\frac{\sigma y}{\sigma x}(X - \bar{x}) \qquad (1)$$

Similarly the equation or the line of regression of X on Y is given by

$$X - \bar{x} = r\frac{\sigma x}{\sigma y}(Y - \bar{Y}) \qquad (2)$$

The regression equation (1) implies that the line of regression of Y on X passes through the point $(\bar{x}, \bar{y})$. Similarly (2) implies that the line of regression X on Y also passes through the point $(\bar{x}, \bar{y})$. In other words, the mean values $(\bar{x}, \bar{y})$ can be obtained as the point of intersection of the two regression lines.

Regression Coefficients

'b' the slope of the line of regression of Y on X is also called the coefficient of regression of Y on X

$$byx = \text{Regression coefficient of } Y \text{ on } X$$

$$= r\frac{\sigma y}{\sigma x}$$

Similarly, the coefficient of regression of X on Y is given by

$$bXy = \frac{\sigma x}{\sigma y}$$

Properties of Regression Coefficients

(a) Correlation coefficient is the geometric mean between the regression coefficients.

Proof We have

$$bxy \times byx = r\frac{\sigma x}{\sigma X} \cdot r\frac{\sigma Y}{\sigma y} = r^2$$

i.e. $\quad bxy\ byx = r^2$

i.e. $\quad r = \pm\sqrt{bxy \cdot byx}$ (*Proved*)

(b) If one of the regression coefficients is greater than unity, the other must be less than unity.

Let one of the regression coefficients say byx be greater then unity, then we have to show that $bxy < 1$

Now $\quad byx > 1 \Rightarrow \frac{1}{byx} < 1$

Also $\quad r^2 \leqslant 1\ bxy\ bxy \leqslant 1$ i.e. $bxy \leqslant \frac{1}{byx} < 1 \Rightarrow bx\bar{y} < 1$

(*Proved*)

(c) Arithmetic mean of the regression coefficients is greater than the correlation coefficients.

Proof We have to prove that

$$\tfrac{1}{2}(byx + bxy \geqslant r$$

$$\frac{1}{2}\left(r\frac{\sigma y}{\sigma x} + r\frac{\sigma x}{\sigma y}\right) \geqslant r$$

$$\frac{\sigma y}{\sigma x} + \frac{\sigma x}{\sigma y} \geqslant 2$$

$$\sigma y^2 + \sigma x^2 - 2\sigma x\ \sigma y \geqslant 0$$

$$\Rightarrow \quad (\sigma Y - \sigma X)^2 \geqslant 0$$

Which is always true, since the square of real quantity is $\geqslant 0$.

(d) Regression coefficients are independent of the change of origin but not of scale.

Solution Let $U = \frac{X-a}{h}, V = \frac{Y-b}{K}$

$$\Rightarrow \quad X = a + Uh \qquad Y = b + VK$$

where a, b h and K are constants.

Then $$\text{Cov}\,(X, Y) = hK\,\text{Cov}\,(U, V)$$

$$\sigma x^2 = h^2\,\sigma v^2 \text{ and } \sigma y^2 = K^2\,\sigma v^2$$

$$bYX = \frac{U_1}{\sigma X^2} = \frac{hK\,\text{Cov}\,(U_1\,V)}{h^2\,\sigma v^2}$$

$$= \frac{K}{h}\,\frac{\text{Cov}\,(U, V)}{\sigma u^2} = \frac{K}{h}\,bVU$$

[For simple calculation see on other page for the proof of this property.]
Similarly we can prove that

$$bXY = \frac{h}{K}\,bVU$$

Hence the result. *(Proved)*

Angle between two lines of Regression

Equation of the lines of regression of Y on X; and X on Y are

$$Y-\bar{y} = r\,\frac{\sigma y}{\sigma x}\,(X-\bar{x}) \tag{1}$$

and $$X-\bar{x} = r\,\frac{\sigma x}{\sigma y}\,(Y-\bar{y})$$

Slope of these lines are $r\,\frac{\sigma y}{\sigma x}$ and $\frac{1}{r}\,\frac{\sigma y}{\sigma x}$. If θ be the angle between the two lines of regression then

$$\tan\theta = \frac{r\,\frac{\sigma y}{\sigma x} \sim \frac{\sigma y}{r\,\sigma x}}{1 + r\,\frac{\sigma y}{\sigma x}\cdot\frac{\sigma y}{r\,\sigma x}} = \frac{1-r^2}{r}\left\{\frac{(\sigma x\,\sigma y)}{\sigma x^2 + \sigma y^2)}\right\}$$

$$\theta = \tan^{-1}\left\{\frac{1-r^2}{r}\,\frac{\sigma x\,\sigma y}{\sigma x^2 + \sigma y^2}\right\}$$

If θ is obtuse then

$$\tan\theta = \frac{\frac{(r^2-1)}{r}\,\frac{\sigma y}{\sigma x}}{\frac{\sigma x^2+\sigma y^2}{\sigma x^2}}$$

$$\tan\theta = \frac{(r^2-1)}{r}\,\frac{\sigma x\,\sigma y}{(\sigma x^2 + \sigma y^2)}$$

$$\theta = \tan^{-1}\left\{\frac{(r^2-1)}{r}\,\frac{\sigma x\,\sigma y}{(\sigma x^2 + \sigma y^2)}\right\}$$

Problem 1 If θ is the angle between the lines of regression of a Bivariate distribution, prove that

$$\tan\theta = \pm \frac{1-r^2}{r} \frac{\sigma x \, \sigma y}{\sigma x^2 + \sigma y^2}$$

where r σx and σy have the usual meanings. [*I.F.S. 83*]

Case I If $r = 0$ then

$$\tan\theta = \infty$$

$$\Rightarrow \quad \theta = \frac{\pi}{2}$$

Thus if the two variables are uncorrelated, the line of regression becomes perpendicular to each other.

Case II $(r = \pm 1)$ If $r = \pm 1$ then

$$\tan\theta = 0 = \tan n\pi \ \tan n = 0, 1$$

$$\Rightarrow \quad \theta = 0 \quad \text{or} \quad \pi$$

In this case the two lines of regression either coincide or they are parallel to each other. But since both the lines of regression pass through the point $(\bar{x}, \bar{y})$, they cannot be parallel. Hence in the case of perfect correlation $(r = \pm 1)$ positive or negative, the two lines of regression coincide.

Remark 1 Whenever two lines intersect there are two angles between them, one acute angle and the other obtuse angle.

Further $\tan\theta > 0$, $0 < \theta < \pi/2$

i.e. θ is obtuse angle and if $\tan\theta < 0$

if $\frac{\pi}{2} < \theta < \pi$ i.e. θ is an obtuse angle and since $0 < r^2 < 1$ the acute angle (θ_1) and obtuse angle θ_2, between the two lines of regression are given by

$$\theta_1 = \text{Acute angle}$$

$$= \tan^{-1}\left\{\frac{\sigma x \, \sigma y}{\sigma x^2 + \sigma y^2} \frac{1-r^2}{r}\right\}$$

and $\theta_2 = \text{obtuse angle} = \tan^{-1}\left\{\frac{\sigma x \, \sigma y}{\sigma x^2 + \sigma y^2} \frac{r^{2-1}}{r}\right\}$

In fact if $r = 0$ (variables un correlated) the two lines of regression are perpendicular to each other and if $r = \pm 1$ $\theta = 0$ i.e. the two lines coincide leads as to the conclusion that for higher degree of correlation between the variables, the angle between the lines is smaller i.e. the two lines of regression are nearer to each other. On the other hand, if the correlation lines of regression make a larger angle. They indicate a poor degree of correlation between the variables and ultimately for $\theta = \pi/2$, $r = 0$ i.e. the lines become perpendicular if no correlation exists between the variables.

Thus by plotting the lines of regression on a graph-paper we can have an approximate about the degree of correlation between the two variables under study.

Two lines coincide $r = -1$

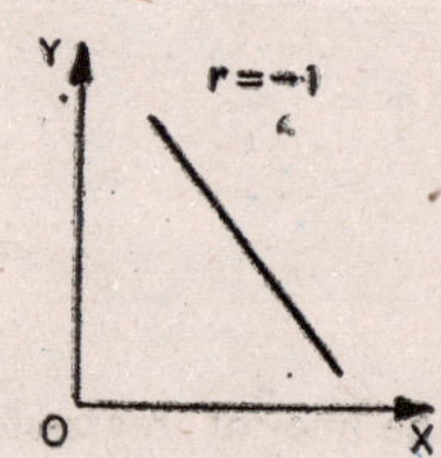

Two lines coincide $r = 1$

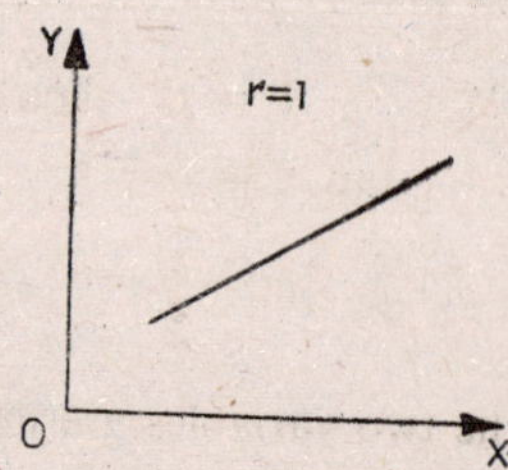

Two lines perpendicular

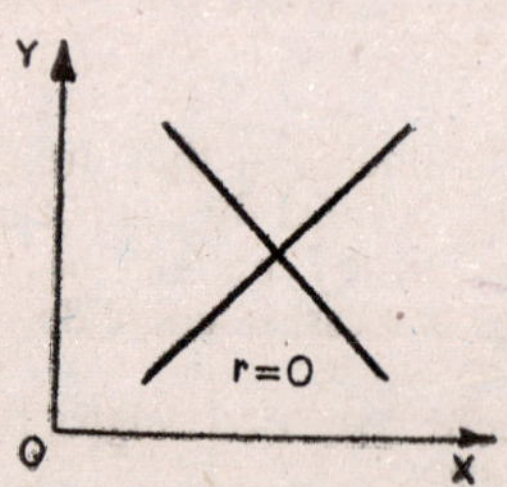

Two lines apart
(lower degree of correlation)

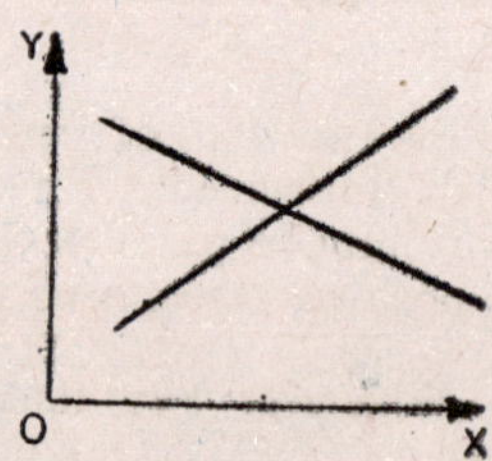

Two lines apart lower degree of correlation

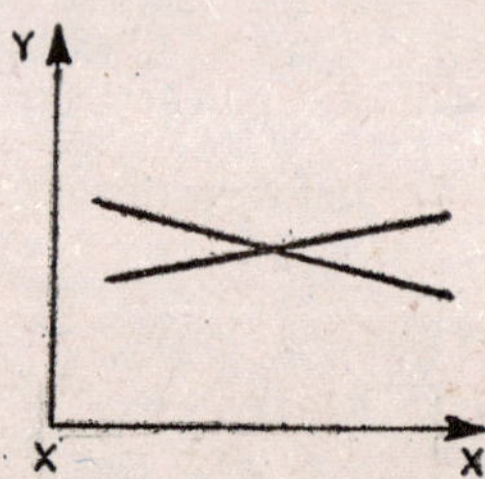

Problem 2 In partially destroyed laboratory record of an analysis of correlation data, the following results only are legible:

Variance of $X = 9$

Regression equations:

$$8X - 10Y + 66 = 0,$$
$$40X - 18Y = 214$$

What were (i) the mean values of X and Y

(ii) the correlation coefficient between X and Y and

(iii) the standard deviation of Y? [*I.F.S. 84*]

Solution The equation of the lines of regression are

$$8X - 10Y + 66 = 0 \quad (1)$$

and
$$40X - 18Y - 214 = 0 \quad (2)$$

Since both the lines pass through the point $(\bar{X}, \bar{Y})$

Then
$$8\bar{X} - 10\bar{Y} + 66 = 0$$

and
$$40\bar{X} - 18\bar{Y} - 214 = 0$$

$$\frac{\bar{X}}{2140 + 1188} = \frac{\bar{Y}}{2640 + 1712} = \frac{1}{-144 + 400}$$

$$\frac{\bar{X}}{3328} = \frac{\bar{Y}}{4352} = \frac{1}{256}$$

$$\bar{X} = \frac{3328}{256} = 13$$

$$\bar{Y} = \frac{4352}{256} = 17$$

(ii) The two lines of regression may be put in the form

$$8X - 10Y + 66 = 0$$

$$\Rightarrow \quad 10Y = 8X + 66$$

$$\Rightarrow \quad Y = \frac{8}{10} X + \frac{66}{10}$$

Thus bYX = regression coefficient of Y on $X = \frac{8}{10}$

$$X = \frac{18Y + 214}{40}$$

$$X = \frac{18}{40} Y + \frac{214}{40}$$

So bXY = regression coefficient of X on $Y = \frac{18}{40}$

We have
$$r^2 = bXY \times bYX$$

$$r^2 = \frac{4}{5} \times \frac{9}{20}$$

$$r^2 = \frac{9}{25} \quad \Rightarrow \quad r = \pm \frac{3}{5} = \pm\, 0.6$$

Since both the regression coefficients are positive

$$r = +\, 0.6$$

(iii) Standard deviation of $Y = \sigma_Y$

If is given that $V(X) = 9$

i.e. $\sigma x^2 = 9$

i.e. $\sigma x = 3$

We have $by\,x = r\,\frac{\sigma y}{\sigma x}$

$$\frac{4}{5} = \frac{3}{5}\,\frac{\sigma y}{3}$$

$$\sigma y = 4$$

i.e. $\sigma_Y = 4$

Thus the standard deviation of $Y = 4$

Variance of $Y = V(Y) = \sigma y^2$

$$= (4)^2 = 16$$

$$V(Y) = 16 \qquad \textbf{Ans.}$$

Problem 3 If the lines of regression of Y on X and X and Y are respectively $a_1 X + b_1 Y + c_1 = 0$ and $a_2 X + b_2 Y + c_2 = 0$,

prove that $a_1 b_2 \leqslant a_2 b_1$

Solution The line of regression of Y on X

i.e. $a_1 X + b_1 Y + c_1 = 0$

i.e. $b_1 Y = -(a_1 X + c_1)$

$\Rightarrow$ $b_1 Y = -a_1 X - c_1$

$\Rightarrow$ $Y = -\frac{a_1}{b_1} X - \frac{c_1}{b_1}$

Here $bYX = -\frac{a_1}{b_1}$ (1)

The line of regression of X and Y

i.e. $a_2 X + b_2 Y + c_2 = 0$

$$a_2 X = -b_2 Y - c_2$$

$$X = -\frac{b_2}{a_2} Y - \frac{c_2}{a_2}$$

Here $bXY = -\frac{b_2}{a_2}$ **(2)**

Again $$r^2 = bYX \cdot bXY$$

$$r^2 = \left(-\frac{a_1}{b_1}\right)\left(-\frac{b_2}{a_2}\right)$$

$$r^2 = \frac{a_1\, b_2}{b_1\, a_2} \quad (3)$$

$$r^2 \leqslant 1 \quad \text{[we know]}$$

$\Rightarrow$ $$\frac{a_1\, b_2}{a_2\, b_1} \leqslant 1$$

$\Rightarrow$ $$a_1\, b_2 \leqslant a_2\, b_1$$ (*Proved*)

Problem 4 Given that $X = 4Y + 5$ and $Y = KX + 4$ are the lines of regression of X on Y and Y on X respectively. Show that $0 < 4K < 1$. If $K = \frac{1}{16}$, find the *means of the two variables* and coefficient of correlation between them.

Solution $X = 4Y + 5$ is the line of regression of X on Y

Then $$bXY = 4$$

Again $Y = KX + 4$ is the line of regression of $\bar{Y}$ on X

Then $bYX = K$

We know that $r^2 = bXY \cdot bYX = 4K$

Again as we know that $0 < r^2 < 1$

[*First part proved*]

$\Rightarrow$ $$0 < 4K < 1$$

If $$K = \frac{1}{16}$$

Then $$r^2 = 4\,\frac{1}{16}$$

$$r^2 = \frac{1}{4}$$

$$r = \pm\,\frac{1}{2}$$

$\Rightarrow$ $$r = +\,\frac{1}{2}$$

Since both the regression coefficients are positive

If $$K = \frac{1}{16}$$

Then the two regression lines are

$$X = 4Y + 5 \tag{1}$$

And $$Y = \frac{1}{16} X + 4 \tag{2}$$

since both the regression lines passes through the mean $\bar{X}$ and $\bar{Y}$ so $(\bar{X}, \bar{Y})$ will satisfy the equation (1) and (2)

So $$\bar{X} = 4\bar{Y} + 5 \qquad 2(a)$$

$$\bar{Y} = \frac{1}{16} \bar{X} + 4$$

$\Rightarrow$ $$16\bar{Y} = \bar{X} + 64 \tag{3}$$

$$4\bar{Y} = \bar{X} - 5$$

$\Rightarrow$ $$16\bar{Y} = 4\bar{X} - 20 \tag{4}$$

From relation (4) and (3)

$$4\bar{X} - 20 - \bar{X} - 64 = 0$$

$$3\bar{X} - 84 = 0$$

$\Rightarrow$ $$3\bar{X} = 84$$

$\Rightarrow$ $$\bar{X} = \frac{84}{3} = 28$$

Putting the value of $\bar{X}$ in equation 2 (a) we have

$$28 = 4\bar{Y} + 5$$

$\Rightarrow$ $$4\bar{Y} = 28 - 5$$

$\Rightarrow$ $$4\bar{Y} = 23$$

$\Rightarrow$ $$\bar{Y} = \frac{23}{4} = 5.75$$

Thus the means of $X\,(\bar{X})$ and $Y\,(\bar{Y})$ are 28 and 5·75 respectively.

Problem 5 The regression lines of Y on X and of X on Y are respectively $Y = aX + b$ and $X = cY + d$, show that

(i) Means are $$\bar{X} = \frac{bc + d}{1 - ac}$$

and $$\bar{Y} = \frac{ad + b}{1 - ac}$$

(ii). Correlation coefficient between X and Y is $\sqrt{ac}$

(iii) For two random variables X and Y with the same mean, the two regression equations are

$$Y = aX + b \quad \text{and} \quad X = \alpha Y + \beta$$

Show that $\dfrac{b}{\beta} = \dfrac{1-a}{1-\alpha}$

Solution The two lines of regression are

$$Y = aX + b \tag{1}$$

and

$$X = cY + d \tag{2}$$

Since both the lines pass through the point (X, Y) so it will satisfy both the equation

$$\bar{Y} = a\bar{X} + b \tag{3}$$

and

$$\bar{X} = c\bar{Y} + d \tag{4}$$

From (4)

$$\frac{\bar{X}-d}{c} = \bar{Y} \tag{5}$$

From (3) and (5) we have

$$a\bar{X} + b = \frac{\bar{X}-d}{c}$$

$$ac\bar{X} + bc = \bar{X} - d$$

$$bc + d = \bar{X}(1-ac)$$

$$\bar{X} = \frac{bc+d}{1-ac}$$

Putting the value of $\bar{X}$ in (4) we have

$$\frac{bc+d}{1-ac} = c\bar{Y} + d$$

$$\frac{bc+d}{1-ac} - d = c\bar{Y}$$

$$\frac{bc+d-d+acd}{1-ac} = c\bar{Y}$$

$$\frac{c(b+ad)}{1-ac} = c\bar{Y}$$

i.e.

$$\bar{Y} = \frac{b+ad}{1-ac}$$

Thus the means of X and Y are $\dfrac{bc+d}{1-ac}$ and $\dfrac{ad+b}{1-ac}$ respectively.

(ii) From the equation of two lines of regression we have the coefficient of regression of Y on X and of X on Y are given by

$$bYX = a$$

$$bXY = c$$

Again $$r^2 = bYX \cdot bXY$$

$$r^2 = ac$$

$\Rightarrow$ $$r = \sqrt{ac}$$

Thus the correlation coefficientis $\sqrt{ac}$ between X and Y.

(b) For X and Y two random variables the means are same

i.e. $$\bar{X} = \bar{Y}$$

Regression equations are

$$Y = aX + b \quad (1)$$

and $$X = \alpha Y + \beta \quad (2)$$

Since both the equation passes through the mean $(\bar{X}, \bar{Y})$ so

$$\bar{Y} = a\bar{X} + b$$

and $$\bar{X} = \alpha \bar{Y} + \beta$$

$$\bar{Y} = a\bar{X} + b$$

$$\bar{Y} = a\bar{Y} + b$$

since $$\bar{X} = \bar{Y}$$

$$\bar{Y}(1-a) = b$$

$\Rightarrow$ $$\bar{Y} = \frac{b}{1-a} \quad (3)$$

$$\bar{X} = \alpha \bar{Y} + \beta$$

[since $\bar{X} = \bar{Y}$]

$$\bar{Y} = \alpha \bar{Y} + \beta$$

$\Rightarrow$ $$(1-\alpha)\bar{Y} = \beta$$

$\Rightarrow$ $$\bar{Y} = \frac{\beta}{1-\alpha} \quad (4)$$

From relation (3) and (4) we have

$$\frac{b}{1-a} = \frac{\beta}{1-\alpha}$$

$\Rightarrow$ $$\frac{b}{\beta} = \frac{1-a}{1-\alpha}$$ *(Proved)*

Probability theory and Theoretical distributions

Probability theory was originated from gambling theory. A large no. of problems exists even today, which are based on the game of chance, such as cointossing, die throwing and playing cards. The utility of probability in business and economics is most emphatically revealed in the field of prediction for future. We have to anticipate consequences of each of these plans and finally we compare the results. Uncertainty, it plays an important role in business and probabily is a concept which measures the degree of uncertainly and that of certainty also as a corollary. The probability when defined in the simplest way is the chance of occuring of a certain event when expressed quantitavely. The probability is defined in the following two different ways.

(i) Mathematical (or a priori) definition.

(ii) Statistical (or empirical) definition.

Before we study the probability theory in details, it is appropriate to give the definition of certain terms, which are essential for the study of probability theroy.

Some improtant terms and concept

(1) Randem Experiment or Trial: An experiment is characterised by the property that its observations under a given set of circumstances do not always lend to some observed out come but rather to different out comes which follow a sort of statistical regularly. It is also called a trial. For example tossing a coin throwing a die.

(2) **Sample space.** Let us toss a coin. The results are either head or tail. Let *1 denote head* and *0 denote tail.* Mark the point 0, 1 on a straight line. Thus we get two different points 0 and 1 on a straight line. These points are called sample points or event points. For a given experiment there are different possible out comes and hence different sample points. The collection of all such sample points is called a sample space. Toss two coins simultaneously then the possible results are four pairs (0, 0), (1, 0), (0, 1) (1, 1) and they can be represented as points in co-ordinate plane. These points constitute a sample space of four sample points similarly, tossing three coins simultaneously, we get points which can be denoted by the triplets (0, 0, 0), (0, 1, 0), (0, 0, 1), (1, 1, 0), (1, 0, 1), (1, 1, 1) (1, 0, 0) (0, 1, 1), these 8 points form a sample space of 3-dimension. In general if we tossing n coins simultaneously we can have n, dimensional sample space consisting of 2^n sample points.

Event. A subcollection of a number of sample points under a definite rule or law is called an event. For example let us e is faces 1, 2, 3, 4, 5, 6 be represented by E_1, E_2, E_3 E_4 E_5, E_6 respectively. Then all the E, are sample points. Let E be event of getting an even number on the die. Obviously $E = \{E_2, E_4, E_6\}$ which is a subset of the set

$$\{E_1, E_2, E_3, E_4, E_5, E_6\}$$

Null Event. An event having no sample point is called a null event and is denoted by ϕ.

Discrete sample space: A sample space whose elements are finite or infinite but countable is called a discrete sample space for example, if we tossacoin as many times as we require for turning up one head then the sequence of points is $S_1 = (1)$, $S_2 = (0, 1)$, $S_3 = (1, 0, 1)$ $S_4 = (0, 0, 0, 1)$ etc. is a discrete sample space.

Continuous sample space. A sample space whose elements are infinite and un-countable or assume all the values on a real line R or an interval of R is called a continuous sample space. In this case the sample points build up a continuum; and the sample space is said to be continuous. For example, all the points on a line or all points on a plane is a sample space.

Exhaustive Cases or Events: It is the total no. of all the possible out comes of an experiment. For example when we throw a die, then any one of the six faces (1, 2, 3, 4, 5, 6) may turn up and therefore, there are six possible outcomes. Hence these are six exhaustive cases or events in throwing a die.

Mutually Exclusive Events. If in an experiment the occurence of an event prealudes or prevents or rules out the happening of all other events in the same experiment, then these events are said to be mutually exclusive events. For example, in tossing a coin, the events. Head or Tail are mutually exclusive because if the out come is head, then the possibility of getting a tail in the same trial is ruled out.

Equally likely. Events are said to be equally likely if there is no reason to expect any one in preference to other. For example in throwing a die. all the six faces (1, 2, 3, 4, 5, 6) are equally likely to occur.

Collectively Exhaustive events: The total number of events in a population exhausts the population. So they are known as collectively exhaustive events.

Equally Probable events. If in an experiment all possible out comes have an equal chance of occurance, then such events are said to be equally. probable. For example, in throwing a coin, the events Head and Tail have equal chances of occurance, therefore, they are equally probable events.

Favourable Cases. The cases which ensures the occurence of an event are said to be favourable to the event.

Independent and Dependent events: When the experiments are conducted in such a way that the occurance of an event in one trial does not have any effect on the occurence of this or other events at a subsequent experiment, then the events are said to be independent. In other words, two or more events are said to be independent if the happening of any one does not depend on the happening of the other. Events which are not independent are called dependent events.

For example. If we draw a card in a Pack of well shuffled cards and again draw a card from the rest of pack of cards (containing 51 cards), then the second drow is dependent on the first. But if on the other hand we draw a second card from the pack by replacing the first card drawn, the second draw is known as independent *of the first.*

Classical Definition of Probability: If an experiment has n mutually exclusive, equally likely and exhaustive cases, out of which m are favourable to the happening of the event A, then the probability of the happening of A is denoted by $P(A)$ and is defined as

$$P(A) = \frac{m}{n} = \frac{\text{No. of cases favourable to } A}{\text{Total (Exhaustive) number of cases}}$$

Problem 1 What is the probability of getting an even number in a single through with a die?

Solution The possible cases in a throw of a die are six

i.e. 1, 2, 3, 4, 5, 6

Favourable cases are those which are marked with 2, 4, 6 and these are three in number.

$\therefore$ Probability of gettieg an even number $= \frac{3}{6} = \frac{1}{2}$.

Note 1. Probability of an event which is certain to occur is 1 and the probability of an impossible event is zero.

Note 2. The possibility of occurence of any event lies between 0 and 1 both inclusive.

Problem 2 What is the probability of getting tail in a throw of a coin.

Solution When we toss a coin, there are two possible out comes head or tail. In this case the number of possible cases $n = 2$.

No. of favourable cases, $= m = 1$

($\therefore$ The out come of tailes favourable event)

$\therefore$ Probability of getting a tail $= \frac{m}{n} = \frac{1}{2}$.

Problem 3 A bag contains 6 white balls, 9 black balls, what is the probability of drawing a black ball?

Solution Total no. of equally likely n (balls) $= 6 + 9 = 15$

Number of favourable cases $m = {}^9c_1 = 9$ [$\because$ No. of black balls]

Probability of drawing a black-ball $= \frac{9}{15} = \frac{3}{5}$ **Ans.**

Problem 4 What is the probability that if a card is drawn at random from an ordinary pack of cards it is

(i) a red card (ii) aclub

(iii) one of the court cards. (*Jack or queen or king*)

Solution No. of exhaustive cases = 52

(i) There are 26 red cards and 26 black cards in an ordinary pack.

$\therefore$ Favourable cases = 26 (m = no. of red cards) probability of getting a red card $= \frac{26}{52} = \frac{1}{2}$

(ii) There are 13 clubs in a pack

Favourable cases = 13 = (No of clubs in a pack)

Probability of getting a club $= \frac{13}{52} = \frac{1}{4}$

(iii) There are $4 \times 3 = 12$ court cards in a pack of cards.

Favourable cases = 12

Probability of getting one of the court cards $= \frac{12}{52} = \frac{3}{13}$. **Ans.**

Problem 5 What is the probability of throwing a number greater than 3 with an ordinary die?

Solution The six faces of a die are marked with numbess 1, 2, 3, 4, 5, 6 and thus there are only 6 exhaustive cases i.e. $n = 6$. There are three numbers 4, 5, 6 which are greater than 3 in a die.

$\therefore$ Favourable cases $= m = 3$

$\therefore$ Probability of getting a number greater than 3 $= \frac{m}{n} = \frac{3}{6} = \frac{1}{2}$.

Ans.

Problem 6 What is the probability of getting a total of 9 in a single throw with two dice?

Solution The number of exhaustive cases when two dice are thrown simultaneously $= 6^2 = 36$

But of these 36 cases there will be only four favourable cases. These are (3, 6), (4, 5), (5, 4) (6, 3)

$\therefore$ Probability $= \frac{4}{36} = \frac{1}{9}$.

Statistical or Emperical definition

Von Mises has given the following statistical or emperical definition of probability.

"If the experiment be repeated a large no. of times under essentially identical conditions, the limiting value of the ratio of the no. of times the event. A happens to the total number of trials of the experiment as the number of trials increases indefinitely is called the probability of happening the event A."

Symbolically Let $P(A)$ denote the probability of the occurance of A. Let m be the number of times in which an event A occurs in a series of n trials, then

$$P(A) = \lim_{n\to\infty} \frac{m}{n}$$

Provided the limit is finite and unique.

Theorems on probability

There are two important theorems of probability, namely.

1. The addition theorem, or the theorem on total probability.
2. The multiplication theorem or theorem on compound probability.

Statement. If the events are mutually exclusive, then the probability of happening of any one of them is equal to the sum of the probabilities of the happening of seperate events i.e. in other words if $E_1, E_2, E_3 \ldots E_n$ be n events and $P(E_1), P(E_2) \ldots$

$P(E_n)$ be their respective probabilities then

$$P(E_1 + E_2 + E_3 + \ldots + E_n) = P(E_1) + P(E_2) + \ldots + E_n$$

Proof Let $E_1, E_2, E_3 \ldots E_n$ be n naturally exclusive events with proabiiities $P(E_1), P(E_2) \ldots P(E_n)$ respectively.

Let N be the total number of trials.

Let $m_1, m_2, m_3 \ldots m_n$ be the cases favourable to events $E_1, E_2, E_3 \ldots E_n$ respectively then.

$$P(E_i) = \frac{m_i}{N}, i = 1, 2 \ldots n$$

Since $E_1, E_2, E_3 \ldots E_n$ been mutually exclusive therefore the cases favourable to the happening of any one of the events $E_1, E_2 \ldots E_n$ is

$$P(E_1 + E_2 + \ldots + E_n) = \frac{m_1 + m_2 + \ldots + m_n}{N}$$

$$= \frac{m_1}{N} + \frac{m_2}{N} + \frac{m_3}{N} + \ldots + \frac{m_n}{N}$$

$$= P(E_1) + P(E_2) + P(E_3) + \ldots + P(E_n)$$

Problem 1 A die is rolled. What is the probability that a number 1 and 6 may appear on the upper face?

Solution The probability of appearing the number 1 on the upper face $= \frac{1}{6}$.

The probability of appearing 6 on the upper face $= \frac{1}{6}$.

$\therefore$ The probability of 1 or 6 may appear on the face

$$= \frac{1}{6} + \frac{1}{6} = \frac{2}{6} = \frac{1}{3}$$

Problem 2 If the probability of the horse A winning the race is 1/5 and the probability of the horse B winning the same race is 1/6. What is the probablity that one of the horses will win the races).

Solution Probability of the winning of the horse $A = \frac{1}{5}$ probability of the winning of the horse $B = \frac{1}{6}$

$$\therefore \qquad P\,(A) + B) = P\,(A) + P\,(B)$$

$$P\,(A + B) = \frac{1}{5} + \frac{1}{6} = \frac{6+5}{30} = \frac{11}{30}$$

Problem 3 In a horse race the odds in favour of four horses. H_1, H_2, H_3, H_4 are 1:3 1:4; 1:5; 1:6 respectively not more than one wins at a time. Find the chance that one of them will win the race.

Solution

$$P\,(H_1) = \frac{1}{1+3} = \frac{1}{4}$$

$$P\,(H_2) = \frac{1}{1+4} = \frac{1}{5}$$

$$P\,(H_3) = \frac{1}{1+5} = \frac{1}{6}$$

$$P\,(H_4) = \frac{1}{1+6} = \frac{1}{7}$$

We know that

$$P\,(H_1 + H_2 + H_3 + H_4) = P\,(H_1) + P\,(H_2) + P\,(H_3) + P\,(H_4)$$

$$= \frac{1}{4} + \frac{1}{5} + \frac{1}{6} + \frac{1}{7} = \frac{319}{420}$$

Multiple theorem or theorem on compound probability.

Simple and compound events:

A single event is called a simple event, where as when two or more than two simple events occur in connection with each other, then their simultaneous occurence is called a compound event. If A and B are two simple events, the simultaneous occurence of A and B is called a compound event and is denoted by AB.

Conditional probability. The probability of the happening of an event A, when it is known that B has already happend: is called the conditional probability of A and is denoted by $P(A/B)$.

(i.e. $P(A/B)$ = conditional probability of A given that B has already occured.

Similarly $P(B/A)$ = conditional probability of B given that A has already occured,

Mutually independent events

An event A is said to be independent of the event B if

$P(A/B) = P(A)$ i.e. the probability of the happening of A is independent of the happening of B.

Theorem on compound probability

The probability of the simultaneous occurence of the two events A and B is equal to the probability of one of the events multiplied by the conditional probability of the other, given the occurence of the first i.e.

$$P(AB) = P(A)\,P(B/A) = P(B) \cdot P(A/B)$$

Problem 1 A card is drawn from a pack of 52 cards and then a second is drawn. What is the probability that both the cards drawn are queens?

Solution *First draw*: Probability of getting a queen $= \frac{4}{52} = \frac{1}{13}$

Second draw: After drawing the first queen we are left with 51 cards having 3 queens.

$\therefore$ Probability of getting a queen in the second draw $= \frac{3}{51} = \frac{1}{17}$

Probability that both the cards are queen $= \frac{1}{13} \times \frac{1}{17} = \frac{1}{221}$ **Ans.**

Problem 2 A bag contains 5 white and 3 black balls. Two balls are drawn one after the other without replacement. Find the probability that both the balls drawn are back.

Solution Let $P(A)$, $P(B/A)$ denote the probability of drawing a black ball in the first and second attempt respectively.

$\therefore$ Probabiiity of drawing a black ball in the first attempt is $P(A)$

where $$P(A) = \frac{3}{3+5} = \frac{3}{8}$$

Probability of drawing the second black ball given the first ball drawn is black is

$$P\left(\frac{B}{A}\right) = \frac{\text{favourable cases}}{\text{total no. of exhaustive}} = \frac{2}{5+2} = \frac{2}{7}$$

Probability that both the balls drawn are black is

$$P(AB) = P(A)\,P(B/A)$$

$$= \frac{3}{8} \times \frac{2}{7} = \frac{6}{56} = \frac{3}{28} \qquad \textbf{Ans.}$$

33

Addition Theorem for Compatible Events

Theorem The probability of the occurence of at least one of the events A and B is given by

$$P(A+B) = P(A) + (B) - P(AB)$$

Proofs. A and B are two events, then the event $A + B$ means the occurence of at least one of the two events A and B. It is the union of the following mutually exclusive events

(i) $A\bar{B}$ which means that A happens but B does not happen

(ii) $\bar{A}B$ which means B happens but A does not happen

(iii) AB which means both A and B occur

$$\therefore \quad A + B = A\bar{B} + \bar{A}B + AB$$

Applying the theorem of addition of probabilities, we have

$$P(A+B) = P(A\bar{B}) + P(\bar{A}B) + P(AB) \qquad (1)$$

But $$A = A\bar{B} + AB$$

$$\therefore \quad P(A) = P(A\bar{B}) + P(AB)$$

$$\Rightarrow \quad P(A\bar{B}) = P(A) - (AB) \qquad \text{(ii)}$$

Again $$B = \bar{A}B + AB$$

$$\Rightarrow \quad P(B) = P(\bar{A}B) + P(AB)$$

$$\Rightarrow \quad P(\bar{A}B) = P(B) - P(AB) \qquad \text{(iii)}$$

So $$P(A+B) = P(A) - P(AB) + P(B) - P(AB) + P(AB)$$

$$= P(A) + P(B) - P(AB)$$

Happening of at least one event

Let A and B be two independent events and P_1 and P_2 be the probabilities of their happening; then the chance that both A and B happen is $P_1 P_2$. Also probabilities of not happening A and B are $1-P_1$, $1-P_2$ respectively and $(1-P_1) X (1-P_2)$ is the probability that both will not happen.

Now the chance that at least one of them happen is

$$P_1 P_2 + P_1 (1-P_2) + P_2 (1-P_1) = 1-(1-P_1)(1-P_2)$$

Thus the above result can be generalised for n events $E_1, E_2 \ldots E_n$ with $P_1, P_2 \ldots P_n$ respective probabilities then the probability that at least one of them happen is

$$1-(1-P_2)(1-P_2)\ldots(1-P_n)$$

Problem 1 Four coins are tossed. Find the probability that at least one head turns up.

Probability of getting *a* head in *a* foss of a coin $= \frac{1}{2}$

Probability of getting a tail in a toss of a coin $= \frac{1}{2}$ (*in each case*)

∴ Probability of getting at least one head

$$= 1-(1-\tfrac{1}{2})\times(1-\tfrac{1}{2})\times(1-\tfrac{1}{2})(1-\tfrac{1}{2})$$

$$= 1-\tfrac{1}{2}\times\tfrac{1}{2}\times\tfrac{1}{2}\times\tfrac{1}{2}$$

$$= 1-\frac{1}{16} = \frac{15}{16} \quad \textbf{Ans.}$$

Problem 2 In a throw of 3 dice, find the probability that at least one dice shows up 1.

Solution P = probability of getting 1 in a throw of a die = 1/6
Probability of getting at least one die shows up 1

$$= 1-\left(1-\frac{1}{6}\right)\left(1-\frac{1}{6}\right)\left(1-\frac{1}{6}\right)$$

$$= 1-\frac{5}{6}\times\frac{5}{6}\times\frac{5}{6}$$

$$= 1-\left(\frac{5}{6}\right)^3 = 1-\frac{125}{216}$$

$$= \frac{216-125}{216} = \frac{91}{216}$$

Problem 3 A problem in Mathmatics is given to three students Dayanand, Ramesh and Naresh and whose chances of solving it are $\frac{1}{2}, \frac{1}{3}, \frac{1}{4}$ respectively, What is the probability that the problem will be solved. (at least by one of them).

Solution The probabilities of Dayanand, Ramesh and Naresh solving the problem are $\frac{1}{2}$, $\frac{1}{3}$ and $\frac{1}{4}$ respectively the probabilities of Dayanand Ramesh and Naresh not solving the problem are $1-\frac{1}{2}=\frac{1}{2}$, $1-\frac{1}{3}=\frac{2}{3}$ and $1-\frac{1}{4}=\frac{3}{4}$ respectively.

The probability that the problem is not solved by any one of them is

$$= \frac{1}{2} \times \frac{2}{3} \times \frac{3}{4} = \frac{1}{4}$$

The probability that the problem will be solved by at least one of them

$$= 1 - \frac{1}{4} = \frac{3}{4} \quad \textbf{Ans.}$$

Problem 4 What is the probability that a leap year selected at random will have 53 sundays ? [*I.F.S. 85*]

Solution There are 366 days in a leap year and it has 52 complete weeks and 2 days over. These two extra days can occur in following possible ways

(i) Sunday and Monday;
(ii) Monday and Tuesday
(iii) Tuesday and Wednesday
(vi) Wednesday and Thursday
(v) Thursday and Friday
(vi) Friday and Saturday
(vii) Saturday and Sunday

$\therefore$ No. of exhaustive Cases = 7

No. of favourable Cases = 2

[There are two cases which have Sunday (i) and (vii)]

$\therefore$ probability = 2/7 **Ans.**

Problem 5 A card is drawn from an ordinary pack of playing cards and a person bets that it is a spade or an ace what are the odds against his winning this bet ?

Solution In a pack of 52 cards, 1 card can be drawn in 52 ways since there are 13 spades and 3 ace (one ace is also present in spade) therefore the favourite cases $m = 13 + 3 = 16$

Probability of getting a spade or an ace

$$= \frac{16}{52} = \frac{4}{13} = \frac{4}{4+9}$$

odds against winning the bet are 9 to 4. **Ans.**

Problem 6 A card is drawn at random from *a* well shuffled pack of 52 cards. Find the probability of getting a two heart or diamond.

Solution Since there is only one two of hearts and only one two of diamonds, therefore the probability of getting a two of hearts = 1/52 and the probability of getting a two of diamonds = 1/52

Since there are mutually, exclusive cases, therefore the probability of getting a two of heart or a two of diamand

$$= \frac{1}{52} + \frac{1}{52} = \frac{2}{52} = \frac{1}{26}$$

Problem 7 A man and his wife appear for an interview for two posts. The probability of the husbands selection is 1/7 and that of the wife's selection is 1/5. What is the probability that only one of them will be selected ?

The probability that husband is not selected $= 1-1/7 = 6/7$

The probability that wife is not selected

$$= 1 - \frac{1}{5} = \frac{5-1}{5} = \frac{4}{5}.$$

The probability that only husband is selected

$$= \frac{1}{7} \times \frac{4}{5} = \frac{4}{35}$$

The probability that only wife is selected

$$= \frac{1}{5} \times \frac{6}{7} = \frac{6}{35}$$

The probability that only one of them is selected

$$= \frac{4}{35} + \frac{6}{35} = \frac{10}{35} = \frac{2}{7}$$

Problem 8 From a pack of 52 cards, two are drawn at random. Find the chance that one is a king and other is a queen.

Soution Total number of ways in which two cards can be drawn out of 52 cards is $52c_2$

Since in a pack of cards there are 4 kings and 4 queens, therefore the number of favourable cases is ${}^4c_1 \times {}^4c_2$

Thus required probability is

$$= \frac{\text{No of favourable Case}}{\text{No of exhaustive Cases}}$$

$$= \frac{{}^4c_1 \times {}^4c_1}{{}^{52}c_2} = \frac{4 \times 4}{\frac{52}{2!\,48!}} = \frac{4 \times 4}{\frac{52 \times 49}{2}}$$

$$= \frac{4 \times 4 \times 2}{52 \times 51} = \frac{4 \times 2}{13 \times 51}$$

The required probability is $= \frac{8}{663}$

Problem 9 Three groups of children contains 3 girls and 1 boy; 2 girls and 2 boys; 1 girls and 3 boys respectively. One child is selected at random from each group. Find the chance that the three selected comprise girl and 2 boys. *[I.F.S. 86]*

Solution The event may happen in any one of the following three mutually exclusive ways.

1. Girl from the first group, boy from the second group, boy from the third group.

The probability of happening is

$$\frac{3}{4} \cdot \frac{2}{4} \cdot \frac{3}{4} = \frac{4}{3} \cdot \frac{1}{2} \cdot \frac{3}{4} = \frac{9}{32}$$

2. Boy from the first group, girl from the second group, Boy from the third group

$$= \frac{1}{4} \cdot \frac{2}{4} \cdot \frac{3}{4} = \frac{1}{4} \times \frac{1}{2} \times \frac{3}{4} = \frac{3}{32}$$

3. Boy from the first group, Boy from the second group, Girl from the third

$$= \frac{1}{4} \cdot \frac{2}{4} \cdot \frac{1}{4} = \frac{1}{4} \times \frac{1}{2} \times \frac{1}{4} = \frac{1}{32}$$

$\therefore$ By the theorem of total probability, the required probability is

$$= \frac{9}{32} + \frac{3}{32} + \frac{1}{32} = \frac{13}{32} \qquad \textbf{Ans.}$$

Problem 10 Four persons are chosen at random from a group containing 3 men, 2 women and 4 children. Show that the chance that exactly two of them will be children is 10/21.

Solution The total no of ways in which four persons can be selected out of 9 persons is ${}^9c_4$.

The no. of ways in which 2 children can be selected out of 4 children $= {}^4c_2$

Now we have to chose only two person from the rest 5

The no of ways in which 2 person can be selected out of 5 $= {}^5c_2$

$\therefore$ The number of favourable cases$= {}^4c_2 \times {}^5c_2$

No. of exhaustive cases $= {}^9c_4$

So the required probability

$$\frac{\text{No of favourable cases}}{\text{Total no of exhaustive cases}} = \frac{{}^4c_2 \times {}^5c_2}{{}^9c_4}$$

$$= \frac{\dfrac{4!}{2!\,2!} \cdot \dfrac{5!}{2!\,3!}}{\dfrac{9!}{4!\,5!}} = \frac{4 \times 3 \times 2!}{2!\,2!} \times \frac{5 \times 4 \times 3!}{2!\,3!} \times \frac{4!\,5!}{9!}$$

$$= \frac{2 \times 3 \times 5 \times 2 \times 4!5!}{9 \times 8 \times 7 \times 6 \times 5!} = \frac{2 \times 3 \times 5 \times 2 \times 4 \times 3 \times 2 \times 1}{9 \times 8 \times 7 \times 6} = \frac{10}{21} \qquad \textbf{Ans.}$$

Problem 11 A bag contains 3 black and 5 white balls. One ball is drawn from the bag. What is the probability that the ball is not black.

Solution The probability of drawing a black from the bag = 3/8

The probability that the drawn ball is not black

$$= 1 - \frac{3}{8} = \frac{8-3}{8} = \frac{5}{8} \quad \textbf{Ans.}$$

Problem 12 In a single throw of two dice find the probability that neither a doublet (same number on the both dice) nor a total of 9 will appear.

Solution Total number of cases in a throw of two dice = 36
No of Cases with doublet = 6

[(1, 1); (2, 2); (3, 3); (4, 4); (5, 5); (6, 6)

No of cases with a total of 9 = 4

[(5, 4); (6, 3); (4, 5) (3, 6)]

∴ Total number of cases in which a doublet or a total of 9

$$= 6 + 4 = 10$$

P (doublet or a total of 9)

$$= P(A) = \frac{10}{36} = \frac{5}{18}$$

P (neither a doublet nor a total of 9)

$$= 1 - P(A) = 1 - \frac{5}{18} = \frac{18-5}{18} = \frac{13}{18} \quad \textbf{Ans.}$$

Problem 13 A bag contains tickets numbered from 1 to 20. Two tickets are drawn. Find the probability that both the numbers are prime.

Solution There are 8 prime numbers from 1 to 20 viz

2, 3, 5, 7, 11, 13, 17, 19

No of success $= 8c_2 = \frac{8!}{2!\ 6!} = \frac{8 \times 7 \times 6!}{2 \times 6!} = 4 \times 7 = 28$

Total number of ways

$$= 20c_2 = \frac{20 \times 19 \times 18!}{2! \times 18!} = 10 \times 19 = 190$$

Probability (both the numbers are prime)

$$= \frac{28}{190} = \frac{14}{95} \quad \textbf{Ans.}$$

Problem 14 Three coins are tossed once. Find the probability of getting exactly 2 heads.

Solution There are three mutually exhaustive and cxclusive cases. Let the coins be A, B and C.

Probability of getting head in a single throw $P = \frac{1}{2}$ probabitity of not getting head in a single throw $q = 1-p = 1-\frac{1}{2}=\frac{1}{2}$

First Case The Coins A and B show a head and coin C shows a tail

The probability of this

$$= \frac{1}{2} \times \frac{1}{2} \times \frac{1}{2} = \frac{1}{8}$$

Second Case The coins B and C show a head and the coin A shows a tail. The probability of this is

$$= \frac{1}{2} \times \frac{1}{2} \times \frac{1}{2} = \frac{1}{8}$$

Third Case The coins A and C shows a head and the coin B shows a tail.

The probability of this $= \frac{1}{2} \times \frac{1}{2} \times \frac{1}{2} = \frac{1}{8}$

∴ Total probability of getting 2 heads and one tail

$$= \frac{1}{8} + \frac{1}{8} + \frac{1}{8} = \frac{3}{8}$$ **Ans.**

Problem 15 In a single throw of two dice, determine the probability of obtaining total of 7 or 9.

Solution Here the number of exhaustive cases when two dice are thrown simultaneously are $6^2 = 36$

The number of favourable cases for obtaining a total of 7 are (1, 6), (2, 5) (3, 4) (4, 3) (5, 2) (6, 1) thus there are 6 favourable cases

The no. of favourable cases for obtaining a total of 9 are (6, 3), (5, 4), (4, 5), (3, 6). Thus there are 4 favourable cases.

∴ Probability $= \frac{4}{36}$

Thus probability of obtaining a total of 7 or 9

$$= \frac{6}{36} + \frac{4}{36} = \frac{1}{6} + \frac{1}{9}$$

$$= \frac{9+6}{54} = \frac{15}{54} = \frac{5}{18}$$ **Ans.**

Problem 16 Two dice are thrown. Find the probability of getting an odd number on the one and a multiple of three on the other.

Solution The possible outcomes of the simultaneous throwing of two dice are 36 odd number in a dice are 1, 3, 5

and the multiple of are 3 are 3, 6

The outcomes which have an odd number on the one and a multiple of 3 on the other are

$$(1, 3), (1, 6), (3, 3), (3, 6), (5, 3), (5, 6)$$

$$(3, 1), (6, 1), (3, 3), (6, 3), (3, 5), (6, 5) = 12$$

But (3, 3) is common so

No of favourable Cases $= 12 - 1 = 11$

Probability of (an odd number on the one and multiple of three (3) on the other) are $= \frac{11}{36}$ **Ans.**

Problem 17 A and B throw a coin alternately till one of them gets a 'head' and wins the game. Find their respective probabilities of winning.

Solution Let $P(A)$, $P(\bar{A})$ be probabilities of A's getting the head and not getting the head respectively, then

$$P(A) = \frac{1}{2}$$

$$P(\bar{A}) = 1 - P(A) = 1 - \frac{1}{2} = \frac{1}{2}$$

Similarly $P(B)$, $P(\bar{B})$ be the probabilities of B's getting the head and not getting the head respectively, then

$$P(B) = \frac{1}{2}$$

$$P(\bar{B}) = 1 - \frac{1}{2} = \frac{1}{2}$$

Let A starts the games. He can win it in the first throw, 3rd throw, 5th throw, 7th throw and so on

Probability of A's winning in first throw

$$P(A) = \frac{1}{2}$$

Probabilities of A's winning in the third throw

$$= P(\bar{A}) \cdot P(\bar{B})\, P(A) = \frac{1}{2} \cdot \frac{1}{2} \cdot \frac{1}{2} = \left(\frac{1}{2}\right)^3$$

Probabilities of A's winning in the 5th through

$$= P(\bar{A}), P(\bar{B}) P(A) P(\bar{B}) P(A)$$

$$= \frac{1}{2} \cdot \frac{1}{2} \cdot \frac{1}{2} \cdot \frac{1}{2} \frac{1}{2} = \left(\frac{1}{2}\right)^5$$

Probabilities of A's winning in the 7th throw

$$= P(\bar{A}) P(\bar{B}) P(\bar{A}) P(\bar{B}) P(\bar{A}) P(\bar{B}) P(A)$$

$$= \frac{1}{2} \cdot \frac{1}{2} \cdot \frac{1}{2} \cdot \frac{1}{2} \cdot \frac{1}{2} \cdot \frac{1}{2} \cdot \frac{1}{2} = \left(\frac{1}{2}\right)^7$$

Since all these cases are mutually exclusive and therefore, the chance of A's winining the game is the sum of the probabilities of these cases

Probability of A's winning the game first is

$$= \frac{1}{2} + \left(\frac{1}{2}\right)^3 + \left(\frac{1}{2}\right)^5 + \left(\frac{1}{2}\right)^7 + \ldots$$

$$= \frac{1}{2}\left[1 + \left(\frac{1}{2}\right)^2 + \left(\frac{1}{2}\right)^4 + \ldots\right.$$

$$= \frac{1}{2}\left[\frac{1}{1-(\frac{1}{2})^2}\right] = \frac{1}{[1-\frac{1}{4}]} = \frac{1}{2} \cdot \frac{1}{\frac{3}{4}}$$

$$= \frac{1}{2} \cdot \frac{4}{3} = \frac{2}{3}$$

Since A and B are mutually exclusive and either of them must happen, so the sum of their probabilities is equal to 1

$\therefore$ The probability of B's winning the game first

$$= 1 - \frac{2}{3} = \frac{3-2}{3} = \frac{1}{3} \qquad \textbf{Ans.}$$

Problem 18 An anticraft gun can take a minimum of four shots at an enemy plane moving away from it. The probability of having the plane at the first, second, third and fourth short are 0.4, 0.3, 0.2 and 0.1 respectively. What is the probabllity that the gun hits the plane.

Solution Let S_1, S_2, S_3, S_4 be the events of hitting the plane by 1st, 2nd, 3rd and 4th shot respectively, then

$$P(S_1) = 0.4 \qquad P(S_2) = 0.3 \qquad P(S_3) = 0.2 \qquad P(S_4) = 0.1$$

Also $P(\bar{S}_1) = 0.6$ $\quad P(\bar{S}_2) = 0.7$, $\quad P(\bar{S}_3) = 0.8$ $\quad P(\bar{S}_4) = 0.9$

Probability that no shot hit the plane is

$$P(\bar{S}_1 \bar{S}_2 \bar{S}_3 \bar{S}_4) = P(\bar{S}_1) P(\bar{S}_2) P(\bar{S}_3) P(\bar{S}_4)$$

$$= 0.6 \times 0.7 \times 0.8 \times 0.9 = 0.3024$$

Probability that at least one shot hit the plane

$$= 1 - P(\bar{S}_1 \bar{S}_2 \bar{S}_3 \bar{S}_4) = 1 - 0.3024 = 0.6976$$

Problem 19 A speaks truth in 75% and B in 80% of the cases. In what percentage of cases are they likely to contradict narrating the same incident?

Solution Let $P(A)$, $P(B)$ be the probability of A and B speaking the truths then

$$P(A) = \frac{75}{100} = \frac{3}{4} \quad P(B) = \frac{80}{100} = \frac{4}{5}$$

$$P(\bar{A}) = (A \text{ tells lie}) = 1 - P(A)$$

$$= 1 - \frac{3}{4} = \frac{4-3}{4} = \frac{1}{4}$$

$$P(\bar{B}) = P(B \text{ tells lie})$$

$$= 1 - \frac{4}{5} = \frac{5-4}{5} = \frac{1}{5}$$

Now P (A and B will contradict)

$$= P(A)\,P(\bar{B}) + P(B)\,P(\bar{A})$$

$$= \frac{3}{4} \cdot \frac{1}{5} + \frac{1}{4} \cdot \frac{4}{5} = \frac{3}{20} + \frac{4}{20} = \frac{7}{20} = 35\%$$

Problem 20 An urn contains 25 balls numbered 1 through 25. Two balls are drawn from the urn with replacement. Find the probability of getting

(a) both odd numbers

(b) one odd and one even number

(c) at least one odd number

(d) no odd number

Solution Total number of cases = 25 let E and D denotes the event of drawing 'even' and 'odd' numbered ball. There are 13 balls numbered odd and 12 ball numbered even.

Then
$$P(E) = \frac{12}{25}$$

$$P(D) = \frac{13}{25}$$

(a) Since the balls are replaced back in the urn, let $P(D, D)$ be the probability of getting both odd numbered balls then

$$P(DD) = P(D).P(D)$$

$$= \frac{13}{25} \cdot \frac{13}{25} = \frac{169}{625}$$

(b) The total number of such cases consists of first odd and second even) + (first even second odd)

$\therefore$ P (one odd and one even)

$$= P(ED) = P(E)\,P(D) + P(D)\,P(E)$$

$$= \frac{12}{25} \cdot \frac{13}{25} + \frac{13}{25} \cdot \frac{12}{25}$$

$$= \frac{156}{625} + \frac{156}{625} = \frac{312}{525}$$

(c) **At least one odd**

Probability of getting both the balls even numbered

$$= P(EE) = P(E)\,.\,P(E)$$

$$= \frac{12}{25} \times \frac{12}{25} = \frac{144}{625}$$

$$P \text{ (at least one odd)} = 1 - \frac{144}{625} = \frac{625-144}{625} = \frac{481}{625}$$

(d) **No odd number**

$$P \text{ (no odd number)} = 1 - P \text{ (at least one odd)}$$

$$= 1 - \frac{481}{625} = \frac{625-481}{625} = \frac{144}{625}$$

or P (no odd number)

$$= P \text{ (both even number) } P = (EE)$$

$$P(E)\,P(E) = \frac{12}{25} \times \frac{12}{25} = \frac{144}{625} \quad \textbf{Ans.}$$

Problem 21 There are two bags one bag contains 4 white and 2 black balls. Second bag contains 5 white and 4 black balls. Two balls are transferred from first bag to second bag. Then one ball is taken from the second bag. Find the probability that it is white.

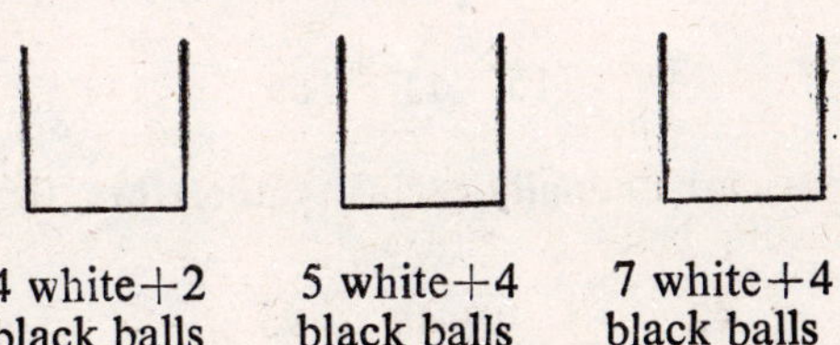

There are mutually exclusive and exhaustive ways in which 2 balls can be transferred from first bag to second bag.

First way Two white balls have been transferred from first bag to second bag so that the probability for that is

$$\frac{\text{Favourable no. of cases}}{\text{Exhaustive no. of cases}} = \frac{{}^4c_2}{{}^6c_2}$$

We have 7 white and 4 black balls and probability of getting a white ball is 7/11

$$\therefore \text{ Required probability} = \frac{{}^4c_2}{{}^6c_2} \times \frac{7}{11} = \frac{4!}{2!\,2!} \times \frac{2!\,4!}{6!} \times \frac{7}{11}$$

$$= \frac{4 \times 3 \times 2!}{2 \times 2!} \times \frac{2!\,4!}{6 \times 5 \times 4!} \times \frac{7}{11} = \frac{42}{165}$$

Second way Two black balls have been transferred from first bag to the second bag so that probability for that is

$$\frac{{}^2c_2}{{}^6c_2} = \frac{1}{\dfrac{6!}{2!\,4!}} = \frac{2!\,4!}{6} = \frac{2!\,4!}{6 \times 5 \times 4!} = \frac{1}{15}$$

Now we have 5 white and 6 black balls and the probability of getting a white ball from the second bag is $\frac{5}{11}$

$$\text{Required probability} = \frac{1}{15} \times \frac{5}{11} = \frac{5}{165}$$

Third way One black and one white ball has been transferred from first bag to the sccond so that the probability for this is

$$\frac{{}^4c_1 \times {}^2c_1}{{}^6c_2} = \frac{8}{15}$$

In the second bag there are 6 white and 5 black balls.

Then the probability of drawing a white ball is $\frac{6}{11}$

$$\text{Required probability} \quad = \frac{8}{15} \times \frac{6}{11} = \frac{48}{165}$$

Since these three cases are mutually exclusive, therefore, the required probability of drawing a white ball

$$= \frac{42}{165} + \frac{5}{165} + \frac{48}{165} = \frac{95}{165}$$

Random Variable and Mathematical Expectation

Random Variable

A random variable x is a real valued function defined on a sample space S of an experiment. In other words to each of the out comes of the experiment E_i (sample point) of S, there corresponds a unique real number x_i, known as the value of the random variable x. The example of random variable are

(i) The number of sixes in a toss of two dice (ii) The number of two tails in a toss of three coins (iii) The number of queens in a draw of two cards from a well shuffled deck.

The random variable is also called a stochastic variable or simply a variable. It is written as $x(E_i) = x_i$, which implies that the random variable x takes the value x_i corresponding to the outcome E_i.

Discrete random variable

A random variable is said to be descrete if it takes only a finite or an infinite but countable number of values.

Continuous random variable

A random variable is said to be continuous if it takes a continuum of values i.e. if takes any value in an interval.

Mathematical expectation

Let x be a discrete random variable which takes $x_1, x_2, x_3, \ldots, x_n$ mutually exclusive values with respective probabilites $p_1, p_2, p_3 \ldots p_n$ then the expectation of x is

$$E(x) = p_1 x_1 + p_2 x_2 + \ldots + p_n x_n$$

$$= \sum_{i=1}^{n} p_i x_i \qquad \text{where} \qquad \sum p_i = 1$$

Mean $E(x)$ is also called the mean or expected value of the discrete random variable x provided the series

$$\sum p_i x_i \text{ is convergent}$$

Variance The quantity $E(x-\bar{x})^2$ is called the variance and it is

$$E(x_i - \bar{x})^2 = \sum_{i=1}^{n} p_i (x_i - \bar{x})^2$$

$$= \sum_{i=1}^{n} p_i [x^2 - 2x_i \bar{x} + \bar{x}^2]$$

$$= \sum_{i=1}^{n} p_i x_i^2 - 2\bar{x} \sum_{i=1}^{n} p_i x_i + \sum_{i=1}^{n} p_i \bar{x}^2$$

$$= \sum_{i=1}^{n} p_i x_i^2 - 2\bar{x}\,\bar{x} + \bar{x}^2 \sum_{i=1}^{n} p_i$$

$$= \sum_{i=1}^{n} p_i x_i^2 - 2\bar{x}^2 + \bar{x}^2 \sum_{i=1}^{n} p_i = 1 \quad \text{(since)}$$

$$= \sum_{i=1}^{n} p_i x_i^2 - \bar{x}^2$$

$$= E(x_i^2) - [E(x)]^2 = E(x^2) - [E(\bar{x})]^2$$

$$= \sum_{i=1}^{n} p_i x_i^2 - \mu^2 \qquad \mu = E(x) = \bar{x}$$

[where $\bar{x} = E(x) =$ mean (or expected value of the random variable x]

Theorem on Mathematical expectations

Theorem 1 The expectation of a sum of two random variable is equal to the sum of their expectations i.e.

$$E(x + y) = E(x) + E(y)$$

where x and y are two discrete random variables

Theorem 2 The expectation of the product of two independent random variables is equal to the product of their expectations i.e.

$$E(x\,y) = E(x) \cdot E(y)$$

where x and y are two discrete random variables.

Problem 1 What is the expectation of the sum of points on a dice?

Solution Here the random variable x is the number of points on the dice which takes up the values 1, 2, 3, 4, 5, 6. These are equi probable events with probability each equal to 1/6 i.e. here $x_1, x_2, x_3, x_4 \ldots x_6$ are values of the random variable x with probability

$$\frac{1}{6}, \frac{1}{6}, \frac{1}{6}, \frac{1}{6}, \frac{1}{6}, \frac{1}{6}$$

Now $$E(x) = p_1 x_1 + p_2 x_2 + p_3 x_3 + p_4 x_4 + p_5 x_5 + p_6 x_6$$

$$= \frac{1}{6} \cdot 1 + \frac{1}{6} \cdot 2 + \frac{1}{6} \cdot 3 + \frac{1}{6} \cdot 4 + \frac{1}{6} \cdot 5 + \frac{1}{6} \cdot 6$$

$$= \frac{1}{6}(1 + 2 + 3 + 4 + 5 + 6)$$

$$= \frac{1}{6} \times 21 = \frac{21}{6} = \frac{7}{2}$$

$$E(x) = \frac{7}{2} \qquad \textbf{Ans.}$$

Problem 2 A and B throws with a dice for a prize of Rs. 11 which is to be won by a player who first throws 6. If A has the first throw, what are the respective expectations.

Solution Let $P(A)$ be the probability that A will win the prize then

$$E(A) = P(A) \times 11$$

Similarly $E(B) = P(B) \times 11$, where $P(B)$ is the probability that B will win the prize.

Now let us find the probability of winning the prize by A i.e. $P(A)$.

A can win the prize at 1st, 3rd, 5th, . . . trials probability of A's winning in the first throw

$$P(A) = \frac{1}{6}$$

Probabilities of A's winning in the third throw

$$= P(\bar{A})\, P(\bar{B})\, P(A)$$

$$= \frac{5}{6} \cdot \frac{5}{6} \cdot \frac{1}{6}$$

$$= \left(\frac{5}{6}\right)^2 \cdot \frac{1}{6}$$

Probabilities of A's winning in the 5th throw

$$= P(\bar{A})\, P(\bar{B})\, P(\bar{A})\, P(\bar{B})\, P(A)$$

$$P(\bar{A}) = 1 - P(A) = 1 - \frac{1}{6}$$

$$P(\bar{B}) = \frac{5}{6} = 1 - \frac{1}{6} = \frac{5}{6}$$

$$P(A) = \frac{1}{6}$$

$$= \frac{5}{6} \cdot \frac{5}{6} \cdot \frac{5}{6} \cdot \frac{5}{6} \cdot \frac{1}{6} = \left(\frac{5}{6}\right)^4 \cdot \frac{1}{6}$$

So the probability of A's winning infinite throw

$$= \frac{1}{6} + \left(\frac{5}{6}\right)^2 \cdot \frac{1}{6} + \left(\frac{5}{6}\right)^4 \cdot \frac{1}{6} + \ldots$$

$$= \frac{1}{6}\left[1 + \left(\frac{5}{6}\right)^2 + \left(\frac{5}{6}\right)^4 + \ldots\right]$$

$$= \frac{1}{6} \cdot \frac{1}{1 - \left(\frac{5}{6}\right)^2} = \frac{1}{6} \cdot \frac{1}{1 - \frac{25}{36}} = \frac{1}{6} \cdot \frac{36}{36 - 25} = \frac{1}{6} \cdot \frac{36}{11} = \frac{6}{11}$$

But $\quad P(A) + P(B) = 1$

$$\Rightarrow \quad P(B) = 1 - \frac{6}{11} = \frac{11 - 6}{11} - \frac{5}{11}$$

A's expectation $\quad = E(A) = P(A) = P(A) \times 11$

$$= \frac{6}{11} \times 11 = \text{Rs. } 6$$

B's expectation $\quad = E(B) = P(B) \times 11$

$$= \frac{5}{11} \times 11 = \text{Rs. } 5$$

34

Probability Distribution

The random variable X taking the values $x_1, x_2, x_3 \ldots x_n$ with probabilities $p_1, p_2, p_3 \ldots p_n$ respectively such that (i) every probability is a non-negative number not greater than 1

i.e. $p_i > 0, i = 1, 2, 3 \ldots n, 0 \leqslant p_i \leqslant 1$

(ii) The sum of all the probabilities is always unity

i.e. $p_1 + p_2 + \ldots + p_n = 1$

is said to possess the probability distribution. It is represented in a tabular form as given below:

X	x_1	x_2	x_3	...	x_r	...	x_n
$P(X)$	p_1	p_2	p_3	...	p_r	...	p_n

Also random variable X will have

$$\text{mean} = \sum_{i=1}^{n} p_i x_i$$

$$\text{variance} = \sigma^2 = \sum_{i=1}^{n} p_i x_i^2 - \mu^2$$

where μ is not a nice number.

Problem 1 Find the probability distribution of the *number of heads*, in two tosses of a coin.

Solution When we toss a coin twice we get the four outcomes viz

(*HH*, *HT*, *TH*, *TT* (*T* for tail, *H* for Haid)

In the above case we notice that the no of heads can be zero one, or two

$$\therefore \quad P\,(\text{zero head}) = \frac{1}{4}$$

$$P\,(\text{one head}) = \frac{2}{4} \qquad P\,(\text{two heads}) = \frac{1}{4}$$

Thus X takes the values 0, 1, 2 (zero head). one head two heads) with probabilities $\frac{1}{4}$, $\frac{2}{4}$, $\frac{1}{4}$ respectively. Thus [we have the probability distributions.

X	0	1	2
$P(X)$	$\frac{1}{4}$	$\frac{2}{4}=\frac{1}{2}$	$\frac{1}{4}$

Problem 2 Two cards are drawn successively with replacement from a well shuffled deck of 52 cards. Find the probability distribution of the number of kings.

Solution Let X denote the number of kings. Here X can take the values 0, 1 or 2.

Now $\quad P\,(\text{king}) = \frac{4}{52} = \frac{1}{13}$

$$P\,(\text{not king}) = 1 - \frac{4}{52} = \frac{52-4}{52} = \frac{48}{52} = \frac{12}{13}$$

$$P\,(X=0) = P\,(\text{not king not king})$$

$$= P\,(\text{not king}) \cdot P\,(\text{not king})$$

$$= \frac{12}{13} \cdot \frac{12}{13} = \frac{144}{169}$$

$$P\,(X=1) = P\,(\text{king and not king}) + P\,(\text{not king and king})$$

$$P\,(X=1) = P\,(\text{king}) \cdot P\,(\text{not king}) + P\,(\text{not king}) \cdot P\,(\text{king})$$

$$P\,(X=1) = \frac{1}{13} \times \frac{12}{13} + \frac{12}{13} \times \frac{1}{13} = \frac{12}{169} + \frac{12}{169} = \frac{24}{169}$$

$$P\,(X=2) = P\,(\text{king and king}) = P\,(\text{king}) \cdot P\,(\text{king})$$

$$= \frac{1}{13} \cdot \frac{1}{13} = \frac{1}{169}$$

$\therefore$ we have the following probability distribution

X	0	1	2
$P(X)$	$\frac{144}{169}$	$\frac{24}{169}$	$\frac{1}{169}$

Problem 3 Find the probability distribution of the number of sixes in three losses of a dice and sketch its graph.

Solution Let X be the number of sixes, then X takes the values 0, 1 or 2.

Now
$$P\,(a \text{ six}) = \frac{1}{6}$$

$$P\,(\text{not six}) = 1 - \frac{1}{6} = \frac{5}{6}$$

$$P\,(X = 0) = \frac{5}{6} \times \frac{5}{6} \times \frac{5}{6} = \frac{125}{216}$$

$$P\,(X = 1) = P\,(\text{six not a six not a six})$$
$$+ P\,(\text{not a six not a six a six})$$
$$+ P\,(\text{not a six} \cdot \text{six not a six})$$
$$= \frac{1}{6}\,\frac{5}{6} \cdot \frac{5}{6} + \frac{5}{6} \cdot \frac{5}{6} \cdot \frac{1}{6} + \frac{5}{6} \cdot \frac{1}{6} \cdot \frac{5}{6}$$
$$= 3\left(\frac{1}{6} \times \frac{5}{6} \times \frac{5}{6}\right) = \frac{25 \times 3}{216} = \frac{75}{216}$$

$$P\,(X = 2) = P\,(\text{six six not a six})$$
$$+ P\,(\text{not a six six and six})$$
$$+ P\,(\text{six not a six six})$$
$$= \frac{1}{6} \cdot \frac{1}{6} \cdot \frac{5}{6} + \frac{5}{6} \cdot \frac{1}{6} \cdot \frac{1}{6} + \frac{1}{6} \times \frac{5}{6} \cdot \frac{1}{6}$$
$$= 3 \times \frac{5}{216} = \frac{15}{216}$$

$$P\,(X = 3) = P\,(\text{six, six, six})$$
$$= \frac{1}{6} \cdot \frac{1}{6} \cdot \frac{1}{6} = \frac{1}{216}$$

We have the required probability distribution as

X	0	1	2	3
$P\,(X)$	$\frac{125}{216}$	$\frac{75}{216}$	$\frac{15}{216}$	$\frac{1}{216}$

and its graph is given by Fig.

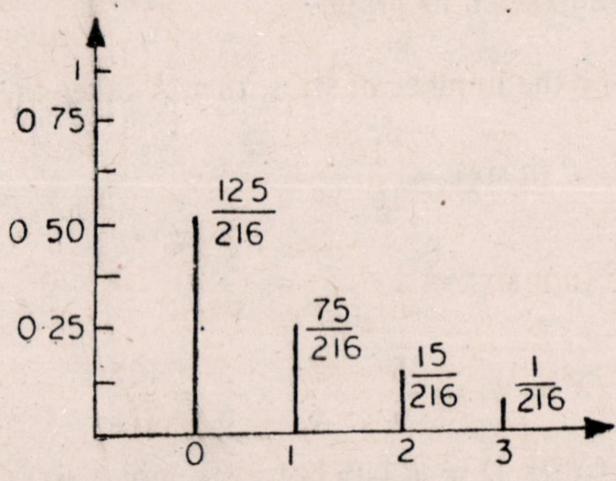

Problem 4 An urn contains 4 white and 3 red balls. Find the probability distribution of the number of red balls in three draws, with replacement, from the urn. Also find its mean and variance.

Solution Let X be the number of red balls in three draws, then X takes the values 0, 1 or 2.

So
$$P\text{ (red ball)} = \frac{3}{7}$$

$$P\text{ (not red ball)} = 1 - \frac{3}{7} = \frac{7-3}{7} = \frac{4}{7}$$

Here
$$P(X = 0) = P\text{ (not any red not red, not red)}$$
$$= P\text{ (not red) } P\text{ (not red) } P\text{ (not red)}$$
$$= \frac{4}{7} \cdot \frac{4}{7} \cdot \frac{4}{7} = \frac{64}{343}$$

$$P(X = 1) = P\text{ (red, not red, not)} + P\text{ (not red, red, not red)} + P\text{ (not red, not red, red)}$$

$$= \frac{3}{7} \cdot \frac{4}{7} \cdot \frac{4}{7} + \frac{4}{7} \cdot \frac{3}{7} \cdot \frac{4}{7} + \frac{4}{7} \cdot \frac{4}{7} \cdot \frac{3}{7}$$

$$= 3\,\frac{3 \cdot 4 \cdot 4}{7 \cdot 7 \cdot 7} = \frac{144}{343}$$

$$P(X = 2) = P\text{ (red red not red)} + P\text{ (red not red, red)} + P\text{ (not red, red, red)}$$

$$= \frac{3}{7} \cdot \frac{3}{7} \cdot \frac{4}{7} + \frac{3}{7} \cdot \frac{4}{7} \cdot \frac{3}{7} + \frac{4}{7} \cdot \frac{3}{7} \cdot \frac{3}{7}$$

$$= \frac{3 \cdot 4 \cdot 3 \cdot 3}{343} = \frac{108}{343}$$

$$P(X=3) = P(\text{red red . red})$$
$$= P(\text{red})\, P(\text{red})\, P(\text{red})$$
$$= \frac{3}{7} \cdot \frac{3}{7} \cdot \frac{3}{7} = \frac{27}{343}$$

∴ The required probability distribution is

X	0	1	2	3
$P(X)$	$\frac{64}{343}$	$\frac{144}{343}$	$\frac{108}{343}$	$\frac{27}{343}$

Now mean $\mu = \sum p_i x_i$

$$= 0 \cdot \frac{64}{343} + 1 \cdot \frac{144}{343} + 2 \cdot \frac{108}{343} + 3 \cdot \frac{27}{343}$$

$$= \frac{1}{343}(145 + 216 + 81) = \frac{441}{343} = \frac{9}{7}$$

Also variation $\sigma^2 = \sum p_i x_i^2 - (\mu)^2$

$$\sigma^2 = 0 \cdot \frac{64}{343} + \frac{144}{343} \cdot 1^2 + \frac{108}{343} \cdot 4 + \frac{27}{343} \cdot 9 - \left(\frac{9}{7}\right)^2$$

$$\sigma^2 = \frac{1}{343}(144 + 432 + 243) - \frac{81}{49}$$

$$\sigma^2 = \frac{819}{343} - \frac{81}{49}$$

$$\sigma^2 = \frac{819 - 81 \times 7}{343} = \frac{819 - 567}{343}$$

$$\sigma^2 = \frac{252}{343} = \frac{36}{49} \qquad \text{Mean} = \frac{9}{7}$$

$$\text{Variance} = \frac{36}{49}$$ **Ans.**

Problem 5 Two cards are drawn with replacement from a will shuffled deck of 52 cards. Find μ and σ for the no. of aces.

Solution Let X denotes the number of aces. There are 4 aces in a pack of cords

Probability of getting an ace $= \frac{4}{52} = \frac{1}{13}$

Probability of not getting an ace $= 1 - \frac{1}{13} = \frac{13-1}{13} = \frac{12}{13}$

The X attains values 0, 1, 2,

$$P(X = 0) = P(\text{not an ace. not an acc})$$

$$= P(\text{not an ace})\ P(\text{not an ace})$$

$$= \frac{12}{13} \cdot \frac{12}{13} = \frac{144}{169}$$

$$P(X = 1) = P(\text{an ace} \cdot \text{not an ace}) + P(\text{not an ace} \cdot \text{an ace})$$

$$= \frac{1}{13} \cdot \frac{12}{13} + \frac{12}{13} \cdot \frac{1}{13}$$

$$= \frac{12}{169} + \frac{12}{169} = \frac{24}{169}$$

$$P(X = 2) = P(\text{an ace}) \cdot \text{an ace}) = P(\text{an ace})\ P(\text{an ace})$$

$$= \frac{1}{13} \cdot \frac{1}{13} = \frac{1}{169}$$

We have the following distribution

X	0	1	2
$P(X)$	$\frac{144}{169}$	$\frac{24}{169}$	$\frac{1}{169}$

Now mean $= \mu = \sum p_i\, x_i$

$$= 0 \,.\, \frac{144}{169} + 1 \,.\, \frac{24}{169} + 2 \,.\, \frac{1}{169}$$

$$= \frac{1}{169}(24 + 2) = \frac{26}{169} = \frac{2}{13}$$

$$\sigma^2 = \sum p_i\, x_i^2 - (\mu)^2$$

$$\sigma^2 = \left(\frac{144}{169} \,.\, 0 + \frac{24}{169} \cdot 1^2 + \frac{1}{169} \,.\, 2^2\right) - \frac{4}{169}$$

$$\sigma^2 = \left(\frac{24}{169} + \frac{4}{169}\right) - \frac{4}{169}$$

$$\sigma^2 = \frac{28}{169} - \frac{4}{169} = \frac{24}{169}$$

$$\sigma = \sqrt{\frac{24}{169}} = \frac{4.9}{13} = 0.377 \qquad \textbf{Ans.}$$

Problem 6 A die is tossed twiee Getting a number greater than 4 is considered a success. Find the variance of the probability distribution of the no. f success.

Solution Let X be the number of success, then X takes the values 0, 1 or 2 The number greater than 4 is 5 or 6.

Let S denote the success in getting 5 or 6

$$P(S) = P(5 \text{ or } 6) = \frac{2}{6} = \frac{1}{3}$$

$$P(\bar{S}) = 1 - \frac{1}{3} = \frac{3-1}{3} = \frac{2}{3}$$

$$P(X=0) = P(\bar{S}\bar{S}) = P(\bar{S}) \,.\, P(\bar{S})$$

$$= \frac{2}{3} \times \frac{2}{3} = \frac{4}{9}$$

$$P(X=1) = P(S\bar{S}) + P(\bar{S}S)$$

$$= \frac{1}{3} \times \frac{2}{3} + \frac{2}{3} \times \frac{1}{3} = \frac{2}{9} + \frac{2}{9} = \frac{4}{9}$$

$$P(X=2) = P(SS) = P(S) \,.\, P(S) = \frac{1}{3} \times \frac{1}{3} = \frac{1}{9}$$

Thus X takes the values 0, 1, 2 with probobilities $\frac{4}{9}, \frac{4}{9}$ and $\frac{1}{9}$ respectively

Here mean $= \mu = \sum p_i x_i$

$$= \frac{4}{9} \,.\, 0 + \frac{4}{9} \,.\, 1 + \frac{1}{9} \,.\, 2 = \frac{1}{9}(4+2) = \frac{6}{9} = \frac{2}{3}$$

Also $\sum p_i x_i^2 = \frac{4}{9} \,.\, 0 + \frac{4}{9} \,.\, 1^2 + \frac{1}{9} \,.\, 2^2 = \frac{4}{9} \,.\, 1 + \frac{1}{9} \,.\, 4 = \frac{8}{9}$

Variance $\sigma^2 = \sum p_i x_i - (\mu)^2$

$$\sigma^2 = \frac{8}{9} - \left(\frac{2}{3}\right)^2$$

$$\sigma^2 = \frac{8}{9} - \frac{4}{9} = \frac{4}{9} \quad \Rightarrow \quad \sigma = \frac{2}{3}$$ **Ans.**

Problem 7 Two bad Oranges are accedently mixed with ten good ones. Three oranges are drawn at random, without replacement from this lot. Find the mean and variance for the number of bad oranges.

Solution Let X be the random variable associated with the drawing the bad oranges without replacement then, obviously, X can take the values 0, 1, 2 (i.e. no bad orange, one bad orange, two bad oranges)

Now $P(X = 0) = \dfrac{^{10}C_3}{^{12}C_3} = \dfrac{10 \cdot 9 \cdot 8 \cdot 7\,!}{3\,! \cdot 7\,!} \times \dfrac{3! \times 9}{12 \times 11 \times 10 \times 9\,!}$

$$= \frac{10 \times 9 \times 8}{12 \times 11 \times 10} = \frac{6}{11}$$

$P(X = 1) = P$ (2 good orange · 1 bad orange)

$$= \frac{^{10}C_2 \cdot {}^{2}C_1}{^{12}C_3} = \frac{9}{22}$$

$P(X = 2) = P$ (2 bad orange one good orange)

$$= \frac{^{2}C_2 \times {}^{10}C_1}{^{12}C_3} = \frac{1}{22}$$

Thus X takes the values 0, 1, 2 with probability $\frac{6}{11}, \frac{9}{22}, \frac{1}{22}$ respectively

Now we have

$$\text{Mean } \mu = \sum p_i x_i = \frac{6}{11} \cdot 0 + \frac{9}{22} \cdot 1 + \frac{1}{22} \cdot 2$$

$$= \frac{1}{22}(9 + 2) = \frac{11}{22} = \frac{1}{2}$$

Variance $\sigma^2 = \sum p_i x_i^2 - (\mu)^2$

$$\sigma^2 = \frac{6}{11} \cdot 0^2 + \frac{9}{22} \cdot 1^2 + \frac{1}{22} \cdot 2^2 - \left(\frac{1}{2}\right)^2$$

$$= 0 + \frac{9}{22} + \frac{4}{22} - \frac{1}{4} = \frac{13}{22} - \frac{1}{4}$$

$$= \frac{26 - 11}{44} = \frac{15}{44} \qquad \text{Variance } \sigma^2 = \frac{15}{44} \qquad \textbf{Ans.}$$

Problem 8 A die is tossed twice A success is getting an odd number on toss. Find the variance of the probability distribution of the number success.

Solution Let X be the random variable associated with the getting an od number. Let $P(S)$ be the probability of getting a success is getting an od number (1 or 3 or 5) in a toss of a die let $P(\bar{S})$ be the probability of n success

$$P(S) = \frac{3}{6} = \frac{1}{2}$$

$$P(\bar{S}) = 1 - \tfrac{1}{2}$$

$$P(X=0) = P\,(\text{not success not success})$$
$$= P\,(\text{not success})\; P\,(\text{not success}) = \tfrac{1}{2}\cdot\tfrac{1}{2} = \tfrac{1}{4}$$
$$P(X=1) = P\,(S\,\bar{S}) + P(\bar{S}S)$$
$$= P(S)\cdot P(\bar{S}) + P(\bar{S})\cdot P(S)$$
$$= \tfrac{1}{2}\cdot\tfrac{1}{2} + \tfrac{1}{2}\cdot\tfrac{1}{2} = \tfrac{1}{4}+\tfrac{1}{4} = \tfrac{2}{3} = \tfrac{1}{2}$$
$$P(X=2) = P(\text{success}\cdot\text{success})$$
$$= P\,(SS) = P(S)\cdot P(S)$$
$$= \tfrac{1}{2}\cdot\tfrac{1}{2} = \tfrac{1}{4}$$

Thus X takes the valuts 0, 1, 2 with respective probabilities $\frac{1}{3}$, $\frac{1}{2}$, $\frac{1}{3}$

We have the table

X	0	1	2
$P(X)$	$\frac{1}{4}$	$\frac{1}{2}$	$\frac{1}{2}$

$$\text{Mean } \mu = \sum p_i x_i = 0\cdot\frac{1}{4} + 1\cdot\frac{1}{2} + 2\cdot\frac{1}{4}$$
$$= \frac{1}{2} + \frac{1}{2} = 1$$

Variance $\quad \sigma^2 = \sum p_i x_i^2 - (\mu)^2$

$$\sigma^2 = \frac{1}{4}\cdot 0^2 + \frac{1}{2}\cdot 1^2 + \frac{1}{4}\cdot 2^2 - 1^2$$
$$\sigma^2 = \frac{1}{2}\cdot 1 + \frac{4}{4} - (1)^2$$
$$\sigma^2 = \frac{1}{2} + 1 - 1 \qquad \sigma^2 = \frac{1}{2} = 0.5$$

Mean = 1 $\qquad$ Variance $\sigma^2 = 0.5$

Problem 9 Calculate the variance of a number obtained as a result of throwing an un biased die.

Solution Here the random variable X takes the values 1, 2, 3, 4, 5, 6, with probabilities $\frac{1}{6}$, $\frac{1}{6}$, $\frac{1}{6}$, $\frac{1}{6}$, $\frac{1}{6}$ respectively

$$\text{Mean} = \mu = \sum_{i=1}^{6} p_i x_i$$

$$= \frac{1}{6}.1 + \frac{1}{6}.2 + \frac{1}{6}.3 + \frac{1}{6}.4 + \frac{1}{6}.5 + \frac{1}{6}.6$$

$$= \frac{1}{6}(1+2+3+4+5+6) = \frac{21}{6} = \frac{7}{2}$$

$$\text{Variance } \sigma^2 = \sum p_i x_i^2 - (\mu)^2$$

$$= \frac{1}{6}.1^2 + \frac{1}{6}.2^2 + \frac{1}{6}.3^2 + \frac{1}{6}.4^2 + \frac{1}{6}.5^2 + \frac{1}{6}.6^2 - \left(\frac{7}{2}\right)^2$$

$$= \frac{1}{6}(1+4+9+16+25+36) - \frac{49}{4}$$

$$= \frac{91}{6} - \frac{49}{4} = \frac{182-147}{12} = \frac{35}{12} = 2.92 \quad \textbf{Ans.}$$

Theoritical Distribution

Binomial Distribution. Binomial distribution is a probability distribution which is obtained when the probability p of happening of an event is same in all the trials. For example, the probability p of getting a head when a coin is tossed a number of times, must remain same in each toss i.e. $\frac{1}{2}$.

Let an experiment consisting af n trials be performed and let the occurance of an even in any trial be called a success and its non occurance a failure Let p is the probability of success and q be the probability of the failure in a single trial, where $q = 1-p$, so that $p + q = 1$.

Let us assume that the trials are independent and the probability of success is same in each trial. Let us claim that we have n trials. than the probability of happening of the event r times and failing $n-r$ times in any specified order is $p^r q^{n-r}$ (By the theorem multiplication of probability).

But the total number of ways in which the event can happen r times exactly in n trials is ${}^nc_r$ ways are equally likely, mutually exclusive and exhaustive.

Therefore the probability of r success and $n-r$ failures in n trials in any order, what soever is ${}^nc_r\, p^r q^{n-r}$

If can also be expressed in the form

$$p(r) = {}^nc_r\, p^r q^{n-r} \qquad r = 0, 1, 2 \ldots n$$

Where $p(r)$ is the probability distribution of the number of success. Giving different values to r i.e. putting $r = 0, 1, 2, 3 \ldots n$ we get the corresponding probabilities ${}^nc_0\, p^0 q^n \quad {}^nc_1\, p^1 q^{n-1} \quad {}^nc_2\, p^2 q^{n-2} \ldots p^n$
which are the different terms in the binomial expression of $(q + p)^n$

As a result of it, the distribution $p(r) = {}^n c_r\, p^r\, q^{n-t}$ is called Binomial probability distribution. The two independent constants n and p in the distribution are called the parameters of the distribution.

Again if the experiment (each consisting n trials) be repeated N times the frequency function of the binomial distribution is given by

$$f(r) = N\,p(r) = N\,{}^n c_r\, p^r\, q^{n-r}$$

The expected frequencies of 0, 1, 2, 3 . . . n success in the above set of experiment are the successive terms in the Binomial expansion $N(q+p)^n$ where $p + q = 1$, which is also called the Binomial Frequency distribution.

Mean and Variance of Binomial Distribution

The probability distribution of Binomial distribution for r success in n trials is given by $\quad p(r) = {}^n c_r\, b^{n-r}\, p^r$

$$\text{Mean} = \mu = E(x) = \sum_{0}^{n} x_i\, p_i$$

$$= 0.{}^n c_0\, q^n + 1\,{}^n c_1\, q^{n-1} p + 2.{}^n c_2\, q^{n-2} p^2 + \ldots + n.1.p^n$$

$$= n\,q^{n-1} p + 2.\frac{n(n-1)}{2\,!}\, q^{n-2} p^2 + \ldots + n^2 1 p_u$$

$$= np\left[q^{n-1} + (n-1)\,q^{n-2} p + \frac{(n-1)(n-2)}{2!}\, q^{n-3} p^2 + \ldots + p^{r-1}\right]$$

$$= np\,(q+p)^{n-1} = np\,(1)^{n-1} = np$$

Mean of Binomial Distribution $= np$

Also variance

$$\sigma^2 = \sum_{r=0}^{n} x_r^2 p_r - (\mu)^2 \qquad\qquad pr = p(r)$$

Here $\quad x_r = r \quad r = 0, 1, 2 \ldots n$ so

That $\quad x_r^2 = r^2 = r + r(r-1);\ r = 0, 1.\ 2 \ldots n$

$$\sigma^2 = \sum_{r=0}^{u} r^2\, p(r) - (np)^2$$

$$\sigma^2 = \sum_{r=0}^{n} [r(r-1) + r]\,{}^n c_r\, q^{n-r} - n^2 p^2$$

$$\sigma^2 = \sum_{r=0}^{n} r(r-1)\frac{n!}{(n-r)!\,r!}\, p^r\, q^{n-r} + \sum_{r=0}^{n} r\,{}^n c_r\, q^{n-r}\, p^r - n^2 p^2$$

$$\sigma^2 = \sum_{r=0}^{n} r \frac{n!}{(n-r)!\,(r-2)!} q^{n-r} p^r + np - n^2 p^2$$

$$\sigma^2 = n(n-1)\,p^2 \sum \frac{(n-2)!}{(n-r)!\,(r-2)!} q^{n-r} p^{r-2} + np - n^2p^2$$

$$\sigma^2 = n(n-1)\,p^2 \sum^{n-2} c_{r-2}\, q^{(n-2)-(r-2)}\, p^{r-2} + np - n^2 p^2$$

$$\sigma^2 = n(n-1)\,p^2 + (q+p)^{n-2} + np - n^2 p^2$$

$$\sigma^2 = n(n-1)\,p^2 + np - n^2p^2 \qquad p + q = 1$$

$$\sigma^2 = -np^2 + np \qquad \Rightarrow \quad 1 - p = q$$

$$\sigma^2 = np\,(1-p)$$

$$\sigma^2 = npq$$

Thus in a Binomial probability distribution

Mean $\mu = np$

Variance $\sigma^2 = npq$

Properties of distribution

1. The shape and location of a Binomial distribution changes as p changes for a given n or as n changes for a given p

2. The Binomial distribution has its

Mean $= np$

Variance $= npq$

or S. D $= \sqrt{npq}$

3. Binomial distribution is symmetrical if $p = q = \frac{1}{2}$

4. The mode of the Binomial distribution is equal to the value of x which has the largest probability

5. Binomial distribution can be represented graphically.

Problem 1 Find the Binomial distribution whose mean is 3 and variance is 2.

Solution Let $(q + p)^n$ be the Binomial distribution. We are given that its mean is 3 and variance is 2.

But Mean $= np = 3$ (1)

Variance $npq = 2$

$$\frac{npq}{nq} = q = \frac{2}{3}$$

$\therefore \qquad p = 1 - q = 1 - \frac{2}{3} - \frac{3-2}{3} = \frac{1}{3}$

Now $\qquad n.\frac{1}{3}.\frac{2}{3} = 2 \qquad n = 9$

Hence the distribution is $(\frac{2}{3} + \frac{1}{3})^6$

Problem 2 Bringout the fallacy, if any, in the ttatement "The mean of a Binomial Distribution is 5 and its variance is 9"

Solution Let $(q + p)^n \qquad q + 1 =$ 1be the Binomial distribution so that

$$\text{Mean} = np = 5$$

$$\text{Variance} = npq = 9$$

$$\frac{npq}{np} = \frac{9}{5}$$

$\Rightarrow q = \frac{9}{5} > 1$ which is wrong because we know that

$0 < q < 1$ Hence the given statement is false.

Problem 3 If the probabiiity of defective bolt is 0.1. Find the mean and standard deviation for the distribution of defective bolt in a total of 500.

Solution $\qquad p = 0.1 \qquad n = 500$

Let $(q + p)^n$ is the Binomial distribution where $q + p = 1$

$$\text{Mean} = np = 0.1 \times 500 = 50$$

$$\Rightarrow \quad q + p = 1$$

$$\Rightarrow \quad q = 1 - 0.1$$

$$\Rightarrow \quad q = 0.9$$

$$\text{Variance} = npq = 500 \times 0.1 \times 0.9 = 9 \times 5 = 45$$

$$6^2 = 45$$

standard deviation $6 = \sqrt{45} = 6{\cdot}7$ **Ans.**

Problem 4 Six dice are thrown 729 times. How many times do you expect at least three dice to show a five or a six.

Solution Let $N (q + p)^n$ $q + p = 1$, be the binomial distribution.

Now $p =$ the probability of getting 5 or 6 with one die $= \frac{2}{6} = \frac{1}{3}$

$\therefore \qquad q = 1 - p = 1 - \frac{1}{3} = \frac{2}{3}$

Here $\qquad N = 729 \qquad n = 6$

Binomial distribution is $N(q+p)^n = 729\left(\frac{2}{3}+\frac{1}{3}\right)^6$

The expected no of times at least three dice showing 5 or 6

$$= 729\left[{}^6c_3\left(\tfrac{2}{3}\right)^3\left(\tfrac{1}{3}\right)^3 + {}^6c_4\left(\tfrac{2}{3}\right)^2\left(\tfrac{1}{3}\right)^4 + {}^6c_5\left(\tfrac{2}{3}\right)\left(\tfrac{1}{3}\right)^5 + {}^6c_9\left(\tfrac{1}{3}\right)^6\right]$$

$$= 729\,[160 + 60 + 12 + 1] = 233$$

Problem 5 A die is tossed thrice. If getting a four is considered a success, find the mean and variance of the probability distribution of the number of success.

Solution Let $(q+p)^n$, $q+p=1$ be the binomial distribution. Here we given that $n = 3$ $p = \dfrac{1}{6}$ $\qquad q = 1 - \dfrac{1}{6} = \dfrac{5}{6}$

$$\text{Mean} = np = 3.\frac{1}{6} = \frac{1}{2}$$

$$\text{Variance} = npq = \frac{3\times 1}{6}\times\frac{5}{6} = \frac{15}{36} = \frac{5}{12}$$

Problem 6 A die is tossed twice. Getting a number greater that 4 is considered a success. Find the variance of the probability distribution of the number of success.

Solution Let $(q+p)^n$, $q+p=1$, be the Binomial distribution $n = 2$

Probability of getting a number greater than (4) i.e getting *a* '5' or 6 is

$$2/6 = \tfrac{1}{3}$$

$$p = \tfrac{1}{3},\ q = 1 - \tfrac{1}{3} = \tfrac{2}{3}$$

$$\text{Mean} = np = 2\,\tfrac{1}{3} = \tfrac{2}{3}$$

$$\text{Variance} = npq = 2\,\frac{1}{3}\,.\frac{2}{3} = \frac{4}{9}$$ **Ans.**

Problem 7 Determine the binomial distribution whose mean is 9 and whose standard deviation is $\dfrac{3}{2}$

Solution Binamial distribution is given by

$$(q+p)^n \text{ where } p + q = 1$$

$$\text{Mean} = 9$$

$$\Rightarrow \quad np = 9 \qquad (1)$$

and $\qquad \text{Varince} = npq$

$$\text{Standard deviation} = \sigma = \frac{3}{2}$$

$$\text{Variance} = \sigma^2 = \frac{9}{4}.$$

So $$npq = \frac{9}{4} \tag{2}$$

dividing (2) with (1) we have

$$\frac{npq}{np} = \frac{4/9}{9} = \frac{9}{4} \times \frac{1}{9} = \frac{1}{9}$$

$$\Rightarrow \quad q = \frac{1}{4}$$

$$p = 1 - q$$

$$p = 1 - \frac{1}{4} = \frac{4-1}{4} = \frac{3}{4}$$

Again $$n \cdot \frac{3}{4} \cdot \frac{1}{4} = \frac{9}{4}$$

$$n = 12$$

Hence the Binomial distribution is

$$\left(\frac{1}{4} + \frac{3}{4}\right)^{12} \quad \textbf{Ans.}$$

Poisson Distribution

Poisson distribution is a limiting form of the Binomial distribution in which n, the number of trials, becomes very large and p, the probability of the success of the event, is very-very small such that np is a finite quantity and not necessarily large. In the Binomial distribution, the probability of x success is $n_{cx}\, p^x\, q^{n-x}$. We require the limiting value of the expression

$$f(x) = {}^nc_x\, p^x\, q^{n-x} \text{ where } p = \frac{m}{n}$$

Where n ultimately tends to ∞ and m is constant. In Binomial distribution.

$$f(x) = {}^nc_x\, p^x\, q^{n-x} = \frac{n\,(n-1)\,(n-2)\,.\,.\,.\,(n-x+1)}{x\,!} p^x\,(1-p)^{n-x}$$

$$\therefore \quad q = 1 - p$$

$$= \frac{n^x\left(1-\frac{1}{n}\right)\left(1-\frac{2}{n}\right)\left(1-\frac{3}{n}\right)\left(1-\frac{x-1}{n}\right)p^x\,(1-p)^{n-x}}{x\,!}$$

Proceeding to limits as $n \to \infty$, $p \to 0$ so that $np = m$

$$\lim_{n\to\infty} f(x) = \lim_{n\to\infty} \frac{\left(1-\frac{1}{n}\right)\left(1-\frac{2}{n}\right)\cdots}{x!} \frac{\left(1-\frac{x-1}{n}\right)}{} \cdot (np)^x \left(1-\frac{np}{n}\right)^{n-x}$$

$$= \frac{m^x}{x!} \lim_{n\to\infty} \left(1-\frac{m}{n}\right)^n \lim_{n\to\infty} \left(1-\frac{m}{n}\right)^x$$

$$= \frac{m^x}{x!} \text{liffi}_{n\to\infty} \left[\left(1-\frac{m}{n}\right)^{-n/m}\right]^{-m} \lim_{n\to\infty} \left(1-\frac{m}{n}\right) = \frac{m^x}{x!} e^{-m}$$

Hence the probability of 0, 1, 2, 3 . . . x . . . success are given by

$$e^{-m}, \frac{e^{-m}\, m}{1!} \frac{e^{-m}\, m^2}{2!} \cdots \frac{e^{-m}\, m^x}{x!} \text{ respeetively}$$

where m is called the parameter of the poisson distribution and

$$e = 2.7183 = 1 + \frac{1}{1!} + \frac{1}{2!} + \frac{1}{3!} + \ldots$$

Def The probability distribution of a random variable X is said to have a poisson distribution if it takes only non-negative values and if its distribution is given by

$$P(X = x) = \frac{m^x\, e^{-m}}{x!}, x = 0, 1, 2 \ldots$$

where m is the parameter.

The poisson distribution can be derived from Binomial distribution under the following conditions.

(i) p, the probability of the occurence of the event is very-very small.

(ii) n is very-very large, where n is the number of trials.

(iii) np is a finite quantity, say $np = m$, then m is called the parameter of the poisson distribution. In poisson distribution the probability of r success is given by $P(r)$,

where $P(r) = \frac{e^{-m}\, m^r}{r!}$.

Mean and Variance of Poisson Distribution

Mean $(= \mu) = E[P(r)]$

$$\Sigma x_i p_i = p_1 x_1 + p_2 x_2 + \ldots + p_n x_n$$

$$= 0\, e^{-m} + 1\, me^{-m} + 2 \cdot \frac{m^2\, e^{-m}}{2!} + 3 \cdot \frac{m^3\, e^{-m}}{3!}$$

$$+ \frac{4m^4\, e^{-m}}{31} + \ldots$$

$$= me^{-m} + m^2 e^{-m} + \frac{m^3 e^{-m}}{2 \cdot 1} + \frac{m^4 e^{-m}}{3 \cdot 2 \cdot 1} + \ldots$$

$$= me^{-m}\left(1 + m + \frac{m^2}{2 \cdot 1} + \frac{m^3}{3 \cdot 2 \cdot 1} + \ldots\right)$$

$$= me^{-m} e^m = me^{-m+m} = me^0 = m$$

Mean $= m$

Variance $(= \sigma^2) = \sum p_i x_i^2 - \mu^2$

Now $\sum p_i x_i^2 = 0 . e^{-m} + 1 \cdot me^{-m} + 2^2 . \frac{m^2 e^{-m}}{2!} + 3^2 \frac{m^3 e^{-m}}{3!}$

$$+ 4^2 \frac{m^4 e^{-m}}{4!} + \ldots$$

$$= me^{-m} + 2m^2 e^{-m} + \frac{3m^3 e^{-m}}{2!} + \frac{4m^4 e^{-m}}{3!} + \ldots$$

$$= me^{-m}\left[1 + 2m + \frac{3}{2} m^2 + \frac{4m^3}{3 \cdot 2 \cdot 1} + \ldots\right]$$

$$= me^{-m}\left[\left(1 + m + \frac{m^2}{2!} + \ldots\right) + \left(m + \frac{2m^2}{2} + \frac{3m^3}{3 \cdot 2 \cdot 1} \ldots\right)\right.$$

$$= me^{-m}\left[e^m + m\left(1 + m + \frac{m^2}{2!} + \frac{m^3}{3!} + \ldots\right)\right]$$

$$= me^{-m}(e^m + me^m) = me^{-m} . e^m (m + 1) = m^2 + m$$

Variance $= \sum p_i x_i^2 - \mu^2 = m(m + 1) - m^2 = m^2 + m - m^2 = m$

Variance $= m$

Standard deviation $= \sqrt{\text{Variance}} = \sqrt{m}$

Recurrence relation: We have

$$P(r) = \frac{m^r e^{-m}}{r!}$$

$$P(r + 1) = \frac{m^{r+1} e^{-m}}{(r + 1)!}$$

Now $\frac{P(r + 1)}{P(r)} = \frac{m^{r+1} e^{-m}}{(r + 1)!} \times \frac{r!}{m^r e^{-m}} = \frac{m}{r + 1}$

i.e. $P(r + 1) = \frac{m}{r + 1} P(r)$

which is recurrence relation with this formula we can find the

$P(1), P(2), P(3), P(4) \ldots$ if $P(0)$ is given.

Problem 1 If the variance of the poisson distirbution is 2, find the distribution for $r = 1, 2, 3, 4$ and 5 from the recurrence relation of the distribution. (use $e^{-2} = 0.1353$)

Solution Here $m = 2$

$$P(0) = c^{-m} = e^{-2} = 0.1353 \text{ (given)}$$

We know that $P(r+1) = \dfrac{m}{r+1} P(r)$

$$P(0+1) = \frac{m}{0+1} P(0)$$

$$P(1) = \frac{2}{1} \times 0.1353$$

$$P(1) = \cdot 2706$$

$$P(2) = \frac{m}{1+1} P(1)$$

$$\Rightarrow \quad P(2) = \frac{2}{2} \times \cdot 2706$$

$$P(2) = \cdot 2706$$

$$P(2+1) = \frac{m}{2+1} P(2)$$

$$P(3) = \frac{2}{3} P(2)$$

$$P(3) = \frac{2}{3} \times \cdot 2706$$

$$P(3) = \frac{\cdot 5412}{3} = \cdot 1804$$

$$P(3+1) = \frac{m}{3+1} P(3)$$

$$P(4) = \frac{2}{4} P(3)$$

$$P(4) = \frac{1}{2} \times \cdot 1804$$

$$P(4) = \cdot 0902$$

$$P(4+1) = \frac{m}{4+1} P(4)$$

$$P(5) = \frac{2}{5} \times P(4)$$

$$P(5) = \frac{2}{3} \times \cdot 0902 = \frac{\cdot 1804}{5} = \cdot 0361$$

Problem 2 If m is the mean of a poisson distribution. Find the probability that the variable takes any one of the values 0 or 1 or 2.

Solution Let $P(X)$ be the probability that the variable X takes any one of the values 0, 1 or 2. We know that

$$P(x) = \frac{e^{-m} m^x}{x!}$$

$$\therefore \quad P(0 \text{ or } 1 \text{ or } 2) = P(0) + P(1) + P(2)$$

$$= \frac{e^{-m} (m)^0}{0!} + \frac{e^{-m} (m)^1}{1!} + e^{-m} \frac{(m)^2}{2!}$$

$$= e^{-m} \left[1 + m + \frac{m^2}{2} \right]$$

Problem 3 Suppose that the chance of an individual coal miner being killed in a mine accident during a year is $\frac{1}{1400}$. Use the poisson distribution to calculate the probability that in a mine emplying 350 miners, there will be atleast fatal accident in a year. (use $e^{-0.25} = 0.78$)

Solution Here $\quad p = \frac{1}{1400}, n = 350$

$$\therefore \text{ Mean} \quad m = np = \frac{350}{1400} = 0.25$$

The poisson distribution is

$$P(r) = \frac{e^{-m} m^r}{r!} = \frac{e^{-0.25} (0.25)^r}{r!}$$

The probability of zero fatal accident

$$= P(0) = \frac{e^{-0.25} (0.25)^0}{0!} = e^{-0.25} = 0.78$$

$\therefore$ P (at least one fatal accident)

$$= 1 - P(0) = 1 - 0.78 = 0.22$$

Problem 4 Six coin are tossed 6400 times. Using the poisson distribution, what is approximate probability of getting six heads x times.

Solution Probability of getting a head in a throw of a coin $= \frac{1}{2}$

Probability of getting six heads in a throw of six coins $= \frac{1}{26} = \frac{1}{64}$

$$\therefore \text{ Mean} = m = np = 6400 \times \frac{1}{64} = 100$$

$$m = 100$$

Hence probability of getting six beads x times according to poisson distribution is

$$P(x) = \frac{e^{-m} m^x}{x!} = \frac{e^{-100}\, 100^x}{x!} \quad \textbf{Ans.}$$

Problem 5 Fit a poisson distribution of the following data and calculate the theoretical frequencies

Death	0	1	2	3	4
Frequencies	122	60	15	2	1

Solution Mean $= \bar{x} = m = \dfrac{\Sigma xf}{\Sigma f} = \dfrac{60 + 30 + 6 + 4}{122 + 60 + 15 + 2 + 1}$

$$= \frac{100}{200} = \frac{1}{2} = 0.5$$

Now $\qquad e^{-m} = e^{-.5} = 1 - 0.5 + \dfrac{(0.5)^2}{2!} - \ldots = 0.61$

Hence the theoretical frequency i.e. the number of r death is given by

$$\frac{200 \times e^{-5} (0\ 5)^r}{r!}$$

where $r = 0, 1, 2, 3, 4,$

Normal Distribution

The normal distribution is also known as Gaussion distribution or a normal curve. It is a continuous distribution. Normal distribution is also a limiting form of the Binomial distribution under the following conditions:

(i) n, the number of trials is indefinitely large i.e. in other words, $n \to \infty$.

(ii) neither p nor q is very small.

The probability function of the normal distribution with mean at the origin is given by

$$P(x) = y = \frac{1}{\sigma\sqrt{2\pi}} e^{-x^2/2\sigma^2}, -\infty \; \infty \leqslant x \leqslant \infty$$

where σ is the standard deviation

The probability function of the normal distribution with mean m is given by

$$P(x) = \frac{1}{\sigma\sqrt{2\pi}} e^{-(x-m)^2/2\sigma^2}, -\infty \leqslant x \leqslant \infty.$$

Properties of normal curve

The normal probability curve with mean m and standard deviation σ has the following properties

1. The equation of the curve is

$$y = \frac{1}{\sigma\sqrt{2\pi}} e^{-(x-m)^2/2\sigma^2} - \infty \leqslant x \leqslant \infty$$

and it is bell shaped.

2. The curve is symmetrical about the line $x = m$ and x ranges from $-\infty$ to $+\infty$.

3. Mean. mode and median coincide at $x = m$.

4. X axis is asymptote to the curve.

5. It can be shown that it has

Arithmetic mean $= m$

Variance $= \sigma^2$

6. The point of infiexion of the curve are at $x = m + \sigma$, $x = m - \sigma$ and the curve changes from concave to convex at $x = m + \sigma$ to $x = m - \sigma$.

7. In the normal distribution

$\sigma : M \cdot AD : Q \cdot D = 1 : 0 \cdot 7979 : 0 \cdot 6745$

where $Q \cdot D$ = Quartile deviation

MAD = Mean absolute deviation and is equal to $\sigma \sqrt{\frac{2}{\pi}}$

8. The total area under the normal curve is equal to unity and the percentage distribution of area under the normal curve is given in the figure.

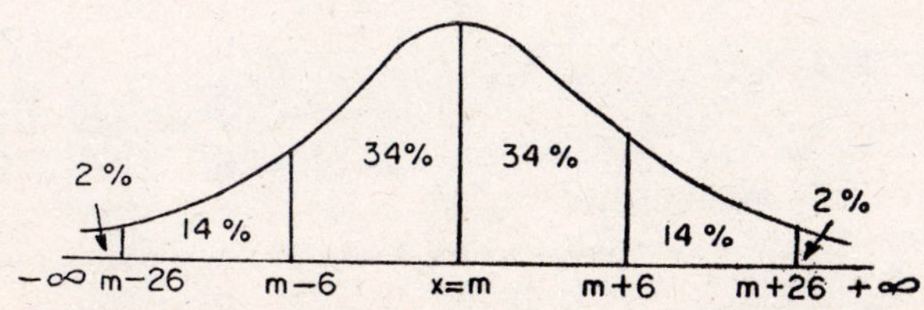

9. The mean deviation from the mean in normal distribution is equal to 4/5 of its standard deviation.

10. All the odd moments about the mean are zero.

11. The maximum ordinate lies at the mean

i.e. at $x = m$.

Examples of normal distribution

(1) The heights of the trees of the same variety and age in the same locality would conform to the laws of normal curve.

(2) The heights of thc men of above 22 years belonging to the same race and living under similar conditions and climate give a normal frequency distribution.

35
Differential Equation

[TYPE : SOLVABLE FOR P]

1. Solve the differential eqn.

$$x\left(\frac{dy}{dx}\right)^2 + (y-x)\frac{dy}{dx} - y = 0$$

Let $\frac{dy}{dx} = p$ so that

$$xp^2 + (y-x)p - y = 0$$

$\therefore$ $p = \frac{(x-y) \pm \sqrt{(x-y)^2 + 4xy}}{2x}$

$= \frac{(x-y) \pm (x+y)}{2x}$ $[\because \sqrt{(x-y)^2 + 4xy} = (x+y)]$

$= \frac{x-y+x+y}{2x}$ and $\frac{x-y-x-y}{2x}$

$p = 1$ and $-y/x$

$\therefore$ $\frac{dy}{dx} = 1$ and $\frac{dy}{dx} = -\frac{y}{x}$

$\Rightarrow$ $dy = dx$ on integrating both sides

$y = x + c$

$\Rightarrow$ $y - x - c = 0$ (1)

Again, $\frac{dy}{y} + \frac{dx}{x} = c$

$\therefore$ $\log y + \log x = k$

$\Rightarrow$ $xy = c$ $[\because \log c = k]$

$\therefore$ $xy - c = 0$ (ii)

Therefore from (i) and (ii) we have

$$(y-x-c)(xy-c) = 0$$

is the Required soln.

2. $y^2 + xyp - x^2 p^2 = 0$

This eqn. reduces to

$x^2 p^2 - xy\,p - y^2 = 0$ is a quadratic eqn. in p

$$\therefore \quad p = \frac{xy \pm \sqrt{x^2 y^2 + 4x^2 y^2}}{2x^2}$$

$$p = \frac{xy \pm \sqrt{5}xy}{2x^2}$$

$$\Rightarrow \quad p = \frac{xy + \sqrt{5}\,xy}{2x^2} \text{ and } \frac{xy - \sqrt{5}xy}{2x^2}$$

$$\therefore \quad p = \frac{xy(1+\sqrt{5})}{2x^2} \text{ and } \frac{xy(1-\sqrt{5})}{2x^2}$$

$$\therefore \quad p = \frac{y}{2x}(1+\sqrt{5})$$

$$\therefore \quad \frac{dy}{dx} = \frac{y}{2x}(1+\sqrt{5}) \text{ and } \frac{y}{2x}(1-\sqrt{5})$$

$$\therefore \quad \int \frac{dy}{y} = \frac{(1+\sqrt{5})}{2}\int \frac{dx}{x}$$

$$\Rightarrow \log y = \frac{(1+\sqrt{5})}{2}\log x + \log c$$

$$\Rightarrow \quad y^2 = (x^{1+\sqrt{5}})\,c$$

$$\Rightarrow \quad y^2 - cx^{(1+\sqrt{5})} = 0 \qquad \text{(i)}$$

and
$$\frac{dy}{dx} = \frac{y}{2x}(1-\sqrt{5})$$

$$\therefore \quad \frac{dy}{y} = \frac{1-\sqrt{5}}{2}\int \frac{dx}{x}$$

$$\Rightarrow \quad y^2 - cx^{1-\sqrt{5}} = 0 \qquad \text{(ii)}$$

From eqn. (i) and (ii) we have

$$[y^2 - cx^{(1+\sqrt{5})}]\,[y^2 - cx^{1-\sqrt{5}}] = 0$$

3.
$$xy\,p^2 - (x^2 + y^2)\,p + xy = 0$$

$$\therefore \quad p = \frac{(x^2+y^2) \pm \sqrt{(x^2+y^2) - 4x^2y^2}}{2xy}$$

$$p = \frac{(x^2+y^2) \pm \sqrt{x^4 + y^4 + 2x^2y^2 - 4x^2y^2}}{2xy}$$

$$p = \frac{(x^2+y^2) \pm (x^2-y^2)}{2xy}$$

$$p = \frac{x^2 + y^2 + x^2 - y^2}{2xy} \text{ and } \frac{x^2 + y^2 - x^2 + y^2}{2xy}$$

$$p = x/y \text{ and } y/x$$

when $dy/dx = x/y$

$$\Rightarrow \int y dy = \int x dx$$

$$\Rightarrow y^2/2 = x^2/2 + c$$

$$\Rightarrow (y^2 - x^2 - 2c) = 0 \qquad \text{(i)}$$

and when $dy/dx = y/x$

$$\Rightarrow \int \frac{dy}{y} = \int \frac{dx}{x}$$

$$\Rightarrow \log y = \log x + \log c$$

$$\Rightarrow y = xc$$

$$\Rightarrow (y - xc) = c \qquad \text{(ii)}$$

Hence from (i) and (ii) we get it it as

$$(y^2 - x^2 - 2c)(y - xc) = 0$$

4. $$x^2 \left(\frac{dy}{dx}\right)^2 + xy \frac{dy}{dx} - 6y^2 = 0$$

Let $dy/dx = p$ we have

$$x^2 p^2 + xy\, p - 6y^2 = 0$$

$$\Rightarrow p = \frac{-xy \pm \sqrt{x^2 y^2 + 24x^2 y^2}}{2x^2}$$

$$p = \frac{xy \pm 5xy}{2x^2}$$

$$\therefore \quad p = \frac{-xy + 5xy}{2x^2} \text{ and } \frac{-xy - 5xx}{2x^2}$$

$$\Rightarrow p = \frac{4xy}{2x^2} \text{ and } \frac{-6xy}{2x^2}$$

$$\Rightarrow p = 2y/x \text{ and } -3y/x$$

When $p = 2y/x$

$$\therefore \quad dy/dx = 2y/x$$

$$\Rightarrow \int \frac{dy}{y} = 2\int \frac{dx}{x}$$

$$\Rightarrow \quad \log y = \log x^2 c$$

$$\Rightarrow \quad y = x^2 c$$

$$(y - x^2 c) = 0 \qquad \text{(i)}$$

Again when $\quad p = -3y/x$

$$\Rightarrow \quad dy/dx = -3y/x$$

$$\Rightarrow \int \frac{dy}{y} + 3\int \frac{dx}{x} = 0$$

$$\Rightarrow \quad \log yx^3 = \log c$$

$$\Rightarrow \quad y\,x^3 - c = 0$$

Hence from eqn. (i) and (ii) we get .

$$(y - x^2 c)\,(yx^3 - c) = 0$$

Problem 5 $\quad p^2 y + (x - y)\,p - x = 0$

$$\Rightarrow \quad p = \frac{(y-x) \pm \sqrt{(x-y)^2 + 4xy}}{2y}$$

$$p = \frac{(y-x) \pm (x+y)}{2y}$$

$$p = \frac{y - x + x + y}{2y} \text{ and } \frac{y - x - x - y}{2y}$$

$$p = \frac{2y}{2y} \text{ and } \frac{-2x}{2y}$$

When $\quad p = dy/dx = 1$

$$\Rightarrow \quad y = x + c$$

$$\Rightarrow (y - x - c) = 0 \qquad \text{(i)}$$

And when $\quad p = \frac{dy}{dy} = -\frac{x}{y}$

$$\Rightarrow \quad \frac{y^2}{2} + \frac{x^2}{2} = c$$

$$\Rightarrow (y^2 + x^2 - c) = 0 \qquad \text{(ii)}$$

From (i) and (ii) we have

$$(y - x - c)\,(x^2 + y^2 - c) = 0$$

Solve the following differential eqn.

[TYPE SOLVABLE FOR x AND y]

Problem 1. $p^2 y + 2px - y = 0$

This eqn. is solvable for x. Hence

$$2px = y - p^2 y = y(1-p^2)$$

$$\therefore \qquad x = \frac{y(1-p^2)}{2p}$$

Now on differentiating both sides w.r.t. y we

$$\frac{dx}{dy} = \frac{y}{2p}\left(-2p\frac{dp}{dy}\right) + (1-p^2)\left[\frac{-y}{2p^2}\frac{dp}{dy} + \frac{1}{2p}\right]$$

$$\frac{1}{p} = -y\frac{dp}{dy} - y\frac{(1-p^2)}{2p^2}\frac{dp}{dy} + \frac{(1-p^2)}{2p}$$

$$\Rightarrow \frac{1}{p} - \frac{(1-p^2)}{2p} = -y\left[1 + \frac{(1-p^2)}{2p^2}\right]\frac{dp}{dy}$$

$$\Rightarrow \frac{2-1+p^2}{2p} = -y\left[\frac{1+p^2}{2p^2}\right]\frac{dp}{dy}$$

$$\Rightarrow \left(\frac{1+p^2}{2p}\right) + y\frac{dp}{dy}\left(\frac{1+p^2}{2p^2}\right) = 0$$

$$\Rightarrow 1 + \frac{y}{p}\frac{dp}{dy} = 0$$

$$\Rightarrow \frac{dy}{y} + \frac{dp}{y} = 0$$

On integrating both sides we get

$$\log y + \log p = \log c$$

$$\Rightarrow py = c \Rightarrow \frac{y}{c} = \frac{1}{p} \Rightarrow p = \frac{c}{y}$$

On substituting the value of p we get x and y

$$x = \frac{y(1-c^2/y^2)}{2c/y} = \frac{c(1-p^2)}{2p^2}$$

Problem 2 $ap^2 + py - x = 0$

$$\Rightarrow x = ap^2 + py$$

On differentiating both sides by w.r.t

$$\frac{dx}{dy} = 2ap\frac{dp}{dy} + p + y\frac{dp}{dy}$$

$$\frac{1}{p} = 2ap\frac{dp}{dy} + y\frac{dp}{dy} + p$$

$$\Rightarrow \frac{1}{p} - p = \frac{dp}{dy}(2ap + y)$$

$$\Rightarrow \frac{1-p^2}{p} = \frac{dp}{dy}(2ap + y)$$

$$\Rightarrow \frac{dy}{dp} = \frac{p(2ap + y)}{(1-p^2)} = \frac{2ap^2}{1-p^2} = \frac{yp}{1+p^2}$$

$$\Rightarrow \frac{dy}{dp} - \frac{p}{1-p^2} y = \frac{2ap^2}{1-p^2}$$

This is a linear eqn. in y

$\therefore$ I.F. $\quad e^{-\int dp/(1-p^2)} = e^{1/2 \log (1-p2)} = \sqrt{1-p^2}$

$$y\sqrt{1-p^2} = \int \frac{2ap^2}{1-p^2} \times \sqrt{1-p^2}\, dp$$

$$y\sqrt{1-p^2} = \int \frac{2ap^2}{\sqrt{1-p^2}}\, dp$$

$$y\sqrt{1-p^2} = a \sin^{-1} p - ap\sqrt{1-p^2}$$

$$y = \frac{a \sin^{-1} p}{\sqrt{1-p^2}} - ap$$

Hence $\quad x = ap^2 + \frac{ap \sin^{-1} p}{\sqrt{1-p^2}} - ap^2$

$$\Rightarrow x = \frac{ap \sin^{-1} p}{\sqrt{1-p^2}}$$

Problem 3 $\left(\frac{dy}{dx}\right)^2 + 4xy\frac{dy}{dx} + 8y^2 = 0$

Let $\quad p = \frac{dy}{dx}$

$\therefore \quad p^3 - 4xy\, p + 8y^2 = 0$

$\therefore \quad p^3 + 8y^2 = 4xy\, p$

$$\Rightarrow \quad x = \frac{p^3 + 8y^2}{4yp} = \frac{p^2}{4y} + \frac{8y}{4p}$$

Differentiating both sides w.r.t. y

$$\frac{dx}{dy} = \frac{1}{4y} \times 2p\frac{dp}{dy} - \frac{p^2}{4}\frac{1}{y^2} - 2y\frac{1}{p^2}\frac{dp}{dy} + \frac{2}{p}$$

$$\Rightarrow \quad \frac{1}{p} - \frac{2}{p} = \frac{p}{2y}\frac{dp}{dy} - \frac{2y}{p^2}\frac{dp}{dy} - \frac{p^2}{4y^2}$$

$$\Rightarrow \frac{p^2}{4y^2} - \frac{1}{p} = \frac{dp}{dy}\left(\frac{p}{2y} - \frac{2y}{p^2}\right)$$

$$\Rightarrow \quad \frac{(p^2-4y^2)}{4py^2} = \frac{dp}{dy}\left(\frac{p^3-4y^2}{2yp^2}\right)$$

$$\Rightarrow \quad \frac{1}{2y} = \frac{dp}{dy}\frac{1}{p}$$

$$\Rightarrow \quad \int\frac{dy}{y} = 2\int\frac{dp}{p}$$

$$\Rightarrow \quad \log y = \log p^2 c$$

$$\Rightarrow \quad y = p^2 c \qquad \text{Let} \qquad \text{const} = c^2$$

$$\Rightarrow \quad p = \frac{\sqrt{y}}{c}$$

Putting $\quad p = \dfrac{\sqrt{y}}{c}$ in eqn. eliminating x

$$\therefore \quad x = \frac{y}{4yc^2} + \frac{8\,yc}{4\sqrt{y}} = \frac{1}{4c^2} + \frac{8\sqrt{y}c}{8}$$

$$x = \frac{1 + 8\sqrt{y}c^3}{4c^2}$$

$$\therefore \quad 4xc^2 - 1 = 8\sqrt{y}c^3$$

$$\Rightarrow \quad \frac{c^2}{c^3}\left(4x - \frac{1}{c}\right) = 8\sqrt{y}$$

$$\Rightarrow \quad \frac{1}{c}\left(4x - \frac{1}{c}\right)^2 = 64y$$

Putting $\quad 1/c = k$ we have

$$k\,(4x-k)^2 = 64y$$

Problem 4 $\left(\dfrac{dy}{dx}\right)^2 y^2 - 2x\dfrac{dy}{dx} + y = 0$

Let $\quad \dfrac{dy}{dx} = p$ we have

$$p^3\,y^2 - 2xp + y = 0$$

$$\Rightarrow \quad \frac{p^3 y^2 + y}{2p} = x$$

$$\Rightarrow \quad x = \frac{p^2 y^2}{2} + \frac{y}{2p}$$

On differentiating both sides w.r.t. y

$$\frac{dx}{dy} = \frac{1}{2}\left[2p^2 y + 2y^2 p\frac{dp}{dy} + \frac{1}{p} - \frac{y}{p^2}\frac{dp}{dy}\right]$$

$$\frac{1}{p} = p^2 y + py^2 \frac{bp}{dy} + \frac{1}{2p} - \frac{y}{2p^2}\frac{dp}{dy}$$

$$\Rightarrow \quad \frac{dp}{dy}\left(\frac{y}{2p^2} - py^2\right) = -\frac{1}{2p} + p^2 y$$

$$\Rightarrow \quad \frac{dp}{dy}\left(\frac{y - 2p^3 y^2}{2p^2}\right) = \frac{-1 + 2p^3 y}{2p}$$

$$\Rightarrow \quad \frac{dp}{dy}\left(\frac{2p^3 y - 1}{2px}\right)(-y) = \frac{(2p^3 y - 1)}{2p}$$

$$\Rightarrow \quad \frac{-y}{p}\frac{dp}{dy} = 1$$

$$\Rightarrow \quad \frac{dp}{p} + \frac{dy}{y} = 0$$

$$\Rightarrow \quad \log p + \log y = \log c$$

$$\Rightarrow \quad p = c/y$$

Therefore $\quad x = \frac{c^2}{2} + \frac{y^2}{2c}$

$$x = \frac{c^3 + y^2}{2c}$$

$$\Rightarrow \quad 2cx = c^3 + y^2$$

5. $\quad 4p^3 + 3xp = y$

Here eliminating x we get

$$x = \frac{y}{3p} - \frac{4p^2}{3}$$

$$\Rightarrow \frac{dx}{dy} = \frac{1}{3p} - \frac{y}{3p^2}\frac{dp}{dy} - \frac{4}{3}\cdot 2p\,\frac{dp}{dy}$$

$$\frac{1}{p} = \frac{1}{3p} - \left(\frac{y}{3p^2} + \frac{8}{3}\,p\right)\frac{dp}{dy}$$

$$\frac{2}{3p} = -\left(\frac{y + 8p^3}{3p^2}\right)\frac{dp}{dy}$$

$$\frac{dy}{dp} + \frac{y}{2p} = -\, 4p^2$$

This is a linear eqn. in y

If $\quad = e^{1/2 \int 1/p\, dp} = p^{7/2}$

$\therefore \quad yp^{1/2} = -4 \int p^2 \cdot p^{1/2}\, dp$

$$yp^{1/2} = -4\int p^{5/2}\, dp = -\, \frac{4 \times 2}{7}\, p^{1/2}$$

$\therefore \quad yp^{1/2} = -\frac{8}{7}\, p^{7/2} + c$

$\Rightarrow \quad y = -\frac{8}{7}\, p^3 + cp^{-1/2}$

Similarly, $x = \dfrac{-8/7\, p^3 + cp^{-1/2} - 4p^3}{3p} = \dfrac{-12}{7} p^2 + \dfrac{c}{3}\, p^{-3/2}$

TYPE CLAIRAUTS FORM r=px+f(p)

Problem 1 $\quad (y - px)\,(p - 1) = p$

$\therefore \quad y = \dfrac{p}{p-1} + px$ which is of the clairauts type

Now diff. both sides w.r.t. x we have

$$p = \frac{dy}{dx} = \frac{p-1-p}{(p-1)^2}\frac{dp}{dx} + p + x\,\frac{dp}{dx}$$

$$\Rightarrow \frac{dp}{dx}\left(\frac{1}{p-1}\right)^2 = x\,\frac{dp}{dx}$$

$$\Rightarrow \frac{dx}{dx}\left[\left(\frac{1}{p-1}\right)^2 - x\right] = 0$$

either $\quad \dfrac{dp}{dx} = 0$

$\therefore\ p = c$ Now putting the value of p in the given problem

$$(y - cx)\,(c - 1) = c$$

2. $\quad y = x\dfrac{py}{dx} + p^2\left[\left(\dfrac{dy}{dx}\right)\right]^2$

Let $\quad \dfrac{dy}{dx} = p$ we have

$$y = xp + + p^2$$

On differentiating w.r.t. x both sides

$$\frac{dy}{dx} = x\,\frac{dp}{dx} + p + 2p\frac{dp}{dx}$$

$$p - p = (x + 2p)\,\frac{dp}{dx}$$

i.e. either $\quad \dfrac{dp}{dx} = 0$

$$\Rightarrow \quad p = c$$

Required soln. is $\quad y = xc + c^2$

Problem 3 $\quad y = x\,\dfrac{dy}{dx} + e^{dy/dx}$

Let $\quad \dfrac{dy}{dx} = p \quad$ hence

$y = xp + e^p$ on differentiating w.r.t. x

$$\frac{dy}{dx} = x\,\frac{dp}{dx} + p + e^p\,\frac{dp}{dx}$$

$$\Rightarrow \quad p = x\,\frac{dp}{dx} + p + e^p\,\frac{dp}{dx}$$

$$\Rightarrow \quad 0 = (x + e^p)\,\frac{dp}{dx}$$

either $\quad \dfrac{dp}{dx} = 0$

or, $\int dp = \text{constant} = c$

$\Rightarrow p = \text{constant} = c$

Hence soln is $\quad y = xc + e^c$

Problem 4 $\quad (px - y)(py + x) = a^2 p$

Let $\quad x^2 = u$ and $y^2 = v$

So that $\quad 2x dx = du$ and $2y\,dy = dv$

$$\therefore \quad \frac{y\,dy}{x\,dx} = \frac{dv}{du}$$

$$\Rightarrow \quad \frac{dy}{dx} = \frac{x\,dv}{y\,du}$$

hence instead of p we will substitute $p = \dfrac{xdv}{ydu}$

$$\therefore \quad \left(\frac{x^2}{y}\frac{dv}{du}-y\right)\left(\frac{xdv}{du}+x\right)=a^2\frac{xdv}{ydu}$$

$$\left(\frac{u}{\sqrt{v}}\frac{dv}{du}-\sqrt{v}\right)\left(\sqrt{u}\cdot\frac{dv}{du}+\sqrt{u}\right)=a^2\frac{\sqrt{u}dv}{\sqrt{v}\,du}$$

$$\Rightarrow \quad \frac{u\sqrt{u}}{\sqrt{v}}\left(\frac{dv}{du}\right)^2+\frac{\sqrt{u}\cdot u}{\sqrt{v}}\frac{dv}{du}-\sqrt{uv}\frac{dv}{du}-\sqrt{uv}=a^2\frac{\sqrt{u}}{\sqrt{v}}\frac{dv}{du}$$

$$\frac{u\sqrt{u}}{\sqrt{v}}p^2+p\left[\frac{\sqrt{u}}{\sqrt{v}}u-\sqrt{uv}-a^2\frac{\sqrt{u}}{v}\right]=\sqrt{uv}$$

$$\frac{u\sqrt{u}}{\sqrt{v}}p^2+p\left[\frac{u\cdot\sqrt{u}-\sqrt{u}\cdot v-a^2\sqrt{u}}{\sqrt{v}}\right]=\sqrt{uv}$$

$$\sqrt{u}\left[\frac{u}{\sqrt{v}}p^2+p\left\{\frac{u-v-a^2}{\sqrt{v}}\right\}\right]=\sqrt{u}\sqrt{v}$$

$$up^2+p\,(u-v-a^2)=v.$$

$$\Rightarrow \quad u\,(p^2+p)-pv-pa^2=v$$

$$v\,(p+1)=pu\,(p+1)-pa^2$$

$$\Rightarrow \quad v=pu-[p/(p+1)]\,a^2$$

Which is in the form of claircuts eqn. and whose soln. is nothing but simply

$p = c$ Therefore soln. is

$$y^2=x^2\,c-\frac{(c)}{(1+c)}a^2.$$

Problem 5 $y + xp \log p = (2 + 3 \log p)\, p^3$

$$y=(2+3\log p)\,p^3-xp\log p.$$

This is not exactly the claircuts eqn. but we may say that it is modified form of clairacuts eqn. on differentiating with respect to x both sides we get

$$\frac{dy}{dx}=3\,(2+3\log p)\,p^2\frac{dp}{dx}+p^3\times\frac{3}{p}\frac{dp}{dx}$$
$$-x\,(1+\log p)\frac{dp}{dx}-p\log p$$

$$p=6p^2\frac{dp}{dx}+9p^2\log p\frac{dp}{dx}+3p^2\frac{dp}{dx}-x\frac{dp}{dx}$$
$$-x\log p\frac{dp}{dx}-p\log p.$$

$$\Rightarrow \quad p\,(1 + \log p) = \frac{dp}{dx}\,[6p^2 + 9p^2 \log p + 3p^2 - x - x \log p]$$

$$\therefore \quad \frac{dx}{dp} = \frac{(9p^2 - x)\,(1 + \log p)}{p\,(1 + \log p)}$$

$$\frac{dx}{dp} + \frac{x}{p} = 9p$$

This is a linear eqn. in x. Hence

$$\text{IF} = e^{\int 1/p\, dp} = p$$

$$\therefore \quad xp = 9 \int p^2\, dp = p^3/3 = 3p^3 + c$$

$$\Rightarrow \quad xp = 3p^2 + cp^{-1}$$

Again $\quad y = (2 + 3 \log p)\, p^3 - 3p^3 \log p + c \log p$

$$= 2p^3 + 3p^3 \log p - 3p^3 \log p + c \log p$$

$$y = 2p^3 + c \log p$$

Problem 6 $y = 2px - p^2$

On differenting both sides w.r.t. x

$$\frac{dy}{dx} = 2p + 2x\,\frac{dp}{dx} - 2p\,\frac{dp}{dx}$$

$$p - 2p = 2\,\frac{dp}{dx}\,(x - p)$$

$$-\frac{p}{2} = \frac{dp}{dx}\,x\,(x - p)$$

$$\frac{dx}{dp} + \frac{2\,(x - p)}{p} = 0$$

$$\Rightarrow \quad \frac{dx}{dp} + \frac{2}{p}\,x = 2$$

$$\text{IF} = e^{2\int 1/p\, dp} = e^{\log p^2} = p^2$$

$$\therefore \quad xp^2 = 2 \int p^2\, dp = 2p^3/3 + c$$

$$\Rightarrow \quad x = \tfrac{2}{3}\, p + cp^{-2}$$

MISCELLANEOUS PROBLEMS

Problem 1 $\quad p^2 + py = x\,(x + y)$

$$p^2 + py - x\,(x + y) = 0$$

$$P = \frac{-y \pm \sqrt{y^2 + 4x^2 + 4xy}}{2}$$

$$P = \frac{-y \pm (y + 2x)}{2}$$

$$\Rightarrow \quad P = \frac{-y + y + 2x}{2} \text{ and } \frac{-y - y - 2x}{2}$$

$$P = x \text{ and } -(x + y)$$

Where $\quad P = \dfrac{dy}{dx}$ we have

$$\int dy = \int x dx$$

$$\Rightarrow \quad y = x^2/2 + c$$

$$\Rightarrow \quad (2y - x^2 - 2c) = 0 \qquad \text{(i)}$$

and $\quad \dfrac{dy}{dx} = -(x + y)$

Let $\quad x + y = u$

$\therefore \quad 1 + \dfrac{dy}{dx} = \dfrac{du}{dx}$

$\therefore \quad \dfrac{dy}{dx} = \dfrac{du}{dx} - 1$

$$\Rightarrow \quad \frac{du}{dx} - 1 = -u$$

$$\Rightarrow \quad \frac{du}{dx} = 1 - u$$

$$\Rightarrow \quad \frac{du}{1-u} = dx$$

$$-\log(1-u) = x + c$$

$$\Rightarrow \quad 1 - u = e^{-x-c} = -e^{-x} \cdot k \cdot [e^{-c} = e^k]$$

$$\Rightarrow 1 - x - y = -ke^{-x}$$

$$\Rightarrow (y + x - 1 - ke^{-x}) = 0 \qquad \text{(ii)}$$

combining (i) and (ii), $(2y - x^2 - 2c)(y + x - 1 - ke^{-x}) = 0$

Problem 2 $\quad p = \sin(x - y)$

$\therefore \quad \dfrac{dy}{dx} = \sin(x - y)$

Let $x-y=t$

$$\Rightarrow \frac{dy}{dx}=-\frac{dt}{dx}+1$$

$$\therefore \quad \frac{dt}{dx}-1=-\sin t$$

$$\Rightarrow \frac{dt}{dx}=-\sin t+1$$

$$\Rightarrow \int\frac{dt}{1-\sin t}=\int dx$$

$$\Rightarrow \int\frac{dt}{1-\cos(\pi/2-t/0)}=x+c$$

$$\Rightarrow \int\frac{dt}{2\cos^2(\pi/4-t/2)}=x+c$$

$$\Rightarrow \tfrac{1}{2}\int dt\operatorname{cosec}^2(\pi/4-t/2)=x+c$$

$$\Rightarrow \cot(\pi/4-t/2)=x+c$$

$$\Rightarrow \quad x+c=\cot(\pi/4-t/2)$$

Putting $t=x-y$ more we get

$$x+c=\cot[\pi/4-\tfrac{1}{2}(x-y)]$$

Problem 3 $p(p-y)=x(x+y)$

$$\Rightarrow \quad p^2-py-x(x+y)=0$$

$$p=\frac{y\pm\sqrt{y^2+4x^2+4xy}}{2}$$

$$p=y\pm(y+2x)/2$$

$$p=\frac{y+y+2x}{2}\text{ and }\frac{y-y-2x}{2}$$

$$p=(x+y)\text{ and}-x$$

When $\frac{dy}{dx}=x+y$

Putting $x+y=z$

$$\frac{dy}{dx}=\frac{dz}{dx}-1$$

$$\Rightarrow \quad \frac{dz}{dx} - 1 = z$$

$$\Rightarrow \quad \int \frac{dz}{1+z} = \int dx$$

$$\Rightarrow \log(1+z) = x + c$$

$$\Rightarrow \quad 1 + z = e^x \cdot e^c$$

$$\Rightarrow \quad (x + y + 1 - ke^x) = 0 \qquad \text{(i)}$$

And when $\quad \frac{dy}{dx} = -x$

$$\Rightarrow \quad y + x^2/2 - c = 0$$

$$\Rightarrow \quad (2y + x^2 - 2c) = 0 \qquad \text{(ii)}$$

Combining (i) and (ii) we get

$$(x + y + 1 - ke^x)(2y + x^2 - 2c) = 0$$

Problem 4 $\quad p^2 xy + p(4x^2 - 3y^2) - 12xy = 0$

$$p = \frac{(3y^2 - 4x^2) \pm \sqrt{(4x^2 - y3^2)^2 + 48x^2 y^2}}{2xy}$$

$$p = \frac{(3y^2 - 4x^2) \pm (4x^2 + 3y^2)}{2xy}$$

$$p = \frac{3y^2 - 4x^2 + 4x^2 + 3y^2}{2xy} \text{ and } \frac{3y^2 - 4x^2 - 4x^2 - 3y^2}{2xy}$$

$$p = \frac{3y}{x} \text{ and } \frac{-4x}{y}$$

When $\quad \frac{dy}{dx} = \frac{3y}{x}$

$$\Rightarrow \quad \int \frac{dy}{y} = 3 \int \frac{dx}{x}$$

$$\Rightarrow \log y = \log x^3 c$$

$$\Rightarrow \quad (y - x^3 c) = 0 \qquad \text{(i)}$$

And when $\quad \frac{dy}{dx} = \frac{-4x}{y}$

$$\Rightarrow \quad \int y\, dy + \int 4x dx = 0$$

$$\Rightarrow \quad \frac{y^2}{2} + 4\frac{x^2}{2} = c$$

$$\Rightarrow \quad y^2 + 2x^2 - c = 0 \qquad \text{(ii)}$$

From (i) and (ii) we have

$$(y-x^3 c)(y^2 + 2x^2-c) = 0$$

Problem 5 $(1 + p^2)\, y = 2\, px.$

Solution $\Rightarrow \quad x = \dfrac{(1 + P^2)\, y}{2P}$

$$\Rightarrow \quad x = \frac{y}{2p} + \frac{py}{2}$$

On differentating both sides w.r.t. y

$$\frac{dx}{dy} = \frac{1}{2p} - \frac{y}{2} - \frac{1}{P^2}\frac{dP}{dy} + \frac{1}{2}P + \frac{y}{2}\frac{dp}{dy}$$

$$\frac{1}{p} - \frac{1}{2} - \frac{p}{2} = \frac{dp}{dy}\left(\frac{y}{2} - \frac{y}{2P^2}\right)$$

$$\frac{2-1-p^2}{2p} = \frac{dp}{dy}\left(\frac{yP^2-y}{2P^2}\right)$$

$$\Rightarrow \quad \frac{1-p^2}{2P} = -y\frac{dP}{dy}\frac{(1-^2)}{2P^2}$$

$$\Rightarrow \quad p + y\frac{dy}{dy} = 0$$

$$\Rightarrow \quad \frac{dy}{y} + \frac{dp}{p} = 0$$

Integrating both sides we get

$$\log yp = \log c$$

$$\Rightarrow \quad p = c/y$$

hence, $\quad x = \dfrac{\left(1 + \dfrac{c^2}{y^2}\right) y}{2\dfrac{c}{y}}$

$$x = \left(\frac{c^2 + y^2}{2c}\right) = c\,\frac{(1 + P^2)}{2P^2}$$

Problem 6 $p^2 x^2-2pxy + y^2 + 4p = 0.$

Solulion This can be rewritten as

$$p^2 x^2-2pxy + y^2 = -4p$$

$$\Rightarrow \quad (px-y)^2 = -4p$$

$$\Rightarrow \quad (px-y)^2 = 4i^2 p$$

$$\Rightarrow \quad px-y = 2ip^{1/2}$$

$$\Rightarrow \quad y = px-2ip^{1/2} \text{ [clairaut's eqn.]}$$

$$\therefore \quad \frac{dy}{dx} = p + x\frac{dp}{dx} - 2i\,\frac{1}{2}\,P^{-1/2}\,\frac{dp}{dx}$$

$$p = p + x\frac{dp}{dx} - \frac{i}{\sqrt{p}}\frac{pd}{dx}$$

$$\Rightarrow \quad \frac{dp}{dx}\,(x-i) = 0$$

i.e. either $\frac{dp}{dx} = 0$

$$\Rightarrow \quad p = c$$

Required soln. is

$$c^2 x^2 - 2cxy + 4c + y^2 = 0$$

Problem 7 $p^2 (p + m) = a (y + mx)$

Solution $\Rightarrow$ $\frac{p^2 (p + m)}{a} - mx = y$

On differentiating both sides w.r.t. x

$$\frac{dy}{dx} = \frac{1}{a}\left[p^2\frac{dp}{dx} + 2(p+m)\,p\frac{dp}{dx}\right] - m$$

$$p = \frac{1}{a}\left[p^2\frac{dp}{dx} + 2p\,(p+m)\,\frac{dp}{dx}\right] - m$$

$$\Rightarrow (p + m) = \frac{p}{\alpha}\frac{dp}{dx}(p + 2p + 2m)$$

$$\Rightarrow (p + m) = \frac{p}{a}\frac{dp}{dx}(3p + 2m)$$

$$\Rightarrow \quad ax = \left[\frac{1}{a}\frac{3p^2}{p+m} + \frac{p}{a}\frac{2m}{p+m}\right] dp$$

$$x = \frac{1}{a}(I_1 + I_2)$$

where $I_1 = \int \frac{3p^2}{p+m}\,dp$

Let $p + m = p$ but $p = u - m$

$$dp = du$$

$$\therefore \quad T_1 = 3\int \frac{(u-m)^2}{u}\,du = 3\int \frac{u^2 + m^2 - 2um}{u}\,du$$

$$= 3\int u\,du - 6m\int du + 3m^2 \int \frac{du}{u}$$

$$= 3\,\frac{u^2}{2} - 6um + 3m^2 \log u$$

and for $I_2 = \int \frac{2pm}{p+m}\,dp = 2m\int \frac{u-m}{u}\,dp$

$$= 2mu - 2m^2 \log u$$

Required total is

$$x = \frac{1}{a}\left[\frac{3u^2}{2} - 4um + m^2 \log u\right] + c$$

$$= \frac{1}{a}\left[\frac{3}{2}(p^2 + m^2 + 2pm) - 4pm - 4m^2 + m^2 \log (p+m)\right] + c$$

$$x = \frac{1}{a}\left[\frac{3}{2}\ p^2 - pm + m^2 \log (p+m)\right] + k$$

where $k = c - \frac{5m^2}{2}$

Hence $y = \frac{1}{a}\left[p^3 - \frac{p^2 m}{2} + m^2 p - m^3 \log (p+m)\right] + c$

$$= \frac{1}{a}\left[p^2\left(p - \frac{m}{2}\right) + m^2 p - m^3 \log (p+m)\right] + c$$

Problem 8 $y = 2px + f(p^2 x)$.

Solution The above function is not exactly clairaut's on differentiating both sides we get

$$\frac{dy}{dx} = 2p + 2x\frac{dp}{dx} + f^1(p^2 x)\left[p^2 + 2px\frac{dp}{dx}\right]$$

$$p = 2p + 2x\frac{dp}{dx} + p^2 f^1(p^2 x) + 2px\, f^1(p^2 x)\ \frac{dp}{dx}$$

$$-p - p^2 f^1(p^2 x) = \frac{dp}{dx}(2x + 2px f^1(p^2 x)$$

$$-p(1 + pf^1(p^2 x)) = 2x \frac{dp}{dx}(1 + pf^1(p^2 x))$$

$$\Rightarrow \quad \frac{dx}{x} + 2\frac{dp}{p} = 0$$

$$\Rightarrow \quad \log x + 2\log p = \log c^2$$

$$\Rightarrow \quad xp^2 = c^2$$

$$\Rightarrow \quad p = \frac{c}{\sqrt{x}}$$

Hence, $\quad y = 2c\sqrt{x} + f(c^2)$

Problem 9 $\quad y = 2px + y^{n-1} p^n$

Solution On differentiating both sides

$$\frac{dy}{dx} = 2p + 2x\frac{dp}{dx} + ny^{n-1} p^{n-1} \frac{dp}{dx} + (n-1) y^{n-2} p^n \frac{dy}{dx}$$

The above eqn. can be written as

$$x = \frac{y}{2p} - \frac{1}{2}(yp)^{n-1}$$

On differentiating both sides w.r.t. y we get

$$\frac{dx}{dy} = \frac{1}{2}\left[-\frac{y}{p^2}\frac{dp}{dy} + \frac{1}{p}\right] - \frac{1}{2}\left[(n-1)(yp^{n-2}\frac{d}{dy}(yp)\right]$$

$$\frac{dx}{dy} = \frac{-1}{2}\frac{y}{p^2}\frac{dp}{dy} + \frac{1}{2p} - \frac{1}{2}(n-1)(yp)^{n-2}\left[y\frac{dp}{dy} + p\right]$$

$$\frac{1}{2p} + \frac{1}{2}(n-1)y^{n-2}p^{n-1} = -\frac{dp}{dy}\left[\frac{y}{2p^2} + \frac{y(n-1)(yp)^{n2}}{2}\right]$$

$$\frac{1 + (n-1)y^{n-2}p^n}{2p} = -y\frac{dp}{dy}\left[\frac{1 + p^n y^{n-2}(n-1)}{2p^2}\right]$$

$$\Rightarrow \quad p + y\frac{dp}{dy} = 0$$

$$\Rightarrow \quad \frac{dy}{y} + \frac{dp}{p} = 0$$

$$\log y + \log p = \log c$$

$$\Rightarrow \quad py = c$$

$$\Rightarrow \quad y = \frac{c}{p} \quad \text{or} \quad p = \frac{c}{y}$$

$$\therefore \quad y = \frac{2c}{y} x + y^{n-1} \frac{c^n}{y^n}$$

$$\Rightarrow \quad y = \frac{2cx + c^n}{y}$$

$$\Rightarrow \quad y^2 = 2cx + c^n$$

Problem 10 Solve the following.

Solution $\qquad e^{3x}(p-1) + p^3 e^{2y} = 0$

Here in this problem,

Putting $\qquad e^x = u \quad$ and $\quad e^y = v$

$$e^x\, dx = du \quad \text{and} \quad e^y\, dy = dv$$

$$\therefore \quad \frac{e^y\, dy}{e^x\, dx} = \frac{dv}{du}$$

$$\Rightarrow \quad \frac{dy}{dx} = \frac{udv}{vdu}$$

$$u^3\left(\frac{u}{v}\frac{dv}{du} - 1\right) + \left(\frac{u}{v}\frac{dv}{du}\right)^3 v^2 = 0$$

$$\frac{u^4}{v}\frac{dv}{du} - u^3 + \frac{u^3}{v^3}\left(\frac{dv}{du}\right)^3 \times v^2 = 0$$

$$\frac{u^4}{v}\frac{dv}{du} + \frac{u^3}{v}\left(\frac{dv}{du}\right)^3 = u^3$$

$$\Rightarrow \quad \frac{u^3}{v}\frac{dv}{du}\left[u + \left(\frac{dv}{du}\right)^2\right] = u^3$$

$$v = u\frac{dv}{du} + \left(\frac{dv}{du}\right)^3$$

This is an eqn. of the clairaut's type hence,

$$\frac{dv}{du} = c.$$

Required solution is

$v = uc + c^3$ putting the values of u and v we have

$$e^y = ce^x + c^3$$

$$e^y = ce^x + c^3$$

Problem 11 Solve completely,

$$y^2(y - px) = x^4 p^2$$

Solution Let $u = \frac{1}{x}$ and $v = \frac{1}{y}$

$$du = -\frac{1}{x^2}\,dx \quad \text{and} \quad dv = -\frac{1}{y^2}\,dy$$

$$\therefore \quad \frac{x^2\,dy}{y^2\,dx} = \frac{du}{du}$$

$$\Rightarrow \quad \frac{dy}{dx} = \frac{u^2\,dv}{v^2\,du}$$

Therefore, $\frac{1}{v^2}\left(\frac{1}{v} - \frac{u^2}{v^2}\,\frac{1}{u}\,\frac{dv}{du}\right) = \frac{1}{u^4}\cdot\frac{u^4}{v^4}\left(\frac{dv}{du}\right)^2$

$$\frac{1}{v^2}\left(\frac{1}{v} - \frac{u}{u^2}\frac{dv}{du}\right) = \frac{1}{v^4}\left(\frac{dv}{du}\right)^2$$

$$\frac{1}{v} = \frac{u}{v^2}\frac{dv}{du} + \frac{1}{v^2}\left(\frac{dv}{du}\right)^2$$

$$\Rightarrow \quad \frac{1}{v} = \frac{1}{v^2}\left[u\,\frac{dv}{du} + \left(\frac{dv}{du}\right)^2\right]$$

$$\Rightarrow \quad v = u\,\frac{dv}{du} + \left(\frac{dv}{du}\right)^2$$

Type of clairaut's equation hence,

$$\frac{dv}{du} = c$$

$$\therefore \quad v = uc + c^2$$

$$\Rightarrow \quad \frac{1}{y} = \frac{1}{x}\,c + c^2$$

$$\Rightarrow \quad x = c^2\,xy + cy$$

LINEAR EQUATION WITH CONSTANT COEFFIGIENTS

Problem 1 $\frac{d^2 y}{dx^2}-3\frac{dy}{dx}+2y=0$

Here $\frac{d^2 y}{dx^3}=D^2 y$

i.e. $(D^2-3D+2)\,y=0.$

The roots of the equation

$D^2-3D+2=0$ arc

2, 1 hence the general solution is

$$y=ae^{2x}+be^{x}$$

Problem 2 $(D^2-D+1)\,y=0$

The roots of the equation

$$D=-\frac{-1\pm\sqrt{1-4}}{2}=-\tfrac{1}{2}\pm\frac{\sqrt{3}i}{2}$$

$$=-\frac{1}{2}\pm\frac{\sqrt{3}i}{2}$$

The general solution is

$$y\,e^{-1/2x}\left(a\cos\frac{\sqrt{3}}{2}x+b\sin\frac{\sqrt{3}}{2}x\right)$$

Problem 3 $9(D^2+12D+4)\,y=0$

$\therefore\quad 9D^2+12D+4=0$

$(3D+2)\,(3D+2)=0$

$\Rightarrow\quad D=-2/3,\ -2/3$

Here the roots are repeating hence the general solution is given as

$$y=(a+bx)\,e^{-2/3x}$$

Problem 4 $(D^2+7D+10)\,y=0$

When $D^2+7D+10=0$

$\Rightarrow D^2+2D+5D+10=0$

$D\,(D+2)+5\,(D+2)=0$

$D=-5,\ -2$

Required general solution is

$$y=ae^{-2x}+be^{-5x}$$

Problem 5 $\frac{d^2 y}{dx^2} + a^2 y = 0$

$$(D^2 + a^2)\, y = 0$$

When $D^3 + a^2 = 0$

$$D = \pm\, ai$$

Required general Solution is

$$y = A \cos ax + B \sin ax.$$

Problem 6 $\frac{d^2 y}{dx^2} + 4\frac{dy}{dx} + 13y = 0$

i.e. $(D^2 + 4D + 13)\, y = 0$

$$D^2 + 4D + 13 = 0$$

$$D = \frac{-4 \pm \sqrt{16-52}}{2} = \frac{-4 \pm 6i}{2}$$

$$D = -2 \pm 3i$$

Required general solution is

$$y = e^{-2x}\,(a \cos 3x + b \sin 3x)$$

Problem 7 $(8D^2 - 6D - 5)\, y = 0$

$$8D^2 - 6D - 5 = 0$$

$$8D^2 + 4D - 10D - 5 = 0$$

$$4D\,(2D + 1) - 5\,(2D + 1) = 0$$

$$D = \frac{5}{4},\ \frac{-1}{2}$$

Required general solution is

$$y = ae^{5/4x} + be^{-(1/2)x}$$

Problem 8 $16\frac{d^2 y}{dx^2} + 24\frac{dy}{dx} + 9y = 0$

$$(16D^2 + 24D + 9)\, y = 0$$

$$(4D + 3)^2\, y = 0$$

i.e. $D = -3/4, -3/4$

Required Solution is $y = (a + bx)e^{-3x/4}$

Problem 9 $\frac{d^4 y}{d^2 4} - y = 0$

$\therefore \quad (D^4 - 1) y = 0$

$(D^2 - 1)(D^2 + 1) = 0$

i.e. $\quad D = +1, -1, i, -i$

Required general solution is

$$y = ae^x + be^{-x} + c \cos x + d \sin x$$

Problem 10 $(D^3 + 3D + 1) y = 0$

i.e. $\quad D = -1, -1, -1$

The root is repeating three times here we have the general solution is

$$y = (a + bx + cx^2) e^{-x}$$

Problem 11 Find the value of y which satisfies the equation

$\frac{d^2 y}{dx^2} + 4 \frac{dy}{dx} - 12y = 0$ given that $y = 0$

and $\quad \frac{dy}{dx} = 1$ when $x = 0$

$$(D^2 + 4D - 12) y = 0$$

$$D^2 + 4D - 12 = 0$$

$$D^2 + 6D - 2D - 12 = 0$$

$$D(D + 6) - 2(D + 6) = 0$$

$$D = 2, -6$$

Required general Solution is

$$y = ae^{2x} + be^{-6x}$$

$$\frac{dy}{dx} = 2ae^{2x} - 6be^{-6x}$$

When $\quad x = 0, \frac{dy}{dx} = 1$

$$1 = 2a - 6b \quad (1)$$

Again when $\quad x = 0 \quad y = 0$

$$0 = a + b \quad (2)$$

Solving equation (1) and (2) we have

$$a-b = 0 \times 2$$

$$2a + 6b = 1$$

$$2a + 2b = 0$$

$$- \quad - \quad -$$

$$-8b = 1 \rightarrow b = -1/8$$

$$\rightarrow \qquad a = +1/8$$

Hence the general Solution is

$$y = +1/8\, e^{2x} - 1/8\, e^{-6x}$$

12. Solve $\dfrac{d^2 y}{dx^2} - 4\dfrac{dy}{dx} + 5y = 0$

$$(D^2 - 4D + 5)\, y = 0$$

$$D^2 - 5D + D + 5 = 0$$

$$(D-5)(D+1) = 0$$

$$D = 5, -1$$

$$y = ae^{5x} + be^{-x}$$

$$\frac{dy}{dx} = 5ae^{5x} - be^{-x}$$

When $\quad x = 0 \;\; \dfrac{dy}{dx} = 2$

i.e. $\quad 2 = 5a - b \qquad (1)$

Again, $\quad y = 1$ when $x = 0$

$$1 = a + b \qquad (2)$$

Solving for equation (1) and (2)

$$5a - b = 2$$

$$a + b = 1$$

$$6a = 3$$

$$\Rightarrow \qquad a = \tfrac{1}{2}$$

$$(D^2 - 4D + 5)\, y = 0$$

i.e. $\quad D = \dfrac{4 \pm \sqrt{16-20}}{2}$

$$= 2 \pm i$$

Required Solution is $y = e^{2x}(a\cos x + b\sin x)$

$$\frac{dy}{dx} = e^{2x}(-a\sin x + b\cos x) + 2(a\cos x + b\sin x)e^{2x}$$

When $x = 0,\ \frac{dy}{dx} = 2$

i.e. $2 = 2a + b$ (1)

When $x = 0,\ y = 0$

$a = 1$ hence, $b = 0$

Therefore, $y = e^{2x}\cos x$

Problem 13 Solve $\frac{d^2x}{dt^2} + \mu x = 0,\ \mu > 0$

Given that $x = a;$ and $\frac{dx}{dt} = 0$

When $t = \frac{\pi}{\sqrt{\mu}}$

$$(D^2 + \mu)x = 0$$

$$\Rightarrow \quad D^2 = -\mu = \mu i^2$$

$$\Rightarrow \quad D = \pm\sqrt{\mu}\, i$$

Required solution is

$$x = A\cos\sqrt{\mu}\, t + A\sin\sqrt{\mu}\, t$$

$$\frac{dx}{dt} = -A\sqrt{\mu}\sin\sqrt{\mu}\, t + B\sqrt{\mu}\cos\sqrt{\mu}\, t$$

When $\frac{dx}{dt} = 0,\ t = \frac{\pi}{\sqrt{\mu}}$

$\Rightarrow \quad 0 = -B\sqrt{\mu} \Rightarrow B = 0$

and when $t = \frac{\pi}{\sqrt{\mu}},\ x = a$

$a = -A$ i.e. $A = -a$

Hence the value of $x = -a\cos\sqrt{\mu t}$

Inverse operators

If X be a function of x then $\frac{1}{D-\alpha}X$ stands for the function such that when $(D-\alpha)$ operates on it the result obtained is the function X.

To evaluate

$$\frac{1}{D-\alpha} X = e^{\alpha x} \int X e^{-\alpha x} dx$$

$\frac{1}{D} X$ means the integral of X

$\frac{1}{(D-\alpha)(D-\beta)} X$ means that when $(D-\alpha)$ is operated $\frac{IX}{(D-\beta)}$ is obtained.

(i) $\frac{1}{D^2} e^{-x} = \frac{1}{D}\left[\frac{e^{-x}}{D}\right] = \frac{1}{D} [\int e^{-x} dx] = \frac{1}{D} - e^{-x}$

$$= - \int e^{-x} dx = e^{-x}$$

(ii) $\frac{1}{(D+1)(D-1)} \cos x = \frac{1}{D+1}\left[\frac{1}{D-1} \cos x\right]$

Here $\frac{1}{D-1} \cos x = e^x \int e^{-x} \cos x dx$

$$= e^x e^{-x} \frac{\cos(x + \tan^{-1} 1)}{\sqrt{2}}$$

$$= \frac{\cos(x + \pi/4)}{\sqrt{2}}$$

Again on this we have to operate $\frac{1}{D+1}$

i.e. $\frac{1}{D+1}\left[\frac{1}{\sqrt{2}} \cos \cdot \left(x + \frac{\pi}{4}\right)\right]$

$$= \frac{1}{\sqrt{2}} e^{-x} \int e^x \cos\left(x + \frac{\pi}{4}\right) dx$$

$$= \frac{\frac{1}{\sqrt{2}} e^{-x}.e^x \cos\left(x + \frac{\pi}{4} - \tan^{-1} 1\right)}{\sqrt{2}}$$

$$= \frac{1}{\sqrt{2}} \times \frac{1}{\sqrt{2}} \cos\left(x + \frac{\pi}{4} - \frac{\pi}{4}\right) = . \frac{1}{2} \cos x$$

(iii) $\frac{1}{D-4} (x + e^x) = \frac{1x}{D-4} + \frac{1}{D-4} e^x$

$$= e^{4x} \int x e^{-4x} dx + e^{4x} \int e^{-4x} e^x dx$$

$$= e^{4x}\left[\frac{-xe^{-4x}}{4} + \frac{1}{4}\int e^{-4x}\,dx\right] - e^{4x}\frac{e^{-3x}}{+3}$$

$$= e^{4x}\left[-\frac{xe^{-4x}}{4} - \frac{e^{-4x}}{16} - \frac{e^{4x}\,e^{-3x}}{3}\right]$$

$$= e^{4x}.e^{-4x}\left[-\frac{1}{4}x - \frac{1}{16} - \frac{e^{-3x}}{3}\right]$$

(iv) $\frac{1}{(D+1)(D-1)}e^{x} = \frac{1}{D+1}\left[\frac{1}{D-1}e^{x}\right]$

$$= \frac{1}{D+1}\left[e^{x}\int e^{-x}e^{x}\,dx\right] = \frac{1}{D+1}[\,xe]^{x}$$

$$= \frac{1}{D-(-1)}(x\,e^{x}) = e^{-x}\int x\,e^{x}\,e^{x}\,dx = e^{-x}\int x\,e^{2x}\,dx$$

$$= e^{-x}\left[\frac{x\,e^{2x}}{2} - \int\frac{e^{2x}}{2}\,dx\right] = e^{-x}\left[\frac{xe^{2x}}{2} - \frac{e^{2x}}{4}\right]$$

$$= \left[\frac{x\,e^{x}}{2} - \frac{e^{x}}{4}\right] = \frac{e^{x}}{4}(2x-1)$$

(v) $\frac{1}{D+2}x^2 = \frac{1}{D-(-2)}x^2 = e^{-2x}\int x^2\,e^{2x}\,dx$

$$= e^{-2x}\left[\frac{x^2\,e^{2x}}{2} - \frac{2}{2}\int x\,e^{2x}\,dx\right]$$

$$= e^{-2x}\left[\frac{x^2\,e^{2x}}{2} - \frac{x\,e^{2x}}{2} + \int\frac{e^{2x}}{2}\,dx\int\right.$$

$$= e^{-2x}\left[\frac{x^2\,e^{2x}}{2} - \frac{x\,e^{2x}}{2} + \frac{e^{2x}}{4}\right] = \left(\frac{x^2}{2} - \frac{x}{2} + \frac{1}{4}\right)$$

(vi) $\frac{1}{(D+3)(D-3)}(\sin 2x + 2e^{3x})$

$$= \frac{\sin 2x}{(D+3)(D-3)} + \frac{2e^{3x}}{(D+3)(D-3)}$$

$$= \frac{1}{D+3}\left[e^{3x}\int e^{-3x}\sin 2x\,dx\right] + \frac{2}{D+3}\left[e^{3x}\int e^{-3x}.e^{3x}.dx\right]$$

$$= \frac{1}{D+3}\left[e^{3x}\,e^{-3x}\frac{\sin(2x+\tan^{-1}2/3)}{\sqrt{13}}\right] + \frac{2}{D+3}[x\,e^{3x}]$$

$$= \frac{1}{D+3}\left[\frac{1}{\sqrt{13}}\sin(2x+\tan^{-1}2/3)\right] + \frac{2}{D+3}x\,[e^{3x}]$$

$$= \frac{1}{\sqrt{13}} e^{-3x} \int e^{3x} \sin\left(2x + \tan^{-1}\frac{2}{3}\right) dx + 2e^{-3x} \int x\, e^{3x} \cdot e^{3x}\, dx$$

$$= \frac{1}{\sqrt{13}} e^{-3x} \frac{e^{3x} \sin(2x + \tan^{-1} 2/3 - \tan^{-1} 2/3)}{\sqrt{13}}$$

$$+ 2e^{-3x} \left[\frac{x\, e^{6x}}{6} - \frac{e^{6x}}{36}\right]$$

$$= \frac{1}{13} \sin 2x + \frac{2}{36} e^{-3x} \cdot e^{6x} (6x - 1)$$

$$= \frac{\sin 2x}{13} + \frac{1}{3} x\, e^{x} + (K)$$

Problem 1 $\frac{9d^2y}{dx^2} - y = e^{-x} \qquad \Rightarrow \qquad (9D^2 - 1)\, y = e^{-x}$

Since the roots of $9D^2 - 1 = 0$ are the complimentary function i.e.

$$D = \pm\, 1/3$$

i.e. $\qquad$ C.F. $= ae^{(1/3)x} + be^{-(1/3)x}$

and $\qquad$ P.I. $= \frac{1}{(3D-1)(3D+1)} e^{-x} = \frac{1}{9} \cdot \frac{1}{(D-1/3)(D+1/3)} e^{-x}$

$$= \frac{1}{9} \cdot \frac{1}{D-1/3} [e^{-(1/3)x} \textstyle\int e^{-x} e^{(1/3)x}\, dx]$$

$$= \frac{1}{9} \cdot \frac{1}{D-1/3} [e^{-(1/3)x} (e^{-(2/3)x}\, dx)]$$

$$= \frac{1}{9} \cdot \frac{1}{D-1/3} [e^{-(1/3)x} \textstyle\int e^{-(2/3)x} dx]$$

$$= \frac{1}{9} \cdot \frac{1}{D-1/3} \left[\frac{-3}{2} e^{-(1/3)x} e^{-(2/3)x}\right]$$

$$= -\frac{1}{6} [e^{(1/3)x} e^{-(1/3)x} e^{-x}\, dx] = \left(-\frac{1}{6}\right) e^{(1/3)x} \textstyle\int e^{-(4/3)x}\, dx]$$

$$= +\frac{1}{6} \times \frac{3}{4} [e^{(1/3)x} e^{-(4/3)x}] = \frac{1}{8} e^{-x}$$

Required general solution is

$$y = ae^{(1/3)x} + be^{-(1/3)x} + (1/8)\, e^{-x}$$

Problem 2 $\frac{d^2y}{dx^2}+\frac{dy}{dx}-2y=2x \qquad \Rightarrow \qquad (D^2+D-2)\,y=2x$

For C.F. $\qquad D^2+D-2=0$

$$D^2+2D-D-2=0$$

$$D\,(D+2)-1\,(D+2)=0$$

$$D=1,\,-2$$

C.F. $\qquad = ae^x+be^{-2x}$

P.I. $\qquad = \frac{1}{(D-1)(D+2)}2x=\frac{2}{D-1}\,(e^{-2x}\int x\,e^{2x}\,dx]$

$$=\frac{2}{D-1}\left[e^{-2x}\left(x\frac{e^{2x}}{2}-\frac{e^{2x}}{4}\right)\right]=\frac{2}{4.(D-1)}\,(2x-1)$$

$$=\frac{1}{2}\,.\,[e^x\int(2x-1)\,e^{-x}\,dx]$$

$$=\frac{1}{2}\,\{e^x\int 2x\,e^{-x}\,dx-\int e^{-x}\,dx\}$$

$$=\frac{1}{2}\left[e^x\left\{\frac{2x\,e^{-x}}{-1}-e^{-x}+e^{-x}\right]=\frac{-2}{2}\,(e^x.e^{-x}\,x]=-x.\right.$$

Complete solution is

$$y=ae^x+be^{-2x}-x.$$

Problem 3 $(D^2-2D+1)\,y=x^2-1$

C.F. $\qquad =(D-1)^2=0 \Rightarrow 1,\,1$ repeated the roots

$\therefore$ C.F. $\qquad =(a+bx)\,e^x$

Then P.I. $=\frac{1}{(D-1)(D-1)}\,(x^2-1)=\frac{1}{(D-1)}\,[e^x\int e^{-x}\,(x^2-1)\,dx]$

$$=\frac{1}{(D-1)}\,[e^x\,\{(1-x^2)\,e^{-x}+2\int x\,e^{-x}\,dx\}]$$

$$=\frac{1}{(D-1)}\,[e^x\,\{(1-x^2)\,e^{-x}+2\,(-x\,e^{-}x-e^{-x})\}]$$

$$=\frac{1}{(D-1)}\,[e^x\,\{(1-x^2)\,e^{-x}+-2e^{-x}\,(x+1)\}]$$

$$=[(1-x^2-2x-2)]=-2x-x^2-1$$

$$=e^x\int e^{-x}\,(-2x-x^2-1)\,dx$$

$$= e^x [e^{-x} (x^2 + 1 + 2x) - \int (2x + 2) e^{-x} dx]$$
$$= e^x [e^{-x} (x^2 + 2x + 1) + (2x + 2) e^{-x} + 2\int -e^{-x} dx]$$
$$= e^x [e^{-x} (x^2 + 2x + 1) + (2x + 2) e^{-x} + 2e^{-x}]$$
$$= (x^2 + 2x + 1 + 2x + 2 + 2) = x^2 + 4x + 5$$

Required integral is

$$y = (a + bx) e^x + (x^2 + 4x + 5)$$

Problem 4 $(6D^2 - D - 2) y = x e^{-x}$

C.F. $= (6D^2 - D - 2) = 0$

$$(6D^2 - 4D + 3D - 2) = 0$$
$$3D (2D + 1) - 2 (2D + 1) = 0$$
$$D = -1/2, 2/3$$

C.F. $= ae^{-1/2x} + be^{2/3x}$

P.I. $= \dfrac{1}{(3D-2)(2D + 1)} x e^{-x}$

$$= \frac{1}{6} \cdot \frac{1}{(D-2/3)(D + 1/2)} x e^{-x}$$
$$= \frac{1}{6} \frac{1}{(D-2/3)} [e^{-1/2x} \int e^{1/2x} x e^{-x} dx]$$
$$= \frac{1}{6} \cdot \frac{1}{(D-2/3)} [e^{-1/2x} \int x e^{-1/2x} dx]$$
$$= \frac{1}{6} \cdot \frac{1}{(D-2/3)} [e^{-1/2x} \{2x e^{-1/2x} - \int -2e^{-(1/2)x}$$

Second method for question 3

P.I. $= \dfrac{1}{(D-1)^2} (x^2 - 1) = \dfrac{1}{(1-D)^2} (x^2 - 1) = (1-D)^{-2} (x^2 - 1)$

$$= (1 + 2D + 3D^2 + \ldots)(x^2 - 1) = x^2 - 1 + 4x + 6$$
$$= (x^2 - 1) + 4x + 6 = x^2 + 4x + 5$$

Required solution is $(a + bx) e^x + (x^2 + 4x + 5)$

$$= \frac{1}{6} \cdot \frac{1}{D-2/3} [e^{-1/2x} \{-2x e^{-1/2x} - 4e^{-1/2x}\}]$$
$$= \frac{1}{6} \cdot \frac{1}{D-2/3} [e^{-x} \{-2x - 4\}] = \frac{-1}{6(D-2/3)} e^{-x} (2x + 4)$$

$$= -\frac{1}{6} e^{2/3x} \int e^{-2/3x} e^{-x} (2x + 4)\, dx$$

$$= \frac{-e^{2/3x}}{6} \left[\oint e^{-5/3x} (2x + 4)\, dx \right]$$

$$= \frac{-e^{2/3x}}{3} \left(\frac{-3}{5} (x + 2)\, e^{-5/3x} - \int \frac{-3}{5} e^{-5/3x}\, dx \right)$$

$$= \frac{-e^{2/3x}}{3} \left(\frac{-3}{5} (x + 2)\, e^{-5/3x} - \frac{3}{5} \times \frac{3}{5} e^{-5/3x} \right)$$

$$= \frac{e^{2/3x}}{3} \cdot e^{-5/3x} \frac{3}{5} \left(x + 2 + \frac{3}{5} \right) = \frac{e^{-x}}{5} \left(x + \frac{13}{5} \right)$$

The solution is then given as

$$y = ae^{-x/2} + be^{2/3x} + \frac{e^{-x}}{5} \left(x + \frac{13}{5} \right).$$

Problem 5 $(D^2 + 4)\, y = \tan 2x$

$$\text{C.F.} = (D^2 + 4) = 0$$

i.e. $\qquad D = \pm\, 2i$

$$\text{C.F.} = a \cos 2x + b \sin 2x$$

While the P.I. $= \dfrac{1}{(D^2 + 4)} \tan 2x = \dfrac{1}{(D - 2i)(D + 2i)} \tan 2x$

$$= \frac{1}{4i} \left(\frac{1}{D - 2i} - \frac{1}{D + 2i} \right) \tan 2x$$

$$= \frac{1}{4i} \left(\frac{1}{D - 2i} \tan 2x - \frac{1}{D + 2i} \tan 2x \right)$$

$$= \frac{1}{4i} \left[e^{2ix} \int e^{-2ix} \tan 2x dx - e^{-2ix} \int e^{2ix} \tan 2x\, dx \right] \qquad \text{(i)}$$

Now $\int e^{-2ix} \tan 2x dx$

$$= \int (\cos 2x - i \sin 2x) \tan 2x\, dx$$

$$= \int \left(\sin 2x - i \sin 2x \frac{\sin 2x}{\cos 2x} \right) dx$$

$$= -\cos 2x - i \int \frac{(1 - \cos^2 2x)}{\cos 2x} dx$$

$$= -\cos 2x - i \int \sec 2x\, dx + i \int \cos 2x\, dx$$

$$= -\frac{\cos 2x}{2} - \frac{i}{2}\log(\sec 2x + \tan 2x) + i\frac{\sin 2x}{2}$$

$$= -\frac{1}{2}(\cos 2x - i\sin 2x) - \frac{i}{2}\log(\sec 2x + \tan 2x)$$

$$= -\frac{1}{2}e^{-2ix} - \frac{i}{2}\log(\sec 2x + \tan 2x)$$

$$= -\frac{1}{2}[e^{-2ix} + i\log(\sec 2x + \tan 2x)]$$

$\therefore \quad e^{2ix}\int e^{-2ix}\tan 2x\,dx = -\frac{1}{2}[1 + ie^{-2ix}\log(\sec 2x + \tan 2x)]$

Similarly $\int e^{2ix}\tan 2x\,dx = \int(\cos 2x + i\sin 2x)\cdot\tan 2x\,dx$

$$= -\frac{\cos 2x}{2} + \frac{i}{2}\log(\sec 2x + \tan 2x) - \frac{i\sin 2x}{2}$$

$$= -\frac{1}{2}[e^{2ix} - i\log(\sec 2x + \tan 2x)$$

$\therefore \quad e^{-2ix}\int e^{2ix}\tan 2x\,dx = -\frac{1}{2}[1 - e^{2ix}\,i\log(\sec 2x + \tan 2x)]$

$\therefore$ The expression (i) reduces to—

$$\frac{1}{4i}[-\tfrac{1}{2}(1 + ie^{-2ix}\log\{\sec 2x + \tan 2x) - 1 + ie^{2ix}\log(\sec 2x + \tan 2x)]$$

$$-\frac{1}{8i}[i\log(\sec 2x + \tan 2x)(\cos 2x - i\sin 2x + \cos 2x + i\sin 2x)$$

$$-\frac{1}{8i}\left(i\log\frac{1 + \cos(\pi/2 - 2x)}{\sin(\pi/2 - 2x)} \times 2\cos 2x\right)$$

$$-\frac{1}{8}\left(\log\frac{2\cos^2(\pi/4 - x)}{\sin\left(\frac{\pi}{4} - x\right)\cos\left(\frac{\pi}{4} - x\right)} \times 2\cos 2x\right)$$

$$-\frac{1}{8}\log\cot(\pi/4 - x)\,2\cos 2x$$

$$\frac{1}{4}\cos 2x\log\frac{1}{\cot(\pi/4 - x)}$$

$$\frac{1}{4}\cos 2x\log\tan(\pi/4 - x)$$

Proceeding

$$\int e^{-2ix} \tan 2x\, dx = \int (\cos 2x - i \sin 2x) \tan 2x\, dx$$

$$= \int \left(\sin 2x - i \frac{\sin^2 2x}{\cos 2x} \right) dx$$

$$= \int \sin 2x\, dx - i \int \frac{(1-\cos^2 2x)}{\cos 2x}\, dx$$

$$= -\frac{\cos 2x}{2} - i\, [\int (\sec 2x - \cos 2x)\, dx]$$

$$= -\frac{\cos 2x}{2} - i\left[\frac{1}{2} \log \tan\left(\frac{\pi}{4} + x\right) - \frac{\sin 2x}{2}\right]$$

$$= -\frac{1}{2} e^{-2ix} - \frac{1}{2} i \log \tan\left(\frac{\pi}{4} + x\right)$$

and similarly for

$$\int e^{2ix} \tan 2x\, dx = \int (\cos 2x + i \sin 2x) \tan 2xd$$

$$= -\frac{\cos 2x}{2} + i\left(\frac{1}{2} \log \tan\left(\frac{\pi}{4} + x\right) - \frac{\sin 2x}{2}\right.$$

$$= -\frac{1}{2}\left(\cos 2x - i \sin 2x\right) + \frac{i}{2} \log \tan\left(\frac{\pi}{4} + x\right)$$

$$= -\frac{1}{2} e^{+2ix} + \frac{i}{2} \log \tan\left(\frac{\pi}{4} + x\right)$$

The exp. (i) is

$$\frac{1}{4i}\left[e^{2ix}\left(-\frac{1}{2}e^{-2ix} - \frac{i}{2} \log \tan\left(\frac{\pi}{4} + x\right)\right)\right]$$

$$-e^{-2ix} - \left[\frac{1}{2}e^{2ix} + \frac{i}{2} \log \tan\left(\frac{\pi}{4} + x\right)\right]$$

$$\frac{1}{4i}\left[-\frac{1}{2} - \frac{i}{2} e^{2ix} \log \tan\left(\frac{\pi}{4} + x\right)\right.$$

$$\left. + \frac{1}{2} - \frac{i}{2} e^{-2ix} \log \tan\left(\frac{\pi}{4} + x\right)\right]$$

$$\frac{1}{4i}\left(-\frac{i}{2} \log [\tan (\pi/4 + x) (\cos 2x + i \sin 2x\right.$$

$$+ \cos 2x - i \sin 2x)]$$

$$-\frac{1}{4i}\left[+\frac{2i}{2} \cos 2x \log \tan\left(\frac{\pi}{4} + x\right)\right]$$

$$-\frac{1}{4} \cos 2x \log \tan\left(\frac{\pi}{4} + x\right)$$

The complete solution is

$$y = a \cos 2x + b \sin 2x - 1/4 \cos 2x \log \tan (\pi/4 + x)$$

6. $\dfrac{d^2y}{ax^2} + a^2y = \sec ax$

$(D^2 + a^2)\, y = \sec^2 ax$

$\therefore \qquad \text{C.F.} = (D^2 + a^2) = 0$

$\Rightarrow \qquad D = \pm\, ai$

$\therefore \qquad \text{C;F.} = A \cos ax + B \sin ax$

and the P.I.

$$= \frac{1}{(D-ai)(D+ai)} \sec ax = \frac{1}{2ai}\left[\frac{1}{D-ai} - \frac{1}{D+ai}\right] \sec ax$$

$$= \frac{1}{2ai} [e^{aix} \int e^{-aix} \sec ax\, dx - e^{-aix} \int e^{aix} \sec ax\, dx]$$

$$= \frac{1}{2ai} [e^{aix} \int (\cos ax - i \sin ax) \sec ax\, dx$$

$$- e^{-aix} \int (\cos ax + i \sin ax) \sec ax\, dx]$$

$$= \frac{1}{2ai} [e^{aix} \int (1 - i \tan ax)\, dx - e^{-aix} \int (1 + i \tan x)\, dx)]$$

$$= \frac{1}{2ai}\left(x\, e^{aix} + \frac{ie^{aix}}{a} \log \cos ax - xe^{-aix} + \frac{ie^{-aix}}{a} \log \cos ax\right]$$

$$= \frac{1}{2ai} (x \cos ax + i \sin ax - \cos ax + i \sin ax)$$

$$+ \frac{i}{a} \log \cos ax\, (\cos ax + i \sin 2ax$$

$$+ \cos ax - i \sin ax]$$

$$= \frac{1}{2ai}\left(2ix \sin ax + \frac{i}{a} \log \cos ax \times 2 \cos ax\right)$$

$$= \frac{x}{a} \sin ax + \frac{1}{a^2} \cos ax \log \cos ax$$

Hence the complete solution is

$$y = A \cos ax + \bar{B} \sin ax + \frac{1}{a}\, x \sin ax + \frac{1}{a^2} \cos ax \log \cos ax$$

Article Differential equation of the form $\frac{1}{f(D)} e^{mx}$

Putting $D = m$ we will be getting the value. But if $(D-m) = 0$ then. The general result is glven in the following manner

i.e. $$\frac{e^{mx}}{(D-m)^r} = \frac{x^r}{r!} e^{-x}$$ [To be Remembered]

Problem 1 $$\frac{6d^2y}{dx^2} + \frac{17dy}{dx} + 12y = e^{-x}$$

I.e. $$(6D^2 + 17D + 12)\, y = e^{-x}$$

For C.F. we have $(6D^2 + 8D + 9D + 12) = 0$

$$2D\,(3D + 4) + 3D\,(3D + 4) = 0$$

$$(2D + 3)\,(3D + 4) = 0$$

i.e. $$D = -\frac{3}{2}, -\frac{4}{3}$$

$$\text{C.F.} = ae^{-3/2x} + he^{-4/3x}$$

And the P.I. $$= \frac{1}{(2D + 3)\,(3D + 4)} e^{-x}$$

here $m = -$ putting is D^r

$$= \frac{1}{(-2 + 3)\,(-3 + 4)} \epsilon^{-x}$$

$$= \frac{1}{1 \times 1} e^{-x} = e^{-x}$$

The complete soln. is

$$y = ae^{-(3/2)x} + be^{-(4/3)x} + e^{-x}$$

Problem 2 $$\frac{d^2y}{dx^2} - \frac{dy}{dx} + y = e^{2x} + e^x$$

$$(D^2 - D + 1)\, y = e^{2x} + e^x$$

For. $CF\,(D^2 - D + 1) = 0$

$$D = \frac{1 \pm \sqrt{1-4}}{2} = \frac{1 \pm \sqrt{3}\, i}{2} = \frac{1}{2} \pm \frac{\sqrt{3}\, i}{2}$$

$$CF = e^{(1/2)x}\left[a \cos \frac{\sqrt{3}}{2} x + b \sin \frac{\sqrt{3}}{2} x\right]$$

And the $$P.I = \frac{e^{2x}}{(D^2-D+1)} + \frac{e^x}{(D^2+1-D)}$$

$$= \frac{e^{2x}}{(4-2+1)} + \frac{e^x}{1+1-1} = \frac{e^{2x}}{3} + e^x$$

Required Solution is $y = e^{1/2x}\left[a\cos\frac{\sqrt{3}}{2}x + b\sin\frac{\sqrt{3}}{2}x\right] + e^x + \frac{e^{2x}}{3}$

Problem 3 $\frac{3d^2y}{dx^2} + 2\frac{dy}{dx} - y = e^{x/2} + 2e^{3x}$

$$3D^2 + 2D - 1 = 0$$

$$3D^2 + 3D - D - 1 = 0$$

$$3D(D+1) - 1(D+1) = 0$$

$\Rightarrow$ $$D = \tfrac{1}{3}, -1$$

$$CF = ae^{-x} + be^{(1/3)x}$$

$$P.I = \frac{e^{x/2}}{(D+1)(3D-1)} + \frac{2e^{3x}}{(D+1)(3D-1)}$$

$$= \frac{e^{x/2}}{(1/2+1)(3/2-1)} + \frac{2e^{3x}}{(3+1)(9-1)}$$

$$= \frac{4}{3}e^{x/2} + \frac{e^{3x}}{16}$$

Required complete solution is

$$y = ae^{-x} + be^{(1/3)x} + \frac{4}{3}e^{x/2} + \frac{e^{3x}}{16}$$

Problem 4 $(D^2-4)y = 3e^{2x} - 4e^{-2x}$

$$CF = ae^{2x} + be^{-2x}$$

$$P.I = \frac{3e^{2x}}{D^2-4} - \frac{4e^{-2x}}{(D^2-4)}$$

$$= \frac{3e^{2x}}{(D-2)(D+2)} - \frac{4e^{-2x}}{(D+2)(D-2)}$$

here Let $$A = \frac{3e^{2x}}{(D-2)(D+2)}$$

and $$B = \frac{4e^{-2x}}{(D+2)(D-2)}$$

In the first one putting $D = 2$ while in second one putting $D = -2$ we get

$$A = \frac{3e^{2x}}{(D-2)(D+2)} = \frac{3}{4}\frac{e^{2x}}{D-2}$$

$$= \frac{3}{4} e^{2x} \int e^{-2x} e^{2x}\, dx = \frac{3}{4} xe^{2x}$$

$$L = \frac{4e^{-2x}}{(D+2)(D-2)} = \frac{4e^{-2x}}{(D+2)(-2-2)}$$

$$= -1 \cdot \frac{e^{-2x}}{D+2} = -1 \cdot e^{-2x} \int e^{2x} e^{-2x}\, dx = -xe^{-2x}$$

Required complete solution is

$$y = ae^{2x} + be^{-2x} + \tfrac{3}{4} xe^{2x} + xe^{-2x}$$

Problem 4 $\frac{d^2 y}{dx^2} - (a+b)\frac{dy}{dx} + a\,by = e^{ax} + e^{bx}$

$$D^2 - (a+b)D + ab = 0$$

$$D^2 - aD - bD + ab = 0$$

$$D(D-a) - b(D-a) = 0$$

$$(D-a)(D-b) = 0$$

$$D = a, b$$

$$CF = Ae^{ax} + Be^{bx}$$

$$PI = \frac{1}{(D-a)(D-b)} e^{ax} + \frac{e^{bx}}{(D-a)(D-b)}$$

$$= \frac{e^{ax}}{(D-a)(a-b)} + \frac{e^{bx}}{(b-a)(D-b)}$$

$$= \frac{1}{(a-b)} e^{ax} \int e^{-ax} e^{ax}\, ax + \frac{1}{(b-a)} e^{bx} \int e^{-bx} e^{bx}\, dx$$

$$= \frac{1}{(a-b)} xe^{ax} + \frac{1}{(b-a)} xe^{bx}$$

Required Solution is

$$y = Ae^{ax} + Be^{bx} + \frac{x}{a-e}(e^{ax} - e^{bx})$$

Problem 5 $\frac{d^2 y}{dx^2} + 2\frac{dy}{dx} + y = e^{x/2} + e^{-x/2}$

$$(D^2 + 2D + 1) = 0$$

i.e. $$(D+1)^2 = 0$$

$$D = -1 \text{ repeated roots}$$

∴ $$\text{CF} = (a+bx)\,e^{-x}$$

$$\text{PI} = \frac{1}{(D+1)^2}\,e^{x/2} + \frac{e^{-x/2}}{(D+1)^2}$$

$$= \frac{e^{x/2}}{(1/2+1)^2} + \frac{e^{-x/2}}{(-1/2+1)^2} = \frac{4}{9}\,e^{x/2} + 4e^{-x/2}$$

The complete solution is

$$y = (a+bx)\,e^{-x} + \frac{4}{9}\,e^{x/2} + 4e^{-x/2}$$

Problem 6 $9 \cdot \dfrac{d^2y}{dx^2} + 12 \cdot \dfrac{dy}{dx} + 4y = e^{-2x/3}$

$$9D^2 + 12D + 4 = 0$$

i.e. $$(3D+2)^2 = 0$$

$$D = -\frac{2}{3},\ -\frac{2}{3} \text{ repeated roots}$$

$$\text{C.F.} = (a+bx)\,e^{-2x/3}$$

$$\text{P.I.} = \frac{1}{(3D+2)}\,e^{-2x/3} = \frac{1}{9}\cdot\frac{1}{(D+2/3)^2}\,e^{-2x/3}$$

$$= \frac{1}{9}\cdot\frac{1}{(D-(-2/3))^2}\,e^{-2x/3} = \frac{1}{9}\cdot\frac{x^2}{2}\,e^{-2x/3} = \frac{x^2}{18}\,e^{-2x/3}$$

Complete solution is

$$y = (a+bx)\,e^{-2x/3} + \frac{x^2}{18}\,e^{-2x/3}$$

Problem 7 $\dfrac{d^3y}{dx^3} - \dfrac{d^2y}{dx^2} - 4\dfrac{dy}{dx} + 4y = e^{2x}$

$$(D^3 - D^2 - 4D + 4) = 0$$

$$(D-1)(D^2-4) = 0$$

$$(D-1)(D-2)(D+2) = 0$$

$$D = 1, 2, -2$$

$$\text{C.F.} = ae^{x} + be^{2x} + ce^{-2x}$$

$$\text{P.I.} = \frac{1}{(D-1)(D+2)(D-2)} e^{2x}$$

$$= \frac{1}{(D-2)(2-1)(2+2)} e^{2x} = \frac{1.1}{4(D-2)} e^{2x}$$

$$= \frac{1}{4} \cdot e^{2x} \int e^{-2x} e^{2x} dx = \frac{xe^{2x}}{6}$$

The complete solution is

$$y = ae^{x} + be^{2x} + ce^{-2x} + \frac{xe^{2x}}{4}$$

Problem 8 $(3D^2 - 4D + 5)\, y = e^{x} - 2e^{2x} + 3e^{3x}$

$$D = \frac{4 \pm \sqrt{16-60}}{6} = \frac{4 \pm 2\sqrt{11}\, i}{6} = \frac{2}{3} \pm \frac{1}{3}\sqrt{11}\, i$$

$$\text{C.F.} = \left(a \cos \frac{\sqrt{11}}{3} x + b \sin \frac{\sqrt{11}}{3} x \right) e^{2/3\, x}$$

$$\text{P.I.} = \frac{e^{x}}{3D^2 - 4D + 3} + \frac{2e^{2x}}{3D^2 - 4D + 5} - \frac{3e^{3x}}{3D^2 - 4D + 5}$$

$$= \frac{e^{x}}{3 - 4 + 5} - \frac{2e^{2x}}{12 - 8 + 5} + \frac{3e^{3x}}{27 - 12 + 5}$$

$$= \frac{e^{x}}{4} - \frac{2e^{2x}}{9} + \frac{3e^{3x}}{20}$$

The complete solution is

$$y = \left(a \cos \frac{\sqrt{11}}{3} x + b \sin \frac{\sqrt{11}}{3} \right) e^{2/3\, x}$$

$$+ \frac{e^{x}}{4} - \frac{2e^{2x}}{9} + \frac{3e^{3x}}{20}$$

Problem 9 $(D-3)^2\, y = 2e^{3x} + e^{-x}$

$(D-3)^2 = 0$

$D = 3, 3$ repeated roots

$\text{C.F.} = e^{3x}(a + bx)$

$$\text{P.I.} = \frac{2e^{3x}}{(D-3)^2} + \frac{e^{-x}}{(D-3)^2} = 2\frac{x^2}{2} e^{3x} + \frac{e^{-x}}{(-1-3)^2}$$

$$= x^2 e^{3x} + \frac{e^{-x}}{16}$$

Required complete solution is

$$y = e^{3x}(a + bx) + x^2 e^{3x} + \frac{e^{-x}}{16}$$

Problem 10 $(D^2-2D+1)\,y = (1+e^{-x})^2$

$$(D^2-2D+1)\,y = 1 + 2e^{-x} + e^{-2x}$$

$$(D-1)^2\,y = 1 + 2e^{-x} + e^{-2x}$$

$$\text{C.F.} = (a+bx)\,e^{x}$$

$$\text{P.I.} = \frac{1}{(D-1)^2} + \frac{2e^{-x}}{(D-1)^2} + \frac{e^{-2x}}{(D-1)^2}$$

$$= \frac{1}{(1-D)^2} + \frac{2e^{-x}}{(-1-1)^2} + \frac{e^{-2x}}{(-2-1)^2}$$

$$= (1-D)^{-2} + \frac{2e^{-x}}{4} + \frac{e^{-2x}}{9}$$

$$= (1+2D+3D^2+\ldots)\,1 + \frac{e^{-x}}{2} + \frac{e^{-2x}}{9}$$

$$= 1 + \frac{e^{-x}}{2} + \frac{e^{-2x}}{9}$$

Required solution is

$$y = (a+bx)\,e^{x} + \frac{e^{-x}}{2} + \frac{e^{-2x}}{9} + 1.$$

Problem 11 Solve

$$(D^2+5D+6)\,y = e^{2x} \text{ given that } y = 0\ \frac{dy}{dx} = 0, \text{ when } x=0$$

$$D^2+5D+6 = 0$$

$$(D+2)(D+3) = 0$$

$$D = -2, -3$$

$$\text{C.F.} = ae^{-2x} + be^{-3x}$$

$$\text{P.I.} = \frac{1}{(D+2)(D+3)}\,e^{2x} = \frac{e^{2x}}{(2+2)(2+3)} = \frac{e^{2x}}{20}$$

$$y = ae^{-2x} + be^{-3x} + \frac{1}{20}\,e^{2x}$$

when $x = 0, \quad y = 0$

$$0 = a + b + 1/20$$

× $a + b = -\,1/20$ (1)

and when $\dfrac{dy}{dx} = 0, \quad x = 0$

i.e. $$\frac{dy}{dx} = -2ae^{-2x} - 3be^{3x} + \frac{1}{10} e^{2x}$$

$$0 = -2a - 3b + 1/10$$

$$\times \qquad 2a + 3b = 1/10 \qquad \text{(ii)}$$

Non solving for (i) and (ii)

$$a + b = -1/20 \; x^2$$

$$2a + 3b = 1/10$$

$$2a + 2b = -1/10$$

$$- \quad - \quad\quad +$$

$$b = 2/10 = 1/5$$

Hence $$a = -1/4$$

Required complete solution is

$$y = -\frac{1}{4} e^{-2x} + \frac{1}{5} e^{-3x} + \frac{1}{20} e^{2x}$$

Problem 12 Solve $(D^2 - 7D + 6)\, y = 2e^{3x}$ given that

$$y = 1, \qquad dy/ax = 0 \qquad \text{when} \qquad x = 0$$

Solution $$(D^2 - 7D + 6)\, y = 2e^{3x}$$

$$(D - 1)(D - 6)\, y = 2e^{3x}$$

$$\text{C.F.} = ae^x + be^{6x}$$

$$P.I. = \frac{1}{(D-1)(D-6)} 2e^{3x} = \frac{2}{(3-1)(3-6)} e^{3x}$$

$$= \frac{2}{-6} e^{3x} = -\frac{e^{3x}}{3}$$

Required solution is,

$$y = ae^x + be^{6x} - \frac{e^{3x}}{3}$$

$$\frac{dy}{dx} = ae^x + 6be^{6x} - e^{3x}$$

when $$x = 0, \qquad dy/dx = 0$$

$$0 = a + 6b - 1 \quad \Rightarrow \quad a + 6b = 1$$

when $$x = 0, \qquad y = 1$$

i.e. $$1 = a + b - \frac{1}{3} \quad \Rightarrow \quad a + b = \frac{4}{3}$$

$\therefore \quad b = -\frac{1}{15} \quad \text{and} \quad a = \frac{7}{5}$

Hence $\quad y = \frac{7}{5} e^x - \frac{1}{15} e^{6x} - \frac{e^{3x}}{3}$

Problem 1 $\frac{d^2y}{dx^2} - 3\frac{dy}{dx} + 2y = \cos 2x$

$$D^2 - 3D + 2 = 0$$

$$(D-1)(D-2) = 0$$

$$D = 1, 2$$

$$\text{C.F.} = ae^x + be^{2x}$$

$$\text{P.I.} = \frac{1}{(D-1)(D-2)} \cos 2x$$

$$= \frac{\cos 2x}{D^2 - 3D + 2} = \frac{\cos 2x}{-4 - 3D + 2}$$

$$= \frac{-(2-3D)\cos 2x}{(2-3D)(2+3D)} = \frac{-(2-3D)\cos 2x}{4 - 9D^2}$$

$$= -\frac{(2-3D)\cos 2x}{4+36} = -\frac{1}{40}(2-3D)\cos 2x$$

$$= -\frac{1}{20}\cos 2x - \frac{3}{20}\sin 2x$$

The complete solution is

$$y = ae^x + be^{2x} - \frac{1}{20}\cos x - \frac{3}{20}\sin 2x$$

Problem 2 $(D^2 + 4D - 3)\, y = 2 \sin 3x$

$$D = \frac{-4 \pm \sqrt{16+12}}{2} = \frac{-4 \pm 2\sqrt{7}}{2} = 2 \pm \sqrt{7}$$

$$\text{C.F.} = a_e\,(-2+\sqrt{7})\,x + be^{(-4-\sqrt{7})\,x}$$

$$\text{P.I.} = \frac{2\sin 3x}{(D^2 + 4D - 3)} = \frac{2\sin 3x}{-9 + 4D - 3} = \frac{2\sin 3x}{4D - 12}$$

$$= \frac{\sin 3x \;(D+3)}{2(D-3)(D+3)} = \frac{1}{2}(D+3)\frac{\sin 3x}{(D^2-9)}$$

$$= \frac{1}{2}(D+3)\frac{\sin 3x}{-9-9} = -\frac{1}{36} \times 3\,[\cos 3x + \sin 3x]$$

$$= -\frac{1}{12}(\text{ccs}\ 3x + \sin 3x)$$

Hence the complete solution is

$$y = ae^{(-2+\sqrt{7})x} + be^{(-2-\sqrt{7})x}$$

$$- \frac{1}{12}(\cos 3x + \sin 3x)$$

3. $\dfrac{d^2 y}{dx^2} + a^2 y = \sin ax$

$$D^2 + a^2 = 0$$

$$D = \pm ai$$

$$\text{C.F.} = a \cos ax + b \sin ax$$

$$\text{P.I.} = \frac{1}{D^2 + a^2} \sin ax$$

Here $(D^2 = -a^2)$ we will replace the D'. become zero hence the other way to solve is

$$\text{P.I.} = \frac{1}{(D-ai)(D+ai)} e^{aix}$$

$$= \frac{1}{2ai} \frac{1}{(D-ai)} e^{aix} = \frac{1}{2ai} \cdot \left[e^{aix} \int e^{-aix} e^{aix} dx \right]$$

$$= \frac{x \cdot e^{aix}}{2ai} = -\frac{i^2}{2ai} x (\cos ax + i \sin ax)$$

$$= -\frac{i}{2a} x (\cos ax + i \sin ax) = -\frac{x \cos ax}{2a}$$

[Because sin ax in the euler's expansion is always an imaginary part While if cos ax will be the question we will be taking the real part]

Hence the complete solution is

$$y = a \cos ax + b \sin ax - \frac{x \cos ax}{2a}$$

4. $\dfrac{d^2 y}{dx^2} + 4y = \cos 3x + \sin 3x$

$$D^2 + 4 = 0$$

$$D = \pm 2i$$

$$\text{C.F.} = a \cos 2x + b \sin 2x$$

$$\text{P.I.} = \frac{\cos 3x}{D^2+4} + \frac{\sin 3x}{D^2+4}$$

$$= \frac{\cos 3x}{-9+4} + \frac{\sin 3x}{-9+4} = -\frac{1}{5}(\cos 3x + \sin 3x)$$

The complete solution is

$$y = a\cos 2x + b\sin 2x - \frac{1}{5}(\cos 3x + \sin 3x)$$

5. $\dfrac{d^2y}{dx^2} + 9y = e^x - \cos 2x$

$$D^2 + 9 = 0 \qquad D = \pm 3i$$

$$\text{C.F.} = a\cos 3x + b\sin 3x$$

$$\text{P.I.} = \frac{e^x}{D^2+9} - \frac{\cos 2x}{D^2+9} = \frac{e^x}{1+9} - \frac{\cos 2x}{-4+9}$$

$$= \frac{e^x}{10} - \frac{\cos 2x}{5} = \frac{1}{10}e^x - \frac{1}{5}\cos 2x$$

Required solution is

$$y = a\cos 3x + b\sin 3x + \frac{e^x}{10} - \frac{\cos 2x}{5}$$

6. $\dfrac{d^2y}{dx^2} - 3\dfrac{dy}{dx} + y = 2\sin 3x$

$$D^2 - 3D + 1 = 0$$

$$D = \frac{3 \pm \sqrt{9-4}}{2} = \frac{3 \pm \sqrt{5}}{2}$$

$$\text{C.F.} = ae^{(3+\sqrt{5})/2\,x} + be^{(3-\sqrt{5})/2x}$$

$$\text{P.I.} = \frac{2\sin 3x}{D^2-3D+1} = \frac{2\sin 3x}{-9-3D+1}$$

$$= \frac{2\sin 3x}{-(3D+8)}\,\frac{(3D-8)}{(3D-8)} = -\frac{2\sin 3x\,(3D-8)}{(9D^2-64)}$$

$$= \frac{-2(3D-8)\sin 3x}{-81-64} = \frac{2}{145}(3D-8)\sin 3x$$

$$= \frac{2}{145}\times 9\cos 3x - \frac{2}{145}\times 8\sin 3x$$

$$= \frac{18}{145}\cos 3x - \frac{16}{145}\sin 3x$$

The complete solution is

$$y = ae^{3+\sqrt{5}/2\,x} + be^{3-\sqrt{5}/2\,x} + \frac{18}{145}\cos 3x - \frac{16}{145}\sin 3x$$

Problem 7 $2\dfrac{d^2y}{dx^2} - 3\dfrac{dy}{dx} + 4y = 3\cos\dfrac{x}{2}$

$$2D^2 - 3D + 4 = 0$$

$$D = \frac{3 \pm \sqrt{9-32}}{4} = \frac{3 \pm \sqrt{2}\,3i}{4}$$

$$\text{C.F.} = e^{3/4\,x}\left(a\cos\frac{\sqrt{23}}{4}x + b\sin\frac{\sqrt{23}}{4}x\right)$$

$$\text{P.I.} = \frac{1}{2D^2 - 3D + 4}\,3\cos\frac{x}{2}$$

$$= \frac{1}{2(-1/4) - 3D + 4}\,3\cos\frac{x}{2}$$

$$= \frac{3\cos x/2}{7/2 - 3D} = \frac{6\cos x/2}{(7-6D)}$$

$$= \frac{6\cos x/2}{(7-6D)} \cdot \frac{7+6D}{7+6D} = \frac{6(7+6D)\cos x/2}{49 - 36D^2}$$

$$= \frac{6\cdot(7+6D)\cos x/2}{49 + 36\times 1/4} = \frac{6(7\cos x/2 - 3\sin x/2)}{58}$$

$$= \frac{3}{29}\left(7\cos\frac{x}{2} - 3\sin\frac{x}{2}\right)$$

The complete solution is

$$y = e^{3/4\,x}\left(a\cos\frac{\sqrt{23}}{4}x + b\sin\frac{\sqrt{23}}{4}x\right) + \frac{3}{29}\left(7\cos\frac{x}{2} - 3\sin\frac{x}{2}\right)$$

Problem 8. $(D^2 - 8D + 9)\,y = 40\sin 5x$

$$D^2 - 8D + 9 = 0$$

$$D = \frac{8 \pm \sqrt{64-36}}{2} = \frac{8 \pm 2\sqrt{7}}{2} = 4 \pm \sqrt{7}$$

$$\text{C.F.} = ae^{(4+\sqrt{7})x} + be^{(4-\sqrt{7})x}$$

$$\text{P.I.} = \frac{40\sin 5x}{D^2 - 8D + 9} = \frac{40\sin 5x}{-25 - 8D + 9}$$

$$= \frac{40\sin 5x}{-16 - 8D} = \frac{40\sin 5x}{-8(2+D)} = \frac{-5\sin 5x}{(D+2)} \cdot \frac{(D-2)}{(D-2)}$$

$$= \frac{-5\,(D-2)\sin 5x}{D^3-4} = \frac{-5\,(D-2)\sin 5x}{-25-4}$$

$$= \frac{5}{29}\,(5\cos 5x - 2\sin 5x)$$

The complete solution is

$$y = a_e{}^{(4+\sqrt{7})\,x} + be^{(4-\sqrt{7})\,x} + \frac{5}{29}(5\cos 2x - 2\sin 5x)$$

$$(4D^2 + 16D - 9)y = 4e^{x/2} + \sin 1/4\,x.$$

$$4D^2 + 16D - 9 = 0$$

$$4D^3 + 18D - 2D - 9 = 0$$

$$2D\,(2D-1) + 9\,(2D-1) = 0$$

$$D = \frac{1}{2}, -\frac{9}{2}$$

$$\text{CF} = ae^{1/2x} + be^{-9/2x}$$

$$\text{PI} = \frac{1}{4D^2 + 16D - 9}\left[4e^{x/2} + 3\sin\frac{1}{4}\,x\right]$$

$$= \frac{4e^{x/2}}{(2D-1)\,(2D+9)}$$

$$= \frac{4e^{x/2}}{(2D-1)\,10} = \frac{2}{52}\,\frac{e^{x/2}}{(D-1/2)}$$

$$= \frac{1}{5}\,.\,e^{+1/2\,x}\int e^{-x/2}\,.\,e^{x/2}\,dx = \frac{xe^{x/2}}{2}$$

and second part $\dfrac{3\sin x/4}{4D^2 + 16D - 9}$

$$= \frac{3\sin x/4}{-4\,.\,1/16 + 16D - 9} = \frac{3\sin x/4}{(16D - 37/4)}$$

$$= \frac{3\,(16D + 37/4)\sin x/4}{256D^2 - 1369/16}$$

$$= \frac{3\,(16D + 37/4)\sin x/4}{-256\times 1/16 - 1369/16}$$

$$= \frac{-3\times 16\,[16/4\cos x/4 + 37/4\sin x/4]}{1625}$$

$$= -\frac{48}{1625}\left[4\cos\frac{x}{4} + \frac{37}{4}\sin\frac{x}{4}\right]$$

Required Solution is

$$y = ae^{x/2} + be^{-9/2\ x} + \frac{1}{5}\ x\ e^{x/2}$$

$$- \frac{48}{1625}\left[4\cos\frac{x}{4} + \frac{37}{4}\ \sin\ \frac{x}{4}\right)$$

Problem 10 $\dfrac{d^2y}{dx^2} - 4y = \cos^2 x$

$$D^2 - 4 = 0$$

$$D = \pm 2$$

$$CF = ae^{2x} + be^{-2x}$$

$$PI = \frac{1}{D^2-4}\cos^2 x = \frac{1+\cos 2x}{2\,(D^2-4)}$$

$$= \frac{1}{2}\left[\frac{1}{D^2-4}\right] + \frac{1}{2}\ \frac{\cos 2x}{(D^2-4)}$$

$$= \frac{1}{2}\left[\frac{1}{D-1}\ e^{-2x}\int e^{2x}\ dx\right] + B$$

$$= \frac{1}{2}\left[\frac{1}{D-2}\ \frac{e^{-2x}\ e^{2x}}{2}\right] + B = \frac{1}{4}\left[e^{2x}\int e^{-2x}\ dx\right] + B$$

$$= -\frac{1}{8}\ e^{2x}\ e^{-2x} + B = -\frac{1}{8} + B$$

$$B = \frac{1}{2}\cdot\frac{\cos 2x}{D^2-4} = \frac{1}{2}\ \frac{\cos 2x}{(-4-4)} = \frac{1}{2}\cdot\frac{\cos 2x}{-8}$$

∴ The required complete solution is

$$y = ae^{2x} + be^{-2x} - \frac{1}{8}\left(1 + \frac{1}{2}\ \cos 2x\right)$$

Problem 11 $(D^2 + D + 1) = (1 + \sin x)^2$

$$(D^2 + D + 1) = 1 + \sin^2 x + 2\sin x$$

$$(D^2 + D + 1)\,y = 1 + \frac{1 - \cos 2x}{2} + 2\sin x$$

$$(D^2 + D + 1)\,y = \frac{3}{2} - \frac{\cos 2x}{2} + 2\sin x$$

$$D^2 + D + 1 = 0$$

$$D = \frac{-1 \pm \sqrt{1-4}}{2} = \frac{-1 \pm \sqrt{3}\,i}{2}$$

$$CF = e^{-1/2}\,[a \cos \sqrt{3}x + b \sin \sqrt{3}x]$$

$$\text{P.I.} = \frac{3}{2} \cdot \frac{1}{(D^2 + D + 1)} - \frac{1}{2} \cdot \frac{\cos 2x}{(D^2 + D + 1)} + \frac{2 \sin x}{(D^2 + D + 1)}$$

$$= \frac{3}{2} \cdot (1 + D + D^2)^{-1} - \frac{1}{2}\ \frac{\cos 2x}{-4+D+1} + \frac{2 \sin x}{-1+D+1}$$

$$= \frac{3}{2} \cdot [1-(D + D^2) + \ldots] \cdot 1 - \frac{1}{2}\,\frac{\cos 2x}{(D-3)} + \frac{2 \sin x}{D}$$

$$= \frac{3}{2} - \frac{1}{2}\,\frac{\cos 2x\,(D + 3)}{(D-3)\,(D+3)} + 2\,(-\cos x)$$

$$= \frac{3}{2} - \frac{1}{2}\,\frac{(D + 3)\,(\cos x)}{-4-9} - 2 \cos x$$

$$= \frac{3}{2} - \frac{1}{-26}\,[-2 \sin 2x + 3 \cos 2x] - 2 \cos x$$

$$= \frac{3}{2} + \frac{1}{26}\,[3 \cos 2x - 2 \sin 2x] - 2 \cos x$$

The complete solution is

$$y = e^{-x/2}\left(a \cos \frac{\sqrt{3}}{2} x + b \sin \frac{\sqrt{3}}{2} x\right) + \frac{3}{2}$$

$$+ \frac{1}{26}\,(3 \cos 2x - 2 \sin 2x) - 2 \cos x$$

Prooblem 12 $D^4 - 2D^2 + 1)\, y = \cos x$

Solution $(D-1)^2\,(D + 1)^2\, y = \cos x$

$$D = -1,\ -1,\ 1,\ 1 \text{ repeated root } x$$

$$C.F. = (a + bx)\, e^{-x} + (c + dx)\, e^{x}$$

$$P.I. = \frac{1}{(D-1)^2\,(D+ 2)^2} \cos x = \frac{\cos x}{D^4 - 2D^2 + 1}$$

replacing $D^2 = -1$ i.e. $D^4 = (-1)^2 = 1$

$$= \frac{\cos x}{1 + 2 + 1} = \frac{\cos x}{4}$$

Required Complete Equation is

$$y = (a + bx)\, e^{-x} + (c + dx)\, e^{x} + \frac{1}{4} \cos x.$$

Problem 13 $(D^3 + D^2 + D + 1)\, y = \sin 2x$

$$D^2 (D + 1) + 1 (D + 1) = 0$$

$$(D^2 + 1)(D + 1) = 0$$

$$D = \pm 2, -1.$$

$$\text{CF} = ae^{-x} + b (\cos x + c \sin x)$$

$$\text{P.I.} = \frac{\sin 2x}{D^3 + D^2 + D + 1} = \frac{\sin 2x}{D^2 \cdot D + D^2 + D + 1}$$

$$= \frac{\sin 2x}{-4D + (-4) + D + 1} = \frac{\sin 2x}{-3-3D} = \frac{\sin 2x}{-3\ (1+D)}$$

$$= -\frac{(1-D) \sin 2x}{3 \cdot (1-D^2)} = -\frac{(1-D) \sin 2x}{3 \cdot 5}$$

$$= -\frac{1}{15} (\sin 2x - 2 \cos 2x)$$

$$= \frac{1}{15} (2 \cos 2x - \sin 2x)$$

Repuired complete solution is

$$y = ae^{-x} + b \cos x + c \sin x + \frac{1}{15} (2 \cos 2x - \sin 2x)$$

14. Solve $\frac{d^2y}{dx^2} + 2\frac{dy}{dx} + 10y + 37 \sin 3x = 0$ and find the value of y when $x = \frac{x}{2}$ if it is given that $y = 3$, $\frac{dy}{dx} = 0$ when $x = 0$

Solution $\frac{d^2y}{dx^2} + 2\frac{dy}{dx} + 10y = -37 \sin 3x$

$$(D^2 + 2D + 10)\, y = -37 \sin 3x$$

$$D = \frac{-2 \pm \sqrt{4-40}}{2} = \frac{-2 \pm 6i}{2}$$

$$= -1 \pm 3i$$

$$\text{C.F.} = e^{x} (a \cos 3x + b \sin 3x)$$

$$P.I. = \frac{-37 \sin 3x}{D^2 + 2D + 10} = \frac{-37 \sin 3x}{-9 + 2D + 10}$$

$$= \frac{-37 \sin 3x}{(1 + 2D)} = \frac{-37 (1-2D) \sin 3x}{1-4D^2}$$

$$= \frac{-37 [\sin 3x - 6 \cos 3x]}{37} = 6 \cos 3x - \sin 3x$$

$$y = e^{-x}(a \cos 3x + b \sin 3x) + 6 \cos 3x - \sin 3x$$

when $y = 3, \quad x = 0$

$$3 = a + 6 \quad \Rightarrow \quad a = -3$$

$$\frac{dy}{dx} = e^{-x}(-3a \sin 3x + 3b \cos 3x)$$

$$-(a \cos 3x + b \sin 3x)\, e^{-x} - 18 \sin 3x - 3 \cos 3x$$

$$\frac{dy}{dx} = 0, \quad \text{when} \quad x = 0,$$

i.e.
$$0 = 3b - a - 3$$

$$3 = 3b - a \qquad (2)$$

$$\Rightarrow \quad 3 = 3b + b \quad \Rightarrow \quad b = 0$$

Hence, $y = -3e^{-x} \cdot \cos 3x + 6 \cos 3x - \sin 3x$

When $x = \frac{\pi}{2}; \quad y = 1$

Problem 1 $\frac{d^2y}{dx^2} + 2\frac{dy}{dx} + y = 2x + x^2$

$$(D^2 + 2D + 1)\, y = 0$$

$$\Rightarrow \quad (D + 1)^2 = 0$$

$$\times \quad D = -1, -1 \text{ (repeated roots)}$$

$$\text{C.F.} = (a + bx)\, e^{-x}$$

$$\text{P.I.} = \frac{2x}{(1 + D^2)} + \frac{x^2}{(1 + D)^2}$$

$$= 2(1 + D)^{-2} x + x^2 (1 + D)^{-2}$$

$$= 2[1 - 2D + 3D^2]\, x + x^2 [1 - 2D + 3D^2 + . .]$$

$$= 2[x - 2] + x^2 - 4x + 6$$

$$= 2x - 4 + x^2 - 4x + 6$$

$$= x^2 - 2x + 2.$$

Required complete solution is

$$y = (a + bx)\, e^{-x} + x^2 - 2x + 2.$$

Problem 2 $\left(\frac{d^3y}{dx^3} - \frac{d^2y}{dx^2} - \frac{6dy}{dx}\right) = 1 + x^2$

Solution $D^3 - D^2 - 6D = 1 + x^2$

$\Rightarrow \quad D(D^2 - D - 6) = 0$

$$D(D-3)(D+2)=0$$

i.e. $$D = 0, 3, -2$$

$$\text{C.F.} = a + bc^{3x} + ce^{-2x}$$

$$\text{P.I.} = \frac{1}{D^3-D^2-6D}\,x^2 + \frac{1}{D^3-D^2-6D}$$

$$= \frac{x^2}{D(D^2-D-6)} + \frac{1}{D(D^2-D-6)}$$

$$= -\frac{1}{6}\,\frac{x^2}{D\left(1+\left(\frac{D^2-D}{-6}\right)\right)} - \frac{1}{6}\,\frac{1}{D}\left(1+\frac{(D^2-D)}{-6}\right)^{-1}$$

$$= -\frac{1}{6}\,\frac{1}{D}\left(1-\left(\frac{D^2-D}{-6}\right)+\ldots\right)x^2$$

$$-\frac{1}{6}\,\frac{1}{D}\left(1-\frac{(D^2-D)}{-6}\right)\Bigg)$$

$$= -\frac{1}{6}\,\frac{1}{D}\left(1+\frac{D^2-D}{6}+\frac{D^2}{36}+\ldots\right)x^2$$

$$-\frac{1}{6}\,\frac{1}{D}\left(1+\frac{D^2-D}{6}+\ldots\right)$$

$$= -\frac{1}{6}\,\frac{1}{D}\;x^2+\frac{1}{6}\times(2-2x)+\frac{1}{36}\;x^2\Big)$$

$$-\frac{1}{6}\,\frac{1}{D}\,[1+\ldots]$$

$$= -\frac{1}{6}\,\frac{1}{D}\left(x^2+\frac{1}{3}+\frac{1}{18}-\frac{x}{3}+1\right)$$

$$= -\frac{1}{6}\,\frac{1}{D}\left(x^2-\frac{x}{3}+\frac{6+1+18}{18}\right)$$

$$= -\frac{1}{6}\,\frac{1}{D}\left(x^2-\frac{x}{3}+\frac{25}{18}\right)$$

$$= -\frac{1}{6}\left(\frac{x^3}{3}-\frac{x^2}{6}+\frac{25}{18}\,x\right)$$

$$= -\frac{1}{6}\left(\frac{25}{18}\,x-\frac{x^2}{6}+\frac{x^3}{3}\right)$$

Complete solution is

$$y = a + be^{3x} + ce^{-2x} - \frac{1}{6}\left(\frac{25}{18}\,x-\frac{x^2}{6}+\frac{x^3}{3}\right)$$

Problem 3 $\dfrac{d^2y}{dx^2} - 4y = x^2$

Solution $D^2 - 4 = 0$

$$(D-2)(D+2) = 0$$

$$D = 2, \; -2$$

$$\text{C.F.} = ae^{2x} + be^{-2x}$$

$$\text{PI} = \frac{1}{4} \frac{1}{[D^2/4 - 1]} x^2 = -1/4\,(1 - D^2/4)^{-1}\, x^2$$

$$= -\frac{1}{4}[1 + D^2/4 \ldots]\, x^2$$

$$= -\frac{1}{4}\left(x^2 + \frac{1}{4} \times 2\right) = -\frac{1}{4}\;\left[x^2 + \frac{1}{2}\right)$$

The complete solution is

$$y = ae^{2x} + be^{-2x} - 1/4\,(x^2 + 1/2)$$

Problem 4 $(D^4 + D^3 + D^2 - D - 2) = x^2$

$$(D^2 - 1)(D^2 + D + 2) = 0$$

$$D = \pm 1, \; D = \frac{-1 + \sqrt{1-8}}{2} = -\frac{1}{2} \pm \sqrt{\frac{7}{2}}\, i$$

$$\text{C.F.} = ae^{x} + be^{-x} + e^{-1/2x}\left(c \cos \sqrt{\frac{7}{2}}\; x + d \sin \sqrt{\frac{7}{2}}\; x\right)$$

$$\text{P.I.} = \frac{1}{(D^4 + D^3 + D^2 - D - 2)}\, x^2$$

$$= \frac{1}{2} \cdot \frac{1}{\left(\dfrac{D^4 + D^3 + D^2 - D}{2} - 1\right)}\, x^2$$

$$= \frac{-1}{2} \frac{x^2}{\left(1 - \dfrac{D^4 + D^3 + D^2 - D}{2}\right)}$$

$$= -\frac{1}{2}\left(1 - \frac{(D^4 + D^3 + D^2 - D)}{2}\right)^{-1} x^2$$

$$= -\frac{1}{2} x^2 \left[1 + \frac{D^4 + D^3 + D^2 - D}{2} + \left(\frac{D^4 + D^3 + D^2 - D}{2}\right)^2 + \ldots\right]$$

$$= -\frac{1}{2}x^2\left[1 + \frac{D^4 + D^3 + D^2 - D}{2} + \frac{1}{4}D^2 + \ldots\right.$$

(rejecting other terms containing D^3, D^4, D^5 . . .)

$$= -\frac{1}{2}\left[x^2 + 1 - x + \frac{1}{4}x^2\right]$$

$$= -\frac{1}{2}\left(x^2 - x + \frac{3}{2}\right)$$

Hence the complete solution is

$$y = ae^x + be^{-x} + e^{-1/2x}\,(c\cos\sqrt{7/2}\,x + d\sin\sqrt{7/2}\,x) - 1/2\,(x^2 - x + 3/2)$$

Article Differential equation of the form

$f(D)\,y = e^{ax}\,V$ where V is the function of x

Problem 1 $(D^2 + 3D + 2)\,y = e^{2x}\sin x$

Solution $D^2 + 3D + 2 = 0$

$$(D + 1)(D + 2) = 3$$

$$D = -1, -2$$

$$\text{C.F.} = ae^{-x} + be^{-2x}$$

$$\text{P.I.} = \frac{1}{D^2 + 3D + 2}\,e^{2x}\sin x$$

$$= e^{2x}\frac{\sin x}{(D + 2)^2 + 3\,(D + 2) + 2}$$

$$= c^x\frac{\sin x}{D^2 + 4 + 4D + 3D + 6 + 2}$$

$$= e^{2x}\frac{\sin x}{D^2 + 7D + 12} = e^{2x}\frac{\sin x}{-1 + 7D + 12}$$

$$= e^{2x}\frac{\sin x}{7D + 11} = e^{2x}\frac{(7D - 11)\sin x}{49D^2 - 121}$$

$$= e^{2x}\frac{\sin x\,(7D - 11)}{-42 - 121} = \frac{e^{2x}\sin x\,(7D - 11)}{-170}$$

$$= \frac{e^{2x}\,(7\cos x - 11\sin x)}{-170} = \frac{e^{2x}\,(11\sin x - 7\cos x)}{170}$$

complete solution is therefore

$$y = ae^{-2x} + be^{-2x} + \frac{1}{170}e^{-2x}\,(11\sin x - 7\cos x)$$

roblem 2 $\frac{d^2y}{dx^2} + 2y = x^2 c^{3x} + e^x \cos 2x$

olution $D^2 + 2 = 0$

$$D = \pm\sqrt{2i}$$

$$\text{C.F.} = a \cos \sqrt{2x} + b \sin \sqrt{2x}$$

$$\text{P.I.} = \frac{x^2 e^{3x}}{D^2 + 2} + \frac{e^x \cos 2x}{D^2 + 2}$$

$$= e^{3x} \frac{x^2}{(D + 3)^2 + 2} + e^x \frac{\cos 2x}{(D + 1)^2 + 2}$$

$$= e^{3x} \frac{x^2}{D^2 + 9 + 6D + 2} + e^x \frac{\cos 2x}{D^2 + 1 + 2D + 2}$$

$$= \frac{e^{3x}}{11} \frac{x^2}{\left(1 + \frac{D^2 + 6D}{11}\right)} + e^x \frac{\cos 2x}{-4 + 2D + 3}$$

$$= \frac{e^{3x}}{11}\left[1 - \frac{D^2 + 6D}{11} + \frac{36D^2}{121} + \ldots\right] x^2$$

$$+ e^x \frac{\cos 2x}{(2D-1)} \times \frac{2D + 1}{2D + 1}$$

$$= \frac{e^{3x}}{11}\left(x^2 - \frac{2}{11} - \frac{6}{11} \times 2x + \frac{36}{121} \times 2\right)$$

$$+ e^x \frac{(2D + 1) \cos 2x}{4D^2 - 1}$$

$$= \frac{e^{3x}}{11}\left[x^2 - \frac{12}{11} x + \frac{50}{121}\right] + \frac{e^x (-4 \sin 2x + \cos x)}{-16-1}$$

$$= \frac{e^{3x}}{11}\left(x^2 - \frac{12}{11} x + \frac{50}{121}\right) - \frac{1}{17} e^x (\cos 2x - 4 \sin 2x)$$

Hence the complete solution is therefore

$$y = a \cos \sqrt{2}\, x + b \sin \sqrt{2}\, x$$

$$+ \frac{e^{3x}}{11}\left(x^2 - \frac{12}{11} x + \frac{50}{121}\right) - \frac{1}{17} e^x\left(\cos 2x - 4 \sin 2x\right)$$

Problem 3 $(D^3 - D^2 + 3D + 5) = e^x \cos 2x$

Solution $D^3 - D^2 + 3D + 5 = 0$

$$(D + 1)(D^2 - 2D + 5) = 0$$

$$D = -1, D = \frac{2 \pm \sqrt{4 - 20}}{2} = 1 \pm 2i$$

$$\text{C.F.} = ae^{-x} + (b \cos 2x + c \sin 2x) e^x$$

$$\text{P.I.} = \frac{e^x \cos 2x}{(D + 1)(D^2 - 2D + 5)}$$

$$= \frac{e^x \cos 2x}{(D + 1)^3 - (D + 1)^2 + 3(D + 1) + 5}$$

$$= \frac{e^x \cos 2x}{D^3 + 4D + 2D^2 + 8}$$

$$= e^x \frac{\cos 2x}{D^3 + 4D + 2D^2 + 8}$$

Since the D^r. is coming out to be zero

Hence we have $\frac{1}{D^3 + 2D^2 + 4D + 8} e^{2ix}$

$$= \frac{e^{2ix}}{(D + 2)(D + 2i)(D - 2i)}$$

$$= \frac{1}{4i} \frac{1}{(D + 2)} \frac{1}{(D - 2i)} e^{2ix}$$

$$= \frac{1}{4i} \frac{1}{(D + 2)} e^{2ix} \int e^{-2ix} e^{2ix} dx$$

$$= \frac{1}{4i} \frac{1}{(D + 2)} xe^{2ix} \qquad \text{putting } D = 2i$$

$$= \frac{1}{4i} \frac{1}{2(1 + i)} x [\cos 2x + i \sin 2x]$$

$$= -\frac{1}{8} \frac{i(1 - i)}{(1 - i^2)} x [\cos 2x + i \sin 2x]$$

$$= -\frac{1}{16} (i + 1) x [\cos 2x + i \sin 2x]$$

$$= +\frac{x}{16} \sin 2x - \frac{1}{16} x \cos 2x$$

$$= -\frac{1}{16} x (\cos 2x - \sin 2x)$$

Required complete solution is

$$y = ae^{-x} + (b \cos 2x + c \sin 2x)\, e^{x} - \frac{1}{16} x \,(\cos 2x - \sin 2x)$$

Problem 4 $(D^3 - 7D - 6)\, y = e^{2x}(1 + x)$

Solution $D^3 - 7D - 6 = 0$

$$(D + 1)(D^2 - D - 6) = 0$$

$$(D + 1)(D - 3)(D + 2) = 0$$

$$D = -1, -2, 3$$

$$\text{C.F.} = ae^{-x} + be^{-2x} + ce^{3x}$$

$$\text{P.I.} = \frac{e^{2x}}{D^3 - 7D - 6} + \frac{xe^{2x}}{(D^3 - 7D - 6)}$$

$$= \frac{e^{2x}}{(2)^3 - 7 \times 2 - 6} + \frac{x\, e^{2x}}{(D + 2)^3 - 7(D + 2) - 6}$$

$$= \frac{e^{2x}}{-12} + \frac{xe^{2x}}{D^3 + 6D^2 + 5D - 12}$$

$$= \frac{e^{2x}}{-12} + \frac{e^{2x}}{12} \frac{x}{\left[\dfrac{D^3 + 6D^2 + 5D}{12} - 1\right]}$$

$$= \frac{e^{2x}}{-12} - \frac{e^{2x}}{12}\left[1 - \frac{(D^3 + 3D^2 + 5D)}{12}\right]^{-1} x$$

$$= \frac{e^{2x}}{-12} - \frac{e^{2x}}{12}\, x \left[1 + \frac{D^3 + 3D^2 + 5D}{12} + \ldots\right]$$

$$= \frac{e^{2x}}{-12} - \frac{e^{2x}}{12}\left[x + \frac{5}{12}\right] = \frac{-e^{2x}}{12}\left(1 + x + \frac{5}{12}\right)$$

$$= -\frac{1}{12}\left(\frac{17}{12} + x\right) e^{2x}$$

The complete solution is

$$y = ae^{-x} + be^{-2}x + ce^{3x} - \frac{1}{12}\left(\frac{17}{12} + x\right)e^{2x}$$

Art. Type $\dfrac{1}{f(D)}\, xV = \left[x - \dfrac{1}{f(D)} f'(D)\right]\dfrac{1}{f(D)}\, V$

where V = function of x.

Problem 1 $(D^2 + 2D + 1)\, y = x \sin x$

$$D^2 + 2D + 1 = 0$$

$$D = -1, -1 \text{ repeated roots}$$

Solution $\quad$ C.F. $= (a + bx)\, e^{-x}$

$$\text{P.I.} = \frac{1}{(D+1)^2}\, x \sin x$$

$$= \left[x - \frac{1}{(D+1)^2} \times 2\,(D+1)\right] \frac{1}{(D+1)^2}$$

$$= \left[x - \frac{2}{D+1}\right] \frac{\sin x}{-1 + 2D + 1}$$

$$= \left[x - \frac{2}{D+1}\right] \frac{1}{2}\, (-\cos x)$$

$$= -\frac{1}{2}\, x \cos x + \frac{1}{D+1} \cos x$$

$$= -\frac{1}{2}\, x \cos x + e^{-x} \int e^{x} \cos x\, dx$$

$$= -\frac{1}{2} x \cos x + e^{-x} \left[e^{x} \cos x + \int \sin x\, e^{x}\, dx\right]$$

$$= -\frac{1}{2}\, x \cos x + e^{-x} \left[\frac{e^{x} \cos x + \sin x\, e^{x}}{2}\right]$$

$$= -\frac{1}{2}\, x \cos x + \frac{1}{2} \cos x + \frac{1}{2} \sin x$$

$$= \frac{1}{2}\, (1 - x) \cos x + \frac{1}{2} \sin x$$

$$\therefore \quad y = (a + bx)\, e^{-x} + \frac{1}{2} (1 - x) \cos x + \frac{1}{2} \sin x$$

Solution $\quad (D^2 + 1)\, y = x^2 \sin 2x$

$$D^2 = -1$$

$$\Rightarrow \quad D = \pm i$$

$$\text{C.F.} = a \cos x + b \sin x$$

$$\text{P.I.} = \frac{1}{(D^2 + 1)}\, x^2 \sin 2x$$

In this problem we will in stead of sin $2x$ use e^{2ix} and lastly consider the imaginary part]

$$= \frac{1}{D^2+1} x^2 e^{2ix}$$

$$= \frac{x^2 e^{2ix}}{(D+2i)^2+1} = \frac{x^2 e^{2ix}}{D^2+4iD-3}$$

$$= e^{2ix} \frac{x^2}{\left(\frac{D^2+4Di}{3}-1\right)} = \frac{-e^{2ix}}{3} \frac{x^2}{\left(1-\frac{D^2+4Di}{3}\right)}$$

$$= \frac{-e^{2ix}}{3}\left[1-\frac{D^2+4Di}{3}\right]^{-1} x^2$$

$$= -\frac{e^{2ix}}{3}\left[1+\frac{D^2+4Di}{3}+\left(\frac{D^2+4Di}{3}\right)^2+\ldots\right] x^2$$

$$= \frac{-e^{2ix}}{3}\left[1+\frac{D^2}{3}+\frac{4}{3} i D-\frac{16}{9} D^2+\ldots\right] x^2$$

$$= \frac{-e^{2ix}}{3}\left(x^2+\frac{1}{3} \times 2+\frac{4}{3} i \times 2x-\frac{16}{9}\cdot 2\right)$$

$$= \frac{-e^{2ix}}{3}\left\{x^2+\frac{2}{3}+\frac{8xi}{3}-\frac{32}{9}\right\}$$

$$= \frac{-e^{2ix}}{3}\left\{x^2+\frac{8}{3} ix-\frac{26}{9}\right\}$$

$$= \frac{-1}{3}(\cos 2x+i \sin 2x)\left\{x^2+\frac{8}{3} ix-\frac{26}{9}\right\}$$

Hence the imaginary part x are

$$= -\frac{8}{9} x \cos 2x-\frac{x^2}{3} \sin 2x+\frac{26}{9\times 3} \sin 2x$$

Hence the complete solution is

$$y = a \cos x+b \sin x-\frac{1}{3}\left\{x^2-\frac{26}{9}\right\} \sin 2x$$
$$-\frac{8}{9} x \cos 2x$$

Art. Homogeneous linear differential equation are the equation of the type

$$x^n \frac{d^n y}{dx^n}+a_1 x^{n-1} \frac{d^{n-1} y}{dx^{n-1}}+\ldots+a_{n-1} x \frac{dy}{dx}+a_n y = X$$

Where X is the function of x

They are transformed by putting $z = \log x$

$\Rightarrow$ $x = e^z$ fot converting them in the different equation with constant coefficient

$$\frac{dy}{dx} = \frac{dy}{dz} \cdot \frac{dz}{dx} = \frac{1}{x}\frac{dy}{dz}$$

$$\frac{d^2y}{dx^2} = \frac{d^2y}{dz^2} \cdot \frac{1}{x^2} - \frac{1}{x^2}\frac{dy}{dz}$$

Lastly, we have

$$[D(D-1)(D-2)\ldots(D-n+1) + \ldots + a_1 D(D-1) + \ldots + \ldots(D-n+2) + \ldots a_n]\, y = Z$$

or $\qquad \phi(D)\, y = Z$

The different equation with constant coefficient

1. $$x^2\frac{d^2y}{dx^2} + 7x\frac{dy}{dx} + 5y = 2x^6$$

Let $\qquad z = \log x$

$\Rightarrow$ $\qquad x = e^z$. The equation becomes

$$[D(D-1) + 7D + 5]\, y = 2(e^z)^6$$

$$[D^3 - D + 7D + 5]\, y = 2e^{6z}$$

Where $\qquad D = \frac{d}{dz}$

$$(D^2 + 6D + 5)\, y = 2e^{6z}$$

$$(D+1)(D+5) = 0$$

$\Rightarrow$ $\qquad D = -1, -5$

$$\text{C.F.} = ae^{-z} + be^{-5z}$$

$$\text{P.I.} = \frac{2e^{6z}}{D^2 + 6D + 5} = \frac{2e^{6z}}{36 + 36 + 5} = \frac{2}{77}e^{6z}$$

The complete solution is therefore

$$y = ae^{-z} + be^{-5z} + \frac{2}{77}e^{6z}$$

$$= ax^{-1} + bx^{-5} + \frac{2}{77}x^6$$

Problem 2 $x^2 \dfrac{d^2 y}{dx^2} + 2 \dfrac{dy}{dx} - 4y = x^3$

Solution Putting $\log x = z \Rightarrow x = e^z$

$$[D(D-1) + D - 4] = 0$$

$$[D^2 - 4] = 0$$

$$D = \pm 2$$

$$\text{CF} = ae^{2z} + be^{-2z} = ax^2 + bx^{-2}$$

$$\text{P.I.} = \frac{(e^z)^3}{D^2 - 4} = \frac{e^{3z}}{D^2 - 4}$$

$$= \frac{e^{3z}}{9 - 4} = \frac{1}{5}(e^z)^3 = \frac{1}{5} x^3$$

The complete solution is

$$y = ax^2 + bx^{-2} + \frac{1}{5} x^3$$

Problem 3 $x^2 \dfrac{d^2 y}{dx^2} + 3x \dfrac{dy}{dx} + y = (1 - x)^2$

Putting $x = e^z$

The equation reduces to

$$[D(D-1) + 3D + 1]\, y = 1 + e^{2z} - 2e^z$$

$$D^2 - D + 3D + 1 = 0$$

$$D^2 + 2D + 1 = 0$$

$$D = -1, -1 \text{ repeated roots}$$

$$\text{C.F.} = (a + bz)\, e^{-z}$$

$$= (a + b \log x)\, x^{-1}$$

$$\text{P.I.} = \frac{1 + e^{2z} - 2e^z}{(D + 1)^2}$$

$$= (1 + D)^{-2} + \frac{e^{2z}}{D^2 + 2D + 1} - \frac{2e^z}{D^2 + 2D + 1}$$

$$[1 - 2D + D + \ldots] + \frac{e^{2z}}{4 + 4 + 1} - \frac{2e^z}{1 + 2 + 1}$$

$$= 1 + \frac{e^{2z}}{2} - \frac{2e^z}{4}$$

$$= 1 + \frac{x^2}{9} - \frac{2x}{4}$$

Required complete solution is

$$y = (a + b \log x)\, x^{-1} + 1 - \frac{1}{2} x + \frac{x^2}{9}$$

Problem 4 $x^2 \dfrac{d^2 y}{dx^2} - 2x \dfrac{dy}{dx} + 2y = x + x^2 \log x + x^2$

Solution Putting $x = e^z$

$$D(D-1) - 2D + 2 = 0$$

$$D^2 - D - 2D + 2 = 0$$

$$D(D-1) - 2(D-1) = 0$$

$$D = 1, 2$$

$$\text{C.F.} = ae^z + be^{2z}$$

$$= ax + bx^2$$

$$\text{P.I.} = \frac{x}{D^2 - 3D + 2} + \frac{x^2 \log x}{D^2 - 3D + 2} + x^2$$

$$= \frac{e^z}{D^2 - 3D + 2} + \frac{ze^{2z}}{D^2 - 3D + 2} + \frac{e^{2z}}{D^2 - 3D + 2}$$

$$= \frac{e^z}{(D-1)(D-2)} + \frac{e^{2z}}{(D-1)(D-2)}$$

$$+ \frac{e^{2z} z}{(D+2)^2 - 3(D+2) + 2}$$

$$= \frac{e^z}{(1-2)(D-1)} + \frac{e^{2z}}{(2-1)(D-2)} + \frac{ze^{2z}}{D^2 + D}$$

$$= -e^z \int e^{-z} e^z \, dz + e^{2z} \int e^{-2z} e^{2z} \, dz + \frac{ze^{2x}}{D(1 + D)}$$

$$= -ze^z + ze^{2z} + \frac{z}{D}(1 - D + D^2 + \ldots) e^{2z}$$

$$= -ze^z + ze^{2z} + \frac{z-1}{D} e^{2z}$$

$$= -ze^z + ze^{2z} + \left(\frac{z^2}{2} - z\right) e^{2z}$$

$$= -x \log x + x^2 \log x + [\tfrac{1}{2} (\log x)^2 - \log x]^2$$

$$= -x \log x + x^2 [\log x - \log x + \tfrac{1}{2} (\log x)^2]$$

Complete solution is

$$y = ax + bx^2 - x \log x + \tfrac{1}{2} x^2 (\log x)^2$$

Problem 5 $x^2 \dfrac{d^2 y}{d\,^2} + 2x \dfrac{dy}{dx} - 20y = (x + 1)^2$

Putting $x = e^z$ i.e. $z = \log x$ we have

$$[D(D-1) + 2D - 20] = 0$$

$$D^2 - D + 2D - 20 = 0$$

$$D^2 + D - 20 = 0$$

$$(D + 5)(D - 4) = 0$$

$$D = 4, -5$$

$$\text{C.F.} = ne^{4z} + be^{-5z} = ax^4 + bx^{-5}$$

$$\text{P.I.} = \frac{(1 + e^z)^2}{D^2 + D - 20} = \frac{1 + e^{2z} + 2e^z}{D^2 + D - 20}$$

$$= -\frac{1}{20} \cdot \left[1 - \frac{D^2 + D}{20}\right]^{-1} + \frac{e^{2z} + 2e^z}{D^2 + D - 20}$$

$$= -\frac{1}{20}\left[1 + \frac{D^2 + D}{20} + \ldots\right]$$

$$+ \frac{e^{2z}}{4 + 2 - 20} + \frac{2e^z}{1 + 1 - 20}$$

$$= -\frac{1}{20} + \frac{e^{2z}}{-14} + \frac{2e^z}{-18} = -\frac{x^2}{14} - \frac{1}{9}x - \frac{1}{20}$$

The complete solution is therefore

$$y = ax^4 + bx^{-1} - \frac{x^2}{14} - \frac{1}{9}x - \frac{1}{20}$$

Problem1 $\dfrac{d^2 y}{dx^2} - 2m\dfrac{dy}{dx} + m^2 y = \sin nx$

Solution $D^2 - 2mD + m^2 = 0$

$$(D - m)^2 = 0$$

$D = m_1\ m$ repeated roots

$$\text{C.F.} = (a + bx)e^{mx}$$

$$\text{P.I.} = \frac{\sin nx}{D^2 - 2mD + m^2}$$

$$= \frac{\sin nx}{-n^2 - 2mD + m^2} = \frac{\sin x^2}{(m^2 - n^2) - 2mD}$$

$$= \frac{[(m^2 - n^2) + 2mD] \sin nx}{(m^2 - n^2)^2 - 4m^2 D^2}$$

$$= \frac{(m^2 - n^2)\sin nx + 2\,mn \cos nx}{(m^2 - n^2)^2 + 4m^2 n^2}$$

$$= \frac{(m^2 - n^2)\sin nx + 2mn \cos nx}{(m^2 + n^2)^2}$$

The complete solution is therefore

$$y = (a + bx)e^{mx} + \frac{(m^2 - n^2)\sin nx + 2mn \cos nx}{(m^3 + n^2)^2}$$

Problem 2 $\dfrac{d^2 y}{dx^2} + 4y = \sin 3x \cos x$

Solution $D^2 + 4 = 0$

$$D = \pm 2i$$

$$\text{C.F.} = a \cos 2x + b \sin 2x$$

$$\text{P.I.} = \frac{1}{2} \frac{2 \sin 3x \cos x}{D^2 + 4}$$

$$= \frac{1}{2} \left[\frac{\sin 4x + \sin 2x}{D^2 + 4} \right]$$

$$= \frac{1}{2} \frac{\sin 4x}{D^2 + 4} + \frac{1}{2} \frac{\sin 2x}{D^2 + 4}$$

$$\frac{\sin 2x}{D^2 + 4} = \frac{1}{(D-2i)(D + 2} e^{2ix}$$

$$= \frac{1}{4i} \frac{e^{2ix}}{(D-2i} = \frac{1}{4i} e^{2ix} \int e^{2ix} e^{-2ix} dx$$

$$= \frac{1}{4i} xe^{2ix} = \frac{-i}{4} xe^{2ix}$$

$$= -\frac{i}{4} x [\cos 2x + i \sin 2x]$$

$$= -\frac{1}{4} x \cos 2x$$

$\therefore$ $$\frac{1}{2} \frac{\sin 2x}{D^2 + 4} = \frac{-1}{8} x \cos 2x$$

$\therefore$ $$\text{P.I.} = \frac{1}{2} \cdot \frac{\sin 4x}{-16 + 4} - \frac{1}{8} x \cos 2x$$

$$= -\frac{\sin 4x}{24} - \frac{1}{8} x \cos 2x$$

Hence the complete solution is

$$y = a \cos 2x + b \sin 2x - \frac{1}{24} \sin 4x \frac{-1}{8} x \cos 2x$$

Problem 3 $\dfrac{d^2 y}{dx^2} - 6 \dfrac{dy}{dx} + 8y = (e^{2x} - 1)^2$

Solution $D^2 - 6D + 8 = 0$

$$D = 4, 2$$

$$\text{C.F.} = ae^{2x} + be^{4x}$$

$$\text{P.I.} = \frac{e^{4x} + 1 - 2e^{2x}}{D^2 - 6D + 8}$$

$$= \frac{e^{4x}}{D^2 - 6D + 1} + \frac{1}{8}\left(1 + \frac{D^2 - 6D}{8}\right)^{-1} - \frac{2e^{2x}}{(D+2)(D-4)} + ,..$$

$$= \frac{e^{4x}}{(D-2)(D-4)} + \frac{1}{8} - \frac{2e^{2x}}{-2(D-2)}$$

$$= \frac{e^{4x}}{2(D-4)} + \frac{1}{8} + e^{2x}\int e^{-2x} e^{2x}\,dx$$

$$= \tfrac{1}{2} e^{4x} \int e^{-4x} e^{4x}\,dx + \frac{1}{8} + xe^{2x}$$

$$= \frac{1}{2} xe^{4a} + \frac{1}{8} - xe^{2x}$$

Required solution

$$y = ae^{2x} + be^{4x} + \frac{1}{8} + \frac{1}{2} xe^{4x} - xe^{2x}$$

Problem 4 Find the solution of the equation

$$\frac{d^2y}{dx^2} - y = 1$$

which vanishes when $x = 0$ and tends to a finite limit as $n \to -\infty$

Solution

$$D^2 - 1 = 0$$

$$D = \pm 1$$

$$\text{C.F.} = ae^x + be^{-x}$$

$$\text{P.I.} = \frac{1}{D^2 - 1} = -\left[\frac{1}{(1 - D^2)}\right]$$

$$= -[(1 - D^2)]^{-1}$$

$$= -[1 + D^2 + \ldots] = -1$$

$$y = ae^x + be^{-x} - 1$$

Now as from the question $y \to 0$ as $x \to 0$

$$0 = a - 1 \quad \Rightarrow \quad a = 1$$

Now when $x \to -\infty$, $e^x \to 0$, and $e^{-x} \to \infty$ therefore in order that y is to be inite $b = 0$

$\therefore$ $$y = e^x - 1$$

Problem 5 $\dfrac{4d^2y}{dx^2} - y = 2 \sin \left(\dfrac{\pi}{3} + x\right)$

$$4D^2 - 1 = 0$$

Solution $D = \pm 1/2$

$$\text{C.F.} = ae^{1/2x} + be^{-1/2x}$$

$$\text{P.I.} = \frac{2 \sin (\pi/3 + x)}{4D^2 - 1} = \frac{2 \sin \pi/3 \cos x + 2 \cos \pi/3 \sin x}{4D^2 - 1}$$

$$= \frac{2\sqrt{3}/2 \cos x}{4D^2 - 1} + \frac{\sin x}{4D^2 - 1} = \frac{\sqrt{3} \cos x}{-5} + \frac{\sin x}{-5}$$

$$= -1/5 (\sin x + \sqrt{3} \cos x)$$

The complete solution is

$$y = ae^{1/2x} + be^{-1/2x} - 1/5 (\sin x + \sqrt{3} \cos x)$$

Problem 6 $d^2y/dx^2 - 4dy/dx - 13y = e^{x/2} - \sin 1/3\, x$

Solution $D^2 - 4D - 13 = 0$

$$D = \frac{4 \pm \sqrt{16 + 52}}{2} = \pm \sqrt{17}$$

$$\text{C.F.} = ae^{(2+\sqrt{7})x} + be^{(2-\sqrt{7})x}$$

$$\text{P.I.} = \frac{e^{x/2}}{D^2 - 4D - 13} - \frac{\sin \frac{1}{3}x}{D^2 - 4D - 13}$$

$$= \frac{e^{x/2}}{\frac{1}{4} - 4.\frac{1}{2} - 13} - \frac{\sin x/3}{-1/9 - 4D - 13}$$

$$= -\frac{4e^{x/2}}{59} - \frac{\sin x/3}{-4D - 118/9}$$

$$= -\frac{4}{59} e^{x/2} + \frac{(4D - 118/9) \sin x/3)}{16D^2 - 13924/81}$$

$$= -\frac{4}{59} e^{x/2} + \frac{[4/3 \cos x/3 - 118/9 \sin x/3]\, 81}{1296\, D^2 - 13924}$$

$$= -\frac{4}{59} e^{x/2} + \frac{[4/3 \cos x/3 - 118/9 \sin x/3]\, 81}{-144 - 13924}$$

$$= -\frac{4}{59} e^{x/2} - \frac{9}{7084} (-59 \sin 1/3\, x + 6 \cos x/3)$$

Required solution is

$$y = ae^{(2+\sqrt{17})x} + be^{(2-\sqrt{17})x} - 4/59\, e^{x/2}$$

$$- \frac{9}{7084} (-59 \sin x/3 + 6 \cos x/3)$$

Problem 7 $4\frac{d^2y}{dx^2}-4\frac{dy}{dx}+2y=\cos^2(x+1/6^x)$

$$4D^2-4D+2=0$$

Solution $$D=\frac{4\pm\sqrt{16-32}}{8}=\frac{1}{2}\pm\frac{1}{2}i$$

$$\text{C.F.}=(a\cos 1/2\,x+b\sin x/2)\,e^{1/2x}$$

$$\text{P.I.}=\frac{\cos^2(x+1/6\,x)}{4D^2-4D+2}=\frac{1}{2}\frac{[1+\cos 2(x+1/6\,x)]}{4D^2+2-4D}$$

$$=\frac{1}{2}\left[\frac{1}{4D^2-4D+2}+\frac{\cos 2x\cos x/3-\sin 2x\sin x/3}{4D^2-4D+2}\right]$$

$$=\frac{1}{2}\cdot\frac{1}{2}\left[\frac{1}{1+\frac{4D^2-4D}{2}}\right.$$

$$\left.+\cdot\frac{2\cos 2x\cos x/3-2\sin 2x\sin x/3}{4D^2-4D+2}\right]$$

$$=\frac{1}{4}\left(1-\frac{4D^2-4D}{2}+\ldots\right)+\ldots$$

$$=\frac{1}{4}+\frac{1}{4}\left(\frac{\cos 7x/3+\cos 5x/3+\cos 7x/3-\cos 5x/3}{4D^2-4D+2}\right)$$

$$=\frac{1}{4}+\frac{1}{4}\times 2\frac{\cos x/3}{4(-1/9)-4D+2}$$

$$=\frac{1}{4}+\frac{1}{2}\frac{\cos x/3}{-4/9-4D+2}=\frac{1}{4}+\frac{9}{2}\frac{\cos x/3}{-(36D+14)}$$

$$=\frac{1}{4}+\frac{9}{4}-\frac{(18D-7)\cos x/3}{[324D^2-196]}$$

$$=\frac{1}{4}-\frac{9}{4}\frac{(18D-7)\cos x/3}{\left(-\frac{324}{9}-196\right)}$$

$$=\frac{1}{4}-\frac{9}{4}\frac{-[18/3\sin x/3-7\cos x/3]}{-2088}$$

$$=\frac{1}{4}-\frac{1}{928}(6\sin x/3-7\cos x/3)$$

$$=\frac{1}{4}-\frac{1}{928}[6\sin x/3-7\cos x/3]$$

Problem 8 $\frac{d^2y}{dx^2} - \frac{4dy}{dx} + y = e^{2x} \sin 2x$

Solution $D^2 - 4D + 1 = 0$

$$D = \frac{4 \pm \sqrt{16-4}}{2} = \frac{4 \pm 2\sqrt{3}}{2} = 2 \pm \sqrt{3}$$

$$\text{C.F.} = ae^{(2+\sqrt{3})x} + be^{(2-\sqrt{3})x}$$

$$\text{P.I.} = \frac{e^{2x} \sin 2x}{D^2 - 4D + 1} = \frac{e^{2x} \sin 2x}{(D+2)^2 - 4(D+2) + 1}$$

$$= \frac{e^{2x} \sin 2x}{D^2 + 4D + 4 - 4D - 8 + 1} = \frac{e^{2x} \sin 2x}{D^2 - 3}$$

$$= e^{2x} \frac{\sin 2x}{-4-3} = -\frac{e^{2x} \sin 2x}{7}$$

$\therefore$ $y = ae^{(2+\sqrt{3})x} + be^{(2-\sqrt{3})x} - 1/7\, e^{2x} \sin 2x$

Problem 9 $\frac{d^4y}{dx^4} - y = e^x \cos x$

Solution $(D^4 - 1)\, y = e^x \cos x$

$\Rightarrow$ $D^5 - 1 = 0$

$(D^2 + 1)(D^2 - 1) = 0$

$$D = -1, +1, \pm i$$

$$\text{C.F.} = ae^x + be^{-x} + (e \cos x + d \sin x)$$

$$\text{P.I.} = \frac{e^x \cos x}{D^4 - 1} = \frac{e^x \cos x}{(D + D^4 - 1}$$

$$= \frac{e^x \cos x}{D^4 + 4D^3 + 6D^2 + 4D} = \frac{e^x \cos x}{D(D^3 + 4D^2 + 6D + 4)}$$

$$= \frac{e^x \cos x}{D(-D - 4 + 6D + 4)} = \frac{e^x \cos x}{D \cdot 5D}$$

$$= \frac{1}{5} e^x \frac{1}{D^2} \cos x = \frac{e^x}{5} \frac{\sin x}{D} = \frac{-e^x}{5} \cos x$$

Required complete solution is

$$y = ae^x + be^{-x} + (c \cos x + d \sin x) - \frac{e^x}{5} \cos x$$

Problem 10 $\dfrac{d^4y}{dx^4} + 2\dfrac{d^2y}{dx^2} + y = x^2 \cos x$

Solution $(D^4 + 2D^2 + 1)\, y = x^2 \cos x$

$$D^4 + 2D^2 + 1 = 0$$

$$(D^2 + 1)^2 = 0$$

$$\Rightarrow \quad D^2 = -1, -1$$

$$D = \pm i, \pm i \qquad \text{(repeated roots)}$$

$$\therefore \quad \text{C.F.} = (a + bx) \cos x + (c + dx) \sin x$$

$$\text{P.I.} = \frac{x^2 \cos x}{D^4 + 2D^2 + 1} = \frac{x^2 e^{ix}}{D^4 + 2D^2 + 1}$$

$$= \frac{x^2 e^{ix}}{(D + i)^4 + 2(D + i)^2 + 1}$$

$$= \frac{x^2 e^{ix}}{D^4 + 4D^3 i - 6D^2 - 4Di + 1 + 2(D^2 + 2iD - 1) + 1}$$

$$= \frac{x^2 e^{ix}}{D^4 + 4D^3 i - 6D^2 - 4Di + 2D^2 + 4iD}$$

$$= \frac{x^2 e^{ix}}{D^4 + 4D^3 i - 4D^2}$$

$$= \frac{x^2 e^{ix}}{D^2 (D^2 + 4Di - 4)} = \frac{1}{4D^2} \frac{x^2 e^{ix}}{\left(\frac{D^2 + 4Di}{4} - 1\right)}$$

$$= -\frac{1}{4D^2}\left[1 - \frac{D^2 + 4Di}{4}\right]^{-1} x^2 e^{ix}$$

$$= -\frac{1}{4D^2}\left[1 + \frac{D^2 + 4Di}{4} - D^2\right] x^2 e^{ix}$$

$$= -\frac{e^{ix}}{4D^2}\left[x^2 + 1/4\,(2 + 8xi) - 2\right]$$

$$= -\frac{e^{ix}}{4D^2}\left[x^2 + 2xi - 3/2\right]$$

$$= -\frac{(\cos x + i \sin x)}{4}\left[\frac{x^4}{12} + \frac{x^3}{3}\, i - \frac{3}{2}\, \frac{x^2}{2}\right]$$

$$= -\frac{1}{4}(\cos x + i \sin x)\left[\frac{x^4}{12} + \frac{x^3}{3}\, i - \frac{3x^2}{4}\right]$$

We have to take for the real number

$$= -\frac{x^4}{48}\cos x + \frac{3x^2}{16}\cos x + \frac{x^3}{12}\sin x$$

$$= \frac{1}{48}(9x^2 - x^4)\cos x + \frac{x^3 \sin x}{12}$$

Hence the complete solution is

$$y = (a + bx)\cos x + (c + dx)\sin x + \frac{1}{48}(9x^2 - x^4)\cos x + \frac{x^3}{12}\sin x$$

Problem 11 $\{D^3 - 1) y = xe^x + \cos^2 x$

Solution $(D-1)(D^2 + D + 1) = 0$

i.e. $$D = 1, \frac{-1 \pm \sqrt{1-4}}{2}$$

$$= 1, -\frac{1}{2} \pm \frac{\sqrt{3}i}{2}$$

$$\text{C.F.} = ae^x + e^{-1/2x}\left(b \cos \frac{\sqrt{3}}{2} x + c \sin \frac{\sqrt{3}}{2} x\right)$$

$$\text{P.I.} = \frac{xe^x}{D^3 - 1} + \frac{1}{2} \cdot \frac{2\cos^2 x}{D^3 - 1}$$

$$= \frac{x e^x}{(D+1)^3 - 1} + \frac{1}{2}\frac{(1 + \cos 2x)}{D^3 - 1}$$

$$= \frac{xe^x}{D^3 + 3D + 3D^2} + \frac{1}{2(D^3 - 1)} + \frac{1}{2}\frac{\cos 2x}{D^3 - 1}$$

$$= \frac{xe^x}{D(D^2 + 3 + 3D)} - \frac{1}{2}(1 - D^3)^{-1} + \frac{1}{2}\frac{\cos 2x}{D - 1}$$

$$= \frac{1 \cdot 1}{3D}\frac{x e^x}{\left(1 + \frac{D^3 + 3D}{3}\right)} - \frac{1}{2} - \frac{1}{2}\frac{(D-1)\cos 2x}{16D^2 - 1}$$

$$= \frac{1}{3D}\left(1 - \frac{D^3 + 3D}{3} + \ldots\right) xe^x - \frac{1}{2}$$

$$+ \frac{1}{130}(-2\sin 2x) - \frac{1}{130}\cos 2x$$

$$= \frac{1}{3D}(x-1)e^x - \frac{1}{2} = \frac{1}{3}\left(\frac{x^2}{2} - x\right)e^x - \frac{1}{2}$$

$$- \frac{\sin x}{4} - \frac{\cos x}{2} - \frac{1}{130}$$

Required complete solution is

$$y = ae^x + \left(b \cos \frac{\sqrt{3}}{2} x + c \sin \frac{\sqrt{3}}{2} x\right) e^{-1/2\, x}$$

$$- \frac{1}{2} + \frac{1}{3} (1/2\, x^2 - x)\, e^x - \frac{1}{130}(2 \sin 2x + \cos 2x)$$

Problem 12 $\dfrac{d^2y}{dx^2} + \dfrac{dy}{dx} + y = \cos 2x + x^2$

Solution $D^2 + D + 1 = 0$

$$D = -\frac{1 \pm \sqrt{1-4}}{2} = -\frac{1}{2} + \frac{\sqrt{3i}}{2}$$

$$\text{C.F.} = e^{-1/2x}\left(a \cos \frac{\sqrt{3}}{2} x + b \sin \frac{\sqrt{3}}{2} x\right)$$

$$\text{P.I.} = \frac{\cos 2x}{D^2 + D + 1} + \frac{x^2}{D^2 + D + 1}$$

$$= \frac{\cos 2x}{-3 + D} + (1 + D^2 + D)^{-1} x^2$$

$$= \frac{(D + 3)(\cos 2x)}{D^2 - 9} + (1 - D^2 - D + D^2)\, x^2$$

$$= -\frac{1}{13}[-2 \sin 2x + 3 \cos 2x] + (x^2 - 2x)$$

$$= -\frac{1}{13}(3 \cos 2x - 2 \sin 2x) + (x^2 - 2x)$$

The complete solution is

$$y = \left(a \cos \frac{\sqrt{3}}{2} x \;\; b \sin \frac{\sqrt{3}}{2} x\right) e^{-1/2x}$$

$$- \frac{1}{13}(3 \cos 2x - 2 \sin 2x) + (x^2 - 2x)$$

Problem 13 $\dfrac{d^2y}{dx^2} + y = x\, e^{2x}$

Solution $D^2 + 1 = 0$

$$D^2 = -1,\; D = \pm i$$

$$\text{C.F.} = a \cos x + b \sin x$$

$$\text{P.I.} = \frac{x\, e^{2x}}{D^2+1} = \frac{x\, e^{2x}}{(D+2)^2+1}$$

$$= \frac{x\, e^{2x}}{D^2+4+4D+1} = \frac{x\, e^{2x}}{D^2+4D+5}$$

$$= \frac{1}{5} \cdot \frac{x\, e^{2x}}{\left(1+\frac{D^2D+4}{5}\right)}$$

$$= \frac{1}{5} e^{2x}\left[1 - \frac{D^2+4D}{5} + \frac{16}{25}D^2\right] x$$

$$= \frac{1}{5} e^{2x}\left(x - \frac{4}{5}\right) = \frac{e^2\,(5x-4)}{25} e^{2x}$$

Required complete solution is

$$y = a \cos x + b \sin x + 1/5\,(x - 4/5)\, e^{2x})$$

Problem 14 $(D^2+4)\, y = x \cos 2x$

Solution $D^2 + 4 = 0$

$$D = \pm 2i$$

$$\text{C.F.} = a \cos 2x + b \sin 2x$$

$$\text{P.I.} = \frac{x \cos 2x}{D^2+4} = \frac{x\, e^{2ix}}{D^2+4}$$

$$= \frac{x\, e^{2ix}}{D^2+4Di-4+4} = \frac{x\, e^{2ix}}{D\,(D+4i)}$$

$$= \frac{1}{4i}\,\frac{1}{D}\,\frac{xe^{2ix}}{\left(1+\frac{D}{4i}\right)}$$

$$= \frac{1}{4i}\,\frac{x\, e^{2ix}}{D}\left(1 - \frac{D}{4i} + \ldots\right)$$

$$= \frac{1}{4i}\,\frac{e^{2ix}}{D}\left(x - \frac{1}{4i}\right)$$

$$= \frac{1}{4i}\, e^{2ix}\left(\frac{x^2}{2} - \frac{1}{4i}\, x\right)$$

$$= -\frac{i}{4}\,(\cos 2x + i \sin 2x)\left(\frac{x^2}{2} - \frac{1}{4i}\, x\right)$$

Whose real part is

$$= \frac{x \cos 2x}{16} + \frac{x^2 \sin 2x}{8}$$

Required complete solution is

$$y = a \cos 2x + b \sin 2x + \frac{x \cos 2x}{16} + \frac{x^2 \sin 2x}{8}$$

Problem 15 $(D^2 + 3D + 2)\, y = x^2 \cos x$

Solution $(D + 1)(D + 2) = 0$

$$D = -1, \; -2$$

$$\text{C.F.} = ae^{-x} + be^{-2x}$$

$$\text{P.I.} = \frac{x^2 \cos x}{D^2 + 3D + 2} = \frac{x^2 e^{ix}}{D^2 + 3D + 2}$$

$$= \frac{x^2 e^{ix}}{(D + i)^2 + 3(D + i) + 2} = \frac{x^2 e^{ix}}{D^2 + D(2i + 3) + (2i)}$$

$$= \frac{c^{ix}}{1 + 3i} \left\{ 1 + \frac{(2i + 3) D + D^2}{1 + 3i} \right\}^{-1} x^2$$

$$= \frac{c^{ix}}{1 + 3i} \left\{ 1 + \frac{1}{10} (1 - 3i) \{(2i + 3) D + D^2\}^{-1} \right\} x^2$$

$$= \frac{(1 - 3i)\, e^{ix}}{10} \left[1 + \frac{1}{10} \{9 - 7i) D + (1 - 3i) D^2\} \right]^{-1}$$

$$= \frac{(1 - 3i)\, e^{ix}}{10} \left[1 - \frac{(9 - 7i) D + (1 - 3i) D^2}{10} + \frac{(9 - 7i)^2 D^2}{100} + \ldots \right] x^2$$

$$= \frac{(1 - 3i)\, e^{ix}}{20} \left\{ x^2 - \frac{1}{5} (9 - 7i)^x - \frac{1}{5} (1 - 3i) + \frac{(9 - 7i)^2}{50} \right]$$

$$= \frac{e^{ix}}{10} \left\{ (1 - 3i)\, x^2 + \frac{1}{5} (34i + 12)\, x + \frac{1}{5} (6i + 8) + \frac{1}{50} (1 - 3i)(32 - 126i) \right\}$$

$$= \frac{(\cos x + i \sin x)}{10} \left\{ (1 - 3i)\, x^2 + \frac{1}{5} (34i + 12)\, x + \frac{1}{5} (6i + 8) + \frac{1}{50} (1 - 3i)(32 - 126i) \right\}$$

In this we have to choose the real part

$$= \frac{(\cos x + i \sin x)}{1}\left[\left(x^2 - \frac{73}{25}\right) + i\left(\frac{89}{25} - 3x^2\right)\right]$$

$$= \frac{1}{10}\left(x^2 - \frac{73}{25}\right)\cos x - \frac{1}{10}\left(\frac{89}{25} - 3x^2\right)\sin x$$

$$= \frac{1}{10}(\cos x + 3\sin x)\,x^2 - \frac{73}{250}\cos x - \frac{89}{250}\sin x$$

$$= \frac{1}{10}(\cos x + 3\sin x)\,x^2 + \left(\frac{60-133}{250}\right)\cos x$$

$$- \frac{1}{250}(170-81)\sin x$$

$$= \frac{1}{10}(\cos x + 3\sin x)\,x^2 - \frac{1}{25}(17\sin x - 6\cos x)$$

$$+ \frac{1}{250}(81\sin x - 133\cos x)$$

Complete solution = P.I. + C.F.

Problem 16 $(D^2 - 4D - 5)\,y = x\,e^{-x}$

Solution $D^2 - 4D - 5 = 0$

$$(D-1)(D+5) = 0$$

$$D = 1,\ -5$$

$$\text{C.F.} = ae^x + be^{-5x}$$

$$\text{P.I.} = \frac{xe^{-x}}{D^2 - 4D - 5} = \frac{xe^{-x}}{(D-1)^2 - 4(D-1) - 5}$$

$$= e^{-x}\frac{x}{D^2 - 6D} = \frac{e^{-x}}{D}\frac{x}{(D-6)}$$

$$= -\frac{e^{-x}}{6D}\frac{x}{(1 - D/6)} = -\frac{e^{-x}}{6D}(1 - D/6)^{-1}x$$

$$= -\frac{e^{-x}}{6D}\left(1 + \frac{D}{6} + \ldots\right)x$$

$$= -\frac{e^{-x}}{6D}\left(x + \frac{1}{6}\right) = -\frac{e^{-x}}{6}\left(\frac{x^2}{2} + \frac{1}{6}x\right)$$

$$= -\frac{1}{36}x(1 + 3x)\,e^{-x}$$

Required complete solution is

$$y = ae^x + be^{-5x} - \frac{1}{36}x(1 + 3x)\,c^{-x}$$

Problem 17 $(D^2 + 9)\,y = \cos^2 \dfrac{3x}{2}$

Solution $$(D^2 + 9)\,y = \frac{1 + \cos 3x}{2}$$

$$D^2 + 9 = 0$$

$$D = \pm\, 3i$$

$$\text{C.F.} = a \cos 3x + b \sin 3x$$

$$\text{P.I.} = \frac{1}{2}\,\frac{1 + \cos 3x}{D^2 + 9}$$

$$= \frac{1}{2}\left[\frac{1}{9}\left(1 + \frac{D^2}{9}\right)^{-1} + \frac{\cos 3x}{D^2 + 9}\right]$$

$$= \frac{1}{18} + \frac{1}{2}\,\frac{\cos 3x}{D^2 + 9}$$

Now $$\frac{\cos 3x}{D^2 + 9} = \frac{e^{3ix}}{(D - 3i)\,(D + 3i)} = \frac{1}{6i}\,\frac{e^{3ix}}{(D - 3i)}$$

$$= \frac{1}{6i}\, e^{3ix} \int e^{-3ix}\, e^{3ix}\, dx = \frac{1}{6i}\, x\, e^{3ix}$$

$$= -\frac{i}{6}\, x\,(\cos 3x + i \sin 3x)$$

whose Real part is given by

$$= \frac{x \sin 3x}{6}$$

Hence the complete solution is

$$y = a \cos 3x + b \sin 3x + \frac{x \sin 3x}{12} + \frac{1}{18}$$

$$= a \cos 3x + b \sin 3x + \frac{1}{36}\,(3x \sin 3x + 2)$$

Problem 18 $(D^5 + D^4 + 4D^3 + 4D^2 + 4D + 4)\,y = \cos 3x \cos x$

Solution $$D^5 + D^4 + 4D^3 + 4D^2 + 4D + 4 = 0$$

$$(D + 1)\,(D^4 + 4D^2 + 4) = 0$$

$$(D + 1)\,(D^2 + 2)^2 = 0$$

Either $D = -1,\ D^2 = -2, -2$ (repeated)

$D = -1,\ D = \pm\sqrt{2}i$ (repeated)

$$\text{C.F.} = ae^{-x} + (b + cx)(\cos\sqrt{2}x + (d+ex)\sin\sqrt{2}\,x$$

$$\text{P.I.} = \frac{\cos 3x \cos x}{(D+1)(D^2+2)^2} = \frac{1}{2}\left(\frac{\cos 4x + \cos 2x}{D+1)(D^2+2)}\right)$$

$$= \frac{1}{2}\,\frac{\cos 4x}{(D+1)(D^2+2)^2} + \frac{1}{2}\,\frac{\cos 2x}{(D+1)(D^2+2)^2}$$

$$= \frac{1}{2}\,\frac{\cos 4x}{(D+1)(-16+2)^2} + \frac{1}{2}\,\frac{\cos 2x}{(D+1)(-4+2)^2}$$

$$= \frac{(D-1)\cos 4x}{2\times 196\,(D^2-1)} + \frac{(D-1)\cos 2x}{4\times 2\,(D^2-1)}$$

$$= \frac{-4\sin 4x - \cos 4x}{-2\times 196\times 17} + \frac{2\sin 2x + \cos 2x}{8\times 5}$$

$$= \frac{(4\sin 4x + \cos 4x)}{6664} + \frac{1}{40}(2\sin 2x + \cos 2x)$$

Hence the complete soln is

$$y = ae^{-x} + (b + cx)\cos\sqrt{2}x + (d + ex)\sin\sqrt{2}x$$

$$+ \frac{1}{6664}(4\sin 4x + \cos 4x) + \frac{1}{40}(2\sin 2x + \cos 2x)$$

Problem 19 $(x^2 D^2 + xD - 4)\,y = x^2$

Let $z = \log x$

$\Rightarrow$ $x = e^z$

$$[D\,(D-1) + D-4]\,y = e^{2z}$$

$$(D^2-4)\,y = e^{2z}$$

Where $D = \dfrac{d}{dz}$

$$D^2 - 4 = 0$$

$$D = \pm 2$$

$$\text{CF} = ae^{2z} + be^{-2z}$$

$$\text{PF} = \frac{e^{2z}}{D^2-4} = \frac{e^{2z}}{(D-2)(D+2)}$$

$$= \frac{1}{4}\,\frac{e^{2z}}{(D-2)} = \frac{1}{4}\,z\cdot e^{2z}$$

Reqd. soln.

$$y = ae^{2z} + be^{-2z} + \tfrac{1}{4}ze^{2z}$$

$$= ax^2 + bx^{-2} + \tfrac{1}{4}x^2 \log x$$

Problem 20 $(x^3 D^3 + 3x^2 D^2 + xD + 1)\, y = x \log x$

Let $\qquad z = \log x \Rightarrow x = e^z$

$$[D\,(D-1)\,D-2) + 3D\,(D-1) + D + 1]\, y = ze^z$$

$$[D^3 - 3D^2 + 2D + 3D^2 - 3D + D + 1]\, y = ze^z$$

$$(D + 1)\,(D^2 - D + 1) = 0$$

$$D = -1, \frac{1 \pm \sqrt{1-4}}{2}$$

$$= -1 \;\; \frac{1 \pm \sqrt{3}i}{2}$$

$$CF = ae^{-}z + e^{-1/2z}\left(b \cos \frac{\sqrt{3}}{2} z + c \sin \frac{\sqrt{3}}{2} \;\; z\right)$$

$$PI = \frac{ze^z}{D^3+1} = \frac{ze^z}{(D + 1)^3 + 1}$$

$$= \frac{e^z.z}{D^3 + 3D + 3D^2 + 2} = \frac{e^z \cdot z}{\frac{2 \cdot (D^3 + 3D + 3D^2 + 1)}{2}}$$

$$= \frac{e^z}{2}\left(1 + \frac{D^3 + 3D^2 + 3D}{2}\right)^{-1} z$$

$$= \frac{e^z}{2}\left(1 - \frac{3D}{2} + \ldots\right) z = \frac{ze^z}{2} - \frac{3}{2}\frac{e^z}{2}$$

Son. is $\qquad y = ae^{-2} + e^{-1/2z}\left(\frac{\sqrt{3}}{2} z + c \sin \frac{\sqrt{3}}{2} \; z\right) + \frac{e^z}{4}(2z - b)$

$$= ax^{-1} + \sqrt{x}\left(b \cos\left(\frac{\sqrt{3}}{2} \log x\right)\right.$$

$$\left. + c \sin\left(\frac{\sqrt{3}}{2} \log x\right)\right] + \frac{x}{4}(2 \log x - 3)$$

Problem 21 $\qquad x \frac{d^3 y}{dx^3} + \frac{d^2 y}{dx^2} = \frac{1}{x}$

Multiplying both sides by x^2 we have

$$x^3 \frac{d^3 y}{ax^3} + x^2 \frac{d^2 y}{dx^2} = x$$

Putting $\qquad \log x = z$

$$[D\,(D-1)\,(D-2) + D\,(D-1\,]\, y = e^z$$

$$D^3 - 3D^2 + 2D + D^2 - D = 0$$

$$D^3-2D^2+D=0$$

$$D(D^2-2D+1)y=0$$

either $\quad D=0 \qquad (D-1)^2=0$

$$D=1 \text{ repeated roots}$$

$$\text{CF}=a+(b+cz)\,e^z$$

$$\text{PI}=\frac{e^z}{D^3-2D^2+D}=\frac{e^z}{D(D^2-2D+1)}$$

$$=\frac{e^z}{D(D-1)(D-1)}=\frac{e^z}{(D-1)(D-1)}$$

$$=\frac{ze^z}{D-1}=e^z\int e^{-z}\cdot ze^z\,dz=\frac{z^2e^z}{2}$$

Soln. is $\quad y=a+(b+cz)\,e^2+\dfrac{z^2}{2}e^z$

$$=a+(b+c\log x)\,x+\tfrac{1}{2}\,x\,(\log x)^2$$

Problem 22 $\quad \dfrac{d^2y}{dx^2}-\dfrac{6}{x^2}y=x\log x$

Solution Multiplying throughout by x^2 we have

$$x^2\frac{d^2y}{dx^2}-6y=x^3\log x$$

Putting $\quad \log x=z\Rightarrow x=e^z$

$$\{D(D-1)-6\}\,y=ze^{3z}$$

$$D^2-D-6=0$$

$$(D-3)(D+2)=0$$

$$\text{i.e., } D=3,\,-2$$

$$y=ae^{3z}+be^{-2z}$$

$$\text{PI}=\frac{z^3e^z}{D^2-D-6}=\frac{ze^{3z}}{(D+3)^2-(D+3)-6}$$

$$=\frac{e^{3z}z}{D^2+5D}$$

$$=\frac{e^{3z}\,z}{D(D+5)}=\frac{e^{3z}\,z}{5D(1+D/5)}=\frac{e^{3z}}{5D}(1+D/5)^{-1}z$$

$$=\frac{e^{3z}}{5D}\left(1-\frac{D}{5}+\ldots\right)z$$

$$=\frac{e^{3z}}{5D}\left(z-\frac{1}{5}\right)=\frac{e^{3z}}{5}\left(\frac{z^2}{2}-\frac{1}{5}\;z\right)=\frac{e^{3z}}{5o}(5z-2)\,z.$$

Hence the soln is

$$y = ae^{3z} + be^{-2z} + \frac{1}{50}(5z-2)\,ze^{3z}$$

$$= ax^3 + bx^{-2} + \frac{1}{50}(5\log x - 2)\,x^3 \log x$$

Problem 23 $(x+1)^2 \frac{d^2y}{dx^2} - 3(x+1)\frac{dy}{dx} + 4y = x^2$

Solutian Let $x + 1 = u \Rightarrow x = u - 1$

$$\Rightarrow u^2 \frac{d^2y}{dx^2} - 3u\frac{dy}{dx} + 4y = (u-1)^2$$

$$(u(u-1) - 3u + 4)\,y = u^2 + 1 - 2u$$

Let $\log u = z \Rightarrow u = e^z$

$\Rightarrow u^2 - 4u + 4 = 0 \qquad = e^{2z} - 2e^z + 1$

$\Rightarrow (u-2)^2 = 0$

$\Rightarrow u = 2, 2$ (repeated roots)

$\therefore y = (a + bz)\,e^{2z}$

Now $$\text{PI} = \frac{e^{2z}}{(u-2)^2} - \frac{2e^z}{(u-2)} + \frac{1}{(u-2)^2}$$

$$= \frac{e^{2z}}{(u+2-2)} - \frac{2e^z}{(u-2)^2} + \frac{1}{4}\frac{1}{(u/2-1)^2}$$

$$= \frac{e^{2z}}{u^2} - 2e^z + \frac{1}{4}\;\frac{1}{(1-u/2)^2} \text{ Where } u = \frac{d}{dz}$$

$$u = \frac{z^2 e^{2z}}{2} - 2e^z + \frac{1}{4}\left(1 + \frac{2u}{2} + \ldots\right)$$

$$= \frac{z^2 e^{2z}}{2} - 2e^z + \frac{1}{4}$$

Soln. is $$y = (a + bz)\,e^{2z} + \frac{e^{2z}\cdot z^2}{2} - 2e^z + \frac{1}{4}\,(\log(x+1)]^2$$

i.e., $$y = [a + b\log(x+1)]\,(x+1)^2 + \tfrac{1}{2}(x+1)^2 - 2(x+1) + \tfrac{1}{4}$$

Problem 24 $x^2 D^2 y - 3xDy + 5y = x^2 \sin(\log x)$

Solution $(x^2 D^2 - 3xD + 5)y = x^2 \sin(\log x)$

Let $\log x = z$

$\Rightarrow x = e^z$ i.e.

$$[D(D-1)-3D+5]\,y = e^{2z}\sin z$$

$$[D^2-D-3D+5]\,y = e^{2z}\sin z$$

i.e.

$$D^2-4D+5=0$$

$$D=\frac{4\pm\sqrt{16-20}}{2}=\frac{4\pm 2i}{2}=2\pm i$$

$\therefore$

$$y = e^{2z}\sin(a\cos z+b\sin z)$$

$$\text{PI}=\frac{e^{2z}\sin z}{D^2-4D+5}=\frac{e^{2z}\sin z}{(D+2)^2-4(D+2)+5}$$

$$=\frac{e^{2z}\sin z}{D^2+1}=\frac{e^{2z}e^{iz}}{D^2+1}\ \text{(imaginary part)}$$

$$=\frac{e^{2z}e^{iz}}{(D+i)^2+1}+\frac{e^{2z}e^{iz}}{D^2+2iD}$$

$$=\frac{e^{2z}e^{iz}}{D(D+2i)}=\frac{e^{2z}}{2i\,D}\ \frac{e^{iz}}{(1+D/2i)}$$

$$=\frac{e^{2z}e^{iz}}{2i\,D}\left(1-\frac{D}{2i}+\ldots\right)1=\frac{e^{2z}}{2iD}(e^{iz})=\frac{e^{2z}e^{iz}}{2i}\,z$$

Therefore the Imaginary part

$$=-\tfrac{1}{2}\,ze^{2z}\cos z$$

Hence the soln. is

$$y=(a\cos z+b\sin z)\,e^{2z}-\tfrac{1}{2}\,ze^{2z}\cos z$$

$$y=x^2\,[a\cos(\log x)+b\sin(\log x)]-\tfrac{1}{2}\,x^2\log\cos(\log x)$$

Problem 25 $\quad (x+3)^2\dfrac{d^2y}{dx^2}-4(x+3)\dfrac{dy}{dx}+6y=x$

Let

$$x+3=t$$

$$\Rightarrow\quad x=(t-3)$$

Putting

$$\log t = z$$

$$\Rightarrow\quad t=e^z$$

$\therefore$

$$\left(t^2\frac{d^2y}{dx^2}-4t\frac{dy}{dx}+6\right)y=e^z-3$$

Now,

$$D(D-1)-4D+6=0$$

$$D^2-5D+6=0$$

$$D^2-3D-2D+6=0$$

$$(D-2)(D-3)=0$$

$$D=2,3$$

if $$y = ae^{2z} + be^{3z}$$

$$\text{PI} = \frac{e^z - 3}{(D-2)(D-3)} = \frac{e^z}{(1-2)(1-3)} - \frac{3}{D^2 - 5D + 6}$$

$$= \frac{e^z}{2} - \frac{3}{6} \Big/ \left(1 + \frac{D^2 - 5D}{6}\right)$$

$$= \frac{e^z}{2} - \frac{1}{2}\left(1 - \frac{D^2 - 5D}{6}\right) = \frac{e^z}{2} - \frac{1}{2}$$

Soln. is $$y = ae^{2z} + be^{3z} + \frac{e^z}{2} - \frac{1}{2}$$

$$= a(x+3)^2 + b(x+3)^2 + \tfrac{1}{2}(x+2)$$

36

Groups

Define group

Let 0 be a binary operation defined over a non empty set G. Then the set G together with the operation '0' satisfying the follcwing postulates is called a 'group'

If $a,b,c \in G$

(i) $aob \in G$ [closure axiom]

(ii) the operatian is associative

ie. $ao\,(boc) = (aob)\,oc$ [Associative axiom]

(iii) There exists an element $e \in G$ such that

$$aoe = eoa = a$$

The element e is called an identify element in G.

(iv) For every $a \in G$, there exists an element $a^{-1} \in G$ such that

$$a^{-1}\,o\,a = aoa^{-1} = e$$

a^{-1} is called the inverse of a in G [Inverse axiom]

Finite and Infinite groups

A group is called a finite group if the number of elements in the group is finite. If the group contains an infinite number of elements, then the group is called an infinite group.

The number of elements in a group is called its order. An infinite group has an infinite order.

Commutative or Abelian group

A group (G, o) is called an abelian or commutative if

$$aob = boa \;\forall\; a, b \in G$$

If the group G does not satisfy commutative axiom $aob = boa$ then G is called non abelian group

General properties of groups

(1) If $a, b, c \in G$ then

(i) $ab = ac \Rightarrow b = c$ (left oancellation law)

(ii) $ba = ca \Rightarrow b = c$ (Right cancellation law)

Proofs. Since $a \in G$

$\Rightarrow a^{-1} \in G$

Given $ab = ac$ (1)

Premultiplying both sides of (1) by a^{-1} we get

$$a^{-1}(ab) = a^{-1}(ae)$$

$$\Rightarrow (a^{-1}a)b = (a^{-1}a)c$$

[since associative land holds good in a group]

$\Rightarrow eb = ec$ [existence of inverse]

$\Rightarrow b = c$ [existence of identity]

(iii) Postmultiplying both sides of $ba = ca$ by a^{-1} we get

$$ba = ca$$

$\Rightarrow (ba)a^{-1} = (ca)a^{-1}$

$\Rightarrow b(aa^{-1}) = c(aa^{-1})$ [Associative axiom]

$\Rightarrow be = ce$ [Existence of invsrse]

$\Rightarrow b = c$ [Existence of identity]

Uniqueness of Identity

Theorem 1 The identity element in a group is unique.

An element $e \in G$ is said to be an identity for the operation in G if

$$ae = ea = a \;\forall\; a \in G$$

We have to prove that e is unique. If passible, let e and e^1 be two identity elements both belonging to G

Then e is an identity element

$\Rightarrow ee^1 = e^1$ (1)

and e^1 is an identify element

$\Rightarrow ee^1 = e$ (2)

(1) and (2) shows that $e^1 = e$ *(Proved)*

Uniqueness of the inverse

(2) The inverse of an element in a group is unique.

Proof. b is said to be an inverse of a if

$$ab = ba = e \in G \qquad \text{for } a, b \in G$$

Let the inverse be not unique

Let b and $c \in G$ be two distinct inverses of a

Then we have $\quad ab = ba = e$

And $\quad ac = ca = e$

Now $\quad (ba)\,c = ec = c \qquad a, b, c \in G$

$$b\,(ac) = be = b$$

Since associative property holds good in a group i.e.

$$(ba)\,c = b\,(ac)$$

$$\Rightarrow \qquad c = b$$

Hence the inverse is unique

Theorem 3 The equation $ax = b$ and $ya = b)$ $a, b, x, y \in G$, have uniqu solution in G.

Proofs: Substituting $a^{-1}\,b$ for x in $ax = b$ we obtain

$$a\,(a^{-1}\,b) = b$$

i.e. $\quad (aa^{-1})\,b = b) \qquad$ (associative axiom)

i.e. $\quad eb = b \qquad$ (existence of Inverse)

i.e. $\quad b = b \qquad$ (existence of identity)

Thus the equation $ax = b$ is satisfied by $x = a^{-1}\,b$

Also $\quad a, b \in G$

$\Rightarrow \quad a^{-1}, b \in G$

$\Rightarrow \quad a^{-1}\,b \in G \qquad$ [since G is closed with respect to the operation]

Furthermore the solution is unique. To prove it, if possible, x_1 and x_2 be two solutions of $ax = b$ then

$$ax_1 = b \text{ and } ax_2 = b$$

$\therefore \quad ax_1 = ax_2$

$\Rightarrow x_1 = x_2 \qquad$ [since cancellation law holds good in a group]

Hence $a^{-1}\,b$ is a unique solution of the equation $ax = b$

Similarly we can show that $ya = b$ has a unique solution ba^{-1}.

Theorem 4 If $a \in G$, then $(a^{-1})^{-1} = a$ i.e. the inverse of the inverse of an element of a group is the element itself.

Proof: The solution of the equation

$$a^{-1} x = e \text{ is } x = ae = a$$

But the solution of $a^{-1} x = e$ is the inverse of a^{-1}, so by the last theorem

$$(a^{-1})^{-1} = a$$

Hence the inverse of a^{-1} is a *(Proved)*

Theorem 5 The inverse of the product of two elements of a group is the product of the inverses of the eiements in the reverse order

i.e. $(ab)^{-1} = b^{-1} a^{-1}$: $a, b \in G$

Proof: We have

$$(ab)(b^{-1} a^{-1}) = [(ab) b^{-1}] a^{-1} \quad \text{[associative axiom]}$$
$$= [a (bb^{-1})] a^{-1} \quad \text{[associative axiom]}$$
$$= [ae] a^{-1} \quad \text{[existence of inverse]}$$
$$= aa^{-1} \quad \text{[existence of identify]}$$
$$= e \quad \text{[existence of inverse]}$$

Again
$$(b^{-1} a^{-1})(ab) = b^{-1} [a^{-1} (ab)] \quad \text{[associative axiom]}$$
$$= b^{-1} [(a^{-1} a) a] \quad \text{[associative axiom]}$$
$$= b^{-1} [eb] \quad \text{[existence of inverse]}$$
$$= b^{-1} (b) \quad \text{[existence of identify]}$$
$$= b \quad \text{[existence of inverse]}$$

Since $(ab)(b^{-1} a^{-1}) = (b^{-1} a^{-1})(ab) = e$

Hence by the deffnition of inverse we have

$$(ab^{-1}) = b^{-1} a^{-1}$$ *(Proved)*

Problem 1 Prove that if $a^2 = a$, then $a = e$, a being an element of a group.

Proof: We have $a^2 = a$

$$\Rightarrow \quad aa = a$$

Post multiplying both sides by a^{-1} we have

$$\Rightarrow \quad (a\,a) a^{-1} = aa^{-1}$$
$$\Rightarrow \quad a (aa^{-1}) = aa^{-1} \quad \text{Associative axiom holds in a group}$$
$$\Rightarrow \quad ae = e \quad \text{[identity holds in a group]}$$
$$\Rightarrow \quad a = e$$ *(Proved)*

Problem 2 Prove that

$(ab)^2 = a^2 b^2$, if and only if the group G is abelian where $a, b \in G$

Proof: Let us at first suppose that G is abelian

$$\Rightarrow \quad \text{if } a, b \in G$$

Then $\quad ab = ba$

Now $\quad (ab)^2 = (ab)(ab)$

$= [a(ba)b]$ by general associative axiom

$= [a(ab)b]$ since $ab = ba$

$= (aa)(bb)$ by general associative axiom

$= a^2 b^2$

Conversely we have

$$\Rightarrow (ab)(ab) = a^2 b^2$$

$$\Rightarrow (ab)(ab) = (aa)(bb)$$

$\Rightarrow a(ba)b = a(ab)b$ (By general associative axiom]

$\Rightarrow ba = ab$ [ξ left and right

Cancellation law which holds good in a group.] (*Proved*)

Subgroups

Let (G, o) be any group and H any subset of G. If the set H together with the operation o forms a group (H, o) then (H, o) is a group of (G, o)

Problem 2 If H be a subgroup of a group G, prove that the identity of H is the same as that of G.

Solution Let e and e^1 be the identities of G and H respectively. Then we have to prove that $\quad e^1 = e$

$$a \in H$$

Then $\quad e^1 a = a$

Since H is a subgroup of the group G, therefore

$$a \in H \Rightarrow a \in G$$

$\Rightarrow \quad ae = a$, by identity axiom

Hence in G we have

$$e^1 a = ea$$

$\Rightarrow \quad e^1 = e$, by right cancellation law

Hence the theorem

Criteria for a subgroup

Theorem 1 A non empty subset H of a group G is a subgroup of G if and only if

(i) $a \in H, b \in H \Rightarrow ab \in H$

(ii) $a \in H \Rightarrow a^{-1} \in H$ where a^{-1} is the inverse of a in G.

Proof : Firstly we shall prove the necessary conditions

Let H be a subgroup of the group G. Then H must possess the closure axiom viz

$$a \in H, b \in H \Rightarrow ab \in H$$

Thus the part (i) is proved

Let $a \in H$ then $a \in G$, as H is a subgroup of G

Let a^{-1} be the inverse of a in G since H is itself a group, therefore a^{-1} must be an element of H

Hence $\quad a \in H \Rightarrow a^{-1} \in H$

Thus the part (ii) is *Proved.*

Now let us suppose that two conditions are true then we have toprove that H is a subgroup of G.

By condition (i) $\quad a \in H, b \in H \Rightarrow ab \in H$

Hence H is closed with respect to multiplication operatian.

Since G is a group, therefore the operation in G is associative. Also since H is a subset of G, therefore all the elements of H must belong to G. Hence it follows that the operation in H must be associative.

Let e be the identity element in G

i.e. $\quad aa^{-1} = e \ \forall \ a \in G$

Again $\quad a \in H \Rightarrow a^{-1} \in H$

Then $\quad a \in H, a^{-1} \in H$

$$\Rightarrow aa^{-1} \in H$$

$$\Rightarrow e \in H$$

Hence e is the identity element of H

Again from (ii) $\quad a \in H \Rightarrow a^{-1} \in H$

Hence each element of H possesses an Inverse.

We find that the set H satisfies all the axioms of group. Hence H is a group.

But H is a subset of the group G.

Hence H is a sub group of G.

Theorem 2 The necessary and sufficient condition that a non-empty subset H of a group G be a sub group is

$$a \in H, b \in H \Rightarrow ab^{-1} \in H$$

Proof Firstly we have to prove the necessary condition.

Let us suppose that H is a subgroup of G. Then we have to prove that

$$a \in H, b \in H \Rightarrow ab^{-1} \in H$$

Let $\quad a \in H, b \in H$

$\Rightarrow \quad b^{-1} \in H$

Since H is a subgroup of G hence it is itself a group.

Since H is a group so it is closed with respect to the binary operation

So $\quad a, b \in H$

$\Rightarrow \quad a, b^{-1} \in H$

$\Rightarrow \quad ab^{-1} \in H$ [*First part proved*]

Now we shall prove the second part

i.e. Let $\quad a \in H, b \in H$

$\Rightarrow \quad ab^{-1} \in H$

Then we have to prove that H is a subgroup of G.

(1) Existence of identity

Let e be the idetity element of G

Since $\quad a, a \in H$

$\Rightarrow \quad aa^{-1} \in H$ [Vide *the given condition*]

$\Rightarrow \quad e \in H$

Hence the identify element exists in H.

(2) Existence of inverse element

Since $\quad e, a \ni H$

$\Rightarrow \quad ea^{-1} \in H$

$\Rightarrow \quad a^{-1} \in H$

Hence every element in H possesses inverse element.

(3) Closure axiom

Let $\quad a, b \in H$

$\Rightarrow \quad a, b^{-1} \in H$ [*Since inverse of each element exists in H*]

$\Rightarrow \quad a(b^{-1})^{-1} \in H$ [Vide *the given condition*]

$\Rightarrow \quad ab \in H$

Therefore the closure axiom is satisfied by H. Since G is a group. So operation in G is associative. The operation in his the same operation G. Since H is a subset of G. So binary operation in H is also associative. So H is a group. Since H is a subset and it is a group so it is a subgroup of G.

(*Proved*)

Theorem 3 Prove that the intersection of any two subgroups of a group is again a subgroup of that group.

Proof Let H_1 and H_2 be any two subgroups of a group G, then we have to prove that $H_1 \cap H_2$ is also a subgroup of G.

We know that the necessary and sufficient condition that a non-empty subset H of a group G, be a subgroup is

$$a \in H, b \in H \Rightarrow ab^{-1} \in H$$

Here Let $\quad a \in H_1 \cap H_2, b \in H_1 \cap H_2$

Then we have to prove that $ab^{-1} \in H_1 \cap H_2$.

Since $\quad a \in H_1 \cap H_2$

$\Rightarrow \quad a \in H_1$ and $a \in H_2$

$b \in H_1 \cap H_2$

Since $a \in H_1$, $b \in H_1$ and H_1 is a subgroup of G. Hence

$$ab^{-1} \in H_1 \tag{1}$$

Again $a \in H_2$, $b \in H_2$ and is a subgroup of G. Hence

$$ab^{-1} \in H_2 \tag{2}$$

From Relation (1) and (2) we have

$$ab^{-1} \in H_1 \cap H_2$$

i.e. $\quad a, b \in H_1 \cap H_2$

$$\Rightarrow \quad ab^{-3} \in H_1 \cap H_2 \tag{3}$$

Since H_1 and H_2 are subgroups of G

$\Rightarrow H_1$ and H_2 are non-empty subset of G.

$\Rightarrow H_1 \cap H_2$ is also a non-empty subset of G. (4)

Relation (4) and (5) shows that $H_1 \cap H_2$ is a subgroup of G. (*Proved*)

Problem Define cyclic-group and prove that every cyclic group is a belian.

Proof Let (G, O) be a group. If there exists $a \in G$ such that

$$G = \{a^i / i \in I\}$$

Where I is the set of all integers, then G is called a cyclic group, a is called the generator of the cyclic group, that is, the group G is said to be cyclic if it is capable of being generated by some element.

Let us consider the cyclic group $G = \{a\}$ whose generator is the element a

i.e. $$\{a\} = \{e, a, a^2 \ldots\}$$

Then we have to prove that the cyclic group G is abelian.

Let m_1 $n \in I$ the set of integers. Then by definition of cyclic group

$$a^m a^n = a^{m+a} = a^{n+m}$$

as $$m + n = n + m \ \forall\ m, n \in I$$

$$= a^n \cdot a^m$$

Hence the cyclic group G is abelian.

Again for the additive composition, we have

$$ma + na = na + ma$$

Hence every cyclic group is abelian. (*Provcd*)

Q. State and prove lagrange's theorem on group.

Statement: The order of a subgroup H of a finite group G is a divisor of the order of G.

Proof Let the order of the finite group G be n and the order of its subgroup H is m,

Let the m members of H be

$$h_1, h_2 \ldots hm ;$$

and let $a \in G$ but $a \notin H$

Then $h_1 a, h_2 a, h_3 a \ldots h_m a$ are m elements of Ha. It is clear that these elements are all different, for

$$h_i a = h_j a \qquad \text{Since} a \in G$$

$$\Rightarrow \quad (h_i a)\, a^{-1} = (h_j a)\, a^{-1} \qquad \Rightarrow a^{-1} \in G$$

$$\Rightarrow \quad h_i (aa^{-1}) = h_j (aa^1) \qquad \text{(inverselem into } f(a) \text{ in } G)$$

$$\Rightarrow \quad h_i e = h_j e \ \Rightarrow h_i = h_j$$

$$\therefore \quad h_i a \neq h_j a$$

Since G is finite therefore the number of such cosets is also finite. Let K be the number of disjoint rightcosets

$$\therefore \quad G = H \cup Ha_1 \cup Ha_2 \ldots \cup Hak$$

$\therefore$ The total no. of elements of G

= number of elements in the K cosets

i.e. $n = mK$, as each coset contains m elements

i.e. order of (G) = (order of H)$\cdot K$

Hence the order of a subgroup is a divisor of the order of the group.

(*Proved*)

Homomorphism and Isomorphism of group Homomorphism

Let (Go) and (G^1, o^1) be any two groups A mapping

$$f : G \to G^1 \text{ satisfying}$$

$$f(aob) = f(a)\ o^1\ f(b)$$

$$\forall\ a, b \in G$$

is called a hamomorphism of G to G^1.

Isomorphism

Let (G, o) and (G^1, o^1) be two groups A one-one on to mapping

$$f : G \to G^1$$

Satisfying $$f(aob) = f(a)\ o^1\ f(b)$$

$$\forall\ a, b \in G$$

is called an isomorphism of G to G^1

If there exists an isomorphism from (G, o) to (G^1, o^1), then we say that (G, o) is isomorphic to (G^1, o^1) symbolically we write it as

$$(G, o) \cong (G^1, o^1)$$

or $$G \cong G^1$$

37

Analytical Geometry of Three Domensions Planes, Straight Lines and Spheres

SPHERE

Formula Equation of a sphere whose centres $(\alpha, \beta. \gamma)$ and radius $= r$

$$(x-\alpha)^2+(y-\beta)^2+(z-\gamma)^2 = r^2 \tag{1}$$

Formula 2 If the centre of the sphere be origin (0, 0, 0) the equation of the sphere becomes

$$x^2 + y^2 + z^2 = r^2 \tag{2}$$

Formula 3 General form of the equation of the sphere be

$$x^2+y^2+z^2+24x+2vy+2wz+d = 0 \tag{3}$$

Centre of this sphere is $(-u, -v, -w)$

and radius is $\sqrt{u^2+v^2+w^2-d}$

Formula 4 The equation of a sphere through four points (x_1, y_1, z_1); (x_2, y_2, z_2); (x_3, y_3, z_3) and (x_4, y_4, z_4) is given by

$$\begin{vmatrix} x^2+y^2+z^2 & x & y & z & 1 \\ x_1^2+y_1^2+z_1^2 & x_1 & y_1 & z_1 & 1 \\ x_2^2+y_2^2+z_2^2 & x_2 & y_2 & z_2 & 1 \\ x_3^2+y_3^2+z_3^2 & x_3 & y_3 & z_3 & 1 \end{vmatrix}$$

Article 1 Equation of a sphere on the join of two given points as diameter. *[IFS 88]*

Let the co-ordinates of the given points A and B be (x_1, y_1, z_1); (x_2, y_2, z_2) respectively

Let $P(x, y, z)$ be any point on the sphere join AP and BP

The direction ratios of the line AP are $x-x_1, y-y_1, z-z_1$ and the direction ratios of the line BP are $x-x_2, y-y_2, z-z_2$

Now, since the line AP and BP are at right angle so

Remember $(x-x_1)(x-x_2)+(y-y_1)(y-y_2)+(z-z_1)(z-z_2)=0$

Which is the required equation of the sphere.

Problem 1 If one end of a diameter of the sphere

$$x^2+y^2+z^2-2x+4y-6z-11=0 \text{ be } (-1, 2, 4);$$

find the co-ordinates of other end

Solution Let the co-ordinate of the other end is (α, β, γ) then the centre of the sphere is

$$\left(-\frac{1+\alpha}{2} \quad \frac{2+\beta}{2}, \quad \frac{4+\gamma}{2}\right)$$

The equation of the sphere is

$$x^2+y^2+z^2-2x+4y-6z-11=0$$

co-ordinate of the centre $(+1, -2, +3)$

Hence we have $\frac{-1+\alpha}{2}=1 \Rightarrow -1+\alpha=2 \Rightarrow \alpha=3$

$$\frac{2+\beta}{2}=-2$$

$$2+\beta=-4$$

$$\beta=-6$$

$$\frac{4+\gamma}{2}=3$$

$$4+\gamma=6$$

$$\gamma=2$$

so co-ordinate of the other end is $(3, -6, 2)$

Problem 2 A sphere of radius r passes through the origin and meets the axes in A, B, C prove that the centroid of the triangle ABC lies on the sphere

$$9(x^2+y^2+z^2)=4r^2$$

Let 0 (0, 0, 0) be the origin

Let the co-ordinate of the points A, B, C be respectively $(a, 0, 0)$, $(0, b, 0)$ and $(0, 0, c)$

There general equation of a sphere is given by

$$x^2+y^2+z^2+2ux+2vy+2wz+d=0 \tag{1}$$

This passes through $(a, 0, 0)$

so $\qquad d=0$

Again (1) passes through $(a, 0, 0)$

so $$a^2 + 2ua = 0$$

$$a^2 = -2ua$$

$$u = -\frac{a}{2}$$

Again equation (1) passes through $(0, b, 0)$

$$b^2 + 2vb = 0 \Rightarrow v = -\frac{b}{2}$$

and similarly $w = -\dfrac{c}{2}$

Putting the values of u, v, w and d in equation (1) the required equation of the sphere is given by

$$x^2 + y^2 + z^2 - ax - by - cz = 0 \tag{2}$$

Radius of this circle is

$$\sqrt{u^2 + v^2 + w^2 - d}$$

$$\sqrt{=\frac{a^2}{4} + \frac{b^2}{4} + \frac{c^2}{4}} = \sqrt{\frac{a^2 + b^2 + c^2}{4}}$$

But the radius of the sphere is given to be r

so $$\frac{a^2 + b^2 + c^2}{4} = r^2$$

$$a^2 + b^2 + c^2 = 4r^2$$

Let centroid of the triangle is (α, β, γ)

$$\alpha = \frac{a + 0 + 0}{3} = \frac{a}{3}$$

$$\beta = \frac{0 + b + 0}{3} = \frac{b}{3}$$

$$\gamma = \frac{0 + 0 + c}{3} = \frac{c}{3}$$

$$\Rightarrow \qquad a = 3\alpha, b = 3\beta, c = 3\gamma$$

Putting the values of a, b and c we have

$$9(\alpha^2 + \beta^2 + \gamma^2) = 4r^2$$

Hence the locus of (α, β, γ) is

$$9(x^2 + y^2 + z^2) = 4r^2$$

(Proved)

Problem 3 A plane passes through a fixed point (f, g, h) and cuts the axis in A, B, C, show that the locus of the centre of the sphere is

$$\frac{f}{x} + \frac{g}{y} + \frac{h}{z} = 2$$

Solution Let the co-ordinates of the points A, B, C be respectively $(a, 0\ 0)$, $(0, b, 0)$ and $(0, 0, c)$

Hence the equation of the plane is

$$\frac{x}{a} + \frac{y}{b} + \frac{z}{c} = 1$$

Since the plane passes through the point (f, g, h) we have

$$\frac{f}{a} + \frac{g}{b} + \frac{h}{c} = 1 \qquad (1)$$

Now the equation of the sphere through the points 0, A, B, C is

$$x^2 + y^2 + z^2 - ax - by - cz = 0$$

The co-ordinate of the centre is given by

$$\alpha = \frac{a}{2}\ \beta = \frac{b}{2}\ \gamma = \frac{c}{2}$$

$$\Rightarrow \qquad a = 2\alpha \qquad b = 2\beta, \qquad c = 2\gamma$$

Substituting the values of a, b, c in equation (1) we have

$$\frac{f}{2\alpha} + \frac{g}{2\beta} + \frac{h}{2\gamma} = 1$$

$$\frac{f}{\alpha} + \frac{g}{\beta} + \frac{h}{\gamma} = 1$$

Hence the locus of (α, β, γ) is

$$\frac{f}{x} + \frac{g}{y} + \frac{h}{z} = 2 \qquad \textit{(Proved)}$$

Problem 4 Obtain the equation of the sphere passing through the points $(1, 0\ 0)$, $(0, 1, 0)$, $(0, 0, 1)$ which has its radius as *small as possible.*

Solution General equation of the sphere is given by

$$x^2 + y^2 + z^2 + 2gx + 2fy + 2wz + d = 0 \qquad (1)$$

As it passes through the points $(1, 0, 0)$; $(0, 1\ 0)$ $(0, 0, 1)$ so these points wili satisfy equation (1)

$$1 + 2g + d = 0 \qquad (2)$$

$$1 + 2f + d = 0 \qquad (3)$$

$$1 + 2w + d = 0 \qquad (4)$$

From equation (2) and (3)

$$2(g-f)=0 \quad \Rightarrow g=f$$

From equation (3) and (4)

$$2(f-w)=0 \quad \Rightarrow f=w$$

$$\Rightarrow \qquad f=g=w=-\frac{d+1}{2}$$

Radius of the sphere $= \sqrt{g^2+f^2+w^2-d}$

$$=\sqrt{3g^2-d} = \sqrt{3\left(\frac{d+1}{2}\right)^2-d}$$

$$=\sqrt{\frac{3(d+1)^2}{4}-d} = \sqrt{\frac{3(d^2+2d-1)}{4}-a}$$

$$=\frac{1}{2}\sqrt{3d^2+6d+3-4d}$$

$$=\frac{1}{2}\sqrt{3d^2+2d+3}$$

$$=\frac{1}{2}\sqrt{3\left(d^2+\frac{2}{3}d+1\right)}$$

$$=\frac{1}{2}\sqrt{3\left\{\left(d+\frac{1}{3}\right)^2+\frac{8}{9}\right\}}$$

$$=\frac{1}{2}\sqrt{3\left(d+\frac{1}{2}\right)^2+\frac{8}{9}}$$

$$=\frac{1}{2}\sqrt{3\left(d+\frac{1}{3}\right)^2+2\frac{2}{3}}$$

$\therefore$ For the radius to be as small as we please we should have

$$d+\tfrac{1}{3}=0$$

$$\Rightarrow \qquad d=-\tfrac{1}{3}$$

$$\therefore \qquad f=g=h=-\frac{d+1}{2}$$

$$=-\frac{-\frac{1}{3}+1}{2}=-\frac{(-1+3)/3}{2}=-\frac{\frac{2}{3}}{2}$$

$$=-\frac{2}{3\times 2}=-\frac{1}{3}$$

∴ The required equation of the sphere is

$$x^2+y^2+z^2+2\left(-\tfrac{1}{3}\right)x+2\left(-\tfrac{1}{3}\right)y+2\left(-\tfrac{1}{3}\right)z-\tfrac{1}{3}=0$$

$$\Rightarrow \quad x^2+y^2+z^2-\tfrac{2}{3}x-\tfrac{2}{3}y-\tfrac{2}{3}z-\tfrac{1}{3}=0$$

$$\Rightarrow \quad 3(x^2+y^2+z^2)-2x-2y-2z-1=0$$

This is the required equation of the *sphere.*

Problem 4 Find the equation of the sphere if the extremeties of its one diameter are the points (3, 4, −2) and (−2, −1, 0). Find also the co-ordinates of its centre and radius.

Solution The equation of a sphere whose diameters are the line joining the tow points (x_1, y_1, z_1) and (x_2, y_2, z_2) is given by

$$(x-x_1)(x-x_2)+(y-y_1)(y-y_2)+(z-z_1)(z-z_2)=0$$

Here $x_1=3,\ y_1=4,\ z_1=-2,\ x_2=-2,\ y_2=-1,\ z_2=0$

$$(x-3)(x+2)+(y-4)(y+1)+(z+2)(z-0)=0$$

$$x^2+2x-3x-6+y^2+y-4y-4+z^2+2z=0$$

$$\Rightarrow \quad x^2-x-6+y^2-3y-4+z^2+2z=0$$

$$\Rightarrow \quad x^2+y^2+z^2-x-3y+2z-10=0$$

Radiusof the sphere

$$=\sqrt{\left(\frac{1}{2}\right)^2+\left(\frac{3}{2}\right)^2+(-1)^2-(-10)}=\sqrt{\frac{1}{4}+\frac{9}{4}+1+10}$$

$$=\sqrt{\frac{1+9+4}{4}+10}=\sqrt{\frac{54}{4}}=\tfrac{1}{2}\sqrt{54}=\tfrac{1}{2}\sqrt{6\times 9}$$

The centre D of the sphere $=\left(\frac{1}{2}, \frac{3}{2}, -1\right)$

Radius of the sphere $=\dfrac{3\sqrt{6}}{2}$ **Ans.**

Problem 5 Find the sphere passing through the point (α, β, γ) and the circle

$$x^2+y^2=a^2,\ z=0$$

Solution The given circle is

$$x^2+y^2=a^2,\ z=0$$

or

$$x^2+y^2+z^2=a^2,\ z=0$$

i.e.

$$S_1 \equiv x^2+y^2+z^2-a^2=0 \quad \text{and } S_2 \equiv z=0$$

Let the equation of the sphere passing through the given circle be

$$S_1+kS_2=0$$

$$(x^2+y^2+z^2-a^2)+kz=0$$

$$x^2+y^2+z^2-a^2+kz=0 \qquad \text{(i)}$$

This sphere passes through a fixed point (α, β, γ) so

$$\alpha^2 + \beta^2 + \gamma^2 - a^2 + k\gamma = 0$$

$$-K\gamma = (\alpha^2 + \beta^2 + \gamma^2 - a^2)$$

$$K = -\frac{1}{\gamma}(\alpha^2 + \beta^2 + \gamma^2 - a^2)$$

Substituting the value of k in equation (1) we have

$$x^2 + y^2 + z^2 - a^2 - \frac{1}{\gamma}(\alpha^2 + \beta^2 + \gamma^2 - a^2)\, z = 0$$

$$\Rightarrow \quad \gamma\,(x^2 + y^2 + z^2 - a^2) - (\alpha^2 + \beta^2 + y^2 - a^2)\, z = 0$$

This is the required equation of the sphere

Problem 6 Find the equation of the sphere which passes through the point (2, 3, 4) and the circle $z = 0$, $x^2 + y^2 = 4$

Solution Equation of the circle

$$x^2 + y^2 = 4 \qquad z = 0$$

or

$$x^2 + y^2 + z^2 = 4 \qquad z = 0$$

The equation of a sphere passing through the given circle is given by

$$(x^2 + y^2 + z^2 - 4) + kz = 0 \tag{1}$$

Again equation (1) passes through the point (2, 3, 4) so

$$4 + 9 + 16 - 4 + k4 = 0$$

$$\Rightarrow \quad 25 + 4k = 0$$

$$\Rightarrow \quad k = -\frac{25}{4}$$

Substituting the value of k in equation (1) we have

$$(x^2 + y^2 + z^2 - 4) - \frac{25}{4} z = 0$$

$$4\,(x^2 + y^2 + z^2 - 4) - 25z = 0$$

$$\Rightarrow \quad 4\,(x^2 + y^2 + z^2) - 16 - 25z = 0$$

$$\Rightarrow \quad 4\,(x^2 + y^2 + z^2) - 25z - 16 = 0$$

This is the required equation of the sphere.

Problem 7 Find the equation of the sphere through the circle

$$x^2 + y^2 + z^2 = 36,\ x + y - z + 1 = 0$$

and the point (1,2, 3).

Solution Equation of the sphere through the given circle is given by

$$x^2 + y^2 + z^2 - 36 + k\,(x + y - z + 1) = 0 \tag{1}$$

Equation (1) passes through the point (1, 2, 3) so we have

$$1 + 4 + 9 - 36 + k(1 + 2 - 3 + 1) = 0$$

i.e.
$$-22 + k = 0$$
$$\Rightarrow \quad k = 22$$

Substituting the value of k in equation (1) we have

$$x^2 + y^2 + z^2 - 36 + 22(x + y - z + 1) = 0$$

i.e.
$$x^2 + y^2 + z^2 + 22x + 22y - 22z - z - 36 + 22 = 0$$
$$\Rightarrow \quad x^2 + y^2 + z^2 + 22x + 22y - 22z - 14 = 0$$

This is the required equation of the *sphere*.

Problem 8 Find the equation of the sphere having the circle

$$x^2 + y^2 + z^2 + 7y - 2z + 2 = 0 ; \ 2x + 3y + 4z = 8$$

As the great circle [*Must Revise Trick*]

Solution Let the equation of the sphere through the given circle be

$$x^2 + y^2 + z^2 + 7y - 2z + 2 + k(2x + 3y + 4z - 8) = 0$$
$$x^2 + y^2 + z^2 + 2kx + (7 + 3k)y - 2(1 - 2k)z + 2 - 8k = 0 \quad (1)$$

so
$$u = k, v = \frac{7 + 3k}{2}$$
$$w = -(1 - 2k) \qquad w = 2k - 1$$

Can be of the sphere $(-u, v, -w)$

$$= \left(-k, -\frac{7 + 3k}{2}, 1 - 2k\right)$$

By question, the given circle is the great circle. Therefore the centre of the sphere must lie on the plane of intersection

$$2x + 3y + 4z = 8$$

$$\therefore \quad 2(-k) + 3\left(-\frac{7 + 3k}{2}\right) + 4(1 - 2k) = 8$$
$$\Rightarrow \quad -2k - 3\frac{(7 + 3k)}{2} + 4(1 - 2k) = 8$$
$$\Rightarrow \quad -4k - 21 - 9k + 8 - 16k = 8 + 8$$
$$\Rightarrow \quad -29k - 29 = 0$$
$$\Rightarrow \quad 29k = -29$$
$$\Rightarrow \quad k = -\frac{29}{29}$$
$$\Rightarrow \quad k = -1$$

Puttiug the value of k in equation (1) we have the equation of the sphere as

$$x^2 + y^2 + z^2 + 2(-1)x + (7 - 3)y - 2(1 + 2)z + 2 + 8 = 0$$
$$x^2 + y^2 + z^2 - 2x + 4y - 6z + 10 = 0$$

Problem 9 Obtain the equation of the sphere having its centre on the line $5x + 2z = 0 = 2x - 3y$, and passing through the points $(0, -2, -4)$ and $(2, -1, -1)$

Solution Let the equation of the sphere be

$$x^2 + y^2 + z^2 + 2ux + 2vy + 2wz + d = 0 \quad (1)$$

Its centre is $(-u, -v. -w)$ and it lies on the line

$$5x + 2z = 0 = 2x - 3y$$

i.e. $$-5u - 2w = 0 \quad (2)$$

and $$-2u + 3v = 0 \quad (3)$$

Equation (2) implies that $5u = -2w$

equation (3) implies that $2u = 3v$

Let $$2u = 3v = 6k$$

$$u = 3k, v = 2k$$

$$15k = -2w \quad w = -\frac{15}{2}k$$

Again sphere (1) passes through the points $(0, -2, -4)$ and $(2, -1, -1)$

so $$4 + 16 - 2.0u - 4v - 8w + d = 0$$

i.e. $$20 - 4v - 8w + d = 0$$

or $$d = 4v + 8w - 20$$

$$d = -20 + 8k - 60k$$

$$d = -20 - 52k$$

Again $$4 + 1 + 1 + 4u - 2v - 2w + d = 0$$

i.e. $$6 + 4u - 2v - 2w + d = 0$$

or $$d = -6 - 4u + 2v + 2w$$

or $$d = -6 - 4\cdot 3k + 2\cdot 2k + 2\left(-\frac{15}{2}k\right)$$

or $$d = -6 - 12k + 4k - 15k$$

or $$d = -6 - 23k \quad (5)$$

Thus from equation (4) and (5) we have

$$-20 - 52k = -6 - 23k$$

$$-20 + 6 = 52k - 23k$$

$$-14 = 29k$$

$$\Rightarrow \quad k = -\frac{14}{29}$$

From (5) $$d = -6 - 23 \times \left(-\frac{14}{29}\right) = \frac{148}{29}$$

$$\therefore \qquad u = \frac{3(-14)}{29} = \frac{-42}{29}$$

i.e.
$$v = \frac{2(-14)}{29} = \frac{-28}{29}$$

$$w = -\frac{15}{2}k = -\frac{15}{2}\left(-\frac{14}{29}\right) = +\frac{105}{29}$$

Substituting the values of u, v, w and d in equation (1) we have

$$x^2 + y^2 + z^2 + 2\left(-\frac{42}{29}\right)x + 2\left(-\frac{28}{29}\right)y$$

$$+ 2\left(\frac{105}{29}\right)z + \frac{148}{29} = 0$$

i.e. $\qquad 29(x^2 + y^2 + z^2) - 84x - 56y + 210z + 148 = 0$

This is the required equation of the sphere.

Problem 10 Show that the plane $2x + y - z = 12$ touches the sphere $x^2 + y^2 + z^2 = 24$ and find its point of contact.

Solution Radius of the sphere $= \sqrt{24} = \sqrt{6 \times 4} = 2\sqrt{6}$

Centre of this sphere is (0, 0, 0) Then the length of perpendicular from (0, 0, 0) to the plane $\quad 2x + y - z = 12$ is

$$\frac{2 \cdot 0 + 0 - 0 - 12}{\sqrt{2^2 + 1^2 + (-1)^2}} = \frac{-12}{\sqrt{4 + 1 + 1}} = -\frac{12}{\sqrt{6}} = -\frac{6 \times 2}{\sqrt{6}}$$

$$= -\frac{\sqrt{6} \times \sqrt{6} \times 2}{\sqrt{6}} = -2\sqrt{6}$$

Taking only the magnitude. The length of perpendicular drawn from (0, 0, 0) to the plane $2x + y - z = 12$ is $2\sqrt{6}$ which is equal to the radius of the sphere. Thus the plane $2x + y - z = 12$ touches the sphere

$$x^2 + y^2 + z^2 = 24$$

Let the plane

$$2x + y - z = 12 \tag{1}$$

touches the sphere $x^2 + y^2 + z^2 = 24$ at the point (x_1, y_1, z_1) i.e. the coordinate of the point of contact is (x_1, y_1, z_1).

Now the equation of the plane can be written as

$$xx_1 + py_1 + zz_1 = 24 \tag{2}$$

Now equatio (1) and (2) represent the same plane hence comparing equation (1) and (2) we have

$$\frac{x_1}{2} = \frac{y_1}{1} = \frac{z_1}{-1} = \frac{24}{12}$$

$$x_1 = \frac{24}{12} \times 2$$

$$x_1 = 4$$

$$y_1 = \frac{24}{12} = 2$$

So $(x_1, y_1, z_1) = (4, 2, -2)$

So the point of contact is $(4, 2, -2)$. **Ans.**

Problem 11 Find the equation of a sphere which touches the sphere

$$x^2 + y^2 + z^2 = 9$$

At the point (1, 2, 2) and passes through thc origin.

Solution Since the required sphere touches the given sphere

$$x^2 + y^2 + z^2 = 9 \text{ at } (1. 2, 2)$$

Therefore these two sphere must have the common tangent plane at (1, 2, 2). The equation of the tangent plane to $x^2 + x^2 + z^2 = 9$ at (1, 2, 2) is

$$x + 2y + 2z = 9$$

Let the equation of the sphere touching the given sphere at (1, 2, 2) be

$$x^2 + y^2 + z^2 - 9 + k\,(x + 2y + 2z - 9) = 0 \qquad (1)$$

Since this sphere passes through origin

So $-9-9k = 0 \Rightarrow k = -1$

Substituting the values of k in equation (1) we have

$$x^2 + y^2 + z^2 - 9 + (-1)\,(x + 2y + 2z - 9) = 0$$

i.e. $$x^2 + y^2 + z^2 - 9 - x - 2y - 2z + 9 = 0$$

$$x^2 + y^2 + z^2 - x - 2y - 2z = 0$$

This is the required equation of the *sphere*.

Problem 12 Obtain the equation of the sphere which touches the sphere $x^2 + y^2 + z^2 = 22$ at (2. 3, -3) and passes through the origin.

Solution Since the required sphere touches the sphere $x^2 + y^2 + z^2 = 22$ at (2, 3, -3). So the two surfaces has the common tangent plane.

Equation of the tangent plane to the sphere $x^2 + y^2 + z^2 = 22$ at the point (2, 3, -3) is given by

$$2x + 3y - 3z - 22 = 0 \qquad (1)$$

Now equation of the sphere passing through the intersection of the sphere and the tangent plane is given by

$$(x^2 + y^2 + z^2 - 22) + k\,(2x + 3y - 3z - 22) = 0 \qquad (2)$$

Since sphere (2) passes through the origin

Hence $-22-22k = 0$

$\Rightarrow \quad 22k = -22$

$\Rightarrow \quad k = -1$

So the equation of the sphere is given by

$$(x^2 + y^2 + z^2 - 22) - 1\,(2x + 3y - 3z - 22) = 0$$

$$\Rightarrow \quad x^2 + y^2 + z^2 - 22 - 2x - 3y + 3z + 22 = 0$$

$$\Rightarrow \quad x^2 + y^2 + z^2 - 2x - 3y + 3z = 0$$

Which is the required equation cf the sphere.

Problem 13 Find the equations of the spheres which pass through the circle

$$x^2 + y^2 + z^2 = 5,$$
$$x + 2y + 3z = 3$$

and touch the plane $4x + 3y = 15$

Solution The equations of the spheres which passes through the circle

$$x^2 + y^2 + z^2 = 5, x + 2y + 3z = 3$$

are given by $x^2 + y^2 + z^2 - 5 + k\,(x + 2y + 3z - 3) = 0$

$$x^2 + y^2 + z^2 - 5 + kx + 2ky + 3kz - 3k = 0$$

$$x^2 + y^2 + z^2 + kx + 2ky + 3kz - (5 + 3k) = 0 \qquad (1)$$

Then $2u = k \Rightarrow u = \frac{k}{2}$

$2v = 2k \Rightarrow v = k$

$2w = 3k \Rightarrow w = \frac{3}{2}k$

$d = -(5+3k)$

Thus the centre of the sphere is given by

$$(-u, -v, -w) = \left(-\frac{k}{2}, -k, -\frac{3}{2}k\right)$$

and the radius of the sphere is

$$\sqrt{u^2 + v^2 + w^2 - d} = \sqrt{\frac{k^2}{4} + k^2 + \frac{9}{4}k^2 + 5 + 3k}$$

$$= \sqrt{\frac{14k^2 + 12k + 20}{4}}$$

This sphere will tuch the plane $4x + 3y = 15$ if the length of perpendicular drawn from the centre of the sphere to the plane must be equal to the radius.

i.e. $$\frac{4\left(-\frac{k}{2}\right)+3(-k)-15}{\sqrt{16+9}} = \sqrt{\frac{14k^2+12k+20}{4}}$$

$$\frac{-2k-3k-15}{5} = \frac{\sqrt{14k^2+12k+20}}{2}$$

$$-\frac{5k-15}{5} = \frac{\sqrt{14k^2+12k+20}}{2}$$

$$-2(k+3) = \sqrt{14k^2+12k+20}$$

Squaring both sides we have

$$4(k^2+6k+9) = 14k^2+12k+20$$

$$\Rightarrow \quad 4k^2+24k+36 = 14k^2+12k+20$$

$$\Rightarrow \quad 10k^2-12k-16 = 0$$

$$\Rightarrow \quad 5\ {}^2-6k-8 = 0$$

$$\Rightarrow \quad 5k^2-10k+4k-8 = 0$$

$$\Rightarrow \quad 5k(k-2)+4(k-2) = 0$$

$$\Rightarrow \quad (5k+4)(k-2) = 0$$

If $$5k+4=0 \Rightarrow k = -\frac{4}{5}$$

$$k-2=4 \Rightarrow k=2$$

substituting the values of k in equation (1) we get

$$x^2+y^2+z^2+2x+4y+6z-11=0 \tag{2}$$

and $$x^2+y^2+z^2-\frac{4}{5}x-\frac{8}{5}y-\frac{12}{5}z-\left(5+3x-\frac{4}{5}\right)=0$$

i.e. $$5(x^2+y^2+z^2)-4x-8y-12z-\left(\frac{25-12}{5}\right)=0$$

i.e. $$5(x^2+y^2+z^2)-4x-8y-12z-13=0 \tag{3}$$

(2) and (3) are the required equations of the spheres. **Ans.**

Problem 14 If the tangent plane to the sphere $x^2+y^2+z^2=r^2$ makes intercepts a, b, c on the coordinate axes, prove that $a^{-2}+b^{-2}+c^{-2}=r^{-2}$

Solution The equation of the sphere is $x^2+y^2+z^2=r^2$ (1)

The equation of the tangent plane to the sphere at (x_1, y_1, z_1) is

$$xx_1+yy_1+zz_1=r^2 \tag{2}$$

This tangent plane makes intercepts a, b, c on the co-ordinate axes.

Therefore $(a, 0, 0)$, $(0, b, 0)$, $(0, 0, c)$ must satisfy (2)

Thus $\qquad ax_1 = r^2 \quad \Rightarrow \quad x_1 = \frac{r^2}{a}$

$\qquad by_1 = r^2 \quad \Rightarrow \quad y_1 = \frac{r^2}{b}$

$\qquad cz_1 = r^2 \quad \Rightarrow \quad z_1 = \frac{r^2}{c}$

The point $(x_1\ y_1, z_1)$ lies on (2)

So
$$x_1^2 + y_1^2 + z_1^2 = r^2$$
$$\frac{r^4}{a^2} + \frac{r^4}{b^2} + \frac{r^4}{c^2} = r^2$$
$$\Rightarrow \quad a^{-2} + b^{-2} + c^{-2} = r^{-2}$$

Problem 15 Prove that the circles
$$x^2 + y^2 + z^2 - 2x + 3y + 4z - 5 = 0,\ 5y + 6z + 1 = 0$$
$$x^2 + y^2 + z^2 - 3x - 4y + 5z - 6 = 0,\ \ x + 2y - 7z = 0$$
lie on the same sphere and find its equation

Solution The equation of the sphere through the first circle is
$$x^2 + y^2 + z^2 - 2x + 3y + 4z - 5 + \lambda\,(5y + 6z + 1) = 0 \qquad (1)$$
The equation of the sphere through the second circle is
$$x^2 + y^2 + z^2 - 3x - 4y + 5z - 6 + \lambda_1\,(x + 2y - 7z) = 0 \qquad (2)$$
If the equations (1) and (2) represent the same sphere, then the coefficients of x, y, z and constant should be the same. Hence on comparing coefficients wə get

$$-2 = -3 + \lambda_1 \qquad \text{i.e.} \qquad \lambda_1 = 1$$

i.e. $\qquad 5\lambda + 3 = -4 + 2\lambda_1 \qquad\qquad 5\lambda + 3 = -2$

$$5\lambda + 3 = -4 + 2 \qquad\qquad \lambda = -\frac{5}{5} = -1$$

So $\qquad \lambda_1 = 1 \qquad \lambda = -1$

and comparing the coefficient we have

$$\left.\begin{aligned} -5 + \lambda &= -6 \\ 4 + 6\lambda &= 5 - 7\lambda_1 \end{aligned}\right\}$$ Both are satlsfied for values of λ and λ_1 found above

i.e. $\qquad -5 - 1 = -6$ (true)

$$4 - 6 = 5 - 7\,(1) = -2 \text{ (True)}$$

Then putting the value of λ in (1) and λ_1 in (2) we get the equation of sphere as
$$x^2 + y^2 + z^2 - 2x + 3y + 4z - 5 + (-1)\,(5y + 6z + 1) = 0$$
$$\Rightarrow \quad x^2 + y^2 + z^2 - 2x + 3y + 4z - 5 - 5y - 6z - 1 = 0$$
$$\Rightarrow \quad x^2 + y^2 + z^2 - 2x - 2y - 2z - 6 = 0$$
which is the required equation of the sphere.

Problem 16 Find the co-ordinates of the centre and the radius of the circle $x^2 + y^2 + z^2 - 2y - 4z = 11,\ x + 2y + 2z = 15$

Solution The equation of the sphere is

$$x^2 + y^2 + z^2 - 2y - 4z = 11 = 0$$

$$(x-0)^2 + (y-1)^2 + (z-2)^2 - 1 - 4 - 11 = 0$$

$$(x-0)^2 + (y-1)^2 + (z-2)^2 = 16$$

$$(x-0)^2 + (y-1)^2 + (z-2)^2 = 4^2$$

Length of the perpendicular from the centre (0, 1, 2) on the given plane

$$x + 2y + 2z = 15 \text{ is}$$

$$\frac{2\cdot 0 + 2.1 + 2\cdot 2 - 15}{\sqrt{1^2 + 2^2 + 2^2}} = -\frac{9}{3} = -3 = 3 \text{ (\textit{in magnitude})}$$

Radius of the circle

$$= \sqrt{(\text{Radius of the sphere})^2 - (\text{length of perpeendicular to the given plane})^2}$$

$$= \sqrt{(4)^2 - (3)^2} = \sqrt{16 - 9} = \sqrt{7}$$

Equation of a line through (0, 1, 2) and perpendicular to the given plane are

$$\frac{x-0}{1} = \frac{y-1}{2} = \frac{z-2}{2} = r \text{ (say)}$$

$$\Rightarrow \quad x = r,\ y = 2r + 1,\ z = 2r + 2$$

i.e. co-ordinate of any point on this line is $(r, 2r + 1, 2r + 2)$

If it is the foot of the perpendicular from the centre of the sphere to the given plane, its co-ordinates must satisfy the equation of the plane

$$r + 2(2r + 1) + 2(2r + 2) = 15$$

$$r + 4r + 2 + 4r + 4 = 15$$

$$9r = 9$$

$$\Rightarrow \quad r = 1$$

Hence the co-ordinates of the centre of the circle are (1, 3, 4) **Ans.**

Problem 17 Prove that the centres of the spheres touch the lines

$$y = mx,\ z = c \quad \text{and} \quad y = -mx,\ z = -c$$

must lie on the conicoid $mxy + c(1 + m^2)z = 0$

Solution Let the sphere

$$x^2 + y^2 + z^2 + 2ux + 2vy + 2wz + d = 0 \qquad (1)$$

touch the line $y = mx,\ z = c$

then $x^2 + m^2 x^2 + c^2 + 2ux + 2vmx + 2wc + d = 0$

$$\Rightarrow \quad (1 + m^2)x^2 + 2(u + vm)x + (c^2 + 2wc + d) = 0$$

The roots of this equation must be equal. The condition for equal roots is

$$[2\{(u + vm)\}]^2 = 4\,(1 + m^2)(c^2 + 2wc + d)$$

$$(u + vm)^2 = (1 + m^2)(c^2 + 2wc + d) \tag{2}$$

Again the sphere (1) touches the line

$$y = -mx, \quad z = c$$

Then $\quad x^2 + m^2\,x^2 + c^2 + 2ux - 2vmx + 2w\,(-c) + d = 0$

i.e. $\quad x^2\,(1 + m^2) + 2\,(u - vm)\,x + (c^2 - 2wc + d) = 0$

The roots of this equation must be equal, then

$$4\,\{u - vm)^2 = 4\,(1 + m^2)(c^2 - 2wc + d)$$

i.e. $\quad (u - vm)^2 = (1 + m^2)(c^2 - 2wc + d) \qquad (3)$

Subtracting (3) from (2) we have

$$(u + vm)^2 - (u - vm)^2 = (1 + m^2)(c^2 + 2wc + d - c^2 + 2wc - d)$$

$$4uvm = (1 + m^2)\,4wc$$

$$uvm = (1 + m^2)\,wc \tag{4}$$

To find the locus of the centre $(-u, \ -v, \ -w)$ of the sphere (1) we replace $-u, \ -v, \ -w$ by x, y, z respectively in (4)

Then $\quad (-x)(-y)(m) = (1 + m^2)(-z)\,c$

$$mxy = -c\,(1 + m^2)\,z$$

i.e. $\quad mxy + c\,(1 + m^2)\,z = 0$

which is *a* conicoid.

Problem 18 A variable plane is parallel to the given plane

$$\frac{x}{a} + \frac{y}{b} + \frac{z}{c} = 0$$

and meets the axes in A, B, C respectively. Prove that the circle ABC lies on the surface

$$\left(\frac{b}{c} + \frac{c}{b}\right) yz + \left(\frac{a}{c} + \frac{c}{a}\right) zx + \left(\frac{a}{b} + \frac{b}{a}\right) xy = 0$$

Solution The given plane is

$$\frac{x}{a} + \frac{y}{b} + \frac{z}{c} = 0 \tag{1}$$

Let the equation of the plane parallel to (1) be

$$\frac{x}{a} + \frac{y}{b} + \frac{z}{c}\ k \tag{2}$$

or

$$\frac{x}{ak} + \frac{y}{bk} + \frac{z}{ck} = 1$$

It meets the axes in A, B, C respectively

$$OA = ak, \; OB = bk, \; OC = ck$$

Therefore A, B, C are respectively

$$(ak, 0, 0); (0, bk, 0); (0, 0, ck)$$

$$OA = ak, \; OB = bk, \; OC = ck$$

Let the equation of the sphere passing through $0\,(0, 0, 0)$, $A\,(ak, 0, 0)$, $B\,(0, bk, 0)$, $C\,(0, 0, ck)$ be

$$x^2 + y^2 + z^2 + 2ux + 2vy + 2wz + d = 0 \tag{3}$$

Since (2) passes througn $0\,(0, 0, 0)$

$\Rightarrow$ $\quad d = 0$

again $\quad a^2 k^2 + 2uak = 0$

$\Rightarrow$ $\quad 2u = -ak$

$\quad b^2 k^2 + 2vbk = 0$

$\Rightarrow$ $\quad 2v = -bk$

$\quad c^2 k^2 + 2wck = 0$

$\Rightarrow$ $\quad 2w = -ck$

Substituting these values in equation (3) we have

$$x^2 + y^2 + z^2 - ak\,x - bky - ckz = 0$$

i.e.
$$x^2 + y^2 + z^2 - k\,(ax + by + cz) = 0 \tag{4}$$

Eliminating k from (2) and (4), we find that the circle ABC lies on the surface

$$x^2 + y^2 + z^2 - \left(\frac{x}{a} + \frac{y}{b} + \frac{z}{c}\right)(ax + by + cz) = 0$$

i.e.
$$x^2 + y^2 + z^2 - \left\{x^2 + \frac{b}{a}\,xy + \frac{c}{a}\,xz + y^2 + \frac{a}{b}\,xy + \frac{c}{b}\,yz + \frac{a}{c}\,zx + \frac{b}{c}\,zy + z^2\right\} = 0$$

i.e.
$$-\left[\left(\frac{a}{b} + \frac{b}{a}\right)xy + \left(\frac{b}{c} + \frac{c}{b}\right)yz + \left(\frac{a}{c} + \frac{c}{a}\right)zx\right] = 0$$

$$\Rightarrow \quad \left(\frac{a}{b} + \frac{b}{a}\right)xy + \left(\frac{b}{c} + \frac{c}{b}\right)yz + \left(\frac{a}{c} + \frac{c}{a}\right)zx = 0$$

(Proved)

Appendix 1

CO-ORDINATE GEOMETRY

Tangents and Normals

1. Equation of tangent at (x_1, y_1).

   (a) With respect to the circle

   $x^2 + y^2 = a^2$ is $xx_1 + yy_1 = a^2$

   (b) Wite tespect to the circle

   $x^2 + y^2 + 2gx + 2fy + c = 0$

   is $xx_1 + yy_1 + g(x + x_1) + f(y + y_1) + c = 0$

   Rule to write the above equations

For x^2	write $x\,x_1$
For y^2	write yy_1
For x	write $\frac{1}{2}(x + x_1)$
For y	write $\frac{1}{2}(y + y_1)$

   Leave the constant term as it is.

Q. 1 Find the condition that $lx + my + n = 0$ is normal to the parabola $y^2 = 4ax$ [88]

2. Equation of the normal to the eircle

$$x^2 + y^2 = a^2 \text{ at } (x_1, y_1) \text{ is}$$

$$\boxed{\frac{x}{x_1} = \frac{y}{y_1}}$$

Remember A line touches the circle if the length of the perpendicular from the centre of the circle on the line equals to the radius of the circle.

Problem 1 To find the condition that the line $y = mx + c$ may touch the circle $x^2 + y^2 = a^2$ and hence, to deduce the equation of the tangent in the slope form.

Solution Equation of the line is $y = mx + c$ (i)

Equation of the circle is $x^2 + y^2 = a^2$ (ii)

Substituting the value of y from (i) in (ii) we get

$$x^2 + (mx + c)^2 = a^2$$

$$x^2 + m^2 x^2 + c^2 + 2\,mxc = a^2$$

$$x^2 (1 + m^2) + 2mxc + (c^2 - a^2) = 0 \quad \text{(iii)}$$

The line will be a tangent to the circle if it meets to the circle in two coincident points

$\therefore$ The equation (iii) has equal roots which requires disminant of (iii) = 0

i.e.
$$B^2 - 4AC = 0$$

$$4m^2 c^2 - 4\,(1 + m^2)\,(c^2 - a^2) = 0$$

or
$$4[m^2 c^2 - (1 + m^2)\,(c^2 - a^2)] = 0$$

i.e.
$$m^2 c^2 - (c^2 - a^2) - m^2 (c^2 - a^2) = 0$$

i.e.
$$m^2 c^2 - c^2 + a^2 - m^2 c^2 + m^2 a^2 = 0$$

i.e.
$$c^2 = a^2 (1 + m^2)$$

or
$$c = \pm a\sqrt{1 + m^2}$$

which is the required condition.

Putting $c = \pm\, a\sqrt{1 + m^2}$ in the equation of the line we have

$$y = mx \pm a\sqrt{1 + m^2}$$

which are the tangents for all real values of m

Since these equations involve on by one parameter 'm' the slope of the tangent, this form of equatins of tangent is known as slope form. The two tangents.

$y = mx \pm a\sqrt{1 + m^2}$ are parallel since their slopes are equal. Therefore these are the tangents at the ends of a diameter.

Note 2 Taking only the +ve sign with the radical equation of any tangent to $x^2 + y^2 = a^2$ in the slope form may be taken as

$$y = mx + a\sqrt{1 + m^2}$$

Formula Equation of the tangent to the parabola $y^2 = 4ax$ at the point (x_1, y_1) is

$$\boxed{yy_1 = 2a\,(x + x_1)} \quad \text{(R)}$$

Problem 2 Find the condition that the line $y = mx + c$ may touch the parabola $y^2 = 4ax$. Find also the co-ordinates of the point of contact:

Solution Equation of line is $y = mx + c$ (i)

Equation of parabola is $y^2 = 4ax$ (ii)

Substituting for y from (i) and (ii) we get $(mx + c)^2 = 4ax$

or $$m^2 x^2 + c^2 + 2\, mx\, c = 4ax$$

$\Rightarrow$ $$m^2 x^2 + 2\,(mc - 2a)\, x + c^2 = 0$$

which is a quadratic in x (i) will be tangent to (ii) if the roots of (iii) are equal

i.e. if $$4\,(mc-2a)^2 - 4m^2 c^2 = 0$$

or if $$(mc-2a)^2 - m^2 c^2 = 0$$

$$m^2 c^2 - 4mca + 4a^2 - m^2 c^2 = 0$$

$$4a^2 = 4mca$$

$$\boxed{c = \frac{a}{m}}$$

which is the required condition.

Putting $c = \dfrac{a}{m}$ in equation (iii) we get

$$m^2 x^2 + 2\left(m\,\frac{a}{m} - 2a\right) x + \frac{a^2}{m^2} = 0$$

$$m^2 x^2 + 2\,(a-2a)\, x + \frac{a^2}{m^2} = 0$$

$$m^2 x^2 - 2ax + \frac{a^2}{m^2} = 0$$

or $$\left(mx - \frac{a}{m}\right)^2 = 0$$

or $$mx - \frac{a}{m} = 0$$

$\therefore$ $$x = \frac{a}{m^2}$$

From (1) $$y = mx + c$$

$\Rightarrow$ $$y = mx + \frac{a}{m}$$

$$y = m \cdot \frac{a}{m^2} + \frac{a}{m}$$

i.e. $$y = \frac{a}{m} + \frac{a}{m}$$

i.e. $$y = 2\frac{a}{m}$$

The point of contact is (x_1, y_1)

i.e. $$\left(\frac{a}{m^2}, \frac{2a}{m}\right)$$

Problem 3 Prove that the straight line $y = mx + c$ touches the parabola

$$y^2 = 4a\,(x + a) \text{ if } c = am + \frac{a}{m}.$$

Solution The given line is $y = mx + c$ (1)

and the parabola is $y^2 = 4a\,(x + a)$ (ii)

(i) meets (ii) where

$$(mx + c)^2 = 4a\,(x + a)$$

or $$m^2 x^2 + c^2 + 2mxc = 4ax + 4a^2$$

or $$m^2 x^2 + 2\,(mc - 2a)\,x + (c^2 - 4a^2) = 0 \quad \text{(iii)}$$

(i) touches (ii) if the roots of (iii) are equal

i.e. if the discriminant of (iii) $= 0$

if $$4\,(mc - 2a)^2 - 4m^2\,(c^2 - 4a^2) = 0$$

or if $m^2c^2 - 4amc + 4a^2 - c^2 m^2 + 4a^2 m^2 = 0$

or if $$-4amc + 4a^2 + 4a^2 m^2 = 0$$

or if $$4a\,[-mc + a + am^2] = 0$$

$$-mc + a + am^2 = 0$$

i.e. $$mc = a + am^2$$

or $$c = \frac{a}{m} + am$$

Problem 4 Show that the line $x \cos\alpha + y \sin\alpha = P$ touches the parabola

$$y^2 = 4a\,(x + a) \text{ if}$$

$$P \cos\alpha + a = 0$$

Solution Equation of the line is

$$x \cos\alpha + y \sin\alpha = P \quad (1)$$

and equation of the parabola is $y^2 = 4a\,(x + a)$ (2)

From equation (1) we have

$$x = \frac{(P - y \sin\alpha)}{\cos\alpha}$$

Substituting the value of x from equation (3) in equation (2) we have

$$y^2 = 4a\left[\frac{(P-y\sin\alpha)}{\cos\alpha}+a\right]$$

$$y^2\cos\alpha = 4a\,[P-y\sin\alpha+a\cos\alpha]$$

$$y^2\cos\alpha + 4ay\sin\alpha - 4a\,(P+a\cos\alpha) = 0 \qquad (4)$$

which is a quadratic equation in (1). Now if (1) touches (2) them two values of y of equation (4) must be coincident i. e. the discriminant is equal to zero $B^2 - 4Ac = 0$

$$[4a\sin\alpha]^2 + 4\cos\alpha\,\{4a\,(P+a\cos\alpha)\} = 0$$

$$16a^2\sin^2\alpha + 16\,a\cos\alpha\,(P+a\cos\alpha) = 0$$

$$16\,[a^2\sin^2\alpha + aP\cos\alpha + a^2\cos^2\alpha] = 0$$

$$[a^2(\sin^2\alpha+\cos^2\alpha) + aP\cos\alpha] = 0$$

$$a^2 + aP\cos\alpha = 0$$

i.e. $a\,[a+P\cos\alpha] = 0$

since $a \neq 0$

$\Rightarrow$ $a + P\cos\alpha = 0$ *(Proved)*

Problem 5 Find the condition that the line $lx+mx+n=0$ may touch the parabola $y^2 = 4ax$ and find co-ordinates of the point of contact.

Solution The equation of the line is

$$lx + my + n = 0 \qquad \text{(i)}$$

and that of the parabola is $y^2 = 4\,ax$ (ii)

Let (i) be a tangent to (ii) at (x_1, y_1)

Equation of tangent to (ii) at (x_1, y_1) is

$$yy_1 = 2a\,(x+x_1)$$

or $2ax - yy_1 + 2ax_1 = 0$ (iii)

Since (i) and (iii) both represent the equation of tangent to (ii) at (x_1, y_1)

$$\frac{2a}{l} = \frac{-y_1}{m} = \frac{2ax_1}{n}$$

$\therefore$ $x_1 = \frac{n}{l}\quad y_1 = -\frac{2au}{l}$

As (x_1, y_1) lies on (ii)

so $y_1^2 = 4ax_1$

$\Rightarrow$ $\frac{4a^2m^2}{l^2} = 4a\frac{n}{l}$

$\Rightarrow$ $am^2 = nl$ which is the required condition.

Co-ordinates of the point of contact aro (x_1, y_1)

i.e. $$\left(\frac{n}{l}, -\frac{2am}{l}\right)$$

or $$\left(\frac{am^2}{l^2}, -\frac{2am}{l}\right) \quad \textbf{Ans.}$$

Problem 6 Prove that the line $lx + my + n = 0$ touches the parabola $y = 4a(x-b)$ if $am^2 = bl^2 + nl$.

[Easy question Try your self]

Problem 7 To show that from any point three normals can be drawn to a parabola and

(i) at least one of the three normals is real

(ii) the algebraic sum of their slopes is zero

(iii) the algebraic sum of the ordinates of their feet is zero. [*I.F.S.* *81, 84*]

Solution Let the equation of the parabola be

$$y^2 = 4ax \tag{1}$$

Let (x_1, y_1) be the given point equation of the tangent at (x_1, y_1) is

$$yy_1 = 2a(x + x_1) \quad \Rightarrow \quad y = \frac{2a}{y_1}(x + x_1)$$

Slope of the tangent is $\frac{2a}{y_1}$ then the slope of the normal is given by $-\frac{y_1}{2a}$

Equation of the normal is

$$(y - y_1) = -\frac{y_1}{2a}(x - x_1)$$

Denoting the slope of the normal by m we have

$$m = -\frac{y_1}{2a} \quad \Rightarrow \quad y_1 = -2am$$

As (x_1, y_1) lies on the parabola

$$y_1^2 = 4ax_1$$

$$x_1 = 4am^2,\ 4a^2m^2 = 4ax_1$$

so the points is $(am^2, -2am)$

Equation of normal $y + 2am = m(x - am^2)$

$$y + 2am = mx - am^3$$

$$y = mx - 2am - am^3 \tag{2}$$

Since it passes through (x_1, y_1)

$$y_1 = mx_1 - 2am - am^3$$

$$am^3 + (2a - x_1)\, m + y_1 = 0$$

This is a cubic in m giving three values of m which are the three normals that pass through the point (x_1, y_1)

Putting these values of m in (2) we get the equations of the three normals which can be drawn from (x_1, y_1) to the parabola.

(i) Equation (3) is a cubic equation in m with all its coefficients real

Since imaginary roots occur in conjugate pairs

$\therefore$ at least one root of (3) must be real.

Hence of the three normals to the parabola, from a point, at least one must be real.

(ii) let the roots of (3) be m_1, m_2, m_3

$$m_1 + m_2 + m_3 = -\frac{0}{a} = 0$$

(iii) the three feets of the normals are

$$(am_1^2, -2am_1);\ (am_2^2, -am_2)$$

and $$(am_3^2, -2am_3)$$

The algebraic sum of the ordinates at the feet of normals

$$= (-2am_1) + (-2am_2) + (-2am_3)$$

$$= -2a\,(m_1 + m_2 + m_3) = -2a \times 0 = 0$$

The ordinate of the centroid of the triangle formed by the fect of the normals is given by

$$y = \frac{(-2am_1) + (-2am_2) + (-2am_3)}{3}$$

$$y = -\frac{2a}{3}(m_1 + m_2 + 3) = -\frac{2a}{3} \times 0 = 0$$

i.e. $$y = 0$$

the centroid lies on x-axis which is also the axis of the parabola.

Formula The equation of the tangent to the ellipse

$\frac{x^2}{a^2} + \frac{y^2}{b^2} = 1$ at the point (x_1, y_1) is given by

$$\frac{xx_1}{a^2} + \frac{yy_1}{b^2} = 1$$

Problem 8 Find the condition that the line $lx + my + n = 0$ may touch the ellipse $\frac{x^2}{a^2} + \frac{y^2}{b^2} = 1$ and find the point of contact.

Solution Let (x_1, y_1) be the point of contact of the line

$$lx + my + n = 0 \qquad \text{(i)}$$

With the ellipse
$$\frac{x^2}{a^2} + \frac{y^2}{b^2} = 1 \qquad \text{(ii)}$$

Equation of the tangent at (x_1, y_1) to (ii) is

$$\frac{xx_1}{a^2} + \frac{yy_1}{b^2} = 1 \qquad \text{(iii)}$$

(i) and (iii) reprefent the same line i.e. tangent at (x_1, y_1)

$\therefore$ Comparing coefficients

$$\frac{x_1/a^2}{l} = \frac{y_1/b^2}{m} = \frac{-1}{n}$$

$$\Rightarrow \qquad x_1 = -\frac{a^2 l}{n};\ y_1 = -\frac{b^2 m}{n}$$

Co-ordinate of the point of contact are

$$\left[-\frac{a^2 l}{n}, -\frac{b^2 m}{n}\right]$$

Since (x_1, y_1) lies on the ellipse

$$\therefore \qquad \frac{x_1^2}{a^2} + \frac{y_1^2}{b^2} = 1$$

i.e.
$$\frac{\left[-\frac{a^2 l}{n}\right]^2}{a^2} + \frac{\left[-\frac{b^2 m}{n}\right]^2}{b^2} = 1$$

$$\frac{a^2 l^2}{n^2} + \frac{b^2 m^2}{n^2} = 1$$

or
$$a^2 l^2 + b^2 m^2 = n^2$$

which is the required condition.

Problem 9 Find the condition that the line $x \cos \alpha + y \sin \alpha = p$ may be a tangent to the ellipse $\frac{x^2}{a^2} + \frac{y^2}{b^2} = 1$

Solution Let (x_1, y_1) be the point of contact of the line

$$x \cos \alpha + y \sin \alpha = p \qquad \text{(i)}$$

With the ellipse $$\frac{x^2}{a^2} + \frac{y^2}{b^2} = 1 \tag{ii}$$

Equation of tangent at (x_1, y_1) to (ii) is

$$\frac{xx_1}{a^2} + \frac{yy_1}{b^2} = 1 \tag{iii}$$

Equation (i) and (iii) represent the same line i.e. the tangent at (x_1, y_1)

$\therefore$ Compairing coefficients

$$\frac{x_1/a^2}{\cos\alpha} = \frac{y_1/b^2}{\sin\alpha} = \frac{1}{p}$$

$$\frac{x_1}{a^2\cos\alpha} = \frac{y_1}{b^2\sin\alpha} = \frac{1}{p}$$

$$\Rightarrow \qquad x_1 = \frac{a^2\cos\alpha}{p}$$

$$y_1 = \frac{b^2\sin\alpha}{p}$$

Since (x_1, y_1) lies on the ellipse

$$\therefore \qquad \frac{x_1^2}{a^2} + \frac{y_1^2}{b^2} = 1,$$

$$\Rightarrow \qquad \frac{a^4\cos^2\alpha}{a^2p^2} + \frac{a^4\sin^2\alpha}{b^2p^2} = 1$$

$$\Rightarrow \qquad \boxed{a^2\cos^2\alpha + b^2\sin^2\alpha = p^2}$$

Problem 10 Find the equation of the normal to the ellipse $\frac{x^2}{a^2} + \frac{y^2}{b^2} = 1$

Solution The equation of tangent at 'θ' i.e. at $(a\cos\theta, b\sin\theta)$ to the ellipse $\frac{x^2}{a^2} + \frac{y^2}{b^2} = 1$ is $\frac{x}{a^2}\cdot a\cos\theta + \frac{y\cdot b\sin\theta}{b^2} = 1$

i.e. $$\frac{x}{a}\cos\theta + \frac{y}{b}\sin\theta = 1$$

Slope of the tangent $= -\frac{\cos\theta}{a}\Big/\frac{\sin\theta}{b} = -\frac{b\cos\theta}{a\sin\theta}$

$\therefore$ Slope of normal $= \frac{a\sin\theta}{b\cos\theta}$

So equation of the normal at 'a' i.e. $(a \cos \theta, b \sin \theta)$ is

$$(y-b \sin \theta) = \frac{a \sin \theta}{b \cos \theta}(x-a \cos \theta)$$

$$by-b^2 \sin \theta = \frac{\sin \theta}{\cos \theta}(ax-a^2 \cos \theta)$$

$$\frac{by}{\sin \theta} - b^2 = \frac{ax}{\cos \theta} - a^2$$

or
$$\boxed{\frac{ax}{\cos \theta} - \frac{by}{\sin \theta} = a^2-b^2}$$

Problem 11 Show that the line $lx + my + n = 0$ is a normal to the ellipse $\frac{x^2}{a^2} + \frac{y^2}{b^2} = 1$ if $\frac{a^2}{l^2} + \frac{b^2}{m^2} = \frac{(a^2-b^2)^2}{n^2}$

Solution The normal to the ellipse $\frac{x^2}{a^2} + \frac{y^2}{b^2} = 1$ at the point 'θ' is

$$\frac{ax}{\cos \theta} - \frac{by}{\sin \theta} = a^2-b^2$$

If it is the same as the line $lx + my = -n$ then comparing coefficients we have

$$\frac{l}{\frac{a}{\cos \theta}} = \frac{m}{\frac{-b}{\sin \theta}} = \frac{-n}{a^2-b^2}$$

$$\frac{l \cos \theta}{a} = \frac{m \sin \theta}{-b} = -\frac{n}{a^2-b^2}$$

$$\Rightarrow \quad \cos \theta = -\frac{an}{l(a^2-b^2)}$$

$$\sin \theta = \frac{bn}{m(a^2-b^2)}$$

Squaring and adding we have

$$\cos^2 \theta + \sin^2 \theta = \frac{a^2 n^2}{l^2 (a^2-b^2)^2} + \frac{b^2 n^2}{m^2 (a^2-b^2)^2}$$

$$\frac{(a^2-b^2)^2}{n^2} = \frac{a^2}{l^2} + \frac{b^2}{m^2}$$

Problem 12 Prove that the line $y = mx + c$ is a normal to

$$\frac{x^2}{a^2} + \frac{y^2}{b^2} = 1 \text{ if } \frac{a^2}{m^2} + b^2 = \frac{(a^2-b^2)^2}{c}$$

Solution The normal to the ellipse $\frac{x^2}{a^2}+\frac{y^2}{b^2}=1$

at the point 'θ' is $\frac{ax}{\cos\theta}-\frac{by}{\sin\theta}=b^2-b^2$ (i)

If it is the same as the line $y = mx + c$

i.e. $mx-y=-c$ (ii)

Then comparing coefficients we have

$$\frac{m}{a/\cos\theta}=\frac{1}{b/\sin\theta}=\frac{-c}{a^2-b^2}$$

$$\frac{m\cos\theta}{a}=\frac{\sin\theta}{b}=-\frac{c}{a^2-b^2}$$

$$\cos\theta=-\frac{ac}{m(a^2-b^2)}$$

$$\sin\theta=-\frac{bc}{(a^2-b^2)}$$

Squaring and adding we have

$$\cos^2\theta+\sin\partial=\frac{a^2c^2}{m^2(a^2-b^2)^2}+\frac{b^2c^2}{(a^2-b^2)^2}$$

$$=\frac{a^2c^2}{m^2(a^2-b^2)^2}+\frac{b^2c^2}{(a^2-b^2)^2}$$

$$\Rightarrow \quad \frac{(a^2-b^2)^2}{c^2}=\frac{a^2}{m^2}+b^2$$

which is the required condition.

Problem 13 Find the condition that the line $x\cos\alpha+y\sin\alpha=p$ may be normal to the ellipse $\frac{x^2}{a^2}+\frac{y^2}{b^2}=1$

Solution Similarly as (12)

$$(a^2-b^2)^2=p^2(a^2\sec^2\alpha+b^2\operatorname{cosec}^2\alpha)$$

which is the required condition. **Ans.**

Problem 14 Find the condition that the line $lx+my+n=0$ may be tangent to the ellipse $\frac{x^2}{a^2}+\frac{y^2}{b^2}=1$

Solution The tangent to the ellipse $\frac{x^2}{a^2}+\frac{y^2}{b^2}=1$ at the point 'θ' is

$$\frac{x}{a}\cos\theta+\frac{y}{b}\sin\theta=1 \qquad \text{(i)}$$

If it is the same as the line $lx + my = -n$ (ii)

Then comparing coefficients we get

$$\frac{\cos\theta}{al} = \frac{\sin\theta}{bm} = -\frac{1}{n}$$

$$\cos\theta = -\frac{al}{n}$$

$$\sin\theta = -\frac{bm}{n}$$

Squaring and adding we have

$$1 = \frac{a^2 l^2}{n^2} + \frac{b^2 m^2}{n^2}$$

or $$\boxed{a^2 l^2 + b^2 m^2 = n^2}$$

which is the required condition.

Formula Equation of the tangent at the point (x_1, y_1) to the hyperbola

$$\frac{x^2}{a^2} - \frac{y^2}{b^2} = 1 \text{ is}$$

$$\boxed{\frac{xx_1}{a^2} - \frac{y_1}{b^2} = 1}$$

Problem 15 To find the equation of normal at the point (x_1, y_1) to the hyperbola $\frac{x^2}{a^2} - \frac{y^2}{b^2} = 1$.

Solution The equation of the tangent to the hyperbola at $p\,(x_1, y_1)$ is

$$\frac{xx_1}{a^2} - \frac{yy_1}{b^2} = 1$$

$$\frac{yy_1}{b^2} = \frac{xx_1}{a^2} - 1$$

$$y = \left(\frac{b^2}{a^2}\frac{x_1}{y_1}\right)x - \frac{b^2}{y_1}$$

Slope of the tangent $= \frac{b^2}{a^2}\frac{x_1}{y_1}$

$\therefore$ Slope of normal $= -\frac{a^2}{b^2}\frac{y_1}{x_1}$

Equation of normal at $p\ (x_1, y_1)$ is

$$(y-y_1) = -\frac{a^2}{b^2}\frac{y_1}{x_1}(x-x_1)$$

$$b^2(y-y_1) = -a^2(x-x_1)\frac{y_1}{x_1}$$

$$\frac{b^2(y-y_1)}{y_1} = -a^2\frac{(x-x_1)}{x_1}$$

or
$$\frac{a^2 x}{x_1} + \frac{b^2 y}{y_1} = a^2 + b^2$$

Problem 16 To find the points of intersection of the line $y = mx + c$ with the hyperbola $\frac{x^2}{a^2} - \frac{y^2}{b^2} = 1$ and to deduce the condition of tengency.

Solution Equation of hyperbola is

$$\frac{x^2}{a^2} - \frac{y^2}{b^2} = 1 \tag{i}$$

Equation of the line is $\quad y = mx + c \qquad$ (ii)

To find their point of intersection we have to solve them simultaneously substituting for y from (ii) in (i) we have

$$\frac{x^2}{a^2} - \frac{y^2}{b^2} = 1$$

i.e.
$$\frac{x^2}{a^2} - \frac{(mx+c)^2}{b^2} = 1$$

i.e.
$$\frac{b^2x^2 - a^2(mx+c)^2}{a^2b^2} = 1$$

i.e.
$$b^2x^2 - a^2(mx+c)^2 = a^2b^2$$

$$b^2x^2 - a^2(m^2x^2 + c^2 + 2mxc) = a^2b^2$$

$$b^2x^2 - a^2m^2x^2 - a^2c^2 - 2mxc\,a^2 = a^2b^2$$

i.e.
$$(b^2 - a^2m^2)x^2 - (2a^2mc)x - a^2(b^2 + c^2) = 0 \tag{iii}$$

This is a quadratic in x. If its root be x_1 and x_2 the corresponding values of y say y_1 and $\bar{y}_2$ can be obtained from equation (ii). Thus the line (ii) meets (i), ingeneral, in two points. The two points are real and distinct co-incident or imaginary according as the roots of (iii) are real and distinct, equal or imaginary.

Condition of tangency

The line (ii) is a tangent to the hyperbola (i) if it meets the hyperbola in two co-incident points. This is so if the roots of (iii) are equal i.e. if.

$$B^2 - 4\,Ae = 0$$

$$4a^4\,m^2\,c^2 + 4\,(b^2 - a^2\,m^2)\,a^2\,(b^2 + c^2) = 0$$

$$a^2\,m^2\,c^2 + (b^2 - a^2\,m^2)\,(b^2 + c^2) = 0$$

$$a^2\,m^2\,c^2 + b^4 - a^2\,b^2\,m^2 + b^2\,c^2 - a^2\,m^2\,c^2 = 0$$

$$b^2 + c^2 - a^2\,m^2 = 0$$

$$c^2 = a^2\,m^2 - b^2$$

or $$c = \pm\sqrt{a^2\,m^2 - b^2}$$

Which is the required condition substituting for c in (ii) if

$$y = mx \pm \sqrt{a^2\,m^2 - b^2}$$

Hence the lines $y = mx \pm \sqrt{a^2\,m^2 - b^2}$ are tangents to the hyperbola $\frac{x^2}{a^2} - \frac{y^2}{b^2} = 1$ for all values of m where m is the slopc of the tangent.

Any tangent to the hyperbola is

$$y = mx + \sqrt{a^2\,m^2 - b^2}$$

Problem 17 To thow that two tangents can be drawn from a point to a hyperbola, which are real and distinct, coincident or imaginary, according as the point is outside, on or inside the hyperbola.

Solution Let the equation of the hyperbola be

$$\frac{x^2}{a^2} - \frac{y^2}{b^2} = 1$$

and let $P\,(x_1, y_1)$ be any point in its plane.
The equation of any tangent to the hyperbola in the slope from is

$$y = mx + \sqrt{a^2\,m^2 - b^2}$$

If it passes through $P\,(x_1\;y_1)$ then

$$y_1 = mx_1 + \sqrt{a^2\;m^2 - b^2}$$

Squaring

$$(y_1 - mx_1)^2 = a^2\,m^2 - b^2$$

$$y_1^2 + m^2\,x_1^2 - 2mx_1\,y_1 = a^2\,m^2 - b^2$$

or $$(x_1^2 - a^2)\,m^2 - 2x_1\,y_1\,m + (y_1^2 + b^2) = 0 \qquad (1)$$

This is a quadratic in m. The two roots of the quadratic are the slopes of the tangents from $P(x_1\ y_1)$ to the hyporbola.

Thus in general, two tangents can be drawn from a point to a hyperbola.

The tangents are real and distinct, concident or imaginary according as the roots of (i) are real and distinct equal or imaginary i.e. according as

$$4x_1^2y_1^2-4(x_1^2-a^2)(y_1^2+b^2)>,=\quad \text{or}\quad <0$$

or

$$x_1^2y_1^2-[x_1^2y_1^2-a^2y_1^2-a^2b^2+x_1^2b^2]=<0$$

$$x_1^2y_1^2-x_1^2y_1^2+a^2y_1^2+a^2b^2-x_1^2b^2>=<0$$

$$a^2y_1^2+a^2b^2-x_1^2b^2>=<0$$

or

$$b^2x_1^2-a^2y_1^2-a^2b^2<=>0$$

or

$$\frac{x_1^2}{a^2}-\frac{y_1^2}{b^2}-1<=>0$$

or according as $P(x_1, y_1)$ lies outside or inside the hyperbola.

Problem 18 To find the equation of the normal at $(a\sec\theta, b\tan\theta)$ to the hyperbola

$$\frac{x^2}{a^2}-\frac{y^2}{b^2}=1$$

Solution Equation of the tangent at 'θ' is

$$\frac{x}{a}\sec\theta-\frac{y}{b}\tan\theta=1$$

$$\frac{y}{b}\tan\theta=\frac{x}{a}\sec\theta-1$$

$$y=\frac{b}{a}\frac{(\sec\theta x)}{\tan\theta}-1$$

Slope of the tangent $=\dfrac{b\sec\theta}{a\tan\theta}$

$\therefore$ Slope of normal $=-\dfrac{a\tan\theta}{b\sec\theta}$

Equation of normal at 'θ' i.e. at $(a\sec\theta, b\tan\theta)$

$$(y-b\tan\theta)=-\frac{a\tan\theta}{b\sec\theta}(x-a\sec\theta)$$

$$by - b^2 \tan\theta = -\frac{\tan\theta}{\sec\theta}(ax - a^2\sec\theta)$$

or
$$\frac{by}{\tan\theta} - b^2 = -\frac{ax}{\sec\theta} + a^2$$

$$\frac{ax}{\sec\theta} + \frac{by}{\tan\theta} = a^2 + b^2$$

Problem 19 Show that the line $lx + my + n = 0$ touches the hyperbola

$$\frac{x^2}{a^2} - \frac{y^2}{b^2} = 1$$

$$a^2 l^2 - b^2 m^2 = n^2$$

Solution Equation of the tangent of the point $(a \sec\theta, b\tan\theta)$ to the parabola is given by

$$\frac{x}{a}\sec\theta - \frac{y}{b}\tan\theta = 1 \qquad (1)$$

Since the line $lx + my + n = 0$ (ii)

Touches the clipse $\frac{x^2}{a^2} - \frac{y^2}{b^2} = 1$

So (i) and (ii) are the same line. So comparing the co-efficients of x in (1) and (ii) we have

$$\frac{\sec\theta}{al} = -\frac{\tan\theta}{mb} = \frac{1}{-n}$$

$$\sec\theta = -\frac{al}{n}$$

$$\tan\theta = \frac{mb}{n}$$

We have
$$\sec^2\theta - \tan^2\theta = 1$$

$\therefore$
$$\frac{a^2 l^2}{n^2} - \frac{b^2 m^2}{n^2} = 1$$

or
$$a^2 l^2 - b^2 m^2 = n^2$$

Which is the required *condition*.

Problem 20 Prove that the line $x \cos\alpha + y \sin\alpha = p$ will be a tangent to the hyperbola $\frac{x^2}{a^2} - \frac{y^2}{b^2} = 1$ if $a^2\cos^2\alpha - b^2\sin^2\alpha = p^2$

Solution Please try yourself.

Problem 21 Prove that the line $lx + my = 1$ will be a normal to the hyperbola $\frac{x^2}{a^2} - \frac{y^2}{b^2} = 1$ if $\frac{a^2}{l^2} - \frac{b^2}{m^2} = (a^2 + b^2)^2$.

Solution Any normal to the parabola

$$\frac{x^2}{a^2} - \frac{y^2}{b^2} = 1$$

is
$$\frac{ax}{\sec \theta} + \frac{by}{\tan \theta} = a^2 + b^2$$

If it is the same as the given line $lx + my = 1$ (ii)

Then compaining co-efficients

$$\frac{\frac{l}{a}}{\sec \theta} = \frac{\frac{m}{b}}{\tan \theta} = \frac{1}{a^2 + b^2}$$

$$\frac{l \sec \theta}{a} = \frac{m \tan \theta}{b} = \frac{1}{a^2 + b^2}$$

$$\sec \theta = \frac{a}{l(a^2 + b^2)}$$

$$\tan \theta = \frac{b}{m(a^2 + b^2}$$

Also $\sec^2 \theta - \tan^2 \theta = 1$

$$\frac{a^2}{l^2 (a^2 + b^2)^2} - \frac{b^2}{m^2 (a^2 + b^2)^2} = 1$$

$$\frac{a^2}{l^2} - \frac{b^2}{m^2} = (a^2 + b^2)^2$$

Which is the required condition.

Appendix 2

ELLIPSE

Important Formulas

1. The standard equation of the ellipse is

$$\frac{x^2}{a^2}+\frac{y^2}{b^2}=1$$

(i) Its centre is 0 (0, 0)

(ii) Its foci s and s' are $(\pm\, ae, 0)$

(iii) Length of major axis $= 2a$
Length of minor axis $= 2b$

(iv) Equation of major axis is $y = 0$
Equation of minor axis is $x = 0$

(v) The equation of the directrices $x = \pm \frac{a}{e}$

(vi) $b^2 = a^2(1-e^2)$

(vii) Equation of latera – Recta $x = \pm\, ae$

(viii) Length of latus rectum $= 2\frac{b^2}{a}$

2. The equation of tangent at (x_1, y_1) to it is

$$\frac{xx_1}{a^2}+\frac{yy_1}{b^2}=1$$

3. The equation of normal at (x_1, y_1) is

$$\frac{x-x_1}{x_1/a^2}=\frac{y-y_1}{y_1/b^2}$$

4. The parametric equation of the ellipse

$$x = a\cos\phi, \qquad y = b\sin\phi$$

5. The equation of normal at 'ϕ' is

$$ax\sec\phi - by\,\mathrm{cosec}\,\phi = a^2-b^2$$

6. $y = mx + \sqrt{a^2 m^2 + b^2}$ is always tangent to the ellipse

7. The polar (or the chord of contact) of $(x_1 . y_1)$ with respect to the ellipse is $$\frac{xx_1}{a^2} + \frac{yy_1}{b^2} = 1$$

8. The equation of its chord whose middle point is (x_1, y_1) is
$$(x_1 - x_1)\frac{x_1}{a^2} + (y - y_1)\frac{y_1}{b^2} = 0$$

9. The equation of the pair of tangents from (x_1, y_1) to it is $SS_1 = T^2$
$$\left(\frac{x^2}{a^2} + \frac{y^2}{b^2} - 1\right)\left(\frac{x_1^2}{a^2} + \frac{y_1^2}{b^2} - 1\right) = \left(\frac{xx_1}{a^2} + \frac{yy_1}{b^2} - 1\right)^2$$

10. If P and Q be the ends of two conjugate diameters and ϕ, ϕ_1 be the eccentric angles of P and Q then $\phi \sim \phi_1 = \frac{\pi}{2}$

Problem 1 Show that the line $3x + 4y + \sqrt{7} = 0$ touches the ellipse $3x^2 + 4y^2 = 1$; find also the point of contact.

Solution Equation of the line is
$$3x + 4y + \sqrt{7} = 0$$
$$\Rightarrow \quad 4y = -(3x + \sqrt{7})$$
$$\Rightarrow \quad y = -\frac{(3x + \sqrt{7})}{4} \tag{1}$$

Substituting the values of y in equation
$$3x^2 + 4y^2 = 1$$
$$3x^2 + 4\frac{(3x + \sqrt{7})^2}{16} = 1$$
$$\Rightarrow \quad 3x^2 + \frac{(3x + \sqrt{7})^2}{4} = 1$$
$$\Rightarrow \quad 12x^2 + (3x + \sqrt{7})^2 = 4$$
$$\Rightarrow \quad 12x^2 + 9x^2 + 6\sqrt{7}x + 7 = 4$$
$$\Rightarrow \quad 21x^2 + 6\sqrt{7}\,x + 3 = 0$$
$$\Rightarrow \quad 21x^2 + 3\sqrt{7}x + 3\sqrt{7}x + 3 = 0$$
$$\Rightarrow \quad \sqrt{7}x(\sqrt{7}\,x + 1) + 3(\sqrt{7}x + 1) = 0$$
$$\Rightarrow \quad (3\sqrt{7}\,x + 3)(\sqrt{7}x + 1) = 0$$

$$\Rightarrow \quad 3(\sqrt{7}x + 1)(\sqrt{7}x + 1) = 0$$

$$\Rightarrow \quad (\sqrt{7}x + 1)^2 = 0$$

$$\Rightarrow \quad x = -\frac{1}{\sqrt{7}} \quad \text{or} \quad -\frac{1}{\sqrt{7}}$$

Since the values of x are same so the given line touches the ellipse

Now substituting the value of $x = -\dfrac{1}{\sqrt{7}}$ is equation (1) we have

$$y = -\frac{\left[3\left(-\frac{1}{\sqrt{7}}\right) + \sqrt{7}\right]}{4}$$

$$y = -\frac{[-3 + 7]}{4\sqrt{7}}$$

$$y = -\frac{4}{4\sqrt{7}} \quad \Rightarrow \quad y = -\frac{1}{\sqrt{7}}$$

So the point of contact is $\left(-\dfrac{1}{\sqrt{7}}, -\dfrac{1}{\sqrt{7}}\right)$ **Ans.**

Problem 2 Find the condition that the line $x \cos \alpha + y \sin \alpha = P$ may tangent to the ellipse $\dfrac{x^2}{a^2} + \dfrac{y^2}{b^2} = 1$ [*Mustrevise*]

Solution Let us suppose that $x \cos \alpha + y \sin \alpha = P$ (1)

is tangent to the ellipse $\dfrac{x^2}{a^2} + \dfrac{y^2}{b^2} = 1$ at the point (x_1, y_1)

Equation of the tangent at the point (x_1, y_1) to the ellipse

$$\frac{x^2}{a^2} + \frac{y^2}{b^2} = 1 \text{ is given by } \frac{xx_1}{a^2} + \frac{yy_1}{b^2} = 1 \quad (2)$$

Since (1) and (2) represent the same straight line so comparing (1) and (2) we have

$$\frac{x_1/b^2}{\cos \alpha} = \frac{y_1/b^2}{\sin \alpha} = \frac{1}{p}$$

$$\Rightarrow \quad \frac{x_1}{a^2 \cos \alpha} = \frac{y_1}{b^2 \sin \alpha} = \frac{1}{p}$$

$$\Rightarrow \quad x_1 = \frac{a^2 \cos \alpha}{p}$$

$$y_1 = \frac{b^2 \sin \alpha}{p}$$

Since (x_1, y_1) is a point on the ellipse

$$\frac{x^2}{a^2}+\frac{y^2}{b^2}=1$$

So
$$\frac{x_1^2}{a^2}+\frac{y_1^2}{b^2}=1$$

$$\Rightarrow \quad \frac{a^4\cos^2\alpha}{a^2p^2}+\frac{b^4\sin^2\alpha}{b^2p^2}=1$$

$$\Rightarrow \quad a^2\cos^2\alpha+b^2\sin^2\alpha=p^2$$

which is the required condition.

Problem 3 Find the condition that the line $lx + my + n = 0$ may touch the ellipse $\frac{x^2}{a^2}+\frac{y^2}{b^2}=1$ *[Must revise]*

Solution We know that the line $y = mx + c$ touches the ellipse

$$\frac{x^2}{a^2}+\frac{y^2}{b^2} \quad \text{if} \quad \boxed{c^2 = a^2m^2+b^2}$$

Equation of the straight line is

$$lx + my + n = 0$$

$$my = -lx - n$$

$$y = -\frac{l}{m}x-\frac{n}{m} \qquad (1)$$

Line (1) will be tangent to the ellipse

$$\frac{x^2}{a^2}+\frac{y^2}{b^2}=1 \quad \text{if} \quad \left(-\frac{n}{m}\right)^2 = a^2\left(-\frac{l}{m}\right)^2+b^2$$

$$\Rightarrow \quad \frac{n^2}{m^2}=\frac{a^2l^2}{m^2}+b^2$$

$$\Rightarrow \quad n^2 = a^2l^2+b^2m^2$$

which is the required condition *(Proved)*

Problem 4 Find the equations to the tangents to the ellipse $4x^2 + 3y^2 = 5$ which are parallel to the line

$$y = 3x + 7$$

(Easy question Try yourself)

Solution
$$y = 3x \pm \sqrt{\frac{155}{12}}$$

at first find parallel line to $y = 3x + 7$

which is
$$y = 3x + c \qquad (1)$$

Now (1) touches the ellipse from the condition $c^2 = a^2m^2 + b^2$ find c and put in equation (1).

Problem 5 Show that the equation of the locus of the foot of the perpendicular from the centre of an ellipse on a tangent is

$$r^2 = a^2 \cos^2 \theta + b^2 \sin^2 \theta;$$

a and b being the semi major and semi-minar axis. [*Must revise*]

Solution Let the equation of the ellipse is

$$\frac{x^2}{a^2} + \frac{y^2}{b^2} = 1 \qquad (1)$$

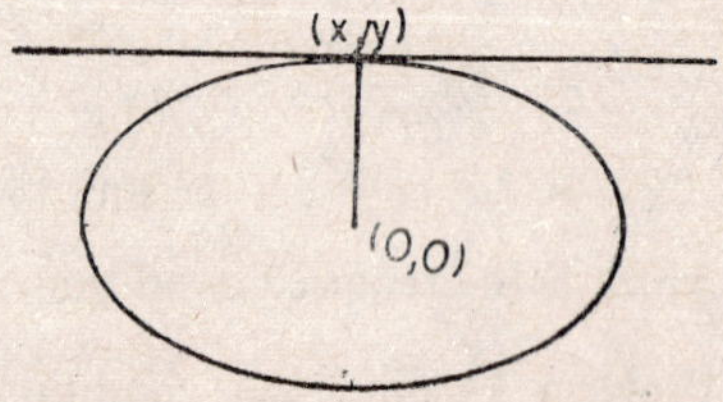

Tangent to the ellipse is given by

$$y = mx \pm \sqrt{a^2 m^2 + b^2} \qquad (1)$$

Now any line perpendicular to (1) and passing through (0, 0) is given by

$$(y-0) = -\frac{1}{m}(x-0)$$

$$\Rightarrow \quad y = -\frac{1}{m}x$$

$$\Rightarrow \quad m = \left(-\frac{x}{y}\right) \qquad (2)$$

$m \times$ slope $= -1$

$\Rightarrow$ slope $= -\dfrac{1}{m}$

Now the foot of the perpendicular on the tangent (1) is (x, y) so for locus we have to find the relation x, y and a, b. So climinating m from (1) and (2) we have

$$y = -\frac{x}{y} \cdot x + \sqrt{\frac{a^2 x^2}{y^2} + b^2}$$

$$y = -\frac{x^2}{y} + \frac{\sqrt{a^2 x^2 + b^2 y^2}}{y}$$

$$\Rightarrow \quad y^2 = -x^2 + \sqrt{a^2 x^2 + b^2 y^2}$$

$$\Rightarrow \quad x^2 + y^2 = \sqrt{a^2 x^2 + b^2 y^2}$$

Squaring both sides we have

$$(x^2 + y^2)^2 = a^2 x^2 + b^2 y^2$$

For polar form let $x = r \cos \theta$, $y = r \sin \theta$

$$\Rightarrow \quad (r^2)^2 = r^2 (a^2 \cos^2 \theta + b^2 \sin^2 \theta)$$

$$\Rightarrow \quad r^2 = a^2 \cos^2 \theta + b^2 \sin^2 \theta$$

(*Proved*)

Problem 6 The feet of the perpendiculars drawn from the foci to any tangent to an ellipse lie on the auxiliary circle prove it. [*Must revise*]

Solution Any tangent to the ellipse $\dfrac{x^2}{a^2} + \dfrac{y^2}{b^2} = 1$,

where $\qquad b^2 = a^2 (1 - e^2)$

is $\qquad y = mx + \sqrt{a^2 m^2 + b^2} \qquad (1)$

The slope of this tangent $= m$

The slope of the line $\perp^r$ to this tangent $= -\dfrac{1}{m}$

The equation of any line $\perp$ to (1) and passing through the focus $(ae, 0)$ is

$$(y-0) = -\frac{1}{m}(x-ae)$$

$$y = -\frac{1}{m}x + \frac{ae}{m}$$

$$my + x = ae \tag{2}$$

and $$y - mx = \sqrt{a^2m^2 + b^2} \tag{3}$$

The point of intersection of (1) and (2) will give the foot of the perpendicular drawn from $(ae, 0)$ to (1). Hence the locus of the foot of perpendicular wil be obtained by eliminating the variable m between (2) and (3).

Squaring and apding equations (2) and (3)

$$(mx + x)^2 + (y - mx)^2 = a^2e^2 + a^2m^2 + b^2$$

$$m^2y^2 + x^2 + y^2 + m^2x^2 = a^2e^2 + a^2m^2 + a^2(1-e^2)$$

$$\Rightarrow y^2(1+m^2) + x^2(1+m^2) = a^2e^2 + a^2m^2 + a^2 - a^2e^2$$

$$\Rightarrow (x^2+y^2)(1+m^2) = a^2(1+m^2)$$

$$\Rightarrow x^2 + y^2 = a^2$$

This is the required auxiliary circle.

Problem 7 Prove that the product of the perpendiculars from the foci on any tangent to anellipse is equal to the square of the semi-minar axis that is, constant.

Solution Let the equation of the eilipse be

$$\frac{x^2}{a^2} + \frac{y^2}{b^2} = 1 \tag{1}$$

where $$b^2 = a^2(1-e^2)$$

Equation of any tangent to the ellipse (1) is

$$y = mx + \sqrt{a^2m^2 + b^2}$$

$$\Rightarrow mx - y + \sqrt{a^2m^2 + b^2} \tag{2}$$

The foci of the ellipse (1) are

$$(ae, 0) \text{ and } (-ae, 0)$$

Let P_1 and P_2 be the lengths of the perpendiculars drawn from $(ae, 0)$ and $(-ae, 0)$ to the tangent (2)

Then
$$P_1 = \frac{mae + \sqrt{a^2 m^2 + b^2}}{\sqrt{1 + m^2}}$$

$$P_2 = \frac{-mae + \sqrt{a^2 m^2 + b^2}}{\sqrt{1 + m^2}}$$

$$P_1 P_2 = \frac{a^2 m^2 + b^2 - m^2 a^2 e^2}{(1 + m^2)}$$

$$P_1 P_2 = \frac{a^2 m^2 + a^2 (1-e^2) - m^2 a^2 e^2}{(1 + m^2)}$$

$$P_1 P_2 = \frac{a^2 m^2 + a^2 - a^2 e^2 - a^2 m^2 e^2}{(1 + m^2)}$$

$$P_1 P_2 = \frac{a^2 (1 + m^2) - a^2 c^2 (1 + m^2)}{(1 + m^2)}$$

$$P_1 P_2 = \frac{a^2 (1-e^2)(1 + m^2)}{(1 + m^2)} = a^2 (1-e^2)$$

$$p_1 p_2 = b^2$$

$p_1 p_2 =$ the square of the semi-minoraxis of the ellipse = constant.

Problem 8 Prove that the locus of the middle points of the portions of the tangents to an ellipse $\frac{x^2}{x^2} + \frac{y^2}{b^2} = 1$ included between the axis the curve

$$\frac{a^2}{x^2} + \frac{b^2}{y^2} = 4$$

Solution *S* Let the equation of the ellipse is

$$\frac{x^2}{a^2} + \frac{y^2}{b^2} = 1$$

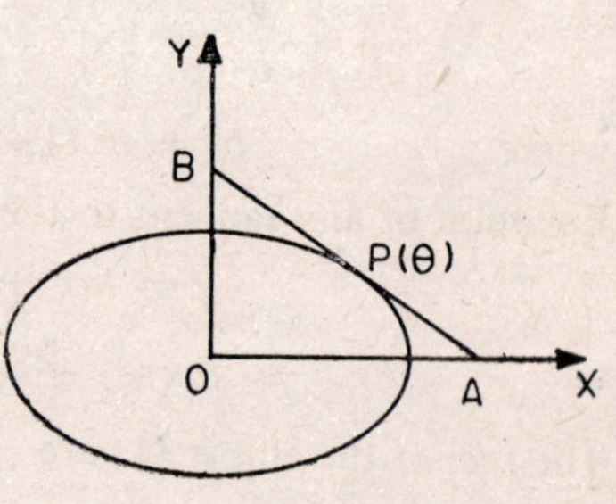

Let the co-ordinate of the point p is

$$(a \cos \theta, b \sin \theta)$$

Then the equation of the tangent at p

$$(a \cos \theta, b \sin \theta)$$

$$\frac{xa \cos \theta}{a^2} + \frac{y \sin \theta}{b^2} = 1$$

$$\Rightarrow \quad \frac{x \cos \theta}{a} + \frac{y \sin \theta}{b} = 1$$

$$\Rightarrow \quad \frac{x}{a/\cos \theta} + \frac{y}{b/\sin \theta} = 1$$

This line cuts the axis In A and B

Then $$OA = \frac{a}{\cos\theta} \quad OB = \frac{b}{\text{sln}\,\theta}$$

Middle point of $$OA = \frac{a}{2\cos\theta}$$

MIddle point of $$OB = \frac{b}{2\sin\theta}$$

The middle point of AB $\left(\frac{a}{2\cos\theta}, \frac{b}{2\sin\theta}\right)$

Let the middle point of AB (tangent) is (α, β)

Then $$\alpha = \frac{a}{2\cos\theta} \qquad \beta = \frac{b}{2\sin\theta}$$

$$\cos\theta = \frac{a}{2\alpha}, \sin\theta = \frac{b}{2\beta}$$

$$\frac{a^2}{4\alpha^2} + \frac{b^2}{4\beta^2} = 1$$

The locus of (α, β) may be obtained by replaing α by x and β by y.

$$\frac{a^2}{4x^2} + \frac{b^2}{4y^2} = 1$$

$$\Rightarrow \quad \frac{a^2}{x^2} + \frac{b_2}{y^2} = 4 \qquad \textit{(Proved)}$$

Problem 9 Problems bosed on the normol of the ellipse.

Find the condition that the line $lx + my + n = 0$ may be a normal to the ellipse $\frac{x^2}{a^2} + \frac{y^2}{b^2} = 1$.

Solution Equation of the normal to the ellipse $\frac{x^2}{a^2} + \frac{y^2}{b^2} = 1$ at 'θ' is

$$ax \sec\theta - by \operatorname{cosec}\theta = a^2 - b^2 \tag{1}$$

If $$lx + my = -n \tag{2}$$

is also normal to the ellipse at the same point then (1) and (2) are the same.

Hence comparing their co-effieients we get

$$\frac{a\sec\theta}{e} = \frac{-b\operatorname{cosec}\theta}{m} = \frac{a^2 - b^2}{-n}$$

$$\Rightarrow \qquad \cos\theta = \frac{-an}{l(a^2-b^2)}$$

$$\sin\theta = \frac{bn}{m(a^2-b^2)}$$

Now $\quad \sin^2\theta + \cos^2\theta = 1$

$$\Rightarrow \qquad \frac{a^2 n^2}{l^2 (a^2-b^2)} + \frac{b^2 n^2}{m^2 (a^2-b^2)} = 1$$

$$\Rightarrow \qquad \frac{a^2}{l^2} + \frac{b^2}{m^2} = \frac{a^2-b^2}{n^2}$$

This is the required equation.

Problem 10 Find the condition so that the line $x \cos\alpha + \sin\alpha = p$ may be normal to the ellipse.

Solution The equation of the ellipse is

$$\frac{x^2}{a^2} + \frac{y^2}{b^2} = 1 \tag{1}$$

We know that the equation of the normal to (1) at $(a\cos\theta, b\sin\theta)$ is

$$ax\sec\theta - by\operatorname{cosec}\theta = a^2-b^2 \tag{2}$$

Let
$$x\cos\alpha + y\sin\alpha = p \tag{3}$$

Touch is the ellipse (1) Then (2) and (3) must represent the same line. Comparing (2) and (3) we get

$$\frac{\cos\alpha}{a\sec\theta} = \frac{\sin\alpha}{-b\operatorname{cosec}\theta} = \frac{p}{a^2-b^2}$$

$$\cos\theta = \frac{ap}{(a^2-b^2)\cos\alpha}$$

$$\sin\theta = \frac{-pb}{(a^2-b^2)\sin\alpha}$$

squaring and adding we have

$$\frac{a^2 p^2}{(a-b^2)^2 \cos^2\alpha)} + \frac{b^2 p^2}{(a^2-b^2)^2 \sin^2\alpha} = 1$$

$$\Rightarrow \qquad \frac{a^2}{\cos^2\alpha} + \frac{b^2}{\sin^2\alpha} = \frac{(a^2-b^2)^2}{p^2}$$

$$\Rightarrow \qquad p^2 (a^2\sec^2\alpha + b^2\operatorname{cosec}^2\alpha) = (a^2-b^2)^2$$

Which is the required condition.

Problem 11 Find the condition that the normals at the points (x_1, y_1), (x_2, y_2), (x_3, y_3) on the ellipse $\frac{x^2}{a^2} + \frac{y^2}{b^2} = 1$ may be concurrent.

Solution The normal to the ellipse $\frac{x^2}{a^2} + \frac{y^2}{b^2} = 1$ at the point (x_1, y_1)

is
$$\frac{x-x_1}{x_1/a^2} = \frac{y-y_1}{y_1/b^2}$$

or
$$(x-x_1)\, y_1\, a^2 = x_1\,(y - y_1)\, b^2$$

$$\Rightarrow \quad xy_1\, a^2 - x_1\, y_1\, a^2 = x_1\, yb^2 - x_1\, y_1\, b^2$$

$$\Rightarrow \quad yb^2\, x_1 - a^2\, xy_1 + (a^2-b^2)\, x_1\, y_1 = 0 \qquad (1)$$

Similarly the normlas at (x_2, y_2) nnd (x_3, y_3) are respectively

$$b^2\, yx_2 - a^2\, xy_2 + (a^2-b^2)\, x_2\, y_2 = 0 \qquad (2)$$

$$b^2\, yx_3 - a^2\, xy_3 + (a^2-b^2)\, x_3\, y_3 = 0 \qquad (3)$$

Eliminating $b^2\, y$, $-a^2\, x$, (a^2-b^2) from (1). (2) and (3) we get the required condition.

$$\begin{vmatrix} x_1 & y_1 & x_1 & y_1 \\ x_2 & y_2 & x_2 & y_2 \\ x_3 & y_3 & x_3 & y_3 \end{vmatrix} = 0$$

Problem 12 If the normal at any point p to the cllips $\frac{x^2}{a^2} + \frac{y^2}{b^2} = 1$ meets the major and minor axis in G and g and if CF be the perpendicular upon this normal, where C is the centie of the ellipse, then prove that $PF \cdot Pg = a^2$

and
$$PF\, PG = b^2$$
[Must revise]

Solution The equation of the ellipse is

$$\frac{x^2}{a^2} + \frac{y^2}{b^2} = 1$$

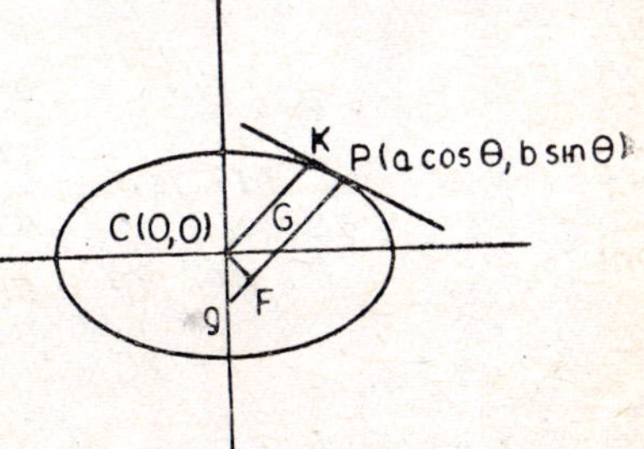

The equation of tangent at p (θ)

i.e. p $(a \cos \theta, b \sin \theta)$ to the ellipse is

$$\frac{x}{a} \cos \theta + \frac{y}{b} \sin \theta = 1 \qquad (1)$$

Ck is the perpendicular from C (0, 0) to the tangent (1) then

$$Ck = \frac{-1}{\sqrt{\frac{x \cos^2 \theta}{a^2} + \frac{\sin^2 \theta}{b^2}}}$$

$$Ck = \frac{-ab}{\sqrt{a^2 \sin^2 \theta + b^2 \cos^2 \theta}}$$

Since $$Ck = PF$$

$$\Rightarrow \quad Ck^2 = PF^2$$

$$PF^2 = \frac{a^2 b^2}{a^2 \sin^2\theta + b^2 \cos^2\theta}$$

The equation of the normal PG at $P(\theta)$ is

$$ax \sec\theta - by \operatorname{cosec}\theta = a^2 - b^2 \tag{2}$$

For the point G, $y = 0 \therefore$ from (2)

$$x = \frac{a^2 - b^2}{a \sec\theta}$$

$$\Rightarrow \quad x = \frac{(a^2 - b^2)\cos\theta}{a}$$

So $$PG^2 = \left[a\cos\theta - \frac{(a^2 - b^2)}{a}\cos\theta\right]^2 + (b\sin\theta - 0)^2$$

$$PG^2 = \frac{[a^2\cos\theta - (a^2 - b^2)\cos\theta]^2}{a^2} + b^2\sin^2\theta$$

$$PG^2 = \frac{a^4\cos^2\theta + (a^2 - b^2)^2\cos^2\theta - 2a^2\cos^2\theta(a^2 - b^2) + a^2 b^2\sin^2\theta}{a^2}$$

$$PG^2 = \frac{a^4\cos^2\theta + (a^4 + b^4 - 2a^2b^2)\cos^2\theta - 2a^4\cos^2\theta + 2a^2b^2\cos^2\theta + a^2b^2\sin^2\theta}{a^2}$$

$$PG^2 = \frac{b^4\cos^2\theta + a^2 b^2\sin^2\theta}{a^2}$$

$$PG^2 = \frac{b^2}{a^2}(b^2\cos^2\theta + a^2\sin^2\theta)$$

$$\Rightarrow \quad PF^2 \cdot PG^2 = \frac{b^2}{a^2}a^2 b^2$$

$$\Rightarrow \quad PF^2\,PG^2 = b^4$$

$$\Rightarrow \quad PF \cdot PG = b^2$$

For the point g $\quad y = 0$

Then $$-by \operatorname{cosec}\theta = a^2 - b^2$$

$$\Rightarrow \quad y = -\frac{a^2 - b^2}{b}\sin\theta$$

The co-ordinate of g $\left(0 \;-\; \frac{a^2 - b^2}{b}\sin\theta\right)$

Hence $$Pg^2 = a^2\cos^2\theta + \left[b\sin\theta + \frac{(a^2-b^2)}{b}\sin\theta\right]^2$$

$$= a^2\cos^2\theta + \frac{[b^2\sin\theta + (a^2-b^2)\sin\theta]^2}{b^2}$$

$$= \frac{a^2b^2\cos^2\theta + b^4\sin^2\theta + (a^2-b^2)^2\sin^2\theta + 2b^2(a^2-b^2)\sin^2\theta}{b^2}$$

$$= \frac{a^2b^2\cos^2\theta + b^4\sin^2\theta + (a^4+b^4-2a^2b^2))\sin^2\theta + 2a^2b^2\sin^2\theta - 2b^4\sin^2\theta}{b^2}$$

$$= \frac{a^4\sin^2\theta + a^2b^2\cos^2\theta}{b^2}$$

$$= \frac{a^2}{b^2}(a^2\sin^2\theta + b^2\cos^2\theta)$$

$$PF^2\cdot Pg^2 = \frac{a^2}{b^2}\cdot a^2b^2$$

$$\Rightarrow \quad PF^2\cdot Pg^2 = a^4$$

$$\Rightarrow \quad PF\cdot Pg = a^2$$ *(Proved)*

Problem 13 If the normal at one end of the latus rectum of an ellipse passes through one extrimity of the minor axis. show that the ecentricity of the curve is given by the equation $e^4 + e^2 - 1 = 0$. *[Must prepare]*

Solution Co-ordinate of S $(ac, 0)$ length of the latus rectum

$$LSL^1 = 2\frac{b^2}{a}$$

Length of semi latus rectum $= \dfrac{b^2}{a}$

So the co-ordinate of C is $\left(ae, \dfrac{b^2}{a}\right)$

The equation of normal at the extremity $L\left(ae, \dfrac{b^2}{a}\right)$ of the latus sectum LSL^1

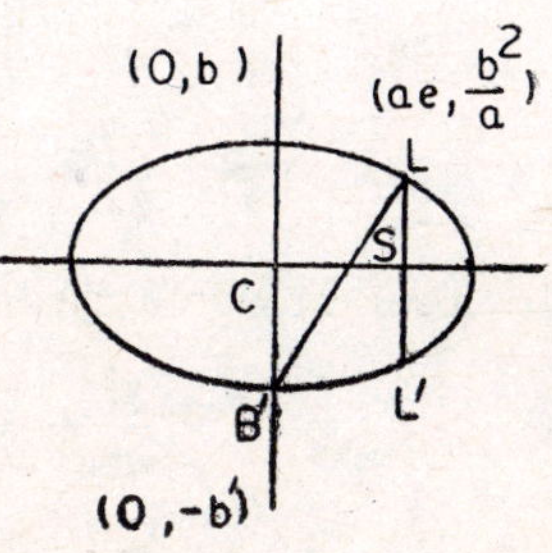

$$\frac{x-ac}{ae/a^2} = \frac{y-\dfrac{b^2}{a}}{a^2/b}$$

$$\Rightarrow \quad a^2\left(\frac{x-ae}{ae}\right) = a\left(y-\frac{b^2}{a}\right)e$$

$$\Rightarrow \quad x-ae = \left(y-\frac{b^2}{a}\right)e$$

If passes through the extremity B^1 (0, $-b$) of the minor axis

$$\therefore \quad -ae = \left(b - \frac{b^2}{a}\right) e$$

$$-a = -\frac{ab - b^2}{a}$$

$$-a^2 = -ab - b^2$$

$$\Rightarrow \quad a^2 = ab + b^2 \qquad (1)$$

Again since we have $\quad b^2 = a^2 (1 - e^2) \qquad (2)$

$\Rightarrow$ Putting the value of b^2 from equation (2) in equation (1)

$$a^2 = aa \sqrt{1 - e^2} + a^2 (1 - e^2)$$

$$a^2 = a^2 \sqrt{1 - e^2} + a^2 (1 - e^2)$$

$$1 = \sqrt{1 - e^2} + 1 - e^2$$

$$1 - 1 + e^2 = \sqrt{1 - e^2}$$

$$\Rightarrow \quad e^2 = \sqrt{1 - e^2}$$

squaring both sides we have

$$e^4 = 1 - e^2$$

$$\Rightarrow \quad e^4 + e^2 - 1 = 0 \qquad (Proved)$$

Problem 14 Show that the locus of the middle points of the chords of an ellipse passing through a fixed point is another ellipse.

Solution Let the ellipse be

$$\frac{x^2}{a^2} + \frac{y^2}{b^2} = 1 \qquad (1)$$

Then the equation of the chord of an ellipse (1) with (x_1, y_1) as middle point is $S_1 = T$

$$\frac{x_1^2}{a^2} + \frac{y_1^2}{b^2} - 1 = \frac{xx_1}{a^2} + \frac{yy_1}{b^2} - 1$$

$$\Rightarrow \quad \frac{x_1^2}{a^2} + \frac{y_1^2}{b^2} = \frac{xx_1}{a^2} + \frac{yy_1}{b^2}$$

It passes through a fixed point α, β so

$$\frac{x_1^2}{a^2} + \frac{y_1^2}{b^2} = \frac{\alpha x_1}{a^2} + \frac{\beta y_1}{b^2}$$

$$\frac{x_1^2}{a^2} - \frac{\alpha x_1}{a^2} = \frac{\beta y_1}{b^2} - \frac{y_1^2}{b^2}$$

$$\frac{x_1^2}{a^2} - \frac{\alpha x}{a^2} + \frac{y_1^2}{b^2} - \frac{\beta y_1}{b^2} = 1$$

$$\frac{x_1^2 - \alpha x_1 + \frac{\alpha^2}{4}}{a^2} + \frac{y_1^2 - \beta y_1 + \frac{\beta^2}{4}}{b^2} = \frac{\alpha^2}{4a^2} + \frac{\beta^2}{4b^2}$$

$$\frac{\left(x_1 - \frac{\alpha}{2}\right)^2}{a^2} + \frac{\left(y_1 - \frac{\beta}{2}\right)^2}{b^2} = \frac{\alpha^2}{4a^2} + \frac{\beta^2}{4b^2}$$

$\therefore$ Locus of (x_1, y_1) is

$$\frac{\left(x - \frac{\alpha}{2}\right)^2}{a^2} + \frac{\left(y - \frac{\beta}{2}\right)^2}{b^2} = \frac{\alpha^2}{4a^2} + \frac{\beta^2}{4b^2}$$

Which evidently represents an ellipse. (*Proved*)

Problem 15 Find the locus of the middle points of the chord of the ellipse which are tangents to $\frac{x^2}{\alpha^2} + \frac{y^2}{\beta^2} = 1$ $\frac{x^2}{a^2} + \frac{y^2}{b^2} = 1$

Solution Let the middle point of the chord of the ellipse

$$\frac{x^2}{\alpha^2} + \frac{y^2}{\beta^2} = 1 \text{ is } (x_1, y_1)$$

Then equation of the chord is given by $S_1 = T$

$$\frac{x_1^2}{a^2} + \frac{y_1^2}{\beta^2} - 1 = \frac{xx_1}{a^2} + \frac{yy_1}{\beta^2} - 1$$

$$\Rightarrow \quad \frac{x_1^2}{\alpha^2} + \frac{y_1^2}{\beta^2} = \frac{xx_1}{\alpha^2} + \frac{yy_1}{\beta^2} \tag{1}$$

$$\Rightarrow \quad \frac{yy_1}{\beta^2} = -\frac{xx_1}{\alpha^2} + \left(\frac{x_1^2}{\alpha^2} + \frac{y_1^2}{\beta^2}\right)$$

$$\Rightarrow \quad y = -\left(\frac{\beta^2}{\alpha^2}\frac{x_1}{y_1}\right)x + \frac{\beta^2}{y_1}\left(\frac{x_1^2}{\alpha^2} + \frac{y_1^2}{\beta^2}\right)$$

Which is of the form $y = mx + c$

$$m = -\frac{\beta^2}{\alpha^2}\frac{x_1}{y_1}$$

$$c = \frac{\beta^2}{y_1}\left(\frac{x_1^2}{\alpha^2} + \frac{y_1^2}{\beta^2}\right)$$

$y = mx + c$ will be targent to

$$\frac{x^2}{a^2}+\frac{y^2}{b^2}=1 \text{ if}$$

$$c^2 = a^2 m^2 + b^2$$

i.e. $$\frac{\beta^4}{y_1^2}\left(\frac{x_1^2}{\alpha^2}+\frac{y_1^2}{\beta^2}\right)^2 = a^2 \frac{\beta^4}{\alpha^4}\frac{x_1^2}{y_1^2}+b^2$$

$$\Rightarrow \left(\frac{x_1^2}{\alpha^2}+\frac{y_1^2}{\beta^2}\right)^2 = \frac{a^2 y_1^2}{\alpha^4 y_1^2}x_1^2 + \frac{b^2 y_1^2}{\beta^4}$$

$$\Rightarrow \left(\frac{x_1^2}{\alpha^2}+\frac{y_1^2}{\beta^2}\right)^2 = \frac{a^2}{\alpha^4}x_1^2 + \frac{b^2 y_1^2}{\beta^4}$$

Hence the locus of (x_1, y_1) is

$$\left(\frac{x^2}{\alpha^2}+\frac{y^2}{\beta^2}\right)^2 = \frac{a^2 x^2}{\alpha^4}+\frac{b^2 y^2}{\beta^4} \quad \textbf{Ans.}$$

Problem 16 Show that the locus of the middle points of the normal chords of the ellipse $\frac{x^2}{a^2}+\frac{y^2}{b^2}=1$ is the curve

$$\left(\frac{x^2}{a^2}+\frac{y^2}{b^2}\right)^2\left(\frac{a^6}{x^2}+\frac{b^6}{y^2}\right) = (a^2-b^2)^2 \quad \text{[Must revise]}$$

Solution Middle point of the chord is (x_1, y_1) then the equation of the chord is given by $S_1 = T$

i.e. $$\frac{x_1^2}{a^2}+\frac{y_1^2}{b^2}-1 = \frac{xx_1}{a^2}+\frac{yy_1}{b^2}-1$$

i.e. $$\frac{x_1^2}{a^2}+\frac{y_1^2}{b^2} = \frac{xx_1}{a^2}+\frac{yy_1}{b^2}$$

i.e. $$\frac{xx_1}{a^2}+\frac{yy_1}{a^2} = \frac{x_1^2}{a^2}+\frac{y_1^2}{b^2} \qquad (1)$$

Now we know that the equation of the normal is

$$ax \sec\theta - by \operatorname{cosec}\theta = a^2 - b^2$$

$$\Rightarrow \frac{ax}{\cos\theta} - \frac{by}{\sin\theta} = a^2 - b^2 \qquad (2)$$

If (1) represent the normal chord then

$$\frac{\frac{x_1}{a^2}}{\frac{a}{\cos\theta}} = \frac{\frac{y_1}{b^2}}{-\frac{b}{\sin\theta}} = \frac{\frac{x_1^2}{a^2}+\frac{y_1^2}{b^2}}{(a^2-b^2)}$$

$$\frac{x_1 \cos\theta}{a^3} = -\frac{y_1 \sin\theta}{b^3} = \frac{\frac{x_1^2}{a^2}+\frac{y_1^2}{b^2}}{(a^2-b^2)}$$

$$\cos\theta = \frac{a^2}{x_1}\frac{\left(\frac{x_1^2}{a^2}+\frac{y_1^2}{b^2}\right)}{(a^2-b^2)} \tag{3}$$

$$\sin\theta = -\frac{b^3}{y_1}\frac{\left(\frac{x_1^2}{a^2}+\frac{y_1^2}{b^2}\right)}{(a^2-b^2)} \tag{4}$$

squaring and adding

$$(a^2-b^2)^2 = \left(\frac{a_6}{x_1^2}+\frac{b^6}{y_1^2}\right)\left(\frac{x_1^2}{a^2}+\frac{y_1^2}{b^2}\right)^2$$

locus of the point (x_1, y_1) can be obtained by replacing x_1 by x and y_1 by y Thus the locus is

$$\left(\frac{x^2}{a^2}+\frac{y^2}{b^2}\right)^2\left(\frac{a^6}{x^2}+\frac{b^6}{y^2}\right) = (a^2-b^2)^2 \qquad \textit{(Proved)}$$

Problem 17 Prove that the locus of the middle points of chords of the ellipse $\frac{x^2}{a^2}+\frac{y^2}{b^2}=1$, which subtands a right angle at the centre.

[Must ravise]

Solution Let the ellipse be $\frac{x^2}{a^2}+\frac{y^2}{b^2}=1$ (1)

Then the equation of the chord of the ellipse (1) with R (x_1, y_1) as middle point is $S_1 = T$

or $$\frac{x_1^2}{a^2}+\frac{y_1^2}{b^2}-1 = \frac{xx_1}{a^2}+\frac{yy_1}{b^2}-1$$

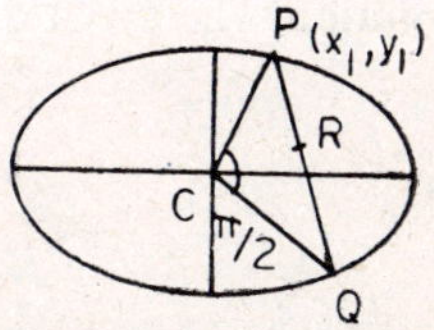

P (x_1, y_1)
R
C
$\pi/2$
Q

or $$\frac{x_1^2}{a^2}+\frac{y_1^2}{b^2} = \frac{xx_1}{a^2}+\frac{yy_1}{b^2}$$

$$\Rightarrow \frac{\frac{xx_1}{a^2}+\frac{yy_1}{b^2}}{\frac{x_1^2}{a^2}+\frac{y_1^2}{b^2}} = 1 \tag{2}$$

Now making (1) homogeneous with the help of (2) we get the equation of pair of lines CP and CQ joining the origin C to the points of intersection P and Q of (1) and (2)

$$\frac{x^2}{a^2}+\frac{y^2}{b^2}=\frac{\left(\frac{xx_1}{a^2}+\frac{yy_1}{b^2}\right)^2}{\left(\frac{x_1^2}{a^2}+\frac{y_1^2}{b^2}\right)^2} \qquad (3)$$

But the chord subtends a right angle at the centre.

$\therefore$ CP and CQ are $\perp$ to each other i.e. the pair of lines given by (3) are at right angles to each other

$\therefore$ The coefficient of x^2 + the coefficient of $y^2 = 0$

or
$$\frac{1}{a^2}\left(\frac{x_1^2}{a^2}+\frac{y_1^2}{b^2}\right)^2-\frac{x_1^2}{a^4}+\frac{1}{b^2}\left(\frac{x_1^2}{a^2}+\frac{y_1^2}{b^2}\right)-\frac{y_1^2}{b^4}=0$$

or
$$\left(\frac{x_1^2}{a^2}+\frac{y_1^2}{b^2}\right)\left(\frac{1}{a^2}+\frac{1}{b^2}\right)=\frac{x_1^2}{a^4}+\frac{y_1^2}{b^4}$$

$\therefore$ locus of $R\,(x_1, y_1)$ is $\dfrac{x^2}{a^4}+\dfrac{y^2}{b^4}=\dfrac{a^2+b^2}{a^2 b^2}\left(\dfrac{x^2}{a^2}+\dfrac{y^2}{b^2}\right)^2$

Hence the result

Problems based on conjugate diameters *of the ellipse.*

Problem 18 For the ellipse $\frac{x^2}{a^2}+\frac{y^2}{b^2}=1$, find the equation of the diameter conjugate to $ax-by=0$

Solution We use the formula in this problem

Product of the slope of the two conjngate diameters $=-\dfrac{b^2}{a^2}$

i.e.
$$\boxed{m_1 m_2=-\frac{b^2}{a^2}}$$
Remember

Solution The given diameter is

$$ax-by=0 \qquad (1)$$

$\therefore$
$$by=ax$$

$$y=\frac{a}{b}x$$

$\Rightarrow$
$$m_1=\frac{a}{b}$$

Let the diameter conjugate to (1) by

$$y=m_2 x \qquad (2)$$

$\therefore$ The condition for this is

$$m_1 m_2 = -\frac{b^2}{a^2}$$

$$\frac{a}{b} \cdot m_2 = -\frac{b^2}{a^2}$$

$$m_2 = -\frac{b^3}{a^3}$$

From (2), the required diameter is

$$y = -\frac{b^3}{a^3} x$$

$$\boxed{a^3 y + b^3 x = 0}$$ **Ans.**

Problem 19 Prove that the polar of any point on a diameter of an ellipse is parallel to the conjugate diameter of the ellipse

Solution Let the ellipse be

$$\frac{x^2}{a^2} + \frac{y^2}{b^2} = 1 \tag{1}$$

Let the two conjugate diameter of (1) be

$$y = m_1 x \tag{2}$$

$$y = m_2 x \tag{3}$$

Where $$m_1 m_2 = -\frac{b^2}{a^2} \tag{4}$$

Let $P(x^1, y^1)$ be any point on (2)

$\therefore$ $$y^1 = mx^1$$

$\therefore$ P becomes $(x^1, m_1 x_1)$

Now polar of $P(x^1, mx^1)$ w.r.t. (1) is

$$\frac{xx^1}{a^2} + \frac{yy_1}{b^2} = 1$$

$$\Rightarrow \quad \frac{xx^1}{a^2} + \frac{y \cdot m_1 x^1}{b^2} = 1$$

$$\text{Its scope} = -\frac{\text{Coefficient of } x}{\text{Coefficient of } y}$$

$$= -\frac{x^1}{a^2} \frac{b^2}{m_1 x^1} = -\frac{b^2}{a^2 m_1} = m_2$$

$$= \text{slope of (3)}$$

Hence the desired result

Problem 20 Prove that the tangents at the extremities of a diameter of an ellipse are parallel to the conjugate diameter.

Solution Let the ellipse be

$$\frac{x^2}{a^2} + \frac{y^2}{b^2} = 1$$

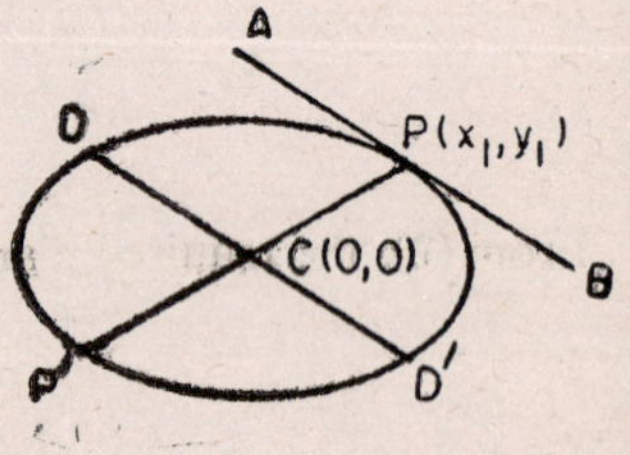

let PP' and DD' be its conjugate diameters whose equations are

$$y = mx \qquad (1)$$

and

$$y = m_1 x \qquad (2$$

respectively where

$$mm_1 = -\frac{b^2}{a^2} \qquad (3)$$

let P be (x_1, y_1). Then $P(x_1, y_1)$ lies on (1)

$\therefore$

$$y_1 = mx_1 \qquad (4)$$

The tangent at $P(x_1, y_1)$ to the ellipse is

$$\frac{xx_1}{a^2} + \frac{yy_1}{b^2} = 1$$

$$\frac{yy_1}{b^2} = -\frac{xx_1}{a^2} + 1$$

$$y = -\frac{b^2}{a^2} \cdot \frac{x_1}{y_1} x + \frac{b^2}{y_1}$$

$$y = -\frac{b^2}{a^2} \frac{1}{m} x + \frac{b^2}{y_1} \qquad \text{from (4)}$$

$$y = \frac{mm_1}{m} x + \frac{b^2}{yt}$$

or

$$y = m_1 x + \frac{b^2}{y_1}$$

which is parallel to (2). Hence the tangent at P is parallel to DD'

Problem 21 If P and D be the ends of conjugate diameters of an ellipse, find the locus of the middle point of PD. [*Must revise*]

Solution Let the ellipse be

$$\frac{x^2}{a^2} + \frac{y^2}{b^2}$$

Let the eccentric angle of P be ϕ, then the eccentric angle of D be $\pi/2 + \phi$

The co-ordinate of P be

$$P\ (a \cos \phi,\ b \sin \phi)$$

and the co-ordinate of D be

$$D\left(a \cos\left(\frac{\pi}{2} + \phi\right),\ b \sin\left(\frac{\pi}{2} + \phi\right)\right)$$

$$D\ (-\ a \sin \phi,\ b \cos \phi)$$

$\therefore$ The co-ordinates of P and D are respectively $(a \cos \phi, b \sin \phi)$ and $(-\ a \sin \phi, b \cos \phi)$

let the mindle point of PD be (h, k)

Then $$h = \frac{a \cos \phi - a \sin \phi}{2} = \frac{a}{2} (\cos \phi - \sin \phi)$$

$$k = \frac{b \sin \phi + b \cos \phi}{2} = \frac{b}{2} (\sin \phi + \cos \phi)$$

$$\frac{2h}{a} = \cos \phi - \sin \phi \quad (1)$$

and $$\frac{2k}{b} = \sin \phi + \cos \phi \quad (2)$$

squaring and adding (1) and (2) we have

$$\frac{4h^2}{a^2} + \frac{4k^2}{b^2} = (\cos \phi - \sin \phi)^2 + (\sin \phi + \cos \phi)^2$$

$$= \cos^2 \phi + \sin^2 \phi + \sin^2 \phi + \cos^2 \phi - 2 \cos \phi \sin \phi + 2 \sin \phi \cos \phi$$

$$\frac{4h^2}{a^2} + \frac{4k^2}{b^2} = 1 + 1$$

$$\frac{4h^2}{a^2} + \frac{4k^2}{b^2} = 2$$

$$\frac{h^2}{a^2} + \frac{k^2}{b^2} = \frac{1}{2}$$

$\therefore$ The locus of (h, k) is

$$\frac{x^2}{a^2} + \frac{y^2}{b^2} = \frac{1}{2}$$

Problem 22 If P and D are the extremities of conjugate diameters of the ellipse $\frac{x^2}{a^2} + \frac{y^2}{b^2} = 1$, show that the tangents at P and D meet on the ellipse $\frac{x^2}{a^2} + \frac{y^2}{b^2} = 2$.

Solution Let the eccentric angle of the end point P be ϕ, then the eccentric angle of the end point Q be $\pi/2 + \phi$.

Then the co-ordinates of the point P is given by

$$P\,(a \cos \phi,\ b \sin \phi)$$

and the co-ordinates of the point Q is given by

$$Q\left(a \cos\left(\frac{\pi}{2} + \phi\right),\ a \sin\left(\frac{\pi}{2} + \phi\right)\right)$$

i.e. $$Q\,(-\,a \sin \phi,\ b \cos \phi)$$

Now the equation of the tangent at the point P $(a \cos \phi, b \sin \phi)$ is given by

$$\frac{xa \cos \phi}{a^2} + \frac{yb \sin \phi}{b^2} = 1$$

$$\Rightarrow \quad \frac{x \cos \phi}{a} + \frac{y \sin \phi}{b} = 1 \qquad (1)$$

Equation of the tangent at the point Q $(-\,a \sin \phi, b \cos \phi)$ is given by

$$\frac{x\,(-a) \sin \phi}{a^2} + \frac{y \cdot b \cos \phi}{b^2} = 1$$

$$\Rightarrow \quad -\frac{x \sin \phi}{a} + \frac{y \cos \phi}{b} = 1 \qquad (2)$$

on solving (1) and (2) a eliminating ϕ we can find the locus of (x, y) which is the meeting point of the two tangents.

Now squaring and adding (1) and (2) we have

$$\frac{x^2}{a^2} + \frac{y^2}{b^2} = 2 \qquad \textit{(Proved)}$$

Problem 23 Show that the sum of the reciprocals of the squares of two diameters of an ellipse, which are at right angles to each other is constant. [*Must revise*]

Solution Let the equation of the ellipse be

$$\frac{x^2}{a^2} + \frac{y^2}{b^2} = 1 \qquad (1)$$

let us express the equation of the ellipse in polar form. Let the centre of the ellipse be taken as pole and the major axis as the initial line.

Putting $x = r \cos \theta$, $y = r \sin \theta$ in equation (1) we get

$$\frac{r^2 \cos^2 \theta}{a^2} + \frac{r^2 \sin^2 \theta}{b^2} = 1$$

$$\frac{\cos^2 \theta}{a^2} + \frac{\sin^2 \theta}{b^2} = \frac{1}{r^2} \qquad (2)$$

Ler r^1 be the radius vector $\perp'$ to r. Then putting $r = r^1$ and $\theta = \frac{\pi}{2} + \theta$ in (2) we get

$$\frac{\cos^2\left(\frac{\pi}{2}+\theta\right)}{a^2}+\frac{\sin^2\left(\frac{\pi}{2}+\theta\right)}{b^2}=\frac{1}{r'^2}$$

$$\frac{\sin^2\theta}{a^2}+\frac{\cos^2\theta}{b^2}=\frac{1}{r'^2} \tag{3}$$

Adding (2) and (3) we get

$$\frac{1}{r^2}+\frac{1}{r'^2}=\frac{1}{a^2}(\cos^2\theta+\sin^2\theta)+\frac{1}{b^2}(\sin^2\theta+\cos^2\theta)$$

or $$\frac{1}{r^2}+\frac{1}{r'^2}=\frac{1}{a^2}+\frac{1}{b^2}$$

or $$\frac{1}{4}\left(\frac{1}{r^2}+\frac{1}{r'^2}\right)=\frac{1}{4}\left(\frac{1}{a^2}+\frac{1}{b^2}\right)$$

or $$\frac{1}{(2r)^2}+\frac{1}{(2r')^2}=\frac{1}{4}\left(\frac{1}{a^2}+\frac{1}{b^2}\right)=\text{constant}$$

Hence the sum of the reciprocals of the squares of two $\perp'$ diameters of an *ellipse is constant.*

Problem 24 If α, β, γ, δ be the eccentric angles of the con-cyclic points of the ellipse $\frac{x^2}{a^2}+\frac{y^2}{b^2}=1$ prove that $\alpha+\beta+\gamma+\delta=2n\pi$ [*Must revise*]

Solution The ellipse is $\frac{x^2}{a^2}+\frac{y^2}{b^2}-1=0$ (1)

The equations of the chords of (1) joining α, β and γ, δ are

$$\frac{x}{a}\cos\frac{\alpha+\beta}{2}+\frac{y}{b}\sin\frac{\alpha+\beta}{2}=\cos\frac{\alpha-\beta}{2} \tag{2}$$

and $$\frac{x}{a}\cos\frac{\gamma+\delta}{2}+\frac{y}{b}\sin\frac{\gamma+\delta}{2}=\cos\frac{\gamma-\delta}{2} \tag{3}$$

The equation of any conic through the intersection of (1) and the chords (2) and (3) is

$$\frac{x^2}{a^2}+\frac{y^2}{b^2}-1+k\left(\frac{x}{a}\cos\frac{\alpha+\beta}{2}+\frac{y}{b}\sin\frac{\alpha+\beta}{2}-\cos\frac{\alpha-\beta}{2}\right)$$
$$\times\left(\frac{x}{a}\cos\frac{\gamma+\delta}{2}+\frac{y}{b}\sin\frac{\gamma+\delta}{2}-\cos\frac{\gamma-\delta}{2}\right)=0$$

This conic will represent a circle of (i) the coefficient of x^2 = the coefficient of y^2 and (ii) the coefficient of $xy = 0$

Considering the condition (ii) we get

$$\cos\frac{\alpha+\beta}{2}\sin\frac{\gamma+\delta}{2}+\sin\frac{\alpha+\beta}{2}\cos\frac{\gamma+\delta}{2}=0$$

$$\sin\frac{(\alpha+\beta+\gamma+\delta)}{2}=0$$

$$\therefore \qquad \frac{\alpha+\beta+\gamma+\delta}{2}=n\pi$$

$$\Rightarrow \qquad \alpha+\beta+\gamma+\delta=2n\pi \qquad \textit{(Proved)}$$

Problem 25 The eccentric angles of two points on the ellipse with $2a$ as the major axis are ϕ and ϕ' and their join intersects the major axis at a distance c from the centre prove that

$$\frac{c-a}{c+a}=\tan\frac{\phi}{2}\tan\frac{\phi'}{2} \qquad \textit{[Must revise]}$$

Solution Let the equation of the ellipse be

$$\frac{x^2}{a^2}+\frac{y^2}{b^2}=1 \qquad (1)$$

Let ϕ and ϕ' be the eccentric angles of the two points on the ellipse. Let $2a$ be the major axis.

The equation of the chord i.e. the joining of ϕ and ϕ' is given yb

$$\frac{x}{a}\cos\frac{\phi+\phi'}{2}+\frac{y}{b}\sin\frac{\phi+\phi'}{2}=\cos\frac{\phi-\phi'}{2} \qquad (2)$$

Since (2) cuts the major axis at a distance c from the centre i.e. at a point $(c, 0)$. So the point $(c, 0)$ will satisfy the equation (2). Hence

$$\frac{c}{a}\cos\frac{\phi+\phi'}{2}=\cos\frac{\phi-\phi'}{2}$$

$$\frac{c}{a}=\frac{\cos\frac{\phi-\phi'}{2}}{\cos\frac{\phi+\phi'}{2}} \qquad (3)$$

Now by companando and dividindo we have

$$\frac{c-a}{c+a}=\frac{\cos\frac{\phi-\phi^1}{2}-\cos\frac{\phi+\phi^1}{2}}{\cos\frac{\phi-\phi}{2}+\cos\frac{\phi+\phi'}{2}}$$

$$\frac{c-a}{c+a}=\frac{2\sin\phi/2\sin\phi'/2}{2\cos\phi'/2\cos\phi'/2}$$

$$\frac{c-a}{c+a}=\tan\phi/2\tan\phi'/2 \qquad \textit{(Proved)}$$

Problem 26 If any pair of the conjugate diameters of an ellipse cut the tangent at P in T and T^1 show that $TP\cdot PT^1 = CD^2$, where CD is the semi diameter conjugate to CP. *[Must revise]*

Solution Let the equation of the ellipse be

$$\frac{x^2}{a^2}+\frac{y^2}{b^2}=1 \tag{1}$$

Let p $(a\cos\theta, b\sin\theta)$ be any point on the ellipse. Let a pair of conjugate diameters cuts the tangent at T and T' respectively. c be the centre (0, 0) of the ellipse.

The equations of the conjugate diameters are given by

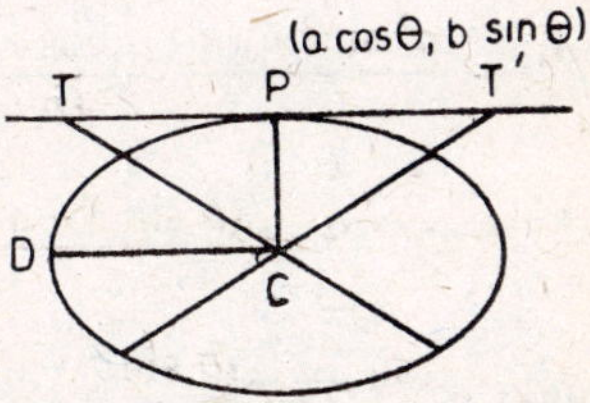

(a cosθ, b sinθ)
T P T'
D
C

$$y = m_1 x \tag{2}$$

and

$$y = m_2 x \tag{3}$$

where

$$m_1 m_2 = -\frac{b^2}{a^2} \tag{4}$$

The equation of the tangent at $(a\cos\theta, b\sin\theta)$ to the ellipse

$$\frac{x^2}{a^2}+\frac{y^2}{b^2}=1$$

is given by

$$\frac{xa\cos\theta}{a^2}+\frac{yb\sin\theta}{b^2}=1$$

$$\frac{x\cos\theta}{a}+\frac{y\sin\theta}{b}=1 \tag{5}$$

The co-ordinates of T and T' can be obtained by the inter-section of equations (2) and (5) and (3) and (5).

From (2) and (5).

We have

$$\frac{x\cos\theta}{a}+\frac{mx\sin\theta}{b}=1$$

$$x(b\cos\theta+m_1 a\sin\theta)=ab$$

$$\Rightarrow \qquad x=\frac{ab}{b\cos\theta+m_1 a\sin\theta}$$

$$y=\frac{m_1 ab}{b\cos\theta+m_1 a\sin\theta}$$

Thus the co-ordinates of the point T be

$$T\left(\frac{ab}{b\cos\theta+m_1 a\sin\theta}, \frac{m_1 ab}{b\cos\theta+m_1 a\sin\theta}\right)$$

Then $$TP^2=\left[a\cos\theta-\frac{ab}{b\cos\theta+m_1 a\sin\theta}\right]^2$$

$$+\left[b\sin\theta-\frac{m_1 ab}{b\cos\theta+m_1 a\sin\theta}\right]^2$$

$$TP^2=\left[\frac{ab\cos^2\theta+m_1 a^2\sin\theta\cos\theta-ab}{b\cos\theta+m_1 a\sin\theta}\right]^2$$

$$+\left[\frac{b^2\sin\theta\cos\theta+m_1 ab\sin^2\theta-m_1 ab}{b\cos\theta+m_1 a\sin\delta}\right]^2$$

$$TP^2=\frac{[m_1a^2\sin\theta\cos\theta-ab\sin^2\theta)^2+[b^2\sin\theta\cos\theta-m_1 ab\cos\theta^2]^2}{(b\cos\theta+m_1 a\sin\theta)^2}$$

$$TP^2=\frac{a^2\sin^2\theta\,(m_1 a\cos\theta-b\sin\theta)^2+b^2\cos^2\theta\,(b\sin\theta-m_1ab^2\cos\theta)}{(b\cos\theta+m_1 a\sin\theta)^2}$$

$$TP^2=\frac{(b\sin\theta-am_1\cos\theta)^2\,(a^2\sin^2\theta+b^2\cos^2\theta)}{(b\cos\theta+m_1 a\sin\theta)^2}$$

Similarly $$T^1P^2=\frac{(b\sin\theta-am_2\cos\theta)^2\,(a^2\sin^2\theta+b^2\cos^2\theta)}{(b\cos\theta+m_1 a\sin\theta)^2}$$

If CP and CD are semiconjugate diameters. So if the eccentric angle of P be $a\cos\theta$, then the eccentric angle of D be $\left(\frac{\pi}{2}+\theta\right)$

The co-ordinates of the point D is $\left(\frac{\pi}{2}+\theta\right)$, $b\sin\left(\frac{\pi}{2}+\theta\right)$

i.e. $$(-a\sin\theta,\ b\cos\theta)$$

So $$CD^2=(-a\sin\theta-0)^2+(b\cos\theta-0)^2$$

$$CD^2=a^2\sin^2\theta+b^2\cos^2\theta$$

$$=\text{since } m_1 m_2=-\frac{b^2}{a^2}$$

$$\Rightarrow\quad m_2=-\frac{b^2}{a^2 m_1}$$

So $$T^1P^2=\frac{\left(b\sin\theta+a\frac{b^2}{a^2 m_1}\cos\theta\right)^2(a^2\sin^2\theta+b^2\cos^2\theta)}{\left(b\cos\theta-\frac{b^2}{a^2 m_1}a\sin\theta\right)^2}$$

$$T^1 P^2 = \frac{(am_1 b \sin\theta + b^2 \cos\theta)^2 (a^2 \sin b^2 + b^2 \cos^2\theta)}{(abm_1 \cos\theta - b^2 \sin\theta)^2}$$

$$T^1 P^2 = \frac{(am_1 \sin\theta + b\cos\theta)^2 (a^2 \sin^2\theta + b^2\cos^2\theta)}{(am_1 \cos\theta - b\sin\theta)^2}$$

$$TP^2\, T^2\, P^2 = (a^2 \sin^2\theta + b^2\cos^2\theta)^2$$

$$TP^2\, T^1\, P^2 = CD^4$$

Taking square root we have

$$TP \cdot T^1 P = CD^2 \qquad \textit{(Proved)}$$

Problem 27 Find the locus of the point of intersection of the normals at the ends of the conjugate diameters of an ellipse. *[For Revision]*

Solution Let the ellipse be

$$\frac{x^2}{a^2} + \frac{y^2}{b^2} = 1 \tag{1}$$

Let P and D be the extremities of the conjugate diameters of (1) let the eceentric angle of P be ϕ. Then the eccentric angle of D be $\left(\frac{\pi}{2} + \phi\right)$.

The equations of the normals at $P(\phi)$

and $D\left(\frac{\pi}{2} + \theta\right)$ to (1) are resperively

$$ax \sec\phi - by \operatorname{cosec}\phi = a^2 - b^2$$

$$\frac{ax}{\cos\phi} - \frac{by}{\sin\phi} = a^2 - b^2$$

$$\frac{ax \sin\phi - by\cos\phi}{\sin\phi\cos\phi} = a^2 - b^2$$

$$ax\sin\phi - by\cos\phi = (a^2 - b^2)\sin\phi\cos\phi \tag{2}$$

and
$$ax \sin\left(\frac{\pi}{2} + \phi\right) - by\cos\left(\frac{\pi}{2} + \phi\right) = (a^2 - b^2)\sin\left(\frac{\pi}{2} + \phi\right)\cos\left(\frac{\pi}{2} + \phi\right)$$

$$ax\cos\phi + by\sin\phi = -(a^2 - b^2)\cos\phi\sin\phi \tag{3}$$

Adding equation (2) and (3) we have

$$\sin\phi\,(ax + by) + \cos\phi\,(ax - by) = 0$$

$$(ax + by)\sin\phi = (by - ax)\cos\phi$$

$$\frac{\sin\phi}{by-ax} = \frac{\cos\phi}{ax+by} = \frac{\sqrt{\sin^2\phi+\cos^2\phi}}{\sqrt{2\,(a^2x^2+b^2y^2)}}$$

$$\frac{\sin\phi}{by-ax} = \frac{\cos\phi}{ax+by} = \frac{1}{\sqrt{2\,(a^2x^2+b^2y^2)}}$$

$$\sin\phi = \frac{by-ax}{\sqrt{\quad{}^2+b^2y^2)}}$$

$$\cos\phi = \frac{ax+by}{\sqrt{2\,(a^2x^2+b^2y^2}}$$

Now substituting the value of $\sin\phi$ and cas ϕ in equation (2) we have

$$\frac{ax\,(by-ax)}{\sqrt{2\,(a^2x^2+b^2y)^2}} - \frac{by\,(ax+by)}{\sqrt{2\,(a^2x^2+b^2y^2)}}$$

$$= (a^2-b^2)\,\frac{(by-ax)\,(ax+by)}{2\,(a^2x^2+b^2y^2)}$$

$$\frac{ax\,(by-ax)-by\,(ax+by)}{\sqrt{2}\,\sqrt{a^2x^2+b^2y^2}} = \frac{(a^2-b^2)\,(b^2y^2-a^2x^2)}{2\,(a^2x^2+b^2y^2)}$$

or

$$-(a^2x^2+b^2y^2) = \frac{(a^2-b^2)\,(b^2y^2-a^2x^2)}{\sqrt{2\,(a^2x^2+by^2)}}$$

Squaring we get

$$2\,(a^2x^2+b^2y^2)^3 = (a^2-b^2)^2\,(b^2y^2-a^2x^2)^2$$

i.e. $2\,(a^2x^2+b^2y^2)^3 = (a^2-b^2)^2\,(a^2x^2-b^2y^2)^2$ **Ans.**

Problem 28 Prove that a chord which joins the end of a pair of conjugate diameteıs of an ellipse always factors a similar ellipse.

Solution Let the ellipse be

$$\frac{x^2}{a^2} + \frac{y^2}{b^2} = 1 \tag{1}$$

Let P and D be the ends of a pair of conjugate diameters of (1)

Let the eccentric angle of P be ϕ and the electric angle D be $\frac{\pi}{2}+\phi$

$\therefore$ Equation of the chord PD is

$$\frac{x}{a}\cos\frac{\phi+\frac{\pi}{2}+\phi}{2} + \frac{y}{b}\sin\frac{\phi+\frac{\pi}{2}+\phi}{2} = \cos\frac{\frac{\pi}{2}+\phi-\phi}{2}$$

i.e. $\frac{x}{a}\cos\left(\frac{\pi}{4}+\phi\right)+\frac{y}{b}\sin\left(\frac{\pi}{4}+\phi\right)=\cos\frac{\pi}{4}$

i.e. $\frac{x}{a}\cos\left(\frac{\pi}{4}+\phi\right)+\frac{y}{b}\sin\left(\frac{\pi}{4}+\phi\right)=\frac{1}{\sqrt{2}}$

$$\frac{x}{a/\sqrt{2}}\cos\left(\frac{\pi}{4}+\phi\right)+\frac{y}{b/\sqrt{2}}\sin\left(\frac{\pi}{4}+\phi\right)=1 \quad (2)$$

or $$\frac{x}{A}\cos\alpha+\frac{y}{P}\sin\alpha=1$$

where $$\alpha=\frac{n}{a}+\phi$$

$$A=\frac{a}{\sqrt{2}},\ B=\frac{b}{\sqrt{2}}$$

Evidently (2) is tangent to the ellipse

$$\frac{x^2}{A^2}+\frac{y^2}{B^2}=1 \quad (3)$$

Let the eccentricity of the ellipse (3) be e'.

Then $B^2 = A^2(1-e'^2)$

$$\frac{b^2}{2}=\frac{a^2}{2}(1-e'^2)$$

$$\Rightarrow \quad b^2 = a^2(1-e'^2) \quad (4)$$

But for ellipse (1)

$$b^2 = a^2(1-e^2) \quad (3)$$

From relation (4) and (5) we have

$$a^2(1-e'^2) = a^2(1-e^2)$$

$$\Rightarrow \quad 1-e^{12} = 1-c^2$$

$$\Rightarrow \quad e'^2 = 1-e^2$$

$$\Rightarrow \quad e' = e$$ *(Proved)*

Problems based on pole and polar

Problem 29 Find the pole of the linc $Ax + By + C = 0$ with respect to the ellipse

$$\frac{x^2}{a^2}+\frac{y^2}{b^2}=1.$$

Solution The ellipse is $\frac{x^2}{a^2}+\frac{y^2}{b^2}=1$ (1)

The given line is $Ax + By + c = 0$ (2)

Let is pole be (x_1, y_1)

Then the polar of (x_1, y_1) with respect to the ellipse (1) is

$$\frac{xx_1}{a^2} + \frac{yy_1}{b^2} = 1$$

Now (2) and (3) represent the same line. Hence comparing their coefficients we obtain

$$\frac{A}{x^1/a^2} = \frac{B}{y^1/b^2} = \frac{c}{-1}$$

$\therefore$
$$x_1 = -\frac{Aa^2}{c}$$

and
$$y_1 = -\frac{Bb^2}{c}$$

Hence the required is $\left(-\frac{Aa^2}{c}, -\frac{Bb^2}{c}\right)$

Problem 30 If a point be sueh that the prependicular from the centre one its polar with respect to the ellipse $\frac{x^2}{a^2} + \frac{y^2}{b^2} = 1$ is constant and equal to c, prove that its loccus is another ellipse.

$$\frac{x^2}{a^4} + \frac{y^2}{b^4} = \frac{1}{c^2}$$

Solution Let the point be (x_1, y_1). Then its polar with respect to the ellipse $\frac{x^2}{a^2} + \frac{y^2}{b^2} = 1$ is given by

$$\frac{xx_1}{a^2} + \frac{yy_1}{b^2} - 1 = 0 \tag{1}$$

Now the $\perp^r$ from centre c (0, 0) to (1) is

$$\frac{0 + 0 - 1}{\sqrt{\frac{x_1^2}{a^4} + \frac{y_1^2}{b^4}}} = c \text{ (constant)}$$

squaring both sides we have

$$\frac{1}{\frac{x_1^2}{a^4} + \frac{y_1^2}{b^4}} = c^2$$

$$\Rightarrow \quad \frac{x_1^2}{a^4} + \frac{y_1^2}{b^4} = \frac{1}{c^2}$$

Hence the locus of the point is

$$\frac{x^2}{a^4} + \frac{y^2}{b^4} = \frac{1}{c^2} \qquad \textit{(Proved)}$$

Problem 31 Find the locus of the poles of the tangents to the ellipse

$$\frac{x^2}{a^2} + \frac{y^2}{b^2} = 1$$

with respect to the parabola $y^2 = 4ax$.

Solution The equation of any tangent to the given ellipse is

$$y = mx + \sqrt{a^2 m^2 + b^2} \qquad (1)$$

Let (x_1, y_1) be the pole of (1)

Then the polar of (x_1, y_1) with respect to $y^2 = 4a$ is

$$yy = 2a(x + x_1)$$

i.e.
$$y = \frac{2a}{y_1}(x + x_1)$$

i.e.
$$y = \frac{2a}{y_1} x + \frac{2a}{y_1} x_1 \qquad (2)$$

Now (1) and (2) represent the same straight line. Hence comparing their coefficients we have

$$m = \frac{2a}{y_1} \quad (3) \qquad \text{and} \qquad \sqrt{a^2 m^2 + b^2} = 2a \frac{x_1}{y_1} \qquad (4)$$

Squaring (4) we have

$$a^2 m^2 + b^2 = 4a^2 \frac{x_1^2}{y_1^2}$$

$$\Rightarrow \qquad a^2 \frac{4a^2}{y_1^2} + b^2 = 4a^2 \frac{x_1^2}{y_1^2}$$

$$\Rightarrow \qquad 4a^4 + b^2 y_1^2 = 4a^2 x_1^2$$

Hence the locus of (x_1, y_1) is

$$b^2 y^2 + 4a^4 = 4a^2 x^2 \qquad \textbf{Ans.}$$

Problem 32 Chords of the ellipse $\frac{x^2}{a^2} + \frac{y^2}{b^2}$ always touch the ellipse $\frac{x^2}{\alpha^2} + \frac{y^2}{\beta^2} = 1$. Sow that the locus of their polar is

$$\frac{\alpha^2 x^2}{a^4} + \frac{\beta^2 y^2}{b^4} = 1$$

Solution Let (x_1, y_1) be the pole. Then the polar of (x_1, y_1) with respect to the ellipse

$$\frac{x^2}{a^2} + \frac{y^2}{b^2} - 1 = 0 \text{ is}$$

$$\frac{xx_1}{a^2} + \frac{yy_1}{b^2} - 1 = 0$$

or
$$\frac{yy_1}{b^2} = -\frac{xx_1}{a^2} + 1$$

$$y = -\frac{b^2}{a^2}\frac{x_1}{y_1}x + \frac{b^2}{y_1} \qquad (1)$$

Which is of the form
$$y = mx + c$$

Here
$$m = -\frac{b^2}{a^2}\frac{x_1}{y_1}$$

and
$$c = \frac{b^2}{y^1}$$

Line (1) touches the ellipse

$$\frac{x^2}{\alpha^2} + \frac{y^2}{\beta^2} = 1$$

The condition for which is $c^2 = a^2 m^2 + b^2$

or
$$\frac{b^4}{y_1^2} = \alpha^2 \frac{b^4}{a^4}\frac{x_1^2}{y_1^2} + {}^2$$

$$a^4 b^4 = \alpha^2 b^4 x_1^2 + a^4 y_1^2 \beta^2$$

$$\Rightarrow \quad \frac{\alpha^2 x_1^2}{a^4} + \frac{\beta^2 y_1^2}{b^4} = 1$$

Hence the locus of (x_1, y_1) is

$$\frac{\alpha^2 x^2}{a^4} + \frac{\beta^2 y^2}{\beta^4} = 1$$

Remember

(1) Equation of the chord of the ellipse $\frac{x^2}{a^2} + \frac{y^2}{b^2} = 1$ whose middle point is (x_1, y_1) is

$$(x - x_1)\frac{x_1}{a^2} + (y - y_1)\frac{y_1}{b^2} = 0$$

(2) The locus of the point of intersection of two perpendicular tangents to an ellipse is a circle called the director circle of the ellipse and its equation is given by

$$\boxed{x^2 + y^2 = a^2 + b^2}$$

(3) Equation of the chord of contact of tangents drown from any point (x_1, y_1) to the ellipse $\boxed{\dfrac{x^2}{a^2} + \dfrac{y^2}{b^2} = 1}$ is given by $\dfrac{xx_1}{a^2} + \dfrac{yy_1}{b^2} = 1$

(4) If through a given point chords of an ellipse be drawn, then the locus of the points of intersection of the tangents at the entermities of chords is called the polar of the point w.r.t. the ellipse and the point is called the pole of the polar.

Polar of the point (x_1, y_1) w.r.t. the ellipse $\dfrac{x^2}{a^2} + \dfrac{y^2}{b^2} = 1$ is given by

$$\boxed{\frac{xx_1}{a^2} + \frac{yy_1}{b^2} = 1}$$

Problem 33 Find the locus of a point the polar of which w.r.t. an ellipse touches its director circle.

Solution Let the ellipse be $\dfrac{x^2}{a^2} + \dfrac{y^2}{b^2} = 1$ (1)

Now the polar of $P\,(h, k)$ w.r.t. (1) is

$$\frac{xh}{a^2} + \frac{yk}{b^2} = 1 \qquad [2)$$

The director circle of (1) is

$$x^2 + y^2 = a^2 + b^2$$

whose centre is (0, 0) and radius is $\sqrt{a^2 + b^2}$

By the equation the line (2) touches the director circle at L (say)

Then
$$CL = \frac{\dfrac{0\cdot h}{a^2} + \dfrac{0\cdot k}{b^2} - 1}{\sqrt{\dfrac{h^2}{a^4} + \dfrac{k^2}{b^4}}}$$

$$CL^2 = \frac{1}{\dfrac{h^2}{a^4} + \dfrac{k^2}{b^4}}$$

CL = radius of the director circle

$$CL = \sqrt{a^2 + b^2}$$

$$CL^2 = a^2 + b^2$$

$$a^2 + b^2 = \frac{1}{\frac{h^2}{a^2} + \frac{k^2}{b^4}}$$

$$\frac{h^2}{a^4} + \frac{k^2}{b^4} = \frac{1}{a^2 + b^2}$$

locus of (h, k) is given by

$$\frac{x^2}{a^4} + \frac{y^2}{b^4} = \frac{1}{a^2 + b^2} \qquad \textbf{Ans.}$$

Problem 34 Find the locus of the pole w.r.t. $\frac{x^2}{a^2} + \frac{y^2}{b^2} = 1$, of any tangent to the circle $x^2 + y^2 = a^2$.

Solution Let (h, k) be the pole. Then the polar of (h, k) with respect to the ellipse $\frac{x^2}{a^2} + \frac{y^2}{b^2} = 1$ is

$$\frac{xh}{a^2} + \frac{yk}{b^2} = 1$$

(1) touches the circle $x^2 + y^2 = a^2$ then

$$CL = \perp^r \text{ from } c\ (0, 0) \text{ upon } (1)$$

$$= \frac{\frac{0 \cdot h}{a^2} + \frac{0k}{b^2} - 1}{\sqrt{\frac{h^2}{a^4} + \frac{k^2}{b^2}}}$$

But $\qquad CL = \text{radius of the circle} = a$

$$a^2 = \frac{1}{\frac{h^2}{a^4} + \frac{k^2}{b^4}}$$

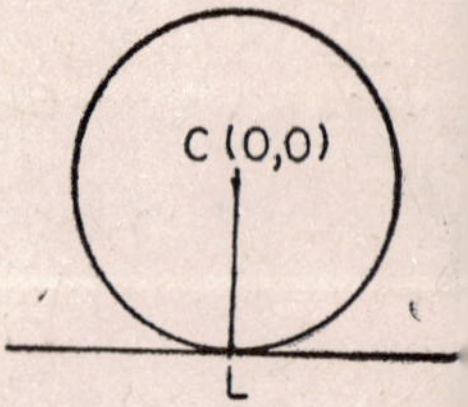

$$\Rightarrow \qquad \frac{h^2}{b^4} + \frac{k^2}{b^4} = \frac{1}{a^2}$$

C (0,0)

L

$\therefore$ locus of (h, k) is

$$\frac{x^2}{a^4} + \frac{y^2}{b^4} = \frac{1}{a^2} \qquad \textbf{Ans.}$$

Problem 35 Prove that the locus of the poles of normal chords of the ellipse $\frac{x^2}{a^2}+\frac{y^2}{b^2}=1$

$$\frac{a^9}{x^2}+\frac{b^6}{y^2}=(a^2-b^2)^2.$$

Solution Equation of the ellipse is

$$\frac{x^2}{a^2}+\frac{y^2}{b^2}=1 \tag{1}$$

The equation of the normal at the point (θ) is given by

$$ax \sec\theta - by \operatorname{cosec}\theta = a^2-b^2 \tag{2}$$

Let the pole of the normal (2) is (h, k)

Then the polar of the pole (h, k) is given by

$$\frac{xh}{a^2}+\frac{yk}{b^2}=1 \tag{3}$$

line (2) and (3) will represent the same straight lines then

$$\frac{a\sec\theta}{h/a^2}=-\frac{b\operatorname{cosec}\theta}{k/b^2}=\frac{a^2-b^2}{1}$$

$$\frac{a^3}{h\cos\theta}=-\frac{b^3}{k\sin\theta}=\frac{a^2-b^2}{1}$$

$$\cos\theta=\frac{a^3}{h(a^2-b^2)} \tag{4}$$

$$\sin\theta=-\frac{b^3}{k(a^2-b^2)} \tag{5}$$

squaring and adding (4) and (5) we have

$$\frac{a^6}{h^2(a^2-b^2)^2}+\frac{b^6}{k^2(a^2-b^2)^2}=1$$

so the locus of (h, k) is given by replacing h by x and k by y

$$\frac{a^6}{x^2(a^2-b^2)^2}+\frac{b^6}{y^2(a^2-b^2)^2}=1$$

$$\Rightarrow \boxed{\frac{a^6}{x^2}+\frac{b^6}{y^2}=(a^2-b^2)^2}$$ *(Proved)*

Problem 36 CP is a variable chord of the ellipse $\frac{x^2}{a^2} + \frac{y^2}{b^2} = 1$ always subtending a right angle at the centre of the ellipse prove that the locus of the pole of CD with respect to the eliipse is another ellipse whose equation

is $$\frac{x^2}{a^4} + \frac{y^2}{b^4} = \frac{1}{a^2} + \frac{1}{b^2}$$

Solution Let the pole of CD be (x_1, y_1). Then CD is the polar of (x_1, y_1) with respect to the ellipse

$$\frac{x^2}{a^2} + \frac{y^2}{b^2} = 1$$

Hence the equation of CD is

$$\frac{xx_1}{a^2} + \frac{yy_1}{b^2} = 1 \tag{2}$$

Now making (1) hamogenous with the help of (2) we get the equation of the pair of lines joining the origin to the points of intersection of (1) and (2) i.e. the points C and D

$$\therefore \quad \frac{x^2}{a^2} + \frac{y^2}{b^2} = \left(\frac{xx_1}{a^2} + \frac{yy_1}{b^2}\right)^2 \tag{3}$$

Since CD subtends a right angle as the centre, therefore

$$\angle COD = \frac{\pi}{2}$$

i.e. $$OC \perp^r OD$$

i.e. the pair of lines given by (3) are at right angles.

$\therefore$ The co-efficients of x^2 + The co-efficients of $y^2 = 0$

or $$\frac{1}{a^2} - \frac{x_1^2}{a^4} + \frac{1}{b^2} - \frac{y_1^2}{b^4} = 0$$

$\therefore$ Locus of (x_1, y_1) is

$$\frac{x^2}{a^4} + \frac{y^2}{b^4} = \frac{1}{a^2} + \frac{1}{b^2}$$

Problem 37 Tangents are drawn from any point on the ellipse

$$\frac{x^2}{a^2} + \frac{y^2}{b^2} = 1$$

to the circle $x^2 + y^2 = r^2$, prove that the chords of contact are tangent to the ellipse $a^2 x^2 + b^2 y^2 = r^4$.

Solution Any point on the ellipse

$$\frac{x^2}{a^2} + \frac{y^2}{b^2} = 1$$

is given by

$$x = a \cos \theta, \; y = b \sin \theta$$

Then from $(a \cos \theta, b \sin \theta)$ tangents are drawn to the circle

$$x^2 + y^2 = r^2$$

Then the equation for the chord of contact is given by

$$x\,a \cos \theta + yb \sin \theta = r^2$$

$$yb \sin \theta = -x\,a \cos \theta + r^2$$

$$y = -\frac{x\,a \cos \theta}{b \sin \theta} + \frac{r^2}{b \sin \theta} \qquad (1)$$

$$y = mx + c$$

$$m = -\frac{a \cos \theta}{b \sin \theta} \qquad c = \frac{r^2}{b \sin \theta}$$

(1) touches the ellipse

$$\frac{x^2}{r^4/a^2} + \frac{y^2}{r^4/b^2} = 1$$

$$\left(\frac{r^2}{b \sin^2 \theta}\right)^2 = \frac{r^4}{a^2} \cdot \left(-\frac{a \cos \theta}{b \sin \theta}\right)^2 + \frac{r^2}{h^2}$$

$$\frac{r^2}{b^2 \sin^2 \theta} = \frac{r^4}{a^2}\,\frac{a^2 \cos^2 \theta}{b^2 \sin^2 \theta} + \frac{r^4}{b^2} = \frac{r^4}{b^2}\left(\frac{\cos^2 \theta}{\sin^2 \theta} + 1\right)$$

$$= \frac{r^4}{b^2}\,\frac{\sin^2 \theta + \cos^2 \theta}{\sin^2 \theta} = \frac{r^4}{b^2}\,\frac{1}{\sin^2 \theta}$$

which is true.

(Hence the statement)

Problem 38 Find the locus of the point, the chord of contact of the tangents drawn from which to the ellipse $\frac{x^2}{a^2} + \frac{y^2}{b^2} = 1$ touches the circle

$$x^2 + y^2 = c^2, \text{ where } a > b > c.$$

Solution Let the given point is (x_1, y_1) then the chord of contact of the tangents from (x_1, y_1) to the given ellipse

$$\frac{x^2}{a^2} + \frac{y^2}{b^2} - 1 = 0$$

i.e. $$\frac{xx_1}{a^2}+\frac{yy_1}{b^2}=1$$

$$\Rightarrow \quad \frac{xx_1}{a^2}+\frac{yy_1}{b^2}-1=0$$

$$\Rightarrow \quad \frac{yy_1}{b^2}=-\frac{xx_1}{a^2}+1$$

$$\Rightarrow \quad y=-\frac{b^2}{a^2}\frac{x^2}{y_1}\cdot x+\frac{b^2}{y_1} \qquad (1)$$

which is of the form $$y=mx+k$$

$$m=-\frac{b^2}{a^2}\frac{x_1}{y_1}$$

$$k=\frac{b^2}{y_1}$$

$y=mx+k$ touches the circle $x^2+y^2=c^2$

$k^2=c^2(1+m^2)$ | $y=mx+a$ touches $x^2+y^2=a^2$ if $c=a\sqrt{1+m^2}$

$$\frac{b^4}{y_1^2}=c^2\left(1+\frac{b^4}{a^4}\frac{x_1^2}{y_1^2}\right)$$

$$\frac{b^4}{y_1^2}=\left(\frac{a^2y_1^2+b^4x_1^2}{a^4y_1^2}\right)$$

$$a^4b^4=c^2(a^4y_1^2+b^4x_1^2)$$

$$\frac{x_1^2}{a^4}+\frac{y_1^2}{b^4}=\frac{1}{c^2}$$

Locus of the point (x_1, y_1) is

$$\frac{x^2}{a^4}+\frac{y^2}{b^4}=\frac{1}{c^2} \qquad \textbf{Ans.}$$

Problem 39 Tangent at right angles are drawn to the ellipse

$$\frac{x^2}{a^2}+\frac{y^2}{b^2}=1$$

Show that the locus of the middle points of the chords of contact is the curve $$\left(\frac{x^2}{a^2}+\frac{y^2}{b^2}\right)^2=\frac{x^2+y^2}{a^2+b^2}$$

Solution Let the ellipse be $\frac{x^2}{a^2}+\frac{y^2}{b^2}=1$ (1)

The equation of the chord PQ with $R\,(x_1, y_1)$ as the middle point is given by

$$(x-x_1)\,\frac{x_1}{a^2} + (y-y_1)\,\frac{y_1}{b^2} = 1$$

i.e. $$\frac{xx_1}{a^2} + \frac{yy_1}{b^2} = \frac{x_1^2}{a^2} + \frac{y_1^2}{b^2} \quad (2)$$

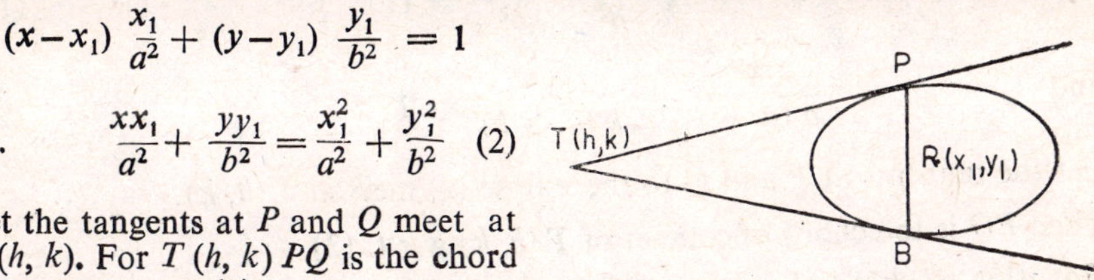

Let the tangents at P and Q meet at $T\,(h, k)$. For $T\,(h, k)$ PQ is the chord of contact w.r.t. (1).

$\therefore$ Equation of chord of contact PQ is

$$\frac{xh}{a^2} + \frac{yk}{b^2} = 1 \tag{3}$$

Equation (2) and (3) will represent the same straight line. Then

$$\frac{x_1/a^2}{h/a^2} = \frac{y_1/b^2}{k/b^2} = \frac{\dfrac{x_1^2}{a^2} + \dfrac{y_1^2}{b^2}}{1}$$

$\therefore$ $$h = \frac{x_1}{\dfrac{x_1^2}{a^2} + \dfrac{y_1^2}{b^2}}, \quad k = \frac{y_1}{\dfrac{x_1^2}{a^2} + \dfrac{y_1^2}{b^2}}$$

Since by question, the tangents at P and Q are at right angles, therefore the intersection (h, k) of the tangents lie on the auxiliary circle

$$x^2 + y^2 = a^2 + b^2$$

$\therefore$ $$h^2 + k^2 = a^2 + b^2$$

$$\frac{x_1^2}{\left(\dfrac{x_1^2}{a^2} + \dfrac{y_1^2}{b^3}\right)^2} + \frac{y_1^2}{\left(\dfrac{x_1^2}{a^2} + \dfrac{y_1^2}{b^2}\right)^2} = a^2 + b^2$$

$$\frac{x_1^2 + y_1^2}{a^2 + b^2} = \left(\frac{x_1^2}{a^2} + \frac{y_1^2}{b^2}\right)^2$$

$\therefore$ Locus of $R\,(x_1, y_1)$ is

$$\left(\frac{x^2}{a^2} + \frac{y^2}{b^2}\right)^2 = \frac{x^2 + y^2}{a^2 + b^2}$$ **Ans.**

Problem 40 A tangent to the ellipse $\dfrac{x^2}{a^2} + \dfrac{y^2}{b^2} = 1$

Meets the ellipse $$\frac{x^2}{a} + \frac{y^2}{b} = (a + b)$$

in P and Q. Prove that the tangents at P and Q are at right angles.

[*Must revise*]

Solution The two ellipse are $\dfrac{x^2}{a^2} + \dfrac{y^2}{b^2} = 1$ (1)

and $$\frac{x^2}{a(a+b)} + \frac{y^2}{b(a+b)} = 1 \quad (2)$$

Let the tangents at P and Q to the ellipse (2) meet at $T(h, k)$.
Then PQ is the chord of contact of $T(h. k)$ w.r.t. (2).
Equation of chord of contact (PQ)

$$\frac{xh}{a(a+b)} + \frac{yk}{b(a+b)} = 1$$

or $$y = -\frac{b(a+b)}{a(a+b)}\frac{h}{k}x + \frac{b(a+b)}{k}$$

But PQ is tangent to (1)

Then $$\frac{b^2(a+b)^2}{k^2} = a^2 \cdot \frac{b^2(a+b)^2}{a^2(a+b)^2}\frac{h^2}{k^2} + b^2$$

$$\frac{b^2(a+b)^2}{k^2} = b^2\frac{h^2}{k^2} + b^2$$

$$b^2(a+b)^2 = b^2(h^2 + k^2)$$

$$\Rightarrow \quad h^2 + k^2 = (a+b)^2$$

Locus of (h, k) is $\quad x^2 + y^2 = (a+b)^2$
which is the director circle of the ellipse (2)
Hence the tangents at P and Q to the ellipse (2) are at right angles.

Appendix 3

HYPERBOLA

Formula

1. The standard equation of the hyperbola is

$$\frac{x^2}{a^2} - \frac{y^2}{b^2} = 1$$

   (i) its centre is 0 (0, 0)
   (ii) its foci stands, are $(\pm ae, 0)$
   (iii) length of transvers axise $= 2a$
   (iv) length of conjugate axis $= 2b$
   (v) e quations of directrix $x = \pm \frac{a}{e}$
   (vi) $b^2 = a^2 (e^2 - 1)$
   (vii) $SS' = 2ae$

2. The equation of tangent at (x_1, y_1) on it is

$$\frac{xx_1}{a^2} - \frac{yy_1}{b^2} = 1$$

3. The equation of piar of tanigents from (x_1, y_1) to it is $SS_1 = T^2$ where

$$S \equiv \frac{x^2}{a^2} - \frac{y^2}{b^2} - 1$$

$$S_1 \equiv \frac{x_1^2}{a^2} - \frac{y_1^2}{b^2} - 1$$

$$T = \frac{xx_1}{a^2} - \frac{yy_1}{b^2} - 1$$

4. $y = mx + \sqrt{a^2m^2 - b^2}$ is always a tangent to it

5. The equation of a rectangular hyperbola is

$$x^2 - y^2 = a^2$$

6. Equation of the assymptotes is

$$\frac{x^2}{a^2} - \frac{y^2}{b^2} = 0$$

7. The equation of the conjuagte hyperbola is

$$\frac{x^2}{a^2} - \frac{y^2}{b^2} = -1$$

8. The equation of the hyperbola with reference to the assymptotes as the axes is
$$xy = c^2$$

9. Length of the latus ractum $= 2\frac{b^2}{a}$

Problem 1 Find the equation of the hyperbola the distance between whose foci is 16 whose eccentricity is $\sqrt{2}$

Solution We have $\qquad e = \sqrt{2}$

In case of a hyperbola

$$b^2 = a^2 (e^2 - 1)$$

$$b^2 = a^2 (2-1)$$

$$b^2 = a^2$$

$$\Rightarrow \qquad b = a$$

Also, the distance between the foci

$$2ae = 16$$

$$2a\sqrt{2} = 16$$

$$a\sqrt{2} = 8$$

$$a = \frac{8}{\sqrt{2}} = 4\sqrt{2}$$

$$b = 4\sqrt{2}$$

Hence the required equation of the hyperbola is

$$\frac{x^2}{a^2} - \frac{y^2}{b^2} = 1$$

$$\Rightarrow \qquad \frac{x^2}{16 \times 2} - \frac{y^2}{16 \times 2} = 1$$

$$\Rightarrow \qquad \frac{x^2}{32} - \frac{y^2}{32} = 1$$

Problem 2 Find the equation of the hyperbola whose focus is (2, 2) eceentricity 2 and directrix $x + y = 9$.

Solution Let $P(x, y)$ be any point on the parabola whose focus is (2, 2) Let PM be the perpendicular from P on the directrix

$$x + y - 9 = 0$$

Then by the distrix

$$\frac{SP}{PM} = e$$

$$SP^2 = e^2 PM^2$$

$$(x - 2)^2 + (y - 2)^2 = 2^2 \left[\frac{x + y - 9}{\sqrt{1 + 1}}\right]^2$$

$$x^2 + y^2 - 4x - 4y + 8 = 4 \frac{(x + y - 9)^2}{2}$$

$$\Rightarrow \quad x^2 + y^2 - 4x - 4y + 8 = 2(x + y - 9)^2$$

$$\Rightarrow \quad x^2 + y^2 - 4x - 4y + 8 = 2x^2 + 2y^2 + 4xy - 36x - 36y + 162$$

$$\Rightarrow \quad x^2 + y^2 + 4xy - 32x - 32y + 154 = 0$$

This is the equation of the hyperbola.

Problem 3 Find the equation of the tangent to the hyperbola $4x^2 - 9y^2 = 1$ which is parallel to the line $4y = 5x + 7$. [*Must rivise*]

Solution A line parallel to

$$4y = 5x + 7 \qquad \text{is given by}$$

$$4y = 5x + K$$

or

$$y = \frac{5x}{4} + \frac{K}{4}$$

If (1) is tangent to

$$4x^2 - 9y^2 = 1$$

or

$$\frac{x^2}{\frac{1}{4}} - \frac{y^2}{\frac{1}{9}} = 1$$

then

$$\frac{k^2}{16} = \frac{1}{4} \times \left(\frac{5}{4}\right)^2 - \frac{1}{9}$$

$$\frac{k^2}{16} = \frac{25}{64} - \frac{1}{9}$$

> If $y = mx + c$ toubles the hyperbola
> $$\frac{x^2}{x^2} - \frac{y^2}{b^2} = 1$$
> then $$c^2 = a^2 m^2 - b^2$$

$$\Rightarrow \quad k^2 = \frac{25}{4} - \frac{16}{9}$$

$$\Rightarrow \quad k^2 = \frac{225 - 64}{36}$$

$$\Rightarrow \quad k^2 = \frac{161}{36}$$

$$\Rightarrow \quad k = \pm \frac{\sqrt{161}}{6}$$

Hence the required equation of the tangent is

$$4y = 5x + \frac{\sqrt{161}}{6} \qquad \textbf{Ans.}$$

Problem 4 Show that the line $21x + 5y = 116$ touches the hyperbola $7x^2 - 5y^2 = 232$ and find the co-ordinates of the point of contact.

Solution Form both the equation calculate the value of x and y. There will be two values of y and the two values of y are the same, therefore the given line touches the given hyperbola. [$y = -2$ or -2]

The co-ordinate of the point of contact is $(6, -2)$.

Problem 5 Find the locus of the middle points of the portions of the tangents to $\frac{x^2}{a^2} - \frac{y^2}{b^2} = 1$ included between the axes. [*Must rivise*]

Solution Equation of the hyperbola

$$\frac{x^2}{a^2} - \frac{y^2}{b^2} = 1 \qquad (1)$$

The equation of the tangent at the point $(a \sec \theta, b \tan \theta)$ is given by

$$\frac{x \cdot a \sec \theta}{a^2} - \frac{y \cdot b \tan \theta}{b^2} = 1$$

$$\Rightarrow \quad \frac{x \sec \theta}{a} - \frac{y \tan \theta}{b} = 1$$

$$\Rightarrow \quad \frac{x}{a \cos \theta} + \frac{y}{(-b) \cot \theta} = 1 \qquad (2)$$

Equation (2) represent a striaght line so the intercepts are

$$a \cos \theta, \; - \; b \cot \theta$$

middle points are

$$\alpha = \frac{a \cos \theta}{2}, \; \beta = -\frac{b \cot \theta}{2}$$

$$\Rightarrow \quad \sec \theta = \frac{a}{2\alpha} \quad \tan \theta = -\frac{b}{2\beta}$$

Now we know that

$$\sec^2 \theta - \tan^2 \theta = 1$$

$$\Rightarrow \quad \frac{a^2}{4\alpha^2} - \frac{b^2}{4\beta^2} = 1$$

$$\Rightarrow \quad \frac{a^2}{\alpha^2} - \frac{b^2}{\beta^2} = 4$$

Hence the locus of the moddle point (α, β) is given by

$$\frac{a^2}{x^2} - \frac{b^2}{y^2} = 4 \qquad \textbf{Ans.}$$

Problem 6 A variable chord of the hyperbola $\frac{x^2}{a^2} - \frac{y^2}{b^2} = 1$ tangent to the circle $x^2 + y^2 = 0$, prove that the locus of its middle points is

$$\left[\frac{x^2}{a^2} - \frac{y^2}{b^2}\right] = c^2 \left[\frac{y^2}{a^4} - \frac{y^2}{b^4}\right] \qquad \text{[\textit{Must revise}]}$$

Solution Equation to the circle is

$$x^2 + y^2 = c^2$$

$$\Rightarrow \quad (x-0)^2 + (y-0)^2 = c^2$$

so the centre of this circle is (0, 0) and the radius is C.

Let (h, K) be the middle point of the variable chord. Then the equation of the chord is

$$T = S_1$$

i.e.

$$\frac{kh}{a^2} - \frac{yK}{b^2} = \frac{h^2}{a^2} - \frac{K^2}{b^2}$$

$$\therefore \quad \frac{\dfrac{h^2}{a^2} - \dfrac{K^2}{b^2}}{\sqrt{\dfrac{h^2}{a^4} + \dfrac{K^2}{b^4}}} = 0$$

Using perpendicular distance from the circle (0, 0) = raidus c.

$$\Rightarrow \qquad \left(\frac{h^2}{a^2} - \frac{K^2}{b^2}\right)^2 = c^2\left(\frac{h^2}{a^4} + \frac{K^2}{b^4}\right) \qquad (1)$$

Now the locus of the middle point h, K) of the chord is obtained by replacing x for b and y for K. lows is

$$\left(\frac{x^2}{a^2} - \frac{y^2}{b^2}\right)^2 = c^2\left(\frac{x^2}{a^4} + \frac{y^2}{b^4}\right)$$

Problem 7 Chords of the circle $x^2 + y^2 = a^2$ touch the hyperbola

$$\frac{x^2}{a^2} - \frac{y^2}{b^2} = 1;$$

prove that there middle points lie on the curve

$$(x^2 + y^2)^2 = a^2 x^2 - b^2 y^2$$

Solution Let the co-ordinate of the middle point of the chord of the circle $x^2 + y^2 = a^2$, is (b, K). Then the equation of the chord is

$$T = S_1$$

$$\Rightarrow \qquad xh + yK = h^2 + K^2$$

$$yK = -hx + (h^2 K^2)$$

$$\Rightarrow \qquad y = -\frac{h}{k}x + \frac{h^2 + k^2}{k}$$

Now line (1) is tangent to the hyperbola

$$\frac{k^2}{a^2} - \frac{y^2}{b^2} = 1$$

condition is

$$c^2 = a^2 m^2 - b^2$$

$$\Rightarrow \qquad \left(\frac{h^2 + K^2}{K}\right)^2 = a^2\left(-\frac{h}{K}\right)^2 - b^2$$

$$\Rightarrow \qquad \left(\frac{h^2 + K^2}{K^2}\right) = \frac{a^2 h^2}{K^2} - b^2$$

$$\Rightarrow \qquad (h^2 + K^2)^2 = a^2 h^2 - b^2 K^2$$

Now the locus of the middle point (h, K) of the chord is given by

$$(x^2 + y^2)^2 = (a^2 x^2 - b^2 y^2) \qquad \textit{(proved)}$$

Problem 8 Prove that the locus of poles with respect to the parabola $y^2 = 4ax$ of the tangents to the hyperbola $x^2 - y^2 = a^2$ is the the ellipse

$$4x^2 + y^2 = 4a^2$$

[Must revise]

Solution Let the pole be (x_1, y_1)

Then the polar of (x_1, y_1) with respect to $y^2 = 4ax$ is

$$yy_1 = 2a(x + x_1)$$

$$\Rightarrow \qquad y = \frac{2a}{y_1} x + \frac{2ax_1}{y_1} \tag{1}$$

If it is tangent to the hyperbola

$$x^2 - y^2 = a^2$$

then

$$\left(\frac{2ax_1}{y}\right)^2 = a^2\left(\frac{2a}{y_1}\right)^2 - a^2$$

| Using $c^2 = a^2 m^2 - a^2$ |

$$\Rightarrow \qquad 4a^2 \frac{x_1^2}{y_1^2} = a^2 \frac{4a^2}{y_1^2} - a^2$$

$$\Rightarrow \qquad 4\frac{x_1^2}{y_1^2} = \frac{4a^2}{y_1^2} - 1$$

$$\Rightarrow \qquad 4x_1^2 = 4a^2 - y_1^2$$

$$\Rightarrow \qquad 4x_1^2 + y_1^2 = 4a^2$$

Hence the locus of the pole (x_1, y_1) is the required ellipse

$$4x^2 + y^2 = 4a^2 \qquad \textit{(proved)}$$

Problem 9 If the polars of (h_1, k_1) and (h_2, k_2) with respect to the hyperbola $\frac{x^2}{a^2} - \frac{y^2}{b^2}$ at right angles then prove that

$$a^4 k_1 k_2 + b^4 h_1 h_2 = 0$$ [*Must revise*]

Solution Polars of (h_1, k_1) with respect to the hyperbola $\frac{x^2}{a^2} - \frac{y^2}{b^2} = 1$

given by $\frac{xh_1}{a^2} + \frac{yk_1}{b^2} = 1$

$$\Rightarrow \qquad \frac{yk_1}{b^2} = \frac{xh_1}{a^2} - 1$$

$$\Rightarrow \qquad y = \frac{b^2}{a^2}\frac{h_1}{k_1} x - \frac{b^2}{k} \tag{1}$$

Again the polar of (h_2, K_2) with respect to the hyperbola

$$\frac{x^2}{a^2} - \frac{y^2}{b^2} = 1$$

is

$$\frac{x \cdot h_2}{a^2} - \frac{y \cdot k_2}{b^2} = 1$$

$$\Rightarrow \quad \frac{yK_2}{b^2} = \frac{xh^2}{a^2} - 1$$

$$\Rightarrow \quad y = \frac{b^2}{a^2}\frac{h^2}{k^2} - \frac{b^2}{k^2} \tag{2}$$

slope of the lines (1) and (2) are

$$m_1 = \frac{b^2}{a^2}\frac{h_1}{k_1}$$

$$m_2 = \frac{b^2}{a^2}\frac{h_2}{k^2}$$

since (1) and (2) are perpendicular to each other hence

$$m_1 \, m_2 = -1$$

$$\frac{b^4}{a^4}\frac{h_1 \, h_2}{k_1 \, k_2} = -1$$

$$\Rightarrow \quad a^4 \, k_1 \, k_2 + b^4 \, h_1 \, h_2 = 0 \qquad \textit{(proved)}$$

Problem 10 Prove that the polar of any point on $\frac{x^2}{a^2} + \frac{y^2}{b^2} - 1 = 0$ with respect to $\frac{x^2}{a^2} - \frac{y^2}{b^2} = 1$ touches $\frac{x^2}{a^2} + \frac{y^2}{b^2} = 1$. [*Must revise*]

Solution Let (α, β) be any point

or $$\frac{x^2}{a^2} + \frac{y^2}{b^2} - 1 = 0$$

$$\Rightarrow \quad \frac{\alpha^2}{a^2} + \frac{\beta^2}{b^2} - 1 = 0$$

$$\Rightarrow \quad \frac{\alpha^2}{a^2} + \frac{\beta^2}{b^2} = 1 \tag{1}$$

Now polar of (α, β) with respect to the hyperbola $\frac{x^2}{a^2} - \frac{y^2}{b^2} = 1$ is given by

$$\frac{x\alpha}{a^2} - \frac{y\beta}{b^2} = 1$$

$$\Rightarrow \quad y = \frac{b^2}{a^2}\frac{\alpha}{\beta}\, x - \frac{b^2}{\beta} \tag{2}$$

line $y = mx + c$ touches the ellipse

$$\frac{x^2}{a^2} + \frac{y^2}{b^2} = 1$$

if $$c^2 = a^2 m^2 + b^2$$

$$\Rightarrow \quad \left(-\frac{b^2}{\beta}\right)^2 = a^2\left(\frac{b^2}{a^2}\ \frac{\alpha}{\beta}\right)^2 + b^2$$

$$\Rightarrow \quad \frac{b^4}{\beta^2} = a^2\ \frac{b^4}{a^4}\ \frac{\alpha^2}{\beta^2} + b^2$$

$$\Rightarrow \quad \frac{b^2}{\beta^2} = \frac{b^2\ \alpha^2}{a^2\ \beta^2} + b$$

$$\Rightarrow \quad \frac{b^2}{\beta^2} = \frac{b^2\ \alpha^2 + a^2\ \beta^2}{a^2\ \beta^2}$$

$$\Rightarrow \quad \frac{\alpha^2}{a^2} + \frac{\beta^2}{b^2} = 1$$

which is true as in equation (1, hence the statement.

Problem 11 If e_1 and e_2 be the eccentricities of a hyperbola and its conjugate prove that

$$\frac{1}{e_1^2} + \frac{1}{e_2^2} = 1$$

Solution Equation of the hyperbola whose eccentricity is e_1 is given by

$$\frac{x^2}{a^2} - \frac{y^2}{b^2} = 1 \tag{1}$$

Then $$b^2 = a^2\,(e_1^2 - 1) \tag{2}$$

Equation of the conjugate of the hyperbola (1) is given by

$$\frac{x^2}{a^2} - \frac{y^2}{b^2} = -1$$

$$\Rightarrow \quad \frac{y^2}{b^2} - \frac{x^2}{a^2} = 1$$

Its eccentricity is e_2

$$\Rightarrow \quad a^2 = b^2\,(e \quad - 1) \tag{3}$$

Now from equation (1) we have,

$$\frac{b^2}{a^2} = e_1^2 - 1$$

$$\frac{b^2}{a^2} + 1 = e_1^2$$

$$\Rightarrow \quad \frac{a^2 + b^2}{a^2} = e_1^2$$

$$\Rightarrow \quad \frac{1}{e_1^2} = \frac{a^2}{a^2 + b^2} \tag{4}$$

Again from equation (3) we have

$$\frac{a^2}{b^2} = e_2^2$$

$$\Rightarrow \quad \frac{a^2}{b^2} + 1 = e_2^2$$

$$\Rightarrow \quad \frac{a^2 + b^2}{b^2} = e_2^2$$

$$\Rightarrow \quad \frac{1}{e_2^2} = \frac{b^2}{a^2 + b^2} \tag{5}$$

$\Rightarrow$ Adding equation (4) and (5) we have

$$\frac{1}{e_1^2} + \frac{1}{e_2^2} = \frac{a^2}{a^2 + b^2} + \frac{b^2}{a^2 + b^2}$$

$$= \frac{a^2 + b^2}{a^2 + b^2} = 1$$

$\Rightarrow \quad \frac{1}{e_1^2} + \frac{1}{e_2^2} = 1$ Remember (*Proved*)

Problem 12 A circle cuts the rectangular hyperbola $xy = 1$ in the points (x_1, yr), $r = 1, 2. 3, 4$ prove that

$$x_1\, x_2\, x_3\, x_4 = y_1\, y_2\, y_3\, y_4$$

Solution Equation of the rectangular hyperbola is

$$xy = 1 \tag{1}$$

Let the equation of the circle is

$$x^2 + y^2 + 2gx + 2fy + c = 0 \tag{2}$$

Circle (2) cuts the hyperbola (1) then from (1)

$$y = \frac{1}{x}$$

$$x^2 + \frac{1}{x^2} + 2gx + 2f\frac{1}{x} + c = 0$$

$$\Rightarrow \quad x^4 + 1 + 2gx^3 + 2fx + cx^2 = 0$$

$$\Rightarrow \quad x^4 + x^3\,(2g) + x^2\,(c) + x\,(2f) + 1 = 0 \tag{3}$$

This is a biquadratic equation in x so

$$x_1\, x_2\, x_3\, x_4 = \frac{1}{1}$$

$$x_1\, x_2\, x_3\, x_4 = 1$$

with respect to x_1, x_2, x_3, x_4 there are points y_1, y_2 y_3, y_4

Since (x_1, y_1); (x_2, y_2); (x_3, y_3) and (x_4, y_4) lies on the hyperbola $xy = 1$

so
$$x_1 y_1 = 1$$
$$x_2 y_2 = 1$$
$$x_3 y_3 = 1$$
$$x_4 y_4 = 1 \quad \Rightarrow \quad x_4 x_2 x_3 x_1 y_1 y_2 y_3 y_4 = 1$$
$$\Rightarrow \quad 1 \cdot y_1 y_2 y_3 y_4 = 1$$
$$\Rightarrow \quad y_1 y_2 y_3 y_4 = 1 \tag{5}$$

Hence from equation (4) and (5) we have

$$x_1 x_2 x_3 x_4 = y_1 y_2 y_3 y_4 = 1 \qquad \textit{(Proved)}$$

Problem 13 Find the equation of a hyperbola whose assymptotes are $2x-y = 3$ and $3x + y-7 = 0$ and which passes through (1, 1).

Solution The equation of the hyperbola with referrence to the assymptotes as the axes is$xy = c^2$

assymptotes are $2x-y = 3$ and $3x + y-7 = 0$

$$\Rightarrow \quad (2x-y-3) = 0 \quad \text{and} \quad (3x + y-7) = 0$$

so equation of the hyperbola is

$$(2x-y-3)\,(3x + y-7) = c^2 \tag{1}$$

(1) passes through (1, 1) so

$$(2-1-3) \times (3 + 1-7) = c^2$$
$$-2x-3 = c^2$$
$$\Rightarrow \quad c^2 = 6$$

so equation of the hyperbola is

$$(2x-y-3)\,(3x + y-7) = 6 \qquad \textbf{Ans.}$$

Reduction of a Second Degree Equation to Standard Form

Some Important Formulaeas

(1) $\phi = ax^2 + 2\,hxy + by^2 + 2gx + 2fy + c = 0$

will represent

(a) a pair of straight line

if
$$\Delta = \begin{vmatrix} a & h & g \\ h & b & f \\ g & f & c \end{vmatrix} = 0$$

i.e.
$$\Delta = abc + 2fgh-af^2-bg^2-ch^2 = 0$$

(b) circle if $a = b$ and $h = 0$

(c) a parabola if $ab^2 = h^2$ and $\Delta \neq 0$

(d) an ellipse if $ab > h^2$ and $\Delta \neq 0$

(3) a hyperbola if $ab < h^2$ and $\Delta \neq 0$

2. The centre of the conic $\phi = 0$ is obtained by solving the equations

$$\frac{\partial \phi}{\partial x} = 0$$

and

$$\frac{\partial \phi}{\partial y} = 0$$

3. The equation of the conic referred to centre as origin is

$$ax^2 + 2hxy + by^2 + c^1 = 0$$

where $c^1 = gx^1 + fy^1 + c$

and (x^1, y^1) is the centre

4. Squares of the semi-axes of the conic

$$ax^2 + 2hxy + by^2 = 1$$

are the roots of

$$\frac{1}{r^4} - (a + b)\frac{1}{r^2} + ab - h^2 = 0$$

The equation of the corresponding axis is

$$\left(a - \frac{1}{r^2}\right)x + hy = 0$$

5. The assymptotes of the conic $S = 0$ are given by

$$S - \frac{\Delta}{ab - h^2} = 0 \text{ Remember}$$

Problem 1 What conics do the following equations represents.

(i) $x^2 + 2xy + y^2 - 2x - 1 = 0$

(ii) $2x^2 + 3y^2 - 4x + 5y + 4 = 0$

(iii) $x^2 + 4xy + y^2 - 2x + 2y - 6 = 0$

Solution We have $x^2 + 2xy + y^2 - 2x - 1 = 0$

Comparing if with $ax^2 + 2hxy + by^2 + 2gx + 2fy + c = 0$ we get

$$a = 1, h = 1, b = 1, g = -1\ f = 0, c = -1$$

Now

$$\Delta = abc + 2fgh - 2f^2 - bg^2 - ch^2$$

$$\Delta = -1 + 2.0 - 0 - 1 - (-1)$$

$$\Delta = -1 - 1 + 1$$

$$\Delta = -1 \neq 2$$

Now $ab = 1, h^2 = 1$

$\Rightarrow$ $ab = h^2$

Hence the given conic is a parabola.

(ii) $2x^2 + 3y^2 - 4x + 5y + 4 = 0$

Comparing it with

$$ax^2 + by^2 + 2hxy + 2gy + 2fy + c = 0$$

$$a = 2 ; b = 3; h = 0\ g = (-2), f = 5/2\ c = 4$$

Now $\Delta = abc + 2fgh - af^2 - bg^2 - ch^2$

$$\Delta = 24 + 0 - 2\cdot\frac{25}{4} - 3(-2)^2 - 4.0$$

$$\Delta = 24 - \frac{25}{2} - 12$$

$$\Delta = 12 - \frac{25}{2} = \frac{24-25}{2} = -\frac{1}{2} \neq 0$$

Now $ab = 2.3 = 6$ and $h^2 = 0$

since $6 > 0$ $ab > h^2$

Thus the given conic is an ellipse.

(iii) $x^2 + 4xy + y^2 - 2x + 2gx + 2y - 6 = 0$

Comparing it with

$$ax^2 + by^2 + 2hxy + 2gx + 2fy + c = 0$$

$$a = 1, b = 1, h = 2; g = -1\ f = 1\ c = -6$$

$$\Delta = abc + 2fgh - 2af^2 - bg^2 - ch^2$$

$$\Delta = -6 + 2.1 - 1 \times 2 - 1(1)^2 - 1(-1)^2 - (-6)(2)^2$$

$$\Delta = -6 - 4 - 1 - 1 + 24$$

$$\Delta = -12 + 24 = 12 \neq 0$$

Again $ab = 1, h^2 = 4$

Here $ab < h^2$

$\Rightarrow$ The given conic represents a hyperbola.

Problem 2 Find the co-ordinates of the centre of the conic.

$$x^2 - 5xy + y^2 + 8x - 20y + 15 = 0$$

Solution Let $\phi(x, y) \equiv x^2 - 5xy + y^2 + 8x - 20y + 15 = 0$

Then $$\frac{\partial\phi}{\partial x} = 2x - 5y + 8$$

and $$\frac{\partial\phi}{\partial y} = 2y - 5x - 20$$

Let (x^1, y^1) be the centre of the conic

Then the centre is given by $\frac{\partial\phi}{\partial x^1} = 0$

and $\frac{\partial\phi}{\partial y^1} = 0$

i.e. $2x^1 - 5y^1 + 8 = 0$

$$-5x^1 + 2y^1 - 20 = 0 \quad (2)$$

We have by cross multiplication

$$\frac{x^1}{100-16} = \frac{y^1}{-40+40} = \frac{1}{4-25}$$

$$\frac{x^1}{84} = \frac{y^1}{0} = \frac{1}{-21}$$

$$x^1 = = \frac{84}{21}, y^1 = 0$$

$$x^1 = -4, y^1 = 0$$

Hence the centre of the conic is $(-4, 0)$

Problem 3 Find the co-ordinates of the centre of the conic

$$x^2 - 4xy - 2y^2 + 10x + 4y = 0$$

and hence find the equation of the conic referred to the centre as origin.

[*Must prepare*]

Solution $\phi(x, y) = x^2 - 4xy - 2y^2 + 10x + 4y = 0$

$$\frac{\partial\phi}{\partial x} = 2x - 4y + 10$$

$$\frac{\partial\phi}{\partial y} = -4y - 4x + 4$$

Let (x^1, y^1) be the centre of the conic then the centre is given by

$$\frac{\partial\phi}{\partial x^1} = 0 \quad \text{and} \quad \frac{\partial\phi}{\partial y^1} = 0$$

i.e. $2x^1 - 4y^1 + 10 = 0$

$$x^1 - 2y^1 + 5 = 0 \quad (1)$$

and $-4y^1 - 4x^1 + 4 = 0$

$$\Rightarrow \quad x^1 + y^1 - x = 0 \quad (2)$$

From (1) and (2) we get by cross-multiplicaton

$$\frac{x^1}{2-5} = \frac{y^1}{5+1} = \frac{1}{1+2}$$

$$\frac{x^1}{-3} = \frac{y^1}{6} = \frac{1}{3}$$

$$\Rightarrow \qquad x^1 = -1; \qquad y^1 = 2$$

Hence the centre of the conic is $(-1, 2)$.

Let the equation of the conic referred to the parallel axes through the centre $(-1, 2)$ be

$$x^2 - 4xy - 2y^2 + c^1 = 0 \tag{3}$$

where $\quad c^1 = gx^1 + fy^1 + c$

$$c^1 = g(-1) + f(2) + c$$

$$c^1 = 5(-1) + 2.2 + 0$$

$$c_1 = -5 + 4 = -1$$

From (3) $\quad x^2 - 4xy - 2y^2 - 1 = 0$

Which is the required equation of the conic referred to the centre as given.
Ans.

Problem 4 What docs thc following equation rcpresent? Find the lengths of the axes of the conic $5x^2 + 6xy + 5y^2 + 12x + 4y - 4 = 0$ what is the entre of this conic.

Solution We have

$$5x^2 + 6xy + 5y^2 + 12x + 4y - 4 = 0$$

Comparing it with $ax^2 + 2hxy + by^2 + 2gx + 2fy + c = 0$

$$a = 5, h = 3, b = 5; g = 6, f = 2\ c = -4$$

Here $\quad \Delta = abc + 2fgh - af^2 - bg^2 - ch^2$

$$\Delta = -100 + 72 - 20 - 180 + 36$$

$$\Delta = -300 + 108$$

$$\Delta = -192 \neq 0$$

Here $\quad ab = 25$

$$h^2 = 9$$

$$ab > h^2$$

The equation represents an ellipse.

Let (x^1, y^1) be the centre of the conic

Then the centre is given by

$$10x^1 + 6y^1 + 12 = 0$$

or $$5x^1 + 3y^1 + 6 = 0 \qquad (1)$$

and $$10y^1 + 6x^1 + 4 = 0$$

or $$3x^1 + 5y^1 + 2 = 0$$

$$5x^1 + 3y^1 + 6 = 0$$

By cross multiplication we have

$$5x^1 + 3y^1 + 6 = 0$$
$$3x^1 + 5y^1 + 2 = 0$$

$$\frac{x^1}{6-30} = \frac{y^1}{18-10} = \frac{1}{25-9}$$

$$\frac{x^1}{-24}; = \frac{y^1}{8} = \frac{1}{16}$$

$$x^1 = -\frac{24}{16} y^1 = \frac{8}{16}$$

$$x^1 = -\frac{3}{2}; y^1 = \frac{1}{2}$$

The equation referred to parallel axis through the centre is given by

$$5x^2 + 6xy + 5y^2 + c^1 = 0$$

where $$c^1 = gx^1 + fy^1 + c$$

$$c^1 = 6\left(-\frac{3}{2}\right) + 2\left(\frac{1}{2}\right) + (-4)$$

$$c^1 = -9 + 1 - 4$$

equations $$c^1 = -13 + 1 = -12$$

$$5x^2 + 6xv + 5y^2 - 12 = 0$$

i.e. $$\frac{5}{12}x^2 + \frac{1}{2}xy + \frac{5}{12}y^2 - 1 = 0$$

The semi-axes of the conic are the roots of the equation.

$$\frac{1}{r^4} - (a+b)\frac{1}{r^2} + ab - h^2 = 0$$

.e. $$\frac{1}{r^4} - \left(\frac{5}{12} + \frac{5}{12}\right)\frac{1}{r^2} + \frac{25}{144} - \frac{1}{16} = 0$$

i.e. $$\frac{1}{r^4} - \frac{5}{6}\frac{1}{r^2} + \frac{16}{144} = 0$$

$$\frac{1}{r^4} - \frac{5}{6}\frac{1}{r^2} + \frac{1}{9} = 0$$

i.e $$\frac{18-15r^2+2r^4}{18r^4}=0$$

$$\Rightarrow \quad 2r^4-15r^2+18=0$$

$$\Rightarrow \quad 2r^4-12r^2-3r^2+18=0$$

$$\Rightarrow \quad 2r^2(r^2-6)-3(r^2-6)=0$$

$$\Rightarrow \quad (2r^2-3)(r^2-6)=0$$

$\Rightarrow$ either $$2r^2-3=0$$

$$\Rightarrow \quad r^2=\frac{3}{2}$$

or $r^2-6=0. \quad r^2=6$

$$r=\sqrt{\frac{3}{2}}=\sqrt{\frac{6}{4}}=\frac{\sqrt{6}}{2}$$

or $r=\sqrt{6}$

Hence the lengths of the semi axes are

$$\sqrt{6}, \frac{\sqrt{6}}{2}$$ **Ans.**

Problem 5 Find the assymptote of the hyperbola

$$3x^2-5xy-2y^2+5x+11y-8=0$$

Solution If the equation of the conic is $S=0$

Then equation of the assymptote is given by

$$S-\frac{A}{ab-b^2}=0$$

ve have $3x^2-5xy-2y^2+5x+11y-8=0$

'omparing it with

$$ax^2+2hxy+by^2+2gx+2fy+c=0$$

$$a=3, \quad h=-\frac{5}{2}, \quad b=-2$$

$$g=\frac{5}{2} \quad f=\frac{11}{2} \quad c=-8$$

$$\Delta=abc+2fgh-af^2-bg^2-ch^2$$

$$\Delta=48+2.\frac{11}{2}.\frac{5}{2}\times\frac{-5}{2}-3.\frac{121}{4}$$

$$-(-2)\frac{25}{4}-(-8)\frac{25}{4}$$

$$\Delta=48-\frac{275}{4}-\frac{363}{4}+\frac{50}{4}+\frac{200}{4}$$

$$\Delta = 48 - \frac{638}{4} + \frac{250}{4}$$

$$\Delta = 48 - \frac{388}{4}$$

$$\Delta = 48 - 97$$

$$\Delta = -49$$

$$ab - h^2 = 3(-2) - \left(-\frac{5}{2}\right)^2$$

$$= -6 - \frac{25}{4} = -\frac{24-25}{4} = -\frac{49}{4}$$

$$\frac{\Delta}{ab-h^2} = \frac{-49}{\frac{-49}{4}} = 4$$

So equation of the assymptote is given by

$$3x^2 - 5xy - 2y^2 + 5x + 11y - 8 - 4 = 0$$

i.e.
$$3x^2 - 5xy - 2y^2 + 5x + 11y - 12 = 0$$

Problem 6 Reduce the equation $14x^2 - 4xy + 11y^2 - 44x - 58y + 71 = 0$ to the standard form.

Solution The given equation is

$$14x^2 - 4xy + 11y^2 - 44x - 58y + 71 = 0$$

The general equation of the conic is

$$ax^2 + 2hxy + by^2 + 2gx + 2fy + c = 0$$

$a = 14$ $\qquad g = -22$

$h = -2$ $\qquad f = -29$

$b = 11$ $\qquad c = 71$

Let $\quad \phi \equiv 14x^2 - 4xy + 11y^2 - 44x - 58y + 71 = 0$

If (x, y_1) be the centre of the conic $\phi = 0$,

Then the centre is given by

$$\frac{\partial \phi}{\partial x_1} = 0 \quad \text{and} \quad \frac{\partial \phi}{\partial y_1} = 0$$

$$28x_1 - 4y_1 - 44 = 0$$

or
$$7x_1 - y_1 - 11 = 0$$

and
$$22y_1 - 4x_1 - 58 = 0$$

or
$$2x_1 - 11y_1 + 29 = 0$$

$$7x_1 - y_1 - 11 = 0 = 0$$

Solving these by cross-coise multiplication we have

$$\frac{x_1}{121 + 29} = \frac{y_1}{203 + 22} = \frac{1}{-2 + 77}$$

$$\frac{x_1}{150} = \frac{y_1}{225} = \frac{1}{75}$$

$$x_1 = 2; \quad y_1 = \frac{225}{75} = 3$$

i.e. $\quad x_1 = 2; \quad y_1 = 3$

The equation referred to parallel axes through the centre is

$$ax^2 + by^2 + 2hxy + c^1 = 0$$

where $c^1 = gx_1 + fy_1 + c$

$$\Rightarrow \quad 14x^2 - 4xy + 11y^2 + c^1 = 0$$

$$c^1 = (-22) \times 2 + (-29) \times 3 + 71$$

$$e^1 = -44 - 87 + 71$$

$$c^1 = -131 + 71$$

$$c^1 = -60$$

So the equation is $\quad 14x^2 - 4xy + 11y^2 - 60 = 0 \quad$ (1)

Now let us rotate the axis about (2, 3) so that the xy term is removed and let the finally transformed equation be

$$ax^2 + by^2 - 60 = 0$$

Then by principle of invariants

$$a + b = a^1 + b^1 = 14 + 11 = 25$$

and $\quad ab = a^1 b^1 - h^{12}$

$$ab = 14 \times 11 - (-2)^2$$

$$ab = 154 - 4$$

$$ab = 150$$

$$a + b = 25 \qquad ab = 150$$

$$(a - b)^2 = (a + b)^2 - 4ab = 625 - 4 \times 150 = 625 - 600 = 25$$

$$a - b = \sqrt{25}$$

$$a - b = 5$$

$$a + b = 25$$
$$a - b = 5$$

adding $2a = 30$, $a = 15$ | $2b = 20$, $b = 10$

Hence the given equation reduces to

$$15x^2 + 10y^2 - 60 = 0$$

$$\Rightarrow \quad 15x^2 + 10y^2 = 60$$

$$\Rightarrow \quad \frac{x^2}{60/15} + \frac{y^2}{60/10} = 1$$

$$\Rightarrow \quad \frac{x^2}{4} + \frac{y^2}{6} = 1$$

which is the standard form of the *given equation.*

Appendix 4

THE SHORTEST DISTANCE

Solid Geometry

Problem 1 Find the shortest distance between the lines

$$\frac{x-3}{3}=\frac{x-8}{-1}=\frac{z-3}{1};$$

$$\frac{x+3}{-3}=\frac{y+7}{2}=\frac{z-6}{4}$$

Solution The equation to the first line AB are

$$\frac{x-3}{3}=\frac{y-1}{-1}=\frac{z-3}{1}=r \text{ (say)}$$

$$x=3r+3;\, y=8-r;\, z=r$$

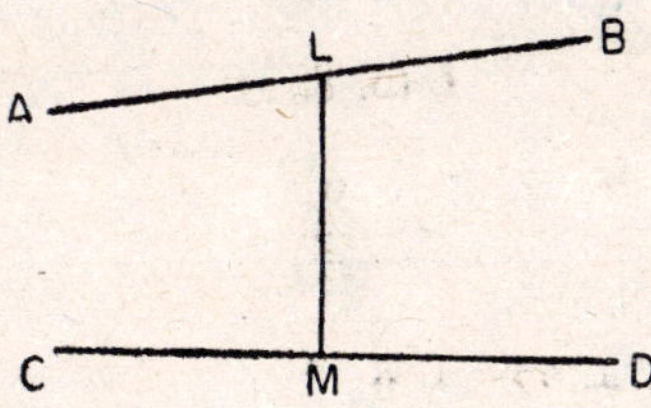

$\therefore$ Any point L on the first line is $(3r+3,\ 8-r,\ r+3)$ (1)

The equation to the second line

$$CD \text{ are } \frac{x+3}{-3}=\frac{y+7}{2}=\frac{z-6}{4}=r_1 \text{ (say)}$$

$\therefore$
$$x=-3-3r_1,\ y=2r_1-7$$
$$z=4r_1+6$$

$\therefore$ Any point M on the second line is

$$(-3-3r_1,\ 2r_1-7,\ 4r_1+6)$$

Hence the direction ratios of $L\,M$ are

$$(3r+3+3+3r_1,\ 8-r-2r_1+7,\ 3+r-4r_1-r)$$

i.e. $$(3r+3r_1+6,\ 15-r-2r_1,\ r-4r_1-3)$$

If LM be perpendicular to both the given lines, then we get

$$3(3r+3r_1+6)-1(15-r-2r_1)+1(r-4r_1-3)=0$$

$$\Rightarrow \quad 9r+9r_1+18-15+r+2r_1+r-4r_1-3=0$$

$$\Rightarrow \quad 11r+7r_1=0$$

i.e. $$r_1=-\frac{11}{7}r \qquad (2)$$

and $$-3(3r+3r_1+6)+2(15-r-2r_1)+4(r-4r_1-3)=0$$

$$-9r-9r_1-18+30-2r-4r_1+4r-16r_1-12=0$$

i.e. $$-7r-29r_1=0$$

$$\Rightarrow \quad 7r=-29r_1$$

i.e. $$7r=-29\left(-\frac{11}{7}r\right)$$

$$\Rightarrow \quad 49r=319r$$

$$\Rightarrow \quad 319r-49r=0$$

$$\Rightarrow \quad 270r=0$$

$$\Rightarrow \quad r=0$$

Hence $$r_1=0$$

Thus $$L(3,8,3)$$

and $$M(-3,-7,6)$$

$$\therefore \quad LM=\sqrt{(3+3)^2+(8+7)^2+(3-6)^2}$$

$$LM=\sqrt{36+225+9}$$

$$LM=\sqrt{270}=\sqrt{9\times 30}=3\sqrt{30}$$

This is the requireds shortest distance.

Problem 2 Find the length and equations of the shortest distance between the lines

$$3x-9y+5z=0=x+y-z \text{ and}$$
$$6x+8y+3z-13=0=x+2y+z-3$$

Solution The first line is

$$3x-9y+5z=0=x+y-z$$

so $$3x-9y+5z=0$$

and $$x+y-z=0$$

By cross-multiplication we have

$$\frac{x}{9-5} = \frac{y}{5+3} = \frac{z}{3+9}$$

i.e.

$$\frac{x}{4} = \frac{y}{8} = \frac{z}{12}$$

$$\Rightarrow \quad \frac{x}{1} = \frac{y}{2} = \frac{z}{3}$$

Now we shall reduce the equation of the second line

$$6x + 8y + 3z - 13 = 0 = x + 2y + z - 3$$

in symmetrical form

Cut this line by aplane $\quad z = 0$

Then $\quad 6x + 8y - 13 = 0$

and $\quad x + 2y - 3 = 0$

By cross-multiplication

$$\frac{x}{-24 + 26} = \frac{y}{-13 + 18} = \frac{1}{12-8}$$

$$\frac{x}{2} = \frac{y}{5} = \frac{1}{4}$$

$$\Rightarrow \quad x = \frac{1}{2}, \quad y = \frac{5}{4}, z = 0$$

Let l, m, n be the direction cosines of the second line

Then $\quad 6l + 8m + 3n = 0$

and $\quad l + 2m + n = 0$

By cross multiplication

$$\frac{l}{8-6} = \frac{m}{3-6} = \frac{n}{12-8}$$

$$\Rightarrow \quad \frac{l}{2} = \frac{m}{-3} = \frac{n}{4}$$

The equations of the second line in symmetrical formula

$$\frac{x - \frac{1}{2}}{2} = \frac{y - \frac{5}{4}}{-3} = \frac{z-0}{4} \qquad (2)$$

Now the equation of the plane through (1) and parallel to (2) is

$$\begin{vmatrix} x & y & z \\ 1 & 2 & 3 \\ 2 & -3 & 4 \end{vmatrix} = 0$$

$\therefore$ $$17x + 2y - 7z = 0$$

$\therefore$ The shortest distance = perpendicular distance of the point

$\left(\frac{1}{2}, \frac{5}{5}, 0\right)$ from (3)

$$= \frac{\frac{17}{2} + \frac{2\times 5}{4} - 7\times 0}{\sqrt{17^2+2^2+(-7)^2}}$$

$$= \frac{\frac{34+10}{4}}{\sqrt{342}} = \frac{11}{\sqrt{342}}$$

The direction cosines of the shortest distance which is perpendicular to (3) are proportional to (17, 2, −7)

The equation of the plane through (1) and the shortest distancc is

$$\begin{vmatrix} x & y & z \\ 1 & 2 & 3 \\ 17 & 2 & -7 \end{vmatrix} = 0$$

or $$10x - 29y + 16z = 0$$

The equation of the plane through (2) and the shortest distance

$$\begin{vmatrix} x-\frac{1}{2} & y-\frac{5}{4} & z \\ 2 & -3 & 4 \\ 17 & 2 & -7 \end{vmatrix} = 0$$

or $$13x + 82y + 55z - 109 = 0$$

Hence the equations to the lines of the shortest distance are

$$10x - 29y + 16z = 0 = 13x + 82y + 55z - 109$$ **Ans.**

Problem 3 Find the shortest distance between axis of z and the line

$$ax + by + cz + d = 1 = a'x + b'y + c'z + d'$$

Solution Any plane passing through the second line is

$$ax+by+cz+d+k\,(a'x+b'y+c'z+d') = 0$$

$$(a+ka')\,x + (b+kb')\,y + (c+kc')\,z + d + kd' = 0 \qquad (1)$$

It will be parallel to the z-axis whose direction cosines are (0, 0, 1) if

$$0\,(a+ka') + 0\,(b+kb') + 1\,(c+kc') = 0$$

$$\Rightarrow \qquad k = -\frac{c}{c'},$$

putting the value of k in (1) equation of the plane becomes

$$(c'a-a'c)\,x + (c'b-b'c)\,y + (dc'-cd') = 0$$

The required shortest distance is the distance of the origin (a point on z axis) from this plane

$$= \frac{dc'-cd'}{\sqrt{(ac'-a'c)^2 + (bc'-b'c)^2}} \qquad \text{Ans}$$

Problem 4 Show that the plane containing the line

$\frac{y}{b} + \frac{z}{c} = 1,\ x = 0$, and parallel to the line

$\frac{x}{a} - \frac{z}{c} = 1,\ y = 0$ is $\frac{x}{a} - \frac{y}{b} - \frac{z}{c} + 1 = 0$

and if $2d$ is the shortest distance between the lines, the

$$d^{-2} = a^{-2} + b^{-2} + c^{-2}$$

Solution Let the equation of the plane containing the line $\frac{y}{b} + \frac{z}{c} = 1$,

$x = 0$ is

$$\frac{y}{b} + \frac{z}{c} - 1 + k\,x = 0 \tag{1}$$

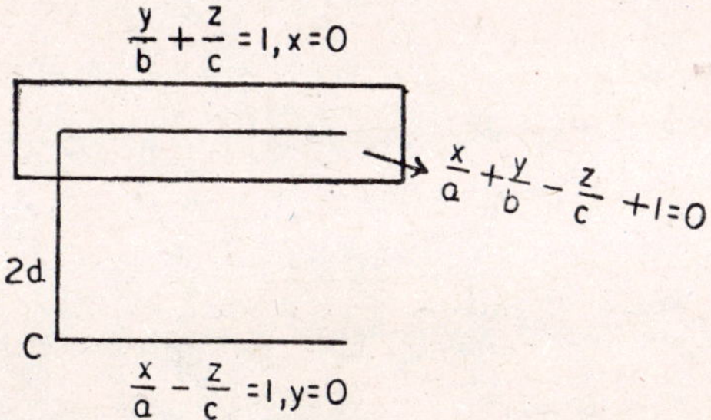

plane (1) is parallel to the line

$$\frac{x}{a} - \frac{z}{c} = 1,\ y = 0$$

making this line symmetrical

$$\frac{x}{a} = 1 + \frac{z}{c}.\ y = 0$$

$$\frac{x}{a} = \frac{z+c}{c}, y = 0$$

i.e. $$\frac{x-0}{a} = \frac{y-0}{0} = \frac{z-(-c)}{c} \quad (1)$$

since (1) is parallel to (2) i.e.

$$a \cdot k + \frac{1}{b} \cdot 0 + \frac{1}{c} \cdot c = 0$$

$$ak = 1$$

$\Rightarrow$ $$k = -\frac{1}{a}$$

Thus equation of the plane is given by

$$\frac{y}{b} + \frac{z}{c} - 1 - \frac{1}{a} \cdot x = 0$$

i.e. $$\frac{x}{a} - \frac{y}{b} - \frac{z}{c} + 1 = 0 \quad \text{(FFP)} \quad (3)$$

Any point of the straight line (2) is $(0. 0, -c)$
since $2d$ is the shortest distance between the lines so
$2d$ = length of 1^r from $(0, 0, -c)$ to the plane (3)

$$\text{i.e. } 2d = \frac{-\left(-\frac{c}{c}\right) + 1}{\sqrt{\frac{1}{a^2} + \frac{1}{b^2} + \frac{1}{c^2}}}$$

i.e. $$2d = \frac{1+1}{\sqrt{\frac{1}{a^2} + \frac{1}{b^2} + \frac{1}{c^2}}}$$

i.e. $$2d = \frac{2}{\sqrt{\frac{1}{a^2} + \frac{1}{b^2} + \frac{1}{c^2}}}$$

$\Rightarrow$ $$\sqrt{\frac{1}{a^2} + \frac{1}{b^2} + \frac{1}{c^2}} = \frac{1}{d}$$

squaring both sides we have

$$\frac{1}{a^2} + \frac{1}{b^2} + \frac{1}{c^2} = \frac{1}{d^2}$$

i.e. $$d^{-2} = a^{-2} + b^{-2} + c^{-2}$$

Problem 5 Find the length of the shortest distance between the lines

$$y = az + b, \qquad z = dx + \beta,$$
$$y = a'z + b', \qquad z = \alpha' x + \beta'$$

Solution Equation of the first straignt line is

$$y = az + b; \quad z = \alpha x + \beta$$

$$y - b = az; \quad \frac{z-0}{\alpha} = \frac{x + \frac{\beta}{\alpha}}{1}$$

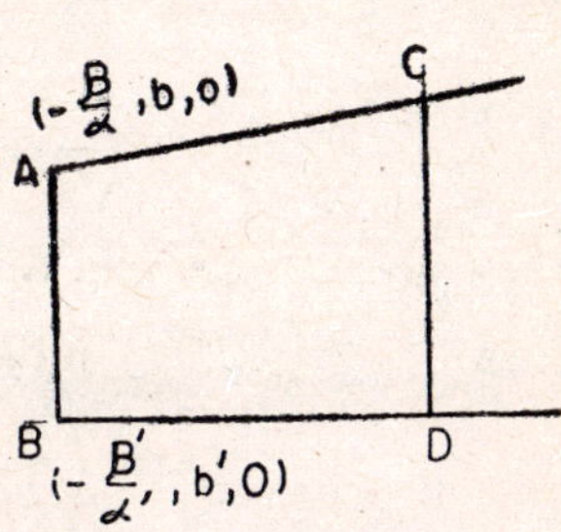

$$\frac{y-b}{a} = z$$

$$\Rightarrow \frac{y-b}{a\alpha} = \frac{z}{\alpha};$$

Thus
$$\frac{x - \left(-\frac{\beta}{\alpha}\right)}{1} = \frac{y-b}{a\alpha} = \frac{z-0}{\alpha}$$

Thus co-ordinate of any point on the first line is $\left(-\frac{\beta}{\alpha}, b, 0\right)$

and the direction 1, $a\alpha$, α

Now the equation of the second straight line is

$$y = a' z + b', z = \alpha' x + \beta'$$

$$\frac{y-b'}{a'} = z, \frac{z}{\alpha'} = \frac{x + \frac{\beta'}{\alpha'}}{1}$$

$$\frac{y-b'}{a' \alpha'} = \frac{z}{\alpha'}; \frac{z}{\alpha'} = \frac{x + \frac{\beta'}{\alpha'}}{1}$$

$$\frac{x + \frac{\beta'}{\alpha'}}{1} = \frac{y-b'}{a^1 \alpha'} = \frac{z-0}{\alpha'}$$

Co-ordinate of any point on the 2nd straight like is

$$\left(-\frac{\beta'}{\alpha'}, b', 0\right)$$

direction ratios are 1, $a' \alpha'$, α'.

Let CD is the shortest distance of the two straight lines let $l, m_1\, n$ are the direction ratios of the line (1) then

$$l \cdot 1 + ma\,\alpha + n\,.\,\alpha = 0$$
$$l\,.\,1 + ma'\,\alpha' + n\,\alpha' = 0$$

By cross multiplication we get

$$\frac{l}{a\alpha\alpha'-a'\alpha'\alpha}=\frac{m}{\alpha-\alpha'}=\frac{n}{a'\alpha'-a\alpha}$$

$$=\frac{\sqrt{l^2+m^2+n^2}}{\sqrt{a^2\alpha'^2(a-a')^2+(\alpha-\alpha')^2+(a'\alpha'-a\alpha)^2}}$$

$$\frac{1}{\sqrt{\alpha^2\alpha'^2(a-a')^2+(\alpha-\alpha')^2+(a'\alpha'-a\alpha)^2}}$$

These gives l, m, n join A and B

Then $\quad CD$ = projection of AB on CD

$$=\left(-\frac{\beta}{\alpha}+\frac{\beta'}{\alpha'}\right)l+(b-b')m+0$$

$$=\frac{\beta^1\alpha-\beta\alpha^1)(a-a^1)+(\alpha-\alpha^1)(b-b^1)}{\sqrt{\alpha^2\alpha'^2(a-a')^2+(\alpha-\alpha')^2+(a'\alpha'-a\alpha)^2}}$$

This is the required shortest distance.

Problem 10 Two straight lines

$$\frac{x-\alpha}{l}=\frac{y-\beta}{m}=\frac{z-\gamma}{n}$$

and

$$\frac{x-\alpha'}{l}=\frac{y-\beta'}{m'}=\frac{z-\gamma'}{n^1}$$

are cut by a third line whose direction cosines are λ, μ, γ. Show that the length intercepted on the third line is given by

$$\begin{vmatrix}\alpha-\alpha' & \beta-\beta' & \gamma-\gamma' \\ l & m & n \\ l^1 & m^1 & n^1\end{vmatrix} \div \begin{vmatrix} l & m & n \\ l^1 & m' & n' \\ \lambda & \mu & \gamma\end{vmatrix}$$

Solution Let the third line cut the two straight lines at the point P and Q. Thedirection cosines of the line PQ is λ, μ, γ the eo-ordinate of the point

A is (α, β, γ) and $AD = r$

The co-ordinate of the point B

is $\quad (\alpha', \beta^1, \gamma')$ and $BQ = r'$

i e. Equation of the first straight line is

$$\frac{x-\alpha}{l}=\frac{y-\beta}{m}=\frac{z-\gamma}{n}=r$$

and the equation of the second straight line

$$\frac{x-\alpha'}{l'}=\frac{y-\beta'}{m'}=\frac{z-\gamma'}{n'}=r'$$

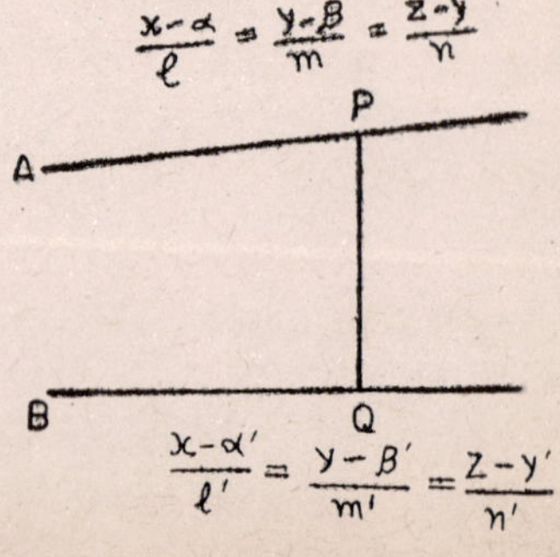

Any point on the first line

is $$P(\alpha + lr, \beta + mr, \gamma + nr)$$

and any point on the second line is

$$Q(\alpha' + l' r^1, \beta' + m' r^1, \gamma' + n' r')$$

The direction ratios of the line PQ is given by

$$\alpha + lr - \alpha^1 - l^1 r^1, \beta + mr - \beta^1 - m^1 r^1$$
$$\gamma + mr - \gamma^1 - n^1 r^1$$

So we have

$$\frac{\lambda}{\eta + lr - \alpha' - l' r^1} = \frac{\mu}{\beta + mr - \beta' - m' r'}$$

$$= \frac{\gamma}{\gamma + nr - \gamma' - n'r'} = \frac{1}{k} \text{ say}$$

$$\Rightarrow \quad \alpha + lr - \alpha' - i' r' = k\lambda$$
$$\beta + mr - \beta' - m' r' = k\mu$$

and $$\gamma + nr - \gamma' - n' r' = k\gamma$$

$$\Rightarrow \quad (\alpha - \alpha') + lr - l' r' = k\lambda$$
$$(\beta - \beta') + mr - m' r' = k\mu$$
$$(\gamma - \gamma') + nr - n' r' = k\gamma$$

$$\Rightarrow \quad (\alpha - \alpha') + lr - l' r' - k\gamma = 0$$
$$(\beta - \beta') + mr - m' r' - k\mu = 0$$
$$(\gamma - \gamma') + nr - n' r' - k\gamma = 0$$

i.e. $$lr - l' r' + (\alpha - \alpha' - k\lambda) = 0$$
$$mr - m' r' + (\beta - \beta' - k\mu) = 0$$
$$nr - n' r^1 + (\gamma - \gamma^1 - k\gamma) = 0$$

Eliminating r and r^1 from (1), (2) and (3) we have.

$$\begin{vmatrix} l & l' & \alpha - \alpha' - k\lambda \\ m & m' & \beta - \beta^1 - k\mu \\ n & n' & \gamma - \gamma' - k\gamma \end{vmatrix} = 0$$

$$\Rightarrow \begin{vmatrix} l & l^1 & \alpha - \alpha' \\ m & m^1 & \beta - \beta' \\ n & n' & \gamma - \gamma' \end{vmatrix} - k \begin{vmatrix} l & l' & \lambda \\ m & m\cdot & \mu \\ n & n' & \gamma \end{vmatrix} = 0$$

$$\Rightarrow \quad k = \frac{\begin{vmatrix} l & l' & \alpha-\alpha' \\ m & m' & \beta-\beta^1 \\ n & n' & \gamma-\gamma' \end{vmatrix}}{\begin{vmatrix} l & l' & \lambda \\ m & m^1 & \mu \\ n & n' & \gamma \end{vmatrix}}$$

Now $PQ^2 = [\alpha+lr-\alpha'-l'\,r']^2+[\beta+mr-\beta'-m'\,r']^2+[\gamma-nr-\gamma'-n^3\,r']^2$

$PQ^2 = k^2\lambda^2 + k^2\mu^2 + k^2\gamma^2$

$PQ^2 = k^2(\lambda^2 + \mu^2 + \bar{y}^2)$

$PQ^2 = k^2-1$ [since $\lambda^2 + \mu^2 + \gamma^2 = 1$]

i.e. $PQ = k$

$$\text{So} \quad PQ = \frac{\begin{vmatrix} l & l' & \alpha-\alpha' \\ m & m^1 & \beta-\beta' \\ n & n' & \gamma-\gamma' \end{vmatrix}}{\begin{vmatrix} l & l\cdot & \lambda \\ m & m' & \mu \\ n & n' & \gamma \end{vmatrix}}$$

Length of intercept on the third line *(Proved)*

Miscelleneous Problems Asked in the Examination

Area of Plane Curves Heading

Problem 1 Find the area enclosed by the poraolas $y^2 = ax$ and $x^2 = 4by$

Solution The vertex of $y^2 = 4ax$ and $x^2 = 4by$ is the origin and their axes are x-axis and y-axis respectively.

Solving $y^2 = 4ax$ and $x^2 = 4by$ we get

$$y^2 = 4a(2b^{1/2}\,y^{1/2})$$

$$y^2 = 8ab^{1/2}\,y^{1/2}$$

$$y^2 - 8ab^{1/2}\,y^{1/2} = 0$$

$$y\,(y - 8ab^{1\,2}\,y^{-1/2}) = 0$$

i.e. either $y = 0$

or $y = 8ab^{1/}\,y^{-1/2} = 0$

$$y - 8b^{1/2}\frac{1}{y^{\frac{1}{2}}} = 0$$

$$y^{3/2} - 8ab^{1/2} = 0$$

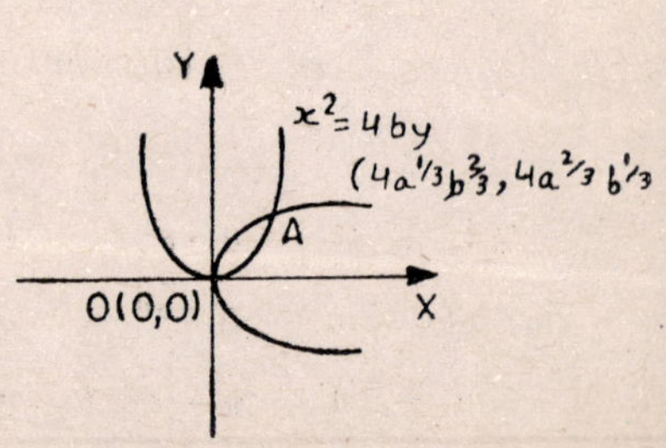

$$y^{3/2} = 8ab^{1/2}$$

$$y = [8ab^{1/2}]^{2/3}$$

$$y = 8^{2/3}\, a^{2/3}\, \frac{2}{b^3 \times 2}$$

$$y = [(2^3)^{/13}]^2\, a^{2/3}\, b^{1/3}$$

$$y = 4a^{2/3}\, b^{1/3}$$

i.e. $y = 0$ or $4a^{2/3}\, b^{1/3}$

Again $x^2 = 4by$

$$x^2 = 4b\, 2\sqrt{ax}$$

$$x^2 = 8ba^{1/2}\, x^{1/2}$$

$$x^2 - 8ba^{1/2}\, x^{1/2} = 0$$

$$x\,[x - 8\, ba^{1/2}\, x^{-1/2}] = 0$$

$\Rightarrow$ $x = 0$

i.e. $x - 8ba^{1/2}\, x^{-1/2} = 0$

i.e. $x - 8ba^{1/2}\dfrac{1}{x^{1/2}} = 0$

i.e. $x^{3/2} = 8ba^{1/2}$

$$x = [8ba^{1/2}]^{2/3}$$

$$x = (8)^{2/3}\, b^{2/3}\, a^{1/3}$$

$$x = 4b^{2/3}\, a^{1/3}$$

i.e. Either $x = 0$ or $x = 4b^{2/3}\, a^{1/2}$

Thus the points of intersection of both the parabolas

$$y^2 = 4ax \quad \text{and} \quad x^2 = 4by$$

are (0, 0) and $(4a^{1/3}\, b^{2/3}, 4a^{2/3}\, b^{1/3})$

So the x-co-ordinates of the points of intersection 0 and A are 0 and $4a^{1/3}\, b^{2/3}$ respectively

$\therefore$ The required area $4a^{l3}\, b^{2/3}$

$$= \int_0^{4a^{1/}\, b^{2/3}} [\phi(x) - \psi(x)]\, dx$$

$$y = \phi(x) = \sqrt{4ax}$$

$$x = \psi(x) = \frac{x^2}{4b}$$

$$x^2 = 4by \quad \Rightarrow \quad y = \frac{x^2}{4b}$$

Therefore the required area

$$= \int_0^{4a^{1/3} b^{2/3}} \left[\sqrt{4ax} - \frac{x^2}{4b}\right] dx$$

$$= \int_0^{4a^{1/3} b^{2/3}} \left[2\sqrt{a}\,\sqrt{x} - \frac{x^2}{4b}\right] dx$$

$$= \left[2\sqrt{a}\ \frac{x^{3/2}}{3/2} - \frac{1}{4b} \cdot \frac{x^3}{3}\right]_0^{4a^{1/3} b^{2/3}}$$

$$= \left[\frac{4}{3}\sqrt{a}\ (4a^{1/3}\ b^{2/3})^{3/2} - \frac{1}{4b \times 3}\ (4a^{1/3}\ 3b^{2/3})^3\right]$$

$$= \left[\frac{4}{3}\ b^{1/2}\ 8a^{1/2}\ b - \frac{1}{4b \times 3}\ 64\ ab^2\right]$$

$$= \left[\frac{32}{3}\ ab - \frac{16}{3}\ ab\right] = ab\left[\frac{32}{3} - \frac{16}{3}\right]$$

$$= ab\left[\frac{32-16}{3}\right] = ab \times \frac{16}{3} = \frac{16\ ab}{3}$$

Problem 8 Compute the $\int \frac{2^x}{1-4^x}\, dx$ [*IFS 83*]

Solution Let $I = \int \frac{2^x}{1-4^x}\, dx$

$$I = \int \frac{2^x\, dx}{1-2^{2x}}$$

Let $2^x = t$

Taking differential we have $2^x \log 2dx = dt$

$$I = \int \frac{dt}{\log 2\,(1-t^2)}$$

$$I = \frac{1}{\log 2} \int \frac{dt}{(1-t^2)}$$

$$I = \frac{1}{\log 2} \times \frac{1}{2} \log \left\{\frac{1+t}{1-t}\right\}$$

$$I = \frac{1}{2 \log 2} \log\left(\frac{1+t}{1-t}\right)$$

$$I = \frac{1}{\log 2} \times \log \left\{\frac{1+2^x}{1-2^x}\right\}$$

$$I = \frac{1}{\log 4} \times \log\left(\frac{1+2^x}{1-2^x}\right)$$

Problem 4 Show that the latus return of the parabola

$$(a^2 + b^2)(x^2 + y^2) = (bx + ay - ab)^2$$

is $$\frac{2ab}{\sqrt{a^2+b^2}}$$ [I.F.S. 81]

Solution $$(a^2 + b^2)(x^2 + y^2) = (bx + ay - ab)^2$$

$$a^2 x^2 + a^2 y^2 + b^2 x^2 + b^2 y^2$$

$$= b^2 x^2 + a^2 y^2 + a^2 b^2 + 2abxy = -2a^2 by - 2ab^2 x$$

$$a^2 x^2 + b^2 y^2 = a^2 b^2 + 2abxy - 2a^2 by - 2ab^2 x$$

$$a^2 x^2 + b^2 y^2 - 2abxy = a^2 b^2 - 2a^2 by - 2ab^2 x$$

$$(ax - by)^2 = -2ab\left(bx + ay - \frac{ab}{2}\right)$$

$$\frac{(ax - by)^2}{a^2 + b^2} \times (a^2 + b^2) = -2ab\left(bx + ay - \frac{ab}{2}\right)$$

$$\left(\frac{ax - by}{\sqrt{a^2 + b^2}}\right)^2 \times (a^2 + b^2) = -2ab\left(bx + ay - \frac{ab}{2}\right)$$

$$\left(\frac{ax - by}{\sqrt{a^2 + b^2}}\right)^2 = -\frac{2ab}{(a^2 + b^2)}\left(bx + ay - \frac{ab}{2}\right)$$

$$\left(\frac{ax - by}{\sqrt{a^2 + b^2}}\right)^2 = -\frac{2ab}{\sqrt{a^2 + b^2}} \frac{\left(bx + ay - \frac{ab}{2}\right)}{\sqrt{a^2 + b^2}}$$

Length of the latus return

$$4A = -\frac{2ab}{\sqrt{a^2 + b^2}}$$

Taking only +ve sign length of the latus return

$$= \frac{2ab}{\sqrt{a^2 + b^2}}$$

Problem 5 The straight line $lx + my = 1$ meets the circle $x^2 + y^2 = 1$ in P and Q. If O is the centre of the circle show that

$$\cos\left(\frac{1}{2} < POQ\right) = \frac{1}{(l^2+m^2)^{1/2}}$$ [I.F.S. 87]

Equation of the circle $x^2 + y^2 = 1$. Equation of the line $lx + my = 1$ $lx + m y = 1$ cuts the circle intwo point P and Q straight line PQ makes angle $\angle POQ$ at the centre. Let OM be the length of $\perp^r$ drawn from O to the line PQ. So OM divides the angle PQQ.

Let $$\angle POM = \theta$$

Then $$\angle QOM = \theta$$

$$OM = \frac{1}{\sqrt{l^2 + m^2}} = \frac{1}{[l^2 + m^2]^{1/2}}$$

$$\cos\theta = \frac{OM}{OP}$$

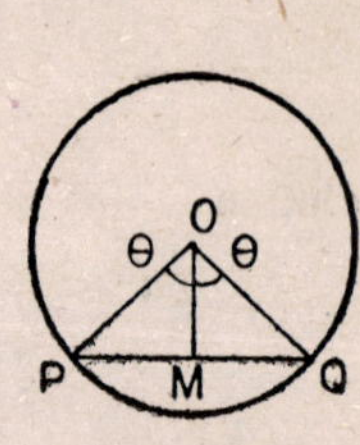

OP = radius of the circle $x^2 + y^2 = 1$ is 1

$$\cos\theta = \frac{1}{(l^2 + m^2)^{1/2}}$$

$$\Rightarrow \qquad \cos\left\{\frac{1}{2} < POQ\right\} = \frac{1}{(l^2 + m^2)^{1/2}}$$

Appendix 5

SET THEORY

Set Theory : Algebera of sets, relation sand function, inverse of a function, composite function, equivalence relation.

(1) Two sets A and B are said to be equal if and only if $A \subseteq B$ and $B \subseteq A$.

i.e. $$A \subseteq B \text{ and } B \subseteq A \Leftrightarrow A = B$$

(2) If $A \subseteq B$, and $B \subseteq C$ then $A \subseteq C$

(3) $A \Delta B =$ Symmetric difference of A and B

$$A \Delta B = (A - B) \cup (B - A)$$

Problems 1 Demorgan's law

let A and B be two sets then

(a) $(A \cup B') = A' \cap B'$

(b) $(A \cap B)' = A' \cup B'$ where the symbols have there usual meaning.

Problem 2 Let A and B be two sets then $A \Delta B = B \Delta A$.

Problem 3 Let A and B be non-empty sets then prove that

$$A \times B = B \times A \text{ iff } A = \bar{B}$$

let $$A \times B = B \times A$$

then we shall prove that $A = B$ i.e. we have to prove that $A \subseteq B$ and $B \subseteq A$

Let $x \in A \Rightarrow (x, b) \in A \times B,$ when $b \in B$

$\Rightarrow (x, b) \in B \times A$ $\quad A \times B = B \times A$

$\Rightarrow x \in B$

Thus $$A \subseteq B \tag{1}$$

Again let y be any arbitrary element of B

$$y \in B \Rightarrow (a, y) \in B \times A$$

$\Rightarrow (a, y) \in B \times A$ vide $A \times B = B \times A$

$\Rightarrow \quad y \in A$

i.e. $y \in B \Rightarrow y \in A$

Thus $\quad B \subseteq A$ (2)

From relation (1) and (2) we have $A = B$

Again let $A = B$ then we shall prove that

$$A \times B = B \times A$$

L.H.S. $= A \times B = A \times A$ as $A = B$

and R.H.S. $= B \times A = A \times A$ as $A = B$

Thus $\quad A \times B = B \times A$ (*proved*)

Relation

Equivalence Relation

Let R be a relation on a set A then Rissaid to be an equivalence relation iff

(i) Ris reflective i.e. $(a, a) \in R \;\forall\; a \in R$

(ii) Ris symmetric i.e. $(a, b) \in R$

$$\Rightarrow (b, a) \in R \;\forall\; a, b \in A$$

(iii) R is transitive i.e.

$$(a, b) \in R, (b, c) \in R$$

$$\Rightarrow (a, c) \in R \quad \forall\; a, b, c \in A$$

Exercise 1 Arelation R is defined on the set $N \times N$ as follows : $(a, b) R (c, d)$ eff $a + d = b + c$ Prove that R is an equivalence relation on $N \times N$.

N is the set of natural numbers then

$$N \times N = \{(a, b) : a, b \in N\}$$

(1) R Satisfies Reflexive property

since $\quad (a + b) = (b + a) \;\forall\; a. b \in N$

i.e. $\quad (a, b) \; R \; (a \, b) \;\forall\; (a \, b) \in N \times N$

(2) R Satisfies Symmetric Property

i.e. we have to prove that

$$(a, b) R (c, d)$$

$$\Rightarrow (c, d) R (a, b)$$

let $\quad (a, b), (c, d) \in N \times N$

$$\Rightarrow a, b, c, d \in N$$

in N we know that

$$b + c = c + b$$
$$a + d = d + a$$

$$(a, b)\ R\ (c, d)$$
$$a + d = b + c$$
$$b + c = a + d$$
$$c + b = d + a$$
$$\Rightarrow \quad (c, d)\ R\ (a, b)$$

Thus $\quad (a, b)\ R\ (c, d) \;\Rightarrow\; (c, d)\ R\ (a, b) \quad \forall\ (a, b), (c, d) \in N \times N$

$\Rightarrow \quad R$ is symmetric

(3) *R* Satisfies Transitive Property

let $\quad (a, b), (c, d), (e, f) \in N \times N$

and $(a, b)\ R\ (c, d)$, $(c, d)\ R\ (e, f)$ then to prove that $(a, b)\ R\ (e f)$

$$(a, b)\ R\ (c, d) \quad \text{and} \quad (c, d)\ R\ (e, f)$$
$$\Rightarrow \quad a + d = b + c \quad (1) \qquad c + f = d + e \quad (2)$$

adding relation (1) and (2) we have

$$a + d + c + f = b + c + d + e$$
$$d + a + f + c = b + d + c + e$$
$$d + (a + f) + c = d + (b + e) + c$$
$$\Rightarrow \quad a + f = b + e$$
$$\Rightarrow \quad (a, b)\ R\ (e, f)$$

Thus R is Trensitive

Since the relation R satisfies Reflexive, symmetric and Transitive property. So R is an equivalence relation.

Example 2. Prove that the relation R congruent madulo mon the set I of integers is an equivalence relation.

$$R = \{(a, b) : a,\ b \in I \;\; a \equiv b \pmod m\}$$
$$= \{(a, b) : a. b \in I \;\; a - b = km\ K \in I\}$$

we have to prove that this relation satisfies (i) Reflexive (ii) Symmetric (iii) and transitive properly.

(i) Reflexivity : $\quad \forall\ a \in I$

$$a - a = 0 = 0\,.\,m \qquad 0 \in I$$

i.e. $\quad a - a = 0\,.\,m \quad \Rightarrow \equiv a \pmod m$

$$\Rightarrow \quad a\ R\ a$$

$\Rightarrow \quad R$ is reflexive.

(ii) Symmetricity :

let $a, b \in I$

and $a\, R\, b$ then we have to prove that $b\, R\, a$

$$a\, R\, b \Rightarrow a \equiv b \pmod m$$

$$\Rightarrow a - b = k_1 m \quad \text{for} \quad k_1 \in I$$

$$\Rightarrow b - a = (-k_1)\, m$$

since $k_1 \in I \Rightarrow -k_1 \in I$

$$\Rightarrow b \equiv a \pmod m$$

$$\Rightarrow b\, R\, a$$ So R is Reflexive.

(iii) Transitivity

Let $a, b, c \in I$ and

$a\, R\, b$, $b\, R\, c$ than we will show that $a\, R\, e$

$$a\, R\, b \Rightarrow a \equiv b \pmod m$$

$$\Rightarrow a - b = k_1 m,\ k \in I$$

$$b\, R\, c \Rightarrow b \equiv c \pmod m$$

$$\Rightarrow b - c = k_2 m \quad k_2 \in I$$

Then $a - b + b - c = (k_1 + k_2)\, m$

$$\Rightarrow a - c = (k_1 + k_2)\, m \qquad k_1 \in I, k_2 \in I$$

$$\Rightarrow a \equiv c \pmod m \qquad \Rightarrow k_1 + k_2 \in I$$

$$\Rightarrow a\, R\, c$$ R is transitive

Since the Relation R is symmetric, Reflexive and transitive. Thus the given relation R is an equivalance relation.

Exercise 3. Is the relation 'a divides b' in the set of all positive integers an equivalence relation ?

(i) Symmetricity $a\, R\, b \Rightarrow$ a divides b

But this does not empley that b divides a.

i.e. $b\, R\, a$ is not true. [a divides b $\Rightarrow$ b divides a in I iff $a = b$, but this condition is not given]

Thus the relation R is not Reflexive.

(ii) Reflexivity in I every enteger divides it self

$$\Rightarrow \text{a divides } a \quad \forall\ a \in I$$

$$\Rightarrow a\, R\, a\ \forall\ a \in I$$

$\Rightarrow$ R is reflexive

(iii) Transitivity : Let $a, b, c \in I$ such that $a R b, b R c$ then we have to prove that $a R c$

$$a R b \Rightarrow a \text{ divides } b$$

$$\Rightarrow b = ak_1 \quad k_1 \in I \qquad (1)$$

$$b R c \Rightarrow b \text{ divide } c$$

$$\Rightarrow c = bk_2 \quad k_2 \in I \qquad (2)$$

$$\Rightarrow c = ak_1 k_2 \qquad k_1, k_2 \in I$$

$$\Rightarrow a \text{ divides } c \qquad \Rightarrow k_1 k_2 \in I$$

$$\Rightarrow a R c \qquad R \text{ is transitive.}$$

Since the relation Res Reflexivc, Transitive but not Symmetric. Thus the relation R is not an equivalence relation.

Example 4 Prove that the relation R defined by

$a R b$ if $|a| = |b|$ where a, b are real number is an equivalence relation.

we have

R (1) Reflexivity

since $\quad |a| = |a| \ \forall\ a \in R$

$$\Rightarrow a R a \ \forall\ a \in R$$

$\Rightarrow$ R is Reflexive.

R (2) Symmetricity :

Let $a R b$ then we have to prove that $b R a$

since $\quad a R b$

$$\Rightarrow |a| = |b| \ \forall\ a, b \in R$$

$$\Rightarrow |c| = |a| \ \forall\ a, b \in R$$

$$\Rightarrow b R a \ \forall\ a, b \in R$$

so R is symmetric.

R (3) Let $a R b$, $b R c$ then we have to prove that $a R c$

$$a R b \Rightarrow |a| = |b| \qquad \text{(i)}$$

$$b R c \Rightarrow |b| = |c| \qquad \text{(ii)}$$

From (i) and (ii) we have

$$|a| = |b| = |c|$$

$$\Rightarrow |a| = |c| \qquad \Rightarrow a R c$$

Thus $a R b$, $b R c \Rightarrow a R c$

so the relation R is an equivalence relation.

Exercise 5 Prove that the relation R defined by $a\,R\,b$ if $a \geqslant b$ is not an equivalence relation; where a, b are real numbers.

(i) Reflexivity : since $\forall\ a \in R \quad a \geqslant a$

$\Rightarrow \quad a\,R\,a$

(2) Symmetricity :

Let $\quad a\,R\,b \quad \forall \quad a, b \in R$

$\Rightarrow \quad a \geqslant b$

$\Rightarrow \quad b \geqslant a \quad \forall \quad a, b \in R$

so the relation R is not symmetric

Thus the relation R is not an equivalence relation.

Exercise 6 Prove that the inverse of an equivalence realtion is again an equivalence relation.

Let R be an equivalence relation defined on the set A. Then we have to prove that R^{-1} is also an equivalence relation. For this we have to prove that

(i) R^{-1} is Reflxive

(ii) R^{-1} is symmetric

(iii) R^{-1} is transitive.

(i) R^{-1} is Reflexive

$(a, a) \in R$ since R is Reflexive

$\Rightarrow \quad (a, a) \in R^{-1} \quad \forall \quad a \in A$

$\Rightarrow \quad R^{-1}$ is Reflexive.

(ii) R^{-1} is symmetric

Let $(a, b) \in R^{-1}$

$\Rightarrow \quad (b, a) \in R$

$\Rightarrow \quad (a, b) \in R \quad$ [since R is symmetric]

$\Rightarrow \quad (b, a) \in R^{-1}$

Thus $(a, b) \in R^{-1} \Rightarrow (b, a) \in R^{-1}$

$\Rightarrow \quad R^{-1}$ is symmetric

(iii) R^{-1} is Transitive :

Let $(a, b) \in R^{-1}$ and $(b, c) \in R^{-1}$ then we have to prove that $(a, c) \in R^{-1}$

$(a, b) \in R^{-1}$

$\Rightarrow$ $(b, a) \in R^{-1}$ [R^{-1} is symmetric]

$\Rightarrow$ $(a, b) \in R$ [By difi.]

Now $(a, b) \in R$, $(b, c) \in$ and R Transitive

$(b, c) \in R^{-1}$

$\Rightarrow$ $(c, b) \in R^{-1}$ [R^{-1} is symmetric]

$\Rightarrow$ $(b, c) \in R$ [By difinition]

$\Rightarrow$ $(a, c) \in R$

$\Rightarrow$ $(c, a) \in R$ [Because R is symmetric]

$\Rightarrow$ $(a, c) \in R^{-1}$ [by defi.]

Thus R^{-1} is *Transitive.*

R^{-1} is an equivalence relation.

Exercise 7. If R and R' be two equivalence relations defined on a set A then prove that

(a) $R \cap R'$ is an equivalence relation on A

(b) $R \cap R'$ is not an equivalence relation on A

R and R' are equivalence relation on A

$$\therefore \quad R \subseteq A \times A \quad \text{and} \quad R' \subseteq A \times A$$

$$\Rightarrow \quad R \cap R' \subseteq A \times A$$

$\Rightarrow$ $R \cap R'$ is a relation on the set A.

Now we shall show that $R \cap R'$ satisfies the three properties.

(R) *Reflexive Property* :

$$(a, a) \in R,\ (a, a) \in R' \ \forall\ a \in A$$

$$\Rightarrow \quad (a, a) \in R \cap R'$$

$\Rightarrow$ $R \cap R'$ is Reflexive.

[S] : Symmetricity :

Let $(a, b) \in R \cap R' \quad \forall \quad a, b \in A$

$$\Rightarrow \quad (a, a) \in R \cap R'$$

$\Rightarrow$ $(a, b) \in R$ and $(a, b) \in R'$

$\Rightarrow$ $(b, a) \in R$ and $(b, a) \in R'$

[since R and R' are symmetric]

$$\Rightarrow \quad (b, a) \in R \cap R'$$

$\Rightarrow$ $R \cap R'$ is symmetric

[T] Transitive :

let $(a, b) \in R \cap R'$ and $(b, c) \in R \cap R'$

$\Rightarrow$ $(a, b) \in R$ and $(a, b) \in R'$

$\Rightarrow$ $(a, b) \in R, (b, c) \in R$

$\Rightarrow$ $(a, c) \in R$

$\Rightarrow$ $(a, c) \in R \cap R'$

$R \cap R'$ is Transitive

$\Rightarrow$ $(a, b) \in R', (b, c) \in R'$

$\Rightarrow$ $(a, b) \in R'$ $(b, c) \in R'$

$\Rightarrow$ $(a, c) \in R'$

which shows that $R \cap R'$ is an equivalence Relation.

(b) Now we will show that $R \cap R'$ is not an equivalence relation.

R, R' are relations

$\Rightarrow$ $R \subseteq A \times A, R' \subseteq A \times A$

$\Rightarrow$ $R \cup R' \subseteq A \times A$

$\Rightarrow$ $R \cup R'$ is a relation:

[*R*] *Reflexive* :

$(a, a) \in R, (a, a) \in R' \ \forall \ a \in A$

$\Rightarrow$ $(a, a) \in R \cup R'$

$\Rightarrow$ $R \cup R'$ is Reflexive,

[*S*] *Symmetric* :

$(a, b) \in R \cup R'$ then to prove that

$(b, a) \in R \cup R'$

since $(a, b) \in R \cup R'$

$\Rightarrow$ $(a, b) \in R$ or $(a, b) \in R'$

$\Rightarrow$ $(b, a) \in R$ or $(b, a) \in R'$

[since R and R' are symmetric]

$\Rightarrow$ $(b, a) \in R \cup R'$

$\Rightarrow$ $R \cup R'$ is symmetric

[*T*] $R \cup R'$ is not transitive. For this we shall give an example.

let $A = \{a, b, c\}$

and $R = \{(a, a), (b, b), (a, b), (b, a) (c, c)\}$

$R' = \{(a, a) (b, b) (b, c) (c, b), (c, c)\}$

then R and R' are equivalence relations.

$R \cup R' = \{(a, b) (b, b), (a, b) (b, a) (b, c), (c, b) (c, c)\}$

$(a, b) \in R \cup R'$ and $(b, c) \in R \cup R'$

But $(a, c) \notin R \cup R'$

Thus $R \cup R'$ is not transitive.

Hence the relation $R \cup R'$ is not an equivalence relation.

Appendix 6

NUMBERS

Complex Numbers, Algebra of Complex Numbers

We denote complex number by z and is defined as $a + i\,b$ where a, b are real numbers.

and $$\sqrt{-1} = i$$

Rational powers of complex numbers

Let z is a complex number then we define

$$z^1 = z \qquad \text{and} \qquad z^n = z \cdot z^{n-1}$$

and $$z^m \cdot z^n = z^{m+n} \qquad (z^m)^n = z^{mn}$$

Problem 1. Let z_1 and z_2 are non-zero complex numbers then

$$(z_1\, z_2)^{-1} = z_2^{-1}\, z_1^{-1}$$

We have $(z_1\, z_2)\,(z_2^{-1}\, z_1^{-1}) = z_1\,(z_2\, z_2^{-1})\, z_1^{-1}$

$$(z_1\, z_2)^{-3} = z_2^{-1}\, z_1^{-1}$$

$$= z_1\,(1)\, z_1^{-1}$$

$$= z_1\, z_1^{-1} = 1 \qquad [z_1 \cdot z_1^{-1} = 1]$$

Thus $$(z_1\, z_2)^{-1} = z_2^{-1} \cdot z^{-1}$$ *(Proved)*

In general $(z_1\, z_2 \ldots z_n)^{-1} = z_1^{-1}\, z_2^{-1} \ldots z_n^{-1}$

Problem 2 Prove that $z \cdot \bar{z} = |z|^2$

where $$z = a + ib$$

Solution

$$z = a + ib \qquad |z| = \sqrt{a^2 + b^2}$$

$$\bar{z} = a - ib$$

Hence $$z\bar{z} = (a + ib)\,(a - ib)$$

$$= a^2 + b^2 = (\sqrt{a^2 + b^2})^2$$

$$z\bar{z} = |z^2|$$ *(Proved)*

Problem 3 Prove that $\frac{1}{z}=\frac{\bar{z}}{|z|^2}=\frac{\bar{z}}{z\cdot\bar{z}}$

where $z=a+ib$

Solution LHS$=\frac{1}{z}=\frac{\bar{z}}{z\cdot\bar{z}}$ [Multiplying the D^r and Ny^r b $y\bar{z}$]

$$\frac{1}{z}=\frac{\bar{z}}{|z|^2} \text{ because } z\cdot\bar{z}=|z|^2$$

Problem 4 If $a^2+b^2+c^2=1$, $b+ic=(1+a)z$ prove that

$$\frac{a+1b}{1+c}=\frac{1+iz}{1-iz}$$

where a, b, c are real nos. and z is a complex number.

Solution Let $z=x+iy$

Then $b+ic=(1+a)(x+iy)$

$$b+ic=(1+a)x+i(1+a)y$$

Equating the real and imaginary part we have

$$(1+a)x=b \quad\Rightarrow\quad x=\frac{b}{1+a}$$

$$(1+a)y=c \quad\Rightarrow\quad y=\frac{c}{1+a}$$

Again $\frac{a+ib}{1+c}=\frac{1+i(x+iy)}{1-j(x+iy)}=\frac{1+ix-y}{1-ix+y}=\frac{(1-y)+ix}{(1+y)-ix}$

$$=\frac{[(1-y)+ix]}{[(1+y)-ix]}\times\frac{[(1+y)+ix]}{[(1+y)+ix]}$$

$$=\frac{[1-y)(1+y)-x^2+2ix]}{(1+y)^2+x^2}=\frac{(1-y^2-x^2)+2ix}{x^2+(1+y)^2}$$

$$\frac{a+ib}{1+c}=\frac{(1-x^2-y^2)}{x^2+(1+y)^2}+\frac{2ix}{x^2+(1+y)^2}$$

Equating real and imaginary parts on both holes we have

$$\frac{a}{1+c}=\frac{1-x^2-y^2}{x^2+(1+y)^2};\ \frac{b}{1+c}=\frac{2x}{x^2+(1+y)^2}$$

$$\frac{a}{b}=\frac{1-\left(\frac{b}{1+a}\right)^2-\left(\frac{c}{1+a}\right)^2}{\frac{2b}{1+a}}$$

$$\frac{a}{b} = \frac{(1+a)^2 - b^2 - c^2}{2b} \times \frac{(1+a)}{(1+a)^2}$$

$$\frac{a}{b} = \frac{(1+a)^2 - b^2 - c^2}{2b} \times \frac{1}{(1+a)}$$

$$2a(1+a) = 1 + a^2 + 2a - b^2 - c^2$$

$$2a + 2a^2 = 1 + a^2 + 2a - b^2 - c^2$$

$$a^2 + b^2 + c^2 = 1 \text{ which is given.}$$

Problem 5 A vareable complex number $z = x + i\,y$ is such that argument of the function $\frac{z-1}{z+1}$ is always equal to $\frac{\pi}{4}$ show that $x^2 + y^2 - 2y = 1$

Solution Let $\alpha = \frac{z-1}{z+1} = \frac{(x+iy)-1}{(x+iy)+1} = \frac{(x-1)+1y}{(x+1)+1y}$

$$= \frac{[(x-1)+iy]}{[(x+1)+iy]} \times \frac{[(x+1)+iy]}{[(x+1)-iy]}$$

$$\alpha = \frac{(x^2-1) - i(x-1)y + iy(x+1) + y^2}{(x+1)^2 + y^2}$$

$$\alpha = \frac{(x^2+y^2-1) - i[xy - y - yx - y]}{(x+1)^2 + y^2}$$

$$\alpha = \frac{(x^2+y^2-1) - i(-2y)}{(x+1)^2 + y^2}; \; \alpha = \frac{(x^2+y^2-1) + 2iy}{(x+1)^2 + y^2}$$

Since RHS is a complex number so

$$\alpha = r\cos\theta + ir\sin\theta$$

$$r\cos\theta + ir\sin\theta = \frac{(x^2+y^2-1) + 2iy}{(x-1)^2 + y^2}$$

Equating the real and imaginary parts we have

$$r\cos\theta = \frac{(x^2+y^2-1)}{(x-1)^2 + y^2} \qquad (1)$$

$$r\sin\theta = \frac{2y}{(x-1)^2 + y^2} \qquad (2)$$

$$\tan\theta = \frac{2y}{x^2+y^2-1}$$

Argument of (θ) $= \frac{\pi}{4}$ i.e $\theta = \frac{\pi}{4}$

$$\text{Tan}\ \frac{\pi}{4} = \frac{2y}{x^2 + y^2 - 1}$$

i.e.
$$1 = \frac{2y}{x^2 + y^2 - 1}$$

$$\Rightarrow \quad x^2 + y^2 - 1 = 2y$$

$$\Rightarrow x^2 + y^2 - 2y = 1$$

(Proved)

Problem 6 Modulus and argument of a complex number

Solution Let $z = x + iy$ *be any complcx no.*

$$x = r\cos\theta, y = r\sin\theta$$

$|z| = \sqrt{x^2 + y^2}$, $|z|$ *is the modulus of* z

$\theta = \tan^{-1}\dfrac{y}{x}$ is called the argument or amplitude of z and written as arg (z)

$$|z| = 0$$

$$\Leftrightarrow x = 0, y = 0$$

Argument of a complex no. is not unique, since if θ be a value of the argument so also $2n\pi + \theta$ where $n = 0, \pm 1, \pm 2, \ldots$

The argument satisfying the inequality $-\pi < \theta < \pi$ is called the principle value of the argument.

Argument (0) is not defined.

Complex Conjugate

$$z = x + iy$$

$\bar{z} = x - 1y$ is known as complex conjugate.

Problem 7 Prove that

$$\text{Arg}\ z + \arg \bar{z} = 2n\pi$$

where n is an integer or *zero*.

Solution
$$z = x + iy$$
$$\bar{z} = x - iy$$

$$\begin{aligned}\text{Arg}\ z + \arg\bar{z} &= \arg z\bar{z}\\ &= \arg(x + iy)(x - iy)\\ &= \arg(x^2 + y^2) = \arg a\end{aligned}$$

$x^2 + y^2 = a$ is a +ve and real

Let $\qquad a = r\cos\theta, \qquad 0 = r\sin\theta \qquad \theta = 0$

$\Rightarrow \qquad \cos\theta = 1$

$\Rightarrow \qquad r = a$

$\cos\theta = 1, \sin\theta = 0$

$\Rightarrow$ The general value of $\theta = 2n\pi$

where n is an *integer*.

Problem 8 Find the loci of the points z satisfying the condition

$$\text{Arg}\left(\frac{z-1}{z+1}\right) = \frac{\pi}{3}$$

Solution
$$\frac{z-1}{z+1} = \frac{(x-1)+iy}{(x+1)+iy}$$

$$= \frac{[(x-1\{+iy]}{(x+1)+iy]} \times \frac{[(x+1)-iy]}{[(x+1)-iy]}$$

$$= \frac{(x^2+y^2-1)+2iy}{(x+1)^2+y^2}$$

$$= \frac{(x^2+y^2-1)}{(x+1)^2+y^2} + i\,\frac{2y}{(x+1)^2+y^2}$$

$$\arg\frac{z-1}{z+1} = \tan^{-1}\frac{2y}{(x^2+y^2-1)}$$

$$\tan^{-1}\frac{2y}{(x^2+y^2-1)} = \frac{\pi}{3}$$

$$\frac{2y}{(x^2+y^2-1)} = \tan\frac{\pi}{3}$$

$$\frac{2y}{(x^2+y^2-1)} = \sqrt{3}$$

$$(x^2+y^2-1) = \frac{2}{\sqrt{3}}\,y$$

$$x^2+y^2-\frac{2}{\sqrt{3}}\,y-1 = 0$$

Which is equation of a *circle*.

Problem 9 Prove that $\left|\frac{a-b}{1-\bar{a}b}\right| < 1$ if $|a| < 1|$ and $|b| < 1$

Solution
$$\left|\frac{a-b}{1-\bar{a}b}\right| < 1$$

$$\Rightarrow \qquad |a-b| < |1-\bar{a}b|$$

$$\Rightarrow \quad |a-b|^2 < |1-\bar{a}b|^2$$

$$\Rightarrow \quad (a-b)(\bar{a}-\bar{b}) < (1-\bar{a}b)(1-a\bar{b})$$

$$\Rightarrow \quad a\bar{a}-a\bar{b}-b\bar{a}+b\bar{b} < 1-\bar{a}b-a\bar{b}+a\bar{a}\,b\bar{b}$$

$$\Rightarrow \quad |a|^2+|b|^2 < 1+|a|^2|b|^2$$

$$\Rightarrow \quad (|a|^2-1)-|b|^2(|a|^2-1) < 0$$

$$\Rightarrow \quad (|a|^2-1)(1-|b|^2) < 0$$

The inequality will held if

$$|a| < 1, \ |b| < 1$$

Problem 10 If $z_1, z_2 \ldots \quad z_n$ are complex numbers such that

$$|z_1| = |z_2| = |z_3| = \ldots |z_n| = 1$$

Then prove that $|z_1+z_2+\ldots+z_n|$

$$= \left|\frac{1}{z_1}+\frac{1}{z_2}+\ldots+\frac{1}{z_n}\right|$$

Solution We have

$$|z_n| = 1$$

$$\Rightarrow \quad |z_n|^2 = 1$$

$$\Rightarrow \quad z_n\bar{z}_n = 1 \qquad \text{for } n = 1, 2, \ldots n$$

$$\Rightarrow \quad \bar{z}_n = \frac{1}{z_n}$$

Now $\quad |z_1+z_2+\ldots+z_n|$

$$= |\overline{(z_1+z_2+\ldots\bar{z}_n}|$$

$$= |\bar{z}_1+\bar{z}_2+\ldots+\bar{z}_n|$$

$$= \left|\frac{1}{z_1}+\frac{1}{z_2}+\ldots+\frac{1}{z_n}\right|$$

$$= \left|\frac{1}{z_1}+\frac{1}{z_2}+\ldots+\frac{1}{z_n}\right| \text{(RHS)} \qquad \textit{[Proved]}$$

Probleml 1 The region of the z plane for which $\left|\frac{z-a}{z+\bar{a}}\right| = 1$ (Re $a \neq 0$) is y axis.

We have $\quad \left|\frac{z-a}{z+\bar{a}}\right| = 1$

$$\Rightarrow \quad |z-a| = |z+\bar{a}|$$

Squaring both sides we have

$$|z-a|^2 = |z+\bar{a}|^2$$

$$\Rightarrow \quad (z-a)(\bar{z}-\bar{a}) = (z+\bar{a})(\bar{z}+a)$$

$$\Rightarrow \quad (z\bar{z}-\bar{a}z-a\bar{z}+a\bar{a}) = (z\bar{z}+az+\bar{a}\bar{z}+a\bar{a})$$

$$\Rightarrow \quad az+\bar{a}\bar{z}+a\bar{z}+a\bar{z} = 0$$

$$\Rightarrow \quad z(a+\bar{a})+\bar{z}(a+\bar{a}) = 0$$

$$\Rightarrow \quad (z+\bar{z})(a+\bar{a}) = 0 \tag{1}$$

Now $\quad (a+\bar{a}) = 2 \text{ Re } a$

Since $\quad \text{Re } a \neq 0$

$$\Rightarrow \quad 2 \text{ Re }(a) \neq 0$$

$$\Rightarrow \quad a+\bar{a} \neq 0$$

Thus the inequality of (1) will give the result

$$z+\bar{z} = 0$$

$$\Rightarrow \quad x+iy+x-iy = 0$$

$$\Rightarrow \quad 2x = 0$$

$$\Rightarrow \quad x = 0$$

Which is the equation of y axis

Problem 12 The one and only one case in which

$$|z_1|+|z_2|+\ldots+|z_n| = |z_1,+z_2+\ldots+z_n|$$

Solution In that in which the numbers $z_1, z_2, z_3 \ldots z_n$ have all the same *amplitude.*

$$\Rightarrow \text{ Let } \quad z_k = r_k(\cos\theta_k + i\sin\theta_k),\ k = 1, 2 \ldots n$$

$$\Rightarrow \quad z_k = r_k e^{i\theta k}$$

$$\Rightarrow \quad |z_k| = r_k\,|e^{1\theta k}|$$

$$\Rightarrow \quad |z_k| = r_k \quad \text{for } k = 1, 2 \ldots n$$

$$\Rightarrow \quad |z_1| = r_1$$

$$|z_2| = r_2 \quad \ldots |z_n| = r_n$$

Let $\quad |z_1+z_2| = |(r_1 \text{ eos } \theta_1 + ir_1\sin\theta_1) + (r_2\cos\theta_2 + i\,r_2\sin\theta_2)|$

$$= |(r_1\cos\theta_1 + r_2\cos\theta_2) + i(r_1\sin\theta_1 + r_2\sin\theta_2)|$$

$$= \sqrt{(r_1\cos\theta_1 + r_2\cos\theta_2)^2 + (r_1\sin\theta_1 + r_2\sin\theta_2)^2}$$

$$= \sqrt{r_1^2 \cos^2 \theta_1 + r_2^2 \cos^2 \theta_2 + 2r_1 r_2 \cos \theta_1 \cos \theta_2 + r_1^2 \sin^2 \theta_1 + r_2^2 \sin^2 \theta_2 + 2r_1 r_2 \sin \theta_1 \sin \theta_2}$$

$$= \sqrt{r_1^2 + r_2^2 + 2r_1 r_2 (\cos \theta_1 \cos \theta_2 + \sin \theta_1 \sin \theta_2)}$$

$$= \sqrt{r_1^2 + r_2^2 + 2r_1 r_2 \{\cos (\theta_1 - \theta_2)\}}$$

$$= \sqrt{r_1^2 + r_2^2 + 2r_1 r_2}$$

$$= \sqrt{(r_1 + r_2)^2} \quad \text{if} \quad \cos (\theta_1 - \theta_2) = 1$$

$$= r_1 + r_2 \quad \text{i.e. if} \quad (\theta_1 - \theta_2) = 0$$

$$= | z_1 | + | z_2 | \quad \text{i.e. if} \quad \theta_1 = \theta_2$$

i.e. $| z_1 + z_2 | = | z_1 | + | z_2 |$

Similarly $| z_1 + z_2 + z_3 | = [r_1^2 + r_2^2 + r_3^2 + 2r_1 r_2 + 2r_2 r_3 + 2r_1 r_3]^{1/2}$

if $\theta_1 = \theta_2 = \theta_3$

Thus $| z_1 + z_2 + z_3 | = [(r_1 + r_2 + r_3)^2]^{1/2}$

$$= r_1 + r_2 + r_3 = | z_1 | + | z_3 | + | z_3 | \text{ etc.}$$

Thus $| z_1 + z_2 + \ldots + z_n | = | z_1 | + | z_2 | + \ldots + | z_n |$

If and only if $\theta_1 = \theta_2 = \theta_3 = \ldots = \theta_n$

i.e. when all of them have the same amplitude.

Problem 13 If $z = x + iy$ and $w = \dfrac{1-iz}{z-i}$; then $| w | = 1$ implies that, in the complex plane z lies on the real axis.

Solution

$$w = \frac{1-iz}{z-i}$$

$$w = \frac{1-i(x+iy)}{x+iy-i}$$

$$w = \frac{1-ix-i^2 y}{x+i(y-1)}$$

$$w = \frac{(1+y)-ix}{x+i(y-1)}$$

$$| \omega | = 1 \quad \Rightarrow \quad \left|\frac{1-iz}{z-i}\right| = 1$$

$$\Rightarrow \quad \left|\frac{1-iz}{z-i}\right| = 1$$

$$\Rightarrow \quad | 1-iz | = | z-i |$$

Squaring both sides we have

$$|1-iz|^2 = |z-i|^2$$

$$\Rightarrow \quad (1-iz)\overline{(1-iz)} = (z-i)\overline{(z-i)}$$

$$\Rightarrow \quad (1-iz)(1+i\bar{z}) = (z-i)(\bar{z}+i)$$

$$\Rightarrow \quad 1 + i\bar{z} - iz + z\bar{z} = z\bar{z} + iz - i\bar{z} + 1$$

$$\Rightarrow \quad + i\bar{z} - iz = iz - i\bar{z}$$

$$\Rightarrow \quad i\bar{z} - iz - iz + i\bar{z} = 0$$

$$\Rightarrow \quad i(\bar{z}-z) + i(\bar{z}-z) = 0$$

$$\Rightarrow \quad 2i(\bar{z}-z) = 0$$

$$\Rightarrow \quad 2i(z-\bar{z}) = 0$$

$$\Rightarrow \quad 2i(2iy) = 0$$

$$\Rightarrow \quad 4i^2 y = 0$$

$$\Rightarrow \quad -4y = 0$$

$$\Rightarrow \quad y = 0$$

which is the equation of real axis.

Problem 14 If z is a complex number then prove that

$$(z^{-1}) = (\bar{z})^{-1}$$

Solution Since z is a complex number so let

$$z = x + iy$$

Then $$\overline{z^{-1}} = \frac{1}{x+iy} = \frac{x-iy}{x^2+y^2}$$

$$z^{-1} = \frac{x+iy}{x^2+y^2} \tag{1}$$

Again $$\bar{z} = x - iy$$

$$(\bar{z})^{-1}) = \frac{1}{x-iy} = \frac{x+iy}{(x-iy)(x+iy)}$$

$$(\bar{z})^{-1} = \frac{x+iy}{x^2+y^2} \tag{2}$$

From equation (1) and (2) we have

$$\overline{(z^{-1})} = (\bar{z})^{-1}$$ *(Proved)*

Problem 15 For any two non-zero complex nos z_1, z_2 prove the inequality.

$$(|z_1| + |z_2|)\left|\frac{z_1}{|z_1|} + \frac{z_2}{|z_2|}\right| \leqslant 2(|z_1| + |z_2|)$$

Solutiou L.H.S. $(|z_1| + |z_2|)\left|\frac{z_1}{|z_1|} + \frac{z_2}{|z_2|}\right|$

$$\leqslant (|z_1| + |z_2|)\left[\left|\frac{z_1}{|z_1|}\right| + \left|\frac{z_2}{|z_2|}\right|\right]$$

$$= (|z_1| + |z_2|)\left[\frac{|z_1|}{|z_1|} + \frac{|z_2|}{|z_2|}\right]$$

$$= (|z_1| + |z_2|)(1 + 1)$$

$$= 2(|z_1| + |z_2|)$$

Thus $(|z_1| + |z_2|\left|\frac{z_1}{|z_1|} + \frac{z_2}{|z_2|}\right| \leqslant 2(|z_1| + |z_2|)$ *(Proved)*

Appendix 7

DIFFERENTIAL EQUATION

Problem 1 Suppose that ammount 'a' and 'b' respectively of two substances are involved in a chemical reaction in which the velocity of transformation $\frac{dx}{dt}$ is proportional to the product $(a-x)(b-x)$. Find 't' in terms of x if $a = 0.6$, $b = 0.4$ and $x = 0.2$ when $t = 300$ seconds.

Solution $$\frac{dx}{dt} = k\,(a-x)(b-x)$$

$$kdt = \frac{dx}{(a-x)(b-x)}$$

$$kdt = \left[\frac{1}{a-x} - \frac{1}{b-x}\right]\frac{1}{(b-a)}\,dx$$

Integrating $$kt = \frac{1}{(b-a)}\,[-\log(a-x) + \log(b-x)] - c$$

$$(kt + c)(b-a) = \log\frac{b-x}{a-x}$$

$$a = .6,\ b = -.4$$

and $$x = .2 \text{ when } t = 300 \text{ second}$$

$$(k\cdot 300 + c)(.4-.6) = \log\frac{.4-.2}{.6-.2}$$

$$(c + 300\,k)(-.2) = \log\frac{.2}{.4} = \log\frac{1}{2}$$

$$(c + 300\,k) \times .2 = \log 2$$

$$c = 5\log 2 - 300\,k$$

$\therefore$ The required solution is

$$(kt + 5\log 2 - 300\,k)(b-a) = \log\frac{b-x}{a-x}$$

$$\therefore \quad kt = \frac{1}{(b-a}\log\frac{b-x}{a-x} + 300\,k - 5\log 2$$

Problem 2 The population of a country increases at a rate proportional to the number of inhabitants. If the population doubles in 30 years, in how many years will it triple.

Solution $\Rightarrow$ x = population in t years

By question $\dfrac{dx}{dt} = kx$ $[k = constant]$

$$\frac{dx}{x} = kdt$$

Integrating $\log x = kt + \log c$

$$\log \frac{x}{c} = kt$$

$$\frac{x}{c} = e^{kt}$$

$$x = ce^{kt}$$

Let $x = x_0$ when $t = 0$

$$c = x_0$$

$\therefore$ $x = x_0 e^{kt}$

when $x = 2x_0$ $t = 30$

$$2x_0 = x_0 e^{30k}$$

$$2 = e^{30k} \qquad (1)$$

when $x = 3x_0$ let $t = T$

$$3x_0 = x_0 e^{Tk}$$

$$3 = e^{Tk} \qquad (2)$$

From (1) $.30k = \log_e 2$ (3)

From (2) $Tk = \log_e 3$

Diving (4) by (3) we have

$$\frac{T}{30} = \frac{\log_e 3}{\log_e 2}$$

$$T = 30 \times \frac{\log_e 3}{\log_e 2}$$

$$T = 47.5 \text{ years}$$

i.e. $T = 48$ years **nearly**

Simple pendulum

Arc $\quad AP = S$

$l =$ length of the pendulum

$S = l\,\theta$

$m =$ mass of the particle suspended

$S =$ displacement

$\frac{ds}{dt} =$ velocity

$\frac{d^2 s}{d^{12}} =$ acceleration directed towards the mean position

$$m \cdot \frac{d^2 s}{dt^2} = -mg \sin \theta$$

$$\frac{d^2 s}{dt^2} = -g \sin \theta$$

If θ be small, then $\sin \theta = \theta$

$$\frac{d^2 s}{dt^2} = -g\theta$$

$$\frac{d^2 s}{dt^2} = -g \frac{s}{l}$$

$$\frac{d^2 s}{dt^2} = -\frac{g}{l} s \qquad \frac{g}{l} = \text{constant} = w^2$$

$$\frac{d^2 s}{dt^2} = -ws^2$$

which is equation of a simple *Harmonic motion.*

$$w^2 = \frac{g}{l}$$

$$w = \sqrt{\frac{g}{l}}$$

$$w = \frac{2\pi}{T} \qquad \text{where} \quad T = \text{time period}$$

$$\frac{2\pi}{T} = \sqrt{\frac{g}{l}}$$

$$T = 2\pi \sqrt{\frac{l}{g}}$$

$$\text{Frequency } n = \frac{1}{T}$$

$$n = \frac{1}{2\pi}\sqrt{\frac{g}{l}}$$

Simple Harmonic motion:

Problem 3 A horizontal shelf is moved up and down with SHM of period $\frac{1}{2}$ sec. What is the greatest amplitude admissible in order that a weight placed on the shelf may not beferked off.

Solution In the case of SHM. The equation of motion is

$$\frac{d^2 x}{dt^2} = -w^2 x$$

Let a be the greatest amplitude then the maximum acceleration $= w^2 a$.

Hence the period $T = \frac{1}{2}$ second

$$T = \frac{2\pi}{w}$$

$$\frac{1}{2} = \frac{2\pi}{w}$$

$$w = 4\pi$$

$$w^2 = 16\,\pi^2$$

The weight placed on the shelf will not be jerked off if the aeceleration of the SHM is less than g or equal to g at the most.

i.e. $$w^2 a = g$$

i.e. $$16\,\pi^2 a = g$$

$$a = \frac{g}{16\pi^2}$$

Problem 4 A particle starts with a velocity V and moves under a retardation equal to k times the space described. Prove that the space transversed before it comes to the rest is equal to $\frac{V}{\sqrt{k}}$.

Solution According to question

$$\frac{d^2 x}{dt^2} = -kx$$

$$v\frac{dv}{dx} = -kx$$

$$vdv = -kx\,dx$$

Integrating both sides we have

$$\frac{v^2}{2} = -k\frac{x^2}{2} + C$$

Since the particle starts with a given velocity V therefore at O, $x=0$ $v=V$

$$\text{so } \frac{V^2}{2} = -k.0 + C$$

$$C = \frac{V^2}{2}$$

$$\frac{v^2}{2} = -k\frac{x^2}{2} + \frac{V^2}{2}$$

$$\frac{V^2}{2} - \frac{v^2}{2} = k\frac{x^2}{2}$$

$$k\frac{x^2}{2} = \frac{V - v^2}{2}$$

when the particle comes at rest then $v = 0$

$$k\frac{x^2}{2} = \frac{V^2 - 0}{2} \qquad \frac{x^2}{2} = \frac{V^2}{2k}$$

$$\Rightarrow \qquad x^2 = \frac{V^2}{k} \qquad \Rightarrow \qquad x = \frac{V}{\sqrt{k}}$$

Hence the required distance is given by $x = \dfrac{V}{\sqrt{k}}$

Problem 5 Show that the particle executing SHM requires one Sixth of its period to prove from the position of maximum displacement to one in which the displaced is half the amplitude.

$\Rightarrow$ equation of rhe SHM is

$$\frac{d^2x}{dt^2} = -\omega^2 x \tag{1}$$

were $\qquad T = \dfrac{2\pi}{\omega}$

Equation (1) can be written as

$$\frac{d^2x}{dt} = -\omega^2 x \qquad \frac{d}{dt}\left(\frac{dx}{dt}\right) = -\omega^2 x$$

$$v\frac{dv}{dx} = -\omega^2 x \qquad v\,dv = -\omega^2 x\,dx$$

Integrating both sides we have

$$\frac{v^2}{2} = -\omega^2 \frac{x^2}{2} + C$$

$$v = 0 \quad \text{when} \quad x = a \text{ amplitude}$$

$$\frac{0^2}{2} = -\omega^2 \frac{a^2}{2} + C$$

$$\Rightarrow \quad C = \omega^2 \frac{a^2}{2}$$

Thus

$$\frac{v^2}{2} = -\omega^2 \frac{x^2}{2} + \omega^2 \frac{a^2}{2}$$

$$\frac{v^2}{2} = \frac{\omega^2 (a^2 - x^2)}{2}$$

$$v = \pm \omega \sqrt{a^2 - x^2}$$

$$v = -\omega \sqrt{a^2 - x^2} \quad \text{(taking −ve sign)}$$

$$\frac{dx}{dt} = -\omega \sqrt{a^2 - x^2}$$

$$\frac{dx}{dt} = -\omega \sqrt{a^2 - x^2}$$

If t be the time from maximum displacement a to $\frac{a}{2}$ we have

$$\int_0^t dt = \frac{1}{\omega} \int_a^{a/2} - \frac{dx}{\sqrt{a^2 - x^2}}$$

$$\Big[t\Big]_0^t = \frac{1}{\omega}\left[\cos^{-1} \frac{x}{a}\right]_a^{a/2}$$

$$t = \frac{1}{\omega}\left[\cos^{-1} \frac{1}{2} - \cos^{-1} 1\right]$$

$$t = \frac{1}{\omega}\left[\frac{\pi}{3} - 0\right] \qquad t = \frac{\pi}{3\omega}$$

we have

$$T = \frac{2\pi}{\omega} \qquad \Rightarrow \qquad \omega = \frac{2\pi}{T}$$

$$t = \frac{\pi}{3 \,.\, \omega} = \frac{\pi}{3 \,.\, \frac{2\pi}{T}} = \frac{T}{6}$$

$$t = \frac{T}{6}$$

(Proved)

oblem 6 Solve $l\left(\frac{d^2\theta}{dt^2}\right)+g\theta=0$, given that $\theta=\theta_0$ and $\frac{d\theta}{dt}=0$ ıen $t=0$

$$\Rightarrow \qquad l\left(\frac{d^2\theta}{dt^2}\right)+g\,\theta=0$$

ıe given equation can be writtenas

$$\left[D^2+\left(\frac{g}{l}\right)\right]\theta=0 \qquad D\equiv\frac{d}{dt}$$

ıe auxiliary equation is

$$m^2+\frac{g}{l}=0 \qquad m^2=-\frac{g}{l}$$

$$\Rightarrow \qquad m=\pm\sqrt{\frac{g}{l}};$$

ıe solution of the given differential equation is

$$\theta=\cos c_1\sqrt{\frac{g}{l}}\,t$$

ıen $t=0$, $\theta=\theta_0$ $\frac{d\theta}{dt}=0$ (given)

$$\theta_0=c_1\cos\sqrt{\frac{g}{t}}\,.\,0$$

$$\theta_0=c_1\,.\cos 0 \qquad \theta_0=c_1$$

$$\theta=\theta_0\cos\left(\sqrt{\frac{g}{l}}\,t\right)$$

rticle 7. Fnd the solution of

$$\frac{d^2 i}{dt^2}+\frac{R\,di}{L\,dt}+\frac{i}{Lc}=0$$

ıere $R^2C=4L$ and R, C, L are constant.

The auxiliary equation can be writers

$$\left[D^2+\left(\frac{R}{L}\right)D+\frac{1}{LC}\right)=0$$

$$D\equiv\frac{d}{dt}\equiv m$$

$$m^2+\frac{R}{L}m+\frac{1}{LC}=0$$

$$m^2 + am + b = 0$$

where $$a = \frac{R}{L}, \quad b = \frac{1}{LC}$$

$$\Rightarrow \quad m = \frac{-a \pm \sqrt{a^2 - 4b}}{2}$$

$$\Rightarrow \quad m = \frac{1}{2}\left[-a \pm \sqrt{a^2 - 4b}\right]$$

$$\Rightarrow \quad m = -\frac{1}{2}\left(\frac{R}{L}\right) \pm \frac{1}{2}\sqrt{\frac{R^2}{L^2} - \frac{4}{LC}}$$

$$\Rightarrow \quad m = -\frac{1}{2}\left(\frac{R}{L}\right) \pm \frac{1}{2}\sqrt{\frac{R^2 C - 4L}{L^2 C}}$$

$$\Rightarrow \quad m = -\frac{L}{2L} \pm 0$$

$$\Rightarrow \quad m = -\frac{R}{2L} \pm 0$$

or $$m = -\frac{R}{2L} \text{ twicc}$$

$\therefore$ The required solution is

$$i = (C_1 + C_2 t)\, e^{-R/2i\ t}$$

where C_1 and C_2 are arbitrary constants.

Appendix 8

SPHERE

roblem 9 Two spheres of radi r_1 and r_2 cut orthogonally. **Prove that** e radius of the common circle is

$$\frac{r_1 r_2}{\sqrt{r_1^2 + r_2^2}}$$

olution Let the equation of the common circle be

$$x^2 + y^2 = a^2, \qquad z = 0 \tag{1}$$

radius is evidently a and we have to evaluate it.

t the equation of the two given sphere through its circle be

$$(x^2 + y^2 - a^2) + 2\lambda z + z^2 = 0 \tag{2}$$

d

$$(x^2 + y^2 - a^2) + 2\mu z + z^2 = 0 \tag{3}$$

ere an extraterm z^2 has been introduced in each equation so that it may present a sphre]

dius of the sphere (2)

$$\sqrt{(-\lambda)^2 - (-a^2)} = \sqrt{\lambda^2 + a^2} = r_1$$

milarly redius of the sphere (3), is given by

$$\sqrt{(-\mu)^2 - (-a^2)} = \sqrt{\mu^2 + a^2} = r_2$$

the sphere (2) and (3) cut each other orthogonally so we have

$$2\lambda\mu = (-a^2) + (-a^2)$$

$$2\lambda\mu = -2a^2$$

uaring both sides

$$4\lambda^2 \mu^2 = 4a^4$$

$$\Rightarrow \quad \lambda^2 \mu^2 = a^4 \quad \Rightarrow \quad (r_1^2 - a^2)(r_2^2 - a^2) = a^4$$

$$\Rightarrow \quad r_1^2 r_2^2 - a^2 (r_1^2 + r_2^2) + a^4 = a^4$$

$$\Rightarrow \quad r_1^2 r_2^2 - a^2 (r_1^2 + r_2^2) = 0$$

$$\Rightarrow \quad a^2 = \frac{r_1^2 r_2^2}{r_1^2 + r_2^2} \quad \Rightarrow \frac{r_1 + r_2}{\sqrt{r_1^2 + r_2^2}} = a$$

Problem 2 Let d be the distance between the centres of two spheres radii r_1 and r_2. Prove that the angle between them is

$$\cos^{-1}\left[\frac{(r_1^2 + r_2^2 - d^2)}{2r_1\ r_2}\right]$$

Solution Let $C_1, C_2 \rightarrow$ centres of the spheres.

$P =$ point of intersection. The angle between the spheres is the an between the radii $c_1\,p$ and $c_2\,p$ in $\Delta\ c_1\,pc_2$

$$c_1\,p = r_1 \qquad c_2\,p = r_2$$

$$c_1\,c_2 = d$$

Let $\theta =$ required angle then

$$\cos\theta = \cos < C_1\,p\,C_2$$

$$= \frac{C_1\,p^2 + C_2\,p^2 - C_1\,C_2^2}{2\ C_1\,p\,.\,C_2\,p}$$

$$\cos\theta = \frac{r_1^2 + r_2^2 - d^2}{2r_1\,r_2}$$

$$\Rightarrow \qquad \theta = \cos^{-1}\left(\frac{r_1^2 + r_2^2 - d^2}{2\,r_1\,r_2}\right)$$

(*Prove*

Problem 3 A sphere of constant radius r passes through region and c the axis in A, B, C. Find the locus of the foot of the perpendicular fr 0 to the plane A, B, C.

Solution Let A, B and C be $(a, 0, 0)$, $(0, b, 0)$ and $(0, 0, C)$

Then the equation through $0, A, B, C$ is

$$x^2 + y^2 + z^2 - ax - by - cz = 0$$

then since r is the radius so

$$r^2 = \left(\frac{a}{2}\right)^2 + \left(\frac{b}{2}\right)^2 + \left(\frac{c}{2}\right)^2$$

$$4r^2 = a^2 + b^2 + c^2$$

Equation of the plane is

$$\frac{x}{a} + \frac{y}{b} + \frac{z}{c} = 1$$

i.e. the direction cosines of the Normal to the plane is

$$\frac{1}{a}, \frac{1}{b}, \frac{1}{c}$$

The equation of the line through 0 (0, 0, 0) and perpendicular to the plane 2) is

$$\frac{x-0}{1/a} = \frac{y-0}{1/b} = \frac{z-0}{1/c}$$

any point on this line is

$$\left(\frac{k}{a}, \frac{k}{b}, \frac{k}{c}\right)$$

If it is the foot (x_1, y_1, z_1) of the prependicular then

$$x_1 = \frac{k}{a}, \quad y_1 = \frac{k}{b}, \quad z_1 = \frac{k}{c}$$

$$a = \frac{k}{x_1} \; b = \frac{k}{y_1}, \; c = \frac{k}{z_1}$$

so we have

$$4r^2 = k^2 x_1^{-2} + k^2 y_1^{-1} + k^2 z_1^{-2}$$

$$4r^2 = k^2 (x_1^{-2} + y_1^{-2} + z_1^{-2}) \qquad (2)$$

we have

$$\frac{x}{1/a} = \frac{y}{1/b} = \frac{z}{1/c} = k$$

$$\frac{x^2}{x/a} = \frac{y^2}{y/b} = \frac{z^2}{z/c} = k$$

$$\frac{x^2 + y^2 + a^2}{x/a + y/b + z/c} = \frac{x^2 + y^2 + z^2}{1}$$

$$\Rightarrow \qquad k = x^2 + y^2 + z^2$$

so the locus of (x_1, y_1, z_1) is given by replacing (x_1, y_1, z_1) by (x, y, z)

$$4r^2 = k^2 (x_1^{-1} + y_1^{-2} + z_1^{-2})$$

$$4r^2 = k^2 (x^{-2} + y^{-2} - z^{-2})$$

$$4r^2 = (x^2 + y^2 + z^2)^2 (x^{-2} + y^{-2} + z^{-2})$$

Appendix 9

INTEGRAL CALCULUS

Problem 1 Evaluate $\int_{c}^{\infty} e-x^2\, dx$

Let $$I = \int_0^{\infty} e-x^2\, dx$$

Putting ax for x we get

$$I = \int_0^{\infty} e-a^2\, x^2\, adx$$

$$I\, e^{-a2} = \int_0^{\infty} e-a^2-a^2\, x^2\, adx$$

$$I\, e^{-a2} = \int_0^{\infty} e-a^2\, {}^{(1+x^2)}\, adx$$

$$I \int_{()}^{\infty} e^{-a2}\, da = \int_0^{\infty} \left\{ \int_0^{\infty} e-a^{2(1+x^2)}\, ada \right\} dx$$

$$I \int_0^{\infty} e^{-a2}\, da = \int_0^{\infty} \left[-\frac{1}{2}\, \frac{e-a^{2(1+x^2)}}{(1+x^2)} \right]_0^{\infty} dx$$

Put $a^2\,(1 + x^2) = t;\ 2a\ 1 + x^2)\, da = dt:\ ada = \dfrac{dt}{2\,(1 + x^2)}$

$$I \int_0^{\infty} e^{-2a}\, da = \int_0^{\infty} \left[-\frac{1}{2}\, \frac{e^{-a^2\,(1+x^2)}}{(1+x^2)} \right]_0^{\infty} dx$$

$$I = \int_0^{\infty} \frac{1}{2}\, \frac{dx}{1 + x^2}$$

$$I^2 = \int_0^{\infty} \frac{dx}{1 + x^2}$$

$$I^2 = \frac{1}{2} \left[\tan^{-1} x \right]_0^{\infty}$$

$$I^2 = \frac{1}{2}\left[\tan^{-1}\infty - \tan^{-1} 0\right]$$

$$I^2 = \frac{1}{2} \cdot \frac{\pi}{2} = \frac{\pi}{4}$$

$$I = \frac{\sqrt{\pi}}{2}$$

Problem 2 $\displaystyle\int_0^{\pi/2} \sin x \log(\sin x)\, dx$

Let $\displaystyle I = \int_0^{\pi/2} \sin x \log(\sin x)\, dx$

$$I = \int_0^{\pi/2} \sin x \log\sqrt{1-\cos^2 x}\, dx$$

Let $\cos x = \theta$

$\Rightarrow \quad -\sin x\, dx = d\theta$

$\Rightarrow \quad \sin x\, dx = -d\theta$

$$I = \int_1^0 -\log\sqrt{1-\theta^2}\, d\theta$$

$$I = -\int_1^0 \log(1-\theta^2)^{1/2}\, d\theta$$

$$I = \frac{1}{2}\int_0^1 \log(1-\theta^2)\, d\theta$$

$$I = \frac{1}{2}\int_0^1 \left[-\theta^2 - \frac{(\theta^2)^2}{2} - \frac{(\theta^2)^3}{3} - \frac{(\theta^2)^4}{4} \ldots\right] d\theta$$

$$I = -\frac{1}{2}\left[\frac{\theta^3}{1.3} + \frac{\theta^5}{2.5} + \frac{\theta^7}{3.7} + \ldots \text{ to } \infty\right]$$

$$= -\left[\frac{1}{2.3} + \frac{1}{4.5} + \frac{1}{6.7} + \ldots \text{ to } \infty\right]$$

$$= -\left[\left(\frac{1}{2} - \frac{1}{3}\right) + \left(\frac{1}{4} - \frac{1}{5}\right) + \ldots \text{ to } \infty\right]$$

$$= -\frac{1}{2} + \frac{1}{3} = \frac{1}{4} + \frac{1}{5} - \ldots \text{ to } \infty$$

$$= \left(1 - \frac{1}{2} + \frac{1}{3} - \frac{1}{4} + \frac{1}{5} - \ldots \text{ to } \infty\right) - 1$$

$$= \log 2 - 1 = \log 2 - \log e = \log\left(\frac{2}{e}\right)$$

Problem 3 Evaluate $\int_0^{\pi/2} \cos x \log(\cos x)\, dx$

$$\int_0^{\pi/2} \frac{\cos x}{\sin x} \log(\cos x)\, dx$$

$$\int_0^{\pi/2} \frac{\cos x}{\sin x} \log \sqrt{1-\sin^2 x}\, dx$$

Solution Let $\sin x = \theta$

$$\cos x\, dx = d\theta$$

$$\int_0^1 \frac{\log \sqrt{1-\theta^2}}{\theta}\, d\theta$$

$$\frac{1}{2}\int_0^1 \frac{\log(1-\theta^2)}{\theta}\, d\theta$$

$$= \frac{1}{2}\int_0^1 \frac{1}{\theta}\left[-\theta^2 - \frac{(\theta^2)^2}{2} - \frac{(\theta^2)^3}{3} - \ldots \text{ to } \infty\right] d\theta$$

$$= -\frac{1}{2}\int_0^1 \left(\theta + \frac{\theta^3}{2} + \frac{\theta^5}{3} + \ldots \text{ to } \infty\right) d\theta$$

$$= = \frac{1}{2}\left[\frac{\theta^2}{2} + \frac{\theta^4}{8} + \frac{\theta^6}{18} + \ldots\right]_0^1$$

$$= -\frac{1}{2}\left[\frac{1}{2} + \frac{1}{8} + \frac{1}{16} + \ldots\right]$$

$$= -\left[\frac{1}{2^2} + \frac{1}{4^2} + \frac{1}{6^2} + \ldots\right]$$

$$= -\frac{\pi^2}{24} \qquad \textbf{Ans.}$$

Problem 4 Evaluate $\int_a^b e^x\, dx$ using the method of definite integral as the limit *of sum.*

Solution we have

$$\int_a^b f(x)\, dx = \lim_{h \to 0} h\,[f(a) + f(a+h) + \ldots + f\{a + (n-1)h\}]$$

where $\quad nh = b - a$

Here $\quad f(x) = e^x$

$$\Rightarrow \quad f(a) = e^a$$

$$f(a+h) = e^{a+h}$$

$$f(a+2h) = e^{a+2h}$$

$$\int_0^b e^x\,dx = \lim_{h\to 0} he^a\,[1 + e^h + e^{2h} + \ldots + e^{(n+1)h}]$$

$$= \lim_{h\to 0} he^a \left[\frac{e^{nh}-1}{e^h-1}\right]$$

$$= \lim_{h\to 0} \left(\frac{h}{e^h-1}\right) e^a\,(e^{nh}-1)$$

$\therefore\ nh = b-a$

$$= \lim_{h\to 0} \left(\frac{h}{e^h-1}\right) e^a\,(e^{b-a}-1)$$

$$= \lim_{h\to 0} \frac{h}{\left[(1+h+\frac{h^2}{2!}+\frac{h^3}{3!}+\ldots)-1\right]}\, e^a\,(e^{b-a}-1)$$

$$= \lim_{h\to 0} \frac{h}{h\left(1+\frac{h}{2!}+\frac{h^2}{3!}+\ldots,\right)}\, e^a\,(e^{b-a}-1)$$

$$= \lim_{h\to 0} \frac{1}{\left(1+\frac{h}{2!}+\frac{h^2}{3!}+\ \ldots\right)}\, e^a\,(e^{b-a}-1)$$

$$= e^a\,(e^{b-a}-1) = e^a \cdot e^{-a}\,(e^{b-a})$$

$${}_a^b\!\int e^x\,dx = e^b - e^a$$

Appendix 10

MISSLANEOUS PROBLEMS

Expectation

Problem 1 Find $E(x)$ if $f(x) = 30x^4 \ (1-x)$ when $0 \leqslant x \leqslant 1$ and zero elsewhere

Solution $E(x) = \int_{-\infty}^{\infty} x f(x)\, dx$

$$= \int_{-\infty}^{0} x\, 30x^4 (1-x)\, dx + \int_{0}^{1} x \cdot 30x^4 (1-x)\, dx$$

$$+ \int_{1}^{\infty} x\, 30x^4 (1-x)\, dx = \int_{0}^{1} x\, 30x^4 (1-x)\, dx$$

$$= 30 \int_{0}^{1} x^5 (1-x)\, dx = 30 \int_{0}^{1} (x^5 - x^6)\, dx$$

$$= 30 \left[\frac{x^6}{6} - \frac{x^7}{7}\right]_0^1 = 30 \left[\frac{1}{6} - \frac{1}{7}\right] = \frac{5}{7}$$

Problem 2 Let X and Y be two random variable such that $Y \leqslant X$ then

$$E(Y) \leqslant E(X)$$

Proved the expectation S exist.

Solution $Y \leqslant X$ we have the random

Vareable $Y - X \leqslant 0$

$\Rightarrow$ $X - Y \geqslant 0$

$\Rightarrow$ $E(X - Y) \geqslant 0$

$\Rightarrow$ $E(X) - E(Y) \geqslant 0$

$\Rightarrow$ $E(X) \geqslant E(Y)$

$\Rightarrow$ $E(Y) \leqslant E(X)$

Problem 3 **Acoin is tossed untill a head appears what is the no. of tosses required?**

Solution X = no. of tosses required to get the first head. X can materialise in the following ways:

Event	x	*Probability*
H	1	$\frac{1}{2}$
TH	2	$\frac{1}{2} \times \frac{1}{2} = \frac{1}{4}$
THH	3	$\frac{1}{2} \times \frac{1}{2} \times \frac{1}{2} = 1/8$

$$\therefore \qquad E(x) = \sum_{=x1}^{\infty} xp(x)$$

$$= 1 \times \tfrac{1}{2} + 2 \times \tfrac{1}{4} + 3 \times 1/8 + \ldots$$

Arithmetic-geometric series with ratio of GP being $\frac{1}{2}$

Let $$S = 1 \cdot \frac{1}{2} + 2 \cdot \frac{1}{4} + 3 \cdot \frac{1}{8} + 4 \cdot \frac{1}{16} + \ldots$$

$$\frac{1}{2} S = \frac{1}{4} + 2 \cdot \frac{1}{8} + 3 \cdot \frac{1}{16} + \ldots$$

Then subtracting we have

$$\frac{1}{2} S = \frac{1}{2} + \frac{1}{4} + \frac{1}{8} + 3 \cdot \frac{1}{16} + \ldots$$

$$\frac{1}{2} S = \frac{\frac{1}{2}}{1-(\frac{1}{2})} = 1$$

$$\Rightarrow \qquad S = 2$$

$$\Rightarrow \qquad E(X) = 2$$

Problem 3 Let x and y be independent non-degenerate variates. Prove that

$$\text{Var}(xy) = \text{var}(x) \cdot \text{var}(y)$$

if $$E(x) = 0, E(y) = 0$$

Solution $$\text{Var}(xy) = E(xy)^2 - [E(xy)]^2$$
$$= E(x^2 y^2) - [E(x) \cdot E(y)]^2$$
$$= E(x^2) \cdot E(y^2) - [E(x)]^2 [E(y)]^2$$

if $$E(x) = 0, E(y) = 0$$

var $$({}^{+}y) = E(x)^2 E(y^2)$$
$$= \text{var}(xy)$$
$$= [E(x)^2) - \{E(x)\}^2] [E(\text{ꞏ})^2 - \{E(y)^2]\}$$
$$= \text{var}(x) \cdot \text{var}(y)$$

i.e. $\text{var}(xy) = \text{var}(x)\,\text{var}(y)$ | Since $E(x) = 0 \quad E(y) = 0$

Problem 4 For any variates x and y show that

$$\{E(x+y)^2\}^{1/2} \leqslant \{E(x^2)\}^{1/2} + \{E(y^2)\}^{1/2}$$

Solution Squaring both sides we have

$$E(x+y)^2 \leqslant [\{E(x^2)\}^{1/2} + \{E(y^2)\}^{1/2}]^2$$

$$\Rightarrow \quad E\{x^2 + y^2 + 2xy) \leqslant E(x^2) + E(y^2) + 2\sqrt{E(x^2) \cdot E(y^2)}$$

$$\Rightarrow \quad E(x^2) + E(y^2) + 2E(xy) \leqslant E(x^2) + E(y^2) + 2\sqrt{E(x^2)\,E(y^2)}$$

$$\Rightarrow \quad 2E(xy) \leqslant 2\sqrt{E(x^2)\,E(y^2)}$$

$$\Rightarrow \quad E(x)\,E(y) \leqslant \sqrt{E(x^2)\,E(y^2)}$$

Squaring both sides

$$[E(xy)]^2 \leqslant E(x^2)\,E(y^2)$$

Which is the Cauchy Schwartz *inequality*.

Problem 1 What is the expectation of the no. of failures preceeding the first success in an infinite series of independent trials with constant probability P of success in each trial? [*IFS 88*]

Solution Let $X =$ denote the number of failure proceeding the first success. Then X can take the values 0, 1, 2 . . . ∞ we have

$$P(x) = P(X = x) = P[x \text{ failures proceed the first success}] = q^x P$$

where $q = 1 - P$ is the probability of fallure in a trial

$$E(X) = \sum_{x=0}^{\infty} x\,P(x) = \sum_{x=0}^{\infty} x\,q^u \cdot P = pq \sum_{0}^{\infty} xq^{x-1}$$

$$= pq\,[1 + 2q + 3q^2 + 4q^3 + \ldots]$$

Let $S = 1 + 2q + 3q^2 + 4q^3 + \ldots$

$$qS = q + 2q^2 + 3q^3 + \ldots$$

Subtracting

$$(1-q)\,S = 1 + q + q^2 + q^3 + \ldots = \frac{1}{(1-q)^2}$$

$$E(X) = \frac{Pq}{(1-q)^2} = \frac{Pq}{P^2} = \frac{q}{P} \qquad \textbf{Ans.}$$

Prablem 2 Two random variables X and Y have the following joint probability density function

$$f(x, y) = 2 - x - y\,;\ 0 \leqslant x \leqslant 1,\ 0 \leqslant y \leqslant 1$$
$$= 0 \qquad \text{otherwise}$$

Find (i) Margi nal probability density function of X and Y

(ii) Var (X) and Var (Y)

(iii) Co-variance between X and Y

Solution $f_X(x) = \int_{-\infty}^{\infty} f(xy)\, dy = \int_{-\infty}^{\infty} (2-x-y)\, dy$

$$= \int_{-\infty}^{0} (2-x-y)\, dy + \int_{0}^{1} (2-x-y)\, dy + \int_{1}^{\infty} (2-x-y)\, dy$$

$$= 0 + \left[2y - xy - \frac{y^2}{2}\right]_0^1 + 0 = 2 - x - \frac{1}{2} = \frac{3}{2} - x$$

$\therefore$ $f_X(x) = \frac{3}{2} - x, \quad 0 < x < 1$

$= 0$ otherwise

Similary $f_Y(Y) = \frac{3}{2} - y \quad 0 < y < 1$

$= 0$ otherwise

Now $E(X) = \int_0^1 x f_X(x)\, dx = \int_0^1 x\left(\frac{3}{2} - x\right) dx = \frac{5}{12}$

$$E(Y) = \int_0^1 y f_Y(Y)\, dy = \int_0^1 Y\left(\frac{3}{2} - Y\right) dy = \frac{5}{12}$$

(iii) $E(X^2) = \int_0^1 x^2\left(\frac{3}{2} - x\right) dx = \left[\frac{3}{6}x^3 - \frac{x^4}{4}\right]_0^1 = \frac{1}{4}$

$$V(X) = E(X^2) - [E(X)]^2$$

$$V(X) = \frac{1}{4} - \left(\frac{5}{12}\right)^2 = \frac{1}{4} - \frac{25}{144} = \frac{1}{16}$$

$$E(XY) = \int_0^1 \int_0^1 xy(2-x-y)\, dx\, dy$$

$$= \int_0^1 \left| 2\frac{x^2 y}{2} - \frac{x^3 y}{3} - \frac{x^2 y^2}{2} \right|_0^1 dy$$

$$= \int_0^1 \left(\frac{2}{3} y - \frac{1}{2} y^2\right) dy = \frac{1}{6}$$

$$\text{COV}(XY) = E(XY) - E(X)\,E(Y) = -\frac{1}{144}$$

Problem 3 What are meant by random sampling. Statistics sampling distribution and standard error.

A random sampling is the process in which each unit of population has an equal chance of being drawn.

Let a sample of size n from a population of size N. Then there are (N_n) possible samples. In the process of random sampling each (N_n) has an equal chance of being selected.

Statistics

Statistical measures computed from sample observation alone are referred to as the statistic e.g. mean $(\bar{x})$ variance (S^2) etc. It is used to avoid verbal *confusion.*

Sample distribution

If a sample of size n is drawn from a population N then the possible sample is

$$(N_n) = \frac{N}{n!\ (N-n)\ !} = G \text{ (let)}$$

For each of these G samples we can compute some statistic in particular mean $\bar{x}$, the variance S^2 etc.

The set of values of the statistic so obtained is called the sampling distribution.

Standard Error

The standard deviation of the sampling distribution of a statistic is known as its standard error. It is denoted by SE.

Standard error enables us to determine the probable limits with which the population parameter may be expected to *lie.*

Problem 4 Find out C, the mathematical expectation and the moment about origin for the random variable with *pdf* given by

$$f(x) = C\,xe^{-x}\ x > 0$$

Solution For the function to be a density function we must have

$$\int_0^\infty f(x)\,dx = \int_0^\infty Cxe^{-x}\,dx = 1$$

$$\Rightarrow \quad C\int_0^\infty x\,e^{-x}\,dx = 1$$

$$\Rightarrow \quad C\int_0^\infty x^{2-1}\,e^{-x}\,dx = 1$$

$$\Rightarrow \quad C\,\Gamma(2) = 1 \quad \Rightarrow \quad C\,\Gamma(1+1) = 1$$

$$\Rightarrow \quad C \cdot 1! = 1 \quad \Rightarrow \quad C = 1$$

Mathematical Expectation $= E[f(x)]$

$$= \int_0^\infty x f(x)\, dx = \int_0^\infty C \cdot x^2 e^{-x}\, dx$$

$\lfloor(n+1) = n!$
$$= \int_0^\infty C x^{3-1} e^{-x}\, dx = C \int_0^\infty x^{3-1} e^{-x}\, dx$$

$$= C\Gamma(3) = C\Gamma(2+1) = C\lfloor 2$$

$$= 2C = 2 \times 1 = 2$$

rth moment about origin

$$\therefore \quad \mu_r^! = \int_0^\infty x^r f(x)\, dx = \int_0^\infty x^r C x e^{-x}\, dx$$

$$= C\int_0^\infty x^{r+1} e^{-x}\, dx = C\int_0^\infty x^{r+2-1} e^{-x}\, dx$$

$$= \Gamma(r+2) = \Gamma(r+1+1)$$

$$= (r+1)! = (r+1)\, r! \qquad \textbf{Ans.}$$

Problem 5 If X and Y are independent binomial variates $b\ (5, \frac{1}{2})$ and $b\ (7, \frac{1}{2})$. Find $P(X + Y = 3)$

Since $\quad X \sim B(5, \frac{1}{2})$

$\quad Y \sim (7, \frac{1}{2})$

Since they are independent, hence $X + Y \sim B(12, \frac{1}{2})$

$$\therefore \quad P(X + Y = r) = {}^{12}C_r\, (\tfrac{1}{2})^r\, (\tfrac{1}{4})^{12-r}$$

$$P(X + Y = 3) = {}^{12}C_3\, (\tfrac{1}{2})^3\, (\tfrac{1}{2})^9 = {}^{12}C_3\, (\tfrac{1}{2})^{12}$$

Problem 6 If X is a normal variate with mean 30 and standard deviation 5, Y is a normal variate with mean 15 and SD 10 prove that

$$P(26 \leqslant x \leqslant 40) = P(7 \leqslant y \leqslant 35)$$

Solution $\quad X \sim N(30, 25) \qquad Y \sim N(15, 100)$

$$\therefore \quad \frac{X-30}{5} \sim N(0, 1) = Z_1$$

and
$$\frac{Y-15}{10} \sim N(0, 1) = Z_2$$

when $\quad X = 26 \qquad Z_1 = \dfrac{22-30}{5} = -0.8$

when $\quad X = 40 \qquad Z_1 = \dfrac{40-30}{5} = 2$

Similarly when $Y = 7$ $\quad Z_2 = \dfrac{7-15}{10} = -0.8$

$$Y = 35 \quad Z_2 = \frac{35-15}{10} = 2$$

$$\therefore \quad P(-0.8 \leqslant x \leqslant 2) = P(-0.8 \leqslant Y \leqslant 2)$$

Problem 7 If X and Y are independent poisson variates with means m_1 and m_2 respectively, prove that $X-Y$ has the value 'r' is the coefficient of t^r in exp. $\{m_1 t + m_2 t^{-1} - m_1 - m_2\}$

Solution $P(X = x) = \dfrac{e^{-m1} m_1^x}{x!}, \quad x = 0, 1 \ldots \infty$

$$P(Y = y) = \frac{e^{-m_2} m_2^y}{y}, \quad y = 0, 1, 2 \ldots \infty$$

$$\therefore \quad P(X-Y = r) = \sum_{s=0}^{\infty} P(X = r + s \cap Y = s)$$

$$= \sum_{s=0}^{\infty} P(X = r + s)\, P(Y = s)$$

[By probability theorem]

$$= \sum_{s=0}^{\infty} \frac{e^{-m_1} m_1^{r+s}}{(r+s)!} \cdot \frac{e^{-m2} m_2^s}{s\,!}$$

$$= e^{-m_1-m_2} \sum_{s=0}^{\infty} \frac{m_1^{r+s} m_2^s}{(r+s)!\, s!} \qquad \text{(ii)}$$

we have $e^{m_1 t+m_2 t-1} = -e^{m_1 t} \times e^{m_2 t-1}$

$$= \left\{1 + m_1 t + \frac{(m_1 t)^2}{2!} + \ldots + \frac{\{m_1 t)^{r+s}}{(r+s)!} + \ldots\right\}$$

$$\times \left\{1 + m_2 t^{-1} + \frac{(m_2 t^{-1})^2}{2!} + \ldots + \frac{(m_2 t^{-1})^s}{s!} + \ldots\right.$$

$$\therefore \quad \text{Coefficient of } t^r \text{ in } e^{m_1 t+m_2 t-1} = \sum_{s=0}^{\infty} \frac{m_1^{r+s} m_2^s}{(r+s)!\, s!}$$

Hence from equation (ii) we get

$$P(X-Y = r) = e^{-m_1-m_2} \times \text{coefficient of } t^r \text{ in } e^{m_1 t+m_2 t-1}$$

$$= \text{coefficient of } t^r \text{ in } e^{-m_1-m_2+m_2 t^{-1}} + m_1 t$$

Required Result.

Problem 8 Find out the expectation, the variance and the normalising factor A, if the density of P distribution is Ae^{-x}, $x \geqslant 0$

Solution For the function to be the distributive we have

$$\int_0^\infty A\, e^{-x} = 1$$

$$\Rightarrow \quad A \int_0^\infty e^{-x}\, dx = 1$$

$$\Rightarrow \quad A \int_0^\infty x^{1-1}\, e^{-x}\, dx = 1$$

$$\Rightarrow \quad A\, \Gamma(1) = 1$$

$$\Rightarrow \quad A = 1$$

Expectation $= \mu_1' = \int_0^\infty A\, x\, e^{-x}\, dx$

$$= \int_0^\infty x\, e^{-x}\, dx = \int_0^\infty x^{2-1}\, e^{-x}\, dx$$

$$= \Gamma(2) = 1 \qquad \textbf{Ans.}$$

$$\mu_2^1 = \int_0^\infty x^2\, e^{-x}\, dx = \Gamma(3) = 2$$

$\therefore \qquad \mu_2 = \mu'_2 - \mu'^2_1 = 2 - 1 \qquad \Rightarrow \quad$ Variance $= 1$

Problem 5 Find the mean of the Binomial distribution

Solution $\quad E(x) = \underset{x=0}{\overset{n}{Z}} xp(x) = \underset{0}{\overset{n}{Z}} x\, {}^n c_x\, q^{n-x}\, p^x$

$$= (0 \cdot q + 1\, {}^n c_1\, q^{n-1}\, p + 2\, {}^n c_2\, q^{n-2}\, p^2 + \ldots np^n]$$

$$= P\,[nq^{n-1} + n\,(n-1)\, q^{n-2}\, p + \ldots + np^{n-1}[$$

$$= np\,[q^{n-1} + (n-1)\, q^{n-2}\, p + \ldots + np^{n-1}]$$

$$= np\,[{}^{n-1}c_0\, q^{n-1} + {}^{n-1}c_1\, q^{n-2}\, p + \ldots + {}^{n-1}c_{n-1}\, p^{n-1}]$$

$$= np\,(q + p)^{n-1} = np\,(1)^{n-1} \qquad \text{asp} + q = 1$$

$$= np$$

Problem 6 If X is $N(1, 4)$ and $y \sim (2, 3)$ are independent variates. Find the distribution of $x + 2y$.

Solution $\quad x \sim N(1, 4)$

$\Rightarrow \quad E(X) = 1 \qquad \text{var}(X) = 4 \quad y$ is $(2, 3)$

$\Rightarrow \quad E(Y) = 2 \;\; \text{var}(Y) = 3$

$$E(X + 2Y) = E(X) + 2\, E(Y) = 1 + 2.2 = 5$$

$$\text{var}(N + 2\overline{Y}) = \text{var}(X) + 2^2\, \text{var}(Y) = 4 + 4 \times 3 = 16$$

$$X + 2Y \sim N(5, 16)$$

$$\boxed{\text{var}(aX + bY) = a^2\, \text{var}(x) + b^2\, \text{var}(Y)}$$

Appendix 11

APPLECATION OF DIFFERENTIAL EQUATION

Problem 7 A body excutes damped forccd vibrations given by the equation

$$\frac{d^2 x}{dt^2} + 2a\frac{dx}{dt} + b^2 x = ce^{-ta} \sin \omega t$$

where the impressed force is damped by a factor e^{-at} equal to the damping factor for natural vibrations. Find the particular integral of this equation if

(i) $\omega \pm \sqrt{b^2 - a^2}$

(ii) $\omega = \sqrt{b^2 - a^2}$ [*I.F.S. 83*]

Solution $PI = \dfrac{1}{(D^2 + 2aD + b^2)} ce^{-at} \sin \omega t$

$$C = \frac{1}{(D^2 + 2aD + b^2)} e^{-at} \sin \omega t$$

$$= Ce^{-at} \frac{1}{[(D-a)^2 + 2a(D-a) + b^2]} \sin \omega t$$

$$= Ce^{-at} \frac{1}{(D^2 - a^2 + b^2)} \sin \omega t$$

$$= Ce^{-at} \frac{1}{(-\omega^2 - a^2 + b^2)} \sin \omega t$$

$$= Ce^{-at} \frac{1}{(b^2 - a^2) - \omega^2} \sin \omega t$$

$f(D^2) = f(-\omega^2)$ if $f(D^2) \neq 0$ only when $\omega \neq \sqrt{b^2 - a^2}$
if $\omega = \sqrt{b^2 - a^2}$ i.e. $\omega^2 = b^2 - a^2 \Rightarrow f(D^2) = 0$

above method fails then

$$PI = Ce^{-at} \frac{1}{(D^2 - a^2 + b^2)} \sin \omega t$$

$$= Ce^{-at}\, t \frac{1}{\frac{d}{dD}(D^2 - a^2 + b^2)} \sin \omega t$$

$$PI = Ce^{-at}\, t\, \frac{1}{2D} \sin \omega t$$

$$PI = -\frac{Ce^{-at}\, t}{2\omega} \cos \omega t \qquad \textbf{Ans.}$$

Problem 8 A cirular disc of mass m and radius r is suspended by a thin wire attached to the centre of one of its flat faces. If the disc is twisted through angle θ, forsionin the wire tends to turn the disc back in the opposite direction. The motion is governed by the differential equation

$$\frac{1}{2} mr^2 \frac{d^2 \theta}{dt^2} = -k\theta$$

[*I.F.S.* 79]

where K is the coefficient of torsion of the wire. Find the motion if

$$\theta = \theta_0 \qquad \text{and} \qquad \frac{d\theta}{\theta t} v_0 \text{ at } t = 0$$

Solution Let $\frac{1}{2} mr^2 = I$ (say), I = moment of inertia of the *disc*

$$\frac{1}{2} mr^2 \frac{d^2 \theta}{dt^2} = -k\theta$$

$$I \frac{d^2 \theta}{dt^2} = -k\theta$$

$$\Rightarrow \quad \frac{d^2 \theta}{dt^2} = -\frac{k}{I}\theta$$

$$\Rightarrow \quad \frac{d^2 \theta}{dt^2} \alpha\, \theta$$

$\Rightarrow$ motion is *SHM*.

$$\frac{d^2 \theta}{dt^2} = -\frac{k}{I}\theta$$

$$\frac{d\theta}{dt} = -\frac{k}{I} \theta t + c$$

$$\boxed{t = 0, \frac{d\theta}{dt} = v_0}$$

$$C = v_0$$

$$\frac{d\theta}{dt} = -\frac{k}{I} \theta t + v_0$$

$$\theta = -\frac{k}{I} \frac{\theta t^2}{2} + v_0 t + c_1$$

$$\boxed{\text{at } t = 0\ \theta = \theta_0}$$

$$\theta_0 = c_1$$

$$\Rightarrow \qquad \theta = -\frac{k}{I}\theta\frac{t^2}{2} + v_0 t + \theta_0$$

$$\Rightarrow \qquad \theta = \frac{-k}{\frac{1}{2}mr^2}\frac{\theta t^2}{2} + v_0 t + \theta_0$$

$$\Rightarrow \qquad \theta = -\frac{k\theta t^2}{mr^2} + v_0 t + \theta_0$$

Problem 9 The rate of radio active deeay is proportional to the quantity x of a substance that has not decayed. Find x as a function of the time t if at the initial instant $t = t_0$ $x = x_0$. Also determine the half life of the radio active substance assuming that the constant of proportionallity k is given. [*I.F.S. 80*]

($-$ve sign because there is decay)

Solution $$-\frac{dx}{dt} \propto x$$

$$-\frac{dx}{dt} = kt$$

$$\Rightarrow \qquad \frac{dx}{x} = -k\,dt$$

integrating $$\log x = -kt + C$$

$$\log x_0 = -kt_0 + C$$

$$t = t_0,\ x = x_0$$

$$C = \log x_0 + kt_0$$

$$\log x = -kt + kt_0 + \log x_0$$

$$\log x - \log x_0 = -k\,(t - t_0)$$

$$\log \frac{x}{x_0} = -k\,(t - t_0)$$

$$\frac{x}{x_0} = e^{-k\,(t-t_0)}$$

$$x = x_0\, e^{-k\,(t-t_0)}$$

Half life is given by $t = T$ i.e. when

$$x = \frac{x_0}{2} \quad [x_0 \text{ at } t_0]$$

$$\frac{x_0}{2} = x_0\, e^{-k\,(T-t_0)}$$

$$e^{k(T-t_0)} = 2$$

$$k(T-t_0) = \log_e 2$$

$$T-t_0 = \frac{\log_e 2}{k}$$

$$T = t_0 + \frac{\log_e 2}{k}$$

Problem 10 A copper ball is heated to a temperature of 100 °C. Then at time $t = 0$, it is placed in water which is maintained at a temperature of 30 °C. At the end of 3 minutes the temperature of the ball is reduced to 70 °C. Find the time at which the temperature of the ball is reduced to 30 °C. Assume that the rate of cooling is proportional to the difference in temperature of the ball from its *surrounding*. [*I.F.S. 81*]

Solution Newton's law of cooling. The rate at which a substance cools in moving air is proportional to the difference between the temperature of the substance and that of the *air*.

$$\frac{dT}{dt} \propto (T-\theta)$$

$$\frac{dT}{dt} = -k(T-\theta)$$

T = tem. of substance

θ = temp. of surrounding

Problem 11 If. temperature of the air is $290k$ and the substance cools from $370k$ to $330k$ in 10 minutes. When the tem. will be $295k$.

Solution

$$\frac{dT}{dt} = -\lambda(T-290)$$

$$\frac{dT}{T-290} = -\lambda dt \qquad (1)$$

$$t = 0.\ T = 370,\ t = 10,\ T = 330$$

$$\int_{370}^{330} \frac{dT}{T-290} = -\lambda \int_0^{10} dt$$

$$\lambda = \frac{\log 2}{10}$$

Now integrating (1) between the limits

$$t = 0,\ T = 370,\ t = t,\ T = 295$$

$$\int_{370}^{295} \frac{dT}{T-290} = -\lambda \int_0^t dt$$

$$t = \frac{1}{\lambda} (\log 16) = \frac{\log 16}{\log 2} \times 10$$

$$t = 40 \text{ minute}$$

Appendix 12

REAL ANALYSIS

Mean Value Theorems

THM. Let f be defined on $[a, b]$ is a function such that

(i) f is continuous on $[a, b]$

(ii) f is derivable on $]a, b[$

(iii) $f(a) = f(b)$

Then there exists a real number c between a and b such that $f'(c) = 0$

Problem 1. Verify the hypothesis and conclusion of Rolle's theorem for the function f defined on $[a, b]$ in each of the following cases.

a. $f(x) = x^2$. $a = -1, b = 1$

$$f(a) = f(-1) = (-1)^2 = 1$$

$$f(b) = f(1) = (1)^2 = 1$$

$\because$ $f(a) = f(b)$

Let us test the derivability of the function

$$R'f'(0) = \lim_{x \to 0+h} \frac{f(0+h) - f(0)}{h-0} \forall x$$

$$= \lim_{\substack{h \to 0 \\ h>0}} \frac{h^2 - 0}{h} = h = 0 = 0$$

$$L f'(0) = \lim_{\substack{h \to 0 \\ h>0}} \frac{f(0-h) - f(0)}{-h-0} = \lim_{\substack{h \to 0 \\ h>0}} \frac{(-h)^2 - 0}{-h} = 0$$

$\because$ $Rf'(0) = Lf'(0)$ therefore the function is derivable in $]-1. 1[$. Since the fuuction is deriable hence it is continuous in $[-1, 1]$. Therefore there exists a real number c such that $f'(c) = 0$

$$a < c < b$$

$\therefore$ $f'(c) = 2c = 0$

$\Rightarrow$ $x = 0 \in [-1, 1]$

i.e., $-1 < 0 < 1$.

(*b*) $f(x) = x^3 - 6x^2 + 11x - 6$, $a = 1, b = 3$

$$f(a) = 1 - 6 + 11 - 6 = 0$$

$$f(b) = 27 - 54 + 33 - 6 = 0$$

Hence $f(a) = f(b)$

The above function is a polynomial hence is continuous in [1, 3] and is differentiable in]1, 3[.

$\because \qquad f(a) = f(b)$

Hence ∃ a real number c such that

$$f'(c) = 0$$

i.e. $\qquad 3x^2 - 12x + 11 = 0$

$\Rightarrow \qquad 3c^2 - 12c + 11 = 0$

$$c = \frac{12 \pm \sqrt{144 - 132}}{6} = \frac{12 \pm 2\sqrt{3}}{6} = \frac{6 \pm \sqrt{3}}{3}$$

$$c = \frac{6 + \sqrt{3}}{3}, \frac{6 - \sqrt{3}}{3} \in [1, 3]$$

(*c*) $\qquad f(x) = \cos x., a = -\pi/2, b = \pi/2$

Let $\qquad x = 0 \in (a, b)$ at which we will test for continuity and derivability of the function.

$$f(0) = \cos(0) = 1$$

$$\text{RHL } f(0 + 0) = \lim_{\substack{h \to 0 \\ h > 0}} \cos h = 1$$

$$\text{LHL } f(0 - 0) = \lim_{\substack{h \to x \\ h > 0}} \cos(-h) = 1$$

Hence is continuous at $x = 0$

Now $\qquad g(x) = \dfrac{f(x) - f(x_0)}{x - x_0}$

$$\therefore \quad Rf'(0) = \lim_{x \to 0 + h} g(x) = \lim_{h \to 0} \frac{\cos h - 1}{h}$$

Problem 2. Examine the validity of the hypotheses and the conclusion of Rolle's theorem for the function f defined on $[a, b]$ in the following cases.

(*a*) $\qquad f(x) = |x|, a = -1, b = 1$

$$Rf'(0) = \lim_{h \to 0} \frac{f(x + h) - f(x)}{x + h - x}$$

$$= \lim_{h \to 0} \frac{|h|}{h} = 1$$

$$Lf'(0) = \lim_{h \to 0} \frac{|h|}{-h} = -1$$

$\because \quad Rf'(0) \neq Lf'(0)$

Hence the function is not derivable at $]-1, 1[$. Therefore the Rolle's theorem is not valid.

(*b*) $\quad f(x) = 2 + (x-1)^{2/3}, a = 0, b = 2$

Let us check the derivability at $x = 1$

$$Rf'(1) = \lim_{h\to 0} \frac{2 + (1 + h - 1)^{2/3} - 2}{1 + h - 1}$$

$$= \lim_{h\to 0} \frac{2 + h^{2/3} - 2}{h} = h^{-1/3} = \infty$$

$$Rf'(1) = \lim_{h\to 0} \frac{2 + (1 - h - 1)^{2/3} - 2}{1 - h - 1} = \lim_{h\to 0} \frac{h^{2/3}}{-h} = -\infty$$

Since the $R'f(1) \neq Lf'(1)$ Hence the function is not derivable at $]0, 2[$ and hence the Rolle's theorem is not valid.

Neither the hypothesis nor conclusion are valid.

(*c*) $\quad f(x) = x^{5/2}\ a = 1, b = 5$

Let a value $2 \in (1, 5)$ on to which we have to check the derivability we have

$$Rf'(2) = \lim_{h\to 0} \frac{(2 + h)^{5/2} - 2^{5/2}}{2 + h - 2} = \lim_{h\to 0} \frac{(2 + h)^{5/2} - 2^{5/2}}{h} = +\infty$$

While $\quad Lf'(2) = \lim\limits_{h\to 0} \dfrac{(2-h)^{5/2} - 2^{5/2}}{-h} = -\infty$

Since $Rf'(2) \neq Lf'(2)$. Hence the function is not derivable on the entire range i.e. $]1, 5[$ and hence the Rolle's theorem is not valid.

(*d*) $\quad f(x) = (x-2)\sqrt{x},\ a = 0, b = 2$

Let $\quad x = 1 \in (0, 2)$

$$Rf'(1) = \lim_{h\to 0} \frac{(1 + h - 2)\sqrt{1 + h} + 1}{h}$$

$$= \lim_{h\to 0} \frac{(h - 1)\sqrt{1 + h} + 1}{h}$$

$$= \mathop{\mathrm{Lim}}_{h\to 0} \frac{(h-1)\left[1 + \frac{h}{2} \text{ Higher terms cont. } h\right] + 1}{h}$$

$$= \lim_{h\to 0} \frac{h - 1 + \frac{h(h-1)}{2} + 0(h) + 1}{h}$$

Where 0 (h) = Higher terms containing h.

$$= \lim_{h\to 0} 1 + \frac{h-1}{2} = \frac{1}{2}$$

While $Lf'(1) = \lim_{h\to 0} \frac{(-h-1)(1-h)^{+1/2}+1}{-h}$

$$= \lim_{h\to 0} \frac{(-h-1)\left[1-\frac{h}{2}+0(h)\right]+1}{-h}$$

$$= \lim_{h\to 0} \frac{-h-1+\frac{(h+1)}{2}+0(h)+1}{-h}$$

$$= \lim_{h\to 0} 1-\frac{1}{2} = \frac{1}{2}$$

$\because$ $Rf'(1) = Lf'(1)$. Hence the function is derivable at every point of (0, 2). Therefore the function is continuous at [0, 2].

Now since, $f(0) = 0$

$f(2) = 0$

Hence, the Hypothesis is valid for the given function.

Problem 3. Prove that if $a_0, a_1 \ldots a_n$ be real numbers such that

$$\frac{a_0}{n+1} + \frac{a_1}{n} + \ldots + \frac{a_{n-1}}{2} + a_n = 0$$

Then there exist at least one real x between 0 and 1 such that

$$a_0 x^n + a_1 x^{n-1} + \ldots + a_n = 0$$

We have since

$$f'(x) = a_0 x^n + a_1 x^{n-1} + \ldots + a_n$$

Hence, $f(x) = \frac{a_0 x^{n+1}}{n+1} + \frac{a_1 x^n}{n} + \ldots + a_n x$

$$f(x) = \frac{a_0 x^{n+1}}{n+1} + \frac{a_1 x^n}{n} + \ldots + \frac{a_{n-1} x^2}{2} + a_n x$$

Since the function is polynomial of degree $n+1$ hence is continuous $\forall\ x$ in [0, 1] while it is derivable $\forall\ x$ in]0, 1 [and

$$f(0) = 0$$

$$f(1) = \frac{a_0}{n+1} + \frac{a_1}{n} + \ldots + \frac{a_{n-1}}{2} + a_n = 0$$

$$f(0) = f(1)$$

Hence ∃ a real number c such that

$$(0 < c < 1), f'(c) = 0$$

Hence, $$a_0 c^n + a_1 c^{n-1} + \ldots + a_n = 0$$

Therefore, at least one real x exist between 0 and 1 such that

$$a_0 x^n + a_1 x^{n-1} + \ldots + a_n = 0$$ [Proved]

Problem 4 Show that there is no real number k for which the eqn. $x^3 - 3x + k = 0$ has two distinct roots in [0, 1]

Let the eqn. has two distinct real roots a, b between 0 and 1 such that $$0 < a < b < 1. \quad (1)$$

Now since $f(x) = x^3 - 3x + k = 0$ is a polynomial of degree of 3 hence it is continuous in [0, 1] and is differentiable in]0, 1[. Hence there exists a real number c in between a and b such that

$$f'(c) = 0$$

i.e., $$3c^2 - 3 = 0$$

$$\Rightarrow \quad c = \pm 1$$

i.e., $x = \pm 1$, i.e., $a < c < b$.

Which contradicts the eqn. (1). Hence it doesn't have two distinct roots.

[Proved]

Problem 5 Prove that if p be any polynomial and p' the derivative of p, then between any two consecutive zeros of p' there lies at the most one zero of p.

— Let α, β ($\alpha < \beta$) be two consecutive zero of p'. Let if possible c_1 and c_2 be two zero of p, such that

$$c_1\ c_2 \in (\alpha, \beta)$$

Since polynomial p is differential and continuous at the prescribed range hence there exist a real number c such that

$$(c_1 < c < c_2)\ f'(c) = 0$$

$$\therefore \quad c_1 < c < c_2$$

i.e., $$\alpha < c < \beta$$

Which contradicts the assumption that α, β be two consecutive zero's of p'. Hence there lies at the most one zero of p.
Hence the Result. [Proved]

ξ LAGRANGE'S MEAN VALUE THM:

Let a function f be defined on $[a, b]$ such that

(i) f is continuous at $]a, b]$

(ii) f is derivable at $]a, b[$

Then there exists a real number c such that

$$\frac{f(b)-f(a)}{b-a} = f'(c)$$

Another statement of LMV Theorem

Let $$b-a=h$$

$$\Rightarrow \quad b = a+h$$

Then c can be written as $a+\theta h$, i.e., for $\theta = 0$, $c = a$ and for $\theta = 1$, $c = b$ where θ is some number such that $0 < \theta < 1$.

L.M V. theorem can be stated as

Let f be defined and continuous on $[a, a+h]$ and is derivable on $[a, a+h]$. Then for some real number θ $(0 < \theta < 1)$

$$f(a+h)-f(a) = h\,f'(a+\theta h)$$

or, $$f(a+h) = f(a) + h\,f'(a+\theta h)$$

Problem 1. Let f be defined and continuous on $[a-h, a+h]$ and derivable on $[a-h, a+h]$. Prove that there is a real number θ between 0 and 1 for which

$$f(a+h)-2f(a)+f(a-h) = h\{f'(a+\theta h)-f'(a-\theta h)\}$$

Let F be the function defined on $[0, 1]$ by setting

$$F(t) = f(a+ht)+f(a-ht) \qquad \forall\ t \in [0, 1]$$

Then F is continuous at $[0, 1]$ and derivable on $]0, 1[$. By L.M.V. theorem there exist a number θ between 0 and 1 such that

$$F(1)-F(0) = F'(\theta)$$

$$F(1) = f(a+h)+f(a-h)$$

$$F(0) = 2f(a)$$

$$F'(\theta) = h[f'[(a+\theta h)-f'(a-\theta h)[$$

Hence, $$f(a+h)+f(a-h)-2f(a)$$

$$= h[f'(a+\theta h)-f'(a-\theta h)]$$

$$\Rightarrow f(a+h)-2f(a)+f(a-h) = h[f'(a+\theta h)+f'(a-\theta h)]$$ *[Proved]*

Problem 2. Find the number θ that appears in the conclusion of Lagrange's mean value theorem in each of the following cases.

(*a*) $f(x) = x^2-2x+3, \quad a = 1,\ h = 1/2$

— The L.M.V. Theorem can be stated as

$$f(a+h) = f(a)+h\,f'(a+\theta h); \qquad 0 < \theta < 1$$

$$f\left(\frac{3}{2}\right) = \frac{9}{4}-3+3 = \frac{9}{4}$$

$$f(a) = f(1) = 1-2+3 = 2$$

$$f'(x) = 2x-2$$

$$f'(a+\theta h) = f'\left(1+\frac{\theta}{2}\right) = 2+\theta-2$$

From L.M.V. theorem

$\therefore$ $$f(a+h) = f(a) + h\,f'(a+\theta h)$$

$\Rightarrow$ $$\frac{9}{4} = 2 + \frac{\theta}{2}$$

$\Rightarrow$ $$\frac{1}{4} = \frac{\theta}{2}$$

$\Rightarrow$ $$\theta = \frac{1}{2}$$

(*b*) $$f(x) = x^3\,;\ a = 1,\ h = \frac{1}{5}$$

$$f(a+h) = f\left(\frac{6}{5}\right) = \frac{216}{125}$$

$$f(a) = f(1) = 1$$

$$f'\left(1+\frac{\theta}{h}\right) = 3x^2 = 3\left(1+\frac{\theta}{5}\right)^2$$

From L.M.V. Theorem $$\frac{216}{125} = 1 + \frac{3}{5}\left(1+\frac{\theta}{5}\right)^2$$

$\Rightarrow$ $$\frac{91}{125} = \frac{3}{5}\left(1+\frac{\theta}{5}\right)^2$$

$\Rightarrow$ $$\frac{91}{3\times 25} = \left(1+\frac{\theta}{5}\right)^2$$

$\Rightarrow$ $$\frac{1}{5}\sqrt{\frac{91}{3}} - 1 = \frac{\theta}{5}$$

$\Rightarrow$ $$\sqrt{\frac{91}{3}} - 5 = \theta.$$

(*c*) $$f(x) = \log_e x;\ a = 1,\ h = 0.1$$

$$f(a+h) = f(1+0.1) = \log_e 1.1$$

$$f(a) = 0$$

$$f'(x) = \frac{1}{x}$$

$\therefore$ $$f'(1+0\,.\,\theta) = \frac{1}{1+0\cdot\theta}$$

Therefore from the L.M.V. theorem

$$\log_e 1 \cdot 1 = \frac{0 \cdot 1}{1+0\cdot\theta}$$

$$\Rightarrow \qquad 1 + 0\cdot\theta = 0\cdot1\ (\log_e 1\cdot1)^{-1}$$

Multiplying by 10 we have

$$10 + 0 = (\log_e 1\cdot1)^{-1}$$

$$\Rightarrow \qquad \theta = (\log_e 1\cdot1)^{-1} - 10.$$

d. $$f(x) = \log_e x;\ a = 1,\ h = e^{-1}$$

$$f(1 + e^{-1}) = \log_e (1 + e^{-1})$$

$$f(a) = 0$$

$$f'(a) = \frac{1}{x}$$

$$\therefore \qquad f'(1 + e^{-1}\ \theta) = \frac{1}{\theta\, e^{-1} + 1}$$

$\therefore$ By L.M.V. Theorem we have,

$$\log_e (1 + e^{-1}) = \frac{e^{-1}}{\theta\, e^{-1} + 1}$$

$$\Rightarrow \qquad \log_e (1 + e^{-1}) = \frac{1}{\theta + e}$$

$$\Rightarrow \qquad [\log_e (1 + e^{-1})]^{-1} = \theta + e$$

$$\Rightarrow \qquad \theta = [\log_e (1 + e^{-1})]^{-1} - e.$$

Problem 3 Verify that on the curve $y = px^2 + qx + r$ (p, q, r bering real, numbers, $p \neq 0$) the chord joining the points which $x = a$, $x = b$ is parallel to the tangent at the point given by $x = \frac{1}{2}(a + b)$

We have the curve,

$$y = px^2 + qx + r \qquad \text{defined on } [a, b]$$

Since the above function is polynomial hence is continuous on $[a, b]$ and is derivable on $]a, b[$. Hence there exist a number c such that $a < c < b$,

$$f'(c) = \frac{f(b) - f(a)}{b - a}$$

i.e., $$y_b = pb^2 + qb + r$$

$$y_a = pa^2 + qa + r$$

$$\therefore \qquad 2pc + q = \frac{pb^2 + qb + r - pa^2 - qa - r}{b - a}$$

$$\Rightarrow \quad 2pc + q = \frac{(b-a)[p(b+a)+q]}{b-a}$$

$$\Rightarrow \quad 2p\,c = p(b+a)$$

$$\Rightarrow \quad c = \tfrac{1}{2}(b+a) \in (a, b)$$

Hence, $x = \frac{1}{2}(b+a)$ which lies in between (a, b)

Problem 4. Prove that for any quadratic function $px^2 + qx + r$ the value of θ in Lagrange's theorem is always $\frac{1}{2}$ whatever p, q, r, a, h may be.

Since the quadration function

$f(x) = px^2 + qx + r$ is a function defined on $[a, a + a]$

and is continuous on $[a, a + h]$. It is derivable on $]a, a + h[$.
Hence there exist a number θ such that $0 < \theta < 1$,

$$f(a+h) = f(a) + hf'(a+\theta h)$$

Here, $\quad f(a+h) = p(a+h)^2 + q(a+h) + r$

$$f(a) = pa^2 + qa + r$$

$$f'(x) = 2px + q$$

$$f'(a+\theta h) = 2p(\theta h + a) + q$$

$$p(a+h)^2 + q(a+h) + r = pa^2 + qa + r + h[2p(a+\theta h) + q]$$

Hence, $p[(a+h-a)(a+h+a) + q[a+h-a] = h[2p(a+\theta h) + q]$

$$ph(2a+h) + qh = h[2p(a+\theta h) + q]$$

$$\Rightarrow \quad q + p(2a+b) = 2p(a+\theta h) + q$$

$$\Rightarrow \quad 2ap + ph = 2ap + 2p\theta h$$

$$1 = 2\theta$$

$$\Rightarrow \quad \theta = \tfrac{1}{2} \in (0, 1)$$

Whatever be the value of p, q, r, a, h may be. [*Proved*]

Problem 5. Let f be defined and continuous on $[a-h, a+h]$ and derivable $]a-h, a+h[$. Prove that there is a real number θ between 0 and 1 such that $\quad f(a+h) - f(a-h) = h\{f'(a+\theta h) + f'(a-\theta h)\}$

Since f is continuous on $[a-h, a+h]$ and is derivable on $]a-h, a+h[$.

Hence let the function $F(t)$ by setting

$$F(t) = f(a+ht) - f(a-ht) \ \forall\ t \in [0, 1]$$

$$\therefore \quad F(0) = f(a) - f(a) = 0$$

$$F(1) = f(a+h) - f(a-h)$$

$$F'(t) = hf'(a+ht) + hf'(a-ht)$$

$$= h[f'(a+ht) + f'(a-ht)]$$

Therefore $\exists$ a number θ $(0 < \theta < 1)$ such that

$$F_{,} = \frac{F(1) - F(0)}{1-0}$$

$$\Rightarrow \quad F'(\theta) = f(a+h) - f(a-h)$$

$$\Rightarrow \quad h\,[f'(a+\theta h) + f'(a-\theta h)] = f(a+h) - f(a-h)$$

$$\Rightarrow \quad f(a+h) - f(a-h) = h\,[f'(a+\theta h) + f'(a-\theta h)] \qquad \textit{(Proved)}$$

Problem 6 If f and g are both defined and continuous on $[a, b]$ and are derivable on $]a, b[$ and if $f'(x) = g'(x)\ \forall\ x$ in $]a, b[$ then prove that $f(x)$ and $g(x)$ differ only by a constant on $[a, b]$.

We have,

f and g are continuous $\forall\ x\ [a, b]$

f and g are derivable $\forall\ x\ ]a, b[$

and if $f'(x) = g'(x)\ \forall\ x \in (a, b)$

We have to show that

$$f(x) - g(x) = \text{constant}$$

Now
$$\lim_{x\to 0} \frac{f(x+h) - f(x)}{h} = \lim_{x\to 0} \frac{g(x+h) - g(x)}{h}$$

$\therefore$
$$\lim_{x\to 0} \frac{1}{h}\,[f(x+h) - f(x) - g(x+h) + g(x)] = 0$$

$\therefore$
$$\lim_{x\to 0} \frac{1}{h}\,[(f-g)(x+h) - (f-g)(x)] = 0$$

Which reduces to $(f-g)'\,x = 0$

i.e., $(f-g)(x) = \text{constant}$

$\Rightarrow$ $f(x) - g(x) = \text{constant}$

Henee the Result. *(Proved)*

CACUHY'S Mean Value Theorem

Theorem Let f and g be functiondefined on $[a, b]$ such that

(i) f and g are continuous on $[a, b]$

(ii) f and g are derivabie on $]a_1\ b[$

(iii) $g'(x)$ does not vanishes at any point of $[a, b]$.

Then there exist a number $c \in\ ]a, b[$ such that

$$\frac{f'(c)}{g'(c)} = \frac{f(b) - f(a)}{g(b) - g(a)}$$

Let g (b) $\neq g(a)$. For if g (a) is not equal $g(b)$ the function g would satisfy all the condition of Rolle's theorem and therefore some x in $]a, b[$ we would have $g'(x) = 0$. Let the function F defined on $[a, b]$ by setting

$$F(x) = f(x) + A\,g(x) \tag{1}$$

Where A is choosen such that the Suitable Result would be obtained.

Since (i) f and g are continuous on $[a_1\, b]$ hence F is continuous on $[a, b]$.

(ii) f and g are derivable on $]a, b[$ therefore F is derivable on $]a, b[$.

(iii) Let us choose A So that $F(a) = F(b)$

i.e.
$$F(a) = f(a) + Ag(a)$$
$$F(b) = f(b) + Ag(b)$$

$\therefore$
$$f(b) - f(a) = -A\,[g(b) - g(a)]$$

$$-A = \frac{f(b)-f(a)}{g(b)-g(a)} \tag{2}$$

From (i) (ii) and (iii), we can say that all the condition of Rolle's theorem is satisfied hence there exist a number c such that

$$a < c < b \qquad F^1(c) = 0$$

i.e. $\quad F^1(x) = f'(x) + Ag'(x)$

i.e. $\quad F^1(c) = 0$

i.e. $\quad f'(c) + Ag'(c) = 0$

$$\Rightarrow \quad -A = \frac{f'(c)}{g'(c)} \tag{3}$$

Hence from (2) and (3) we have,

$$\frac{f'(c)}{g'(c)} = \frac{f(b)-f(\text{a})}{g(b)-g(a)}$$

Since from our statement it is clear that $g'(x) \neq 0$ for any x in $]a, b[$. Hence division by $g^1(c)$ is permissible.

Another form of Cauchy's Theorem

By putting $b - a = h$, the existed c, changes to $a + \theta h$ such that $0 < \theta < 1$. Hence, the theorem can be given as

$$\frac{f^1(a+\theta a)}{g^1(a+\theta h)} = \frac{f(a+h)-f(a)}{g(a+h)-g(a)}$$

Geometrical Interpretation

The ratio of the mean rates of increases of two function in an interval is equal to the ratio of the actual rates of increases of the function at some point within the interval.

Theorem (Generalised mean value). If f, g and h are continuous on $[a, b]$ and derivable on $]a, b[$ then there exist a real number c in $]a, b[$ such that

$$\begin{vmatrix} f^1(c) & g^1(c) & h^1(c) \\ f(a) & g(a) & h(a) \\ f(b) & g(b) & h(b) \end{vmatrix} = 0$$

– Let the function F is defined by setting

$$F(x) = \begin{vmatrix} f(x) & g(x) & h(x) \\ f(a) & g(a) & h(a) \\ f(b) & g(b) & h(b) \end{vmatrix} \; \forall \; x \text{ in } [a: b]$$

Since, f, g and h are continuous in $[a, b]$ hence F is also continuous in $[a, b]$ as f, g and h are derivable in $]a, b[$ therefore F is also derivable in $]a, b[$ Hence there exists a real number c in (a, b) such that

$$F'(c) = 0$$

i.e.
$$F^1(x) = \begin{vmatrix} f'(x) & g^1(x) & h'(x) \\ f(a) & g(a) & h(a) \\ f(b) & g(b) & h(b) \end{vmatrix}$$

i.e.
$$\begin{vmatrix} f'(c) & g^1(c) & h'(c) \\ f(a) & g(a) & h(a) \\ f(b) & g(b) & h(b) \end{vmatrix} = 0 \qquad \textit{(Proved)}$$

As a particular case If we take $h(x) = 1$ in (a, b) the above one reduces to the Cauchey's Theorem. While if we take $h(x) = 1$ in (a, b) and $g(x) = x \; \forall \; x$ in $[a, b]$ it reduces to LMV.

Q 4. If f'' be continuous on $[a, b]$ and derivable on $]a, b[$ then prove that

$$f(b) - f(a) - \tfrac{1}{2}(b-a)\{f'(a) + f'(b)\} = -\frac{(b-a)^3}{12} f'''(d)$$

— Let the function is setting by

$$g(x) = f(x) - f(a) - \tfrac{1}{2}(x-a)\{f'(a) + f^1(x)\{ + A(x-a)^3$$

Where A is a constant is to be determined in such a way that $g(x)$ satisfies all the condition.

The function g is continuous in $[a, b]$ and is derivable in $]a, b[$. Hence there exist a real number c such that

$$g(a) = g(b) \qquad \text{and } g'(c) = 0$$

Since $\quad g(a) = 0$

Hence $\quad g(b) = 0$

i.e. $\quad f(b) - f(a) - \frac{1}{2}(b-a)\{f'(a) + f'(b)\{ + A(x-a)^3 = 0$

Now since,

$$g'(x) = f'(x) - \tfrac{1}{2}(x-a) f''(x) - \tfrac{1}{2}\{f'(a) + f'(x)\{ + 3(x-a)^2 A$$

i.e. $g'(c) = f'(c) - \frac{1}{2}(c-a) f''(c) - \frac{1}{2}\{f'(a) + f'(c)\{ + 3(x-a)^2 A = 0$

i.e. $\quad \frac{1}{2}\{f'(c) - f'(a)\} - \frac{1}{2}(c-a) f''(c) + 3A(c-a)^2 = 0$

Again let $h(x) = \frac{1}{2}\{f'(x) - f'(a) - \frac{1}{2}(x-a) f'' + 3A(x-a)^2 = 0$

$$\forall\, x \text{ in } [a, c]$$

(i) $h(x)$ is continuous in $[a, c]$

(ii) $h(x)$ is derivable in $]a, c[$

(iii) and $h(c) = 0$ So that $h(a) = 0$.

Since it satisfies ail the condition of Rolle's theorem hence there ex:st a number d.

Such that $\qquad a < d < c, h'(d) = 0$

Thefefore,

$$h'(x) = \tfrac{1}{2} f''(x) - \tfrac{1}{2}(x-a) f'''(x) - \tfrac{1}{2} f''(x) + 6A(x-a) = 0$$

i.e. $\qquad h'(d) = -\frac{1}{2}(d-a) f'''(d) + 6A(d-a) = 0$

$\Rightarrow \qquad 6A(d-a) = \frac{1}{2}(d-a) f'''(d)$

Since $\qquad d \neq a$ hence,

$$A = \frac{1}{12} f'''(d)$$

Therefore we have,

$$f(b) - f(a) - \tfrac{1}{2}(b-a)\{f'(a) + f'(b)\{ = -\frac{1}{12}(x-a)^3 f'''(d)$$

(Proved)

Q. 5 If $f(0) = 0$ and $f''(x)$ exists on $[0, \infty]$ show that

$$f'(x) - \frac{f(x)}{x} = \frac{1}{2} x f''(\xi), 0 <" 0 < x$$

and deduce that if $f''(x)$ is positive for positive value of x then $f(x)/x$ is strictly increases in $]0, \infty[$.

Let the Rearrangement is given as

$$f'(x) - \frac{f(x)}{x} = \frac{1}{2} x f''(\xi)$$

$$\Rightarrow \qquad xf'(x) - f(x) = \tfrac{1}{2} x^2 f''(\xi)$$

i.e. $f(x) - xf'(x) + \frac{1}{2} x^2 f''(\xi) = 0$ (1)

We may therefore consider the function F as

$$F(x) = f(x) - xf'(x) + A(x^2) \qquad (2)$$

Where A is to be suitably choosen.

Let c be a real number such that $0 < c < \infty$.

Since $F(x)$ is continuous on $[0, c]$

$F(x)$ is derivable on $]0, c]$.

Since $F\{0) = 0$ hence $F(c) = 0$

Such that $F(0) = F(c)$ it satisfies all the condition of Rolle's theorem. Therefore, there exists a number ξ such that

$$0 < \xi < c \qquad f'(\xi) = 0$$

i.e. $F'(x) = f'(x) - x f''(x) - f'(x) + 2Ax$

$$F'(\xi) = -\xi f''(\xi) + 2A\xi$$

$$0 = -\xi f''(\xi) + 2A\xi$$

$$\Rightarrow \qquad A = \tfrac{1}{2} f''(\xi)$$

and since $F(c) = 0$

Hence $f(c) - cf'(c) + \frac{1}{2} c^2 f''(\xi) = 0$

$$\Rightarrow \qquad f'(c) - \frac{f(c)}{c} = \frac{1}{2} cf''(\xi)$$

Hence the Result is established

i.e. $$f'(x) - \frac{f(x)}{x} = \frac{1}{2} x f''(\xi),\ 0 < \xi < x.$$

Let $$G(x) = \frac{f(x)}{x}$$

$\therefore$ $$G'(x) = \frac{xf'(x) - f(x)}{x^2}$$

$$G'(x) = \frac{f'(x)}{x} - \frac{f(x)}{x^2}$$

$$\Rightarrow \qquad G'(x) = f'(x) - \frac{f(x)}{x} = \frac{1}{2} x f''(\xi$$

Assuming that $f''(x) > 0$ whenever $x > 0$

Hence $G'(x) > 0$ whenever $x > 0$

Let x_1 and x_2 be two positive real numbers such that $x_2 > x_1$ then applying the mean value theorem to G on $[x_1\ x_2]$ i.e.

$$G(x_2) - G(x_1) = (x_2 - x_1)\, G'(\eta)$$

where η is a real number such that

$$x_1 < \eta < x_2$$

Since $\qquad G'(\eta) > 0$ hence

$$G(x_2) > G(x_1)$$

Therefore $f(x)/x$ is strictly increasing in $]0, \infty[$.

Q, 6 If $f'(x)$ and $g'(x)$ exist for all x in $[a, b]$ and if $g'(x)$ does not vanishes any where in $]a, b[$ then prove that for some c between a and b.

$$\frac{f(c) - f(a)}{g(b) - g(c)} = \frac{f'(c)}{g'(c)}$$

Let the function $F(x)$ in $[a, b]$ is given by

$$F(x) = f(x)\, g(x) - f(a)\, g(x) - g(b)\, f(x)$$

Since $f'(x)$ and $g'(x)$ exists $\forall$ x in $[a, b]$ i.e. $f(x)$ and $g(x)$ are continuous in $[a, b]$ and isderivable in $]a, b[$. Hence, $F(x)$ is also continuous in $[a, b]$ and is derivable in $]a, b[$ and as

$$F(a) = f(a)\, g(a) - f(a)\, g(a) - g(b)\, f(a)$$
$$= -g(b)\, f(a)$$
$$F(b) = f(b)\, g(b) - f(a)\, g(b) - g(b)\, f(b)$$
$$= -g(b)\, f(a)$$

$\because \qquad F(a) = F(b)$.

All the condition of Rolle's theorem is satisfied.

Hence there exists a real number c in $[a, b]$

Such that $\qquad F'(c) = 0$

$$F'(x) = f(x)\, g'(x) + g(x)\, f'(x) - f(a)\, g'(x) - g(b)\, f'(x)$$

i.e. $\qquad f(c)\, g'(c) + g(c)\, f'(c) - f(a)\, g'(c) - g(b)\, f'(c) = 0$

$\Rightarrow \qquad g'(c)\, [f(c) - f(a)] = f'(c)\, [g(b) - g(c)]$

$\Rightarrow \qquad \dfrac{f(c) - f(a)}{g(b) - g(c)} = \dfrac{f'(c)}{g'(c)}$ *(Proved)*

Q. 7 Show that

$$\frac{f(b) - f(a) - (b-a)\, f'(a)}{g(b) - g(a) - (b-a)\, g'(a)} = \frac{f''(x_1)}{g''(x_1)}$$

where $a < x_1 < b$. Stating the condition under which the result is valid.

Let $\quad F(x) = f(x) - (b-x) f'(x)$

and $\quad G(x) = g(x) - (b-x) g'(x)$

Here, $\quad F(a) = f(a) - (b-a) f'(a)$

$F(b) = f(b)$

$G(a) = g(a) - (b-a) g'(x)$

$G(b) = g(b)$

Also, $\quad F'(x) = f'(x) - (b-x) f''(x) - f'(x)$

$= -(b-x) f''(x)$

$G'(x) = g'(x) - (b-x) g''(x) - g^1(x)$

$= -(b-x) g''(x)$

$\therefore \quad \dfrac{F'(x)}{G'(x)} = \dfrac{f''(x)}{g''(x)}$

If we assume that,

$f'(x)$ and $g'(x)$ exists in $[a, b]$ and they are derivable in $]a, b[$ i.e. $f''(x)$ and $g''(x)$ exits

in $]a, b[$. and $g''(x) \neq 0$ in $]a, b[$.

Then there exist a real number x_1 in $a < x_1 < b$ such that

$$\frac{F'(x_1)}{G'(x_1)} = \frac{F(b) - F(a)}{G(b) - G(a)}$$

$$\Leftarrow \quad \frac{f''(x_1)}{g''(x_1)} = \frac{f(b) - f(a) + (b-a) f'(a)}{g(b) - g(a) + (b-a) g'(a)} \qquad \textit{(Proved)}$$

Q. 8 If f' is continuous on $[a, a+h]$ and derivabie on $]a, a+h[$. then prove that there exists a real number c between a and $a+h$ such that

$$f(a+h) = f(a) + hf'(a) + \frac{h^2}{2} f''(c)$$

Let the function $F(x)$ on $[a, b]$ is given as

$$F(x) = f(b) - f(x) - (b-x) f'(x) - (b-x)^2 A$$

Where A is to be suitably choosen

$$F(a) = f(b) - f(a) - (b-a) f'(a) - (b-a)^2 A = 0 \qquad (1)$$

$$F(b) = 0.$$

Since f is continuous on $[a, b]$ hence F is continuous on $[a, b]$ and f is derivable on $]a, b[$ hence F is also derivable on $]a, b[$ as $F(b) = 0$ If $F(a) = 0$ the function F, Satisfies all the condition of Rolle's theorem hence there exist a real number c in $[a, b]$ such that $F'(c) = 0$.

i.e. $$F'(x) = -f'(x) - [(b-x)f''(x) - f'(x)] + 2A(b-x)$$

$$F'(x) = -f'(x) - (b-x)f''(x) + f'(x) + 2A(b-x)$$

$$\Rightarrow \quad F'(x) = -(b-x)f''(x) + 2A(b-x)$$

i.e. $$F'(c) = -(b-c)f''(c) + 2A(b-c) = 0$$

$\because$ $b \neq c$ hence, $(b-c) \neq 0$

$$\Rightarrow \quad \tfrac{1}{2}f''(c) = A$$

From eqn. (1) we have,

$$f(b) - f(a) - (b-a)f'(a) - \frac{(b-a)^2}{2}f''(c) = 0$$

i.e. $$f(b) = f(a) + (b-a)f'(a) + \tfrac{1}{2}(b-a)^2 f''(c)$$

Now putting $b-a = h$

$$\Rightarrow \quad b = a + h$$

Therefore, $f(a+h) = f(a) + hf'(a) + \dfrac{h^2}{2}f''(c)$. *(Proved)*

Problem 9 If f' is continuous on $[a, a+h]$, f'' exists in $[a, a+h]$ f'' is continuous at $x = a$ and if $f''(a) \neq 0$ then prove that the number θ tends to $\frac{1}{2}$ as h tends to zero.

Since f' is continuous on $[a, a+h]$ and is derivable on $]a, a+h[$, Hence,

$$f(a+h) = f(a) + hf'(a) + \frac{h^2}{2}f''(a+\theta_1 h) \qquad (1)$$

We can from the Lagrange's Mean Value Theorem

$$f(a+h) = f(a) + hf'(a+\theta h) \qquad (2)$$

Subtracting (1) and (2)

$$h[f'(a+\theta h) - f'(a)] = \frac{h^2}{2}f''(a+\theta_1 h)$$

$$\Rightarrow [f'(a+\theta h) - f'(a)] = \frac{h}{2}f''(a+\theta_1 h) \qquad (3)$$

Again since f' is derivable on $]a, a+h[$ hence from mean value theorem (Lagranges)

$$f'(a+\theta h) = f'(a) + \theta h f''(a+\theta_2 \theta h)$$

i.e. $$f'(a+\theta h) - f'(a) = \theta h f''(a+\theta_2 \theta h) \qquad (4)$$

From (3) and (4) we have

$$\frac{h}{2}f''(a+\theta_1 h) = \theta h f''(a+\theta_2 \theta h)$$

$$\Rightarrow \quad \tfrac{1}{2} f''(a+\theta_1 h) = f''(a+\theta_2 \theta h)$$

as $\quad h \to 0, \quad \theta_1 h \to 0 \quad \theta_2 \theta h \to 0,$

therefore $\quad f''(a+\theta_1 h) = f''(a)$

and $\quad f''(a+\theta_2 \theta h) = f''(a)$

Now we have given that f'' is continuous at $x = a$ i.e.

$$\lim_{h\to 0} f''(a+\theta_1 h) = \lim_{h\to 0} f''(a+\theta_2 \theta h) = f''(a) \neq 0$$

Therefore, $\quad \lim_{h\to 0} \theta = \frac{1}{2}$ *(Proved)*

Taylor's theorem: [With Lagranges multiplier].

Let f be a function defined on $[a, b]$ such that

(i) f^{n-1} is continuous on $[a, b]$.

(ii) f^{n-1} is derivable on $]a, b[$

Then there exist a real number c such that

$$f(b) = f(a) + (b-a) f'(a) + \frac{(b-a)^2}{2!} f''(a) + \ldots + \frac{(b-a)^{n-1}}{(n-1)!} f^{n-1}(a) + \frac{(b-a)^n}{n!} f^n(c)$$

Let the function defined on $[a, b]$ by setting

$$F(x) = f(b) - f(x) - (b-x) f'(x) - \ldots - \frac{(b-x)^{n-1}}{(n-1)!} f^{n-1}(x) - A(b-x)^n$$

Since f^{n-1} is continuous and is derivable on the closed and open interval, i.e. we should observe that $f', f'', f''' \ldots f^{n-1}$ are all defined and exist. Hence F is continuous on $[a, b]$, F is derivable on $]a, b[$ and $F(b) = 0$ if $F(a) = 0$ then it will satisfy all the condition of Rolle's theorem, Hence there will exist a real number c such that $F'(c) = 0$ if $F(a) = 0$

i.e. $$f(b) - f(a) - (b-a) f'(a) - \ldots \frac{(b-a^{n-1})}{(n-1)!} f^{n-1}(a) - A(b-a)^n = 0 \qquad (1)$$

$$F'(x) = -\frac{(b-x)^{n-1}}{(n-1)!} f^n(x) + An(b-x)^{n-1}$$

i.e. $\quad F'(c) = 0$

i.e. $\quad A = \frac{f^n(c)}{}$

Now from (1) we have,

$$f(b) = f(a) + (b-a) f'(a) + \ldots + \frac{(b-a)^{n-1}}{(n-1)!} f^{n-1}(a) + \frac{(b-a)^n}{n!} f^n(c)$$

Another form putting $b = a + h$ i.e. $b - a = h$

$$f(a+h) = f(a) + hf'(a) + \ldots + \frac{h^{n-1}}{(n-1)!} f^{n-1}(a) + \frac{h^n}{n!} f^n(a + \theta h)$$

Where $0 < \theta < 1$ defined on $[a, a + h]$
putting $x - a = h$

i.e. $$f(x) = f(a) + (x-a) f'(a) + \ldots + \frac{(x-a)^{n-1}}{(n-1)!} f^{n-1}(a) + \frac{(x-a)^n}{n!} f^n[a + \theta(x-a)]$$

defined on $[a-h, a + h]$
putting $a = 0$ in the above eqn. is called the Maclaurins theorem.

$$f(x) = f(0) + xf'(0) + \ldots + \frac{x^{n-1}}{(n-1)!} f^{n-1}(0) + \frac{x^n}{n!} f^n(\theta x)$$

defined on $[-h, h]$
Taylor's theorem with Cauchy Remainder.
Let a function f is defined on $[a, b]$ such that
(i) f^{n-1} is continuous on $[a, b]$
(ii) f^{n-1} is derivable on $]a, b[$
Then there exist a real number c such that

$$f(b) = f(a) + (b-a) f'(a) + \frac{(b-a)^2}{2!} f''(a) + \ldots + \frac{(b-a)^{n-1}}{(n-1)!} f^{n-1}(a) + \frac{(b-c)^{n-1}(b-a)}{(n-1)!} f^n(c)$$

Let F and G be two function defined as

$$F(x) = f(b) - f(x) - (b-x) f'(x) + \ldots + \frac{(b-x)^{n-1}}{(n-1)!} f^{n-1}(x)$$

and $G(x) = b - x$

Now, since, $f', f'' \ldots f^{n-1}$ are continuous on $[a, b]$ hence $F(x)$ is continuous on $[a, b]$ similarly that of $G(x)$ i.e. continuous on $[a, b]$ and is derivable on $]a, b[$. Since $G'(x) \neq 0$. Hence we can apply the Cauchy's mean value theorem such that

$$\frac{F'(c)}{G'(c)} = \frac{f'(c)}{g'(c)} = \frac{F(b) - F(a)}{G(b) - G(a)}$$

$$G'(c) = -1$$

$$F'(c) = -\frac{(b-c)^{n-1}}{(n-1)!} f^n(c)$$

Therefore,

$$b-a)\frac{(b-c)^{n-1}}{(n-1)!}f^n(c)=f(b)-(a)-(b-a)f'(a)\ldots-\frac{(b-a)^{n-1}}{(n-1)!}f^{n-1}(a)$$

$$\Rightarrow f(b)=f(a)+(b-a)f'(a)+\ldots+\frac{(b-a)^{n-1}}{(n-1)!}+f^{n-1}(a)$$

$$+\frac{(b-c)^{n-1}}{(n-1)!}\frac{(b-(a)}{f^n(c)}$$

Putting $b = a + h$. We have another form

$$f(a+h)=f(a)+hf(a)+\frac{h^2}{2!}f''(a)+\ldots+\frac{h^{n-1}}{(n-1)!}f^{n-1}(a)$$

$$+\frac{h^{n-1}h^1}{(n-1)!}(1-\theta)^n f^n(a+\theta h)$$

$$(a+\theta h)=f(a)+hf'(a)+\ldots+\frac{h^{n-1}f^{n-1}(a)}{(n-1)!}+\frac{h^n}{(n-1)!}(1-\theta)^n f^n(a+\theta h)$$

defined on $[a, a+h]$

If defined on $[a-h, a+h]$

$$f(x)=f(a)+(x-a)f'(a)+\ldots+\frac{(x-a)^n}{(n-1)!}f^{n-1}(a)$$

$$+\frac{(x-a)^n}{(n-1)!}(1-\theta)^{n-1}f^n[a+\theta(n-a)]$$

putting $a = 0$, defined on $[-h, h]$

$$f(x)=f(0)+xf'(0)+\ldots+\frac{x^n}{(n-1)!}f^{n-1}(0)+\frac{x^n}{(n-1)!}(1-\theta)^{n-1}f^n(a+\theta n)$$

This eqnuation is called a Maclourins theorem with Caucy's remainder.

Problem 6 Show that the number θ which occurs in Lagrange's remainder after n terms in Taylors expansion of a function f in the interval $[a, a+h]$ approaches $\frac{1}{n+1}$ as $h \to 0$ provided

(i) f^n is continuous in $[a, a+h]$

(ii) f^{n+1} exists in $]a, a+h[$

(iii) f^{n+1} is continuous at $x = a$

(iv) $f^{n+1}(a) \neq 0$

Taylors theorem for Lagranges remainder in which f^n is continuous on $[a, a+h]$ and is derivable on $]a, a+h[$ is given as

$$f(a+h)=f(a)+hf'(a)+\ldots+\frac{h^n}{n!}f^n(a+\theta h)$$

Now since f^n is continuous in $[a, a+h]$ and f^{n+1} exists in $]a, a+h[$

i.e. Taylors thm. for $(n+1)$ Lagrangian remainder is given as

$$f(a+h) = f(a) + hf'(a) + \frac{h^n}{n} f^n(a) + \frac{h^{n+1}}{(n+1)!} f^{n+1}(a + \theta_1 h)$$

where $0 < \theta_1 < 1$

We have from these two eqn.

$$\frac{h^n}{n!} f^n(a+\theta h) - f^n(a) = \frac{h^n \cdot h}{(n+1)\, n!} f^{n+1}(a+\theta h) - f^n(a)$$

$$\Rightarrow \quad f^n(a+\theta h) - f^n(a) = \frac{h}{n+1} f^{n+1}(a + \theta_1 h)$$

$$\Rightarrow f^n(a+\theta h) - f^n(a) = \frac{h}{n+1} f^{n+1}(a + \theta_1 h) \qquad \text{(a)}$$

Now since f^n is continuous in $[a, a+h]$, and f^{n+1} exists in $]a, a+h[$
Hence it satisfies all the hypothesis of L.M.V. Therefore,

$$f^n(a+\theta h) = f^n(a) + \theta h\, f^{n+1}(a + \theta_2\, \theta h) \qquad \text{(A)}$$

where $\quad 0 < \theta_2 < 1$

i.e. $\quad f^n(a+\theta h) - f^n(a) = \theta h\, f^{n+1}(a + \theta_2\, \theta h) \qquad$ (A)

Therefore, from eqn. (a) and (A) we have

$$\theta f^{n+1}(a + \theta_2\, \theta h) = \frac{1}{n+1} f^{n+1}(a + \theta_1 h)$$

$\because \; h \to 0, \qquad \theta_1 h \to 0, \theta_2\, \theta h \to 0$

and since f^{n+1} is continuous at $\quad x = a$

and is $f^{n+1}(a) \neq 0$ Hence,

$$\lim_{h\to 0} f^{n+1}(a + \theta_2\, \theta h) = \lim_{n\to 0} f^{n+1}(a + \theta_1 h)$$

$$= f^{n+1}(a) \neq 0$$

Hence $\qquad \lim_{h\to 0} \theta = \frac{1}{n+1}$ *(Proved)*

Power series:

The Maclaurins expansion is called the Power series. i.e.

$$f(x) = f(0) + x f'(0) + \ldots + \frac{x^n}{n!} f'(\theta x) \quad \forall \quad x$$

defined on on $[-h, h]$

Some expansions *(standard)*

Problem 1 Let $\qquad f(x) = e^x$

$$f'(x) = e^x$$

$$f''(x) = e^x$$
$$\ldots f^n(x) = e^x$$

Now According to Maeluarin's theorem

$$f(x) = f(0) + xf'(0) + \frac{x^2}{2!} f''(0) + \ldots + \frac{x^{n-1}}{(n-1)!} f^{n-1}(0) + \frac{x^n}{n!} f^n(\theta_n n)$$

we have, $f(0) = e^0 = 1$

$f'(0) = e^0 = 1$

$f^{n-1}(0) = e^0 = 1$

and $f^n(0) = e^0 = 1$ Therefore

$$f(x) = 1 + x + \frac{x^2}{2!} + \ldots + \frac{x^{n-1}}{(n-1)!} + \frac{x^n}{n!} f^n(\theta_n x)$$

$$\Rightarrow \quad e^x = 1 + x + \frac{x^2}{2!} + \ldots + \frac{x^{n-1}}{(n-1)!} + R_n$$

where $R_n = \frac{x^n}{n!} e^{\theta nx}$

Now as $n \to \infty$, $R_n \to 0$

Therefore the series continues to the infinity, i.e.,

$$e^x = 1 + x + \frac{x^2}{2!} + \ldots + \frac{x^{n-1}}{(n-1)!} + \ldots, \quad \forall \quad x$$

Problem 2 Let $f(x) = (1 + x)^m$

$f'(x) = m(1 + x)^{m-1}$

$f''(x) = m(m-1)(1 + x)^{m-2}$

$\ldots f^n(x) = m(m-1)(m-2)\ldots(m-n+1)(1+x)^{m-x}$

$\therefore \quad f'(0) = m$

$f''(0) = m(m-1)$

$\therefore f^n(0) = m(m-1)(m-2)\ldots(m-n+1)$

Now from the Maclaurin's theorem

$$f(x) = f(0) + xf'(0) + \frac{x^2}{2!} f''(0) + \ldots$$
$$+ \frac{x^{n-1}}{(n-1)!} f^{n-1}(0) + \frac{x^n}{n!} f^n(\theta_n x)$$

i.e., $$(1 + x)^m = 1 + xm + \frac{x^2}{2!} m(m-1) + \ldots$$
$$+ \frac{x^{n-1}}{(n-1)!} m(m-1)\ldots(m-n+1) + \frac{x^n}{n!} f^n(\theta_n x)$$

Therefore, $(1 + x)^m = 1 + mx + m(m-1)\frac{x^2}{2!} + \ldots$

$$+ \frac{x^{n-1}}{(n-1)!} m(m-1)\ldots(m-n+2) + R_n$$

Where $$R_n = \frac{x^n}{n!} m(m-1)(m-2)\ldots(m-n+1)(1+\theta_n x)$$

$$\lim_{n\to\infty} R_n = 0$$

i.e., when $n \to \infty$, $R_n \to 0$

Hence, the expansion continued to infinity

$$(1 + x)^m = 1 + mx + m(m-1)\frac{x^2}{2!} + \ldots,$$

$$+ m(m-1)\ldots(m-n+2)\frac{x^{n-1}}{(n-1)}$$

$$= 1 + mx + \frac{m(m-1)}{2!}x^2 + \ldots$$

$$+ \frac{m(m-1)(m-2)\ldots(m-n+1)x^n}{n!}$$

where $|x| < 1$

i.e., $-1 < x < 1$.

Problem 3 $f(x) = \log(1 + x)$

$$f'(x) = \frac{1}{1+x}$$

$$f''(x) = -\frac{1}{(1+x)^2}$$

$$\ldots f^n(x) = \frac{(-1)^{n-1}(n-1)!}{(1+x)^n}$$

$$f^n(x) = \frac{(-1)^{n-1}(n-1)!}{(1+x)^n}$$

$$f'(0) = 1$$

$$f''(0) = -1$$

$$\ldots f^n(0) = (-1)^{n-1}(n-1)!$$

and $$f^n(\theta_n x) = \frac{(-1)^{n-1}(n-1)!}{(1+\theta_n x)^n}$$

Now from the Maclaurin's theorem

$$f(x) = f(0) + xf'(0) + \frac{x^2}{2!} f''(0) + \ldots$$

$$+ \frac{x^{n-1}}{(n-1)!} f^{n-1}(0) + \frac{x^n}{n!} f^n(\theta_n x)$$

$$\Rightarrow \quad \log(1+x) = x + \frac{x^2}{2!}(-1) \ldots + \frac{x^{n-1}}{(n-1)!}(-1)^{n-2}(n-2)!$$

$$+ \frac{x^n}{n!}(-1)^{n-1} \frac{(n-1)!}{(1+\theta_n x)^n}$$

$$\Rightarrow \quad \log(1+x) = x - \frac{x^2}{2!} + \ldots + \frac{(-1)^{n-2} x^{n-1}}{(n-1)} + R_n$$

where $\quad R_n = \frac{(-1)^{n-1}(n-1)!}{(1+\theta_n x)^n} \frac{x^n}{n!}$

$\lim_{n \to \infty} R_n = 0$ Therefore it continued to infinity

$$\left[\because \lim_{n \to \infty} \frac{x^n}{n!} = 0\right]$$

$$\therefore \quad \log(1+x) = x - \frac{x^2}{2!} + \frac{x^3}{3!} + \ldots \quad \text{where} \quad |x| < |$$

i.e., $-1 < x \leqslant 1$.

Problem 4 Let $f(x) = \sin x$

$$f''(x) = \cos x$$

$$f''(x) = -\sin x$$

$$\ldots f^n(x) = \sin(x + n\pi/2)$$

$$f^n(0) = \sin(\tfrac{1}{2} n\pi) = 0 \quad \text{or} \quad \pm 1 \text{ as } n \text{ is even or odd}$$

Let $\quad n = 2m + 1$

Now from Maclaurin's series

$$f(x) = f(0) + xf'(0) + \frac{x^2}{2!} f''(0) + \ldots$$

$$+ \frac{x^{n-1}}{(n-1)!} f^{n-1}(0) + \frac{x^n}{n!} f^n(\theta_n x)$$

$$\Rightarrow \quad \sin x = x - \frac{x^2}{2!} X 0 + \frac{x^3}{3!} -1) + \ldots$$

$$+ \frac{x^{n-1}}{(n-1)!} f^{n-1}(0) + R_n$$

where $$R^n = \frac{x^n}{n!} f^n (\theta^n x)$$

$$\lim_{n \to \infty} R^n = 0$$

Therefore, $\sin x = x - \frac{x^3}{3!} + \frac{x^5}{5!} + \ldots \quad \forall \quad x \in R.$

Problem 5 Let $f(x) = \cos x$

$$f'(x) = -\sin x$$

$$f''(x) = -\cos x$$

$$\ldots f^n(x) = \cos\left(x + \frac{n}{2}\pi\right)$$

$$f^n(0) = 0 \quad \text{or} \quad \pm 1 \text{ as } n \text{ is odd or even.}$$

Let $n = 2m$

Now from Macluarin's theorem

$$f(x) = f(0) + x f'(0) + \frac{x^2}{2!} f''(0) + \ldots$$

$$+ \frac{x^{n-1}}{(n-1)!} f^{n-1}(0) + \frac{x^n}{n!} f^n(\theta_n x)$$

$$\Rightarrow \quad \cos x = 1 - \frac{x^2}{2!} + \frac{x^4}{4!} + \ldots + \frac{x^{n-1}}{(n-1)} f^{n-}(0) + R_n$$

where $$R_n = \frac{x^n}{n!} f^n(\theta_n x)$$

$$\text{Lt}_{n \to \infty} R_n = 0$$

Hence the expansion continued to ∞

i.e., $\cos x = 1 - \frac{x^2}{2!} + \frac{x^4}{4!} + \ldots \quad \forall \quad x \in R$

Appendix 13

INFINITE SERIES

Remark 1 Geometric series test

The geometric series $a + ar + ar^2 + \ldots$ is

(i) convergent if $|r| < 1$

(ii) divergent if $r \geqslant 1$

(iii) oscillatory if $r \leqslant -1$.

Remark 2 p. series test

The positive term series

$$\sum \frac{1}{n^p} = \frac{1}{1^p} + \frac{1}{2^p} + \frac{1}{3^p} + \ldots \text{ is}$$

(i) convergent if $p > 1$

(ii) divergent if $p \leqslant 1$

Remark 3 Comparison test

Let two positive term $\sum u_n$ and $\sum v_n$ such that

$$\lim_{n \to \infty} \frac{u_n}{v_n} = \text{finite } (\neq 0) \quad \text{then}$$

u_n and v_n behaves alike.

Remark 4 Cauchy's root test

If $\sum u_n$ be a positive term series such that

$$\lim_{n \to \infty} (u_n)^{1/n} = 1 \quad \text{then the series}$$

(i) converges if $l < 1$

(ii) diverges if $l > 1$

(iii) the test fails if $l = 1$.

Remark 5 D. Alembert's Ratio Test

If $\sum u_n$ is a positive term series such that

$$\lim_{n \to \infty} \frac{u_n}{u_n + 1} = l \quad \text{then the series is}$$

(i) convergent if $l > 1$
(ii) divergent if $l < 1$
(iii) the test fails if $l = 1$

If u_n involves increasing powers of x then we should start with ratio test. The test is also useful when u_n contains factorials.

Remark 6 Raabe's test

If $\sum u_.$ is a positive term series such that

$$\lim_{n\to\infty} n\left(\frac{u_n}{u^{n+1}} - 1\right) = l \text{ then the series is}$$

(i) convergent if $l > 1$
(ii) divergent if $l < 1$
(iii) test fails if $l = 1$

Remark 7 Logarithmic test

If $\sum u_n$ is a positive term series such that

$$\lim_{n\to\infty} n \log \frac{u_n}{u_{n+1}} = l \quad \text{then the series}$$

(i) converges if $l > 1$
(ii) diverges if $l < 1$
(iii) test fails if $l = 1$

Remark 8 Cauchy's condensation test

If $\sum u_n$ is a positive term series such that
$u_{n+1} < u_n$ then the series $\sum u_n$ and E $a^n u_a n$ $(a = 2, 3, 4 \ldots)$ behaves alike.

Remark 9 Lerbnitz's test

The alternating series $u_1 - u_2 + u_3 - u_4 \ldots$ is a convergent if
(i) $u_{n+1} < u_n$ i.e., $u_1 > u_2 > u_3 \ldots$
(ii) and $\lim_{n\to\infty} u_n = 0$

Solved Examples

Ex. 1 Show that the series $1 + \frac{2}{3} + \left(\frac{2}{3}\right)^2 + \ldots + \left(\frac{2}{3}\right)^{n-1} + \ldots$ converges

Here $$S_n = 1 + \frac{2}{3} + \left(\frac{2}{3}\right)^2 + \ldots + \left(\frac{2}{3}\right)^{n-1}$$

$$= \frac{1-(2/3)^n}{1-2/3} = 3 - 3\,(2/3)^n$$

Since the given series converges to 3, thevefore the given series is convergent

Ex. 2 Show that the series $1 + 2 + 3 + \ldots + n$ diverges

Here $$S_n = 1 + 2 + 3 + \ldots + n$$

$$S_n = \frac{n(n+1)}{2}$$

$$S_{n+1} = \tfrac{1}{2}(n+1)(n+2)$$

$$\therefore \quad S_{n+1} - S_n = n + 1 > 0 \quad \forall \quad n$$

Here $< S_n >$ is monotonically increasing sequence.
Therefore, it will either diverge or converge but will never oscillate.

$$\underset{n\to\infty}{\text{Lt}} S_n = \infty \text{ Hence the series diverges}$$

Ex. 3 Show that the series $2 - 2 + 2 - 2 \ldots$

$$S_n = 0 \text{ when } n \text{ is even} = 2 \text{ if } n \text{ is odd}$$

Therefore the sequence $< S_n >$ oscillate

Ex. 4 Show that the series $1 + \frac{1}{2} + \frac{1}{3} + \ldots \frac{1}{n} + \ldots$ does not converge

Let the series converges. Taking $\epsilon = \frac{1}{4}$. By Cauchy's sequence we have

$$| S_n - S_m | < \epsilon \quad \forall \quad n > m$$

i.e. $$\frac{1}{m+1} + \frac{1}{m+2} + \ldots + \frac{1}{n} < \frac{1}{4} \quad \forall \quad n \geqslant m$$

But by taking $n = 2m$

$$\frac{1}{m+1} + \frac{1}{m+2} + \ldots + \frac{1}{n} = \frac{1}{m+1} + \frac{1}{m+2} + \ldots + \frac{1}{2m}$$

$$> m\frac{1}{2m} > \frac{1}{2}$$

Therefore, we have a contradiction
Hence the given series does not converge

Remark 10 Gauss test
If the following can be expressed

$$\frac{u_n}{u_{n+1}} = 1 + \frac{a}{n} + \frac{a^m}{n^k}$$

$$= 1 + \frac{a}{n} + \text{higher powers of both}$$

then convergent if $a > 1$ divergent if $a \leqslant 1$

Ex. 5 Show that the series

$$\sqrt{\frac{1}{4}} + \sqrt{\frac{2}{6}} + \ldots + \sqrt{\frac{n}{2(n+1)}} + \ldots$$

does not converge

Here $$u_n = \sqrt{\frac{n}{2(n+1)}} = \frac{1}{\sqrt{2}}\sqrt{\frac{n}{n+1}}$$

$$u_n = \frac{1}{\sqrt{2}}\sqrt{\frac{1}{1+1/n}}$$

Now $$\operatorname*{Lt}_{n\to\infty} u_n = \frac{1}{\sqrt{2}} \neq 0$$

Hence the given series does not converge

Ex. 7 Test for convergence the series

$$\frac{1}{5} + \frac{\sqrt{2}}{7} + \frac{\sqrt{3}}{9} + \frac{\sqrt{4}}{11} + \ldots$$

Here, $$u_n = \frac{\sqrt{n_n}}{2n+3} > 0 \quad \forall \quad n$$

Let $$v_n = \frac{1}{\sqrt{n}}$$

i.e. $$\frac{u_n}{v_n} = \frac{n}{2n+3}$$

i.e. $$\operatorname*{Lt}_{u\to\infty} \frac{u_n}{v_n} = \frac{1}{2+3/n} = \frac{1}{2} \neq 0$$

Now according to comparison test u_n and v_n behaves alike

Now for $$v_n = \frac{1}{n^{1/2}} \qquad \text{Here} \qquad p = \frac{1}{2} < 1$$

i.e., v_n diverges. Hence u_n also diverges

i.e., $$u_n = \frac{\sqrt{n}}{2n+3} \text{ is a divergent one.}$$

Ex. 8 Test for convergence of the series whose nth term is $\sqrt{n^4+1} - n^2$

We have $u_n = \sqrt{n^4+1} - n^2$

$$\therefore \quad u_n = \sqrt{n^4+1} - n^2 \times \frac{\sqrt{n^4+1} + n^2}{\sqrt{n^4+1} + n^2}$$

$$u_n = \frac{n^4 + 1 - n^4}{\sqrt{n^4 + 1} + n^2}$$

$$u_n = \frac{1}{\sqrt{n^4 + 1} + n^2}$$

Let $\quad u_n = \frac{1}{n^2} \quad$ such that

$$\frac{u_n}{v_n} = \frac{n^2}{\sqrt{n^4 + 1} + n^2}$$

$$\frac{u_n}{v_n} = \frac{1}{\sqrt{1 + 1/n^4} + 1}$$

$$\underset{n \to \infty}{\text{Lt}} \frac{u_n}{u_n} = \frac{1}{2} \neq 0$$

Hence according to comparison test v_n and u_n behaves alike

But for $\quad v_n = \frac{1}{n^2}$ the series converges.

Since $p > 1$. Therefore u_n also converges.

Ex. 9 Test for convergence the series

$$\frac{1}{\log 2} + \frac{1}{\log 3} + \ldots + \frac{1}{\log n} + \ldots$$

We have, $\quad u_n = \sum_{n=2}^{\infty} \frac{1}{\log n}$

We know that $n > \log n \ \forall \ n \geqslant 2$

i.e., $$\frac{1}{n} < \frac{1}{\log n}$$

Now according to comparison test let $v_n = 1/n$ i.e., we should test $1/n$. If it diverges u_n also diverges and if it converges u_n also converges.

Here $\quad v_n = \frac{1}{n}$ diverges and so

$$u_n = \frac{1}{\log n} \text{ diverges } \forall \ n \geqslant 2$$

Ex. 10 Test for convergence of the series

$$1 + \frac{1}{2^2} + \frac{1}{3^3} + \frac{1}{4^4} + \ldots + \frac{1}{n^n}$$

Let $$u_n = \frac{1}{n^n}$$

If $n > 2$ then $n^n > 2^n$

i.e., $$\frac{1}{n^n} < \frac{1}{2^n}$$

Let $$v_n = \frac{1}{2^n}$$

Since v_n is a geometric series with common ratio 1/2.
Therefore it must converge

[$\because$ G.P. cvgs. if $|r| < 1$]

Therefore from comparison test $u_n = \frac{1}{n^n}$ also converges

Problem 11 Test for convergence of the series

$$\frac{1}{3.7} + \frac{1}{4.9} + \frac{1}{5.11} + \ldots$$

Here $$n_n = \frac{1}{(n+2)(2n+5)}$$

Let $$v_n = \frac{1}{n^2}$$

$$\frac{u_n}{v^n} = \frac{n^2}{(n+2)(2n+5)} = \frac{1}{(1+2/n)(2+5/n)}$$

$$\underset{n\to\infty}{\text{Lt}} \frac{u_n}{v_n} = \frac{1}{2} \neq 0$$

Hence from comparison test u_n and v_n both behaves alike since v_n converges
Hence, u_n also converges

Problem 2 $$\frac{1}{1.3.5} + \frac{1}{2.4.6} + \frac{1}{3.5.7} + \ldots$$

The general term of the series

$$u_n = \frac{1}{n\,.\,(n+2)(n+4)}$$

Let $$v_n = \frac{1}{n^3}$$

and $$\frac{u_n}{v_n} = \frac{n^3}{n^3(1+2/n)(1+4/n)}$$

$$\frac{u_n}{v_n} = \frac{1}{(1 + 2/n)(1 + 4/n)}$$

$$\underset{n \to \infty}{\text{Lt}} \frac{u_n}{v_n} = 1 \neq 0$$

u_n and v_n behaves alike.
Since v_n converges [$\because$ $p > 1$]

u_n also converges

Problem 13 $\frac{1}{1 \cdot 2 \cdot 6} + \frac{1}{2 \cdot 3 \cdot 7} + \frac{1}{3 \cdot 4 \cdot 8} + \ldots$

General term of the series

$$u_n = \frac{1}{n(n + 1)(n + 2)}$$

$$u_n = \frac{1}{n^3 (1 + 1/n)(1 + 5/n)}$$

$$\text{Let} \quad u_n = \frac{1}{n^3}$$

$$\underset{n \to \infty}{\text{Lt}} \quad u_n = \frac{u_n}{v_n} = \frac{1}{(1 + 1/n)(1 + 5/n)}$$

According to comparison test u_n and v_n behaves alike v_n converges with $p > 1$ hence u_n also converges.

Problem 4 $\frac{1}{\sqrt{3 \cdot 4}} + \frac{1}{\sqrt{4\ 5}} + \frac{1}{\sqrt{5 \cdot 6}} + \frac{1}{\sqrt{6 \cdot 7}} + \ldots$

General term

$$u_n = \frac{1}{\sqrt{(n + 2)(n + 3)}}$$

$$u_n = \frac{1}{n \sqrt{(1 + 2/n)(1 + 3/n)}}$$

$$\text{Let} \quad v_n = \frac{1}{n} \quad \text{which is a positive term series.}$$

$$\underset{n \to \infty}{\text{Lt}} \quad \frac{u_n}{v_n} = \frac{n}{n \sqrt{(1 + 2/n)(1 + 3/n)}} = 1 \neq 0$$

According to comparison test, u_n and v_n both either converges or diverges. But since v_n diverges therefore u_n diverges, too.

Problem 15 $\frac{1}{4\,6} + \frac{\sqrt{3}}{6\cdot 8} + \frac{\sqrt{5}}{8\cdot 10} + \frac{\sqrt{7}}{10\cdot 12} + \ldots$

The general term

$$u_n = \frac{(2n-1)^{1/2}}{(2n+2)(2n+4)}$$

$$u_n = \frac{n^{1/2}(2-1/n)^{1/2}}{n^2(2+2/n)(2+4/n)}$$

Now let v_n an auxiliary positive term

Series with general term $\quad v_n = \frac{1}{n^{3/2}}$

$$\frac{u_n}{v_n} = \frac{(2-1/n)^{1/2}}{(2+2/n)(2+4/n)}$$

$$\underset{n\to\infty}{\text{Let}} \frac{u_n}{v_n} = \frac{\sqrt{2}}{2.2} = \frac{1}{2\sqrt{2}} \neq 0$$

They behaves alike. But $\quad v_n = \frac{1}{n^{3/2}}, p > 1.$

Converges therefore u_n is a convergent series.

Problem 16 $\frac{\sqrt{2}-1}{3^3-1} + \frac{\sqrt{3}-1}{4^3-1} + \frac{\sqrt{4}-1}{5^3-1} + \ldots$

General term $\qquad u_n = \frac{\sqrt{n+1}-1}{(n+2)^3-1}$

$$u_n = \frac{\sqrt{n}\,[(1+1/n)^{1/2}-1/\sqrt{n}]}{n^2[(1+2/n)^3-1/n^3]}$$

$$u_n = \frac{[(1+1/n)^{1/2}-1/\sqrt{n}]}{n^{5/2}[(1+2/n)^3-1/n^3]}$$

Let $\quad v_n = \frac{1}{n^{5/2}}$

be an auxiliary positive term series i.e.,

$$\frac{u_n}{v_n} = \frac{n^{5/2}[(1+1/n)^{1/2}-1/\sqrt{n}]}{n^{5/2}[(1+2/n)^3-1/n^3]}$$

$$\underset{n\to\infty}{\text{Lt}} \frac{u_n}{v_n} = 1 \neq 0$$

u_n and v_n either converges or diverges. But since v_n converges. Hence u_n is also convergent sequence.

Problem 17 $\frac{1}{\sqrt{2}+\sqrt{3}}+\frac{1}{\sqrt{3}+\sqrt{4}}+\frac{1}{\sqrt{4}+\sqrt{5}}+\ldots$

The general term $u_n = \frac{1}{\sqrt{n+1}+\sqrt{n+2}}$

$$u_n = \frac{1}{\sqrt{n}\,(1+1/n)^{1/2}+\sqrt{n}\,(1+2/n)^{1/2}}$$

$$u_n = \frac{1}{\sqrt{n}\,[(1+1/n)^{1/2}+(1+2/n)^{1/2}]}$$

Let $v_n = \frac{1}{\sqrt{n}}$ be auxiliary positive term series.

So that $$\frac{u_n}{v_n} = \frac{1}{[(1+1/n)^{1/2}+(1+2/n)^{1/2}}$$

$$\underset{n\to\infty}{\text{Lt}}\ \frac{u_n}{v_n} = \frac{1}{\sqrt{2}} \neq 0$$

u_n and v_n either converge or diverge.
But v_n diverges for $p < 1$ therefore, u_n is a divergent series.

Problem 18 $\sum_{n=1}^{\infty}\frac{1}{3^n+x}$ for all positive values of x.

$$u_n = \frac{1}{3^n+x} = \frac{1}{3^n\left[1+\frac{x}{3^n}\right]}$$

Let $v_n = \frac{1}{3^n}$ So that we have,

$$\frac{u_n}{v_n} = \frac{3^n}{3^n\,[1+x/3^n]} = \frac{1}{1+x/3^n}$$

$$\underset{n\to\infty}{\text{Let}}\ \frac{u_n}{v_n} = 1 \neq 0.$$

According to comparison test u_n and v_n behaves alike. But for $v_n = 1/3^n$ the series is a G, P with common ration $r = 1/3 < 1$ therefore v_n converges. Hence the series u_n is convergent.

Problem 19 $\sum_{n=1}^{\infty}\frac{n^2}{n^3+5}$

Hence, $$u_n = \frac{n^2}{n^3+5}$$

$$\text{Let} \quad v_n = \frac{1}{n}$$

Such that
$$\frac{u_n}{v_n} = \frac{n^3}{n^3 + 5}$$

$$\lim_{n\to\infty} \frac{u_n}{v_n} = \lim_{n\to\infty} \frac{1}{1 + 5/n^3} = 1 \neq 0$$

Hence from comparison test it is clear that they behaves alike.

Since $v_n = \frac{1}{n}$ diverges hence

$$u_n = \frac{n^2}{n^3 + 5} \quad \text{also diverges.}$$

Problem 20 $\sum_{n=1}^{\infty} \frac{1}{(2n-1)^p}$

General term
$$u_n = \frac{1}{(2n-1)^p} = \frac{1}{n^p\,(2-1/n)^p}$$

$$\text{Let} \quad v_n = \frac{1}{n^p}$$

be an auxiliary positive term series. Such that

$$\frac{u_n}{v_n} = \frac{n^p}{n^p\,(2-1/n)^p} + \frac{1}{(2-1/n)^p}$$

$$\underset{n\to\infty}{\text{Lt}} \frac{u_n}{v_n} = \underset{n\to\infty}{\text{Lt}} \frac{1}{(2-1/n)^p} = \frac{1}{2^p}$$

Now according to comparison test u_n and v_n both either converge or diverge together. But, sinee $v_n = \frac{1}{n^p}$ is a p-th series, which converges

when $p > 1$

and diverges when $p \leqslant 1$.

therefore u_n cvgs when $p > 1$

u_n dvgs when $p \leqslant 1$.

Problem 21 Test for convergence of the series whose nth term is

(a) $\sqrt{n + 1} - \sqrt{n}$

(b) $(n^3 + 1)^{1/3} - n$

(c) $\sqrt{n^3 + 1} - \sqrt{n^3}$

(d) $\sqrt{n^4 + 1} - \sqrt{n^4 - 1}$

(e) $\sqrt{n^2 + 1} - n$.

(a)

$$u_n = \sqrt{n+1} - \sqrt{n} + \frac{\sqrt{n+1} + \sqrt{n}}{\sqrt{n+1} + \sqrt{n}}$$

$$u_n = \frac{n+1-n}{\sqrt{n+1} + \sqrt{n}}$$

$$u_n = \frac{1}{\sqrt{n}\,[(1+1/n)^{1/2}+1]} = \frac{1}{\sqrt{n}\,[(1+1/n)^{1/2}+1]}$$

Let $v_n = \dfrac{1}{\sqrt{n}}$ be an auxiliary positive term series such that

$$\frac{u_n}{v_n} = \frac{1}{[(1+1/n)^{1/2}+1]}$$

$$\underset{n\to\infty}{\text{Lt}} \frac{u_n}{v_n} = \underset{n\to\infty}{\text{Lt}} \frac{1}{[(1+1/n)^{1/2}+1]} = \frac{1}{2} \neq 0$$

Therefore u_n behaves like that of v_n. But
Since v_n is a divergent sequence
Hence u_n is a divergent sequence

(b)

$$u_n = 3\sqrt{n^3+1} - n$$

$$= (n^3+1)^{1/3} - n$$

$$= n\,(1+1/n^3)^{1/3} - n$$

$$u_n = n\,[(1+1/n^3)^{1/3} - 1]$$

$$= n\left[1 + \frac{1}{3}\frac{1}{n^3} + \frac{\frac{1}{3}\left(\frac{1}{3}-1\right)}{2.1}\frac{1}{n^6} + \ldots\right]$$

$$= n\left[\frac{1}{3}\frac{1}{n^3} + \frac{\frac{1}{3}\left(\frac{1}{3}-1\right)}{2.1}\frac{1}{n^6} + \ldots\right]$$

$$u_n = \frac{1}{3}\cdot\frac{1}{n^2} + \frac{\frac{1}{3}\left(\frac{1}{3}-1\right)}{2.1}\frac{1}{n^5} + \ldots$$

Let $v_n = \dfrac{1}{n^2}$ be an auxiliary positive term series such that

$$\frac{u_n}{v_n} = \frac{1}{3} + \frac{\frac{1}{3}\left(\frac{1}{3}-1\right)}{2.1}\frac{1}{n^3} + \ldots$$

$$\underset{n\to\infty}{\text{Lt}} \frac{u_n}{v_n} = \frac{1}{3} \neq 0$$

u_n and v_n either converges or diverges together. But since v_n converges hence u_n is also a convergent series.

(c) $$u_n = \sqrt{n^3+1} - \sqrt{n^3} + \frac{\sqrt{n^3+1}+\sqrt{n^3}}{\sqrt{n^3+1}+\sqrt{n^3}}$$

$$u_n = \frac{n^3+1-n^3}{\sqrt{n^3+1}+\sqrt{n^3}} = \frac{1}{n^{3/2}\,[(1+1/n^3)^{1/2}+1]}$$

Now let $$v_n = \frac{1}{n^{3/2}} \text{ such that}$$

$$\frac{u_n}{v_n} = \frac{1}{[(1+1/n^3)^{1/2}+1]}$$

$$\lim_{n\to\infty} \frac{u_n}{v_n} = \frac{1}{2} \neq 0$$

Here u_n and v_n either converges or diverges together. But since,

$$v_n = \frac{1}{n^{3/2}} [\because \; p > 1]$$

Therefore, $u_n = \sqrt{n^3+1} - \sqrt{n^3}$ is also a convergent series.

(d) $$u_n = \sqrt{n^4+1} - \sqrt{n^4-1} \times \frac{\sqrt{n^4+1}+\sqrt{n^4-1}}{\sqrt{n^4+1}+\sqrt{n^4-1}}$$

$$u_n = \frac{n^4+1-n^4+1}{\sqrt{n^4+1}+\sqrt{n^4-1}}$$

$$= \frac{2}{n^2\,[(1+1/n^4)^{1/2}+(1+1/n^4)^{1/2}}$$

$$u_n = \frac{2}{n^2\,[(1+1/n^4)^{1/2}+(1-1/n^4)^{1/2}]}$$

Let $v_n = \dfrac{1}{n^2}$ be an auxiliary positive term series such that

$$\frac{u_n}{v_n} = \frac{2}{[(1+1/n^4)^{1/2}+(1-1/n^4)^{1/2}]}$$

$$\lim_{n\to\infty} \frac{u_n}{v_n} = \lim_{n\to\infty} \frac{2}{[(1+1/n^4)^{1/2}+(1-1/n^4)^{1/2}]}$$

$$= \frac{2}{2} = 1 \neq 0$$

Therefore we conclude that u_n and v_n both either converges or diverges together. But since $v_n = 1/n^2$ be a convergent series. Hence u_n is also a convergent series.

(e)
$$u_n = \sqrt{n^2+1} - n = n\,(1 + 1/n^2)^{1/2} - n$$
$$= n\left[1 + \frac{1}{2n^2} + \frac{\frac{1}{2}\left(\frac{1}{2}-1\right)}{2\cdot 1}\frac{1}{n^4}\ldots - 1\right]$$
$$= \frac{1}{2n} + \frac{\frac{1}{2}\left(\frac{1}{2}-1\right)}{2\cdot 1}\frac{1}{n^3} + \ldots$$

Let
$$u_n = \frac{1}{n} \text{ such that}$$
$$\frac{u_n}{v_n} = \frac{1}{2} + \frac{\frac{1}{2}\left(\frac{1}{2}-1\right)}{2.1}\frac{1}{n^2} + \ldots$$
$$\underset{n\to\infty}{\text{Lt}} \frac{u_n}{v_n} = \frac{1}{2} \neq 0$$

i.e. u_n and v_n either converges or diverges together. But since, $v_n = 1/n$ diverges for $p = 1$. Therefore, u_n is also a divergent series.

Problem 22 Prove that the series $\sum_{n=2}^{\infty} \frac{1}{n^2 \log n}$ converges.

$$u_n = \frac{1}{n^2 \log n} \qquad \forall\, n \geqslant 2$$
$$\left[\begin{array}{lll} \text{since} & n^2 < n^2 \log n & \forall\, n \geqslant 3 \\ \text{i.e.,} & \dfrac{1}{n^2} > \dfrac{1}{n^2 \log n} & \end{array}\right]$$
$$u_{n+1} = \frac{1}{(n+1)^2 \log (n+1)}$$

Hence, Applying Ratio test
$$\frac{u_n}{u_{n+1}} = \frac{(n+1)^2}{n^2}\,\frac{\log (n+1)}{\log n}$$
$$= (1+1/n)^2 \frac{\log (1+n)}{\log n}$$
$$\underset{n\to\infty}{\text{Lt}} \frac{u_n}{u_{n+1}} = \underset{n\to\infty}{\text{Lt}}\ (1 + 1/n)^2 \frac{\log (1+n)}{\log n}$$
$$= \underset{n\to\infty}{\text{Lt}} \frac{\log \{n\,(1+1/n)\}}{\log n}$$
$$= \underset{n\to\infty}{\text{Lt}} \frac{\log n + \log (1+1/n)}{\log n}$$

$$= \underset{n\to\infty}{\text{Let}}\ 1 + \frac{\left[\frac{1}{n} - \frac{1}{2n^2} + \ldots\right]}{\log n}$$

$$= 1 + \frac{1}{n \log n} - \frac{1}{2n^2 \log n} + \ldots = 1$$

Therefore Ratio test fails.
we proceeds for Raabe's test

$$n\left[\frac{u_n}{u_{n+1}} - 1\right] = n\frac{\left[\frac{1}{n} - \frac{1}{2n^2} + \ldots\right]}{\log n} = \frac{1 - \frac{1}{2n} + \ldots}{\log n}$$

$$= \lim_{n\to\infty}\left[\frac{1}{\log n} - \frac{1}{2n \log n} + \ldots\right] = 0 < 1.$$

From Raabe's test therefore the series converges.

Problem 23 Test for convergence of the series $\sum_{n=1}^{n=\infty} \cos\left(\frac{1}{n}\right)$

Here $$u_n = \cos\frac{1}{n}$$

Let $$x = \frac{1}{n} \text{ so that}$$

$$\cos x = 1 - \frac{x^2}{2!} + \frac{x^4}{4!}\ldots$$

$\therefore$ $$\cos\left(\frac{1}{n}\right) = 1 - \frac{1}{2n^2} + \frac{1}{24n^4}\ldots$$

Now $$\underset{n\to\infty}{\text{Lt}} \cos\frac{1}{n} = \underset{n\to\infty}{\text{Lt}}\left[1 - \frac{1}{2n^2} + \frac{1}{24n^4}\right] = 1 \neq 0.$$

Therefore from the theorem, that a series is said to be convergent if $\lim_{n\to\infty} u_n = 0$, the given series diverges.

Problem 24 Show that the series $\sum_{n=1}^{\infty} (1/n)^{1/n}$ diverges.

Here $$u_n = \left(\frac{1}{n}\right)^{1/n}$$

$\because$ $$n^{1/n} < n$$

$\therefore$ $$\frac{1}{n^{1/n}} > \frac{1}{n}$$

Now from the comparison test $\frac{1}{n^{1/n}}$ behaves alike as $\frac{1}{n}$. But since $v_n = \frac{1}{n}$ diverges

Hence, $$u_n = \left(\frac{1}{n}\right)^{1/m} \text{ is divergent series.}$$

Problem 25 Assuming that $\sin \theta < \theta$ whenever $\theta < \pi/2$, $\theta > 0$ show that $\sum_{n=1}^{\infty} \sin\left(\frac{1}{n^2}\right)$ converges.

Let $$u_n = \sin\left(\frac{1}{n^2}\right)$$

Since, $n \to \infty$ therefore $\frac{1}{n^2} \to 0$

New let $v_n = \frac{1}{n^2}$ such that

$$\underset{n\to\infty}{\text{Lt}} \frac{u_n}{v_n} = \underset{1/n\to 0}{\text{Lt}} \frac{\sin(1/n^2)}{(1/n^2)} = 1 \neq 0$$

From comparison test, we say that u_n and v_n behaves alike.

But $v_n = 1/n^2$ converges hence u_n also converges.

Problem 26 Test the convergence the series whose *n*th term in

$$\frac{\sqrt{n+1} - \sqrt{n-1}}{n}$$

$$u_n = \frac{\sqrt{n+1} - \sqrt{n-1}}{n} \times \frac{\sqrt{n+1} + \sqrt{n-1}}{\sqrt{n+1} + \sqrt{n-1}}$$

$$= \frac{n+1-n+1}{n[\sqrt{n+1} + \sqrt{n-1}]} = \frac{2}{n[\sqrt{n+1} + \sqrt{n-1}]}$$

$$= \frac{2}{n[\sqrt{n}(1+1/n)^{1/2} + \sqrt{n}(1-1/n)^{1/2}]}$$

$$= \frac{2}{n^{3/2}[(1+1/n)^{1/2} + (1-1/n)^{1/2}]}$$

Let $v_n = \frac{1}{n^{3/2}}$ be an auxiliary positive term series such that

$$\frac{u_n}{v_n} = \frac{2}{[(1+1/n)^{1/2} + (1-1/n)^{1/2}]}$$

$$\lim_{n\to\infty} \frac{u_n}{v_n} = \lim_{n\to\infty} \frac{2}{[(1 + 1/n)^{1/2} + (1-1/n)^{1/2}]}$$

$$= \frac{2}{2} = 1 \neq 0$$

Therefore from comparison test they behaves alike i.e., u_n and v_n either converges on diverge

But since $v_n = \frac{1}{n^{3/2}}, p > 1$ Hence the series converges.

Problem 28 Test for convergence the series whose nth term is

$$\frac{n^{n2}}{(n + 1)^{n2}}$$

$$u_n = \frac{n^{n2}}{(n + 1)^{n2}} = \left(\frac{1}{n + 1}\right)^{n2}$$

i.e. $$u_n = (1 + 1/n)^{-n2}$$

Now from cauchy's nth root test we have,

$$\lim_{n\to\infty} (u_n)^{1/n} = \underset{n\to\infty}{\text{Lt}} (1 + 1/n)^{-n2\times 1/n}$$

$$= \lim_{n\to\infty} (1 + 1/n)^{-n} = \underset{n\to\infty}{\text{Lt}} \frac{1}{(1 + 1/n)^n} = 1/e < 1$$

Therefore the series converges.

Problem 29 Does the series whose nth term is $(n^{1+1/n})^{-1}$ converges or diverges.

We have, $$u_n = (n^{1+1/n})^{-1}$$

$$u_n = \frac{1}{n^{1+1/n}} = \frac{1}{n^n \cdot n^{1/n}}$$

Let $v_n = \frac{1}{n^n}$ be an auxiliary positive term series such that

$$\frac{u_n}{v_n} = \frac{1}{n^{1/n}}$$

Now $$\underset{n\to\infty}{\text{Let}} \frac{u_n}{v_n} = \underset{n\to\infty}{\text{Lt}} \frac{1}{n^{1/n}} = 1 \neq 0$$

$$\left[\because \lim_{n\to\infty} \frac{\log n}{n} = 0\right.$$

$$\therefore \lim_{n\to\infty} \log n^{1/n} = 0$$

$$\Rightarrow \lim_{n\to\infty} n^{1/n} = e^0 = 1 \Big]$$

Therefore according to comparison test u_n and v_n either converges or diverges together.

But $v_n = \frac{1}{n}$ diverges. Hence u_n is a divergent series.

Problem 30 Assuming that $\lim_{n\to\infty} \left(\frac{n^n}{n\,!}\right)^{1/n} = e$

find whether the series $\sum_{n=1}^{\infty} \frac{n^n}{n\,!}$ converges or diverges

We have $$u_n = \frac{n^n}{n\,!}$$

From cauchy's with root test we haves,

$$(u_n)^{1/n} = \left(\frac{n^n}{n\,!}\right)^{1/n}$$

$$\lim_{n\to\infty} (u_n)^{1/n} = \lim_{n\to\infty} \left(\frac{n^n}{n\,!}\right)^{1/n} = e > 1$$

Hence, series diverges.

Problem 31 Test for converges the series $\sum_{n=2}^{\infty} \frac{1}{(\log n)^n}$

Hence, $$u_n = \frac{1}{(\log n)^n}$$

From cauchy's nth root test

$$\operatorname*{Lt}_{n\to\infty} (u_n)^{1/n} = \operatorname*{Lt}_{n\to\infty} \frac{1}{(\log n)^{n\times 1/n}} = \operatorname*{Lt}_{n\to\infty} \frac{1}{\log n} = 0 < 1$$

Hence the series is convergent.
Test each of the series 1-7 for convergence

Problem 32 $\frac{1}{3} + \frac{1\cdot 2}{3\cdot 5} + \frac{1\cdot 2\cdot 3}{3\cdot 5\cdot 7} + \frac{1\cdot 2\cdot 3\cdot 4}{3\cdot 5\cdot 7\cdot 9} + \ldots$

$$u_n = \frac{1\cdot 2\cdot 3\ldots n}{3\cdot 5\cdot 7\ldots(2n+1)}$$

$$u_{n+1} = \frac{1 \cdot 2 \ldots n \cdot (n+1)}{3 \cdot 5 \cdot 7 \ldots (2n+1)(2n+3)}$$

from D.A Lembert's Ratio test

$$\frac{u_n}{u_{n+1}} = \frac{2n+3}{n+1}$$

$$\underset{n \to \infty}{\text{Lt}} \frac{u_n}{u_{n+1}} = \underset{n \to \infty}{\text{Lt}} \frac{(2 + 3/n)}{(1 + 1/n)} = 2 > 1$$

Therefore the series converges.

Problem 33 $\frac{1}{5} + \frac{2!}{5^2} + \frac{3!}{5^3} + \frac{4!}{5^4} + \ldots$

General term $\quad u_n = \frac{n!}{5^n}$

$\therefore \quad u_{n+1} = \frac{(n+1)!}{5^{n+1}}$

From D. Alembert's Ratio test

$$\frac{u_n}{n_{n+1}} = \frac{n!\, 5^{n+1}}{5^n\,(n+1)!}$$

$$\frac{u_n}{u_{n+1}} = \frac{5}{n+1}$$

$$\therefore \quad \underset{n \to \infty}{\text{Lt}} \frac{u_n}{u_{n+1}} = \underset{n \to \infty}{\text{Lt}} \frac{5}{n+1} = 0 < 1$$

Therefore the given series diverges.

Problem 34 $\frac{1}{2} + \frac{2}{2^2} + \frac{3}{2^3} + \ldots$

$$u_n = \frac{n}{2^n}$$

$$u_{n+1} = \frac{n+1}{2^{n+1}}$$

$$\therefore \quad \frac{u_n}{u_{n+1}} = \frac{n\, 2^n \times 2}{2^n \cdot (n+1)} = \frac{2n}{n+1}$$

$$\underset{n \to \infty}{\text{Lim}} \frac{u_n}{u_{n+1}} = \underset{n \to \infty}{\text{Lim}} \frac{2}{1 + 1/n} = 2 > 1$$

Therefore the series is convergent.

Problem 35 $\frac{1}{2} + \frac{2!}{8} + \frac{3!}{32} + \ldots$

$$u_n = \frac{n!}{2 \cdot 4^{n-1}}$$

$$u_{n+1} = \frac{(n+1)!}{2 \cdot 4^n}$$

Applying D. Alembert's ratio test

$$\frac{u_n}{u_{n+1}} = \frac{n!\, 2 \cdot 4^n}{2 \cdot 4^{n-1}(n+1)!} = \frac{4}{(n+1)}$$

$$\lim_{n \to \infty} \frac{u_n}{u_{n+1}} = \lim_{n \to \infty} \frac{4}{n+1} = 0 < 1$$

Therefore the series diverges.

Problem 36 $\sum_{n=1}^{\infty} \frac{5^n}{n+5}$

$$u_n = \frac{5^n}{n+5}$$

$$u_{n+1} = \frac{5^{n+1}}{n+6} = \frac{5^n \cdot 5}{n+6}$$

From D. Alembert's Ratio test

$$\frac{u_n}{u_{n+1}} = \frac{5^n (n+6)}{(n+5)\, n^n \cdot 5} = \frac{(n+6)}{5(n+5)}$$

$$\lim_{n \to \infty} \frac{u_n}{u_{n+1}} = \lim_{n \to \infty} \frac{(1 + 6/n)}{5(1 + 5/n)} = \frac{1}{5} < 1$$

Therefore the given series is divergent one.

Problem 37 $\sum_{n=1}^{\infty} \frac{2^{n-1}}{3^n + 1}$

$$u_n = \frac{2^{n-1}}{3^n + 1}$$

and
$$u_{n+1} = \frac{2^n}{3^{n+1} + 1} = \frac{2^n}{3^n \cdot 3 + 1}$$

Therefore from Ratio test.

$$\frac{u_n}{u_{n+1}} = \frac{2^n\,(3^n\,.\,3 + 1)}{2\,.\,(3^n + 1)\,2^n}$$

$$\lim_{n\to\infty} \frac{u_n}{u_{n+1}} = \mathop{\mathrm{Lt}}_{n\to\infty} \frac{3^n\,(3 + 1/3^n)}{3^n\,(1 + 1/3^n)} = 3 > 1$$

Therefore the given series is said to be convergent.

Problem 38 $\sum_{n=1}^{\infty} \frac{n\,!}{n^n}$

$$u_n = \frac{n\,!}{n^n}$$

$$u_{n+1} = \frac{(n+1)\,!}{(n+1)^{n+1}} = \frac{(n+1)\,!}{(n+1)^n\,(n+1)} = \frac{n\,!}{(n+1)^n}$$

From D. Alembert's ratio test

$$\frac{u_n}{u_{n+1}} = \frac{n\,!\,(n+1)^n}{n^n\;n\,!} = \left(\frac{n+1}{n}\right)^n$$

$$\lim_{n\to\infty} \frac{u_n}{u_{n+1}} = \mathop{\mathrm{Lt}}_{n\to\infty} (1 + 1/n)^n = e > 1$$

Hence the given series is said to be convergent.

Problem 39 $x + \frac{x^2}{2} + \frac{x^3}{3} + \frac{x^4}{4} + \ldots$

$$u_n = \frac{x^n}{n}$$

$$u_{n+1} = \frac{x^{n+1}}{n+1}$$

From Ratio test we get,

$$\frac{u_n}{u_{n+1}} = \frac{x^n\,(n+1)}{n\,.\,x^n\,.\,x} = \left(\frac{n+1}{n}\right)\frac{1}{x}$$

$$\lim_{n\to\infty} \frac{u_n}{u_{n+1}} = \lim_{n\to\infty} \left(1 + \frac{1}{n}\right)\frac{1}{x} = \frac{1}{x}$$

The given series cvgs if $\frac{1}{x} > 1$ i.e. $x < 1$

given series dvgs if $\frac{1}{x} < 1$ i.e. $x > 1$

test fails at $x = 1$

However at $x = 1$ we have series reduces to

$$u_n = 1 + \tfrac{1}{2} + \tfrac{1}{3} + \ldots,$$

$$u_n = 1/n \text{ which is a divergent series}$$

cvg if $\quad x < 1$

dvgs if $\quad x \geqslant 1$

Problem 40 $\quad \dfrac{x}{\sqrt{5}} + \dfrac{x^3}{\sqrt{7}} + \dfrac{x^5}{\sqrt{9}} + \dfrac{x^7}{\sqrt{11}} + \ldots$

General term $\quad u_n = \dfrac{x^{2n-1}}{\sqrt{(2n+3)}}$

$$u_{n+1} = \frac{x^{2n+1}}{\sqrt{2n+5}}$$

From Ratio test

$$\underset{n\to\infty}{\text{Lt}} \frac{u_n}{u_{n+1}} = \underset{n\to\infty}{\text{Lt}} \frac{x^{2n}}{x(2n+3)^{1/2}} \times \frac{(2n+5)^{1/2}}{x^{2n}\,.\,x}$$

$$= \underset{n\to\infty}{\text{Lt}} \frac{1}{x^2}\left(\frac{1+5/2n}{1+3/2n}\right)^{1/2} = \frac{1}{x^2}$$

Series cvgs if $\dfrac{1}{x^2} > 1 \quad$ i.e. $\quad x^2 < 1 \quad \Rightarrow \quad x < 1$

Series dvgs if $\dfrac{1}{x^2} < 1 \quad$ i.e. $\quad x^2 > 1 \quad \Rightarrow \quad x > 1$

Test fails if $\quad x^2 = 1 \quad$ i.e. $\quad x = 1$

However, series is

$$\frac{1}{\sqrt{5}} + \frac{1}{\sqrt{7}} + \frac{1}{\sqrt{9}} + \ldots$$

$$u_n = \frac{1}{\sqrt{2n+3}} = \frac{1}{\sqrt{n}\,(2+3/n)^{1/2}}$$

Let $\quad v_n = \dfrac{1}{\sqrt{n}}$ be an auxiliary positive term series

$$\underset{n\to\infty}{\text{Lim}} \frac{u_n}{v_n} = \frac{1}{(2+3/n)^{1/2}} = \frac{1}{2} \neq 0$$

u_n diverges since v_n is a divergent.

Reqd. series therefore is said to be

convergent if $x < 1$

divergent if $\quad x \geqslant 1$

Problem 41 $\frac{x}{1.3}+\frac{x^2}{2.4}+\frac{x^2}{3.5}+\ldots$

$$u_n = \frac{x^n}{n\,.\,(n+2)}$$

$$u_{n+1} = \frac{x^{n+1}}{(n+1)\,(n+3)}$$

$$\therefore \quad \frac{u_n}{u_{n+1}} = \frac{x^n\,(n+1)\,(n+3)}{n\,.\,(n+2)\,x^n\,.\,x}$$

$$= \frac{n^2\,(1+1/n)\,(1+3/n)}{n^2\,(1+2/n)\,x}$$

$$\lim_{n\to\infty} \frac{n_n}{u_{n+1}} = \lim_{n\to\infty} \frac{(1+1/n)\,(1+3/n)}{(1+2/n)\,x} = \frac{1}{x}$$

The given series cvgs if $\frac{1}{x} > 1$ i.e. $x < 1$

series dvgs if $\frac{1}{x} < 1$ i.e. $x > 1$

test fails at $x = 1$

However the series reduces to

$$u_n = \frac{1}{1\cdot 3}+\frac{1}{2\cdot 4}+\frac{1}{3\cdot 5}+\ldots = \frac{1}{n\cdot(n+2)}$$

Let $v_n = \frac{1}{n^2}$ such that from comparison test

$$\lim_{n\to\infty} \frac{u_n}{v_n} = \mathop{\mathrm{Lt}}_{n\to\infty} \frac{n^2}{n^2\,(1+2/n)} = 1 \neq 0$$

Therefore, u_n and v_n either converges or diverges together since v_n converges

Hence u_n is also a convergent series at $x = 1$

Reqd. series is therefore said to be

convergent if $x \leqslant 1$

divergent if $x > 1$

Problem 42 $\frac{x^2}{2\sqrt{1}}+\frac{x^3}{3\sqrt{2}}+\frac{x^4}{4\sqrt{3}}+\ldots$

General term of the series is

$$u_n = \frac{x^{n+1}}{(n+1)\,n^{1/2}}$$

and

$$u_{n+1} = \frac{x^{n+2}}{(n+2)\,(n+1)^{1/2}}$$

Applying the Ratio test we have

$$\frac{u_n}{u_{n+1}} = \frac{x^n \cdot x}{(n+1)\, n^{1/2}} \quad \frac{(n+2)(n+1)^{1/2}}{x^n \cdot x^2}$$

$$= \frac{1}{x}\left[\frac{(1+2/n)}{(1+1/n)}\ (1+1/n)^{1/2}\right]$$

$$\lim_{n\to\infty} \frac{u_n}{u_{n+1}} = \lim_{n\to\infty} \frac{1}{x}\left[\frac{(1+2/n)\,(1+1/n)^{1/2}}{(1+1/n)}\right] = \frac{1}{x}$$

Series cvgs if $\frac{1}{x} > 1$ i.e. $x < 1$

Series dvgs if $\frac{1}{x} < 1$ i.e. $x > 1$

at $x = 1$. Ratio test fails then we have

$$u_n = \frac{1}{(n+1)\, n^{1/2}} = \frac{1}{n^{1/2}\ (1+1/n)^{1/2}}$$

Let $$v_n = \frac{1}{u^{3/2}}$$

From comparison test we have

$$\lim_{n\to\infty} \frac{u_n}{v_n} = \lim_{n\to\infty} \frac{1}{(1+1/n)^{1/2}} \neq 0$$

Hencc, u_n and v_n both either converges or diverges but since, v_n is a convergent series

Hence u_n also converges
Reqd. series is therefore said to be
(i) dvgt if $x > 1$
(ii) convergent if $x \leqslant 1$.

Problem 43 $\frac{x}{2\sqrt{3}} + \frac{x^2}{3\sqrt{3}} + \frac{x^3}{4\sqrt{5}}$ ..

– General term $u_n = \frac{x^n}{(n+1)\,(n+2)^{1/2}}$

$$u_n = \frac{x^n}{n^{3/2}\,(1+1/n)\,(1+2/n)^{1/2}}$$

and $$u_{n+1} = \frac{x^{n+1}}{(n+2)\,(n+3)^{1/2}}$$

From Ratio test test we have

$$\frac{u_n}{u_{n+1}} = \frac{x^n (n+2)(n+3)^{1/2}}{(n+1)(n+2)^{1/2}} = \frac{1}{x}\left[\frac{(1+2/n)(1+3/n)^{1/2}}{(1+1/n)(1+2/n)^{1/2}}\right]$$

$$\lim_{n\to\infty} \frac{u_n}{u_n+1} = \frac{1}{x} \lim_{n\to\infty}\left[\frac{(1+2/n)(1+3/n)^{1/2}}{(1+1/n)(1+2/n)^{1/2}}\right] = \frac{1}{x}$$

convergent if $\frac{1}{x} > 1$ i.e. $x \lhd 1$

divergent if $\frac{1}{x} < 1$ i.e. $x > 1$

at $x = 1$ the series reduces to

$$u_n = \frac{1}{(n+1)(n+2)^{1/2}} = \frac{1}{n^{3/2}(1+1/n)(1+2/n)^{1/2}}$$

Therefore from comparison test u_n converges since $p > 1$
Hence the series is said to be

convergent if $x \leqslant 1$

divergent if $x > 1$

Problem 44 $1 + \frac{x}{2} + \frac{x^2}{5} + \ldots \frac{x^n}{n^2+1} + \ldots$

$$u_n = \frac{x^n}{n^2+1}$$

$$u_{n+1} = \frac{x^{n+1}}{(n+1)^2+1}$$

According to Ratio test

$$\frac{u_n}{u_{n+1}} = \frac{x^n (n+1)^2 + 1}{(n^2+1)\, x^n \cdot x} = \frac{1}{x}\left[\frac{n^2\{(1+1/n)^2 + 1/n^2\}}{n^2\{1 + 1/n^2\}}\right]$$

$$\lim_{n\to\infty} \frac{u_n}{u_n+1} = \frac{1}{x} \operatorname*{Lt}_{n\to\infty} \frac{(1+1/n)^2 + 1/n^2}{(1+1/n^2)} = \frac{1}{x}$$

cvgs. if $\frac{1}{x} > 1$ i.e. $x < 1$

dvgs if $\frac{1}{x} < 1$ i.e. $x > 1$

at $x = 1,\ u_n = \frac{1}{n^2+1}$

i.e. $u_n = \frac{1}{n^2(1+1/n^2)}$

Let $\quad v_n = 1/n^2 \quad$ such that

$$\underset{n \to \infty}{\text{Lt}} \frac{u_n}{v_n} = \underset{n \to \infty}{\text{Lt}} \frac{1}{1 + 1/n^2} \neq 0$$

Since, v_n converges and hence u_n is a convergent series at $x = 1$.

$$\left.\begin{array}{l} \text{cvgs if } x \leqslant 1 \\ \text{dvg if } x > 1 \end{array}\right]$$

Problem 45 $1 + \frac{2}{5} x + \frac{6}{9} x^2 + \frac{19}{17} x^3 + \ldots + \frac{2^n - 2}{2^n + 1} x^{n-1} + \ldots$

General term $u_n = \dfrac{2^n - 2}{2^n + 1} x^{n-1}$

and $\quad u_{n+1} = \dfrac{2^{n+1} - 2}{2^{n+1} + 1} x^n$

Applying Ration test we have

$$\frac{u^n}{u_n + 1} = \left[\frac{2^n - 2}{2^n + 1}\right]\left[\frac{2^{n+1} + 1}{2^{n+1} - 2}\right]\frac{x^{n-1}}{x^n}$$

$$\underset{n \to \infty}{\text{Lim}} \frac{u_n}{u_n + 1} = \underset{n \to \infty}{\text{Lt}} \frac{(1 - 2/2^n)}{(1 + 1/2^n)} \frac{(1 + 2/2^n)}{(1 - 2/2^n)} \frac{1}{x} = \frac{1}{x}$$

series cvgs i f $\dfrac{1}{x} > 1$ i.e. $x < 1$

dvgs if $\quad \dfrac{1}{x} < 1$ i.e. $x > 1$

at $\quad x = 1$, the Ratio test fails

However series reduces to

$$u_n = \frac{2^n - 2}{2^n + 1}$$

$$\underset{n \to \infty}{\text{Lim}} u_n = \underset{n \to \infty}{\text{Lt}} \frac{(1 - 2/2^n)}{(1 + 1/2^n)} = 1 \neq 0$$

Hence the series diverges. Therefore the given series cvgs. if $x < 1$
and dvgs if $x \geqslant 1$

Problem 46 Test for convergence the series $\sum_{n=1}^{\infty} \dfrac{r^n}{n\,!}$ where r is any positive number

$$u^n = \frac{r^n}{n\,!}$$

$$u_{n+1} = \frac{r^n + 1}{(n+1)\,!} = \frac{r^n \cdot r}{(n+1)\,!}$$

By Ratio test,

$$\frac{u^n}{u^n + 1} = \frac{r^n\,(n+1)\,!}{n\,!\,r^n \cdot r}$$

$$\underset{n\to\infty}{\text{Lt}} \frac{u_n}{u_{n+1}} = \underset{n\to\infty}{\text{Lt}} \frac{(n+1)}{r} = \infty$$

Hence from Ratio test
the series converges $\forall\ r > 0$.

Problem 47 Test for convergence the series whose nth them is

$$\frac{\sqrt{n-1}}{\sqrt{n^2+1}}\ x^n,\ x > 0$$

$$u_n = \frac{\sqrt{n-1}}{\sqrt{n^3+1}}\,x^n$$

$$u_{n+1} = \frac{\sqrt{n}}{\sqrt{(n+1)^3+1}}\ x^{n+1}$$

Applying Ratio test

$$\underset{n\to\infty}{\text{Lim}} \frac{u_n}{u_{n+1}} = \underset{n\to\infty}{\text{Lt}} \frac{1}{x}\left[\frac{\sqrt{n-1}\ \ \sqrt{(n+1)^3+1}}{\sqrt{n^3+1}\ \sqrt{n}}\right]$$

$$= \underset{n\to\infty}{\text{Lim}} \frac{1}{x}\left[\sqrt{1-\frac{1}{n}}\ \sqrt{\frac{n^3+3n^2+3n+2}{n^3+1}}\right]$$

$$= \underset{n\to\infty}{\text{Lim}} \frac{1}{x}\left[\sqrt{1-1/n}\ \sqrt{1+\frac{3n^2+3n+1}{n^3+1}}\right]$$

$$= \underset{n\to\infty}{\text{Lim}} \frac{1}{x}\left[\sqrt{1-1/n}\ \sqrt{1+\frac{(3+3/n+1/n^2)}{n\,(1+1/n^3)}}\right]$$

$$= \frac{1}{x}\,[1] = \frac{1}{x}$$

cvgs if $\dfrac{1}{x} > 1 \ \Rightarrow\ x < 1$

dvgs if $\dfrac{1}{x} < 1 \ \Rightarrow\ x > 1$

at $x = 1$ the Ratio test fails. However, the series reduces to

$$u_n = \frac{\sqrt{n-1}}{\sqrt{n^3+1}}$$

$$u_n = \frac{1}{n}\sqrt{\frac{1-1/n}{1+1/n^3}}$$

Let $v_n = 1/n$ be auxitary positive term series. Therefore applying comparison test

$$\lim_{n\to\infty} \frac{u_n}{v_n} = 1 \neq 0$$

Hence u_n and v_n both cvgs or dvgs together.
But v_n diverges. Hence u_n diverges at $x = 1$.
i.e. series cvgs if $x < 1$
dvgs if $x \geqslant 1$.

Problem 48 Test for convergence the series $\sum_{n=1}^{\infty} \frac{\sqrt{n}}{\sqrt{n^2+1}} x^n$

for positive value of x.
General term of the series

$$u_n = \frac{\sqrt{n}}{\sqrt{n^2+1}} x^n$$

$$u_{n+1} = \frac{\sqrt{n+1}}{\sqrt{(n+1)^2+1}} x^{n+1}$$

$$\therefore \operatorname*{Lt}_{n\to\infty} \frac{u_n}{u_{n+1}} = \frac{x^2\sqrt{n}}{x^n \cdot x\sqrt{n^2+1}} \frac{\sqrt{(n+1)^2+1}}{\sqrt{n+1}}$$

$$= \frac{1}{x}\left[\frac{\sqrt{n^2+2n+2}}{\sqrt{n^2+1}} \frac{1}{(1+1/n)^{1/2}}\right]$$

$$= \frac{1}{x} \lim_{n\to\infty}\left[\frac{(1+2/n+2/n^2)^{1/2}}{(1+1/n^2)^{1/2}} \frac{1}{(1+1/n)^{1/2}}\right] = \frac{1}{n}$$

Series converges if $\frac{1}{x} > 1$ i.e. $x < 1$

Series diverges if $\frac{1}{x} < 1$ i.e. $x > 1$

at $x = 1$ we have

$$u_n = \frac{\sqrt{n}}{\sqrt{n^2 + 1}}$$

$$u_n = \frac{\sqrt{n}}{n\sqrt{1 + 1/n^2}} = \frac{1}{\sqrt{n\,(1 + 1/n^2)}}$$

Let $v_n = \dfrac{1}{\sqrt{n}}$ be an auxiilary positive term series. Such that

$$\operatorname*{Lt}_{n\to\infty} \frac{u_n}{v_n} = \operatorname*{Lt}_{n\to\infty} \frac{1}{(1 + 1/n^2)^{1/2}} = 1 \neq 0$$

From comparison test u_n and v_n either converges or diverges together. Bu since v_n diverges hence, u_n is divergent series.
Therefore, the gives series
converges if $x < 1$
diverges if $x \geqslant 1$

Problem 49 Test for convergence the series

$$1 + \frac{2^p}{2\,!} + \frac{3^p}{3!} + \frac{4^p}{3\,!} + \ldots$$

General term $u_n = \dfrac{n^p}{n\,!}$

i.e. $u_{n+1} = \dfrac{(n + 1)^n}{(n + 1)\,!}$

Applying Ratio test

$$\frac{u_n}{u_{n+1}} = \frac{n^p\,(n + 1)\,!}{n\,!\,(n + 1)^p}$$

$$\operatorname*{Lim}_{n\to\infty} \frac{u_n}{u_{n+1}} = \operatorname*{Lim}_{n\to\infty} \left(\frac{n}{n + 1}\right)^p \frac{(n + 1)\,n\,!}{n\,!}$$

$$= \operatorname*{Lim}_{n\to\infty} \frac{1}{(1 + 1/n)^p}\,(n + 1) = \infty$$

Therefore, the series converges.

Problem 50 It the series

$$\frac{1^2 \cdot 2^2}{1\,!} + \frac{2^2\,.\,3^2}{2\,!} + \frac{3^2 \cdot 4^2}{3\,!} + \ldots$$

t Le $u_n = \dfrac{n^2 \cdot (n + 1)^2}{n\,!}$

$$u_{n+1} = \frac{(n+1)^2 (n+2)^2}{(n+1)!}$$

Applying Ratio test

$$\frac{u_n}{u_{n+1}} = \left(\frac{1}{n+1}\right)^2 \left(\frac{n+1}{n+2}\right)^2 (n+1)$$

$$\underset{n\to\infty}{\text{Lt}} \left(\frac{1}{1+1/n}\right)^2 \left(\frac{1+1/n}{1+2/n}\right)^2 (n+1) = \infty$$

Hence the series is convergent.

Problem 51 Is the series $\sum_{n=1}^{\infty} \frac{n^5}{(n+1)!}$ convergent or divergent

General terms

$$u_n = \frac{n^5}{(n+1)!}$$

and $$n_{n+1} = \frac{(n+1)^5}{(n+2)!}$$

Applying Ratio test.

$$\underset{n\to\infty}{\text{Lim}} \frac{u_n}{u_{n+1}} = \underset{n\to\infty}{\text{Lt}} \frac{n^5}{(n+1)^5} \frac{(n+2)!}{(n+1)!}$$

$$= \underset{n\to\infty}{\text{Lim}} \left(\frac{n}{n+1}\right)^5 (n+2)$$

$$= \underset{n\to\infty}{\text{Lim}} \left(\frac{1}{1+1/n}\right)^5 (n+2) = \infty$$

Therefore the series is convergent.

Some More Problem [in papers] Apart from All Above

Problem 52 $x^2 + \frac{2^2}{3.4} x^4 + \frac{2^2 . 4^2}{3.4.5.6} x^6 + \ldots$

The general terms

$$u_n = \frac{2^2 \cdot 4^2 \ldots (2n-2)^2}{3 \cdot 4 \cdot 5 \ldots (2n-2)(2n-1)} x^{2n}$$

$$= \frac{2^2.4^2 \ldots (2n-2)^2}{3.4.5 \ldots (2n-2)(2n-1)} x^{2n}$$

$$u_{n+1} = \frac{2^2.4^2 \ldots (2n-2)^2 (2n)^2}{3.4.5 \ldots (2n-2)(2n-1)(2n)(2n+1)} x^{2n+2}$$

Applying Ratio test

$$\frac{u_n}{u_{n+1}} = \frac{2n\,(2n+1)}{(2n)^2}\,\frac{1}{x^2}$$

$$\lim_{n\to\infty} \frac{u_n}{u_{n+1}} = \lim_{n\to\infty} (1 + 1/2n)\,\frac{1}{x^2}$$

Series converges if $\frac{1}{x^2} > 1$ i.e. $x^2 < 1$

$$\Rightarrow \quad x > -1 \qquad Or \qquad x < 1$$

Series diverges if $\frac{1}{x^2} < 1$ i.e. $x^2 > 1$

$$\Rightarrow \quad x > 1 \qquad Or \qquad x < -1.$$

If $x^2 = 1$ The Ratio test failes and

Hence proceed for Raabe's test i.e.

$$\mathop{\mathrm{Lt}}_{n\to\infty} n\left[\frac{u_n}{u_{n+1}} - 1\right] = n\left[\frac{2_{n+1}}{2n} - 1\right]$$

$$= \lim_{n\to\infty} n\left[\frac{1}{2n}\right] < 1\Big]$$

Hence the series diverges

Problem 53 $\frac{3}{7}\,x + \frac{3.6}{7.10}\,x^2 + \frac{3.6.9}{7.10.13}\,x^3 + \ldots$

Here the General term of the series

$$u_n = \frac{3.6.9\ldots 3n}{7.10.13\ldots(3n+4)}\,x^n$$

$$u_{n+1} = \frac{3.6.9\ldots 3n\,(3x+3)}{7.10.13\ldots 3n+4\,(3x+7)}\,x^{n+1}$$

Applying the Ratio test we get

$$\lim_{n\to\infty} \frac{u_n}{u_{n+1}} = \lim_{n\to\infty} \frac{(3n+7)}{(3n+3)}\,\frac{1}{x}$$

$$= \lim_{n\to\infty} \frac{(1+7/3n)}{(1+3/3n)}\,\frac{1}{x} = \frac{1}{x}$$

convergent if $\frac{1}{x} > 1$ i.e. $x < 1$

divergent if $\frac{1}{x} < 1$ i.e. $x > 1$

at $x = 1$ the test fails and we proceed for Raabe's test i.e.

$$\lim_{n\to\infty} n\left[\frac{u_n}{u_{n+1}}\right] = \lim_{n\to\infty} n\left[\frac{3n+7}{3n+3} - 1\right]$$

$$= \lim_{n\to\infty} n\left[\frac{3n+7-3n-3}{3n+3}\right]$$

$$= \lim_{n\to\infty} \frac{4n}{3n+3} = \frac{4}{3} > 1$$

Hence the series is said to be convergent at $x = 1$.

Problem 54 Test convergence of the following positive term series.

$$1 + \frac{(1+\alpha)}{(1+\beta)} + \frac{(1+\alpha)(2+\alpha)}{(1+\beta)(2+\beta)} + \ldots$$

The general term of the series in

$$u_n = \frac{(1+\alpha)(2+\alpha)\ldots(\alpha+n-1)}{(1+\beta)(2+\beta)\ldots(\beta+n-1)}$$

and $\quad u_{n+1} = \dfrac{(1+\alpha)(2+\alpha)\ldots(\alpha+n-1)(\alpha+n)}{(1+\beta)(2+\beta)\ldots(\beta+n-1)(\beta+n)}$

Applying Ratio test we get

$$\lim_{n\to\infty} \frac{u_n}{u_{n+1}} = \lim_{n\to\infty} \left(\frac{\beta+n}{\alpha+n}\right)$$

$$= \lim_{n\to\infty} \frac{(1+\beta/n)}{(1+\alpha/n)} = 1$$

the test fails we proced for Raabe's test

$$\mathop{\mathrm{Lt}}_{n\to\infty} n\left[\frac{u_n}{u_{n+1}} - 1\right] = \lim_{n\to\infty} n\left[\frac{\beta+n-\alpha-n}{\alpha+n}\right]$$

$$= \lim_{n\to\infty} \frac{(\beta-\alpha)}{(1+\alpha/n)} = (\beta-\alpha)$$

Hence the given series cvg if $\beta - \alpha > 1$

i.e. $\beta > \alpha + 1$

diverges if $\beta - \alpha < 1 \Rightarrow \beta < 1 + \alpha$ and at $\beta - \alpha = 1$ again test fails. Now we proceed for Gauss test i.e. to express

$$\frac{u_n}{u_{n+1}} = 1 + \frac{a}{n} + \frac{a^2}{n^2} + \ldots$$

When $\qquad \beta - \alpha = 1$

$\Rightarrow$ $\beta = 1 + \alpha$ the series reduces to

$$u_n = 1 + \frac{\beta}{1+\beta} + \frac{\beta}{\beta+2} + \ldots$$

$$u_n = \frac{\beta}{\beta + n-1}$$

and $$u_{n+1} = \frac{\beta}{\beta + n}$$

$\therefore$ $$\frac{u_n}{u_n + 1} = \frac{\beta + n}{\beta + n - 1} = \left(1 + \frac{\beta}{n}\right)\left(1 + \frac{\beta}{n} - \frac{1}{n}\right)^{-1}$$

$$= \left(1 + \frac{\beta}{n}\right)\left(1 + \frac{1}{n} - \frac{\beta}{n} + ..\right)$$

$$= 1 + \frac{\beta}{n} - \frac{\beta^2}{n^2} + \frac{1}{n} - \frac{\beta}{n} + \frac{\beta}{n^2} \ldots$$

$$= 1 + \frac{1}{n} - 0 \text{ (higher power containing } n)$$

$\because$ $a = 1$ Hence the series diverges at

$$\alpha = \beta - 1$$

or $$\beta = 1 + \alpha$$

Problem 55 $$\frac{2^2}{3^2} + \frac{2^2 \cdot 4^2}{3^2\, 5^2} + \ldots$$

$$u_n = \frac{2^2 \cdot 4^2 \ldots (2n)^2}{3^2 \cdot 5^2 \ldots (2n+1)^2}$$

and $$u_{n+1} = \frac{2^2 \cdot 4^2 \ldots (2n)^2\,(2n+2)^2}{3^2 \cdot 5^2 \ldots (2n+1)^2\,(2n+3)^2}$$

Applying Ratio test we have

$$\underset{a \to \infty}{\text{Lt}} \frac{u_n}{n_{n+1}} = \underset{n \to \infty}{\text{Lt}} \left(\frac{2n+3}{2n+2}\right)^2$$

$$= \underset{n \to \infty}{\text{Lt}} \frac{(1 + 3/2n)^2}{(1 + 2/2n)^2} = 1$$

The Ratio test fails proceed for Raabe's test

i.e. $$\underset{n\to\infty}{\text{Lt}} \text{ is } \left[\frac{u_n}{u_{n+1}} - 1\right] = \underset{n\to\infty}{\text{Lt}}\ n\left[\frac{(2n+3)^2-(2n+2)^2}{(2n+2)^2}\right]$$

$$\underset{n\to\infty}{\text{Lt}}\ n\left[\frac{4n^2+9+12n-4n^2-4-8n}{(2n+2)^2}\right]$$

$$= \underset{n\to\infty}{\text{Lt}}\ n\frac{[4n+n]}{(2n+2)^2} = \underset{n\to\infty}{\text{Lt}} \frac{n^2(4+5/n)}{n^2(2+2/n)^2}$$

$$= \frac{4}{4} = 1$$

the test fails

Now proceeding for Gauss's test

$$\frac{u_n}{u_n+1} = \frac{4n^2(1+3/2n)^2}{4n^2(1+2/2n)^2} = \left(1+\frac{3}{2n}\right)^2\left(1+\frac{2}{2n}\right)^{-2}$$

$$= \left(1+\frac{3}{n}\right)\left(1-\frac{2}{n} + \text{higher power}\right)$$

$$= 1 - \frac{2}{n} + \frac{3}{n} + 0\text{ (higher powers)}$$

$$= 1 + \frac{1}{n} + 0\text{ (higher powers)}$$

$\because$ $a = 1$ Hence the series diverges.

Problem 56 Test for the convergence of the series

$$\frac{1}{2}x + \frac{1}{2}\cdot\frac{3}{4}\cdot x^2 + \frac{1}{2}\cdot\frac{3}{4}\cdot\frac{5}{6}\cdot x^3 + \ldots$$

General term, $$u_n = \frac{1.3.5\ldots(2n-1)}{2.4.6\ldots2n}x^n$$

$$u_{n+1} = \frac{1.3.5\ldots(2n-1)(2n+1)}{2.4.6\ldots2n(2n+2)}x^{n+1}$$

Applying Ratio test

$$\underset{n\to\infty}{\text{Lt}} \frac{u_n}{n_{n+1}} = \underset{n\to\infty}{\text{Lt}} \frac{(2n+2)}{(2n+1)}\frac{1}{x} = \underset{n\to\infty}{\text{Lt}} \frac{\left(1+\frac{1}{n}\right)}{\left(1+\frac{1}{2_n}\right)}\cdot\frac{1}{x}$$

he series cvgs if $\frac{x}{x} > 1 \Rightarrow x < 1$

eries dvgs if $\frac{1}{x} < 1 \Rightarrow x > 1$

t $x = 1$ the Ratio test fails then we proceed for Raabe's test

$$\underset{n\to\infty}{\text{Lt}}\ n\left[\frac{u_n}{u_{n+1}} - 1\right] = \underset{n\to\infty}{\text{Lt}}\ n\left[\frac{2n+2-2n-1}{2n+1}\right]$$

$$= \underset{n\to\infty}{\text{Lt}}\ \frac{n}{2n+1} = \frac{1}{2} < 1$$

Ience at $x = 1$ the series diverges.

lternating series

. Leibnitz's test: A series is said to be convergent if

(i) It is monotonically decreasing function.

(ii) and $\underset{n\to\infty}{\text{Lim}}\ u_n = 0.$

Def. Absolute eonvergence

n alternating series $\sum u_n$ is said to be absolutely convergent if the positive rm series $\sum u_n$ 1 converges.

e. The series $\frac{1}{1^2} - \frac{1}{2^2} + \frac{1}{3^2} - \frac{1}{4^2} \cdots$

bsolutely converges because its positive term converges i.e.

$$|u_n| = \frac{1}{n^2}$$

sult. Every absolute convergent series is convergent. But the converse the theorem is not true, i.e. A series may be convergent without being bsolutely convergent.

The process Is known as the conditional convergence.

roblem 57 Show that the series

$$\frac{\log 2}{2^2} - \frac{\log 3}{3^2} + \frac{\log 4}{4^2} \ldots \text{converges}$$

Solution The above series is an alternating series with general term

$$u_n = \frac{\log(n+1)}{(n+1)^2}$$

$$\underset{n\to\infty}{\text{Lim}}\ u_n = \underset{n\to\infty}{\text{Lim}}\ \frac{\log(n+1)}{n+1)}\ \frac{1}{(n+1)} = 0\left[\because \underset{n\to\infty}{\text{Lim}}\ \frac{\log n}{n} = 0\right]$$

Now we should check for the monotonic decreasing of the function i.e.

$$u_{n+1} \leqslant u_n \ \forall \ n$$

Let $\qquad f(x) = \dfrac{\log x}{x^2}$

$$\therefore \qquad f'(x) = \frac{\frac{1}{x} \cdot x^2 - 2x \log x}{x^4} = \frac{x - 2x \log x}{x^4} = \frac{1 - \log x^2}{x^3} < 0$$

Whenever $\qquad x > e^{1/2}$

Therefore $f(x)$ is monotonically decreasing function.

All the condition of Leibnitz test has been satisfied. Hence the series is convergent,

Problem 58 Show that the series

$$x - \frac{x^3}{3} + \frac{x^5}{5} \cdots$$

Converges iff $\qquad -1 \leqslant x \leqslant 1.$

Solution The general term,

$$u_n = (-1)^{n-1} \frac{x^{2n-1}}{(2n+1)}$$

$$\therefore \qquad u_{n+1} = (-1)^n \frac{x^{2n+1}}{2n+1}$$

Therefore $\left|\dfrac{u_n}{u_n + 1}\right| = \dfrac{2n+1}{2n-1} \dfrac{1}{x^2}$

So that $\qquad \lim\limits_{n \to \infty} \left|\dfrac{u_n}{u_n + 1}\right| = \dfrac{1}{x^2}$

By D. Alemberts ratio test $\sum | u_n |$ converges if $\dfrac{1}{x^2} > 1$ i.e. if $| x | < 1$ and diverges if $| x | > |$, Since every absolutely convergent series is convergent therefore u_n converges if $| x | < 1$.

When $x = -1$, the series reduces $-1 + \dfrac{2}{3} - \dfrac{1}{5} \cdots$

which is convergent

When $x = +1$ the series reduces to $1 - \dfrac{1}{3} + \dfrac{1}{5} - \dfrac{1}{7}$

Which is convergent.

Thus $= u_n$ converges iff $-1 \leqslant x \leqslant 1$.

Problem 59 Show that the series $1-\frac{1}{3}+\frac{1}{5}-\frac{1}{7}+\ldots$ is conditionally convergent.

We have from Leibnitzs test the series is convorgent.

But $|u_n| \sum \frac{1}{2n-1}$, Let $|v_n|$ be an auxiliary positive term with $|v_n| = \frac{1}{n}$

So that $\underset{n\to\infty}{\text{Lt}} \left|\frac{u_n}{v_n}\right| = \frac{1}{2} \neq 0$

Hence, $|v_n|$ and $|u_n|$ behaves a like. But since $|v_n|$ diverges hence $|u_n|$ diverges.

Therefore, we say that the series is conditionally convergent.

Problem 60 $\frac{1}{2}-\frac{1}{4}+\frac{1}{6}-\frac{1}{8}+\ldots$

The given series is an alte rnating series

Here $\qquad u_{n+1} \leqslant u_n \ \forall\ n$

i.e $\qquad \frac{1}{2} > \frac{1}{4} > \frac{1}{6} > \frac{1}{8} \ldots$

Therefore we may say that it is a monotonically decrcasing functlon

$$u_n = \frac{1}{2n}$$

$$\underset{n\to\infty}{\text{Lt}}\ u_n = \underset{n\to\infty}{\text{Lt}}\ \frac{1}{2n} = 0$$

Hence the series is said to be convergent.

But for the absolute convergence we have

$$u_n = (-1)^{n-1}\frac{1}{2n}$$

$$\therefore \qquad u_{n+1} = (-1)^n \frac{1}{2n+2}$$

$$\underset{n\to\infty}{\text{Lt}} \left|\frac{u_n}{u_n+1}\right| = \frac{2n+2}{2n} = 1$$

Ratio test fails, hence we proceed for Raabe's test. This test also fails. Proceeding for Gauss test

$$\underset{n\to\infty}{\text{Lt}} \left|\frac{u_n}{u_n+1}\right| = \left(1+\frac{1}{n}\right) = 1+\frac{1}{n}$$

Comparing to with $1 + 1/n + 0$ (higher power) hence, $a = 1$. Therefor it diverges.

Hence, the series is conditionally convergent.

Problem 61 $\frac{1}{\log 2} - \frac{1}{\log 3} + \frac{1}{\log 4} - \frac{1}{\log 5} + \ldots$

Solution $u_n = (-1)^{n+1} \frac{1}{\log (n+1)}$

$$\therefore \quad |u_n| = \frac{1}{\log (n+1)}$$

and $$|u_{n+1}| = \frac{1}{\log (n+2)}$$

$$\therefore \quad \left|\frac{u_n}{u_{n+1}}\right| = \frac{\log (n+2)}{\log (n+1)}$$

$$= \frac{\log (n+1)}{\log (n+1)} = \frac{\log (n+1)\{1 + 1/n+1\}}{\log (n+1)}$$

$$= \frac{\log (n+1) + \log \{1 + 1/n+1\}}{\log (h+1)}$$

$$= \frac{1 + \frac{1}{n+1} - \frac{1}{2(n+1)^2} + \ldots}{\log (n+1)}$$

$$\lim_{n\to\infty} \frac{u_n}{u_n+1} = 1 + \frac{1}{(n+1)\log (n+1)} - \frac{1}{2(n+1)^2 \log (n+1)}$$

$$= 1$$

test fails we proceed for Rabe's test

i.e., $$n\left[\frac{u_n}{u_{n+1}} - 1\right] = \frac{n}{n+1} \quad \frac{1}{\log (n+1)} = 0 < 1$$

Therefore the given series is conditionally convergent

Problem 62 $\sum_{n=1}^{\infty} \frac{(-1)^{n-1}}{2n+3}$

We have, $$u_n = \frac{(-1)^{n-1}}{2n+3}$$

$$|u_n| = \frac{1}{2n+3}$$

Let $\quad |v_n| = \frac{1}{n}$ be an auxiliary positive series so that

$$\frac{|u_n|}{|v_n|} = \underset{n\to\infty}{\text{Lt}} \frac{n}{2n+3}$$

$$= \underset{n\to\infty}{\text{Lt}} \frac{1}{2+3/n} = \frac{1}{2} \neq 0$$

Therefore the $|u_n|$ diverges. Hence, the given series is conditionally convergent.

Since every condition of Leibnitz test is fulfilled

and $\quad \lim_{n\to\infty} u_n = 0.$

Problem 63. $\quad \sum_{n=1}^{\infty} (-1)^n \frac{\sin n\alpha}{n^3}$, α being real

The expansion of $\sin n\alpha$ is gives as

$$\sin n\alpha = n\alpha - \frac{(n\alpha)^3}{3!} + \frac{(n\alpha)^5}{5!} \ldots$$

i.e., $\quad u_n = \frac{(n\alpha)^{2n-1}}{(2n-1)!}(-1)^{n-1}$

Reqd. General term of the series reduces to

$$u_n = \frac{(-1)^{2n-1}(n\alpha)^{2n-1}}{(2n-1)!} \cdot \frac{1}{n^3}$$

$$\therefore \quad |u_n| = \frac{(n\alpha)^{2n-1}}{(2n-1)!} \cdot \frac{1}{n^3} = \frac{h^{2n}\alpha^{2h-1}}{n^4(2n-1)!} = \frac{n^{2n-4}\alpha^{2n-1}}{(2n-1)!}$$

$$\therefore \quad |u_{n+1}| = \frac{(n+1)^{2n-2}\alpha^{2n+1}}{(2n+1)!} = \frac{\alpha^{2n+1}(n+1)^{2n-2}}{(2n+1)!}$$

$$\therefore \quad \frac{|u_n|}{|u_{n+1}|} = \frac{(2n+1)!}{(2n-1)!} \frac{n^{2n-4}}{(n+1)^{2n-2}} \frac{1}{\alpha^2}$$

$$= \frac{2n(2n+1)}{\alpha^2}\left(\frac{1}{1+1/n}\right)^{2n-2} \frac{1}{n^2}$$

$$\lim_{n\to\infty} \frac{4n^2(1+1/2n)}{n^2} \frac{1}{(1+1/n)^{2n-2}} \frac{1}{\alpha^2} = \frac{4}{\alpha^2}$$

The series converges if $\frac{4}{\alpha^2} > 1 \Rightarrow 4 > \alpha^2$

i.e., $$|\alpha| < 2$$

$$\text{at } \alpha = \pm 2.$$

We have, series converges hence, the given series is absolutely convergent.

Problem 64 $\sum_{n=1}^{\infty} (-1)^n \frac{\cos n\alpha}{n\sqrt{n}}$, α being real.

Expansion of $\cos n\alpha$ is

$$\cos n\alpha = \frac{1-(n\alpha)^2}{2!} + \frac{(n\alpha)^4}{4!} + \ldots$$

$$u_n = \frac{(-1)^{n-1} x^{2n-2}}{(2n-2)!}$$

The general term of the series reduces to

$$u_n = \frac{(-1)^{2n-1} x^{2n-2}}{(2n-2)!\, n\sqrt{n}}$$

$$\therefore \qquad |u_n| = \frac{x^{2h-2}}{h\sqrt{n}\,(2n-2)!}$$

$$|u_{n+1}| = \frac{x^{2n}}{(n+1)(n+1)^{1/2}(2n)!}$$

Applying *D*. *A*lembert's ratio test

$$\frac{|u_n|}{|u_{n+1}|} = \lim_{n\to\infty} \frac{x^{2h}(h+1)(n+1)^{1/2}(2n)!}{x^2 n\sqrt{n}\,(2n-2)!x^{2h}}$$

$$= \operatorname*{Lt}_{h\to\infty} \frac{(1+1/n)(1+n)^{1/2}\, 2n(2n-1)}{x^2} = \infty$$

Hence the series is convergent $\forall\, x$.
Therefore, the gives series is Absoluceely ing.

Problem 65 $1 - \frac{1}{2^p} + \frac{1}{3^p} - \frac{1}{4^p} + \ldots$

Solution $u_n = \frac{(-1)^{n-1}}{n^p} \Rightarrow |u_n| = \frac{1}{n^p}$

The given series converges if $p > 1$ diverges if $p \leqslant 1$.
Therefore, for $p > 1$ the series is absolutely convergent.

When $\qquad 0 < p \leqslant 1,$

$$u_n = \frac{(-1)^{n-1}}{n^p}$$

It is a monotonically decreasing function and

$$\lim_{n\to\infty} u_n = \underset{n\to\infty}{\text{Lt}} \frac{(-1)^{n+1}}{n^p} = 0$$

Therefore the series is conditionally cnvg

When $\qquad p = 0$, the series changes to

$$u_n = 1 - + 1 - 1 \ldots$$

Which is an oscillatyry series.

Problem 66 Test for convergence the series

$$\sum_{n=1}^{\infty} (-1)^{n+1} \left[\frac{1}{n^2} + \frac{1}{(n+1)^2}\right]$$

$$|u_n| = \left[\frac{1}{n^2} + \frac{1}{(n+1)^2}\right]$$

and $\qquad |u_{n+1}| = \left[\frac{1}{(n+1)^2} + \frac{1}{(n+2)^2}\right]$

Applying *D*. Alembest's Ratio test

$$\left|\frac{u_n}{u_{n-1}}\right| = \frac{[(n+1)^2 + n^2]\,[(n+1)^2\,(n+2)^2]}{n^2\,(n+1)^2\,[(n+2)^2 + (n+1)^2]}$$

$$= [(1 + 1/n)^2 + 1]\left[\frac{1}{1+\dfrac{(n+1)^2}{(n+2)^2}}\right]$$

$$\underset{h\to\infty}{\text{Lt}} \left|\frac{u^{n-1}}{u_{n+1}}\right| = \underset{n\to\infty}{\text{Lt}} [(1+1/n)^2 + 1]\left[\frac{1}{1+\dfrac{(1+1/n)^2}{(1+2/n)^2}}\right] = 1$$

Ratio test fails. We proceed for Raabe's test

$$\underset{n\to\infty}{\text{Lt}}\ n\left[\left|\frac{u_n}{u_{n+1}}\right| - 1\right] = n.\frac{(n+1)^2\,[n^2+4+4n-n^2]}{n^2\,[(n+2)^2 + (n+1)^2]}$$

$$= \frac{n \cdot 4\,(1+n)^3}{n^2\,[(n+2)^2 + (n+1)^2]} = \frac{4n^3\,(1+1/n)^3}{n^3\,[(1+2/n)^2 + (1+1/n)^2]}$$

$$= 2 > 1$$

Hence the series is Absolutely convergent.

Problem 67 Test for convergence the series

$$\sum_{n=1}^{\infty} (-1)^n \frac{n+2}{2n+5}$$

$\therefore$

$$|u_n| = \frac{n+2}{2n+5}$$

$$|u_{n+1}| = \frac{n+3}{2^{n+1}+5}$$

Applying Ratio test

$$\left|\frac{u_n}{u_{n+1}}\right| = \underset{n\to\infty}{\text{Lt}} \frac{(n+2)(2^{n+1}+5}{(n+3)(2^n+5)} = \underset{n\to\infty}{\text{Lt}} \frac{(n+2)(2^n\cdot 2+5)}{(n+3)(2^n+5)}$$

$$= \underset{n\to\infty}{\text{Lt}} \frac{(1+2/n)(2+5/2^n)}{(1+3/n)(1+5/2^n)} = \frac{1\times 2}{1\times 1} = 2 > 1$$

The series converges absolutely.

Appendix 14

REPRODUCTIVE PROPERTY FOR DIFFERENT DISTRIBUTIONS

(1) Additive property of Binomial distribution.

Q. Prove that ingeneral the sum of independent binominal variates is not a binomial varire.

Or

Prove that binomial distribution does not possess the additive or reproductive property.

We know that if

$$M_{X+Y}(t) = M_X(t) \cdot M_Y(t)$$

then it shows reproduetive property.

Ans. Let $X \sim B(n_1, p_1)$ and $Y \sim B(n_2 \cdot p_2)$ be independent random variables. Then we know that the moment generating function for Binomal distribution is given by

$$M_X(t) = (q_1 + p_1 e^t)^{n1} \text{ remember} \quad (1)$$

and $$M_Y(t) = (q_2 + p_2 e^t)^{n2} \text{ remember} \quad (2)$$

Then $$M_{X+Y}(t) = M_X(t)\, M_Y(t)$$

$$(q_1 + p_1 e^t)^{n1} \cdot (q_2 + p_2 e^t)^{n2} \quad (3)$$

since equation (3) cannot be put in form $(q + p\, e^t)^n$

$\Rightarrow$ $X + Y$ is not Bionomial variate.

Special Case

Prove that the binomial distribution possesses the additive or reproductive property if $p_1 = p_2$

Proof Let us take $p_1 = p_2 = p$

then $$M_X(t) = (q_1 + p_1 e^t)^{n_1}$$

$$= (q + p\, e^t)^{n1}$$

and $$M_Y(t) = (q_2 + p_2 e^t)^{n_2}$$

$$= (q + p\, e^t)^{n_2}$$

Then $\quad M_{X+Y}(t) = M_X(t) \cdot M_Y(t)$

$$M_{X+Y}(t) = (q + p\,e^t)^{n_1} \cdot (q + p\,e^t)^{n_2}$$

$$M_{X+Y}(t) = (q + p\,e^t)^{n_1+n_2}$$

then $\quad X + Y \sim B(n_1 + n_2, p)$

Q. 2 State and prove Reproductive property of poisson variable.

Or

If X and Y are independent poisson variates prove sum i.e. $X + Y$ is also possion-variate.

Or

If $X \sim p(\lambda_1)$ and $Y \sim p(\lambda_2)$

$$\Rightarrow \quad X + Y \sim p(\lambda_1 + \lambda_2)$$

where X and Y are independent.

Proof We know that the moment Generating function of the poisson variate is given by

$$M_X(t) = e^{\lambda\,(e^t-1)}$$

where λ is a parameter let X and Y are any two independent poisson variates then

$$X \sim p(\lambda_1) \text{ and}$$

$$Y \sim p(\lambda_2)$$

where λ_1 and λ_2 are parameters for X and Y

$$M_X(t) = e^{\lambda_1\,(e^t-1)}$$

$$M_K(t) = e^{\lambda_2\,(e^t-)})$$

Now $\quad M_{X+Y}(t) = M_X(t) \cdot M_Y(t)$

$$= e\lambda_1(e^t-1).\; e\;\lambda_2(e^t-1)$$

$$= e\lambda_1\,(e^t-1) + \lambda_2\,(e^t-1) = e$$

$$= e(\lambda_1 + \lambda_2)\,(e^t-1)$$

$$\Rightarrow \quad X + Y \sim p(\lambda_1 + \lambda_2)$$

Thus $X + Y$ is also a poisson variate whose parameter is $\lambda_1 + \lambda_2$

In general case we can show that if

$$X_i \sim p(\lambda_i)$$

Then $\quad \sum X_i \sim p(\sum \lambda_i)$

As $\quad M_{\Sigma X_i}(t)$

$$= M_{X_1} \cdot M_{X_2}(t)\, M_{X_3}(t_1 \ldots$$

$$= e^{\lambda_1\,(e^t-1)} \cdot e^{\lambda_2\,(e^t-1)}\; e^{\lambda_3\,(e^t-1)}$$

$$= e(\lambda_1+\lambda_2+\ldots)(e^t-1)$$

$$= e^{(\Sigma\lambda_i)\,(e^t-1)}$$

Thus $\qquad \sum X_i \sim p(\sum X_i)$

Thus we can write that the sum of independent poisson variate is again a poisson variate. [*Proved*]

Q 3 Show that the difference of two independent poisson variate is not a poisson variate.

Proof Let X_1 and X_2 be two independent poisson variate, then we have to show that $X_1 - X_2$ is not a poisson variate.

$$X_1 \sim p(\lambda_1)$$

$$X_2 \sim p(\lambda_2)$$

Then $M_{X_1 - X_2}(t) = M_{X_1 + (-X_2)}(t)$

$$= M_{X_1}(t)\, M_{(-X_2)}(t)$$

$$= M_{X_1}(t)\; M_{X_2}(-t) = e^{\lambda_2 (e^t - 1)} \cdot e^{\lambda_2 (e^{-t} - 1)}$$

so the expression cannot be put in the form $e^{\lambda(e^t - 1)}$

so the difference of two end posion variate is not again a poisson variate. [*Proved*]

Q. 4 Prove that a linear combination of independent normal variates is also a normal variate.

Proof Let $X_i (i = 1, 2 \ldots n$ be n-independent normal variates with mean μ_1 and variance σ_i^2 respectively. Then Moment generating function is given by

$$M_{Xi}(t) = e^{[\mu_i (t) + (\sigma i^2 t^2)/2]}$$

i.e. $\qquad X_i \sim N(\mu i, \sigma_i^2)$

where μ_i, is the mean and σ^2 is the variance of the normal distribution

The moment generating function of their liner combination $\sum a_i, x_i \ldots$ where $a_1, a_2 \ldots a_n$ are constants is given by

$$M_{\Sigma a_i X_i}(t)$$

$$= M_{a_1 X_1 + a_2 X_2 + \ldots + a_1 X_n}$$

$$= M_{a_1 X_1}(t)\, M_{a_2 X_2}(t) \ldots M_{a_n X_n}(t)$$

[$\because$ X is are independent]

$$= M_{X_1}(a_1 t)\, M_{X_2}(a_2 t) \ldots M_{X_n}(a_n t)$$

since $\qquad M_{cX}(t) = M_X(ct).$

$$= e^{(a_1\mu_1 t + (\sigma_1^2 a_1^2 t^2)/2)} \, e^{(a_2\mu_2 t + \sigma_2^2 (a_2^2 t^2/2))}$$

$$\ldots e^{(a_n\mu_n t + \sigma_n^2 (a_{2n} t^2/2))}$$

$$= e^{a_1\mu_1 t + a_2\mu_2 t + a_3\mu_3 t + \ldots, + a_n\mu_n t + t^2/2(\sigma_1^2 a_1^2 + \ldots + \sigma_n^2 a_2^2)}$$

$$= e^{\, t(a_1\mu_1 + a_3\mu_2 + a_3\mu_3 + \ldots + a_n\mu_n) + (t^2/2)(\sigma_1^2 + \delta_2^2 a^2 + \ldots)}$$

Thus $\qquad \sum a_i x_i \sim \sum_{i=1}^{n} a_i \mu_i \sum_{i=1}^{n} a_i^2 \sigma^2)$

Remark If we take $a_1 = a_2 = 1 \qquad a_3 = a_4 = \ldots 0$

$$X_1 + X \sim (\mu_1 + \mu_2, \sigma_1^2 + \sigma_2^2)$$

If we take

$$a_1 = 1, \qquad a_2 = -1 \qquad a_3 = a_4 = \ldots 0$$

then $\qquad X_1 - X_2 \, (\mu_1 - \mu_2, \sigma_1^2 + \sigma_2)$

Thus we see that the sum as well as the difference of two independent normal variates is also a normal variate. This result provides a sharp contrast to the poisson variate in which case though the sum of independent poisson variate is a poisson variate, the difference is not a poisson variate.

Q. 5 Prove the Additive property of x^2-variate [I.F.S. 85]

Or

Prove that the sum of independent chi-square variate is also *a* x^2 Variate More precisely if X_i^2 $(i = 1, 2 \ldots k)$ are independent. X^2 variates

with n_i degree of freedom respectively them the sum $\sum_{i=1}^{n} X_i$ is also a chi-

square variate with $\sum_{i=1}^{n} n_i$ degree of freedom.

Proof We have (Moment generating function)

$$M_{X_1^2}(t) = (1-2t)^{ni/2} \, ; \, i = 1, 2 \ldots$$

Then moment generating function of the sum $\sum_{i=1}^{n} X_i^2$ is given by

$= M_{X_1}(t) \cdot M_{X_2}(t) \ldots$

[$\because$ X^2 is are independent]

$= (1-2t)^{-n_1/2}\ (1-2t)^{-n_2/2} \ldots (1-2t)^{-n_k/2}$

$= (1-2t)^{-(n_1+n_2+\ldots+n_k)/2}$

which is *mgf* of a X^2 variate with $(n_1 + n_2 + \ldots + n_k)$ degree of freedom. Hence by uniqueness theorem of *mgf*'s $\sum_{i=1}^{k}$ is a X_i^2 is a X^2 variate

with $\sum_{i=1}^{k} n_i$ degree of freedom.